Current Law

Case Citator

2007

THOMSON

™

SWEET & MAXWELL

AUSTRALIA
LBC Information Services
Sydney

CANADA and USA
Carswell
Toronto

NEW ZEALAND
Brooker's
Auckland

SINGAPORE and MALAYSIA
Sweet & Maxwell Asia
Singapore and Kuala Lumpur

Current Law

Case Citator

2007

SWEET & MAXWELL

EDITORIAL TEAM

Sadie Allanson
Catherine Aylward
Sam Chubb
Zoe Ciereszko
Marie Clare
Dominic Howell
Gerry Howell
Harjeet Jutle
Dylan Llewellyn-Nunes
Jackie Pearson
Alix Robinson
Colette Rybicki
Martin Syrett
Nina Taylor
Amy Thomas
Lisa Thwaites
Pat Williams

PRODUCTION TEAM

Steve Casling
Roger Greenwood
Lisa Thwaites
Debra Wade

THOMSON

™

SWEET & MAXWELL

Published in 2008 by
Sweet & Maxwell Limited of
100 Avenue Road, Swiss Cottage, London NW3 3PF.
Typeset by Sweet & Maxwell Ltd, Mytholmroyd, Hebden Bridge, West Yorkshire.
Printed in Germany by Bercker.

A CIP catalogue record for this book is available from the British
Library.

ISBN 978-1-84703-538-7

No forests were destroyed to make this product; only farmed
timber was used and re-planted.

CONTENTS

CONTENTS

PREFACE

The Sweet & Maxwell Current Law Service

The Current Law Service began in 1947 and provides a comprehensive guide to developments in case law, primary legislation and secondary legislation in the UK and mainland Europe. The Current Law Service presently consists of the Monthly Digests, the Year Book, Current Law Statutes, the Statute Citator, the Statutory Instrument Citator, the Case Citator, Current Law Week and European Current Law.

Also available is the Current Legal Information CD, which contains an archive of Year Books dating back to 1947, the present year's accumulated Monthly Digests and the English and Scottish Case Citators from 1947 to the current month, as well as a range of other Sweet & Maxwell current awareness products such as the Current Law Legislation Citators, Legal Journals Index and Financial Journals Index.

The Case Citators

The Current Law Case Citators comprise four cumulative volumes covering the years 1947-1976, 1977-1997, 1998-2001, 2002-2004 and single volumes covering 2005, 2006 and 2007. Together they provide a comprehensive reference guide to case law after 1946.

How to use the Citators

When searching for a case, users should consult the most recent citator volume first, since it provides the most comprehensive and authoritative information. The current volume contains a guide to the complete history of cases digested or judicially considered in 2007. For earlier case law not considered since 2006, users should consult either the previous citator volumes (2006, 2005, 2002-2004, 1998-2001, 1977-1997, and 1947-1976) or the Current Legal Information CD.

The material in this volume is arranged in alphabetical order in three sections:

English Citator
Scottish Citator
Ships' Names Index

The details in each entry can be used on a number of different levels, including identifying law report series in which a full report of a case can be found, the judicial history of a case and the location of an abstract of a case within a Current Law Yearbook. The following information is provided:

(a) The full name of any case reported between 1947 and 2007

Cases are listed alphabetically by the first party's name, giving the most recent Current Law Year Book paragraph reference to the appropriate digest. Most references have a year before the paragraph number, e.g. 07/**239** alludes to the 2007 Year Book, paragraph 239. If no year is given, the case is contained in the Current Law Consolidation 1947-1951. (For Scotland see the Scottish Year Books 1948-1951.)

(b) An extensive list of references to the law reports and journals reporting each case

Each entry gives details about one case, beginning with the case name and any joined cases or other names by which the case might be known, followed by the reports in descending order of authority and the court in which the case was heard. Where cases go on to an appellate court, the entry states whether the higher court affirmed or reversed the decision of the lower court.

(c) The judicial history of a case

If a case has been applied, considered, approved, distinguished, overruled, etc., since it was decided, Current Law Year Book references to digests of cases in which the judicial consideration took place are provided. These references are in normal type while the paragraph number of the actual digest of each case is given in bold.

(d) Details of Scottish cases

Part II of the Citator contains details of cases decided or judicially considered in the Scottish Courts. References to English cases judicially considered in Scotland are also included in this part, so subscribers wishing to follow the full history of an English case should consult both parts of the Citator. Scottish cases published in English Law Reports are included in both the Scottish and English sections.

(e) Ships' Names Index

This is an alphabetical listing of all ships' names and their law report citations to assist where only the ship's name is known by the user. The official party names for these cases will be located in the main body of the Citator.

Whilst every effort has been made to ensure that details of cases in this citator are correct, there may be occasions when a citation is wrong. The editor would be grateful for notification of any errors to enable them to be rectified on the database from which this volume was derived.

Case Citator Editor
Sweet & Maxwell Ltd
The Hatchery
Hall Bank Lane
Mytholmroyd, Hebden Bridge
West Yorkshire
HX7 5HQ
email: smg.casecitatoreditor@thomson.com

TABLE OF ABBREVIATIONS

Courts Abbreviations

AAT = Administrative Appeals Tribunal (Australia)

AD = Anotato Dikastirio (Cyprus)

Afr Comm HPR = African Commission on Human and Peoples Rights

AG = Amtsgericht (Germany)

AGO = Advocate Generals Opinion

AIT = Asylum and Immigration Tribunal

APDPK = Arkhe Prostasias Dedomenon Prosopikou Kharaktera (Greece)

App (B) = Cour d'Appel (Belgium)

App (I) = Corte di Appello (Italy)

App Person = Trade Marks Registry (Appointed Person)

Ar Pag = Areios Pagos (Greece)

ArbG = Arbeitsgericht (Germany)

ARRS = Afdeling Rechtspraak van de Raad van State (NL)

As Huk Mah = Asliye Hukuk Mahkemesi (Turkey)

Aꜱ Tic Mah = Asliye Ticaret Mahkemesi (Turkey)

AT = Augstakas Tiesas (Latvia)

ATMC = Administrative Trade Mark Committee (Greece)

Aud = Audiencia Provincial (Spain)

BAG = Bundesarbeitsgericht (Germany)

Bd of Trade = Board of Trade

BezG = Bezirksgericht (Switzerland)

BFH = Bundesfinanzhof (Germany)

BG = Bundesgericht (Switzerland)

BGH = Bundesgerichtshof (Germany)

BKA = Bundeskartellamt (Germany)

BPG = Bundespatentgericht (Germany)

BRB = Burgerlijke Rechtbank (Belgium)

BsozG = Bundessozialgericht (Germany)

BverfG = Bundesverfassungsgericht (Germany)

BverwG = Bundesverwaltungsgericht (Germany)

C Adm A = Cour Administrative d'Appel (Belgium/France)

C Concurrence = Conseil de la Concurrence (Belgium/France)

C Cost = Corte Costituzionale (Italy)

C d'A = Cour d'Appel (France/Luxembourg)

CA = Court of Appeal

CA (Civ Div) = Court of Appeal (Civil Division)

CA (Crim Div) = Court of Appeal (Criminal Division)

CAC = Central Arbitration Committee

CAEW = Central Authority for England and Wales

Care Standards Tr = Care Standards Tribunal

Cass = Cour de Cassation (Belgium/France/Luxembourg)

CAT = Competition Appeal Tribunal

CC = County Court

CCA = Court of Criminal Appeal

CCAT = Competition Commission Appeal Tribunal

CCP = Court of Common Pleas

CE = Conseil d'Etat (Belgium/France)

CEC = Commission of the European Communities

Cent Crim Ct = Central Criminal Court (Ireland)

Central Crim Ct = Central Criminal Court

CFA (HK) = Court of Final Appeal (Hong Kong)

CFI = Court of First Instance

CFI (HK) = Court of First Instance of the High Court (Hong Kong Special Administrative Region)

CFI (Phl) = Court of First Instance (Philippines)

Charity Comm = Charity Commissioners

Ch D = Chancery Division

Ch D (Bankruptcy Ct) = Chancery Division (Bankruptcy Court)

Ch D (Companies Ct) = Chancery Division (Companies Court)

Ch D (Irl) = Chancery Division (Ireland)

Ch D (NI) = Chancery Division (Northern Ireland)

Ch D (Patents Ct) = Chancery Division (Patents Court)

Ch D (RPC) = Chancery Division (Restrictive Practices Court)

CICA = Criminal Injuries Compensation Authority

CICAP = Criminal Injuries Compensation Appeals Panel

CICB = Criminal Injuries Compensation Board

Circ Ct = Circuit Court (Ireland)

CJ = Court of Justice

CJ (Gen Div) (Ont) = Ontario Court of Justice (General Division)

CMAC = Courts Martial Appeal Court

CollvB = College van Beroep voor het Bedrijfsleven (NL)

Comm Cartels = Commission des Cartels (Switzerland)

Comm Conc = Commission de la Concurrence (France)

Comm Ministers = Committee of Ministers

Commr Pat = Commissioner of Patents (Australia)

Comm Sec Cons (F) = Commission de la Securite des Consommateurs

Comm Tributaria PG = Commissione Tributaria di Primo Grado (Italy)

Comm Tributaria SG = Commissione Tributaria di Secondo Grado (Italy)

Comp Auth = Competition Authority (Ireland)

Cons Const = Conseil Constitutionnel (France)

Cons Ct = Consistory Court

Cons Stato = Consiglio di Stato (Italy)

Const Ct = Constitutional Court

Cour d'Arb = Cour d'Arbitrage (Belgium)

CP = Court of Protection

CPD = Common Pleas Division

CRC = Commission Federale de Recours en Matiere de Contributions (Switzerland)

Crim CA = Criminal Court of Appeal (Ireland)

CRvB = Centrale Raad van Beroep (Netherlands)

CS = Court of Session

CSJ = Cour Superieure de Justice (Luxembourg)

CST = Civil Service Tribunal

Ct Sup = Corte Suprema de Justicia (Argentina)

DC = Divisional Court

DR = District Registry

EAT = Employment Appeal Tribunal

EC Council = European Council

Eccl Ct = Court of Ecclesiastical Causes Reserved

ECHR = European Court of Human Rights

ECHR (Grand Chamber) = European Court of Human Rights (Grand Chamber)

ECJ = European Court of Justice

ECSR = European Committee of Social Rights

ED = Eparhiako Dikastrio (Cyprus)

EFTA = EFTA Court of Justice

Epit Antag = Epitropi Antagonismou (Greece)

EPO = European Patent Office

ERGI (Swi) = Eidgenossische Rekurskommission fur Geistiges Eigentum (Switzerland)

TABLE OF ABBREVIATIONS

ES = Eidgenossisches Steuerrekurskommission (Switzerland)
ET = Employment Tribunal
Eur Comm HR = European Commission on Human Rights
Ex Chamber = Court of Exchequer Chamber
Ex Ct = Court of Exchequer
Ex Div = Extra Division
Fam Ct = Family Court
Fam Div = Family Division
FAS Mosk Okr (RF) = Federalnyi Arbitrazhnyi Sud Moskovskogo Okruga (Russian Federation)
Fed CA = Federal Court of Appeal
Fed Ct = Federal Court
Fed HC = Federal High Court
FG = Finanzgericht (Germany)
FSMT = Financial Services & Markets Tribunal
GC = Giudice Conciliatore (Italy)
HC = High Court
HCJ = High Court of Justiciary
HD = Hogsta Domstolen (Finland/Sweden)
HerrR = Herredsrett (Norway)
HFD = Hogsta forvaltningsdomstolen (Finland)
HL = House of Lords
HO = Hovioikeus/Hovratt (Finland)
Hof = Gerechtshof (Netherlands)
HR (DK) = Hojesteret (Denmark)
HR (N) = Hoyesterett (Norway)
HR (NL) = Hoge Raad (NL)
HR (Swe) = Hovratt (Sweden)
HR Ch = Human Rights Chamber for Bosnia and Herzegovina
HvB = Hof van Beroep (Belgium)
HvC = Hof van Cassatie (Belgium)
IA Comm HR = Inter American Commission on Human Rights
IACHR = Inter American Court of Human Rights
IAT = Immigration Appeal Tribunal
ICC = International Chamber of Commerce, Arbitration Tribunal
ICJ = International Court of Justice
ICTA Tr = Tribunal constituted under the Income and Corporation Taxes Act 1988 s.706
IH = Inner House
IH = Court of Session (Inner House)
IH (1 Div) = Court of Session (Inner House, First Division)
IH (2 Div) = Court of Session (Inner House, Second Division)
IH (Ex Div) = Court of Session (Inner House, Extra Division)
IPT = Investigatory Powers Tribunal
IT = Industrial Tribunal
ITAT (Ind) = Income Tax Appellate Tribunal (India)
It Cass = Corte di Cassazione (Italy)
J de Paix = Justices de la Paix (Luxembourg)
JP = Juge de Paix (Belgium)
JPI = Juzgado de Primera Instancia (Spain)
KBD = King's Bench Division
KBD (Comm) = King's Bench Division (Commercial Court)
KBD (Irl) = King's Bench Division (Ireland)
KBD (NI) = King's Bench Division (Northern Ireland)
KG (Ger) = Kammergericht (Germany)
KG (Swi) = Kassationsgericht (Switzerland)
KHO = Korkein Hallinto-Oikeus (Finland)
KKO = Korkein Oikeus (Finland)
KO = Kihlakunnanoikeus/Haradsratt (Finland)
Ktg = Kantongerecht (Netherlands)

Lab Ct = Labour Court (Ireland)
Land Ct (IoM) = Land Court (Isle of Man)
LArbG = Landesarbeitsgericht (Germany)
LCD = Lord Chancellors Department
Legf Bir = Legfelsobb Birosag (Hungary)
LG (A) = Landesgericht (Austria)
LG (Ger) = Landgericht (Germany)
LGO = Local Government Ombudsman
LJ in Lunacy = Lords Justices sitting in Lunacy
LR = Lagmannsrett (Norway)
LSozG = Landessozialgericht (Germany)
LVAC = Lands Valuation Appeal Court
LVT = Leasehold Valuation Tribunal
MC = Magistrates Court
MCLC = Mayor's and City of London Court
MD = Marknadsdomstolen (Sweden)
MMC = Monopolies and Mergers Commission
MR = Markedsradet (Norway)
Nat Ct = National Court
NI Comm = National Insurance Commissioner
NIRC = National Industrial Relations Court
NO = Naringsfrihetotombudsman (Swe)
NS CR = Nejvyssi soud Ceske republiky (Czech Republic)
NSA (PL) = Naczelny Sad Administracyjny (Poland)
ObG = Obergericht (Switzerland)
ODEI = Office of the Director of Equality Investigations (Ireland)
OGH = Oberster Gerichtshof (Austria)
OH = Outer House
OHIM = Office for Harmonization in the Internal Market
Okr Sod = Okrozno Sodisce (Slovenia)
OL = Ostre Landsret (Denmark)
OLG = Oberlandesgericht (Austria/Germany)
OPM = Oberster Patent- und Markensenat (Austria)
OR = Official Referee
OVG = Oberverwaltungsgericht (Germany)
Pat App Tr = Patents Appeal Tribunal
Pat Val Apel Pad = Patentu Valdes Apelacijas Padome (Latvia)
PC = Privy Council
PCA = Parliamentary Commissioner for Administration
PCC = Patents County Court
PDAD = Probate, Divorce & Admiralty Division
PO = Patent Office
Prer Ct = Prerogative Court
Pret = Pretura (Italy)
PVO = Plant Variety Office
PVST = Plant Varieties & Seeds Tribunal
QB = Court of Queen's Bench
QBD = Queen's Bench Division
QBD (Admin) = Queen's Bench Division (Administrative Court)
QBD (Admlty) = Queen's Bench Division (Admiralty Court)
QBD (Comm) = Queen's Bench Division (Commercial Court)
QBD (Merc) = Queen's Bench Division (Mercantile Court)
QBD (NI) = Queen's Bench Division (Northern Ireland)
QBD (OR) = Queen's Bench Division (Official Referee)
QBD (TCC) = Queen's Bench Division (Technology & Construction Court)
QBD (UK-Irl) = Queen's Bench Division (UK - Ireland)
R = Riigikohus (Estonia)
RB (B) = Tribunal de Premiere Instance (Belgium)
RB (NL) = Arrondissementsrechtbank (Netherlands)
RDAT = Registered Designs Appeal Tribunal

TABLE OF ABBREVIATIONS

Refugees Status Apps = Refugees Status Appeals Authority (New Zealand)
Rel = Tribunal de Relacao (Portugal)
RP Comm = Restrictive Practices Commission (Ireland)
RPC = Restrictive Practices Court
RR = Regeringsratten (Sweden)
RvK = Rechtbank van Koophandel (Belgium)
Ry & Canal Comm = Railway and Canal Commission
Ry Rates Tr = Railway Rates Tribunal
Sad Apel = Sad Apelacyjny (Poland)
Sad Rej = Sad Rejonowy (Poland)
SCSL (UN) = Special Court for Sierra Leone (Appeals Chamber)
SENT = Special Educational Needs Tribunal
SH = So- og Handelsret (Denmark)
Sh Ct = Sheriff Court
Sh Pr = Sheriff Principal
Solicitors Disc Ctte (SC) = Solicitors Discipline (Scotland) Committee
SozG = Sozialgericht (Germany)
Sp Comm = Special Commissioners
Sp Imm App Comm = Special Immigration Appeals Commission
Spec Crim Ct = Special Criminal Court (Ireland)
SS Comm = Social Security Commissioner
Sup Ct = Supreme Court
Sup Trib = Supremo Tribunal de Justica (Portugal)
Sup Trib Admin = Supremo Tribunal Administrativo (Portugal)
Sym Ep = Symvoulio tis Epikrateias (Greece)
TAR = Tribunale Amministrativo (Italy)
TMR = Trade Marks Registry
Tr = Tribunal
TR = Tingsratt (Sweden)
Transport Arb Tr = Transport Arbitration Tribunal
Trib = Tribunale (Italy)
Trib Ad = Tribunal Administratif (France)
Trib Civil = Tribunal Civil (Belgium)

Trib Comm = Tribunal de Commerce (Belgium/France)
Trib Comp = Tribunal de Defensa de la Competencia (Spain)
Trib Const = Tribunal Constitucional (Spain)
Trib Corr = Tribunal Correctionnel (France)
Trib Correct = Tribunal Correctionnel (Belgium)
Trib d'Arr = Tribunal d'Arrondissement (Luxembourg)
Trib Fed = Tribunal Federal (Switzerland)
Trib Gde Inst = Tribunal de Grande Instance (Belgium/France)
Trib Police = Tribunal de Police (France)
Trib Prem Inst = Tribunal de Premiere Instance (Monaco)
Trib Sup = Tribunal Supremo (Spain)
Trib Travail = Tribunal du Travail (Belgium)
Tryb Konst = Trybunal Konstytucyjny (Poland)
UN CAT = UN Committee Against Torture
UN CEDW = UN Committee on the Elimination of Discrimination against Women
UN CERD = UN Committee on the Elimination of Racial Discrimination
UN HRC = UN Human Rights Committee
UN ICT = UN International Criminal Tribunal
Ur Last = Urad Republike Slovenije za Intelektualno Lastnino (Slovenia)
US CR = Ustavni Soud Ceske Republiky (Czech Republic)
US Ct = US Court
V&D Tr = VAT and Duties Tribunal
VAC = Valuation Appeal Court
VfGH = Verfassungsgerichtshof (Austria)
VGH = Verwaltungsgericht (Germany/Switzerland)
Visje Sod = Visje Sodisce (Slovenia)
VL = Vestre Landsret (Denmark)
VrS = Vrchni soud (Prague)
VT = Valuation Tribunal
VwGH = Verwaltungsgerichtshof (Austria)
Yrg = Yargitay (Turkey)

Jurisdiction Abbreviations

A = Austria
Abu = Abu Dhabi (United Arab Emirates)
ACT = Australian Capital Territory
Afg = Afghanistan
AI = Ascension Island (St Helena)
AL = Albania
Ald = Alderney
Alg = Algeria
Alta = Alberta
And = Andorra
Ang = Anguilla
Ango = Angola
Ant = Antigua and Barbuda
Arg = Argentina
Arm = Armenia (CIS)
Aus = Australia
Aze = Azerbaijan (CIS)
B = Belgium
Bah = Bahamas
Bahr = Bahrain
Bang = Bangladesh
Bar = Barbados
BC = British Columbia
BEL = Belarus (CIS)
Ben = Benin
Ber = Bermuda
BF = Burkina Faso

BG = British Guiana
BH = British Honduras
Bhu = Bhutan
BIH = Bosnia Herzegovina
Bol = Bolivia
Bots = Botswana
Bru = Brunei
Bul = Bulgaria
Bur = Burundi
BVI = British Virgin Islands
Bze = Belize
Bzl = Brazil
Camb = Cambodia
Camn = Cameroon
Can = Canada
Canary I = Canary Islands (Spain)
Cape = Cape of Good Hope
CAR = Central African Republic
Cey = Ceylon
CI = Cayman Islands
CIS = Commonwealth of Independent States
Com = Comoros
Con = Congo
Cook I = Cook Islands
CR = Costa Rica
CV = Cape Verde
Cy = Cyprus

TABLE OF ABBREVIATIONS

CZ = Czech Republic
Dji = Djibouti
DK = Denmark
Dom = Dominica
DomR = Dominican Republic
Dub = Dubai
EA = Eastern Africa
EC = European Communities
ECHR = European Commission on Human Rights
Ecu = Ecuador
Egy = Egypt
EIS = El Salvador
EPO = European Patent Office
EqG = Equatorial Guinea
Eri = Eritrea
Eth = Ethiopia
EU = European Union
EW = Estonia
F = France
FI = Falkland Islands
Fin = Finland
FL = Lichtenstein/Liechtenstein
FMS = Federated Malay States
FRY = Yugoslavia
Gab = Gabon
Gam = Gambia, The
GBi = Guinea Bissau
Geo = Georgia (CIS)
Ger = Germany
Gha = Ghana
Gib = Gibraltar
Gld = Greenland (Denmark)
GR = Greece
Gren = Grenada
Gua = Guatemala
Gue = Guernsey
Gui = Guinea
Guy = Guyana
H = Hungary
HK = Hong Kong
Hon = Honduras
HR = Croatia
I = Italy
Ind = India
Indo = Indonesia
IoM = Isle of Man
Iran = Iran
Iraq = Iraq
Irl = Ireland
IS = Iceland
Isr = Israel
Ivo = Ivory Coast
Jam = Jamaica
Jer = Jersey
Jor = Jordan
Jpn = Japan
Kaz = Kazakhstan (CIS)
Ken = Kenya
Kir = Kiribati
Kuw = Kuwait
Kyr = Kyrgyzstan (CIS)
L = Luxembourg
LA = Latvia
Leb = Lebanon
Les = Lesotho
Libe = Liberia
Libya = Libya
LT = Lithuania
M = Malta

Mace = Macedonia
Mad = Madagascar
Made = Madeira (Portugal)
Mal = Malaysia
Man = Manitoba
Mar = Martinique
Marshall I = Marshall Islands (Micronesia)
Mau = Mauritius
MC = Monaco
Mex = Mexico
Mic = Micronesia
Mnegro = Montenegro
Mnia = Mauritania
Mol = Moldova (CIS)
Mong = Mongolia
Mor = Morocco
Moz = Mozambique
Mrat = Montserrat
Mves = Maldives
Mwi = Malawi
Mya = Myanmar
N = Norway
Nam = Namibia
NAnt = Netherlands Antilles
Nau = Nauru
NB = New Brunswick
Nfld = Newfoundland
NI = Northern Ireland
Nic = Nicaragua
Nig = Nigeria
NK = North Korea
NL = Netherlands
NS = Nova Scotia
NSW = New South Wales
NT = Northern Territory
NWT = North West Territories
NZ = New Zealand
OAS = Organisation of American States
OAU = Organisation of African Unity
Oman = Oman
Ont = Ontario
P = Portugal
Pak = Pakistan
Pal = Palestine
Pan = Panama
Par = Paraguay
PEI = Prince Edward Island
Phl = Philippines
PI = Pitcairn Islands (New Zealand)
PL = Poland
PNG = Papua New Guinea
Poly = Polynesia
PR = Puerto Rico
PRC = People's Republic of China
Qat = Qatar
Qld = Queensland
Que = Quebec
RF = Russian Federation
Rho = Rhodesia
RI = Rhode Island
RO = Romania
Rwa = Rwanda
SA = South Africa
Sask = Saskatchewan
Saudi = Saudi Arabia
SAus = South Australia
SC = Scotland
Sen = Senegal
Serb = Serbia

Sey = Seychelles
Sing = Singapore
SK = South Korea
SL = Sierra Leone
Slo = Slovakia
Slove = Slovenia
Smld = Somaliland
Sol = Solomon Islands
Som = Somalia
Sp = Spain
SrL = Sri Lanka
StC = Saint Christopher and Nevis
StH = St Helena
StL = Saint Lucia
StV = Saint Vincent and the Grenadines
Sud = Sudan
Sur = Surinam
Swa = Swaziland
Swe = Sweden
Swi = Switzerland
Syria = Syria
Tai = Taiwan
Taj = Tajikistan (CIS)
Tan = Tanzania
Tas = Tasmania
TCI = Turks and Caicos Islands
TDC = Tristan Da Cunha (St Helena)
Thai = Thailand
Tka = Tanganyika
Ton = Tonga

TR = Turkey
Trin = Trinidad and Tobago
Tun = Tunisia
Turkn = Turkmenistan (CIS)
Tuv = Tuvalu
UAE = United Arab Emirates
Ug = Uganda
UK = United Kingdom
UK-Irl = UK - Ireland (pre 1922)
UKEW = England and Wales
UKR = Ukraine (CIS)
UN = United Nations
UN ICT = United Nations International Criminal Tribunal
Uru = Uruguay
US = United States
Uzb = Uzbekistan (CIS)
Van = Vanuatu
Ven = Venezuela
VI = Virgin Islands
Vic = Victoria
Viet = Vietnam
WA = Western Australia
WI = West Indies
Wind = Windward Islands
WS = Western Samoa
WSah = Western Sahara
YT = Yukon Territory
Zai = Zaire
Zam = Zambia
Zim = Zimbabwe

Law Report/Journal Abbreviations

A.2d = Atlantic Reporter 2nd
A.B.C. = Australian Bankruptcy Cases
A.C. = Appeal Cases
A.C.D. = Administrative Court Digest
A.C.L.C. = Australian Company Law Cases
A.C.L.R. = Australian Company Law Reports
A.C.S.R. = Australian Companies and Securities Reports
A.C.T.R. = Australian Capital Territory Reports
A.D. = Appellate Division Reports (NY)
A.D.2d = Appellate Division Reports 2nd (NY)
A.F.T.R. = American Federal Tax Reports
A.I.R. All. = All India Reporter, Allahabad Series
A.I.R. Bom. = All India Reporter, Bombay Series
A.I.R. Delhi = All India Reporter, Delhi Series
A.I.R. Mad. = All India Reporter, Madras Series
A.I.R. P.C. = All India Reporter, Privy Council Series
A.I.R. S.C. = All India Reporter, Supreme Court Series
A.L.J. = Australian Law Journal
A.L.J.R. = Australian Law Journal Reports
A.L.M.D. = Australian Legal Monthly Digest
A.L.R. = Australian Law Reports
A.L.R. = American Law Reports (1919-48)
A.L.R. (C.N.) = Argus Law Reports, Current Notes (Australia)
A.L.R. Fed. = American Law Reports Federal
A.L.R.2d = American Law Reports 2nd (1948-65)
A.L.R.3d = American Law Reports 3rd (1965-80)
A.M.C. = American Maritime Cases
A.R. = Alberta Reports (Canada)
A.T.C. = Annotated Tax Cases
A.T.R. = Australian Tax Reports
Act. = Acton's Prize Causes Reports
Ad. & El. = Adolphus & Ellis' Reports
Adam = Adam's Justiciary Reports (Scotland)

Add. = Addams' Ecclesiastical Reports
Admin. L.R. = Administrative Law Reports
Al. = Aleyn's Select Cases
All E.R. = All England Law Reports
All E.R. (Comm) = All England Law Reports (Commercial Cases)
All E.R. (EC) = All England Law Reports (European Cases)
All E.R. Rep. = All England Law Reports Reprints
All N.L.R. = All Nigeria Law Reports
Am.Dec. = American Decisions
Am.Rep. = American Reports
Am.St.Rep. = American State Reports
Amb. = Ambler's Chancery Reports
And. = Anderson's Common Pleas Reports
Andr. = Andrews' King's Bench Reports
Anst. = Anstruther's Exchequer Reports
Ark. = Arkley's Justiciary Reports (Scotland)
Asp. = Aspinall's Maritime Cases (1870-1940)
Atk. = Atkyn's Chancery Reports
B. & Ad. = Barnewall and Adolphus's King's Bench Reports
B. & Ald. = Barnewall and Alderson's King's Bench Reports
B. & C. = Barnewall and Cresswell's King's Bench Reports
B. & C.R. = Reports of Bankruptcy and Companies (Winding up) Cases (1918-41)
B. & S. = Best and Smith's Queen's Bench Reports
B.C.C. = British Company Cases
B.C.L.C. = Butterworths Company Law Cases
B.C.L.R. = British Columbia Law Reports (Canada)
B.H.R.C. = Butterworths Human Rights Cases
B.L.G.R. = Butterworths Local Government Reports
B.L.R. = Building Law Reports

TABLE OF ABBREVIATIONS

B.M.L.R. = Butterworths Medico Legal Reports
B.N.C. = Brooke's New Cases
B.P.I.R. = Bankruptcy and Personal Insolvency Reports
B.R. = Bankruptcy Reporter
B.T.C. = British Tax Cases
B.V.C. = British VAT Cases
B.W.C.C. = Butterworths Workmen's Compensation Cases
BCCA = Court of Appeal of British Columbia (media neutral cite)
BCSC = Supreme Court of British Columbia (media neutral cite)
Ball & B. = Ball and Beatty's Irish Chancery Reports
Bank. L.R. = Banking Law Reports
Bankr.Ct.Dec. = Bankruptcy Court Decisions (CRR)
Barn. Ch. = Barnardiston's Chancery Reports
Barn. K.B. = Barnardiston's King's Bench Reports
Barnes = Barnes' Notes of Cases in Common Pleas
Beat. = Beatty's Irish Chancery Reports
Beav. = Beavan's Rolls Court Reports
Bel. = Bellewe's Reports (Les Ans du Roy Richard le Second)
Bell C.C. = Bell's Crown Cases Reserved
Belt's Supp. = Belt's Supplement to Vesey Senior's Reports
Benl. = Benloe's Reports
Benl. & Dal. Benloe = Benloe & Dalison's Reports (Benloe)
Benl. & Dal. Dalison = Benloe & Dalison's Reports (Dalison)
Bing. = Bingham's Common Pleas Reports
Bing. N.C. = Bingham, New Cases, English Common Pleas
Binn. = Binney's Reports (U.S.A.)
Bli. = Bligh's House of Lords Reports
Bli. N.S. = Bligh's House of Lords Reports, New Series
Bos. & P. = Bosanquet and Puller's Common Pleas Reports
Bos. & P. N.R. = Bosanquet and Puller's New Reports, Common Pleas
Bott P.L. = Bott's Poor Law Cases
Br. & Col. Pri. Cas. = British and Colonial Prize Cases
Bro. C.C. = W. Brown's Chancery Reports
Bro. P.C. = J. Brown's Parliamentary Cases
Brod. & Bing. = Broderip and Bingham's Common Pleas Reports
Broun = Broun's Justiciary Reports (Scotland)
Brown. & Lush. = Browning and Lushington's Admiralty Reports
Brownl. = Brownlow and Goldesborough's Common Pleas Reports
Bull. N.P. = Buller's Nisi Prius Reports
Bulst. = Bulstrode's King's Bench Reports
Bunb. = Bunbury's Exchequer Reports
Burr. = Burrow's King's Bench Reports tempore Mansfield
Burrell = Burrell's Admiralty Reports
Bus. L.R. = Business Law Reports
Bus. L.R. D = Business Law Reports Digest Pages
C. Rob. = Christopher Robinson's Admiralty Reports
C.B. = Common Bench Reports (Manning)
C.B. N.S. = Common Bench Reports (Manning), New Series
C.C.C. = Canadian Criminal Cases
C.C.C. (2d) = Canadian Criminal Cases, 2nd Series
C.C.C. (3d) = Canadian Criminal Cases, 3rd Series
C.C.L. Rep. = Community Care Law Reports
C.C.L.R. = Consumer Credit Law Reports
C.C.L.T. = Canadian Cases on the Law of Torts

C.C.P.A. = Court of Customs & Patent Appeals Reports
C.E.C. = European Community Cases
C.I.L.L. = Construction Industry Law Letter
C.I.L.R. = Cayman Islands Law Reports
C.L.C. = Commercial Law Cases
C.L.R. = Commonwealth Law Reports
C.M.L. Rev. = Common Market Law Review
C.M.L.R. = Common Market Law Reports
C.M.L.R. D = Common Market Law Reports Restrictive Practices Supplement
C.M.L.R. M = Common Market Law Reports Merger Decisions
C.O.D. = Crown Office Digest
C.P. Rep. = Civil Procedure Reports
C.P.C. (2d) = Carswell's Practice Cases, Second Series
C.P.C. (3d) = Carswell's Practice Cases, Third Series
C.P.L. = Current Property Law (1952-53)
C.P.L.R. = Civil Practice Law Reports
C.P.R. = Canadian Patent Reporter
C.P.R. (2d) = Canadian Patent Reporter, 2nd Series
C.P.R. (3d) = Canadian Patent Reporter, 3rd Series
C.P.R. (4th) = Canadian Patent Reporter, 4th Series
C.R. = Criminal Reports (Canada, 1946-67)
C.R. N.S. = Criminal Reports (New Series) (Canada, 1967-78)
C.R.R. = Canadian Rights Reporter
C.S. = Rapports Judiciaires de Quebec, Cour Superieure
CAT = Competition Commission Appeal Tribunal (media neutral cite)
CJ C.A.R. = Colorado Appellate Report
CSIH = Court of Session, Inner House (media neutral cite)
CSOH = Court of Session, Outer House (media neutral cite)
Cab. & Ell. = Cababe and Ellis' Queen's Bench Reports
Cal. = California Reports
Cal. Daily Op. Serv. = California Daily Opinion Service
Cal.3d = California Reports 3rd
Cal.4th = California Reports, 4th Series
Cal.Rptr.2d = California Reporter 2d (West's)
Cald. M.C. = Caldecott's Magistrates Cases
Calth. = Calthrop's City of London Special Cases
Camp. = Campbell's Nisi Prius Reports
Can. B.R. = Canadian Bar Review
Car. & K. = Carrington and Kirwan's Nisi Prius Reports
Car. & M. = Carrington and Marshman's Nisi Prius Reports
Car. & P. = Carrington and Payne's Nisi Prius Reports
Carswell For = Carswell Foreign
Cart. = Carter's Common Pleas Reports
Carth. = Carthew's King's Bench Reports
Cary = Cary's Chancery Reports
Cas. t. Hard. = Lee's King's Bench Cases tempore Hardwicke
Cas. t. Talb. = Cases in Equity tempore Talbot
Ch. = Chancery Division
Ch. Cas. = Cases Argued and Decreed in Chancery (Select Cases in Chancery)
Ch. Cas. in Ch. = Choyce Cases in Chancery
Chit. = Chitty's King's Bench Practice and Pleading Reports
Cl. & F. = Clark and Finnelly's House of Lords Reports
Clark's Rep. = Clark's Reports (Jamaica)
Clay. = Clayton's Reports and Pleas of Assises at Yorke
Clunet = Journal du Droit International (France)
Co. Rep. = Coke's King's Bench Reports
Coll. = Collyer's Chancery Cases tempore Bruce
Colles = Colles' Parliament Reports

TABLE OF ABBREVIATIONS

Com. = Comyns' King's Bench, Common Pleas and Exchequer Reports
Com. Cas. = Commercial Cases
Com. L.R. = Commercial Law Reports
Comb. = Comberbach's King's Bench Reports
Comp. A.R. = Competition Appeal Reports
Con. L.R. = Construction Law Reports
Const. L.J. = Construction Law Journal
Cooke = Cooke's Common Pleas Reports
Coop. Pr. Cas. = Cooper's Practice Cases
Coop. t. Brough. = Cooper's Select Cases of Lord Brougham
Coop. t. Cott. = Cooper's Chancery Reports tempore Cottenham
Costs L.R. = Costs Law Reports
Costs L.R. (Core Vol.) = Costs Law Reports, Core Volume
Coup. = Couper's Justiciary Reports (Scotland)
Cowp. = Cowper's King's Bench Reports
Cox C.C. = Cox's Criminal Cases
Cox Eq. Cas. = Cox's Equity Cases
Cr. & J. = Crompton and Jervis' Exchequer Reports
Cr. & M. = Crompton and Meeson's Exchequer Reports
Cr. & Ph. = Craig and Phillip's Chancery Reports
Cr. App. R. = Criminal Appeal Reports
Cr. App. R. (S.) = Criminal Appeal Reports (Sentencing)
Cr. M. & R. = Crompton, Meeson and Roscoe's Exchequer Reports
Cr. S. & P. = Craigie, Stewart and Paton's Scottish Appeal Cases
Cranch = Cranch's United States Supreme Court Reports
Crim. L.R. = Criminal Law Review
Cro. Car. = Croke's King's Bench Reports tempore Charles
Cro. Eliz. = Croke's King's Bench Reports tempore Elizabeth
Cro. Jac. = Croke's King's Bench Reports tempore James
Cun. = Cunningham's King's Bench Reports
Curt. = Curteis' Ecclesiastical Reports
D. = Dunlop, Bell and Murray's Reports, Session Cases, 2nd series (Scotland)
D. & R. = Decisions and Reports of the European Commission of Human Rights
D. (H.L.) = Dunlop's Session Cases, 2nd Series (House of Lords cases, Scotland)
D.L.R. = Dominion Law Reports (Canada, 1912-55)
D.L.R. (2d) = Dominion Law Reports (2d) (Canada, 1956-68)
D.L.R. (3d) = Dominion Law Reports (3d) (Canada, 1969-84)
D.L.R. (4th) = Dominion Law Reports (4th) (Canada, 1985-94)
D.R.A. = De-rating Appeals
D.T.C. = Dominion Tax Cases
Daily Telegraph = Daily Telegraph
Dan. = Daniell's Exchequer Reports
Dav. = Davis' Irish Reports
De G. = De Gex's Bankruptcy Reports
De G. & J. = De Gex and Jones' Chancery Reports
De G. & Sm. = De Gex and Smale's Chancery Reports
De G.F. & J. = De Gex, Fisher and Jones' Chancery Reports
De G.J. & S. = De Gex, Jones and Smith's Chancery Reports
De G.M. & G. = De Gex, Macnaghten and Gordons' Chancery Reports

Dea. & Sw. = Deane and Swabey's Ecclesiastical Reports
Deac. & Ch. = Deacon and Chitty's Bankruptcy Reports
Dears. = Dearsley's Crown Cases Reserved
Dears. & B. = Dearsley and Bell's Crown Cases Reserved
Den. = Denison and Pearce's Crown Cases Reserved
Dick. = Dickens' Chancery Reports
Disc. L.R. = Discrimination Law Reports
Dods. = Dodson's Admiralty Reports
Donn. = Donnelly's Chancery Cases
Doug. K.B. = Douglas' King's Bench Reports
Dow = Dow's House of Lords Cases
Dow. & Cl. = Dow and Clark's House of Lords Reports
Dowl. & L. = Dowling and Lowndes' Bail Court Reports
Dowl. & Ry. K.B. = Dowling and Ryland's King's Bench Reports
Dowl. & Ry. N.P. = Dowling and Ryland's Nisi Prius Cases
Dowl. N.S. = Dowling's Bail Court Reports, New Series
Dowl. Pr. Cas. = Dowling's Bail Court Practice Cases
Dr. & War. = Drury and Warren's Irish Chancery Reports
Dr. t. Sug. = Drury's Irish Chancery Cases tempore Sugden
Drew. = Drewry's Chancery Reports tempore Kindersley
Drew. & Sm. = Drewry and Smales' Chancery Reports
Dyer = Dyer's King's Bench Reports
E.A. = East African Law Reports
E.A.C.A. = Law Reports of the Court of Appeals for Eastern Africa
E.A.T.C. = East African Tax Cases
E.B.L.R. = Electronic Business Law Reports
E.C.C. = European Commercial Cases
E.C.D.R. = European Copyright and Design Reports
E.C.D.R. CN = European Copyright and Design Reports Case Notes
E.C.R. = European Court Reports
E.C.R. IA = European Court Reports
E.G. = Estates Gazette
E.G.C.S. = Estates Gazette Case Summaries
E.G.D. = Estates Gazette Digest of Cases
E.G.L.R. = Estates Gazette Law Reports (Bound Volume)
E.H.L.R. = Environmental Health Law Reports
E.H.L.R. Dig. = Environmental Health Reports Digest Pages
E.H.R.R. = European Human Rights Reports
E.H.R.R. CD = European Human Rights Reports, Commission Decisions
E.H.R.R. SE = European Human Rights Reports, Summaries and Extracts
E.L.R. = Education Law Reports
E.M.L.R. = Entertainment and Media Law Reports
E.N.P.R. = European National Patent Reports
E.P.O.R. = European Patent Office Reports
E.P.O.R. A = European Patent Office Reports A (1979-85, J decisions)
E.P.O.R. B = European Patent Office Reports B (1979-85, T decisions)
E.P.O.R. C = European Patent Office Reports C (1979-85, T decisions)
E.R. = English Reports
E.T.M.R. = European Trade Mark Reports
E.T.M.R. CN = European Trade Mark Reports Case Notes
ERC = Environment Reporter Cases (BNA)

TABLE OF ABBREVIATIONS

EWCA Civ = Court of Appeal (Civil)
EWCA Crim = Court of Appeal (Criminal)
EWHC = High Court
EWHC Admin = High Court (Administrative Court)
East = East's King's Bench Reports
East P.C. = East's Pleas of the Crown
Ed. C.R. = Education Case Reports
Ed. Law Rep. = Education Law Reporter
Eden = Eden's Chancery Reports
Edw. = Edward's Admiralty Reports
El. & Bl. = Ellis and Blackburn's Queen's Bench Reports
El. & El. = Ellis and Ellis' Queen's Bench Reports
El. Bl. & El. = Ellis, Blackburn and Ellis' Queen's Bench Reports
Emp. L.R. = Employment Law Reports
Employee Benefits Cas. = Employee Benefits Cases
Env. L.R. = Environmental Law Reports
Env. L.R. D = Environmental Law Reports Digest Pages
Envtl. L. Rep. = Environmental Law Reporter (ELR) (cases only)
Eq. Cas. Abr. = Abridgment of Cases in Equity
Eq. Rep. = Equity Reports
Esp. = Espinasse's Nisi Prius Reports
Eu. L.R. = European Law Reports
Ex. = Exchequer Reports (Welsby, Hurlstone and Gordon)
Ex. C.R. = Canada Law Reports, Exchequer Court
Extradition L.R. = Extradition Law Reports
F. = Federal Reporter (U.S.A.)
F. = Fraser's Session Cases, 5th Series (Scotland)
F. & F. = Foster and Finlason's Nisi Prius Reports
F. (Ct. of Sess.) = Faculty Decisions, Court of Session (Scotland)
F. (H.L.) = Fraser's Session Cases, 5th Series (House of Lords, Scotland)
F. (J.) = Fraser's Session Cases, 5th Series (Justiciary cases, Scotland)
F.2d = Federal Reporter, 2nd Series (U.S.A.)
F.3d = Federal Reporter, 3rd Series (U.S.A.)
F.C. = Canada Law Reports, Federal Court
F.C.R. = Family Court Reporter
F.L.R. = Family Law Reports
F.R.D. = Federal Rules Decisions (U.S.A.)
F.S.R. = Fleet Street Reports
F.Supp. = Federal Supplement (U.S.A.)
F.Supp.2d = Federal Supplement, Second Series
F.T.L.R. = Financial Times Law Reports
F.T.R. = Federal Trial Reports
FCA = Federal Court of Australia (media neutral cite)
FCA = Federal Court of Appeal of Canada (media neutral cite)
FCAFC = Federal Court of Australia, Full Court (media neutral cite)
Fam. = Family Division
Fam. L.R. = Family Law Reports (Scotland)
Fam. Law = Family Law
FamCA = Family Court of Australia (media neutral cite)
Fed. L.R. = Federal Law Reports (Australia)
Fed. R. Evid. Serv. = Federal Rules of Evidence Service (Callaghan's)
Fed. Sec. L. Rep. P = Federal Securities Law Reports (CCH)
Fed.R.Serv.2d = Federal Rules Service 2nd (Callaghan's)
Fed.R.Serv.3d = Federal Rules Service 3rd (Callaghan's)
Fed.Sent.R. = Federal Sentencing Reporter (U.S.A.)
Fin. L.R. = Financial Law Reports
Financial Times = Financial Times

Fitzg. = Fitz-Gibbons' King's Bench Reports
Fla. L. Weekly Fed. S = Florida Law Weekly, United States Supreme Court
Forr. = Forrest's Exchequer Reports
Fort. = Fortescue's Courts of Westminster Hall Reports
Fost. = Foster's Crown Cases
Freem. Ch. = Freeman's Chancery Reports
Freem. K.B. = Freeman's King's Bench and Common Pleas Reports
G. Coop. = Cooper's Chancery Reports
G.W.D. = Green's Weekly Digest (Scotland)
GRUR = Gewerblicher Rechtsschutz und Urheberrecht
Ga. = Georgia Reports
Giff. = Giffard's Chancery Reports
Gilb. Ch. = Gilbert's Cases in Equity
Gilb. K.B. = Gilbert's King's Bench Cases
Gl. & J. = Glyn and Jameson's Bankruptcy Reports
Godb. = Godbolt's Courts of Record at Westminster Reports
Gould. = Gouldsborough's King's Bench Reports
Gow = Gow's Nisi Prius Reports
Guardian = Guardian
H. & Tw. = Hall and Twells' Chancery Reports
H. Bl. = H. Blackstone's Common Pleas Reports
H.B.R. = Hansell's Bankruptcy Reports (1915-17)
H.K. Cases = Hong Kong Cases
H.K.L.R. = Hong Kong Law Reports
H.K.L.R.D. = Hong Kong Law Reports and Digest
H.L. Cas. = Clark's House of Lords Cases
H.L.R. = Housing Law Reports
H.R.C.D. = Human Rights Case Digest
H.R.L.R. = Human Rights Law Reports - UK Cases
HCA = High Court of Australia (media neutral cite)
HCJAC = High Court of Justiciary, Appeal (media neutral cite)
HCJT = High Court of Justiciary, Trial (media neutral cite)
Hag. Adm. = Haggard's Admiralty Reports
Hag. Con. = Haggard's Consistorial Reports
Hag. Ecc. = Haggard's Ecclesiastical Reports
Har. & Woll. = Harrison and Wollaston's King's Bench and Bail Court Reports
Hardres = Hardres' Exchequer Reports
Hare = Hare's Chancery Reports
Hay & M. = Hay and Marriott's Admiralty Reports
Hayes = Hayes' Irish Exchequer Reports
Hayes & J. = Hayes and Jones' Irish Exchequer Reports
Hem. & M. = Hemming and Miller's Chancery Reports
Het. = Hetley's Reports
Hob. = Hobart's Reports (Common Pleas and King's Bench)
Hodg. = Hodges' Common Pleas Reports
Holt Eq. = Holt's Equity Reports
Holt K.B. = Holt's King's Bench Reports
Holt N.P. = Holt's Nisi Prius Reports
Hous. L.R. = Housing Law Reports (Scottish)
Hov. Supp. = Hovenden's Supplement to Vesey Junior's Reports
How. = Howard's United States Supreme Court Reports
Hume = Hume's Session Cases (Scotland)
Hurl. & C. = Hurlstone and Coltman's Exchequer Reports
Hurl. & N. = Hurlstone and Norman's Exchequer Reports
Hut. = Hutton's Reports
I.C.L.R. = Irish Common Law Reports, Second Series (1850-66)
I.C.R. = Industrial Cases Reports

TABLE OF ABBREVIATIONS

I.H.R.R. = International Human Rights Reports
I.L.Pr. = International Litigation Procedure
I.L.R. = International Law Reports
I.L.R.M. = Irish Law Reports Monthly
I.L.T. = Irish Law Times
I.L.T.R. = Irish Law Times Reports
I.N.L.R. = Immigration and Nationality Law Reports
I.P.D. = Intellectual Property Decisions
I.P.L.R. = Industrial Property Law Reports (India)
I.P.R. = Intellectual Property Reports (Australia)
I.R. = Irish Reports
I.R. C.L. = Irish Reports, Common Law
I.R.L.R. = Industrial Relations Law Reports
I.T.C. = Srinivasan's Reports of Income Tax Cases (India)
I.T.C.L.R. = IT & Communications Law Reports
I.T.E.L.R. = International Trust and Estate Law Reports
I.T.L. Rep. = International Tax Law Reports
I.T.R. = Industrial Tribunal Reports
IEHC = High Court of Ireland (media neutral cite)
IESC = Supreme Court of Ireland (media neutral cite)
ITRD = International Trade Reporter Decisions (BNA)
III.2d = Illinois Reports, 2nd Series
III.Dec. = Illinois Decisions
Imm. A.R. = Immigration Appeal Reports
Ind. = Indiana Reports
Ind. Cas. = Indian Cases
Ind. L.R. = Indian Law Reports
Ind. L.R. All. = Indian Law Reports, Allahabad Series
Ind. L.R. Cal. = Indian Law Reports, Calcutta Series
Ind. L.R. Mad. = Indian Law Reports, Madras Series
Ind. L.R. Pat. = Indian Law Reports, Patna Series
Independent = Independent
Info. T.L.R. = Information Technology Law Reports
Inquest L.R. = Inquest Law Reports
Ir. Ch. R. = Irish Chancery Reports (1850-66)
Ir. Eq. = Irish Reports, Equity (1866-77)
Ir. Eq. R. = Irish Equity Reports, First Series (1838-50)
Ir. Jur. Rep. = Irish Jurist Reports
Ir. L.J. = Irish Law Journal
Ir. L.R. = Irish Law Reports
Irvine = Irvine's High Court and Circuit Courts of
   Justiciary Reports (Scotland)
J. & Lat. = Jones and La Touche's Irish Chancery
   Reports (1844-46)
J. Bridg. = Sir John Bridgman's Reports
J.C. = Justiciary Cases (Scotland)
J.J. = Jersey Judgments
J.L.R. = Jamaica Law Reports
J.P. = Justice of the Peace Reports
J.P. Rep. = Local Government Review Reports
J.P.I. Law = Journal of Personal Injury Law
J.P.I.L. = Journal of Personal Injury Litigation
J.P.L. = Journal of Planning & Environment Law
J.P.N. = Justice of the Peace Notes of Cases
Jac. = Jacob's Chancery Reports
Jac. & W. = Jacob and Walker's Chancery Reports
Jebb. & Sym. = Jebb and Syme's Queen's Bench
   Reports (Ireland, 1838-41)
Jenk. = Jenkins' Eight Centuries of Reports
Jer. L.R. = Jersey Law Reports
John. = Johnson's Chancery Reports
John. & H. = Johnson and Hemming's Chancery
   Reports
Jur. = Jurist
Jur. N.S. = Jurist, New Series
K.B. = King's Bench
K.I.R. = Knight's Industrial Law Reports
Kay = Kay's Chancery Reports
Kay & J. = Kay and Johnson's Chancery Reports

Keb. = Keble's King's Bench Reports
Keen = Keen's Rolls Court Reports
Keil. = Keilwey's Reports
Kel. = Kelyng's Divers Cases
Kel.W. = W Kelynge's King's Bench and Chancery
   Reports
Keny. = Kenyon's King's Bench Reports
Kn. = Knapp's Privy Council Appeal Cases
Ky. = Kentucky Reports
L. & T.R. = Landlord and Tenant Reports
L.D.B. = Legal Decisions Affecting Bankers
L.Ed. = Lawyers' Edition, United States Supreme Court
   Reporter
L.Ed.2d = Lawyers' Edition 2nd Series, United States
   Supreme Court Reporter
L.G. Rev. = Local Government Review
L.G.L.R. = Local Government Law Reports
L.G.R. = Local Government Reports
L.G.R.A. = Local Government Reports of Australia
L.J. = Law Journal (Newspaper)
L.J. Bcy. = Law Journal Reports, Bankruptcy (1832-
   80)
L.J. C.P. = Law Journal Reports, Common Pleas (1831-
   75)
L.J. Ch. = Law Journal Reports, Chancery (1831-1946)
L.J. Ex. = Law Journal Reports, Exchequer (1831-75)
L.J. K.B. = Law Journal Reports, King's Bench (1831-
   1946)
L.J. M.C. = Law Journal Reports, Magistrates Cases
   (1831-96)
L.J. N.C. = Law Journal, Notes of Cases
L.J. N.C.C.R. = Law Journal, County Court Reports
   (1934-47)
L.J. N.S. = Law Journal Reports, New Series (1832-
   1946)
L.J. O.S. = Law Journal Reports, Old Series (1822-31)
L.J. P. = Law Journal Reports, Probate, Divorce and
   Admiralty (1875-1946)
L.J. P. & M. = Law Journal Reports, Probate, Divorce
   and Matrimonial (1858-59, 1866-75)
L.J. P.C. = Law Journal Reports, Privy Council (1831-
   1946)
L.J. P.M. & A. = Law Journal Reports, Probate,
   Matrimonial and Admiralty (1860-65)
L.J. Q.B. = Law Journal Reports, Queen's Bench
   (1831-1946)
L.J.R. = Law Journal Reports (1947-49)
L.M.C.L.Q. = Lloyd's Maritime and Commercial Law
   Quarterly
L.R. A. & E. = Admiralty and Ecclesiastical Cases
   (1865-75)
L.R. App. Cas. = Appeal Cases (1875-90)
L.R. C.C.R. = Crown Cases Reserved
L.R. C.P. = Common Pleas (1865-75)
L.R. C.P.D. = Common Pleas Division (1875-80)
L.R. Ch. App. = Chancery Appeals (1865-75)
L.R. Ch. D. = Chancery Division (1875-90)
L.R. Eq. = Equity Cases
L.R. Ex. = Exchequer (1865-75)
L.R. Ex. D. = Exchequer Division (1875-80)
L.R. H.L. = English and Irish Appeals (1866-75)
L.R. Ind. App. = Indian Appeals
L.R. Ir. = Ireland
L.R. P. & D. = Probate and Divorce (1865-75)
L.R. P.C. = Privy Council
L.R. P.D. = Probate Division (1875-90)
L.R. Q.B. = Queen's Bench (1865-75)
L.R. Q.B.D. = Queen's Bench Division (1875-90)
L.R. R.P. = Restrictive Practices (1958-72)

TABLE OF ABBREVIATIONS

L.R. Sc. = Scotch and Divorce Appeals
L.R.B. = Law Reports of the Bahamas
L.R.C. = Law Reports of the Commonwealth
L.R.C. (Const) = Law Reports of the Commonwealth (Constitutional & Administrative Reports)
L.R.L.R. = Lloyd's Reinsurance Law Reports
L.R.R.M. (BNA) = Labor Relations Reference Manual (BNA)
L.S.G. = Law Society Gazette
L.T. = Law Times (1859-1965)
L.T. O.S. = Law Times (Old Series) (1843-59)
L.T.R. = Law Times Reports (1859-1947)
LS Law Medical = LS Law Medical
Lab.Cas. P = Labor Cases (CCH)
Lane = Lane's Exchequer Reports
Lat. = Latch's King's Bench Reports
Ld. Raym. = Lord Raymond's King's Bench Reports
Le. & Ca. = Leigh and Cave's Crown Cases Reserved
Leach = Leach's Cases in Crown Law
Lee = Lee's Ecclesiastical Reports
Leo. = Leonard's Reports of the Courts at Westminster
Lev. = Levinz's King's Bench and Common Pleas Reports
Lewin = Lewin's Crown Cases Reserved
Ley = Ley's Court of Wards Reports
Lil. = Lilly's Assise Cases
Litt. = Littleton's Common Bank and Exchequer Reports
Ll. & G. t Sug. = Lloyd and Goold's Reports of Chancery in Ireland tempore Sugden
Ll. L. Pr. Cas. = Lloyd's List Prize Cases (1914-24)
Ll. L. Pr. Cas. (N.S.) = Lloyd's List Prize Cases, Second Series (1939-53)
Ll. L. Rep. = Lloyd's List Law Reports (1919-50)
Lloyd's List = Lloyd's List
Lloyd's Rep. = Lloyd's Law Reports (1951-)
Lloyd's Rep. Bank. = Lloyd's Law Reports Banking
Lloyd's Rep. I.R. = Lloyd's Law Reports, Insurance & Reinsurance
Lloyd's Rep. Med. = Lloyd's Law Reports Medical
Lloyd's Rep. P.N. = Lloyd's Law Reports Professional Negligence
Lofft = Lofft's King's Bench Reports
Lush. = Lushington's Admiralty Reports
Lut. = Lutwyche's Reports (Livre des Entries)
Lut. Reg. Cas. = Lutwyche's Entries and Reports, Common Pleas (Registration Cases)
M'Cle. = M'Cleland's Exchequer Reports
M'Cle. & Y. = M'Cleland and Younge's Exchequer Reports
M. = Macpherson's Session Cases, 3rd Series (Scotland)
M. & S. = Maule and Selwyn's King's Bench Reports
M. & W. = Meeson and Welsby's Exchequer Reports
M. (H.L.) = Macpherson's Session Cases, 3rd Series (House of Lords cases, Scotland)
M.C.C. = MacGillivray's Copyright Cases
M.H.L.R. = Mental Health Law Reports
M.L.J. = Malaysian Law Journal
M.P.L.R. = Municipal and Planning Law Reports (Canada)
M.P.R. = Maritime Provinces Reports (Canada)
M.R. = Mauritius Reports
Mac. & G. = Macnaghten and Gordon's Chancery Reports
Macl. & R. = Maclean and Robinson's House of Lords Cases
Macq. = Macqueen's Scottish Appeal Cases
Madd. = Maddock's Chancery Reports

Man. & G. = Manning and Granger's Common Pleas Reports
Man. & Ry. K.B. = Manning and Ryland's King's Bench Reports
Man. & Ry. M.C. = Manning and Ryland's Magistrates Cases Reports
Man. Law = Managerial Law
Mans. = Manson's Bankruptcy and Companies Winding up Cases (1894-1913)
Manx L.R. = Manx Law Reports
March N.C. = March's New Cases
Masons C.L.R. = Masons Computer Law Reports
Masons C.L.R. Rep. = Masons Computer Law Reports Reprints (Case Digests, 1994-97)
Mass. = Massachusetts Reports
Med. L.R. = Medical Law Reports
Media L. Rep. = Media Law Reporter (BNA)
Mer. = Merivale's Chancery Reports
Misc. = New York Miscellaneous Reports
Misc.2d = Miscellaneous Reports, 2nd Series (New York)
Mod. = Modern Reports
Mol. = Molloy's Chancery Reports (Ireland, 1927-31)
Mont. D. & De G. = Montagu, Deacon and De Gex's Bankruptcy Reports
Moo. Ind. App. = Moore's Appeals from the East Indies Reports
Moo. K.B. = Moore's King's Bench Reports
Moo. P.C. = Moore's Privy Council Cases
Moo. P.C. N.S. = Moore's Privy Council Cases, New Series
Mood. & M. = Moody and Malkin's Nisi Prius Reports
Mood. & R. = Moody and Robinson's Nisi Prius Reports
Mood. C.C. = Moody's Crown Cases Reserved
Mor. Dic. = Morison's Dictionary of Decisions (Scotland)
Morr. = Morrell's Bankruptcy Reports
Mos. = Moseley's Chancery Reports
My. & C. = Mylne and Craig's Chancery Reports
My. & K. = Mylne and Keen's Chancery Reports
N.B. Eq. = New Brunswick Equity Reports
N.B.R. = National Bankruptcy Register Reports
N.B.R. 2d = New Brunswick Reports, 2nd Series
N.C. = Notes of Cases, Ecclesiastical and Maritime (ed. Thornton)
N.E. = North Eastern Reporter (U.S.A.)
N.E.2d = North Eastern Reporter 2nd
N.H. = New Hampshire Reports
N.I. = Northern Ireland Law Reports
N.I.J.B. = Northern Ireland Judgment Bulletin
N.I.L.Q. = Northern Ireland Legal Quarterly
N.J. = New Jersey Reports
N.L.J. = New Law Journal
N.L.J. Rep. = New Law Journal Reports
N.L.R. = New Law Reports (Sri Lanka)
N.P.C. = New Property Cases
N.R. = National Reporter (Canada)
N.S.R. 2d = Nova Scotia Reports, 2nd Series
N.S.W.L.R. = New South Wales Law Reports
N.S.W.R. = New South Wales Reports (1960-70)
N.W. = North Western Reporter (U.S.A.)
N.W.2d = North Western Reporter, 2nd Series (U.S.A.)
N.Y. = New York Reports
N.Y.2d = New York Reports, 2nd Series
N.Y.S. = New York Supplement Reporter
N.Y.S.2d = New York Supplement Reporter, 2nd Series
N.Z.L.R. = New Zealand Law Reports
NDLR P = National Disability Law Reporter

TABLE OF ABBREVIATIONS

NICA = Court of Appeal (Northern Ireland) (media neutral cite)

NICh = Chancery Division (Northern Ireland) (media neutral cite)

NIFam = Family Division (Northern Ireland) (media neutral cite)

NIQB = Queen's Bench Division (Northern Ireland) (media neutral cite)

NSWCA = Court of Appeal of New South Wales (media neutral cite)

NSWSC = Supreme Court of New South Wales (media neutral cite)

NZCA = Court of Appeal of New Zealand (media neutral cite)

NZSC = Supreme Court of New Zealand (media neutral cite)

Nels. = Nelson's Chancery Reports

Nev. & M. K.B. = Neville and Manning's King's Bench Reports

New Rep. = New Reports

Nfld. & P.E.I.R. = Newfoundland and Prince Edward Island Reports

Noy = Noy's Reports

O'M. & H. = O'Malley and Hardcastle's Election Cases

O. Bridg. = Sir Orlando Bridgman's Reports

O.F.L.R. = Offshore Financial Law Reports

O.J. E.P.O. = Official Journal of the European Patent Office

O.L.R. = Ontario Law Reports (1901-30)

O.P.L.R. = Occupational Pensions Law Reports

O.R. = Ontario Reports (1882-1900, 1931-)

O.R. (2d) = Ontario Reports, 2nd Series

O.R. (3d) = Ontario Reports, 3rd Series

Owen = Owen's King's Bench and Common Pleas Reports

P. = Pacific Reporter (U.S.A.)

P. = Probate

P. & C.R. = Property, Planning and Compensation Reports

P. & C.R. D = Property and Compensation Reports Digest Pages

P. & C.R. DG = Property, Planning and Compensation Reports Digest Pages

P.Wms. = Peere Williams' Chancery Reports

P.2d = Pacific Reporter, 2nd Series (U.S.A.)

P.A.D. = Planning Appeal Decisions

P.C.C. = Palmer's Company Cases

P.I.Q.R. P = Personal Injury and Quantum Reports

P.I.Q.R. Q = Personal Injury and Quantum Reports

P.L.C.R. = Planning Law Case Reports

P.L.R. = Planning Law Reports

P.N.G.L.R. = Papua New Guinea Law Reports

P.N.L.R. = Professional Negligence and Liability Reports

Pal. L.R. = Palestine Law Reports

Palm. = Palmer's Reports

Park on Ins. = Park on Insurance, 8th ed.

Park. = Parker's Exchequer Reports

Pat. = Paton's Scottish Appeals, House of Lords

Peake = Peake's Nisi Prius Reports

Peake Add. Cas. = Peake's Additional Cases

Pens. App. R. = Pensions Appeal Reports

Pens. L.R. = Pensions Law Reports

Perry & K. = Perry and Knapp's Election Cases

Ph. = Phillips' Chancery Reports

Phil. Ecc. = Phillimore's Ecclesiastical Reports

Plow. = Plowden's Commentaries

Po. L.R. = Police Law Reports

Pollex. = Pollexfen's Special Cases

Pop. = Sir John Popham's Reports

Prec. Ch. = Precedents in Chancery

Price = Price's Exchequer Reports

Prison L.R. = Prison Law Reports

Q.B. = Queen's Bench

Q.B. = Queen's Bench Reports (1841-1856)

Q.J.P. = Queensland Justice of the Peace Reports

Q.L.J. = Queensland Law Journal Reports (1897-1901)

Q.R. = Quantum Reports (Kemp & Kemp)

Q.S.R. = Queensland State Reports (1902-57)

Q.W.N. = Queensland Law Reporter and Weekly Notes (1908-72)

QCA = Court of Appeal of Queensland (media neutral cite)

QSC = Supreme Court of Queensland (media neutral cite)

Qd. R. = Queensland State Reports (1958-)

R. = Retties Session Cases, 4th Series (Scotland)

R. & I.T. = Rating and Income Tax Reports

R. (H.L.) = Retties Session Cases, 4th Series (House of Lords cases, Scotland)

R. (J.) = Retties Session Cases, 4th Series (Justiciary cases, Scotland)

R.A. = Rating Appeals

R.C.N. = Rating Case Notes

R.F.L. = Reports of Family Law (Canada)

R.I.C.S. = Royal Institution of Chartered Surveyors, Scottish Lands Valuation Appeal Reports

R.J.Q. B.R. = Rapports Judiciares de Quebec, Cour du Banc du Roi (1875-91)

R.L.R. = Road Law Reports

R.P.C. = Reports of Patent Cases

R.P.R. = Real Property Reports (Canada)

R.R.C. = Ryde's Rating Cases

R.T.R. = Road Traffic Reports

R.V.R. = Rating and Valuation Reporter

RICO Bus. Disp. Guide = RICO Business Disputes Guide (CCH)

Ram. = Ramanathan's Reports, Sri Lanka

Re. L.R. = Reinsurance Law Reports

Recueil = Recueil de la Jurisprudence de la Cour (ECJ)

Rep. Ch. = Reports of Cases in Chancery

Rep. L.R. = Reparation Law Reports (Scottish)

Rep. L.R. (Quantum) = Reparation Law Reports, Quantum Cases (Scottish)

Rep. t. Finch = Reports in Chancery tempore Finch

Ridge. t. Hard. = Ridgeway's King's Bench and Chancery Reports tempore Hardwicke

Rob. = Robinson's Scottish Appeal Cases, House of Lords

Rob. Ecc. = Robertson's Ecclesiastical Reports

Roll. Abr. = Rolle's Abridgment des Plusieurs Cases

Rolle = Rolle's King's Bench Reports

Rose = Rose's Bankrupty Cases

Russ. = Russell's Chancery Reports

Russ. & M. = Russell and Mylne's Chancery Reports

Russ. & Ry. = Russell and Ryan's Crown Cases Reserved

Russ. Cr. = Russell on Crime

Ry. & M. = Ryan and Moody's Nisi Prius Reports

S. = Shaw's Session Cases, 1st Series (Scotland)

S.A. = South African Law Reports

S.A. (A.D.) = South African Law Reports (Appellate Division)

S.A. (T.P.D.) = South African Law Reports (Transvaal Provincial Division)

S.A.C.R. = South African Criminal Law Reports

S.A.L.J. = South African Law Journal

S.A.S.R. = South Australian State Reports

TABLE OF ABBREVIATIONS

S.C. = Session Cases (Scotland)
S.C. (H.L.) = Session Cases (House of Lords cases, Scotland)
S.C. (J.) = Session Cases (Justiciary 1907-16, Scotland)
S.C. (P.C.) = Session Cases (Privy Council Cases, Scotland)
S.C. (S.A.) = Supreme Court Reports (South Africa)
S.C.C.R. = Scottish Criminal Case Reports
S.C.C.R. (Supp.) = Scottish Criminal Case Reports Supplement
S.C.L.R. = Scottish Civil Law Reports
S.C.R. = Canada Law Reports, Supreme Court
S.Ct. = Supreme Court Reporter
S.E. = South Eastern Reporter (U.S.A.)
S.E.2d = South Eastern Reporter, 2nd Series (U.S.A.)
S.J. = Solicitors Journal (Old)
S.J.L.B. = Solicitors Journal Law Brief
S.L.C.R. = Scottish Land Court Reports
S.L.C.R. App. = Scottish Land Court Reports (Appendix)
S.L.L.P. = Scottish Licensing Law and Practice
S.L.R. = Scottish Law Reporter (1865-1924)
S.L.T. = Scots Law Times
S.L.T. (Land Ct) = Scots Law Times (Land Court Reports)
S.L.T. (Land Ct.) = Scots Law Times (Land Ct)
S.L.T. (Lands Tr) = Scots Law Times (Lands Tribunal Reports)
S.L.T. (Lands Tr.) = Scots Law Times (Lands Tr)
S.L.T. (Lyon Ct) = Scots Law Times (Lyon Court Reports)
S.L.T. (Lyon Ct.) = Scots Law Times (Lyon Ct)
S.L.T. (Notes) = Scots Law Times (Notes)
S.L.T. (P.L.) = Scots Law Times (Poor Law Reports)
S.L.T. (Sh Ct) = Scots Law Times (Sheriff Court Reports)
S.L.T. (Sh Ct.) = Scots Law Times (Sheriff Court)
S.L.T. (Sh. Ct.) = Scots Law Times (Sheriff Court)
S.N. = Session Notes
S.R. (N.S.W.) = New South Wales State Reports (1901-)
S.S.L.R. = Straits Settlements Law Reports (Malaysia)
S.T.C. = Simons Tax Cases
S.T.C. (S.C.D.) = Simons Tax Cases: Special Commissioners Decisions
S.T.I. = Simon's Tax Intelligence
S.W.2d = South Western Reporter, 2nd Series (U.S.A.)
SCC = Supreme Court of Canada (media neutral cite)
SGCA = Court of Appeal of Singapore (media neutral cite)
SGHC = High Court of Singapore (media neutral cite)
Salk. = Salkeld's King's Bench Reports
Sask. R. = Saskatchewan Reports
Saund. = Saunder's King's Bench Reports
Sav. = Savile's Common Bench Reports
Say. = Sayer's King's Bench Reports
Sc. Jur. = Scottish Jurist
Sch. & L. = Schoales and Lefroy's Irish Chancery Reports
Scotsman = Scotsman
Scott N.R. = Scott's New Common Pleas Reports
Sel. Cas. Ch. = Select Cases in Chancery tempore King
Sess. Cas. K.B. = Session Cases touching settlements (England, 1710-48)
Sh. App. = Shaw's Scottish Appeal Cases, House of Lords
Sh. Ct. Rep. = Scottish Law Review, Sheriff Court Reports (1885-1963)

Shaw = Shaw's Justiciary Cases (Scotland)
Ship. Gaz. = Shipping Gazette
Show. K.B. = Shower's King's Bench Reports
Show. Parl. Cas. = Shower's Cases in Parliament
Sid. = Siderfin's King's Bench Reports
Sim. = Simon's Vice Chancellors Reports
Sim. & St. = Simon and Stuart's Chancery Reports
Sim. N.S. = Simon's Vice Chancellors Reports, New Series
Skin. = Skinner's King's Bench Reports
Sm. & G. = Smales and Giffard's Chancery Reports
Smith & B. = Smith and Batty's King's Bench Reports (Ireland, 1824-25)
Smith L.C. = Smith's Leading Cases on Various Branches of the Law
Sneed (TN) = Sneed's Tennessee Reports
So.2d = Southern Reporter, 2nd Series (U.S.A.)
Sol. = The Solicitor
Sp. Ecc. & Ad. = Spinks' Ecclesiastical and Admiralty Reports
Sp. Pri. Cas. = Spinks' Admiralty Prize Court Reports
St. Tr. = Cobbett and Howell's State Trials
St. Tr. (N.S.) = MacDonnell's State Trials, New Series
Stark. = Starkie's Nisi Prius Reports
Str. = Strange's King's Bench Reports
Sty. = Style's Modern Reports
Sw. = Swabey's Admiralty Reports
Sw. & Tr. = Swabey and Tristram's Reports
Swans. = Swanston's Chancery Reports
Syme = Syme's Justiciary Reports (Scotland)
T. Jones = Sir Thomas Jones' King's Bench Reports
T. Raym. = Sir Thomas Raymond's King's Bench Reports
T.C. = Tax Cases
T.C.L.R. = Technology and Construction Law Reports
T.L.R. = Times Law Reports
T.R. = Taxation Reports (1939-81)
T.S. = Transvaal Supreme Court Reports (South Africa)
TCC = Tax Court of Canada (media neutral cite)
Taml. = Tamlyn's Chancery Reports
Tang. L.R. (R.) = Tanganyika Law Reports
Tas. R. = Tasmanian Reports (1979-)
Tas. S.R. = Tasmanian State Reports (1941-98)
Taunt. = Taunton's Common Pleas Reports
Tenn. = Tennessee Reports
Term Rep. = Durnford and East's Term Reports
Times = Times
Toth. = Tothill's Chancery Transactions
Tr. Consist. J. = Tristram's Consistory Judgments
Tr. L. = Trading Law
Tr. L.R. = Trading Law Reports
Traff. Cas. = Traffic Cases
Trin. L.R. = Trinidad Law Reports
Turn. & R. = Turner and Russell's Chancery Reports
Tyr. = Tyrwhitt's Exchequer Reports
U.C.R. = Upper Canada Reports
U.K.C.L.R. = UK Competition Law Reports
U.K.H.R.R. = United Kingdom Human Rights Reports
U.K.T. = UK Transcripts
U.S. = United States Supreme Court Reports
U.S.App.D.C. = United States District Court for the District of Columbia
U.S.P.Q. = United States Patent Quarterly (BNA)
U.S.P.Q.2d = United States Patent Quarterly 2nd (BNA)
UCC Rep.Serv. = Uniform Commercial Code Reporting Service (Callaghan's)
UKAIT = Asylum and Immigration Tribunal (media neutral cite)

TABLE OF ABBREVIATIONS

UKHL = House of Lords
UKIAT = Immigration Appeal Tribunal
UKPC = Privy Council
UKPC D = Privy Council (Devolution)
USLW = United States Law Week
V. & B. = Vesey and Beames' Chancery Reports
V. & D.R. = Value Added Tax and Duties Reports
V.A.T.T.R. = Value Added Tax Tribunal Reports
V.L.R. = Victorian Law Reports (1875-1956)
V.R. = Victorian Reports (1957 -)
VSC = Supreme Court of Victoria (media neutral cite)
Va. = Virginia Reports
Vaugh. = Vaughan's Common Pleas Reports
Vent. = Ventris' King's Bench Reports
Vern. = Vernon's Chancery Reports
Ves. Jr. = Vesey Junior's Chancery Reports
Ves. Sen. = Vesey Senior's Chancery Reports
W. & S. = Wilson and Shaw's Scottish Appeal Cases, House of Lords
W. Jones = Sir William Jones' Reports
W. Rob. = W. Robinson's Admiralty Reports
W.A.C.A. = West African Court of Appeal Reports
W.A.L.R. = Western Australian Law Reports (1875-1956)
W.A.R. = Western Australian Reports (1957-)
W.I.R. = West Indian Reports
W.L.R. = Weekly Law Reports
W.N. = Weekly Notes (1866-1952)
W.N. (N.S.W.) = Weekly Notes, New South Wales
W.P.A.R. = War Pensions Appeal Reports

W.P.C. = Webster's Patent Cases
W.R. = Weekly Reporter (1853-1906)
W.T.L.R. = Wills & Trusts Law Reports
W.W.R. = Western Weekly Law Reports (Canada)
Wall. = Wallace's United States Supreme Court Reports
West H.L. = West's House of Lords Cases
West t. Hard. = West's Chancery Reports tempore Hardwicke
Wheat. = Wheaton's Supreme Court Reports (U.S.A.)
White = White's Justiciary Reports (Scotland)
Wight. = Wightwick's Exchequer Reports
Will. Woll. & Dav. = Willmore, Wollaston and Davison's Queen's Bench Reports
Willes = Willes' Common Pleas Reports
Wilm. = Wilmot's Notes and Opinions, King's Bench
Wils. Ch. = Wilson's Chancery Reports
Wils. Ex. = Wilson's Exchequer in Equity Reports
Wils. K.B. = Wilson's King's Bench Reports
Winch = Winch's Reports
Wm. Bl. = W. Blackstone's King's Bench Reports
Y. = Younge's Exchequer in Equity Reports
Y. & C. Ch. = Younge and Collier's Chancery Cases
Y. & C. Ex. = Younge and Collier's Exchequer Reports
Y. & J. = Younge and Jervis' Exchequer Reports
Y.B. = Year Books
Y.B. (R.S.) = Year Books, Rolls Series
Y.B. (S.S.) = Year Books, Selden Society
Yel. = Yelverton's King's Bench Reports
Yer. = Yerger's Tennessee Reports
Z.L.R. = Zimbabwe Law Reports

CURRENT LAW

PART I

CASE CITATOR 2007 (ENGLAND)

The Current Law Case Citator comprises in a single table:

(i) Full case name of cases reported in 2007

(ii) The judicial history of any case of whatever date which has been considered, applied, overruled, etc., in 2007

Note: Figures appearing in bold type indicate the paragraph in the Current Law Year Book at which the case is digested

1st Property Finance Ltd v Martin & Haigh (A Firm) [2006] P.N.L.R. 29, Ch D ...... *Digested*, 07/**3396**

3C Waste Ltd v Mersey Waste Holdings Ltd [2006] EWHC 2598 (Comm); [2007] Env. L.R. 17; [2007] J.P.L. 880, QBD (Comm) .... *Digested*, 07/**1522**
3M I/Withdrawal of application (J37/03) [2007] E.P.O.R. 28, EPO (Legal Bd App) .. *Digested*, 07/**2574**

7E Communications Ltd v Vertex Antennentechnik GmbH [2007] EWCA Civ 140; [2007] 1 W.L.R. 2175; [2007] 2 All E.R. (Comm) 798; [2007] 2 Lloyd's Rep. 411; [2007] C.P. Rep. 23; [2007] 1 C.L.C. 417; [2007] I.L.Pr. 18; *Times*, March 19, 2007, CA (Civ Div); affirming (Unreported, March 29, 2006), QBD .... *Digested*, 07/**364**

64-70 Holywell Lane, London, EC2, Re see Spirerose Ltd v Transport for London

83 Tower Hill, Upper Dormington, Hereford, Re see White v Herefordshire Council

566935 BC Ltd v Allianz Insurance Co of Canada [2007] Lloyd's Rep. I.R. 503, CA (BC)

A v A [2004] EWHC 2818 (Fam); [2006] 2 F.L.R. 115; [2006] Fam. Law 435, Fam Div .... *Applied*, 07/1689
A v A; *sub nom* NA v MA [2006] EWHC 2900 (Fam); [2007] 1 F.L.R. 1760; [2007] Fam. Law 295, Fam Div .... *Digested*, 07/**1708**
A vA [2007] EWHC 99 (Fam); [2007] 2 F.L.R. 467; [2007] Fam. Law 791, Fam Div
A v B [2006] EWHC 2006 (Comm); [2007] 1 All E.R. (Comm) 591; [2007] 1 Lloyd's Rep. 237; [2007] 2 C.L.C. 157, QBD (Comm) .... *Digested*, 07/**237**: *Applied*, 07/353
A v B (A Firm) see A v B Plc
A v B (Costs) [2007] EWHC 54 (Comm); [2007] 1 All E.R. (Comm) 633; [2007] 1 Lloyd's Rep. 358; [2007] 2 C.L.C. 203; [2007] Bus. L.R. D59, QBD (Comm) . *Digested*, 07/**396**
A v B (Damages: Paternity) [2007] EWHC 1246 (QB); [2007] 2 F.L.R. 1051; [2007] 3 F.C.R. 861; [2007] Fam. Law 909; (2007) 104(16) L.S.G. 26, QBD
A v B Hospitals NHS Trust [2006] EWHC 1178 (Admin), QBD (Admin) .... *Applied*, 07/3071
A v B Hospitals NHS Trust [2006] EWHC 2833 (Admin); [2007] LS Law Medical 303; (2007) 95 B.M.L.R. 240, QBD (Admin) .... *Digested*, 07/**3061**: *Applied*, 07/3081

A v B Plc; *sub nom* B and C v A; A v B (A Firm) [2002] EWCA Civ 337; [2003] Q.B. 195; [2002] 3 W.L.R. 542; [2002] 2 All E.R. 545; [2002] E.M.L.R. 21; [2002] 1 F.L.R. 1021; [2002] 2 F.C.R. 158; [2002] H.R.L.R. 25; [2002] U.K.H.R.R. 457; 12 B.H.R.C. 466; [2002] Fam. Law 415; (2002) 99(17) L.S.G. 36; (2002) 152 N.L.J. 434; (2002) 146 S.J.L.B. 77; *Times*, March 13, 2002; *Independent*, March 19, 2002; *Daily Telegraph*, March 11, 2002, CA (Civ Div); reversing [2001] 1 W.L.R. 2341; [2002] 1 All E.R. 449; [2002] E.M.L.R. 7; [2002] 1 F.L.R. 179; [2002] 1 F.C.R. 369; [2002] Fam. Law 100; (2001) 98(41) L.S.G. 34; (2001) 145 S.J.L.B. 235; *Times*, November 2, 2001; *Independent*, November 16, 2001, QBD . . . . *Digested*, 02/**3220**:
Applied, 03/297, 04/1391, 04/1496: *Approved*, 04/2673:
Considered, 02/3219, 03/2923, 03/2941, 07/2250, 07/2887:
Distinguished, 03/1217

A v Essex CC; *joined cases* J v Worcestershire CC; S v Hertfordshire CC; B v Suffolk CC; A2/2007/1792, CA (Civ Div); affirming [2007] EWHC 1652 (QB); [2007] H.R.L.R. 38; [2007] E.L.R. 521, QBD
A v Germany (10482/83) (1984) 6 E.H.R.R. CD587, Eur Comm HR . . . . *Considered*, 07/2193
A v Headteacher and Governors of Lord Grey School see Ali v Lord Grey School Governors
A v Hertfordshire CC see R. (on the application of A) v Hertfordshire CC
A v HM Treasury see M v HM Treasury
A v Rothschild Trust Cayman Ltd [2006] W.T.L.R. 1129; (2006-07) 9 I.T.E.L.R. 307, Grand Court (CI) . . . . *Digested*, 06/**4398**
A v Secretary of State for the Home Department see RA (Iraq) v Secretary of State for the Home Department
A v Secretary of State for the Home Department; *sub nom* X v Secretary of State for the Home Department [2004] UKHL 56; [2005] 2 A.C. 68; [2005] 2 W.L.R. 87; [2005] 3 All E.R. 169; [2005] H.R.L.R. 1; [2005] U.K.H.R.R. 175; 17 B.H.R.C. 496; [2005] Imm. A.R. 103; (2005) 155 N.L.J. 23; (2005) 149 S.J.L.B. 28; *Times*, December 17, 2004; *Independent*, December 21, 2004, HL; reversing [2002] EWCA Civ 1502; [2004] Q.B. 335; [2003] 2 W.L.R. 564; [2003] 1 All E.R. 816; [2003] H.R.L.R. 3; [2002] U.K.H.R.R. 1141; 13 B.H.R.C. 394; [2003] A.C.D. 10; (2002) 99(46) L.S.G. 33; (2002) 146 S.J.L.B. 246; *Times*, October 29, 2002, CA (Civ Div); affirming [2002] H.R.L.R. 45; [2002] A.C.D. 98, Sp Imm App Comm . . . . *Digested*, 05/**2105**:
Applied, 04/2004, 05/1139, 07/2171: *Considered*, 06/656, 07/2172, 07/2300
A v Secretary of State for the Home Department; *joined cases* D v Secretary of State for the Home Department; C v Secretary of State for the Home Department [2005] UKHL 71; [2006] 2 A.C. 221; [2005] 3 W.L.R. 1249; [2006] 1 All E.R. 575; [2006] H.R.L.R. 6; [2006] U.K.H.R.R. 225; 19 B.H.R.C. 441; (2005) 155 N.L.J. 1924; *Times*, December 9, 2005; *Independent*, December 14, 2005, HL; reversing [2004] EWCA Civ 1123; [2005] 1 W.L.R. 414; [2004] H.R.L.R. 38; (2004) 154 N.L.J. 1291; (2004) 148 S.J.L.B. 1029; *Times*, October 5, 2004, CA (Civ Div) . . . . *Digested*, 06/**2200**:
Applied, 06/2621: *Followed*, 07/3691
A v Secretary of State for the Home Department [2006] EWCA Civ 149; [2006] Imm. A.R. 455, CA (Civ Div) . . . . *Digested*, 07/**2273**
A v South Staffordshire Magistrates see R. (on the application of A) v South Staffordshire Magistrates Court
A v United Kingdom see R v United Kingdom (A/121)
A v United Kingdom (10358/83) (1984) 6 E.H.R.R. CD587, Eur Comm HR . . . . *Applied*, 07/2193
A v X AG (4C.371/2005) [2007] E.T.M.R. 47, BG (Swi) . . . . *Digested*, 07/**2670**
A Ahlstrom Osakeyhtio v Commission of the European Communities (C89/85); *sub nom* Wood Pulp Cartel, Re (C89/85) [1993] E.C.R. I-1307; [1993] 4 C.M.L.R. 407; *Financial Times*, April 6, 1993, ECJ (5th Chamber) . . . . *Digested*, 93/**4254**:
Considered, 98/726, 06/603, 07/605
A & B v C & D [1982] 1 Lloyd's Rep. 166, QBD (Comm) . . . . *Digested*, 82/**2571**:
Applied, 07/237: *Distinguished*, 06/198
A Brunsteiner GmbH v Bayerische Motorenwerke AG (BMW) (C-376/05) [2006] E.C.R. I-11383; [2007] R.T.R. 20; [2007] 4 C.M.L.R. 7, ECJ (3rd Chamber) . . . *Digested*, 07/**1568**
A Hospital v SW see A Hospital v W
A Hospital v W; *sub nom* A Hospital v SW [2007] EWHC 425 (Fam); [2007] LS Law Medical 273, Fam Div . . . . *Digested*, 07/**1986**
A Local Authority v MA see SA (Vulnerable Adult with Capacity: Marriage), Re
A Local Authority v N see K, Re
A Local Authority v W see W (Children) (Identification: Restrictions on Publication), Re
A Solicitor (No.7 of 2007), Re [2007] EWCA Civ 840; (2007) 151 S.J.L.B. 1263, CA (Civ Div)
A Trust, Re see FM v ASL Trustee Co Ltd
A (A Child), Re [2007] EWCA Civ 1058; *Times*, October 16, 2007, CA (Civ Div)
A (A Child) (Abduction: Habitual Residence), Re; *sub nom* W v F [2007] EWHC 779 (Fam); [2007] 2 F.L.R. 129; [2007] Fam. Law 676; (2007) 104(18) L.S.G. 28; (2007) 151 S.J.L.B. 503, Fam Div . . . . *Digested*, 07/**1737**

A (A Child) (Change of Residence), Re [2007] EWCA Civ 899; [2007] Fam. Law 1061; (2007) 151 S.J.L.B. 807; *Times*, June 27, 2007, CA (Civ Div) . . . . *Digested*, 07/**1792**

A (A Child) (Custody Decision after Maltese Non-Return Order: Brussels II Revised), Re [2006] EWHC 3397 (Fam); [2007] 1 F.L.R. 1923; [2007] 1 F.C.R. 402; [2007] Fam. Law 290, Fam Div . . . . *Digested*, 07/**1739**

A (A Child) (Wardship: Habitual Residence), Re [2006] EWHC 3338 (Fam); [2007] 1 F.L.R. 1589; [2007] 1 F.C.R. 390; [2007] Fam. Law 401, Fam Div . . . . *Digested*, 07/**1827**

A (Brussels II Revised: Article (11) 7 Application), Re see HA v MB (Brussels II Revised: Article (11) 7 Application)

A (Children) (Care Proceedings: Asylum Seekers), Re [2003] EWHC 1086 (Fam); [2003] 2 F.L.R. 921; [2003] Fam. Law 806; *Times*, May 26, 2003, Fam Div . . . . *Digested*, 04/**2028**:
Considered, 07/1735: *Followed*, 06/2243

A (Children) (Split Hearings: Practice), Re [2006] EWCA Civ 714; [2007] 1 F.L.R. 905; [2007] Fam. Law 16; *Times*, September 7, 2006, CA (Civ Div) . . . . *Digested*, 06/**1667**

A (Iraq) v Secretary of State for the Home Department [2005] EWCA Civ 1438; [2006] Imm. A.R. 114; [2006] I.N.L.R. 97; *Independent*, December 6, 2005, CA (Civ Div) . . . . *Digested*, 06/**2205**:
Considered, 06/2278: *Followed*, 07/2335

A/S Tankexpress v Compagnie Financiere Belge des Petroles SA [1949] A.C. 76; [1948] 2 All E.R. 939; (1948-49) 82 Ll. L. Rep. 43; [1949] L.J.R. 170; (1949) 93 S.J. 26, HL; affirming (1947) 80 Ll. L. Rep. 365, CA; reversing (1946) 79 Ll. L. Rep. 451, KBD . . . . *Digested*, 47-51/**9487**:
Applied, 79/50: *Considered*, 07/3420: *Distinguished*, 71/10880

AA v Secretary of State for the Home Department see AS v Secretary of State for the Home Department

AA v Secretary of State for the Home Department; *sub nom* AA (Third Party Maintenance: R297 (V): Bangladesh), Re; Entry Clearance Officer, Dhaka v AA [2005] UKAIT 105; [2005] Imm. A.R. 328; [2006] I.N.L.R. 1, AIT . . . . *Digested*, 06/**2267**:
Applied, 07/2326: *Followed*, 07/2335

AA v Secretary of State for the Home Department; *sub nom* AA (Involuntary Returns to Zimbabwe), Re; LK (AA Applied: Zimbabwe), Re; *joined case* LK v Secretary of State for the Home Department [2006] EWCA Civ 401; [2007] 1 W.L.R. 3134; [2007] 2 All E.R. 160; [2006] I.N.L.R. 401; (2006) 156 N.L.J. 681; *Times*, April 17, 2006, CA (Civ Div); reversing [2005] UKIAT 144, IAT . . . . *Digested*, 06/**2238**

AA (Afghanistan) v Secretary of State for the Home Department [2007] EWCA Civ 12; *Times*, February 2, 2007, CA (Civ Div)

AA (DP 3/96 - Commencement of Enforcement Action: Pakistan), Re see AA (Pakistan) v Secretary of State for the Home Department

AA (Involuntary Returns to Zimbabwe), Re see AA v Secretary of State for the Home Department

AA (Pakistan) v Secretary of State for the Home Department (2007) 151 S.J.L.B. 125, CA (Civ Div)

AA (Pakistan) v Secretary of State for the Home Department; *sub nom* AA (DP 3/96 - Commencement of Enforcement Action: Pakistan), Re [2007] UKAIT 16; [2007] Imm. A.R. 525, AIT

AA (Somalia) v Secretary of State for the Home Department; *joined case* AH (Iran) v Secretary of State for the Home Department [2007] EWCA Civ 1040, CA (Civ Div) . . . . *Applied*, 07/926

AA (Third Party Maintenance: R297 (V): Bangladesh), Re see AA v Secretary of State for the Home Department

AAH Pharmaceuticals Ltd v Pfizer Ltd [2007] EWHC 565 (Ch); [2007] U.K.C.L.R. 1561, Ch D

Aalborg Portland A/S v Commission of the European Communities (C-204/00 P) [2004] E.C.R. I-123; [2005] 4 C.M.L.R. 4, ECJ (5th Chamber) . . . . *Digested*, 05/**1435**:
Applied, 07/605, 07/612, 07/644: *Followed*, 07/611

Aaron v Shelton [2004] EWHC 1162 (QB); [2004] 3 All E.R. 561; [2004] 3 Costs L.R. 488; (2004) 154 N.L.J. 853, QBD . . . . *Digested*, 04/**327**:
Applied, 05/379: *Doubted*, 07/391

AB v British Coal Corp see AB v Department of Trade and Industry

AB v Department of Trade and Industry; *sub nom* AB v British Coal Corp [2006] EWCA Civ 1357; [2007] P.I.Q.R. P8; (2006) 103(42) L.S.G. 34; (2006) 150 S.J.L.B. 1429, CA (Civ Div) . . . . *Digested*, 07/**3077**

AB (A Firm) v Revenue and Customs Commissioners [2007] S.T.C. (S.C.D.) 99; [2007] S.T.I. 157, Sp Comm . . . . *Digested*, 07/**4056**

AB (Jamaica) v Secretary of State for the Home Department [2007] EWCA Civ 1302; [2007] U.K.H.R.R. 1177, CA (Civ Div)

AB (Risk: Return: Israel Check Points: Palestine), Re [2005] UKIAT 46, IAT . . . . *Considered*, 07/2343

Abaco Machines (Australasia) Pty Ltd's Patent Application [2007] EWHC 347 (Pat); [2007] Bus. L.R. 897; (2007) 30(5) I.P.D. 30035, Ch D (Patents Ct) . . . . *Digested*, 07/**2628**

ABB AG v Hochtief Airport GmbH [2006] EWHC 388 (Comm); [2006] 1 All E.R. (Comm) 529; [2006] 2 Lloyd's Rep. 1, QBD (Comm) . . . . *Digested*, 06/**217**:
Applied, 07/253

ABB Asea Brown Boveri Ltd *v* Commission of the European Communities (C-213/02 P) see Dansk Rorindustri A/S *v* Commission of the European Communities (C-189/02 P)

ABB Asea Brown Boveri Ltd *v* Commission of the European Communities (T-31/99) [2002] E.C.R. II-1881, CFI . . . . *Applied*, 07/1589:
Subsequent proceedings, 06/574

Abbey Life Assurance Co Ltd *v* Tansell see MHC Consulting Services Ltd *v* Tansell

Abbey National Plc *v* Customs and Excise Commissioners (C-169/04) [2006] S.T.C. 1136; [2006] E.C.R. I-4027; [2006] 2 C.M.L.R. 65; [2006] C.E.C. 1089; [2006] S.T.I. 1493; *Times*, June 6, 2006, ECJ (3rd Chamber) . . . . *Digested*, 06/**4495**:
Applied, 07/4335

Abbey National Plc *v* Fairbrother [2007] I.R.L.R. 320, EAT. *Digested*, 07/**1318**:
Distinguished, 07/1317

Abbott *v* Richardson [2006] EWHC 1291 (Ch); [2006] W.T.L.R. 1567, Ch D . . . . *Digested*, 07/**3959**

ABC Ltd *v* M (Inspector of Taxes) see Barclays Mercantile Business Finance Ltd *v* Mawson (Inspector of Taxes)

Abdi *v* Barnet LBC see Barnet LBC *v* Ismail

Abdi *v* Secretary of State for the Home Department see R. (on the application of Nadarajah) *v* Secretary of State for the Home Department

Abdirahman *v* Leicester City Council see Abdirahman *v* Secretary of State for Work and Pensions

Abdirahman *v* Secretary of State for Work and Pensions; *joined cases* Ullusow *v* Secretary of State for Work and Pensions; Abdirahman *v* Leicester City Council [2007] EWCA Civ 657; [2007] 4 All E.R. 882; [2007] 3 C.M.L.R. 37; [2007] Eu. L.R. 814, CA (Civ Div) . . . . *Digested*, 07/**3824**

Abdullah *v* City of Westminster (2007) 151 S.J.L.B. 857, CA (Civ Div)

Abdullah *v* Shropshire CC see R. *v* Barnet LBC Ex p. Shah (Nilish)

Abercromby Motor Group Ltd *v* Revenue and Customs Commissioners [2007] S.T.I. 1702, V&DTr (Edinburgh)

Aberdeen Journals Ltd *v* Director General of Fair Trading [2003] CAT 11; [2003] Comp. A.R. 67, CCAT . . . . *Digested*, 04/**527**:
Applied, 06/590: *Considered*, 07/2723

Ablack *v* Inner London Education Authority see R. *v* Barnet LBC Ex p. Shah (Nilish)

Able (UK) Ltd *v* Revenue and Customs Commissioners [2007] EWCA Civ 1207; [2007] S.T.I. 2700; [2007] N.P.C. 125, CA (Civ Div); affirming [2006] EWHC 3046 (Ch); [2007] S.T.C. 1738; [2007] R.V.R. 101; [2006] S.T.I. 2345, Ch D . . *Digested*, 07/**4061**

Abnett *v* British Airways Plc; *joined case* Sidhu *v* British Airways Plc [1997] A.C. 430; [1997] 2 W.L.R. 26; [1997] 1 All E.R. 193; [1997] 2 Lloyd's Rep. 76; 1997 S.C. (H.L.) 26; 1997 S.L.T. 492; 1997 S.C.L.R. 114; (1997) 94(2) L.S.G. 26; (1996) 146 N.L.J. 1851; (1997) 141 S.J.L.B. 26; *Times*, December 13, 1996; *Independent*, December 17, 1996, HL; affirming [1995] P.I.Q.R. P427, CA (Civ Div) . . . . *Digested*, 97/**220**:
Applied, 97/879, 01/949, 07/297: *Considered*, 00/5164, 02/243, 04/375:
Referred to, 95/5499

Abou-Rahmah *v* Abacha [2006] EWCA Civ 1492; [2007] Bus. L.R. 220; [2007] 1 All E.R. (Comm) 827; [2007] 1 Lloyd's Rep. 115; [2007] W.T.L.R. 1; (2006-07) 9 I.T.E.L.R. 401; *Independent*, November 14, 2006, CA (Civ Div); affirming [2005] EWHC 2662 (QB); [2006] 1 All E.R. (Comm) 247; [2006] 1 Lloyd's Rep. 484; [2006] W.T.L.R. 377, QBD . . . . *Digested*, 07/**4237**

Abu-Qulbain *v* Secretary of State for the Home Department see Huang *v* Secretary of State for the Home Department

AC *v* RM see C (Responsible Authority), Re

AC Yule & Son Ltd *v* Speedwell Roofing & Cladding Ltd [2007] EWHC 1360 (TCC); [2007] B.L.R. 499; [2007] C.I.L.L. 2489, QBD (TCC)

Accent Foundation Ltd *v* Lee; *sub nom* Lee *v* Accent Foundation Ltd [2007] EWCA Civ 665; (2007) 104(26) L.S.G. 34; (2007) 151 S.J.L.B. 806, CA (Civ Div)

Accurate Financial Consultants Pty Ltd *v* Koko Black Pty Ltd [2007] VSC 40; (2007-08) 10 I.T.E.L.R. 536, Sup Ct (Vic)

Acereda Herrera *v* Servicio Cantabro de Salud (C-466/04) [2006] E.C.R. I-5341; [2006] 3 C.M.L.R. 24; [2006] C.E.C. 978, ECJ (1st Chamber) . . . . *Digested*, 07/**3854**

Achilles Paper Group Ltd *v* Office of Fair Trading [2006] CAT 24; [2007] Comp. A.R. 1, CAT. . . . . *Digested*, 07/**645**

Achour *v* France (67335/01) (2007) 45 E.H.R.R. 2, ECHR (Grand Chamber)

Ackroyd *v* Mersey Care NHS Trust (No.2) see Mersey Care NHS Trust *v* Ackroyd (No.2)

Acrylic Glass Cartel, Re (COMP/F/38.645) [2007] 5 C.M.L.R. 10, CEC

Actavis Ltd *v* Merck & Co Inc A3/2007/1625; A3/2007/1650, CA (Civ Div); reversing [2007] EWHC 1311 (Pat); (2007) 30(7) I.P.D. 30049, Ch D (Patents Ct)

Acton *v* Birmingham South West Circuit Methodist Church Manses Trust [2006] 3 E.G.L.R. 101; [2006] 39 E.G. 184; [2007] R.V.R. 78, Lands Tr . . . . *Digested*, 07/**3418**

AD *v* Bury MBC see D *v* Bury MBC

Adam Opel AG *v* Autec AG (C-48/05) [2007] C.E.C. 204; [2007] E.T.M.R. 33, ECJ (1st Chamber) . . . . *Digested*, 07/**2653**

Adami *v* Malta (17209/02) (2007) 44 E.H.R.R. 3; 20 B.H.R.C. 703, ECHR . . . . *Digested*, 07/**2265**

Adams *v* Adams [1892] 1 Ch. 369, CA. . . . . *Applied*, 07/**4255**

Adams v Bracknell Forest BC; *sub nom* Bracknell Forest BC v Adams [2004] UKHL
29; [2005] 1 A.C. 76; [2004] 3 W.L.R. 89; [2004] 3 All E.R. 897; [2004] E.L.R.
459; [2005] P.I.Q.R. P2; (2004) 101(26) L.S.G. 28; (2004) 148 S.J.L.B. 761;
Times, June 24, 2004, HL; reversing [2003] EWCA Civ 706; [2003] E.L.R. 409;
(2003) 100(26) L.S.G. 39; (2003) 147 S.J.L.B. 599; *Times,* May 14, 2003;
Independent, May 15, 2003, CA (Civ Div)............................ *Digested,* 04/**372**:
          Applied, 05/438, 07/473, 07/474, 07/483: *Considered,* 07/475
Addison v Babcock FATA Ltd; *sub nom* Babcock FATA Ltd v Addison [1988] Q.B.
280; [1987] 3 W.L.R. 122; [1987] 2 All E.R. 784; [1987] I.C.R. 805; [1987]
I.R.L.R. 173; [1987] 1 F.T.L.R. 505; (1987) 84 L.S.G. 1409, CA (Civ Div);
reversing [1987] I.C.R. 45; [1986] I.R.L.R. 388; (1986) 83 L.S.G. 2568; *Times,*
July 10, 1986, EAT .... *Digested,* 87/**1388**:
          Applied, 05/1331, 07/1425: *Considered,* 88/1335, 88/1336:
          Distinguished, 06/1388: *Followed,* 93/1816
Adealon International Corp Proprietary Ltd v Merton LBC [2007] EWCA Civ 362;
[2007] 1 W.L.R. 1898; (2007) 151 S.J.L.B. 577, CA (Civ Div); affirming [2006]
EWHC 1075 (Ch); [2006] 2 E.G.L.R. 1; [2006] 29 E.G. 134; (2006) 150 S.J.L.B.
575; [2006] 2 P. & C.R. DG13, Ch D .... *Digested,* 07/**3399**
Adekunle v Ritchie [2007] B.P.I.R. 1177; [2007] W.T.L.R. 1505; (2007) 104(35) L.S.G.
36; [2007] 2 P. & C.R. DG20, CC (Leeds)
Adelson v Associated Newspapers Ltd [2007] EWCA Civ 701; [2007] 4 All E.R. 330;
[2007] C.P. Rep. 40; *Times,* July 18, 2007, CA (Civ Div); affirming [2007] EWHC
997 (QB); *Times,* May 10, 2007, QBD .... *Digested,* 07/**534**
Adeneler v Ellinikos Organismos Galaktos (ELOG) (C-212/04) [2007] All E.R. (EC)
82; [2006] E.C.R. I-6057; [2006] 3 C.M.L.R. 30; [2006] I.R.L.R. 716, ECJ... *Digested,* 07/**1370**:
          Considered, 07/1420: *Distinguished,* 07/1332, 07/1386
Adidas-Salomon AG v Draper [2006] EWHC 2262 (Ch); (2007) 30(1) I.P.D. 30004,
Ch D
Adidas-Salomon AG v Fitnessworld Trading Ltd (C-408/01) [2004] Ch. 120; [2004]
2 W.L.R. 1095; [2003] E.C.R. I-12537; [2004] 1 C.M.L.R. 14; [2004] C.E.C. 3;
[2004] E.T.M.R. 10; [2004] F.S.R. 21; *Times,* October 31, 2003, ECJ (6th
Chamber) .... *Digested,* 04/**2390**:
          Applied, 05/2562: *Considered,* 06/2586, 07/2666, 07/2673
Adidas-Salomon AG v Nike Europe Holding BV [2007] E.T.M.R. 12, RB (Den Haag)... *Digested,* 07/**2673**
Adkins v Revenue and Customs Commissioners [2007] S.T.C. (S.C.D.) 323; [2007]
S.T.I. 558, Sp Comm. .... *Digested,* 07/**4135**
Administration de l'Enregistrement et des Domaines v Eurodental Sarl (C-240/05)
[2007] S.T.C. 275; [2006] S.T.I. 2745, ECJ (3rd Chamber)
Administration des Douanes et Droits Indirects v Rioglass SA (C-115/02) [2003] E.C.R.
I-12705; [2006] 1 C.M.L.R. 12; [2004] E.T.M.R. 38; [2004] F.S.R. 35, ECJ
(6th Chamber)... *Digested,* 04/**1412**:
          Considered, 07/2638
Admissibility of Art.226 EC Action (C-195/04), Re see Commission of the European
Communities v Finland (C-195/04)
Adria Wien Pipeline GmbH v Finanzlandesdirektion fur Karnten (C-143/99) [2002] All
E.R. (EC) 306; [2001] E.C.R. I-8365; [2002] 1 C.M.L.R. 38, ECJ (5th
Chamber) .... *Digested,* 02/**616**:
          Applied, 07/650: *Distinguished,* 07/1646: *Followed,* 05/2380
Adubofour v Latif (t/a A1 Kebabish) (Unreported, May 3, 2006), CC (Ilford) [*Ex rel.*
Nicholas Preston, Barrister, Clerksroom, 199 Strand, London]............ *Digested,* 07/**3211**
Advanced Medical Solutions Group Plc v Revenue and Customs Commissioners [2007]
S.T.I. 389, V&DTr (Manchester)
Advocate General for Scotland v General Commissioners for Aberdeen City see
Revenue and Customs Commissioners, Petitioners
Advocate General for Scotland v MacDonald; *sub nom* MacDonald v Ministry of
Defence; Secretary of State for Defence v MacDonald; MacDonald v Advocate
General for Scotland; *joined case* Pearce v Mayfield Secondary School
Governing Body [2003] UKHL 34; [2004] 1 All E.R. 339; 2003 S.C. (H.L.) 35;
2003 S.L.T. 1158; 2003 S.C.L.R. 814; [2003] I.C.R. 937; [2003] I.R.L.R. 512;
[2003] E.L.R. 655; (2003) 100(29) L.S.G. 36; (2003) 147 S.J.L.B. 782; 2003
G.W.D. 23-677; *Times,* June 20, 2003, HL; affirming 2002 S.C. 1; 2001 S.L.T.
819; 2001 S.C.L.R. 795; [2002] I.C.R. 174; [2001] I.R.L.R. 431; [2001] Emp.
L.R. 793; 2001 G.W.D. 19-731, IH (Ex Div); reversing [2001] 1 All E.R. 620;
[2001] I.C.R. 1; [2000] I.R.L.R. 748; [2001] Emp. L.R. 105; [2001] H.R.L.R. 5;
Independent, November 27, 2000, EAT............................... *Digested,* 03/**1309**:
          Applied, 05/1298, 06/1303, 07/1402: *Considered,* 01/2315, 07/1334
Advocaten voor de Wereld VZW v Leden van de Ministerraad (C-303/05) [2007] 3
C.M.L.R. 1, ECJ (Grand Chamber) .... *Considered,* 07/**1657**
Aectra Refining & Marketing Inc v Exmar NV (The New Vanguard and The Pacifica)
[1994] 1 W.L.R. 1634; [1995] 1 All E.R. 641; [1995] 1 Lloyd's Rep. 191; *Times,*
August 15, 1994; *Independent,* August 22, 1994, CA (Civ Div)............ *Digested,* 95/**4213**:
          Applied, 06/692, 07/238: *Considered,* 05/206, 06/211

AEI Rediffusion Music Ltd *v* Phonographic Performance Ltd (Costs); *sub nom* Phonographic Performance Ltd *v* AEI Rediffusion Music Ltd (Costs) [1999] 1 W.L.R. 1507; [1999] 2 All E.R. 299; [1999] C.P.L.R. 551; [1999] E.M.L.R. 335; [1999] R.P.C. 599; (1999) 22(5) I.P.D. 22046; (1999) 96(12) L.S.G. 33; (1999) 143 S.J.L.B. 97; *Times*, March 3, 1999; *Independent*, February 24, 1999, CA (Civ Div); affirming [1999] E.M.L.R. 129; (1998) 21(12) I.P.D. 21130, Ch D; reversing [1998] E.M.L.R. 459, Copyright Tr . . . . *Digested*, 99/**3456**:
Applied, 04/500, 07/386: *Considered*, 00/396, 00/457, 01/470, 02/371, 02/2837, 03/360, 03/3583, 05/357: *Followed*, 01/460
Aerlink Leisure Ltd *v* Three Rivers DC [2007] P.A.D. 54, Planning Inspector
Aeroports de Paris *v* Commission of the European Communities (C-82/01 P) [2002] E.C.R. I-9297; [2003] 4 C.M.L.R. 12, ECJ (6th Chamber) . . . . *Digested*, 03/**550**:
Applied, 07/652: *Considered*, 05/575
Aerospace Publishing Ltd *v* Thames Water Utilities Ltd [2007] EWCA Civ 3; [2007] Bus. L.R. 726; 110 Con. L.R. 1; [2007] 3 Costs L.R. 389; [2007] C.I.L.L. 2429; (2007) 104(4) L.S.G. 32; (2007) 151 S.J.L.B. 123; [2007] N.P.C. 5; *Times*, January 22, 2007, CA (Civ Div); reversing in part [2005] EWHC 2987 (QB), QBD . . . . *Digested*, 07/**1059**
Aerotel Ltd *v* Telco Holdings Ltd; *joined case* Macrossan's Patent Application (No.0314464.9) [2006] EWCA Civ 1371; [2007] Bus. L.R. 634; [2007] 1 All E.R. 225; [2006] Info. T.L.R. 215; [2007] R.P.C. 7; (2007) 30(4) I.P.D. 30025; (2006) 156 N.L.J. 1687; *Independent*, November 15, 2006, CA (Civ Div); reversing [2006] EWHC 997 (Pat); (2006) 29(7) I.P.D. 29055, Ch D (Patents Ct) . . . . *Digested*, 07/**2615**:
Applied, 07/2627, 07/2635
Aerts *v* Belgium (2000) 29 E.H.R.R. 50; 5 B.H.R.C. 382; (2000) 53 B.M.L.R. 79; [1998] H.R.C.D. 749, ECHR . . . . *Digested*, 99/**3094**:
Considered, 07/2232: *Distinguished*, 03/2118
AF *v* Secretary of State for the Home Department [2007] EWHC 2001 (Admin); (2007) 104(34) L.S.G. 26, QBD (Admin)
AF Blakemore & Son Ltd *v* Machin see AF Blakemore & Son Ltd Staff Retirement Benefit Scheme, Re
AF Blakemore & Son Ltd Staff Retirement Benefit Scheme, Re; *sub nom* AF Blakemore & Son Ltd *v* Machin [2007] EWHC 963 (Ch); [2007] Pens. L.R. 189, Ch D *Digested*, 07/**3027**
AF Noonan (Architectural Practice) Ltd *v* Bournemouth & Boscombe Athletic Community Football Club Ltd; *sub nom* Bournemouth & Boscombe Athletic Community Football Club Ltd, Re [2007] EWCA Civ 848; [2007] 1 W.L.R. 2614; [2007] C.P. Rep. 44; (2007) 151 S.J.L.B. 923; *Times*, July 12, 2007, CA (Civ Div); affirming [2006] EWHC 2113 (Ch), Ch D . . . . *Digested*, 07/**506**
AF (A Minor) (Abduction), Re see F (A Minor) (Child Abduction), Re
Afro Caribbean Housing Association Ltd *v* Revenue and Customs Commissioners [2006] V. & D.R. 124; [2006] S.T.I. 1374, V&DTr (London) . . . . *Digested*, 07/**4349**
Afsar *v* Revenue and Customs Commissioners [2007] S.T.I. 2814, Sp Comm
AG *v* Mental Health Tribunal for Scotland [2007] M.H.L.R. 1, Sh Pr
AG (Eritrea) *v* Secretary of State for the Home Department [2007] EWCA Civ 801; [2007] I.N.L.R. 407; (2007) 157 N.L.J. 1235, CA (Civ Div)
Agapitos *v* Agnew (The Aegeon) (No.1) [2002] EWCA Civ 247; [2003] Q.B. 556; [2002] 3 W.L.R. 616; [2002] 1 All E.R. (Comm) 714; [2002] 2 Lloyd's Rep. 42; [2002] C.L.C. 886; [2002] Lloyd's Rep. I.R. 573; (2002) 99(16) L.S.G. 38; (2002) 146 S.J.L.B. 66, CA (Civ Div); affirming [2002] Lloyd's Rep. I.R. 191, QBD (Comm) . . . . *Digested*, 02/**2732**:
Considered, 05/2359, 06/432, 07/363: *Referred to*, 05/2387
AGF Insurance Ltd *v* Lexington Insurance Co see Wasa International Insurance Co Ltd *v* Lexington Insurance Co
AGF Kosmos Assurances Generales *v* Surgil Trans Express [2007] I.L.Pr. 24, Cass (F) . *Digested*, 07/**680**
AGILENT TECHNOLOGIES INC/Altering light signal (T1123/04) [2007] E.P.O.R. 7, EPO (Technical Bd App)
AGM-COS.MET Srl *v* Finland (C-470/03); *sub nom* AGM-COS.MET Srl *v* Suomen Valtio [2007] All E.R. (EC) 1126; [2007] 2 C.M.L.R. 41, ECJ . . . . *Digested*, 07/**1650**
AGM-COS.MET Srl *v* Suomen Valtio see AGM-COS.MET Srl *v* Finland (C-470/03)
Agorastoudis *v* Goodyear Hellas AVEE (C-187/05) [2006] E.C.R. I-7775, ECJ . . . . . . *Considered*, 07/**1554**
Agraz SA *v* Commission of the European Communities (C-243/05 P) [2007] 1 C.M.L.R. 27; [2006] E.C.R. IA-10833, ECJ (1st Chamber)
AGREVO/Triazole sulphonamides (T939/92) [1996] E.P.O.R. 171, EPO (Technical Bd App) *Applied*, 98/**3477**:
Considered, 07/2601
AGRUPACION OLCINA SL/Correction under Rule 88 (J5/06) [2007] E.P.O.R. 21, EPO (Legal Bd App) . . . . *Digested*, 07/**2575**
Agulian *v* Cyganik see Cyganik *v* Agulian
AH *v* Secretary of State for the Home Department; *sub nom* AH (Scope of s.103A Reconsideration: Sudan), Re [2006] UKAIT 38; [2006] Imm. A.R. 504; [2006] I.N.L.R. 517, AIT . . . . *Digested*, 07/**2334**:
Applied, 07/2276: *Followed*, 07/2335
AH (Iran) *v* Secretary of State for the Home Department see AA (Somalia) *v* Secretary of State for the Home Department

AH (Scope of s.103A Reconsideration: Sudan), Re see AH v Secretary of State for the Home Department

AH (Sudan) v Secretary of State for the Home Department; *sub nom* Secretary of State for the Home Department v AH (Sudan) [2007] UKHL 49; [2007] 3 W.L.R. 832; (2007) 151 S.J.L.B. 1500; *Times*, November 15, 2007, HL; reversing [2007] EWCA Civ 297; [2007] Imm. A.R. 584; (2007) 151 S.J.L.B. 469, CA (Civ Div)

Ahmad v United States; *joined case* Aswat v United States [2006] EWHC 2927 (Admin); [2007] H.R.L.R. 8; [2007] U.K.H.R.R. 525; [2006] Extradition L.R. 276; [2007] A.C.D. 54; (2006) 156 N.L.J. 1882; *Times*, December 5, 2006, DC . . . . *Digested*, 07/**1671**

Ahmed v Governing Body of the University of Oxford see Ahmed v University of Oxford

Ahmed v Mogul Eastern Foods [2005] EWHC 3532 (Ch); [2007] B.P.I.R. 975, Ch D

Ahmed v University of Oxford; *sub nom* Ahmed v Governing Body of the University of Oxford [2002] EWCA Civ 1907; [2003] 1 W.L.R. 995; [2003] 1 All E.R. 915; [2003] I.C.R. 733; (2003) 100(10) L.S.G. 27; *Times*, January 17, 2003; *Independent*, January 22, 2003, CA (Civ Div) . . . . *Digested*, 03/**1296**: *Applied*, 07/1184

Ahmed v Wingrove [2006] EWHC 1918 (Ch); [2007] 1 P. & C.R. D15, Ch D

Ahmed v Wingrove [2007] EWHC 1777 (Ch); [2007] 31 E.G. 81 (C.S.); [2007] 2 P. & C.R. DG24, Ch D

Ahmed Saeed Flugreisen v Zentrale zur Bekampfung Unlauteren Wettbewerbs eV (66/86); *joined case* Silver Line Reiseburo GmbH v Zentrale zur Bekampfung Unlauteren Wettbewerbs eV (66/86) [1989] E.C.R. 803; [1990] 4 C.M.L.R. 102; *Times*, April 13, 1989, ECJ . . . . *Digested*, 91/**3786**: *Considered*, 07/639

Ahmed (Iftikhar) v Secretary of State for the Home Department; *sub nom* Secretary of State for the Home Department v Ahmed (Iftikhar) [2000] I.N.L.R. 1; *Times*, December 8, 1999, CA (Civ Div) . . . . *Digested*, 00/**3313**: *Applied*, 05/2164, 07/2297: *Considered*, 05/2140, 06/2227

Ahmed (t/a New Touch) v Revenue and Customs Commissioners [2007] B.V.C. 2402, V&DTr (London)

Ahokainen v Virallinen Syyttaja (C-434/04) see Criminal Proceedings against Ahokainen (C-434/04)

Ahsan v University Hospitals Leicester NHS Trust [2006] EWHC 2624 (QB); [2007] P.I.Q.R. P19, QBD . . . . *Digested*, 07/**3062**

AI (Pakistan) v Secretary of State for the Home Department [2007] EWCA Civ 386; [2007] Imm. A.R. 712; [2007] I.N.L.R. 425; *Times*, May 22, 2007, CA (Civ Div) . . . . *Digested*, 07/**2353**

AIC Ltd v ITS Testing Services (UK) Ltd (The Kriti Palm) [2006] EWCA Civ 1601; [2007] 1 All E.R. (Comm) 667; [2007] 1 Lloyd's Rep. 555; [2007] 2 C.L.C. 223; *Times*, December 21, 2006, CA (Civ Div); affirming [2005] EWHC 2122 (Comm); [2006] 1 Lloyd's Rep. 1; [2005] 2 C.L.C. 490, QBD (Comm) . . . . *Digested*, 07/**482**

AIC Ltd v Marine Pilot Ltd (The Archimidis) A3/2007/1176/1189, CA (Civ Div); reversing in part [2007] EWHC 1182 (Comm); [2007] 2 All E.R. (Comm) 189; [2007] 2 Lloyd's Rep. 101; [2007] 1 C.L.C. 762; (2007) 157 N.L.J. 743, QBD (Comm) . . . . *Digested*, 07/**3817**

AIC Ltd v Nigeria [2003] EWHC 1357 (QB); *Independent*, July 28, 2003, QBD . . . . . . *Considered*, 07/239: *Followed*, 06/195

Aid to Olympic Airways, Re (C-415/03) see Commission of the European Communities v Greece (C-415/03)

Aiden Shipping Co Ltd v Interbulk Ltd (The Vimeira) (No.2) [1986] A.C. 965; [1986] 2 W.L.R. 1051; [1986] 2 All E.R. 409; [1986] 2 Lloyd's Rep. 117; (1986) 130 S.J. 429, HL; reversing [1985] 1 W.L.R. 1222; [1985] 3 All E.R. 641; [1986] 1 Lloyd's Rep. 107; (1985) 82 L.S.G. 3529; (1985) 135 N.L.J. 1165; (1985) 129 S.J. 812; *Financial Times*, October 16, 1985, CA (Civ Div); reversing [1985] 2 Lloyd's Rep. 377, QBD (Comm) . . . . *Digested*, 86/**2606**: *Applied*, 87/2991, 89/2938, 92/3454, 93/49, 94/3591, 95/3994, 96/710: *Considered*, 87/2942, 88/296, 90/3604, 91/2823, 92/2535, 92/2570, 93/3153, 93/3175, 94/3579, 97/607, 97/3113, 99/390, 01/1817, 02/393, 02/394, 07/361: *Followed*, 96/3541, 99/392, 99/417

Aids to the Textile Industry, Re (173/73) see Italy v Commission of the European Communities (173/73)

AIG Europe (Ireland) Ltd v Faraday Capital Ltd [2007] EWCA Civ 1208; [2007] 2 C.L.C. 844, CA (Civ Div); reversing [2006] EWHC 2707 (Comm); [2007] 1 All E.R. (Comm) 527; [2006] 2 C.L.C. 770; [2007] Lloyd's Rep. I.R. 267, QBD (Comm) . . . . *Digested*, 07/**2502**

Ainsworth v Inland Revenue Commissioners see Inland Revenue Commissioners v Ainsworth

Air Canada v British Columbia (1989) 59 D.L.R. (4th) 161; [1989] 1 S.C.R. 1161; [1989] 4 W.W.R. 97, Sup Ct (Can) . . . . *Considered*, 07/3439: *Followed*, 94/6018

Air Canada v Lee [1978] I.C.R.1202; [1978] I.R.L.R. 392; (1978) 13 I.T.R. 574, EAT . . .   *Digested*, 79/**931**:
                                       Applied, 79/932: *Distinguished*, 07/1397

Air Great Lakes Pty Ltd v KS Easter (Holdings) Pty Ltd (1985) 2 N.S.W.L.R. 309, CA
    (NSW) . . . .   *Distinguished*, 07/1396

Air Liquide Industries Belgium SA v Province de Liege (C-41/05) see Air Liquide
    Industries Belgium SA vVille de Seraing (C-393/04)

Air Liquide Industries Belgium SA vVille de Seraing (C-393/04); *joined case* Air Liquide
    Industries Belgium SA v Province de Liege (C-41/05) [2006] 3 C.M.L.R. 23,
    ECJ (2nd Chamber) . . . .   *Digested*, 07/**650**:
                                        Considered, 07/649: *Followed*, 07/1044

Air One SpA v Commission of the European Communities (T-395/04) [2006] E.C.R.
    II-1343; [2006] 3 C.M.L.R. 20, CFI (4th Chamber) . . . .   *Digested*, 07/**647**

Airbus UK Ltd vWebb A2/2007/0477, CA (Civ Div); reversing [2007] I.C.R. 956, EAT   *Digested*, 07/**1432**

Aird v Prime Meridian Ltd [2006] EWCA Civ 1866; [2007] C.P. Rep. 18; [2007]
    B.L.R. 105; 111 Con. L.R. 209; (2007) 104(2) L.S.G. 31; (2007) 151 S.J.L.B. 60;
    Times, February 14, 2007, CA (Civ Div); affirming [2006] EWHC 2338 (TCC);
    [2006] B.L.R. 494; [2006] T.C.L.R. 8; 108 Con. L.R. 1; [2006] C.I.L.L. 2393,
    QBD (TCC) . . . .   *Digested*, 07/**460**

Airedale NHS Trust v Bland [1993] A.C. 789; [1993] 2 W.L.R. 316; [1993] 1 All E.R.
    821; [1993] 1 F.L.R. 1026; [1994] 1 F.C.R. 485; [1993] 4 Med. L.R. 39; (1993)
    12 B.M.L.R. 64; [1993] Fam. Law 473; (1993) 143 N.L.J. 199; *Times*, February 5,
    1993; *Independent*, February 5, 1993; *Guardian*, February 5, 1993, HL;
    affirming (1992) 142 N.L.J. 1755; *Times*, December 10, 1992; *Independent*,
    December 10, 1992, CA (Civ Div); affirming (1992) 142 N.L.J. 1648; *Times*,
    November 23, 1992; *Independent*, November 20, 1992, Fam Div . . . .   *Digested*, 93/**2712**:
                Applied, 94/3015, 95/4266, 01/2934, 05/3946, 07/1986:
           Considered, 94/1004, 95/4104, 97/2593, 97/6070, 98/958, 00/3246,
            01/2662, 01/2935: *Distinguished*, 97/5783: *Followed*, 98/2650, 98/2651,
                                             01/3571, 02/1888

Airey v Cordell [2006] EWHC 2728 (Ch); [2007] Bus. L.R. 391; [2007] B.C.C. 785;
    (2006) 150 S.J.L.B. 1150, Ch D . . . .   *Digested*, 07/**435**

Airtours Plc v Commission of the European Communities (T342/99) [2002] All E.R.
    (EC) 783; [2002] E.C.R. II-2585; [2002] U.K.C.L.R. 642; [2002] 5 C.M.L.R. 7,
    CFI (5th Chamber) . . . .   *Applied*, 07/635

AJ Bekhor & Co Ltd v Bilton [1981] Q.B. 923; [1981] 2 W.L.R. 601; [1981] 2 All E.R.
    565; [1981] 1 Lloyd's Rep. 491; [1981] Com. L.R. 50; (1981) 125 S.J. 203, CA
    (Civ Div) . . . .   *Digested*, 81/**2159**:
              Applied, 82/2463, 89/2074, 89/2989, 07/455: *Considered*, 87/2885, 91/871:
                        Distinguished, 82/2511: *Followed*, 85/2674, 94/3738, 95/4122

AJ (A Child) (Adoption Order or Special Guardianship Order), Re; *sub nom* JJ v AT
    [2007] EWCA Civ 55; [2007] 1 F.L.R. 507; [2007] 1 F.C.R. 308; [2007] Fam.
    Law 387; (2007) 104(8) L.S.G. 38, CA (Civ Div) . . . .   *Digested*, 07/**1681**

AK v Secretary of State for the Home Department; *sub nom* AK (Tribunal Appeal: Out
    of Time: Bulgaria), Re [2004] UKIAT 201; [2004] Imm. A.R. 486; [2004]
    I.N.L.R. 549, IAT . . . .   *Digested*, 05/**2221**:
                                         Considered, 07/2284

AK v Secretary of State for the Home Department [2006] EWCA Civ 1117; [2007]
    Imm. A.R. 81; [2007] I.N.L.R. 195, CA (Civ Div) . . . .   *Digested*, 07/**2343**

AK (Bangladesh) v Secretary of State for the Home Department; *sub nom* AK (Long-
    term third party support: Bangladesh), Re [2006] UKAIT 69; [2007] Imm. A.R.
    177, AIT . . . .   *Digested*, 07/**2335**

AK (Bangladesh) v Secretary of State for the Home Department; *sub nom* AK (WHM:
    Maximum 12 Months' Work: Bangladesh), Re [2007] UKAIT 64; [2007] Imm.
    A.R. 767, AIT

AK (Long-term third party support: Bangladesh), Re see AK (Bangladesh) v Secretary of
    State for the Home Department

AK (Tribunal Appeal: Out of Time: Bulgaria), Re see AK v Secretary of State for the Home
    Department

AK (WHM: Maximum 12 Months' Work: Bangladesh), Re see AK (Bangladesh) v Secretary
    of State for the Home Department

Akaeke v Secretary of State for the Home Department; *sub nom* Secretary of State for
    the Home Department v Akaeke [2005] EWCA Civ 947; [2005] Imm. A.R. 701;
    [2005] I.N.L.R. 575; *Times*, September 23, 2005, CA (Civ Div) . . . .   *Digested*, 05/**2211**:
                                           Applied, 07/2307

Akaroglu v Romania; *joined case* R. (on the application of Akaroglu) v Secretary of
    State for the Home Department [2007] EWHC 367 (Admin); *Times*, March 9,
    2007, DC . . . .   *Digested*, 07/**1669**

Akbarali v Brent LBC see R. v Barnet LBC Ex p. Shah (Nilish)

Akhtar v Arif [2006] EWHC 2726 (Ch); [2006] 3 F.C.R. 526; [2007] W.T.L.R. 35;
    [2007] 2 P. & C.R. DG3, Ch D . . . .   *Digested*, 07/**3434**

Akram v Adam [2004] EWCA Civ 1601; [2005] 1 W.L.R. 2762; [2005] 1 All E.R. 741; [2005] C.P. Rep. 14; [2005] H.L.R. 14; [2005] L. & T.R. 9; [2004] 50 E.G. 84 (C.S.); (2005) 102(5) L.S.G. 28; (2004) 148 S.J.L.B. 1433; [2004] N.P.C. 182; [2005] 1 P. & C.R. DG13; *Times*, December 29, 2004, CA (Civ Div) . . . . *Digested*, 05/**467**: *Distinguished*, 07/370
Aksoy v Turkey (21987/93) (1997) 23 E.H.R.R. 553; 1 B.H.R.C. 625, ECHR . . . . *Digested*, 97/**2824**: *Applied*, 98/3162, 06/2162, 07/2203: *Followed*, 98/3073, 02/2482
Aktiebolaget NN v Skatteverket (C-111/05) [2007] 2 C.M.L.R. 40; [2007] S.T.I. 1167, ECJ (3rd Chamber) . . . . *Digested*, 07/**4341**
Aktionsgemeinschaft Recht und Eigentum eV v Commission of the European Communities (T-114/00) [2002] E.C.R. II-5121, CFI . . . . *Reversed*, 07/1564
Akyuz v Secretary of State for the Home Department see R. (on the application of Ozturk) v Secretary of State for the Home Department
AKZO Chemie BV v Commission of the European Communities (C-62/86) [1991] E.C.R. I-3359; [1993] 5 C.M.L.R. 215; [1994] F.S.R. 25; *Times*, October 7, 1991, ECJ (5th Chamber) . . . . *Digested*, 91/**3834**: *Applied*, 97/854, 06/590: *Considered*, 04/527, 07/1548: *Followed*, 98/716
Akzo Nobel Chemicals Ltd v Commission of the European Communities (T-125/03) [2007] 4 C.M.L.R. 23, CFI . . . . *Digested*, 07/**2799**
Akzo Nobel Chemicals Ltd v Commission of the European Communities (T-125/03); *joined case* Akzo Nobel Chemicals Ltd v Commission of the European Communities (T-253/03) [2007] C.I.L.L. 2513, CFI (1st Chamber)
Akzo Nobel Chemicals Ltd v Commission of the European Communities (T-253/03) see Akzo Nobel Chemicals Ltd v Commission of the European Communities (T-125/03)
Akzo Nobel NV v Commission of the European Communities (T-330/01) [2007] 4 C.M.L.R. 3, CFI (3rd Chamber)
Akzo NV's European Patent (EP 0 389 035) see Arrow Generics Ltd, Petitioners
Al Gouri v Achkar (Unreported, November 21, 2006), QBD [*Ex rel.* Simon Edwards, 39 Essex Street, London] . . . . *Digested*, 07/**3079**
AL (Nigeria) v Secretary of State for the Home Department see DK (Serbia) v Secretary of State for the Home Department
AL (Serbia) v Secretary of State for the Home Department [2006] EWCA Civ 1619; [2007] H.R.L.R. 7; [2007] U.K.H.R.R. 564; [2007] Imm. A.R. 369; [2007] I.N.L.R. 136; (2006) 150 S.J.L.B. 1606, CA (Civ Div). . . . . *Digested*, 07/**2293**
Al-Amoudi v Brisard [2006] EWHC 1062 (QB); [2007] 1 W.L.R. 113; [2006] 3 All E.R. 294; (2006) 150 S.J.L.B. 856, QBD . . . . *Digested*, 06/**1041**
Al-Fagih v HH Saudi Research & Marketing (UK) Ltd [2001] EWCA Civ 1634; [2002] E.M.L.R. 13, CA (Civ Div); reversing 1996-A-No. 1535, QBD . . . . *Digested*, 02/**959**: *Applied*, 06/1049, 07/1075: *Considered*, 03/951, 06/1047, 07/1076
Al-Fayed v Deputy Coroner of the Queen's Household and Assistant Deputy Coroner for Surrey see Paul v Deputy Coroner of the Queen's Household and Assistant Deputy Coroner for Surrey
Al-Fayed v Hamilton (Costs) see Hamilton v Al-Fayed (Costs)
Al-H (Rashid) v F (Sara) [2001] EWCA Civ 186; [2001] 1 F.L.R. 951; [2001] 1 F.C.R. 385; *Times*, March 2, 2001, CA (Civ Div) . . . . *Digested*, 01/**2676**: *Applied*, 04/1471, 06/1641: *Considered*, 07/1750, 07/1827
Al-Koronky v Time Life Entertainment Group Ltd [2006] EWCA Civ 1123; [2006] C.P. Rep. 47; [2007] 1 Costs L.R. 57; *Times*, August 28, 2006, CA (Civ Div); affirming [2005] EWHC 1688 (QB), QBD . . . . *Digested*, 06/**501**
Al-Mehdawi v Secretary of State for the Home Department see R. v Secretary of State for the Home Department Ex p. Al-Mehdawi
Al-Moayad v Germany (Admissibility) (35865/03) (2007) 44 E.H.R.R. SE22, ECHR
Al's Bar and Restaurant Ltd v Wandsworth LBC (Unreported, October 28, 2002) . . . . *Followed*, 07/3496
Alagon v Secretary of State for the Home Department 1995 S.L.T. 381; [1993] Imm. A.R. 336, OH. . . . . *Digested*, 95/**6024**: *Considered*, 07/2325: *Not followed*, 97/6141
Alan Phillips Associates Ltd v Dowling (t/a Joseph Dowling Partnership) [2007] EWCA Civ 64; [2007] B.L.R. 151; (2007) 151 S.J.L.B. 122, CA (Civ Div) . . . . *Digested*, 07/**422**
Alawiye v Mahmood (t/a Amsons) [2006] EWHC 277; [2007] 1 W.L.R. 79; [2006] 3 All E.R. 668, Ch D . . . . *Digested*, 06/**461**
Albacom SpA v Ministero del Tesoro, del Bilancio e della Programmazione Economica (C-292/01) [2003] E.C.R. I-9449; [2003] Info. T.L.R. 446, ECJ (5th Chamber) . . . . *Digested*, 05/**4183**: *Applied*, 07/1579: *Considered*, 06/4323
Albany Building Ltd, Re [2007] B.C.C. 591, Ch D (Birmingham)
Albatros Feeds v Minister for Agriculture and Food, Ireland [2007] Eu. L.R. 485, Sup Ct (Irl)

9

Albert v Lavin; *sub nom* Lavin v Albert [1982] A.C. 546; [1981] 3 W.L.R. 955; [1981] 3 All E.R. 878; (1982) 74 Cr. App. R. 150; (1981) 125 S.J. 860; *Times*, December 4, 1981, HL; affirming [1981] 2 W.L.R. 1070; [1981] 1 All E.R. 628; (1981) 72 Cr. App. R. 178; [1981] Crim. L.R. 238; (1981) 125 S.J. 114; (1981) 125 S.J. 860; *Times*, December 5, 1980, QBD . . . . *Digested*, 82/**683**:
Applied, 85/512, 87/753: *Considered*, 84/504, 04/3144:
Disapproved, 84/502.3: *Followed*, 96/1508, 07/3317

Albert Ruckdeschel & Co v Hauptzollamt Hamburg-St Annen (117/76); *joined case* Diamalt AG v Hauptzollamt Itzehoe (16/77) [1977] E.C.R. 1753; [1979] 2 C.M.L.R. 445, ECJ. . . . . *Digested*, 78/**1225**:
Considered, 07/1508: *Followed*, 00/2640

Albion Water Ltd v Water Services Regulation Authority (formerly Director General of Water Services) [2006] CAT 33; [2007] Comp. A.R. 325, CAT

Albion Water Ltd v Water Services Regulation Authority (formerly Director General of Water Services) [2006] CAT 36; [2007] Comp. A.R. 328, CAT . . . . *Digested*, 07/**638**

Albion Water Ltd v Water Services Regulation Authority (formerly Director General of Water Services) C1/2007/0373 & C1/2007/0374, CA (Civ Div); affirming [2006] CAT 23; [2007] Comp. A.R. 22, CAT . . . . *Digested*, 07/**655**

Albion Water Ltd v Water Services Regulation Authority (formerly Director General of Water Services); *joined case* Aquavitae (UK) Ltd v Water Services Regulation Authority (formerly Director General of Water Services) [2006] CAT 25; [2007] Comp. A.R. 264, CAT. . . . . *Digested*, 07/**637**

Albion Water Ltd v Water Services Regulation Authority (formerly Director General of Water Services) [2007] CAT 2; [2007] Comp. A.R. 553, CAT

Albion Water Ltd v Water Services Regulation Authority (formerly Director General of Water Services) [2007] CAT 5; [2007] Comp. A.R. 564, CAT

Albion Water Ltd v Water Services Regulation Authority (formerly Director General of Water Services) [2007] CAT 1; [2007] Comp. A.R. 505, CAT

Albion Water Ltd v Water Services Regulation Authority (formerly Director General of Water Services) [2007] CAT 8; [2007] Comp. A.R. 567, CAT

Albion Water Ltd v Water Services Regulation Authority (Leave to Appeal) [2007] U.K.C.L.R. 1577, CA (Civ Div)

Albon (t/a NA Carriage Co) v Naza Motor Trading Sdn Bhd [2007] EWHC 9 (Ch); [2007] 1 W.L.R. 2489; [2007] 2 All E.R. 719; [2007] 1 All E.R. (Comm) 795; [2007] 1 Lloyd's Rep. 297; [2007] Bus. L.R. D87, Ch D . . . . *Digested*, 07/**520**

Albon (t/a NA Carriage Co) v Naza Motor Trading Sdn Bhd [2007] EWCA Civ 1124; [2007] 2 C.L.C. 782, CA (Civ Div); affirming [2007] EWHC 1879 (Ch); [2007] 2 Lloyd's Rep. 420, Ch D

Albon (t/a NA Carriage Co) v Naza Motor Trading Sdn Bhd [2007] EWHC 665 (Ch); [2007] 2 All E.R. 1075; [2007] 2 All E.R. (Comm) 513; [2007] 2 Lloyd's Rep. 1, Ch D . . . . *Digested*, 07/**529**

Albon (t/a NA Carriage Co) v Naza Motor Trading Sdn Bhd [2007] EWHC 2613 (Ch); (2007) 157 N.L.J. 1615, Ch D

Albon (t/a NA Carriage Co) v Naza Motor Trading Sdn Bhd [2007] EWHC 327 (Ch); [2007] 1 All E.R. (Comm) 813, Ch D . . . . *Digested*, 07/**519**

Alcock v Chief Constable of South Yorkshire; *sub nom* Jones v Wright; *joined cases* Penk v Wright; Jones v Chief Constable of South Yorkshire; Copoc v Chief Constable of South Yorkshire [1992] 1 A.C. 310; [1991] 3 W.L.R. 1057; [1991] 4 All E.R. 907; [1992] P.I.Q.R. P1; (1992) 89(3) L.S.G. 34; (1991) 141 N.L.J. 166; (1992) 136 S.J.L.B. 9; *Times*, November 29, 1991; *Independent*, November 29, 1991; *Guardian*, December 11, 1991, HL; affirming [1991] 3 All E.R. 88; *Times*, May 6, 1991; *Independent*, May 10, 1991; *Guardian*, May 9, 1991, CA (Civ Div); affirming [1991] 2 W.L.R. 814; [1991] 1 All E.R. 353; (1990) 140 N.L.J. 1717; *Independent*, December 7, 1990, QBD . . . . *Digested*, 92/**3250**:
Applied, 92/3253, 93/2972, 95/6157, 98/3938, 00/531, 01/5352, 01/6665, 02/948, 03/5828: *Considered*, 95/3682, 97/2615, 98/4035, 99/4059, 00/4213, 00/4220, 00/6598, 03/3132, 03/5844, 05/2834, 07/4654:
Distinguished, 03/3028

Alcon Inc v Office for Harmonisation in the Internal Market (Trade Marks and Designs) (OHIM) (C-412/05 P) [2007] E.T.M.R. 68; [2007] Bus. L.R. D85, ECJ

Aldi Stores Ltd v WSP Group Plc [2007] EWCA Civ 1260; 115 Con. L.R. 49; (2007) 104(48) L.S.G. 24; [2007] N.P.C. 128; *Times*, December 4, 2007, CA (Civ Div); reversing [2007] EWHC 55 (TCC); [2007] B.L.R. 113, QBD (TCC). . . . . *Digested*, 07/**346**

Alecansan SL v Office for Harmonisation in the Internal Market (Trade Marks and Designs) (OHIM) (T-202/03) [2006] E.T.M.R. 93, CFI (1st Chamber) . . . . *Digested*, 07/**2641**

Alevizos v Ipourgos Ikonomikon (C-392/05) [2007] 2 C.M.L.R. 51, ECJ (4th Chamber) . . . . *Digested*, 07/**1575**

Alexander v Bridgen Enterprises Ltd [2006] I.C.R. 1277; [2006] I.R.L.R. 422, EAT . . . *Digested*, 06/**1308**:
Applied, 07/1431: *Followed*, 06/1335

Alexander v Standard Telephones & Cables Ltd (No.2); *joined case* Wall v Standard Telephones & Cables Ltd (No.2) [1991] I.R.L.R. 286; *Independent*, July 31, 1989, Ch D . . . . *Digested*, 91/**1620**:
Applied, 98/2107: *Considered*, 04/1200, 07/1396: *Followed*, 98/2110

Alexander's Application, Re see Scottish Ministers v Scottish Information Commissioner

Alfa Vita Vissilopoulos AE (formerly Trofo Super-Markets AE) *v* Greece (C-158/04)
    [2006] E.C.R. I-8135; [2007] 2 C.M.L.R. 2, ECJ (1st Chamber)
Alford *v* West Bromwich Building Society see Investors Compensation Scheme Ltd *v*
    West Bromwich Building Society (No.1)
Alhamrani *v* Russa Management Ltd [2007] W.T.L.R. 1317, Royal Ct (Jer)
Ali *v* Lane [2006] EWCA Civ 1532; [2007] 1 P. & C.R. 26; [2007] 2 E.G. 126; [2006]
    48 E.G. 231 (C.S.); [2006] N.P.C. 124; *Times*, December 4, 2006, CA (Civ Div)   *Digested*, 07/**3364**:
    Applied, 07/3365

Ali *v* Lord Grey School Governors; *sub nom* A *v* Headteacher and Governors of Lord
    Grey School [2006] UKHL 14; [2006] 2 A.C. 363; [2006] 2 W.L.R. 690;
    [2006] 2 All E.R. 457; [2006] H.R.L.R. 20; [2006] U.K.H.R.R. 591; 20 B.H.R.C.
    295; [2006] E.L.R. 223; *Times*, March 27, 2006; *Independent*, March 28,
    2006, HL; reversing [2004] EWCA Civ 382; [2004] Q.B. 1231; [2004] 2 W.L.R.
    1442; [2004] 4 All E.R. 628; [2005] B.L.G.R. 212; [2004] E.L.R. 169; (2004)
    101 (14) L.S.G. 25; (2004) 148 S.J.L.B. 417; *Times*, April 9, 2004; *Independent*,
    April 1, 2004, CA (Civ Div); reversing in part [2003] EWHC 1533 (QB); [2003]
    4 All E.R. 1317; [2003] E.L.R. 517; (2003) 100(34) L.S.G. 29; *Times*, August
    14, 2003, QBD. . . . .   *Digested*, 06/**1139**:
    Applied, 07/1179: *Considered*, 04/1023, 06/1145
Ali *v* Pattni see Pattni *v* Ali
Ali *v* Smith (Unreported, October 6, 2006), CC (Brentford) . . . .   *Digested*, 07/**524**
Ali *v* Southwark LBC [1988] I.C.R. 567; [1988] I.R.L.R. 100, Ch D . . . .   *Digested*, 88/**1253**:
    Applied, 07/1380
Ali (t/a Vakas Balti) *v* Revenue and Customs Commissioners [2006] EWCA Civ 1572;
    [2007] S.T.C. 618; [2007] B.T.C. 5003; [2006] S.T.I. 2530, CA (Civ Div);
    reversing [2006] EWHC 23 (Ch); [2006] S.T.C. 1872; [2006] B.T.C. 5116;
    [2006] B.V.C. 185; [2006] S.T.I. 233, Ch D . . . .   *Digested*, 07/**4297**
Alker *v* Collingwood Housing Association [2007] EWCA Civ 343; [2007] 1 W.L.R.
    2230; [2007] H.L.R. 29; [2007] L. & T.R. 23; [2007] 25 E.G. 184; *Times*,
    February 14, 2007, CA (Civ Div) . . . .   *Digested*, 07/**2738**
Allaway *v* Reilly [2007] I.R.L.R. 864, EAT (SC)
Allen *v* Exel Logistics Ltd (Unreported, October 16, 2006), CC (Newbury) [*Ex rel.*
    Fentons Solicitors, 5th Floor, Trafftord House, Chester Road, Old Trafford,
    Manchester] . . . .   *Digested*, 07/**2079**
Allen *v* Flood; *sub nom* Flood *v* Jackson [1898] A.C. 1, HL; reversing [1895] 2 Q.B.
    21, CA . . . .   *Applied*, 52/3507:
    68/3954: *Considered*, 62/3063, 64/3703, 67/3981, 07/4190
Allen *v* Matthews [2007] EWCA Civ 216; [2007] B.P.I.R. 281; [2007] 2 P. & C.R. 21;
    [2007] N.P.C. 30, CA (Civ Div) . . . .   *Digested*, 07/**3353**
Allen (Deceased), Re; *sub nom* Lewis *v* Vincent (2007-08) 10 I.T.E.L.R. 506, HC (NZ)
Alliance & Leicester Building Society *v* Paul Robinson & Co CHANF 1999/0164/A3, CA
    (Civ Div); affirming 95-A-7546, Ch D . . . .   *Considered*, 07/1057
Alliance & Leicester Plc *v* Revenue and Customs Commissioners [2007] V. & D.R. 240;
    [2007] S.T.I. 1703, V&DTr (Manchester)
Allied Domecq Retailing Ltd *v* Williams (Valuation Officer) see Williams (Valuation
    Officer) *v* Scottish & Newcastle Retail Ltd
Allied Maples Group Ltd *v* Simmons & Simmons [1995] 1 W.L.R. 1602; [1995] 4 All
    E.R. 907; [1996] C.L.C. 153; 46 Con. L.R. 134; [1955-95] P.N.L.R. 701; (1995)
    145 N.L.J. 1646; [1995] N.P.C. 83; (1995) 70 P. & C.R. D14, CA (Civ Div) . . . .   *Digested*, 96/**4489**:
    Applied, 97/3832, 98/1447, 98/3604, 00/4266, 00/4276, 03/946, 03/3015,
    05/2880, 05/3419, 06/1026, 07/1316: *Considered*, 96/4482, 96/4505,
    97/3839, 97/3903, 00/4264, 02/1318, 06/2900: *Distinguished*, 03/3121,
    04/913: *Followed*, 05/2877: *Not applied*, 01/537: *Referred to*, 97/3917
Allmark *v* Burnham; *sub nom* Distinct Services Ltd, Re [2005] EWHC 2717 (Ch);
    [2006] 2 B.C.L.C. 437, Ch D (Companies Ct) . . . .   *Digested*, 07/**593**
Allnutt *v* Allnutt see Allnutt *v* Wilding
Allnutt *v* Wilding; *sub nom* Strain (Deceased), Re; Allnutt *v* Allnutt [2007] EWCA Civ
    412; [2007] B.T.C. 8003; [2007] W.T.L.R. 941; (2006-07) 9 I.T.E.L.R. 806, CA
    (Civ Div); affirming [2006] EWHC 1905 (Ch); [2006] B.T.C. 8040; [2006]
    W.T.L.R. 1317; (2006-07) 9 I.T.E.L.R. 381; (2006) 150 S.J.L.B. 1057, Ch D . . . .   *Digested*, 07/**4247**
Allsports Ltd *v* Office of Fair Trading see JJB Sports Plc *v* Office of Fair Trading
Almatrans SA *v* Steamship Mutual Underwriting Association (Bermuda) Ltd (The
    Tutova) [2006] EWHC 2223 (Comm); [2007] 1 Lloyd's Rep. 104, QBD
    (Comm) . . . .   *Digested*, 07/**2500**
Almond *v* Ash Bros & Heaton see Dawkins (Valuation Officer) *v* Ash Bros & Heaton
    Ltd
Aloe Vera of America Inc *v* United States 9 I.T.L. Rep. 727, US Court
Alpha Club (UK) Ltd, Re; *joined case* Marketing Services Worldwide (UK) Ltd, Re
    [2002] EWHC 884 (Ch); [2004] B.C.C. 754; [2002] 2 B.C.L.C. 612, Ch D . . .   *Digested*, 03/**2413**:
    Not followed, 07/2463

Alphacell Ltd v Woodward [1972] A.C. 824; [1972] 2 W.L.R. 1320; [1972] 2 All E.R. 475; 70 L.G.R. 455; [1972] Crim. L.R. 41; (1972) 116 S.J. 431, HL; affirming [1972] 1 Q.B. 127; [1971] 3 W.L.R. 445; [1971] 2 All E.R. 910; 69 L.G.R. 561; (1971) 115 S.J. 464, QBD . . . . *Digested,* 72/**3549**:
Applied, 75/2750, 95/5131, 95/5132, 95/5136, 97/2346: *Considered,* 84/950, 87/117, 89/3783, 89/3789, 94/2032, 95/5133, 95/5135, 07/1528: *Followed,* 81/3731

Alpro Ltd v Revenue and Customs Commissioners [2007] S.T.I. 387, V&DTr (London)

Alrosa Co Ltd v Commission of the European Communities (T-170/06) [2007] 5 C.M.L.R. 7, CFI (4th Chamber)

Altitude Scaffolding Ltd, Re; *joined case* T&N Ltd, Re [2006] EWHC 1401 (Ch); [2006] B.C.C. 904; [2007] 1 B.C.L.C. 199, Ch D (Companies Ct) . . . . *Digested,* 07/**2449**

Altmark Trans GmbH v Nahverkehrsgesellschaft Altmark GmbH (C-280/00) [2005] All E.R. (EC) 610; [2003] E.C.R. I-7747; [2003] 3 C.M.L.R. 12, ECJ . . . . *Digested,* 03/**4444**:
Applied, 04/551, 07/1621: *Considered,* 06/624, 07/649

Aluminium Silicon Mill Products GmbH v Council of the European Union (T-107/04) [2007] 2 C.M.L.R. 37, CFI (3rd Chamber). . . . . *Digested,* 07/**1584**

AM (3rd Party Support not Permitted r281 (v): Ethiopia), Re see AM (Ethiopia) v Secretary of State for the Home Department

AM (Ethiopia) v Secretary of State for the Home Department; *sub nom* AM (3rd Party Support not Permitted r281 (v): Ethiopia), Re [2007] UKAIT 58; [2007] Imm. A.R. 627, AIT

AM (Serbia) v Secretary of State for the Home Department see MA (Pakistan) v Secretary of State for the Home Department

Amann v Switzerland (27798/95) (2000) 30 E.H.R.R. 843, ECHR. . . . . *Digested,* 01/**3585**:
Applied, 07/2241, 07/2258: *Considered,* 00/921: *Distinguished,* 01/980

Amare v Secretary of State for the Home Department [2005] EWCA Civ 1600; [2006] Imm. A.R. 217, CA (Civ Div) . . . . *Digested,* 07/**2296**:
Applied, 06/2227

Amat-G Ltd v Georgia (2507/03) (2007) 45 E.H.R.R. 35, ECHR

Amec Developments Ltd v Jury's Hotel Management (UK) Ltd [2002] T.C.L.R. 13; (2001) 82 P. & C.R. 22; [2001] 1 E.G.L.R. 81; [2001] 07 E.G. 163; [2000] E.G. 138 (C.S.); [2000] N.P.C. 125, Ch D . . . . *Digested,* 01/**1549**:
Applied, 05/2693: *Considered,* 06/1018, 06/1019, 07/1060

Amendment to Game and Lottery Law, Re (E-1/06) see EFTA Surveillance Authority v Norway (E-1/06)

Amicus v MacMillan Publishers Ltd [2007] I.R.L.R. 378, CAC . . . . *Digested,* 07/**1378**

Amicus v MacMillan Publishers Ltd [2007] I.R.L.R. 885; (2007) 151 S.J.L.B. 1058, EAT

Amjad v Steadman-Byrne see Steadman-Byrne v Amjad

Amoako v DPP see R. (on the application of Amoako) v DPP

AMP (UK) Plc v Barker [2001] O.P.L.R. 197; [2001] Pens. L.R. 77; [2001] W.T.L.R. 1237; (2000-01) 3 I.T.E.L.R. 414, Ch D . . . . *Digested,* 01/**4595**:
Applied, 05/3420, 06/2986: *Considered,* 07/4247: *Followed,* 05/2990

Amurta SGPS v Inspecteur van de Belastingdienst/Amsterdam (C-379/05) [2007] S.T.I. 2648, ECJ (1st Chamber)

Amuur v France (1996) 22 E.H.R.R. 533, ECHR . . . . *Digested,* 97/**2766**:
Applied, 01/3620, 07/2229: *Considered,* 00/3248

Amwell View School Governors v Dogherty [2007] I.C.R. 135; [2007] I.R.L.R. 198; *Times,* October 5, 2006, EAT . . . . *Digested,* 06/**1302**

AN v Barclays Private Bank & Trust (Cayman) Ltd [2007] W.T.L.R. 565; (2006-07) 9 I.T.E.L.R. 630, Grand Ct (CI) . . . . *Digested,* 07/**4255**

An NHS Trust v D [2005] EWHC 2439 (Fam); [2006] 1 F.L.R. 638; [2006] Lloyd's Rep. Med. 193; (2006) 87 B.M.L.R. 119; [2006] Fam. Law 100, Fam Div . . . . . *Digested,* 06/**1852**:
Considered, 07/1986

An NHS Trust v J see B NHS Trust v J

An NHS Trust v MB [2006] EWHC 507 (Fam); [2006] 2 F.L.R. 319; (2006) 9 C.C.L. Rep. 568; [2006] Lloyd's Rep. Med. 323; [2006] Fam. Law 445, Fam Div. . . . *Digested,* 06/**1847**:
Considered, 07/1984

Anders & Kern UK Ltd (t/a Anders & Kern Presentation Systems) v CGU Insurance Plc (t/a Norwich Union Insurance) [2007] EWCA Civ 1481, CA (Civ Div); affirming [2007] EWHC 377 (Comm); [2007] 2 All E.R. (Comm) 1160; [2007] Lloyd's Rep. I.R. 555, QBD. . . . . *Digested,* 07/**2478**

Anderson v Customs and Excise Commissioners see Hughes v Customs and Excise Commissioners

Anderson v Revenue and Customs Commissioners [2007] V. & D.R. 137, V&DTr (London)

Anderton v Clwyd CC see Phelps v Hillingdon LBC

Anderton *v* Clwyd CC; *sub nom* Cummins *v* Shell International Trading & Shipping Ltd; Home Office *v* Dorgan; Bryant *v* Pech; *joined cases* Cummins *v* Shell International Manning Services Ltd; Chambers *v* Southern Domestic Electrical Services Ltd; Dorgan *v* Home Office; Bryant *v* Mike Beer Transport Ltd [2002] EWCA Civ 933; [2002] 1 W.L.R. 3174; [2002] 3 All E.R. 813; [2002] C.P. Rep. 71; (2002) 99(35) L.S.G. 38; (2002) 152 N.L.J. 1125; (2002) 146 S.J.L.B. 177; *Times,* July 16, 2002; *Independent,* July 11, 2002, CA (Civ Div); reversing [2001] C.P. Rep. 110, QBD . . . .   *Digested,* 02/**491**:
                                                   Applied, 02/476, 03/455, 03/456, 04/412, 07/371, 07/433:
                                                   Considered, 03/2724, 04/383, 06/347: *Followed,* 05/341
Andrews *v* Cunningham [2007] EWCA Civ 762; [2007] N.P.C. 93, CA (Civ Div)
Angel Airlines SA *v* Dean & Dean Solicitors [2006] EWCA Civ 1505; [2007] 3 Costs L.R. 355; *Times,* November 28, 2006, CA (Civ Div)
Angelikotonou *v* National Westminster Bank Plc see National Westminster Bank Plc *v* Kotonou (Costs)
Angelov *v* Finland (Admissibility) (26832/03) (2007) 44 E.H.R.R. SE2, ECHR
Angelova *v* Bulgaria (55523/00) 23 B.H.R.C. 61, ECHR
Angiotech Pharmaceuticals Inc *v* Conor Medsystems Inc see Conor Medsystems Inc *v* Angiotech Pharmaceuticals Inc
Angiotech Pharmaceuticals Inc's Patent (No.706376) see Conor Medsystems Inc *v* Angiotech Pharmaceuticals Inc
Anglo Petroleum Ltd *v* TFB (Mortgages) Ltd; *joined cases* TFB (Mortgages) Ltd *v* Sutton; TFB (Mortgages) Ltd *v* Anglo Petroleum Ltd [2007] EWCA Civ 456; [2007] B.C.C. 407, CA (Civ Div); affirming [2006] EWHC 258 (Ch), Ch D . . .   *Digested,* 07/**576**
Anglo-Northern Trading Co Ltd *v* Emlyn Jones & Williams see Countess of Warwick Steamship Co *v* Le Nickel SA
Angonese *v* Cassa di Risparmio di Bolzano SpA (C-281/98) [2000] All E.R. (EC) 577; [2000] E.C.R. I-4139; [2000] 2 C.M.L.R. 1120; [2000] C.E.C. 374, ECJ . .   *Digested,* 00/**2387**:
                                                                                 Followed, 07/3830
Angora Trust, Re see Schmidt *v* Rosewood Trust Ltd
Anheuser-Busch Inc *v* Budejovicky Budvar Narodni Podnik (C-245/02) [2004] E.C.R. I-10989; [2005] E.T.M.R. 27, ECJ. . . . .   *Digested,* 05/**2587**:
                                                                                 Applied, 07/2679
Anheuser-Busch Inc *v* Budejovicky Budvar NP [2006] E.T.M.R. 77, HD (Swe). . . . . . .   *Digested,* 07/**2664**:
                                                                          Subsequent related litigation, 07/2664
Anheuser-Busch Inc *v* Portugal (73049/01) [2006] E.T.M.R. 43; (2007) 44 E.H.R.R. 42, ECHR . . . .   *Digested,* 06/**2122**
Anheuser-Busch Inc *v* Portugal (73049/01) [2007] E.T.M.R. 24; (2007) 45 E.H.R.R. 36; 23 B.H.R.C. 307, ECHR (Grand Chamber) . . . .   *Digested,* 07/**2636**
Anheuser-Busch Inc's Community Trade Mark Application (R234/2005-2) [2007] E.T.M.R. 23, OHIM (2nd Bd App) . . . .   *Digested,* 07/**2650**
Aniagwu *v* Hackney LBC; *joined case* Aniagwu *v* Owens [1999] I.R.L.R. 303, EAT . . .   *Digested,* 99/**2099**:
                                                   Disapproved, 02/1400: *Distinguished,* 00/2128: *Doubted,* 07/1389
Aniagwu *v* Owens see Aniagwu *v* Hackney LBC
Anklagemyndigheden *v* Festersen (C-370/05) see Criminal Proceedings against Festersen (C-370/05)
Annable *v* Southern Derbyshire HA see Heil *v* Rankin
ANOTIO/Right to submit observations (T47/04) [2006] E.P.O.R. 35, EPO (Technical Bd App) . . . .   *Digested,* 07/**2560**
Ansar *v* Lloyds TSB Bank Plc [2006] EWCA Civ 1462; [2007] I.R.L.R. 211, CA (Civ Div); affirming [2006] I.C.R. 1565, EAT. . . . .   *Digested,* 07/**1343**
Ansell (Inspector of Taxes) *v* Brown [2001] S.T.C. 1166; 73 T.C. 338; [2001] B.T.C. 381; [2001] S.T.I. 847; (2001) 98(31) L.S.G. 37; *Times,* June 20, 2001, Ch D . . . . . .   *Digested,* 01/**5242**:
                                                                                 Considered, 07/4052
Ansul BV *v* Ajax Brandbeveiliging BV (C-40/01) [2005] Ch. 97; [2004] 3 W.L.R. 1048; [2003] E.C.R. I-2439; [2005] 2 C.M.L.R. 36; [2003] E.T.M.R. 85; [2003] R.P.C. 40; (2005) 28(4) I.P.D. 28022, ECJ . . . .   *Digested,* 04/**2386**:
                                                   Applied, 04/2416, 05/2540, 05/2582, 06/2553: *Considered,* 03/2635,
                                                                              04/2416: *Followed,* 07/2676
Antartica Srl *v* Office for Harmonisation in the Internal Market (Trade Marks and Designs) (OHIM) (T-47/06) [2007] E.T.M.R. 77, CFI (3rd Chamber)
Antonelli *v* Secretary of State for Trade and Industry [1998] Q.B. 948; [1998] 2 W.L.R. 826; [1998] 1 All E.R. 997; (1998) 10 Admin. L.R. 75; [1998] 1 E.G.L.R. 9; [1998] 14 E.G. 133; [1998] C.O.D. 178; (1997) 94(35) L.S.G. 35; (1997) 141 S.J.L.B. 198; [1997] N.P.C. 123; *Times,* October 3, 1997; *Independent,* October 14, 1997, CA (Civ Div); affirming [1996] 2 E.G.L.R. 229; [1995] C.O.D. 334; [1995] N.P.C. 68, QBD. . . . .   *Digested,* 97/**82**:
                                                                                 Applied, 06/2219, 07/1952
Antoni *v* Antoni [2007] UKPC 10; [2007] W.T.L.R. 1335, PC (Bah) . . . .   *Digested,* 07/**4236**
Antoniades *v* East Sussex Hospitals NHS Trust [2007] EWHC 517 (QB); (2007) 95 B.M.L.R. 62, QBD . . . .   *Digested,* 07/**2921**

Anufrijeva v Southwark LBC; *sub nom* R. (on the application of Anufrijeva) v Southwark LBC; *joined cases* R. (on the application of N) v Secretary of State for the Home Department; R. (on the application of M) v Secretary of State for the Home Department [2003] EWCA Civ 1406; [2004] Q.B. 1124; [2004] 2 W.L.R. 603; [2004] 1 All E.R. 833; [2004] 1 F.L.R. 8; [2003] 3 F.C.R. 673; [2004] H.R.L.R. 1; [2004] U.K.H.R.R. 1; 15 B.H.R.C. 526; [2004] H.L.R. 22; [2004] B.L.G.R. 184; (2003) 6 C.C.L. Rep. 415; [2004] Fam. Law 12; (2003) 100(44) L.S.G. 30; *Times*, October 17, 2003; *Independent*, October 23, 2003, CA (Civ Div); affirming in part [2002] EWHC 3163 (QB); (2003) 6 C.C.L. Rep. 25, QBD . . . . *Digested*, 04/**1986**:
       Applied, 03/2246, 05/3947, 07/1717: *Considered*, 07/54, 07/2238:
       Previous proceedings, 03/2246

Anyanwu v South Bank Students Union [2001] UKHL 14; [2001] 1 W.L.R. 638; [2001] 2 All E.R. 353; [2001] I.C.R. 391; [2001] I.R.L.R. 305; [2001] Emp. L.R. 420; [2001] E.L.R. 511; (2001) 98(21) L.S.G. 39; (2001) 151 N.L.J. 501; (2001) 145 S.J.L.B. 110; *Times*, March 27, 2001; *Independent*, March 28, 2001, HL; reversing [2000] 1 All E.R. 1; [2000] I.C.R. 221; [2000] I.R.L.R. 36; [2000] E.L.R. 229; (1999) 96(43) L.S.G. 34; (1999) 143 S.J.L.B. 271; *Times*, November 4, 1999; *Independent*, December 13, 1999, CA (Civ Div); reversing (Unreported, January 21, 1998), EAT . . . . *Digested*, 01/**2300**:
       Applied, 06/1363: *Considered*, 07/1428: *Followed*, 01/3492

AP v Vale of Glamorgan CC see P (Children) (Care Proceedings: Split Hearing), Re

AP (Citizens Directive Article 3(2): Discretion: Dependence: India), Re see AP (India) v Secretary of State for the Home Department

AP (India) v Secretary of State for the Home Department; *sub nom* AP (Citizens Directive Article 3(2): Discretion: Dependence: India), Re [2007] UKAIT 48; [2007] Imm. A.R. 692, AIT

Apex Frozen Foods Ltd (In Liquidation) v Ali [2007] EWHC 469 (Ch); [2007] 5 Costs L.R. 818; [2007] B.P.I.R. 1437, Ch D

Appellant v South African Revenue Service Commissioner 10 I.T.L. Rep. 446

Appiah v Bishop Douglass Roman Catholic High School Governors [2007] EWCA Civ 10; [2007] I.C.R. 897; [2007] I.R.L.R. 264; [2007] E.L.R. 217, CA (Civ Div) . .   *Digested*, 07/**1184**

Apple and Pear Development Council v Customs and Excise Commissioners; *sub nom* Customs and Excise Commissioners v Apple and Pear Development Council [1986] S.T.C. 192; [1987] 2 C.M.L.R. 634, HL; affirming in part [1985] S.T.C. 383; (1985) 82 L.S.G. 1643; (1985) 129 S.J. 300, CA (Civ Div); affirming [1984] S.T.C. 296, DC; affirming [1984] 2 C.M.L.R. 217; [1983] V.A.T.T.R. 142, VAT Tr . . . . *Digested*, 86/**3485**:
       Applied, 90/4626, 90/4627, 03/4553, 07/4309: *Considered*, 90/4626, 98/4922

Appleton v Garrett [1996] P.I.Q.R. P1; [1997] 8 Med. L.R. 75; (1997) 34 B.M.L.R. 23, QBD . . . . *Digested*, 97/**3798**:
       Considered, 04/914, 07/1060

Aquavitae (UK) Ltd v Water Services Regulation Authority (formerly Director General of Water Services) see Albion Water Ltd v Water Services Regulation Authority (formerly Director General of Water Services)

Aquavitae (UK) Ltd v Water Services Regulation Authority (formerly Director General of Water Services) [2007] CAT 4; [2007] Comp. A.R. 609, CAT

Aquila Design (GRB) Products v Cornhill Insurance (1987) 3 B.C.C. 364; [1988] B.C.L.C. 134, CA (Civ Div) . . . . *Digested*, 87/**2952**:
       Applied, 07/416

Arab African Energy Corp v Olie Producten Nederland BV [1983] 2 Lloyd's Rep. 419; [1983] Com. L.R. 195, QBD (Comm) . . . . *Digested*, 83/**139**:
       Applied, 00/217: *Considered*, 07/233

Aramis, The [1989] 1 Lloyd's Rep. 213; *Financial Times*, November 22, 1988, CA (Civ Div); reversing [1987] 2 Lloyd's Rep. 58, QBD (Admlty) . . . . *Digested*, 90/**4057**:
       Applied, 06/1315, 07/1347

Arbeitsgemeinschaft der Offentlich Rechtlichen Rundfunkanstalten der Bundesrepublik Deutschland (ARD) v Commission of the European Communities (T158/00) [2003] E.C.R. II-3825; [2004] 5 C.M.L.R. 14, CFI (3rd Chamber) . . . .   *Applied*, 07/639

Arbory Group Ltd v West Craven Insurance Services [2007] Lloyd's Rep. I.R. 491; [2007] P.N.L.R. 23, QBD (Leeds) . . . . *Digested*, 07/**2480**

Arbuthnot v Gulututan (Unreported, May 30, 2007), CC (Ilford) [*Ex rel*. Nigel Ffitch, Barrister, Phoenix Chambers, Gray's Inn, London] . . . . *Digested*, 07/**3098**

Arbuthnot Latham Bank Ltd v Trafalgar Holdings Ltd; *joined case* Chishty Coveney & Co v Raja [1998] 1 W.L.R. 1426; [1998] 2 All E.R. 181; [1998] C.L.C. 615; *Times*, December 29, 1997, CA (Civ Div) . . . . *Digested*, 98/**619**:
       Applied, 00/608, 03/473: *Considered*, 98/611, 00/344, 00/4656, 01/671, 07/3957: *Followed*, 98/3363, 00/348

Arbuthnott v Fagan (Discovery); *joined case* Arbuthnott v Feltrim Underwriting Agencies Ltd (In Liquidation) (Discovery) [1996] L.R.L.R. 143; *Independent*, July 11, 1994, CA (Civ Div); affirming [1994] C.L.C. 659, QBD (Comm) . . . . . . *Digested*, 96/**3585**:
       Applied, 07/439: *Considered*, 98/340

Arbuthnott *v* Feltrim Underwriting Agencies Ltd (In Liquidation) (Discovery) see
  Arbuthnott *v* Fagan (Discovery)

Arcelor Atlantique et Lorraine, Re [2007] 2 C.M.L.R. 28, CE (F) . . . .   *Digested,* 07/**1569**

ARCH/Copper pyrithione (T178/03) [2006] E.P.O.R. 41, EPO (Technical Bd App). . . .   *Digested,* 07/**2564**

Archer Daniels Midland Co *v* Commission of the European Communities (C-397/03 P)
  [2006] E.C.R. I-4429; [2006] 5 C.M.L.R. 4, ECJ (1st Chamber) . . . .   *Digested,* 07/**607**

Archer Daniels Midland Co *v* Commission of the European Communities (T-329/01);
  sub nom Sodium Gluconate Cartel, Re (T-329/01) [2007] 4 C.M.L.R. 2, CFI
  (3rd Chamber)

Archer Daniels Midland Co *v* Commission of the European Communities (T-59/02); *sub
  nom* Citric Acid Cartel, Re (T-59/02) [2006] 5 C.M.L.R. 28, CFI (3rd
  Chamber) . . . .   *Digested,* 07/**610**

Archer Daniels Midland Co *v* Commission of the European Communities (T224/00)
  [2003] E.C.R. II-2597; [2003] 5 C.M.L.R. 12, CFI (4th Chamber) . . . .   *Digested,* 04/**502**:
                                             Preliminary ruling given, 07/607

Architects of Wine Ltd *v* Barclays Bank Plc [2007] EWCA Civ 239; [2007] 2 All E.R.
  (Comm) 285; [2007] 2 Lloyd's Rep. 471; (2007) 151 S.J.L.B. 431; [2007] Bus.
  L.R. D37, CA (Civ Div); affirming [2006] EWHC 1648 (QB); [2007] 1 All E.R.
  (Comm) 152; [2007] 1 Lloyd's Rep. 55; [2007] 1 B.C.L.C. 218, QBD (Comm) .   *Digested,* 07/**300**

ARCO Chemie Nederland Ltd *v* Minister van Volkshuisvesting, Ruimtelijke Ordening en
  Milieubeheer (C-418/97); *sub nom* Epon, Re (C-419/97); *joined case* Vereniging
  Dorpsbelang Hees *v* Directeur van de dienst Milieu en Water van de provincie
  Gelderland (C-419/97) [2002] Q.B. 646; [2002] 2 W.L.R. 1240; [2003] All
  E.R. (EC) 237; [2000] E.C.R. I-4475; [2003] Env. L.R. 2; [2001] Env. L.R. D6,
  ECJ (5th Chamber) . . . .   *Digested,* 02/**1519**:
      Applied, 02/1520, 02/1521: *Considered,* 01/2413, 05/1362, 07/1518:
                                             Followed, 05/1414

ArcorAG & Co KG (formerly ISIS Multimedia Net GmbH & Co KG) *v* Germany (C-422/04)
  see I-21 Germany GmbH *v* Germany (C-392/04)

Ardenglen Developments Ltd *v* Revenue and Customs Commissioners [2007] S.T.I.
  385, V&DTr (Edinburgh)

Arduino *v* Compagnia Assicuratrice RAS SpA (C35/99) see Criminal Proceedings
  against Arduino (C35/99)

Argos Ltd *v* Office of Fair Trading [2004] CAT 24; [2005] Comp. A.R. 588, CAT . . . . .   *Digested,* 06/**602**:
                                      Subsequent related litigation, 07/621

Argos Ltd *v* Office of Fair Trading; *joined case* JJB Sports Plc *v* Office of Fair Trading
  [2006] EWCA Civ 1318; [2006] U.K.C.L.R. 1135; (2006) 103(42) L.S.G. 32;
  (2006) 150 S.J.L.B. 1391, CA (Civ Div) . . . .   *Digested,* 07/**621**:
                                        Previous proceedings, 06/602

Argos Ltd *v* Office of Fair Trading (Penalties) [2005] CAT 13; [2005] Comp. A.R. 834,
  CAT. . . . .   *Digested,* 06/**603**:
                                      Subsequent related litigation, 07/621

Aribisala *v* St James Homes (Grosvenor Dock) Ltd [2007] EWHC 1694 (Ch); [2007]
  37 E.G. 234; [2007] 25 E.G. 183 (C.S.); [2007] 2 P. & C.R. DG25, Ch D . . . . .   *Digested,* 07/**3394**

Arif (t/a Trinity Fisheries) *v* Revenue and Customs Commissioners [2006] EWHC 1262
  (Ch); [2006] S.T.C. 1989; [2006] B.T.C. 5759; [2006] B.V.C. 829; [2006] S.T.I.
  1619, Ch D; affirming [2006] S.T.I. 286, V&DTr . . . .   *Digested,* 07/**4283**

Arjona *v* Instituto Nacional de la Seguridad Social (INSS) (C-31/96); *joined cases*
  Instituto Nacional de la Seguridad Social (INSS) *v* Lazaro (C-33/96); Mateos *v*
  Instituto Nacional de la Seguridad Social (INSS) (C-32/96) [1997] E.C.R. I-
  5501, ECJ . . . .   *Applied,* 07/1626

Arkin *v* Borchard Lines Ltd (Costs Order) [2005] EWCA Civ 655; [2005] 1 W.L.R.
  3055; [2005] 3 All E.R. 613; [2005] 2 Lloyd's Rep. 187; [2005] C.P. Rep. 39;
  [2005] 4 Costs L.R. 643; (2005) 155 N.L.J. 902; *Times,* June 3, 2005;
  Independent, June 7, 2005, CA (Civ Div); reversing in part [2003] EWHC 2844
  (Comm); [2004] 1 Lloyd's Rep. 88; [2004] 2 Costs L.R. 231; (2003) 153
  N.L.J. 1903, QBD (Comm) . . . .   *Digested,* 05/**385**:
                                Applied, 07/405: *Considered,* 07/421

Armah *v* Ghana (No.1); *sub nom* R. *v* Governor of Brixton Prison Ex p. Armah (No.1);
  Kwesi Armah, Re [1968] A.C. 192; [1966] 3 W.L.R. 828; [1966] 3 All E.R. 177;
  (1967) 131 J.P. 43; (1966) 110 S.J. 890, HL; reversing [1966] 3 W.L.R. 23;
  [1966] 2 All E.R. 1006; (1966) 110 S.J. 468, QBD . . . .   *Digested,* 66/**5069**:
                                      Applied, 91/1756, 07/1672

Armitage *v* West Bromwich Building Society see Investors Compensation Scheme Ltd
  v West Bromwich Building Society (No.1)

Armory *v* Delamirie 93 E.R. 664; (1722) 1 Str. 505, KB . . . .   *Applied,* 05/**957**,
                  07/**1058**: *Considered,* 95/3262, 06/297

Armstrong *v* Newcastle upon Tyne NHS Hospital Trust [2005] EWCA Civ 1608;
  [2006] I.R.L.R. 124, CA (Civ Div); affirming UKEAT/0158/04/DZM, EAT . . . . .   *Digested,* 07/**1360**:
                    Considered, 07/1364: *Doubted,* 06/1368

Arnander *v* Revenue and Customs Commissioners [2007] R.V.R. 208; [2006] S.T.C.
  (S.C.D.) 800; [2007] W.T.L.R. 51; [2006] S.T.I. 2460, Sp Comm . . . .   *Digested,* 07/**4105**

Arnold v National Westminster Bank Plc (No.1) [1991] 2 A.C. 93; [1991] 2 W.L.R.
  1177; [1991] 3 All E.R. 41; (1991) 62 P. & C.R. 490; [1991] 2 E.G.L.R. 109; [1991]
  30 E.G. 57; [1991] E.G. 49 (C.S.); (1991) 135 S.J. 574; Times, April 26, 1991,
  HL; affirming [1990] Ch. 573; [1990] 2 W.L.R. 304; [1990] 1 All E.R. 529;
  (1990) 59 P. & C.R. 389; [1990] 01 E.G. 58; (1990) 87(7) L.S.G. 35; (1990)
  134 S.J. 1010; Times, November 20, 1989; Independent, November 24, 1989, CA
  (Civ Div); affirming [1989] Ch. 63; [1988] 3 W.L.R. 1229; [1988] 3 All E.R.
  977; (1989) 58 P. & C.R. 175; [1988] 45 E.G. 106; [1988] E.G. 101 (C.S.);
  (1988) 85(46) L.S.G. 41; (1988) 138 N.L.J. Rep. 218; (1988) 132 S.J. 1639;
  Times, July 11, 1988; Independent, July 7, 1988, Ch D . . . . Digested, 91/**1736**:
         Applied, 91/203, 95/3781, 97/487, 00/3772, 03/1579, 06/2591, 07/3225:
           Considered, 92/2742, 96/2578, 97/766, 97/3886: Distinguished, 98/2162:
                                                  Followed, 99/370: Referred to, 94/2807

Arnold (Inspector of Taxes) v G-Con Ltd [2006] EWCA Civ 829; [2006] S.T.C. 1516;
  [2007] B.T.C. 244; [2006] S.T.I. 1517; Times, June 9, 2006, CA (Civ Div);
  affirming [2005] EWHC 2456 (Ch); [2006] S.T.C. 693; [2006] B.T.C. 383;
  [2005] S.T.I. 364; (2005) 102(18) L.S.G. 24; Times, March 14, 2005, Ch D . . . Digested, 06/**4212**:
                                                                  Applied, 06/4136

Arnup v MW White Ltd B3/2007/0740, CA (Civ Div); reversing in part [2007] EWHC
  601 (QB); [2007] P.I.Q.R. Q6; [2007] Pens. L.R. 135, QBD . . . . Digested, 07/**1056**

Arrow Generics Ltd v Akzo Nobel NV see Ivax Pharmaceuticals UK Ltd v Akzo Nobel
  BV

Arrow Generics Ltd v Merck & Co Inc [2007] EWHC 1900 (Pat); [2007] F.S.R. 39;
  (2007) 30(9) I.P.D. 30058, Ch D (Patents Ct)

Arrow Generics Ltd v Warner-Lambert Co see Ranbaxy UK Ltd v Warner-Lambert Co

Arrow Generics Ltd, Petitioners; sub nom Akzo NV's European Patent (EP 0 389 035)
  [2006] CSOH 146; 2006 S.L.T. 919; [2007] R.P.C. 11; 2006 G.W.D. 29-649,
  OH . . . . Digested, 06/**5538**

Arrowdell Ltd v Coniston Court (North) Hove Ltd [2007] R.V.R. 39, Lands Tr . . . . Digested, 07/**3370**

Arsenal Football Club Plc v Reed (C-206/01) [2003] Ch. 454; [2003] 3 W.L.R. 450;
  [2003] All E.R. (EC) 1; [2002] E.C.R. I-10273; [2003] 1 C.M.L.R. 12; [2003]
  C.E.C. 3; [2003] E.T.M.R. 19; [2003] R.P.C. 9; (2002) 152 N.L.J. 1808; Times,
  November 18, 2002, ECJ . . . . Digested, 02/**2912**:
                            Applied, 07/2653, 07/5324: Considered, 06/2595

Arsenal Football Club Plc v Reed (No.1) [2001] 2 C.M.L.R. 23; [2001] E.T.M.R. 77;
  [2001] R.P.C. 46; (2001) 24(6) I.P.D. 24037; Times, April 26, 2001; Daily
  Telegraph, April 17, 2001, Ch D . . . . Digested, 01/**4041**:
                      Distinguished, 02/2886, 07/2689: Preliminary ruling given, 02/2912

Arsenal Football Club Plc v Reed (No.2) [2003] EWCA Civ 696; [2003] 3 All E.R.
  865; [2003] 2 C.M.L.R. 25; [2003] Eu. L.R. 641; [2003] E.T.M.R. 73; [2003]
  R.P.C. 39; (2003) 26(7) I.P.D. 26045; (2003) 147 S.J.L.B. 663; Times, May 22,
  2003, CA (Civ Div); reversing [2002] EWHC 2695 (Ch); [2003] 1 All E.R. 137;
  [2003] 1 C.M.L.R. 13; [2002] Eu. L.R. 806; [2003] E.T.M.R. 36; (2003) 26(2)
  I.P.D. 26008; (2003) 100(3) L.S.G. 32; (2002) 152 N.L.J. 1923; Times,
  December 17, 2002; Independent, February 10, 2003, Ch D . . . . Digested, 03/**2640**:
                                                              Considered, 07/2674

Artesian Residential Developments Ltd v Beck; sub nom Artesian Residential
  Investments Ltd v Beck [2000] Q.B. 541; [2000] 2 W.L.R. 357; [1999] 3 All
  E.R. 113; (2000) 32 H.L.R. 107; [1999] L. & T.R. 278; [1999] 2 E.G.L.R. 30;
  [1999] 22 E.G. 145; [1999] E.G. 46 (C.S.); [1999] N.P.C. 41, CA (Civ Div) . . . . Digested, 99/**3710**:
                                                              Applied, 07/2718

Artesian Residential Investments Ltd v Beck see Artesian Residential Developments Ltd
  v Beck

Arthrex Inc's Community Trade Mark Application (R 154/2006-2) [2007] E.T.M.R. 14,
  OHIM (2nd Bd App) . . . . Digested, 07/**2657**

Arthur v London Eastern Railway Ltd (t/a One Stansted Express) [2006] EWCA Civ
  1358; [2007] I.C.R. 193; [2007] I.R.L.R. 58; (2006) 103(43) L.S.G. 30, CA (Civ
  Div) . . . . Digested, 07/**1440**

Arthur JS Hall & Co v Simons; sub nom Harris v Scholfield Roberts & Hall; Barratt v
  Ansell (t/a Woolf Seddon); joined cases Barratt v Woolf Seddon; Cockbone v
  Atkinson Dacre & Slack; Harris v Scholfield Roberts & Hill [2002] 1 A.C. 615;
  [2000] 3 W.L.R. 543; [2000] 3 All E.R. 673; [2000] B.L.R. 407; [2000] E.C.C.
  487; [2000] 2 F.L.R. 545; [2000] 2 F.C.R. 673; [2001] P.N.L.R. 6; [2000]
  Fam. Law 806; [2000] E.G. 99 (C.S.); (2000) 97(32) L.S.G. 38; (2000) 150
  N.L.J. 1147; (2000) 144 S.J.L.B. 238; [2000] N.P.C. 87; Times, July 21, 2000;
  Independent, July 25, 2000, HL; affirming [1999] 3 W.L.R. 873; [1999] 1 F.L.R.
  536; [1999] 2 F.C.R. 193; [1999] Lloyd's Rep. P.N. 47; [1999] P.N.L.R. 374;
  [1999] Fam. Law 215; [1998] N.P.C. 162; Times, December 18, 1998;
  Independent, December 18, 1998, CA (Civ Div); affirming [1998] 2 F.L.R. 679;
  [1999] P.N.L.R. 208; [1998] Fam. Law 524, QBD . . . . Digested, 00/**4269**:
                   Applied, 00/597, 03/509, 05/363, 05/2869: Cited, 01/525, 07/2946:
                                                              Considered, 01/4515

Artyomov v Russia (Admissibility) (17582/05) (2007) 44 E.H.R.R. SE16, ECHR

Arun DC v First Secretary of State; *sub nom* R. (on the application of Arun DC) v First
Secretary of State; First Secretary of State v Arun DC [2006] EWCA Civ 1172;
[2007] 1 W.L.R. 523; [2007] 1 P. & C.R. 10; [2007] J.P.L. 237; (2006) 156
N.L.J. 1477; *Times*, September 21, 2006, CA (Civ Div); reversing [2005] EWHC
2520 (Admin); [2006] 1 W.L.R. 365; [2006] 1 P. & C.R. 23; [2006] J.P.L.
654; *Times*, October 13, 2005, QBD (Admin) . . . . *Digested*, 06/**3294**
AS v Hungary (4/2004) (2007) 45 E.H.R.R. SE1, UN CEDW
AS v Secretary of State for the Home Department; *sub nom* AS and AA (Effect of
Previous Linked Determination: Somalia), Re; *joined case* AA v Secretary of
State for the Home Department [2006] UKAIT 52; [2006] Imm. A.R. 586, AIT *Digested*, 07/**2305**
AS and AA (Effect of Previous Linked Determination: Somalia), Re see AS v Secretary of
State for the Home Department
Asda Stores Ltd v Wandsworth LBC [2007] EWHC 433 (Admin); (2007) 104(7)
L.S.G. 26; *Times*, February 22, 2007, QBD
Ash v McKennitt see McKennitt v Ash
Ashan v Watt (formerly Carter) see Carter v Ahsan (No.1)
Ashe v National Westminster Bank Plc; *sub nom* National Westminster Bank Plc v
Ashe; A3/2007/0805, CA (Civ Div); affirming [2007] EWHC 494 (Ch); [2007]
B.P.I.R. 988; [2007] 2 P. & C.R. 27; [2007] 12 E.G. 155 (C.S.); [2007] N.P.C.
36, Ch D
Ashiagbor (Deceased), Re see Kuenyehia v International Hospitals Group Ltd
Ashley v Chief Constable of Sussex [2006] EWCA Civ 1085; [2007] 1 W.L.R. 398;
[2006] Po. L.R. 227; (2006) 103(32) L.S.G. 20; *Times*, August 30, 2006, CA
(Civ Div); reversing [2005] EWHC 415 (QB); [2005] Po. L.R. 48, QBD . . . . . . *Digested*, 06/**4341**
Ashley v Revenue and Customs Commissioners [2007] S.T.I. 2237, Sp Comm
Ashman (Setting of Minimum Term), Re see Jones (Setting of Minimum Term), Re
Ashton Investments Ltd v OJSC Russian Aluminium (Rusal) [2006] EWHC 2545
(Comm); [2007] 1 All E.R. (Comm) 857; [2007] 1 Lloyd's Rep. 311; [2006] 2
C.L.C. 739; [2006] Info.T.L.R. 269; *Times*, October 31, 2006, QBD (Comm) . . *Digested*, 07/**684**
Ashworth v Newnote Ltd [2007] EWCA Civ 793; [2007] B.P.I.R. 1012, CA (Civ Div) . *Digested*, 07/**2453**
Ashworth Hospital Authority v MGN Ltd; *sub nom* Ashworth Security Hospital v MGN
Ltd [2002] UKHL 29; [2002] 1 W.L.R. 2033; [2002] 4 All E.R. 193; [2002]
C.P.L.R. 712; [2002] E.M.L.R. 36; [2002] H.R.L.R. 41; [2002] U.K.H.R.R. 1263;
12 B.H.R.C. 443; [2003] F.S.R. 17; (2002) 67 B.M.L.R. 175; (2002) 99(30)
L.S.G. 37; (2002) 146 S.J.L.B. 168; *Times*, July 1, 2002; *Independent*, July 3,
2002, HL; affirming [2001] 1 W.L.R. 515; [2001] 1 All E.R. 991; [2001] E.M.L.R.
11; [2001] F.S.R. 33; (2001) 61 B.M.L.R. 48; (2001) 98(6) L.S.G. 46; (2001)
145 S.J.L.B. 20; *Times*, January 10, 2001; *Independent*, January 18, 2001; *Daily
Telegraph*, January 9, 2001, CA (Civ Div); affirming HQ 0000397, QBD . . . . . . *Digested*, 02/**3221**:
Applied, 06/990: *Considered*, 02/415, 05/2064: *Distinguished*, 03/2922,
06/2096: *Followed*, 07/486
Ashworth Security Hospital v MGN Ltd see Ashworth Hospital Authority v MGN Ltd
Asian Institute of Technology (AIT) v Commission of the European Communities (C-
547/03 P) [2006] E.C.R. I-845; [2006] 2 C.M.L.R. 29, ECJ (2nd Chamber) . . *Digested*, 06/**1529**:
Followed, 07/1647
Asklepios Kliniken GmbH v Commission of the European Communities (T-167/04)
[2007] 3 C.M.L.R. 34, CFI (4th Chamber)
ASM Shipping Ltd v Harris [2007] EWHC 1513 (Comm); [2007] 1 C.L.C. 1017; (2007)
23 Const. L.J. 533; [2007] Bus. L.R. D105; *Times*, August 6, 2007, QBD
(Comm) . . . . *Digested*, 07/**248**
ASM Shipping Ltd of India v TTMI Ltd of England [2005] EWHC 2238 (Comm);
[2006] 2 All E.R. (Comm) 122; [2006] 1 Lloyd's Rep. 375; [2006] 1 C.L.C. 656,
QBD (Comm) . . . . *Digested*, 06/**207**:
Considered, 07/251
ASM Shipping Ltd of India v TTMI Ltd of England [2007] EWHC 927 (Comm); [2007]
2 Lloyd's Rep. 155; [2007] 1 C.L.C. 555, QBD (Comm) . . . . *Digested*, 07/**241**
ASM Shipping Ltd of India v TTMI Ltd of England (Permission to Appeal) [2006] EWCA
Civ 1341; [2007] 1 Lloyd's Rep. 136; [2007] C.P. Rep. 5; [2006] 2 C.L.C. 471,
CA (Civ Div) . . . . *Digested*, 07/**249**:
Considered, 07/233, 07/240
ASML Netherlands BV v Semiconductor Industry Services GmbH (Semis) (C-283/05)
[2007] 1 All E.R. (Comm) 949; [2007] C.E.C. 246; [2007] I.L.Pr. 4, ECJ (1st
Chamber) . . . . *Digested*, 07/**1577**
ASNEF-EQUIFAX Servicios de Informacion sobre Solvencia y Credito SL v Asociacion de
Usuarios de Servicios Bancarios (AUSBANC) (C-238/05) [2006] E.C.R. I-
11125; [2007] 4 C.M.L.R. 6, ECJ (3rd Chamber) . . . . *Digested*, 07/**1550**
Asociacion Nacional de Empresas Forestales (ASEMFO) v Transformacion Agraria SA
(TRAGSA) (C-295/05) [2007] 2 C.M.L.R. 45, ECJ . . . . *Digested*, 07/**1642**
Aspinall v Revenue and Customs Commissioners see Postlethwaite's Executors v
Revenue and Customs Commissioners
Aspinall's Club Ltd v Al-Zayat [2007] EWCA Civ 1001; *Times*, October 31, 2007, CA
(Civ Div); reversing [2007] EWHC 362 (Comm); [2007] Bus. L.R. D92, QBD
(Comm)

Aspinden Holdings Ltd v Chief Assessor and Comptroller of Property Tax [2006]
    SGCA 31; [2007] R.A. 291, CA (Sing)
Asscher v Staatssecretaris van Financien (C-107/94) [1996] All E.R. (EC) 757; [1996]
    S.T.C. 1025; [1996] E.C.R. I-3089; [1996] 3 C.M.L.R. 61; [1996] C.E.C. 834;
    Times, July 15, 1996, ECJ (5th Chamber) . . . .   Digested, 96/**3341**:
                                          Applied, 02/4433, 07/1616: Considered, 04/3760
Assenov v Bulgaria (24760/94) (1999) 28 E.H.R.R. 652; [1998] H.R.C.D. 986, ECHR
    (1996) 22 E.H.R.R. CD163, Eur Comm HR . . . .   Digested, 00/**3197**:
                                          Applied, 02/2543, 07/2231: Considered, 07/2306
Assicurazioni Generali SpA v Arab Insurance Group (BSC) [2002] EWCA Civ 1642;
    [2003] 1 W.L.R. 577; [2003] 1 All E.R. (Comm) 140; [2003] 2 C.L.C. 242;
    [2003] Lloyd's Rep. I.R. 131; (2003) 100(3) L.S.G. 34; Times, November 29,
    2002, CA (Civ Div); affirming [2002] C.L.C. 164; [2002] Lloyd's Rep. I.R. 633,
    QBD (Comm) . . . .   Digested, 03/**2480**:
                            Applied, 03/257, 05/10, 06/766, 07/3432: Considered, 03/2725, 07/4213
Assicurazioni Generali SpA v CGU International Insurance Plc [2004] EWCA Civ 429;
    [2004] 2 All E.R. (Comm) 114; [2004] 2 C.L.C. 122; [2004] Lloyd's Rep. I.R.
    457; (2004) 148 S.J.L.B. 475, CA (Civ Div); affirming [2003] EWHC 1073
    (Comm); [2003] 2 All E.R. (Comm) 425; [2003] 2 C.L.C. 852; [2003] Lloyd's
    Rep. I.R. 725, QBD (Comm) . . . .   Digested, 04/**2242**:
                                          Applied, 07/2504: Considered, 07/2505: Followed, 07/2507
Assistant Deputy Coroner for Inner West London v Channel 4 Television Corp [2007]
    EWHC 2513 (QB); Times, December 11, 2007, QBD . . . .   Digested, 07/**25**
Assistant Director of Income Tax v Green Emirate Shipping & Travels 9 I.T.L. Rep. 1, ITAT
    (Ind)
Associated Japanese Bank (International) Ltd v Credit du Nord SA [1989] 1 W.L.R.
    255; [1988] 3 All E.R. 902; [1989] Fin. L.R. 117; (1989) 86(8) L.S.G. 43; (1988)
    138 N.L.J. Rep. 109; (1989) 133 S.J. 81, QBD . . . .   Digested, 89/**430**:
                                          Applied, 94/572, 01/954, 07/2468, 07/2715
Associated Newspapers Ltd v Burstein [2007] EWCA Civ 600; [2007] 4 All E.R. 319;
    [2007] E.M.L.R. 21; (2007) 151 S.J.L.B. 856, CA (Civ Div) . . . .   Digested, 07/**1071**
Associated Newspapers Ltd v HRH Prince of Wales see HRH Prince of Wales v
    Associated Newspapers Ltd
Associated Society of Locomotive Engineers & Firemen (ASLEF) v United Kingdom
    (11002/05) [2007] I.R.L.R. 361; (2007) 45 E.H.R.R. 34; 22 B.H.R.C. 140; Times,
    March 9, 2007, ECHR . . . .   Digested, 07/**2179**
Association de la Presse Internationale ASBL (API) v Commission of the European
    Communities (T-36/04) [2007] 3 C.M.L.R. 51, CFI
Association Greenpeace France v Ministere de l'Agriculture et de la Peche (C6/99)
    [2001] All E.R. (EC) 791; [2000] E.C.R. I-1651; [2001] 2 C.M.L.R. 45, ECJ . . .   Digested, 01/**2504**:
                                                                                        Applied, 07/552
Association of British Travel Agents Ltd v Civil Aviation Authority see R. (on the
    application of Association of British Travel Agents Ltd (ABTA)) v Civil Aviation
    Authority
Association of British Travel Agents Ltd v Director General of Fair Trading (Costs) see
    Institute of Independent Insurance Brokers v Director General of Fair Trading
    (Costs)
Associazione Nazionale Autotrasporto Viaggiatori (ANAV) v Comune di Bari (C-410/04)
    [2006] E.C.R. I-3303; [2006] 2 C.M.L.R. 63, ECJ (1st Chamber) . . . .   Digested, 07/**3325**
Astall v Revenue and Customs Commissioners [2007] S.T.I. 2128, Sp Comm
Aston v Aston [2007] W.T.L.R. 1349, CC (Guildford)
Aston v Swindon BC see Swindon BC (formerly Thamesdown BC) v Aston
Aston Cantlow and Wilmcote with Billesley Parochial Church Council v Wallbank; sub
    nom Wallbank v Aston Cantlow and Wilmcote with Billesley Parochial Church
    Council [2003] UKHL 37; [2004] 1 A.C. 546; [2003] 3 W.L.R. 283; [2003] 3
    All E.R. 1213; [2003] H.R.L.R. 28; [2003] U.K.H.R.R. 919; [2003] 27 E.G. 137
    (C.S.); (2003) 100(33) L.S.G. 28; (2003) 153 N.L.J. 1030; (2003) 147 S.J.L.B.
    812; [2003] N.P.C. 80; Times, June 27, 2003, HL; reversing [2001] EWCA Civ
    713; [2002] Ch. 51; [2001] 3 W.L.R. 1323; [2001] 3 All E.R. 393; [2002] 1 P. &
    C.R. 5; 4 I.T.L. Rep. 353; [2002] S.T.I. 168; [2001] 21 E.G. 167 (C.S.); (2001)
    98(22) L.S.G. 37; (2001) 98(25) L.S.G. 46; (2001) 145 S.J.L.B. 140; Times,
    June 15, 2001, Independent, May 24, 2001, CA (Civ Div); reversing (2001) 81 P.
    & C.R. 14; [2000] 2 E.G.L.R. 149; (2000) 97(17) L.S.G. 32; (2000) 144
    S.J.L.B. 181; [2000] N.P.C. 33; Times, March 30, 2000, Ch D . . . .   Digested, 03/**968**:
                                          Applied, 03/68, 03/68, 06/2108, 06/2114: Considered, 06/4044, 07/3912
Aston Cantlow and Wilmcote with Billesley Parochial Church Council v Wallbank, Times,
    February 21, 2007, Ch D . . . .   Digested, 07/**1082**
AstraZeneca Insurance Co Ltd v CGU International Insurance Plc (Permission to
    Appeal) see CGU International Insurance Plc v AstraZeneca Insurance Co Ltd
    (Permission to Appeal)
ASTROPOWER/Divisional (G1/05) [2007] E.P.O.R. 46, EPO (Enlarged Bd App)
Aswat v United States see Ahmad v United States
AT v Hungary (2/2003) (2007) 44 E.H.R.R. SE14, UN CEDW

AT (Guinea) v Secretary of State for the Home Department [2006] EWCA Civ 1889; [2007] Imm. A.R. 481, CA (Civ Div)

ATBM v SITMB; *sub nom* Fire in the Mont Blanc Tunnel, Re [2007] I.L.Pr. 45, Cass (F)

ATC (Cayman) Ltd v Rothschild Trust Cayman Ltd [2007] W.T.L.R. 951; (2006-07) 9 I.T.E.L.R. 36, Grand Ct (CI) . . . . *Digested*, 07/**4263**

Atherton (Inspector of Taxes) v British Insulated & Helsby Cables Ltd see British Insulated & Helsby Cables Ltd v Atherton (Inspector of Taxes)

Athinaiki Chartopoiia AE v Panagiotidis (C-270/05) [2007] I.R.L.R. 284, ECJ (1st Chamber) . . . . *Digested*, 07/**1554**

Athletic Union of Constantinople (AEK) v National Basketball Association (Application to Strike Out); *sub nom* National Basketball Association v Athletic Union of Constantinople (AEK) (Application to Strike Out); Athletic Union of Constantinople (AEK) v National Basketball Association (No.2) [2002] EWCA Civ 830; [2002] 1 W.L.R. 2863; [2002] 3 All E.R. 897; [2002] 2 All E.R. (Comm) 385; (2002) 99(29) L.S.G. 33; (2002) 146 S.J.L.B. 153; *Times*, June 13, 2002; *Independent*, June 13, 2002, CA (Civ Div) . . . . *Digested*, 02/**209**:
Applied, 07/240

Athletic Union of Constantinople (AEK) v National Basketball Association (No.2) see Athletic Union of Constantinople (AEK) v National Basketball Association (Application to Strike Out)

Atkinson v Secretary of State for Transport [2006] EWHC 995 (Admin); [2007] Env. L.R. 5, QBD (Admin) . . . . *Digested*, 07/**1500**

Atkinson v United States; *sub nom* R. v Brixton Prison Governor Ex p. Atkinson; *joined case* United States v Atkinson [1971] A.C. 197; [1969] 3 W.L.R. 1074; [1969] 3 All E.R. 1317; (1969) 113 S.J. 901, HL; affirming [1969] 2 All E.R. 1146; (1969) 133 J.P. 617; (1969) 113 S.J. 690, QBD . . . . *Digested*, 69/**2155**:
Applied, 69/1452, 71/7105, 91/1750, 93/1871, 05/1362: *Considered*, 85/2128, 90/2267, 94/1115, 07/1663: *Distinguished*, 02/1593

ATOTECH/Correction (G02/95) [1997] E.P.O.R. 77, EPO (Enlarged Bd App) . . . . *Applied*, 07/2575

Attheraces Ltd v British Horseracing Board Ltd [2007] EWCA Civ 38; [2007] U.K.C.L.R. 309; [2007] E.C.C. 7; [2007] Info. T.L.R. 41; [2007] Bus. L.R. D77, CA (Civ Div); affirming [2005] EWHC 3015 (Ch); [2006] U.K.C.L.R. 167; [2006] E.C.C. 24; [2006] Eu. L.R. 654; [2006] E.C.D.R. 13; [2006] Info. T.L.R. 423; [2006] F.S.R. 20; (2006) 29(2) I.P.D. 29011, Ch D . . . . *Digested*, 07/**634**

Attorney General v BBC [2007] EWCA Civ 280; [2007] C.P. Rep. 26; (2007) 104(13) L.S.G. 25, CA (Civ Div) . . . . *Digested*, 07/**452**

Attorney General v Blake [2001] 1 A.C. 268; [2000] 3 W.L.R. 625; [2000] 4 All E.R. 385; [2000] 2 All E.R. (Comm) 487; [2001] I.R.L.R. 36; [2001] Emp. L.R. 329; [2000] E.M.L.R. 949; [2000] 23(12) I.P.D. 23098; (2000) 97(32) L.S.G. 37; (2000) 150 N.L.J. 1230; (2000) 144 S.J.L.B. 242; *Times*, August 3, 2000; *Independent*, November 6, 2000, HL; affirming [1998] Ch. 439; [1998] 2 W.L.R. 805; [1998] 1 All E.R. 833; [1998] E.M.L.R. 309; (1998) 95(4) L.S.G. 33; (1998) 148 N.L.J. 15; (1998) 142 S.J.L.B. 35; *Times*, December 22, 1997; *Independent*, December 19, 1997, CA (Civ Div); reversing [1997] Ch. 84; [1996] 3 W.L.R. 741; [1996] 3 All E.R. 903; [1996] E.M.L.R. 382; [1996] F.S.R. 727; (1996) 19(7) I.P.D. 19066; *Times*, April 23, 1996, Ch D . . . . *Digested*, 00/**797**:
Applied, 00/2132, 06/1018: *Considered*, 03/717, 04/912, 05/956, 07/1054

Attorney General v D see Attorney General's Reference (No.4 of 2004), Re

Attorney General v Scotcher [2005] UKHL 36; [2005] 1 W.L.R. 1867; [2005] 3 All E.R. 1; [2005] 2 Cr. App. R. 35; [2005] U.K.H.R.R. 637; [2005] Crim. L.R. 791; (2005) 155 N.L.J. 828; *Times*, May 20, 2005, HL; affirming [2003] EWHC 1380 (Admin); [2004] A.C.D. 2, QBD (Admin) . . . . *Digested*, 05/**849**:
Considered, 07/992

Attorney General v Wilts United Dairies Ltd (1922) 38 T.L.R. 781, HL; affirming (1921) 37 T.L.R. 884, CA . . . . *Applied*, 76/22:
Considered, 92/4327.a: *Distinguished*, 47-51/4649, 62/491, 90/4450, 07/4298: *Explained*, 52/1195

Attorney General v Zaoui [2005] NZSC 38; 19 B.H.R.C. 147, Sup Ct (NZ) . . . . *Digested*, 07/**2362**

Attorney General of New Zealand v Ortiz [1984] A.C. 1; [1983] 2 W.L.R. 809; [1983] 2 All E.R. 93; [1983] 2 Lloyd's Rep. 265; (1983) 133 N.L.J. 537; (1983) 127 S.J. 307, HL; affirming [1982] 3 W.L.R. 570; [1982] 3 All E.R. 432; [1982] 2 Lloyd's Rep. 224; [1982] Com. L.R. 156; (1982) 79 L.S.G. 919; (1982) 126 S.J. 429, CA (Civ Div); reversing [1982] Q.B. 349; [1982] 2 W.L.R. 10; [1982] 1 Lloyd's Rep. 173; (1981) 125 S.J. 530; *Times*, July 8, 1981, QBD (Comm) . . . . *Digested*, 83/**2015**:
Applied, 88/408, 03/621: *Considered*, 07/4200

Attorney General of the British Virgin Islands v Hartwell [2004] UKPC 12; [2004] 1 W.L.R. 1273; [2004] P.I.Q.R. P27; [2004] Inquest L.R. 89; [2004] Po. L.R. 141; (2004) 101(12) L.S.G. 37; (2004) 148 S.J.L.B. 267; *Times*, February 27, 2004, PC (BVI) . . . . *Digested*, 04/**2712**:
Applied, 07/4201

Attorney General of Trinidad and Tobago v Phillip [1995] 1 A.C. 396; [1994] 3 W.L.R.
1134; [1995] 1 All E.R. 93; (1994) 91(41) L.S.G. 43; (1994) 144 N.L.J. 1549;
(1994) 138 S.J.L.B. 208; *Times*, October 11, 1994; *Independent*, October 19,
1994, PC (Trin) . . . . *Digested*, 95/**899**:
Applied, 07/53: *Followed*, 01/1072

Attorney General of Tuvalu v Philatelic Distribution Corp Ltd [1990] 1 W.L.R. 926;
[1990] 2 All E.R. 216; [1990] B.C.C. 30; [1990] B.C.L.C. 245; (1990) 134 S.J.
832; *Times*, October 24, 1989; *Independent*, October 25, 1989; *Financial Times*,
November 1, 1989; *Daily Telegraph*, November 6, 1989, CA (Civ Div) . . . . *Digested*, 90/**3580**:
Applied, 07/717

Attorney General's Reference (Nos.14 and 24 of 1993), Re; *sub nom* R. v Shepherd (Peter
James); R. v Wernet (Robert Stewart) [1994] 1 W.L.R. 530; [1994] 2 All E.R.
242; (1994) 99 Cr. App. R. 39; (1994) 15 Cr. App. R. (S.) 640; [1994] R.T.R. 49;
(1994) 138 S.J.L.B. 23; *Times*, December 27, 1993, CA (Crim Div) . . . . *Digested*, 94/**1193**:
Applied, 95/1319, 02/4026: *Approved*, 96/1836: *Considered*, 95/4427,
96/1756, 96/1757, 96/1762, 96/1763, 96/1767, 96/1822, 96/1824, 96/1826,
96/1827, 96/1828, 96/1829, 96/1835, 97/1662, 97/1668, 97/1669, 97/1671,
97/1673, 99/1326, 00/1197, 00/1364, 03/3645, 05/3766:
Distinguished, 96/1759: *Followed*, 96/1761, 97/1678, 07/3590:
Referred to, 95/1344, 97/1661, 97/1665, 97/1667

Attorney General's Reference (No.32 of 1996), Re; *sub nom* R. v Whittaker (Steven Alan)
[1997] 1 Cr. App. R. (S.) 261; [1996] Crim. L.R. 917; (1996) 93(38) L.S.G. 42;
Times, July 24, 1996, CA (Crim Div) . . . . *Digested*, 96/**1912**:
Applied, 07/3687, 07/3691: *Considered*, 98/1233, 98/1346, 98/1405,
99/1251, 99/1255, 99/1308, 02/3878, 02/4029, 03/3791, 03/3876,
06/3730, 06/3898: *Followed*, 99/1254

Attorney General's Reference (No.33 of 1996), Re; *sub nom* R. v Latham (Daniel George)
[1997] 2 Cr. App. R. (S.) 10; [1997] Crim. L.R. 140; *Times*, November 15, 1996;
Independent, November 12, 1996, CA (Crim Div) . . . . *Digested*, 97/**1622**:
Applied, 97/1163: *Considered*, 97/1623, 98/1288, 00/1267, 02/4028,
03/3794, 03/3796, 03/3800, 06/3762, 07/3674: *Distinguished*, 99/1259:
Followed, 97/1621, 03/3790

Attorney General's Reference (No.1 of 1997), Re; *sub nom* R. v Wheeler (Glen); R. v
Wheeler (Ian) [1998] 1 Cr. App. R. (S.) 54, CA (Crim Div) . . . . *Digested*, 97/**1402**:
Considered, 00/1131, 00/1135, 02/3875, 06/3645, 07/3578

Attorney General's Reference (No.50 of 1997), Re; *sub nom* R. v V (David Victor) [1998]
2 Cr. App. R. (S.) 155, CA (Crim Div) . . . . *Digested*, 98/**1249**:
Considered, 00/1287, 07/3611

Attorney General's Reference (Nos.78, 79 and 85 of 1998), Re; *sub nom* R. v Russell
(Robert John); R. v O (Jason Patrick) (A Juvenile); R. v M (Sarah Ruth) (A
Juvenile) [2000] 1 Cr. App. R. (S.) 371, CA (Crim Div) . . . . *Digested*, 00/**1132**:
Applied, 07/3578: *Considered*, 00/1130, 01/1375, 05/3658

Attorney General's Reference (No.19 of 1999), Re; *sub nom* R. v Kitchener (Marvine
Wayne) [2000] 1 Cr. App. R. (S.) 287, CA (Crim Div) . . . . *Digested*, 99/**1259**:
Considered, 05/3664, 07/3674

Attorney General's Reference (Nos.86 and 87 of 1999), Re; *sub nom* R. v Webb (Robert
Edward); R. v Simpson (Moira) [2001] 1 Cr. App. R. (S.) 141; [2001] Crim. L.R.
58; *Times*, November 8, 2000; *Independent*, December 11, 2000, CA (Crim
Div) . . . . *Digested*, 00/**1186**:
Applied, 07/3597: *Considered*, 03/3770

Attorney General's Reference (No.3 of 2000), Re; *sub nom* R. v Loosley (Grant Spencer)
(No.2); R. v G (Entrapment); R. v Loosely (Grant Spencer); *joined case* R. v
Looseley (Grant Spencer) (No.2) [2001] UKHL 53; [2001] 1 W.L.R. 2060;
[2001] 4 All E.R. 897; [2002] 1 Cr. App. R. 29; [2002] H.R.L.R. 8; [2002]
U.K.H.R.R. 333; [2002] Crim. L.R. 301; (2001) 98(45) L.S.G. 25; (2001) 145
S.J.L.B. 245; *Times*, October 29, 2001; *Independent*, November 2, 2001; *Daily
Telegraph*, November 6, 2001, HL; *reversing* [2001] EWCA Crim 1214; [2001] 2
Cr. App. R. 26; [2001] H.R.L.R. 47; [2001] Crim. L.R. 645; *Times*, June 27,
2001; *Independent*, May 25, 2001, CA (Crim Div) . . . . *Digested*, 01/**992**:
Applied, 05/1487, 07/849: *Considered*, 06/2200, 07/1953

Attorney General's Reference (No.4 of 2000), Re; *sub nom* R. v GC [2001] EWCA Crim
780; [2001] 2 Cr. App. R. 22; [2001] R.T.R. 27; [2001] Crim. L.R. 578; *Times*,
March 27, 2001, CA (Crim Div) . . . . *Digested*, 01/**1031**:
Considered, 07/862

Attorney General's Reference (No.7 of 2000), Re [2001] EWCA Crim 888; [2001] 1 W.L.R.
1879; [2001] 2 Cr. App. R. 19; [2001] H.R.L.R. 41; [2001] B.P.I.R. 953; [2001] Crim.
L.R. 736; (2001) 98(22) L.S.G. 35; (2001) 145 S.J.L.B. 109; *Times*, April 12, 2001,
CA (Crim Div) . . . . *Digested*, 01/**974**:
Considered, 06/499: *Followed*, 07/855

Attorney General's Reference (No.15 of 2000), Re; *sub nom* R. v G (Richard) [2001] 1
Cr. App. R. (S.) 23, CA (Crim Div) . . . . *Digested*, 00/**1286**:
Considered, 07/3664

Attorney General's Reference (No.47 of 2000), Re; *sub nom* R. *v* Harvey (Calvin David)
[2001] 1 Cr. App. R. 471; [2001] 1 Cr. App. R. (S.) 134, CA (Crim Div) . . . .   *Digested*, 01/**1214**:
Considered, 07/3578

Attorney General's Reference (No.2 of 2001), Re; *sub nom* R. *v* J (Unreasonable Delay)
[2003] UKHL 68; [2004] 2 A.C. 72; [2004] 2 W.L.R. 1; [2004] 1 All E.R.
1049; [2004] 1 Cr. App. R. 25; [2004] H.R.L.R. 16; [2004] U.K.H.R.R. 193; 15
B.H.R.C. 472; [2004] Crim. L.R. 574; (2004) 101(4) L.S.G. 30; (2004) 148
S.J.L.B. 25; *Times*, December 12, 2003; *Independent*, December 16, 2003, HL;
affirming [2001] EWCA Crim 1568; [2001] 1 W.L.R. 1869; [2002] 1 Cr. App. R.
24; [2001] U.K.H.R.R. 1265; [2002] Crim. L.R. 207; (2001) 98(32) L.S.G. 36;
(2001) 145 S.J.L.B. 172; *Times*, July 12, 2001, CA (Crim Div) . . . .   *Digested*, 04/**884**:
Applied, 03/820, 03/3385, 07/1953: *Considered*, 04/3439:
Followed, 06/535

Attorney General's Reference (Nos.19, 20 and 21 of 2001), Re; *sub nom* R. *v* Field (Jason);
R. *v* C (Craig) (A Juvenile); R. *v* Byrne (Alan) [2001] EWCA Crim 1432;
[2002] 1 Cr. App. R. (S.) 33, CA (Crim Div) . . . .   *Digested*, 02/**4032**:
Applied, 03/3786, 05/3758: *Considered*, 01/1434, 03/3794, 05/3670,
07/3781: *Distinguished*, 03/3797: *Followed*, 03/3790

Attorney General's Reference (No.27 of 2001), Re; *sub nom* R. *v* R (Malcolm James)
[2001] EWCA Crim 1283; [2002] 1 Cr. App. R. (S.) 42, CA (Crim Div) . . . .   *Digested*, 02/**3977**:
Considered, 06/3656, 07/3664

Attorney General's Reference (Nos.4 and 7 of 2002), Re; *sub nom* R. *v* Lobban (Adrian
Michael); R. *v* Sawyers (Christopher); *joined case* R. *v* Q. (Steven James) (A
Juvenile) [2002] EWCA Crim 127; [2002] 2 Cr. App. R. (S.) 77; [2002] Crim.
L.R. 333; *Times*, February 11, 2002, CA (Crim Div) . . . .   *Digested*, 02/**4066**:
Applied, 02/4008, 03/3762, 03/3764, 04/802: *Considered*, 02/4057,
03/3763, 03/3839, 04/874, 04/3432, 04/3433, 04/3435, 05/3726,
05/3735, 05/3777, 05/3780, 06/3903, 07/3795: *Followed*, 03/3848,
03/3849, 03/3850, 03/3858

Attorney General's Reference (No.152 of 2002), Re see R. *v* Cooksley (Robert Charles)

Attorney General's Reference (No.52 of 2003), Re; *sub nom* R. *v* Webb (Ian David)
[2003] EWCA Crim 3731; [2004] Crim. L.R. 306; *Times*, December 12, 2003,
CA (Crim Div) . . . .   *Digested*, 04/**3443**:
Considered, 05/3743, 07/3736

Attorney General's Reference (No.2 of 2004), Re; *sub nom* R. *v* Neville (Daniel John)
[2004] EWCA Crim 1280; [2005] 1 Cr. App. R. (S.) 14, CA (Crim Div) . . . .   *Digested*, 05/**3604**:
Considered, 07/3643

Attorney General's Reference (No.3 of 2004), Re [2005] EWCA Crim 1882; [2006] Crim.
L.R. 63, CA (Crim Div) . . . .   *Digested*, 06/**862**:
Considered, 07/877

Attorney General's Reference (No.4 of 2004), Re; *sub nom* Attorney General *v* D [2005]
EWCA Crim 889; [2005] 1 W.L.R. 2810; [2005] 2 Cr. App. R. 26; [2005]
Crim. L.R. 799; *Times*, May 17, 2005, CA (Crim Div) . . . .   *Digested*, 05/**814**:
Approved, 07/911: *Followed*, 06/875

Attorney General's Reference (No.9 of 2004), Re; *sub nom* R. *v* Uddin (Alim); Attorney
General's Reference (No.9 of 2005), Re [2005] EWCA Crim 812; [2005] 2 Cr.
App. R. (S.) 105, CA (Crim Div) . . . .   *Digested*, 05/**3671**:
Applied, 06/3744: *Followed*, 07/3797

Attorney General's Reference (No.25 of 2004), Re; *sub nom* R. *v* Gay (Alan Thomas)
[2004] EWCA Crim 1203; [2005] 1 Cr. App. R. (S.) 15, CA (Crim Div) . . . .   *Digested*, 05/**3565**:
Considered, 07/3643

Attorney General's Reference (No.98 of 2004), Re; *sub nom* R. *v* Meakin (Joel) [2004]
EWCA Crim 2769; [2005] 1 Cr. App. R. (S.) 125, CA (Crim Div) . . . .   *Digested*, 05/**3777**:
Considered, 07/3795

Attorney General's Reference (No.104 of 2004), Re; *sub nom* R. *v* Garvey (Wayne)
[2004] EWCA Crim 2672; [2005] 1 Cr. App. R. (S.) 117; [2005] Crim. L.R. 150;
(2004) 148 S.J.L.B. 1283; *Times*, October 29, 2004; *Independent*, December
16, 2004, CA (Crim Div) . . . .   *Digested*, 04/**3285**:
Considered, 06/3666, 06/3837, 06/3846, 07/3604: *Followed*, 05/3532

Attorney General's Reference (Nos.120 and 121 of 2004), Re; *sub nom* R. *v* Herbert
(Stephen Ronald); R. *v* Beard (Gary Colin) [2005] EWCA Crim 890; [2006] 1
Cr. App. R. (S.) 7, CA (Crim Div) . . . .   *Digested*, 05/**3609**:
Considered, 07/3647

Attorney General's Reference (No.9 of 2005), Re see Attorney General's Reference (No.9 of
2004), Re

Attorney General's Reference (Nos.117 and 118 of 2005), Re; *sub nom* R. *v* Byfield
(Wayne Leonard); R. *v* Swaby (Errol Rio) [2006] EWCA Crim 1157; [2007] 1 Cr.
App. R. (S.) 22, CA (Crim Div) . . . .   *Digested*, 06/**3688**

Attorney General's Reference (No.6 of 2006), Re; *sub nom* R. *v* Farish (Michael John)
[2006] EWCA Crim 1043; [2007] 1 Cr. App. R. (S.) 12; [2006] Crim. L.R. 772,
CA (Crim Div) . . . .   *Digested*, 06/**3690**

Attorney General's Reference (Nos.14 and 15 of 2006), Re; *sub nom* R. *v* Webster (Alan); R. *v* French (Tanya) [2006] EWCA Crim 1335; [2007] 1 All E.R. 718; [2007] 1 Cr. App. R. (S.) 40; [2006] Crim. L.R. 943; *Times*, June 20, 2006, CA (Crim Div). . . . . *Digested*, 06/**3662**:
Applied, 06/3701, 07/3664: *Considered*, 07/3749

Attorney General's Reference (Nos.24, 25, 26, 27, 28 and 29 of 2006), Re; *sub nom* R. *v* Artan (Abdekhader); R. *v* Mohammed (Liban); R. *v* Glanville (Peter); R. *v* Holder (Keiffer); R. *v* Orr (Ross); R. *v* Banks (Joel) [2007] EWCA Crim 2217; (2007) 151 S.J.L.B. 1299, CA (Crim Div)

Attorney General's Reference (Nos.24, 25, 26, 27, 28 and 41 of 2006), Re; *sub nom* R. *v* B (Ivan Leon); R. *v* F (Nathan Leon); R. *v* X (Andrew Goldwyne); R. *v* J (Dennis Jerome); R. *v* P (Courtney); R. *v* O (Seun) [2006] EWCA Crim 1617; [2007] 1 Cr. App. R. (S.) 50, CA (Crim Div). . . . . *Digested*, 06/**3901**

Attorney General's Reference (No.32 of 2006), Re; *sub nom* R. *v* Riding (Ashley Cuncliffe) [2006] EWCA Crim 1500; [2007] R.T.R. 4, CA (Crim Div) . . . . . *Digested*, 06/**3878**

Attorney General's Reference (No.34 of 2006), Re; *sub nom* R. *v* Cluff (Allan Keith) [2006] EWCA Crim 1278; [2007] 1 Cr. App. R. (S.) 19, CA (Crim Div) . . . . . . *Digested*, 06/**3868**

Attorney General's Reference (No.35 of 2006), Re; *sub nom* R. *v* Green (Ashley) [2006] EWCA Crim 1940; [2007] 1 Cr. App. R. (S.) 36, CA (Crim Div) . . . . *Digested*, 06/**3883**

Attorney General's Reference (No.36 of 2006), Re; *sub nom* R. *v* Hussain (Imtiaz) [2006] EWCA Crim 1372; [2007] 1 Cr. App. R. (S.) 38, CA (Crim Div) . . . . *Digested*, 06/**3845**

Attorney General's Reference (No.39 of 2006), Re; *sub nom* R. *v* J (Rodney Clive) [2006] EWCA Crim 1431; [2007] 1 Cr. App. R. (S.) 34, CA (Crim Div) . . . . *Digested*, 06/**3660**

Attorney General's Reference (No.39 of 2006), Re; *sub nom* R. *v* B (Christopher) [2006] EWCA Crim 1578; [2007] 1 Cr. App. R. (S.) 41, CA (Crim Div) . . . . *Digested*, 06/**3891**

Attorney General's Reference (Nos.42, 43 and 44 of 2006), Re; *sub nom* R. *v* Richards (Nelson); R. *v* Davis (Aaron Christopher); R. *v* Clemow (William Alfred) [2006] EWCA Crim 2053; [2007] 1 Cr. App. R. (S.) 80, CA (Crim Div) . . . . *Digested*, 07/**3706**

Attorney General's Reference (No.47 of 2006), Re [2006] EWCA Crim 1762; [2007] 1 Cr. App. R. (S.) 63, CA (Crim Div) . . . . *Digested*, 06/**3859**

Attorney General's Reference (No.48 of 2006), Re; *sub nom* R. *v* Farrow (Andrew) [2006] EWCA Crim 2396; [2007] 1 Cr. App. R. (S.) 90, CA (Crim Div) . . . . . . *Digested*, 07/**3646**

Attorney General's Reference (No.49 of 2006), Re; *sub nom* R. *v* J (SJ) [2006] EWCA Crim 2387, CA (Crim Div) . . . . *Digested*, 07/**3604**

Attorney General's Reference (Nos.52 and 53 of 2006), Re; *sub nom* R. *v* Rance (Ryan); R. *v* Toth (Mark) [2006] EWCA Crim 2571; (2006) 150 S.J.L.B. 1332, CA (Crim Div) . . . . *Digested*, 07/**3728**

Attorney General's Reference (No.54 of 2006), Re; *sub nom* R. *v* Guang Jie Li [2006] EWCA Crim 2117; [2007] 1 Cr. App. R. (S.) 86, CA (Crim Div)

Attorney General's Reference (No.55 of 2006), Re [2006] EWCA Crim 3167, CA (Crim Div)   *Digested*, 07/**3753**

Attorney General's Reference (No.56 of 2006), Re; *sub nom* R. *v* Sharrock (Michael Dean) [2006] EWCA Crim 2296; [2007] 1 Cr. App. R. (S.) 96; [2007] Crim. L.R. 96, CA (Crim Div) . . . . *Digested*, 06/**3830**

Attorney General's Reference (No.58 of 2006), Re; *sub nom* R. *v* Richer (Joseph); R. *v* Finch (David) [2006] EWCA Crim 2827, CA (Crim Div) . . . . *Digested*, 07/**3649**

Attorney General's Reference (No.59 of 2006), Re; *sub nom* R. *v* Doe (Nelson) [2006] EWCA Crim 2096, CA (Crim Div) . . . . *Digested*, 06/**3667**:
Applied, 07/3792

Attorney General's Reference (No.64 of 2006), Re see R. *v* Johnson (Paul Anthony)

Attorney General's Reference (Nos.66 and 67 of 2006), Re; *sub nom* R. *v* C; *joined case* R. *v* R [2006] EWCA Crim 2777; (2006) 103(44) L.S.G. 27, CA (Crim Div) . . . *Digested*, 07/**3757**:
Considered, 07/3633, 07/3756

Attorney General's Reference (No.72 of 2006), Re; *sub nom* R. *v* Latham (Craig) [2006] EWCA Crim 2607; [2007] 1 Cr. App. R. (S.) 108, CA (Crim Div). . . . . *Digested*, 07/**3749**

Attorney General's Reference (No.74 of 2006), Re [2006] EWCA Crim 2531, CA (Crim Div)   *Digested*, 07/**3790**

Attorney General's Reference (No.76 of 2006), Re [2006] EWCA Crim 3250, CA (Crim Div). . . . . *Digested*, 07/**3750**

Attorney General's Reference (No.77 of 2006), Re; *sub nom* R. *v* PW [2006] EWCA Crim 2384, CA (Crim Div) . . . . *Digested*, 07/**3664**

Attorney General's Reference (No.78 of 2006), Re; *sub nom* R. *v* Donohue (Ryan) [2006] EWCA Crim 2793; [2007] 1 Cr. App. R. (S.) 114, CA (Crim Div) . . . . . . *Digested*, 07/**3782**

Attorney General's Reference (No.79 of 2006) (Application for Leave to Make Reference), Re; *sub nom* R. *v* Whitte (Adam George) [2006] EWCA Crim 2626; [2007] 1 Cr. App. R. (S.) 122, CA (Crim Div) . . . . *Digested*, 07/**3748**

Attorney General's Reference (No.81of 2006), Re [2006] EWCA Crim 2637, CA (Crim Div)   *Digested*, 07/**3580**

Attorney General's Reference (No.85 of 2006), Re; *sub nom* R. *v* Workman (David Paul) [2006] EWCA Crim 2623; [2007] 1 Cr. App. R. (S.) 104, CA (Crim Div) . . . . . *Digested*, 07/**3755**

Attorney General's Reference (No.86 of 2006), Re; *sub nom* R. *v* Shaw (Michael Phillip) [2006] EWCA Crim 2570; [2007] Bus. L.R. 906; [2007] 1 Cr. App. R. (S.) 101; [2007] I.C.R. 1047; (2006) 150 S.J.L.B. 1329, CA (Crim Div) . . . . *Digested*, 07/**3676**

Attorney General's Reference (No.87 of 2006), Re; *sub nom* R. *v* Geddes (Daniel Peter) [2006] EWCA Crim 2722, CA (Crim Div) . . . . *Digested*, 07/**3708**

Attorney General's Reference (Nos.88, 89, 90 and 91 of 2006), Re; *sub nom* R. *v* Meehan
(Brian John); R. *v* McCallister (Gerard Martin); R. *v* Sangha (Bhovinder Singh);
R. *v* Burch (David William) [2006] EWCA Crim 3254; [2007] 2 Cr. App. R. (S.)
28, CA (Crim Div) . . . . *Digested*, 07/**3598**
Attorney General's Reference (Nos.90 and 91 of 2006), Re; *sub nom* R. *v* Botchett
(Darren); R. *v* Richards (Ian) [2006] EWCA Crim 3252; [2007] 2 Cr. App. R.
(S.) 31, CA (Crim Div) . . . . *Digested*, 07/**3672**
Attorney General's Reference (No.92 of 2006), Re; *sub nom* R. *v* Morrison (Matthew
James) [2006] EWCA Crim 2926, CA (Crim Div) . . . . *Digested*, 07/**3756**
Attorney General's Reference (No.93 of 2006), Re; *sub nom* R. *v* Mohamed (Abdi
Ahmed) [2006] EWCA Crim 3212; [2007] 2 Cr. App. R. (S.) 6, CA (Crim Div) . *Digested*, 07/**3798**
Attorney General's Reference (No.96 of 2006), Re [2006] EWCA Crim 3251; [2007] 2 Cr.
App. R. (S.) 30, CA (Crim Div) . . . . *Digested*, 07/**3773**
Attorney General's Reference (No.97 of 2006), Re [2006] EWCA Crim 2757, CA (Crim Div) *Digested*, 07/**3629**
Attorney General's Reference (Nos.98 and 99 of 2006), Re; *sub nom* R. *v* Wells (Scott);
R. *v* McGarry (Michael) [2006] EWCA Crim 3177; [2007] 2 Cr. App. R. (S.)
19, CA (Crim Div) . . . . *Digested*, 07/**3784**
Attorney General's Reference (No.100 of 2006), Re; *sub nom* R. *v* Amies (Marie Mandy)
[2006] EWCA Crim 3286, CA (Crim Div) . . . . *Digested*, 07/**3767**
Attorney General's Reference (Nos.102 and 103 of 2006), Re [2006] EWCA Crim 3247, CA
(Crim Div) . . . . *Digested*, 07/**3794**
Attorney General's Reference (Nos.104, 105 and 106 of 2006), Re; *sub nom* R. *v* Tilley
(Darren David); R. *v* Phelps (David); R. *v* Hathaway (Scott) [2006] EWCA Crim
3065, CA (Crim Div) . . . . *Digested*, 07/**3727**
Attorney General's Reference (No.107 of 2006), Re (2007) 151 S.J.L.B. 164, CA (Crim Div)
Attorney General's Reference (Nos.108, 109, 110 and 111 of 2006), Re; *sub nom* R. *v* Miah
(Tutu); R. *v* Hoque (Abdul); R. *v* JM; R. *v* Juhel (Abdul) [2006] EWCA Crim
2925, CA (Crim Div) . . . . *Digested*, 07/**3633**
Attorney General's Reference (No.111 of 2006), Re; *sub nom* R. *v* Hussain (Ghulam)
[2006] EWCA Crim 3269; [2007] 2 Cr. App. R. (S.) 26, CA (Crim Div) . . . . . . *Digested*, 07/**3677**
Attorney General's Reference (No.112 of 2006), Re; *sub nom* R. *v* Glover (Ian Robert)
[2006] EWCA Crim 3385; [2007] 2 Cr. App. R. (S.) 39, CA (Crim Div) . . . . . . *Digested*, 07/**3766**
Attorney General's Reference (No.113 of 2006), Re; *sub nom* R. *v* L [2006] EWCA Crim
3292; [2007] 2 Cr. App. R. (S.) 29, CA (Crim Div) . . . . *Digested*, 07/**3797**
Attorney General's Reference (Nos.118 and 119 of 2006), Re; *sub nom* R. *v* Rodrigo De
Oliveira (Werleson); R. *v* Jesus (Lucas) [2007] EWCA Crim 121; (2007) 151
S.J.L.B. 128, CA (Crim Div)
Attorney General's Reference (No.121 of 2006), Re [2007] EWCA Crim 181, CA (Crim Div) *Digested*, 07/**3608**
Attorney General's Reference (No.123 of 2006), Re; *sub nom* R. *v* Sharp (Charles)
[2006] EWCA Crim 3375; [2007] 2 Cr. App. R. (S.) 38, CA (Crim Div) . . . . . . *Digested*, 07/**3589**
Attorney General's Reference (Nos.125 and 126 of 2006), Re; *sub nom* R. *v* Tomney
(Simon); R. *v* Tomney (Jake Colin) [2007] EWCA Crim 174; [2007] 2 Cr. App. R.
(S.) 47, CA (Crim Div) . . . . *Digested*, 07/**3795**
Attorney General's Reference (No.126 of 2006), Re; *sub nom* Attorney General's
Reference (No.127 of 2006), Re; R. *v* H [2007] EWCA Crim 53; [2007] 1 All
E.R. 1254; [2007] 2 Cr. App. R. (S.) 59; [2007] M.H.L.R. 64; [2007] Crim. L.R.
399; (2007) 151 S.J.L.B. 200; *Times*, February 13, 2007, CA (Crim Div) . . . . . . *Digested*, 07/**3787**
Attorney General's Reference (No.127 of 2006), Re see Attorney General's Reference
(No.126 of 2006), Re
Attorney General's Reference (Nos.129 and 132 of 2006), Re; *sub nom* R. *v* Delgado-
Fernandez (Elisabeth); R. *v* Thanh Hue Thi; R. *v* Zammit (Godwin) [2007] EWCA
Crim 762; [2007] 2 Cr. App. R. (S.) 85; [2007] Crim. L.R. 651, CA (Crim Div) . *Digested*, 07/**3765**
Attorney General's Reference (No.130 of 2006), Re; *sub nom* R. *v* Jones (Kate Elizabeth)
[2007] EWCA Crim 147; [2007] 2 Cr. App. R. (S.) 53, CA (Crim Div) . . . . *Digested*, 07/**3654**
Attorney General's Reference (No.133 of 2006), Re; *sub nom* R. *v* Tuzzio (Daryll Dale)
[2007] EWCA Crim 809; [2007] 2 Cr. App. R. (S.) 91; (2007) 151 S.J.L.B. 398,
CA (Crim Div) . . . . *Digested*, 07/**3671**
Attorney General's Reference (No.134 of 2006), Re; *sub nom* R. *v* Bennett (Adam)
[2007] EWCA Crim 309; [2007] 2 Cr. App. R. (S.) 54, CA (Crim Div) . . . . *Digested*, 07/**3609**
Attorney General's Reference (No.142 of 2006), Re; *sub nom* R. *v* Herbert (William
Andrew) [2007] EWCA Crim 662; [2007] 2 Cr. App. R. (S.) 84, CA (Crim Div) *Digested*, 07/**3588**
Attorney General's Reference (Nos.143 and 144 of 2006), Re; *sub nom* R. *v* Brown
(Deland Anthony); R. *v* Carty (Donnel Marcus) [2007] EWCA Crim 1245;
[2007] Crim. L.R. 735; *Times*, June 5, 2007, CA (Crim Div) . . . . *Digested*, 07/**3783**
Attorney General's Reference (No.145 of 2006), Re; *sub nom* R. *v* Carter (Stephen)
Times, March 20, 2007, CA (Crim Div)
Attorney General's Reference (No.146 of 2006), Re; *sub nom* R. *v* Vandermeulen (Yvan)
[2007] EWCA Crim 570; [2007] 2 Cr. App. R. (S.) 74, CA (Crim Div) . . . . *Digested*, 07/**3591**
Attorney General's Reference (No.147 of 2006), Re; *sub nom* R. *v* Gunner (James)
[2007] EWCA Crim 961, CA (Crim Div) . . . . *Digested*, 07/**3733**
Attorney General's Reference (No.149 of 2006), Re; *sub nom* R. *v* Pollard (Stephen)
[2007] EWCA Crim 965; [2007] 2 Cr. App. R. (S.) 96, CA (Crim Div) . . . . *Digested*, 07/**3699**
Attorney General's Reference (No.196 of 2006), Re; *sub nom* R. *v* Hatton (Christoher)
[2006] EWCA Crim 3273, CA (Crim Div) . . . . *Digested*, 07/**3650**

Attorney General's Reference (No.1 of 2007), Re; *sub nom* R. v Hardy (James Andrew) [2007] EWCA Crim 760; [2007] 2 Cr. App. R. (S.) 86; *Times,* April 12, 2007, CA (Crim Div) . . . . *Digested,* 07/**3715**
Attorney General's Reference (No.7 of 2007), Re; *sub nom* R. v Bradstock (Oliver) [2007] EWCA Crim 902; [2007] 2 Cr. App. R. (S.) 101, CA (Crim Div) . . . . *Digested,* 07/**3718**
Attorney General's Reference (No.8 of 2007), Re; *sub nom* R. v Krivec (Danielle) [2007] EWCA Crim 922; [2007] Crim. L.R. 642; *Times,* April 27, 2007, CA (Crim Div) . *Digested,* 07/**3628**
Attorney General's Reference (Nos.32, 33 and 34 of 2007), Re; *sub nom* R. v Bate (Dean) [2007] EWCA Crim 1375; [2007] Crim. L.R. 815, CA (Crim Div)
Attorney General's Reference (Nos.59 and 60 of 2007), Re; *sub nom* R. v Shrimpton (Alan); R. v Perry (Darren Michael) [2007] EWCA Crim 1993; (2007) 104(30) L.S.G. 34, CA (Crim Div)
Attorney General's Reference (No.66 of 2007), Re; *sub nom* R. v Russell (Leon) [2007] EWCA Crim 2630; (2007) 104(40) L.S.G. 26, CA (Crim Div)
Attorney General's Reference (Nos.68 and 92 of 2007), Re; *sub nom* R. v Harding (Paul William); *joined case* R. v Hawkes (John Clayton) [2007] EWCA Crim 2634; *Times,* December 11, 2007, CA (Crim Div) . . . . *Digested,* 07/**3632**
Attorney General's Reference (Nos.74 and 83 of 2007), Re; *sub nom* R. v F; R. v F [2007] EWCA Crim 2550; *Times,* November 16, 2007, CA (Crim Div)
Attridge Law (A Firm) v Coleman [2007] 2 C.M.L.R. 24; [2007] I.C.R. 654; [2007] I.R.L.R. 88; *Times,* January 12, 2007, EAT . . . . *Digested,* 07/**1330**
Auchterarder Golf Club v Revenue and Customs Commissioners [2007] S.T.I. 386, V&DTr (Edinburgh)
AUKOL/Financial records (T690/06) [2007] E.P.O.R. 39, EPO (Technical Bd App) . . . *Digested,* 07/**2630**
Auntie's Cafe Ltd v Revenue and Customs Commissioners [2007] S.T.C. (S.C.D.) 306; [2007] S.T.I. 554, Sp Comm. . . . . *Digested,* 07/**4134**
Auroux v Commune de Roanne (C-220/05) [2007] All E.R. (EC) 918, ECJ
Austin v Commissioner of Police of the Metropolis [2007] EWCA Civ 989; (2007) 104(42) L.S.G. 32; (2007) 151 S.J.L.B. 1367; *Times,* October 29, 2007, CA (Civ Div); affirming [2005] EWHC 480 (QB); [2005] H.R.L.R. 20; [2005] U.K.H.R.R. 1039; [2005] Po. L.R. 68; (2005) 155 N.L.J. 515; *Times,* April 14, 2005, QBD . . . . *Digested,* 07/**3316**
Austin v Rea (Unreported, June 27, 2006), CC (Horsham) [*Ex rel.* CS2 Lawyers, Millennium Way, Chesterfield, Derbyshire] . . . . *Digested,* 07/**3074**
Australia and New Zealand Banking Group Ltd v Compagnie Noga d'Importation et d'Exportation SA [2007] EWHC 293 (Comm); [2007] 1 Lloyd's Rep. 487, QBD (Comm) . . . . *Digested,* 07/**787**
Australian Broadcasting Corp v O'Neill [2006] HCA 46; 22 B.H.R.C. 305, HC (Aus) . . *Digested,* 07/**2182**
AUSTRALIAN NATIONAL UNIVERSITY/Detection of glaucoma (T1197/02) [2007] E.P.O.R. 9, EPO (Technical Bd App) . . . . *Digested,* 07/**2597**
Austria v Huber (C-336/00) [2002] E.C.R. I-7699, ECJ (5th Chamber) . . . . *Applied,* 07/**1563**
Auto Lease Holland BV v Bundesamt fur Finanzen (C-185/01) [2005] S.T.C. 598; [2003] E.C.R. I-1317; [2005] B.T.C. 5151; [2005] B.V.C. 182; [2003] S.T.I. 202, ECJ (5th Chamber) . . . . *Digested,* 05/**4395**: *Applied,* 07/4305: *Considered,* 04/4021: *Distinguished,* 04/3992, 07/4310
Automatic Fire Detection, Re (C-254/05) see Commission of the European Communities v Belgium (C-254/05)
Avalon Trust, Re [2007] W.T.L.R. 1693; (2006-07) 9 I.T.E.L.R. 450, Royal Ct (Jer) . . . . *Digested,* 07/**4254**
Aveat Heating Ltd v Jerram Falkus Construction Ltd [2007] EWHC 131 (TCC); [2007] T.C.L.R. 3; 113 Con. L.R. 13, QBD (TCC)
AVERY DENNISON/Fluid absorbing adhesive (T876/06) [2007] E.P.O.R. 49, EPO (Technical Bd App)
Avis v Turner [2007] EWCA Civ 748; [2007] 4 All E.R. 1103; [2007] 2 F.C.R. 695; [2007] B.P.I.R. 663; [2007] 48 E.G. 146; [2007] W.T.L.R. 1521; [2007] Fam. Law 979; [2007] 30 E.G. 132 (C.S.); (2007) 104(31) L.S.G. 24; (2007) 151 S.J.L.B. 986; [2007] N.P.C. 91; *Times,* August 22, 2007, CA (Civ Div); affirming [2007] B.P.I.R. 6, Ch D . . . . *Digested,* 07/**3431**
Avowal Administrative Attorneys Ltd v North Shore District Court 10 I.T.L. Rep. 84, HC (NZ)
Avraamides v Colwill [2006] EWCA Civ 1533; [2007] B.L.R. 76; (2006) 103(46) L.S.G. 31; [2006] N.P.C. 120; *Times,* December 8, 2006, CA (Civ Div) . . . . *Digested,* 07/**788**
AWB (Geneva) SA v North America Steamships Ltd [2007] EWCA Civ 739; [2007] 2 Lloyd's Rep. 315; [2007] 2 C.L.C. 117; [2007] B.P.I.R. 1023; (2007) 104(31) L.S.G. 27, CA (Civ Div); reversing [2007] EWHC 1167 (Comm); [2007] 1 C.L.C. 749, QBD (Comm) . . . . *Digested,* 07/**530**
Awoyomi v Radford [2007] EWHC 1671 (QB); [2007] P.N.L.R. 34; (2007) 157 N.L.J. 1046; *Times,* July 23, 2007, QBD . . . . *Digested,* 07/**2946**
AXA Equity & Law Life Assurance Society Plc (No.2), Re; *joined case* Axa Sun Life Plc (No.2), Re [2001] 1 All E.R. (Comm) 1010; [2001] 2 B.C.L.C. 447; (2001) 98(10) L.S.G. 43; (2001) 145 S.J.L.B. 51; *Times,* January 31, 2001, Ch D . . . . . *Digested,* 01/**3804**: *Considered,* 07/2481

Axa Sun Life Plc (No.2), Re see AXA Equity & Law Life Assurance Society Plc (No.2), Re
Ayegh v Sweden (Admissibility) (4701/05) (2007) 44 E.H.R.R. SE7, ECHR
Aylesbury Vale DC v Florent [2007] EWHC 724 (QB); (2007) 151 S.J.L.B. 505, QBD

Ayliffe v DPP see R. v Jones (Margaret)

Ayres & Sun Timber Co Ltd v Leeds City Council (Unreported, July 17, 1980), Crown Ct
(Leeds) . . . .   *Considered*, 07/3294

Azam v Iqbal see I, Re

Aziz, Re see Law Society v Shah

Aziz v Aziz [2007] EWCA Civ 712; [2007] Fam. Law 1047; *Times*, July 17, 2007, CA
(Civ Div) . . . .   *Digested*, 07/**2699**

Aziz v Crown Prosecution Service see Crown Prosecution Service v Aziz

Azmi v Kirklees MBC [2007] I.C.R. 1154; [2007] I.R.L.R. 484; [2007] E.L.R. 339;
Times, April 17, 2007, EAT; affirming [2007] E.L.R. 125, ET . . . .   *Digested*, 07/**1399**

B, Re see R. v B

B, Re see R. (on the application of Hoxha) v Special Adjudicator

B v A [2007] I.R.L.R. 576, EAT . . . .   *Digested*, 07/**1402**

B v A County Council [2006] EWCA Civ 1388; [2007] 1 F.L.R. 1189; [2006] 3 F.C.R.
568; [2007] P.I.Q.R. P17; [2007] Fam. Law 292; (2006) 150 S.J.L.B. 1571, CA
(Civ Div) . . . .   *Digested*, 07/**1682**

B v Attorney General of New Zealand [2003] UKPC 61; [2003] 4 All E.R. 833;
[2003] Lloyd's Rep. Med. 527, PC (NZ) . . . .   *Digested*, 03/**3006**:
Applied, 03/3004, 07/2934

B v B see MB v KB

B v B [2007] EWHC 594 (Fam); [2007] 2 F.C.R. 127, Fam Div . . . .   *Digested*, 07/**1686**

B v DPP see R v DPP

B v Harrow LBC (No.1); *sub nom* F v Harrow LBC; F v Special Education Needs
Tribunal; B v Special Educational Needs Tribunal [2000] 1 W.L.R. 223; [2000] 1
All E.R. 876; [2000] 3 F.C.R. 1; [2000] B.L.G.R. 162; [2000] Ed. C.R. 188;
[2000] E.L.R. 109; (2000) 97(6) L.S.G. 34; (2000) 144 S.J.L.B. 83; *Times*,
January 28, 2000; *Independent*, February 2, 2000, HL; reversing [1998] 3
F.C.R. 231; [1999] B.L.G.R. 144; [1998] Ed. C.R. 176; [1998] E.L.R. 351; (1998)
42 B.M.L.R. 88; (1998) 95(17) L.S.G. 32; (1998) 142 S.J.L.B. 134; *Times*,
March 26, 1998, CA (Civ Div); reversing [1998] Ed. C.R. 1; *Times*, December 29,
1997, QBD . . . .   *Digested*, 00/**1946**:
Considered, 98/1983, 02/1165, 07/5121

B v Reading BC; *sub nom* L v Reading BC [2007] EWCA Civ 1313; *Times*, December
27, 2007, CA (Civ Div); reversing [2006] EWHC 3206 (QB), QBD

B v Secretary of State for the Home Department see R. (on the application of Hoxha)
v Special Adjudicator

B v Special Educational Needs Tribunal see B v Harrow LBC (No.1)

B v Suffolk CC see A v Essex CC

B v Torbay Council [2007] 1 F.L.R. 203; [2006] Fam. Law 924, Fam Div . . . .   *Digested*, 07/**1713**:
Doubted, 07/1727

B v United Kingdom (36337/97); *joined case* P v United Kingdom (35974/97) [2001]
2 F.L.R. 261; [2001] 2 F.C.R. 221; (2002) 34 E.H.R.R. 19; 11 B.H.R.C. 667;
[2001] Fam. Law 506; *Times*, May 15, 2001, ECHR . . . .   *Digested*, 01/**2628**:
Applied, 03/428, 06/345: *Cited*, 04/1511: *Distinguished*, 07/1774

B and C v A see A v B Plc

B and O (Children), Re see B (Children) (Allegation of Sexual Abuse: Child's Evidence), Re

B Borough Council v S [2006] EWHC 2584 (Fam); [2007] 1 F.L.R. 1600; [2007] 1
F.C.R. 574; (2006) 9 C.C.L. Rep. 596; (2007) 93 B.M.L.R. 1; [2007] Fam. Law
119, Fam Div . . . .   *Digested*, 07/**360**

B City Council v S [2006] EWHC 3065 (Fam); [2007] 1 F.L.R. 1223; [2007]
U.K.H.R.R. 588; [2007] Fam. Law 300, Fam Div . . . .   *Digested*, 07/**1723**

B NHS Trust v J; *sub nom* An NHS Trust v J [2006] EWHC 3152 (Fam); (2007) 94
B.M.L.R. 15, Fam Div . . . .   *Digested*, 07/**1985**

B Trust, Re [2007] W.T.L.R. 1361; (2006-07) 9 I.T.E.L.R. 783, Royal Ct (Jer)

B (A Child), Re [2006] EWCA Civ 1906; (2007) 151 S.J.L.B. 25, CA (Civ Div)

B (A Child) v Ealing Family Housing Association (Unreported, December 5, 2006), CC
(Uxbridge) [*Ex rel.* Tim Sharpe, Barrister, 1 Temple Gardens, London] . . . .   *Digested*, 07/**3167**

B (A Child) v Heath (Unreported, May 24, 2006), CC (Coventry) [*Ex rel.* Stephen
Garner, No.8 Chambers, Fountain Court, Steelhouse Lane, Birmingham] . . . . .   *Digested*, 07/**3133**

B (A Child) v JJB Sports Plc (Unreported, November 23, 2006), CC (Wigan) [*Ex rel.*
Tom Gosling, Barrister, Oriel Chambers, 14 Water Street, Liverpool] . . . .   *Digested*, 07/**4195**

B (A Child) v Maidstone and Tunbridge Wells NHS Trust (Unreported, October 17,
2006), CC (Tunbridge Wells) [*Ex rel.* Adam Walker, Barrister, Lamb Chambers,
Lamb Building, Elm Court, Temple, London] . . . .   *Digested*, 07/**3200**

B (A Child) (Care Proceedings: Expert Witness), Re [2007] EWCA Civ 556; [2007] 2 F.L.R.
979; [2007] Fam. Law 798; (2007) 151 S.J.L.B. 673, CA (Civ Div)

B (A Child) (Child Support: Reduction of Contact), Re [2006] EWCA Civ 1574; [2007] 1
F.L.R. 1949; [2007] Fam. Law 114; (2006) 103(47) L.S.G. 28; (2006) 150 S.J.L.B.
1569; *Times*, January 5, 2007, CA (Civ Div) . . . .   *Digested*, 07/**1767**

B (A Child) (Contact: Permission to Appeal), Re see O (Children) (Contact: Permission to
Appeal), Re

B (A Child) (Disclosure), Re see Kent CC v B (A Child)

B (A Child) (Prohibited Steps Order), Re [2007] EWCA Civ 1055; *Times*, October 10, 2007,
CA (Civ Div) . . . . *Digested*, 07/**1788**
B (Appeal: Lack of Reasons), Re [2003] EWCA Civ 881; [2003] 2 F.L.R. 1035; [2003]
Fam. Law 716, CA (Civ Div) . . . . *Applied*, 05/1533:
Considered, 07/466
B (Children) (Allegation of Sexual Abuse: Child's Evidence), Re; *joined case* B and O
(Children), Re [2006] EWCA Civ 773; [2006] 2 F.L.R. 1071; [2006] 2 F.C.R.
386; [2006] Fam. Law 847, CA (Civ Div) . . . . *Digested*, 07/**1720**
B (Children) (Emergency Protection Orders), Re see X Local Authority *v* B (Emergency
Protection Orders)
B (Children) (Indemnity Costs), Re [2007] EWCA Civ 921; [2007] Fam. Law 1065; (2007)
151 S.J.L.B. 296, CA (Civ Div)
B (Children Act Proceedings: Issue Estoppel), Re see B (Minors) (Care Proceedings: Issue
Estoppel), Re
B (Leave to Remove), Re; *sub nom* K *v* B [2006] EWHC 1783 (Fam); [2007] 1 F.L.R.
333; [2006] Fam. Law 1032, Fam Div . . . . *Digested*, 07/**1794**
B (Minors) (Care Proceedings: Evidence), Re see B (Minors) (Care Proceedings: Issue
Estoppel), Re
B (Minors) (Care Proceedings: Issue Estoppel), Re; *sub nom* B (Minors) (Care
Proceedings: Evidence), Re; B (Minors: Issue Estoppel), Re; B (Children Act
Proceedings: Issue Estoppel), Re [1997] Fam. 117; [1997] 3 W.L.R. 1; [1997] 2
All E.R. 29; [1997] 1 F.L.R. 285; [1997] 1 F.C.R. 477; [1997] Fam. Law 235;
(1997) 161 J.P.N. 358; (1996) 93(44) L.S.G. 30; (1996) 140 S.J.L.B. 252;
Times, December 16, 1996; *Independent*, November 25, 1996, Fam Div . . . . . . *Digested*, 96/**685**:
Applied, 07/1685: *Considered*, 98/1981
B (Minors) (Care Proceedings: Practice), Re; *sub nom* CB and JB (Minors) (Care
Proceedings: Guidelines), Re [1999] 1 W.L.R. 238; [1998] 2 F.L.R. 211; [1998] 2
F.C.R. 313; [1998] Fam. Law 454; *Times*, May 13, 1998, Fam Div . . . . *Digested*, 98/**2401**:
Applied, 03/1517: *Considered*, 05/1559, 07/1728: *Followed*, 99/2358
B (Minors: Issue Estoppel), Re see B (Minors) (Care Proceedings: Issue Estoppel), Re
Baars *v* Inspecteur der Belastingdienst Particulieren/Ondernemingen Gorinchem (C-
251/98) [2000] E.C.R. I-2787; [2002] 1 C.M.L.R. 49; 2 I.T.L. Rep. 660, ECJ
(5th Chamber) . . . . *Digested*, 02/**4374**:
Applied, 07/1617, 07/1624
Babcock FATA Ltd *v* Addison see Addison *v* Babcock FATA Ltd
Babcock International Ltd *v* National Grid Co Plc see Fairchild *v* Glenhaven Funeral
Services Ltd (t/a GH Dovener & Son)
Babula *v* Waltham Forest College [2007] EWCA Civ 174; [2007] I.C.R. 1026; [2007]
I.R.L.R. 346; (2007) 104(12) L.S.G. 32; (2007) 151 S.J.L.B. 396; *Times*, April 17,
2007, CA (Civ Div); reversing UKEAT/0635/05/SM, EAT . . . . *Digested*, 07/**1441**
BACTIGUARD and Device Trade Mark, Re see Fenchurch Environmental Group Ltd *v*
Bactiguard AG
Baden *v* Smith (No.1) see Baden's Deed Trusts (No.1), Re
Baden's Deed Trusts (No.1), Re; *sub nom* McPhail *v* Doulton; Baden *v* Smith (No.1)
[1971] A.C. 424; [1970] 2 W.L.R. 1110; [1970] 2 All E.R. 228; (1970) 114 S.J.
375, HL; reversing [1969] 2 Ch. 388; [1969] 3 W.L.R. 12; [1969] 1 All E.R. 1016;
(1969) 113 S.J. 149, CA (Civ Div); affirming [1967] 1 W.L.R. 1457; [1967] 3 All
E.R. 159; (1967) 111 S.J. 773, Ch D . . . . *Digested*, 70/**2635**:
Applied, 71/10652, 72/3163, 77/2695, 91/2726, 02/249, 07/318:
Considered, 69/1746, 80/228, 86/2804: *Distinguished*, 04/3951:
Subsequent proceedings, 71/10652
BADIA I FARRE/Seat furniture (T763/04) [2007] E.P.O.R. 48, EPO (Technical Bd App)
Baghli *v* France (34374/97) (2001) 33 E.H.R.R. 32, ECHR . . . . *Digested*, 02/**2517**:
Distinguished, 07/2262
Bahin *v* Hughes (1886) L.R. 31 Ch. D. 390, CA . . . . *Applied*, 07/4248
Baigent *v* Random House Group Ltd [2007] EWCA Civ 247; [2007] F.S.R. 24;
(2007) 104(15) L.S.G. 21, CA (Civ Div); affirming [2006] EWHC 719 (Ch);
[2006] E.M.L.R. 16; [2006] F.S.R. 44; (2006) 29(5) I.P.D. 29039, Ch D . . . . *Digested*, 07/**2521**
Bailey (t/a Elite Angling Products) *v* Haynes (t/a RAGS) [2007] F.S.R. 10, PCC . . . . . . *Digested*, 07/**2537**
Bain *v* Brand (1875-76) L.R. 1 App. Cas. 762; (1876) 3 R. (H.L.) 16, HL; reversing
(1874) 2 R. 258, IH (2 Div) . . . . *Considered*, 07/5285:
Explained, 86/4106: *Followed*, 81/3242, 89/4524
Bainbridge *v* Redcar and Cleveland BC; *joined case* Redcar and Cleveland BC *v*
Williams [2007] I.R.L.R. 494, EAT . . . . *Digested*, 07/**1365**
Baird *v* Byrne Bros (Formwork) Ltd see Byrne Bros (Formwork) Ltd *v* Baird
Baird Textile Holdings Ltd *v* Marks & Spencer Plc [2001] EWCA Civ 274; [2002] 1 All
E.R. (Comm) 737; [2001] C.L.C. 999, CA (Civ Div); affirming 2000 Folio No.
22, QBD (Comm) . . . . *Digested*, 01/**931**:
Applied, 06/2704: *Considered*, 07/2952
Bajrami *v* Albania (35853/04) [2007] 1 F.L.R. 1629; [2007] 1 F.C.R. 91; [2007] Fam.
Law 386, ECHR . . . . *Digested*, 07/**1773**
Bajwa *v* Pannu 2007 BCCA 260; (2007-08) 10 I.T.E.L.R. 47, CA (BC)

Baker v Baker [1995] 2 F.L.R. 829; [1996] 1 F.C.R. 567; [1996] Fam. Law 80, CA
(Civ Div) . . . . *Digested*, 95/**2342**:
Applied, 03/1586: *Considered*, 07/1686
Baker v Baker (2007-08) 10 I.T.E.L.R. 897, Ch D
Baker v Baker (No.2) [1997] 1 F.L.R. 148; [1997] 2 F.C.R. 249; [1997] Fam. Law 163,
CA (Civ Div) . . . . *Digested*, 97/**2484**:
Applied, 07/1698
Baker v Black Sea & Baltic General Insurance Co Ltd; *sub nom* Black Sea & Baltic
General Insurance Co Ltd v Baker [1998] 1 W.L.R. 974; [1998] 2 All E.R. 833;
[1998] C.L.C. 820; [1998] Lloyd's Rep. I.R. 327; (1998) 95(23) L.S.G. 26;
(1998) 148 N.L.J. 782; (1998) 142 S.J.L.B. 171; *Times*, May 21, 1998, HL;
reversing in part [1996] L.R.L.R. 353; [1996] 5 Re. L.R. 202, CA (Civ Div);
affirming [1995] L.R.L.R. 261, QBD (Comm) . . . . *Digested*, 98/**3407**:
Applied, 07/2504
Baker v Potter [2004] EWHC 1422 (Ch); [2005] B.C.C. 855, Ch D (Companies Ct) . . *Digested*, 06/**568**:
Considered, 07/1709
Baker v Willoughby [1970] A.C. 467; [1970] 2 W.L.R. 50; [1969] 3 All E.R. 1528; 7
K.I.R. 457; (1970) 114 S.J. 15, HL; reversing [1969] 2 W.L.R. 489; [1969] 2 All
E.R. 549; 6 K.I.R. 5; (1968) 113 S.J. 37; *Times*, December 11, 1968, CA (Civ Div);
reversing [1969] 1 Q.B. 38; [1968] 2 W.L.R. 1138; [1968] 2 All E.R. 236;
(1968) 112 S.J. 234, QBD . . . . *Digested*, 70/**1862**:
Applied, 71/3255, 72/2531, 76/2671, 00/6163, 07/330: *Cited*, 00/1482:
Considered, 70/737, 70/1862: *Distinguished*, 78/718, 80/1885,
81/278.u: *Doubted*, 81/1835: *Followed*, 77/2011, 79/683, 98/6103
Baker Refractories Ltd v Bishop see Barber v Somerset CC
Baker (Valuation Officer) v Citibank NA [2007] R.A. 93, Lands Tr
Balans Ltd v Hounslow LBC [2007] P.A.D. 7, Planning Inspector
Baldwin v Brighton and Hove City Council [2007] I.C.R. 680; [2007] I.R.L.R. 232,
EAT . . . . *Digested*, 07/**1320**
Balfour Beatty Power Networks Ltd v Wilcox [2006] EWCA Civ 1240; [2007] I.R.L.R.
63, CA (Civ Div); affirming [2006] I.R.L.R. 258, EAT . . . . *Digested*, 07/**1415**
BALI Trade Mark (No.1) see Berlei (UK) Ltd v Bali Brassiere Co Inc (No.1)
Ballast Plc, Re; *sub nom* St Paul Travelers Insurance Co Ltd v Dargan [2006] EWHC
3189 (Ch); [2007] B.C.C. 620; [2007] B.P.I.R. 117; [2007] Lloyd's Rep. I.R.
742, Ch D . . . . *Digested*, 07/**2441**
Ballast Plc (In Administration), Re [2004] EWHC 2356 (Ch); [2005] 1 W.L.R. 1928; [2005]
1 All E.R. 630; [2005] B.C.C. 96; [2005] 1 B.C.L.C. 446; (2004) 101(44) L.S.G. 33;
Times, October 28, 2004, Ch D (Companies Ct) . . . . *Digested*, 04/**2115**:
Considered, 06/2316, 07/2387
Balmoral Group Ltd v Borealis (UK) Ltd [2006] EWHC 1900 (Comm); [2006] 2
Lloyd's Rep. 629; [2006] 2 C.L.C. 220, QBD (Comm) . . . . *Digested*, 07/**3566**
Bamber v Eaton; *sub nom* Osea Road Campsites Ltd, Re [2004] EWHC 2437 (Ch);
[2005] 1 W.L.R. 760; [2005] 1 All E.R. 820; [2007] B.C.C. 877; (2004)
101(40) L.S.G. 28; *Times*, October 22, 2004, Ch D . . . . *Digested*, 05/**453**
Banbury Visionplus Ltd v Revenue and Customs Commissioners [2006] EWHC 1024
(Ch); [2006] S.T.C. 1568; [2006] B.T.C. 5482; [2006] B.V.C. 552; [2006] S.T.I.
1511; *Times*, June 12, 2006, Ch D; affirming [2006] B.V.C. 2246; [2005] V. &
D.R. 337; [2006] S.T.I. 283, V&D Tr (London) . . . . *Digested*, 06/**4454**:
Applied, 07/4333: *Considered*, 07/5569
Banca Popolare di Cremona Sarl v Agenzia Entrate Ufficio Cremona (C-475/03) [2006]
E.C.R. I-9373; [2007] 1 C.M.L.R. 31, ECJ . . . . *Digested*, 07/**1581**
Banco de Credito Industrial SA v Ayuntamiento de Valencia (C387/92) see Banco
Exterior de Espana SA v Ayuntamiento de Valencia (C387/92)
Banco Exterior de Espana SA v Ayuntamiento de Valencia (C387/92); *sub nom* Banco
de Credito Industrial SA v Ayuntamiento de Valencia (C387/92) [1994] E.C.R. I-
877; [1994] 3 C.M.L.R. 473, ECJ . . . . *Digested*, 94/**4949**:
Applied, 97/2399, 07/650
Banco Nacional de Comercio Exterior SNC v Empresa de Telecomunicaciones de Cuba
SA [2007] EWHC 2322 (Comm); [2007] 2 C.L.C. 690; [2007] I.L.Pr. 59, QBD
(Comm) . . . . *Digested*, 07/**508**
Banco Nacional de Comercio Exterior SNC v Empresa de Telecomunicationes de Cuba
SA [2007] EWCA Civ 662; [2007] 2 All E.R. (Comm) 1093; [2007] 2 Lloyd's
Rep. 484; [2007] C.P. Rep. 39; [2007] 2 C.L.C. 34; [2007] I.L.Pr. 51; (2007)
104(29) L.S.G. 22; (2007) 151 S.J.L.B. 923, CA (Civ Div); affirming [2007]
EWHC 19 (Comm); [2007] 2 All E.R. (Comm) 46; [2007] I.L.Pr. 16, QBD
(Comm) . . . . *Digested*, 07/**457**
Bandwith Shipping Corp v Intaari (A Firm) (The Magdalena Oldendorff) [2007]
EWCA Civ 998; [2007] 2 C.L.C. 537; *Times*, October 31, 2007, CA (Civ Div);
affirming [2006] EWHC 2532 (Comm), QBD (Comm) . . . . *Digested*, 07/**253**
Bangla Television Ltd (In Liquidation), Re see Valentine v Bangla TV Ltd
Bank Austria Creditanstalt AG v Commission of the European Communities (T-198/03)
[2006] E.C.R. II-1429; [2006] 5 C.M.L.R. 10, CFI (2nd Chamber) . . . . *Digested*, 07/**1588**

27

Bank Line Ltd v Arthur Capel & Co [1919] A.C. 435, HL . . . .   *Applied*, 47-51/1742,
            47-51/1745, 47-51/9504, 56/874, 80/194: *Considered*, 81/2496, 90/4065,
                                                             06/3919, 07/3815

Bank of Credit and Commerce International SA (In Liquidation) v Ali (No.1) [2001] UKHL
     8; [2002] 1 A.C. 251; [2001] 2 W.L.R. 735; [2001] 1 All E.R. 961; [2001] I.C.R.
     337; [2001] I.R.L.R. 292; [2001] Emp. L.R. 359; (2001) 98(15) L.S.G. 32;
     (2001) 151 N.L.J. 351; (2001) 145 S.J.L.B. 67; (2001) 145 S.J.L.B. 70; *Times*,
     March 6, 2001, HL; affirming [2000] 3 All E.R. 51; [2000] I.C.R. 1410; [2000]
     I.R.L.R. 398; *Times*, May 10, 2000, CA (Civ Div); reversing [1999] 2 All E.R.
     1005; [1999] I.C.R. 1068; [1999] I.R.L.R. 226; (1999) 96(7) L.S.G. 35; (1999)
     149 N.L.J. 53; *Times*, January 25, 1999, Ch D . . . .   *Digested*, 01/**2228**:
                  Applied, 02/207, 02/217, 03/2723, 06/203, 06/2411, 07/2760:
                           Considered, 07/2500: *Distinguished*, 02/703

Bank of Credit and Commerce International (Overseas) Ltd v Akindele; *sub nom* BCCI v
     Chief Labode Onadimaki Akindele [2001] Ch. 437; [2000] 3 W.L.R. 1423;
     [2000] 4 All E.R. 221; [2000] Lloyd's Rep. Bank. 292; [2000] B.C.C. 968;
     [2000] W.T.L.R. 1049; (1999-2000) 2 I.T.E.L.R. 788; (2000) 97(26) L.S.G. 36;
     (2000) 150 N.L.J. 950; *Times*, June 22, 2000; *Independent*, June 29, 2000,
     CA (Civ Div); affirming [1999] B.C.C. 669, Ch D . . . .   *Digested*, 00/**2315**:
                                   Applied, 03/529, 05/3444, 07/3438

Bank of Credit and Commerce International (Overseas) Ltd (In Liquidation) v Ernst &
     Whinney see Bank of Credit and Commerce International (Overseas) Ltd (In
     Liquidation) v Price Waterhouse (No.3)

Bank of Credit and Commerce International (Overseas) Ltd (In Liquidation) v Price
     Waterhouse (No.3); *joined case* Bank of Credit and Commerce International
     (Overseas) Ltd (In Liquidation) v Ernst & Whinney [1998] Ch. 84; [1997] 3
     W.L.R. 849; [1997] 4 All E.R. 781; [1997] 6 Bank. L.R. 216; [1998] B.C.C. 511;
     Times, June 25, 1997, Ch D . . . .   *Digested*, 97/**316**:
                                        Doubted, 00/274, 07/439

Bank of Dubai Ltd v Abbas [1997] I.L.Pr. 308, CA (Civ Div); reversing (Unreported,
     December 5, 1994), QBD . . . .   *Applied*, 07/517

Bank of England v Riley [1992] Ch. 475; [1992] 2 W.L.R. 840; [1992] 1 All E.R. 769;
     Times, November 1, 1990, CA (Civ Div) . . . .   *Digested*, 92/**977**:
                               Applied, 07/437: *Considered*, 92/2558

Bank of Ireland v Hollicourt (Contracts) Ltd see Hollicourt (Contracts) Ltd (In
     Liquidation) v Bank of Ireland

Bank of Ireland Mortgage Bank v Coleman (t/a Coleman & Co) [2006] IEHC 337;
     [2007] P.N.L.R. 16, HC (Irl)

Bank of Nova Scotia v Hellenic Mutual War Risk Association (Bermuda) Ltd (The Good
     Luck) [1992] 1 A.C. 233; [1991] 2 W.L.R. 1279; [1991] 3 All E.R. 1; [1991] 2
     Lloyd's Rep. 191; (1991) 141 N.L.J. 779; *Times*, May 17, 1991; *Independent*, May
     31, 1991; *Financial Times*, May 21, 1991, HL; reversing [1990] 1 Q.B. 818; [1990]
     2 W.L.R. 547; [1989] 3 All E.R. 628; [1989] 2 Lloyd's Rep. 238; (1990)
     87(10) L.S.G. 34; *Times*, April 20, 1989, CA (Civ Div); reversing [1988] 1 Lloyd's
     Rep. 514, QBD (Comm) . . . .   *Digested*, 91/**3261**:
                 Applied, 02/2753, 06/2428: *Considered*, 95/4125, 96/681:
                         Distinguished, 07/2470: *Followed*, 95/754, 03/2483

Bank of Scotland v Bennett see Royal Bank of Scotland Plc v Etridge (No.2)

Bank of Scotland v Euclidian (No.1) Ltd [2007] EWHC 1732 (Comm); (2007) 157
     N.L.J. 1083, QBD (Comm)

Bank of Scotland v Neath Port Talbot CBC [2006] EWHC 2276 (Ch); [2007] Env. L.R.
     D15, Ch D

Bankers & Securities Dealers Association of Iceland v EFTA Surveillance Authority (E9/
     04) [2006] 2 C.M.L.R. 50, EFTA . . . .   *Digested*, 07/**1648**

Bankovic v Belgium (Admissibility) (52207/99); *sub nom* Bankovic v United Kingdom
     (Admissibility) (52207/99) 11 B.H.R.C. 435; (2007) 44 E.H.R.R. SE5, ECHR . .   *Digested*, 02/**2535**:
                 Applied, 05/2065, 05/2129, 06/2163, 07/2212, 07/2239:
                         Considered, 03/2162, 04/2008

Bankovic v United Kingdom (Admissibility) (52207/99) see Bankovic v Belgium
     (Admissibility) (52207/99)

Banks v Goodfellow (1869-70) L.R. 5 Q.B. 549, QB . . . .   *Applied*, 47-51/10958,
         01/5165, 01/5167, 02/4328, 05/3971, 06/4093, 06/4094, 06/4096, 06/4108,
                                   07/3958: *Considered*, 78/351.u

Banks v National Westminster Bank Plc [2005] EWHC 3479 (Ch); [2006] W.T.L.R.
     1693, Ch D . . . .   *Digested*, 07/**3962**

Banks v Theatre Royal de la Monnaie (C-178/97) [2000] Q.B. 865; [2000] 3 W.L.R.
     1069; [2000] All E.R. (EC) 324; [2000] E.C.R. I-2005; [2000] 2 C.M.L.R. 754;
     [2000] C.E.C. 256; *Times*, April 5, 2000, ECJ (5th Chamber) . . . .   *Digested*, 00/**4817**:
                                        Applied, 07/1634

Banks v United Kingdom (Admissibility) (21387/05) (2007) 45 E.H.R.R. SE2, ECHR

Bannatyne (General Assembly of the Free Church) v Baron Overtoun see General
     Assembly of Free Church of Scotland v Lord Overtoun

Banque Bruxelles Lambert SA (BBL) v Belgium (C-8/03) [2004] S.T.C. 1643; [2004]
E.C.R. I-10157; [2005] 1 C.M.L.R. 13; [2004] C.E.C. 485; [2007] B.T.C. 5132;
[2007] B.V.C. 101; [2004] S.T.I. 2256, ECJ (1st Chamber) . . . .   *Digested*, 05/**4412**

Banque Saudi Fransi v Lear Siegler Services Inc [2006] EWCA Civ 1130; [2007] 1 All
E.R. (Comm) 67; [2007] 2 Lloyd's Rep. 47, CA (Civ Div); affirming [2005]
EWHC 2395 (Comm); [2006] 1 Lloyd's Rep. 273, QBD (Comm) . . . .   *Digested*, 07/**311**

Bansi v Alpha Flight Services [2007] I.C.R. 308, EAT . . . .   *Digested*, 07/**1434**:
                                                         Applied, 07/1319

Bar 24 Ltd v Sheffield City Council [2007] P.A.D. 37, Planning Inspector

Barbados Trust Co Ltd (formerly CI Trustees (Asia Pacific) Ltd) v Bank of Zambia [2007]
EWCA Civ 148; [2007] 2 All E.R. (Comm) 445; [2007] 1 Lloyd's Rep. 495;
[2007] 1 C.L.C. 434; (2006-07) 9 I.T.E.L.R. 689, CA (Civ Div); affirming [2006]
EWHC 222 (Comm); [2006] 1 Lloyd's Rep. 723; [2006] 1 C.L.C. 311; (2005-
06) 8 I.T.E.L.R. 739, QBD (Comm) . . . .   *Digested*, 07/**305**

Barber v CI Ltd [2006] B.C.C. 927, Ch D . . . .   *Digested*, 07/**2430**

Barber v DPP [2006] EWHC 3137 (Admin); [2007] R.T.R. 25, QBD (Admin) . . . . .   *Digested*, 07/**3539**

Barber v Guardian Royal Exchange Assurance Group (C-262/88) [1991] 1 Q.B. 344;
[1991] 2 W.L.R. 72; [1990] 2 All E.R. 660; [1990] E.C.R. I-1889; [1990] 2
C.M.L.R. 513; [1990] I.C.R. 616; [1990] I.R.L.R. 240; [1990] 1 P.L.R. 103;
(1990) 140 N.L.J. 925; *Times*, May 18, 1990; *Independent*, May 23, 1990;
Financial Times, May 25, 1990; *Guardian*, July 12, 1990, ECJ . . . .   *Digested*, 90/**1915**:
                Applied, 91/1636, 91/1669, 92/1979, 93/1751, 95/1997, 95/1998, 95/2001,
                98/2240, 98/4133, 01/2277, 01/2281, 02/1367, 02/3380, 04/2799,
                05/3000: *Cited*, 92/1940, 92/1968, 95/2095, 00/4382:
                Considered, 94/4814, 94/4822, 94/4826, 95/2000, 95/2039, 96/2629,
                96/4609, 97/5378, 01/4605, 05/1257, 06/2960, 06/2987, 06/2993,
                07/3043: *Followed*, 00/2159: *Referred to*, 97/2214, 97/3947

Barber v RJB Mining (UK) Ltd [1999] 2 C.M.L.R. 833; [1999] I.C.R. 679; [1999]
I.R.L.R. 308; (1999) 143 S.J.L.B. 141; *Times*, March 8, 1999; *Independent*, March
22, 1999, QBD . . . .   *Digested*, 99/**2072**:
                                                         Applied, 07/2941

Barber v Somerset CC; *sub nom* Jones v Sandwell MBC; Hatton v Sutherland; Bishop
v Baker Refractories Ltd; Somerset CC v Barber; *joined cases* Baker Refractories
Ltd v Bishop; Sutherland v Hatton; Sandwell MBC v Jones [2004] UKHL 13;
[2004] 1 W.L.R. 1089; [2004] 2 All E.R. 385; [2004] I.C.R. 457; [2004]
I.R.L.R. 475; [2004] E.L.R. 199; [2004] P.I.Q.R. P31; (2004) 77 B.M.L.R. 219;
(2004) 101(18) L.S.G. 34; (2004) 148 S.J.L.B. 419; *Times*, April 5, 2004, HL;
reversing [2002] EWCA Civ 76; [2002] 2 All E.R. 1; [2002] I.C.R. 613; [2002]
I.R.L.R. 263; [2002] Emp. L.R. 288; [2002] P.I.Q.R. P21; (2002) 68 B.M.L.R.
115; (2002) 99(12) L.S.G. 34; (2002) 146 S.J.L.B. 43; *Times*, February 12,
2002; *Independent*, February 13, 2002; *Daily Telegraph*, February 14, 2002, CA
(Civ Div) . . . .   *Digested*, 04/**2713**:
            Applied, 03/3134, 03/3135, 04/1194, 04/2860, 05/2883, 05/2884, 06/2891,
            06/2892, 06/2916, 07/1316, 07/2940, 07/2941: *Considered*, 03/5830,
                                  05/2883, 07/1322: *Explained*, 07/2942

Barclays Bank of Swaziland Ltd v Hahn [1989] 1 W.L.R. 506; [1989] 2 All E.R. 398;
[1991] R.V.R. 58, HL; affirming [1989] 1 W.L.R. 13; [1989] 1 All E.R. 193; (1988)
132 S.J. 1698, CA (Civ Div) . . . .   *Digested*, 89/**3099**:
                              Applied, 97/705: *Considered*, 07/516

Barclays Bank Plc v Coleman see Royal Bank of Scotland Plc v Etridge (No.2)

Barclays Bank Plc v Harris see Royal Bank of Scotland Plc v Etridge (No.2)

Barclays Bank Plc v Revenue and Customs Commissioners; *sub nom* Revenue and
Customs Commissioners v Barclays Bank Plc [2007] EWCA Civ 442; [2007]
B.T.C. 338; [2007] S.T.I. 1436; (2007) 151 S.J.L.B. 675; *Times*, June 5, 2007, CA
(Civ Div); affirming [2006] EWHC 2118 (Ch); [2007] S.T.C. 747; [2006] B.T.C.
771; [2006] S.T.I. 2131; (2006) 150 S.J.L.B. 1115; *Times*, September 12, 2006,
Ch D; reversing [2006] S.T.C. (S.C.D.) 100; [2006] S.T.I. 589, Sp Comm . . . . .   *Digested*, 07/**4092**

Barclays Mercantile Business Finance Ltd v Mawson (Inspector of Taxes); *sub nom* ABC
Ltd v M (Inspector of Taxes) [2004] UKHL 51; [2005] 1 A.C. 684; [2004] 3
W.L.R. 1383; [2005] 1 All E.R. 97; [2005] S.T.C. 1; 76 T.C. 446; [2004] B.T.C.
414; 7 I.T.L. Rep. 383; [2004] S.T.I. 2435; (2004) 154 N.L.J. 1830; (2004) 148
S.J.L.B. 1403; *Times*, November 27, 2004, HL; affirming [2002] EWCA Civ
1853; [2003] S.T.C. 66; [2003] B.T.C. 81; [2002] S.T.I. 1809; (2003) 100(9)
L.S.G. 29; *Times*, December 27, 2002; *Independent*, December 18, 2002, CA
(Civ Div); reversing [2002] EWHC 1527 (Ch); [2002] S.T.C. 1068; [2002] B.T.C.
388; [2002] S.T.I. 1066; (2002) 99(38) L.S.G. 34; *Times*, August 26, 2002,
Ch D; affirming [2002] S.T.C. (S.C.D.) 78; [2002] S.T.I. 47, Sp Comm . . . .   *Digested*, 05/**3988**:
            Applied, 06/4213, 07/3992, 07/4085: *Considered*, 06/4257:
                 Distinguished, 06/4125: *Followed*, 05/4022

Barclays Private Bank & Trust (Cayman) Ltd v Chamberlain [2007] W.T.L.R. 1697;
(2006-07) 9 I.T.E.L.R. 302, Grand Ct (CI)

Baring Securities (Hong Kong) Ltd v Inland Revenue Commissioner 10 I.T.L. Rep. 196,
CFA (HK); reversing [2006] 3 H.K.L.R.D. 315, CA (HK); reversing 7 I.T.L. Rep.
873, CFI (HK)

Barke v Seetec Business Technology Centre Ltd [2005] EWCA Civ 578; [2005] I.C.R. 1373; [2005] I.R.L.R. 633; *Times*, May 26, 2005, CA (Civ Div) . . . .   *Digested*, 05/**1256**:
Applied, 07/1319: *Considered*, 06/2226

Barker v Bromley LBC (C-290/03) see R. (on the application of Barker) v Bromley LBC (C-290/03)

Barkhuizen v Napier 22 B.H.R.C. 717, Const Ct (SA)

Barking and Dagenham LBC v MG see Barking and Dagenham LBC v Special Educational Needs and Disability Tribunal (SENDIST)

Barking and Dagenham LBC v Special Educational Needs and Disability Tribunal (SENDIST); *sub nom* R. (on the application of Barking and Dagenham LBC) v SENDIST; *joined case* Barking and Dagenham LBC v MG [2007] EWHC 343 (Admin); [2007] B.L.G.R. 742, QBD (Admin)

Barlow Clowes International Ltd (In Liquidation) v Eurotrust International Ltd [2005] UKPC 37; [2006] 1 W.L.R. 1476; [2006] 1 All E.R. 333; [2006] 1 All E.R. (Comm) 478; [2006] 1 Lloyd's Rep. 225; [2005] W.T.L.R. 1453; (2005-06) 8 I.T.E.L.R. 347; (2005) 102(44) L.S.G. 32; [2006] 1 P. & C.R. DG16, PC (IoM) .   *Digested*, 06/**4381**:
Applied, 06/2545, 07/4238: *Considered*, 06/4380, 07/4237

Barnes v DPP see Revitt v DPP

Barnes v St Helens MBC; *sub nom* St Helens MBC v Barnes [2006] EWCA Civ 1372; [2007] 1 W.L.R. 879; [2007] 3 All E.R. 525; [2007] C.P. Rep. 7; [2007] P.I.Q.R. P10; *Times*, November 17, 2006; *Independent*, October 27, 2006, CA (Civ Div) .   *Digested*, 07/**477**:
Applied, 07/373

Barnes v Tomlinson [2006] EWHC 3115 (Ch); [2007] W.T.L.R. 377, Ch D . . . .   *Digested*, 07/**4238**

Barnes v Wigan MBC C970280, Ch 1996 B1890, Ch D . . . .   *Distinguished*, 07/1329

Barnet LBC v Abdi see Barnet LBC v Ismail

Barnet LBC v Ismail; *sub nom* Ismail v Barnet LBC; Abdi v Barnet LBC; *joined case* Barnet LBC v Abdi [2006] EWCA Civ 383; [2006] 1 W.L.R. 2771; [2007] 1 All E.R. 922; [2006] I.N.L.R. 295; [2006] H.L.R. 23; [2006] B.L.G.R. 559; *Times*, April 25, 2006, CA (Civ Div) . . . .   *Digested*, 06/**2011**

Barnet LBC v Y see X, Re

Barnet Primary Care Trust v X [2006] EWHC 787 (QB); (2006) 92 B.M.L.R. 17, QBD .   *Digested*, 07/**1971**

Barnetson v Framlington Group Ltd; *sub nom* Framlington Group Ltd v Barnetson [2007] EWCA Civ 502; [2007] 1 W.L.R. 2443; [2007] 3 All E.R. 1054; [2007] C.P. Rep. 42; [2007] I.C.R. 1439; [2007] I.R.L.R. 598; (2007) 23 Const. L.J. 665; *Times*, June 11, 2007, CA (Civ Div) . . . .   *Digested*, 07/**343**

Barnett v Brabyn (Inspector of Taxes) [1996] S.T.C. 716; 69 T.C. 133; *Times*, July 5, 1996, Ch D . . . .   *Digested*, 96/**3406**:
Distinguished, 07/4001

Barnett v Lambeth LBC see Kay v Lambeth LBC

Barnstaple Boat Co Ltd v Jones [2007] EWCA Civ 727; (2007) 151 S.J.L.B. 987, CA (Civ Div)

Barracks v Coles see Coles v Barracks

Barracks v Commissioner of Police of the Metropolis see Coles v Barracks

Barratt v Ansell (t/a Woolf Seddon) see Arthur JS Hall & Co v Simons

Barratt v Woolf Seddon see Arthur JS Hall & Co v Simons

Barret McKenzie v Escada (UK) Ltd see Barrett McKenzie & Co Ltd v Escada (UK) Ltd

Barrett v Enfield LBC [2001] 2 A.C. 550; [1999] 3 W.L.R. 79; [1999] 3 All E.R. 193; [1999] 2 F.L.R. 426; [1999] 2 F.C.R. 434; (1999) 1 L.G.L.R. 829; [1999] B.L.G.R. 473; (1999) 11 Admin. L.R. 839; [1999] Ed. C.R. 833; (1999) 2 C.C.L. Rep. 203; [1999] P.I.Q.R. P272; (1999) 49 B.M.L.R. 1; [1999] Fam. Law 622; (1999) 96(28) L.S.G. 27; (1999) 143 S.J.L.B. 183; *Times*, June 18, 1999, HL; reversing [1998] Q.B. 367; [1997] 3 W.L.R. 628; [1997] 3 All E.R. 171; [1997] 2 F.L.R. 167; [1997] 3 F.C.R. 145; (1998) 10 Admin. L.R. 230; (1997) 37 B.M.L.R. 16; [1997] Fam. Law 534; *Times*, April 22, 1997, CA (Civ Div) . . . . . .   *Digested*, 99/**3966**:
Applied, 99/1889, 00/4212: *Considered*, 99/3967, 03/3004, 07/2937:
Distinguished, 99/3963: *Followed*, 98/3944, 99/1765, 04/2725

Barrett v Revenue and Customs Commissioners [2007] S.T.I. 2416, Sp Comm

Barrett McKenzie & Co Ltd v Escada (UK) Ltd; *sub nom* Barret McKenzie v Escada (UK) Ltd [2001] E.C.C. 50; [2001] Eu. L.R. 567; *Times*, May 15, 2001, QBD . . .   *Digested*, 02/**66**:
Considered, 07/68

Barrington v Sloane Properties Ltd [2007] 40 E.G. 268, Lands Tr . . . .   *Digested*, 07/**2759**

Barros D'Sa v University Hospital Coventry and Warwickshire NHS Trust; *sub nom* Barros D'Sa v Walsgrave Hospital NHS Trust [2001] EWCA Civ 983; [2001] I.R.L.R. 691; [2001] Lloyd's Rep. Med. 442; (2001) 62 B.M.L.R. 39; *Daily Telegraph*, June 26, 2001, CA (Civ Div) . . . .   *Digested*, 01/**2244**:
Followed, 07/458

Barros D'Sa v Walsgrave Hospital NHS Trust see Barros D'Sa v University Hospital Coventry and Warwickshire NHS Trust

Barry v Midland Bank Plc [1999] 1 W.L.R. 1465; [1999] 3 All E.R. 974; [1999] I.C.R. 859; [1999] I.R.L.R. 581; (1999) 96(31) L.S.G. 36; (1999) 149 N.L.J. 1253; (1999) 143 S.J.L.B. 221; *Times*, July 23, 1999; *Independent*, October 25, 1999; HL; affirming [1998] 1 All E.R. 805; [1999] I.C.R. 319; [1998] I.R.L.R. 138; *Times*, December 29, 1997, CA (Civ Div); affirming [1997] I.C.R. 192; *Times*, October 25, 1996, EAT . . . .
Digested, 99/**2117**:
Applied, 02/**3362**, 07/**1404**

Bartoline Ltd v Royal & Sun Alliance Insurance Plc; *sub nom* Bartoline Ltd v Royal Sun Alliance Plc [2006] EWHC 3598 (QB); [2007] 1 All E.R. (Comm) 1043; [2007] Lloyd's Rep. I.R. 423, QBD (Merc)
Digested, 07/**2501**

Bartoline Ltd v Royal Sun Alliance Plc see Bartoline Ltd v Royal & Sun Alliance Insurance Plc

Barton v Brown (t/a Cardbar Ltd) [2007] R.A. 377, Lands Tr . . . .
Digested, 07/**3371**

Barton v Golden Sun Holidays Ltd (In Liquidation) [2007] I.L.Pr. 57; (2007) 151 S.J.L.B. 1128, QBD

Barton Henderson Rasen v Merrett and Ernst & Young [1993] 1 Lloyd's Rep. 540, QBD (Comm) . . . .
Digested, 93/**3099**:
Applied, 07/369

BASF AG v Commission of the European Communities (T-15/02); *sub nom* Vitamins Cartel, Re (T-15/02) [2006] 5 C.M.L.R. 2, CFI (4th Chamber) . . . .
Digested, 07/**1546**

BASF/Incrustation inhibitors (T123/85) [1989] E.P.O.R. 476, EPO (Technical Bd App)
Applied, 04/2322, 07/2564

Basford Developments Ltd v Ellesmere Port and Neston BC [2007] P.A.D. 1, Planning Inspector

Basildon DC v Wahlen; *sub nom* Basildon DC v Whalen [2006] EWCA Civ 326; [2006] 1 W.L.R. 2744; [2007] 1 All E.R. 734; [2006] H.L.R. 34; (2006) 103(15) L.S.G. 24; [2006] N.P.C. 38; *Times*, April 17, 2006; *Independent*, March 31, 2006, CA (Civ Div) . . . .
Digested, 06/**2044**

Basildon DC v Whalen see Basildon DC v Wahlen

Basingstoke Press Ltd (In Administration) v Clarke [2007] I.C.R. 1284; [2007] I.R.L.R. 588, EAT. . . . .
Digested, 07/**1410**

BAT Industries Plc, Re; *sub nom* BAT Industries Plc v BAT Reconstructions Ltd; No.001165 of 1998, Ch D . . . .
Digested, 98/**658**:
Considered, 07/2447

BAT Industries Plc v BAT Reconstructions Ltd see BAT Industries Plc, Re

Bath and North East Somerset DC v Connors [2006] EWHC 1595 (QB); [2006] N.P.C. 82, QBD . . . .
Digested, 07/**3260**

Bati v Turkey (33097/96) (2006) 42 E.H.R.R. 37, ECHR . . . .
Digested, 06/**2162**:
Applied, 07/2203

Battery Specialists (Five Star) Ltd, Re (Unreported, February 23, 1998), Ch D . . . . . .
Applied, 07/436

Baumbast v Secretary of State for the Home Department (C-413/99) [2002] E.C.R. I-7091; [2002] 3 C.M.L.R. 23; [2003] I.C.R. 1347; [2003] I.N.L.R. 1; *Times*, October 8, 2002, ECJ . . . .
Digested, 02/**2628**:
Applied, 07/1611, 07/3824: *Considered*, 06/1589: *Distinguished*, 05/3856:
Followed, 05/2204

Baustahlgewebe GmbH v Commission of the European Communities (C-185/95 P) [1998] E.C.R. I-8417; [1999] 4 C.M.L.R. 1203; (1999) 18 Tr. L.R. 87, ECJ. . . . .
Digested, 99/**2242**:
Applied, 07/614, 07/1589: *Followed*, 01/768

Baverstock (A Bankrupt), Re see Shah v Baverstock

Baxall Securities Ltd v Sheard Walshaw Partnership; *sub nom* Blaxhall Securities Ltd v Sheard Walshaw Partnership [2002] EWCA Civ 9; [2002] B.L.R. 100; [2002] T.C.L.R. 18; 83 Con. L.R. 164; [2002] Lloyd's Rep. P.N. 231; [2002] P.N.L.R. 24; [2002] 1 E.G.L.R. 73; [2002] 17 E.G. 158; (2002) 18 Const. L.J. 481; [2002] 5 E.G. 130 (C.S.), CA (Civ Div); reversing in part [2001] C.L.C. 188; [2001] B.L.R. 36; (2001) 3 T.C.L.R. 8; 74 Con. L.R. 116; [2001] Lloyd's Rep. P.N. 85; [2001] P.N.L.R. 9; (2001) 17 Const. L.J. 150; *Daily Telegraph*, November 14, 2000, QBD (TCC) . . . .
Digested, 02/**3285**:
Applied, 06/2895: *Not applied*, 07/2915

Baxendale-Walker v Law Society [2007] EWCA Civ 233; [2007] 3 All E.R. 330; [2007] 3 Costs L.R. 475; (2007) 104(13) L.S.G. 24; (2007) 157 N.L.J. 439, CA (Civ Div); affirming [2006] EWHC 643 (Admin); [2006] 3 All E.R. 675; [2006] 5 Costs L.R. 696; (2006) 156 N.L.J. 601; *Times*, May 17, 2006; *Independent*, April 5, 2006, QBD (Admin) . . . .
Digested, 07/**2800**:
Considered, 07/2802

Baxi Group Ltd v Revenue and Customs Commissioners [2007] EWCA Civ 1378, CA (Civ Div); affirming [2006] EWHC 3353 (Ch); [2007] B.T.C. 5298; [2007] B.V.C. 267; [2007] S.T.I. 114; (2007) 104(4) L.S.G. 33, Ch D; reversing [2006] B.V.C. 2553; [2006] S.T.I. 1369, V&D Tr . . . .
Digested, 07/**4316**

Baybut v Eccle Riggs Country Park Ltd, *Times*, November 13, 2006, Ch D . . . .
Digested, 07/**756**

Bayer AG v Commission of the European Communities (C-2/01 P) see Bundesverband der Arzneimittel Importeure eV v Bayer AG (C-2/01 P)

Bayer AG v Commission of the European Communities (T41/96) [2001] All E.R. (EC)
1; [2000] E.C.R. II-3383; [2001] 4 C.M.L.R. 4; [2001] I.C.R. 735; (2002) 63
B.M.L.R. 71; *Times*, February 9, 2001, CFI (5th Chamber) . . . . *Digested*, 01/**776**:
Affirmed, 04/494: *Applied*, 03/556, 04/487, 05/555, 06/602, 07/644

Bayerische Motorenwerke AG v ALD Auto-Leasing D GmbH (C-70/93) [1995] E.C.R.
I-3439; [1996] 4 C.M.L.R. 478, ECJ. . . . . *Digested*, 96/**1066**:
Considered, 07/1543

BBC v CAFCASS Legal see Ward (A Child), Re
BBC v Rochdale MBC [2005] EWHC 2862 (Fam); [2006] E.M.L.R. 6; [2007] 1
F.L.R. 101; [2006] Fam. Law 929, Fam Div . . . . *Digested*, 06/**445**

BBC v Sugar; *joined cases* R. (on the application of Sugar) v Information
Commissioner; R. (on the application of BBC) v Information Tribunal; C1/2007/
1078, CA (Civ Div); affirming [2007] EWHC 905 (Admin); [2007] 1 W.L.R.
2583; [2007] 4 All E.R. 518; [2007] A.C.D. 87; *Times*, May 22, 2007, QBD
(Admin) . . . . *Digested*, 07/**2892**

BC v A see Reading BC v D (Angela)
BCCI v Chief Labode Onadimaki Akindele see Bank of Credit and Commerce
International (Overseas) Ltd v Akindele
BCCI SA, Re see Malik v Bank of Credit and Commerce International SA (In
Liquidation)

BEA Hotels NV v Bellway LLC [2007] EWHC 1363 (Comm); [2007] 2 Lloyd's Rep.
493; [2007] 1 C.L.C. 920, QBD (Comm). . . . . *Digested*, 07/**235**

Beale v Harvey [2003] EWCA Civ 1883; [2004] 2 P. & C.R. 18, CA (Civ Div) . . . . *Digested*, 04/**3195**:
Distinguished, 07/3364, 07/3365

Beam Tube Products Ltd, Re; *sub nom* Fanshawe v Amav Industries Ltd [2006] EWHC
486 (Ch); [2006] B.C.C. 615; [2007] 2 B.C.L.C. 732, Ch D (Companies Ct) . . *Digested*, 06/**2325**

Bearman (A Bankrupt), Re see Saunders (A Bankrupt), Re
Beattie v Dunbar; *sub nom* SB v Dunbar 2006 S.C.L.R. 777; [2007] M.H.L.R. 7; 2006
G.W.D. 10-180, Sh Pr . . . . *Digested*, 07/**5413**

Beaumont v Amicus [2007] I.C.R. 341, EAT . . . . *Digested*, 07/**1412**
Beauvale Group Ltd (In Administration), Re [2006] B.C.C. 912, Ch D . . . . *Followed*, 07/2395
Becciev v Moldova (9190/03) (2007) 45 E.H.R.R. 11, ECHR . . . . *Digested*, 07/**2230**

Becker v Finanzamt Munster-Innenstadt (8/81) [1982] E.C.R. 53; [1982] 1 C.M.L.R.
499, ECJ. . . . . *Digested*, 82/**1333**:
Applied, 91/3640, 98/2111, 99/4984, 00/5321, 03/4559, 03/4568, 03/4568,
07/1565, 07/4351: *Cited*, 00/5317: *Considered*, 06/4475: *Followed*, 04/1206

Beckett Investment Management Group Ltd v Hall [2007] EWCA Civ 613; [2007] I.C.R.
1539; [2007] I.R.L.R. 793; (2007) 151 S.J.L.B. 891; *Times*, July 11, 2007, CA
(Civ Div); reversing [2007] EWHC 241 (QB), QBD . . . . *Digested*, 07/**1327**:
Considered, 07/351

Beckwith-Moore v Novak [2007] E.T.M.R. 39, Arbitration . . . . *Digested*, 07/**2541**
Bedford v TUI UK Ltd (t/a Austravel) (Unreported, October 12, 2006), CC (Oldham)
[*Ex rel*. Benjamin Gold, Barrister, 1 Chancery Lane, London] . . . . *Digested*, 07/**2126**

Bedford BC v Stanbridge [2007] P.A.D. 88, Planning Inspector
Bee v Jenson [2006] EWHC 2534 (Comm); [2007] R.T.R. 9; [2007] Lloyd's Rep. I.R.
451, QBD (Comm) . . . . *Digested*, 07/**2489**

Bee v Jenson [2007] EWCA Civ 923; [2007] 4 All E.R. 791; [2007] 2 All E.R.
(Comm) 1172; (2007) 104(37) L.S.G. 34; (2007) 151 S.J.L.B. 1228; *Times*,
October 17, 2007, CA (Civ Div); affirming [2006] EWHC 3359 (Comm); [2007]
R.T.R. 32; (2007) 104(4) L.S.G. 33; (2007) 157 N.L.J. 66; *Times*, January 16,
2007, QBD (Comm). . . . . *Digested*, 07/**2497**

Beggs v Scottish Ministers [2007] UKHL 3; [2007] 1 W.L.R. 455; 2007 S.L.T. 235;
2007 S.C.L.R. 287; (2007) 151 S.J.L.B. 258; 2007 G.W.D. 5-72; *Times*, February
8, 2007, HL . . . . *Digested*, 07/**717**

Beggs v Scottish Ministers (Contempt of Court) 2005 1 S.C. 342; 2005 S.L.T. 305;
2005 S.C.L.R. 640; 2005 G.W.D. 10-145, IH (1 Div) . . . . *Digested*, 05/**5026**:
Subsequent related litigation, 07/717

Begum v Barnes (Unreported, February 15, 2007), CC (Manchester) [*Ex rel*. Chris
Middleton, Barrister, Oriel Chambers, 14 Water Street, Liverpool] . . . . *Digested*, 07/**3138**

Begum v Gerrard [2006] B.P.I.R. 1351, Ch D . . . . *Digested*, 07/**3432**

Begum v Tower Hamlets LBC; *sub nom* Tower Hamlets LBC v Begum (Runa) [2003]
UKHL 5; [2003] 2 A.C. 430; [2003] 2 W.L.R. 388; [2003] 1 All E.R. 731;
[2003] H.R.L.R. 16; [2003] U.K.H.R.R. 419; 14 B.H.R.C. 400; [2003] H.L.R. 32;
[2003] B.L.G.R. 205; 2003 Hous. L.R. 20; [2003] A.C.D. 41; (2003) 100(13)
L.S.G. 28; (2003) 147 S.J.L.B. 232; [2003] N.P.C. 21; *Times*, February 17, 2003;
Independent, February 18, 2003, HL; affirming [2002] EWCA Civ 239; [2002]
1 W.L.R. 2491; [2002] 2 All E.R. 668; [2002] H.R.L.R. 24; [2002] U.K.H.R.R.
1014; [2002] H.L.R. 29; [2002] B.L.G.R. 417; [2002] A.C.D. 72; (2002) 99(16)
L.S.G. 37; (2002) 146 S.J.L.B. 67; [2002] N.P.C. 35; *Times*, April 4, 2002;
Independent, March 14, 2002; *Daily Telegraph*, March 6, 2002, CA (Civ Div) . . *Digested*, 03/**55**:
Applied, 03/3446, 03/4104, 03/4975, 06/1812, 07/3915:
Considered, 02/3740, 03/2073, 03/2632, 07/2772

Begum (Amirun) v Tower Hamlets LBC see R. (on the application of Begum (Amirun))
v Tower Hamlets LBC

Behrami v France (Admissibility) (71412/01); *joined case* Saramati v France (Admissibility) (78166/01) 22 B.H.R.C. 477; (2007) 45 E.H.R.R. SE10, ECHR

Belchev v Bulgaria (39270/98) (Unreported, April 8, 2004), ECHR

Belfast City Council v Miss Behavin' Ltd [2007] UKHL 19; [2007] 1 W.L.R. 1420; [2007] 3 All E.R. 1007; [2007] N.I. 89; [2007] H.R.L.R. 26; (2007) 104(19) L.S.G. 27; (2007) 151 S.J.L.B. 575; *Times*, May 1, 2007, HL ....   *Applied*, 07/2230

Belfield Furnishings Ltd, Re see Isaacs v Belfield Furnishings Ltd   *Digested*, 07/**2816**

Belgacom Mobile SA v Commune de Schaerbeek (C-545/03) see Mobistar SA v Commune de Fleron (C-544/03)

Belgium v Commission of the European Communities (C-75/97) [1999] E.C.R. I-3671; [2000] 1 C.M.L.R. 791, ECJ (6th Chamber) ....   *Digested*, 00/**731**:
           Applied, 07/1646: *Followed*, 03/588

Belgium v Recolta Recycling SPRL (C-440/04) see Kittel v Belgium (C-439/04)

Belgium v Ryanair Ltd [2006] IEHC 213; [2007] Eu. L.R. 28, HC (Irl)

Belgium v Temco Europe SA (C-284/03) [2005] S.T.C. 1451; [2004] E.C.R. I-11237; [2005] 1 C.M.L.R. 23; [2005] C.E.C. 20; [2007] B.T.C. 5339; [2007] B.V.C. 308; [2004] S.T.I. 2399; *Times*, November 25, 2004, ECJ (1st Chamber) .....   *Digested*, 05/**4351**:
           Applied, 06/4493

Belgium v Van Calster (C261/01) [2003] E.C.R. I-12249; [2004] 1 C.M.L.R. 18, ECJ ..   *Digested*, 04/**547**:
           Applied, 07/649

Bell v Lever Brothers Ltd; *sub nom* Lever Bros Ltd v Bell [1932] A.C. 161, HL; reversing [1931] 1 K.B. 557, CA. ....   *Applied*, 47-51/9247,
    47-51/9254, 53/3290, 57/596, 80/592, 83/430, 89/430, 91/408, 91/425,
    02/720, 06/767, 06/2926, 07/2715: *Considered*, 47-51/8914, 68/3999,
    69/1819, 99/2111, 07/339: *Distinguished*, 66/1854, 68/2240, 83/1254,
           03/518, 05/524

Bell v United Kingdom (41534/98) (2007) 45 E.H.R.R. 24, ECHR

BELL MASCHINENFABRIK/Withdrawal of appeal (G08/91); *sub nom* BELL MASCHINENFABRIK/Withdrawal of appeal (T695/89) [1993] E.P.O.R. 445, EPO (Enlarged Bd App) ....   *Considered*, 07/2572

BELL MASCHINENFABRIK/Withdrawal of appeal (T695/89) see BELL MASCHINENFABRIK/Withdrawal of appeal (G08/91)

Bell Scaffolding (Aust) Pty Ltd v Rekon Ltd [2006] EWHC 2656; [2007] C.I.L.L. 2405, QBD (TCC)

Bellinger v Bellinger [2003] UKHL 21; [2003] 2 A.C. 467; [2003] 2 W.L.R. 1174; [2003] 2 All E.R. 593; [2003] 1 F.L.R. 1043; [2003] 2 F.C.R. 1; [2003] H.R.L.R. 22; [2003] U.K.H.R.R. 679; 14 B.H.R.C. 127; (2003) 72 B.M.L.R. 147; [2003] A.C.D. 74; [2003] Fam. Law 485; (2003) 153 N.L.J. 594; (2003) 147 S.J.L.B. 472; *Times*, April 11, 2003; *Independent*, April 15, 2003, HL; affirming [2001] EWCA Civ 1140; [2002] Fam. 150; [2002] 2 W.L.R. 411; [2002] 1 All E.R. 311; [2001] 2 F.L.R. 1048; [2001] 3 F.C.R. 1; (2002) 64 B.M.L.R. 1; [2001] Fam. Law 807; (2001) 98(33) L.S.G. 30; (2001) 145 S.J.L.B. 207; *Times*, August 15, 2001, CA (Civ Div); affirming [2001] 1 F.L.R. 389; (2001) 58 B.M.L.R. 52; [2001] Fam. Law 107; *Times*, November 22, 2000; *Independent*, December 18, 2000, Fam Div. ....   *Digested*, 03/**2169**:
     Applied, 03/1310: *Considered*, 02/2532, 02/2533, 07/2261

Bellinger v TUI UK Ltd (Unreported, August 21, 2006), CC (Central London) [*Ex rel.* Benhamin Gold, Barrister, No. 1 Chancery Lane, London] ....   *Digested*, 07/**2125**

Belvedere's Trade Mark Application [2007] E.T.M.R. 18, PO (Irl). ....   *Digested*, 07/**2683**

Benatti v WPP Holdings Italy Srl see WPP Holdings Italy Srl v Benatti

Bendenoun v France (A/284) (1994) 18 E.H.R.R. 54, ECHR. ....   *Digested*, 94/**2397**:
     Applied, 98/3144, 99/3141, 06/2146: *Considered*, 97/2817, 07/2226

Benfield Greig Group Plc, Re see Nugent v Benfield Greig Group Plc

Benham v United Kingdom (19380/92) (1996) 22 E.H.R.R. 293; *Times*, June 24, 1996; *Independent*, June 19, 1996, ECHR (1994) 18 E.H.R.R. CD105, Eur Comm HR ....   *Digested*, 96/**3155**:
     Applied, 97/2765, 06/2157, 07/948: *Cited*, 96/16: *Followed*, 00/3221

Benmax v Austin Motor Co Ltd [1955] A.C. 370; [1955] 2 W.L.R. 418; [1955] 1 All E.R. 326; (1955) 72 R.P.C. 39; (1955) 99 S.J. 129, HL; affirming (1953) 70 R.P.C. 284, CA; reversing (1953) 70 R.P.C. 143, Ch D ....   *Digested*, 55/**2078**:
     Applied, 59/431, 73/2505, 77/1392, 85/1089, 94/2730, 00/660, 07/1720:
     Approved, 66/8132: *Considered*, 59/77, 60/2603, 61/2987, 74/2785,
           94/3439

Bennett, Re; *sub nom* Jones v Bennett [1896] 1 Ch. 778, CA ....   *Distinguished*, 07/4241

Bennett v Horseferry Road Magistrates Court see R. v Horseferry Road Magistrates Court Ex p. Bennett (No.1)

Bennett v Revenue and Customs Commissioners [2007] S.T.C. (S.C.D.) 158; [2007] S.T.I. 220, Sp Comm. ....   *Digested*, 07/**4055**

Bensaid v United Kingdom (44599/98) (2001) 33 E.H.R.R. 10; 11 B.H.R.C. 297; [2001] I.N.L.R. 325; [2001] M.H.L.R. 287, ECHR ....   *Digested*, 02/**2514**:
     Applied, 03/2225, 04/2032, 06/2245, 06/2246: *Considered*, 03/2246,
       04/2009, 06/2223, 07/2301: *Followed*, 04/2029

Bentinck v Bentinck [2007] EWCA Civ 175; [2007] I.L.Pr. 32; [2007] 2 F.L.R. 1;
   [2007] 2 F.C.R. 267; [2007] Fam. Law 495; (2007) 104(12) L.S.G. 36; *Times*,
   April 12, 2007, CA (Civ Div) . . . .   *Digested*, 07/**661**
Bentley v Secretary of State for Trade and Industry see Rutherford v Secretary of State
   for Trade and Industry
Bentley v United States [2005] EWHC 1078 (Admin); [2005] Extradition L.R. 65,
   QBD (Admin) . . . .   *Considered*, 07/5169
Berck Ltd v Revenue and Customs Commissioners [2007] S.T.I. 1697, V&DTr
   (Manchester)
Berecova v Slovakia (74499/01) [2007] 2 F.C.R. 207, ECHR . . . .   *Digested*, 07/**2245**
Beresford v Royal Insurance Co Ltd [1938] A.C. 586, HL; affirming [1937] 2 K.B. 197,
   CA . . . .   *Applied*, 47-51/10073,
           64/3228, 71/2470, 71/5180, 71/6012: *Considered*, 53/3273, 70/594, 07/2485:
                  Distinguished, 56/8303, 57/967: *Explained*, 87/2051
Berghoefer GmbH & Co KG v ASA SA (221/84) [1985] E.C.R. 2699; [1986] 1
   C.M.L.R. 13; *Times*, July 29, 1985, ECJ (5th Chamber) . . . .   *Digested*, 86/**1386**:
                      Applied, 96/1093: *Considered*, 07/349
Berkeley v North & South Trust Co see North & South Trust Co v Berkeley
Berkeley v Secretary of State for the Environment, Transport and the Regions (No.3)
   [2001] EWCA Civ 1012; [2001] 3 C.M.L.R. 11; [2002] Env. L.R. 14; [2002] 1 P.
   & C.R. 21; [2002] J.P.L. 224; (2001) 98(30) L.S.G. 38; [2001] N.P.C. 107;
   Times, October 19, 2001; *Daily Telegraph*, July 10, 2001, CA (Civ Div); affirming
   [2001] Env. L.R. 32; [2001] J.P.L. 660, QBD (Admin) . . . .   *Digested*, 01/**4700**:
                      Considered, 07/3268
Berkeley Community Villages Ltd v Pullen [2007] EWHC 1330 (Ch); [2007] 24 E.G.
   169 (C.S.); [2007] N.P.C. 71, Ch D
Berlei (UK) Ltd v Bali Brassiere Co Inc (No.1); *sub nom* BALI Trade Mark (No.1) [1969]
   1 W.L.R. 1306; [1969] 2 All E.R. 812; [1969] F.S.R. 288; [1969] R.P.C. 472;
   (1969) 113 S.J. 720, HL; reversing [1968] F.S.R. 1; [1968] R.P.C. 426, CA (Civ
   Div); reversing [1966] F.S.R. 8; [1966] R.P.C. 387, Ch D . . . .   *Digested*, 69/**3565**:
            Applied, 74/3830, 75/3432, 97/4893, 99/3537, 00/3770, 03/2629,
           04/2399, 07/2662: *Considered*, 72/3435, 93/3990, 96/5723, 98/3534,
           98/3539, 98/3540, 00/3795: *Followed*, 95/4946, 97/4899, 00/3774,
                  00/3786, 05/2577: *Referred to*, 00/3795
Bermingham v United States of America see R. (on the application of Bermingham) v
   Director of the Serious Fraud Office
Bernard v Attorney General of Jamaica [2004] UKPC 47; [2005] I.R.L.R. 398; (2004)
   148 S.J.L.B. 1281, PC (Jam) . . . .   *Digested*, 05/**4200**:
           Applied, 05/4199, 06/2916: *Distinguished*, 07/4201
Bernard v Trinidad and Tobago [2007] UKPC 34; [2007] 2 Cr. App. R. 22, PC (Trin) . . .   *Digested*, 07/**1027**
Bernhard Schulte GmbH & Co KG v Nile Holdings Ltd [2004] EWHC 977 (Comm);
   [2004] 2 Lloyd's Rep. 352, QBD (Comm). . . . .   *Digested*, 05/**309**:
                      Considered, 07/1077
Berry v British Transport Commission [1962] 1 Q.B. 306; [1961] 3 W.L.R. 450; [1961]
   3 All E.R. 65; (1961) 105 S.J. 587, CA; reversing in part [1961] 1 Q.B. 149;
   [1960] 3 W.L.R. 666; [1960] 3 All E.R. 322; (1960) 104 S.J. 826, QBD . . . . . .   *Digested*, 61/**5397**:
                 Applied, 01/478: *Considered*, 03/3041, 07/396
Besix SA v Wasserreinigungsbau Alfred Kretzschmar GmbH & Co KG (WABAG)
   (C256/00) [2003] 1 W.L.R. 1113; [2004] All E.R. (EC) 229; [2004] 1 All E.R.
   (Comm) 521; [2002] E.C.R. I-1699; [2003] I.L.Pr. 8, ECJ . . . .   *Digested*, 04/**578**:
                    Applied, 05/604, 07/657
Bessant v South Cone Inc see REEF Trade Mark
Best Beat Ltd v Rossall [2006] EWHC 1494 (Ch); [2006] B.P.I.R. 1357; [2006]
   C.I.L.L. 2343, Ch D . . . .   *Digested*, 07/**255**
Betterment Properties (Weymouth) Ltd v Dorset CC 2007/0876, CA (Civ Div);
   affirming [2007] EWHC 365 (Ch); [2007] 2 All E.R. 1000; [2007] N.P.C. 26,
   Ch D . . . .   *Digested*, 07/**3422**
Beximco Pharmaceuticals Ltd v Shamil Bank of Bahrain EC see Shamil Bank of Bahrain
   EC v Beximco Pharmaceuticals Ltd (No.1)
Bexley LBC v Downes [2007] P.A.D. 58, Planning Inspector
Bexley LBC v Eastwood [2007] P.A.D. 47, Planning Inspector
Bexley LBC v Maison Maurice Ltd [2006] EWHC 3192 (Ch); [2007] B.L.G.R. 645;
   [2007] 10 E.G. 184; [2007] R.V.R. 30; [2007] 2 E.G. 124 (C.S.); [2006] N.P.C.
   134, Ch D . . . .   *Digested*, 07/**3466**
BFS Group Ltd v Secretary of State for Defence; *sub nom* BSF Group Ltd v Secretary
   of State for Defence [2006] EWHC 1513 (Ch); [2006] Eu. L.R. 1101; (2006) 150
   S.J.L.B. 892, Ch D . . . .   *Digested*, 07/**3329**
Bhamjee v Forsdick [2003] EWCA Civ 1113; [2004] 1 W.L.R. 88; [2003] C.P. Rep.
   67; [2003] B.P.I.R. 1252; (2003) 100(36) L.S.G. 41; *Times*, July 31, 2003;
   Independent, July 29, 2003, CA (Civ Div). . . . .   *Digested*, 03/**482**:
                 Applied, 04/282: *Considered*, 04/281, 07/368
Bhatia v CIT (International Taxation) Mumbai see Meman v CIT (International Taxation)
   Mumbai
Bhikha v Leicester City Council see R. v Wandsworth LBC Ex p. O

Bic *v* Turkey (55955/00) (2007) 44 E.H.R.R. 38, ECHR . . . .   *Digested*, 07/**2233**
Biggin & Co Ltd *v* Permanite Ltd [1951] 2 K.B. 314; [1951] 2 All E.R. 191; [1951] 2
    T.L.R. 159; (1951) 95 S.J. 414, CA; reversing in part [1951] 1 K.B. 422; [1950] 2
    All E.R. 859; (1950) 66 T.L.R. (Pt. 2) 944, KBD . . . .   *Digested*, 47-51/**2491**:
                    Applied, 53/3273, 84/3104, 99/1379, 99/1400, 00/826: *Considered*, 75/179,
                    76/58u, 82/230, 99/244, 99/789, 03/670, 04/677, 07/745:
                    Followed, 85/3479
Bignell (t/a Just Employment) *v* Just Employment Law Ltd [2007] EWHC 2203 (Ch);
    (2007) 30(10) I.P.D. 30064, Ch D (Patents Ct)
Bigum *v* Denmark (Admissibility) (2404/05) (2007) 44 E.H.R.R. SE11, ECHR
Bikeworld Ltd *v* Commissioner of Income Tax see Bikeworld Ltd *v* Director General of
    Mauritius Revenue Authority
Bikeworld Ltd *v* Director General of Mauritius Revenue Authority; *sub nom* Bikeworld
    Ltd *v* Commissioner of Income Tax [2007] UKPC 5; [2007] S.T.I. 260, PC
    (Mau)
Bim Kemi AB *v* Blackburn Chemicals Ltd (No.1) [2001] EWCA Civ 457; [2001] 2
    Lloyd's Rep. 93; [2001] C.L.C. 1166, CA (Civ Div) . . . .   *Digested*, 01/**941**:
                    Applied, 07/238
Binomugisha *v* Southwark LBC [2006] EWHC 2254 (Admin); [2007] 1 F.L.R. 916;
    [2007] 3 F.C.R. 457; [2007] A.C.D. 35; [2007] Fam. Law 117; (2006) 150
    S.J.L.B. 1291, QBD (Admin) . . . .   *Digested*, 07/**2313**
Biogen Inc *v* Medeva Plc [1997] R.P.C. 1; (1997) 38 B.M.L.R. 149; (1997) 20(1) I.P.D.
    20001; *Times*, November 1, 1996, HL; affirming [1995] F.S.R. 4; [1995] R.P.C.
    25; *Independent*, November 28, 1994, CA (Civ Div); reversing [1993] R.P.C.
    475; *Times*, December 1, 1992, Ch D (Patents Ct) . . . .   *Digested*, 96/**4549**:
                    Applied, 96/4554, 99/3518, 02/2820, 06/2503, 07/2614:
                    Considered, 00/3599, 02/2816: *Distinguished*, 97/3890: *Followed*, 02/2847,
                    04/2283
Bioid AG (In Liquidation) *v* Office for Harmonisation in the Internal Market (Trade Marks
    and Designs) (OHIM) (C-37/03) [2005] E.C.R. I-7975, ECJ . . . .   *Applied*, 07/1547
Birch *v* University of Liverpool see University of Liverpool *v* Humber and Birch
Bircham & Co Nominees (No.2) Ltd *v* Clarke see Earl Cadogan *v* Sportelli
Bird *v* Philpott [1900] 1 Ch. 822, Ch D . . . .   *Applied*, 47-51/719:
                    Followed, 07/2406
Bird *v* Sylvester [2007] EWCA Civ 1052; (2007) 151 S.J.L.B. 1297, CA (Civ Div)
Birkdale School Sheffield *v* Revenue and Customs Commissioners CH/2007/APP/0297,
    Ch D; reversing [2007] B.V.C. 2426, V&DTr (Manchester)
Birkett *v* James [1978] A.C. 297; [1977] 3 W.L.R. 38; [1977] 2 All E.R. 801; (1977)
    121 S.J. 444, HL. . . . .   *Digested*, 77/**2410**:
                    Applied, 78/310.u, 78/2237, 78/2426, 81/113, 81/1966, 83/2209, 83/3068,
                    84/2739, 92/3495, 93/1764, 93/3336, 94/2902, 95/2963, 96/366, 96/900,
                    97/785, 00/616: *Considered*, 77/2407, 77/2408, 77/2411, 79/1663, 79/1665,
                    79/2191, 81/2201, 82/1849, 82/2461, 82/2553, 83/3073, 85/2683,
                    85/2728, 87/133, 87/2985, 88/2934, 89/2963, 89/3070, 89/3071, 91/2971,
                    92/190, 92/2813, 92/3610, 92/3611, 93/3338, 94/3644, 94/3788, 94/3904,
                    97/489, 97/644, 97/759, 97/761, 97/1314, 97/3024, 98/611, 98/612, 98/613,
                    98/619, 00/348, 00/4656, 06/5096, 07/3957: *Disapproved*, 89/3075,
                    00/626: *Distinguished*, 78/1848, 78/2425, 80/2194, 81/868, 88/2838,
                    90/3644, 94/3635, 95/3888, 96/909, 98/614: *Followed*, 78/311.u, 78/2423,
                    96/898, 97/1007, 99/3356: *Not followed*, 99/367: *Referred to*, 97/754,
                    97/1037, 00/605, 00/617
Birmingham City Council *v* Aweys see R. (on the application of Aweys) *v* Birmingham
    City Council
Birmingham City Council *v* Crook [2007] EWHC 1415 (QB); [2007] 5 Costs L.R. 732;
    (2007) 157 N.L.J. 939, QBD (Birmingham)
Birmingham City Council *v* H [2006] EWHC 3062 (Fam); (2007) 95 B.M.L.R. 159,
    Fam Div. . . . .   *Digested*, 07/**1724**
Birmingham City Council *v* R see R (A Child) (Special Guardianship Order), Re
Birmingham City Council *v* Walker see Walker *v* Birmingham City Council
Birmingham City Council *v* Wetherill see Wetherill *v* Birmingham City Council
Birmingham City Football Club Plc *v* Revenue and Customs Commissioners [2007]
    B.V.C. 2439; [2007] V. & D.R. 149; [2007] S.T.I. 2245, V&DTr (Manchester)
Bishop *v* Baker Refractories Ltd see Barber *v* Somerset CC
Bishop *v* TNT UK Ltd (Unreported, November 27, 2006), CC (Romford) [*Ex rel.*
    Andrew Spencer, Barrister, 1 Chancery Lane, London] . . . .   *Digested*, 07/**768**
Bishop's Stortford and Stansted Park & Ride *v* East Hertfordshire DC [2007] P.A.D. 19,
    Planning Inspector
Bizspace (NE) Ltd *v* Baird Corporatewear Ltd [2007] 17 E.G. 174, Ch D . . . .   *Digested*, 07/**2719**
Bjorklund *v* Finland (41909/02) (Admissibility) (2007) 45 E.H.R.R. SE6, ECHR
BK (Spouses: Marriage: Meaning of Subsisting: Turkey), Re see BK (Turkey) *v* Secretary of
    State for the Home Department
BK (Turkey) *v* Secretary of State for the Home Department; *sub nom* BK (Spouses:
    Marriage: Meaning of Subsisting: Turkey), Re [2005] UKIAT 174, IAT . . . .   *Not followed*, 07/2333
Blaby DC *v* Harlequins Private Day Nursery [2007] P.A.D. 31, Planning Inspector

Black v Sumitomo Corp [2001] EWCA Civ 1819; [2002] 1 W.L.R. 1562; [2003] 3 All
 E.R. 643; [2002] 1 Lloyd's Rep. 693; [2002] C.P.L.R. 148; *Times*, January 25,
 2002; *Independent*, December 13, 2001, CA (Civ Div); reversing TNS, QBD
 (Comm) . . . .   *Digested,* 02/**422**:
            Applied, 02/426, 05/456, 06/430, 06/431, 07/500, 07/503:
                                                  Considered, 07/502
Black v United Kingdom (56745/00) (2007) 45 E.H.R.R. 25, ECHR
Black Horse Ltd v Langford [2007] EWHC 907 (QB); [2007] R.T.R. 38, QBD (Leeds)   *Digested,* 07/**762**
Black Sea & Baltic General Insurance Co Ltd v Baker see Baker v Black Sea & Baltic
 General Insurance Co Ltd
Blackburn v Revenue and Customs Commissioners CH/2007/APP/0298, Ch D;
 reversing [2007] S.T.C. (S.C.D.) 519, Sp Comm
Blackburn Rovers Football & Athletic Club Plc vAvon Insurance Plc [2006] EWHC 840
 (QB); [2007] Lloyd's Rep. I.R. 1; (2006) 150 S.J.L.B. 574, QBD . . . .   *Digested,* 07/**2471**
Blackburn-Smith v Lambeth LBC [2007] EWHC 767 (Admin); (2007) 10 C.C.L. Rep.
 352, QBD (Admin) . . . .   *Digested,* 07/**3941**
Blacklock v Revenue and Customs Commissioners [2007] V. & D.R. 225; [2007]
 S.T.I. 2247,V&DTr (Manchester)
Blackspur Group Plc, Re; *sub nom* Eastaway v Secretary of State forTrade and Industry
 [2007] EWCA Civ 425; [2007] B.C.C. 550; [2007] U.K.H.R.R. 739, CA (Civ
 Div); affirming [2006] EWHC 299 (Ch); [2006] 2 B.C.L.C. 489; [2006]
 U.K.H.R.R. 620, Ch D (Companies Ct) . . . .   *Digested,* 07/**564**
Blackwell v Mills 26 T.C. 468. . . . .   *Applied,* 69/1738:
                                                  Considered, 07/4057
Blake v United Kingdom (68890/01) (2007) 44 E.H.R.R. 29; *Times*, October 11, 2006,
 ECHR . . . .   *Digested,* 07/**2224**
Blake & Lyons v Lewis Berger & Sons [1951] 2 T.L.R. 605; [1951] W.N. 425; (1951)
 95 S.J. 514 . . . .   *Digested,* 47-51/**3231**:
                                                  Considered, 07/2757
Blakey v Excel Airways Ltd (Unreported, April 27, 2007), CC (Altrincham) [*Ex rel.*
 ChristopherTaft, Barrister, St James's Chambers, 68 Quay Street, Manchester] .   *Digested,* 07/**3132**
Blanchard v Lancashire CC (Unreported, September 11, 2006), CC (Burnley) [*Ex rel.*
 Karim Sabry, Barrister, 8 King Street Chambers, 8 King Street, Manchester] . . .   *Digested,* 07/**3170**
Blanco v Scottish Ministers see Somerville v Scottish Ministers
Bland v Chief Supplementary Benefit Officer [1983] 1 W.L.R. 262; [1983] 1 All E.R.
 537; (1983) 127 S.J. 53, CA (Civ Div) . . . .   *Digested,* 83/**3482**:
            Applied, 86/3142, 95/2735, 07/3897: *Considered,* 95/4566, 95/4794:
                                                  Disapproved, 90/3733
Blaxhall Securities Ltd v Sheard Walshaw Partnership see Baxall Securities Ltd v
 SheardWalshaw Partnership
Blights Builders Ltd, Re [2006] EWHC 3549 (Ch); [2007] Bus. L.R. 629; [2007] 3 All E.R.
 776; [2007] B.C.C. 712, Ch D (Birmingham) . . . .   *Digested,* 07/**2464**
Bloomberg LLP's Patent Application (No.GB2395941A) see Cappellini's Patent
 Application (No.GB2381884A)
Bloxham v Freshfields Bruckhaus Deringer [2007] Pens. L.R. 375, ET . . . .   *Digested,* 07/**1310**
Bluck v Information Commissioner (2007) 98 B.M.L.R. 1, InformationTr
Blue Station Ltd v Kamyab [2007] EWCA Civ 1073; (2007) 151 S.J.L.B. 1296, CA (Civ
 Div); affirming [2007] EWHC 262 (Ch), Ch D
Blum v DPP; *joined cases* Shaer v DPP; Evans v DPP; Rai v CPS [2006] EWHC 3209
 (Admin); [2007] U.K.H.R.R. 233; [2007] A.C.D. 40; (2007) 104(3) L.S.G. 29,
 QBD (Admin) . . . .   *Digested,* 07/**879**
Blundell v St Andrew's Catholic Primary School Governors [2007] I.C.R. 1451; [2007]
 I.R.L.R. 652, EAT
Blyth v Birmingham Waterworks Co 156 E.R. 1047; (1856) 11 Ex. 781, Ex Ct . . . .   *Applied,* 47-51/6897,
                                                  52/368, 55/2702, 07/4051
BO v Secretary of State for the Home Department; *sub nom* BO (Extension of Time
 for Appealing: Nigeria), Re [2006] UKAIT 35; [2006] Imm. A.R. 441; [2006]
 I.N.L.R. 436, AIT . . . .   *Digested,* 07/**2284**
BO (Extension of Time for Appealing: Nigeria), Re see BO v Secretary of State for the
 Home Department
Boake Allen Ltd v Revenue and Customs Commissioners; *sub nom* NEC Semi
 Conductors Ltd v Revenue and Customs Commissioners [2007] UKHL 25;
 [2007] 1 W.L.R. 1386; [2007] 3 All E.R. 605; [2007] S.T.C. 1265; [2007] 3
 C.M.L.R. 6; [2007] Eu. L.R. 701; [2007] B.T.C. 414; 9 I.T.L. Rep. 995; [2007]
 S.T.I. 1585; (2007) 104(23) L.S.G. 30; (2007) 151 S.J.L.B. 707; *Times*, May 24,
 2007, HL; affirming [2006] EWCA Civ 25; [2006] S.T.C. 606; [2006] Eu. L.R.
 755; [2006] B.T.C. 266; 8 I.T.L. Rep. 819; [2006] S.T.I. 321; (2006) 156 N.L.J.
 240; *Times*, February 10, 2006; *Independent*, February 8, 2006, CA (Civ Div);
 reversing in part [2003] EWHC 2813 (Ch); [2004] S.T.C. 489; [2004] Eu. L.R.
 351; [2004] B.T.C. 208; 6 I.T.L. Rep. 416; [2003] S.T.I. 2221; (2004) 101(4)
 L.S.G. 32; *Times*, December 5, 2003, Ch D . . . .   *Digested,* 07/**3972**:
                                                  Considered, 06/4163, 06/4163

Board of Trade v Owen; *sub nom* R. v Owen (Henry Geoffrey); *joined case* R. v Seth-Smith (Patrick Sidney) [1957] A.C. 602; [1957] 2 W.L.R. 351; [1957] 1 All E.R. 411; (1957) 41 Cr. App. R. 11; (1957) 121 J.P. 177; (1957) 101 S.J. 186, HL; affirming [1957] 1 Q.B. 174; [1956] 3 W.L.R. 739; [1956] 3 All E.R. 432; (1956) 120 J.P. 553; (1956) 100 S.J. 769, CCA [1956] 3 W.L.R. 252; (1956) 40 Cr. App. R. 103; (1956) 100 S.J. 454, Central Crim Ct . . . .   *Digested*, 57/**697**:
Applied, 69/1453, 75/591, 81/1204, 83/574, 85/527: *Considered*, 72/590, 00/952, 07/923: *Distinguished*, 68/652

Boardman v Phipps; *sub nom* Phipps v Boardman [1967] 2 A.C. 46; [1966] 3 W.L.R. 1009; [1966] 3 All E.R. 721; (1966) 110 S.J. 853, HL; affirming [1965] Ch. 992; [1965] 2 W.L.R. 839; [1965] 1 All E.R. 849; (1965) 109 S.J. 197, CA; affirming [1964] 1 W.L.R. 993; [1964] 2 All E.R. 187; (1964) 108 S.J. 619, Ch D . . . . . .   *Digested*, 66/**11052**:
Applied, 72/361, 72/487, 78/3060, 81/2624, 94/2083, 01/5525, 03/520, 04/456, 05/2812, 05/4307, 07/1536: *Considered*, 77/2708, 84/388, 87/3552, 87/3553, 89/459, 90/487, 01/951: *Distinguished*, 88/311, 04/3940

Bock v Germany (A/150) (1990) 12 E.H.R.R. 247, ECHR . . . .   *Applied*, 98/3135, 07/2219

Boehringer Ingelheim KG v Swingward Ltd (C-348/04) [2007] Bus. L.R. 1100; [2007] 2 C.M.L.R. 52; [2007] C.E.C. 652; [2007] E.T.M.R. 71; (2007) 98 B.M.L.R. 16, ECJ (2nd Chamber)

Boehringer Ingelheim Ltd v Vetplus Ltd [2007] EWCA Civ 583; [2007] Bus. L.R. 1456; [2007] E.T.M.R. 67; [2007] H.R.L.R. 33; [2007] F.S.R. 29; (2007) 97 B.M.L.R. 1; (2007) 30(8) I.P.D. 30052; (2007) 30(9) I.P.D. 30055; *Times*, June 27, 2007, CA (Civ Div); affirming [2007] EWHC 972 (Ch); [2007] F.S.R. 28; (2007) 30(6) I.P.D. 30043, Ch D . . . .   *Digested*, 07/**2672**

Boehringer Mannheim GmbH v Commission of the European Communities (7/72) [1972] E.C.R. 1281; [1973] C.M.L.R. 864, ECJ . . . .   *Digested*, 74/**1513**:
Considered, 07/607

Bohning v United States [2005] EWHC 2613 (Admin); [2007] 1 W.L.R. 362; [2006] 3 All E.R. 394; [2005] Extradition L.R. 121, QBD (Admin) . . . .   *Digested*, 06/**1610**

Bolam v Friern Hospital Management Committee [1957] 1 W.L.R. 582; [1957] 2 All E.R. 118; [1955-95] P.N.L.R. 7; (1957) 101 S.J. 357, QBD . . . .   *Digested*, 57/**2431**:
Applied, 67/2729, 83/2548, 84/2322, 84/2326, 85/2318, 87/2601, 87/2605, 91/2654, 93/2999, 94/3399, 95/3679, 97/3789, 97/3797, 99/3997, 00/2779, 00/4250, 01/4513, 02/1120, 04/996, 04/2742, 05/2839, 05/2854, 06/2869, 06/2872, 07/2926: *Approved*, 75/245: *Cited*, 00/4248, 00/4283, 03/1161: *Considered*, 88/2453, 89/3044, 93/2712, 94/1535, 94/3359, 95/3714, 96/3580, 02/1637, 03/2958, 04/2705, 07/2953: *Distinguished*, 74/265, 92/3242, 93/233, 96/4469: *Followed*, 97/2142, 98/3986, 99/789, 99/4056: *Not applied*, 99/3992, 99/3995

Bolitho (Deceased) v City and Hackney HA [1998] A.C. 232; [1997] 3 W.L.R. 1151; [1997] 4 All E.R. 771; [1998] P.I.Q.R. P10; [1998] Lloyd's Rep. Med. 26; (1998) 39 B.M.L.R. 1; [1998] P.N.L.R. 1; (1997) 94(47) L.S.G. 30; (1997) 141 S.J.L.B. 238; *Times*, November 27, 1997, HL; affirming [1993] P.I.Q.R. P334; [1993] 4 Med. L.R. 381, CA (Civ Div) . . . .   *Digested*, 97/**3789**:
Applied, 98/3977, 99/3994, 01/4263, 01/4542, 02/3294, 03/5826, 04/2698, 06/2869, 07/2917, 07/2926: *Considered*, 96/4459, 98/3986, 03/2989, 07/2923, 07/3068: *Distinguished*, 98/3969, 05/2863: *Followed*, 98/3963, 99/3989

Bollore SA v Commission of the European Communities (T-109/02) [2007] 5 C.M.L.R. 2, CFI

Bols Distilleries BV (t/a Bols Royal Distilleries) v Superior Yacht Services Ltd [2006] UKPC 45; [2007] 1 W.L.R. 12; [2007] 1 All E.R. (Comm) 461; [2007] 1 Lloyd's Rep. 683; [2007] 1 C.L.C. 308; [2007] I.L.Pr. 46, PC (Gib) . . . .   *Digested*, 07/**349**

Bolton v Law Society [1994] 1 W.L.R. 512; [1994] 2 All E.R. 486; [1994] C.O.D. 295; *Times*, December 8, 1993, CA (Civ Div). . . . .   *Digested*, 94/**4220**:
Applied, 98/3724, 03/1724, 05/1807, 05/3349: *Approved*, 03/1733: *Considered*, 07/2800: *Followed*, 97/3375, 05/1805

Bolton v Stone; *sub nom* Stone v Bolton [1951] A.C. 850; [1951] 1 All E.R. 1078; [1951] 1 T.L.R. 977; 50 L.G.R. 32; (1951) 95 S.J. 333, HL; reversing [1950] 1 K.B. 201; [1949] 2 All E.R. 851; 65 T.L.R. 683; 48 L.G.R. 107; (1949) 93 S.J. 710, CA; reversing [1949] 1 All E.R. 237, KBD . . . .   *Digested*, 47-51/**6897**:
Applied, 47-51/6863, 47-51/9605, 47-51/9855, 53/2524, 57/2376, 57/2416, 61/5875, 62/2033, 69/2400, 74/3364, 98/3994, 07/4196: *Considered*, 62/2083, 70/1067, 75/2291, 75/2324, 77/2146, 77/2597, 81/275.bu, 87/4737, 95/3659: *Distinguished*, 66/3445

Bolton MBC v Municipal Mutual Insurance Ltd [2006] EWCA Civ 50; [2006] 1 W.L.R. 1492; [2006] 1 C.L.C. 242; [2007] Lloyd's Rep. I.R. 173; (2006) 103(9) L.S.G. 31; (2006) 150 S.J.L.B. 226; *Times*, February 9, 2006; *Independent*, February 9, 2006, CA (Civ Div); affirming in part [2006] Lloyd's Rep. I.R. 15, QBD . . . . .   *Digested*, 06/**2431**

Bolton Pharmaceutical Co 100 Ltd v Doncaster Pharmaceuticals Group Ltd; *sub nom* Doncaster Pharmaceuticals Group Ltd v Bolton Pharmaceutical Co 100 Ltd; *joined case* Bolton Pharmaceutical Co 100 Ltd v Swinghope Ltd [2006] EWCA Civ 661; [2006] E.T.M.R. 65; [2007] F.S.R. 3, CA (Civ Div); reversing [2005] EWHC 1600 (Ch); (2005) 28(9) I.P.D. 28066, Ch D . . . . *Digested,* 06/**2606**

Bolton Pharmaceutical Co 100 Ltd v Swinghope Ltd see Bolton Pharmaceutical Co 100 Ltd v Doncaster Pharmaceuticals Group Ltd

Bolton School v Evans [2006] EWCA Civ 1653; [2007] I.C.R. 641; [2007] I.R.L.R. 140; (2006) 103(46) L.S.G. 30; (2006) 150 S.J.L.B. 1532, CA (Civ Div); affirming [2006] I.R.L.R. 500; [2006] E.L.R. 255, EAT . . . . *Digested,* 07/**1438**

Bombay Province v Bombay Municipal Corp [1947] A.C. 58; 62 T.L.R. 643; [1947] L.J.R. 380, PC (Ind) . . . . *Digested,* 47-51/**1656**:
Applied, 07/875: *Considered,* 86/1934: *Distinguished,* 88/3845:
Followed, 49/4357

Bond House Systems Ltd v Customs and Excise Commissioners [2004] V. & D.R. 125, Ch D [2003] B.V.C. 2319; [2003] V. & D.R. 210; [2003] S.T.I. 1431, V&DTr (Manchester). . . . . *Digested,* 05/**4368**:
Referred to, 07/4302

Bond House Systems Ltd v Customs and Excise Commissioners (C-484/03) see Optigen Ltd v Customs and Excise Commissioners (C-354/03)

Bondi v Bank of America NA (C-341/04) see Eurofood IFSC Ltd, Re (C-341/04)

Bone v Fabcon Projects Ltd [2007] 1 All E.R. 1071; [2006] I.C.R. 1421; [2006] I.R.L.R. 908, EAT. . . . . *Digested,* 07/**1358**

Bonham v Blake Lapthorn Linell [2006] EWHC 2513 (Ch); [2007] W.T.L.R. 189, Ch D
. . . . *Digested,* 07/**4259**

Bonham v Fishwick A3/2007/1936, CA (Civ Div); affirming [2007] EWHC 1859 (Ch); (2007-08) 10 I.T.E.L.R. 329, Ch D . . . . *Digested,* 07/**4257**

Bonifacti v Italy (C-9/90) see Francovich v Italy (C-6/90)

Bonnard v Perryman [1891] 2 Ch. 269; [1891-94] All E.R. Rep. 965, CA . . . . *Applied,* 59/3338,
75/1950, 79/1656, 86/1990, 05/970: *Considered,* 69/2078, 86/2598,
91/2885, 98/1773, 07/2182, 07/2672: *Distinguished,* 87/2298:
Followed, 68/3133

Boodhoo, Re [2007] EWCA Crim 14; [2007] 4 All E.R. 762; [2007] 3 Costs L.R. 433; [2007] 1 Cr. App. R. 32; [2007] P.N.L.R. 20; [2007] Crim. L.R. 714; *Times,* February 5, 2007, CA (Crim Div) . . . . *Digested,* 07/**963**

Bookit Ltd v Customs and Excise Commissioners see Bookit Ltd v Revenue and Customs Commissioners

Bookit Ltd v Revenue and Customs Commissioners; *sub nom* Bookit Ltd v Customs and Excise Commissioners [2006] EWCA Civ 550; [2006] S.T.C. 1367; [2006] B.T.C. 5535; [2006] B.V.C. 605; [2006] S.T.I. 1513, CA (Civ Div); affirming [2005] EWHC 1689 (Ch); [2005] S.T.C. 1481; [2005] B.T.C. 5581; [2005] B.V.C. 612; [2004] S.T.I. 1337, Ch D; reversing [2004] B.V.C. 2229; [2004] V. & D.R. 421; [2004] S.T.I. 1949, V&DTr (London) . . . . *Digested,* 06/**4435**:
Applied, 07/5568

Booth v Bradford MDC see Bradford MDC v Booth

Boparan v Revenue and Customs Commissioners [2007] S.T.C. (S.C.D.) 297; [2007] S.T.I. 552, Sp Comm. . . . . *Digested,* 07/**4138**

Borchert v Revenue and Customs Commissioners [2006] S.T.C. (S.C.D.) 500; [2006] S.T.I. 1797, Sp Comm . . . . *Digested,* 07/**4097**

Borg v DPP see Revitt v DPP

Borrowdale v Secretary of State for Work and Pensions see Secretary of State for Work and Pensions v Morina

Bosanquet v Allen see Carver v Duncan (Inspector of Taxes)

Boston Scientific Ltd v Palmaz see Palmaz v Boston Scientific BV

Boswell (Steels), Re; *sub nom* Company (No.001567 of 1988), Re (1989) 5 B.C.C. 145, Ch D (Companies Ct) . . . . *Digested,* 89/**353**:
Considered, 07/459

Bot v Prefecture du Val-de-Marne (C-241/05) [2006] E.C.R. I-9627; [2007] 1 C.M.L.R. 18, ECJ . . . . *Digested,* 07/**1613**

Botham v Ministry of Defence see Lawson v Serco Ltd

Bothma (t/a DAB Builders) v Mayhaven Healthcare Ltd [2007] EWCA Civ 527; 114 Con. L.R. 131, CA (Civ Div)

Bott v Macaulay [2007] W.T.L.R. 235, Sup Ct (Can)

Bottomley v Todmorden Cricket Club [2003] EWCA Civ 1575; [2004] P.I.Q.R. P18; (2003) 100(48) L.S.G. 18; (2003) 147 S.J.L.B. 1309; *Times,* November 13, 2003, CA (Civ Div) . . . . *Digested,* 03/**2990**:
Considered, 07/2935: *Distinguished,* 04/2707

Bottrill v Secretary of State for Trade and Industry see Secretary of State for Trade and Industry v Bottrill

Bouanich v Skatteverket (C-265/04) [2006] E.C.R. I-923; [2006] 3 C.M.L.R. 14; 8 I.T.L. Rep. 433; [2006] S.T.I. 203, ECJ (3rd Chamber) . . . . *Digested,* 06/**4252**:
Considered, 07/3974

Bouchelkia v France (23078/93) (1998) 25 E.H.R.R. 686, ECHR . . . . *Digested,* 98/**3152**:
Distinguished, 07/2262

Boudhiba v Central Examining Court No.5 of the National Court of Justice, Madrid see
Boudhiba v Spain
Boudhiba v Spain; *sub nom* Boudhiba v Central Examining Court No.5 of the National
Court of Justice, Madrid [2006] EWHC 167 (Admin); [2007] 1 W.L.R. 124;
[2006] 3 All E.R. 574; [2006] Extradition L.R. 20; [2006] A.C.D. 54, QBD
(Admin) . . . . *Digested*, 06/**1595**
Boujlifa v France (2000) 30 E.H.R.R. 419; [1998] H.R.C.D. 21, ECHR . . . . *Digested*, 01/**3554**:
Distinguished, 07/2262
Boultif v Switzerland (54273/00) [2001] 2 F.L.R. 1228; (2001) 33 E.H.R.R. 50;
[2001] Fam. Law 875, ECHR . . . . *Digested*, 02/**2516**:
Applied, 06/2178, 06/2180, 07/2252: *Considered*, 04/2063, 05/2120,
07/2262: *Distinguished*, 06/5522
Bourhill v Young; *sub nom* Bourhill v Young's Executor [1943] A.C. 92; [1942] 2 All
E.R. 396; 1942 S.C. (H.L.) 78; 1943 S.L.T. 105, HL; affirming 1941 S.C. 395; 1941
S.L.T. 364, IH (2 Div) . . . . *Applied*, 47-51/6897,
52/917, 53/2525, 55/2194, 61/2343, 80/3416, 07/5426: *Approved*, 82/2153:
Considered, 62/2033, 64/2520, 67/2674, 70/1849, 72/2397, 76/1858,
81/1849, 87/2608, 87/4737, 92/3250, 94/3380, 95/3682:
Distinguished, 47-51/6812, 59/886, 60/873, 68/2663, 84/2330:
Followed, 53/964
Bourhill v Young's Executor see Bourhill v Young
Bournemouth & Boscombe Athletic Community Football Club Ltd, Re see AF Noonan
(Architectural Practice) Ltd v Bournemouth & Boscombe Athletic Community
Football Club Ltd
Bournemouth Symphony Orchestra v Customs and Excise Commissioners see
Bournemouth Symphony Orchestra v Revenue and Customs Commissioners
Bournemouth Symphony Orchestra v Revenue and Customs Commissioners; *sub nom*
Longborough Festival Opera v Revenue and Customs Commissioners (Leave to
Appeal); Bournemouth Symphony Orchestra v Customs and Excise
Commissioners; *joined case* Revenue and Customs Commissioners v
Longborough Festival Opera (Leave to Appeal) [2006] EWCA Civ 1281; [2007]
S.T.C. 198; [2006] B.T.C. 5769; [2006] B.V.C. 839; [2006] S.T.I. 2299; (2006)
150 S.J.L.B. 1431; *Times*, November 9, 2006, CA (Civ Div); affirming [2005]
EWHC 1566 (Ch); [2005] S.T.C. 1406; [2005] B.T.C. 5516; [2005] B.V.C. 547;
[2005] S.T.I. 1311; *Times*, September 6, 2005, Ch D; affirming [2005] S.T.I. 117,
V&DTr . . . . *Digested*, 07/**4291**:
Subsequent related litigation, 06/4441
Bouverie No.1 Ltd v De Vere Hotels & Leisure Ltd [2006] EWHC 2242 (Ch); (2006)
103(37) L.S.G. 31; [2006] N.P.C. 101, Ch D . . . . *Digested*, 07/**2119**
Bovale Ltd v Monmouthshire CC [2007] P.A.D. 43, Planning Inspector
Bovemij Verzekeringen NV v Benelux-Merkenbureau (C-108/05) [2006] E.C.R. I-7605;
[2007] E.T.M.R. 29, ECJ (1st Chamber) . . . . *Digested*, 07/**2665**
Bovril Ltd v Bodega Co Ltd. . . . . *Considered*, 07/2546
Bowe v Queen, The; *sub nom* R. v Bowe (Forrester); R. v Davies (Trono); *joined case*
Davies v Queen, The [2006] UKPC 10; [2006] 1 W.L.R. 1623; 21 B.H.R.C. 43,
PC (Bah) . . . . *Digested*, 06/**3686**:
Applied, 07/3625
Bowman v Fels [2005] EWCA Civ 226; [2005] 1 W.L.R. 3083; [2005] 4 All E.R.
609; [2005] 2 Cr. App. R. 19; [2005] 2 C.M.L.R. 23; [2005] 2 F.L.R. 247;
[2005] W.T.L.R. 481; [2005] Fam. Law 546; (2005) 102(18) L.S.G. 24; (2005)
155 N.L.J. 413; (2005) 149 S.J.L.B. 357; [2005] N.P.C. 36; *Times*, March 14,
2005, CA (Civ Div) . . . . *Digested*, 05/**811**:
Considered, 07/999
Boyden v Canty see Canty v Canty
Boylan v Boylan [1988] 1 F.L.R. 282; [1988] F.C.R. 689; [1988] Fam. Law 62;
(1988) 152 J.P.N. 770 . . . . *Digested*, 88/**1646**:
Considered, 07/1706: *Followed*, 96/2872
Boyland & Son Ltd v Rand [2006] EWCA Civ 1860; [2007] H.L.R. 24; *Times*, January
18, 2007, CA (Civ Div) . . . . *Digested*, 07/**543**
BPS Advertising Ltd v Barnet LBC [2006] EWHC 3335 (Admin); (2007) 171 J.P. 223;
(2007) 171 J.P.N. 441, QBD (Admin) . . . . *Digested*, 07/**961**
BR (Iran) v Secretary of State for the Home Department; *joined case* MD (Iran) v
Secretary of State for the Home Department [2007] EWCA Civ 198; [2007] 1
W.L.R. 2278; [2007] 3 All E.R. 318; [2007] I.N.L.R. 297; (2007) 157 N.L.J.
438, CA (Civ Div) . . . . *Digested*, 07/**540**
Bracken v East Hertfordshire DC [2000] P.L.C.R. 434; [2000] C.O.D. 366; (2000)
97(19) L.S.G. 45; [2000] N.P.C. 52, DC . . . . *Digested*, 01/**4690**:
Considered, 07/3233
Bracken Bay Kitchens Ltd v Office of Communications [2007] CAT 22; [2007] Comp.
A.R. 811, CAT
Bracknell Forest BC v Adams see Adams v Bracknell Forest BC
Bracknell Forest BC v Princegate Estates Plc [2007] P.A.D. 89, Planning Inspector
Bradbury v London & Cambridge Properties Ltd (Unreported, February 2, 2007), CC
(Kingston upon Hull) . . . . *Digested*, 07/**2778**

Bradford v West Devon BC [2007] P.A.D. 45, Planning Inspector

Bradford & Bingley Plc v Rashid [2006] UKHL 37; [2006] 1 W.L.R. 2066; [2006] 4 All E.R. 705; [2006] 2 All E.R. (Comm) 951; [2006] 29 E.G. 132 (C.S.); (2006) 103(30) L.S.G. 30; (2006) 156 N.L.J. 1172; (2006) 150 S.J.L.B. 983; *Times*, July 14, 2006, HL; reversing [2005] EWCA Civ 1080, CA (Civ Div) . . . . — *Digested*, 06/**280**: *Followed*, 07/343

Bradford MDC v Booth; *sub nom* Booth v Bradford MDC (2000) 164 J.P. 485; (2001) 3 L.G.L.R. 8; [2000] C.O.D. 338; (2000) 164 J.P.N. 801; *Times*, May 31, 2000, DC . . . . — *Digested*, 00/**395**: *Applied*, 06/2761, 06/2778, 07/2800, 07/2802

Bradford MDC v Pratt [2007] I.R.L.R. 192, EAT . . . . — *Digested*, 07/**1406**

Bradley Egg Farm Ltd v Clifford [1943] 2 All E.R. 378, CA . . . . — *Applied*, 07/4253

Bradley's Application, Re [1995] N.I. 192, QBD (NI) . . . . — *Considered*, 07/4372

Bradstock Group Pension Scheme Trustees Ltd v Bradstock Group Plc [2002] EWHC 651 (Ch); [2002] I.C.R. 1427; [2002] O.P.L.R. 281; [2002] Pens. L.R. 327; [2002] W.T.L.R. 1281; (2002) 99(36) L.S.G. 40; *Times*, July 10, 2002, Ch D . . — *Digested*, 02/**3388**: *Considered*, 07/3025

Brady (Inspector of Taxes) v Group Lotus Car Companies Plc [1987] 3 All E.R. 1050; [1987] S.T.C. 635; [1987] 2 F.T.L.R. 453; 60 T.C. 359; (1987) 84 L.S.G. 2536, CA (Civ Div); affirming [1987] 2 All E.R. 674; [1987] S.T.C. 184; (1987) 84 L.S.G. 657, Ch D . . . . — *Digested*, 87/**541**: *Applied*, 06/4189, 07/4363

Braid v Walsall MBC (1999) 78 P. & C.R. 94; [1998] E.G. 41 (C.S.); [1998] N.P.C. 35, CA (Civ Div) . . . . — *Digested*, 99/**3725**: *Applied*, 07/2727

Brain v Yorkshire Rider Ltd [2007] Lloyd's Rep. I.R. 564, CC (Leeds) . . . . — *Digested*, 07/**1066**

Brampton Manor (Leisure) Ltd v McLean [2006] EWHC 2983 (Ch); [2007] B.C.C. 640, Ch D . . . . — *Digested*, 07/**303**

Brander v Revenue and Customs Commissioners [2007] S.T.C. (S.C.D.) 582; [2007] S.T.I. 1647, Sp Comm

Brannigan v Office of Fair Trading [2006] CAT 28; [2007] Comp. A.R. 420, CAT . . . . — *Digested*, 07/**600**

Brannigan v Office of Fair Trading [2007] CAT 23; [2007] Comp. A.R. 956, CAT

Branson v Bower (No.1) [2001] EWCA Civ 791; [2001] E.M.L.R. 32, CA (Civ Div); affirming TS/01/0012, QBD . . . . — *Digested*, 01/**1822**: *Applied*, 07/1071

Branston & Gothard Ltd, Re; *sub nom* Hill v Phillips [1999] 1 All E.R. (Comm) 289; [1999] Lloyd's Rep. Bank. 251; [1999] B.P.I.R. 466; [2007] W.T.L.R. 85, Ch D . — *Digested*, 99/**3304**

Braspetro Oil Services Co v FPSO Construction Inc [2007] EWHC 1359 (Comm); [2007] 2 All E.R. (Comm) 924, QBD (Comm)

Brasserie du Pecheur SA v Germany (C-46/93); *joined case* R. v Secretary of State for Transport Ex p. Factortame Ltd (C-48/93) [1996] Q.B. 404; [1996] 2 W.L.R. 506; [1996] All E.R. (EC) 301; [1996] E.C.R. I-1029; [1996] 1 C.M.L.R. 889; [1996] C.E.C. 295; [1996] I.R.L.R. 267; *Times*, March 7, 1996, ECJ . . . . — *Digested*, 96/**2803**: *Applied*, 98/2321, 99/144, 99/2565, 00/2383, 01/5581, 06/1526, 07/622, 07/1650, 07/3021: *Considered*, 96/101, 96/292, 96/2596, 96/5648, 97/80, 99/2259, 07/2490: *Followed*, 02/1571, 04/1426: *Remitting to*, 97/2393: *Subsequent related litigation*, 97/468

Brasserie Nationale SA v Commission of the European Communities (T49/02); *sub nom* Luxembourg Brewers Cartel, Re (T49/02) [2005] E.C.R. II-3033; [2006] 4 C.M.L.R. 8, CFI (3rd Chamber) . . . . — *Digested*, 06/**578**: *Applied*, 07/605

Brassford v Patel [2007] B.P.I.R. 1049, Ch D

Breakspear v Ackland (2007-08) 10 I.T.E.L.R. 852, Ch D

Brebbia v New Forest DC [2007] P.A.D. 79, Planning Inspector

Brecknell v United Kingdom (32457/04); *joined cases* O'Dowd v United Kingdom (34622/04); Reavey v United Kingdom (34640/04); McGrath v United Kingdom (34651/04); McCartney v United Kingdom (34575/04) *Times*, December 7, 2007, ECHR

Breckon v DPP [2007] EWHC 2013 (Admin); (2007) 104(35) L.S.G. 35, DC

Breen v Slater see Goodwood Recoveries Ltd v Breen

Brelec Installations Ltd, Re see Welsby v Brelec Installations Ltd (In Liquidation)

Bremner (Robert John) v Westwater 1994 J.C. 25; 1994 S.L.T. 707; 1993 S.C.C.R. 1023, HCJ . . . . — *Digested*, 94/**6241**: *Approved*, 07/1006

Brennan v ECO Composting Ltd [2006] EWHC 3153 (QB); [2007] 1 W.L.R. 773; [2007] 3 All E.R. 67; (2006) 156 N.L.J. 1919; *Times*, January 1, 2007, QBD . . . — *Digested*, 07/**489**

Brent LBC [2007] R.V.R. 233, LGO

Brent LBC v Doughan [2007] EWCA Civ 135; [2007] H.L.R. 28, CA (Civ Div) . . . . . . — *Digested*, 07/**498**

Brent LBC v K [2007] EWHC 1250 (Fam); [2007] 2 F.L.R. 914; [2007] Fam. Law 691, Fam Div

Breslin v McKenna [2007] NICA 14; [2007] N.I. 201, CA (NI)

Brett v Reading University see Brett (Deceased), Re

Brett (Deceased), Re; *sub nom* Brett v Reading University [2007] EWCA Civ 88; (2007) 104(9) L.S.G. 31; (2007) 151 S.J.L.B. 261, CA (Civ Div)

Brewer *v* Commissioner of Police of the Metropolis [1969] 1 W.L.R. 267; [1969] 1 All E.R. 513; (1969) 53 Cr. App. R. 157; (1969) 133 J.P. 185; (1968) 112 S.J. 1022; *Times*, December 14, 1968, DC . . . .
Digested, 69/3175:
Considered, 69/3177, 07/882

Brewer *v* Moreplay Ltd (Unreported, May 9, 2007), CC (Basingstoke) [*Ex rel.* Richard Wheeler, Barrister, 3 Paper Buildings, 4 St Peters Street, Winchester, Hants] . . .
*Digested, 07/**3105***

Brick Farm Management Ltd *v* Richmond Housing Partnership Ltd [2006] EWHC 1004 (Ch); [2007] L. & T.R. 1; [2006] 2 E.G.L.R. 46; [2006] 27 E.G. 236, Ch D . . .
*Digested, 07/**3368***

Brickfield Properties *v* Newton; *joined case* Rosebell Holdings *v* Newton [1971] 1 W.L.R. 862; [1971] 3 All E.R. 328; (1971) 115 S.J. 307, CA (Civ Div) . . . .
*Digested, 71/**9434**:*
Applied, 92/2829: Considered, 75/401.u, 82/1851: Followed, 07/492

Bridge UK.Com Ltd (t/a Bridge Communications) *v* Abbey Pynford Plc [2007] EWHC 728 (TCC); [2007] C.I.L.L. 2465, QBD (TCC)

Brigden *v* American Express Bank Ltd [2000] I.R.L.R. 94, QBD . . . .
*Digested, 00/**2117**:*
Applied, 04/1199: Disapproved, 07/1321

Brikom Investments Ltd *v* Carr; *joined cases* Brikom Investments Ltd *v* Roddy; Brikom Investments Ltd *v* Hickey [1979] Q.B. 467; [1979] 2 W.L.R. 737; [1979] 2 All E.R. 753; (1979) 38 P. & C.R. 326; (1979) 251 E.G. 359, CA (Civ Div) . . . .
*Digested, 79/**1598**:*
Applied, 01/3855, 07/2735: Considered, 90/2775

Brikom Investments Ltd *v* Hickey see Brikom Investments Ltd *v* Carr
Brikom Investments Ltd *v* Roddy see Brikom Investments Ltd *v* Carr
Brill & Co *v* Penn see Penn *v* Bristol and West Building Society
Bristol and West Building Society *v* Saunders see Saunders (A Bankrupt), Re
Bristol City Council *v* Glastonbury see Bristol City Council *v* Hassan
Bristol City Council *v* Hassan; *joined case* Bristol City Council *v* Glastonbury [2006] EWCA Civ 656; [2006] 1 W.L.R. 2582; [2006] 4 All E.R. 420; [2006] C.P. Rep. 37; [2006] H.L.R. 31; [2006] L. & T.R. 17; [2006] 22 E.G. 176 (C.S.); (2006) 103(23) L.S.G. 33; [2006] N.P.C. 61; [2006] 2 P. & C.R. DG20; *Times*, July 17, 2006, CA (Civ Div) . . . .
*Digested, 06/**2716**:*
Considered, 07/2718

Bristol City Council *v* Lovell [1998] 1 W.L.R. 446; [1998] 1 All E.R. 775; (1998) 30 H.L.R. 770; [1999] L. & T.R. 66; [1998] R.V.R. 133; [1998] E.G. 29 (C.S.); (1998) 95(14) L.S.G. 23; (1998) 95(9) L.S.G. 30; (1998) 148 N.L.J. 329; (1998) 142 S.J.L.B. 116; [1998] N.P.C. 31; *Times*, February 27, 1998, HL; reversing (1997) 29 H.L.R. 528; [1996] E.G. 140 (C.S.); [1996] N.P.C. 130, CA (Civ Div) . . . .
*Digested, 98/**3055**:*
Applied, 06/2044, 07/2767: Considered, 05/2674: Followed, 98/3056

Brit Syndicates Ltd *v* Grant Thornton International see Brit Syndicates Ltd *v* Italaudit SpA (In Liquidation) (formerly Grant Thornton SpA)

Brit Syndicates Ltd *v* Italaudit SpA (In Liquidation) (formerly Grant Thornton SpA); *sub nom* Brit Syndicates Ltd *v* Grant Thornton International [2006] EWCA Civ 1661; [2007] 1 All E.R. (Comm) 785; [2007] 1 Lloyd's Rep. 329; [2006] 2 C.L.C. 974; [2007] Lloyd's Rep. I.R. 343, CA (Civ Div); reversing [2006] EWHC 341 (Comm); [2006] Lloyd's Rep. I.R. 487, QBD (Comm) . . . .
*Digested, 07/**2498***

Britannia Alloys & Chemicals Ltd *v* Commission of the European Communities (C-76/06 P) [2007] 5 C.M.L.R. 3; [2007] Bus. L.R. D75, ECJ (4th Chamber)

Britannia Car Hire Service *v* Hardman (Unreported, March 21, 2006), CC (Bury) [*Ex rel.* Carl Chapman Solicitors, 20/22 Bowkers Row, Nelson Square, Bolton] . . . . . .
*Digested, 07/**487***

Britannia HeatTransfer Ltd (In Administration), Re [2007] B.C.C. 470; [2007] B.P.I.R. 1038, Ch D (Birmingham) . . . .
*Digested, 07/**2421***

British Aggregates Association *v* Commission of the European Communities (T-210/02) [2007] Env. L.R. 11, CFI (2nd Chamber) . . . .
*Digested, 07/**1646***

British Airways Plc *v* Apogee Enterprises Inc [2007] EWHC 93 (TCC); 111 Con. L.R. 200, QBD (TCC)

British Airways Plc *v* Commission of the European Communities (C-95/04 P) [2007] 4 C.M.L.R. 22; [2007] C.E.C. 607, ECJ (3rd Chamber) . . . .
*Digested, 07/**1547***

British Airways Plc *v* Commission of the European Communities (T-219/99) [2004] All E.R. (EC) 1115; [2003] E.C.R. II-5917; [2004] 4 C.M.L.R. 19, CFI (1st Chamber) . . . .
*Digested, 05/**575**:*
Applied, 07/1548

British Anzani (Felixstowe) Ltd *v* International Marine Management (UK) Ltd [1980] Q.B. 137; [1979] 3 W.L.R. 451; [1979] 2 All E.R. 1063; (1980) 39 P. & C.R. 189; (1978) 250 E.G. 1183; (1979) 123 S.J. 64, QBD . . . .
*Digested, 79/**1633**:*
Applied, 03/2775, 07/2716: Considered, 85/1283, 85/2604, 92/2700, 93/2519, 94/2797, 99/3723

British Aviation Insurance Co Ltd, Re [2005] EWHC 1621 (Ch); [2006] B.C.C. 14; [2006] 1 B.C.L.C. 665, Ch D (Companies Ct) . . . .
*Digested, 06/**2381**:*
Applied, 06/2382: Considered, 07/2448

British Coal Corp *v* Commission of the European Communities (T-367/94) see National Power Plc, Re (C-151/97 P (I))

41

British Coal Corp v Smith; *joined case* Ratcliffe v North Yorkshire CC [1996] 3 All E.R. 97; [1996] I.C.R. 515; [1996] I.R.L.R. 399; (1996) 93(25) L.S.G. 28; (1996) 140 S.J.L.B. 134; *Times*, May 23, 1996; *Independent*, June 13, 1996, HL; affirming [1994] I.C.R. 810; [1994] I.R.L.R. 342; *Times*, May 11, 1994; *Independent*, May 11, 1994, CA (Civ Div); reversing [1993] I.C.R. 529; [1993] I.R.L.R. 308; *Times*, February 23, 1993, EAT . . . . *Digested*, 96/**2549**:
Distinguished, 07/1362: *Subsequent related litigation*, 95/1995

British Energy Power & EnergyTrading Ltd v Credit Suisse A3/2007/1620/1621, CA (Civ Div); affirming [2007] EWHC 1428 (Comm); [2007] 2 Lloyd's Rep. 427, QBD (Comm)

British Home Stores Ltd v Burchell [1980] I.C.R. 303; [1978] I.R.L.R. 379; (1978) 13 I.T.R. 560, EAT . . . . *Digested*, 80/**1004**:
Applied, 80/1005, 80/1006, 82/2856, 83/1348, 90/1929, 90/1975, 97/2286, 97/6017, 99/2139, 03/1312, 03/1340, 07/1422: *Approved*, 00/2237:
Considered, 84/1304, 84/1312, 87/1395, 90/1949.a, 91/1696, 97/2289, 02/1387, 05/5218, 06/1384: *Referred to*, 89/1504, 96/2656

British Industrial Plastics Ltd v Ferguson [1940] 1 All E.R. 479, HL . . . . *Applied*, 05/4198, 07/4190

British Insulated & Helsby Cables Ltd v Atherton (Inspector of Taxes); *sub nom* Atherton (Inspector of Taxes) v British Insulated & Helsby Cables Ltd [1926] A.C. 205; 10 T.C. 155, HL; affirming [1925] 1 K.B. 421, CA. . . . . *Applied*, 47-51/4727, 53/1699, 53/1702, 54/1561, 59/1529, 06/4140, 07/4053: *Considered*, 64/1782, 65/1922, 65/1937, 86/453: *Distinguished*, 47-51/4729, 47-51/4732, 53/1703, 00/4934: *Doubted*, 89/534

British Medical Association v Chaudhary (No.2) [2007] EWCA Civ 788; [2007] I.R.L.R. 800; [2007] LS Law Medical 554; (2007) 97 B.M.L.R. 15; (2007) 151 S.J.L.B. 1021, CA (Civ Div); reversing UKEAT/1351/01/DA, UKEAT/0804/02/DA, EAT . . . . *Digested*, 07/**1390**:
Subsequent related litigation, 03/1294

British Phonographic Industry Ltd v Mechanical-Copyright Protection Society Ltd (2007) 30(9) I.P.D. 30059, CopyrightTr

British Racing Drivers Club Ltd v Hextall Erskine & Co [1996] 3 All E.R. 667; [1996] B.C.C. 727; [1997] 1 B.C.L.C. 182; [1996] P.N.L.R. 523, Ch D . . . . *Digested*, 96/**4492**:
Considered, 06/556: *Followed*, 07/2944

British Sky Broadcasting Group Plc v Sky Home Services Ltd [2006] EWHC 3165 (Ch); [2007] 3 All E.R. 1066; [2007] F.S.R. 14; [2007] Bus. L.R. D41, Ch D . . *Digested*, 07/**2546**

British South Africa Co v Companhia de Mocambique; *sub nom* Companhia de Mocambique v British South Africa Co; *joined case* De Sousa v British South Africa Co [1893] A.C. 602; [1891-94] All E.R. Rep. 640, HL; reversing [1892] 2 Q.B. 358, CA. . . . . *Applied*, 90/609, 99/731, 07/510: *Approved*, 67/128: *Considered*, 77/341, 97/901:
Distinguished, 47-51/9624, 04/2255: *Followed*, 78/286

British Sugar Plc v James Robertson & Sons Ltd [1997] E.T.M.R. 118; [1996] R.P.C. 281; (1996) 19(3) I.P.D. 19023; *Times*, February 17, 1996, Ch D . . . . *Digested*, 96/**5708**:
Applied, 99/3544, 00/3791, 07/2683: *Considered*, 97/4906, 98/3537, 98/3538, 99/3584, 99/3589, 00/3758, 02/2898, 03/2646:
Followed, 98/3541, 03/2638: *Referred to*, 97/4891, 97/4895, 99/3542, 99/3566, 99/3581

British Telecommunications Plc v James Thomson & Sons (Engineers) Ltd [1999] 1 W.L.R. 9; [1999] 2 All E.R. 241; 1999 S.C. (H.L.) 9; 1999 S.L.T. 224; 1999 S.C.L.R. 126; [1999] B.L.R. 35; (1999) 1 T.C.L.R. 1; 61 Con. L.R. 1; [1999] Lloyd's Rep. I.R. 105; (1999) 96(4) L.S.G. 40; (1999) 143 S.J.L.B. 28; [1998] N.P.C. 161; 1999 G.W.D. 1-47; *Times*, December 11, 1998, HL; reversing 1997 S.C. 59; 1997 S.L.T. 767; 1997 S.C.L.R. 228; 82 B.L.R. 1; 54 Con. L.R. 108; [1997] 6 Re. L.R. 325; 1997 Rep. L.R. 23; (1997) 13 Const. L.J. 332; 1997 G.W.D. 3-77; *Times*, January 28, 1997, IH (2 Div); affirming 49 Con. L.R. 163, OH . . . . *Digested*, 99/**5783**:
Applied, 01/4469: *Considered*, 07/745

British Telecommunications Plc v One in a Million Ltd; *joined cases* Marks & Spencer Plc v One in a Million Ltd; Virgin Enterprises Ltd v One in a Million Ltd; J Sainsbury Plc v One in a Million Ltd; Ladbroke Group Plc v One in a Million Ltd [1999] 1 W.L.R. 903; [1998] 4 All E.R. 476; [1999] E.T.M.R. 61; [1997-98] Info. T.L.R. 423; [1998] I.T.C.L.R. 146; [2001] E.B.L.R. 2; [1999] F.S.R. 1; [1998] Masons C.L.R. 165; (1998) 95(37) L.S.G. 37; (1998) 148 N.L.J. 1179; *Times*, July 29, 1998; *Independent*, July 31, 1998, CA (Civ Div); affirming [1997-98] Info. T.L.R. 316; [1998] I.T.C.L.R. 7; [1998] F.S.R. 265; (1997) 16 Tr. L.R. 554; [1998] Masons C.L.R. 116; (1998) 21(2) I.P.D. 21016; (1997) 147 N.L.J. 1809; *Times*, December 2, 1997, Ch D . . . . *Digested*, 98/**3520**:
Applied, 04/2272, 06/2593, 07/2545: *Considered*, 98/3501, 00/3592, 01/5357, 02/2782, 02/2891, 03/2648, 07/2674: *Referred to*, 99/3587

British Telecommunications Plc v Sun Life Assurance Society Plc [1996] Ch. 69; [1995] 3 W.L.R. 622; [1995] 4 All E.R. 44; (1997) 73 P. & C.R. 475; [1995] 2 E.G.L.R. 44; [1995] 45 E.G. 133; (1995) 145 N.L.J. 1366; (1995) 139 S.J.L.B. 203; [1995] N.P.C. 140; *Times*, August 3, 1995; *Independent*, September 12, 1995, CA (Civ Div); affirming (1995) 69 P. & C.R. 305; [1994] 43 E.G. 158; [1994] E.G. 117 (C.S.); (1994) 68 P. & C.R. D14, Ch D . . . .
Digested, 96/3817:
Applied, 98/3051, 98/3623: Considered, 07/2737
British Vita Unlimited v British Vita Pension Fund Trustees Ltd [2007] EWHC 953 (Ch); [2007] Pens. L.R. 157, Ch D . . . .
Digested, 07/3011
British Waterways v Kennet DC [2007] P.A.D. 42, Planning Inspector
British Waterways Board v Severn Trent Water Ltd [2001] EWCA Civ 276; [2002] Ch. 25; [2001] 3 W.L.R. 613; [2001] 3 All E.R. 673; [2001] Env. L.R. 45; [2002] E.H.L.R. 1; (2001) 98(13) L.S.G. 43; (2001) 98(16) L.S.G. 34; [2001] N.P.C. 53; *Times*, March 23, 2001; *Independent*, March 14, 2001, CA (Civ Div); reversing [2001] Ch. 32; [2000] 3 W.L.R. 1; [2000] 1 All E.R. 347; [2000] Env. L.R. 284; (1999) 96(42) L.S.G. 41; (1999) 143 S.J.L.B. 249; [1999] N.P.C. 120; *Times*, October 26, 1999; *Independent*, November 29, 1999, Ch D . . . .
Digested, 01/5632:
Considered, 07/2961
Broadway Investments Hackney Ltd v Grant [2006] EWCA Civ 1709; [2007] H.L.R. 23; [2007] 1 P. & C.R. 18; [2007] L. & T.R. 11; (2007) 104(2) L.S.G. 31; [2007] N.P.C. 1, CA (Civ Div) . . . .
Digested, 07/2749
Brock v Minerva Dental Ltd [2007] I.C.R. 917, EAT . . . .
Digested, 07/1339
Brogan v United Kingdom (11209/84) see Brogan v United Kingdom (A/145-B)
Brogan v United Kingdom (A/145-B); *sub nom* Brogan v United Kingdom; Brogan v United Kingdom (11209/84); *joined cases* McFadden v United Kingdom (11365/85); Coyle v United Kingdom (11266/84) (1989) 11 E.H.R.R. 117; *Times*, November 30, 1988; *Independent*, November 30, 1988; *Guardian*, December 7, 1988, ECHR (1987) 9 E.H.R.R. CD378, Eur Comm HR . . . .
Digested, 88/1804:
Applied, 03/2157, 05/2130, 07/2231: Followed, 98/3073
Bromley LBC v Special Educational Needs Tribunal (No.2) [1999] 3 All E.R. 587; (1999) 1 L.G.L.R. 970; [1999] B.L.G.R. 747; [1999] Ed. C.R. 907; [1999] E.L.R. 260; (1999) 2 C.C.L. Rep. 239; [1999] C.O.D. 409; *Times*, June 14, 1999; *Independent*, June 17, 1999, CA (Civ Div); affirming (Unreported, December 18, 1998), QBD . . . .
Digested, 99/1890:
Applied, 02/1167, 07/1266: Considered, 03/1123, 07/1262
Bromley LBC v Watts Farm [2007] P.A.D. 56, Planning Inspector
Bromor Properties Ltd's Application, Re (1995) 70 P. & C.R. 569, Lands Tr . . . .
Digested, 96/5009:
Cited, 07/3423
Bronson v Inker (Unreported, December 7, 2006), CC (Brighton) [*Ex rel.* Richard Wheeler, Barrister, 3 Paper Buildings, 4 St Peters Street, Winchester, Hants] . . .
Digested, 07/3183
Brook Street Bureau (UK) Ltd v Dacas see Dacas v Brook Street Bureau (UK) Ltd
Brooker v Police [2007] NZSC 30; 22 B.H.R.C. 408, Sup Ct (NZ)
Brooks v Commissioner of Police of the Metropolis [2005] UKHL 24; [2005] 1 W.L.R. 1495; [2005] 2 All E.R. 489; [2005] Po. L.R. 157; (2005) 155 N.L.J. 653; *Times*, April 26, 2005, HL; reversing [2002] EWCA Civ 407; [2002] Po. L.R. 88; *Daily Telegraph*, April 11, 2002, CA (Civ Div) . . . .
Digested, 05/3342:
Applied, 07/2934: Considered, 06/2880: Distinguished, 06/2171:
Previous proceedings, 05/3342
BROTHER/Admissibility of appeal (T1474/05) [2006] E.P.O.R. 55, EPO (Technical Bd App) . . . .
Digested, 07/2567
Brotherton v Aseguradora Colseguros SA (No.2); *sub nom* Brotherton v La Previsora SA Compania de Seguros [2003] EWCA Civ 705; [2003] 2 All E.R. (Comm) 298; [2003] 2 C.L.C. 629; [2003] Lloyd's Rep. I.R. 746; (2003) 147 S.J.L.B. 658, CA (Civ Div); affirming [2003] EWHC 335 (Comm); [2003] 1 All E.R. (Comm) 774, QBD (Comm) . . . .
Digested, 03/2476:
Applied, 07/2484: Followed, 05/614
Brotherton v La Previsora SA Compania de Seguros see Brotherton v Aseguradora Colseguros SA (No.2)
Brown, Re see Brown (formerly Bajinya) v Governor of Belmarsh Prison
Brown v Bennett [1999] B.C.C. 525; [1999] 1 B.C.L.C. 649, CA (Civ Div); affirming [1999] B.C.C. 91; [1998] 2 B.C.L.C. 97; *Times*, January 3, 1998, Ch D . . . .
Digested, 99/3288:
Applied, 07/3438
Brown v Clark see Cityspan Ltd, Re
Brown v Croydon LBC [2007] EWCA Civ 32; [2007] I.C.R. 909; [2007] I.R.L.R. 259, CA (Civ Div); affirming (2006) 150 S.J.L.B. 572, EAT . . . .
Digested, 07/1388
Brown v Executors of the Estate of HM Queen Elizabeth the Queen Mother B4/2007/1702/FAFMF, CA (Civ Div); reversing [2007] EWHC 1607 (Fam); [2007] W.T.L.R. 1129, Fam Div . . . .
Digested, 07/3967
Brown v Revenue and Customs Commissioners [2007] S.T.I. 381, V&DTr (Manchester)
Brown v Rice [2007] EWHC 625 (Ch); [2007] B.P.I.R. 305; [2007] C.I.L.L. 2467, Ch D . . . .
Digested, 07/1078

43

Brown v Russell Young & Co [2007] EWCA Civ 43; [2007] 2 All E.R. 453; [2007] 4
Costs L.R. 552; (2007) 157 N.L.J. 222; (2007) 151 S.J.L.B. 196; *Times*, February
13, 2007, CA (Civ Div); affirming (Unreported, April 12, 2006), Sup Ct Costs
Office . . . . *Digested*, 07/**415**
Brown v Secretary of State for Work and Pensions [2007] EWCA Civ 89; (2007)
104(9) L.S.G. 33; *Times*, April 4, 2007, CA (Civ Div) . . . . *Digested*, 07/**3886**
Brown v Simion see Simion v Brown
Brown (formerly Bajinya) v Governor of Belmarsh Prison; *sub nom* Brown, Re; R. (on
the application of Brown) v Governor of Belmarsh Prison; *joined cases* R. (on the
application of Nteziryayo) v Governor of Belmarsh Prison; R. (on the
application of Ugirashebuja) v Governor of Belmarsh Prison; R. (on the
application of Munaneza) v Governor of Belmarsh Prison [2007] EWHC 498
(Admin); [2007] Q.B. 838; [2007] 2 W.L.R. 1184; [2007] 2 All E.R. 633;
(2007) 104(14) L.S.G. 23; *Times*, May 15, 2007, DC . . . . *Digested*, 07/**1666**
Brown's Operating System Services Ltd v Southwark Roman Catholic Diocesan Corp
[2007] EWCA Civ 164; [2007] L. & T.R. 25; (2007) 104(11) L.S.G. 33; (2007)
151 S.J.L.B. 335; [2007] N.P.C. 25, CA (Civ Div)
Browne v Associated Newspapers Ltd [2007] EWCA Civ 295; [2007] 3 W.L.R. 289;
[2007] C.P. Rep. 29; [2007] E.M.L.R. 20; (2007) 157 N.L.J. 671, CA (Civ Div);
reversing in part [2007] EWHC 202 (QB); [2007] E.M.L.R. 19; (2007) 157
N.L.J. 670, QBD . . . . *Digested*, 07/**2893**
Broxbourne BC v Zog 2 Ltd [2007] P.A.D. 91, Planning Inspector
Bruce v Dignity Funerals Ltd; *sub nom* Dignity Funerals Ltd v Bruce 2005 1 S.C. 59;
2004 S.L.T. 1223; 2005 S.C.L.R. 951; [2005] I.R.L.R. 189; (2004) 148 S.J.L.B.
1313; 2004 G.W.D. 32-662, IH (2 Div); reversing EATS/0015/02, EAT (SC) . . . *Digested*, 05/**5217**:
Considered, 07/1317

Brugg Rohrsysteme GmbH v Commission of the European Communities (C-207/02 P)
see Dansk Rorindustri A/S v Commission of the European Communities (C-
189/02 P)
Brunel Motor Co Ltd v Revenue and Customs Commissioners CH/2007/APP/0319, Ch
D; affirming [2007] S.T.I. 1706, V&DTr (Manchester)
Brunel University v Vaseghi; *sub nom* Brunel University v Webster [2007] EWCA Civ
482; [2007] I.R.L.R. 592; (2007) 151 S.J.L.B. 709, CA (Civ Div); affirming
(Unreported, August 17, 2006), EAT . . . . *Digested*, 07/**1376**
Brunel University v Webster see Brunel University v Vaseghi
Brunel University v Webster see Wong v Igen Ltd (formerly Leeds Careers Guidance)
Brunsden v Humphrey (1884-85) L.R. 14 Q.B.D. 141, CA; reversing (1882-83) L.R. 11
Q.B.D. 712, QBD . . . . *Applied*, 64/1370,
98/533: *Considered*, 99/431, 07/2919: *Disapproved*, 68/2639:
Distinguished, 47-51/7913: *Followed*, 61/1377, 89/2724

BRUTT Trade Marks see Target Fixings Ltd v Brutt Beteiligungsgesellschaft MBH
Brutus v Cozens [1973] A.C. 854; [1972] 3 W.L.R. 521; [1972] 2 All E.R. 1297; (1972)
56 Cr. App. R. 799; [1973] Crim. L.R. 56; (1972) 116 S.J. 647, HL; reversing
[1972] 1 W.L.R. 484; [1972] 2 All E.R. 1; (1972) 116 S.J. 217, QBD . . . . *Digested*, 72/**706**:
Applied, 73/602, 73/655, 73/655, 74/2726, 79/2532, 93/977, 93/4067,
98/4669, 04/770, 05/796, 07/863: *Considered*, 73/602, 74/2726, 82/632,
82/632, 86/1238, 89/3395, 89/3602, 90/4372, 91/2373, 91/2373, 93/4067,
95/5116, 95/5116, 95/5119, 96/1506, 03/4560: *Distinguished*, 90/4372:
Followed, 97/2863

Bryan v Arpan see Starlight Developers Ltd, Re
Bryan (Setting of Minimum Term), Re; *sub nom* R. v Bryan (Alsent); R. v Bryan (Leslie)
[2006] EWCA Crim 1660; [2007] 1 Cr. App. R. (S.) 53; [2006] Crim. L.R.
942, CA (Crim Div) . . . . *Digested*, 07/**3731**
Bryant v Mike Beer Transport Ltd see Anderton v Clwyd CC
Bryant v Munro (Unreported, April 24, 2006), CC (Altrincham) [*Ex rel.* Karim Sabry,
Barrister, 8 King Street Chambers, 3rd Floor, 8 King Street, Manchester] . . . . . *Digested*, 07/**3156**
Bryant v Pech see Anderton v Clwyd CC
Brzezinski v Dyrektor Izby Celnej w Warszawie (C-313/05) [2007] 2 C.M.L.R. 4;
[2007] C.E.C. 432, ECJ (1st Chamber) . . . . *Digested*, 07/**1607**
BS (India) v Entry Clearance Officer [2007] EWCA Civ 1235; (2007) 104(45) L.S.G.
32, CA (Civ Div)
BS&N Ltd (BVI) v Micado Shipping Ltd (Malta) (The Seaflower) (No.2) [2000] 2 All
E.R. (Comm) 169; [2000] 2 Lloyd's Rep. 37; [2000] C.L.C. 802, QBD
(Comm) . . . . *Digested*, 00/**4702**:
Considered, 07/3816

BSF Group Ltd v Secretary of State for Defence see BFS Group Ltd v Secretary of
State for Defence
BSW Ltd v Balltec Ltd [2006] EWHC 822 (Pat); [2007] F.S.R. 1; (2006) 29(6) I.P.D.
29050, Ch D (Patents Ct) . . . . *Digested*, 07/**500**
BTP Tioxide Ltd v Armada Marine SA see Pioneer Shipping Ltd v BTP Tioxide Ltd (The
Nema) (No.2)
BTP Tioxide Ltd v Pioneer Shipping Ltd see Pioneer Shipping Ltd v BTP Tioxide Ltd
(The Nema) (No.2)

Buchberger v Austria (32899/96) (2003) 37 E.H.R.R. 13, ECHR . . . .   *Digested*, 03/**2195**:
     Considered, 07/1774
Buck v Nottinghamshire Healthcare NHS Trust [2006] EWCA Civ 1576; (2007) 93
     B.M.L.R. 28; [2006] M.H.L.R. 351; (2006) 103(47) L.S.G. 28; (2006) 150
     S.J.L.B. 1568; *Times*, December 1, 2006, CA (Civ Div) . . . .   *Digested*, 07/**2953**
Buckley v Dalziel [2007] EWHC 1025 (QB); [2007] 1 W.L.R. 2933; [2007] E.M.L.R.
     23; *Times*, June 7, 2007, QBD . . . .   *Digested*, 07/**1073**
Bucknell v DPP; *sub nom* MB v DPP [2006] EWHC 1888 (Admin); (2007) 171 J.P. 10;
     (2007) 171 J.P.N. 267, DC . . . .   *Digested*, 07/**864**
Budd Scott v Daniell [1902] 2 K.B. 351, KBD . . . .   *Applied*, 47-51/5368:
     Distinguished, 07/2752
Buddington v Secretary of State for the Home Department see R. (on the application
     of Buddington) v Secretary of State for the Home Department
Budge v AF Budge (Contractors) Ltd (In Receivership and Liquidation) [1997] B.P.I.R.
     366, CA (Civ Div) . . . .   *Digested*, 97/**3031**:
     Applied, 06/2385: *Followed*, 07/2452
Buehler AG v Chronos Richardson Ltd [1998] 2 All E.R. 960; [1998] R.P.C. 609;
     (1998) 21(7) I.P.D. 21076; (1998) 95(16) L.S.G. 25; (1998) 142 S.J.L.B. 133;
     Times, April 3, 1998, CA (Civ Div) . . . .   *Digested*, 98/**3456**:
     Applied, 03/5748, 07/2677
Buffrey v Buffrey (2006-07) 9 I.T.E.L.R. 455, Sup Ct (NSW) . . . .   *Digested*, 07/**4252**
Bugdaycay v Secretary of State for the Home Department; *sub nom* R. v Secretary of
     State for the Home Department Ex p. Bugdaycay; *joined cases* Musisi v
     Secretary of State for the Home Department; Norman v Secretary of State for
     the Home Department; Nelidow Santis v Secretary of State for the Home
     Department [1987] A.C. 514; [1987] 2 W.L.R. 606; [1987] 1 All E.R. 940;
     [1987] Imm. A.R. 250; (1987) 84 L.S.G. 902; (1987) 137 N.L.J. 199; (1987) 131
     S.J. 297, HL; affirming [1986] 1 W.L.R. 155; [1986] 1 All E.R. 458; [1986]
     Imm. A.R. 8; (1986) 83 L.S.G. 700; (1986) 130 S.J. 129; *Times*, November 12,
     1985, CA (Civ Div); affirming *Times*, July 11, 1985, DC . . . .   *Digested*, 87/**1989**:
     Applied, 89/1951, 89/1954, 92/2402, 92/2450, 93/2233, 94/2452,
     96/3220, 97/4111, 01/3421, 03/3944, 07/2344: *Cited*, 94/2498, 95/2695:
     Considered, 87/23, 87/1983, 88/14, 91/1965, 94/2455, 96/3231, 96/3236,
     96/3278, 05/3882: *Followed*, 97/2929, 98/3196, 07/2295:
     Referred to, 89/1939, 95/2676
Bulk Trading SA v Moeller [2006] EWCA Civ 1294; [2007] 1 Lloyd's Rep. 61, CA (Civ
     Div) . . . .   *Digested*, 07/**417**
Bull v Devon AHA [1993] 4 Med. L.R. 117, CA (Civ Div) . . . .   *Considered*, 01/4502,
     07/2929
Bull v Nottinghamshire and City of Nottingham Fire and Rescue Authority; *joined case*
     Lincolnshire CC v Fire Brigades Union [2007] EWCA Civ 240; [2007] I.C.R.
     1631; [2007] B.L.G.R. 439; (2007) 151 S.J.L.B. 333, CA (Civ Div); affirming
     [2006] EWHC 2749 (QB), QBD . . . .   *Digested*, 07/**1323**
Bunce v Lovatt (Unreported, July 31, 2006), CC (Coventry) [*Ex rel.* Stephen Garner,
     Barrister, No.8 Chambers, Fountain Court, Steelhouse Lane, Birmingham] . . . .   *Digested*, 07/**3104**
Bunce v Postworth Ltd (t/a Skyblue) [2005] EWCA Civ 490; [2005] I.R.L.R. 557,
     CA (Civ Div); affirming UKEAT/0052/04/MH, EAT . . . .   *Digested*, 05/**1214**:
     Applied, 07/1345, 07/4073
Bundeskartellamt v Volkswagen AG (C-266/93) [1995] E.C.R. I-3477, ECJ . . . .   *Digested*, 96/**1048**:
     Applied, 07/599, 07/642
Bundesverband der Arzneimittel Importeure eV v Bayer AG (C-2/01 P); *sub nom* Bayer
     AG v Commission of the European Communities (C-2/01 P) [2004] All E.R.
     (EC) 500; [2004] E.C.R. I-23; [2004] 4 C.M.L.R. 13; [2004] E.T.M.R. 100;
     [2005] I.C.R. 834; (2004) 78 B.M.L.R. 91, ECJ . . . .   *Digested*, 04/**494**:
     Considered, 07/621
Bunney v Burns Anderson Plc; *joined case* Cahill v Timothy James & Partners Ltd
     [2007] EWHC 1240 (Ch); [2007] 4 All E.R. 246; (2007) 104(25) L.S.G. 36;
     Times, June 20, 2007, Ch D . . . .   *Digested*, 07/**51**
Bunt v Tilley [2006] EWHC 407 (QB); [2007] 1 W.L.R. 1243; [2006] 3 All E.R. 336;
     [2006] E.M.L.R. 18; [2006] Info. T.L.R. 151; (2006) 103(14) L.S.G. 29, QBD . .   *Digested*, 06/**1046**
BUPA Care Homes (CFC Homes) Ltd v Muscolino [2006] I.C.R. 1329, EAT. . . . .   *Digested*, 07/**1429**
BUPA Purchasing Ltd v Customs and Excise Commissioners (No.1) [2003] EWHC
     1957 (Ch); [2003] S.T.C. 1203; [2004] B.T.C. 5003; [2004] B.V.C. 63; [2003]
     S.T.I. 1398, Ch D; affirming [2003] B.V.C. 2086; [2003] S.T.I. 442, V&DTr. . . . .   *Digested*, 03/**4553**:
     Followed, 07/4309
BUPA Purchasing Ltd v Customs and Excise Commissioners (No.2) see BUPA
     Purchasing Ltd v Revenue and Customs Commissioners
BUPA Purchasing Ltd v Revenue and Customs Commissioners; *sub nom* BUPA
     Purchasing Ltd v Customs and Excise Commissioners (No.2); Revenue and
     Customs Commissioners v BUPA Purchasing Ltd [2007] EWCA Civ 542;
     [2007] B.T.C. 5635; [2007] B.V.C. 603; *Times*, July 5, 2007, CA (Civ Div);
     reversing [2005] EWHC 2117 (Ch); [2006] S.T.C. 388; [2005] B.T.C. 5637;
     [2005] B.V.C. 668; [2005] S.T.I. 1675, Ch D . . . .   *Digested*, 07/**4282**

Burden v United Kingdom (13378/05) [2007] S.T.C. 252; [2007] 1 F.C.R. 69; (2007)
  44 E.H.R.R. 51; 21 B.H.R.C. 640; 9 I.T.L. Rep. 535; [2007] W.T.L.R. 607; [2007]
  S.T.I. 106; *Times*, January 19, 2007, ECHR. . . . . *Digested*, 07/**2205**
Burdis v Livsey see Lagden v O'Connor
Burdle v Secretary of State for the Environment [1972] 1 W.L.R. 1207; [1972] 3 All
  E.R. 240; 70 L.G.R. 511; (1972) 24 P. & C.R. 174; (1972) 116 S.J. 507, QBD. . . . . *Digested*, 72/**3335**:
                                                Applied, 82/3130, 89/3559, 90/4333, 97/4089, 99/4220, 07/3226:
                                                Considered, 83/3649, 92/4172, 93/182, 93/3860, 96/4766, 01/4656,
                                                                                                      03/3382: *Distinguished*, 83/3683
Burdov v Russia (59498/00) (2004) 38 E.H.R.R. 29, ECHR . . . . *Digested*, 04/**1948**:
                                                                                                      Applied, 07/2209

Bureau Rik Decan-Business Research & Development NV (BRD) v Belgium (C-401/95)
  see Garage Molenheide BVBA v Belgium (C-286/94)
Burford Midland Properties Ltd v Marley Extrusions Ltd [1994] B.C.C. 604; [1995] 1
  B.C.L.C. 102; [1995] 2 E.G.L.R. 15; [1994] E.G. 108 (C.S.), Ch D . . . . *Digested*, 95/**2843**:
                                                                      Applied, 07/2422: *Considered*, 96/3518
Burge v Swarbrick [2007] HCA 17; [2007] F.S.R. 27, HC (Aus)
Burgess v Rawnsley [1975] Ch. 429; [1975] 3 W.L.R. 99; [1975] 3 All E.R. 142;
  (1975) 30 P. & C.R. 221; (1975) 119 S.J. 406, CA (Civ Div) . . . . *Digested*, 75/**3115**:
                                                                      Applied, 07/3963: *Considered*, 79/2420, 85/2944, 95/2364
Burlo v Langley; *sub nom* Langley v Burlo; Langley v Burso [2006] EWCA Civ 1778;
  [2007] 2 All E.R. 462; [2007] I.C.R. 390; [2007] I.R.L.R. 145; (2007) 104(2)
  L.S.G. 30; (2007) 151 S.J.L.B. 61, CA (Civ Div); affirming [2006] 2 All E.R. 1104;
  [2006] I.C.R. 850; [2006] I.R.L.R. 460; *Times*, April 3, 2006, EAT. . . . . *Digested*, 07/**1425**
Burnden Group Plc v Northstar Systems Ltd (In Liquidation) see Ultraframe (UK) Ltd v
  Fielding
Burnley BC v Stansfield [2007] P.A.D. 11, Planning Inspector
Burrows v East Hampshire DC [2007] P.A.D. 80, Planning Inspector
Burrows v Vauxhall Motors Ltd; *joined case* Mongiardi v IBC Vehicles [1998] P.I.Q.R.
  P48; (1997) 94(47) L.S.G. 31; (1997) 147 N.L.J. 1723; (1997) 141 S.J.L.B. 237;
  Times, December 17, 1997, CA (Civ Div) . . . . *Digested*, 98/**477**:
                                                Considered, 07/403: *Distinguished*, 98/441: *Followed*, 98/491
Burton v De Vere Hotels Ltd [1997] I.C.R. 1; [1996] I.R.L.R. 596; *Times*, October 3,
  1996; *Independent*, November 4, 1996, EAT . . . . *Digested*, 96/**2587**:
                                                Applied, 98/2194, 03/1299: *Considered*, 00/2206, 01/2316, 07/1334:
                                                                                                      Disapproved, 03/1309
Burton Allton & Johnson Ltd v Peck [1975] I.C.R. 193; [1975] I.R.L.R. 87, QBD . . . . . *Digested*, 75/**1141**:
                                                Applied, 00/6215, 07/1398: *Distinguished*, 84/1214, 85/1150
Buschau v Rogers Communications Inc 2006 SCC 28; (2006-07) 9 I.T.E.L.R. 73, Sup
  Ct (Can) . . . . *Digested*, 07/**3036**
Bushell v Secretary of State for the Environment [1981] A.C. 75; [1980] 3 W.L.R. 22;
  [1980] 2 All E.R. 608; 78 L.G.R. 269; (1980) 40 P. & C.R. 51; [1980] J.P.L. 458;
  (1981) 125 S.J. 168, HL; reversing 78 L.G.R. 10; (1980) 39 P. & C.R. 341;
  [1980] J.P.L. 27; (1979) 123 S.J. 605, CA (Civ Div); reversing 76 L.G.R. 460;
  (1978) 36 P. & C.R. 363; [1978] J.P.L. 310; (1978) 122 S.J. 110, QBD . . . . *Digested*, 80/**1337**:
                                                Applied, 80/308, 84/1614, 02/6041: *Considered*, 83/38, 86/2017, 87/35,
                                                87/3162, 88/3604, 96/4751, 05/59: *Distinguished*, 94/1874, 07/1506:
                                                                                                      Followed, 95/4845: *Referred to*, 91/5756
Business Environment Bow Lane Ltd v Deanwater Estates Ltd [2007] EWCA Civ 622;
  [2007] L. & T.R. 26; [2007] 32 E.G. 90; [2007] 27 E.G. 303 (C.S.); [2007]
  N.P.C. 79, CA (Civ Div); reversing [2006] EWHC 3363 (Ch); [2007] L. & T.R.
  12; [2007] 19 E.G. 166, Ch D . . . . *Digested*, 07/**2735**
Business Transfers, Re (C-382/92) see Commission of the European Communities v
  United Kingdom (C-382/92)
Busk Madsen v Denmark see Kjeldsen v Denmark (A/23)
Bute v Revenue and Customs Commissioners [2007] S.T.I. 2415, Sp Comm
Butland v Powys CC [2007] EWCA Civ 1298, CA (Civ Div); reversing [2007] EWHC
  734 (Admin); [2007] Env. L.R. 30; (2007) 104(14) L.S.G. 22, QBD (Admin) . . *Digested*, 07/**515**
Butler v Woodman (t/a DCW Surfacing Contractors) (Unreported, November 7,
  2005), CC (Bristol) [*Ex rel*. James Hogg, Pupil Barrister, St James Chambers, 68
  Quay Street, Manchester] . . . . *Digested*, 07/**3171**
Butler Machine Tool Co v Ex-cell-o Corp (England) [1979] 1 W.L.R. 401; [1979] 1 All
  E.R. 965; (1977) 121 S.J. 406, CA (Civ Div) . . . . *Digested*, 79/**338**:
                                                                      Applied, 07/3569: *Considered*, 05/654
Butler (Inspector of Taxes) v Wildin [1989] S.T.C. 22; 62 T.C. 666; [1988] B.T.C. 475;
  (1988) 85(46) L.S.G. 43; *Times*, November 16, 1988; *Independent*, November
  21, 1988, Ch D . . . . *Digested*, 89/**2033**:
                                                                      Applied, 07/4100: *Distinguished*, 06/4226
Butlin v Butlin (Rectification) see Butlin's Settlement Trusts (Rectification), Re
Butlin's Settlement Trusts (Rectification), Re; *sub nom* Butlin v Butlin (Rectification)
  [1976] Ch. 251; [1976] 2 W.L.R. 547; [1976] 2 All E.R. 483; (1975) 119 S.J.
  794, Ch D . . . . *Digested*, 76/**2508**:
                                                Applied, 98/4873, 01/5510: *Considered*, 07/4247: *Followed*, 01/4595
Butlins Skyline Ltd v Beynon [2007] I.C.R. 121, EAT. . . . . *Digested*, 07/**1357**

Butterworth v Soutter [2000] B.P.I.R. 582, Ch D . . . . *Digested*, 01/**3717**:
Applied, 05/2270, 07/2410
Buyco Ltd v Revenue and Customs Commissioners [2006] V. & D.R. 57, V&DTr
(London). . . . . *Digested*, 07/**4286**
BVBA Management Training & Consultancy v Benelux-Merkenbureau (C-239/05)
[2007] E.T.M.R. 35, ECJ (2nd Chamber) . . . . *Digested*, 07/**2647**
Bwllfa and Merthyr Dare Steam Collieries (1891) Ltd v Pontypridd Waterworks Co; *sub
nom* Bwllfa and Merthyr Dare Steam Collieries (1891) Ltd and Pontypridd
Waterworks Co's Arbitration, Re [1903] A.C. 426, HL; reversing [1902] 2 K.B.
135, CA; reversing [1901] 2 K.B. 798, KBD . . . . *Applied*, 62/2560,
68/1862, 68/4074, 75/3666, 79/297, 03/3023, 07/3816: *Considered*, 69/433,
82/20.au, 95/4829, 03/1230, 05/2671: *Distinguished*, 79/2873, 83/3143,
91/3062
Bwllfa and Merthyr Dare Steam Collieries (1891) Ltd and Pontypridd Waterworks Co's
Arbitration, Re see Bwllfa and Merthyr Dare Steam Collieries (1891) Ltd v
Pontypridd Waterworks Co
Byblos Bank SAL v Al-Khudhairy (1986) 2 B.C.C. 99549, CA (Civ Div) . . . . *Applied*, 07/303
Byrne v Mental Health Tribunal for Scotland [2007] M.H.L.R. 2; 2006 G.W.D. 10-179,
Sh Pr
Byrne v Motor Insurers Bureau A2/2007/1622 & A2/2007/1627, CA (Civ Div);
affirming [2007] EWHC 1268 (QB); [2007] 3 All E.R. 499; [2007] 3 C.M.L.R.
15; [2007] Eu. L.R. 739; [2007] P.I.Q.R. P25; (2007) 104(25) L.S.G. 38;
(2007) 157 N.L.J. 858; (2007) 151 S.J.L.B. 811; *Times*, June 15, 2007, QBD . . . *Digested*, 07/**2496**
Byrne Bros (Formwork) Ltd v Baird; *sub nom* Baird v Byrne Bros (Formwork) Ltd
[2002] I.C.R. 667; [2002] I.R.L.R. 96; [2002] Emp. L.R. 567, EAT . . . . *Digested*, 02/**1378**:
Applied, 06/1313, 07/1345
Byrzykowski v Poland (11562/05) [2006] Lloyd's Rep. Med. 505; [2006] Inquest
L.R. 125, ECHR . . . . *Digested*, 07/**2235**
Bysermaw Properties Ltd v Revenue and Customs Commissioners [2007] S.T.I. 2811,
Sp Comm

C v C (Abduction: Rights of Custody Abroad) [1989] 1 W.L.R. 654; [1989] 2 All E.R.
465; [1989] 1 F.L.R. 403; [1989] F.C.R. 197; [1989] Fam. Law 228; (1989) 153
J.P.N. 236; (1989) 133 S.J. 660; *Times*, December 19, 1988; *Independent*,
January 2, 1989, CA (Civ Div) . . . . *Digested*, 89/**2437**:
Applied, 90/3155, 91/2527, 93/2789: *Approved*, 07/1775:
Considered, 95/3431, 96/534, 97/402, 03/1503, 04/1470:
Distinguished, 94/3151, 95/5533, 02/1632: *Followed*, 94/5440, 98/2383,
98/5842
C v C (Maintenance Pending Suit: Legal Costs) [2006] 2 F.L.R. 1207; [2006] Fam.
Law 739, Fam Div . . . . *Approved*, 07/1707
C v C (Privilege) [2006] EWHC 336 (Fam); [2007] W.T.L.R. 753, Fam Div . . . . *Digested*, 07/**470**
C v D [2007] EWCA Civ 1282; [2007] 2 C.L.C. 930; 116 Con. L.R. 230, CA (Civ
Div); affirming [2007] EWHC 1541 (Comm); [2007] 2 All E.R. (Comm) 557;
[2007] 2 Lloyd's Rep. 367; [2007] 1 C.L.C. 1038, QBD (Comm) . . . . *Digested*, 07/**353**
C v Lancashire CC see Crane v Lancashire CC
C v M see C (Responsible Authority), Re
C v R. 2005 SCC 61; 21 B.H.R.C. 435, Sup Ct (Can)
C v S (Minors) (Abduction: Illegitimate Child) see J (A Minor) (Abduction: Custody
Rights), Re
C v Secretary of State for the Home Department see A v Secretary of State for the
Home Department
C v W; *sub nom* JPC v SLW [2007] EWHC 1349 (Fam); [2007] 2 F.L.R. 900; [2007]
3 F.C.R. 243; [2007] Fam. Law 886, Fam Div . . . . *Digested*, 07/**1745**
C Czarnikow Ltd v Koufos (The Heron II) see Koufos v C Czarnikow Ltd (The Heron II)
C Inc Plc v L [2001] 2 All E.R. (Comm) 446; [2001] 2 Lloyd's Rep. 459; [2001] C.L.C.
1054; (2001) 151 N.L.J. 535; *Times*, May 4, 2001, QBD (Comm) . . . . *Digested*, 01/**46**:
Applied, 02/450, 07/456
C Melchers & Co v Commission of the European Communities (101/80) see Musique
Diffusion Francaise SA v Commission of the European Communities (100/80)
C Plc v P; *sub nom* W v P [2007] EWCA Civ 493; [2007] 3 W.L.R. 437; [2007] 3 All
E.R. 1034; [2007] C.P. Rep. 35; *Times*, May 28, 2007, CA (Civ Div); affirming
[2006] EWHC 1226 (Ch); [2006] Ch. 549; [2006] 3 W.L.R. 273; [2006] 4 All
E.R. 311; (2006) 156 N.L.J. 988; *Times*, June 8, 2006, Ch D . . . . *Digested*, 07/**855**
C (A Child), Re see C (A Child) v XYZ CC
C (A Child), Re; *sub nom* P, Re; P v South Gloucestershire Council; C (Breach of
Human Rights: Damages), Re [2007] EWCA Civ 2; [2007] 1 F.L.R. 1957; [2007]
3 F.C.R. 288; [2007] H.R.L.R. 14; [2007] U.K.H.R.R. 602; [2007] Fam. Law
393; (2007) 104(3) L.S.G. 28; (2007) 151 S.J.L.B. 61; *Times*, February 1, 2007,
CA (Civ Div) . . . . *Digested*, 07/**1717**
C (A Child), Re [2007] EWCA Civ 866; [2007] Fam. Law 990; (2007) 151 S.J.L.B. 925, CA
(Civ Div)

C (A Child) v Davies (Unreported, January 29, 2007), CC (Warrington) [*Ex rel.* Horwich Farrelly Solicitors, National House, 36 St. Ann Street, Manchester] . . .   *Digested*, 07/**407**

C (A Child) v Humphreys (Unreported, May 26, 2006), CC (Edmonton) [*Ex rel.* Joanna Kerr, Barrister, Lamb Chambers, Temple, London] . . . .   *Digested*, 07/**3146**

C (A Child) v Northampton General Hospital NHS Trust (Unreported, February 15, 2005), QBD DR [*Ex rel.* Wilson Browne, Solicitors, PO Box No 8, 41 Meadow Road, Kettering, Northamptonshire] . . . .   *Digested*, 07/**3218**

C (A Child) v Retail Variations Group (Unreported, September 26, 2006), CC (Coventry) [*Ex rel.* Stephen Garner, Barrister, No 8 Chambers, Fountain Court, Steelhouse Lane, Birmingham] . . . .   *Digested*, 07/**3173**

C (A Child) v XYZ CC; *sub nom* C (A Child), Re [2007] EWCA Civ 1206; [2007] 3 F.C.R. 659; *Times*, December 5, 2007, CA (Civ Div) . . . .   *Digested*, 07/**1676**

C (A Child) (Child Abduction: Settlement), Re [2006] EWHC 1229 (Fam); [2006] 2 F.L.R. 797; [2007] 1 F.C.R. 649; [2006] Fam. Law 828, Fam Div . . . .   *Digested*, 07/**1746**

C (A Child) (Financial Provision), Re [2007] 2 F.L.R. 13; [2007] Fam. Law 303, Fam Div

C (A Minor) v DPP; *sub nom* Curry v DPP [1996] A.C. 1; [1995] 2 W.L.R. 383; [1995] 2 All E.R. 43; [1995] 2 Cr. App. R. 166; (1995) 159 J.P. 269; [1995] R.T.R. 261; [1995] 1 F.L.R. 933; [1995] Crim. L.R. 801; [1995] Fam. Law 400; (1995) 159 J.P.N. 248; (1995) 145 N.L.J. 416; *Times*, March 17, 1995; *Independent*, March 21, 1995, HL; affirming [1994] 3 W.L.R. 888; [1994] 3 All E.R. 190; [1995] 1 Cr. App. R. 118; (1994) 158 J.P. 389; [1994] R.T.R. 341; [1994] Crim. L.R. 523; (1994) 158 J.P.N. 319; (1994) 138 S.J.L.B. 91; *Times*, March 30, 1994; *Independent*, March 30, 1994; *Guardian*, April 4, 1994, QBD . . . .   *Digested*, 95/**1108**:
           Considered, 96/1398, 96/1400, 96/1404, 96/1641, 97/1197, 07/1023:
           Followed, 96/1399

C (A Minor) (Adoption: Parental Agreement: Contact), Re [1993] 2 F.L.R. 260; [1994] 2 F.C.R. 485; [1993] Fam. Law 612, CA (Civ Div) . . . .   *Digested*, 94/**3087**:
           Applied, 07/1681, 07/3906: *Considered*, 98/2365, 00/2430, 01/2529:
           Followed, 07/4550

C (A Minor) (Detention for Medical Treatment), Re see C (A Minor) (Medical Treatment: Court's Jurisdiction), Re

C (A Minor) (Interim Care Order: Residential Assessment), Re; *sub nom* C (A Minor) (Local Authority: Assessment), Re [1997] A.C. 489; [1996] 3 W.L.R. 1098; [1996] 4 All E.R. 871; [1997] 1 F.L.R. 1; [1997] 1 F.C.R. 149; [1997] Fam. Law 228; (1997) 161 J.P.N. 62; (1997) 94(1) L.S.G. 23; (1996) 146 N.L.J. 1777; (1997) 141 S.J.L.B. 12; *Times*, November 29, 1996; *Independent*, December 4, 1996, HL; reversing [1996] 2 F.L.R. 708; (1996) 93(39) L.S.G. 27; (1996) 140 S.J.L.B. 221; *Times*, October 3, 1996; *Independent*, November 11, 1996, CA (Civ Div) . . . .   *Digested*, 97/**365**:
           Applied, 98/2410, 07/1725, 07/1751: *Followed*, 98/2408, 99/2361, 04/1477

C (A Minor) (Leave to Seek Section 8 Orders), Re [1994] 1 F.L.R. 26; [1994] 1 F.C.R. 837; (1994) 158 J.P.N. 191, Fam Div . . . .   *Digested*, 95/**3549**:
           Disapproved, 07/1679

C (A Minor) (Local Authority: Assessment), Re see C (A Minor) (Interim Care Order: Residential Assessment), Re

C (A Minor) (Medical Treatment: Court's Jurisdiction), Re; *sub nom* C (A Minor) (Detention for Medical Treatment), Re [1997] 2 F.L.R. 180; [1997] 3 F.C.R. 49; [1997] Fam. Law 474; (1997) 94(13) L.S.G. 29; (1997) 141 S.J.L.B. 72; *Times*, March 21, 1997; *Independent*, March 20, 1997, Fam Div . . . .   *Digested*, 97/**428**:
           Considered, 07/3911

C (A Minor) (Secure Accommodation Order: Bail), Re [1994] 2 F.L.R. 922; [1994] 2 F.C.R. 1153; [1995] Fam. Law 19; (1994) 158 J.P.N. 732; *Times*, July 5, 1994; *Independent*, August 29, 1994, Fam Div . . . .   *Digested*, 95/**3566**:
           Applied, 96/544: *Considered*, 07/3940

C (Abduction: Settlement) (No.1), Re see Cannon v Cannon

C (Breach of Human Rights: Damages), Re see C (A Child), Re

C (Children) (Appointment of Guardian), Re see C (Children) (Contact: Moratorium: Change of Gender), Re

C (Children) (Contact: Moratorium: Change of Gender), Re; *sub nom* C (Children) (Appointment of Guardian), Re [2006] EWCA Civ 1765; [2007] 1 F.L.R. 1642; [2007] Fam. Law 396; (2006) 150 S.J.L.B. 1605, CA (Civ Div) . . . .   *Digested*, 07/**1769**:
           Considered, 07/1784

C (Responsible Authority), Re; *sub nom* C v M; AC v RM [2005] EWHC 2939 (Fam); [2006] 1 F.L.R. 919; [2006] Fam. Law 270, Fam Div . . . .   *Digested*, 07/**1791**

C&K Meats Ltd v Mid-Suffolk DC [2007] P.A.D. 63, Planning Inspector

C&W Berry Ltd v Armstrong-Moakes [2007] EWHC 2101 (QB); [2007] B.P.I.R. 1199, QBD

C-J (Section 91(14) Order), Re; *sub nom* DJ v MS [2006] EWHC 1491 (Fam); [2006] 2 F.L.R. 1213, Fam Div . . . .   *Digested*, 07/**1783**

CA Blackwell (Contractors) Ltd v Gerling Allegemeine Verischerungs-AG; *sub nom* CA Blackwell (Contractors) Ltd v Gerling General Insurance Co [2007] EWCA Civ 1450, CA (Civ Div); affirming [2007] EWHC 94 (Comm); [2007] Lloyd's Rep. I.R. 511, QBD (Comm) . . . .   *Digested*, 07/**2479**

CA Blackwell (Contractors) Ltd v Gerling General Insurance Co see CA Blackwell (Contractors) Ltd v Gerling Allegemeine Verischerungs-AG

Cable & Wireless Plc v IBM UK Ltd see Cable & Wireless Plc v IBM United Kingdom Ltd

Cable & Wireless Plc v IBM United Kingdom Ltd; *sub nom* Cable & Wireless Plc v IBM UK Ltd [2002] EWHC 2059 (Comm); [2002] 2 All E.R. (Comm) 1041; [2002] C.L.C. 1319; [2003] B.L.R. 89; [2002] Masons C.L.R. 58; (2002) 152 N.L.J. 1652, QBD (Comm) . . . . *Digested,* 03/**965**:
Applied, 07/528: *Considered,* 04/184

Cable & Wireless Plc v Muscat; *sub nom* Muscat v Cable & Wireless Plc [2006] EWCA Civ 220; [2006] I.C.R. 975; [2006] I.R.L.R. 354; (2006) 103(12) L.S.G. 30; (2006) 150 S.J.L.B. 362; *Times,* April 10, 2006; *Independent,* March 15, 2006, CA (Civ Div); affirming UKEAT/0661/04/LA, EAT . . . . *Digested,* 06/**1315**:
Considered, 07/3999: *Explained,* 07/1346

Cabletron Systems Ltd v Revenue Commissioners (C-463/98) [2001] E.C.R. I-3495, ECJ . . . . *Considered,* 07/1033

Cabour SA v Arnor (SOCO) Sarl (C230/96); *sub nom* Cabour SA v Automobiles Peugeot SA (C230/96) [1998] E.C.R. I-2055; [1998] 5 C.M.L.R 679, ECJ (6th Chamber) . . . . *Applied,* 07/626

Cabour SA v Automobiles Peugeot SA (C230/96) see Cabour SA v Arnor (SOCO) Sarl (C230/96)

Cadbury Schweppes Plc v Halifax Share Dealing Ltd [2006] EWHC 1184 (Ch); [2006] B.C.C. 707; [2007] 1 B.C.L.C. 497; (2006) 103(24) L.S.G. 29; (2006) 150 S.J.L.B. 739, Ch D

Cadbury Schweppes Plc v Inland Revenue Commissioners (C-196/04) [2007] Ch. 30; [2006] 3 W.L.R. 890; [2007] All E.R. (EC) 153; [2006] S.T.C. 1908; [2006] E.C.R. I-7995; [2007] 1 C.M.L.R. 2; [2006] C.E.C. 1026; 9 I.T.L. Rep. 89; [2006] S.T.I. 2201; *Times,* September 20, 2006, ECJ (Grand Chamber) . . . . *Digested,* 07/**4145**:
Applied, 07/1614, 07/1617

Cadbury Schweppes Plc v Williams (Inspector of Taxes) [2006] EWCA Civ 657; [2007] S.T.C. 106; [2006] B.T.C. 402; [2006] S.T.I. 1572; *Times,* July 19, 2006, CA (Civ Div); affirming [2005] EWHC 1610; [2006] S.T.C. 210; [2005] B.T.C. 436; [2005] S.T.I. 1313, Ch D; affirming [2005] S.T.C. (S.C.D.) 151; [2004] S.T.I. 2440, Sp Comm . . . . *Digested,* 06/**4300**

Cadman v Health and Safety Executive (C-17/05) [2007] All E.R. (EC) 1; [2006] E.C.R. I-9583; [2007] 1 C.M.L.R. 16; [2007] C.E.C. 318; [2006] I.C.R. 1623; [2006] I.R.L.R. 969; *Times,* October 6, 2006, ECJ . . . . *Digested,* 07/**1367**

Cadman (Setting of Minimum Term), Re; *sub nom* R. v Cadman (John Richard) [2006] EWHC 586 (QB); [2006] 3 All E.R. 1255; *Times,* May 26, 2006, QBD . . . . *Digested,* 06/**3752**:
Approved, 07/3692

Caesar v Trinidad and Tobago (12.147) 21 B.H.R.C. 305, IACHR . . . . *Digested,* 07/**2196**

Caffoor (Trustees of the Abdul Gaffoor Trust) v Income Tax Commissioner (Colombo); *sub nom* Gaffoor (Abdul) Trustees v Ceylon Commissioner of Income Tax; Trustees of Abdul Gaffoor Trust v Income Tax Commissioner, Colombo [1961] A.C. 584; [1961] 2 W.L.R. 794; [1961] 2 All E.R. 436; (1961) 40 A.T.C. 93; [1961] T.R. 97; (1961) 105 S.J. 383, PC (Cey) . . . . *Digested,* 61/**943**:
Applied, 01/5291: *Considered,* 66/5957, 70/158: *Distinguished,* 07/4001:
Followed, 88/247

Cahill v Timothy James & Partners Ltd see Bunney v Burns Anderson Plc

Caines (Setting of Minimum Term), Re; *sub nom* R. v Caines (Timothy Carlton); *joined case* R. v Roberts (David Wynne) (Application for Permission to Appeal) [2006] EWCA Crim 2915; [2007] 1 W.L.R. 1109; [2007] 2 All E.R. 584; *Times,* December 7, 2006, CA (Crim Div) . . . . *Digested,* 07/**3692**

Cairns v Visteon UK Ltd [2007] I.C.R. 616; [2007] I.R.L.R. 175, EAT . . . . *Digested,* 07/**1347**

Caister on Sea Joint Burial Committee, Re see Norfolk CC v Knights

Calabar Properties Ltd v Stitcher [1984] 1 W.L.R. 287; [1983] 3 All E.R. 759; (1984) 11 H.L.R. 20; (1984) 47 P. & C.R. 285; (1983) 268 E.G. 697; (1983) 80 L.S.G. 3163; (1983) 127 S.J. 785, CA (Civ Div) . . . . *Digested,* 84/**1892**:
Applied, 84/1962, 86/1843, 88/2019, 93/2462, 95/1575, 06/1016:
Considered, 87/2142, 89/2195, 90/2764, 07/2747: *Distinguished,* 89/2116,
99/3663

Calderdale MBC v Gorringe see Gorringe v Calderdale MBC

Calderdale MBC v S [2004] EWHC 2529 (Fam); [2005] 1 F.L.R. 751; [2005] Fam. Law 353; (2004) 101(47) L.S.G. 30; *Times,* November 18, 2004, Fam Div . . . . *Digested,* 05/**1629**:
Applied, 07/1725

Calfa, Re (C-348/96) see Criminal Proceedings against Calfa (C-348/96)

Callard v Pringle (2007) 151 S.J.L.B. 1128, CA (Civ Div)

Callery v Gray (No.1); *joined case* Russell v Pal Pak Corrugated Ltd (No.1) [2002] UKHL 28; [2002] 1 W.L.R. 2000; [2002] 3 All E.R. 417; [2002] 2 Costs L.R. 205; [2003] R.T.R. 4; [2003] Lloyd's Rep. I.R. 203; [2002] P.I.Q.R. P32; (2002) 152 N.L.J. 1031; *Times,* July 2, 2002; *Independent,* July 2, 2002; *Daily Telegraph,* July 11, 2002, HL; affirming [2001] EWCA Civ 1117; [2001] 1 W.L.R. 2112; [2001] 3 All E.R. 833; [2001] 2 Costs L.R. 163; [2001] Lloyd's Rep. I.R. 743; [2001] P.I.Q.R. P32; (2001) 151 N.L.J. 1129; *Times,* July 18, 2001; *Independent,* July 24, 2001; *Daily Telegraph,* July 24, 2001, CA (Civ Div); reversing in part [2002] R.T.R. 10, CC (Chester) [*Ex rel.* Amelans, Solicitors, Barlow House, 708-710 Wilmslow Road, Manchester] . . . . *Digested,* 02/**360**:
Applied, 02/322, 03/330, 03/332, 05/2704: *Cited,* 03/331:
Considered, 05/2703, 06/402, 06/2739, 06/2740, 06/2741, 06/2742,
07/389: *Distinguished,* 04/2552

Calltell Telecom Ltd v Revenue and Customs Commissioners [2007] B.V.C. 2544, V&DTr (Manchester)

Calor Gas Ltd v Homebase Ltd [2007] EWHC 1173 (Ch); (2007) 151 S.J.L.B. 742, Ch D

Calvelli v Italy (32967/96) (Unreported), ECHR . . . . *Applied,* 07/2235:
Considered, 05/34: *Distinguished,* 05/2113

Calvin v Carr [1980] A.C. 574; [1979] 2 W.L.R. 755; [1979] 2 All E.R. 440; (1979) 123 S.J. 112, PC (Aus) . . . . *Digested,* 79/**14**:
Applied, 80/315, 89/1500, 02/704, 05/720: *Considered,* 87/3162, 95/3252,
00/6628, 07/1143: *Followed,* 97/63: *Referred to,* 81/108

Calzaturificio Brennero SAS v Wendel GmbH Schuhproduktion International (C-258/ 83) [1984] E.C.R. 3971; [1986] 2 C.M.L.R. 59, ECJ (4th Chamber) . . . . *Digested,* 86/**1392**:
Considered, 07/457

Cambridge Gas Transport Corp v Official Committee of Unsecured Creditors of Navigator Holdings Plc; *sub nom* Cambridge Gas Transportation Corp v Official Committee of Unsecured Creditors of Navigator Holdings Plc [2006] UKPC 26; [2007] 1 A.C. 508; [2006] 3 W.L.R. 689; [2006] 3 All E.R. 829; [2006] 2 All E.R. (Comm) 695; [2006] B.C.C. 962; [2007] 2 B.C.L.C. 141, PC (IoM) . . . . . *Digested,* 06/**2360**:
Considered, 07/448

Cambridge Gas Transportation Corp v Official Committee of Unsecured Creditors of Navigator Holdings Plc see Cambridge Gas Transport Corp v Official Committee of Unsecured Creditors of Navigator Holdings Plc

Cambridgeshire CC v Kama [2006] EWHC 3148 (Admin); (2007) 171 J.P. 194; (2007) 171 J.P.N. 428, DC . . . . *Digested,* 07/**2814**

Camden LBC v Mortgage Times Group Ltd [2006] EWHC 1615 (Admin); [2007] Env. L.R. 4; [2007] J.P.L. 57; [2006] N.P.C. 78; *Times,* August 15, 2006, DC . . . . . . *Digested,* 06/**1452**

Camden Lock (London) Ltd v Camden LBC [2007] EWHC 495 (Admin); [2007] N.P.C. 32, QBD (Admin)

Camden Primary Care Trust v Atchoe [2007] EWCA Civ 714; (2007) 151 S.J.L.B. 672, CA (Civ Div); affirming UKEAT/0172/06/DM, EAT

Cameron v Network Rail Infrastructure Ltd (formerly Railtrack Plc) [2006] EWHC 1133 (QB); [2007] 1 W.L.R. 163; [2007] 3 All E.R. 241; [2006] H.R.L.R. 31; [2007] U.K.H.R.R. 245; [2006] P.I.Q.R. P28; (2006) 156 N.L.J. 881; (2006) 150 S.J.L.B. 739; *Times,* June 14, 2006, QBD . . . . *Digested,* 06/**2108**:
Applied, 07/2961

Camm v Camm (1983) 4 F.L.R. 577; (1983) 13 Fam. Law 112, CA (Civ Div) . . . . *Digested,* 83/**1100**:
Applied, 95/2340: *Cited,* 00/2519: *Considered,* 07/1830: *Followed,* 95/2341,
05/1688

Campaign for Nuclear Disarmament v Prime Minister of the United Kingdom see R. (on the application of Campaign for Nuclear Disarmament) v Prime Minister

Campbell v Frisbee [2002] EWCA Civ 1374; [2003] I.C.R. 141; [2003] E.M.L.R. 3; (2002) 146 S.J.L.B. 233, CA (Civ Div); reversing [2002] EWHC 328 (Ch); [2002] E.M.L.R. 31, Ch D . . . . *Digested,* 02/**724**:
Considered, 07/2510

Campbell v Meyer (Unreported, September 12, 2006), CC (Stockport) [*Ex rel.* David Calvert, Barrister, St James's Chambers, 68 Quay Street, Manchester] . . . . *Digested,* 07/**3129**

Campbell v MGN Ltd see Campbell v Mirror Group Newspapers Ltd

Campbell v MGN Ltd (Unreported, March 8, 2006) . . . . *Considered,* 07/389

Campbell v MGN Ltd (Costs) see Campbell v Mirror Group Newspapers Ltd (Costs)

Campbell v MGN Ltd (No.2) see Campbell v Mirror Group Newspapers Ltd (Costs)

Campbell v Mirror Group Newspapers Ltd; *sub nom* Campbell v MGN Ltd [2004] UKHL 22; [2004] 2 A.C. 457; [2004] 2 W.L.R. 1232; [2004] 2 All E.R. 995; [2004] E.M.L.R. 15; [2004] H.R.L.R. 24; [2004] U.K.H.R.R. 648; 16 B.H.R.C. 500; (2004) 101(21) L.S.G. 36; (2004) 154 N.L.J. 733; (2004) 148 S.J.L.B. 572; *Times*, May 7, 2004; *Independent*, May 11, 2004, HL; reversing [2002] EWCA Civ 1373; [2003] Q.B. 633; [2003] 2 W.L.R. 80; [2003] 1 All E.R. 224; [2003] E.M.L.R. 2; [2003] H.R.L.R. 2; (2002) 99(42) L.S.G. 38; (2002) 146 S.J.L.B. 234; *Times*, October 16, 2002; *Independent*, October 18, 2002, CA (Civ Div); reversing [2002] EWHC 499 (QB); [2002] E.M.L.R. 30; [2002] H.R.L.R. 28; (2002) 99(19) L.S.G. 28; (2002) 146 S.J.L.B. 107; *Times*, March 29, 2002; *Daily Telegraph*, April 11, 2002, QBD . . . . *Digested*, 04/**2673**:
Applied, 03/1217, 05/2121, 05/2812, 06/2853, 06/3400, 06/3400, 07/2189, 07/2247, 07/2510: *Considered*, 03/2923, 06/2440, 07/2250, 07/2887: *Distinguished*, 07/2383: *Followed*, 05/979, 06/456, 06/2096

Campbell v Mirror Group Newspapers Ltd (Costs); *sub nom* Campbell v MGN Ltd (Costs); Campbell v MGN Ltd (No.2) [2005] UKHL 61; [2005] 1 W.L.R. 3394; [2005] 4 All E.R. 793; [2006] 1 Costs L.R. 120; [2006] E.M.L.R. 1; [2006] H.R.L.R. 2; 21 B.H.R.C. 516; (2005) 102(42) L.S.G. 23; (2005) 155 N.L.J. 1633; *Times*, October 21, 2005, HL . . . . *Digested*, 06/**2739**:
Distinguished, 07/383

Campbell v South Northamptonshire DC [2004] EWCA Civ 409; [2004] 3 All E.R. 387; [2004] H.L.R. 43; (2004) 148 S.J.L.B. 476; *Times*, April 23, 2004; *Independent*, April 22, 2004, CA (Civ Div) . . . . *Digested*, 04/**3579**:
Applied, 07/3875: *Considered*, 07/3867

Campbell-James v Guardian Media Group Plc [2005] EWHC 893 (QB); [2005] E.M.L.R. 24, QBD . . . . *Digested*, 05/**972**:
Applied, 07/1074

Campina GmbH & Co v Hauptzollamt Frankfurt (Oder) (C-45/06) [2007] 2 C.M.L.R. 26, ECJ (5th Chamber) . . . . *Digested*, 07/**1578**

Campina Melkunie BV v Benelux-Merkenbureau (C-265/00) [2004] E.C.R. I-1699; [2005] 2 C.M.L.R. 9; [2005] C.E.C. 676; [2004] E.T.M.R. 58, ECJ (6th Chamber) . . . . *Digested*, 05/**2564**:
Applied, 07/2648

Cancellation of Registered Design for Chocolate Interior, Re [2007] E.C.D.R. 3, Sad Rej (PL)

Cannito v Fondiaria Sai SpA (C-296/04) see Manfredi v Lloyd Adriatico Assicurazioni SpA (C-295/04)

Cannon v Cannon; *sub nom* C (Abduction: Settlement) (No.1), Re [2004] EWCA Civ 1330; [2005] 1 W.L.R. 32; [2005] 1 F.L.R. 169; [2004] 3 F.C.R. 438; [2005] Fam. Law 8; (2004) 101(44) L.S.G. 31; *Times*, October 28, 2004, CA (Civ Div); reversing [2004] EWHC 1245 (Fam); [2005] 1 F.L.R. 127; [2004] Fam. Law 782, Fam Div . . . . *Digested*, 05/**1539**:
Applied, 07/1746: *Considered*, 07/1736, 07/1736: *Subsequent related litigation*, 05/1546

Canon Kabushiki Kaisha v Metro Goldwyn Mayer Inc (C-39/97) [1998] All E.R. (EC) 934; [1998] E.C.R. I-5507; [1999] 1 C.M.L.R. 77; [1998] C.E.C. 920; [1999] E.T.M.R. 1; [1999] F.S.R. 332; [1999] R.P.C. 117; *Times*, October 10, 1998, ECJ . *Digested*, 98/**3526**:
Applied, 00/3742, 00/3748, 01/3987, 01/4025, 01/4036, 05/2540, 05/2559, 06/2579, 07/2641, 07/2658, 07/2683: *Considered*, 99/3531, 00/3728, 03/2651, 06/2601, 07/2640: *Followed*, 00/3701, 01/4029, 06/2556: *Not followed*, 99/3544: *Referred to*, 01/4024

CANON/Searching image data (T643/00) [2007] E.P.O.R. 1, EPO (Technical Bd App)   *Followed*, 07/2591

Cantor Gaming Ltd v GameAccount Global Ltd [2007] EWHC 2381 (Ch); (2007) 104(39) L.S.G. 30, Ch D

Cantor Gaming Ltd v GameAccount Global Ltd [2007] EWHC 1914 (Ch); [2007] E.C.C. 24, Ch D . . . . *Digested*, 07/**2520**

Canty v Canty; *sub nom* Boyden v Canty [2007] EWCA Civ 241; [2007] B.P.I.R. 299, CA (Civ Div) . . . . *Digested*, 07/**377**

Canwest Mediaworks Inc v Canada 10 I.T.L. Rep. 551, CA (Can); reversing 2006 TCC 579; 9 I.T.L. Rep. 189, Tax Ct (Can)

Caparo Industries Plc v Dickman [1990] 2 A.C. 605; [1990] 2 W.L.R. 358; [1990] 1 All
E.R. 568; [1990] B.C.C. 164; [1990] B.C.L.C. 273; [1990] E.C.C. 313; [1955-
95] P.N.L.R. 523; (1990) 87(12) L.S.G. 42; (1990) 140 N.L.J. 248; (1990) 134
S.J. 494; *Times,* February 12, 1990; *Independent,* February 16, 1990; *Financial
Times,* February 13, 1990; *Guardian,* February 15, 1990; *Daily Telegraph,* February
15, 1990, HL; affirming [1989] Q.B. 653; [1989] 2 W.L.R. 316; [1989] 1 All
E.R. 798; (1989) 5 B.C.C. 105; [1989] B.C.L.C. 154; [1989] P.C.C. 125; (1988)
138 N.L.J. Rep. 289; (1989) 133 S.J. 221; *Times,* August 8, 1988; *Independent,*
August 10, 1988; *Financial Times,* August 5, 1988; *Daily Telegraph,* August 26,
1988, CA (Civ Div); reversing in part (1988) 4 B.C.C. 144; [1988] B.C.L.C. 387,
QBD . . . .   *Digested,* 90/**3266**:
        Applied, 90/3265, 90/3281, 91/2650, 91/2652, 92/1915, 92/2605, 93/2982,
        94/3365, 95/2906, 95/3668, 95/3686, 95/3701, 95/4519, 95/4730,
        96/4440, 96/4484, 97/331, 97/3778, 97/3816, 98/3997, 99/3956, 99/3963,
        99/3966, 99/4025, 99/5435, 00/679, 00/4201, 00/4246, 00/4249,
        00/6162, 00/6586, 01/1509, 01/1989, 01/4462, 01/4464, 01/4541, 04/658,
        04/2119, 04/2704, 05/2845, 05/2848, 05/2851, 05/2861, 05/2868,
        06/684, 06/2885, 06/4380, 07/1682: *Cited,* 00/4218, 07/1755:
        Considered, 91/35, 91/2657, 93/2044, 93/2958, 93/2983, 93/2994,
        93/2997, 95/3452, 95/3652, 95/3667, 98/3921, 98/3951, 98/3999,
        99/3953, 00/4205, 01/550, 03/5821, 04/386, 04/5103, 05/2891, 06/2880,
        06/5590, 06/5600, 07/2937, 07/2952: *Distinguished,* 91/2653:
        Followed, 93/5553, 97/424, 97/4087, 98/3930, 98/3987, 99/3959, 99/4015,
        00/4219, 00/4224, 01/4470: *Referred to,* 92/6078, 94/6386, 95/5841,
        99/4023

Cape Durasteel Ltd v Rosser and Russell Building Services Ltd 46 Con. L.R. 75, QBD .   *Digested,* 96/**1130**:
        Applied, 07/528

Cape Plc, Re [2006] EWHC 1316 (Ch); [2007] Bus. L.R. 109; [2006] 3 All E.R. 1222;
[2007] 2 B.C.L.C. 546; *Times,* July 5, 2006, Ch D (Companies Ct) . . . .   *Digested,* 06/**2362**
Capelloni and Aquilini v Pelkmans (C-119/84) [1985] E.C.R. 3147; [1986] 1 C.M.L.R.
388, ECJ (4th Chamber) . . . .   *Digested,* 86/**1379**:
        Considered, 07/457

Capewell v Customs and Excise Commissioners; *sub nom* Capewell v Revenue and
Customs Commissioners [2007] UKHL 2; [2007] 1 W.L.R. 386; [2007] 2 All
E.R. 370; [2007] 2 Costs L.R. 287; [2007] B.P.I.R. 678; (2007) 104(7) L.S.G.
26; (2007) 157 N.L.J. 223; (2007) 151 S.J.L.B. 198; *Times,* February 1, 2007, HL;
reversing [2005] EWCA Civ 964; [2006] C.P. Rep. 5; [2005] B.P.I.R. 1266;
Times, September 20, 2005, CA (Civ Div) . . . .   *Digested,* 07/**1014**
Capewell v Revenue and Customs Commissioners see Capewell v Customs and
Excise Commissioners
Capita Trust Co (Channel Islands) Ltd v Chatham Maritime J3 Developments Ltd [2006]
EWHC 2596 (Ch); [2007] L. & T.R. 2; (2006) 103(36) L.S.G. 36, Ch D . . . . .   *Digested,* 07/**2721**
Capital Bank AD v Bulgaria (49429/99) (2007) 44 E.H.R.R. 48, ECHR. . . . .   *Digested,* 07/**2214**
Capital Cabs Ltd v Blackmore see Richardson v Blackmore
Capital Structures Plc v Time & Tide Construction Ltd [2006] EWHC 591 (TCC);
[2006] B.L.R. 226; [2006] C.I.L.L. 2345, QBD (TCC) . . . .   *Digested,* 07/**742**
Cappellini's Patent Application (No.GB2381884A); *joined case* Bloomberg LLP's Patent
Application (No.GB2395941A) [2007] EWHC 476 (Pat); [2007] Info. T.L.R.
97; [2007] F.S.R. 26; (2007) 30(5) I.P.D. 30034, Ch D (Patents Ct) . . . .   *Digested,* 07/**2627**
Carbide/Graphite Group Inc v Commission of the European Communities (T252/01)
see Tokai Carbon Co Ltd v Commission of the European Communities (T-236/
01)
Carbotermo SpA v Comune di Busto Arsizio (C-340/04) [2006] E.C.R. I-4137;
[2006] 3 C.M.L.R. 7, ECJ (1st Chamber). . . . .   *Digested,* 07/**3328**
Card Protection Plan Ltd v Customs and Excise Commissioners [2001] UKHL 4;
[2002] 1 A.C. 202; [2001] 2 W.L.R. 329; [2001] 2 All E.R. 143; [2001] 1 All E.R.
(Comm) 438; [2001] S.T.C. 174; [2001] 2 C.M.L.R. 2; [2001] B.T.C. 5083;
[2001] B.V.C. 158; [2001] S.T.I. 151; (2001) 98(9) L.S.G. 41; (2001) 145 S.J.L.B.
60; *Times,* February 6, 2001, HL; reversing [1994] S.T.C. 199; [1994] 1
C.M.L.R. 756, CA (Civ Div); affirming [1992] S.T.C. 797, QBD . . . .   *Digested,* 01/**5600**:
        Applied, 94/4602, 04/3992, 06/4449: *Considered,* 98/4961, 07/5568:
        Preliminary ruling given, 99/4972: *Referred to,* 95/5039, 95/5093

Card Protection Plan Ltd v Customs and Excise Commissioners (C-349/96) [1999] 2
A.C. 601; [1999] 3 W.L.R. 203; [1999] All E.R. (E.C.) 339; [1999] S.T.C. 270;
[1999] E.C.R. I-973; [1999] 2 C.M.L.R. 743; [1999] C.E.C. 133; [1999] B.T.C.
5121; [1999] B.V.C. 155; *Times,* March 18, 1999, ECJ (6th Chamber) . . . .   *Digested,* 99/**4972**:
        Applied, 00/5343, 00/5346, 00/5369, 02/4745, 02/4750, 02/4782,
        03/4538, 03/4545, 03/4576, 03/4580, 04/3968, 04/4009, 04/4354,
        05/4355, 05/4397, 06/4449, 06/4476, 06/4514, 07/4341, 07/4342:
        Considered, 01/5599, 03/4537, 03/4558, 04/3977, 04/4018, 05/4419,
        06/4438: *Distinguished,* 00/5294, 01/5564, 05/4394, 06/4490:
        Followed, 99/4983, 00/5344, 04/3981, 06/4501: *Referred to,* 04/4020:
        Subsequent proceedings, 01/5600

Cardiff CC v National Assembly for Wales [2006] EWHC 1412 (Admin); [2007] 1 P. &
  C.R. 9; [2007] J.P.L. 60; [2006] A.C.D. 99, QBD (Admin) . . . .   *Digested*, 07/**3267**
Cardigan v Curzon-Howe (1885) L.R. 30 Ch. D. 531, Ch D . . . .   *Considered*, 07/**4249**
Cardile v LED Builders Pty Ltd [1999] HCA 18; 198 C.L.R. 380, HC (Aus) . . . .   *Considered*, 07/**456**
Carillion Construction Ltd v Devonport Royal Dockyard Ltd [2005] EWCA Civ 1358;
  [2006] B.L.R. 15; 104 Con. L.R. 1; (2005) 102(47) L.S.G. 26; *Times*, November
  24, 2005, CA (Civ Div); affirming [2005] EWHC 778 (TCC); [2005] B.L.R.
  310; 102 Con. L.R. 167, QBD (TCC) . . . .   *Digested*, 06/**670**:
                                                  Applied, 07/**395**: *Followed*, 06/**666**
Carleton (Earl of Malmesbury) v Strutt & Parker (A Partnership) [2007] EWHC 2199
  (QB); [2007] 42 E.G. 294 (C.S.), QBD
Carleton (Earl of Malmesbury) v Strutt & Parker (A Partnership) [2007] EWHC 999
  (QB); 116 Con. L.R. 38; [2007] P.N.L.R. 29; [2007] 21 E.G. 130 (C.S.), QBD . .   *Digested*, 07/**2947**
Carltona Ltd v Commissioners of Works [1943] 2 All E.R. 560, CA . . . .   *Applied*, 47-51/**1530**,
               47-51/**8203**, 54/**46**, 61/**7385**, 68/**3426**, 69/**276**, 76/**279**, 96/**7374**, 02/**2593**,
               02/**3761**, 03/**4042**, 07/**717**: *Cited*, 07/**2811**: *Considered*, 83/**2708**, 87/**4112**,
               91/**1981**, 93/**1662**, 00/**5396**, 07/**5436**: *Distinguished*, 97/**4123**:
                                                  Followed, 90/**4713**, 96/**2961**
Carmarthenshire CC v Edward Ware Homes (Burry Port) Ltd [2007] P.A.D. 71,
  Planning Inspector
Carmarthenshire CC v Evans [2007] P.A.D. 68, Planning Inspector
Carmel Southend Ltd v Strachan & Henshaw Ltd [2007] EWHC 1289 (TCC); [2007]
  35 E.G. 136; [2007] 24 E.G. 168 (C.S.), QBD (TCC) . . . .   *Digested*, 07/**2730**
Carmichael v National Power Plc [1999] 1 W.L.R. 2042; [1999] 4 All E.R. 897; [1999]
  I.C.R. 1226; [2000] I.R.L.R. 43; (1999) 96(46) L.S.G. 38; (1999) 143 S.J.L.B.
  281; *Times*, November 23, 1999; *Independent*, November 25, 1999, HL; reversing
  [1998] I.C.R. 1167; [1998] I.R.L.R. 301; (1998) 95(19) L.S.G. 23; (1998) 142
  S.J.L.B. 140; *Times*, April 2, 1998, CA (Civ Div) . . . .   *Digested*, 99/**2002**:
                Applied, 03/**1280**, 05/**667**, 05/**1213**, 06/**1286**: *Considered*, 01/**2262**:
                                  Distinguished, 06/**1312**, 07/**1396**: *Followed*, 03/**1257**
Carnegie v Drury; *sub nom* Drury v BBC [2007] EWCA Civ 497; [2007] E.M.L.R. 24;
  Times, June 11, 2007, CA (Civ Div) . . . .   *Digested*, 07/**518**
Carpenter (Setting of Minimum Term), Re; *sub nom* R. v Carpenter (Agnes Jane) [2006]
  EWHC 3122 (QB); [2007] M.H.L.R. 32, QBD . . . .   *Digested*, 07/**3680**
Carphone Warehouse UK Ltd v Malekout [2006] EWCA Civ 767; [2007] H.L.R. 3;
  [2006] 2 E.G.L.R. 35; [2006] 31 E.G. 90; [2006] 25 E.G. 209 (C.S.); (2006)
  150 S.J.L.B. 812; [2006] N.P.C. 68; *Times*, June 28, 2006, CA (Civ Div) . . . . .   *Digested*, 06/**2723**
Carr v Isard [2007] W.T.L.R. 409, Ch D . . . .   *Digested*, 07/**3963**
Carrick DC v Micclechester [2007] P.A.D. 15, Planning Inspector
Carroll v Mertz (2007-08) 10 I.T.E.L.R. 643, US Court
Carruthers v South Norfolk DC; *sub nom* Curruthers v South Norfolk DC [2006]
  EWHC 478 (Admin); [2007] R.V.R. 203; [2006] N.P.C. 33, QBD (Admin) . . . . . .   *Digested*, 07/**52**
Carson v Metroline Travel (Unreported, February 15, 2007), CC (Brentford) [*Ex rel.*
  Hannah Sherlock, Barrister, 4 King's Bench Walk, Temple, London] . . . .   *Digested*, 07/**3152**
Carson v Secretary of State for Work and Pensions see R. (on the application of
  Carson) v Secretary of State for Work and Pensions
Carter v Ahsan (No.1); *sub nom* Watt (formerly Carter) v Ahsan; Labour Party v Ahsan;
  Ashan v Watt (formerly Carter) [2007] UKHL 51; (2007) 157 N.L.J. 1694; *Times*,
  November 27, 2007, HL; reversing [2005] EWCA Civ 990; [2005] I.C.R. 1817;
  Times, August 23, 2005, CA (Civ Div); reversing [2004] I.C.R. 938, EAT . . . . .   *Digested*, 05/**429**
Carter v Basildon and Thurrock University Hospitals NHS Foundation Trust [2007]
  EWHC 1882 (QB); [2007] LS Law Medical 657, QBD . . . .   *Digested*, 07/**2927**
Carter v DPP [2006] EWHC 3328 (Admin); [2007] R.T.R. 22, DC . . . .   *Digested*, 07/**844**
Carter Lauren Construction Ltd v Revenue and Customs Commissioners [2007] S.T.C.
  (S.C.D.) 482; [2007] S.T.I. 1329, Sp Comm . . . .   *Digested*, 07/**4001**
Cartwright v Derbyshire CC (Unreported, July 20, 2006), CC (Mansfield) [*Ex rel.*
  Browne Jacobson LLP, Solicitors, 44 Castlegate, Nottingham] . . . .   *Digested*, 07/**2870**
Cartwright v Superintendent of HM Prison [2004] UKPC 10; [2004] 1 W.L.R. 902;
  (2004) 148 S.J.L.B. 232, PC (Bah) . . . .   *Digested*, 04/**1437**:
                            Applied, 05/**1488**: *Considered*, 05/**1486**: *Overruled*, 07/**1672**
Carver v Duncan (Inspector of Taxes); *joined case* Bosanquet v Allen [1985] A.C.
  1082; [1985] 2 W.L.R. 1010; [1985] 2 All E.R. 645; [1985] S.T.C. 356; 59 T.C.
  125; (1985) 129 S.J. 381, HL; affirming [1984] 3 W.L.R. 1209; [1984] S.T.C.
  556; (1984) 81 L.S.G. 2624; (1984) 128 S.J. 704, CA (Civ Div); reversing
  [1983] 1 W.L.R. 494; [1983] S.T.C. 310, Ch D . . . .   *Digested*, 85/**3132**:
                                                  Applied, 04/**2766**, 07/**4241**
Cascades SA v Commission of the European Communities (T-308/94) [1998] E.C.R.
  II-925, CFI . . . .   *Considered*, 07/**1589**
Casey v Cartwright [2006] EWCA Civ 1280; [2007] 2 All E.R. 78; [2007] C.P. Rep. 3;
  [2007] R.T.R. 18; [2007] P.I.Q.R. P6; (2006) 103(40) L.S.G. 34; (2006) 150
  S.J.L.B. 1331; *Times*, October 10, 2006; *Independent*, October 11, 2006, CA (Civ
  Div) . . . . *Digested*, 07/**2954**
Casio Keisanki Kabushiki Kaisha (Casio Computer Co Ltd), Re (R 1421/2006-3) [2007]
  E.C.D.R. 13, OHIM (3rd Bd App)

Casting Book Ltd (t/a Independent Posters) v Office of Fair Trading [2006] CAT 35;
　[2007] Comp. A.R. 446, CAT. . . . . 　*Digested*, 07/**620**
Castle Cement Ltd v Environment Agency; *sub nom* R. (on the application of Castle
　Cement Ltd) v Environment Agency; R. v Environment Agency Ex p. Castle
　Cement Ltd [2001] EWHC Admin 224; [2001] 2 C.M.L.R. 19; [2001] Env. L.R.
　46; [2002] J.P.L. 43; (2001) 98(14) L.S.G. 42; [2001] N.P.C. 64, QBD
　(Admin) . . . . 　*Digested*, 02/**1520**:
　　　　　　　　　　　　　　　　　　　　　　　　　　　　　　　　　Considered, 07/1518
Castle House Investments Ltd (In Voluntary Liquidation) v Bradford MDC [2007] R.V.R.
　277, Lands Tr
Catalyst Recycling Ltd v Nickelhutte AUE GmbH A2/2007/1498, CA (Civ Div);
　affirming [2007] EWHC 866 (QB), QBD. . . . . 　*Digested*, 07/**790**
Catholic Care (Diocese of Leeds) v Y (Kevin Raymond); *sub nom* Y (Kevin Raymond) v
　Catholic Care (Diocese of Leeds); Y (Kevin Raymond) v South Tyneside MBC;
　joined case Home Office v Y (Kevin Raymond) [2006] EWCA Civ 1534; [2007]
　Q.B. 932; [2007] 2 W.L.R. 1192; [2007] 1 All E.R. 895; [2007] P.I.Q.R. P15;
　(2006) 103(46) L.S.G. 33; (2006) 156 N.L.J. 1802; (2006) 150 S.J.L.B. 1531;
　Times, November 22, 2006, CA (Civ Div) . . . . 　*Digested*, 07/**473**:
　　　　　　　　　　　　　　　　　　　　　　　　　　　　　　　　　Applied, 07/483
Catlin Syndicate Ltd v Adams Land & Cattle Co [2006] EWHC 2065 (Comm); [2006]
　2 C.L.C. 425; [2007] Lloyd's Rep. I.R. 96, QBD (Comm) . . . . 　*Digested*, 07/**673**
Cattley v Pollard [2006] EWHC 3130 (Ch); [2007] Ch. 353; [2007] 3 W.L.R. 317;
　[2007] 2 All E.R. 1086; [2007] P.N.L.R. 19; [2007] W.T.L.R. 245; (2007-08) 10
　I.T.E.L.R. 1; *Times*, January 23, 2007, Ch D . . . . 　*Digested*, 07/**476**
Cavanagh v Hussain (Unreported, April 16, 2007), CC (Oldham) [*Ex rel.* Heather
　Belbin, Barrister, Oriel Chambers, 14 Water Street, Liverpool] . . . . 　*Digested*, 07/**3111**
Cave v Robinson Jarvis & Rolf; *sub nom* Robinson Jarvis & Rolf v Cave [2002] UKHL
　18; [2003] 1 A.C. 384; [2002] 2 W.L.R. 1107; [2002] 2 All E.R. 641; [2003] 1
　C.L.C. 101; 81 Con. L.R. 25; [2002] P.N.L.R. 25; [2002] 19 E.G. 146 (C.S.);
　(2002) 99(20) L.S.G. 32; (2002) 152 N.L.J. 671; (2002) 146 S.J.L.B. 109;
　Times, May 7, 2002; *Independent*, April 30, 2002, HL; reversing [2001] EWCA
　Civ 245; [2002] 1 W.L.R. 581; [2001] C.P. Rep. 66; 78 Con. L.R. 1; [2001]
　Lloyd's Rep. P.N. 290; [2001] P.N.L.R. 23; (2001) 17 Const. L.J. 262; [2001] 9
　E.G. 229 (C.S.); [2001] N.P.C. 36; *Independent*, April 9, 2001, CA (Civ Div) . . . 　*Digested*, 02/**466**:
　　　　　　Applied, 04/380, 04/381, 05/461, 07/471: *Considered*, 04/377, 07/479
Cavendish v Relay Roads Ltd see Charlesworth v Relay Roads Ltd (No.2)
Cawsand Fort Management Co Ltd v Stafford [2007] EWCA Civ 1187; [2007] 48 E.G.
　145 (C.S.); [2007] N.P.C. 124, CA (Civ Div); affirming [2007] L. & T.R. 13;
　[2007] 5 E.G. 308, Lands Tr
Cawthorne v Hamdan [2007] EWCA Civ 6; [2007] Ch. 187; [2007] 2 W.L.R. 185;
　[2007] 2 All E.R. 116; [2007] 2 P. & C.R. 1; [2007] L. & T.R. 14; [2007] 11 E.G.
　162; [2007] 5 E.G. 306 (C.S.); (2007) 104(6) L.S.G. 31; [2007] N.P.C. 8, CA
　(Civ Div); affirming [2006] 3 E.G.L.R. 183, Lands Tr. . . . . 　*Digested*, 07/**3369**
CB and JB (Minors) (Care Proceedings: Guidelines), Re see B (Minors) (Care Proceedings:
　Practice), Re
CC v AB [2006] EWHC 3083 (QB); [2007] E.M.L.R. 11; [2007] 2 F.L.R. 301; [2007]
　Fam. Law 591, QBD . . . . 　*Digested*, 07/**2189**
Ce.MON v Dano-Invest [2007] E.C.C. 10, App (Brussels) . . . . 　*Digested*, 07/**636**
Celesio AG v Office of Fair Trading (Costs) [2006] CAT 20; [2007] Comp. A.R. 269,
　CAT. . . . . 　*Digested*, 07/**627**
Celine Sarl v Celine SA (C-17/06) [2007] E.T.M.R. 80, ECJ (Grand Chamber)
CELLTECH PHARMA EUROPE/Pharmaceutical compositions (T265/03) [2007] E.P.O.R.
　41, EPO (Technical Bd App) . . . . 　*Digested*, 07/**2551**
Cellular Solutions (T Wells) Ltd v Revenue and Customs Commissioners [2007] S.T.I.
　383, V&D Tr (London)
Cemex UK Cement Ltd v Department for the Environment, Food and Rural Affairs
　[2006] EWHC 3207 (Admin); [2007] Env. L.R. 21, QBD (Admin) . . . . 　*Digested*, 07/**1508**
Cenbauer v Croatia (73786/01) (2007) 44 E.H.R.R. 49, ECHR . . . . 　*Digested*, 07/**2198**
Cenir v Entry Clearance Officer [2003] EWCA Civ 572, CA (Civ Div) . . . . 　*Considered*, 07/2325
Centaur Clothes Group Ltd v Walker (Inspector of Taxes) see Walker (Inspector of Taxes)
　v Centaur Clothes Group Ltd
Center Parcs (UK) Group Plc v Revenue and Customs Commissioners [2007] S.T.I. 375,
　V&D Tr (Manchester)
Central Broadcasting Services Ltd v Attorney General of Trinidad and Tobago [2006]
　UKPC 35; [2006] 1 W.L.R. 2891; 21 B.H.R.C. 577, PC (Trin) . . . . 　*Digested*, 06/**2844**
Central Examining Court, Madrid v Sander see R. (on the application of United States)
　v Bow Street Magistrates Court
Central London Property Trust Ltd v High Trees House Ltd [1947] K.B. 130 . . . . 　*Considered*, 07/2746
Centralan Property Ltd v Customs and Excise Commissioners (C-63/04) [2006] S.T.C.
　1542; [2005] E.C.R. I-11087; [2007] B.T.C. 5430; [2007] B.V.C. 341; [2006]
　S.T.I. 158; [2006] 3 E.G. 120 (C.S.), ECJ (3rd Chamber). . . . . 　*Digested*, 07/**4305**
Centre Public d'Aide Sociale, Courcelles v Lebon (C-316/85) [1987] E.C.R. 2811;
　[1989] 1 C.M.L.R. 337; *Times*, September 9, 1987, ECJ . . . . 　*Digested*, 90/**2209**:
　　　　　　Considered, 95/4617, 07/1652: *Followed*, 97/4605: *Not followed*, 04/3597

Centre Reinsurance International Co v Curzon Insurance Ltd; *joined cases* Centre
　　Reinsurance International Co v Freakley; Freakley v Centre Reinsurance
　　International Co [2006] UKHL 45; [2007] Bus. L.R. 284; [2006] 1 W.L.R.
　　2863; [2006] 4 All E.R. 1153; [2006] 2 All E.R. (Comm) 943; [2006] B.C.C.
　　971; [2007] 1 B.C.L.C. 85; [2006] B.P.I.R. 1405; [2007] Lloyd's Rep. I.R. 32;
　　(2006) 103(41) L.S.G. 35; (2006) 156 N.L.J. 1613; (2006) 150 S.J.L.B. 1395;
　　Times, October 16, 2006, HL; reversing [2005] EWCA Civ 115; [2005] 2 All E.R.
　　(Comm) 65; [2006] 1 B.C.L.C. 225; [2005] 1 C.L.C. 78; [2006] B.P.I.R. 1122;
　　[2005] Lloyd's Rep. I.R. 303; *Times*, February 28, 2005, CA (Civ Div); affirming
　　in part [2004] EWHC 200 (Ch); [2004] 2 All E.R. (Comm) 28; [2006] 1
　　B.C.L.C. 187; [2004] 2 C.L.C. 586; [2004] Lloyd's Rep. I.R. 622; (2004)
　　101 (11) L.S.G. 34; *Times*, February 27, 2004, Ch D . . . .   *Digested*, 06/**2318**
Centre Reinsurance International Co v Freakley see Centre Reinsurance International Co
　　v Curzon Insurance Ltd
Centro Equestre da Leziria Grande Lda v Bundesamt fur Finanzen (C-345/04) [2007]
　　All E.R. (EC) 680; [2007] 2 C.M.L.R. 18; [2007] C.E.C. 564; [2007] S.T.I. 343,
　　ECJ (3rd Chamber) . . . .   *Digested*, 07/**1633**
Centros Ltd v Erhvervs- og Selskabsstyrelsen (C-212/97) [2000] Ch. 446; [2000] 2
　　W.L.R. 1048; [2000] All E.R. (EC) 481; [1999] E.C.R. I-1459; [1999] B.C.C.
　　983; [2000] 2 B.C.L.C. 68; [1999] 2 C.M.L.R. 551; [2000] C.E.C. 290, ECJ . .   *Digested*, 99/**2253**:
　　　　　　　　　　　　　　　　　　　　Applied, 01/2498, 07/4145: *Followed*, 06/1569
Cereal Investments Co (CIC) SA v ED&F Man Sugar Ltd [2007] EWHC 2843 (Comm);
　　[2007] 2 C.L.C. 959, QBD (Comm)
Ceredigion CC v Jones; *sub nom* R. (on the application of Jones) v Ceredigion CC
　　(No.2); R. (on the application of Jones) v Ceredigion CC [2007] UKHL 24;
　　[2007] 1 W.L.R. 1400; [2007] 3 All E.R. 781; (2007) 104(23) L.S.G. 32; (2007)
　　157 N.L.J. 778; (2007) 151 S.J.L.B. 706; *Times*, May 24, 2007, HL; affirming
　　[2005] EWCA Civ 986; [2005] 1 W.L.R. 3626; [2006] 1 All E.R. 138; [2005]
　　C.P. Rep. 48; [2005] E.L.R. 565; [2006] A.C.D. 3; *Times*, September 16, 2005,
　　CA (Civ Div) . . . .   *Digested*, 07/**469**
Cetelem SA v Roust Holdings Ltd [2005] EWCA Civ 618; [2005] 1 W.L.R. 3555;
　　[2005] 4 All E.R. 52; [2005] 2 All E.R. (Comm) 203; [2005] 2 Lloyd's Rep.
　　494; [2005] 1 C.L.C. 821; *Times*, June 13, 2005, CA (Civ Div); affirming [2004]
　　EWHC 3175 (QB), QBD . . . .   *Digested*, 05/**325**:
　　　　　　　　　　　　　　　　　　　Considered, 07/233: *Distinguished*, 07/249
CFA Institute v Chartered Insurance Institute; *sub nom* CFA Institute's Trade Mark
　　Application [2007] E.T.M.R. 76, TMR
CFA Institute's Trade Mark Application see CFA Institute v Chartered Insurance Institute
CFPH LLC's Patent Applications (Nos.0226884.3 and 0419317.3) [2005] EWHC 1589
　　(Pat); [2006] R.P.C. 5; (2005) 28(9) I.P.D. 28070, Ch D (Patents Ct) . . . .   *Digested*, 06/**2528**:
　　　　　　　　　　　　　　　　　　　Applied, 06/2468, 07/2632: *Considered*, 06/2535
CFW Architects v Cowlin Construction Ltd [2006] EWHC 6 (TCC); 105 Con. L.R. 116;
　　[2006] C.I.L.L. 2335, QBD (TCC) . . . .   *Digested*, 07/**750**
CGU International Insurance Plc v AstraZeneca Insurance Co Ltd (Permission to
　　Appeal); *sub nom* AstraZeneca Insurance Co Ltd v CGU International Insurance
　　Plc (Permission to Appeal) [2006] EWCA Civ 1340; [2007] Bus. L.R. 162;
　　[2007] 1 All E.R. (Comm) 501; [2007] 1 Lloyd's Rep. 142; [2007] C.P. Rep. 4;
　　[2006] 2 C.L.C. 441; [2006] H.R.L.R. 43; *Times*, November 3, 2006;
　　Independent, October 24, 2006, CA (Civ Div). . . . .   *Digested*, 06/**204**:
　　　　　　　　　　　　　　　　　　　　　　　　　　　　Applied, 07/240
Chacon Navas v Eurest Colectividades SA (C-13/05) [2007] All E.R. (EC) 59; [2006]
　　E.C.R. I-6467; [2006] 3 C.M.L.R. 40; [2007] I.C.R. 1; [2006] I.R.L.R. 706;
　　Times, August 9, 2006, ECJ . . . .   *Digested*, 07/**1333**:
　　　　　　　　　　　　　　　Applied, 07/1332: *Considered*, 07/1386, 07/1420
Chadwick v Beardsmore (Unreported, May 24, 2006), CC (Liverpool) [*Ex rel.* Patrick
　　McCarthy, National House, 36 St Ann's Street, Manchester] . . . .   *Digested*, 07/**342**
Chahal v United Kingdom (22414/93) (1997) 23 E.H.R.R. 413; 1 B.H.R.C. 405; *Times*,
　　November 28, 1996; *Independent*, November 20, 1996, ECHR (1995) 20
　　E.H.R.R. CD19, Eur Comm HR . . . .   *Digested*, 96/**3130**:
　　　　　　　　　　　　Applied, 97/2764, 05/2167, 07/2230: *Considered*, 03/2256:
　　　　　　　　　　　　　　　　　　　　　　Followed, 98/3069, 04/2034
Chambelin Solicitors v Emokpae see Wong v Igen Ltd (formerly Leeds Careers
　　Guidance)
Chamberlain v Boodle & King [1982] 1 W.L.R. 1443; [1982] 3 All E.R. 188; (1981) 125
　　S.J. 257; *Times*, April 1, 1981, CA (Civ Div); affirming (1980) 124 S.J. 186, QBD.   *Digested*, 82/**3080**:
　　　　　　　　　　　　　　　　　　　　　　Applied, 07/2460: *Cited*, 00/451
Chamberlin Solicitors v Emokpae see Emokpae v Chamberlin Solicitors
Chambers v Chambers [2007] EWCA Civ 1165; (2007) 151 S.J.L.B. 1299, CA (Civ
　　Div)
Chambers v Southern Domestic Electrical Services Ltd see Anderton v Clwyd CC
Chambers v Starkings see Sage v Double A Hydraulics Ltd
Chandi (Setting of Minimum Term), Re see Jones (Setting of Minimum Term), Re
Chandler v Secretary of State for Communities and Local Government [2007] EWHC
　　1000 (Admin); [2007] 2 P. & C.R. 24; [2007] N.P.C. 59, QBD (Admin) . . . . . .   *Digested*, 07/**3266**

Chandler v Secretary of State for Work and Pensions [2007] EWCA Civ 1211; (2007)
104(48) L.S.G. 22; (2007) 151 S.J.L.B. 1564, CA (Civ Div)
Chanel Ltd v FW Woolworth & Co Ltd [1981] 1 W.L.R. 485; [1981] 1 All E.R. 745;
[1981] F.S.R. 196; (1981) 125 S.J. 202; *Times*, November 14, 1980, CA (Civ
Div) . . . . *Digested*, 81/**2126**:
Applied, 92/576, 93/587: *Considered*, 93/3211, 94/3675:
Distinguished, 87/3031, 97/2721, 07/437: *Followed*, 97/3904:
Referred to, 95/4240, 99/435

Channel Tunnel Group Ltd v Balfour Beatty Construction Ltd; *joined case* France
Manche SA v Balfour Beatty Construction Ltd [1993] A.C. 334; [1993] 2
W.L.R. 262; [1993] 1 All E.R. 664; [1993] 1 Lloyd's Rep. 291; 61 B.L.R. 1; 32
Con. L.R. 1; [1993] I.L.Pr. 607; (1993) 137 S.J.L.B. 36; [1993] N.P.C. 8; *Times*,
January 25, 1993, HL; affirming [1992] Q.B. 656; [1992] 2 W.L.R. 741; [1992] 2
All E.R. 609; [1992] 2 Lloyd's Rep. 7; 56 B.L.R. 23; (1992) 8 Const. L.J. 150;
(1992) 136 S.J.L.B. 54; [1992] N.P.C. 7; *Times*, January 23, 1992; *Financial
Times*, January 29, 1992, CA (Civ Div) . . . . *Digested*, 93/**151**:
Applied, 95/4180, 97/939, 07/528: *Considered*, 94/478, 95/4184, 97/271,
01/46, 06/446, 06/759: *Distinguished*, 99/1639

Chaoulli v Attorney General of Quebec 2005 SCC 35; 21 B.H.R.C. 93, Sup Ct (Can)
Chapman v Simon [1994] I.R.L.R. 124, CA (Civ Div) . . . . *Digested*, 94/**1967**:
Applied, 98/2183, 03/1297, 03/1300: *Considered*, 01/2320, 07/1404:
Distinguished, 00/2236

Chapman v United Kingdom (27238/95) (2001) 33 E.H.R.R. 18; 10 B.H.R.C. 48;
Times, January 30, 2001, ECHR (1998) 25 E.H.R.R. CD64, Eur Comm HR . . . . *Digested*, 01/**4744**:
Applied, 02/3684, 03/3380, 03/3485, 05/3285, 06/2823:
Considered, 02/3686, 03/3424, 04/1376, 04/3040, 04/3095, 06/3331,
07/2137, 07/2879, 07/3293: *Distinguished*, 02/3069, 04/1992:
Followed, 06/3381

Chapter Group Plc v London Regional Transport [2006] R.V.R. 242, Lands Tr. . . . . *Digested*, 07/**3384**:
Considered, 07/3228

Charalambous v Cyprus (43151/04) [2007] 2 F.C.R. 661; [2007] Fam. Law 1067,
ECHR . . . . *Digested*, 07/**2221**
Charalambous v Earle see Earle v Charalambous (Addendum to Judgment)
CHARBONNAGES/Venturi (T204/83) [1986] E.P.O.R. 1, EPO (Technical Bd App) . . . *Applied*, 07/2580
Charkham (Deceased) v Inland Revenue Commissioners [2000] R.V.R. 7, Lands Tr . . . *Digested*, 00/**5026**:
Considered, 07/4109, 07/4110

Charles v Staatssecretaris van Financien (C-434/03) [2006] S.T.C. 1429; [2005]
E.C.R. I-7037; [2005] 3 C.M.L.R. 38; [2005] S.T.I. 1258, ECJ . . . . *Digested*, 06/**4430**:
Considered, 07/4309

Charles Church Developments Ltd v Stent Foundations Ltd [2006] EWHC 3158 (TCC);
[2007] 1 W.L.R. 1203; [2007] B.L.R. 81; [2007] T.C.L.R. 2; [2007] C.I.L.L.
2408; *Times*, January 4, 2007, QBD (TCC) . . . . *Digested*, 07/**350**
Charles Church Developments Ltd v Stent Foundations Ltd [2007] EWHC 855 (TCC);
[2007] C.I.L.L. 2477, QBD (TCC)
Charleston v News Group Newspapers Ltd [1995] 2 A.C. 65; [1995] 2 W.L.R. 450;
[1995] 2 All E.R. 313; [1995] E.M.L.R. 129; (1995) 145 N.L.J. 490; (1995) 139
S.J.L.B. 100; *Times*, March 31, 1995; *Independent*, March 31, 1995, HL;
affirming [1994] E.M.L.R. 186; *Times*, January 12, 1994; *Independent*, January
14, 1994; *Guardian*, February 26, 1994, CA (Civ Div) . . . . *Digested*, 95/**3126**:
Applied, 07/5098: *Considered*, 95/5: *Followed*, 99/1634

Charlesworth v Relay Roads Ltd (No.2); *sub nom* Cavendish v Relay Roads Ltd
[2000] 1 W.L.R. 230; [1999] 4 All E.R. 397; [2000] C.P. Rep. 37; [2000]
C.P.L.R. 109; [2000] R.P.C. 300; (1999) 22(11) I.P.D. 22104; (1999) 96(32)
L.S.G. 33; (1999) 149 N.L.J. 1254; (1999) 143 S.J.L.B. 222; *Times*, August 31,
1999; *Independent*, October 18, 1999, Ch D . . . . *Digested*, 99/**502**:
Applied, 01/582, 07/495: *Followed*, 99/453

Charlesworth v Smith (Unreported, March 21, 2007), CC (Worthington) [*Ex rel.* Alison
Griffiths, 4 King's Bench Walk, Temple, London] . . . . *Digested*, 07/**3137**
Charman v Charman [2005] EWCA Civ 1606; [2006] 1 W.L.R. 1053; [2006] 2 F.L.R.
422; [2006] W.T.L.R. 1; (2006-07) 9 I.T.E.L.R. 43; [2006] Fam. Law 516;
(2006) 103(5) L.S.G. 28; *Independent*, January 13, 2006, CA (Civ Div);
affirming [2005] EWHC 2406 (Fam), Fam Div . . . . *Digested*, 06/**1625**
Charman v Charman [2006] EWCA Civ 1791; [2007] 1 F.L.R. 1237; [2007] Fam. Law
208, CA (Civ Div)
Charman v Charman [2007] EWCA Civ 503; [2007] 1 F.L.R. 1246; [2007] 2 F.C.R.
217; [2007] W.T.L.R. 1151; (2006-07) 9 I.T.E.L.R. 913; [2007] Fam. Law 682;
(2007) 157 N.L.J. 814; (2007) 151 S.J.L.B. 710, CA (Civ Div); affirming [2006]
EWHC 1879 (Fam); [2007] 1 F.L.R. 593; [2007] 1 F.C.R. 33; [2006] W.T.L.R.
1349; (2006-07) 9 I.T.E.L.R. 173; [2006] Fam. Law 1018; (2006) 103(35)
L.S.G. 33; (2006) 150 S.J.L.B. 1111, Fam Div . . . . *Digested*, 07/**1691**:
Considered, 07/1692

Charman v Orion Publishing Group Ltd [2007] EWCA Civ 972; (2007) 104(41) L.S.G.
26, CA (Civ Div); reversing [2006] EWHC 1756 (QB); [2007] 1 All E.R. 622,
QBD . . . . *Digested*, 07/**1076**

Chartbrook Ltd v Persimmon Homes Ltd A3/2007/0621, CA (Civ Div); affirming
    [2007] EWHC 409 (Ch); [2007] 1 All E.R. (Comm) 1083; [2007] 2 P. & C.R. 9;
    [2007] 11 E.G. 160 (C.S.), Ch D . . . .   *Digested,* 07/**806**
Charter Plc v City Index Ltd see City Index Ltd v Gawler
Charter Plc v City Index Ltd; *sub nom* City Index Ltd v Gawler [2006] EWHC 2508
    (Ch); [2007] 1 W.L.R. 26; [2007] 1 All E.R. 1049; [2007] P.N.L.R. 15; [2006]
    W.T.L.R. 1705; (2006-07) 9 I.T.E.L.R. 276; *Times,* October 27, 2006, Ch D . . . .   *Digested,* 07/**4248**
Chateignier v Office National de l'Emploi (ONEM) (C-346/05) [2006] E.C.R. I-10951;
    [2007] 1 C.M.L.R. 20; [2007] C.E.C. 341, ECJ (5th Chamber) . . . .   *Digested,* 07/**1558**
Chatha v Revenue and Customs Commissioners [2007] S.T.I. 2240, V&DTr
Chaudhary v Chaudhary [1985] Fam. 19; [1985] 2 W.L.R. 350; [1984] 3 All E.R. 1017;
    [1985] Fam. Law 26; (1984) 81 L.S.G. 2855; (1984) 128 S.J. 736, CA (Civ
    Div); affirming (1983) 13 Fam. Law 177; *Times,* May 18, 1983, Fam Div . . . .   *Digested,* 85/**1080**:
                                    Applied, 03/2285, 07/1809: *Distinguished,* 93/4834: *Followed,* 00/2505:
                                                                                           Not followed, 83/1126
Chaudhry v Revenue and Customs Commissioners [2007] EWHC 1805 (Admin);
    [2007] B.T.C. 5810; [2007] B.V.C. 757; [2007] S.T.I. 1868; *Times,* August 2,
    2007, DC
Cheall v United Kingdom (10550/83) (1986) 8 E.H.R.R. CD74, Eur Comm HR . . . . . .   *Applied,* 07/2179
Checkpoint Ltd v Strathclyde Pension Fund [2003] EWCA Civ 84; [2003] L. & T.R.
    22; [2003] 1 E.G.L.R. 1; [2003] 14 E.G. 124; [2003] 8 E.G. 128 (C.S.); (2003)
    100(12) L.S.G. 29; (2003) 147 S.J.L.B. 233; [2003] N.P.C. 23; *Times,* February
    12, 2003, CA (Civ Div); affirming [2002] EWHC 439 (Ch); [2002] 2 E.G.L.R.
    97; [2002] 13 E.G. 101 (C.S.), Ch D . . . .   *Digested,* 03/**190**:
                                                Applied, 03/2778, 07/252: *Considered,* 05/2678
Cheesman v R Brewer Contracts Ltd [2001] I.R.L.R. 144; [2001] Emp. L.R. 143, EAT .   *Digested,* 01/**2333**:
                                                                               Applied, 03/1329, 07/1416
Cheil Jedang Corp v Commission of the European Communities (T-220/00) [2003]
    E.C.R. II-2473, CFI . . . .   *Applied,* 07/**1589**
Chellaram v Chellaram (No.2) [2002] EWHC 632 (Ch); [2002] 3 All E.R. 17; [2002]
    W.T.L.R. 675; (2001-02) 4 I.T.E.L.R. 729; (2002) 152 N.L.J. 639, Ch D . . . . . .   *Digested,* 02/**633**:
                                                                                           Disapproved, 07/516
Chelmsford BC v First Secretary of State see R. (on the application of Chelmsford BC)
    v First Secretary of State
CHEMI/Phosphatidylserine (T1425/05) [2007] E.P.O.R. 8, EPO (Technical Bd App) . .   *Digested,* 07/**2595**
Chen v Secretary of State for the Home Department (C-200/02); *joined case* Zhu v
    Secretary of State for the Home Department (C-200/02) [2005] Q.B. 325;
    [2004] 3 W.L.R. 1453; [2005] All E.R. (EC) 129; [2004] E.C.R. I-9925; [2004]
    3 C.M.L.R. 48; [2004] C.E.C. 503; [2004] Imm. A.R. 754; [2005] I.N.L.R. 1;
    Times, October 21, 2004, ECJ . . . .   *Digested,* 05/**2207**:
                                    Applied, 07/1611: *Considered,* 06/1589, 07/1652, 07/2367:
                                                                                           Distinguished, 07/2368
Chepelev v Russia (58077/00) [2007] 2 F.C.R. 649, ECHR
Cherney v Deripaska [2007] EWHC 965 (Comm); [2007] 2 All E.R. (Comm) 785;
    [2007] I.L.Pr. 49, QBD (Comm) . . . .   *Digested,* 07/**517**
Cherwell DC v First Secretary of State [2006] EWHC 2704 (Admin); [2007] J.P.L.
    897, QBD (Admin) . . . .   *Digested,* 07/**3235**
Cheryl Investments Ltd v Saldanha; *joined case* Royal Life Saving Society v Page
    [1978] 1 W.L.R. 1329; [1979] 1 All E.R. 5; (1979) 37 P. & C.R. 349; (1978) 248
    E.G. 591; (1978) 122 S.J. 777, CA (Civ Div) . . . .   *Digested,* 78/**1771**:
                                    Applied, 91/2217: *Considered,* 85/1908, 89/2154, 89/2156, 89/2169,
                                                                        89/2171, 96/3846: *Followed,* 07/2749
Cheshire CC v S see S (Children), Re
Chessington World of Adventures Ltd v Reed [1998] I.C.R. 97; [1997] I.R.L.R. 556, EAT   *Digested,* 98/**2194**:
                                                                                           Considered, 07/1334
Chester City Council v Arriva Plc [2007] EWHC 1373 (Ch); [2007] U.K.C.L.R. 1582;
    (2007) 151 S.J.L.B. 855, Ch D
Chesterton Commercial Holdings v Wycombe DC [2007] P.A.D. 49, Planning Inspector
Cheung v Lau (2007-08) 10 I.T.E.L.R. 112, CA (HK)
Cheverny Consulting Ltd v Whitehead Mann Ltd [2006] EWCA Civ 1303; [2007] 1 All
    E.R. (Comm) 124, CA (Civ Div); reversing [2005] EWHC 2431 (Ch), Ch D . . .   *Digested,* 07/**802**
Chichester DC v First Secretary of State [2006] EWHC 1876 (Admin); [2007] J.P.L.
    389, QBD (Admin). . . . .   *Digested,* 07/**3275**:
                                                                                           Considered, 07/3252
Chichester DC v Searle see South Buckinghamshire DC v Porter (No.1)
Chief Adjudication Officer v Gibbon see Chief Adjudication Officer v Quinn
Chief Adjudication Officer v Quinn; *joined case* Chief Adjudication Officer v Gibbon
    [1996] 1 W.L.R. 1184; [1996] 4 All E.R. 72; (1997-98) 1 C.C.L. Rep. 529; (1996)
    93(37) L.S.G. 27; (1996) 146 N.L.J. 1150; (1996) 140 S.J.L.B. 207; *Times,*
    August 8, 1996, HL . . . .   *Digested,* 96/**5473**:
                                                                                           Considered, 07/3910
Chief Constable of Cumbria v Wright [2006] EWHC 3574 (Admin); [2007] 1 W.L.R.
    1407, DC . . . .   *Digested,* 07/**375**

Chief Constable of Greater Manchester v I [2007] EWHC 1837 (Fam); [2007] Fam. Law 900, Fam Div

Chief Constable of Merseyside v Harrison [2006] EWHC 1106 (Admin); [2007] Q.B. 79; [2006] 3 W.L.R. 171; (2006) 170 J.P. 523; [2006] Po. L.R. 198; [2006] A.C.D. 67; (2006) 170 J.P.N. 914; *Times*, April 14, 2006, DC . . . .   *Digested*, 06/**316**

Chief Constable of Northern Ireland v Cassells [2007] NICA 12; [2007] N.I. 194, CA (NI)

Chief Constable of Thames Valley v Hepburn see Hepburn v Chief Constable of Thames Valley

Chief Constable of Thames Valley v Kellaway [2000] I.R.L.R. 170, EAT . . . .   *Digested*, 00/**2147**:
                                           Considered, 03/1260, 07/1319

Chief Constable of the West Midlands v Billingham [1979] 1 W.L.R. 747; [1979] 2 All E.R. 182; [1979] R.T.R. 446; [1979] Crim. L.R. 256; (1979) 123 S.J. 98, QBD . .   *Digested*, 79/**2311**:
                                    Applied, 05/755: *Considered*, 07/1006

Chief Constable of West Yorkshire v Khan; *sub nom* Khan v Chief Constable of West Yorkshire [2001] UKHL 48; [2001] 1 W.L.R. 1947; [2001] 4 All E.R. 834; [2001] I.C.R. 1065; [2001] I.R.L.R. 830; [2001] Emp. L.R. 1399; (2001) 98(42) L.S.G. 37; (2001) 145 S.J.L.B. 230; *Times*, October 16, 2001; *Daily Telegraph*, October 16, 2001, HL; reversing [2000] I.C.R. 1169; [2000] I.R.L.R. 324; (2000) 150 N.L.J. 308; *Times*, March 15, 2000; *Independent*, March 3, 2000, CA (Civ Div); affirming (Unreported, July 28, 1998), EAT . . . .   *Digested*, 01/**2302**:
            Applied, 05/1232, 05/1235, 07/1390, 07/1402: *Cited*, 00/2186:
                             Considered, 06/1365: *Followed*, 03/1354

Chief Constable of West Yorkshire v Vento (No.2) see Vento v Chief Constable of West Yorkshire

Chillcott v WM Armstrong (Longtown) Ltd (Unreported, April 30, 2007), CC (Chester) [*Ex rel.* Clare Harrington, Barrister, 13 King's Bench Walk, Temple, London] . . . .   *Digested*, 07/**3078**

Chiltern DC v Hodgetts see Hodgetts v Chiltern DC

Chime Corp Ltd, Re (Unreported), CFA (HK) . . . .   *Applied*, 07/592

Chiniah v Income Tax Commissioner [2007] UKPC 23; [2007] Bus. L.R. 1167; [2007] S.T.I. 1358, PC (Mau) . . . .   *Digested*, 07/**4167**

Chirkinian v Larcom Trustees Ltd [2006] EWHC 1917 (Ch); [2006] B.P.I.R. 1363; [2006] W.T.L.R. 1523, Ch D . . . .   *Digested*, 07/**4239**

Chirnside v Fay [2006] P.N.L.R. 7, CA (NZ) [2006] NZSC 68; [2007] P.N.L.R. 6; (2007-08) 10 I.T.E.L.R. 226, Sup Ct (NZ) . . . .   *Digested*, 07/**1536**

Chishty Coveney & Co v Raja see Arbuthnot Latham Bank Ltd v Trafalgar Holdings Ltd

Chittenden v Pepper; *sub nom* Newlands (Seaford) Educational Trust (In Administration), Re [2006] EWHC 1511 (Ch); [2007] B.C.C. 195; [2006] B.P.I.R. 1230; [2006] 2 E.G.L.R. 7; [2006] 33 E.G. 100; [2006] 27 E.G. 234 (C.S.); [2006] N.P.C. 75, Ch D . . . .   *Digested*, 06/**2370**

Chmelir v Czech Republic (64935/01) (2007) 44 E.H.R.R. 20, ECHR

Cho Yang Shipping Co Ltd v Commission of the European Communities (Order II) (C-361/00 P(R)) [2000] E.C.R. I-11657; [2001] 4 C.M.L.R. 32, ECJ . . . .   *Digested*, 01/**2453**:
                                             Applied, 07/1549

Choudhry v Jabar & Motor Insurers' Bureau (Unreported, May 2, 2006), CC (Luton) [*Ex rel.* Nicholas Preston, Barrister, Clerksroom, Third Floor, 218 Strand, London] . . . .   *Digested*, 07/**2495**

CHP Property Group Ltd v Wigan MBC [2007] R.V.R. 326, Lands Tr . . . .   *Digested*, 07/**3390**

Chrisostomou v Manchester City Council [2007] R.V.R. 207, Lands Tr

Christian v Queen, The; *sub nom* R. v Christian (Stevens Raymond) [2006] UKPC 47; [2007] 2 A.C. 400; [2007] 2 W.L.R. 120; (2006) 150 S.J.L.B. 1464; *Times*, November 15, 2006; *Independent*, November 9, 2006, PC (PI) . . . .   *Digested*, 07/**2808**

Christian Democratic People's Party v Moldova (28793/02) (2007) 45 E.H.R.R. 13, ECHR . . . .   *Digested*, 07/**2178**

Christie v Department for Constitutional Affairs [2007] I.C.R. 1553; *Times*, September 4, 2007, EAT . . . .   *Digested*, 07/**1386**

Christie v Leachinsky; *sub nom* Leachinsky v Christie [1947] A.C. 573; [1947] 1 All E.R. 567; 63 T.L.R. 231; (1947) 111 J.P. 224; [1947] L.J.R. 757; 176 L.T. 443, HL; affirming [1946] K.B. 124, CA . . . .   *Digested*, 47-51/**6152**:
            Applied, 71/10199, 75/2960, 75/2964, 80/2304, 82/2715, 86/638, 04/891,
           07/2292: *Considered*, 68/3982, 76/402, 80/2312, 81/2328, 90/4323,
                             98/4286: *Distinguished*, 47-51/6159: *Followed*, 81/2090:
                                         Referred to, 93/4889

Christmas v Hampshire CC (Duty of Care) see X (Minors) v Bedfordshire CC

Christoph-Dornier-Stiftung fur Klinische Psychologie v Finanzamt Giessen (C-45/01) [2005] S.T.C. 228; [2003] E.C.R. I-12911; [2004] 1 C.M.L.R. 30; [2004] C.E.C. 144; [2005] B.T.C. 5232; [2005] B.V.C. 263; [2003] S.T.I. 1935, ECJ (5th Chamber) . . . .   *Digested*, 04/**3975**:
                                           Applied, 07/4346

Christophe X v PMA France Sarl [2007] E.C.C. 15, Cass (F)

Chrulew v Borm-Reid & Co [1992] 1 W.L.R. 176; [1992] 1 All E.R. 953; (1991) 141 N.L.J. 744; *Times*, May 28, 1991, QBD . . . .   *Digested*, 92/**3449**:
                                     Applied, 07/378: *Considered*, 96/697

Church Commissioners for England v Baines see WellcomeTrust Ltd v Hamad
Church Commissioners for England v Meya [2006] EWCA Civ 821; [2007] H.L.R. 4; [2007] L. & T.R. 3; [2006] 2 E.G.L.R. 39; [2006] 34 E.G. 90; [2006] 26 E.G. 155 (C.S.); [2006] N.P.C. 69; [2007] 1 P. & C.R. DG4; *Times*, July 4, 2006, CA (Civ Div); reversing 5CL52582, CC (London) . . . .   *Digested*, 06/**2672**
Church of Jesus Christ of Latter-Day Saints v Gallagher (Valuation Officer) see Gallagher (Valuation Officer) v Church of Jesus Christ of Latter-Day Saints
Church of Jesus Christ of Latter-Day Saints v Henning (Valuation Officer) [1964] A.C. 420; [1963] 3 W.L.R. 88; [1963] 2 All E.R. 733; (1963) 127 J.P. 481; 61 L.G.R. 565; [1963] R.A. 177; [1963] R.V.R. 422; 10 R.R.C. 99; (1963) 107 S.J. 455, HL; affirming [1962] 1 W.L.R. 1091; [1962] 3 All E.R. 364; (1962) 126 J.P. 483; 60 L.G.R. 414; [1962] R.A. 425; [1962] R.V.R. 504; 9 R.R.C. 196; (1962) 106 S.J. 589, CA . . . .   *Digested*, 63/**2959**:
    Applied, 06/3448, 07/2878: *Considered*, 63/2959: *Distinguished*, 06/3447
Church of Scientology's Application for Registration as a Charity [2005] W.T.L.R. 1151, Charity Comm . . . .   *Applied*, 07/323
Churchill v First Independent Factors & Finance Ltd see First Independent Factors & Finance Ltd v Churchill
Churchill Car Insurance v Kelly; *sub nom* Kelly v Churchill Car Insurance [2007] EWHC 18 (QB); [2007] R.T.R. 26, QBD . . . .   *Digested*, 07/**334**
CI LawTrustees Ltd v Minwalla [2006] W.T.L.R. 807; (2006–07) 9 I.T.E.L.R. 601, Royal Ct (Jer) . . . .   *Digested*, 07/**4245**:
    Considered, 07/4244
CI Ltd v Joint Liquidators of Sonatacus Ltd see Sonatacus Ltd, Re
Cia de Seguros Imperio v Heath (REBX) Ltd (formerly CE Heath & Co (America) Ltd); *sub nom* Companhia de Seguros Imperio v Heath (REBX) Ltd [2001] 1 W.L.R. 112; [2000] 2 All E.R. (Comm) 787; [2000] C.L.C. 1543; [2001] Lloyd's Rep. I.R. 109; [2000] Lloyd's Rep. P.N. 795; (2000–01) 3 I.T.E.L.R. 134; *Times*, September 26, 2000; *Independent*, October 23, 2000, CA (Civ Div); affirming [1999] 1 All E.R. (Comm) 750; [1999] C.L.C. 997; [1999] Lloyd's Rep. I.R. 571; [1999] Lloyd's Rep. P.N. 571; *Independent*, May 3, 1999, QBD (Comm) . . . . . .   *Digested*, 00/**513**:
    Applied, 05/314: *Considered*, 07/472
Cimber Air A/S v Skatteministeriet (C-382/02) [2005] S.T.C. 547; [2004] E.C.R. I-8379; [2004] 3 C.M.L.R. 55; [2007] B.T.C. 5357; [2007] B.V.C. 326; [2004] S.T.I. 2120, ECJ (2nd Chamber) . . . .   *Digested*, 05/**4344**
Cimenteries CBR SA v Commission of the European Communities (T-25/95) [2000] E.C.R. II-491; [2000] 5 C.M.L.R. 204, CFI (4th Chamber) . . . .   *Digested*, 00/**710**:
    Considered, 06/596, 07/1545: *Followed*, 05/553: *Reversed*, 05/1435
Cinar Corp v Panju [2006] EWHC 2557 (QB); [2007] 1 All E.R. (Comm) 373, QBD . .   *Digested*, 07/**455**
Cinema Press Ltd v Pictures & Pleasures Ltd [1945] K.B. 356; [1945] 1 All E.R. 440, CA . . . .   *Applied*, 55/362,
    57/2783, 07/388
Cinpres Gas Injection Ltd v Melea Ltd [2006] EWHC 2950 (Ch); [2007] Bus. L.R. 20; (2007) 30(1) I.P.D. 30008; *Times*, December 5, 2006, Ch D (Patents Ct) . . . . .   *Digested*, 07/**2623**
Ciola v Land Vorarlberg (C-224/97) [1999] E.C.R. I-2517; [1999] 2 C.M.L.R. 1220, ECJ . . . .   *Digested*, 99/**2252**:
    Considered, 07/1640
CIPC (Ocean View) Ltd Partnership v Churchill International Property Corp; *joined case* Langridge v Evans 2006 BCSC 1127; (2006–07) 9 I.T.E.L.R. 157, Sup Ct (BC) . .   *Digested*, 07/**4261**
Cipolla v Fazari (C-94/04); *joined case* Macrino v Meloni (C-202/04) [2007] All E.R. (EC) 699; [2007] 4 C.M.L.R. 8, ECJ. . . . .   *Digested*, 07/**617**
Circle Trust, Re see HSBC International Trustee Ltd v Wong Kit Wan
Circuit Systems Ltd (In Liquidation) v Zuken-Redac (UK) Ltd see Norglen Ltd (In Liquidation) v Reeds Rains Prudential Ltd
Citco Banking Corp NV v Pusser's Ltd [2007] UKPC 13; [2007] Bus. L.R. 960; [2007] B.C.C. 205; [2007] 2 B.C.L.C. 483, PC (BVI) . . . .   *Digested*, 07/**589**
Citibank NA v Citybond Holdings Plc; *sub nom* Citybond Holdings Plc's Trade Mark Application (No.2210663) [2007] R.P.C. 13, App Person; reversing in part (Unreported, May 18, 2005), TMR . . . .   *Digested*, 07/**2679**
Citibank NA v MBIA Assurance SA; *sub nom* Citibank NA v QVT Financial LP [2007] EWCA Civ 11; [2007] 1 All E.R. (Comm) 475; [2007] 1 C.L.C. 113, CA (Civ Div); affirming [2006] EWHC 3215 (Ch), Ch D . . . .   *Digested*, 07/**304**
Citibank NA v QVT Financial LP see Citibank NA v MBIA Assurance SA
CITIBANK/Integrated account (T368/05) [2007] E.P.O.R. 54, EPO (Technical Bd App)
Citric Acid Cartel, Re (T-59/02) see Archer Daniels Midland Co v Commission of the European Communities (T-59/02)
City & Country Properties Ltd v Kamali see Kamali v City & Country Properties Ltd
City & Country Properties Ltd v Plowden Investments Ltd [2007] L. & T.R. 15, CC (Guildford)
City Index Ltd v Gawler see Charter Plc v City Index Ltd
City Index Ltd v Gawler; *sub nom* Charter Plc v City Index Ltd [2007] EWCA Civ 1382; [2007] 2 C.L.C. 968, CA (Civ Div)

City Inn (Jersey) Ltd v Ten Trinity Square Ltd A3/2007/1480, CA (Civ Div); affirming
   [2007] EWHC 1829 (Ch); [2007] 46 E.G. 178; [2007] 26 E.G. 162 (C.S.), Ch
   D

City Motors Groep NV v Citroen Belux NV (C-421/05) [2007] 4 C.M.L.R. 12, ECJ (3rd
   Chamber) . . . .   *Digested,* 07/**626**

City of Belfast Warehousing Ltd v Revenue and Customs Commissioners [2007] S.T.I.
   2250, V&DTr (Belfast)

City Truck Group Ltd, Re; *sub nom* Secretary of State for Trade and Industry v Gee
   [2006] B.C.C. 384, Ch D (Companies Ct) . . . .   *Digested,* 07/**397**

City Truck Group Ltd, Re; *sub nom* Secretary of State for Trade and Industry v Gee
   [2007] EWHC 350 (Ch); [2007] 2 B.C.L.C. 649, Ch D (Companies Ct)

City Vintners Ltd, Re; *joined case* Goldman Williams Ltd, Re; Nos. 7219 & 7220 of
   2001, Ch D (Companies Ct) . . . .   *Considered,* 07/**2951**

City Wall Properties (Scotland) Ltd v Pearl Assurance Plc [2007] CSIH 79; [2007]
   N.P.C. 114, IH (Ex Div); affirming 2005 G.W.D. 35-666, OH

Citybond Holdings Plc's Trade Mark Application (No.2210663) see Citibank NA v
   Citybond Holdings Plc

Cityhook Ltd v Office of Fair Trading [2006] CAT 32; [2007] Comp. A.R. 459, CAT . .   *Digested,* 07/**641**

Cityhook Ltd v Office of Fair Trading [2007] CAT 10; [2007] Comp. A.R. 612, CAT

Cityhook Ltd v Office of Fair Trading [2007] CAT 18; [2007] Comp. A.R. 813, CAT

Cityhook Ltd v Office of Fair Trading (Time Extension) [2006] CAT 26; [2007] Comp.
   A.R. 279, CAT

Cityspan Ltd, Re; *sub nom* Brown v Clark [2007] EWHC 751 (Ch); [2007] 2 B.C.L.C.
   522, Ch D . . . .   *Digested,* 07/**2429**

CKE Engineering Ltd (In Administration), Re [2007] B.C.C. 975, Ch D (Birmingham)

Claim for Damages Caused by Vitamin Cartel, Re (13 O 55/02) [2007] I.L.Pr. 55, LG (Ger)

Claim for Maintenance by the State against Parent Resident in Switzerland, Re (21 UF 381/
   06) [2007] I.L.Pr. 41, OLG (Ger)

Claims Direct Test Cases (Case Management), Re [2002] EWCA Civ 428; [2002] P.I.Q.R.
   Q11; *Times,* April 4, 2002, CA (Civ Div) . . . .   *Digested,* 02/**289**:
                                                               Applied, 05/452, 07/364

Clan Real Estate v Islington LBC [2007] P.A.D. 6, Planning Inspector

Clancy v Cannock Chase Technical College; *joined case* Clancy v Parker [2001]
   I.R.L.R. 331; [2001] Emp. L.R. 1001; [2001] O.P.L.R. 297; [2001] Pens. L.R. 175,
   EAT . . . .   *Digested,* 01/**2342**:
                                                               Applied, 07/**1424**

Clancy v Parker see Clancy v Cannock Chase Technical College

Clark v Ardington Electrical Services see Lagden v O'Connor

Clark v Bowlt [2006] EWCA Civ 978; [2007] P.I.Q.R. P12; (2006) 150 S.J.L.B. 886,
   CA (Civ Div) . . . .   *Digested,* 07/**203**

Clark v Chief Constable of Cleveland [2000] C.P. Rep. 22; (1999) 96(21) L.S.G. 38;
   Times, May 13, 1999, CA (Civ Div) . . . .   *Digested,* 99/**1392**:
                                                               Applied, 07/**1051**

Clark v Chief Constable of Essex [2006] EWHC 2290 (QB); (2006) 103(38) L.S.G.
   32; (2006) 150 S.J.L.B. 1253, QBD . . . .   *Digested,* 07/**2940**

Clark v Novacold Ltd see Clark v TDG Ltd (t/a Novacold Ltd)

Clark v TDG Ltd (t/a Novacold Ltd); *sub nom* Clark v Novacold Ltd [1999] 2 All E.R.
   977; [1999] I.C.R. 951; [1999] I.R.L.R. 318; [1999] Disc. L.R. 240; (1999) 48
   B.M.L.R. 1; *Times,* April 1, 1999, CA (Civ Div); reversing [1998] I.C.R. 1044;
   [1998] I.R.L.R. 420; [1999] Disc. L.R. 22; (1998) 42 B.M.L.R. 101; *Times,* June
   11, 1998, EAT . . . .   *Digested,* 99/**2022**:
              Applied, 99/2024, 01/2239, 01/2240, 01/6461, 03/5477, 04/1077, 04/1220,
                         05/1229: *Distinguished,* 07/2765: *Followed,* 00/2127

Clark v Tull (t/a Ardington Electrical Services) see Lagden v O'Connor

Clark v University of Lincolnshire and Humberside [2000] 1 W.L.R. 1988; [2000] 3 All
   E.R. 752; [2000] Ed. C.R. 553; [2000] E.L.R. 345; [2000] C.O.D. 293;
   (2000) 150 N.L.J. 616; (2000) 144 S.J.L.B. 220; *Times,* May 3, 2000;
   Independent, May 3, 2000, CA (Civ Div) . . . .   *Digested,* 00/**2001**:
                 Applied, 05/2497, 06/1227, 07/1281: *Considered,* 07/51

Clark (A Child), Re; *sub nom* EC (Child Abduction: Stayed Proceedings), Re [2006]
   EWCA Civ 1115; [2007] 1 F.L.R. 57; [2006] Fam. Law 918; *Times,* July 19, 2006,
   CA (Civ Div) . . . .   *Digested,* 07/**1807**

Clarke v Arriva Kent Thameside Ltd EAT/0341/00, EAT . . . .   *Applied,* 07/**1352**

Clarke v Birkin [2006] EWHC 340 (Ch); [2006] B.P.I.R. 632, Ch D . . . .   *Digested,* 07/**2412**

Clarke v Brothwood [2006] EWHC 2939 (Ch); [2007] W.T.L.R. 329, Ch D . . . .   *Digested,* 07/**3966**

Clarke v General Accident Fire & Life Assurance Corp Plc see Clarke v Kato

Clarke v Harlowe [2005] EWHC 3062 (Ch); [2007] 1 F.L.R. 1; [2007] 3 F.C.R. 726;
   [2006] B.P.I.R. 636; [2005] W.T.L.R. 1473; [2006] Fam. Law 846; [2006] 1 P.
   & C.R. DG11, Ch D . . . .   *Digested,* 06/**4391**:
                                                               Considered, 07/**3359**

Clarke v Kato; *sub nom* Clarke v General Accident Fire & Life Assurance Corp Plc; *joined case* Cutter v Eagle Star Insurance Co Ltd [1998] 1 W.L.R. 1647; [1998] 4 All E.R. 417; (1999) 163 J.P. 502; [1999] R.T.R. 153; [1999] P.I.Q.R. P1; (1998) 95(43) L.S.G. 31; (1998) 148 N.L.J. 1640; (1998) 142 S.J.L.B. 278; [1998] N.P.C. 142; *Times*, October 23, 1998; *Independent*, October 27, 1998, HL; reversing [1997] 1 W.L.R. 208; [1997] R.T.R. 264; [1997] P.I.Q.R. P27; *Times*, December 11, 1996, CA (Civ Div) . . . . *Digested*, 98/**3395**: *Applied*, 01/4449, 04/738: *Considered*, 07/3458, 07/3527

Clarke v Swaby [2007] UKPC 1; [2007] 2 P. & C.R. 2, PC (Jam) . . . . *Digested*, 07/**2762**

Clarkson v Barclays Private Bank & Trust (Isle of Man) Ltd [2007] W.T.L.R. 1703, CLD (IoM)

Class International BV v Colgate-Palmolive Co (C-405/03) [2006] Ch. 154; [2006] 2 W.L.R. 507; [2005] E.C.R. I-8735; [2006] 1 C.M.L.R. 14; [2006] C.E.C. 193; [2006] E.T.M.R. 12, ECJ. . . . . *Digested*, 06/**2464**: *Applied*, 06/2581: *Considered*, 07/2638

Claughton (Liquidator of Hollicourt (Contracts) Ltd) v Bank of Ireland see Hollicourt (Contracts) Ltd (In Liquidation) v Bank of Ireland

Claussen v Yeates see Cranfield v Bridgegrove Ltd

Clavering v Ellison 11 E.R. 282; (1859) 7 H.L. Cas. 707, QB . . . . *Applied*, 47–51/10845, 52/2247, 52/3644, 54/2119, 68/3586: *Considered*, 62/1948, 07/4255: *Distinguished*, 67/4101

Clay, Re; *sub nom* Clay v Booth; Deed of Indemnity, Re [1919] 1 Ch. 66, CA . . . . *Applied*, 47–51/7798: *Cited*, 03/296: *Considered*, 75/104, 87/2984: *Distinguished*, 70/11, 07/2555

Clay v Booth see Clay, Re

Claymore Dairies Ltd v Office of Fair Trading (Costs) (No.2) [2006] CAT 5; [2006] Comp. A.R. 568, CAT . . . . *Digested*, 07/**4985**

Claymore Dairies Ltd v Office of Fair Trading (formerly Director General of Fair Trading) [2006] CAT 31; [2007] Comp. A.R. 467, CAT. . . . . *Digested*, 07/**602**

Claymore Dairies Ltd v Office of Fair Trading (Further Stay of Proceedings) [2006] CAT 6; [2006] Comp. A.R. 574, CAT . . . . *Digested*, 07/**4997**

Claymore Services Ltd v Nautilus Properties Ltd [2007] EWHC 805 (TCC); [2007] B.L.R. 452, QBD (TCC)

Clayton v Clayton [2006] EWCA Civ 878; [2006] Fam. 83; [2006] 3 W.L.R. 599; [2007] 1 All E.R. 1197; [2007] E.M.L.R. 3; [2007] 1 F.L.R. 11; [2006] 2 F.C.R. 405; [2006] H.R.L.R. 34; [2007] U.K.H.R.R. 264; [2006] Fam. Law 926; (2006) 103(28) L.S.G. 28; (2006) 156 N.L.J. 1101; (2006) 150 S.J.L.B. 890; *Times*, July 4, 2006; *Independent*, June 29, 2006, CA (Civ Div); reversing [2005] EWHC 3451 (Fam), Fam Div . . . . *Digested*, 06/**1687**: *Followed*, 07/1732

Cleanaco Ltd v Revenue and Customs Commissioners [2007] V. & D.R. 21, V&DTr (London)

Cleansing Service Group Ltd v Vehicle & Operator Services Agency [2006] EWHC 662; [2007] R.T.R. 15, QBD (Admin) . . . . *Digested*, 07/**4207**

Clegg v Andersson (t/a Nordic Marine) [2003] EWCA Civ 320; [2003] 1 All E.R. (Comm) 721; [2003] 2 Lloyd's Rep. 32; (2003) 100(20) L.S.G. 28; *Times*, April 14, 2003, CA (Civ Div); reversing [2002] EWHC 943 (QB), QBD . . . . *Digested*, 03/**3617**: *Considered*, 07/3568

Clement (Listing Officer) v Bryant [2003] EWHC 422 (Admin); [2003] R.A. 133, QBD (Admin) . . . . *Applied*, 03/2868, 07/2835

Clements v Henry Hadaway Organisation Ltd see HHO Licensing Ltd (In Liquidation), Re

Clements (Deceased), Re see Durling's Application, Re

Clifford v First American Corp see First American Corp v Sheikh Zayed Al-Nahyan

Clifford v Phillips see Clifford v Timms

Clifford v Timms; *joined cases* Clifford v Phillips; Hill v Clifford [1908] A.C. 12, HL; affirming [1907] 2 Ch. 236, CA; reversing [1907] 1 Ch. 420, Ch D . . . . *Applied*, 78/2827, 07/1429: *Considered*, 06/2926, 07/339

Clifton v Karle (Unreported, March 1, 2007), CC (Birmingham) [*Ex rel.* Jonas Roy Bloom Solicitors, Citadel, 190 Corporation Street, Birmingham] . . . . *Digested*, 07/**1067**

Clifton v Revenue and Customs Commissioners [2007] S.T.C. (S.C.D.) 386; [2007] S.T.I. 1178, Sp Comm . . . . *Digested*, 07/**4072**

Clingham v Kensington and Chelsea RLBC see R. (on the application of McCann) v Manchester Crown Court

Clockfair Ltd v Harrington (Valuation Officer) [2006] R.A. 286, Lands Tr . . . . *Digested*, 07/**3344**

Clowes v Hilliard (1876-77) L.R. 4 Ch. D. 413, Ch D . . . . *Distinguished*, 07/2633

CLT-UFA SA v Finanzamt Koln-West (C-253/03) [2007] S.T.C. 1303; [2006] 2 C.M.L.R. 27; [2006] S.T.I. 530, ECJ (3rd Chamber) . . . . *Digested*, 06/**4155**

Club Kaede Ltd v Revenue and Customs Commissioners [2007] S.T.I. 2251, V&DTr (London)

Clydesdale v Driver and Vehicle Testing Agency [2002] N.I. 421, CA (NI) . . . . *Distinguished*, 07/4518

CMA CGM v Commission of the European Communities (T-213/00); *sub nom* Fettcsa
Agreement, Re (T-213/00) [2003] E.C.R. II-913; [2003] 5 C.M.L.R. 4, CFI (3rd
Chamber) .... *Digested*, 04/**486**:
Applied, 07/1589: *Followed*, 07/1590: *Preliminary ruling given*, 05/545

CMS Peripherals Ltd v Revenue and Customs Commissioners [2007] EWHC 1128
(Ch); [2007] B.T.C. 5679; [2007] B.V.C. 647; [2007] S.T.I. 1563, Ch D   *Digested*, 07/**4326**

CN v Secretary of State for the Home Department see MM v Secretary of State for
the Home Department

CNA Insurance Co Ltd v Office Depot International (UK) Ltd [2005] EWHC 456
(Comm); [2005] Lloyd's Rep. I.R. 658; [2007] Lloyd's Rep. I.R. 89, QBD
(Comm) .... *Digested*, 06/**329**

Co-operative Group (CWS) Ltd v Office of Fair Trading [2007] CAT 24; [2007] Comp.
A.R. 899, CAT

Coal Mining Contractors v Davies; *sub nom* Davies v Department of Trade and Industry
[2006] EWCA Civ 1360; [2007] 1 W.L.R. 3232; [2007] 1 All E.R. 518; [2007]
C.P. Rep. 17; [2007] P.I.Q.R. P13; (2006) 150 S.J.L.B. 1428, CA (Civ Div) ....   *Digested*, 07/**451**

Coard v Attorney General [2007] UKPC 7, PC (Gren) ....   *Digested*, 07/**3625**

Coast Lines Ltd v Societa Nazionale di Navigazione di Genoa (The Fagernes) see
Fagernes, The

Coaten v PBS Corp [2006] EWHC 1781 (Ch); [2006] 3 E.G.L.R. 43; [2006] 44 E.G.
198; [2007] 1 P. & C.R. DG11, Ch D ....   *Digested*, 07/**3357**

Cobbe v Yeoman's Row Management Ltd; *sub nom* Yeoman's Row Management Ltd v
Cobbe [2006] EWCA Civ 1139; [2006] 1 W.L.R. 2964; [2007] 1 P. & C.R. 8;
[2006] 3 E.G.L.R. 107; [2006] W.T.L.R. 1473; [2007] 1 P. & C.R. DG14, CA (Civ
Div); affirming [2005] EWHC 266 (Ch); [2005] W.T.L.R. 625; [2005] N.P.C.
29; [2005] 2 P. & C.R. DG1, Ch D ....   *Digested*, 06/**769**:
Distinguished, 07/1537

Cobzaru v Romania (48254/99) 23 B.H.R.C. 36, ECHR

Cockbone v Atkinson Dacre & Slack see Arthur JS Hall & Co v Simons

Coco v AN Clark (Engineers) Ltd [1968] F.S.R. 415; [1969] R.P.C. 41, Ch D ....   *Digested*, 68/**1458**:
Applied, 88/3403, 99/3437, 01/4415, 03/1217, 07/4190: *Considered*, 87/1294,
03/2923: *Referred to*, 73/2498

Codent Ltd v Lyson Ltd [2005] EWCA Civ 1835; [2006] C.P. Rep. 33; [2007] 2
Costs L.R. 185, CA (Civ Div) ....   *Digested*, 06/**358**

Cofacredit SA v Morris [2006] EWHC 353 (Ch); [2007] 2 B.C.L.C. 99, Ch D ....   *Digested*, 07/**2434**

Coffee Republic Plc v Revenue and Customs Commissioners [2007] S.T.I. 2245, V&DTr
(London)

Cofidis SA v Jean-Louis Fredout (C-473/00) [2002] E.C.R. I-10875, ECJ ....   *Followed*, 07/256

Coflexip SA v Stolt Offshore MS Ltd [2004] EWCA Civ 213; [2004] F.S.R. 34; (2004)
27(5) I.P.D. 27047; (2004) 148 S.J.L.B. 297, CA (Civ Div); affirming [2003]
EWHC 1892 (Pat); [2004] F.S.R. 7; (2003) 26(10) I.P.D. 26066, Ch D (Patents
Ct) .... *Digested*, 04/**2338**:
Considered, 05/2505, 07/2606, 07/2677: *Followed*, 05/329

Cofresco Frischalteprodukte GmbH & Co KG v Controller of Patents, Designs and Trade
Marks [2007] IEHC 187; [2007] E.T.M.R. 63, HC (Irl)

COGNIS/Glycosides (T715/01) [2007] E.P.O.R. 13, EPO (Technical Bd App)

Cohen v Davis; *sub nom* International Championship Management Ltd, Re; Mall
Corporate Events Ltd, Re; *joined case* Cohen v Dubey [2006] EWHC 768 (Ch);
[2007] B.C.C. 95; [2007] 2 B.C.L.C. 274; [2006] P.N.L.R. 33, Ch D
(Companies Ct) .... *Digested*, 06/**2379**

Cohen v Dubey see Cohen v Davis

Cohen v Kingsley Napley (A Firm) [2006] EWCA Civ 66; [2006] P.N.L.R. 22; (2006)
103(9) L.S.G. 31, CA (Civ Div); reversing in part [2005] EWHC 899 (QB);
[2005] P.N.L.R. 37, QBD ....   *Digested*, 06/**2900**:
Followed, 07/479

Coker v Diocese of Southwark see Diocese of Southwark v Coker

Colchester Estates (Cardiff) v Carlton Industries Plc [1986] Ch. 80; [1984] 3 W.L.R.
693; [1984] 2 All E.R. 601; (1984) 271 E.G. 778; (1984) 81 L.S.G. 2699, Ch D   *Digested*, 84/**2588**:
Applied, 02/4488, 07/2392, 07/2395: *Approved*, 95/2983:
Considered, 86/366, 88/2067, 92/2555: *Not followed*, 98/4029

Cole v Davis-Gilbert [2007] EWCA Civ 396; (2007) 151 S.J.L.B. 335; *Times*, April 6,
2007, CA (Civ Div) ....   *Digested*, 07/**2933**

Cole v Lambeth LBC see Kay v Lambeth LBC

Coles v Barracks; *sub nom* Barracks v Commissioner of Police of the Metropolis;
Barracks v Coles [2006] EWCA Civ 1041; [2007] I.C.R. 60; [2007] I.R.L.R. 73;
[2006] Po. L.R. 217; *Times*, August 7, 2006, CA (Civ Div); affirming [2005] Po.
L.R. 233, EAT ....   *Digested*, 06/**1351**

Coles v Passmore (Unreported, March 10, 2006), CC (Bristol) [*Ex rel.* Rachel Russell,
Barrister, St John's Chambers, 101 Victoria Street, Bristol]. ....   *Digested*, 07/**767**

Collector of Stamp Revenue v Arrowtown Assets Ltd 6 I.T.L. Rep. 454, CFA (HK) ....   *Applied*, 07/**3992**:
Considered, 05/4084

Collee v Finanzamt Limburg an der Lahn (C-146/05) [2007] S.T.I. 2213, ECJ (3rd
Chamber)

Colley *v* Revenue and Customs Commissioners [2007] S.T.C. (S.C.D.) 236; [2007] S.T.I. 417, Sp Comm

Collidge *v* Freeport Plc A2/2007/1280, A2/2007/1280 B, CA (Civ Div); affirming [2007] EWHC 1216 (QB); (2007) 104(25) L.S.G. 35, QBD

Collier *v* P & MJ Wright (Holdings) Ltd [2007] EWCA Civ 1329; [2007] B.P.I.R. 1452; [2007] N.P.C. 136, CA (Civ Div)

Collier *v* Williams; *joined cases* Marshall *v* Maggs; Leeson *v* Marsden; Glass *v* Surrendran [2006] EWCA Civ 20; [2006] 1 W.L.R. 1945; [2007] 1 All E.R. 991; [2006] C.P. Rep. 22; [2006] P.I.Q.R. P18; (2006) 103(7) L.S.G. 23; (2006) 150 S.J.L.B. 128; *Times*, February 3, 2006, CA (Civ Div) . . . .   *Digested*, 06/**348**:
Applied, 07/464: *Considered*, 07/480

Collins *v* Hilton (Unreported, April 20, 2007), CC (Manchester) [*Ex rel.* James Hogg, Pupil Barrister, St James's Chambers, Manchester] . . . .   *Digested*, 07/**3107**

Collins & Aikman Europe SA, Re [2006] EWHC 1343 (Ch); [2006] B.C.C. 861; [2007] 1 B.C.L.C. 182; [2007] I.L.Pr. 2, Ch D (Companies Ct) . . . .   *Digested*, 07/**2386**

Colls *v* Home & Colonial Stores Ltd; *sub nom* Home & Colonial Stores Ltd *v* Colls [1904] A.C. 179, HL; reversing [1902] 1 Ch. 302, CA . . . .   *Applied*, 64/1200, 70/825, 71/3750, 79/797, 84/1150, 85/1085, 05/3434: *Considered*, 00/4633: *Explained*, 07/2962

Colonial Mutual Life Assurance Society *v* Producers and Citizens Co-operative Assurance Co of Australia Ltd 46 C.L.R. 41 . . . .   *Considered*, 07/2943

Color Drack GmbH *v* Lexx International Vertriebs GmbH (C-386/05) [2007] I.L.Pr. 35, ECJ . . . .   *Digested*, 07/**1576**

Coloroll Pension Trustees Ltd *v* Russell (C-200/91) [1995] All E.R. (EC) 23; [1994] E.C.R. I-4389; [1995] I.C.R. 179; [1994] I.R.L.R. 586; [1994] O.P.L.R. 179; *Times*, November 30, 1994; *Financial Times*, October 4, 1994, ECJ . . . .   *Digested*, 95/**2001**:
Applied, 02/3380: *Considered*, 96/2562, 07/3024

Columbus Container Services BVBA & Co *v* Finanzamt Bielefeld-Innenstadt (C-298/05) 10 I.T.L. Rep. 366; [2007] S.T.I. 2846, ECJ (1st Chamber)

Colzani *v* RUWA Polstereimaschinen GmbH (C-24/76) see Estasis Salotti di Colzani Aimo e Gianmario Colzani *v* RUWA Polstereimaschinen GmbH (C-24/76)

Comfort Hotels *v* Wembley Stadium [1988] 1 W.L.R. 872; [1988] 3 All E.R. 53; (1988) 132 S.J. 967, Ch D . . . .   *Digested*, 88/**2957**:
Applied, 91/2870, 91/2984: *Considered*, 91/2986, 07/999

Comite International de la Rayonne et des Fibres Synthetiques (CIRFS) *v* Commission of the European Communities (C-313/90) [1993] E.C.R. I-1125, ECJ (5th Chamber) . . . .   *Digested*, 93/**4393**:
Applied, 98/2334, 06/1545: *Considered*, 07/1540: *Distinguished*, 07/1564: *Followed*, 02/1554

Commercial Veneer Co Ltd *v* Printing House Properties Ltd [1957] E.G.D. 119 . . . .   *Considered*, 07/2722

Commerzbank AG *v* Keen see Keen *v* Commerzbank AG

Commission of the European Communities *v* Aktionsgemeinschaft Recht und Eigentum eV (ARE) (C-78/03 P) [2005] E.C.R. I-10737; [2006] 2 C.M.L.R. 48, ECJ. . . .   *Digested*, 07/**1564**

Commission of the European Communities *v* Anic Partecipazioni SpA (C-49/92 P) [1999] E.C.R. I-4125; [2001] 4 C.M.L.R. 17, ECJ (6th Chamber) . . . .   *Digested*, 01/**758**:
Applied, 03/558, 07/1545: *Considered*, 07/605: *Distinguished*, 04/494: *Followed*, 05/1435

Commission of the European Communities *v* Austria (C-209/04) [2006] E.C.R. I-2755; [2006] Env. L.R. 39, ECJ (2nd Chamber) . . . .   *Digested*, 07/**1470**

Commission of the European Communities *v* Austria (C-29/04); *sub nom* Modling Waste Disposal Contract, Re (C-29/04) [2005] E.C.R. I-9705; [2006] 1 C.M.L.R. 40, ECJ. . . . .   *Digested*, 06/**3420**:
Followed, 07/3325

Commission of the European Communities *v* Belgium (C-254/05); *sub nom* Automatic Fire Detection, Re (C-254/05) [2007] 3 C.M.L.R. 13, ECJ (4th Chamber)

Commission of the European Communities *v* Belgium (C-304/88) [1990] E.C.R. I-2801, ECJ . . . .   *Applied*, 07/1605

Commission of the European Communities *v* Belgium (C-408/03); *sub nom* Conditions of Residence and Deportation, Re (C-408/03) [2006] All E.R. (EC) 725; [2006] E.C.R. I-2647; [2006] 2 C.M.L.R. 41; [2006] C.E.C. 850, ECJ . . . . . .   *Digested*, 07/**1611**

Commission of the European Communities *v* Belgium (C-422/05); *sub nom* Night Flight Restrictions, Re (C-422/05) [2007] 3 C.M.L.R. 19, ECJ (3rd Chamber)

Commission of the European Communities *v* Belgium (C-437/04) [2007] S.T.I. 1052, ECJ

Commission of the European Communities *v* Belgium (C-522/04) [2007] Pens. L.R. 247, ECJ

Commission of the European Communities *v* Belgium (C-87/94) [1996] E.C.R. I-2043, ECJ (5th Chamber) . . . .   *Considered*, 06/3418, 07/2795

Commission of the European Communities *v* CAS Succhi di Frutta SpA (C-496/99 P) [2004] E.C.R. I-3801, ECJ . . . .   *Applied*, 07/2795

Commission of the European Communities v Council of the European Communities
(45/86); *sub nom* Generalised Tariff Preferences, Re (45/86) [1987] E.C.R.
1493; [1988] 2 C.M.L.R. 131; *Times*, April 25, 1987, ECJ . . . .   *Digested*, 89/**1577**:
         Applied, 07/1556

Commission of the European Communities v Council of the European Communities (C-
300/89); *sub nom* Titanium Dioxide Directive, Re (C-300/89) [1991] E.C.R. I-
2867; [1993] 3 C.M.L.R. 359; *Times*, August 21, 1991, ECJ . . . .   *Digested*, 91/**3857**:
         Considered, 03/1455, 07/1563

Commission of the European Communities v Council of the European Union (C-281/
01); *sub nom* Energy Star Agreement, Re (C-281/01) [2002] E.C.R. I-12049;
[2003] 1 C.M.L.R. 15, ECJ (5th Chamber) . . . .   *Digested*, 03/**1425**:
         Applied, 07/1563

Commission of the European Communities v Council of the European Union (C-533/
03) [2007] S.T.C. 1121; [2006] E.C.R. I-1025; [2006] S.T.I. 234, ECJ (2nd
Chamber)

Commission of the European Communities v Council of the European Union (C-94/03)
[2006] Env. L.R. 45, ECJ (2nd Chamber) . . . .   *Digested*, 07/**1563**

Commission of the European Communities v Cresson (C-432/04) [2007] All E.R. (EC)
752; [2006] E.C.R. I-6387, ECJ

Commission of the European Communities v Denmark (C-150/04); *sub nom* Taxation of
Pension Contributions, Re (C-150/04) [2007] S.T.C. 1392; [2007] 2 C.M.L.R.
16; [2007] S.T.I. 254, ECJ . . . .   *Digested*, 07/**1618**

Commission of the European Communities v Denmark (C-192/01); *sub nom* Prohibition
of Marketing of Enriched Foods, Re (C-192/01) [2003] E.C.R. I-9693; [2003]
3 C.M.L.R. 29, ECJ . . . .   *Digested*, 04/**1600**:
         Applied, 05/1450: *Followed*, 05/1732, 07/1606

Commission of the European Communities v Finland (C-195/04); *sub nom* Admissibility
of Art.226 EC Action (C-195/04), Re [2007] 2 C.M.L.R. 50, ECJ (2nd
Chamber) . . . .   *Digested*, 07/**1541**

Commission of the European Communities v Finland (C-54/05); *sub nom* Motor Vehicle
Transfer Licences, Re (C-54/05) [2007] 2 C.M.L.R. 33, ECJ (2nd Chamber) . .   *Digested*, 07/**1605**

Commission of the European Communities v France (C-232/05) [2006] E.C.R. I-10071;
[2007] 3 C.M.L.R. 3, ECJ (1st Chamber) . . . .   *Digested*, 07/**1649**

Commission of the European Communities v France (C-255/04); *sub nom* Law on
Licensing System of Performing Artists Agents, Re (C-255/04) [2007] All E.R.
(EC) 435; [2006] E.C.R. I-5251; [2006] 3 C.M.L.R. 25, ECJ (1st Chamber) . . .   *Digested*, 07/**1634**

Commission of the European Communities v France (C-304/02); *sub nom* Control
Measures for Fishing Activities, Re (C-304/02) [2005] E.C.R. I-6263; [2005] 3
C.M.L.R. 13, ECJ . . . .   *Digested*, 06/**1525**:
         Followed, 07/1628

Commission of the European Communities v France (C-334/02); *sub nom* Levy to
Income on Investments, Re (C-334/02) [2007] S.T.C. 54; [2004] E.C.R. I-
2229; [2005] 2 C.M.L.R. 24; [2006] 1 C.M.L.R. 44; [2006] B.T.C. 55; 6 I.T.L.
Rep. 642; [2004] S.T.I. 558, ECJ (5th Chamber) . . . .   *Digested*, 04/**3772**

Commission of the European Communities v France (C-340/02) [2004] E.C.R. I-9845,
ECJ . . . .   *Applied*, 07/2795

Commission of the European Communities v France (C-97/00) [2001] E.C.R. I-2053,
ECJ . . . .   *Applied*, 07/1574

Commission of the European Communities v France (C177/04) [2006] E.C.R. I-2461,
ECJ . . . .   *Followed*, 07/1628

Commission of the European Communities v France (C35/97) [1998] E.C.R. I-5325,
ECJ (5th Chamber) . . . .   *Followed*, 05/3860,
         07/3830

Commission of the European Communities v Germany (C-191/95) [1999] All E.R. (EC)
483; [1998] E.C.R. I-5449; [1999] 2 C.M.L.R. 1265; *Times*, October 10, 1998,
ECJ. . . . .   *Digested*, 98/**2313**:
         Considered, 03/1431, 07/1587

Commission of the European Communities v Germany (C-318/05) [2007] S.T.I. 2188;
Times, October 11, 2007, ECJ (Grand Chamber)

Commission of the European Communities v Germany (C-387/99); *sub nom* Vitamin
Supplements, Re (C-387/99) [2004] E.C.R. I-3751; [2006] 3 C.M.L.R. 16, ECJ
(6th Chamber) . . . .   *Digested*, 07/**1606**:
         Followed, 05/1447

Commission of the European Communities v Germany (C-401/06) [2007] S.T.I. 2848,
ECJ (3rd Chamber)

Commission of the European Communities v Germany (C-427/98); *sub nom* Coupon
Scheme, Re (C-427/98) [2003] S.T.C. 301; [2002] E.C.R. I-8315; [2003] 1
C.M.L.R. 4; [2003] B.T.C. 5149; [2003] B.V.C. 205; [2003] S.T.I. 101, ECJ . . . .   *Applied*, 03/4579:
         Considered, 05/4341: *Distinguished*, 07/4310

Commission of the European Communities v Germany (C-431/92); *sub nom*
Grosskrotzenburg Power Station, Re (C-431/92) [1995] E.C.R. I-2189; [1996]
1 C.M.L.R. 196, ECJ . . . .   *Digested*, 96/**2718**:
         Applied, 07/1470: *Followed*, 00/4460

Commission of the European Communities *v* Germany (C-503/04); *sub nom* Waste Water Contract, Re (C-503/04) [2007] 3 C.M.L.R. 40, ECJ (2nd Chamber)

Commission of the European Communities *v* Germany (C-98/03) [2006] E.C.R. I-53; [2006] Env. L.R. 36, ECJ (2nd Chamber) . . . .   *Digested,* 07/**1476**

Commission of the European Communities *v* Germany (C209/00) [2002] E.C.R. I-11695, ECJ . . . .   *Applied,* 07/1649

Commission of the European Communities *v* Greece (C-13/06) [2007] S.T.C. 194; [2006] S.T.I. 2747, ECJ (4th Chamber) . . . .   *Digested,* 07/**1598**

Commission of the European Communities *v* Greece (C-156/04); *sub nom* Temporary Importation of Motor Vehicles, Re (C-156/04) [2007] 3 C.M.L.R. 11, ECJ (1st Chamber)

Commission of the European Communities *v* Greece (C-331/94) [1996] S.T.C. 1168; [1996] E.C.R. I-2675; [1997] B.T.C. 5079; [1997] B.V.C. 190, ECJ (5th Chamber) . . . .   *Applied,* 07/4341

Commission of the European Communities *v* Greece (C-387/97) [2000] E.C.R. I-5047; [2001] Env. L.R. D2; *Times,* July 7, 2000, ECJ . . . .   *Digested,* 00/**2301**:
                 Considered, 06/1525: *Followed,* 07/1628

Commission of the European Communities *v* Greece (C-415/03); *sub nom* Aid to Olympic Airways, Re (C-415/03) [2005] E.C.R. I-3875; [2005] 3 C.M.L.R. 10, ECJ (2nd Chamber) . . . .   *Digested,* 06/**1588**:
                 Applied, 07/1649

Commission of the European Communities *v* Greece (C-65/05) [2007] All E.R. (EC) 738; [2006] E.C.R. I-10341; [2007] 1 C.M.L.R. 26; [2007] C.E.C. 306, ECJ (2nd Chamber)

Commission of the European Communities *v* Greencore Group Plc (C-123/03 P) [2004] E.C.R. I-11647; [2005] 4 C.M.L.R. 1, ECJ (2nd Chamber) . . . .   *Applied,* 06/1548:
                Considered, 07/1587

Commission of the European Communities *v* Ireland (C-175/05) [2007] E.C.D.R. 8, ECJ (6th Chamber) . . . .   *Digested,* 07/**2519**

Commission of the European Communities *v* Ireland (C-183/05) [2007] Env. L.R. 23, ECJ . . . .   *Digested,* 07/**1596**

Commission of the European Communities *v* Ireland (C-216/05) [2006] E.C.R. I-10787; [2007] Env. L.R. 18, ECJ . . . .   *Digested,* 07/**1574**

Commission of the European Communities *v* Ireland (C-282/02) [2005] E.C.R. I-4653; [2006] Env. L.R. 21, ECJ (2nd Chamber) . . . .   *Applied,* 07/1596

Commission of the European Communities *v* Ireland (C-459/03); *sub nom* Dispute over MOX Plant, Re (C-459/03) [2006] All E.R. (EC) 1013; [2006] E.C.R. I-4635; [2006] 2 C.M.L.R. 59, ECJ . . . .   *Digested,* 07/**1594**

Commission of the European Communities *v* Italy (C-119/04); *sub nom* Employment Conditions of Foreign-Language Assistants, Re (C-119/04) [2006] E.C.R. I-6885; [2006] 3 C.M.L.R. 43, ECJ . . . .   *Digested,* 07/**1628**

Commission of the European Communities *v* Italy (C-134/05); *sub nom* Licensing of Debt Collection Services, Re (C-134/05) [2007] 3 C.M.L.R. 36, ECJ (1st Chamber)

Commission of the European Communities *v* Italy (C-135/05) [2007] Env. L.R. 33, ECJ (3rd Chamber)

Commission of the European Communities *v* Italy (C-207/05) (Unreported, June 1, 2006), ECJ . . . .   *Applied,* 07/1649

Commission of the European Communities *v* Italy (C-212/99) [2001] E.C.R. I-4923, ECJ (6th Chamber) . . . .   *Followed,* 07/1628

Commission of the European Communities *v* Italy (C-260/04) [2007] 3 C.M.L.R. 50, ECJ (4th Chamber)

Commission of the European Communities *v* Italy (C-270/02) [2004] E.C.R. I-1559; [2004] 3 C.M.L.R. 26, ECJ (3rd Chamber) . . . .   *Digested,* 05/**687**:
               Applied, 07/1605: *Followed,* 06/1759

Commission of the European Communities *v* Italy (C-388/01); *sub nom* Museum Admission Rates, Re (C-388/01) [2003] E.C.R. I-721; [2003] 1 C.M.L.R. 40; *Times,* January 30, 2003, ECJ (6th Chamber) . . . .   *Digested,* 03/**1447**:
                 Followed, 07/3830

Commission of the European Communities *v* Italy (C-420/01) [2003] E.C.R. I-6445, ECJ . . . .   *Applied,* 07/1605

Commission of the European Communities *v* Italy (C-486/04) [2007] Env. L.R. D10; [2006] E.C.R. IA-11025, ECJ

Commission of the European Communities *v* Italy (C35/96); *sub nom* Customs Agents, Re (C35/96) [1998] E.C.R. I-3851; [1998] 5 C.M.L.R. 889, ECJ (5th Chamber) . . . .   *Applied,* 07/653:
                 Followed, 01/761

Commission of the European Communities *v* Jego-Quere et Cie SA (C-263/02 P) [2005] Q.B. 237; [2005] 2 W.L.R. 179; [2004] All E.R. (EC) 983; [2004] E.C.R. I-3425; [2004] 2 C.M.L.R. 12; [2004] C.E.C. 284, ECJ (6th Chamber) .   *Digested,* 05/**1470**:
               Applied, 07/1591: *Followed,* 05/942

Commission of the European Communities *v* Luxembourg (C-32/05) [2007] Env. L.R. 22, ECJ . . . .   *Digested,* 07/**1597**

Commission of the European Communities v Netherlands (C-3/96) [1998] E.C.R. I-
3031; [1999] Env. L.R. 147, ECJ . . . .   *Digested*, 99/**2155**:
                                   Applied, 07/1470: *Considered*, 04/3041
Commission of the European Communities v Netherlands (C-50/06); *sub nom*
Expulsion of Foreign Nationals, Re (C-50/06) [2007] 3 C.M.L.R. 8, ECJ (3rd
Chamber) . . . .   *Digested*, 07/**1559**
Commission of the European Communities v Netherlands (C-523/04); *sub nom* Dutch
Air Transport Agreement, Re (C-523/04) [2007] 2 C.M.L.R. 48, ECJ
Commission of the European Communities v Portugal (C-191/05) [2006] E.C.R. I-
6853; [2007] Env. L.R. D2, ECJ (2nd Chamber)
Commission of the European Communities v Portugal (C-239/04) [2007] Env. L.R. D4;
[2006] E.C.R. IA-10183, ECJ
Commission of the European Communities v Portugal (C-53/05); *sub nom*
Implementation of Art.5(3) of the Rental Rights Directive, Re (C-53/05) [2006]
E.C.R. I-6215; [2006] 3 C.M.L.R. 35; [2006] E.C.D.R. 24, ECJ (3rd Chamber)   *Digested*, 07/**2525**:
                                               Applied, 07/2519
Commission of the European Communities v Portugal (C-61/05) [2006] E.C.R. I-6779;
[2006] 3 C.M.L.R. 36; [2006] E.C.D.R. 25, ECJ (3rd Chamber) . . . .   *Digested*, 07/**2526**
Commission of the European Communities v SGL Carbon AG (C-301/04 P); *sub nom*
Graphite Electrodes Cartel Appeal, Re (C-301/04 P) [2006] 5 C.M.L.R. 15, ECJ
(2nd Chamber) . . . .   *Digested*, 07/**609**:
                                            Previous proceedings, 05/552
Commission of the European Communities v Spain (C-195/02) [2004] E.C.R. I-7857;
[2005] R.T.R. 23; *Times*, October 11, 2004, ECJ. . . . .   *Digested*, 06/**3528**:
                                               Followed, 07/1628
Commission of the European Communities v Spain (C-404/00) [2003] E.C.R. I-6695,
ECJ. . . . .   *Applied*, 07/1649
Commission of the European Communities v Spain (C-503/03) [2007] All E.R. (EC)
797; [2006] E.C.R. I-1097, ECJ
Commission of the European Communities v Sweden (C-104/06) [2007] 2 C.M.L.R. 5;
[2007] S.T.I. 194, ECJ . . . .   *Digested*, 07/**1612**
Commission of the European Communities v United Kingdom (124/81); *sub nom* Ultra
Heat Treated Milk, Re (124/81) [1983] E.C.R. 203; [1983] 2 C.M.L.R. 1; *Times*,
July 26, 1982, ECJ. . . . .   *Digested*, 83/**1531**:
                                Applied, 07/1605: *Considered*, 07/1604
Commission of the European Communities v United Kingdom (C-127/05) [2007] All
E.R. (EC) 986; [2007] 3 C.M.L.R. 20; [2007] I.C.R. 1393; [2007] I.R.L.R. 720;
Times, June 25, 2007, ECJ (3rd Chamber) . . . .   *Digested*, 07/**1567**
Commission of the European Communities v United Kingdom (C-199/04) [2007] Env.
L.R. D12, ECJ
Commission of the European Communities v United Kingdom (C-305/03) [2007]
S.T.C. 1211; [2006] S.T.I. 383; *Times*, February 24, 2006, ECJ (3rd Chamber)
Commission of the European Communities v United Kingdom (C-33/03) [2005] S.T.C.
582; [2005] E.C.R. I-1865; [2005] 2 C.M.L.R. 26; [2005] C.E.C. 661; [2007]
B.T.C. 5917; [2007] B.V.C. 864; [2005] S.T.I. 366; *Times*, March 15, 2005, ECJ
(1st Chamber) . . . .   *Applied*, 06/4442
Commission of the European Communities v United Kingdom (C-382/92); *sub nom*
Business Transfers, Re (C-382/92) [1994] E.C.R. I-2435; [1995] 1 C.M.L.R.
345; [1994] I.C.R. 664; [1994] I.R.L.R. 392; *Times*, June 27, 1994; *Financial
Times*, June 14, 1994, ECJ . . . .   *Digested*, 94/**4926**:
                      Considered, 95/2031, 96/2596, 96/2641, 04/1299, 07/1394
Commission of the European Communities v United Kingdom (C-383/92) [1994]
E.C.R. I-2479, ECJ. . . . .   *Applied*, 07/1393
Commission of the European Communities v United Kingdom (C-484/04); *sub nom* UK
Working Time Guidelines, Re (C-484/04) [2006] E.C.R. I-7471; [2006] 3
C.M.L.R. 48; [2007] C.E.C. 56; [2007] I.C.R. 592; [2006] I.R.L.R. 888; *Times*,
September 21, 2006, ECJ (3rd Chamber) . . . .   *Digested*, 07/**1442**
Commission of the European Communities v United Kingdom (C-508/03) [2006] Q.B.
764; [2006] 3 W.L.R. 492; [2006] E.C.R. I-3969; [2007] Env. L.R. 1; [2006]
J.P.L. 1673; [2006] 19 E.G. 172 (C.S.); [2006] N.P.C. 52, ECJ (1st Chamber) . .   *Digested*, 07/**3269**:
                                       Applied, 07/3271, 07/3272
Commission of the European Communities v United Kingdom (C-6/04) [2005] E.C.R.
I-9017; [2006] Env. L.R. 29; *Times*, October 27, 2005, ECJ (2nd Chamber) . . .   *Digested*, 06/**1537**:
                                               Applied, 07/1476
Commission of the European Communities v Volkswagen AG (C-74/04 P); *sub nom*
Volkswagen AG v Commission of the European Communities (C-74/04 P)
[2007] Bus. L.R. 35; [2006] E.C.R. I-6585; [2007] R.T.R. 12; [2007] I.C.R. 217,
ECJ. . . . .   *Digested*, 07/**1543**
Commissioner of Police of the Metropolis v Hendricks; *sub nom* Hendricks v
Commissioner of Police of the Metropolis [2002] EWCA Civ 1686; [2003] 1 All
E.R. 654; [2003] I.C.R. 530; [2003] I.R.L.R. 96; (2003) 100(5) L.S.G. 30;
(2002) 146 S.J.L.B. 274; *Times*, December 6, 2002, CA (Civ Div); reversing
[2002] Emp. L.R. 32, EAT . . . .   *Digested*, 03/**1298**:
                                         Considered, 05/1229, 07/1440

Commissioner of Police of the Metropolis v Hurst see R. (on the application of Hurst) v HM Coroner for Northern District London

Commissioner of Police of the Metropolis v Kay see Kay v Commissioner of Police of the Metropolis

Commonwealth Store (Slough) Ltd, Re (Unreported, May 3, 1971) . . . . *Considered, 07/2440*

Commune de Macot la Plagne v Sebluxl SA [2007] I.L.Pr. 12, Cass (F) . . . . *Digested, 07/**681***

Compagnie de Saint-Gobain, Zweigniederlassung Germany v Finanzamt Aachen-Innenstadt (C-307/97) [2000] S.T.C. 854; [1999] E.C.R. I-6161; [2001] 3 C.M.L.R. 34, ECJ . . . . *Digested, 01/**5212**:*
Applied, 02/1572: Considered, 06/4157, 07/3974: Followed, 04/2831

Compagnie Gervais Danone SA v Piotrowski (ICD2954) [2007] E.T.M.R. 42, OHIM (Cancellation Div) . . . . *Digested, 07/**1555***

Compagnie Nouvelle France Navigation SA v Compagnie Navale Afrique du Nord (The Oranie and The Tunisie) [1966] 1 Lloyd's Rep. 477; 116 N.L.J. 948, CA . . . . *Digested, 66/**380**:*
Considered, 07/229

Compagnie Royale Asturienne des Mines SA v Commission of the European Communities (29/83) [1984] E.C.R. 1679; [1985] 1 C.M.L.R. 688, ECJ (4th Chamber) . . . . *Digested, 85/**1314**:*
Applied, 07/1545

Companhia de Mocambique v British South Africa Co see British South Africa Co v Companhia de Mocambique

Companhia de Seguros Imperio v Heath (REBX) Ltd see Cia de Seguros Imperio v Heath (REBX) Ltd (formerly CE Heath & Co (America) Ltd)

Compania Espanola para la Fabricacion de Aceros Inoxidables SA (ACERINOX) v Commission of the European Communities (C-57/02 P) [2005] E.C.R. I-6689; [2005] 5 C.M.L.R. 15, ECJ (1st Chamber) . . . . *Digested, 06/**573**:*
Applied, 07/603

Company A v Revenue and Customs Commissioners [2007] S.T.C. (S.C.D.) 466; [2007] S.T.I. 1326, Sp Comm . . . . *Digested, 07/**4066***

Company (No.001567 of 1988), Re see Boswell (Steels), Re

Company (No.000709 of 1992), Re see O'Neill v Phillips

Company (No.003025 of 1997), Re see Galileo Group Ltd, Re

Company (No.0005945 of 2006), Re [2006] EWHC 3436 (Ch); [2007] B.P.I.R. 1; (2006) 150 S.J.L.B. 1153, Ch D . . . . *Digested, 07/**2461***

COMPARATIVE VISUAL ASSESSMENTS/Assessment system (T125/04) [2007] E.P.O.R. 33, EPO (Technical Bd App) . . . . *Not followed, 07/2591*

Compass Trustees Ltd v McBarnett [2003] W.T.L.R. 461; (2002-03) 5 I.T.E.L.R. 44, Royal Ct (Jer) . . . . *Digested, 03/**4471**:*
Considered, 07/4244

Competition Authority v O'Regan [2007] IESC 22; [2007] E.C.C. 22, Sup Ct (Irl)

Computershare Investor Services Plc v Jackson [2007] EWCA Civ 1065; (2007) 104(44) L.S.G. 32; (2007) 151 S.J.L.B. 1434, CA (Civ Div); affirming UKEAT/0503/06/CEA, EAT

COMVIK/Two identities (T641/00) [2004] E.P.O.R. 10, EPO (Technical Bd App) . . . . . *Digested, 04/**2329**:*
Applied, 05/2484, 07/2630: Followed, 07/2589

Comyn Ching & Co (London) Ltd v Oriental Tube Co Ltd [1981] Com. L.R. 67; 17 B.L.R. 47, CA (Civ Div). . . . . *Digested, 81/**304**:*
Considered, 07/745

Concordia Bus Finland Oy AB (formerly Stagecoach Finland Oy AB) v Helsingin Kaupunki (C-513/99) [2004] All E.R. (EC) 87; [2002] E.C.R. I-7213; [2003] 3 C.M.L.R. 20, ECJ . . . . *Digested, 04/**3162**:*
Applied, 07/3327: Followed, 05/3354

Concurrence SA v Sony France SA [2007] E.C.C. 27, Trib Comm (F)

Conde Nast Publications Ltd v Customs and Excise Commissioners; sub nom Conde Nast Publications Ltd v Revenue and Customs Commissioners [2006] EWCA Civ 976; [2006] S.T.C. 1721; [2007] 2 C.M.L.R. 35; [2006] Eu. L.R. 1152; [2006] B.T.C. 5555; [2006] B.V.C. 625; [2006] S.T.I. 1881; (2006) 103(30) L.S.G. 30; Times, July 28, 2006, CA (Civ Div); reversing [2005] EWHC 1167 (Ch); [2005] S.T.C. 1327; [2005] Eu. L.R. 1014; [2005] B.T.C. 5447; [2005] B.V.C. 478; [2005] S.T.I. 1093, Ch D; affirming [2005] B.V.C. 2259, V&DTr . . . . *Digested, 06/**4465**:*
Applied, 06/4460: Considered, 07/4360

Conde Nast Publications Ltd v Revenue and Customs Commissioners see Conde Nast Publications Ltd v Customs and Excise Commissioners

Conde Nast Publications Ltd v Revenue and Customs Commissioners see Fleming (t/a Bodycraft) v Customs and Excise Commissioners

Conditions of Residence and Deportation, Re (C-408/03) see Commission of the European Communities v Belgium (C-408/03)

Condron v National Assembly for Wales see R. (on the application of Condron) v National Assembly for Wales

Conduit Europe SA v Telefonica de Espana SAU [2007] E.C.C. 17, Aud (Sp)

Confederacion Espanola de Empresarios de Estaciones de Servicio v Compania Espanola de Petroleos SA (C-217/05) [2007] 4 C.M.L.R. 5; [2007] C.E.C. 143, ECJ (3rd Chamber) . . . . *Digested, 07/**642***

Confederation Generale du Travail (CGT) *v* Premier Ministre (C-385/05) see Confederation Generale du Travail (CGT) *v* Prime Minister (C-385/05)

Confederation Generale du Travail (CGT) *v* Prime Minister (C-385/05); *sub nom* Confederation Generale du Travail (CGT) *v* Premier Ministre (C-385/05) [2007] 2 C.M.L.R. 6; [2007] C.E.C. 457, ECJ (2nd Chamber) . . . .   *Digested*, 07/**1393**

Conijn *v* Finanzamt Hamburg-Nord (C-346/04) [2006] E.C.R. I-6137; [2006] 3 C.M.L.R. 34; [2006] C.E.C. 1013, ECJ (3rd Chamber) . . . .   *Digested*, 07/**4026**

CONJUCHEM/Fusion peptide inhibitors (T433/05) [2007] E.P.O.R. 52, EPO (Technical Bd App)

Conlon *v* Simms; *sub nom* Simms *v* Conlon [2006] EWCA Civ 1749; [2007] 3 All E.R. 802; *Times*, January 17, 2007, CA (Civ Div); reversing [2006] EWHC 401 (Ch); [2006] 2 All E.R. 1024; (2006) 103(13) L.S.G. 25, Ch D . . . .   *Digested*, 07/**339**: *Considered*, 07/471

Conn *v* Sunderland City Council; *sub nom* Sunderland City Council *v* Conn [2007] EWCA Civ 1492; *Times*, November 23, 2007, CA (Civ Div) . . . .   *Digested*, 07/**1377**

Connolly *v* DPP [2007] EWHC 237 (Admin); [2007] 2 All E.R. 1012; [2007] 2 Cr. App. R. 5; [2007] H.R.L.R. 17; [2007] Crim. L.R. 729; (2007) 157 N.L.J. 295; *Times*, February 28, 2007, DC . . . .   *Digested*, 07/**898**

Connolly *v* Sellers Arenascene Ltd (No.2) see Sellers Arenascene Ltd *v* Connolly (No.2)

Connolly *v* Tasker see Heil *v* Rankin

Connor *v* Chief Constable of Merseyside [2006] EWCA Civ 1549; [2007] H.R.L.R. 6; [2007] U.K.H.R.R. 621; [2006] Po. L.R. 281; (2006) 103(47) L.S.G. 29; *Times*, December 4, 2006, CA (Civ Div) . . . .   *Digested*, 07/**4191**

Connors *v* United Kingdom (40086/98) see Ezeh *v* United Kingdom (39665/98)

Connors *v* United Kingdom (66746/01) (2005) 40 E.H.R.R. 9; 16 B.H.R.C. 639; [2004] H.L.R. 52; [2004] 4 P.L.R. 16; [2004] N.P.C. 86; *Times*, June 10, 2004, ECHR . . . .   *Digested*, 04/**1992**: *Applied*, 06/2173, 06/2708: *Considered*, 06/1649, 06/2046: *Distinguished*, 05/190, 07/2242: *Explained*, 05/3424

Conor Medsystems Inc *v* Angiotech Pharmaceuticals Inc; *sub nom* Angiotech Pharmaceuticals Inc *v* Conor Medsystems Inc; Angiotech Pharmaceuticals Inc's Patent (No.706376) [2007] EWCA Civ 5; [2007] R.P.C. 20; (2007) 94 B.M.L.R. 122; [2007] 30(5) I.P.D. 30031, CA (Civ Div); affirming [2006] EWHC 260 (Pat); [2006] R.P.C. 28; (2006) 29(5) I.P.D. 29042, Ch D (Patents Ct) . .   *Digested*, 07/**2619** *Applied*, 53/159,

Conquer *v* Boot [1928] 2 K.B. 336, KBD . . . . 83/130: *Considered*, 76/96, 07/1365

Conseil General de la Vienne *v* Directeur General des Douanes et Droits Indirects (C-419/04) [2006] 3 C.M.L.R. 27, ECJ (3rd Chamber) . . . .   *Digested*, 07/**1031**

Consett Iron Co Ltd *v* Assessment Committee for No.5 or North-Western Area of County of Durham see Consett Iron Co Ltd *v* Durham Assessment Committee

Consett Iron Co Ltd *v* Durham Assessment Committee; *sub nom* Consett Iron Co Ltd *v* Assessment Committee for No.5 or North-Western Area of County of Durham [1931] A.C. 396, HL . . . .   *Applied*, 07/**3342**

Consistent Group Ltd *v* Kalwak; *sub nom* Consistent Group Ltd *v* Welsh Country Foods Ltd; A2/2007/1211, CA (Civ Div); reversing [2007] I.R.L.R. 560, EAT . .   *Digested*, 07/**1345**

Consistent Group Ltd *v* Welsh Country Foods Ltd see Consistent Group Ltd *v* Kalwak

Consoft SA *v* Consoft GmbH Computertechnik (R742/2005-2) [2007] E.T.M.R. 22, OHIM (2nd Bd App) . . . .   *Digested*, 07/**2649**

Consolidated Criminal Practice Direction (Amendment No.14: Forms for Use in Criminal Proceedings) [2007] 1 W.L.R. 1535; [2007] 1 Cr. App. R. 22, Sup Ct . . . .   *Digested*, 07/**1010**

Consolidated Criminal Practice Direction (Amendment No.15: Treatment of Vulnerable Defendants, Binding Over Orders and Conditional Discharges, Settling the Indictment, Management of Cases to be Heard in the Crown Court and Forms for Use in Criminal Proceedings) [2007] 2 Cr. App. R. 20, Sup Ct

Consolidated Criminal Practice Direction (Amendment No.4) (Guidance to Jurors) see Practice Direction (Crown Ct: Guidance to Jurors)

Consorzio Industrie Fiammiferi (CIF) *v* Autorita Garante della Concorrenza e del Mercato (C198/01) [2004] All E.R. (EC) 380; [2003] E.C.R. I-8055; [2003] 5 C.M.L.R. 16, ECJ . . . .   *Digested*, 04/**495**: *Followed*, 07/643

Constantine *v* Lambeth LBC see Kay *v* Lambeth LBC

Constitutionality of Framework Decision on the European Arrest Warrant, Re [2007] 3 C.M.L.R. 24, US CR (CZ)

Contex Drouzhba *v* Wiseman [2007] EWCA Civ 1201; (2007) 157 N.L.J. 1695, CA (Civ Div); affirming [2006] EWHC 2708 (QB); [2007] 1 B.C.L.C. 758, QBD . . .   *Digested*, 07/**4188**

Continental Assurance Co of London Plc (In Liquidation), Re see Singer *v* Beckett

Continental Contractors Ltd *v* Medway Oil and Storage Co Ltd see Medway Oil and Storage Co Ltd *v* Continental Contractors Ltd

Continental Property Ventures Inc *v* White [2007] L. & T.R. 4; [2006] 1 E.G.L.R. 85; [2006] 16 E.G. 148, Lands Tr . . . .   *Digested*, 06/**2722**

Continental Shelf 128 Ltd *v* Hebrew University of Jerusalem; *sub nom* Continental Shelf 128 Ltd's Trade Mark; EINSTEIN Trade Mark [2007] R.P.C. 23, App Person; reversing [2007] E.T.M.R. 6, TMR . . . .   *Digested*, 07/**2686**

Continental Shelf 128 Ltd's Trade Mark see Continental Shelf 128 Ltd v Hebrew University of Jerusalem

Contour Homes Ltd v Rowan see Contour Homes Ltd v Rowen

Contour Homes Ltd v Rowen; *sub nom* Contour Homes Ltd v Rowan [2007] EWCA Civ 842; [2007] 1 W.L.R. 2982; [2007] L. & T.R. 27; (2007) 151 S.J.L.B. 895; *Times*, July 13, 2007, CA (Civ Div)

Control Measures for Fishing Activities, Re (C-304/02) see Commission of the European Communities v France (C-304/02)

Cooke v Gaylo (Unreported, April 25, 2007), CC (Macclesfield) [*Ex rel.* Chris Middleton, Barrister, Oriel Chambers, 14 Water Street, Liverpool] . . . . *Digested*, 07/**3121**

Cookeson v Government of Australia [2001] EWHC Admin 149, QBD (Admin) . . . . . . *Distinguished*, 07/1668

Coombes v DPP [2006] EWHC 3263 (Admin); (2007) 171 J.P. 271; [2007] R.T.R. 31; (2007) 171 J.P.N. 547; *Times*, December 29, 2006, DC . . . . *Digested*, 07/**3538**

Coombes v Revenue and Customs Commissioners [2007] EWHC 3160 (Ch); [2007] S.T.I. 2701, Ch D

Cooney v Lancashire CC (Unreported, January 18, 2007), CC (Preston) [*Ex rel.* James Hogg, Barrister, St James's Chambers, 68 Quay Street, Manchester] . . . . *Digested*, 07/**3198**

Cooper v Director of Personnel Administration [2006] UKPC 37; [2007] 1 W.L.R. 101, PC (Trin) . . . . *Digested*, 07/**695**

Cooper v Houston see Cooper (A Bankrupt), Re

Cooper v United Kingdom (48843/99) (2004) 39 E.H.R.R. 8; [2004] Crim. L.R. 577; *Times*, January 12, 2004, ECHR . . . . *Digested*, 04/**1945**:
Applied, 05/234: *Distinguished*, 07/2216

Cooper (A Bankrupt), Re; *sub nom* Cooper v Houston [2005] NICh 1; [2006] N.I. 103; [2007] B.P.I.R. 1206, Ch D (NI)

Cooperatieve Vereniging Suiker Unie UA v Commission of the European Communities (40/73); *sub nom* European Sugar Cartel, Re (40/73); Suiker Unie v Commission of the European Communities (40/73) [1975] E.C.R. 1663; [1976] 1 C.M.L.R. 295; [1976] F.S.R. 443; *Times*, December 23, 1975, ECJ . . . . *Digested*, 76/**1055**:
Applied, 07/642: *Considered*, 78/1257, 05/570, 07/643:
Distinguished, 05/549

Cooperatieve Verkoop- en Productievereniging van Aardappelmeel en Derivaten Avebe BA v Commission of the European Communities (T-314/01) [2007] 4 C.M.L.R. 1, CFI (3rd Chamber)

Cooperative Insurance Society Ltd v Argyll Stores (Holdings) Ltd [1998] A.C. 1; [1997] 2 W.L.R. 898; [1997] 3 All E.R. 297; [1997] C.L.C. 1114; [1997] 1 E.G.L.R. 52; [1997] 23 E.G. 141; [1997] E.G. 81 (C.S.); (1997) 94(26) L.S.G. 30; (1997) 147 N.L.J. 845; (1997) 141 S.J.L.B. 131; [1997] N.P.C. 79; *Times*, May 26, 1997; *Independent*, June 5, 1997, HL; reversing [1996] Ch. 286; [1996] 3 W.L.R. 27; [1996] 3 All E.R. 934; (1996) 72 P. & C.R. 130; [1996] 1 E.G.L.R. 71; [1996] 09 E.G. 128; [1995] N.P.C. 199; *Times*, December 29, 1995; *Independent*, January 25, 1996, CA (Civ Div) . . . . *Digested*, 97/**3260**:
Considered, 07/245: *Followed*, 02/728

Coors Brewers Ltd v Adcock [2007] EWCA Civ 19; [2007] I.C.R. 983; [2007] I.R.L.R. 440; (2007) 151 S.J.L.B. 160, CA (Civ Div); reversing UKEAT/0460/05/DZM, EAT . . . . *Digested*, 07/**1356**

Coors Holdings Ltd v Dow Properties Ltd [2007] EWCA Civ 255; [2007] 2 P. & C.R. 22; [2007] N.P.C. 37, CA (Civ Div) . . . . *Digested*, 07/**2727**

Copland v United Kingdom (62617/00) (2007) 45 E.H.R.R. 37; *Times*, April 24, 2007, ECHR

Copoc v Chief Constable of South Yorkshire see Alcock v Chief Constable of South Yorkshire

Copyright in Architectural Drawings, Re (4 OB 41/06 T) [2007] E.C.C. 28, OGH (A)

Corbett v South Yorkshire Strategic HA [2006] EWCA Civ 1797; (2007) 151 S.J.L.B. 27, CA (Civ Div)

Corbett v South Yorkshire Strategic HA [2007] LS Law Medical 430, QBD (Sheffield) *Digested*, 07/**3063**:
Considered, 07/3065

Cordle v Cordle [2001] EWCA Civ 1791; [2002] 1 W.L.R. 1441; [2002] 1 F.L.R. 207; [2002] 1 F.C.R. 97; [2002] Fam. Law 174; (2002) 99(1) L.S.G. 19; (2001) 145 S.J.L.B. 262; *Times*, December 7, 2001; *Independent*, November 22, 2001, CA (Civ Div) . . . . *Digested*, 01/**2630**:
Applied, 06/1633, 07/1706

Coreck Maritime GmbH v Handelsveem BV (C-387/98); *sub nom* Handelsveem BV v Coreck Maritime GmbH (C-387/98) [2000] E.C.R. I-9337; [2001] C.L.C. 550; [2001] I.L.Pr. 39; *Times*, December 1, 2000, ECJ (5th Chamber) . . . . *Digested*, 01/**795**:
Applied, 06/764, 07/349: *Considered*, 06/438

Corkindale v Police Medical Appeal Board [2006] EWHC 3362 (Admin); *Times*, January 18, 2007, QBD (Admin)

Corner v Salford City Council [2007] R.V.R. 241, Lands Tr

Cornick v Cornick (No.2) [1995] 2 F.L.R. 490, CA (Civ Div) . . . . *Digested*, 96/**2872**:
Considered, 07/1706: *Subsequent related litigation*, 02/1687

Cornick v Cornick (No.3) [2001] 2 F.L.R. 1240; [2001] Fam. Law 871; (2002) 99(9) L.S.G. 27, Fam Div . . . . *Digested*, 02/**1687**:
Considered, 07/1706: *Disapproved*, 03/1595

Cornwall CC v Prater; *sub nom* Prater v Cornwall CC [2006] EWCA Civ 102; [2006] 2 All E.R. 1013; [2006] I.C.R. 731; [2006] I.R.L.R. 362; [2006] B.L.G.R. 479; (2006) 156 N.L.J. 372; *Independent*, February 28, 2006, CA (Civ Div); affirming UKEAT0055/05/SM, EAT . . . . *Digested*, 06/**1312**: *Applied*, 07/4132

Corporacion Habanos SA v Mastercigars Direct Ltd see Mastercigars Direct Ltd v Hunters & Frankau Ltd
Corporate Development Partners LLC v E-Relationship Marketing Ltd [2007] EWHC 436 (Ch); (2007) 104(14) L.S.G. 24, Ch D
Corr v IBC Vehicles Ltd [2006] EWCA Civ 331; [2007] Q.B. 46; [2006] 3 W.L.R. 395; [2006] 2 All E.R. 929; [2006] I.C.R. 1138; (2006) 103(16) L.S.G. 24; *Times*, April 21, 2006; *Independent*, April 6, 2006, CA (Civ Div); reversing [2005] EWHC 895 (QB); [2006] P.I.Q.R. P11, QBD . . . . *Digested*, 06/**2893**
Corus UK Ltd v Erewash BC [2006] EWCA Civ 1175; [2006] C.P. Rep. 41; [2007] 1 P. & C.R. 22, CA (Civ Div); affirming [2005] EWHC 2821 (Admin); [2005] N.P.C. 145, QBD (Admin) . . . . *Digested*, 07/**444**
Corus UK Ltd v Mainwaring (2007) 151 S.J.L.B. 1298, EAT
Cosgrove v Northern Ireland Ambulance Service [2006] NICA 44; [2007] I.R.L.R. 397, CA (NI) . . . . *Digested*, 07/**4507**
Cosgrove v Pattison [2001] C.P. Rep. 68; [2001] C.P.L.R. 177; *Times*, February 13, 2001, Ch D . . . . *Digested*, 01/**690**:
Applied, 07/336: *Cited*, 01/689: *Distinguished*, 03/476: *Followed*, 04/346
Costain Ltd v Wilson [2007] EWHC 713 (QB); (2007) 151 S.J.L.B. 502, QBD
Cotswold Computer Components Ltd v Revenue and Customs Commissioners [2007] S.T.I. 375, V&D Tr
Cott UK Ltd v FE Barber Ltd [1997] 3 All E.R. 540, QBD . . . . *Digested*, 97/**271**:
Applied, 07/528

Coulter v HM Advocate see Montgomery v HM Advocate
Coulthard v Disco Mix Club Ltd [2000] 1 W.L.R. 707; [1999] 2 All E.R. 457; [1999] E.M.L.R. 434; [1999] F.S.R. 900; *Times*, March 25, 1999; *Independent*, March 8, 1999, Ch D . . . . *Digested*, 99/**458**:
Considered, 07/472

Council for the Regulation of Health Care Professionals v General Medical Council; *sub nom* Ruscillo v Council for the Regulation of Health Care Professionals; Council for the Regulation of Health Care Professionals v Truscott; *joined case* Council for the Regulation of Health Care Professionals v Nursing and Midwifery Council [2004] EWCA Civ 1356; [2005] 1 W.L.R. 717; [2005] Lloyd's Rep. Med. 65; [2005] A.C.D. 69; [2004] 148 S.J.L.B. 1248; *Times*, October 27, 2004; *Independent*, October 28, 2004, CA (Civ Div); affirming [2004] EWHC 527 (Admin); [2004] 1 W.L.R. 2068; [2004] Lloyd's Rep. Med. 365; [2005] A.C.D. 46; (2004) 101(16) L.S.G. 28; *Times*, April 8, 2004, QBD (Admin) . . . . *Digested*, 05/**1796**:
Applied, 05/1801, 05/1919, 07/1953
Council for the Regulation of Health Care Professionals v Nursing and Midwifery Council see Council for the Regulation of Health Care Professionals v General Medical Council
Council for the Regulation of Health Care Professionals v Truscott see Council for the Regulation of Health Care Professionals v General Medical Council
Council for the Regulation of Healthcare Professionals v General Dental Council; *sub nom* Council for the Regulation of Healthcare Professionals v Marshall [2006] EWHC 1870 (Admin); (2006) 92 B.M.L.R. 36; [2007] A.C.D. 18, QBD (Admin) *Digested*, 07/**1938**
Council for the Regulation of Healthcare Professionals v General Medical Council; *sub nom* Council for the Regulation of Healthcare Professionals v Saluja; Saluja, Re [2006] EWHC 2784 (Admin); [2007] 1 W.L.R. 3094; [2007] 2 All E.R. 905; [2007] LS Law Medical 237; (2006) 92 B.M.L.R. 153; [2007] A.C.D. 29; (2006) 156 N.L.J. 1767, QBD (Admin) . . . . *Digested*, 07/**1953**
Council for the Regulation of Healthcare Professionals v Marshall see Council for the Regulation of Healthcare Professionals v General Dental Council
Council for the Regulation of Healthcare Professionals v Saluja see Council for the Regulation of Healthcare Professionals v General Medical Council
Council of Civil Service Unions v Minister for the Civil Service [1985] A.C. 374; [1984] 3 W.L.R. 1174; [1984] 3 All E.R. 935; [1985] I.C.R. 14; [1985] I.R.L.R. 28; (1985) 82 L.S.G. 437; (1984) 128 S.J. 837, HL; reversing [1984] I.R.L.R. 353, CA (Civ Div); reversing [1984] I.R.L.R. 309, DC . . . . *Digested*, 85/**12**:
Applied, 86/3554, 87/2460, 88/1843, 88/3553, 89/17, 89/4022, 94/75,
94/1947, 94/2485, 95/5905, 97/2785, 00/4114: *Considered*, 85/656,
86/950, 86/2017, 86/2934, 87/10, 87/12, 87/20, 87/47, 88/6, 88/2713,
88/3510, 90/4, 91/55, 91/76, 93/31, 94/8, 94/4984, 95/20, 95/67, 95/88,
95/3252, 95/4255, 95/4413, 96/316, 97/6229, 00/4447:
Distinguished, 96/2520, 06/39, 07/45: *Followed*, 87/14, 93/5413, 96/1994:
Referred to, 87/2524, 92/5981, 93/5483, 95/2543, 95/4820
Countess Bathurst v Kleinwort Benson (Channel Islands) Trustees Ltd; *sub nom* Wesley v Kleinwort Benson (Channel Islands) Trustees Ltd [2007] W.T.L.R. 959, Royal Ct (Gue) . . . . *Digested*, 07/**4242**

Countess of Warwick Steamship Co v Le Nickel SA; *joined case* Anglo-Northern Trading
Co Ltd v Emlyn Jones & Williams [1918] 1 K.B. 372, CA; affirming [1917] 2
K.B. 78, KBD . . . . *Considered,* 07/3815
Country & Metropolitan Homes Surrey Ltd v Topclaim Ltd [1996] Ch. 307; [1996] 3
W.L.R. 525; [1997] 1 All E.R. 254, Ch D . . . . *Digested,* 96/**5023**:
Considered, 07/3394
County Personnel (Employment Agency) Ltd v Alan R Pulver & Co [1987] 1 W.L.R. 916;
[1987] 1 All E.R. 289; [1986] 2 E.G.L.R. 246; (1987) 84 L.S.G. 1409; (1986)
136 N.L.J. 1138; (1987) 131 S.J. 474; *Times,* October 29, 1986, CA (Civ Div) . . . *Digested,* 87/**3551**:
Applied, 91/1315, 91/1319, 93/2989, 00/1483, 07/2947: *Considered,* 89/1199,
90/1567, 92/1533, 94/1758, 96/4502, 99/4031: *Distinguished,* 98/4018,
05/2866: *Followed,* 98/3959, 98/4025
Coupers Partnership Ltd v Basarik (t/a Uppers Bistro) [2007] EWCA Civ 40; [2007]
R.V.R. 116; [2007] 6 E.G. 164 (C.S.); (2007) 151 S.J.L.B. 195, CA (Civ Div) . . . . *Digested,* 07/**783**
Coupon Scheme, Re (C-427/98) see Commission of the European Communities v
Germany (C-427/98)
Courage Ltd v Crehan (C453/99); *sub nom* Crehan v Courage Ltd (C453/99) [2002]
Q.B. 507; [2001] 3 W.L.R. 1646; [2001] All E.R. (EC) 886; [2001] E.C.R. I-
6297; [2002] U.K.C.L.R. 171; [2001] 5 C.M.L.R. 28; [2001] C.E.C. 297; [2002]
I.C.R. 457; *Times,* October 4, 2001; *Daily Telegraph,* September 25, 2001, ECJ . . *Digested,* 01/**783**:
Applied, 07/626: *Considered,* 06/2592
Couronne v Crawley BC see R. (on the application of Couronne) v Crawley BC
Courtaulds Northern Spinning v Sibson [1988] I.C.R. 451; [1988] I.R.L.R. 305, CA
(Civ Div); reversing [1987] I.C.R. 329, EAT . . . . *Digested,* 88/**1247**:
Complaint dismissed, 94/2413: *Considered,* 07/1325
Coutts & Co v Passey [2007] B.P.I.R. 323, Ch D
Couwenbergh v Valkova [2004] EWCA Civ 676; [2004] C.P. Rep. 38; [2004]
W.T.L.R. 937; (2004) 148 S.J.L.B. 694, CA (Civ Div); reversing (Unreported,
July 31, 1998), Ch D . . . . *Digested,* 04/**255**:
Distinguished, 07/510
Coventry v Coventry see Coventry (Deceased), Re
Coventry CC v Enodis Group Ltd [2007] P.A.D. 83, Planning Inspector
Coventry (Deceased), Re; *sub nom* Coventry v Coventry [1980] Ch. 461; [1979] 3
W.L.R. 802; [1979] 3 All E.R. 815; (1979) 123 S.J. 606, CA (Civ Div); affirming
[1979] 2 W.L.R. 853; [1979] 2 All E.R. 408; (1979) 123 S.J. 406; *Times,*
November 14, 1978, Ch D . . . . *Digested,* 79/**2807**:
Applied, 81/2887, 83/3919, 83/3920, 95/5147, 03/4123: *Considered,* 82/206,
82/3385, 83/3921, 84/2464, 84/3665, 86/3549, 92/4584, 95/2355,
07/4112: *Followed,* 96/5551
Cowan v Cowan [2001] EWCA Civ 679; [2002] Fam. 97; [2001] 3 W.L.R. 684;
[2001] 2 F.L.R. 192; [2001] 2 F.C.R. 331; [2001] Fam. Law 498; *Times,* May 17,
2001, CA (Civ Div) . . . . *Digested,* 01/**2633**:
Applied, 06/1621: *Considered,* 07/1691, 07/1704: *Distinguished,* 03/1590
Cowley v Cheshire and Merseyside Strategic HA [2007] EWHC 48 (QB); [2007] LS
Law Medical 160; (2007) 94 B.M.L.R. 29, QBD . . . . *Digested,* 07/**3068**
Cox v Cox [2006] EWHC 1077 (Ch); [2006] B.C.C. 890, Ch D . . . . *Digested,* 07/**1709**
Cox v MGN Ltd [2006] EWHC 1235 (QB); [2006] 5 Costs L.R. 764, QBD . . . . *Digested,* 07/**389**
Coyle v United Kingdom (11266/84) see Brogan v United Kingdom (A/145-B)
Coys of Kensington (Sales) Ltd v McDonald see Cressman v Coys of Kensington
(Sales) Ltd
CP v Secretary of State for the Home Department; *sub nom* CP (Section 86(3) and
(5): Wrong Immigration Rule: Dominica), Re [2006] UKAIT 40; [2006] Imm.
A.R. 525; [2006] I.N.L.R. 450, AIT. . . . . *Digested,* 07/**2351**
CP (Section 86(3) and (5): Wrong Immigration Rule: Dominica), Re see CP v Secretary of
State for the Home Department
Crabb v Arun DC [1976] Ch. 179; [1975] 3 W.L.R. 847; [1975] 3 All E.R. 865; (1976)
32 P. & C.R. 70; (1975) 119 S.J. 711, CA (Civ Div) . . . . *Digested,* 75/**1191**:
Applied, 77/2509, 79/1083, 79/1085, 79/2635, 81/2732, 82/1149, 07/2762,
07/3466: *Considered,* 80/1073, 82/150.u, 86/1901, 86/3551, 93/1852,
94/2109, 95/4560, 96/4949, 98/123, 02/4319
Craig (Deceased), Re see Price v Craig
Cranage Parish Council v First Secretary of State [2004] EWHC 2949 (Admin);
[2005] 2 P. & C.R. 23; [2005] J.P.L. 1176; [2005] A.C.D. 79, QBD (Admin) . . *Digested,* 05/**3295**:
Applied, 07/3289
Crane v Lancashire CC; *sub nom* C v Lancashire CC [1997] 3 F.C.R. 587; [1997]
E.L.R. 377; (1997) 94(22) L.S.G. 31; *Times,* May 16, 1997; *Independent,* June 9,
1997, QBD. . . . . *Digested,* 97/**2141**:
Applied, 06/1218: *Considered,* 07/1267
Crane v Sky In-Home Service Ltd; *sub nom* Crane v Sky In-Home Services Ltd
[2007] EWHC 66 (Ch); [2007] 2 All E.R. (Comm) 599; [2007] 1 C.L.C. 389;
[2007] E.C.C. 25; [2007] Eu. L.R. 549; [2007] Bus. L.R. D47, Ch D . . . . *Digested,* 07/**69**
Crane v Sky In-Home Services Ltd see Crane v Sky In-Home Service Ltd

Cranfield v Bridgegrove Ltd; *joined cases* Claussen v Yeates; McManus v Sharif; Murphy v Staples UK Ltd; Smith v Hughes [2003] EWCA Civ 656; [2003] 1 W.L.R. 2441; [2003] 3 All E.R. 129; [2003] C.P. Rep. 54; [2003] 21 E.G. 191 (C.S.); (2003) 147 S.J.L.B. 599; [2003] N.P.C. 66; *Times*, May 16, 2003, CA (Civ Div) . . . . *Digested*, 03/**455**:
Applied, 05/467, 05/485, 07/371: *Considered*, 06/347
Cranswick Country Foods Plc v Beall [2007] I.C.R. 691, EAT . . . . *Digested*, 07/**1394**
Cranway Ltd v Playtech Ltd [2007] EWHC 182 (Pat); [2007] R.P.C. 22; (2007) 30(3) I.P.D. 30022, Ch D (Patents Ct) . . . . *Digested*, 07/**2548**
Crawley BC v Attenborough [2006] EWHC 1278 (Admin); (2006) 170 J.P. 593; (2007) 171 J.P.N. 69, QBD (Admin) . . . . *Digested*, 06/**2778**
Cream Holdings Ltd v Banerjee [2004] UKHL 44; [2005] 1 A.C. 253; [2004] 3 W.L.R. 918; [2004] 4 All E.R. 617; [2005] E.M.L.R. 1; [2004] H.R.L.R. 39; [2004] U.K.H.R.R. 1071; 17 B.H.R.C. 464; (2005) 28(2) I.P.D. 28001; (2004) 101(42) L.S.G. 29; (2004) 154 N.L.J. 1589; (2004) 148 S.J.L.B. 1215; *Times*, October 15, 2004, HL; reversing [2003] EWCA Civ 103; [2003] Ch. 650; [2003] 3 W.L.R. 999; [2003] 2 All E.R. 318; [2003] E.M.L.R. 16; [2003] H.R.L.R. 18; (2003) 100(15) L.S.G. 25; *Times*, February 28, 2003; *Independent*, April 7, 2003, CA (Civ Div) . . . . *Digested*, 05/**2041**:
Applied, 04/1924, 05/4191, 06/454, 06/1037, 07/2189, 07/2672, 07/2887, 07/2893: *Considered*, 05/970, 06/456: *Not applied*, 04/928
Creating Careers v Revenue and Customs Commissioners [2006] B.V.C. 2643; [2006] V. & D.R. 46; [2006] S.T.I. 1423, V&DTr (Manchester) . . . . *Digested*, 07/**4289**
Credit & Industrial Bank v Czech Republic (Admissibility) (29010/95) (1998) 26 E.H.R.R. CD88, Eur Comm HR . . . . *Applied*, 07/2214
Credit Suisse Fides Trust SA v Cuoghi [1998] Q.B. 818; [1997] 3 W.L.R. 871; [1998] 1 W.L.R. 474; [1997] 3 All E.R. 724; [1997] C.L.C. 1187; [1998] I.L.Pr. 41; *Times*, July 3, 1997, CA (Civ Div) . . . . *Digested*, 97/**893**:
Applied, 03/413, 07/457: *Considered*, 98/563, 00/490
Credit Suisse Financial Products v Societe Generale d'Enterprises [1996] 5 Bank. L.R. 220; [1997] C.L.C. 168; [1997] I.L.Pr. 165, CA (Civ Div) . . . . *Digested*, 96/**1097**:
Applied, 07/364
CREEDNZ Inc v Governor General [1981] 1 N.Z.L.R. 172, CA (NZ) . . . . *Applied*, 85/2,
07/4378: *Considered*, 84/2756, 91/94, 95/3098
Crehan v Courage Ltd (C453/99) see Courage Ltd v Crehan (C453/99)
Crehan v Inntrepreneur Pub Co (CPC); *sub nom* Inntrepreneur Pub Co (CPC) v Crehan [2006] UKHL 38; [2007] 1 A.C. 333; [2006] 3 W.L.R. 148; [2006] 4 All E.R. 465; [2006] U.K.C.L.R. 1232; [2007] E.C.C. 2; [2006] Eu. L.R. 1189; [2006] I.C.R. 1344; [2006] 30 E.G. 103 (C.S.); (2006) 150 S.J.L.B. 983; [2006] N.P.C. 85; *Times*, July 20, 2006, HL; reversing [2004] EWCA Civ 637; [2004] 2 C.L.C. 803; [2004] U.K.C.L.R. 1500; [2004] E.C.C. 28; [2004] Eu. L.R. 693; [2004] 3 E.G.L.R. 128; [2004] 23 E.G. 120 (C.S.); (2004) 148 S.J.L.B. 662; [2004] N.P.C. 83; *Times*, May 28, 2004, CA (Civ Div); reversing [2003] EWHC 1510 (Ch); [2003] U.K.C.L.R. 834; [2004] E.C.C. 8; [2003] Eu. L.R. 663; [2003] 27 E.G. 138 (C.S.); (2003) 100(27) L.S.G. 39; (2003) 100(33) L.S.G. 28; *Times*, August 13, 2003, Ch D . . . . *Digested*, 06/**585**
Creighton v HM Advocate (1904) 6 F. (J.) 72; (1904) 12 S.L.T. 36, HCJ . . . . *Considered*, 07/5051
Cressey v E Timm & Son Ltd [2005] EWCA Civ 763; [2005] 1 W.L.R. 3926; [2006] I.C.R. 282; [2006] P.I.Q.R. P9; (2005) 102(28) L.S.G. 33; *Times*, July 25, 2005, CA (Civ Div) . . . . *Digested*, 05/**439**:
Distinguished, 07/480
Cressman v Coys of Kensington (Sales) Ltd; *sub nom* Coys of Kensington (Sales) Ltd v McDonald; McDonald v Coys of Kensington Holdings Ltd [2004] EWCA Civ 47; [2004] 1 W.L.R. 2775; (2004) 101(10) L.S.G. 29; (2004) 148 S.J.L.B. 182; *Times*, February 13, 2004, CA (Civ Div) . . . . *Digested*, 04/**3266**:
Applied, 07/4248
Cresswell v DPP; *joined case* Currie v DPP [2006] EWHC 3379 (Admin); (2007) 171 J.P. 233; (2007) 171 J.P.N. 500; [2007] Env. L.R. D8, DC . . . . *Digested*, 07/**875**
Crewe Services & Investment Corp v Silk (2000) 79 P. & C.R. 500; [1998] 2 E.G.L.R. 1; [1998] 35 E.G. 81; [1997] E.G. 170 (C.S.); [1997] N.P.C. 170; *Times*, January 2, 1998, CA (Civ Div) . . . . *Digested*, 98/**122**:
Applied, 07/2736: *Considered*, 00/1449
Criminal Proceedings against Ahokainen (C-434/04); *sub nom* Ahokainen v Virallinen Syyttaja (C-434/04) [2007] 1 C.M.L.R. 11; [2006] E.C.R. IA-9171, ECJ (3rd Chamber) . . . . *Digested*, 07/**1604**:
Applied, 07/1605
Criminal Proceedings against Arduino (C35/99); *sub nom* Arduino v Compagnia Assicuratrice RAS SpA (C35/99) [2002] E.C.R. I-1529; [2002] 4 C.M.L.R. 25, ECJ . . . . *Digested*, 02/**573**:
Considered, 07/617
Criminal Proceedings against Bernaldez (C-129/94) [1996] All E.R. (EC) 741; [1996] E.C.R. I-1829; [1996] 2 C.M.L.R. 889; *Times*, May 6, 1996, ECJ (5th Chamber)   *Digested*, 96/**3614**:
Considered, 07/3458: *Followed*, 00/3547

Criminal Proceedings against Brugge (C-385/01) see Criminal Proceedings against
    Gozutok (C-187/01)
Criminal Proceedings against Calfa (C-348/96); *sub nom* Calfa, Re (C-348/96) [1999]
    All E.R. (EC) 850; [1999] E.C.R. I-11; [1999] 2 C.M.L.R. 1138; [1999] C.E.C.
    477; [1999] I.N.L.R. 333; (1999) 96(19) L.S.G. 30; *Times*, January 21, 1999,
    ECJ . . . .   *Digested*, 99/**1132**:
                                        Applied, 07/1620: *Followed*, 05/1462
Criminal Proceedings against dell'Orto (C-467/05) [2007] 3 C.M.L.R. 29, ECJ (3rd
    Chamber)
Criminal Proceedings against Festersen (C-370/05); *sub nom* Anklagemyndigheden *v*
    Festersen (C-370/05) [2007] 2 C.M.L.R. 7, ECJ (3rd Chamber) . . . .   *Digested*, 07/**1602**
Criminal Proceedings against Franzen (C-189/95) [1997] E.C.R. I-5909; [1998] 1
    C.M.L.R. 1231, ECJ . . . .   *Applied*, 06/619:
                                        Considered, 99/2222, 07/1604: *Followed*, 00/2400
Criminal Proceedings against Gambelli (C-243/01) [2003] E.C.R. I-13031; [2006] 1
    C.M.L.R. 35; *Times*, December 4, 2003, ECJ . . . .   *Digested*, 06/**1568**:
                                        Applied, 07/1619, 07/1620
Criminal Proceedings against Gasparini (C-467/04) [2006] E.C.R. I-9199; [2007] 1
    C.M.L.R. 12, ECJ (1st Chamber)
Criminal Proceedings against Gozutok (C-187/01); *joined case* Criminal Proceedings
    against Brugge (C-385/01) [2003] E.C.R. I-1345; [2003] 2 C.M.L.R. 2, ECJ .   *Applied*, 07/1573
Criminal Proceedings against Heinonen (C-394/97) [1999] E.C.R. I-3599; [2000] 2
    C.M.L.R. 1037, ECJ (5th Chamber) . . . .   *Digested*, 00/**2400**:
                                                                                        Considered, 07/1604
Criminal Proceedings against Kraaijenbrink (C-367/05) [2007] 3 C.M.L.R. 44, ECJ (2nd
    Chamber)
Criminal   Proceedings   against   Lindqvist   (C-101/01);   *sub   nom*   Lindqvist   *v*
    Aklagarkammaren i Jonkoping (C-101/01) [2004] Q.B. 1014; [2004] 2 W.L.R.
    1385; [2004] All E.R. (EC) 561; [2003] E.C.R. I-12971; [2004] 1 C.M.L.R. 20;
    [2004] C.E.C. 117; [2004] Info. T.L.R. 1; *Times*, November 13, 2003, ECJ . . . . . . *Digested*, 03/**1428**:
                                        Applied, 07/1572: *Considered*, 07/2383
Criminal Proceedings against Placanica (C-338/04) [2007] All E.R. (EC) 827; [2007] 2
    C.M.L.R. 25, ECJ . . . .   *Digested*, 07/**1620**
Criminal Proceedings against Pupino (C-105/03) [2006] Q.B. 83; [2005] 3 W.L.R. 1102;
    [2006] All E.R. (EC) 142; [2005] E.C.R. I-5285; [2005] 2 C.M.L.R. 63; [2006]
    C.E.C. 448; *Times*, July 14, 2005, ECJ . . . .   *Digested*, 06/**1581**:
                                                                                        Applied, 07/1657
Criminal Proceedings against van Bennekom (C-227/82) see Officer van Justitie *v* Van
    Bennekom (C-227/82)
Criminal Proceedings against Van Esbroeck (C-436/04); *sub nom* Van Esbroeck *v*
    Openbaar Ministerie (C-436/04) [2006] E.C.R. I-2333; [2006] 3 C.M.L.R. 6,
    ECJ (2nd Chamber) . . . .   *Digested*, 07/**1573**
Cripps *v* Trustee Solutions Ltd see Trustee Solutions Ltd *v* Dubery
Crofton *v* NHS Litigation Authority [2007] EWCA Civ 71; [2007] 1 W.L.R. 923;
    [2007] B.L.G.R. 507; (2007) 10 C.C.L. Rep. 123; [2007] P.I.Q.R. Q3; [2007] LS
    Law Medical 254; (2007) 104(8) L.S.G. 36; (2007) 151 S.J.L.B. 262; *Times*,
    February 15, 2007, CA (Civ Div); reversing [2006] Lloyd's Rep. Med. 168, QBD   *Digested*, 07/**1065**
Crofton *v* Yeboah; *sub nom* Yeboah *v* Crofton [2002] EWCA Civ 794; [2002] I.R.L.R.
    634; *Times*, June 20, 2002, CA (Civ Div); reversing EAT/475/00, EAT/1352/98,
    EAT/1353/98, EAT/1354/98, EAT/1356/98, EAT . . . .   *Digested*, 02/**1398**:
                                        Applied, 04/1309, 07/1316, 07/1391: *Considered*, 06/1369
Crofts *v* Veta Ltd see Lawson *v* Serco Ltd
Croke *v* Hydro Aluminium Worcester Ltd [2007] I.C.R. 1303, EAT . . . . *Digested*, 07/**1344**
Croke (A Minor) *v* Wiseman [1982] 1 W.L.R. 71; [1981] 3 All E.R. 852, CA (Civ Div) . .   *Digested*, 82/**787**:
                                        Applied, 84/1042: *Distinguished*, 07/3071
Crompton (t/a David Crompton Haulage) *v* Department of Transport North Western Area
    [2003] EWCA Civ 64; [2003] R.T.R. 34; *Times*, February 7, 2003, CA (Civ
    Div) . . . .   *Digested*, 03/**4413**:
                                        Applied, 06/1812: *Considered*, 05/3458, 07/2815: *Distinguished*, 07/1944
Crompton's Leisure Machines Ltd, Re [2006] EWHC 3583 (Ch); [2007] B.C.C. 214; *Times*,
    December 27, 2006, Ch D . . . .   *Digested*, 07/**2395**
Cronin (t/a Cronin Driving School) *v* Customs and Excise Commissioners [1991] S.T.C.
    333; [1991] B.T.C. 5064; [1992] C.O.D. 91, QBD . . . .   *Digested*, 92/**4549**:
                                                                                        Distinguished, 94/4597, 07/4344
Crookdake *v* Drury see Sowden *v* Lodge
Croom's Trade Mark Application; *sub nom* McQUEEN CLOTHING CO Trade Mark
    [2005] R.P.C. 2, App Person . . . .   *Digested*, 05/**2560**:
                                        Applied, 07/2679: *Considered*, 05/2565
Crosby *v* Fleetwood Travel (Unreported, October 18, 2006), CC (West London) [*Ex
    rel.* Clara Johnson, Barrister, 3 Hare Court, Temple, London] . . . . *Digested*, 07/**2127**
Cross Construction Sussex Ltd *v* Tseliki [2006] EWHC 1056 (Ch); [2006] B.P.I.R. 888,
    Ch D . . . .   *Digested*, 06/**2350**:
                                                                                        Considered, 07/2411

Crossland (Inspector of Taxes) v Hawkins [1961] Ch. 537; [1961] 3 W.L.R. 202; [1961] 2 All E.R. 812; 39 T.C. 493; (1961) 40 A.T.C. 126; [1961] T.R. 113; (1961) 105 S.J. 424, CA; reversing 53 R. & I.T. 758; (1960) 39 A.T.C. 461; [1960] T.R. 297, Ch D . . . . *Digested*, 61/**4252**:
Applied, 05/4101, 07/4100: *Considered*, 74/1870: *Distinguished*, 06/4226

Crossman, Re see Inland Revenue Commissioners v Crossman

Crow v Waters [2007] 2 P. & C.R. DG14, Ch D

Crowley v Ashland (UK) Chemicals Ltd (Unreported, April 20, 1979), EAT. . . . . *Considered*, 07/1435

Crowley (t/a Contraband Discount Stores) v Liverpool PSDA Ltd [2007] R.V.R. 125, Lands Tr . . . . *Digested*, 07/**3386**

Crown Prosecution Service v Aziz; *sub nom* Aziz v Crown Prosecution Service [2006] EWCA Civ 1136; [2007] I.C.R. 153; (2006) 103(33) L.S.G. 24; (2006) 150 S.J.L.B. 1054; *Times*, August 30, 2006, CA (Civ Div); reversing UKEAT/0646/04/DM, EAT . . . . *Digested*, 06/**1350**

Crown Prosecution Service v Benye [2007] EWHC 772 (Admin); [2007] N.P.C. 48, QBD (Admin)

Crown Prosecution Service v CE [2006] EWCA Crim 1410, CA (Crim Div) . . . . *Considered*, 07/858

Crown Prosecution Service v Greenacre; *sub nom* DPP v Greenacre [2007] EWHC 1193 (Admin); (2007) 171 J.P. 411; (2007) 171 J.P.N. 723, QBD (Admin) . . . . . . *Digested*, 07/**950**

Crown Prosecution Service v J see Jennings v CPS

Crown Prosecution Service v P; *sub nom* DPP v P [2007] EWHC 946 (Admin); [2007] 4 All E.R. 628; (2007) 171 J.P. 349; (2007) 171 J.P.N. 659, QBD (Admin) . . . . *Digested*, 07/**1023**:
Considered, 07/934

Crown Prosecution Service v P; *sub nom* DPP v P [2007] EWHC 1144 (Admin); [2007] 4 All E.R. 648, QBD (Admin)

Crown Prosecution Service v Picton [2006] EWHC 1108 (Admin); (2006) 170 J.P. 567; (2006) 170 J.P.N. 954, QBD (Admin) . . . . *Digested*, 06/**988**:
Considered, 07/1029

Crown Prosecution Service v T; *sub nom* DPP v T [2006] EWHC 728 (Admin); [2007] 1 W.L.R. 209; [2006] 3 All E.R. 471; (2006) 170 J.P. 470; [2006] 3 F.C.R. 184; [2007] A.C.D. 71; (2006) 170 J.P.N. 835; *Times*, April 13, 2006, DC . . . . *Digested*, 06/**328**

Crowther v Kirklees MDC (Unreported, October 13, 2006), CC (Huddersfield) [*Ex rel.* Thompsons Solicitors, Acresfield, 8 Exchange Street, Manchester] . . . . *Digested*, 07/**2958**

Crucial Music Corp (formerly Onemusic Corp) v Klondyke Management AG (formerly Point Classics AG) [2007] EWHC 1782 (Ch); [2007] I.L.Pr. 54, Ch D . . . . *Digested*, 07/**669**

Crusader v Revenue and Customs Commissioners [2007] S.T.I. 2418, Sp Comm

Crystal Palace FC (2000) Ltd v Dowie [2007] EWHC 1392 (QB); [2007] I.R.L.R. 682, QBD . . . . *Digested*, 07/**812**

CS v Secretary of State for the Home Department; *sub nom* CS (Race Discrimination: Proper Approach: Effect: Jamaica), Re [2006] UKAIT 4; [2006] Imm. A.R. 289, AIT . . . . *Digested*, 07/**2331**

CS (Race Discrimination: Proper Approach: Effect: Jamaica), Re see CS v Secretary of State for the Home Department

CT v Bristol City Council see L (A Child), Re

CTI Group Inc v Transclear SA (The Mary Nour) [2007] EWHC 2070 (Comm); [2007] 2 C.L.C. 518; (2007) 104(38) L.S.G. 35, QBD (Comm)

CTI Group Inc v Transclear SA (The Mary Nour) [2007] EWHC 2340 (Comm); [2007] 2 C.L.C. 530, QBD (Comm)

Cubitt Building & Interiors Ltd v Fleetglade Ltd [2006] EWHC 3413 (TCC); 110 Con. L.R. 36; [2007] C.I.L.L. 2431, QBD (TCC) . . . . *Digested*, 07/**732**

Cuddy v Hawkes see Hawkes v Cuddy

Cuddy v Hawkes; *sub nom* Neath Rugby Ltd, Re; Hawkes v Cuddy [2007] EWCA Civ 1072; [2007] B.P.I.R. 1217; *Times*, November 13, 2007, CA (Civ Div)

Cullen v General Medical Council [2005] EWHC 353 (Admin), QBD (Admin) . . . . *Considered*, 07/1954

Cullin v London Fire and Civil Defence Authority; *sub nom* White v London Fire and Civil Defence Authority; Sheehan v London Fire and Civil Defence Authority [1999] P.I.Q.R. P314, CA (Civ Div); affirming (Unreported, March 31, 1999), QBD [*Ex rel.* Thompsons Solicitors, Congress House, Great Russell Street, London] . . . . *Digested*, 99/**3980**:
Considered, 07/4654

Cumbria CC v Carlisle-Morgan [2007] I.R.L.R. 314, EAT . . . . *Digested*, 07/**1437**

Cummings v Weymouth and Portland BC [2007] EWHC 1601 (Admin); [2007] 2 P. & C.R. 25, QBD (Admin) . . . . *Digested*, 07/**3247**

Cummins v Shell International Manning Services Ltd see Anderton v Clwyd CC

Cummins v Shell International Trading & Shipping Ltd see Anderton v Clwyd CC

Cumpana v Romania (33348/96) (2005) 41 E.H.R.R. 14, ECHR (Grand Chamber) . . . *Digested*, 06/**2095**:
Applied, 07/2186

Cundall Johnson & Partners LLP v Whipps Cross University Hospital NHS Trust [2007] EWHC 2178 (TCC); [2007] B.L.R. 520; 115 Con. L.R. 125; [2007] C.I.L.L. 2516, QBD (TCC) . . . . *Digested*, 07/**504**

Cunningham v Collett & Farmer (A Firm) [2006] EWHC 1771 (TCC); 113 Con. L.R. 142, QBD (TCC)

Curistan *v* Times Newspapers Ltd A2/2007/0979 & 0989, CA (Civ Div); affirming
  [2007] EWHC 926 (QB); [2007] 4 All E.R. 486; *Times*, May 10, 2007, QBD . . .　　*Digested*, 07/**1070**
Currey *v* Currey [2006] EWCA Civ 1338; [2007] 2 Costs L.R. 227; [2007] 1 F.L.R.
  946; [2007] Fam. Law 12; (2006) 156 N.L.J. 1651; (2006) 150 S.J.L.B. 1393;
  Times, November 3, 2006; *Independent*, October 25, 2006, CA (Civ Div) . . . .　　*Digested*, 07/**1707**
Currie *v* DPP see Cresswell *v* DPP
Curruthers *v* South Norfolk DC see Carruthers *v* South Norfolk DC
Curry *v* DPP see C (A Minor) *v* DPP
Curry *v* Revenue and Customs Commissioners [2007] S.T.I. 1698, V&DTr (London)
CUSSONS/Cleaning compositions (T447/03) [2006] E.P.O.R. 42, EPO (Technical Bd
  App) . . . .　　*Digested*, 07/**2573**
Customs Agents, Re (C35/96) see Commission of the European Communities *v* Italy
  (C35/96)
Customs and Excise Commissioners *v* Apple and Pear Development Council see Apple
  and Pear Development Council *v* Customs and Excise Commissioners
Customs and Excise Commissioners *v* Barclays Bank Plc [2006] UKHL 28; [2007] 1
  A.C. 181; [2006] 3 W.L.R. 1; [2006] 4 All E.R. 256; [2006] 2 All E.R. (Comm)
  831; [2006] 2 Lloyd's Rep. 327; [2006] 1 C.L.C. 1096; (2006) 103(27) L.S.G.
  33; (2006) 156 N.L.J. 1060; (2006) 150 S.J.L.B. 859; *Times*, June 22, 2006,
  HL; reversing [2004] EWCA Civ 1555; [2005] 1 W.L.R. 2082; [2005] 3 All E.R.
  852; [2005] 1 Lloyd's Rep. 165; (2004) 154 N.L.J. 1831; (2004) 148 S.J.L.B.
  1402; [2004] N.P.C. 175; *Independent*, December 2, 2004, CA (Civ Div);
  reversing [2004] EWHC 122 (Comm); [2004] 1 W.L.R. 2027; [2004] 2 All E.R.
  789; [2004] 1 All E.R. (Comm) 960; [2004] 1 Lloyd's Rep. 572; [2004] 2
  C.L.C. 1; (2004) 101(7) L.S.G. 35; (2004) 154 N.L.J. 224; *Times*, February 11,
  2004, QBD (Comm) . . . .　　*Digested*, 06/**2880**:
　　　　　　　　　　　　　　　　　　　　　　　Applied, 07/1755, 07/4144
Customs and Excise Commissioners *v* British Telecommunications Plc [1999] 1 W.L.R.
  1376; [1999] 3 All E.R. 961; [1999] S.T.C. 758; [1999] B.T.C. 5273; [1999] B.V.C.
  306; (1999) 96(28) L.S.G. 27; *Times*, July 5, 1999; *Independent*, July 8, 1999,
  HL; reversing [1998] S.T.C. 544; [1998] B.T.C. 5155; [1998] B.V.C. 186; (1998)
  95(17) L.S.G. 30; *Times*, March 24, 1998, CA (Civ Div); reversing [1997] S.T.C.
  475; [1997] B.T.C. 5111; [1997] B.V.C. 222; *Independent*, March 17, 1997, QBD .　　*Digested*, 99/**4993**:
　　　　　　　　　　Applied, 02/4785, 03/4580, 06/4449, 07/4316: *Considered*, 03/4576:
　　　　　　　　　　　　　　　　　　　　　　　　　　Distinguished, 98/835
Customs and Excise Commissioners *v* DFDS A/S (C-260/95) [1997] 1 W.L.R. 1037;
  [1997] All E.R. (EC) 342; [1997] S.T.C. 384; [1997] E.C.R. I-1005; [1997] B.T.C.
  5167; [1997] B.V.C. 279; (1997) 94(27) L.S.G. 24; *Times*, February 24, 1997,
  ECJ (5th Chamber) . . . .　　*Digested*, 97/**5021**:
　　　　　　　　　　　　　Applied, 04/3993: *Considered*, 98/4963, 07/4348
Customs and Excise Commissioners *v* Federation of Technological Industries (C-384/
  04); *sub nom* Federation of Technological Industries *v* Customs and Excise
  Commissioners (C-384/04) [2006] S.T.C. 1483; [2006] E.C.R. I-4191; [2006]
  3 C.M.L.R. 11; [2006] C.E.C. 669; [2007] B.T.C. 5614; [2007] B.V.C. 582;
  [2006] S.T.I. 1514; *Times*, May 29, 2006, ECJ (3rd Chamber). . . . .　　*Digested*, 07/**4320**:
　　　　　　　　　　　　　　　　　　　　　　　　　Applied, 07/4318
Customs and Excise Commissioners *v* Ferrero UK Ltd [1997] S.T.C. 881; [1997] B.T.C.
  5294; [1997] B.V.C. 408; *Times*, May 19, 1997; *Independent*, May 19, 1997, CA
  (Civ Div); reversing [1996] S.T.C. 866, QBD . . . .　　*Digested*, 97/**5047**:
　　　　　　　　　　　　　　Applied, 07/4363: *Followed*, 05/4418
Customs and Excise Commissioners *v* Hubbard Foundation Scotland [1981] S.T.C. 593;
  1981 S.C. 244; 1982 S.L.T. 277, IH (1 Div) . . . .　　*Digested*, 82/**4440**:
　　　　　　　　　　　　　　Considered, 07/4322: *Followed*, 98/4878
Customs and Excise Commissioners *v* Lord Fisher; *sub nom* Lord Fisher DSC *v*
  Customs and Excise Commissioners [1981] 2 All E.R. 147; [1981] S.T.C. 238,
  QBD; affirming [1979] V.A.T.T.R. 227, VAT Tr . . . .　　*Digested*, 81/**2849**:
　　　　　　　　Applied, 84/3038, 03/4606, 05/4383: *Considered*, 88/3454, 06/4429,
　　　　　　　　　　　　　　　　　　　　　　　　　　07/4336
Customs and Excise Commissioners *v* Loyalty Management UK Ltd see Revenue and
  Customs Commissioners *v* Loyalty Management UK Ltd
Customs and Excise Commissioners *v* Madgett (t/a Howden Court Hotel) (C-308/96)
  see Madgett (t/a Howden Court Hotel) *v* Customs and Excise Commissioners
  (C-308/96)
Customs and Excise Commissioners *v* Morrison's Academy Boarding Houses
  Association [1978] S.T.C. 1; 1977 S.C. 279; 1977 S.L.T. 197, IH (1 Div) . . . .　　*Digested*, 77/**3812**:
　　　　　　Applied, 79/2743, 95/5121, 07/4364: *Considered*, 01/5579:
　　　　　　　　　　　　　　　　　　　　　　　　Distinguished, 98/6219
Customs and Excise Commissioners *v* Newbury [2003] EWHC 702 (Admin); [2003] 1
  W.L.R. 2131; [2003] 2 All E.R. 964; [2003] Eu. L.R. 476; (2003) 100(23)
  L.S.G. 38; *Times*, April 18, 2003, QBD (Admin) . . . .　　*Digested*, 03/**926**:
　　　　　　　　　　　　　　　　　　　　　　　Considered, 07/1048

Customs and Excise Commissioners v Plantiflor Ltd; *sub nom* Plantiflor Ltd v Customs and Excise Commissioners [2002] UKHL 33; [2002] 1 W.L.R. 2287; [2002] S.T.C. 1132; [2002] 3 C.M.L.R. 5; [2002] B.T.C. 5413; [2002] B.V.C. 572; [2002] S.T.I. 1093; (2002) 99(36) L.S.G. 39; (2002) 152 N.L.J. 1385; *Times*, July 31, 2002; *Independent*, November 11, 2002, HL; reversing [2000] S.T.C. 137; [2000] B.T.C. 5050; [2000] B.V.C. 103; [2000] S.T.I. 128; *Times*, February 10, 2000, CA (Civ Div); reversing [1999] S.T.C. 51; [1999] B.T.C. 5038; [1999] B.V.C. 37; *Times*, November 25, 1998; *Independent*, November 23, 1998, QBD; reversing [1997] B.V.C. 2380; [1997] V. & D.R. 301; [1997] S.T.I. 998, V&DTr . .   *Digested*, 02/**4785**: *Applied*, 04/3992, 05/4346, 07/4310: *Approved*, 98/4916: *Cited*, 07/4293: *Followed*, 07/4293

Customs and Excise Commissioners v Redrow Group Plc [1999] 1 W.L.R. 408; [1999] 2 All E.R. 1; [1999] S.T.C. 161; [1999] B.T.C. 5062; [1999] B.V.C. 96; [1999] E.G. 20 (C.S.); (1999) 96(9) L.S.G. 32; (1999) 143 S.J.L.B. 58; [1999] N.P.C. 18; *Times*, February 18, 1999; *Independent*, February 18, 1999, HL; reversing [1997] S.T.C. 1053; [1997] B.T.C. 5347; [1997] B.V.C. 461; [1997] E.G. 92 (C.S.); *Times*, July 3, 1997; *Independent*, July 14, 1997, CA (Civ Div); reversing [1996] S.T.C. 365; [1995] E.G. 202 (C.S.), QBD; affirming [1995] V. & D.R. 115, VAT Tr (Manchester). . . . .   *Digested*, 99/**4994**: *Applied*, 02/4774, 04/3992, 05/4346, 05/4375, 06/5741, 07/4310: *Considered*, 03/4529: *Distinguished*, 05/4379, 06/4468

Customs and Excise Commissioners v Robertson's Electrical Ltd see Robertson's Electrical Ltd v Customs and Excise Commissioners

Customs and Excise Commissioners v Royal Bank of Scotland Plc see Oval 1742 Ltd (In Creditors Voluntary Liquidation), Re

Customs and Excise Commissioners v Rysaffe Trustee Co (CI) Ltd see Rysaffe Trustee Co (CI) Ltd v Inland Revenue Commissioners

Customs and Excise Commissioners v Smith see Revenue and Customs Commissioners v Smith

Customs and Excise Commissioners v Sooner Foods Ltd; *sub nom* Sooner Foods Ltd v Customs and Excise Commissioners [1983] S.T.C. 376, QBD; reversing in part [1982] V.A.T.T.R. 70, VAT Tr . . . .   *Digested*, 83/**3862**: *Applied*, 07/4282: *Considered*, 06/4426

Customs and Excise Commissioners v Total Network SL; *sub nom* Total Network SL v Revenue and Customs Commissioners; Revenue and Customs Commissioners v Total Network SL [2007] EWCA Civ 39; [2007] 2 W.L.R. 1156; [2007] S.T.C. 1005; [2007] B.T.C. 5150; [2007] B.V.C. 119; [2007] S.T.I. 291; (2007) 104(8) L.S.G. 39; *Times*, February 6, 2007, CA (Civ Div); reversing [2005] EWHC 1 (QB); [2005] S.T.C. 637; [2005] B.T.C. 5273; [2005] B.V.C. 304; [2005] S.T.I. 105, QBD . . . .   *Digested*, 07/**4298**

Customs and Excise Commissioners v Weller see Revenue and Customs Commissioners v Weller

Customs and Excise Commissioners v Yarburgh Children's Trust see Yarburgh Children's Trust v Customs and Excise Commissioners

Customs and Excise Commissioners v Zoological Society of London (C-267/00) see Zoological Society of London v Customs and Excise Commissioners (C-267/00)

Cutler v Walters (Unreported, August 24, 2006), CC (Salford) [*Ex rel.* Anna Short, Barrister, 8 King Street, Manchester] . . . .   *Digested*, 07/**3157**

Cutter v Eagle Star Insurance Co Ltd see Clarke v Kato

Cutts v Head [1984] Ch. 290; [1984] 2 W.L.R. 349; [1984] 1 All E.R. 597; (1984) 81 L.S.G. 509; (1984) 128 S.J. 117; *Times*, December 14, 1983, CA (Civ Div) . . . . .   *Digested*, 84/**2608**: *Applied*, 86/1517, 92/3449, 99/349, 02/312, 03/277, 03/287, 04/260, 07/343: *Considered*, 85/2702, 89/1701, 94/3674, 96/697, 96/1276, 04/266: *Followed*, 94/3561, 00/319

Cyganik v Agulian; *sub nom* Agulian v Cyganik [2006] EWCA Civ 129; [2006] 1 F.C.R. 406; [2006] W.T.L.R. 565; (2005-06) 8 I.T.E.L.R. 762, CA (Civ Div); reversing [2005] EWHC 444 (Ch); [2005] W.T.L.R. 1049; (2004-05) 7 I.T.E.L.R. 831, Ch D . . . .   *Digested*, 06/**4082**: *Considered*, 07/4068

Cyprus v Konstantinou [2007] 3 C.M.L.R. 42, AD (Cy)

Cytec Norge KS, Re; *sub nom* Cytec Overseas Corp NUF v Assessment Committee of Nedre Romerike 10 I.T.L. Rep. 464, LR (Eidsivating)

Cytec Overseas Corp NUF v Assessment Committee of Nedre Romerike see Cytec Norge KS, Re

Czech Republic v European Media Ventures SA [2007] EWHC 2851 (Comm); [2007] 2 C.L.C. 908, QBD (Comm)

Czech Sugar Quotas, Re [2006] 3 C.M.L.R. 15, US CR (CZ) . . . .   *Digested*, 07/**83**

D, Re see Reading BC v D (Angela)

D v B (Flawed Sexual Abuse Inquiry) [2006] EWHC 2987 (Fam); [2007] 1 F.L.R. 1295; [2007] 1 F.C.R. 369; [2007] Fam. Law 122, Fam Div . . . .   *Digested*, 07/**1754**

D v Bury MBC; *sub nom* AD v Bury MBC; *joined case* H v Bury MBC [2006] EWCA
Civ 1; [2006] 1 W.L.R. 917; [2006] 2 F.L.R. 147; [2006] 1 F.C.R. 148; [2006]
A.C.D. 45; [2006] Fam. Law 348; (2006) 103(6) L.S.G. 30; *Times,* January 24,
2006, CA (Civ Div) . . . .   *Digested,* 06/**1662**:
Applied, 07/2916

D v D see D (A Child) (Abduction: Rights of Custody), Re
D v D [2007] EWHC 278 (Fam); [2007] 2 F.L.R. 653; [2007] 1 F.C.R. 603; [2007]
Fam. Law 685, Fam Div . . . .   *Digested,* 07/**1689**

D v East Berkshire Community NHS Trust see JD v East Berkshire Community Health
NHS Trust
D v Secretary of State for Health see R. (on the application of D) v Secretary of State
for Health
D v Secretary of State for the Home Department see A v Secretary of State for the
Home Department
D v Soho House UK Ltd (Unreported, September 4, 2006), MCLC [*Ex rel.* Russell
Cooke, Solicitors, 2 Putney Hill, Putney, London] . . . .   *Digested,* 07/**3073**

D v Southwark LBC see R. (on the application of D) v Southwark LBC
D (A Child) v Barclay (Unreported, June 21, 2006), CC (Reading) [*Ex rel.* Richard
Wheeler, Barrister, 3 Paper Buildings, 4 St Peters Street, Winchester, Hants] . . .   *Digested,* 07/**3116**

D (A Child) v Brayshaw (Unreported, May 15, 2007), CC (Bradford) [*Ex rel.* Leila
Benyounes, Barrister, Park Lane Chambers, Leeds] . . . .   *Digested,* 07/**3087**

D (A Child) v Bristol City Council (Unreported, June 5, 2007), CC (Bristol) [*Ex rel.*
Andrew Granville Stafford, Barrister, 4 King's Bench Walk, Temple, London] . . . .   *Digested,* 07/**3201**

D (A Child) v De Silva (Unreported, April 11, 2007), CC (King's Lynn) [*Ex rel.* Shabham
Walji, Barrister, Regency Chambers, Cathedral Square, Peterborough] . . . .   *Digested,* 07/**3095**

D (A Child) v Hadfield (Unreported, January 8, 2007), CC (Peterborough) [*Ex rel.*
Shabnam Walji, Barrister, Regency Chambers, Cathedral Square, Peterborough
PE1 1XW] . . . .   *Digested,* 07/**3179**

D (A Child) v Lowe (Unreported, December 13, 2006), CC (Liverpool) [*Ex rel.* William
Rankin (Senior), Barrister, Oriel Chambers, 14 Water Street, Liverpool] . . . . . .   *Digested,* 07/**3097**

D (A Child) v Rossendale BC (Unreported, November 22, 2005), CC (Preston) [*Ex rel.*
James Hogg, Pupil Barrister, St James Chambers, 68 Quay Street, Manchester]   *Digested,* 07/**3195**

D (A Child) (Abduction: Foreign Custody Right), Re see D (A Child) (Abduction: Rights of
Custody), Re
D (A Child) (Abduction: Rights of Custody), Re; *sub nom* D (A Child) (Abduction:
Foreign Custody Right), Re; D v D [2006] UKHL 51; [2007] 1 A.C. 619; [2006]
3 W.L.R. 989; [2007] 1 All E.R. 783; [2007] 1 F.L.R. 961; [2007] 1 F.C.R. 1;
[2007] Fam. Law 102; (2006) 103(46) L.S.G. 29; (2006) 156 N.L.J. 1803;
(2006) 150 S.J.L.B. 1532; *Times,* November 17, 2006; *Independent,* November
21, 2006, HL; reversing [2006] EWCA Civ 830, CA (Civ Div) . . . .   *Digested,* 07/**1775**:
Considered, 07/1736

D (A Child) (Paternity), Re [2006] EWHC 3545 (Fam); [2007] 2 F.L.R. 26; [2007] Fam.
Law 590, Fam Div
D (Children) (Article 13 (b): Non-Return), Re [2006] EWCA Civ 146; [2006] 2 F.L.R. 305;
[2006] Fam. Law 438, CA (Civ Div) . . . .   *Digested,* 07/**1744**

D (Sexual Abuse Allegations: Evidence of Adult Victim), Re [2002] 1 F.L.R. 723; [2002]
Fam. Law 259, Fam Div . . . .   *Digested,* 02/**1639**:
Considered, 07/332

D&H Travel Ltd v Foster [2006] I.C.R. 1537, EAT . . . .   *Digested,* 07/**1382**

D'Ambumenil v Customs and Excise Commissioners (C-307/01) [2004] Q.B. 1179;
[2004] 3 W.L.R. 174; [2005] S.T.C. 650; [2003] E.C.R. I-13989; [2004] 2
C.M.L.R. 18; [2004] C.E.C. 47; [2005] B.T.C. 5710; [2005] B.V.C. 741; [2003]
S.T.I. 2181, ECJ (5th Chamber) . . . .   *Digested,* 04/**3984**:
Applied, 05/4353, 05/4355, 07/4346

D'Arcy v Revenue and Customs Commissioners see Revenue and Customs
Commissioners v D'Arcy
D'Hoop v Office National de l'Emploi (C-224/98); *sub nom* D'Hoop v Rijksdienst voor
Arbeidsvoorziening (C-224/98) [2003] All E.R. (EC) 527; [2002] E.C.R. I-
6191; [2002] 3 C.M.L.R. 12; [2002] C.E.C. 642; [2004] I.C.R. 137, ECJ . . . . . .   *Digested,* 03/**1445**:
Applied, 05/3922, 07/1610: *Considered,* 06/4008, 07/1625:
Followed, 05/4008, 06/4010

D'Hoop v Rijksdienst voor Arbeidsvoorziening (C-224/98) see D'Hoop v Office
National de l'Emploi (C-224/98)
Da Silva v Netherlands (50435/99); *joined case* Hoogkamer v Netherlands (50435/
99) [2006] 1 F.C.R. 229; [2007] 44 E.H.R.R. 34, ECHR . . . .   *Digested,* 06/**2192**

Dabas v High Court of Justice, Madrid see Dabas v Spain
Dabas v Spain; *sub nom* Dabas v High Court of Justice, Madrid [2007] UKHL 6;
[2007] 2 A.C. 31; [2007] 2 W.L.R. 254; [2007] 2 All E.R. 641; [2007] 2
C.M.L.R. 39; (2007) 104(11) L.S.G. 33; (2007) 151 S.J.L.B. 333; *Times,* March
5, 2007, HL; affirming [2006] EWHC 971 (Admin); [2007] 1 W.L.R. 145;
[2006] Extradition L.R. 123; [2006] A.C.D. 90; *Times,* June 2, 2006, QBD
(Admin) . . . .   *Digested,* 07/**1657**:
Applied, 07/1659, 07/1660

Dacas v Brook Street Bureau (UK) Ltd; *sub nom* Brook Street Bureau (UK) Ltd v
    Dacas [2004] EWCA Civ 217; [2004] I.C.R. 1437; [2004] I.R.L.R. 358; *Times*,
    March 19, 2004, CA (Civ Div); reversing [2003] I.R.L.R. 190, EAT . . . .   *Digested*, 04/**1204**:
                   Applied, 05/1214, 06/1315, 07/1347: *Considered*, 07/3999:
                            Distinguished, 06/4135: *Explained*, 07/1346
Dacorum BC v Fourth Avenue Estates [2007] P.A.D. 81, Planning Inspector
Dadourian Group International Inc v Simms; *sub nom* Dadourian Group International Inc
    v Simms (No.2) [2006] EWCA Civ 1745; [2007] 1 W.L.R. 2967; [2007] 2 All
    E.R. 329; [2007] 2 All E.R. (Comm) 498; [2007] C.P. Rep. 15; (2007) 157
    N.L.J. 107; *Times*, January 17, 2007, CA (Civ Div) . . . .   *Digested*, 07/**454**
Dadourian Group International Inc v Simms (No.2) see Dadourian Group International
    Inc v Simms
Daiber v Hauptzollamt Reutlingen (200/84) [1985] E.C.R. 3363; *Times*, October 21,
    1985, ECJ . . . .   *Digested*, 85/**1418**:
                         Applied, 07/1032: *Considered*, 99/4661
Daiichi Pharmaceutical Co Ltd v Commission of the European Communities (T-26/02);
    sub nom Vitamins Cartel, Re (T-26/02) [2006] 5 C.M.L.R. 3, CFI (4th
    Chamber) . . . .   *Digested*, 07/**1589**
Daimlerchrysler AG v Commission of the European Communities (T-325/01) [2005]
    E.C.R. II-3319; [2007] 4 C.M.L.R. 15, CFI (5th Chamber) . . . .   *Digested*, 07/**599**
Daktaras v Lithuania (42095/98) (2002) 34 E.H.R.R. 60, ECHR . . . .   *Digested*, 02/**2395**:
                                       Applied, 07/2227
Daley v Allied Suppliers [1983] I.C.R. 90; [1983] I.R.L.R. 14; (1983) 80 L.S.G. 213,
    EAT . . . .   *Digested*, 83/**1264**:
                                    Considered, 07/1392
Dallison v Caffery [1965] 1 Q.B. 348; [1964] 3 W.L.R. 385; [1964] 2 All E.R. 610;
    (1964) 128 J.P. 379; (1964) 108 S.J. 560, CA; affirming *Times*, July 3, 1963,
    HC . . . .   *Digested*, 64/**2337**:
            Applied, 93/3077, 01/1143, 07/4191: *Considered*, 68/941, 76/402, 90/1020,
                                  97/3417, 06/4341: *Followed*, 98/4257
Daly v Smith (Unreported, June 7, 2007), CC (Milton Keynes) [*Ex rel.* Alison Griffiths,
    4 King's Bench Walk, Temple, London] . . . .   *Digested*, 07/**3099**
Damhar v Arriva London Ltd (Unreported, January 8, 2007), CC (Bow) [*Ex rel.* Lucy
    MacKinnon, Hailsham Chambers, 4 Paper Buildings, Temple, London EC4Y
    7EX] . . . .   *Digested*, 07/**423**
Dampskibsselskabet AF 1912 A/S v Motis Exports Ltd see Motis Exports Ltd v
    Dampskibsselskabet AF 1912 A/S (No.1)
Danesh v Kensington and Chelsea RLBC; *sub nom* Kensington and Chelsea RLBC v
    Danesh [2006] EWCA Civ 1404; [2007] 1 W.L.R. 69; [2007] H.L.R. 17; (2006)
    103(40) L.S.G. 34; (2006) 150 S.J.L.B. 1329, CA (Civ Div) . . . .   *Digested*, 07/**2156**
Daniels v Griffiths [1998] E.M.L.R. 489; (1997) 94(48) L.S.G. 29; (1997) 147 N.L.J.
    1809; (1998) 142 S.J.L.B. 22; *Times*, December 2, 1997; *Independent*,
    December 3, 1997, CA (Civ Div) . . . .   *Digested*, 98/**1778**:
                                      Considered, 07/1073
Danninger v Bus Atha Cliath [2007] IEHC 29; [2007] Eu. L.R. 605, HC (Irl)
Dansk Rorindustri A/S v Commission of the European Communities (C-189/02 P);
    joined cases ABB Asea Brown Boveri Ltd v Commission of the European
    Communities (C-213/02 P); LR AF 1998 (Deutschland) GmbH v Commission of
    the European Communities (C-208/02 P); Brugg Rohrsysteme GmbH v
    Commission of the European Communities (C-207/02 P); LR af 1998 A/S v
    Commission of the European Communities (C-206/02 P); KE KELIT
    Kunststoffwerk GmbH v Commission of the European Communities (C-205/02
    P); Isoplus Fernwarmetechnik Vertriebsgesellschaft mbH v Commission of the
    European Communities (C-202/02 P) [2005] E.C.R. I-5425; [2005] 5
    C.M.L.R. 17, ECJ . . . .   *Digested*, 06/**574**:
                   Applied, 07/607, 07/609, 07/612: *Followed*, 07/610
Danzer v Council of the European Union (T-47/02) [2006] E.C.R. II-1779; [2006] 3
    C.M.L.R. 21, CFI (3rd Chamber) . . . .   *Digested*, 07/**552**
Darker v Chief Constable of the West Midlands; *sub nom* Docker (Deceased) v Chief
    Constable of the West Midlands [2001] 1 A.C. 435; [2000] 3 W.L.R. 747;
    [2000] 4 All E.R. 193; [2000] Po. L.R. 305; (2000) 97(32) L.S.G. 38; (2000)
    150 N.L.J. 1421; (2000) 144 S.J.L.B. 243; *Times*, August 1, 2000; *Independent*,
    November 6, 2000, HL; reversing (1998) 95(17) L.S.G. 31; (1998) 142 S.J.L.B.
    134; *Times*, April 29, 1998, CA (Civ Div) . . . .   *Digested*, 00/**4543**:
                            Applied, 01/401, 06/313: *Considered*, 07/340
Darlington Building Society v O'Rourke James Scourfield & McCarthy [1999] Lloyd's
    Rep. P.N. 33; [1999] P.N.L.R. 365; *Times*, November 20, 1998, CA (Civ Div) . .   *Digested*, 98/**601**:
                                    Considered, 01/626, 07/492
Darnton v University of Surrey [2003] I.C.R. 615; [2003] I.R.L.R. 133, EAT . . . .   *Digested*, 03/**1345**:
                                        Applied, 07/1441
Dasema Trading Ltd's Trade Mark [2007] E.T.M.R. 15, TMR . . . .   *Digested*, 07/**2678**
Dashwood (formerly Kaye) v Fleurets Ltd [2007] EWHC 1610 (QB); [2007] 34 E.G.
    84; [2007] 28 E.G. 120 (C.S.), QBD . . . .   *Digested*, 07/**803**

Dass v Revenue and Customs Commissioners; *sub nom* Dass v Special Commissioner
    [2006] EWHC 2491 (Ch); [2007] S.T.C. 187; [2006] B.T.C. 866; [2006] S.T.I.
    2298, Ch D; affirming [2007] S.T.C. (S.C.D.) 79; [2007] S.T.I. 138, Sp Comm. .   *Digested*, 07/**4053**
Dass v Special Commissioner see Dass v Revenue and Customs Commissioners
Dass (Setting of Minimum Term), Re; *sub nom* R. v Dass (Rajesh Kumar) [2006] EWHC
    3254 (QB); [2007] M.H.L.R. 37, QBD . . . .   *Digested*, 07/**3695**
Dassonville v Commission of the European Communities (8/74) see Procureur du Roi
    v Dassonville (8/74)
Datec Electronic Holdings Ltd v United Parcels Service Ltd [2007] UKHL 23; [2007]
    Bus. L.R. 1291; [2007] 1 W.L.R. 1325; [2007] 4 All E.R. 765; [2007] 2 All E.R.
    (Comm) 1067; [2007] 2 Lloyd's Rep. 114; [2007] 1 C.L.C. 720; [2007] R.T.R.
    40; (2007) 151 S.J.L.B. 670; *Times*, May 18, 2007, HL; affirming [2005] EWCA
    Civ 1418; [2006] 2 All E.R. (Comm) 350; [2006] 1 Lloyd's Rep. 279; [2005] 2
    C.L.C. 1025, CA (Civ Div); reversing [2005] EWHC 221 (Comm); [2005] 1
    Lloyd's Rep. 470, QBD (Comm) . . . .   *Digested*, 07/**4213**
Davenham Trust Plc v CV Distribution (UK) Ltd; *sub nom* Taylor (A Bankrupt), Re
    [2006] EWHC 3029 (Ch); [2007] Ch. 150; [2007] 2 W.L.R. 148; [2007] 3 All
    E.R. 638; [2007] B.P.I.R. 175, Ch D (Manchester) . . . .   *Digested*, 07/**374**
Davey v Aylesbury Vale DC; *sub nom* R (on the application of Davey) Aylesbury Vale
    DC [2007] EWCA Civ 1166; [2007] 47 E.G. 168 (C.S.); (2007) 151 S.J.L.B.
    1498; [2007] N.P.C. 123; *Times*, November 21, 2007, CA (Civ Div); affirming
    [2007] EWHC 116 (QB); [2007] 3 Costs L.R. 452, QBD . . . .   *Digested*, 07/**402**
David M Aaron (Personal Financial Planners) Ltd, Re; *sub nom* Secretary of State for
    Trade and Industry v Aaron (2007) 157 N.L.J. 859, Ch D
David Truex (A Firm) v Kitchin; *sub nom* Truex v Kitchin [2007] EWCA Civ 618; [2007]
    4 Costs L.R. 587; [2007] 2 F.L.R. 1203; [2007] P.N.L.R. 33; [2007] Fam. Law
    903; (2007) 157 N.L.J. 1011; (2007) 151 S.J.L.B. 926; [2007] N.P.C. 87; *Times*,
    August 29, 2007, CA (Civ Div) . . . .   *Digested*, 07/**2777**
Davidson v Scottish Ministers (Incidental Petition: Dismissal of Appeal); *sub nom*
    Davidson, Petitioner (No.3) 2005 1 S.C. (H.L.) 1, HL . . . .   *Digested*, 06/**5114**:
                                                                                              Considered, 07/4855
Davidson, Petitioner (No.3) see Davidson v Scottish Ministers (Incidental Petition:
    Dismissal of Appeal)
Davies v Bramwell [2007] EWCA Civ 821; (2007) 151 S.J.L.B. 1264, CA (Civ Div)
Davies v Department of Trade and Industry see Coal Mining Contractors v Davies
Davies v Meadwestvaco Calmar Ltd see Davies v Saint-Golbain Calmar Ltd
Davies v Muldoon (Unreported, June 29, 2007), CC (Basildon) [*Ex rel.* Alison
    Griffiths, Barrister, 4 King's Bench Walk, Temple, London] . . . .   *Digested*, 07/**3182**
Davies v Queen, The see Bowe v Queen, The
Davies v Saint-Golbain Calmar Ltd; *sub nom* Davies v Meadwestvaco Calmar Ltd; A3/
    2007/0668, CA (Civ Div); affirming [2007] EWHC 438 (Ch); [2007] Pens.
    L.R. 217, Ch D . . . .   *Digested*, 07/**3002**
Davies (Inspector of Taxes) v Hicks see Hicks v Davies (Inspector of Taxes)
Daw v Intel Corp (UK) Ltd; *sub nom* Intel Corp (UK) Ltd v Daw [2007] EWCA Civ
    70; [2007] 2 All E.R. 126; [2007] I.C.R. 1318; [2007] I.R.L.R. 355; (2007)
    104(8) L.S.G. 36; (2007) 157 N.L.J. 259; (2007) 151 S.J.L.B. 259, CA (Civ
    Div); affirming [2006] EWHC 1097 (QB), QBD . . . .   *Digested*, 07/**2942**
Dawkins (Valuation Officer) v Ash Bros & Heaton Ltd; *sub nom* Almond v Ash Bros &
    Heaton [1969] 2 A.C. 366; [1969] 2 W.L.R. 1024; [1969] 2 All E.R. 246; (1969)
    133 J.P. 319; 67 L.G.R. 499; (1969) 113 S.J. 345, HL; affirming [1968] 1
    W.L.R. 133; [1967] 3 All E.R. 952; (1968) 132 J.P. 49; 66 L.G.R. 35; 13 R.R.C.
    181; (1967) 111 S.J. 757, CA (Civ Div); affirming (1966) 119 E.G. 275; [1966]
    R.A. 533; [1966] R.V.R. 624; 12 R.R.C. 268, Lands Tr . . . .   *Digested*, 69/**3019**:
                                 Applied, 07/3341: *Considered*, 70/1500, 85/2932, 87/3193, 00/4613
Dawson v Broughton (2007) 151 S.J.L.B. 1167, CC (Manchester)
Dawson v Stonham Housing Association see Dunnachie v Kingston upon Hull City
    Council
Day v Brighton and Hove City Council [2006] EWHC 2928 (Admin); [2007] Env.
    L.R. D6, QBD (Admin)
Day v Haine [2007] EWHC 2691 (Ch); [2007] B.P.I.R. 1470; *Times*, December 28,
    2007, Ch D (Companies Ct)
Daymond v Enterprise South Devon UKEAT/0005/07/DA, EAT . . . .   *Applied*, 07/1427
Days Healthcare UK Ltd (formerly Days Medical Aids Ltd) v Pihsiang Machinery
    Manufacturing Co Ltd [2006] EWHC 1444 (QB); [2006] 4 All E.R. 233; [2007]
    C.P. Rep. 1; [2006] 5 Costs L.R. 788, QBD . . . .   *Digested*, 06/**386**
DCC Holdings (UK) Ltd v Revenue and Customs Commissioners [2007] S.T.C. (S.C.D.)
    592; [2007] S.T.I. 1649, Sp Comm . . . .   *Digested*, 07/**4017**
DCM (Optical Holdings) Ltd v Revenue and Customs Commissioners [2007] CSIH 58;
    2007 S.C. 813; 2007 S.L.T. 705; [2007] B.T.C. 5786; [2007] B.V.C. 733;
    [2007] S.T.I. 1813; 2007 G.W.D. 22-377, IH (1 Div); reversing [2006] B.V.C.
    2708; [2006] S.T.I. 1716, V&DTr . . . .   *Digested*, 07/**5569**
DDT Trucks of North America Ltd v DDT Holdings Ltd [2007] EWHC 1542 (Comm);
    [2007] 2 Lloyd's Rep. 213, QBD (Comm) . . . .   *Digested*, 07/**242**
DE, Re see JE v DE

De Cavel v De Cavel (120/79) [1980] E.C.R. 731; [1980] 3 C.M.L.R. 1, ECJ (3rd
   Chamber) . . . . *Digested,* 81/**1036**:
                                                     Applied, 07/1697
De Cavel v De Cavel (C-143/78) [1979] E.C.R.1055; [1979] 2 C.M.L.R. 547, ECJ . . .   *Digested,* 79/**1130**:
                        Applied, 07/1697: *Considered,* 03/1585, 03/1585, 04/1535, 05/1682
De Coster v College des Bourgmestre et Echevins de Watermael Boitsfort (C-17/00)
   [2002] All E.R. (EC) 154; [2001] E.C.R. I-9445; [2002] 1 C.M.L.R. 12, ECJ (5th
   Chamber) . . . . *Digested,* 02/**1582**:
                                            Applied, 06/4322, 07/2798
De Cuyper v Office National de l'Emploi (ONEM) (C-406/04) [2006] All E.R. (EC)
   947; [2006] E.C.R. I-6947; [2006] 3 C.M.L.R. 44; [2006] C.E.C. 937; [2007]
   I.C.R. 317, ECJ . . . . *Digested,* 07/**1625**:
                                             Followed, 07/1608
De Dampierre v De Dampierre [1988] A.C. 92; [1987] 2 W.L.R. 1006; [1987] 2 All
   E.R. 1; [1987] 2 F.L.R. 300; [1987] Fam. Law 418; (1987) 84 L.S.G. 1493;
   (1987) 131 S.J. 471, HL; reversing [1987] 1 F.L.R. 511; [1986] Fam. Law 361, CA
   (Civ Div) . . . . *Digested,* 87/**399**:
                  Applied, 92/475, 95/2334, 99/2403, 02/628, 03/1554, 05/1623:
                        Considered, 94/3256, 97/2453, 07/1810: *Followed,* 92/5695:
                                               Referred to, 95/2303
De Francesco v Barnum (1890) L.R. 45 Ch. D. 430, Ch D . . . . *Considered,* 07/4197
De Freitas v Permanent Secretary of Ministry of Agriculture, Fisheries, Lands and
   Housing [1999] 1 A.C. 69; [1998] 3 W.L.R. 675; 4 B.H.R.C. 563; (1998) 142
   S.J.L.B. 219, PC (Ant) . . . . *Digested,* 98/**3084**:
                                      Applied, 07/2340: *Considered,* 03/3813
De Groot v Staatssecretaris van Financien (C-385/00); *sub nom* FWL de Groot v
   Inspecteur van de Belastingdienst Particulieren/Ondernemingen te Haarlem (C-
   385/00) [2004] S.T.C. 1346; [2002] E.C.R. I-11819; [2004] 3 C.M.L.R. 21;
   [2004] B.T.C. 437; 5 I.T.L. Rep. 711; [2003] S.T.I. 172, ECJ (5th Chamber) . . . . . *Digested,* 03/**4148**:
                              Applied, 07/1612, 07/1614: *Considered,* 06/1573
De Landtsheer Emmanuel SA v Comite Interprofessionnel du Vin de Champagne (C-
   381/05) [2007] Bus. L.R. 1484; [2007] 2 C.M.L.R. 43; [2007] E.T.M.R. 69,
   ECJ (1st Chamber) . . . . *Digested,* 07/**1571**
De Lasteyrie du Saillant v Ministere de l'Economie, des Finances et de l'Industrie (C-9/
   02) [2005] S.T.C. 1722; [2004] E.C.R. I-2409; [2004] 3 C.M.L.R. 39; [2006]
   B.T.C. 105; 6 I.T.L. Rep. 666; [2004] S.T.I. 890, ECJ (5th Chamber) . . . . *Digested,* 04/**3697**:
                              Applied, 07/1612: *Considered,* 06/4157, 07/1624
De Longhi SpA's Trade Mark Applications . . . . *Applied,* 07/2679
De Meyere v Belgium (A/43) see Le Compte v Belgium (A/43)
De Nemethy v Revenue and Customs Commissioners [2007] S.T.I. 2127, Sp Comm
De Sousa v British South Africa Co see British South Africa Co v Companhia de
   Mocambique
Deadman v Bristol City Council [2007] EWCA Civ 822; [2007] I.R.L.R. 888; (2007)
   104(32) L.S.G. 26, CA (Civ Div) . . . . *Digested,* 07/**1322**
Deakin v First Secretary of State [2006] EWHC 3402 (Admin); [2007] J.P.L. 1073,
   QBD (Admin) . . . . *Digested,* 07/**3231**
Dean & Dean Solicitors v Angel Airlines SA [2007] EWHC 399 (QB); [2007] 5 Costs
   L.R. 795, QBD
Dearlove (t/a Diddy) v Combs (t/a Sean Puffy Combs, Puffy and P Diddy) [2007]
   EWHC 375 (Ch); (2007) 30(4) I.P.D. 30029, Ch D
Debaecker v Bouwman (49/84) [1985] E.C.R. 1779; [1986] 2 C.M.L.R. 400, ECJ
   (4th Chamber) . . . . *Digested,* 86/**1394**:
                                           Applied, 06/463, 07/462
Debenhams Plc v Westminster City Council [1987] A.C. 396; [1986] 3 W.L.R. 1063;
   [1987] 1 All E.R. 51; 85 L.G.R. 190; [1987] 1 E.G.L.R. 248; [1986] R.A. 249;
   (1987) 151 L.G. Rev. 188; (1987) 84 L.S.G. 341; (1986) 136 N.L.J. 1185; (1986)
   130 S.J. 985, HL; reversing [1986] 1 E.G.L.R. 189; (1986) 278 E.G. 974;
   [1986] R.A. 114; [1986] J.P.L. 671; (1986) 83 L.S.G. 1479; (1986) 130 S.J. 483,
   CA (Civ Div); affirming [1985] 1 E.G.L.R. 159; (1985) 274 E.G. 826; [1985]
   R.A. 265, QBD . . . . *Digested,* 87/**3195**:
                  Applied, 92/4288, 93/3900, 07/3339: *Considered,* 00/4473, 02/3694:
                                                  Followed, 99/4327
Debtor (No.88 of 1991), Re [1993] Ch. 286; [1992] 3 W.L.R. 1026; [1992] 4 All E.R. 301;
   (1992) 142 N.L.J. 1039; (1992) 136 S.J.L.B. 206; *Times,* July 10, 1992;
   Independent, July 10, 1992, Ch D . . . . *Digested,* 92/**4101**:
                                        Applied, 03/2369, 07/2460
Debtor (No.303 of 1997), Re see Hurst v Bennett (No.1)
Debtor (No.101 of 1999) (No.1), Re [2001] 1 B.C.L.C. 54; [2000] B.P.I.R. 998; (2000)
   97(30) L.S.G. 40; *Times,* July 27, 2000, Ch D . . . . *Digested,* 00/**3473**:
                                        Considered, 07/2422
Decision CIS/3573/2005 (Unreported, May 12, 2006), SS Comm . . . . *Applied,* 07/3868
Deed of Indemnity, Re see Clay, Re
Deforche (Societe) v Tomacrau (Societe) [2007] I.L.Pr. 25, Cass (F) . . . . *Digested,* 07/**687**

DEG-Deutsche Investitions und Entwicklungsgesellschaft mbH v Koshy (Account of
   Profits: Limitations); *sub nom* Gwembe Valley Development Co Ltd (In
   Receivership) v Koshy (Account of Profits: Limitations) [2003] EWCA Civ 1048;
   [2004] 1 B.C.L.C. 131; [2004] W.T.L.R. 97; (2003) 147 S.J.L.B. 1086; *Times,*
   September 9, 2003, CA (Civ Div); affirming in part [2002] 1 B.C.L.C. 478; *Times,*
   December 10, 2001, Ch D . . . .   *Digested,* 03/**519**:
                                          Applied, 07/471: *Considered,* 06/470, 06/4076
Del Cerro Alonso v Osakidetza-Servicio Vasco de Salud (C-307/05) [2007] 3 C.M.L.R.
   54; [2007] I.R.L.R. 911, ECJ (2nd Chamber)
Del Grosso v Payne & Payne (A Firm) [2007] EWCA Civ 340; (2007) 151 S.J.L.B.
   336, CA (Civ Div)
Delaney v Staples (t/a De Montfort Recruitment) [1992] 1 A.C. 687; [1992] 2 W.L.R.
   451; [1992] 1 All E.R. 944; [1992] I.C.R. 483; [1992] I.R.L.R. 191; (1992) 142
   N.L.J. 384; *Times,* March 16, 1992; *Independent,* March 13, 1992, HL; affirming
   [1991] 2 Q.B. 47; [1991] 2 W.L.R. 627; [1991] 1 All E.R. 609; [1991] I.C.R. 331;
   [1991] I.R.L.R. 112; (1991) 141 N.L.J. 581, CA (Civ Div); reversing in part
   [1990] I.C.R. 364; [1990] I.R.L.R. 86; (1990) 87(10) L.S.G. 35, EAT . . . .   *Digested,* 92/**2028**:
                      Applied, 95/1981, 95/2040, 97/2294, 98/2208, 98/2245, 04/1267, 05/2262,
                              05/4093, 06/4218, 07/1356: *Considered,* 98/5827, 00/2247, 01/5274:
                      Distinguished, 96/2675, 98/5827: *Followed,* 99/2017: *Not followed,* 90/1985,
                                                                                          91/1709
Delhi Electric Supply & Traction Co Ltd, Re see India v Taylor
Dellar v Zivy [2007] EWHC 2266 (Ch); [2007] I.L.Pr. 60, Ch D . . . .   *Digested,* 07/**3961**
Demirel v Tasarruff Mevduati Sigorta Fonu see Tasarruf Mevduati Sigorta Fonu v
   Demirel
Demon Internet Ltd v Young (Inspector of Taxes) [2005] S.T.C. (S.C.D.) 233; [2005]
   S.T.I. 108, Sp Comm . . . .   *Digested,* 05/**4102**:
                                                                                    Not followed, 07/4072
Dempster (t/a Boulevard) v Revenue and Customs Commissioners see Revenue and
   Customs Commissioners v Dempster (t/a Boulevard)
Denfleet International Ltd v TNT Global SpA see TNT Global SpA v Denfleet
   International Ltd
Denison Mines Ltd v Ontario Hydro (2002) 56 O.R. (3d) 181, CA (Ont) . . . .   *Considered,* 07/233
Denkavit Internationaal BV v Ministre de l'Economie, des Finances et de l'Industrie (C-
   170/05) [2007] S.T.C. 452; [2007] 1 C.M.L.R. 40; [2007] C.E.C. 172; [2007]
   Pens. L.R. 1; 9 I.T.L. Rep. 560; [2007] S.T.I. 109, ECJ (1st Chamber) . . . .   *Digested,* 07/**1615**
Denkavit Nederland BV v Commission of the European Communities (T-20/99)
   [2000] E.C.R. II-3011; [2000] 3 C.M.L.R. 1014, CFI (1st Chamber). . . . .   *Digested,* 01/**2502**:
                                                                    Applied, 05/1425, 07/1539
Dennard v Plant see Lagden v O'Connor
Dennis v Lloyds Bank Plc see Dennis (Deceased), Re
Dennis (Deceased), Re; *sub nom* Dennis v Lloyds Bank Plc [1981] 2 All E.R. 140;
   (1980) 124 S.J. 885; *Times,* November 14, 1980, Ch D . . . .   *Digested,* 81/**2887**:
                                          Applied, 03/4123: *Considered,* 00/2528, 07/4112
Denton v Southwark LBC [2007] EWCA Civ 623; (2007) 104(29) L.S.G. 22; (2007)
   151 S.J.L.B. 925; [2007] N.P.C. 85, CA (Civ Div)
Denyer v Revenue and Customs Commissioners; *sub nom* Revenue and Customs
   Commissioners v Denyer [2007] EWHC 2750 (Ch); [2007] S.T.I. 2702; [2007]
   49 E.G. 103 (C.S.), Ch D; reversing 20121, V&DTr (London)
Department for Constitutional Affairs v Jones [2007] EWCA Civ 894, CA (Civ Div);
   affirming UKEAT/0333/06/DM, EAT . . . .   *Applied,* 07/1375
Department for Environment, Food and Rural Affairs v Feakins see Secretary of State for
   the Environment, Food and Rural Affairs v Feakins
Department for the Environment, Food and Rural Affairs v Robertson see Robertson v
   Department for the Environment, Food and Rural Affairs
Department for the Environment, Food and Rural Affairs v Rockall see Rockall v
   Department for the Environment, Food and Rural Affairs
Department of Transport v North West Water Authority [1984] A.C. 336; [1983] 3
   W.L.R. 707; [1983] 3 All E.R. 273; 82 L.G.R. 207; (1983) 133 N.L.J. 1016;
   (1983) 127 S.J. 713, HL; reversing [1983] 3 W.L.R. 105; [1983] 1 All E.R. 892;
   81 L.G.R. 599; (1983) 127 S.J. 426; *Times,* December 9, 1982, QBD. . . . .   *Digested,* 83/**2749**:
                                                  Applied, 07/2752: *Considered,* 93/432
Deputy Commissioner of Income Tax v Patni Computer Systems 10 I.T.L. Rep. 53, ITAT
   (Ind)
Deputy Commissioner of Income Tax, Special Range 26 v Roxon OY 9 I.T.L. Rep. 1045,
   ITAT (Ind)
Deputy Director of Income Tax v SET Satellite (Singapore) Pte Ltd 9 I.T.L. Rep. 962,
   ITAT (Ind)
Der Grune Punkt - Duales System Deutschland v Commission of the European
   Communities (T-151/01) [2001] E.C.R. II-3295, CFI . . . .   *Applied,* 07/1549
Der Grune Punkt - Duales System Deutschland GmbH v Commission of the European
   Communities (T-151/01) [2007] 5 C.M.L.R. 4; [2007] E.T.M.R. 60, CFI (1st
   Chamber)

Der Grune Punkt - Duales System Deutschland GmbH v Commission of the European
    Communities (T-289/01) [2007] 5 C.M.L.R. 5, CFI (1st Chamber)
Derby & Co Ltd v Weldon (No.7) [1990] 1 W.L.R. 1156; [1990] 3 All E.R. 161, Ch D ..   *Digested*, 91/**2859**:
    Applied, 07/470: *Considered*, 91/781
Derbyshire v Mackman see O'Reilly v Mackman
Derbyshire v St Helens MBC see St Helens MBC v Derbyshire
Derbyshire CC v Fallon [2007] EWHC 1326 (Ch); [2007] 45 E.G. 164; [2007] 25 E.G.
    182 (C.S.), Ch D ....   *Digested*, 07/**3412**
Derin v Landkreis Darmstadt-Dieburg (C-325/05) [2007] 3 C.M.L.R. 41; [2007]
    I.C.R. 1706, ECJ (1st Chamber)
Derry City Council's Application for Judicial Review, Re [2007] NIQB 5; [2007] N.I. 164,
    QBD (NI)
Designer Room Ltd, Re [2004] EWHC 720 (Ch); [2005] 1 W.L.R. 1581; [2004] 3 All E.R.
    679; [2004] B.C.C. 904, Ch D ....   *Digested*, 04/**2112**:
    Considered, 07/2392, 07/2395
Designers Guild Ltd v Russell Williams (Textiles) Ltd (t/a Washington DC) [2000] 1
    W.L.R. 2416; [2001] 1 All E.R. 700; [2001] E.C.D.R. 10; [2001] F.S.R. 11; (2001)
    98(3) L.S.G. 42; (2000) 144 S.J.L.B. 290; *Times*, November 28, 2000, HL;
    reversing [2000] F.S.R. 121; (1999) 22(7) I.P.D. 22067, CA (Civ Div); reversing
    [1998] F.S.R. 803; (1998) 21(6) I.P.D. 21064, Ch D ....   *Digested*, 01/**3859**:
    Applied, 03/2508, 05/2427: *Considered*, 02/2776, 07/2521:
    Explained, 07/2514: *Followed*, 06/2441
Desnousse v Newham LBC [2006] EWCA Civ 547; [2006] Q.B. 831; [2006] 3
    W.L.R. 349; [2007] 2 All E.R. 547; [2006] H.L.R. 38; [2007] B.L.G.R. 368;
    [2006] N.P.C. 58; *Times*, June 28, 2006; *Independent*, May 19, 2006, CA (Civ
    Div)..   *Digested*, 06/**2046**
Deutsch v Credit Lyonnais SA (R232/2005-1) [2007] E.T.M.R. 4, OHIM (1st Bd App)
Deutsche Genossenschaftsbank v Brasserie du Pecheur (148/84) [1985] E.C.R. 1981;
    [1986] 2 C.M.L.R. 496, ECJ (5th Chamber) ....   *Digested*, 86/**1382**:
    Applied, 07/462

Deutsche Morgan Grenfell Group Plc v Inland Revenue Commissioners; *sub nom* Inland
    Revenue Commissioners v Deutsche Morgan Grenfell Group Plc; Deutsche
    Morgan Grenfell Plc v Revenue and Customs Commissioners [2006]
    UKHL 49; [2007] 1 A.C. 558; [2006] 3 W.L.R. 781; [2007] 1 All E.R. 449;
    [2007] S.T.C. 1; [2007] 1 C.M.L.R. 14; [2007] Eu. L.R. 226; 78 T.C. 120; [2006]
    B.T.C. 781; 9 I.T.L. Rep. 201; [2006] S.T.I. 2386; (2006) 103(43) L.S.G. 29;
    (2006) 150 S.J.L.B. 1430; *Times*, October 26, 2006, HL; reversing [2005]
    EWCA Civ 78; [2006] Ch. 243; [2006] 2 W.L.R. 103; [2005] 3 All E.R. 1025;
    [2005] S.T.C. 329; [2005] Eu. L.R. 553; [2005] B.T.C. 126; 7 I.T.L. Rep. 476;
    [2005] S.T.I. 194; (2005) 102(10) L.S.G. 30; [2005] N.P.C. 18; *Times*, February
    15, 2005, CA (Civ Div); reversing in part [2003] EWHC 1779 (Ch); [2003] 4
    All E.R. 645; [2003] S.T.C. 1017; [2003] Eu. L.R. 838; [2003] B.T.C. 497; 5 I.T.L.
    Rep. 1067; [2003] S.T.I. 1269; (2003) 100(36) L.S.G. 41; (2003) 153 N.L.J.
    1171; *Times*, July 30, 2003, Ch D ....   *Digested*, 07/**3973**:
    Applied, 04/3173, 07/4298: *Considered*, 06/4141, 07/3990:
    Reversed, 07/3973

Deutsche Morgan Grenfell Group Plc v Revenue and Customs Commissioners see
    Deutsche Morgan Grenfell Group Plc v Inland Revenue Commissioners
Deutz Energy GmbH v Quebecor World Europe [2007] I.L.Pr. 27, Cass (F) ....   *Digested*, 07/**663**
Devaseelan v Secretary of State for the Home Department [2002] UKIAT 702; [2003]
    Imm. A.R. 1, IAT ....   *Digested*, 04/**2013**:
    Applied, 02/2577, 04/2009, 07/926: *Considered*, 04/2015, 05/2152, 07/2283
Develey Holding GmbH & Co Beteiligungs KG v Office for Harmonisation in the Internal
    Market (Trade Marks and Designs) (OHIM) (T-129/04) [2006] E.T.M.R. 85,
    CFI (2nd Chamber) ....   *Digested*, 07/**2660**
Devenish Nutrition Ltd v Sanofi-Aventis SA [2007] EWHC 2394 (Ch); (2007) 151
    S.J.L.B. 1398, Ch D
Devi v Roy [1946] A.C. 508; 62 T.L.R. 549; [1947] L.J.R. 26; 176 L.T. 209, PC (Ind) ..   *Digested*, 47-51/**7967**:
    Applied, 06/3462, 07/363: *Followed*, 53/2920
Devine v Designer Flowers Wholesale Florist Sundries [1993] I.R.L.R. 517, EAT ......   *Digested*, 94/**2011**:
    Cited, 00/6218: *Considered*, 07/1317
Devlin v Baslington see Giles v Thompson
Dexter Ltd (In Administrative Receivership) v Vlieland-Boddy [2003] EWCA Civ 14;
    (2003) 147 S.J.L.B. 117, CA (Civ Div); affirming [2002] EWHC 1561 (Ch), Ch D
    ....   *Applied*, 07/346
Dexter Montague & Partners v Legal Services Commission see R. (on the application of
    Law Society) v Legal Services Commission

Dextra Accessories Ltd v MacDonald (Inspector of Taxes); *sub nom* MacDonald (Inspector of Taxes) v Dextra Accessories Ltd [2005] UKHL 47; [2005] 4 All E.R. 107; [2005] S.T.C. 1111; [2005] Pens. L.R. 395; 77 T.C. 146; [2005] B.T.C. 355; [2005] S.T.I. 1235; (2005) 102(29) L.S.G. 33; *Times,* July 11, 2005, HL; affirming [2004] EWCA Civ 22; [2004] S.T.C. 339; [2004] B.T.C. 88; [2004] S.T.I. 234; (2004) 101(9) L.S.G. 32; (2004) 148 S.J.L.B. 150; *Times,* February 3, 2004, CA (Civ Div); reversing [2003] EWHC 872 (Ch); [2003] S.T.C. 749; [2003] B.T.C. 472; [2003] W.T.L.R. 675; (2003) 100(25) L.S.G. 47; *Times,* April 25, 2003, Ch D; affirming [2002] S.T.C. (S.C.D.) 413; [2003] W.T.L.R. 349; [2002] S.T.I. 1335, Sp Comm . . . . *Digested,* 05/**4026**:
Considered, 07/4085

DGT Steel & Cladding Ltd v Cubitt Building & Interiors Ltd [2007] EWHC 1584 (TCC); [2007] B.L.R. 371; [2007] T.C.L.R. 8; 116 Con. L.R. 118; [2007] C.I.L.L. 2492; (2007) 104(33) L.S.G. 27, QBD (TCC) . . . . *Digested,* 07/**528**

Dhesi v Chief Constable of Kent see R. v Manchester Stipendiary Magistrate Ex p. Hill

Diab v Regent Insurance Co Ltd [2006] UKPC 29; [2007] Bus. L.R. 915; [2007] 1 W.L.R. 797; [2006] 2 All E.R. (Comm) 704; [2006] 1 C.L.C. 1084; [2006] Lloyd's Rep. I.R. 779, PC (Bze) . . . . *Digested,* 06/**2406**:
Considered, 07/2470

Diageo Pension Trust v Merthyr Tydfil Council [2007] P.A.D. 65, Planning Inspector

Diagnostic Methods (G1/04) [2006] E.P.O.R. 15, EPO (Enlarged Bd App) . . . . *Digested,* 06/**2511**:
Applied, 07/2596, 07/2597

Diagnostiko & Therapeftiko Kentro Athinon (Ygeia AE) v Ypourgos Oikonomikon (C-394/04) [2006] S.T.C. 1349; [2005] E.C.R. I-10373; [2005] S.T.I. 1904, ECJ (3rd Chamber) . . . . *Followed,* 07/4295

Diamalt AG v Hauptzollamt Itzehoe (16/77) see Albert Ruckdeschel & Co v Hauptzollamt Hamburg-St Annen (117/76)

Diamond v Mansfield [2006] EWHC 3290; (2007) 104(3) L.S.G. 28, QBD

Dibro v Hore [1990] I.C.R. 370; [1990] I.R.L.R. 129; (1990) 87(13) L.S.G. 43; *Times,* January 24, 1990, EAT . . . . *Digested,* 90/**1875**:
Applied, 07/1365

Dickson v United Kingdom (44362/04) [2006] 2 F.L.R. 449; [2006] 2 F.C.R. 1; (2007) 44 E.H.R.R. 21; 21 B.H.R.C. 236; [2006] Fam. Law 532; *Times,* May 16, 2006, ECHR . . . . *Digested,* 06/**2196**

Dickson v United Kingdom (44362/04) [2007] 3 F.C.R. 877; 24 B.H.R.C. 19; (2007) 157 N.L.J. 1766; *Times,* December 21, 2007, ECHR (Grand Chamber)

Digby v East Cambridgeshire DC [2007] I.R.L.R. 585, EAT

Dignity Funerals Ltd v Bruce see Bruce v Dignity Funerals Ltd

Dillenkofer v Germany (C-178/94); *joined cases* Knor v Germany (C-190/94); Heuer v Germany (C-189/94); Schulte v Germany (C-188/94); Erdmann v Germany (C-179/94) [1997] Q.B. 259; [1997] 2 W.L.R. 253; [1996] All E.R. (EC) 917; [1996] E.C.R. I-4845; [1996] 3 C.M.L.R. 469; [1997] I.R.L.R. 60; *Times,* October 14, 1996, ECJ . . . . *Digested,* 96/**2802**:
Applied, 99/5274, 01/5581: *Considered,* 07/2490: *Followed,* 97/4672

Diment v NH Foot Ltd [1974] 1 W.L.R. 1427; [1974] 2 All E.R. 785; (1974) 28 P. & C.R. 163; (1974) 118 S.J. 810, Ch D . . . . *Digested,* 74/**1081**:
Followed, 07/3428

Dimmock v Secretary of State for Children, Schools and Families; *sub nom* R. (on the application of Dimmock) v Secretary of State for Education and Skills; Dimmock v Secretary of State for Education and Skills [2007] EWHC 2288 (Admin); [2007] A.C.D. 96; (2007) 157 N.L.J. 1462, QBD (Admin)

Dimmock v Secretary of State for Education and Skills see Dimmock v Secretary of State for Children, Schools and Families

Dimond v Lovell [2002] 1 A.C. 384; [2000] 2 W.L.R. 1121; [2000] 2 All E.R. 897; [2000] R.T.R. 243; [2000] C.C.L.R. 57; 2000 Rep. L.R. 62; (2000) 97(22) L.S.G. 47; (2000) 150 N.L.J. 740; *Times,* May 12, 2000; *Independent,* May 17, 2000, HL; affirming [2000] Q.B. 216; [1999] 3 W.L.R. 561; [1999] 3 All E.R. 1; [1999] R.T.R. 297; [1999] C.C.L.R. 46; (1999) 96(21) L.S.G. 40; (1999) 149 N.L.J. 681; (1999) 143 S.J.L.B. 181; *Times,* May 3, 1999, CA (Civ Div); reversing (Unreported, May 1, 1998), CC (Sheffield) [*Ex rel.* Cottrill Stone Lawless Solicitors, 18 Lloyd Street, Albert Square, Manchester] . . . . *Digested,* 00/**2566**:
Applied, 99/2470, 99/2471, 99/2475, 99/2478, 99/2481, 00/2570, 00/2587, 00/2587, 01/881, 01/900, 01/1527, 07/2497: *Cited,* 99/2458, 99/2461, 99/2476, 99/2499, 00/425, 00/425, 00/2574, 00/2580, 00/2592, 00/2593, 01/896, 01/899, 01/3830, 02/685: *Considered,* 99/532, 99/2453, 99/2454, 99/2454, 99/2459, 99/2460, 99/2466, 99/2467, 99/2468, 99/2477, 99/2496, 00/311, 00/2570, 00/2589, 01/885, 01/888, 01/890, 01/898, 06/702: *Distinguished,* 99/535, 99/2452, 99/2482, 99/2491, 99/2504, 00/2578, 00/2585, 00/2597, 01/893, 01/894, 02/932, 04/630: *Followed,* 99/2463, 99/2489, 00/2565, 00/2577, 00/2579, 01/657, 01/887, 01/901, 04/628: *Referred to,* 99/2451, 99/2464, 99/2465, 99/2472, 99/2473, 99/2474, 99/2483, 99/2485, 99/2487, 99/2490, 00/2562, 00/2589, 01/1542

Dingmar v Dingmar [2006] EWCA Civ 942; [2007] Ch. 109; [2006] 3 W.L.R. 1183; [2007] 2 All E.R. 382; [2007] 1 F.L.R. 210; [2006] 2 F.C.R. 595; [2006] W.T.L.R. 1171; [2006] Fam. Law 1025; [2006] N.P.C. 83, CA (Civ Div) . . . . *Digested, 06/**4088***

Diocese of Southwark v Coker; sub nom Coker v Diocese of Southwark [1998] I.C.R. 140; (1997) 94(29) L.S.G. 29; (1997) 141 S.J.L.B. 169; *Times*, July 17, 1997, CA (Civ Div); affirming [1996] I.C.R. 896; *Times*, April 4, 1996, EAT; reversing [1995] I.C.R. 563; *Independent*, March 16, 1995, IT . . . . *Digested, 97/**2293**: Applied, 02/5576: Considered, 07/1326*

Dionik Anonimi Etairia Emporias I/I, Logismikou & Parokhis Ipiresion Mikhanografisis v Epitropi Kefalaiagoras (C-430/05) [2007] 3 C.M.L.R. 35, ECJ (1st Chamber)

Dionsynth Ltd v Thomson see Thomson v Diosynth Ltd

Director General of Fair Trading v First National Bank Plc [2001] UKHL 52; [2002] 1 A.C. 481; [2001] 3 W.L.R. 1297; [2002] 1 All E.R. 97; [2001] 2 All E.R. (Comm) 1000; [2002] 1 Lloyd's Rep. 489; [2002] E.C.C. 22; (2001) 151 N.L.J. 1610; *Times*, November 1, 2001; *Daily Telegraph*, October 30, 2001, HL; reversing [2000] Q.B. 672; [2000] 2 W.L.R. 1353; [2000] 2 All E.R. 759; [2000] 1 All E.R. (Comm) 371; [2000] Lloyd's Rep. Bank. 130; [2000] C.C.L.R. 31; (2000) 97(7) L.S.G. 39; *Times*, March 14, 2000, CA (Civ Div); reversing [2000] 1 W.L.R. 98; [2000] 1 All E.R. 240; [1999] Lloyd's Rep. Bank. 427; [2000] E.C.C. 169; (1999) 18 Tr. L.R. 245; *Times*, September 21, 1999; *Independent*, November 8, 1999, Ch D . . . . *Digested, 01/**910**: Applied, 01/3832, 03/664, 04/618, 07/766: Considered, 03/2456, 05/194: Followed, 05/721*

Director General of Fair Trading v Proprietary Association of Great Britain; sub nom Medicaments and Related Classes of Goods (No.2), Re [2001] 1 W.L.R. 700; [2001] U.K.C.L.R. 550; [2001] I.C.R. 564; [2001] H.R.L.R. 17; [2001] U.K.H.R.R. 429; (2001) 3 L.G.L.R. 32; (2001) 98(7) L.S.G. 40; (2001) 151 N.L.J. 17; (2001) 145 S.J.L.B. 29; *Times*, February 2, 2001; *Independent*, January 12, 2001, CA (Civ Div); reversing (2001) 98(2) L.S.G. 41; (2000) 144 S.J.L.B. 289, Ch D (RPC) . . . . *Digested, 01/**14**: Applied, 01/692, 01/856, 01/857, 02/1618, 02/1838, 03/642, 03/2217, 03/4604, 04/30, 04/2754, 05/647: Considered, 02/452: Distinguished, 02/3100, 07/248: Followed, 02/1105*

Director of Income Tax (International Taxation), Mumbai v Morgan Stanley & Co Inc; sub nom Morgan Stanley & Co Inc v Director of Income Tax (International Taxation), Mumbai 9 I.T.L. Rep. 1124, Sup Ct (Ind)

Director of the Assets Recovery Agency v McCormack [2007] EWHC 908 (QB); [2007] S.T.I. 1275, QBD

Director of the Assets Recovery Agency v Olupitan; sub nom Olupitan v Director of the Assets Recovery Agency; C1/2007/0538, CA (Civ Div); affirming [2007] EWHC 162 (QB); (2007) 157 N.L.J. 258; [2007] N.P.C. 17, QBD . . . . *Digested, 07/**509***

Director of the Serious Fraud Office v A [2007] EWCA Crim 1927; (2007) 151 S.J.L.B. 1058, CA (Civ Div)

Diriye v Secretary of State for the Home Department see Saad v Secretary of State for the Home Department

Dispit Ltd v Revenue and Customs Commissioners [2007] S.T.C. (S.C.D.) 194; [2007] S.T.I. 349, Sp Comm. . . . . *Digested, 07/**4002***

Dispute over MOX Plant, Re (C-459/03) see Commission of the European Communities v Ireland (C-459/03)

Distinct Services Ltd, Re see Allmark v Burnham

District Court of Vilnius City v Barcys see Lithuania v Barcys

Division of Jurisdiction between Constitutional Tribunal and European Court of Justice, Re (P37/05) [2007] 3 C.M.L.R. 48, Tryb Konst (PL)

Dixon v Hodgson [2007] 4 E.G. 188, CC (Carlisle) . . . . *Digested, 07/**3400***

Dizman v Turkey (27309/95) (2007) 44 E.H.R.R. 25, ECHR

DJ v MS see C-J (Section 91(14) Order), Re

DJ&C Withers (Farms) Ltd v Ambic Equipment Ltd see English v Emery Reimbold & Strick Ltd

Djebbar v Secretary of State for the Home Department [2004] EWCA Civ 804; [2004] Imm. A.R. 497; [2004] I.N.L.R. 466; (2004) 101(33) L.S.G. 36; *Times*, July 12, 2004, CA (Civ Div) . . . . *Digested, 04/**2015**: Applied, 07/926*

DK (Serbia) v Secretary of State for the Home Department; joined cases SP (Serbia) v Secretary of State for the Home Department; PE (Nigeria) v Secretary of State for the Home Department; AL (Nigeria) v Secretary of State for the Home Department; MS (Somalia) v Secretary of State for the Home Department; JN (Uganda) v Secretary of State for the Home Department [2006] EWCA Civ 1747; [2007] 2 All E.R. 483; [2007] Imm. A.R. 411; [2007] I.N.L.R. 166; *Times*, January 10, 2007, CA (Civ Div) . . . . *Digested, 07/**2276***

DKLL Solicitors v Revenue and Customs Commissioners [2007] EWHC 2067 (Ch); [2007] B.C.C. 908, Ch D

DO v LP see S (A Child) (Adoption Order or Special Guardianship Order), Re

Do v Immigration Appeal Tribunal see R. (on the application of Ullah) v Special Adjudicator

Do v Secretary of State for the Home Department see R. (on the application of Ullah) v Special Adjudicator

Dobbin v Redpath [2007] EWCA Civ 570; [2007] 4 All E.R. 465; (2007) 104(20) L.S.G. 29, CA (Civ Div) . . . . *Digested,* 07/**3423**

Dobson v Thames Water Utilities Ltd [2007] EWHC 2021 (TCC); [2007] B.L.R. 465; [2007] T.C.L.R. 7; 116 Con. L.R. 135; [2007] H.R.L.R. 45; [2007] C.I.L.L. 2518; [2007] N.P.C. 102, QBD (TCC) . . . . *Digested,* 07/**2961**

Docker (Deceased) v Chief Constable of the West Midlands see Darker v Chief Constable of the West Midlands

DOCUMOTION RESEARCH/Tamper-evident form (T354/05) [2007] E.P.O.R. 29, EPO (Technical Bd App) . . . . *Digested,* 07/**2581**

Dodds v Walker [1981] 1 W.L.R. 1027; [1981] 2 All E.R. 609; (1981) 42 P. & C.R. 131; (1981) 125 S.J. 463, HL; affirming [1980] 1 W.L.R. 1061; [1980] 2 All E.R. 507; (1980) 40 P. & C.R. 487; (1980) 255 E.G. 53; (1980) 124 S.J. 575, CA (Civ Div) . . . . *Digested,* 81/**1518**:
Applied, 85/1847, 05/892, 07/2354: *Considered,* 04/4594, 05/5214: *Followed,* 04/440

Dogan v Secretary of State for the Home Department; *sub nom* R. (on the application of the Secretary of State for the Home Department) v Chief Asylum Support Adjudicator [2003] EWCA Civ 1673; [2004] H.L.R. 25, CA (Civ Div) . . . . *Digested,* 04/**2016**:
Considered, 07/2288

Doheny v New India Assurance Co Ltd [2004] EWCA Civ 1705; [2005] 1 All E.R. (Comm) 382; [2005] Lloyd's Rep. I.R. 251, CA (Civ Div); affirming (Unreported, May 21, 2004), QBD . . . . *Digested,* 05/**2365**:
Applied, 07/2483

Doherty v Birmingham City Council [2006] EWCA Civ 1739; [2007] H.L.R. 32; [2007] B.L.G.R. 165; (2007) 151 S.J.L.B. 62; [2007] N.P.C. 2, CA (Civ Div). . . *Digested,* 07/**2242**

Dokter v Minister van Landbouw, Natuur en Voedselkwaliteit (C-28/05) [2006] E.C.R. I-5431; [2006] 3 C.M.L.R. 26, ECJ (3rd Chamber) . . . . *Digested,* 07/**1566**

Dollar Land (Manhattan) Ltd, Re see El-Ajou v Dollar Land (Manhattan) Ltd

Dolphin Quays Developments Ltd v Mills [2006] EWHC 931 (Ch); [2007] 1 P. & C.R. 12, Ch D . . . . *Digested,* 07/**3395**

Dolphin Quays Developments Ltd v Mills; *sub nom* Mills v Birchall; A3/2007/1191, CA (Civ Div); affirming [2007] EWHC 1180 (Ch); [2007] 4 All E.R. 503; [2007] B.P.I.R. 1482; [2007] N.P.C. 62, Ch D . . . . *Digested,* 07/**420**

Domsalla (t/a Domsalla Building Services) v Dyason [2007] EWHC 1174 (TCC); [2007] B.L.R. 348; [2007] T.C.L.R. 5; 112 Con. L.R. 95; [2007] C.I.L.L. 2501, QBD (TCC) . . . . *Digested,* 07/**724**

Donaldson v Smith [2007] W.T.L.R. 421; (2006) 150 S.J.L.B. 744; [2007] 1 P. & C.R. DG2, Ch D . . . . *Digested,* 07/**3429**

Doncaster Pharmaceuticals Group Ltd v Bolton Pharmaceutical Co 100 Ltd see Bolton Pharmaceutical Co 100 Ltd v Doncaster Pharmaceuticals Group Ltd

Donegal International Ltd v Zambia [2007] EWHC 197 (Comm); [2007] 1 Lloyd's Rep. 397, QBD (Comm)

Donkin v Law Society [2007] EWHC 414 (Admin); (2007) 157 N.L.J. 402, DC

Donnelly v Weybridge Construction Ltd (No.2) [2006] EWHC 2678 (TCC); 111 Con. L.R. 112; [2006] 46 E.G. 208 (C.S.), QBD (TCC) . . . . *Digested,* 07/**797**

Donoghue v Stevenson; *sub nom* McAlister v Stevenson [1932] A.C. 562; 1932 S.C. (H.L.) 31; 1932 S.L.T. 317; [1932] W.N. 139, HL . . . . *Applied,* 47-51/6681, 47-51/6693, 47-51/6761, 47-51/6881, 47-51/6897, 52/1563, 52/2362, 53/639, 53/2422, 56/904, 57/1415, 57/2371, 61/825, 62/2028, 62/2188, 63/2362, 64/1670, 65/416, 65/2669, 68/4511, 69/2403, 70/1493, 70/1850, 72/1104, 72/2350, 72/2352, 72/2408, 72/2409, 74/2579, 75/933, 75/3994, 77/2025, 78/2065, 78/3538, 81/1849, 82/2135, 85/2301, 87/2579, 88/3410, 89/1286, 01/4509, 04/2747, 07/5426: *Considered,* 47-51/351, 47-51/6734, 47-51/9691, 54/2200, 55/1839, 57/2369, 62/2083, 62/3080, 65/2663, 65/2671, 69/1157, 70/1849, 72/2528, 74/363, 74/3638, 75/2343, 76/228, 87/2580, 88/2418, 88/2433, 88/3376, 88/3409, 91/2657, 91/2661, 93/2983, 93/2997, 94/5335, 95/4519, 98/3995, 99/3960, 00/4227: *Distinguished,* 51/3988, 47-51/6584, 47-51/6705, 47-51/7886, 52/4290, 57/2366, 57/2639, 63/330, 63/2360, 64/2516, 66/6884, 72/2361, 83/2746: *Followed,* 76/3296, 85/4437: *Referred to,* 79/1866

Donohue v Armco Inc [2001] UKHL 64; [2002] 1 All E.R. 749; [2002] 1 All E.R. (Comm) 97; [2002] 1 Lloyd's Rep. 425; [2002] C.L.C. 440, HL; reversing [2000] 1 All E.R. (Comm) 641; [2000] 1 Lloyd's Rep. 579; [2000] C.L.C. 1090; [2001] I.L.Pr. 48, CA (Civ Div); reversing [2000] 1 All E.R. (Comm) 425; [1999] 2 Lloyd's Rep. 649; [1999] C.L.C. 1748; [2000] I.L.Pr. 321, QBD (Comm) . . . . *Digested,* 02/**643**:
Applied, 04/193, 05/2406, 06/330, 06/649: *Considered,* 03/593, 05/625, 05/2371: *Distinguished,* 04/2344: *Followed,* 07/355

Donovan v Staffordshire CC see Staffordshire CC v Donovan

Doodes v Gotham see Gotham v Doodes

Dooley v Havering LBC [2007] P.A.D. 82, Planning Inspector

Dooley v Law Society (Application to Set Aside Intervention) HC 0002868, Ch D . . . *Considered,* 07/2801

Dootson v Blackburn with Darwen BC [2007] P.A.D. 24, Planning Inspector
Dorgan v Home Office see Anderton v Clwyd CC
Dornoch Ltd v Mauritius Union Assurance Co Ltd [2006] EWCA Civ 389; [2006] 2
    All E.R. (Comm) 385; [2006] 2 Lloyd's Rep. 475; [2006] 1 C.L.C. 714; [2006]
    Lloyd's Rep. I.R. 786, CA (Civ Div); affirming [2005] EWHC 1887 (Comm);
    [2006] Lloyd's Rep. I.R.127; (2005) 102(35) L.S.G. 42, QBD (Comm) . . . . . .   *Digested*, 06/**642**:
                                             Considered, 07/2492
Dornoch Ltd v Mauritius Union Assurance Co Ltd [2007] EWHC 155 (Comm); [2007]
    Lloyd's Rep. I.R. 350, QBD (Comm) . . . .   *Digested*, 07/**2506**
Dornoch Ltd v Royal & Sun Alliance Insurance Plc see Royal & Sun Alliance Insurance
    Plc v Dornoch Ltd
Dosanjh (Setting of Minimum Term), Re see Jones (Setting of Minimum Term), Re
Dostenko v City of Westminster [2007] EWCA Civ 1325; [2007] N.P.C. 134, CA (Civ
    Div)
Dott v Brown [1936] 1 All E.R. 543. . . . .   *Considered*, 07/4093
Dougan v Mackman see O'Reilly v Mackman
Douglas v Hello! Ltd see OBG Ltd v Allan
Douglas v Hello! Ltd (No.6); *sub nom* Douglas v Hello! Ltd (Trial Action: Breach of
    Confidence) (No.3) [2005] EWCA Civ 595; [2006] Q.B. 125; [2005] 3 W.L.R.
    881; [2005] 4 All E.R. 128; [2005] E.M.L.R. 28; [2005] 2 F.C.R. 487; [2005]
    H.R.L.R. 27; (2005) 28(8) I.P.D. 28057; (2005) 155 N.L.J. 828; *Times*, May 24,
    2005; *Independent*, May 26, 2005, CA (Civ Div); reversing in part [2003]
    EWHC 786 (Ch); [2003] 3 All E.R. 996; [2003] E.M.L.R. 31; (2003) 153 N.L.J.
    595; *Independent*, June 16, 2003, Ch D . . . .   *Digested*, 05/**2812**:
          Applied, 03/1217, 05/4188, 07/2510: *Approved*, 04/1391:
                 Considered, 06/2440: *Reversed*, 07/4190
Douglas v Hello! Ltd (Trial Action: Breach of Confidence) (No.3) see Douglas v Hello!
    Ltd (No.6)
Dougoz v Greece (40907/98) (2002) 34 E.H.R.R. 61; 10 B.H.R.C. 306; [2001] Prison
    L.R. 136, ECHR . . . .   *Digested*, 01/**3566**:
                                          Applied, 07/2230
DOW GLOBAL/Unity (W7/06) [2007] E.P.O.R. 27, EPO (Technical Bd App) . . . .   *Digested*, 07/**2593**
Dowden v Stack see Stack v Dowden
Down Lisburn Health & Social Services Trust v H [2006] UKHL 36; [2007] 1 F.L.R. 121;
    [2006] Fam. Law 920; (2006) 150 S.J.L.B. 986, HL (NI) . . . .   *Digested*, 07/**4550**
Downey v Charles Evans Shopfitters Ltd see Grieves v FT Everard & Sons Ltd
Downs' Application for Review of Opinion (2007) 30(3) I.P.D. 30024, PO
Doyle v United Kingdom (Admissibility) (30158/06) (2007) 45 E.H.R.R. SE3, ECHR
DPP v Bayer; *joined cases* DPP v Whistance; DPP v Snook; DPP v Hart [2003] EWHC
    2567 (Admin); [2004] 1 W.L.R. 2856; [2004] 1 Cr. App. R. 38; (2003) 167
    J.P. 666; [2004] Env. L.R. 23; [2004] Crim. L.R. 663; [2004] A.C.D. 67;
    (2004) 168 J.P.N. 15; (2003) 100(47) L.S.G. 21; *Times*, November 7, 2003,
    QBD (Admin) . . . .   *Digested*, 04/**769**:
                                        Considered, 07/875
DPP v Chand [2007] EWHC 90 (Admin); (2007) 171 J.P. 285; (2007) 171 J.P.N. 565,
    DC . . . .   *Digested*, 07/**824**
DPP v Clutterbuck [2006] EWHC 3447 (Admin); [2007] 2 Cr. App. R. (S.) 16, DC . . .   *Digested*, 07/**3611**
DPP v Collins [2006] UKHL 40; [2006] 1 W.L.R. 2223; [2006] 4 All E.R. 602;
    [2007] 1 Cr. App. R. 5; (2006) 170 J.P. 712; [2007] Crim. L.R. 98; (2007) 171
    J.P.N. 162; (2006) 156 N.L.J. 1212; (2006) 150 S.J.L.B. 987; *Times*, July 21,
    2006, HL; reversing [2005] EWHC 1308 (Admin); [2006] 1 W.L.R. 308;
    [2005] 3 All E.R. 326; [2005] 2 Cr. App. R. 39; [2005] Crim. L.R. 794; (2005)
    155 N.L.J. 1010, QBD (Admin) . . . .   *Digested*, 06/**832**
DPP v Cottier [1996] 1 W.L.R. 826; [1996] 3 All E.R. 126; [1996] 2 Cr. App. R. 410;
    [1996] Crim. L.R. 804; *Times*, February 22, 1996, DC . . . .   *Digested*, 96/**1638**:
                      Considered, 07/1026: *Followed*, 96/1637
DPP v Everest; *sub nom* R. (on the application of DPP) v Everest [2005] EWHC 1124
    (Admin); (2005) 169 J.P. 345; (2005) 169 J.P.N. 537, QBD (Admin) . . . .   *Digested*, 05/**828**:
                                          Considered, 07/988
DPP v Greenacre see Crown Prosecution Service v Greenacre
DPP v Hall [2005] EWHC 2612 (Admin); [2006] 1 W.L.R. 1000; [2006] 3 All E.R.
    170; (2006) 170 J.P.11; (2006) 170 J.P.N.12, DC . . . .   *Digested*, 06/**3802**:
                                          Applied, 07/358
DPP v Hart see DPP v Bayer
DPP v Haw [2007] EWHC 1931 (Admin); [2007] H.R.L.R. 43; [2007] U.K.H.R.R.
    1194; (2007) 104(33) L.S.G. 26; (2007) 157 N.L.J. 1198; *Times*, September 11,
    2007, DC. . . . .   *Digested*, 07/**2811**
DPP v Holden [2006] EWHC 658 (Admin); [2007] R.T.R. 5, QBD (Admin). . . . .   *Digested*, 07/**1007**
DPP v Lawrence [2007] EWHC 2154 (Admin); (2007) 171 J.P. 656; (2007) 151
    S.J.L.B. 1261, DC . . . .   *Digested*, 07/**835**
DPP v M [2004] EWHC 1453 (Admin); [2004] 1 W.L.R. 2758; [2005] Crim. L.R.
    392; (2004) 148 S.J.L.B. 660; *Times*, July 23, 2004, QBD (Admin) . . . .   *Digested*, 04/**771**:
                 Applied, 05/814: *Approved*, 07/911: *Considered*, 06/875

DPP v Majewski; *sub nom* R. v Majewski (Robert Stefan) [1977] A.C. 443; [1976] 2 W.L.R. 623; [1976] 2 All E.R. 142; (1976) 62 Cr. App. R. 262; [1976] Crim. L.R. 374; (1976) 120 S.J. 299, HL; affirming [1975] 3 W.L.R. 401; [1975] 3 All E.R. 296; (1976) 62 Cr. App. R. 5; [1975] Crim. L.R. 570; (1975) 119 S.J. 560, CA (Crim Div) . . . . *Digested*, 76/**487**:
Applied, 77/637, 82/680, 84/656, 93/755: *Considered*, 76/487, 77/488, 79/398, 85/692, 87/824, 89/584, 90/1126, 94/1074, 94/1125, 07/876:
Distinguished, 80/450

DPP v Meaden [2003] EWHC 3005 (Admin); [2004] 1 W.L.R. 945; [2004] 4 All E.R. 75; [2004] Po. L.R. 8; [2004] Crim. L.R. 587; *Times*, January 2, 2004, QBD (Admin) . . . . *Applied*, 07/4191

DPP v Milton [2006] EWHC 242 (Admin); (2006) 170 J.P. 319; [2006] R.T.R. 21; [2007] A.C.D. 17; (2006) 28 J.P.N. 533; (2006) 150 S.J.L.B. 166, QBD (Admin) . . . . *Digested*, 06/**877**

DPP v P see Crown Prosecution Service v P

DPP v P see Crown Prosecution Service v P

DPP v Pal [2000] Crim. L.R. 756, DC . . . . *Considered*, 07/911

DPP v Snook see DPP v Bayer

DPP v T see Crown Prosecution Service v T

DPP v Whistance see DPP v Bayer

DPP of Mauritius v Hurnam see Mauritius v Hurnam

DR v Secretary of State for the Home Department; *sub nom* DR (ECO: Post Decision Evidence: Morocco), Re [2005] UKIAT 38; [2005] Imm. A.R. 205; [2005] I.N.L.R. 117, IAT . . . . *Digested*, 05/**2212**:
Considered, 07/2330

DR (ECO: Post Decision Evidence: Morocco), Re see DR v Secretary of State for the Home Department

Dragon Futures Ltd v Revenue and Customs Commissioners [2006] V. & D.R. 348; [2007] S.T.I. 373, V&DTr (London) . . . . *Digested*, 07/**4318**

Dragon Futures Ltd v Revenue and Customs Commissioners (Stay of Appeal) [2005] EWHC 2534 (Ch); [2006] B.T.C. 5444; [2006] B.V.C. 507; [2005] S.T.I. 1718, Ch D . . . . *Digested*, 07/**4302**

Drax Holdings Ltd, Re; *joined case* InPower Ltd, Re [2003] EWHC 2743 (Ch); [2004] 1 W.L.R. 1049; [2004] 1 All E.R. 903; [2004] B.C.C. 334; [2004] 1 B.C.L.C. 10, Ch D (Companies Ct) . . . . *Digested*, 04/**2190**:
Applied, 06/2361: *Considered*, 06/550, 07/2448

Drescher v Drescher Estate (2007-08) 10 I.T.E.L.R. 679, Sup Ct (NS)

Dresdner Bank AG v Commission of the European Communities (T-44/02) [2007] 4 C.M.L.R. 13, CFI (4th Chamber) . . . . *Digested*, 07/**644**

Drinkall v Whitwood [2003] EWCA Civ 1547; [2004] 1 W.L.R. 462; [2004] 4 All E.R. 378; (2003) 100(47) L.S.G. 21; (2003) 147 S.J.L.B. 1308; *Times*, November 13, 2003, CA (Civ Div) . . . . *Digested*, 04/**417**:
Applied, 07/489

Driskel v Peninsula Business Services Ltd [2000] I.R.L.R. 151, EAT. . . . . *Digested*, 00/**2208**:
Applied, 07/1405: *Considered*, 05/1305

Drummond v Revenue and Customs Commissioners [2007] S.T.C. (S.C.D.) 682; [2007] S.T.I. 1818, Sp Comm

Drury v BBC see Carnegie v Drury

DS v HM Advocate; *sub nom* HM Advocate v DS [2007] UKPC D1; 2007 S.C. (P.C.) 1; 2007 S.L.T. 1026; 2007 S.C.C.R. 222; [2007] H.R.L.R. 28; *Times*, June 12, 2007, PC (Sc) . . . . *Digested*, 07/**5019**

DSG Retail Ltd v Stockton on Tees BC [2006] EWHC 3138 (Admin); [2007] A.C.D. 38, DC

DSM Kunststoffen BV v Commission of the European Communities (C-244/99 P) see Limburgse Vinyl Maatschappij NV (LVM) v Commission of the European Communities (C-238/99 P)

DSR Senator Lines GmbH v Commission of the European Communities (C-364/99 P (R)) [1999] E.C.R. I-8733; [2000] 5 C.M.L.R. 600, ECJ. . . . . *Digested*, 01/**754**:
Applied, 06/1550: *Considered*, 07/1549

DT v FL [2006] IEHC 98; [2007] I.L.Pr. 56, HC (Irl)

DTE Financial Services Ltd v Wilson (Inspector of Taxes) [2001] EWCA Civ 455; [2001] S.T.C. 777; 74 T.C. 14; [2001] B.T.C. 159; [2001] S.T.I. 670; (2001) 98(21) L.S.G. 40; *Times*, May 3, 2001; *Daily Telegraph*, April 10, 2001, CA (Civ Div); affirming [1999] S.T.C. 1061; [1999] B.T.C. 415; (1999) 96(44) L.S.G. 41; (1999) 143 S.J.L.B. 270; *Times*, November 9, 1999, Ch D; affirming [1999] S.T.C. (S.C.D.) 121, Sp Comm. . . . . *Digested*, 01/**5237**:
Applied, 07/4085: *Distinguished*, 03/4233

Dubai Aluminium Co Ltd v Amhurst Brown Martin & Nicholson see Dubai Aluminium Co Ltd v Salaam

Dubai Aluminium Co Ltd v Salaam; *joined case* Dubai Aluminium Co Ltd v Amhurst Brown Martin & Nicholson [2002] UKHL 48; [2003] 2 A.C. 366; [2002] 3 W.L.R. 1913; [2003] 1 All E.R. 97; [2003] 2 All E.R. (Comm) 451; [2003] 1 Lloyd's Rep. 65; [2003] 1 B.C.L.C. 32; [2003] 1 C.L.C. 1020; [2003] I.R.L.R. 608; [2003] W.T.L.R. 163; (2003) 100(7) L.S.G. 36; (2002) 146 S.J.L.B. 280; *Times*, December 6, 2002; *Independent*, December 10, 2002, HL; reversing [2001] Q.B. 113; [2000] 3 W.L.R. 910; [2000] 2 Lloyd's Rep. 168; [2000] Lloyd's Rep. P.N. 497; [2000] P.N.L.R. 578; *Times*, April 21, 2000, CA (Civ Div); reversing [1999] 1 Lloyd's Rep. 415; (1998) 148 N.L.J. 1301; *Times*, September 4, 1998, QBD (Comm) . . . . *Digested*, 03/**3046**:
Applied, 01/4267, 03/3033, 03/3045, 05/4199, 05/4200, 06/543, 06/1337, 06/2915, 07/4248: *Distinguished*, 03/3613

Dubai Aluminium Co Ltd v Salaam [2007] B.P.I.R. 690, Ch D
Dubey v Hall see Dubey v Revenue and Customs Commissioners
Dubey v Revenue and Customs Commissioners; *sub nom* Dubey v Hall; Farepak Food and Gifts Ltd (In Administration), Re [2006] EWHC 3272 (Ch); [2007] 2 B.C.L.C. 1; [2007] W.T.L.R. 1407, Ch D (Companies Ct) . . . . *Digested*, 07/**2388**
Dudgeon v United Kingdom (7525/76) (1981) 3 E.H.R.R. 40, Eur Comm HR . . . . *Considered*, 07/108
Duffy, Re see Duffy's Application for Judicial Review, Re
Duffy v Revenue and Customs Commissioners [2007] S.T.C. (S.C.D.) 377; [2007] S.T.I. 1176, Sp Comm . . . . *Digested*, 07/**4162**
Duffy's Application for Judicial Review, Re; *sub nom* Duffy, Re [2006] NICA 28; [2007] N.I. 12, CA (NI) . . . . *Digested*, 07/**4378**
Duijnstee (Liquidator) v Lodewijk Goderbauer (C-288/82) [1983] E.C.R. 3663; [1985] 1 C.M.L.R. 220; [1985] F.S.R. 221, ECJ (4th Chamber) . . . . *Digested*, 85/**1454**:
Applied, 07/2617: *Considered*, 98/3455
Duke of Westminster (Deceased) v Regis Group (Barclays) Ltd [2007] 38 E.G. 204, Lands Tr
Dulwich Estate v Baptiste [2007] EWHC 410 (Ch); [2007] 8 E.G. 137 (C.S.); *Times*, February 22, 2007, Ch D
Dumford Trading AG v OAO Atlantrybflot [2005] EWCA Civ 24; [2005] 1 Lloyd's Rep. 289, CA (Civ Div); reversing [2004] EWHC 1099 (Comm); [2004] 2 Lloyd's Rep. 157, QBD (Comm) . . . . *Digested*, 05/**710**:
Applied, 07/2500

Dunbar v Plant [1998] Ch. 412; [1997] 3 W.L.R. 1261; [1997] 4 All E.R. 289; [1998] 1 F.L.R. 157; [1997] 3 F.C.R. 669; [1998] Fam. Law 139; (1997) 94(36) L.S.G. 44; (1997) 141 S.J.L.B. 191; *Times*, August 13, 1997, CA (Civ Div) . . . . *Digested*, 97/**4729**:
Applied, 07/3026: *Followed*, 06/4075
Duncan v British Coal Corp see White v Chief Constable of South Yorkshire
Duncan (t/a G Duncan Motor Services) v Revenue and Customs Commissioners [2007] V. & D.R. 114; [2007] S.T.I. 1704, V&D Tr (Edinburgh)
Dunn v Ward see Hollins v Russell
Dunnachie v Kingston upon Hull City Council; *sub nom* Kingston Upon Hull City Council v Dunnachie (No.1); *joined cases* Williams v Southampton Institute; Dawson v Stonham Housing Association [2004] UKHL 36; [2005] 1 A.C. 226; [2004] 3 W.L.R. 310; [2004] 3 All E.R. 1011; [2004] I.C.R. 1052; [2004] I.R.L.R. 727; (2004) 101(33) L.S.G. 34; (2004) 154 N.L.J. 1156; (2004) 148 S.J.L.B. 909; *Times*, July 16, 2004; *Independent*, July 21, 2004, HL; reversing [2004] EWCA Civ 84; [2004] 2 All E.R. 501; [2004] I.C.R. 481; [2004] I.R.L.R. 287; (2004) 101(10) L.S.G. 27; (2004) 154 N.L.J. 248; (2004) 148 S.J.L.B. 233; *Times*, February 26, 2004; *Independent*, February 18, 2004, CA (Civ Div); reversing [2003] I.C.R. 1294; [2003] I.R.L.R. 384; *Times*, June 9, 2003, EAT . . *Digested*, 04/**1303**:
Applied, 03/1337, 06/1388, 07/1425: *Considered*, 05/1322, 05/1331: *Followed*, 04/1307

DUNS LICENSING ASSOCIATES/Estimating sales activity (T154/04) [2007] E.P.O.R. 38, EPO (Technical Bd App) . . . . *Digested*, 07/**2626**
Dunster Properties Ltd v First Secretary of State [2007] EWCA Civ 236; [2007] 2 P. & C.R. 26; [2007] J.P.L. 1464; (2007) 151 S.J.L.B. 336, CA (Civ Div); reversing [2006] EWHC 2079 (Admin), QBD (Admin) . . . . *Digested*, 07/**3278**:
Considered, 07/3283

Dunwood Travel Ltd v Revenue and Customs Commissioners; *sub nom* Revenue and Customs Commissioners v Dunwood Travel Ltd; A3/2007/0587, CA (Civ Div); affirming [2007] EWHC 319 (Ch); [2007] B.T.C. 5387; [2007] B.V.C. 406; [2007] S.T.I. 444, Ch D; reversing [2006] S.T.I. 2107, V&D Tr (Manchester) . . . . *Digested*, 07/**4287**
Duomatic Ltd, Re [1969] 2 Ch. 365; [1969] 2 W.L.R. 114; [1969] 1 All E.R. 161; (1968) 112 S.J. 922, Ch D . . . . *Digested*, 69/**412**:
Applied, 74/321, 80/268, 80/269, 99/607, 00/654, 01/748, 03/540, 04/472:
Considered, 98/704, 02/556, 04/458, 05/470: *Distinguished*, 90/487, 07/321
DUPONT TEIJIN FILMS/Polyester film (T882/03) [2006] E.P.O.R. 48, EPO (Technical Bd App) . . . . *Digested*, 07/**2585**
Durant v Financial Services Authority (Disclosure) [2003] EWCA Civ 1746; [2004] F.S.R. 28; *Times*, January 2, 2004, CA (Civ Div) . . . . *Digested*, 04/**1551**:
Considered, 07/4889

Durferrit GmbH v Office for Harmonisation in the Internal Market (Trade Marks and Designs) (OHIM) (T-224/01) [2003] E.C.R. II-1589; [2004] E.T.M.R. 32, CFI (4th Chamber) . . . . *Digested,* 04/**2388**: *Applied,* 06/2568, 07/2641

Durkin v Texaco Ltd (Unreported, May 3, 2007), CC (Walsall) [*Ex rel.* Stephen Garner, Barrister, No. 8 Chambers, Fountain Court, Steelhouse Lane, Birmingham] . . . . 　*Digested,* 07/**3123**

Durling's Application, Re; *sub nom* Clements (Deceased), Re [2007] W.T.L.R. 1717, Sup Ct (NS)

Durmic v Serbia and Montenegro (29/2003) 23 B.H.R.C. 11, UN CERD

Dutch Air Transport Agreement, Re (C-523/04) see Commission of the European Communities v Netherlands (C-523/04)

Dutch Bitumen Cartel, Re (COMP/F/38.456) [2007] 5 C.M.L.R. 9, CEC

Dutch Books, Re (C-43/82 and C-63/82) see VBVB and VBBB v Commission of the European Communities (C-43/82 and C-63/82)

DV v General Medical Council [2007] EWHC 1497 (Admin); [2007] LS Law Medical 603, QBD (Admin)

Dwr Cymru Cyfyngedig (Welsh Water) v Corus UK Ltd [2007] EWCA Civ 285; [2007] 14 E.G. 105 (C.S.), CA (Civ Div); reversing in part [2006] EWHC 1183 (Ch), Ch D

Dwyer v Rodrick (1983) 80 L.S.G. 3003; (1983) 127 S.J. 806; *Times,* November 12, 1983, CA (Civ Div); reversing (Unreported, February 10, 1982), QBD . . . . 　*Digested,* 83/**2557**: *Applied,* 07/2928

Dymny v Lambeth LBC see Kay v Lambeth LBC

Dymocks Franchise Systems (NSW) Pty Ltd v Todd (Costs) [2004] UKPC 39; [2004] 1 W.L.R. 2807; [2005] 4 All E.R. 195; [2005] 1 Costs L.R. 52; (2004) 154 N.L.J. 1325; (2004) 148 S.J.L.B. 971, PC (NZ) . . . . 　*Digested,* 04/**328**: *Applied,* 06/395, 07/379, 07/405, 07/420: *Considered,* 06/374, 06/417, 07/387, 07/404, 07/421, 07/428

Dyson v Leeds City Council (No.2) see Fairchild v Glenhaven Funeral Services Ltd (t/a GH Dovener & Son)

Dyson Ltd v Registrar of Trade Marks (C-321/03) [2007] Bus. L.R. 787; [2007] 2 C.M.L.R. 14; [2007] C.E.C. 223; [2007] E.T.M.R. 34; [2007] R.P.C. 27, ECJ (3rd Chamber) . . . . 　*Digested,* 07/**1580**

Dyson Technology Ltd v Strutt [2005] EWHC 2814 (Ch), Ch D . . . . 　*Cited,* 07/388

Dyson Technology Ltd v Strutt [2007] EWHC 1756 (Ch); [2007] 4 Costs L.R. 597, Ch D . . . . 　*Digested,* 07/**388**

E v E [2007] EWHC 276 (Fam); [2007] 1 F.L.R. 1977; [2007] Fam. Law 480, Fam Div . . . . 　*Digested,* 07/**1738**

E v Newham LBC; *sub nom* R. (on the application of E) v Newham LBC [2003] EWCA Civ 9; [2003] B.L.G.R. 547; [2003] E.L.R. 286; (2003) 147 S.J.L.B. 113; *Independent,* January 29, 2003, CA (Civ Div) . . . . 　*Digested,* 03/**1123**: *Applied,* 05/1143: *Considered,* 07/1263: *Followed,* 07/1264

E v Secretary of State for the Home Department; *joined case* R v Secretary of State for the Home Department [2004] EWCA Civ 49; [2004] Q.B. 1044; [2004] 2 W.L.R. 1351; [2004] I.N.L.R. 268; [2004] B.L.G.R. 463; (2004) 101(7) L.S.G. 35; (2004) 148 S.J.L.B. 180; *Times,* February 9, 2004; *Independent,* February 4, 2004, CA (Civ Div) . . . . 　*Digested,* 04/**2030**: *Applied,* 05/2208, 05/2213, 06/1216, 06/2269, 07/1256: *Considered,* 06/2212, 06/2225: *Followed,* 05/2215, 05/2224

E LBC v AK see K (Order Delay), Re

E (A Child), Re see L (A Child), Re

E (A Child), Re see S (Children) (Permission to Seek Relief), Re

E (A Child) v Scholes (Unreported, October 16, 2006), CC (Stafford) [*Ex rel.* Adam Walker, Barrister, Lamb Chambers, Lamb Building, Elm Court, Temple, London]. 　*Digested,* 07/**3191**

E (A Juvenile) v DPP [2002] EWHC 433 (Admin); [2002] Crim. L.R. 737, QBD (Admin) . . . . 　*Applied,* 03/787, 06/849: *Considered,* 03/786, 07/886

E (A Minor) v Dorset CC (Appeal) see X (Minors) v Bedfordshire CC

E (Minors) (Residence: Imposition of Conditions), Re; *sub nom* E (Minors) (Residence Orders), Re [1997] 2 F.L.R. 638; [1997] 3 F.C.R. 245; [1997] Fam. Law 606; (1997) 161 J.P.N. 937; *Times,* May 16, 1997, CA (Civ Div) . . . . 　*Digested,* 97/**444**: *Considered,* 03/1547, 07/1788: *Followed,* 01/2667

E (Minors) (Residence Orders), Re see E (Minors) (Residence: Imposition of Conditions), Re

EA (Nigeria) v Secretary of State for the Home Department; *sub nom* EA (Section 85(4) Explained: Nigeria), Re [2007] UKAIT 13; [2007] Imm. A.R. 487; [2007] I.N.L.R. 310, AIT

EA (Section 85(4) Explained: Nigeria), Re see EA (Nigeria) v Secretary of State for the Home Department

Eagle Distribuidora de Bebidas SA v Second Group of the Revenue Department in Brasilia 9 I.T.L. Rep. 627

Eagle Star Insurance Co Ltd, Re [2006] EWHC 1850 (Ch); [2007] 1 B.C.L.C. 21, Ch D
(Companies Ct) . . . . *Digested,* 07/**2481**
Ealing LBC v Surdonja see Mohamed v Hammersmith and Fulham LBC
Ealing LBC v White see White v Aldridge (President of the Special Educational Needs
Tribunal)
Earl Cadogan v 26 Cadogan Square Ltd see Howard de Walden Estates Ltd v Aggio
Earl Cadogan v 27/29 Sloane Gardens Ltd see Earl Cadogan v Sportelli
Earl Cadogan v Atlantic Telecasters Ltd see Pitts v Earl Cadogan
Earl Cadogan v Grandeden Property Management Ltd see Earl Cadogan v Sportelli
Earl Cadogan v Sportelli; *joined cases* Earl Cadogan v 27/29 Sloane Gardens Ltd; Earl
Cadogan v Grandeden Property Management Ltd; Howard de Walden Estates
Ltd v Maybury Court Freehold Co Ltd; Bircham & Co Nominees (No.2) Ltd v
Clarke [2007] EWCA Civ 1042; [2007] R.V.R. 314; [2007] 44 E.G. 180 (C.S.);
(2007) 151 S.J.L.B. 1402; [2007] N.P.C. 110, CA (Civ Div); affirming [2006]
R.V.R. 382, Lands Tr . . . . *Digested,* 07/**2743**
Earle v Charalambous [2006] EWCA Civ 1090; [2007] H.L.R. 8; (2006) 150 S.J.L.B.
1056; [2006] N.P.C. 92; [2007] 1 P. & C.R. DG10, CA (Civ Div) . . . . *Digested,* 07/**2747**
Earle v Charalambous (Addendum to Judgment); *sub nom* Charalambous v Earle
[2006] EWCA Civ 1090; [2007] H.L.R. 8; [2006] 42 E.G. 245 (C.S.); (2006)
150 S.J.L.B. 1396; [2006] N.P.C. 109; *Times,* November 15, 2006, CA (Civ Div) *Digested,* 07/**2737**
East v Bennett Bros Ltd [1911] 1 Ch. 163, Ch D . . . . *Considered,* 07/2449:
Distinguished, 69/388
East v Pantiles (Plant Hire) [1982] 2 E.G.L.R. 111; (1982) 263 E.G. 61, CA (Civ Div) . . . *Digested,* 82/**1803:**
Applied, 02/3028, 07/2748: *Considered,* 96/3798
East Ayrshire Council v Robertson [2007] R.V.R. 158; 2006 G.W.D. 26-581, Sh Pr. . . . *Digested,* 07/**4977**
East Dorset DC v Eaglebeam Ltd [2006] EWHC 2378 (QB); [2007] Env. L.R. D9,
QBD . . . . *Digested,* 07/**1531**
East Dorset DC v Ward [2007] P.A.D. 55, Planning Inspector
East Sussex CC v Reprotech (Pebsham) Ltd see R. (on the application of Reprotech
(Pebsham) Ltd) v East Sussex CC
Eastaway v Secretary of State for Trade and Industry see Blackspur Group Plc, Re
Eastman Photographic Materials Co Ltd v Comptroller General of Patents, Designs and
Trade Marks [1898] A.C. 571, HL . . . . *Applied,* 69/213:
Considered, 07/2662

Eastwood v Magnox Electric Plc; *joined case* McCabe v Cornwall CC [2004] UKHL
35; [2005] 1 A.C. 503; [2004] 3 W.L.R. 322; [2004] 3 All E.R. 991; [2004]
I.C.R. 1064; [2004] I.R.L.R. 733; (2004) 101(32) L.S.G. 36; (2004) 154 N.L.J.
1155; (2004) 148 S.J.L.B. 909; *Times,* July 16, 2004; *Independent,* October 11,
2004, HL; reversing [2002] EWCA Civ 463; [2003] I.C.R. 520; [2002] I.R.L.R.
447; [2002] Emp. L.R. 795, CA (Civ Div) . . . . *Digested,* 04/**1183:**
Considered, 03/1246, 07/1317
Easyjet Airline Co Ltd v Commission of the European Communities (T-177/04) [2006]
E.C.R. II-1931; [2006] 5 C.M.L.R. 11, CFI (2nd Chamber) . . . . *Digested,* 07/**639**
Easynet Group Plc v Easygroup IP Licensing Ltd [2006] EWHC 1872 (Pat); [2007]
R.P.C. 6; (2006) 29(8) I.P.D. 29063; (2006) 150 S.J.L.B. 1190, Ch D (Patents
Ct)
Eaton Ltd v King see King v Eaton Ltd (No.2)
EB v France (43546/02) 23 B.H.R.C. 741, ECHR (Grand Chamber)
EB Central Services Ltd v Revenue and Customs Commissioners; *sub nom* Revenue
and Customs Commissioners v EB Central Services Ltd (formerly Excess
Baggage Plc); A3/2007/0476, CA (Civ Div); reversing [2007] EWHC 201 (Ch);
[2007] B.T.C. 5498; [2007] B.V.C. 466; [2007] S.T.I. 342, Ch D; reversing in
part [2006] S.T.I. 2112, V&D Tr (London) . . . . *Digested,* 07/**4365**
EB (Kosovo) v Secretary of State for the Home Department see HB (Ethiopia) v
Secretary of State for the Home Department

eBay Canada Ltd v Canada 10 I.T.L. Rep. 159, Fed Ct (Can)
Ebied v Hopkins see Wellcome Trust Ltd v Hamad
Ebury (Valuation Officer), Re [2007] R.A. 157, Lands Tr. . . . . *Digested,* 07/**3350**
EC (Child Abduction: Stayed Proceedings), Re see Clark (A Child), Re
Eckardt v Germany (23947/03) (Admissibility) (2007) 45 E.H.R.R. SE7, ECHR
Eckle v Germany (A/51) (1983) 5 E.H.R.R. 1, ECHR . . . . *Applied,* 98/3132,
98/3150, 99/3130, 00/6074, 00/6090, 02/5515, 07/4358:
Considered, 00/6083, 03/5407, 03/5408
Ecuador v Occidental Exploration & Production Co [2007] EWCA Civ 656; [2007] 2
Lloyd's Rep. 352; [2007] 2 C.L.C. 16, CA (Civ Div); affirming [2006] EWHC
345 (Comm); [2006] 1 Lloyd's Rep. 773; [2006] 2 C.L.C. 1; 8 I.T.L. Rep. 948,
QBD (Comm) . . . . *Digested,* 07/**247**
ED&F Man Sugar Ltd v Lendoudis [2007] EWHC 2268 (Comm); [2007] 2 Lloyd's
Rep. 579, QBD (Comm)
Eder v Revenue and Customs Commissioners [2007] S.T.C. (S.C.D.) 334; [2007] S.T.I.
560, Sp Comm . . . . *Digested,* 07/**4163**

Edgar v Edgar [1980] 1 W.L.R. 1410; [1980] 3 All E.R. 887; (1981) 2 F.L.R. 19; (1980)
   11 Fam. Law 20; (1980) 124 S.J. 809; *Times*, July 24, 1980, CA (Civ Div) . . . . .   *Digested*, 80/**791**:
             Applied, 91/1794, 95/2340, 95/2344, 96/2857, 07/1708: *Cited*, 04/1514:
             Considered, 83/2622, 87/1743, 94/2166, 95/2336, 03/1580, 07/1830:
             Distinguished, 83/1100, 96/2875, 97/2477, 99/4635: *Followed*, 84/1118,
                        05/1688: *Referred to*, 87/1750, 93/5228
Edgebrough Building Co v Woking UDC (1966) 198 E.G. 581. . . . .   *Considered*, 07/3294
EDI Services Ltd v Revenue and Customs Commissioners [2006] S.T.C. (S.C.D.) 392;
   [2006] S.T.I. 1588, Sp Comm . . . .   *Digested*, 06/**4257**:
                                     Considered, 07/4085
EDICO/Multiple subtitles (T190/03) [2007] E.P.O.R. 15, EPO (Technical Bd App) . . . .   *Digested*, 07/**2601**
Edinburgh City Council v Secretary of State for Scotland; *joined cases* Revival
   Properties Ltd v Edinburgh City Council; Secretary of State for Scotland v
   Revival Properties Ltd [1997] 1 W.L.R. 1447; [1998] 1 All E.R. 174; 1998 S.C.
   (H.L.) 33; 1998 S.L.T. 120; 1997 S.C.L.R. 1112; [1997] 3 P.L.R. 71; [1998] J.P.L.
   224; [1997] E.G. 140 (C.S.); (1997) 94(42) L.S.G. 31; (1997) 141 S.J.L.B. 228;
   [1997] N.P.C. 146; 1997 G.W.D. 33-1693; *Times*, October 31, 1997, HL; affirming
   in part 1996 S.C.L.R. 600, IH (2 Div). . . . .   *Digested*, 97/**6350**:
             Applied, 99/4178, 06/3289, 07/5464: *Considered*, 99/4218, 01/4743,
                        05/3295: *Followed*, 97/4116, 99/6411
Editions Plon v France (58148/00) (2006) 42 E.H.R.R. 36, ECHR . . . .   *Digested*, 06/**2100**:
                                     Considered, 07/2187
Eduardo Lafuente Nieto v Instituto Nacional de la Seguridad Social (Inss) and Tesoreria
   General de la Seguridad Social (Tgss) (C-251/94) [1996] E.C.R. I-4187, ECJ . .   *Applied*, 07/1626,
                                       07/1626
Edwards v Bailey (Unreported, July 26, 2007), CC (Bromley) [*Ex rel.* Joanna Kerr,
   Barrister, Lamb Chambers, Temple, London] . . . .   *Digested*, 07/**3141**
Edwards v Edwards see Edwards (Deceased), Re
Edwards v Environment Agency see R. (on the application of Edwards) v Environment
   Agency (No.2)
Edwards v Golding [2007] EWCA Civ 416; *Times*, May 22, 2007, CA (Civ Div);
   affirming [2006] EWHC 1684 (QB), QBD . . . .   *Digested*, 07/**480**
Edwards v Governors of Hanson School SLJ 1999/6858/A1, CA (Civ Div) . . . .   *Considered*, 07/1430
Edwards v United Kingdom (46477/99) (2002) 35 E.H.R.R. 19; 12 B.H.R.C. 190;
   [2002] M.H.L.R. 220; [2002] Po. L.R. 161; *Times*, April 1, 2002, ECHR . . . .   *Digested*, 02/**3348**:
              Applied, 06/2934: *Considered*, 04/3126, 06/2933, 07/2980:
                                  Followed, 03/2167
Edwards v United States [2007] EWHC 1877 (Admin); *Times*, October 5, 2007, QBD
   (Admin) . . . .   *Digested*, 07/**1659**
Edwards (Deceased), Re; *sub nom* Edwards v Edwards [2007] EWHC 1119 (Ch);
   [2007] W.T.L.R. 1387, Ch D (Cardiff) . . . .   *Digested*, 07/**3968**
Edwards (Inspector of Taxes) v Bairstow; *joined case* Edwards (Inspector of Taxes) v
   Harrison [1956] A.C. 14; [1955] 3 W.L.R. 410; [1955] 3 All E.R. 48; 48 R. & I.T.
   534; 36 T.C. 207; (1955) 34 A.T.C. 198; [1955] T.R. 209; (1955) 99 S.J. 558,
   HL; reversing (1954) 47 R. & I.T. 340; (1954) 33 A.T.C. 131; [1954] T.R. 155, CA;
   affirming 46 R. & I.T. 177; (1954) 33 A.T.C. 58; [1954] T.R. 65, QBD . . . .   *Digested*, 55/**417**:
          Applied, 56/4272, 59/1529, 62/1506, 66/6154, 67/1949, 71/999, 71/3949,
          74/320, 76/250, 77/2446, 82/476, 82/1617, 82/1647, 83/1225, 83/1976,
          84/460, 89/125, 89/3189, 90/754, 90/2675, 92/3364, 92/2274, 95/391,
          95/876, 98/2137, 98/2140, 98/4622, 99/3066, 99/6471, 03/4251, 06/4189,
            06/4278, 07/4068: *Considered*, 56/4853, 74/283.u, 74/485, 74/1816,
          74/1834, 74/1873, 74/2097, 82/3282, 84/3218, 84/3253, 87/3193, 90/1864,
          91/2373, 92/164, 94/7, 94/357, 95/7, 95/155, 95/896, 95/5020, 98/4604,
              99/4660, 99/4663, 06/215, 06/4118, 07/4348: *Followed*, 03/4190
Edwards (Inspector of Taxes) v Harrison see Edwards (Inspector of Taxes) v Bairstow
Edwinton Commercial Corp v Tsavliris Russ (Worldwide Salvage & Towage) Ltd (The
   Sea Angel) [2007] EWCA Civ 547; [2007] 2 All E.R. (Comm) 634; [2007] 2
   Lloyd's Rep. 517; [2007] 1 C.L.C. 876, CA (Civ Div); affirming [2006] EWHC
   1713 (Comm); [2007] 1 All E.R. (Comm) 407; [2007] 1 Lloyd's Rep. 335;
   [2006] 2 C.L.C. 600, QBD (Comm) . . . .   *Digested*, 07/**3815**
Efax Ltd v Protus IP Solutions Inc; *sub nom* Efax Ltd's Trade Mark Application
   (No.2349223) [2007] R.P.C. 26, TMR . . . .   *Digested*, 07/**2669**
Efax Ltd's Trade Mark Application (No.2349223) see Efax Ltd v Protus IP Solutions Inc
EFTA Surveillance Authority v Norway (E-1/06); *sub nom* Amendment to Game and
   Lottery Law, Re (E-1/06) [2007] 2 C.M.L.R. 27, EFTA . . . .   *Digested*, 07/**1619**
EFTA Surveillance Authority v Norway (E-2/06); *sub nom* Monopoly on Hydropower
   Resources, Re (E-2/06) [2007] 3 C.M.L.R. 22, EFTA
EFTA Surveillance Authority v Norway (E3/05); *sub nom* Finmark Family Allowance
   Supplement, Re (E3/05) [2006] 2 C.M.L.R. 66, EFTA . . . .   *Digested*, 07/**3830**
Egan v Motor Services (Bath) Ltd [2007] EWCA Civ 1002; (2007) 151 S.J.L.B. 1364;
   Times, December 24, 2007, CA (Civ Div)
Egana v Normore (2007-08) 10 I.T.E.L.R. 813, CJ (Gen Div) (Ont)
EH Humphries (Norton) Ltd v Fire Alarm Fabrication Services Ltd see Gray v Fire Alarm
   Fabrication Services Ltd

Ehrari (A Child) v Curry [2007] EWCA Civ 120; [2007] R.T.R. 42; (2007) 151 S.J.L.B.
  299, CA (Civ Div); affirming [2006] EWHC 1319 (QB), QBD . . . .   *Digested*, 07/**2932**
EINSTEIN Trade Mark see Continental Shelf 128 Ltd v Hebrew University of Jerusalem
Eisai Ltd v National Institute for Health and Clinical Excellence (NICE); *sub nom* R. (on
  the application of Eisai Ltd) v National Institute for Health and Clinical
  Excellence; C1/2007/2219 & 2227, CA (Civ Div); reversing [2007] EWHC 1941
  (Admin); (2007) 10 C.C.L. Rep. 638; [2007] LS Law Medical 617; (2007) 98
  B.M.L.R. 70; [2007] A.C.D. 77, QBD (Admin) . . . .   *Digested*, 07/**1982**
El Corte Ingles SA v Office for Harmonisation in the Internal Market (Trade Marks and
  Designs) (OHIM) (T-443/05) [2007] E.T.M.R. 81, CFI (4th Chamber)
El-Ajou v Dollar Land (Manhattan) Ltd; *sub nom* Dollar Land (Manhattan) Ltd, Re
  [2005] EWHC 2861 (Ch); [2007] B.C.C. 953, Ch D
El-Ajou v Dollar Land Holdings Plc (No.1) [1994] 2 All E.R. 685; [1994] B.C.C. 143;
  [1994] 1 B.C.L.C. 464; [1993] N.P.C. 165; *Times*, January 3, 1994, CA (Civ Div);
  reversing [1993] 3 All E.R. 717; [1993] B.C.C. 698; [1993] B.C.L.C. 735, Ch D   *Digested*, 94/**416**:
            Applied, 99/3288, 01/4529, 04/456, 07/3438: *Considered*, 02/4667, 07/439
El-Ajou v Stern [2006] EWHC 3067 (Ch); [2007] B.P.I.R. 693, Ch D . . . .   *Digested*, 07/**527**
El-Boujaidi v France (2000) 30 E.H.R.R. 223, ECHR . . . .   *Digested*, 00/**3240**:
                                                                    Distinguished, 07/2262
El-Fadl v El-Fadl [2000] 1 F.L.R. 175; [2000] 1 F.C.R. 685; [2000] Fam. Law 84, Fam
  Div . . . .   *Digested*, 00/**2505**:
                                                                    Applied, 07/1809
El-Farargy v El-Farargy [2007] EWCA Civ 1149; [2007] 3 F.C.R. 711; (2007) 104(46)
  L.S.G. 26; (2007) 151 S.J.L.B. 1500; *Times*, November 23, 2007, CA (Civ Div) .   *Digested*, 07/**31**
Elahi v United Kingdom (30034/04) (2007) 44 E.H.R.R. 30; *Times*, July 21, 2006,
  ECHR . . . .   *Digested*, 06/**2181**
Electrocoin Automatics Ltd v Coinworld Ltd [2004] EWHC 1498 (Ch); [2005]
  E.T.M.R. 31; [2005] F.S.R. 7; (2004) 27(8) I.P.D. 27084, Ch D . . . .   *Digested*, 05/**2574**:
                                                                    Applied, 07/2679
ELECTROMAGNETICGEOSERVICES/Subterraneanreservoirs (T136/05) [2006] E.P.O.R.
  47, EPO (Technical Bd App) . . . .   *Digested*, 07/**2602**
Elektrim SA v Vivendi Universal SA [2007] EWHC 11 (Comm); [2007] 2 All E.R.
  (Comm) 365; [2007] 1 Lloyd's Rep. 693; [2007] 1 C.L.C. 16; [2007] Bus. L.R.
  D69, QBD (Comm)
Elektrim SA v Vivendi Universal SA [2007] EWHC 571 (Comm); [2007] 2 Lloyd's Rep.
  8; [2007] 1 C.L.C. 227, QBD (Comm) . . . .   *Digested*, 07/**230**
ELI LILLY/Naphthyl compounds (T278/00) [2004] E.P.O.R. 13, EPO (Technical Bd App)   *Digested*, 04/**2309**:
                                                                    Considered, 07/2602
Elias v Secretary of State for Defence see R. (on the application of Elias) v Secretary
  of State for Defence
Elida Gibbs Ltd v Customs and Excise Commissioners (C-317/94) [1997] Q.B. 499;
  [1996] S.T.C. 1387; [1996] E.C.R. I-5339; [1996] C.E.C. 1022; [1997] B.V.C. 80;
  Times, November 12, 1996, ECJ (6th Chamber) . . . .   *Digested*, 96/**5908**:
            Applied, 07/4323: *Considered*, 01/5556, 03/4569, 04/3983, 04/4024:
                                                                    Distinguished, 01/5614, 04/3981
Elizabeth Court (Bournemouth) Ltd v Revenue and Customs Commissioners [2007]
  S.T.I. 2853, Sp Comm
ELKERMESCONTROLLEDTHERAPEUTICSINC/Preparation of microparticles (T1193/05)
  [2007] E.P.O.R. 11, EPO (Technical Bd App) . . . .   *Digested*, 07/**2561**
Ella v Ella [2007] EWCA Civ 99; [2007] 2 F.L.R. 35; [2007] 3 F.C.R. 768; [2007]
  Fam. Law 483; (2007) 104(5) L.S.G. 31; (2007) 151 S.J.L.B. 125, CA (Civ
  Div) . . . .   *Digested*, 07/**1810**
Elles v Hambros Bank Ltd see Galileo Group Ltd, Re
Elli Poluhas Dodsbo v Sweden (61564/00) (2007) 45 E.H.R.R. 22, ECHR
Ellis v Bristol City Council [2007] EWCA Civ 685; [2007] I.C.R. 1614; [2007] P.I.Q.R.
  P26; *Times*, August 21, 2007, CA (Civ Div) . . . .   *Digested*, 07/**2081**
Elrify v Westminster City Council [2007] EWCA Civ 332; [2007] H.L.R. 36, CA (Civ
  Div) . . . .   *Digested*, 07/**2161**
Elsholz v Germany (25735/94) [2000] 2 F.L.R. 486; [2000] 3 F.C.R. 385; (2002) 34
  E.H.R.R. 58; [2000] Fam. Law 800, ECHR . . . .   *Digested*, 01/**3556**:
            Considered, 03/2198, 07/1774, 07/2253: *Followed*, 01/6510
Elstone's Application, Re see Scottish Ministers v Scottish Information Commissioner
EM (Lebanon) v Secretary of State for the Home Department [2006] EWCA Civ 1531;
  [2007] 1 F.L.R. 991; [2007] 3 F.C.R. 1; [2007] U.K.H.R.R. 1; [2007] Imm. A.R.
  347; [2007] Fam. Law 398; (2006) 150 S.J.L.B. 1570; *Times*, November 29,
  2006, CA (Civ Div) . . . .   *Digested*, 07/**2309**
EMAG Handel Eder OHG v Finanzlandesdirektion fur Karnten (C-245/04) [2007] S.T.C.
  1461; [2006] E.C.R. I-3227; [2006] C.E.C. 809; [2006] S.T.I. 1267, ECJ (1st
  Chamber) . . . .   *Digested*, 07/**4306**
Eman v College van Burgemeester en Wethouders van den Haag (C-300/04) [2007]
  All E.R. (EC) 486; [2006] E.C.R. I-8055; [2007] 1 C.M.L.R. 4, ECJ . . . .   *Digested*, 07/**1582**
Emap Active Ltd v Hill [2007] EWHC 1592 (Ch); [2007] B.P.I.R. 1228, Ch D
Emezie v Emokpae see Emokpae v Chamberlin Solicitors

EMI Group Plc v Revenue and Customs Commissioners [2007] S.T.I. 2252, V&DTr
(London)

Emin v Secretary of State for the Environment (1989) 58 P. & C.R. 416; [1989] J.P.L.
909; [1989] E.G. 16 (C.S.), QBD . . . .　　*Digested*, 90/**4357**:
　　　　　　　　　　　　　　　　　Applied, 05/3262, 07/3248: *Considered*, 91/3433

Emmott v Attorney General (C-208/90) see Emmott v Minister for Social Welfare (C-
208/90)

Emmott v Minister for Social Welfare (C-208/90); *joined case* Emmott v Attorney
General (C-208/90) [1991] E.C.R. I-4269; [1991] 3 C.M.L.R. 894; [1993] I.C.R.
8; [1991] I.R.L.R. 387, ECJ . . . .　　*Digested*, 92/**4840**:
　　　　　　　Considered, 95/2112, 96/2573, 96/2577, 06/4028, 07/2490:
　　　　　　Distinguished, 95/4639, 97/3983, 99/5284, 07/1639, 07/1640:
　　　　　　　　　　　　　　　　　　　　　　　　Followed, 92/1974

Emmott Based Challenge to Limitation Period, Re (V R 51/05) [2007] 2 C.M.L.R. 11, BFH
(Ger) . . . .　　*Digested*, 07/**1639**

Emokpae v Chamberlin Solicitors see Wong v Igen Ltd (formerly Leeds Careers
Guidance)

Emokpae v Chamberlin Solicitors; *sub nom* Chamberlin Solicitors v Emokpae; *joined
case* Emezie v Emokpae [2004] I.C.R. 1476; [2004] I.R.L.R. 592, EAT . . . . . .　　*Applied*, 07/1402:
　　　　　　　　　　　　　　　　　　　　　　　　Overruled, 05/1221

Emperor of Austria v Day 45 E.R. 861; (1861) 3 De G.F. & J. 217, QB . . . .　　*Considered*, 86/1297,
　　　　　　　　　　　　　　　　　　　　　　　　87/501, 07/4200

Employment Conditions of Foreign-Language Assistants, Re (C-119/04) see Commission
of the European Communities v Italy (C-119/04)

Empowerment Enterprises Ltd v Customs and Excise Commissioners; *sub nom*
Revenue and Customs Commissioners v Empowerment Enterprises Ltd [2006]
CSIH 46; 2007 S.C. 123; 2006 S.L.T. 955; [2007] B.T.C. 5931; [2007] B.V.C.
878; [2006] S.T.I. 2344; 2006 G.W.D. 32-682, IH (Ex Div); reversing [2005]
B.V.C. 2445; [2005] S.T.I. 876, V&DTr (Edinburgh) . . . .　　*Digested*, 06/**5739**

Emunefe v Secretary of State for the Home Department [2005] EWCA Civ 1002;
[2005] I.N.L.R. 587, CA (Civ Div) . . . .　　*Digested*, 06/**2299**:
　　　　　　　　　　　　　　　　　　　　　　　　Considered, 07/2331

Encia Remediation Ltd v Canopius Managing Agents Ltd [2007] EWHC 916 (Comm);
[2007] 2 All E.R. (Comm) 947; [2007] 1 C.L.C. 818; [2007] Env. L.R. D17, QBD
(Comm) . . . .　　*Digested*, 07/**2499**

Energie Steiermark Holding AG v Finanzlandesdirektion fur Steiermark (C-339/99)
[2002] E.C.R. I-8837, ECJ . . . .　　*Applied*, 07/3985

Energotech Sarl, Re [2007] B.C.C. 123, Trib Gde Inst (F)

Energy Financing Team Ltd v Director of the Serious Fraud Office see R. (on the
application of Energy Financing Team Ltd) v Bow Street Magistrates Court

Energy Star Agreement, Re (C-281/01) see Commission of the European Communities v
Council of the European Union (C-281/01)

Enertrag UK v East Northamptonshire DC [2007] P.A.D. 84, Planning Inspector

Enfield LBC v McKeon [1986] 1 W.L.R. 1007; [1986] 2 All E.R. 730; (1986) 18 H.L.R.
330; 85 L.G.R. 24; (1986) 83 L.S.G. 2243; (1986) 136 N.L.J. 631; (1986) 130
S.J. 504, CA (Civ Div) . . . .　　*Digested*, 86/**1645**:
　　　　　　　Applied, 07/2767: *Considered*, 93/2108: *Distinguished*, 90/2519

Enfield Technical Services Ltd v Payne; *joined case* Grace v BF Components Ltd; A2/
2007/1874; A2/2007/1931, CA (Civ Div); affirming [2007] I.R.L.R. 840, EAT . .　　*Digested*, 07/**1427**

Enforcement of a Default Judgment, Re [2007] I.L.Pr. 13, BGH (Ger) . . . .　　*Digested*, 07/**678**

Engel v Netherlands (A/22) (1979-80) 1 E.H.R.R. 647, ECHR . . . .　　*Applied*, 88/2973,
98/3119, 00/3235, 02/3349, 03/866, 03/925, 03/4604, 05/2909, 05/4164,
06/4640, 07/2172, 07/2226: *Considered*, 01/98, 02/2470, 02/2619, 03/2141,
　　　　　　　04/2777, 04/3144, 06/5128, 07/54, 07/953, 07/2171

Engelbrecht v Road Accident Fund 22 B.H.R.C. 682, Const Ct (SA)

Engil Sociedade de Construcao Civil SA v Urlaubs- und Lohnausgleichskasse der
Bauwirtschaft (C-71/98) see Finalarte Sociedade de Construcao Civil Lda v
Urlaubs- und Lohnausgleichskasse der Bauwirtschaft (C-49/98)

England v Magill see Porter v Magill

English v Emery Reimbold & Strick Ltd; *joined cases* Verrechia (t/a Freightmaster
Commercials) v Commissioner of Police of the Metropolis; DJ&C Withers
(Farms) Ltd v Ambic Equipment Ltd [2002] EWCA Civ 605; [2002] 1 W.L.R.
2409; [2002] 3 All E.R. 385; [2002] C.P.L.R. 520; [2003] I.R.L.R. 710; [2002]
U.K.H.R.R. 957; (2002) 99(22) L.S.G. 34; (2002) 152 N.L.J. 758; (2002) 146
S.J.L.B. 123; *Times*, May 10, 2002; *Independent*, May 7, 2002, CA (Civ Div) . . .　　*Digested*, 02/**301**:
　　　　　Applied, 02/371, 04/2698, 05/950, 05/1212, 05/1256, 06/498, 06/1335,
　　　06/4090, 07/249, 07/1434: *Considered*, 03/847, 03/1544, 05/2213, 06/468,
　　　　　　　　06/2226, 07/466, 07/2453: *Distinguished*, 05/1138

English & American Insurance Co Ltd v Axa Re SA [2007] EWCA Civ 1178, CA (Civ
Div); affirming [2006] EWHC 3323 (Comm); [2007] 1 C.L.C. 1; [2007] Lloyd's
Rep. I.R. 359, QBD (Comm) . . . .　　*Digested*, 07/**2505**

English Welsh and Scottish Railway Ltd v E.ON UK Plc [2007] EWHC 599 (Comm);
[2007] U.K.C.L.R. 1653; [2007] Eu. L.R. 633, QBD . . . .　　*Digested*, 07/**809**

Enkler v Finanzamt Homburg (C-230/94) [1996] S.T.C. 1316; [1996] E.C.R. I-4517;
[1997] 1 C.M.L.R. 881; [1996] C.E.C. 858; [1997] B.V.C. 24, ECJ (4th
Chamber) . . . .   *Applied*, 07/**4305**

Enterprise Oil Ltd v Strand Insurance Co Ltd [2006] EWHC 58 (Comm); [2006] 1
Lloyd's Rep. 500; [2006] 1 C.L.C. 33; [2007] Lloyd's Rep. I.R. 186, QBD
(Comm) . . . .   *Digested*, 06/**2414**

Entry Clearance Officer, Dhaka v AA see AA v Secretary of State for the Home
Department

Entwistle Pearson (Manchester) v Chorley BC (1993) 66 P. & C.R. 277; [1993] R.V.R.
220, Lands Tr . . . .   *Digested*, 93/**424**:
Applied, 07/3246

Environment Agency v Anti-Waste Ltd see R. (on the application of Anti-Waste Ltd) v
Environment Agency

Environment Agency v Biffa Waste Services Ltd [2006] EWHC 1102 (Admin); [2006]
Env. L.R. 47, QBD (Admin) . . . .   *Digested*, 07/**1528**

Environment Agency v Biffa Waste Services Ltd [2006] EWHC 3495 (Admin); [2007]
Env. L.R. 16; *Times*, December 20, 2006, DC

Environment Agency v Lewin Fryer [2006] EWHC 1597 (TCC); (2006) 22 Const. L.J.
574, QBD (TCC) . . . .   *Digested*, 07/**419**

Environment Agency v Milford Haven Port Authority (The Sea Empress); *sub nom* R. v
Milford Haven Port Authority [2000] 2 Cr. App. R. (S.) 423; [2000] Env. L.R.
632; [2000] J.P.L. 943, CA (Crim Div); reversing in part [1999] 1 Lloyd's Rep.
673, Crown Ct (Cardiff) . . . .   *Digested*, 00/**2291**:
Considered, 07/3655

EO (Deportation Appeals: Scope and Process: Turkey), Re see EO (Turkey) v Secretary of
State for the Home Department

EO (Turkey) v Secretary of State for the Home Department; *sub nom* EO (Deportation
Appeals: Scope and Process: Turkey), Re [2007] UKAIT 62; [2007] Imm. A.R.
645, AIT

Epon, Re (C-419/97) see ARCO Chemie Nederland Ltd v Minister van Volkshuisvesting,
Ruimtelijke Ordening en Milieubeheer (C-418/97)

Epping Electrical Co Ltd v Briggs & Forrester (Plumbing Services) Ltd [2007] EWHC 4
(TCC); [2007] B.L.R. 126; 113 Con. L.R. 1; (2007) 23 Const. L.J. 239; [2007]
C.I.L.L. 2438, QBD (TCC) . . . .   *Digested*, 07/**727**

Equal Opportunities Commission v Secretary of State for Trade and Industry; *sub nom*
R. (on the application of Equal Opportunities Commission) v Secretary of State
for Trade and Industry [2007] EWHC 483 (Admin); [2007] 2 C.M.L.R. 49;
[2007] I.C.R. 1234; [2007] I.R.L.R. 327; [2007] A.C.D. 74; (2007) 104(13)
L.S.G. 25, QBD (Admin) . . . .   *Digested*, 07/**1405**

Equatorial Guinea v Royal Bank of Scotland International [2006] UKPC 7, PC (Gue) . .   *Considered*, 07/4200

Equitas Ltd v Horace Holman & Co Ltd [2007] EWHC 903 (Comm); [2007] Lloyd's
Rep. I.R. 567, QBD (Comm) . . . .   *Digested*, 07/**381**

ERDC Group Ltd v Brunel University [2006] EWHC 687 (TCC); [2006] B.L.R. 255;
109 Con. L.R. 114; [2006] C.I.L.L. 2348, QBD (TCC) . . . .   *Digested*, 06/**679**

Erdel v Germany (Admissibility) (30067/04) 44 E.H.R.R. SE23, ECHR

Erdmann v Germany (C-179/94) see Dillenkofer v Germany (C-178/94)

ERG Raffinerie Mediterranee SpA v Chevron USA Inc (t/a Chevron Texaco Global
Trading) [2007] EWCA Civ 494; [2007] 2 All E.R. (Comm) 548; [2007] 2
Lloyd's Rep. 542; [2007] 1 C.L.C. 807, CA (Civ Div); affirming [2006] EWHC
1322 (Comm); [2006] 2 All E.R. (Comm) 913; [2006] 2 Lloyd's Rep. 543, QBD
(Comm) . . . .   *Digested*, 07/**810**

Erkner v Austria (9616/81) see Erkner v Austria (A/117)

Erkner v Austria (A/117); *sub nom* Erkner v Austria (9616/81) (1987) 9 E.H.R.R. 464,
ECHR (1986) 8 E.H.R.R. CD520, Eur Comm HR . . . .   *Applied*, 07/**2224**

Erlanger v New Sombrero Phosphate Co; *sub nom* New Sombrero Phosphate Co v
Erlanger (1877-78) L.R. 3 App. Cas. 1218, HL; affirming (1877) L.R. 5 Ch. D. 73,
CA . . . .   *Applied*, 53/**2071**,
71/1318, 77/1207, 84/388, 95/842, 06/743: *Considered*, 96/4972, 07/799

Eroglu v Eroglu [1994] 2 F.L.R. 287; [1994] 2 F.C.R. 525; [1994] Fam. Law 495, Fam
Div . . . .   *Digested*, 95/**2304**:
Considered, 07/1809

Erven Warnink BV v J Townend & Sons (Hull) Ltd (No.1) [1979] A.C. 731; [1979] 3
W.L.R. 68; [1979] 2 All E.R. 927; [1979] F.S.R. 397; [1980] R.P.C. 31; (1979)
123 S.J. 47, HL; reversing [1978] F.S.R. 473, CA (Civ Div); reversing [1978]
F.S.R. 1, Ch D . . . .   *Digested*, 79/**2690**:
Applied, 80/2728, 81/2789, 84/3531, 94/4293, 95/4938, 95/6459,
98/3523, 02/2770: *Considered*, 83/475, 84/3534, 84/3536, 90/4319,
96/3637, 96/3638, 07/2674: *Followed*, 99/6314: *Referred to*, 94/4290,
97/4902

Eskelinen v Finland (43083/98) (2007) 45 E.H.R.R. 1, ECHR . . . .   *Digested*, 07/**2213**

Eskelinen v Finland (63235/00) (2007) 45 E.H.R.R. 43; (2007) 157 N.L.J. 598,
ECHR (Grand Chamber)

Eski v Austria (21949/03) [2007] 1 F.L.R. 1650; [2007] 1 F.C.R. 453; [2007] Fam.
Law 481, ECHR . . . .   *Digested*, 07/**2246**

Essex CC v Premier Recycling Ltd [2006] EWHC 3594 (TCC); [2007] B.L.R. 233,
  QBD (TCC) . . . .   *Digested,* 07/**232**
Essex CC v Special Educational Needs and Disability Tribunal (SENDIST) [2006]
  EWHC 1105 (Admin); [2006] E.L.R. 452, QBD (Admin) . . . .   *Digested,* 07/**1267**
Essex County Showground Group Ltd v Essex CC [2006] R.V.R. 336, Lands Tr . . . . . .   *Digested,* 07/**3389**
Estasis Salotti di Colzani Aimo e Gianmario Colzani v RUWA Polstereimaschinen GmbH
  (C–24/76); *sub nom* Colzani v RUWA Polstereimaschinen GmbH (C–24/76)
  [1976] E.C.R. 1831; [1977] 1 C.M.L.R. 345; *Times,* December 20, 1976, ECJ . . .   *Digested,* 77/**1242**:
                    Applied, 85/1452, 89/4512, 01/800, 01/3838, 07/364: *Considered,* 96/1097
Esure Insurance Ltd v Direct Line Insurance Plc [2007] EWHC 1557 (Ch); (2007)
  30(8) I.P.D. 30053, Ch D
Etablissements Consten Sarl v Commission of the European Economic Community
  (56/64); *joined case* Grundig-Verkaufs GmbH v Commission of the European
  Economic Community (58/64) [1966] E.C.R. 299; [1966] C.M.L.R. 418, ECJ .   *Digested,* 67/**1552**:
             Applied, 68/1511, 07/614, 07/642: *Considered,* 67/1550, 74/1531, 06/2592:
                               Followed, 67/1554, 74/1555
ETERNA Trade Mark (I ZR 162/03) [2007] E.T.M.R. 25, BGH (Ger)
Etna France v France Telecom [2007] E.C.C. 6, Cass (F)
Eton College v Windsor and Maidenhead RLBC [2007] P.A.D. 30, Planning Inspector
Eurocruit Europe Ltd (In Liquidation), Re; *sub nom* Goldfarb v Poppleton [2007] EWHC
  1433 (Ch); [2007] B.C.C. 916; [2007] 2 B.C.L.C. 598; *Times,* July 16, 2007,
  Ch D . . . .   *Digested,* 07/**2442**
Eurofood IFSC Ltd, Re (C–341/04); *sub nom* Bondi v Bank of America NA (C–341/04)
  [2006] Ch. 508; [2006] 3 W.L.R. 309; [2006] All E.R. (EC) 1078; [2006]
  E.C.R. I–3813; [2006] B.C.C. 397; [2007] 2 B.C.L.C. 151; [2006] I.L.Pr. 23;
  [2006] B.P.I.R. 661, ECJ . . . .   *Digested,* 07/**2428**:
                                         Applied, 07/2411
Eurohypo AG v Office for Harmonisation in the Internal Market (Trade Marks and
  Designs) (OHIM) (T–439/04) [2006] E.C.R. II–1269; [2006] 3 C.M.L.R. 12, CFI
  (3rd Chamber) . . . .   *Digested,* 07/**2645**
European Parliament v Council of the European Union (C–164/97) [1999] E.C.R. I–
  1139; [1999] Env. L.R. 604, ECJ (5th Chamber) . . . .   *Digested,* 99/**2609**:
                                        Considered, 07/1563
European Parliament v Council of the European Union (C–317/04); *joined case*
  European Parliament v Council of the European Union (C–318/04) [2007] All
  E.R. (EC) 278; [2006] E.C.R. I–4721; [2006] 3 C.M.L.R. 9, ECJ . . . .   *Digested,* 07/**1572**
European Parliament v Council of the European Union (C–318/04) see European
  Parliament v Council of the European Union (C–317/04)
European Parliament v Council of the European Union (C–436/03); *sub nom* Validity of
  Regulation 1435/2003, Re (C–436/03) [2006] E.C.R. I–3733; [2006] 3
  C.M.L.R. 3, ECJ . . . .   *Digested,* 07/**1556**
European Parliament v Council of the European Union (C–540/03); *sub nom* Validity of
  Directive 2003/86, Re (C–540/03) [2007] All E.R. (EC) 193; [2006] E.C.R. I–
  5769; [2006] 3 C.M.L.R. 28; [2006] 2 F.C.R. 461, ECJ . . . .   *Digested,* 06/**2301**
European Sugar Cartel, Re (40/73) see Cooperatieve Vereniging Suiker Unie UA v
  Commission of the European Communities (40/73)
Europeenne et Luxembourgeoise d'Investissements SA (ELISA) v Directeur General des
  impots (C–451/05) [2007] S.T.I. 2399, ECJ (4th Chamber)
Europemballage Corp v Commission of the European Communities (6/72) [1973]
  E.C.R. 215; [1973] C.M.L.R. 199, ECJ . . . .   *Digested,* 73/**1245**:
                                    Applied, 06/613, 07/639
EUROTEC/Control system (T347/04) [2007] E.P.O.R. 20, EPO (Technical Bd App) . . .   *Digested,* 07/**2612**
Evaldsson v Sweden (75252/01) 23 B.H.R.C. 335, ECHR
Evans v Cherry Tree Finance Ltd (Unreported, April 13, 2007), Ch D (Leeds) [*Ex rel.*
  John Pugh, Barrister, 707 The Corn Exchange, Fenwick Street, Liverpool] . . . .   *Digested,* 07/**766**
Evans v Clarke [2007] Lloyd's Rep. I.R. 16, CC (Swansea) . . . .   *Digested,* 07/**2493**
Evans v DPP see Blum v DPP
Evans v Hughes [1972] 1 W.L.R. 1452; [1972] 3 All E.R. 412; (1972) 56 Cr. App. R.
  813; [1972] Crim. L.R. 558; (1972) 116 S.J. 842, QBD . . . .   *Digested,* 72/**689**:
                Applied, 74/666, 77/621, 07/998: *Considered,* 73/583, 73/584, 84/1534,
                                04/769: *Distinguished,* 89/866
Evans v Kosmar Villa Holiday Plc [2007] EWCA Civ 1003; (2007) 104(43) L.S.G. 31;
  (2007) 151 S.J.L.B. 1404; [2007] N.P.C. 109, CA (Civ Div); reversing [2006]
  EWHC 3417 (Comm), QBD (Comm)
Evans v Motor Insurers Bureau see White (Brian) v White
Evans v Pontypridd Roofing Ltd [2001] EWCA Civ 1657; [2002] P.I.Q.R. Q5, CA (Civ
  Div) . . . .   *Digested,* 02/**3494**:
                     Applied, 04/2851, 07/3071: *Considered,* 04/2846
Evans v Secretary of State for the Environment, Transport and the Regions (C–63/01)
  [2005] All E.R. (EC) 763; [2003] E.C.R. I–14447; [2004] R.T.R. 32; [2004] 1
  C.M.L.R. 47; [2004] Lloyd's Rep. I.R. 391; *Times,* December 9, 2003, ECJ (5th
  Chamber) . . . .   *Digested,* 04/**2230**:
                                  Applied, 07/2469, 07/2496
Evans v TNT Logistics Ltd [2007] Lloyd's Rep. I.R. 708, CC (Pontypridd) . . . .   *Digested,* 07/**1062**

Evans v United Kingdom (6339/05) [2007] 1 F.L.R. 1990; [2007] 2 F.C.R. 5; 22
B.H.R.C. 190; (2007) 95 B.M.L.R. 107; [2007] Fam. Law 588; (2007) 157
N.L.J. 599; *Times*, May 2, 2007, ECHR (Grand Chamber) . . . .   *Digested*, 07/**2260**
Evanturel v Evanturel (1874-75) L.R. 6 P.C. 1, PC (Can) . . . .   *Considered*, 07/4255
Everest Trust, Re see Schmidt v Rosewood Trust Ltd
Evolution Trading Group Ltd v Baris (UK) Ltd see Keisner v Terrus Group Ltd
Ewart v Cochrane (1861) 4 Macq. 117 . . . .   *Considered*, 07/5277
Ewing v Davis see R. (on the application of Ewing) v Davis
Ewing v Office of the Deputy Prime Minister see R. (on the application of Ewing) v
Office of the Deputy Prime Minister
Excelsior Commercial & Industrial Holdings Ltd v Salisbury Hamer Aspden & Johnson
(Costs) [2002] EWCA Civ 879; [2002] C.P. Rep. 67; [2002] C.P.L.R. 693;
Independent, June 18, 2002, CA (Civ Div) . . . .   *Digested*, 02/**353**:
          Applied, 06/384, 07/399: *Considered*, 06/380, 07/398
Executors of Lady Fox v Inland Revenue Commissioners see Gray v Inland Revenue
Commissioners
Exeter City Council v Bairstow see Trident Fashions Plc, Re
Exeter City Council v Bairstow; *sub nom* Trident Fashions Plc, Re [2007] EWHC 400
(Ch); [2007] Bus. L.R. 813; [2007] 4 All E.R. 437; [2007] B.C.C. 236; [2007] 2
B.C.L.C. 455; [2007] 2 P. & C.R. 8; [2007] R.A. 109; [2007] N.P.C. 28; *Times*,
April 6, 2007, Ch D (Companies Ct) . . . .   *Digested*, 07/**2393**
EXFLUOR/Perfluorocarbons (T877/04) [2006] E.P.O.R. 38, EPO (Technical Bd App) .   *Digested*, 07/**2563**
Expandable Grafts Partnership v Boston Scientific BV see Palmaz v Boston Scientific
BV
Experience Hendrix LLC v PPX Enterprises Inc [2003] EWCA Civ 323; [2003] 1 All
E.R. (Comm) 830; [2003] E.M.L.R. 25; [2003] F.S.R. 46; (2003) 26(7) I.P.D.
26046; (2003) 100(22) L.S.G. 29; (2003) 147 S.J.L.B. 509; *Times*, April 19,
2003, CA (Civ Div); reversing [2002] EWHC 1353 (QB); *Daily Telegraph*, July
18, 2002, QBD . . . .   *Digested*, 03/**717**:
          Applied, 06/1018: *Cited*, 07/1054
Experience Hendrix LLC v Purple Haze Records Ltd [2007] EWCA Civ 501; [2007]
F.S.R. 31; (2007) 104(23) L.S.G. 29; (2007) 151 S.J.L.B. 712, CA (Civ Div);
affirming [2006] EWHC 968 (Ch); [2006] E.M.L.R. 25, Ch D . . . .   *Digested*, 07/**2527**:
          Considered, 06/2544
Expert Clothing Service & Sales Ltd v Hillgate House Ltd [1987] 1 E.G.L.R. 65; (1987)
282 E.G. 715, HL; affirming in part [1986] Ch. 340; [1985] 3 W.L.R. 359;
[1985] 2 All E.R. 998; (1985) 50 P. & C.R. 317; [1985] 2 E.G.L.R. 85; (1985)
275 E.G. 1011; (1985) 82 L.S.G. 2010; (1985) 129 S.J. 484, CA (Civ Div). . . .   *Digested*, 87/**2146**:
       Applied, 99/5407: *Considered*, 85/1844, 87/2156, 91/2226, 91/2226,
       92/2664, 92/2664, 94/2760, 94/2760, 96/3744, 01/4195, 06/2683,
       07/2725: *Followed*, 00/3944
Expulsion of Foreign Nationals, Re (C-50/06) see Commission of the European
Communities v Netherlands (C-50/06)
Extramet Industrie SA v Council of the European Communities (C-358/89) [1991]
E.C.R. I-2501; [1993] 2 C.M.L.R. 619; *Financial Times*, June 16, 1992, ECJ (6th
Chamber) . . . .   *Digested*, 92/**4643**:
        Applied, 07/1584: *Distinguished*, 02/1541, 02/1587: *Followed*, 02/1556
EXXON/Fuel oils (T409/91) [1994] E.P.O.R. 149, EPO (Technical Bd App) . . . .   *Applied*, 07/2576
Eyeson v Milton Keynes Council [2005] EWHC 1160 (Admin); [2005] H.L.R. 38,
QBD (Admin) . . . .   *Digested*, 05/**3917**:
          Considered, 07/3898
Eyres v Atkinsons Bathrooms Ltd see Eyres v Atkinsons Kitchens & Bedrooms Ltd
Eyres v Atkinsons Kitchens & Bedrooms Ltd; *sub nom* Eyres v Atkinsons Bathrooms
Ltd [2007] EWCA Civ 365; (2007) 151 S.J.L.B. 576; *Times*, May 21, 2007, CA
(Civ Div); reversing (Unreported, May 25, 2006), QBD . . . .   *Digested*, 07/**2955**
Ezeh v United Kingdom (39665/98); *joined case* Connors v United Kingdom (40086/
98) (2004) 39 E.H.R.R. 1; 15 B.H.R.C. 145; [2004] Prison L.R. 95; [2004]
Crim. L.R. 472; *Times*, October 30, 2003, ECHR (Grand Chamber) . . . .   *Digested*, 03/**2141**:
          Applied, 05/2909, 07/2226
Ezsias v North Glamorgan NHS Trust [2007] EWCA Civ 330; [2007] 4 All E.R. 940;
[2007] I.C.R. 1126; [2007] I.R.L.R. 603; (2007) 104(12) L.S.G. 34; *Times*,
March 19, 2007, CA (Civ Div); affirming UKEAT/0705/05/SM, UKEAT/0612/
05/SM, EAT . . . .   *Digested*, 07/**1428**
Ezzouhdi v France (47160/99) (Unreported, February 13, 2001), ECHR . . . .   *Considered*, 07/2259

F v Birmingham City Council [2006] EWCA Civ 1427; [2007] H.L.R. 18; (2006)
103(45) L.S.G. 29; (2006) 150 S.J.L.B. 1466; [2006] N.P.C. 119, CA (Civ Div)   *Digested*, 07/**2135**
F v Harrow LBC see B v Harrow LBC (No.1)
F v M see F (Children) (Contact: Change of Name), Re
F v Special Education Needs Tribunal see B v Harrow LBC (No.1)
F v Switzerland (A/128) (1988) 10 E.H.R.R. 411, ECHR . . . .   *Applied*, 07/2221

F Hoffmann La Roche & Co AG *v* Commission of the European Communities (85/76)
　　[1979] E.C.R. 461; [1979] 3 C.M.L.R. 211; [1980] F.S.R. 13, ECJ . . . . 　*Digested,* 79/**1204**:
　　　　　　　　　　　Applied, 03/5306, 07/1547, 07/1548: *Considered,* 05/575, 07/2723:
　　　　　　　　　　　　　　　　　　　　　　　　　　　　　Followed, 07/616
F Loendersloot Internationale Expeditie NV *v* Revenue and Customs Commissioners
　　[2006] V. & D.R. 149, V&DTr (London) . . . . 　*Digested,* 07/**1039**
F Primary School Governing Body *v* T [2006] EWHC 1250 (Admin); [2006] E.L.R. 465,
　　QBD (Admin) . . . . 　*Digested,* 07/**1254**
F (A Child) (Abduction: Child's Wishes), Re [2007] EWCA Civ 468; [2007] 2 F.L.R. 697;
　　[2007] Fam. Law 677; (2007) 151 S.J.L.B. 434, CA (Civ Div) . . . . 　*Digested,* 07/**1743**
F (A Child) (Abduction: Joinder of Child as Party), Re; *sub nom* F (A Child) (Application
　　for Child Party Status), Re [2007] EWCA Civ 393; [2007] 2 F.L.R. 313; [2007]
　　Fam. Law 679, CA (Civ Div) . . . . 　*Digested,* 07/**1742**
F (A Child) (Application for Child Party Status), Re see F (A Child) (Abduction: Joinder of
　　Child as Party), Re
F (A Child) (Care Proceedings), Re; *sub nom* Somerset CC *v* DFM [2007] EWCA Civ
　　810; [2007] Fam. Law 1059; (2007) 151 S.J.L.B. 1060, CA (Civ Div)
F (A Child) (Indirect Contact), Re [2006] EWCA Civ 1426; [2007] 1 F.L.R. 1015; [2006] 3
　　F.C.R. 553; [2007] Fam. Law 109; (2006) 150 S.J.L.B. 1465; *Independent,*
　　November 7, 2006, CA (Civ Div) . . . . 　*Digested,* 07/**1771**
F (A Minor) (Child Abduction), Re; *sub nom* AF (A Minor) (Abduction), Re [1992] 1
　　F.L.R. 548; [1992] F.C.R. 269; [1992] Fam. Law 195; *Independent,* October 7,
　　1991, CA (Civ Div) . . . . 　*Digested,* 93/**2797**:
　　　　　　　　　　　　　　　Applied, 05/1547: *Considered,* 96/534, 07/1737
F (Abduction: Unborn Child), Re; *sub nom* J, Re [2006] EWHC 2199 (Fam); [2007] 1
　　F.L.R. 627; [2007] Fam. Law 103, Fam Div . . . . 　*Digested,* 07/**1750**
F (Adult: Court's Jurisdiction), Re; *sub nom* F (Adult Patient), Re [2001] Fam. 38;
　　[2000] 3 W.L.R. 1740; [2000] 2 F.L.R. 512; [2000] 3 F.C.R. 30; [2000]
　　U.K.H.R.R. 712; (2000) 3 C.C.L. Rep. 210; [2000] Lloyd's Rep. Med. 381;
　　(2000) 55 B.M.L.R. 81; [2000] M.H.L.R. 120; [2000] Fam. Law 709; (2000)
　　97(35) L.S.G. 37; (2000) 97(36) L.S.G. 41; *Times,* July 25, 2000; *Independent,*
　　July 6, 2000, CA (Civ Div) . . . . 　*Digested,* 00/**4171**:
　　　　　　　　　　　　　　　Applied, 01/2662, 04/3648: *Followed,* 07/3911
F (Adult Patient), Re see F (Adult: Court's Jurisdiction), Re
F (Children), Re; *sub nom* F (Children) (Interim Care Order), Re [2007] EWCA Civ 516;
　　[2007] 2 F.L.R. 891; [2007] 2 F.C.R. 639; [2007] Fam. Law 687, CA (Civ
　　Div) . . . . 　*Digested,* 07/**1764**
F (Children) (Adoption: Natural Parents), Re [2006] EWCA Civ 1345; [2007] 1 F.L.R. 363;
　　[2006] Fam. Law 1015; (2006) 150 S.J.L.B. 1394; *Times,* November 16, 2006, CA
　　(Civ Div) . . . . 　*Digested,* 07/**1683**
F (Children) (Contact: Change of Name), Re; *sub nom* F *v* M [2007] EWHC 2543
　　(Fam); [2007] 3 F.C.R. 832, Fam Div
F (Children) (Contact: Lack of Reasons), Re [2006] EWCA Civ 792; [2007] 1 F.L.R. 65;
　　[2006] 2 F.C.R. 399; [2006] Fam. Law 837, CA (Civ Div) . . . . 　*Digested,* 07/**1766**
F (Children) (Contact Orders: Domestic Violence), Re; *sub nom* F (Children)
　　(Restrictions on Applications), Re [2005] EWCA Civ 499; [2005] 2 F.L.R. 950;
　　[2005] 2 F.C.R. 176; [2005] Fam. Law 694, CA (Civ Div) . . . . 　*Digested,* 05/**1587**:
　　　　　　　　　　　　　　　　　　　　　　　　　　　　　Applied, 07/1783
F (Children) (Interim Care Order), Re see F (Children), Re
F (Children) (Paternity: Jurisdiction), Re [2007] EWCA Civ 873; [2007] Fam. Law 984;
　　(2007) 151 S.J.L.B. 1022; *Times,* August 6, 2007, CA (Civ Div) . . . . 　*Digested,* 07/**1784**
F (Children) (Restrictions on Applications), Re see F (Children) (Contact Orders: Domestic
　　Violence), Re
F (Mongolia) *v* Secretary of State for the Home Department; *sub nom* R. (on the
　　application of F (Mongolia)) *v* Asylum and Immigration Tribunal [2007] EWCA
　　Civ 769; [2007] 1 W.L.R. 2523; [2007] H.R.L.R. 40; *Times,* August 28, 2007,
　　CA (Civ Div) . . . . 　*Digested,* 07/**2300**
F...SP.Z.O.O's Trade Mark Application [2007] E.T.M.R. 16, Sad Rej (PL)
Faaborg-Gelting Linien A/S *v* Finanzamt Flensburg (C-231/94) [1996] All E.R. (EC)
　　656; [1996] S.T.C. 774; [1996] E.C.R. I-2395; [1996] 3 C.M.L.R. 535; [1996]
　　C.E.C. 587; *Times,* May 9, 1996, ECJ (6th Chamber) . . . . 　*Digested,* 96/**5902**:
　　　　　　　　　　　Applied, 06/4501, 07/4341: *Considered,* 98/4904, 06/4449
Fadeyeva *v* Russia (55723/00) (2007) 45 E.H.R.R. 10, ECHR . . . . 　*Digested,* 07/**2256**:
　　　　　　　　　　　　　　　　　　　　　　　　　　　　　Considered, 07/2961
Fagan *v* Commissioner of Police of the Metropolis [1969] 1 Q.B. 439; [1968] 3
　　W.L.R. 1120; [1968] 3 All E.R. 442; (1968) 52 Cr. App. R. 700; (1969) 133 J.P.
　　16; (1968) 112 S.J. 800, DC . . . . 　*Digested,* 68/**633**:
　　　　　　　　　　　Applied, 76/404: *Considered,* 76/561, 81/362, 07/904: *Explained,* 82/507
Fagernes, The; *sub nom* Coast Lines Ltd *v* Societa Nazionale di Navigazione of Genoa
　　(The Fagernes) [1927] P. 311; (1927) 28 Ll. L. Rep. 261, CA; reversing [1926] P.
　　185; (1926) 25 Ll. L. Rep. 179, PDAD . . . . 　*Applied,* 07/**2808**:
　　　　　　　　　　　　　　　　　　　　　　　　　　　　　Considered, 67/3755
Fagg *v* Rushton [2007] EWHC 657 (Ch); [2007] B.P.I.R. 1059, Ch D . . . . 　*Digested,* 07/**306**
FAI General Insurance Co Ltd, Re see HIH Casualty & General Insurance Ltd, Re

FAI Insurances Ltd, Re see HIH Casualty & General Insurance Ltd, Re

Fairchild v Glenhaven Funeral Services Ltd (t/a GH Dovener & Son); *joined cases* Pendleton v Stone & Webster Engineering Ltd; Dyson v Leeds City Council (No.2); Matthews v Associated Portland Cement Manufacturers (1978) Ltd; Fox v Spousal (Midlands) Ltd; Babcock International Ltd v National Grid Co Plc; Matthews v British Uralite Plc [2002] UKHL 22; [2003] 1 A.C. 32; [2002] 3 W.L.R. 89; [2002] 3 All E.R. 305; [2002] I.C.R. 798; [2002] I.R.L.R. 533; [2002] P.I.Q.R. P28; [2002] Lloyd's Rep. Med. 361; (2002) 67 B.M.L.R. 90; (2002) 152 N.L.J. 998; *Times,* June 21, 2002; *Independent,* June 25, 2002; *Daily Telegraph,* June 27, 2002, HL; reversing [2001] EWCA Civ 1881; [2002] 1 W.L.R. 1052; [2002] I.C.R. 412; [2002] I.R.L.R. 129; [2002] P.I.Q.R. P27; *Times,* December 13, 2001; *Independent,* December 21, 2001; *Daily Telegraph,* December 20, 2001, CA (Civ Div); affirming 00/TLQ/1284, QBD . . . . *Digested,* 02/**2225**:
                                         Applied, 04/2693, 04/2755, 06/2867, 07/5100: *Considered,* 02/3245,
                                         02/3247, 03/2990, 05/2841, 05/4199: *Followed,* 06/2866

Fairey v Southampton CC [1956] 2 Q.B. 439; [1956] 3 W.L.R. 354; [1956] 2 All E.R. 843; (1956) 120 J.P. 434; 54 L.G.R. 388; (1956) 100 S.J. 509, CA; affirming [1956] 2 W.L.R. 517; [1956] 1 All E.R. 419; 54 L.G.R. 135; (1956) 100 S.J. 133, QBD . . . . *Digested,* 56/**3869**:
                        Applied, 99/2886, 07/3421: *Cited,* 04/1817: *Considered,* 97/2338, 06/3495

Fairfax Gerrard Holdings Ltd v Capital Bank Plc [2007] EWCA Civ 1226; [2007] 2 C.L.C. 896, CA (Civ Div); reversing [2006] EWHC 3439 (Comm); [2007] 1 Lloyd's Rep. 171; [2007] B.P.I.R. 330, QBD (Comm) . . . . *Digested,* 07/**782**

Fairmount Investments Ltd v Secretary of State for the Environment; *sub nom* Fairmount Investments Ltd v Southwark LBC [1976] 1 W.L.R. 1255; [1976] 2 All E.R. 865; 75 L.G.R. 33; (1976) 120 S.J. 801, HL; affirming (1975) 238 E.G. 337; [1976] J.P.L. 161; (1975) 119 S.J. 866, CA (Civ Div); reversing [1975] J.P.L. 285, QBD . . . . *Digested,* 76/**305**:
                        Applied, 79/1367, 80/313, 82/288, 91/2030, 04/3080: *Considered,* 76/2676,
                                         86/2017, 87/3658, 87/3736, 93/431, 07/3247

Fairmount Investments Ltd v Southwark LBC see Fairmount Investments Ltd v Secretary of State for the Environment

Falanga v Italy [2007] EWHC 268 (Admin), DC . . . . *Digested,* 07/**1668**

Fanshawe v Amav Industries Ltd see Beam Tube Products Ltd, Re

Faraday Capital Ltd v Copenhagen Reinsurance Co Ltd [2006] EWHC 1474 (Comm); [2007] Lloyd's Rep. I.R. 23, QBD (Comm) . . . . *Digested,* 07/**2507**

Farah Constructions Pty Ltd v Say-Dee Pty Ltd [2007] HCA 22; (2007-08) 10 I.T.E.L.R. 136, HC (Aus)

Farepak Food and Gifts Ltd (In Administration), Re see Dubey v Revenue and Customs Commissioners

Farley v Buckley [2007] EWCA Civ 403; (2007) 104(21) L.S.G. 27, CA (Civ Div); affirming (Unreported, June 8, 2006), QBD (Manchester)

Farley v Child Support Agency; *sub nom* Farley v Secretary of State for Work and Pensions (No.2) [2006] UKHL 31; [2006] 1 W.L.R. 1817; [2006] 3 All E.R. 935; (2006) 170 J.P. 650; [2006] 2 F.L.R. 1243; [2006] 2 F.C.R. 713; [2006] Fam. Law 735; (2007) 171 J.P.N. 105; (2006) 103(28) L.S.G. 28; (2006) 150 S.J.L.B. 889; *Times,* June 29, 2006; *Independent,* June 30, 2006, HL; reversing [2005] EWCA Civ 869; [2006] C.P. Rep. 4; [2005] 2 F.L.R. 1075; [2005] 3 F.C.R. 343; [2005] A.C.D. 94; [2005] Fam. Law 772; (2005) 102(40) L.S.G. 26; *Times,* June 30, 2005; *Independent,* June 28, 2005, CA (Civ Div) . . . . *Digested,* 06/**1648**

Farley v Secretary of State for Work and Pensions (No.2) see Farley v Child Support Agency

Farmizer (Products) Ltd, Re; *sub nom* Moore v Gadd [1997] B.C.C. 655; [1997] 1 B.C.L.C. 589; (1997) 94(8) L.S.G. 27; (1997) 141 S.J.L.B. 45; *Times,* February 17, 1997; *Independent,* March 10, 1997, CA (Civ Div); affirming [1995] B.C.C. 926; [1995] 2 B.C.L.C. 462; *Independent,* June 19, 1995, Ch D (Companies Ct) . . . . *Digested,* 97/**3056**:
                              Considered, 07/2442: *Distinguished,* 01/3784

Farrell v Whitty (C-356/05) [2007] 2 C.M.L.R. 46; [2007] C.E.C. 718; [2007] Lloyd's Rep. I.R. 525, ECJ . . . . *Digested,* 07/**1565**

Farrell Matthews & Weir v Hansen [2005] I.C.R. 509; [2005] I.R.L.R. 160, EAT . . . . . *Digested,* 05/**1196**:
                                                                          Applied, 07/1356

Fatnani v General Medical Council; *sub nom* R. (on the application of Fatnani) v General Medical Council; *joined case* Raschid v General Medical Council [2007] EWCA Civ 46; [2007] 1 W.L.R. 1460; [2007] I.C.R. 811; (2007) 104(5) L.S.G. 29; (2007) 151 S.J.L.B. 127, CA (Civ Div); reversing [2006] EWHC 1573 (Admin), QBD (Admin) . . . . *Digested,* 07/**1943**

Fazenda Publica v L SA 10 I.T.L. Rep. 26, Sup Trib Admin (P)

Fazenda Publica v Solisnor-Estaleiros Navais SA (C-130/96) [1998] S.T.C. 191; [1997] E.C.R. I-5053; [1998] C.E.C. 599; [1998] B.T.C. 5371; [1998] B.V.C. 350, ECJ (1st Chamber) . . . . *Digested,* 98/**4944**:
                                                             Applied, 01/5276, 07/1581

FB *v* Secretary of State for the Home Department; *sub nom* FB (HC 395 Para 284:
　Six Months: Bangladesh), Re [2006] UKAIT 30; [2006] Imm. A.R. 400; [2006]
　I.N.L.R. 457, AIT . . . . *Digested,* 07/**2354**
FB (HC 395 Para 284: Six Months: Bangladesh), Re see FB *v* Secretary of State for the
　Home Department
FCUK Trade Mark see Woodman *v* French Connection Ltd
Feakins *v* Department for Environment, Food and Rural Affairs see Secretary of State
　for the Environment, Food and Rural Affairs *v* Feakins
Federacion Espanola de Empresas de Tecnologia Sanitaria (FENIN) *v* Commission of the
　European Communities (C-205/03 P) [2006] E.C.R. I-6295; [2006] 5
　C.M.L.R. 7, ECJ . . . . *Digested,* 07/**653**
Federacion Nacional de Empresas de Instrumentacion Cientifica Medica Tecnica y Dental
　(FENIN) *v* Commission of the European Communities (T319/99) [2004] All
　E.R. (EC) 300; [2003] E.C.R. II-357; [2003] 5 C.M.L.R. 1; (2003) 72 B.M.L.R.
　128, CFI (1st Chamber) . . . . *Digested,* 04/**524**:
　　　　　　　　　　　　　　　　　　　　　　　　　　　　　　　Affirmed, 07/653
Federation Against Copyright Theft (FACT) *v* Broomhall (Costs) [2007] 4 Costs L.R.
　640, Sup Ct Costs Office
Federation of Technological Industries *v* Customs and Excise Commissioners (C-384/
　04) see Customs and Excise Commissioners *v* Federation of Technological
　Industries (C-384/04)
Federation of Tour Operators *v* HM Treasury see R. (on the application of Federation of
　Tour Operators) *v* HM Treasury
Fedotov *v* Russia (5140/02) (2007) 44 E.H.R.R. 26, ECHR
Feld *v* Barnet LBC; *joined case* Pour *v* Westminster City Council [2004] EWCA Civ
　1307; [2005] H.L.R. 9; [2005] B.L.G.R. 411; [2005] A.C.D. 49; (2004) 101 (42)
　L.S.G. 30; (2004) 148 S.J.L.B. 1247; *Times,* October 26, 2004, CA (Civ Div) . . 　*Digested,* 04/**1904**:
　　　　　　　　　　　　　　　　　　　　　　　　　　　　　　　Applied, 07/2142
Fenchurch Environmental Group Ltd *v* Bactiguard AG; *sub nom* BACTIGUARD and
　Device Trade Mark, Re [2007] R.P.C. 31, TMR
Ferag AG *v* Muller Martini Ltd [2007] EWCA Civ 15; (2007) 151 S.J.L.B. 163, CA (Civ
　Div); reversing [2006] EWHC 225, Ch D (Patents Ct)
Ferchimex SA *v* Council of the European Union (T-164/94) [1995] E.C.R. II-2681, CFI 　*Applied,* 07/1584
Ferguson *v* Welsh [1987] 1 W.L.R. 1553; [1987] 3 All E.R. 777; [1988] I.R.L.R. 112; 86
　L.G.R. 153; (1987) 137 N.L.J. 1037; (1987) 131 S.J. 1552, HL . . . . 　*Digested,* 87/**2612**:
　　　　　　　　　　　　Applied, 03/2990: *Considered,* 07/2935: *Distinguished,* 00/4206
Ferras *v* United States [2006] 2 S.C.R. 77, Sup Ct (Can) . . . . 　*Considered,* 07/1667
Ferriby Construction (UK) Ltd *v* Revenue and Customs Commissioners [2007] S.T.I.
　2411, Sp Comm
Ferriere Nord SpA *v* Commission of the European Communities (T-153/04) [2006] 5
　C.M.L.R. 24, CFI (1st Chamber) . . . . 　*Digested,* 07/**1590**
Ferring SA *v* Agence Centrale des Organismes de Securite Sociale (ACOSS) (C53/00)
　[2001] E.C.R. I-9067; [2003] 1 C.M.L.R. 34, ECJ (6th Chamber) . . . . 　*Considered,* 02/4420:
　　　　　　　　　　　　　　　　　　　　　　　　　　　　　　　Followed, 07/649
Fettcsa Agreement, Re (T-213/00) see CMA CGM *v* Commission of the European
　Communities (T-213/00)
FI (Nigeria) *v* Secretary of State for the Home Department see HB (Ethiopia) *v*
　Secretary of State for the Home Department
Fidelity Investments Canada Ltd *v* Canada (Revenue Agency) 9 I.T.L. Rep. 11, Fed Ct
　(Can)
Fidelity Management SA *v* Myriad International Holdings BV [2005] EWHC 1193
　(Comm); [2005] 2 All E.R. (Comm) 312; [2005] 2 Lloyd's Rep. 508, QBD
　(Comm) . . . . 　*Digested,* 05/**195**:
　　　　　　　　　　　　　　　　　　　　　　　　　　　　　　　Applied, 07/254
Fidium Finanz AG *v* Bundesanstalt fur Finanzdienstleistungsaufsicht (C-452/04)
　[2007] All E.R. (EC) 239; [2006] E.C.R. I-9521; [2007] 1 C.M.L.R. 15, ECJ . . . 　*Digested,* 07/**1599**:
　　　　　　　　　　　　　　　　　　　　　　　　　　　　　　　Applied, 07/1617
Film Finance Inc *v* Royal Bank of Scotland [2007] EWHC 195 (Comm); [2007] 1
　Lloyd's Rep. 382, QBD (Comm) . . . . 　*Digested,* 07/**234**
Filmer *v* DPP [2006] EWHC 3450 (Admin); [2007] R.T.R. 28, DC . . . . 　*Digested,* 07/**983**
Finalarte Sociedade de Construcao Civil Lda *v* Urlaubs- und Lohnausgleichskasse der
　Bauwirtschaft (C-49/98); *joined cases* Urlaubs- und Lohnausgleichskasse der
　Bauwirtschaft *v* Santos & Kewitz Construcoes Lda (C-69/98); Urlaubs- und
　Lohnausgleichskasse der Bauwirtschaft *v* Duarte dos Santos Sousa (C-68/98);
　Urlaubs- und Lohnausgleichskasse der Bauwirtschaft *v* Turiprata Construcoes
　Civil SA (C-54/98); Urlaubs- und Lohnausgleichskasse der Bauwirtschaft *v*
　Tecnamb-Tecnologia do Ambiante Lda (C-53/98); Urlaubs- und
　Lohnausgleichskasse der Bauwirtschaft *v* Tudor Stone Ltd (C-52/98); Urlaubs-
　und Lohnausgleichskasse der Bauwirtschaft *v* Amilcar Oliveira Rocha (C-50/
　98); Engil Sociedade de Construcao Civil SA *v* Urlaubs- und
　Lohnausgleichskasse der Bauwirtschaft (C-71/98); Portugaia Construcoes Lda
　v Urlaubs- und Lohnausgleichskasse der Bauwirtschaft (C-70/98) [2001]
　E.C.R. I-7831; [2003] 2 C.M.L.R. 11, ECJ (5th Chamber) . . . . 　*Digested,* 03/**1283**:
　　　　　　　　　　　　　　　　　　　　　　　　　Considered, 05/1466, 07/1634

Financing of a Fraudulent Investment Project, Re [2007] E.C.C. 8, BGH (Ger)
Finanzamt Arnsberg *v* Stadt Sundern (C-43/04) [2005] E.C.R. I-4491; [2007] B.T.C.
   5815; [2007] B.V.C. 784, ECJ (3rd Chamber)
Finanzamt Bergisch Gladbach *v* HE (C-25/03) [2007] S.T.C. 128; [2005] E.C.R. I-
   3123; [2005] 2 C.M.L.R. 38; [2007] B.T.C. 5942; [2007] B.V.C. 889; [2005]
   S.T.I. 864, ECJ (2nd Chamber) . . . . *Digested*, 06/**4458**
Finanzamt Dinslaken *v* Meindl (C-329/05) [2007] S.T.C. 314; [2007] 2 C.M.L.R. 12;
   [2007] C.E.C. 192; [2007] S.T.I. 218, ECJ (1st Chamber) . . . . *Digested*, 07/**1622**
Finanzamt Eisleben *v* Feuerbestattungsverein Halle eV (C-430/04) [2006] S.T.C.
   2043; [2006] E.C.R. I-4999; [2006] S.T.I. 1619, ECJ (2nd Chamber) . . . . *Digested*, 07/**4351**
Finanzamt Gladbeck *v* Linneweber (C-453/02); *joined case* Finanzamt Herne-West *v*
   Akritidis (C-462/02) [2005] E.C.R. I-1131; [2005] 1 C.M.L.R. 53; [2005] C.E.C.
   548; [2007] B.T.C. 5258; [2007] B.V.C. 227; [2005] S.T.I. 255, ECJ (2nd
   Chamber) . . . . *Digested*, 05/**4348**:
                            Cited, 07/1640: *Considered*, 07/1639
Finanzamt Gross-Gerau *v* MKG-Kraftfahrzeuge-Factoring GmbH (C-305/01); *sub nom*
   MKG-Kraftfahrzeuge-Factory GmbH *v* Finanzamt Gross-Gerau (C-305/01)
   [2004] All E.R. (EC) 454; [2003] S.T.C. 951; [2003] E.C.R. I-6729; [2003] 3
   C.M.L.R. 2; [2003] C.E.C. 466; [2003] B.T.C. 5561; [2003] B.V.C. 616; [2003]
   S.T.I. 1148, ECJ (6th Chamber) . . . . *Digested*, 03/**4548**:
                                     Applied, 07/4335
Finanzamt Herne-West *v* Akritidis (C-462/02) see Finanzamt Gladbeck *v* Linneweber
   (C-453/02)
Finanzamt Koln-Altstadt *v* Schumacker (C-279/93) [1996] Q.B. 28; [1995] 3 W.L.R.
   498; [1995] All E.R. (E.C.) 319; [1995] S.T.C. 306; [1995] E.C.R. I-225; [1996]
   2 C.M.L.R. 450; *Times*, February 24, 1995, ECJ . . . . *Digested*, 95/**2773**:
           Applied, 02/4433, 05/1469, 07/1601, 07/1616, 07/1622, 07/4026:
                   Considered, 96/3341: *Followed*, 95/2786, 01/5245, 02/1577
Finanzamt Offenbach am Main-Land *v* Keller Holding GmbH (C-471/04) [2007] S.T.C.
   962; [2006] 2 C.M.L.R. 28; [2006] S.T.I. 533, ECJ (1st Chamber) . . . . *Digested*, 06/**4154**
Finanzamt Rendsburg *v* Harbs (C-321/02) [2006] S.T.C. 340; [2004] E.C.R. I-7101;
   [2007] B.T.C. 5114; [2007] B.V.C. 83; [2004] S.T.I. 1656, ECJ . . . . *Digested*, 06/**4424**
Finanzamt Uelzen *v* Armbrecht (C-291/92) [1995] All E.R. (E.C.) 882; [1995] S.T.C.
   997; [1995] E.C.R. I-2775; *Times*, October 26, 1995, ECJ . . . . *Digested*, 96/**5859**:
                                 Applied, 06/4430, 07/4305
Findlay, Re; *sub nom* Findlay *v* Secretary of State for the Home Department [1985]
   A.C. 318; [1984] 3 W.L.R. 1159; [1984] 3 All E.R. 801; [1985] Crim. L.R. 154;
   (1985) 82 L.S.G. 38; (1984) 128 S.J. 816, HL; affirming *Times*, July 7, 1984, CA
   (Civ Div); affirming *Times*, May 23, 1984, DC . . . . *Digested*, 84/**2756**:
          Applied, 94/4983, 99/5221, 00/4490, 07/4378: *Cited*, 94/2469:
          Considered, 87/20, 87/3617, 94/43, 95/3098, 95/3099, 95/3252, 99/2684,
                                 06/2224: *Followed*, 97/3934
Findlay *v* Secretary of State for the Home Department see Findlay, Re
Findlay *v* United Kingdom (22107/93) (1997) 24 E.H.R.R. 221; *Times*, February 27,
   1997; *Independent*, March 4, 1997, ECHR (1996) 21 E.H.R.R. CD7, Eur Comm
   HR . . . . *Digested*, 97/**2807**:
        Applied, 97/2808, 05/2104, 06/5003: *Considered*, 97/288, 00/3227, 01/366,
               03/5307, 04/1945, 05/234, 06/3750: *Distinguished*, 01/358:
          Explained, 98/256: *Followed*, 99/3090, 99/3091, 00/3215, 07/2216
Findlay's Executor *v* West Lothian Council; *sub nom* Findlay's Executor, Petitioner
   [2006] CSOH 188; [2007] R.V.R. 263; 2006 G.W.D. 40-769, OH
Findlay's Executor, Petitioner see Findlay's Executor *v* West Lothian Council
Fine *v* Abergavenny Magistrates' Court see Robinson *v* Abergavenny Magistrates'
   Court
Finelist Ltd, Re see Secretary of State for Trade and Industry *v* Swan
Finlan *v* Eyton Morris Winfield (A Firm) [2007] EWHC 914 (Ch); [2007] 4 All E.R.
   143, Ch D . . . . *Digested*, 07/**2920**
Finmark Family Allowance Supplement, Re (E3/05) see EFTA Surveillance Authority *v*
   Norway (E3/05)
Finn No AS *v* Supersok AS [2007] E.C.D.R. 12, HerrR (N)
Fiona Trust & Holding Corp *v* Privalov; *sub nom* Premium Nafta Products Ltd *v* Fili
   Shipping Co Ltd [2007] UKHL 40; [2007] Bus. L.R. 1719; [2007] 4 All E.R. 951;
   [2007] 2 All E.R. (Comm) 1053; [2007] 2 C.L.C. 553; 114 Con. L.R. 69;
   [2007] C.I.L.L. 2528; (2007) 104(42) L.S.G. 34; (2007) 151 S.J.L.B. 1364;
   Times, October 25, 2007, HL; affirming [2007] EWCA Civ 20; [2007] Bus. L.R.
   686; [2007] 1 All E.R. (Comm) 891; [2007] 2 Lloyd's Rep. 267; [2007] 1
   C.L.C. 144; (2007) 23 Const. L.J. 307; (2007) 104(6) L.S.G. 33; *Times*, January
   29, 2007, CA (Civ Div); reversing [2006] EWHC 2583 (Comm); [2007] 1 All
   E.R. (Comm) 81, QBD (Comm) . . . . *Digested*, 07/**792**
FIORELLI Trade Mark see Lunan Group Ltd *v* Edwin Co Ltd
Fire in the Mont Blanc Tunnel, Re see ATBM *v* SITMB
Firle Investments Ltd *v* Datapoint International Ltd [2001] EWCA Civ 1106; [2001] C.P.
   Rep. 101; [2001] N.P.C. 106, CA (Civ Div); reversing HT-99-119, QBD (TCC) . . . *Digested*, 01/**502**:
                            Applied, 02/356: *Considered*, 07/2736

First American Corp v Al-Nahyan see First American Corp v Sheikh Zayed Al-Nahyan
First American Corp v Sheikh Zayed Al-Nahyan; *sub nom* First American Corp v Al-Nahyan; *joined case* Clifford v First American Corp [1999] 1 W.L.R. 1154; [1998] 4 All E.R. 439; [1998] Lloyd's Rep. Bank. 213; [1998] C.L.C. 1225; [1999] I.L.Pr. 179; *Times*, August 17, 1998, CA (Civ Div) . . . . *Digested, 98/350*: *Applied, 01/406, 07/341*
First DCS Pte Ltd v Chief Assessor [2007] SGHC 82; [2007] R.A. 394, HC (Sing)
First Independent Factors & Finance Ltd v Churchill; *sub nom* Churchill v First Independent Factors & Finance Ltd [2006] EWCA Civ 1623; [2007] Bus. L.R. 676; [2007] B.C.C. 45; [2007] 1 B.C.L.C. 293; [2007] B.P.I.R. 14; (2006) 150 S.J.L.B. 1606; *Times*, January 11, 2007, CA (Civ Div); affirming 4RH01828, CC (Canterbury) . . . . *Digested, 07/2427*
First National Telecom Services Ltd v Revenue and Customs Commissioners [2007] B.V.C. 2038; [2006] S.T.I. 2226, V&DTr (London)
First National Tricity Finance Ltd v Ellis see OT Computers Ltd (In Administration), Re
First National Tricity Finance Ltd v OT Computers Ltd (In Administration) see OT Computers Ltd (In Administration), Re
First Secretary of State v Arun DC see Arun DC v First Secretary of State
First Secretary of State v James Hay Pension Trustees Ltd see James Hay Pension Trustees Ltd v First Secretary of State
First Secretary of State v Sainsbury's Supermarkets Ltd see MR Dean & Sons (Edgware) Ltd v First Secretary of State
Firth v Everitt [2007] EWHC 1979 (Ch); (2007) 104(39) L.S.G. 30, Ch D
Fishenden v Higgs & Hill (1935) 153 L.T. 128 . . . . *Approved, 69/2866*: *Considered, 92/3602, 07/2962*
Fisher v Brooker A2/2007/0157, CA (Civ Div); reversing in part [2006] EWHC 3239 (Ch); [2007] E.M.L.R. 9; [2007] F.S.R. 12, Ch D . . . . *Digested, 07/2523*
Fishers Bistro v Lothian Assessor [2007] CSIH 41; 2007 S.C. 671; [2007] R.A. 384; 2007 G.W.D. 19-342, LVAC
Fisk v Brian Thornhill & Son (A Firm) [2007] EWCA Civ 152; [2007] Lloyd's Rep. I.R. 699; [2007] P.N.L.R. 21; (2007) 151 S.J.L.B. 334, CA (Civ Div) . . . . *Digested, 07/2476*
Fiskano AB v Commission of the European Communities (C-135/92) [1994] E.C.R. I-2885; [1995] 3 C.M.L.R. 795, ECJ (5th Chamber) . . . . *Digested, 94/4856*: *Applied, 07/1645*
Fitzpatrick v Inland Revenue Commissioners (No.2) 1992 S.C. 207; 1993 S.L.T. 54, IH (1 Div) . . . . *Digested, 93/5419*: *Considered, 07/4057*: *Subsequent proceedings, 94/5928*
Fitzpatrick v Stinton (Unreported, March 13, 2007), CC (Birmingham) [*Ex rel.* Stephen Garner, Barrister, No. 8 Chambers, Fountain Court, Steelhouse Lane, Birmingham] . . . . *Digested, 07/3126*
Five Oaks Properties Ltd v Revenue and Customs Commissioners [2006] S.T.C. (S.C.D.) 769; [2006] S.T.I. 2405, Sp Comm . . . . *Digested, 07/4005*
FKI Engineering Ltd v DE Wind Holdings Ltd A3/2007/0523, CA (Civ Div); affirming [2007] EWHC 72 (Comm); [2007] I.L.Pr. 17, QBD (Comm) . . . . *Digested, 07/686*
FKP Scorpio Konzertproduktionen GmbH v Finanzamt Hamburg-Eimsbuttel (C-290/04) [2007] S.T.C. 1069; [2006] E.C.R. I-9461; [2007] 1 C.M.L.R. 33; [2006] S.T.I. 2274, ECJ . . . . *Digested, 07/1635*
Flaherty v National Greyhound Racing Club Ltd; *sub nom* National Greyhound Racing Club Ltd v Flaherty [2005] EWCA Civ 1117; (2005) 102(37) L.S.G. 31; *Times*, October 5, 2005, CA (Civ Div); reversing [2004] EWHC 2838 (Ch), Ch D . . . *Digested, 05/720*: *Applied, 07/3264*
Flashing Badge Co Ltd v Groves (t/a Flashing Badges by Virgo and Virgo Distribution) [2007] EWHC 1372 (Ch); [2007] E.C.D.R. 17; [2007] F.S.R. 36, Ch D . . . . *Digested, 07/2517*
Fleming v Diosynth Ltd see Thomson v Diosynth Ltd
Fleming v Xaniar Ltd (In Liquidation) 1998 S.C. 8; 1998 S.L.T. 703; [1997] I.R.L.R. 682; 1997 G.W.D. 31-1582, IH (1 Div) . . . . *Digested, 98/5812*: *Applied, 07/1348*: *Followed, 98/2188*
Fleming (t/a Bodycraft) v Customs and Excise Commissioners; *sub nom* Fleming (t/a Bodycraft) v Revenue and Customs Commissioners; *joined case* Conde Nast Publications Ltd v Revenue and Customs Commissioners [2006] EWCA Civ 70; [2006] S.T.C. 864; [2006] Eu. L.R. 864; [2006] B.T.C. 5241; [2006] B.V.C. 310; [2006] S.T.I. 457; (2006) 103(10) L.S.G. 25; *Times*, March 1, 2006; *Independent*, February 17, 2006, CA (Civ Div); reversing [2005] EWHC 232 (Ch); [2005] S.T.C. 707; [2005] Eu. L.R. 735; [2005] B.T.C. 5215; [2005] B.V.C. 246, Ch D; affirming in part [2004] V. & D.R. 172; [2004] S.T.I. 1560, V&DTr (London) . . . . *Digested, 06/4470*: *Applied, 06/4465*: *Considered, 07/4360*: *Followed, 05/4367*
Fleming (t/a Bodycraft) v Revenue and Customs Commissioners see Fleming (t/a Bodycraft) v Customs and Excise Commissioners
Fletamentos Maritimos SA v Effjohn International BV (No.2) [1997] 1 Lloyd's Rep. 644 (Note); [1997] 2 Lloyd's Rep. 302, CA (Civ Div); affirming [1997] 1 Lloyd's Rep. 295; *Times*, October 8, 1996; *Independent*, October 28, 1996, QBD (Comm) . . . . *Digested, 97/265*: *Considered, 07/251*

Fletcher v Brent LBC [2006] EWCA Civ 960; [2007] H.L.R. 12; (2006) 150 S.J.L.B. 920; [2006] N.P.C. 81, CA (Civ Div) . . . . *Digested*, 07/**2766**

Fletcher v Lewis (Unreported, May 14, 2007), CC (Redditch) [*Ex rel.* Stephen Garner, Barrister, No.8 Chambers, Fountain Court, Steelhouse Lane, Birmingham] . . . . *Digested*, 07/**3149**

Fletcher v Midland Bank Plc (No.2) see Preston v Wolverhampton Healthcare NHS Trust (No.2)

Fletcher v Midland Bank Plc (No.3) see Preston v Wolverhampton Healthcare NHS Trust (No.3)

Fletcher v Midland Bank Plc (No.3) see Powerhouse Retail Ltd v Burroughs

Fletcher v Sheffield City Council (Postponement of Order) [2007] EWHC 419 (Ch); [2007] H.L.R. 26, Ch D

Floe Telecom Ltd v Office of Communications [2006] EWCA Civ 768; [2007] Bus. L.R. 338; [2006] 4 All E.R. 688; [2006] E.C.C. 30; (2006) 103(26) L.S.G. 27; (2006) 150 S.J.L.B. 808; *Times*, July 26, 2006; *Independent*, June 23, 2006, CA (Civ Div) . . . . *Digested*, 06/**601**

Floe Telecom Ltd (In Liquidation) v Office of Communications [2007] CAT 15; [2007] Comp. A.R. 679, CAT

Floe Telecom Ltd (In Liquidation) v Office of Communications [2007] CAT 16; [2007] Comp. A.R. 688, CAT

Flood v Jackson see Allen v Flood

Flora v Wakom (Heathrow) Ltd (formerly Abela Airline Catering Ltd) [2006] EWCA Civ 1103; [2007] 1 W.L.R. 482; [2006] 4 All E.R. 982; [2007] P.I.Q.R. Q2; [2007] LS Law Medical 62; (2006) 156 N.L.J. 1289, CA (Civ Div); affirming [2005] EWHC 2822 (QB); [2006] P.I.Q.R. Q7; [2006] Lloyd's Rep. Med. 80; (2006) 150 S.J.L.B. 130, QBD . . . . *Digested*, 07/**3064**: *Applied*, 07/3063, 07/3067: *Followed*, 07/3066

Flower v Lloyd (No.1) (1877) L.R. 6 Ch. D. 297, CA . . . . *Considered*, 97/640, 02/294, 07/510

Floyd v Revenue and Customs Commissioners [2007] S.T.I. 2816, Sp Comm

Floyd v Scott (Unreported, October 31, 2006), CC (Brighton) [*Ex rel.* David Giles, Barrister, 1 Gray's Inn Square, Ground Floor, London] . . . . *Digested*, 07/**2716**

FM v ASL Trustee Co Ltd; *sub nom* A Trust, Re (2006-07) 9 I.T.E.L.R. 127, Royal Ct (Jer) . . . . *Digested*, 07/**4244**

FO (Children: Settlement - OM distinguished: Nigeria), Re see FO (Nigeria) v Secretary of State for the Home Department

FO (Nigeria) v Secretary of State for the Home Department; *sub nom* FO (Children: Settlement - OM distinguished: Nigeria), Re [2006] UKAIT 89; [2007] Imm. A.R. 382, AIT . . . . *Digested*, 07/**2332**

Foenander v Allan [2006] EWHC 2101 (Ch); [2006] B.P.I.R. 1392, Ch D . . . . *Digested*, 07/**2405**

Fogg v Secretary of State for Defence see R. (on the application of Fogg) v Secretary of State for Defence

Folgero v Norway (15472/02) 23 B.H.R.C. 227; [2007] E.L.R. 557, ECHR (Grand Chamber)

Folkstone Corp v Brockman [1914] A.C. 338, HL . . . . *Considered*, 94/5335: *Superseded*, 07/3421

Fonden Marselisborg Lystbadehavn v Skatteministeriet (C-428/02) [2006] S.T.C. 1467; [2005] E.C.R. I-1527; [2007] B.T.C. 5839; [2007] B.V.C. 808; [2005] S.T.I. 360, ECJ (3rd Chamber) . . . . *Digested*, 06/**4447**

Football League Ltd v Edge Ellison (A Firm) [2006] EWHC 1462 (Ch); [2007] P.N.L.R. 2; (2006) 150 S.J.L.B. 890, Ch D . . . . *Digested*, 07/**2950**

Foots v Southern Cross Mine Management Pty Ltd [2007] HCA 56; [2007] B.P.I.R. 1498, HC (Aus)

Forbes v Director of the Assets Recovery Agency [2007] S.T.C. (S.C.D.) 1; [2006] S.T.I. 2510, Sp Comm . . . . *Digested*, 07/**4049**

Forbes v Director of the Assets Recovery Agency [2007] S.T.C. (S.C.D.) 653; [2007] S.T.I. 1695, Sp Comm

Forbes v Secretary of State for the Home Department [2006] EWCA Civ 962; [2006] 1 W.L.R. 3075; [2006] 4 All E.R. 799; [2007] 1 Cr. App. R. (S.) 72; [2006] U.K.H.R.R. 1053; [2006] Crim. L.R. 1085; (2006) 103(30) L.S.G. 30; *Times*, August 11, 2006, CA (Civ Div); affirming [2005] EWHC 1597 (QB), QBD . . . . . *Digested*, 06/**2943**

Ford v Revenue and Customs Commissioners [2007] Pens. L.R. 399; [2007] S.T.I. 2410, Sp Comm . . . . *Digested*, 07/**4093**

Ford Motor Co Ltd v Revenue and Customs Commissioners [2006] V. & D.R. 114; [2006] S.T.I. 1365, V&DTr (London) . . . . *Digested*, 07/**4322**

Ford Motor Co Ltd v Revenue and Customs Commissioners [2007] EWCA Civ 1370, CA (Civ Div); affirming [2007] EWHC 1014 (Ch); [2007] S.T.C. 1783; [2007] B.T.C. 5511; [2007] B.V.C. 479; [2007] S.T.I. 1045, Ch D; affirming [2007] B.V.C. 2146; [2006] S.T.I. 2584, V&DTr . . . . *Digested*, 07/**4290**

Ford of Europe Inc v Commission of the European Communities see Ford Werke AG v Commission of the European Communities (C-25/84)

Ford Werke AG v Commission of the European Communities (C-25/84); *joined case* Ford of Europe Inc v Commission of the European Communities [1985] E.C.R. 2725; [1985] 3 C.M.L.R. 528, ECJ . . . . *Digested*, 85/**1333**: *Considered*, 07/1543

Ford-Camber Ltd v Deanminster Ltd [2007] EWCA Civ 458; (2007) 151 S.J.L.B. 713,
CA (Civ Div); affirming [2006] EWHC 1961 (Ch); [2006] 3 E.G.L.R. 81; [2006]
40 E.G. 248, Ch D . . . . *Digested*, 07/**3352**
Forder v Forder see Swindale v Forder
Foreningen af Arbejdsledere i Danmark v Daddy's Dance Hall A/S (324/86) [1988]
E.C.R. 739; [1989] 2 C.M.L.R. 517; [1988] I.R.L.R. 315, ECJ (3rd Chamber) . . *Digested*, 90/**2226.d**:
Applied, 98/2216, 98/2217, 06/1379: *Considered*, 96/2646, 01/2332,
06/1362, 07/1414
Fornah v Secretary of State for the Home Department see K v Secretary of State for
the Home Department
Forrest v Reigate and Banstead BC see R. (on the application of McLellan) v Bracknell
Forest BC
Forrest & Sons Ltd v CGU Insurance Plc [2006] Lloyd's Rep. I.R. 113, QBD (Merc) . . . *Digested*, 06/**2410**:
Distinguished, 07/2470
Forsakringsaktiebolaget Skandia v Riksskatteverket (C-422/01); *sub nom* Ramstedt v
Riksskatteverket (C-422/01) [2003] All E.R. (EC) 831; [2003] S.T.C. 1361;
[2003] E.C.R. I-6817; [2004] 1 C.M.L.R. 4; [2003] C.E.C. 484; [2004] O.P.L.R.
253; [2003] Pens. L.R. 189; [2003] B.T.C. 435; 5 I.T.L. Rep. 1042; [2003]
S.T.I. 1874, ECJ (5th Chamber) . . . . *Digested*, 03/**3100**:
Applied, 07/1616
Forsdick v Humphreys (Unreported, March 9, 2007), CC (Dartford) [*Ex rel.* Nigel
Ffitch, Barrister, Phoenix Chambers, Gray's Inn Chambers, Gray's Inn, London]. *Digested*, 07/**2956**
Fosberry v Revenue and Customs (2007) 104(24) L.S.G. 27, Ch D
Foss v Harbottle 67 E.R. 189; (1843) 2 Hare 461, Ct of Chancery . . . . *Applied*, 56/1149,
64/465, 78/241, 78/366, 82/330: *Cited*, 01/6300: *Considered*, 68/445,
82/331, 85/3514, 85/3534, 91/414, 94/421, 96/1213, 96/5732, 02/619,
06/2324, 07/435: *Distinguished*, 63/411, 66/1409, 72/3459
Foster v British Gas Plc (C-188/89) [1991] 1 Q.B. 405; [1991] 2 W.L.R. 258; [1990]
3 All E.R. 897; [1990] E.C.R. I-3313; [1990] 2 C.M.L.R. 833; [1991] I.C.R. 84;
[1990] I.R.L.R. 353; *Times*, July 13, 1990, ECJ. . . . . *Digested*, 91/**1672.a**:
Applied, 92/1977, 95/2070, 95/5037, 98/2111, 07/1565, 07/2496:
Approved, 91/1673: *Considered*, 95/2031, 06/2108: *Followed*, 96/2625:
Referred to, 97/2277
Foster v Lyons & Co Ltd [1927] 1 Ch. 219, Ch D . . . . *Considered*, 07/2757
Foster Bryant Surveying Ltd v Bryant [2007] EWCA Civ 200; [2007] Bus. L.R. 1565;
[2007] B.C.C. 804; [2007] 2 B.C.L.C. 239; [2007] I.R.L.R. 425; [2007] 12 E.G.
154 (C.S.); (2007) 104(13) L.S.G. 24, CA (Civ Div). . . . . *Digested*, 07/**562**
Fotiadis v Plato Learning Inc (1018C 002468593/1) see Fotiadis's Community Trade
Mark (No.2468593)
Fotiadis's Community Trade Mark (No.2468593); *sub nom* Fotiadis v Plato Learning Inc
(1018C 002468593/1) [2007] E.T.M.R. 73, OHIM (Cancellation Div)
Foulser v MacDougall (Inspector of Taxes) [2007] EWCA Civ 8; [2007] S.T.C. 973;
[2007] Eu. L.R. 509; [2007] B.T.C. 95; [2007] S.T.I. 196; (2007) 104(5) L.S.G.
29; (2007) 151 S.J.L.B. 128; *Times*, January 24, 2007, CA (Civ Div); affirming
[2005] EWHC 2958 (Ch); [2006] S.T.C. 311; [2006] 1 C.M.L.R. 41; [2006] Eu.
L.R. 622; [2006] B.T.C. 131; [2006] S.T.I. 44; *Times*, January 13, 2006, Ch D;
affirming [2005] S.T.C. (S.C.D.) 374; [2005] S.T.I. 835, Sp Comm . . . . *Digested*, 07/**3989**
Fourie v Le Roux; *sub nom* Herlan Edmunds Engineering (Pty) Ltd, Re [2007] UKHL
1; [2007] Bus. L.R. 925; [2007] 1 W.L.R. 320; [2007] 1 All E.R. 1087; [2007] 1
All E.R. (Comm) 571; [2007] B.P.I.R. 24; (2007) 157 N.L.J. 178; *Times*, January
25, 2007, HL; affirming [2005] EWCA Civ 204; [2006] 2 B.C.L.C. 531; *Times*,
April 25, 2005, CA (Civ Div); affirming in part [2004] EWHC 2260 (Ch); *Times*,
October 8, 2004, Ch D . . . . *Digested*, 07/**453**:
Previous proceedings, 05/416
Fox v Spousal (Midlands) Ltd see Fairchild v Glenhaven Funeral Services Ltd (t/a GH
Dovener & Son)
Foyle v Turner [2007] B.P.I.R. 43, Ch D . . . . *Digested*, 07/**2403**
FP (Iran) v Secretary of State for the Home Department; *joined case* MB (Libya) v
Secretary of State for the Home Department [2007] EWCA Civ 13; [2007] Imm.
A.R. 450; [2007] I.N.L.R. 224; *Times*, January 26, 2007, CA (Civ Div) . . . . *Digested*, 07/**2274**
Framlington Group Ltd v Barnetson see Barnetson v Framlington Group Ltd
France Manche SA v Balfour Beatty Construction Ltd see Channel Tunnel Group Ltd v
Balfour Beatty Construction Ltd
France Telecom SA (formerly Wanadoo Interactive SA) v Commission of the European
Communities (T-340/03) [2007] 4 C.M.L.R. 21, CFI (5th Chamber) . . . . *Digested*, 07/**1548**
Franchet v Commission of the European Communities (T-391/03) [2006] E.C.R. II-
2023; [2006] 3 C.M.L.R. 37, CFI (3rd Chamber). . . . . *Digested*, 07/**1585**
Francis v Revenue and Customs Commissioners [2006] V. & D.R. 487; [2007] S.T.I.
388, V&DTr (London)
Francis v Secretary of State for Work and Pensions [2005] EWCA Civ 1303; [2006] 1
W.L.R. 3202; [2006] 1 All E.R. 748; [2005] 3 F.C.R. 526; [2006] H.R.L.R. 9;
Times, November 17, 2005; *Independent*, November 17, 2005, CA (Civ Div) . . . *Digested*, 06/**4009**:
Distinguished, 07/3867
Francis v United Kingdom (25624/02) see O'Halloran v United Kingdom (15809/02)

Francis v United Kingdom (C3346/02) [2003] M.H.L.R. 245; [2007] Inquest L.R. 171, ECHR

Francovich v Italy (C-6/90); *joined case* Bonifacti v Italy (C-9/90) [1991] E.C.R. I-5357; [1993] 2 C.M.L.R. 66; [1995] I.C.R. 722; [1992] I.R.L.R. 84; *Times*, November 20, 1991, ECJ . . . . *Digested*, 92/**4815**:
Applied, 98/2570, 98/3396, 99/3620: *Cited*, 00/2380: *Considered*, 92/2904, 94/3046, 95/2031, 96/2566, 96/2596, 96/2597, 96/2629, 96/2792, 96/2803, 97/4627, 07/2490: *Followed*, 97/2265, 02/1571

Franks v Sinclair [2006] EWHC 3365 (Ch); [2007] W.T.L.R. 439, Ch D . . . . *Digested*, 07/**3969**

Franks v Sinclair (Costs) [2006] EWHC 3656 (Ch); [2007] W.T.L.R. 785, Ch D . . . . . *Digested*, 07/**399**

Franses v Al Assad [2007] EWHC 2442 (Ch); [2007] B.P.I.R. 1233, Ch D

Fraser v BN Furman (Productions) Ltd [1967] 1 W.L.R. 898; [1967] 3 All E.R. 57; [1967] 2 Lloyd's Rep. 1; 2 K.I.R. 483; (1967) 111 S.J. 471, CA (Civ Div) . . . . *Digested*, 67/**2037**:
Applied, 79/1501, 84/1812, 94/2661, 94/2702, 94/2703, 99/6308: *Considered*, 69/1828, 73/3756, 74/1882, 75/1882, 97/6167, 03/2473: *Distinguished*, 07/1058: *Followed*, 89/2051, 98/6016

Fraser v Canterbury Diocesan Board of Finance [2007] EWHC 1590 (Ch); [2007] W.T.L.R. 1735; [2007] 28 E.G. 121 (C.S.), Ch D

Fraser v Chester (Unreported, February 19, 2007), CC (Salford) [*Ex rel*. Gareth Thompson, Barrister, St John's Buildings, 24A-28 St John Street, Manchester] . *Digested*, 07/**3158**

Fraser v HLMAD Ltd [2006] EWCA Civ 738; [2007] 1 All E.R. 383; [2006] I.C.R. 1395; [2006] I.R.L.R. 687; (2006) 103(26) L.S.G. 29; (2006) 150 S.J.L.B. 809; *Independent*, June 20, 2006, CA (Civ Div) . . . . *Digested*, 06/**1407**:
Applied, 06/1357

Fraser v Oystertec Plc (Proposed Amendments) [2004] EWHC 2225 (Ch); [2005] B.P.I.R. 389, Ch D . . . . *Digested*, 05/**392**:
Applied, 07/4315

Fratelli Pardini SpA v Ministero del Commercio con l'Estero and Banca Toscana (Lucca Branch) (C-338/85) [1988] E.C.R. 2041, ECJ . . . . *Applied*, 95/4201, 07/2798

Freakley v Centre Reinsurance International Co see Centre Reinsurance International Co v Curzon Insurance Ltd

Freeman v Home Office [1984] Q.B. 524; [1984] 2 W.L.R. 802; [1984] 1 All E.R. 1036; (1984) 81 L.S.G. 1045; (1984) 128 S.J. 298, CA (Civ Div); affirming [1984] 2 W.L.R. 130; [1983] 3 All E.R. 589; (1983) 133 N.L.J. 726; (1983) 127 S.J. 825, QBD . . . . *Digested*, 84/**3570**:
Applied, 07/2898

Freeman v Lockett [2006] EWHC 102 (QB); [2006] P.I.Q.R. P23; [2006] Lloyd's Rep. Med. 151; (2006) 150 S.J.L.B. 265, QBD . . . . *Digested*, 06/**3065**:
Considered, 07/1065

Freeport Plc v Arnoldsson (C-98/06) [2007] I.L.Pr. 58, ECJ (3rd Chamber)

Freistaat Bayern v Blijdenstein (C-433/01) [2004] All E.R. (EC) 591; [2004] E.C.R. I-981; [2004] C.E.C. 172; [2004] I.L.Pr. 8, ECJ (5th Chamber) . . . . *Digested*, 04/**561**:
Applied, 07/657

French Connection Ltd's Trade Mark Application (No.81862) see Woodman v French Connection Ltd

FRESNIUS/Haemodialysis apparatus (T380/04) [2006] E.P.O.R. 43, EPO (Technical Bd App) . . . . *Digested*, 07/**2600**

Fressoz v France (29183/95) (2001) 31 E.H.R.R. 2; 5 B.H.R.C. 654, ECHR . . . . *Digested*, 99/**3105**:
Considered, 05/2030, 07/2187

Frewin v Consignia Plc EAT/0981/02/LA, EAT . . . . *Considered*, 07/1430

Friend v Lord Advocate; *sub nom* Whaley v Lord Advocate [2007] UKHL 53; 2007 S.L.T. 1209; (2007) 151 S.J.L.B. 1565; 2007 G.W.D. 39-680, HL; affirming 2006 S.C. 121; 2005 G.W.D. 30-577, IH (Ex Div); affirming 2004 S.C. 78; 2004 S.L.T. 425; 2003 G.W.D. 22-651, OH . . . . *Digested*, 04/**4480**

Friends of the Earth's Application for Judicial Review [2006] NIQB 48; [2007] N.I. 33; [2007] Env. L.R. 7, QBD (NI) . . . . *Digested*, 07/**4544**

Friends Provident Life Office v Hillier Parker May & Rowden [1997] Q.B. 85; [1996] 2 W.L.R. 123; [1995] 4 All E.R. 260; [1995] C.L.C. 592; (1996) 71 P. & C.R. 286; [1995] E.G. 64 (C.S.); [1995] N.P.C. 63; *Times*, April 15, 1995, CA (Civ Div) . . . *Digested*, 96/**2781**:
Considered, 02/326, 03/3613: *Distinguished*, 00/1448: *Followed*, 07/4248

Fritz Werner Industrie Ausrustungen GmbH v Germany (C-70/94) [1995] E.C.R. I-3189, ECJ . . . . *Digested*, 96/**3679**:
Considered, 07/1563

Front Carriers Ltd v Atlantic and Orient Shipping Corp (Double Happiness) [2007] EWHC 421 (Comm); [2007] 2 Lloyd's Rep. 131, QBD (Comm) . . . . *Digested*, 07/**3801**

Frost v Chief Constable of South Yorkshire see White v Chief Constable of South Yorkshire

Frost v John Summers & Sons Ltd see John Summers & Sons Ltd v Frost

Frydlender v France (30979/96) (2001) 31 E.H.R.R. 52, ECHR . . . . *Digested*, 01/**3523**:
Applied, 07/2218, 07/2220, 07/2221, 07/2222, 07/2225, 07/2249

Fujitsu Ltd's Patent Application (No.9204959.2) [1997-98] Info.T.L.R.103; [1997] R.P.C.
608; (1997) 16 Tr. L.R. 352; [1998] Masons C.L.R. Rep. 99; (1997) 20(7) I.P.D.
20060; *Times*, March 14, 1997, CA (Civ Div); affirming [1997-98] Info. T.L.R.
101; [1996] R.P.C. 511; [1998] Masons C.L.R. Rep. 112; (1996) 19(9) I.P.D.
19078;*Times*, June 18, 1996, Ch D (Patents Ct) . . . .   *Digested*, 97/**3915**:
    Applied, 05/2490, 06/2468: *Cited*, 03/2519: *Considered*, 05/2492, 06/2521,
    07/2632: *Followed*, 05/2446, 07/2615: *Referred to*, 02/2846

Fulcrum Electronics Ltd v Customs and Excise Commissioners (C-355/03) see
Optigen Ltd v Customs and Excise Commissioners (C-354/03)

Fulcrum Trading Co (UK) Ltd (In Liquidation) v Customs and Excise Commissioners see
Optigen Ltd v Customs and Excise Commissioners

Fulham Football Club Ltd v Cabra Estates Plc [1992] B.C.C. 863; [1994] 1 B.C.L.C.
363; (1993) 65 P. & C.R. 284; [1993] 1 P.L.R. 29; (1992) 136 S.J.L.B. 267;
Times, September 11, 1992; *Independent*, September 17, 1992, CA (Civ Div);
reversing [1992] N.P.C. 115; *Times*, July 1, 1992, Ch D . . . .   *Digested*, 93/**3835.a**:
    Considered, 07/787

Fulham Leisure Holdings Ltd v Nicholson Graham & Jones (A Firm) A3/2006/2255,
CA (Civ Div); reversing in part [2006] EWHC 2017 (Ch); [2006] 4 All E.R. 1397
(Note); [2007] P.N.L.R. 5, Ch D . . . .   *Digested*, 07/**2948**

Funnell v Adams & Remer (A Partnership) [2007] EWHC 2166 (QB); (2007) 104(40)
L.S.G. 27, QBD

Futura Participations SA v Administration des Contributions (C-250/95) [1997] S.T.C.
1301; [1997] E.C.R. I-2471; [1997] 3 C.M.L.R. 483; *Times*, June 23, 1997, ECJ .   *Digested*, 97/**1076**:
    Applied, 07/1633: *Considered*, 06/4157: *Distinguished*, 04/3729

Futures London Ltd v Stratford (Valuation Officer) [2006] R.A. 75, Lands Tr . . . .   *Digested*, 06/**3445**:
    Applied, 07/3349

FWL de Groot v Inspecteur van de Belastingdienst Particulieren/Ondernemingen te
Haarlem (C-385/00) see De Groot v Staatssecretaris van Financien (C-385/
00)

G v A Local Authority see R (Children) (Care Proceedings: Maternal Grandmother's
Applications), Re

G v Burnley Magistrates Court see R. (on the application of G) v Burnley Magistrates
Court

G v Chief Constable of West Yorkshire see R. (on the application of G) v Chief
Constable of West Yorkshire

G v G [2006] EWCA Civ 1670; (2006) 103(44) L.S.G. 30; (2006) 150 S.J.L.B. 1466;
Times, November 22, 2006, CA (Civ Div) . . . .   *Digested*, 07/**3703**

G v G (Minors: Custody Appeal) [1985] 1 W.L.R. 647; [1985] 2 All E.R. 225; [1985]
F.L.R. 894; [1985] Fam. Law 321; (1985) 82 L.S.G. 2010; (1985) 83 L.S.G.
2010; (1985) 135 N.L.J. 439; (1985) 129 S.J. 315, HL. . . . .   *Digested*, 85/**2594**:
    Applied, 86/2145, 86/2196, 87/1773, 87/2489, 87/2490, 87/2519, 87/2527,
    91/2553, 92/3032, 95/3372, 95/3390, 95/3469, 95/3486, 95/3489,
    95/3493, 95/3561, 96/563, 96/604, 96/607, 96/614, 96/6976, 02/498,
    02/3270, 06/1670, 07/1800: *Approved*, 98/2398: *Considered*, 86/2182,
    88/2952, 89/2410, 89/2459, 90/3125, 95/67, 95/3386, 95/3498, 95/3532,
    96/608, 97/384, 00/2489, 04/2134, 07/4550: *Distinguished*, 88/2935:
    Explained, 87/2439: *Followed*, 86/1099, 86/2068, 86/2201, 96/560,
    96/609: *Referred to*, 86/3641, 94/3220

G v G (Role of FDR Judge) [2006] EWHC 1993 (Fam); [2007] 1 F.L.R. 237; [2006]
Fam. Law 922, Fam Div . . . .   *Digested*, 07/**1693**

G Middleton Ltd v Berry Creek Overseas Development Ltd [2007] EWHC 318 (TCC);
[2007] T.C.L.R. 4; 113 Con. L.R. 23, QBD (TCC) . . . .   *Digested*, 07/**526**

G Pohl-Boskamp GmbH & Co KG v Gemeinsamer Bundesausschuss (C-317/05) [2007]
1 C.M.L.R. 24; [2006] E.C.R. IA-10611, ECJ (5th Chamber)

G (A Child), Re see Phelps v Hillingdon LBC

G (A Child), Re [2006] EWCA Civ 1507; [2007] 1 F.L.R. 1663; [2007] Fam. Law 110; (2006)
103(40) L.S.G. 36; (2006) 150 S.J.L.B. 1328, CA (Civ Div) . . . .   *Digested*, 07/**1776**

G (A Child), Re; *sub nom* G (A Child) (Parental Responsibility Order), Re [2006]
EWCA Civ 745; [2006] 2 F.L.R. 1092; [2006] Fam. Law 744; (2006) 150
S.J.L.B. 666, CA (Civ Div) . . . .   *Digested*, 07/**1786**

G (A Child), Re; *sub nom* G&B (Children), Re [2007] EWCA Civ 358; [2007] 2 F.L.R.
140; [2007] Fam. Law 687, CA (Civ Div) . . . .   *Digested*, 07/**1680**

G (A Child) v Bromley LBC see Phelps v Hillingdon LBC

G (A Child) v Chhaganlal (Unreported, September 6, 2006), CC (Burton on Trent) [*Ex
rel.* Irwin Mitchell Solicitors, Riverside West, 1 Millsands, Sheffield] . . . .   *Digested*, 07/**394**

G (A Child) v Quintain Ltd (Unreported, April 12, 2007), CC (Birmingham) [*Ex rel.*
Adam Farrer, Barrister, No. 5 Fountain Court, Birmingham] . . . .   *Digested*, 07/**3196**

G (A Child) (Adoption: Disclosure), Re see H (A Child) (Adoption: Consultation of
Unmarried Fathers), Re

G (A Child) (Interim Care Order: Residential Assessment), Re; *sub nom* G (A Child)
(Interim Care Orders: Inpatient Assessment), Re; Kent CC *v* G [2005] UKHL 68;
[2006] 1 A.C. 576; [2005] 3 W.L.R. 1166; [2006] 1 All E.R. 706; [2006] 1
F.L.R. 601; [2005] 3 F.C.R. 621; [2006] Fam. Law 91; (2005) 102(47) L.S.G.
28; *Times*, November 25, 2005; *Independent*, November 29, 2005, HL; reversing
[2004] EWCA Civ 24; [2004] 1 F.L.R. 876; [2004] 1 F.C.R. 317; [2004] Fam.
Law 325; (2004) 101(9) L.S.G. 31; *Times*, January 29, 2004, CA (Civ Div) ...   *Digested*, 06/**1654**:
                         Applied, 07/1725: *Distinguished*, 07/1751
G (A Child) (Interim Care Orders: Inpatient Assessment), Re see G (A Child) (Interim Care
Order: Residential Assessment), Re
G (A Child) (Maintenance Pending Suit), Re [2006] EWHC 1834 (Fam); [2007] 1 F.L.R.
1674; [2007] Fam. Law 215, Fam Div
G (A Child) (Parental Responsibility Order), Re see G (A Child), Re
G (ET) (A Patient), Re; *sub nom* G (TJ) (A Patient), Re [2007] EWHC 1861 (Ch);
[2007] 2 P. & C.R. DG21, CP
G (TJ) (A Patient), Re see G (ET) (A Patient), Re
G&B (Children), Re see G (A Child), Re
G-Tech Construction Ltd, Re [2007] B.P.I.R. 1275, Ch D
GA *v* Secretary of State for the Home Department; *sub nom* GA (Subsisting Marriage:
Ghana), Re [2006] UKAIT 46; [2006] Imm. A.R. 543, AIT ....   *Digested*, 07/**2333**
GA (Subsisting Marriage: Ghana), Re see GA *v* Secretary of State for the Home
Department
Gaafar *v* Secretary of State for the Home Department see Januzi *v* Secretary of State
for the Home Department
GAB Robins (UK) Ltd *v* Triggs 2007/1687, CA (Civ Div); reversing [2007] 3 All E.R.
590; [2007] I.C.R. 1424; [2007] I.R.L.R. 857, EAT ....   *Digested*, 07/**1317**
Gabem Management Ltd *v* Revenue and Customs Commissioners [2007] S.T.C.
(S.C.D.) 247; [2007] S.T.I. 545, Sp Comm. ....   *Digested*, 07/**3998**
Gaffoor (Abdul) Trustees *v* Ceylon Commissioner of Income Tax see Caffoor (Trustees
of the Abdul Gaffoor Trust) *v* Income Tax Commissioner (Colombo)
Gaines-Cooper *v* Revenue and Customs Commissioners [2007] EWHC 2617 (Ch);
[2007] B.T.C. 704; 10 I.T.L. Rep. 255; [2007] S.T.I. 2651, Ch D; affirming [2007]
S.T.C. (S.C.D.) 23; 9 I.T.L. Rep. 274; [2007] W.T.L.R. 101; [2006] S.T.I. 2532,
Sp Comm ....   *Digested*, 07/**4068**
Galandauer *v* Snaresbrook Crown Court; *sub nom* R. (on the application of
Galandauer) *v* Snaresbrook Crown Court [2006] EWHC 1633 (Admin); [2007]
2 Costs L.R. 205; *Times*, August 15, 2006, DC ....   *Digested*, 06/**922**
Galaxy Showers Ltd *v* Wilson [2006] I.R.L.R. 83, EAT ....   *Digested*, 06/**1373**:
                                      Considered, 07/1408
Gale's Patent Application [1991] R.P.C. 305; *Financial Times*, December 18, 1990, CA
(Civ Div) ....   *Digested*, 92/**3279**:
             Considered, 06/2521: *Followed*, 07/2615: *Referred to*, 02/2846
Galgate Cricket Club *v* Doyle (Valuation Officer) [2001] R.A. 21, Lands Tr ....   *Digested*, 01/**4830**:
                                      Considered, 07/3346
Galileo Group Ltd, Re; *sub nom* Company (No.003025 of 1997), Re; Elles *v* Hambros
Bank Ltd [1999] Ch. 100; [1998] 2 W.L.R. 364; [1998] 1 All E.R. 545; [1998]
B.C.C. 228; [1998] 1 B.C.L.C. 318; (1997) 94(46) L.S.G. 30; (1998) 142
S.J.L.B. 21; *Times*, December 10, 1997, Ch D ....   *Digested*, 98/**306**:
                                      Considered, 07/439
Galinski *v* McHugh (1989) 21 H.L.R. 47; (1989) 57 P. & C.R. 359; [1989] 1 E.G.L.R.
109; [1989] 05 E.G. 89; [1988] E.G. 127 (C.S.); (1988) 138 N.L.J. Rep. 303;
Times, October 13, 1988, CA (Civ Div) ....   *Digested*, 89/**2162**:
            Applied, 02/3010, 03/2724, 03/2757: *Distinguished*, 07/2755
Gallagher (Valuation Officer) *v* Church of Jesus Christ of Latter-Day Saints; *sub nom*
Church of Jesus Christ of Latter-Day Saints *v* Gallagher (Valuation Officer)
[2006] EWCA Civ 1598; [2007] R.A. 1; (2006) 150 S.J.L.B. 1572; [2006]
N.P.C. 126; [2007] 2 P. & C.R. DG6, CA (Civ Div); affirming [2006] R.A. 1,
Lands Tr ....   *Digested*, 07/**2878**
Galloway *v* Telegraph Group Ltd [2006] EWCA Civ 17; [2006] E.M.L.R. 11; [2006]
H.R.L.R. 13; (2006) 150 S.J.L.B. 131; *Times*, February 6, 2006; *Independent*,
January 27, 2006, CA (Civ Div); affirming [2004] EWHC 2786 (QB); [2005]
E.M.L.R. 7; (2004) 148 S.J.L.B. 1436; *Times*, January 13, 2005, QBD ....   *Digested*, 06/**1047**:
                                      Considered, 07/1076
Galoo Ltd *v* Bright Grahame Murray [1994] 1 W.L.R. 1360; [1995] 1 All E.R. 16; [1994]
B.C.C. 319; *Times*, January 14, 1994, CA (Civ Div) ....   *Digested*, 95/**3691**:
        Applied, 96/3588, 00/4186, 03/4958, 07/2918: *Considered*, 95/2562,
          97/2661, 98/4002, 98/4989, 00/4249, 01/938, 01/5900, 04/386:
              Distinguished, 03/2997: *Referred to*, 96/1272, 97/4871
Gamboa-Garzon *v* Langer [2006] EWCA Civ 1246; [2007] 2 F.L.R. 518; [2007] Fam.
Law 690, CA (Civ Div). ....   *Digested*, 07/**390**
Game Group Plc *v* First Internet Technology Ltd [2007] E.T.M.R. 78, Arbitration
Gamlestaden Fastigheter AB *v* Baltic Partners Ltd [2007] UKPC 26; [2007] Bus. L.R.
1521; [2007] 4 All E.R. 164; [2007] B.C.C. 272, PC (Jer) ....   *Digested*, 07/**592**

Gan Insurance Co Ltd v Tai Ping Insurance Co Ltd (No.2) [2001] EWCA Civ 1047;
[2001] 2 All E.R. (Comm) 299; [2001] C.L.C. 1103; [2001] Lloyd's Rep. I.R.
667, CA (Civ Div) . . . .
Digested, 01/**3839**:
Applied, 07/2478

Garage Molenheide BVBA v Belgium (C-286/94); *joined cases* Sanders BVBA v
Belgium (C-47/96); Bureau Rik Decan-Business Research & Development NV
(BRD) v Belgium (C-401/95); Schepens v Belgium (C-340/95) [1998] All E.R.
(E.C.) 61; [1998] S.T.C. 126; [1997] E.C.R. I-7281; [1998] 1 C.M.L.R. 1186;
[1998] C.E.C. 208; [1998] B.T.C. 5088; [1998] B.V.C.106, ECJ (5th Chamber)
Digested, 98/**4931**:
Applied, 00/5356, 04/4001, 05/4373, 05/4420, 07/4303:
Considered, 03/4566: *Followed*, 02/4737

Garcia v Bundesanstalt fur Arbeit (C-266/95) [1997] E.C.R. I-3279; [1998] I.C.R. 715,
ECJ . . . .
Digested, 98/**4518**:
Considered, 03/3951: *Followed*, 07/3830

Garcia v Canada 2007 TCC 548; 10 I.T.L. Rep. 179, Tax Ct (Can)

Garcia Avello v Belgium (C-148/02) [2004] All E.R. (EC) 740; [2003] E.C.R. I-11613;
[2004] 1 C.M.L.R. 1, ECJ . . . .
Digested, 04/**1417**:
Considered, 07/1608

Garland v Morris see Garland v Morris (Deceased), Re

Garland (Deceased), Re; *sub nom* Garland v Morris [2007] EWHC 2 (Ch); [2007] 2
F.L.R. 528; [2007] W.T.L.R. 797; [2007] Fam. Law 585, Ch D . . . .
Digested, 07/**3954**

Garrett v Halton BC see Myatt v National Coal Board

Garrod v North Devon NHS Primary Care Trust [2006] EWHC 850; [2007] P.I.Q.R.
Q1, QBD

Gartukayev v Russia (71933/01) (2007) 44 E.H.R.R. 58, ECHR . . . .
Digested, 07/**2191**

Gascoyne v Customs and Excise Commissioners [2004] EWCA Civ 1162; [2005] Ch.
215; [2005] 2 W.L.R. 222, CA (Civ Div); affirming [2003] EWHC 257 (Ch);
[2003] Ch. 292; [2003] 2 W.L.R. 1311; (2003) 100(16) L.S.G. 27; *Times*, March
28, 2003, Ch D . . . .
Digested, 05/**953**:
Applied, 04/904: *Considered*, 07/1041

Gaskin v United Kingdom (10454/83) see Gaskin v United Kingdom (A/160)

Gaskin v United Kingdom (A/160); *sub nom* Gaskin v United Kingdom (10454/83)
[1990] 1 F.L.R. 167; (1990) 12 E.H.R.R. 36; *Times*, August 28, 1989, ECHR
(1989) 11 E.H.R.R. CD402, Eur Comm HR . . . .
Digested, 90/**2560**:
Applied, 07/2179: *Considered*, 02/2510, 02/2512

Gastronome (UK) Ltd v Anglo Dutch Meats (UK) Ltd [2006] EWCA Civ 1233; [2006]
2 Lloyd's Rep. 587, CA (Civ Div); affirming [2005] EWHC 3237 (QB), QBD . . .
Digested, 07/**779**

Gasus Dosier und Fordertechnik GmbH v Netherlands (15375/89) see Gasus Dosier
und Fordertechnik GmbH v Netherlands (A/306-B)

Gasus Dosier und Fordertechnik GmbH v Netherlands (A/306-B); *sub nom* Gasus
Dosier und Fordertechnik GmbH v Netherlands (15375/89) (1995) 20 E.H.R.R.
403, ECHR (1993) 15 E.H.R.R. CD14, Eur Comm HR . . . .
Digested, 96/**3162**:
Applied, 98/3133, 01/3522, 04/4001, 07/3977: *Considered*, 06/2112

Gater Assets Ltd v Nak Naftogaz Ukrainiy [2007] EWCA Civ 988; [2007] 2 Lloyd's
Rep. 588; [2007] 2 C.L.C. 567, CA (Civ Div); reversing [2007] EWHC 697
(Comm); [2007] 2 All E.R. (Comm) 208; [2007] 1 Lloyd's Rep. 522, QBD
(Comm) . . . .
Digested, 07/**514**

Gateshead MBC v Northumbrian Water Group Plc see Gateshead MBC v Secretary of
State for the Environment

Gateshead MBC v Secretary of State for the Environment; *joined case* Gateshead MBC
v Northumbrian Water Group Plc [1995] Env. L.R. 37; (1996) 71 P. & C.R. 350;
[1994] 1 P.L.R. 85; [1995] J.P.L. 432; [1994] E.G. 92 (C.S.), CA (Civ Div);
affirming [1994] Env. L.R. 11; (1994) 67 P. & C.R. 179; [1993] 3 P.L.R. 101;
[1994] J.P.L. 255, QBD . . . .
Digested, 96/**4786**:
Applied, 03/3407, 06/3330, 07/3236: *Considered*, 94/4404

Gator Shipping Corp v Trans-Asiatic Oil SA (The Odenfeld) [1978] 2 Lloyd's Rep. 357,
QBD (Comm) . . . .
Digested, 78/**2712**:
Considered, 07/2726

Gaughan v Revenue and Customs Commissioners [2007] S.T.C. (S.C.D.) 148; [2007]
S.T.I.139, Sp Comm . . . .
Digested, 07/**4101**

Gault v United Kingdom (1271/05), *Times*, November 28, 2007, ECHR

Gauntlett v Law Society [2006] EWHC 1954 (Ch); [2006] B.P.I.R. 1412, Ch D . . . . . .
Digested, 07/**2804**

Gaynor v Central West London Buses Ltd [2006] EWCA Civ 1120; [2007] 1 W.L.R.
1045; [2007] 1 All E.R. 84; [2007] 1 Costs L.R. 33; (2006) 156 N.L.J. 1324;
Times, August 25, 2006; *Independent*, October 5, 2006, CA (Civ Div) . . . .
Digested, 06/**2738**

GC Trading Ltd v Revenue and Customs Commissioners [2007] S.T.I. 2231, Sp Comm

GC (China) v Secretary of State for the Home Department; *sub nom* GC (Citizens
Directive: UK National's Spouse: China), Re [2007] UKAIT 56; [2007] Imm.
A.R. 667, AIT

GC (Citizens Directive: UK National's Spouse: China), Re see GC (China) v Secretary of
State for the Home Department

Ge Bowra Group Ltd v Thanet DC [2007] EWHC 1077 (Admin); [2007] R.V.R. 120,
QBD (Admin) . . . .
Digested, 07/**3339**

GE Capital Finance Pty Ltd v Commissioner of Taxation [2007] FCA 558; 9 I.T.L. Rep.
   1083, Fed Ct (Aus) (Sgl judge)
Gebhard v Consiglio dell'Ordine degli Avvocati e Procuratori di Milano (C-55/94)
   [1996] All E.R. (EC) 189; [1995] E.C.R. I-4165; [1996] 1 C.M.L.R. 603; [1996]
   C.E.C. 175; *Times*, December 13, 1995, ECJ . . . . *Digested,* 96/**3902**:
                      Applied, 07/1624: *Followed,* 02/1571, 05/1462, 05/1468
Gebroeders Beentjes BV v Netherlands (C-31/87) [1988] E.C.R. 4635; [1990] 1
   C.M.L.R. 287, ECJ (4th Chamber) . . . . *Digested,* 91/**3987**:
                      Applied, 07/3327: *Considered,* 96/4151

Gelle v Denmark (34/2004) 23 B.H.R.C. 1, UN CERD
Gemeente Leusden v Staatssecretaris van Financien (C-487/01); *joined case* Holin
   Groep BV cs v Staatssecretaris van Financien (C-7/02) [2007] S.T.C. 776;
   [2004] E.C.R. I-5337; [2006] B.T.C. 5670; [2006] B.V.C. 740; [2004] S.T.I.
   1199, ECJ (5th Chamber)
General Accident Fire & Life Assurance Corp Ltd v Tanter (The Zephyr) [1985] 2 Lloyd's
   Rep. 529; *Financial Times*, July 30, 1985, CA (Civ Div); reversing in part [1984]
   1 W.L.R. 100; [1984] 1 All E.R. 35; [1984] 1 Lloyd's Rep. 58; (1984) 134 N.L.J.
   35; (1983) 127 S.J. 733, QBD (Comm) . . . . *Digested,* 86/**1785**:
           Applied, 86/2620, 06/429: *Considered,* 95/4184, 03/4558, 07/2467
General Assembly of Free Church of Scotland v Lord Overtoun; *sub nom* Bannatyne
   (General Assembly of the Free Church) v Baron Overtoun; *joined case*
   Macalister v Young [1904] A.C. 515; (1904) 7 F. (H.L.) 1; (1904) 12 S.L.T. 297,
   HL; reversing (1902) 4 F. 1083; (1902) 10 S.L.T. 200, IH (2 Div) . . . . *Applied,* 07/**4260**:
                                    Distinguished, 06/297

GENERAL ELECTRIC/Electron beam apparatus (T1179/05) [2007] E.P.O.R. 50, EPO
   (Technical Bd App)
General Feeds Inc Panama v Slobodna Plovidba Yugoslavia (The Krapan J) [1999] 1
   Lloyd's Rep. 688, QBD (Comm) . . . . *Digested,* 99/**244**:
                                  Considered, 07/745

General Issue & Investment Co, Re see Test Holdings (Clifton), Re
General Issues and Investment Co, Re see Test Holdings (Clifton), Re
General Medical Council v Hiew [2007] EWCA Civ 369; [2007] 1 W.L.R. 2007;
   [2007] 4 All E.R. 473; [2007] LS Law Medical 309; *Times*, June 15, 2007, CA
   (Civ Div); affirming [2006] EWHC 2699 (Admin), QBD (Admin) . . . . *Digested,* 07/**1951**
General Medical Council v Meadow see Meadow v General Medical Council
General Motors Acceptance Corp (UK) Plc v Revenue and Customs Commissioners
   [2007] B.V.C. 2302, V&DTr (London)
General Motors BV (formerly General Motors Nederland BV) v Commission of the
   European Communities (C-551/03 P) [2006] E.C.R. I-3173; [2006] 5 C.M.L.R.
   1, ECJ (5th Chamber) . . . . *Digested,* 07/**614**
General Motors Corp v Royal & Sun Alliance Insurance Plc [2007] EWHC 2206
   (Comm); [2007] 2 C.L.C. 507; (2007) 104(40) L.S.G. 28, QBD (Comm)
General Motors Nederland BV v Commission of the European Communities (T368/00)
   [2003] E.C.R. II-4491; [2004] 4 C.M.L.R. 23, CFI (2nd Chamber) . . . . *Subsequent proceed-*
                                     ings, 07/614

GENERAL MOTORS/Refusal of reimbursement (J32/95) [2000] E.P.O.R. 289, EPO
   (Legal Bd App) . . . . *Digested,* 00/**3656**:
                                Considered, 07/2605

Generalised Tariff Preferences, Re (45/86) see Commission of the European Communities
   v Council of the European Communities (45/86)
Generics (UK) Ltd v H Lundbeck A/S; *sub nom* H Lundbeck A/S v Generics (UK) Ltd;
   A3/2007/1326; A3/2007/1387, CA (Civ Div); reversing [2007] EWHC 1040
   (Pat); [2007] R.P.C. 32, Ch D (Patents Ct) . . . . *Digested,* 07/**2614**
Genetic Systems v Roche Diagnostics GmbH (G2/03) see PPG/Disclaimer (G1/03)
Genetic Systems/Disclaimer (G2/03) see PPG/Disclaimer (G1/03)
Genosyis Technology Management Ltd, Re; *sub nom* Wallach v Secretary of State for
   Trade and Industry [2006] EWHC 989 (Ch); [2007] 1 B.C.L.C. 208, Ch D . . . . *Digested,* 07/**567**
George Wimpey UK Ltd v Tewkesbury BC [2007] EWHC 628 (Admin); (2007) 151
   S.J.L.B. 506, QBD (Admin)
Georgian Labour Party v Georgia (Admissibility) (9103/04) (2007) 45 E.H.R.R. SE12,
   ECHR
Georgiou (t/a Marios Chippery) v Customs and Excise Commissioners; *sub nom* Marios
   Chippery, Re [1996] S.T.C. 463, CA (Civ Div); affirming [1995] S.T.C. 1101;
   Times, October 19, 1995, QBD; affirming [1994] V.A.T.T.R. 125, VAT Tr
   (Manchester) . . . . *Digested,* 96/**5905**:
                                 Applied, 07/4283

Geraets-Smits v Stichting Ziekenfonds VGZ (C-157/99); *joined case* Peerbooms v
   Stichting CZ Groep Zorgverzekeringen (C-157/99) [2002] Q.B. 409; [2002] 2
   W.L.R. 154; [2003] All E.R. (EC) 481; [2001] E.C.R. I-5473; [2002] 2 C.M.L.R.
   21; (2001) 62 B.M.L.R. 101; *Times*, September 4, 2001, ECJ . . . . *Digested,* 01/**5133**:
           Applied, 07/1981: *Considered,* 03/1799, 04/1688, 07/1632:
                              Followed, 05/1849, 06/3056
Germany v Council of the European Union (C-380/03) see Germany v European
   Parliament (C-380/03)

Germany v European Parliament (C-376/98); *joined case* R. v Secretary of State for Health Ex p. Imperial Tobacco Ltd (C-74/99) [2000] All E.R. (EC) 769; [2000] E.C.R. I-8419; [2000] 3 C.M.L.R. 1175; *Times*, October 10, 2000, ECJ . . . .   *Digested,* 00/**2417**: *Applied,* 07/1552

Germany v European Parliament (C-380/03); *sub nom* Tobacco Advertising Directive 2003/33, R-e (C-380/03); Germany v Council of the European Union (C-380/ 03) [2007] All E.R. (EC) 1016; [2007] 2 C.M.L.R. 1, ECJ (Grand Chamber) . . .   *Digested,* 07/**1552**

Gesellschaft fur Antriebstechnik mbH & Co KG (GAT) v Lamellen und Kupplungsbau Beteiligungs KG (LuK) (C-4/03) [2006] E.C.R. I-6509; [2007] I.L.Pr. 34; [2006] F.S.R. 45, ECJ (1st Chamber) . . . .   *Digested,* 07/**2617**

Gestoras Pro Amnistia v Council of the European Union (C-354/04 P) [2007] 2 C.M.L.R. 22, ECJ (Grand Chamber) . . . .   *Digested,* 07/**1592**

Geurts v Administratie van de BTW, Registratie en Domeinen (C-464/05) [2007] S.T.I. 2517, ECJ (4th Chamber)

Geven v Land Nordrhein-Westfalen (C-213/05) [2007] 3 C.M.L.R. 45; [2007] C.E.C. 909, ECJ (Grand Chamber)

GH (formerly KAZ: Country Conditions: Effect: Iraq CG), Re see GH (Iraq) v Secretary of State for the Home Department

GH (Iraq) v Secretary of State for the Home Department; *sub nom* GH (formerly KAZ: Country Conditions: Effect: Iraq CG), Re [2005] EWCA Civ 1182; [2006] Imm. A.R. 19; [2006] I.N.L.R. 26; (2005) 102(42) L.S.G. 25, CA (Civ Div); affirming [2004] UKIAT 248; [2004] Imm. A.R. 707, IAT . . . .   *Digested,* 06/**2248**: *Distinguished,* 07/2343

Ghaidan v Godin-Mendoza; *sub nom* Mendoza v Ghaidan; Ghaidan v Mendoza; Godin-Mendoza v Ghaidan [2004] UKHL 30; [2004] 2 A.C. 557; [2004] 3 W.L.R. 113; [2004] 3 All E.R. 411; [2004] 2 F.L.R. 600; [2004] 2 F.C.R. 481; [2004] H.R.L.R. 31; [2004] U.K.H.R.R. 827; 16 B.H.R.C. 671; [2004] H.L.R. 46; [2005] 1 P. & C.R. 18; [2005] L. & T.R. 3; [2004] 2 E.G.L.R. 132; [2004] Fam. Law 641; [2004] 27 E.G. 128 (C.S.); (2004) 101(27) L.S.G. 30; (2004) 154 N.L.J. 1013; (2004) 148 S.J.L.B. 792; [2004] N.P.C. 100; [2004] 2 P. & C.R. DG17; *Times*, June 24, 2004, HL; affirming [2002] EWCA Civ 1533; [2003] Ch. 380; [2003] 2 W.L.R. 478; [2002] 4 All E.R. 1162; [2002] 3 F.C.R. 591; [2003] U.K.H.R.R. 254; 13 B.H.R.C. 608; [2003] H.L.R. 35; [2003] L. & T.R. 14; [2003] A.C.D. 12; [2003] Fam. Law 87; [2002] 46 E.G. 197 (C.S.); (2003) 100(1) L.S.G. 24; (2002) 152 N.L.J. 1718; (2002) 146 S.J.L.B. 253; [2002] N.P.C. 138; [2003] 1 P. & C.R. DG14; *Times*, November 14, 2002; *Independent*, November 22, 2002, CA (Civ Div) . . . .   *Digested,* 04/**2538**: *Applied,* 04/1889, 05/2118, 05/2641, 06/4484, 07/3293, 07/4358: *Considered,* 04/707, 04/1312, 05/2129, 06/871, 06/1004, 06/1649, 06/4470, 07/5431

Ghaidan v Mendoza see Ghaidan v Godin-Mendoza

Ghassemian v Secretary of State for Trade and Industry [2006] EWHC 1715 (Ch); [2007] B.C.C. 229, Ch D . . . .   *Digested,* 07/**571**

Ghazilian's Trade Mark Application; *sub nom* TINY PENIS Trade Mark [2002] E.T.M.R. 57; [2002] R.P.C. 33, App Person; affirming [2002] E.T.M.R. 56; [2001] R.P.C. 33; (2001) 24(4) I.P.D. 24027, TMR . . . .   *Digested,* 02/**2920**: *Considered,* 07/2681

GHE Realisations Ltd (formerly Gatehouse Estates Ltd), Re [2005] EWHC 2400 (Ch); [2006] 1 W.L.R. 287; [2006] 1 All E.R. 357; [2006] B.C.C. 139; *Times*, November 11, 2005, Ch D (Companies Ct) . . . .   *Digested,* 06/**2316**: *Applied,* 07/2389: *Considered,* 07/2391

Ghosh v General Medical Council [2001] UKPC 29; [2001] 1 W.L.R. 1915; [2001] U.K.H.R.R. 987; [2001] Lloyd's Rep. Med. 433; *Times*, June 25, 2001, PC (UK)   *Digested,* 01/**2894**: *Applied,* 02/5954, 07/1943: *Considered,* 02/1837

Giacomelli v Italy (59909/00) (2007) 45 E.H.R.R. 38, ECHR . . . .   *Considered,* 07/204

Gibbins v Max Edwards Ltd (Unreported, August 22, 2006), CC (Southport) [*Ex rel.* Browne Jacobson Solicitors 44 Castle Gate, Nottingham] . . . .   *Digested,* 07/**410**

Gibbon v Mitchell [1990] 1 W.L.R. 1304; [1990] 3 All E.R. 338, Ch D . . . .   *Digested,* 91/**1724**: *Applied,* 05/3420: *Considered,* 02/4713, 05/4304, 07/4247

Gibbs v Harding see Harding (Deceased), Re

Gibraltar European Elections, Re (C-145/04) see Spain v United Kingdom (C-145/04)

Gibson v United States [2007] UKPC 52; [2007] 1 W.L.R. 2367; *Times*, August 3, 2007, PC (Bah) . . . .   *Digested,* 07/**1672**

Gibson's Settlement Trusts, Re; *sub nom* Mellors v Gibson [1981] Ch. 179; [1981] 2 W.L.R. 1; [1981] 1 All E.R. 233; (1981) 125 S.J. 48; *Times*, May 20, 1980, Ch D .   *Digested,* 81/**2136**: *Applied,* 95/4030: *Considered,* 85/2636, 99/3676, 02/4808, 06/402: *Distinguished,* 07/4263

GIE Group Concorde v Master of the Vessel Suhadiwarno Panjan (C440/97) see GIE Groupe Concorde v Master of the Vessel Suhadiwarno Panjan (C440/97)

GIE Groupe Concorde v Master of the Vessel Suhadiwarno Panjan (C440/97); *sub nom* GIE Group Concorde v Master of the Vessel Suhadiwarno Panjan (C440/97) [2000] All E.R. (EC) 865; [1999] 2 All E.R. (Comm) 700; [1999] E.C.R. I-6307; [1999] C.L.C. 1976; [2000] I.L.Pr. 626, ECJ . . . .   *Digested,* 00/**764**: *Applied,* 05/604, 07/657: *Considered,* 04/578

GIE Reunion Europeenne v Zurich Seguros [2007] I.L.Pr. 19, Cass (F)

Giersch v Google Inc (B 795 569) [2007] E.T.M.R. 41, OHIM (Opposition Div) . . . . . .   *Digested*, 07/**2639**

Gil v Spain (56673/00) see Iglesias Gil v Spain (56673/00)

Gilbert v Spoor [1983] Ch. 27; [1982] 3 W.L.R. 183; [1982] 2 All E.R. 576; (1982) 44
P. & C.R. 239; (1982) 126 S.J. 260, CA (Civ Div) . . . .   *Digested*, 82/**2664**:
Cited, 07/3423: *Considered*, 96/5009

Gilbert Ash (Northern) Ltd v Modern Engineering (Bristol) Ltd; *sub nom* Modern
Engineering (Bristol) Ltd v Gilbert Ash (Northern) Ltd [1974] A.C. 689; [1973] 3
W.L.R. 421; [1973] 3 All E.R. 195; 1 B.L.R. 73; 72 L.G.R. 1; (1973) 117 S.J. 745,
HL; reversing 71 L.G.R. 162, CA (Civ Div) . . . .   *Digested*, 73/**262**:
Applied, 74/268, 81/188, 85/218, 88/461, 92/312, 93/2361:
Considered, 75/3180, 85/2604, 93/2519, 94/2797, 07/5011:
Distinguished, 74/267, 84/2722: *Followed*, 82/3441, 83/3961, 86/202,
93/301

Gilboy v Liverpool City Council see R. (on the application of Gilboy) v Liverpool City
Council

Gilby v Westminster City Council [2007] EWCA Civ 604; [2007] N.P.C. 81, CA (Civ
Div)

Giles v Law Society (1996) 8 Admin. L.R. 105; (1995) 92(38) L.S.G. 25; *Times*,
October 20, 1995, CA (Civ Div) . . . .   *Digested*, 96/**3917**:
Applied, 05/2730: *Approved*, 07/2801: *Considered*, 03/2824

Giles v Rhind A3/2007/0753, CA (Civ Div); affirming [2007] EWHC 687 (Ch);
[2007] Bus. L.R. 1470; [2007] 2 B.C.L.C. 531; [2007] B.P.I.R. 713, Ch D . . . . .   *Digested*, 07/**494**

Giles v Thompson; *joined cases* Devlin v Baslington; Sanders v Templar [1994] 1 A.C.
142; [1993] 2 W.L.R. 908; [1993] 3 All E.R. 321; [1993] R.T.R. 289; (1993) 143
N.L.J. 884; (1993) 137 S.J.L.B. 151; *Times*, June 1, 1993, HL; affirming (1993)
143 N.L.J. 284; *Times*, January 13, 1993, CA (Civ Div) . . . .   *Digested*, 93/**3332**:
Applied, 97/3159, 98/1453, 98/2497, 98/2505, 99/2454, 99/2455, 03/718,
07/1066, 07/4313: *Cited*, 99/2489: *Considered*, 95/1617, 96/2145, 97/960,
98/1454, 99/1406, 99/2462: *Distinguished*, 99/3411, 00/1460:
Followed, 97/1803, 99/392, 02/363: *Referred to*, 97/1787, 00/464

Gill v Lewis [1956] 2 Q.B. 1; [1956] 2 W.L.R. 962; [1956] 1 All E.R. 844; (1956) 100
S.J. 299, CA . . . .   *Digested*, 56/**4743**:
Applied, 62/1698, 65/2237: *Considered*, 82/152.u, 85/1877, 88/2030,
06/2674, 07/2725: *Distinguished*, 62/2478

Gillan v DPP; *sub nom* R. (on the application of Gillan) v DPP; R. (on the application
of Gillan) v Crown Court at Winchester [2007] EWHC 380 (Admin); [2007] 1
W.L.R. 2214; [2007] 2 Cr. App. R. 12; [2007] 2 Cr. App. R. (S.) 75; (2007) 171
J.P. 330; [2007] Crim. L.R. 486; (2007) 171 J.P.N. 676; *Times*, March 26,
2007, DC. . . . .   *Digested*, 07/**989**

Gillbard v Caradon DC [2006] EWHC 3233 (Admin); [2007] Env. L.R. D5, DC

Gillette Co v LA-Laboratories Oy [2007] E.T.M.R. 17, KKO (Fin) . . . .   *Digested*, 07/**2675**

Gilly v Directeur des Services Fiscaux du Bas-Rhin (C-336/96) [1998] All E.R. (EC)
826; [1998] S.T.C. 1014; [1998] E.C.R. I-2793; [1998] 3 C.M.L.R. 607; [1998]
B.T.C. 335; 1 I.T.L. Rep. 29, ECJ. . . . .   *Digested*, 98/**4638**:
Applied, 06/4252: *Considered*, 03/4148, 07/3974

Gingi v Secretary of State for Work and Pensions [2001] EWCA Civ 1685; [2002] 1
C.M.L.R. 20; [2002] Eu. L.R. 37, CA (Civ Div) . . . .   *Digested*, 02/**4208**:
Applied, 07/3875

Giniewski v France (64016/00) (2007) 45 E.H.R.R. 23, ECHR . . . .   *Considered*, 07/2185

Girling v Parole Board see R. (on the application of Girling) v Parole Board

Girling (Deceased) v Secretary of State for the Home Department see R. (on the
application of Girling) v Parole Board

GKN Bolts & Nuts Ltd (Automotive Division) Birmingham Works Sports & Social Club, Re;
sub nom Leek v Donkersley [1982] 1 W.L.R. 774; [1982] 2 All E.R. 855;
(1982) 79 L.S.G. 953; (1982) 126 S.J. 327, Ch D . . . .   *Digested*, 82/**283**:
Applied, 07/4264

Gladwell v Secretary of State for Trade and Industry [2007] I.C.R. 264, EAT. . . . .   *Digested*, 07/**1352**:
Applied, 07/1348, 07/1353

Glasgow Airport v Kirkman & Bradford [2007] CSIH 47; 2007 S.C. 742; [2007]
C.I.L.L. 2506; 2007 G.W.D. 18-316, IH (Ex Div); affirming 2007 G.W.D. 9-160,
OH

Glasgow City Council v McNab [2007] I.R.L.R. 476, EAT (SC) . . . .   *Digested*, 07/**5147**

Glass v Surrendran see Collier v Williams

Glaxo Group Ltd v Dowelhurst Ltd [2004] EWCA Civ 290; [2005] E.T.M.R. 104;
(2004) 27(6) I.P.D. 27059, CA (Civ Div); reversing in part [2004] E.T.M.R. 39;
(2004) 27(1) I.P.D. 27004, Ch D . . . .   *Digested*, 06/**2607**:
Distinguished, 07/2651

Glaxo Group Ltd v Genentech Inc A3/2007/1305, CA (Civ Div); affirming [2007]
EWHC 1416 (Pat); [2007] F.S.R. 35; (2007) 30(7) I.P.D. 30048, Ch D (Patents
Ct)

GlaxoSmithKline Biologicals SA v Sanofi Pasteur SA (t/a Aventis Pasteur) [2006]
EWHC 2333 (Pat); (2007) 30(1) I.P.D. 30005, Ch D (Patents Ct)

GlaxoSmithKline Ltd *v* Department of Health [2007] EWHC 1470 (Comm); [2007] 2
    All E.R. (Comm) 1140, QBD (Comm)
GlaxoSmithKline Services Unlimited *v* Commission of the European Communities (T-
    168/01) [2006] 5 C.M.L.R. 29, CFI (4th Chamber) . . . .   *Digested*, 07/**643**
Gleeson *v* RJ Hussey & Son (Unreported, May 5, 2007), CC (Swindon) [*Ex rel.*
    Andrew Granville Stafford, Barrister, 4 King's Bench Walk, Temple, London] . . . .   *Digested*, 07/**3139**
Glen International Ltd *v* Triplerose Ltd [2007] EWCA Civ 388; [2007] L. & T.R. 28;
    [2007] 26 E.G. 164, CA (Civ Div) . . . .   *Digested*, 07/**2755**
Glenboig Union Fireclay Co *v* Inland Revenue Commissioners 1922 S.C. (H.L.) 112;
    1922 S.L.T. 182; 12 T.C. 427, HL. . . . .   *Applied*, 52/**1669**:
                                    Considered, 07/4061: *Distinguished*, 62/2560, 67/1943
Glencore International AG *v* Alpina Insurance Co Ltd [2003] EWHC 2792 (Comm);
    [2004] 1 All E.R. (Comm) 766; [2004] 1 Lloyd's Rep. 111, QBD (Comm) . . . . .   *Digested*, 04/**2227**:
                                              Applied, 07/2506
Glencore International AG *v* Exter Shipping Ltd see Glencore International AG *v* Metro
    Trading International Inc (No.3)
Glencore International AG *v* Metro Trading International Inc (No.3); *sub nom* Glencore
    International AG *v* Exter Shipping Ltd [2002] EWCA Civ 528; [2002] 2 All E.R.
    (Comm) 1; [2002] C.L.C. 1090, CA (Civ Div); affirming (Unreported,
    November 8, 2001), QBD (Comm) . . . .   *Applied*, 07/355
Global Active Holdings Ltd *v* Revenue and Customs Commissioners [2006] V. & D.R.
    190; [2006] S.T.I. 2577, V&DTr . . . .   *Digested*, 07/**4313**
Global Multimedia International Ltd *v* ARA Media Services [2006] EWHC 3107 (Ch);
    [2007] 1 All E.R. (Comm) 1160; *Times*, August 1, 2006, Ch D . . . .   *Digested*, 07/**347**
Global Plant Ltd *v* Secretary of State for Health and Social Security; *sub nom* Global
    Plant Ltd *v* Secretary of State for Social Services [1972] 1 Q.B. 139; [1971] 3
    W.L.R. 269; [1971] 3 All E.R. 385; (1971) 11 K.I.R. 284; (1971) 115 S.J. 506,
    QBD . . . .   *Digested*, 71/**3949**:
                   Applied, 72/1184, 73/2963, 74/1188, 75/2262, 75/2913, 83/1207, 84/1203:
                           Considered, 07/4073: *Followed*, 76/878, 79/2532
Global Plant Ltd *v* Secretary of State for Social Services see Global Plant Ltd *v*
    Secretary of State for Health and Social Security
Globe Equities Ltd *v* Globe Legal Services Ltd; *joined cases* Globe Equities Ltd *v*
    Kotrie; Kotrie *v* Globe Equities Ltd [2000] C.P.L.R. 233; [1999] B.L.R. 232;
    Times, April 14, 1999; *Independent*, March 15, 1999, CA (Civ Div) . . . .   *Digested*, 99/**390**:
                     Applied, 00/423, 07/420: *Considered*, 02/393, 06/374
Globe Equities Ltd *v* Kotrie see Globe Equities Ltd *v* Globe Legal Services Ltd
Glover *v* Staffordshire Police Authority [2006] EWHC 2414 (Admin); [2007] I.C.R.
    661; [2007] A.C.D. 60; *Times*, October 24, 2006, QBD (Admin) . . . .   *Digested*, 07/**3026**
GM (EU National: Establishing Self-sufficiency: France), Re see GM (France) *v* Secretary
    of State for the Home Department
GM (France) *v* Secretary of State for the Home Department; *sub nom* GM (EU
    National: Establishing Self-sufficiency: France), Re [2006] UKAIT 59; [2007]
    Imm. A.R. 18, AIT . . . .   *Digested*, 07/**2368**
GMB *v* Allen [2007] I.R.L.R. 752; (2007) 104(33) L.S.G. 26; (2007) 151 S.J.L.B.
    1129, EAT . . . .   *Digested*, 07/**1404**
GMB (A Trade Union) *v* Securicor Omega Express Ltd see Securicor Omega Express
    Ltd *v* GMB (A Trade Union)
GO (Colombia) *v* Secretary of State for the Home Department; *sub nom* Ocampo *v*
    Secretary of State for the Home Department [2006] EWCA Civ 1276; [2007]
    Imm. A.R. 225; [2007] I.N.L.R. 49; (2006) 103(40) L.S.G. 36; *Times*, October
    27, 2006, CA (Civ Div). . . . .   *Digested*, 07/**2283**
Goatley (Stephen Maurice) *v* HM Advocate [2006] HCJAC 55; 2007 S.L.T. 14; 2006
    S.C.C.R. 463; [2007] Eu. L.R. 42; 2006 G.W.D. 33-690, HCJ . . . .   *Digested*, 07/**5168**
Godfrey *v* Torpey [2006] EWHC 1423 (Ch); [2007] B.P.I.R. 1063, Ch D
Godfrey *v* Torpy [2007] EWHC 919 (Ch); [2007] Bus. L.R. 1203; [2007] B.P.I.R.
    1538; *Times*, May 16, 2007, Ch D . . . .   *Digested*, 07/**2456**
Godin-Mendoza *v* Ghaidan see Ghaidan *v* Godin-Mendoza
Godwin *v* Swindon BC [2001] EWCA Civ 1478; [2002] 1 W.L.R. 997; [2001] 4 All
    E.R. 641; [2002] C.P. Rep. 13; *Independent*, October 19, 2001, CA (Civ Div) . . .   *Digested*, 01/**653**:
                       Considered, 02/476, 02/478, 02/491, 06/347, 07/433:
                             Distinguished, 02/1360: *Followed*, 02/291
Goel *v* Pick; *sub nom* Pick (Virdi's Trustee) *v* Goel [2006] EWHC 833 (Ch); [2007] 1
    All E.R. 982; [2006] R.T.R. 28; [2006] B.P.I.R. 827; *Times*, June 28, 2006, Ch D
    . . . .   *Digested*, 06/**2336**
Gokce *v* Scottish Ambulance Service (2007) 151 S.J.L.B. 1227, EAT
Gold Coast Ltd *v* Naval Gijon SA (The Hull 53) [2006] EWHC 1044; [2007] 1 All E.R.
    (Comm) 237; [2006] 2 Lloyd's Rep. 400, QBD (Comm) . . . .   *Digested*, 06/**214**
Golden Fleece Maritime Inc *v* ST Shipping and Transport Inc (The Elli); *sub nom* Golden
    Fleece Maritime Inc *v* ST Shipping and Transport Inc (The Frixos); A3/2007/
    2220, CA (Civ Div); affirming [2007] EWHC 1890 (Comm); [2007] 2 C.L.C.
    648, QBD (Comm)
Golden Fleece Maritime Inc *v* ST Shipping and Transport Inc (The Frixos) see Golden
    Fleece Maritime Inc *v* ST Shipping and Transport Inc (The Elli)

Golden Rabbit Trade Mark (I ZR 37/04) [2007] E.T.M.R. 30, BGH (Ger) . . . .   *Digested,* 07/**2659**

Golden Strait Corp v Nippon Yusen Kubishika Kaisha (The Golden Victory) [2007] UKHL 12; [2007] 2 A.C. 353; [2007] Bus. L.R. 997; [2007] 2 W.L.R. 691; [2007] 3 All E.R. 1; [2007] 2 All E.R. (Comm) 97; [2007] 2 Lloyd's Rep. 164; [2007] 1 C.L.C. 352; (2007) 157 N.L.J. 518; (2007) 151 S.J.L.B. 468; *Times,* March 30, 2007, HL; affirming [2005] EWCA Civ 1190; [2006] 1 W.L.R. 533; [2006] 1 All E.R. (Comm) 235; [2005] 2 Lloyd's Rep. 747; [2005] 2 C.L.C. 576; (2005) 102(43) L.S.G. 31; *Times,* October 21, 2005, CA (Civ Div); affirming [2005] EWHC 161 (Comm); [2005] 1 All E.R. (Comm) 467; [2005] 1 Lloyd's Rep. 443; [2005] 1 C.L.C. 138; *Times,* March 4, 2005, QBD (Comm) . . . .   *Digested,* 07/**3816**

Goldfarb v Poppleton see Eurocruit Europe Ltd (In Liquidation), Re

Goldman Williams Ltd, Re see City Vintners Ltd, Re

Goldsmiths (Jewellers) Ltd v Customs and Excise Commissioners (C-330/95) [1997] S.T.C. 1073; [1997] E.C.R. I-3801; [1997] 3 C.M.L.R. 978; [1997] B.T.C. 5380; [1997] B.V.C. 494; *Times,* July 25, 1997, ECJ (6th Chamber) . . . .   *Digested,* 97/**4974**:
Considered, 07/4323: *Subsequent proceedings,* 00/5285

Gomes v Trinidad and Tobago see Goodyer v Trinidad and Tobago

Gooch v Basildon DC (Unreported, April 20, 2007), CC (Southend) [*Ex rel.* Jonathan Pennington-Legh] . . . .   *Digested,* 07/**2410**

Goodchild v Bradbury [2006] EWCA Civ 1868; [2007] W.T.L.R. 463, CA (Civ Div) . .   *Digested,* 07/**3435**

Goode v Martin [2001] EWCA Civ 1899; [2002] 1 W.L.R. 1828; [2002] 1 All E.R. 620; [2002] C.P. Rep. 16; [2002] C.P.L.R. 74; [2002] C.L.C. 420; [2002] P.I.Q.R. P24; (2002) 152 N.L.J. 109; *Times,* January 24, 2002; *Independent,* January 16, 2002, CA (Civ Div); reversing [2001] 3 All E.R. 562, QBD (Admlty) . . . .   *Digested,* 02/**487**:
Applied, 07/350, 07/491: *Considered,* 02/486: *Distinguished,* 01/419

Goodes v East Sussex CC [2000] 1 W.L.R. 1356; [2000] 3 All E.R. 603; [2000] R.T.R. 366; (2001) 3 L.G.L.R. 6; [2000] B.L.G.R. 465; [2000] P.I.Q.R. P148; [2001] J.P.L. 70; [2000] E.G. 75 (C.S.); (2000) 97(26) L.S.G. 38; (2000) 150 N.L.J. 949; [2000] N.P.C. 65; *Times,* June 16, 2000; *Independent,* June 20, 2000, HL; reversing [1999] R.T.R. 210; (1999) 1 L.G.L.R. 364; (1999) 96(5) L.S.G. 36; (1999) 143 S.J.L.B. 38; *Times,* January 7, 1999, CA (Civ Div) . . . . . .   *Digested,* 00/**4237**:
Applied, 02/3314, 06/3533: *Considered,* 03/1947, 04/1818, 07/2870:
Followed, 01/4499, 04/2720

Goodeve-Docker v Leonard Ross & Craig see Yudt v Leonard Ross & Craig (A Firm)

Goodman v Goodman [2006] EWHC 1757 (Ch); [2006] W.T.L.R. 1807, Ch D . . . . . .   *Digested,* 07/**3965**

Goodman v Secretary of State for Constitutional Affairs [2006] EWHC 3669 (QB); [2007] 3 Costs L.R. 366, QBD . . . .   *Digested,* 07/**958**

Goodman (Setting of Minimum Term), Re; *sub nom* R. v Goodman (Aaron Leonard) [2006] EWHC 3435 (Admin), QBD (Admin) . . . .   *Considered,* 07/1041

Goodwin v Patent Office [1999] I.C.R. 302; [1999] I.R.L.R. 4; [1999] Disc. L.R. 104; *Times,* November 11, 1998, EAT . . . .   *Digested,* 98/**2114**:
Applied, 00/2125, 01/2242, 04/1209, 05/1147: *Considered,* 07/5115

Goodwin v United Kingdom (28957/95) [2002] I.R.L.R. 664; [2002] 2 F.L.R. 487; [2002] 2 F.C.R. 577; (2002) 35 E.H.R.R. 18; 13 B.H.R.C. 120; (2002) 67 B.M.L.R. 199; [2002] Fam. Law 738; (2002) 152 N.L.J. 1171; *Times,* July 12, 2002, ECHR . . . .   *Digested,* 02/**2532**:
Applied, 03/1310: *Considered,* 04/1261, 04/2814, 07/2261:
Followed, 02/1419, 03/2169

Goodwood Recoveries Ltd v Breen; *joined case* Breen v Slater [2005] EWCA Civ 414; [2006] 1 W.L.R. 2723; [2006] 2 All E.R. 533; [2007] 2 Costs L.R. 147, CA (Civ Div) . . . .   *Digested,* 06/**374**:
Applied, 06/395: *Considered,* 07/387, 07/404

Goodyer v Trinidad and Tobago; *joined case* Gomes v Trinidad and Tobago [2007] EWHC 2012 (Admin); (2007) 104(35) L.S.G. 34, QBD (Admin)

Google Inc v Copiepresse SCRL [2007] E.C.D.R. 5, RB (Brussels) . . . .   *Digested,* 07/**2515**

Gopakumar v General Medical Council C1/2007/0124(A); C1/2007/0124, CA (Civ Div); affirming [2006] EWHC 729 (Admin); [2007] LS Law Medical 228, QBD (Admin) . . . .   *Digested,* 07/**1950**

Gordon v Mitchell [2007] EWHC 1854 (Ch); [2007] 2 P. & C.R. DG22, Ch D

Gorman v Lambeth LBC see Kay v Lambeth LBC

Gorringe v Calderdale MBC; *sub nom* Calderdale MBC v Gorringe [2004] UKHL 15; [2004] 1 W.L.R. 1057; [2004] 2 All E.R. 326; [2004] R.T.R. 27; [2004] P.I.Q.R. P32; (2004) 101(18) L.S.G. 35; (2004) 148 S.J.L.B. 419; *Times,* April 2, 2004, HL; affirming [2002] EWCA Civ 595; [2002] R.T.R. 27; (2002) 99(22) L.S.G. 36; (2002) 146 S.J.L.B. 124; *Times,* May 16, 2002, CA (Civ Div) . . . .   *Digested,* 04/**2752**:
Applied, 04/1818, 05/2850, 05/2891, 06/3533, 07/4144:
Considered, 07/2870, 07/2939

Gorshkov v Monmouthshire CC [2007] P.A.D. 78, Planning Inspector

Gory v Kolver NO 21 B.H.R.C. 613, Const Ct (SA)

Gorzelik v Poland (44158/98) (2004) 38 E.H.R.R. 4, ECHR . . . .   *Digested,* 04/**1918**:
Applied, 07/2192: *Subsequent proceedings,* 05/2040

Goshawk Dedicated Ltd v Tyser & Co Ltd [2006] EWCA Civ 54; [2006] 1 All E.R. (Comm) 501; [2006] 1 Lloyd's Rep. 566; [2006] 1 C.L.C. 198; [2007] Lloyd's Rep. I.R. 224; *Times,* April 4, 2006; *Independent,* February 16, 2006, CA (Civ Div); reversing [2005] EWHC 461 (Comm); [2005] 2 All E.R. (Comm) 115; [2005] Lloyd's Rep. I.R. 379, QBD (Comm) . . . . *Digested,* 06/**2422**

Gosscott (Groundworks) Ltd, Re (1988) 4 B.C.C. 372; [1988] B.C.L.C. 363; [1988] P.C.C. 297; [1988] 2 F.T.L.R. 80, Ch D (Companies Ct) . . . . *Digested,* 88/**296**:
Applied, 07/**2440**

Gotham v Doodes; *sub nom* Doodes v Gotham [2006] EWCA Civ 1080; [2007] 1 W.L.R. 86; [2007] 1 All E.R. 527; [2007] 1 F.L.R. 373; [2007] 2 F.C.R. 712; [2006] B.P.I.R. 1178; [2007] Fam. Law 15; (2006) 156 N.L.J. 1325; [2006] N.P.C. 89; *Times,* August 14, 2006, CA (Civ Div); reversing [2005] EWHC 2576 (Ch); [2006] 1 W.L.R. 729; [2006] 2 F.L.R. 844; [2006] B.P.I.R. 36; [2006] Fam. Law 519; [2005] N.P.C. 134; *Times,* November 25, 2005, Ch D . . . . *Digested,* 06/**335**

Gould (t/a Garry's Private Hire) v Revenue and Customs Commissioners [2007] S.T.C. (S.C.D.) 502; [2007] S.T.I. 1334, Sp Comm. . . . . *Digested,* 07/**4161**

Gouldsmith v Mid Staffordshire General Hospitals NHS Trust [2007] EWCA Civ 397; [2007] LS Law Medical 363, CA (Civ Div) . . . . *Digested,* 07/**2917**

Gover v Propertycare Ltd [2006] EWCA Civ 286; [2006] 4 All E.R. 69; [2006] I.C.R. 1073; *Times,* May 1, 2006, CA (Civ Div); affirming UKEAT/0458/05/ZT, EAT . . *Digested,* 06/**1387**:
Applied, 07/**1423**: *Considered,* 07/**1426**

Governor of Wandsworth Prison v Kinderis; *sub nom* R. (on the application of Governor of Wandsworth Prison) v Kinderis [2007] EWHC 998 (Admin); *Times,* June 26, 2007, DC. . . . . *Digested,* 07/**1658**

Gowans v Lambert (Unreported, February 22, 2007), CC (Preston) [*Ex rel.* James Hogg, Barrister, St James's Chambers, 68 Quay Street, Manchester] . . . . *Digested,* 07/**3109**

Gower v Duffett (Unreported, April 13, 2007), CC (Guildford) [*Ex rel.* Alison Griffiths, 4 King's Bench Walk, Temple, London] . . . . *Digested,* 07/**3127**

Gower v Gower [1938] P. 106, PDAD . . . . *Applied,* 07/**241**

GP Noble Trustees Ltd v Berkeley Berry Birch Plc [2006] EWHC 982 (Ch); [2007] B.P.I.R. 1271, Ch D

Grace v BF Components Ltd see Enfield Technical Services Ltd v Payne

Gracechurch Management Services Ltd v Revenue and Customs Commissioners; *sub nom* Revenue and Customs Commissioners v Gracechurch Management Services Ltd [2007] EWHC 755 (Ch); [2007] B.T.C. 5468; [2007] B.V.C. 379; [2007] S.T.I. 1173; (2007) 151 S.J.L.B. 507; [2007] N.P.C. 39, Ch D; reversing [2007] B.V.C. 2192; [2006] V. & D.R. 330; [2006] S.T.I. 2588, V&DTr (London) . . . . *Digested,* 07/**4309**

GrafTech International Ltd v Commission of the European Communities (T246/01) see Tokai Carbon Co Ltd v Commission of the European Communities (T-236/01)

Graham v Western Bank (1865) 3 M. 617 . . . . *Considered,* 07/**4979**

Grant v Crown Prosecution Service . . . . *Doubted,* 07/**912**

Grant v Electro Centre Ltd (Unreported, June 22, 2006), CC (North Shields) [*Ex rel.* Professor David Grant, Northumbria University, Sutherland Building, Newcastle upon Tyne]. . . . . *Digested,* 07/**763**

Grant v Jamaica see Grant v Queen, The

Grant v Queen, The; *sub nom* Grant v Jamaica [2006] UKPC 2; [2007] 1 A.C. 1; [2006] 2 W.L.R. 835; 20 B.H.R.C. 243; [2006] Crim. L.R. 837, PC (Jam) . . . . *Digested,* 06/**807**

Grant v United Kingdom (32570/03) (2007) 44 E.H.R.R. 1, ECHR . . . . *Digested,* 07/**2261**

Graphite Electrodes Cartel Appeal, Re (C-289/04 P) see Showa Denko KK v Commission of the European Communities (C-289/04 P)

Graphite Electrodes Cartel Appeal, Re (C-301/04 P) see Commission of the European Communities v SGL Carbon AG (C-301/04 P)

Graphite Electrodes Cartel Appeal, Re (C-308/04 P) see SGL Carbon AG v Commission of the European Communities (C-308/04 P)

Graves v Graves [2007] EWCA Civ 660; [2007] 3 F.C.R. 26; (2007) 151 S.J.L.B. 926, CA (Civ Div) . . . . *Digested,* 07/**2715**

Gravier v Liege (293/83) [1985] E.C.R. 593; [1985] 3 C.M.L.R. 1, ECJ . . . . *Digested,* 85/**1412**:
Applied, 07/1630: *Considered,* 85/2790, 86/3524, 90/2154, 06/1231:
Referred to, 89/1621, 90/2120

Gray v Fire Alarm Fabrication Services Ltd; *sub nom* EH Humphries (Norton) Ltd v Fire Alarm Fabrication Services Ltd [2006] EWCA Civ 1496; [2007] I.C.R. 247; *Times,* November 22, 2006, CA (Civ Div); reversing [2006] EWHC 849 (QB), QBD . . . . *Digested,* 07/**2935**

Gray v Inland Revenue Commissioners; *sub nom* Executors of Lady Fox v Inland Revenue Commissioners; Lady Fox's Executors v Inland Revenue Commissioners [1994] S.T.C. 360; [1994] 38 E.G. 156; [1994] R.V.R. 129; [1994] S.T.I. 208; [1994] E.G. 32 (C.S.); [1994] N.P.C. 15; *Times,* February 24, 1994, CA (Civ Div); reversing [1992] 1 E.G.L.R. 211; [1992] 19 E.G. 173; [1992] 20 E.G. 121; [1991] E.G. 116 (C.S.), Lands Tr . . . . *Digested,* 95/**534**:
Applied, 96/443, 06/4240: *Considered,* 06/4245, 07/4066

Gray v Marlborough College [2006] EWCA Civ 1262; [2006] E.L.R. 516; (2006) 150 S.J.L.B. 1289, CA (Civ Div) . . . . *Digested,* 07/**1143**

Gray & Sons Builders (Bedford) Ltd v Essential Box Co Ltd [2006] EWHC 2520 (TCC);
108 Con. L.R. 49; [2006] C.I.L.L. 2395, QBD (TCC) . . . . *Digested,* 07/**395**
Grayan Building Services Ltd (In Liquidation), Re; *sub nom* Secretary of State for Trade
and Industry v Gray [1995] Ch. 241; [1995] 3 W.L.R. 1; [1995] B.C.C. 554;
[1995] 1 B.C.L.C. 276; (1995) 92(1) L.S.G. 36; (1994) 138 S.J.L.B. 227; *Times,*
November 24, 1994; *Independent,* December 12, 1994, CA (Civ Div) . . . .   *Digested,* 95/**582**:
       Applied, 00/660, 07/2418: *Considered,* 96/985, 99/610: *Followed,* 97/824
Great North Eastern Railway Ltd v JLT Corporate Risks Ltd [2006] EWHC 1478
(Comm); [2007] Lloyd's Rep. I.R. 38; [2006] P.N.L.R. 34, QBD (Comm) . . . . .   *Digested,* 06/**478**:
       Considered, 07/479
Great North Eastern Railway Ltd v Office of Rail Regulation [2006] EWHC 1942
(Admin); [2007] A.C.D. 13, QBD (Admin)
Greater Glasgow Health Board's Application, Re [1996] R.P.C. 207; (1996) 19(1) I.P.D.
19003, Ch D (Patents Ct) . . . .   *Digested,* 96/**4565**:
       Applied, 07/2556
Green v Durham City Council [2007] 43 E.G. 202, Lands Tr
Green v Gaul; *sub nom* Loftus (Deceased), Re [2006] EWCA Civ 1124; [2007] 1
W.L.R. 591; [2006] 4 All E.R. 1110; [2006] W.T.L.R. 1391; (2006-07) 9 I.T.E.L.R.
107; (2006) 156 N.L.J. 1365; [2007] 1 P. & C.R. DG12; *Times,* September 1,
2006, CA (Civ Div); affirming [2005] EWHC 406 (Ch); [2005] 1 W.L.R. 1890;
[2005] 2 All E.R. 700; [2005] W.T.L.R. 1325; (2004-05) 7 I.T.E.L.R. 640;
(2005) 102(22) L.S.G. 26; *Times,* March 28, 2005, Ch D . . . .   *Digested,* 06/**4076**:
       Applied, 07/476: *Considered,* 06/4383
Green v United Kingdom (63468/00) see Hobbs v United Kingdom (63684/00)
Green Lane Products Ltd v PMS International Group Ltd A3/2007/1867 and 1867A,
CA (Civ Div); affirming [2007] EWHC 1712 (Pat); [2007] E.C.C. 29; [2007]
E.C.D.R. 16; (2007) 30(8) I.P.D. 30054, Ch D (Patents Ct) . . . .   *Digested,* 07/**2533**
Greenhoff v Barnsley MBC [2006] I.C.R. 1514, EAT . . . .   *Digested,* 07/**1424**
Greenlands Ltd v Wilmshurst see London Association for the Protection of Trade v
Greenlands Ltd
Greensill v Greensill [2007] EWCA Civ 680; [2007] 2 F.L.R. 1127; [2007] Fam. Law
899, CA (Civ Div)
Greenweb Ltd v Wandsworth LBC [2007] 50 E.G. 110; [2007] R.V.R. 349, Lands Tr
Greenwich LBC v S [2007] EWHC 820 (Fam); [2007] 2 F.L.R. 154; [2007] 2 F.C.R.
141; [2007] Fam. Law 697, Fam Div . . . .   *Digested,* 07/**1826**
Gregg v Ashbrae Ltd [2006] NICA 17; [2006] N.I. 300, CA (NI) . . . .   *Digested,* 07/**4654**
Gregg v Scott [2005] UKHL 2; [2005] 2 A.C. 176; [2005] 2 W.L.R. 268; [2005] 4
All E.R. 812; [2005] P.I.Q.R. P24; [2005] Lloyd's Rep. Med. 130; (2005) 82
B.M.L.R. 52; (2005) 149 S.J.L.B. 145; *Times,* January 28, 2005; *Independent,*
February 3, 2005, HL; affirming [2002] EWCA Civ 1471; [2003] Lloyd's Rep.
Med. 105; (2003) 71 B.M.L.R. 16; (2002) 99(48) L.S.G. 27; (2002) 99(49)
L.S.G. 19; (2002) 146 S.J.L.B. 247; *Times,* November 4, 2002, CA (Civ Div) . . .   *Digested,* 05/**2837**:
       Applied, 07/2919
Gregory v Law Society [2007] EWHC 1724 (Admin); (2007) 104(28) L.S.G. 27, DC
Grendon v First Secretary of State; *sub nom* R. (on the application of Grendon) v First
Secretary of State [2006] EWHC 1711 (Admin); [2007] J.P.L. 275; [2006]
N.P.C. 90, QBD (Admin) . . . .   *Digested,* 07/**3250**
Greville v Venables [2007] EWCA Civ 878; (2007) 104(37) L.S.G. 36, CA (Civ Div)
Grieve v Revenue and Customs Commissioners [2007] S.T.I. 2244, V&D Tr
Grieves v FT Everard & Sons Ltd; *joined cases* Quinn v George Clark & Nem Ltd;
Mears v RG Carter Ltd; Jackson v Brock Plc; Rothwell v Chemical & Insulating
Co Ltd; Downey v Charles Evans Shopfitters Ltd; Storey v Clellands
Shipbuilders Ltd; Topping v Benchtown Ltd (formerly Jones Bros (Preston) Ltd);
Johnston v NEI International Combustion Ltd; Hindson v Pipe House Wharf
(Swansea) Ltd [2007] UKHL 39; [2007] 3 W.L.R. 876; [2007] 4 All E.R. 1047;
[2007] I.C.R. 1745; (2007) 104(42) L.S.G. 34; (2007) 157 N.L.J. 1542;
(2007) 151 S.J.L.B. 1366; *Times,* October 24, 2007, HL; affirming [2006] EWCA
Civ 27; [2006] 4 All E.R. 1161; [2006] I.C.R. 1458; (2006) 90 B.M.L.R. 88;
(2006) 103(7) L.S.G. 25; (2006) 156 N.L.J. 185; (2006) 150 S.J.L.B. 164;
Times, January 31, 2006; *Independent,* January 31, 2006, CA (Civ Div);
reversing [2005] EWHC 88 (QB); [2005] P.I.Q.R. P25; *Times,* March 22, 2005,
QBD . . . .   *Digested,* 07/**2919**:
       Cited, 06/325
Griffiths v Cork [2007] EWHC 1827 (Ch); (2007-08) 10 I.T.E.L.R. 313; [2007] 2 P. &
C.R. DG23, Ch D . . . .   *Digested,* 07/**3360**
Griffiths v DPP [2007] EWHC 619 (Admin); [2007] R.T.R. 44, QBD (Admin) . . . . . .   *Digested,* 07/**3537**
Griffiths v Solutia UK Ltd; *sub nom* Solutia UK Ltd (formerly Monsanto Chemicals UK
Ltd) v Griffiths [2001] EWCA Civ 736; [2001] C.P. Rep. 92; [2001] C.P.L.R.
419; [2001] 2 Costs L.R. 247; [2002] P.I.Q.R. P16, CA (Civ Div); affirming
[2001] 1 Costs L.R. 99, QBD . . . .   *Digested,* 01/**523**:
       Considered, 05/367, 07/385

Griffiths *v* St Helens MBC [2006] EWCA Civ 160; [2006] 1 W.L.R. 2233; [2006]
H.L.R. 29; (2006) 103(13) L.S.G. 24; (2006) 150 S.J.L.B. 364; [2006] N.P.C.
28; [2006] 2 P. & C.R. DG9; *Times*, April 24, 2006; *Independent*, March 9,
2006, CA (Civ Div) . . . .   *Digested,* 06/**2031**:
                             Considered, 07/2140
Grimes *v* Uttlesford DC [2007] P.A.D. 26, Planning Inspector
Grimmer *v* KLM Cityhopper UK [2005] I.R.L.R. 596, EAT . . . .   *Digested,* 05/**1279**:
                             Applied, 07/1349
Grosskrotzenburg Power Station, Re (C-431/92) see Commission of the European
Communities *v* Germany (C-431/92)
Groupe Danone *v* Commission of the European Communities (C-3/06 P) [2007] 4
C.M.L.R. 18, ECJ (2nd Chamber) . . . .   *Digested,* 07/**612**
Growth Management Ltd *v* Mutafchiev [2006] EWHC 2774 (Comm); [2007] 1
B.C.L.C. 645, QBD (Comm) . . . .   *Digested,* 07/**800**
Grundig-Verkaufs GmbH *v* Commission of the European Economic Community (58/
64) see Etablissements Consten Sarl *v* Commission of the European Economic
Community (56/64)
Grundy *v* British Airways Plc [2007] EWCA Civ 1020; (2007) 104(43) L.S.G. 33;
(2007) 151 S.J.L.B. 1401, CA (Civ Div)
Gschwind *v* Finanzamt Aachen-Aussenstadt (C-391/97) [2001] S.T.C. 331; [1999]
E.C.R. I-5451; [2001] 1 C.M.L.R. 3; [2000] B.T.C. 294; 2 I.T.L. Rep. 113, ECJ . .   *Digested,* 01/**5245**:
              Applied, 05/1469: *Distinguished,* 07/1622
Guccio Gucci SpA *v* Turkish Patent Institute [2007] E.T.M.R. 57, As Tic Mah (TR)
Guenat *v* Switzerland (24722/94) (Unreported), ECHR . . . .   *Applied,* 05/**3339**:
                             Considered, 07/3316
Guerin Automobiles *v* Commission of the European Communities (C-282/95 P)
[1997] E.C.R. I-1503; [1997] 5 C.M.L.R. 447, ECJ . . . .   *Followed,* 00/2367,
                             07/611
Guernsey *v* Jersey Fishermen's Association Ltd see Jersey Fishermen's Association Ltd
v Guernsey
Guildford BC *v* Brook (Valuation Officer) [2006] R.V.R. 333, VT . . . .   *Digested,* 07/**3343**
Guincho *v* Portugal (8990/80) see Guincho *v* Portugal (A/81)
Guincho *v* Portugal (A/81); *sub nom* Guincho *v* Portugal (8990/80) (1985) 7
E.H.R.R. 223, ECHR (1983) 5 E.H.R.R. CD274, Eur Comm HR . . . .   *Applied,* 07/2224
Guinness Mahon & Co Ltd *v* Kensington and Chelsea RLBC [1999] Q.B. 215; [1998] 3
W.L.R. 829; [1998] 2 All E.R. 272; [1998] Lloyd's Rep. Bank. 109; [1998]
C.L.C. 662; (1998) 95(13) L.S.G. 28; (1998) 148 N.L.J. 366; (1998) 142
S.J.L.B. 92; *Times*, March 2, 1998, CA (Civ Div) . . . .   *Digested,* 98/**304**:
                             Applied, 07/3438
Gulf Import and Export Co *v* Bunge SA [2007] EWHC 2667 (Comm); [2007] 2 C.L.C.
853, QBD (Comm)
Gulf Offshore NS Ltd *v* Canada 2007 FCA 302; 10 I.T.L. Rep. 172, CA (Can); affirming
2006 TCC 246; 8 I.T.L. Rep. 1097, Tax Ct (Can)
Gull *v* Gull [2007] EWCA Civ 900; [2007] Fam. Law 1063; (2007) 104(36) L.S.G.
30, CA (Civ Div)
Gupta (Prabha) *v* General Medical Council [2001] UKPC 61; [2002] 1 W.L.R. 1691;
[2002] I.C.R. 785; [2002] Lloyd's Rep. Med. 82; (2002) 64 B.M.L.R. 56; *Times*,
January 9, 2002, PC (UK) . . . .   *Digested,* 02/**1837**:
              Applied, 07/1943: *Considered,* 06/1808
Guzeli *v* Oberburgermeister der Stadt Aachen (C-4/05) [2006] E.C.R. I-10279;
[2007] 1 C.M.L.R. 25, ECJ (1st Chamber)
Guzzardi *v* Italy (A/39) (1981) 3 E.H.R.R. 333, ECHR . . . .   *Applied,* 06/2078,
      06/3409, 07/2172, 07/3913: *Considered,* 97/2766, 04/3152, 05/2030, 07/953,
                          07/3316: *Distinguished,* 98/3078
GW *v* Oldham MBC see W *v* Oldham MBC
Gwembe Valley Development Co Ltd (In Receivership) *v* Koshy (Account of Profits:
Limitations) see DEG-Deutsche Investitions und Entwicklungsgesellschaft mbH
v Koshy (Account of Profits: Limitations)
Gwynedd CC *v* ASDA Group [2007] P.A.D. 69, Planning Inspector
Gyamfi *v* WM Morrisons Supermarket Plc (Unreported, November 30, 2006), CC
(Epsom) [*Ex rel.* Nicholas Preston, Barrister, Clerksroom, First Floor, 199 Strand,
London] . . . .   *Digested,* 07/**3085**

H *v* Bury MBC see D *v* Bury MBC
H *v* DPP; *sub nom* R. (on the application of H) *v* DPP [2003] EWHC 878 (Admin);
(2003) 167 J.P. 486; (2003) 167 J.P.N. 732, QBD (Admin) . . . .   *Digested,* 03/**787**:
                        Considered, 06/849, 07/886
H *v* H [2007] EWHC 459 (Fam); [2007] 2 F.L.R. 548; [2007] Fam. Law 578; (2007)
151 S.J.L.B. 503, Fam Div . . . .   *Digested,* 07/**1700**

H v H (Child Abduction: Acquiescence); *sub nom* H (Minors) (Abduction: Acquiescence), Re [1998] A.C. 72; [1997] 2 W.L.R. 563; [1997] 2 All E.R. 225; [1997] 1 F.L.R. 872; [1997] 2 F.C.R. 257; [1997] Fam. Law 468; *Times*, April 17, 1997; *Independent*, April 15, 1997, HL; reversing [1996] 2 F.L.R. 570; [1996] 3 F.C.R. 425; [1996] Fam. Law 718; (1996) 93(35) L.S.G. 33; (1996) 140 S.J.L.B. 207; *Times*, August 14, 1996, CA (Civ Div) . . . .   *Digested*, 97/**387**:
         Applied, 07/1741: *Considered*, 99/2315, 00/2441, 03/5524:
         Followed, 99/2317

H v H (Validity of Japanese Divorce) [2006] EWHC 2989 (Fam); [2007] 1 F.L.R. 1318; [2007] 2 F.C.R. 39; [2007] Fam. Law 302, Fam Div. . . . .   *Digested*, 07/**1809**

H v L [2006] EWHC 3099 (Fam); [2007] 2 F.L.R. 162; [2007] 1 F.C.R. 430; *Times*, February 19, 2006, Fam Div . . . .   *Digested*, 07/**332**

H v M (Abduction: Rights of Custody) see Hunter v Murrow

H v Secretary of State for Health see R. (on the application of H) v Secretary of State for Health

H and R (Child Sexual Abuse: Standard of Proof), Re see H (Minors) (Sexual Abuse: Standard of Proof), Re

H Lundbeck A/S v Generics (UK) Ltd see Generics (UK) Ltd v H Lundbeck A/S

H Trust, Re see X Trust Co Ltd v RW

H (A Child), Re see L (A Child), Re

H (A Child), Re [2006] EWCA Civ 896; [2007] 1 F.L.R. 1028; [2007] Fam. Law 111, CA (Civ Div). . . . .   *Digested*, 07/**1770**

H (A Child), Re [2007] EWCA Civ 222; [2007] 2 F.L.R. 317; [2007] Fam. Law 706; (2007) 151 S.J.L.B. 260, CA (Civ Div)

H (A Child) v Adesina (Unreported, October 13, 2006), CC (Milton Keynes) [*Ex rel.* Nicholas J H Preston, Barrister, Clerksroom, 218 Strand, London] . . . .   *Digested*, 07/**3162**

H (A Child) v Alchin (Unreported, March 22, 2006), CC (Pontypridd) [*Ex rel.* Peter Collins, Clarendon Chambers, 1 Plowden Buildings, Temple, London] . . . .   *Digested*, 07/**3092**

H (A Child) v Binley Park Inn (Unreported, March 22, 2007), CC (Coventry) [*Ex rel.* Stephen Garner, Barrister, No. 8 Chambers, Fountain Court, Steelhouse Lane, Birmingham] . . . .   *Digested*, 07/**3205**

H (A Child) v First Choice Holidays & Flights Ltd (Unreported, June 13, 2007), CC (Coventry) [*Ex rel.* Stephen Garner, Barrister, No. 8 Chambers, Fountain Court, Steelhouse Lane, Birmingham] . . . .   *Digested*, 07/**3199**

H (A Child) v Jester Pub (Unreported, October 17, 2006), CC (Rawtenstall) [*Ex rel.* David Calvert, Barrister, St James Chambers, 68 Quay Street, Manchester] . . .   *Digested*, 07/**3197**

H (A Child) v Merck & Co Inc see Horne-Roberts v SmithKline Beecham Plc

H (A Child) v Merk & Co Inc see Horne-Roberts v SmithKline Beecham Plc

H (A Child) v SmithKline Beecham Plc see Horne-Roberts v SmithKline Beecham Plc

H (A Child) (Adoption: Consultation of Unmarried Fathers), Re; *sub nom* H (A Child) (Adoption: Disclosure), Re; *joined case* G (A Child) (Adoption: Disclosure), Re [2001] 1 F.L.R. 646; [2001] 1 F.C.R. 726; [2001] Fam. Law 175; *Times*, January 5, 2001, Fam Div . . . .   *Digested*, 01/**2541**:
         Considered, 07/1723

H (A Child) (Adoption: Disclosure), Re see H (A Child) (Adoption: Consultation of Unmarried Fathers), Re

H (A Child) (Care Order: Appropriate Local Authority), Re; *sub nom* H (A Child) (Care Proceedings: Designation of Local Authority), Re [2003] EWCA Civ 1629; [2004] Fam. 89; [2004] 2 W.L.R. 419; [2004] 1 F.L.R. 534; [2004] 1 F.C.R. 282; [2004] Fam. Law 105; (2004) 101(2) L.S.G. 27; *Times*, November 26, 2003; *Independent*, November 26, 2003, CA (Civ Div) . . . .   *Digested*, 04/**1456**:
         Applied, 07/1826: *Followed*, 04/1455

H (A Child) (Care Proceedings: Designation of Local Authority), Re see H (A Child) (Care Order: Appropriate Local Authority), Re

H (A Child) (Child Abduction), Re [2006] EWCA Civ 1247; [2007] 1 F.L.R. 242; [2007] 1 F.C.R. 345; [2006] Fam. Law 1014; (2006) 150 S.J.L.B. 1189, CA (Civ Div). . .   *Digested*, 07/**1734**:
         Applied, 07/1742

H (A Child) (Interim Care Order), Re [2002] EWCA Civ 1932; [2003] 1 F.C.R. 350, CA (Civ Div). . . . .   *Digested*, 03/**1515**:
         Applied, 07/1714: *Considered*, 06/1657

H (A Child) (Removal from Jurisdiction), Re see H (A Minor) (Abduction: Rights of Custody), Re

H (A Minor) (Abduction: Rights of Custody), Re; *sub nom* H (A Child) (Removal from Jurisdiction), Re [2000] 2 A.C. 291; [2000] 2 W.L.R. 337; [2000] 2 All E.R. 1; [2000] 1 F.L.R. 374; [2000] 1 F.C.R. 225; [2000] Fam. Law 310; (2000) 97(7) L.S.G. 40; (2000) 144 S.J.L.B. 101; *Times*, February 8, 2000; *Independent*, February 8, 2000, HL; affirming [2000] 1 F.L.R. 201; [2000] Fam. Law 80; (1999) 96(47) L.S.G. 30; (1999) 143 S.J.L.B. 283; *Times*, November 16, 1999; *Independent*, November 17, 1999, CA (Civ Div) . . . .   *Digested*, 00/**2447**:
         Applied, 07/1775

H (Abduction: Dominica: Corporal Punishment), Re; *sub nom* H (Abduction: Non-Convention Application), Re [2006] EWCA Civ 871; [2007] 1 F.L.R. 72; [2006] Fam. Law 829, CA (Civ Div); affirming [2006] EWHC 199 (Fam); [2006] 2 F.L.R. 314; [2006] Fam. Law 522, Fam Div. . . . .   *Digested*, 07/**1749**

H (Abduction: Non-Convention Application), Re see H (Abduction: Dominica: Corporal Punishment), Re

H (Children), Re; *sub nom* H (Children) (Residence Order), Re [2007] EWCA Civ 529; [2007] 2 F.C.R. 621, CA (Civ Div) . . . .   *Digested,* 07/**1793**

H (Children) (Residence Order), Re see H (Children), Re

H (Children) (Residence Order: Condition), Re see H (Children: Residence Order: Relocation), Re

H (Children: Residence Order: Relocation), Re; *sub nom* H (Children) (Residence Order: Condition), Re [2001] EWCA Civ 1338; [2001] 2 F.L.R. 1277; [2001] 3 F.C.R. 182; [2001] Fam. Law 870; *Times,* August 29, 2001, CA (Civ Div) . . . .   *Digested,* 01/**2597**: *Considered,* 07/1788

H (Minors) (Abduction: Acquiescence), Re see H v H (Child Abduction: Acquiescence)

H (Minors) (Abduction: Custody Rights), Re; *joined case* S (Minors) (Abduction: Custody Rights), Re [1991] 2 A.C. 476; [1991] 3 W.L.R. 68; [1991] 3 All E.R. 230; [1991] 2 F.L.R. 262; [1992] F.C.R. 45; [1991] Fam. Law 427; (1991) 141 N.L.J. 891; (1991) 135 S.J.L.B. 52, HL; affirming [1991] 2 W.L.R. 62; [1991] 1 All E.R. 836; [1991] 1 F.L.R. 95; [1991] F.C.R. 243; [1991] Fam. Law 177; (1990) 140 N.L.J. 1192; *Independent,* August 20, 1990, CA (Civ Div) . . . .   *Digested,* 91/**2528**: *Applied,* 95/3444, 07/1741: *Considered,* 94/3156

H (Minors) (Child Abuse: Threshold Conditions), Re see H (Minors) (Sexual Abuse: Standard of Proof), Re

H (Minors) (Sexual Abuse: Standard of Proof), Re; *sub nom* H (Minors) (Child Abuse: Threshold Conditions), Re; H and R (Child Sexual Abuse: Standard of Proof), Re [1996] A.C. 563; [1996] 2 W.L.R. 8; [1996] 1 All E.R. 1; [1996] 1 F.L.R. 80; [1996] 1 F.C.R. 509; [1996] Fam. Law 74; (1995) 145 N.L.J. 1887; (1996) 140 S.J.L.B. 24; *Times,* December 15, 1995; *Independent,* January 17, 1996, HL; affirming [1995] 1 F.L.R. 643; [1995] 2 F.C.R. 384; [1995] Fam. Law 401; (1995) 159 J.P.N. 338, CA (Civ Div) . . . .   *Digested,* 96/**632**: *Applied,* 96/490, 96/496, 98/2401, 00/949, 01/1975, 01/2566, 02/1636, 04/1463, 04/1481, 05/570, 05/1529, 05/1559, 05/1560, 05/4191, 06/1043, 06/2435, 06/2859, 06/4107, 07/2680: *Considered,* 96/482, 96/482, 96/610, 01/721, 01/2549, 06/1680: *Distinguished,* 01/2550: *Followed,* 02/1105, 04/1458, 05/2825

HA v MB (Brussels II Revised: Article (11)7 Application); *sub nom* A (Brussels II Revised: Article (11)7 Application), Re [2007] EWHC 2016 (Fam); [2007] Fam. Law 1058; (2007) 104(36) L.S.G. 28; *Times,* November 2, 2007, Fam Div . . . .   *Digested,* 07/**1735**

Haahr Petroleum Ltd v Abenra Havn (C-90/94) [1997] E.C.R. I-4085; [1998] 1 C.M.L.R. 771; [1998] C.E.C. 68, ECJ (6th Chamber) . . . .   *Digested,* 98/**4634**: *Applied,* 00/2405, 07/1607

Habib Bank Ltd v Central Bank of Sudan [2006] EWHC 1767 (Comm); [2007] 1 W.L.R. 470; [2007] 1 All E.R. (Comm) 53; [2006] 2 Lloyd's Rep. 412; [2006] 2 C.L.C. 176; *Times,* September 11, 2006, QBD (Comm) . . . .   *Digested,* 06/**504**

Hachette Filipacchi Presse SA v Saprotex International (Proprietary) Ltd [2007] EWHC 63 (Ch); (2007) 30(3) I.P.D. 30019, Ch D

Hackney LBC v Rottenberg see R. (on the application of Hackney LBC) v Rottenberg

Hackney LBC v Sagnia UKEAT/0600/03/DM, UKEAT/0135/04/DM, EAT . . . .   *Considered,* 07/1343

Haden Bill Electrical Ltd, Re see R&H Electric Ltd v Haden Bill Electrical Ltd

Haderer v Finanzamt Wilmersdorf (C-445/05) [2007] 3 C.M.L.R. 17; [2007] C.E.C. 881; [2007] S.T.I. 1734, ECJ (3rd Chamber)

Hadkinson v Hadkinson [1952] P. 285; [1952] 2 All E.R. 567; [1952] 2 T.L.R. 416, CA   *Digested,* 52/**2648**: *Applied,* 65/3225, 84/2660, 85/3504, 85/3513, 97/2484, 05/1645, 05/1664: *Considered,* 82/2936, 84/1671, 84/2593, 86/2835, 90/3581, 07/1698: *Distinguished,* 79/1399

Hadley v Baxendale 156 E.R. 145; (1854) 9 Ex. 341, Ex Ct . . . .   *Applied,* 47-51/5368, 47-51/5562, 53/3775, 55/2559, 56/50, 66/3146, 66/11174, 66/12340, 67/3623, 77/2881, 79/2391, 80/640, 81/138, 86/980, 90/2764, 91/1316, 93/517, 93/4846, 98/4384, 99/1379, 01/1507, 03/5438, 05/959: *Considered,* 47-51/9490, 61/2343, 67/3615, 68/1013, 69/881, 73/3466, 87/2429, 90/670, 94/5413, 96/401, 96/1196, 97/989, 97/3839, 00/5981, 07/1064: *Distinguished,* 47/2561, 47-51/2561, 47-51/2566, 85/1282, 99/3946: *Followed,* 67/3527, 69/3379, 88/1065, 98/1472: *Referred to,* 76/155.u, 83/4027

Hafner v Secretary of State for the Home Department see R. (on the application of Hafner) v Secretary of State for the Home Department

Haftpflichtverband der Deutsche IndustrieVersicherungsverein auf Gegenseitigkeit (HDI) v Societe Axa France IARD [2007] I.L.Pr. 28, Cass (F) . . . .   *Digested,* 07/**660**

Haggerstone v Burns (Unreported, November 21, 2006), CC (Salford) [*Ex rel.* James Hogg, Pupil Barrister, St James Chambers, 68 Quay Street, Manchester] . . . . .   *Digested,* 07/**3143**

Hague v NamTai Electronics Inc [2006] UKPC 52; [2007] 2 B.C.L.C. 194, PC (BVI) . .   *Digested,* 07/**549**

Haim v Kassenzahnarztliche Vereinigung Nordrhein (C-424/97) [2000] E.C.R. I-5123; [2002] 1 C.M.L.R. 11, ECJ . . . .   *Digested,* 02/**1571**: *Applied,* 07/1650

Haines v Hill see Hill v Haines

Haji-Ioannou v Frangos [2006] EWCA Civ 1663; [2007] 3 All E.R. 938; [2007] C.P.
    Rep. 14; [2007] 2 Costs L.R. 253; (2006) 156 N.L.J. 1918, CA (Civ Div);
    affirming [2006] EWHC 279 (Ch); [2006] 2 Costs L.R. 315; Times, April 7,
    2006, Ch D . . . .   *Digested*, 07/**463**:
                                                                    Cited, 07/463: *Considered*, 07/403
Hakansson v Sweden (11855/85) see Hakansson v Sweden (A/171)
Hakansson v Sweden (A/171); *sub nom* Sturesson v Sweden (A/171); Hakansson v
    Sweden (11855/85) (1991) 13 E.H.R.R. 1, ECHR (1989) 11 E.H.R.R. CD52, Eur
    Comm HR . . . .   *Applied*, 98/3064,
                                                         98/3145, 01/564, 07/2226: *Distinguished*, 98/3121
Haladjian Freres SA v Commission of the European Communities (T-204/03) [2007] 4
    C.M.L.R. 27, CFI (1st Chamber)
Hale v Hants and Dorset Motor Services Ltd [1947] 2 All E.R. 628; (1948) 112 J.P. 47;
    46 L.G.R. 50; (1948) 92 S.J. 26, CA. . . . .   *Digested*, 47-51/**4436**:
                                                                              Considered, 07/3465
Hale v Waldock; *sub nom* Metropolis Motorcycles Ltd, Re [2006] EWHC 364 (Ch);
    [2007] 1 B.C.L.C. 520, Ch D (Companies Ct) . . . .   *Digested*, 07/**586**
Halifax Life Ltd v Equitable Life Assurance Society [2007] EWHC 503 (Comm);
    [2007] 2 All E.R. (Comm) 672; [2007] 1 Lloyd's Rep. 528; (2007) 23 Const.
    L.J. 373; [2007] 17 E.G. 172 (C.S.); [2007] Bus. L.R. D101, QBD (Comm) . . . .   *Digested*, 07/**1077**
Halifax Plc v Customs and Excise Commissioners (C-255/02) [2006] Ch. 387;
    [2006] 2 W.L.R. 905; [2006] S.T.C. 919; [2006] E.C.R. I-1609; [2006] 2
    C.M.L.R. 36; [2006] C.E.C. 690; [2006] B.T.C. 5308; [2006] B.V.C. 377;
    [2006] S.T.I. 501; Times, February 27, 2006, ECJ. . . . .   *Digested*, 06/**4467**:
                                                     Applied, 06/4462, 07/4308: *Considered*, 06/5131, 07/4159
Halifax Plc v Okin [2007] EWCA Civ 567; (2007) 151 S.J.L.B. 706, CA (Civ Div)
Hall Hunter Partnership v Waverley BC [2007] P.A.D. 40, Planning Inspector
Hall (David) v DPP see Knuller (Publishing, Printing and Promotions) Ltd v DPP
Halliburton Energy Services Inc v Smith International (North Sea) Ltd; *sub nom*
    Halliburton Energy Services Inc's Patent [2006] EWCA Civ 185; [2006] R.P.C.
    26, CA (Civ Div) . . . .   *Digested*, 07/**2631**
Halliburton Energy Services Inc v Smith International (North Sea) Ltd [2006] EWCA
    Civ 1599; [2007] Bus. L.R. 460; [2007] R.P.C. 17; (2007) 30(1) I.P.D. 30002,
    CA (Civ Div) . . . .   *Digested*, 07/**2625**
Halliburton Energy Services Inc v Smith International (North Sea) Ltd [2006] EWCA
    Civ 1715; (2007) 30(2) I.P.D. 30009, CA (Civ Div); affirming [2005] EWHC
    1623 (Pat); [2005] Info. T.L.R. 323; [2006] R.P.C. 2, Ch D (Patents Ct) . . . . . .   *Digested*, 05/**2441**:
                                                     Applied, 06/2468, 07/2632: *Considered*, 06/2535
Halliburton Energy Services Inc's Patent see Halliburton Energy Services Inc v Smith
    International (North Sea) Ltd
Halpern v Halpern [2006] EWHC 1728 (Comm); [2007] Q.B. 88; [2006] 3 W.L.R.
    946; [2006] 3 All E.R. 1139; [2006] 2 All E.R. (Comm) 484; [2006] 2 C.L.C.
    479; (2006) 156 N.L.J. 1137; Times, July 18, 2006, QBD (Comm) . . . .   *Digested*, 06/**743**
Halpern v Halpern [2007] EWCA Civ 291; [2007] 3 W.L.R. 849; [2007] 3 All E.R.
    478; [2007] 2 All E.R. (Comm) 330; [2007] 2 Lloyd's Rep. 56; [2007] 1 C.L.C.
    527; Times, May 14, 2007, CA (Civ Div); affirming [2006] EWHC 603 (Comm);
    [2006] 2 All E.R. (Comm) 251; [2006] 2 Lloyd's Rep. 83; [2006] 3 F.C.R. 76,
    QBD (Comm) . . . .   *Digested*, 07/**799**
Halsey (Inspector of Taxes) v Marks & Spencer Plc see Marks & Spencer Plc v Halsey
    (Inspector of Taxes)
Hamid v Secretary of State for the Home Department see Januzi v Secretary of State
    for the Home Department
Hamilton v Al-Fayed (Costs); *sub nom* Hamilton v Fayed (Costs); Al-Fayed v Hamilton
    (Costs) [2002] EWCA Civ 665; [2003] Q.B. 1175; [2003] 2 W.L.R. 128; [2002]
    3 All E.R. 641; [2002] C.P. Rep. 48; [2002] 3 Costs L.R. 389; [2002]
    E.M.L.R. 42; (2002) 99(25) L.S.G. 34; (2002) 146 S.J.L.B. 143; Times, June 17,
    2002; Independent, July 1, 2002, CA (Civ Div); affirming Times, July 25, 2001,
    QBD . . . .   *Digested*, 02/**393**:
                                                         Considered, 04/288, 04/313, 04/328, 07/361
Hamilton v Allied Domecq Plc [2007] UKHL 33; 2007 S.C. (H.L.) 142; 2007 S.L.T.
    697; (2007) 151 S.J.L.B. 984; 2007 G.W.D. 23-390, HL; affirming 2006 S.C.
    221; 2005 S.L.T. 1151; 2005 G.W.D. 37-697, IH (2 Div); reversing 2004 S.L.T. 191;
    2003 G.W.D. 31-877, OH . . . .   *Digested*, 06/**5162**
Hamilton v Fayed (Costs) see Hamilton v Al-Fayed (Costs)
Hamilton v GMB (Northern Region) [2007] I.R.L.R. 391, EAT. . . . .   *Digested*, 07/**1351**
Hamilton v Malcolm Group Ltd (Unreported, November 17, 2006), CC (Birmingham)
    [Ex rel. Stephen Garner, 8 Fountain Court, Steelhouse Lane, Birmingham] . . . .   *Digested*, 07/**2083**
Hamilton v Malcolm Group Ltd (Quantum) (Unreported, November 17, 2006), CC
    (Birmingham) [Ex rel. Stephen Garner, Barrister, 8 Fountain Court, Steelhouse
    Lane, Birmingham]. . . . .   *Digested*, 07/**3093**
Hamilton v Tandberg Television Ltd EAT/65/02/ST, EAT . . . .   *Applied*, 07/**1318**
Hamling v Coxlease School Ltd [2007] I.C.R. 108; [2007] I.R.L.R. 8, EAT. . . . .   *Digested*, 07/**1349**
Hammersmith and Fulham LBC v Pivcevic [2006] EWHC 1709 (Admin); [2006] E.L.R.
    594, QBD (Admin). . . . .   *Digested*, 07/**1261**

Hammerton v Hammerton [2007] EWCA Civ 248; [2007] 2 F.L.R. 1133; [2007] 3
F.C.R. 107; [2007] Fam. Law 798; *Times*, April 12, 2007, CA (Civ Div) . . . .   *Digested*, 07/**948**
Hammond v Commissioner of Police of the Metropolis [2004] EWCA Civ 830;
[2004] I.C.R. 1467; [2005] P.I.Q.R. P1; (2004) 101(27) L.S.G. 30; (2004) 148
S.J.L.B. 758; *Times*, June 24, 2004, CA (Civ Div) . . . .   *Digested*, 04/**1814**:
                                                            Applied, 07/5270: *Considered*, 07/2082
Hammonds (A Firm) v Pro-fit USA Ltd [2007] EWHC 1998 (Ch); (2007) 104(35)
L.S.G. 38, Ch D (Companies Ct)
Hampshire CC v Beer (t/a Hammer Trout Farm) see R. (on the application of Beer (t/a
Hammer Trout Farm)) v Hampshire Farmers Markets Ltd
Hampshire CC v Supportways Community Services Ltd see R. (on the application of
Supportways Community Services Ltd) v Hampshire CC
Hampson v Department of Education and Science [1991] 1 A.C. 171; [1990] 3 W.L.R.
42; [1990] 2 All E.R. 513; [1990] I.C.R. 511; [1990] I.R.L.R. 302; (1990) 154
L.G. Rev. 811; (1990) 140 N.L.J. 853; (1990) 134 S.J. 1123, HL; reversing [1990]
2 All E.R. 25; [1989] I.C.R. 179; [1989] I.R.L.R. 69; (1989) 86(13) L.S.G. 43;
(1989) 133 S.J. 151, CA (Civ Div); affirming [1988] I.C.R. 278; [1988] I.R.L.R.
87, EAT . . . .   *Digested*, 90/**80**:
                                    Applied, 91/452, 99/2029, 99/2029: *Considered*, 91/1672, 07/2338:
                                                                         Referred to, 93/1774
Hanbury Charity v Revenue and Customs Commissioners [2007] S.T.I. 2238, V&DTr
(Manchester)
Hancock v Security Industry Authority see Nicholds v Security Industry Authority
Handels- og Kontorfunktionaerernes Forbund i Danmark v Dansk Arbejdsgiverforening
Ex p. Danfoss A/S (109/88); *sub nom* Union of Clerical and Commercial
Employees v Danish Employers Association Ex p. Danfoss A/S (109/88) [1989]
E.C.R. 3199; [1991] 1 C.M.L.R. 8; [1991] I.C.R. 74; [1989] I.R.L.R. 532; *Times*,
October 28, 1989, ECJ . . . .   *Digested*, 91/**4078**:
                                    Applied, 96/6958, 07/1367: *Considered*, 90/1915, 98/5825, 05/1261:
                                                                         Followed, 04/1254
Handelsveem BV v Coreck Maritime GmbH (C-387/98) see Coreck Maritime GmbH v
Handelsveem BV (C-387/98)
Handelswekerij GJ Bier BV v Mines de Potasse d'Alsace SA (21/76) [1978] Q.B. 708;
[1977] 3 W.L.R. 479; [1976] E.C.R. 1735; [1977] 1 C.M.L.R. 284; (1977) 121 S.J.
677; *Times*, December 6, 1976, ECJ . . . .   *Digested*, 77/**1283**:
                          Considered, 92/2790, 96/7098, 06/646, 07/666: *Distinguished*, 02/629:
                                            Followed, 95/705, 98/770, 06/631: *Referred to*, 97/895
Handi-Craft Co v B Free World Ltd [2007] EWHC 10 (Pat); [2007] E.C.D.R. 21, Ch D
(Patents Ct) . . . .   *Digested*, 07/**2547**
Hankinson v Revenue and Customs Commissioners [2007] S.T.I. 2854, Sp Comm
Hannon v 169 Queens Gate Ltd [2000] 1 E.G.L.R. 40; [2000] 09 E.G. 179; *Times*,
November 23, 1999, Ch D . . . .   *Digested*, 99/**3697**:
                                                                         Applied, 07/2729
Hans Brochier Holdings Ltd v Exner [2006] EWHC 2594 (Ch); [2007] B.C.C. 127,
Ch D . . . .   *Digested*, 07/**2420**
Hanson v Middlesbrough BC; *sub nom* R. (on the application of Hanson) v
Middlesbrough BC [2006] EWHC 1700 (Admin); [2006] R.A. 320, QBD
(Admin) . . . .   *Digested*, 07/**2842**
Hape v R. 22 B.H.R.C. 585, Sup Ct (Can)
Harcourt v FEF Griffin [2007] EWHC 1500 (QB); [2007] P.I.Q.R. Q9, QBD . . . .   *Digested*, 07/**511**
Harding v Revenue and Customs Commissioners CH/2007/APP/0269, Ch D; affirming
[2007] S.T.C. (S.C.D.) 553; [2007] S.T.I. 1437, Sp Comm. . . . .   *Digested*, 07/**3986**
Harding v Wealands [2006] UKHL 32; [2007] 2 A.C. 1; [2006] 3 W.L.R. 83; [2006] 4
All E.R. 1; [2006] 2 C.L.C. 193; [2006] R.T.R. 35; (2006) 156 N.L.J. 1136;
(2006) 150 S.J.L.B. 917; *Times*, July 6, 2006, HL; reversing [2004] EWCA Civ
1735; [2005] 1 W.L.R. 1539; [2005] 1 All E.R. 415; [2005] 2 C.L.C. 411; [2005]
R.T.R. 20; (2005) 155 N.L.J. 59; *Times*, January 5, 2005, CA (Civ Div);
reversing [2004] EWHC 1957 (QB), QBD . . . .   *Digested*, 06/**635**:
                                                                         Considered, 06/641
Harding (Deceased), Re; *sub nom* Gibbs v Harding [2007] EWHC 3 (Ch); [2007] 1 All
E.R. 747; [2007] W.T.L.R. 479; (2006–07) 9 I.T.E.L.R. 563, Ch D . . . .   *Digested*, 07/**3960**
Hardy v Pembrokeshire CC (Permission to Appeal) [2006] EWCA Civ 240; [2006]
Env. L.R. 28; [2007] J.P.L. 284; [2006] N.P.C. 34, CA (Civ Div) . . . .   *Digested*, 06/**519**
Hardy v Sefton MBC [2006] EWHC 1928 (Admin); [2007] R.A. 140, QBD (Admin) . .   *Digested*, 07/**2832**
Hardys & Hansons Plc v Lax [2005] EWCA Civ 846; [2005] I.C.R. 1565; [2005]
I.R.L.R. 726; (2005) 102(29) L.S.G. 31; *Times*, July 26, 2005, CA (Civ Div) . . .   *Digested*, 05/**1300**:
                                                            Applied, 05/1290, 07/1399
Haresfield Court Tenants Association v Revenue and Customs Commissioners see
Wanklin v Revenue and Customs Commissioners
Haringey LBC v C (A Child) [2006] EWHC 1620 (Fam); [2007] 1 F.L.R. 1035; [2006]
Fam. Law 1016; (2006) 103(34) L.S.G. 32, Fam Div . . . .   *Digested*, 07/**1675**
Haringey LBC v Kurtoglu [2007] P.A.D. 57, Planning Inspector
Haringey LBC v S [2006] EWHC 2001 (Fam); [2007] 1 F.L.R. 387, Fam Div . . . .   *Digested*, 07/**1730**

Harland & Wolff Pension Trustees Ltd v Aon Consulting Financial Services Ltd [2006]
EWHC 1778 (Ch); [2007] I.C.R. 429; [2006] Pens. L.R. 201, Ch D . . . .   *Digested*, 06/**2960**

Harland & Wolff Plc v McIntyre see McIntyre v Harland & Wolff Plc

Harouki v Kensington and Chelsea RLBC [2007] EWCA Civ 1000; [2007] N.P.C. 108;
Times, November 12, 2007, CA (Civ Div) . . . .   *Digested*, 07/**2163**

Harper v Interchange Group Ltd [2007] EWHC 1834 (Comm); (2007) 104(36) L.S.G.
28, QBD (Comm)

Harper (t/a Tee Time Catering) v Revenue and Customs Commissioners [2007] S.T.I.
2248, V&DTr (Manchester)

Harris v Scholfield Roberts & Hall see Arthur JS Hall & Co v Simons

Harris v Scholfield Roberts & Hill see Arthur JS Hall & Co v Simons

Harris & Russell v Slingsby [1973] 3 All E.R. 31; [1973] I.C.R. 454; [1973] I.R.L.R. 221;
15 K.I.R. 157; (1973) 8 I.T.R. 433, NIRC . . . .   *Digested*, 73/**1131**:
        Applied, 07/1339: *Considered*, 86/1267

Harris Calnan Construction Co Ltd v Ridgewood (Kensington) Ltd [2007] EWHC 2738
(TCC); [2007] C.I.L.L. 2525, QBD (TCC)

Harris Patent [1985] R.P.C. 19, Ch D (Patents Ct) . . . .   *Considered*, 96/**4564**,
        07/2556: *Referred to*, 93/3145, 96/4565

Harrison v Revenue and Customs Commissioners [2006] EWHC 2844 (Ch); [2007]
R.T.R. 13; *Times*, January 8, 2007, Ch D . . . .   *Digested*, 07/**1043**

Harrison v Secretary of State for the Home Department see R. (on the application of
Harrison) v Secretary of State for the Home Department

Harrods Ltd v Baker (Valuation Officer) [2007] R.A. 247, Lands Tr

Harrow LBC v Qazi see Qazi v Harrow LBC

Harrow LBC v Quazi see Qazi v Harrow LBC

Hart Investments Ltd v Fidler [2006] EWHC 2857 (TCC); [2007] B.L.R. 30; [2007]
T.C.L.R. 1; 109 Con. L.R. 67; [2006] C.I.L.L. 2397, QBD (TCC) . . . .   *Digested*, 07/**433**

Hart Investments Ltd v Fidler (t/a Terence Fidler Partnership); *joined case* Hart
Investments Ltd v Larchpark Ltd (In Liquidation) [2007] EWHC 1058 (TCC);
[2007] B.L.R. 526; 112 Con. L.R. 33; [2007] P.N.L.R. 26, QBD (TCC) . . . .   *Digested*, 07/**752**

Hart Investments Ltd v Larchpark Ltd [2007] EWHC 291 (TCC); [2007] B.C.C. 541;
[2007] B.L.R. 160; 112 Con. L.R. 23, QBD (TCC) . . . .   *Digested*, 07/**512**

Hart Investments Ltd v Larchpark Ltd (In Liquidation) see Hart Investments Ltd v Fidler
(t/a Terence Fidler Partnership)

Hartley v Magill see Porter v Magill

Harwood v Wrexham CBC [2007] P.A.D. 74, Planning Inspector

Hasan v Bulgaria (30985/96) (2002) 34 E.H.R.R. 55; 10 B.H.R.C. 646, ECHR . . . . .   *Digested*, 01/**3486**:
        Applied, 06/1239, 07/2192

Hasan v Commissioner of Police of the Metropolis [2006] Po. L.R. 295, EAT . . . . . .   *Digested*, 07/**1340**

HASASIT & ALZA/Treatment of multi-drug resistant cancer (T923/03) [2007] E.P.O.R. 14,
EPO (Technical Bd App) . . . .   *Digested*, 07/**2577**

Hasham v Zenab (Executrix of Harji) [1960] A.C. 316; [1960] 2 W.L.R. 374; (1960)
104 S.J. 125, PC (EA) . . . .   *Digested*, 60/**3282**:
        Applied, 01/3418: *Considered*, 07/472

Hassan v Barnet LBC see R. (on the application of Mei Ling Lin) v Barnet LBC

Hasselblad (GB) Ltd v Commission of the European Communities (86/82) [1984]
E.C.R. 883; [1984] 1 C.M.L.R. 559; [1984] F.S.R. 321; *Times*, February 25, 1984,
ECJ . . . .   *Digested*, 84/**1378**:
        Considered, 07/621

Hastens Sangar AB v Rock Raamsveld BV [2006] E.T.M.R. 68, RB (Den Haag) . . . . . .   *Digested*, 07/**2642**

Hastings-Bass Trustees v Inland Revenue Commissioners see Hastings-Bass
(Deceased), Re

Hastings-Bass (Deceased), Re; *sub nom* Hastings-Bass Trustees v Inland Revenue
Commissioners [1975] Ch. 25; [1974] 2 W.L.R. 904; [1974] 2 All E.R. 193;
[1974] S.T.C. 211; [1974] T.R. 87; (1974) 118 S.J. 422, CA (Civ Div) . . . .   *Digested*, 74/**993**:
        Applied, 83/3364, 01/5515, 03/4497, 04/2802, 05/4304, 05/4305,
        06/4398: *Considered*, 01/5508, 03/4501, 05/2997, 07/3429

Hatton v Chafes (A Firm) [2003] EWCA Civ 341; [2003] P.N.L.R. 24; (2003) 147
S.J.L.B. 356, CA (Civ Div) . . . .   *Applied*, 03/**431**:
        Followed, 07/479

Hatton v Hopkins [2005] EWHC 3337 (Ch); [2007] 2 Costs L.R. 172, Ch D . . . .   *Digested*, 07/**392**

Hatton v Sutherland see Barber v Somerset CC

Hatton v United Kingdom (36022/97) [2002] 1 F.C.R. 732; (2002) 34 E.H.R.R. 1; 11
B.H.R.C. 634; *Times*, October 8, 2001, ECHR . . . .   *Digested*, 01/**5378**:
        Applied, 07/2263: *Subsequent proceedings*, 04/1984

Hatton v United Kingdom (36022/97) (2003) 37 E.H.R.R. 28; 15 B.H.R.C. 259;
Times, July 10, 2003, ECHR (Grand Chamber) . . . .   *Digested*, 04/**1984**:
        Applied, 04/1373: *Considered*, 04/2763, 04/3042: *Distinguished*, 07/3256:
        Previous proceedings, 01/5378

Haupl v Lidl Stiftung & Co KG (C246/05) [2007] E.T.M.R. 61; [2007] Bus. L.R. D89,
ECJ (3rd Chamber) . . . .   *Digested*, 07/**2676**

Hautala v Council of the European Union (T-14/98) [1999] E.C.R. II-2489; [1999] 3
C.M.L.R. 528, CFI . . . .   *Digested*, 00/**2393**:
        Affirmed, 02/1547: *Applied*, 07/1539

Havering LBC v Special Educational Needs and Disability Tribunal; *sub nom* R. (on the application of Havering LBC) v Special Educational Needs and Disability Tribunal [2006] EWHC 2344 (Admin); [2007] E.L.R. 24; (2006) 150 S.J.L.B. 1289, QBD (Admin) . . . . *Digested, 07/1257*

Haw v Westminster Magistrates Court [2007] EWHC 2960 (Admin); *Times,* December 31, 2007, QBD (Admin)

Haward v Fawcetts (A Firm) [2006] UKHL 9; [2006] 1 W.L.R. 682; [2006] 3 All E.R. 497; [2006] P.N.L.R. 25; [2006] 10 E.G. 154 (C.S.); [2006] N.P.C. 25; *Times,* March 3, 2006, HL; reversing [2004] EWCA Civ 240; [2004] P.N.L.R. 34; (2004) 148 S.J.L.B. 355, CA (Civ Div); reversing [2003] P.N.L.R. 36, QBD . . . *Digested, 06/472*:
Considered, 07/475

Hawk Insurance Co Ltd, Re [2001] EWCA Civ 241; [2002] B.C.C. 300; [2001] 2 B.C.L.C. 480, CA (Civ Div); reversing [2001] B.C.C. 57, Ch D (Companies Ct) . . . . *Digested, 02/2714*:
Applied, 02/2715, 03/2440, 07/2448: Considered, 06/2362, 06/2381:
Followed, 05/2333

Hawkes v Cuddy see Cuddy v Hawkes

Hawkes v Cuddy; *sub nom* Neath Rugby Ltd, Re; *joined case* Cuddy v Hawkes [2007] EWHC 1789 (Ch); [2007] B.C.C. 671; *Times,* August 14, 2007, Ch D . . . *Digested, 07/563*

Hawkes Hill Publishing Co Ltd (In Liquidation), Re; *sub nom* Ward v Perks [2007] B.C.C. 937; [2007] B.P.I.R. 1305; (2007) 151 S.J.L.B. 743, Ch D

Haycocks v Neville [2007] EWCA Civ 78; [2007] 12 E.G. 156; [2007] 4 E.G. 186 (C.S.), CA (Civ Div) . . . . *Digested, 07/3365*

Hayden v Hayden [1992] 1 W.L.R. 986; [1993] 2 F.L.R. 16; [1992] P.I.Q.R. Q111; [1993] Fam. Law 466; *Times,* April 8, 1992, CA (Civ Div) . . . . *Digested, 93/1395*:
Distinguished, 98/931, 07/1056

Hayes v Humberside Valuation Tribunal [1998] R.A. 37, CA (Civ Div); affirming [1997] R.A. 236; [1997] E.G. 6 (C.S.); [1997] N.P.C. 4, QBD [*Ex rel. -*] . . . . *Digested, 98/4299*:
Applied, 07/2835

HB (Albania) v Secretary of State for the Home Department [2007] EWCA Civ 569; [2007] Imm. A.R. 756, CA (Civ Div)

HB (Ethiopia) v Secretary of State for the Home Department; *joined cases* JL (Sierra Leone) v Secretary of State for the Home Department; EB (Kosovo) v Secretary of State for the Home Department; FI (Nigeria) v Secretary of State for the Home Department [2006] EWCA Civ 1713; [2007] Imm. A.R. 396; [2007] I.N.L.R. 150; (2007) 104(1) L.S.G. 12, CA (Civ Div) . . . . *Digested, 07/2307*

HBC Hamburg Bulk Carriers Gmbh & Co KG v Tangshan Haixing Shipping Co Ltd (The Fu Ning Hai) [2006] EWHC 3250 (Comm); [2007] 1 All E.R. (Comm) 1127; [2007] 2 Lloyd's Rep. 223, QBD (Comm) . . . . *Digested, 07/3802*

HBOS Plc v Revenue and Customs Commissioners [2007] B.V.C. 2394, V&DTr (Edinburgh)

HE v Secretary of State for the Home Department; *sub nom* HE (DRC: Credibility and Psychiatric Reports), Re [2004] UKIAT 321; [2005] Imm. A.R. 119, IAT . . . . . . *Digested, 06/2222*:
Considered, 07/337

HE (DRC: Credibility and Psychiatric Reports), Re see HE v Secretary of State for the Home Department

Healthcare at Home Ltd v Genzyme Ltd [2006] CAT 29; [2007] Comp. A.R. 474, CAT *Digested, 07/628*

Healthcare at Home Ltd v Genzyme Ltd [2006] CAT 30; [2007] Comp. A.R. 500, CAT *Digested, 07/619*

Healthcare Leasing Ltd v Revenue and Customs Commissioners [2007] B.V.C. 2529, V&DTr (London)

Hearn v Younger [2002] EWHC 963 (Ch); [2003] O.P.L.R. 45; [2005] Pens. L.R. 49; [2002] W.T.L.R. 1317, Ch D . . . . *Digested, 04/2802*:
Considered, 07/3044

Heath v Commissioner of Police of the Metropolis [2004] EWCA Civ 943; [2005] I.C.R. 329; [2005] I.R.L.R. 270; [2004] Po. L.R. 259; (2004) 148 S.J.L.B. 913; *Times,* July 22, 2004, CA (Civ Div); affirming [2003] Po. L.R. 273, EAT . . . . . . *Digested, 04/1221*:
Considered, 07/1439: Distinguished, 07/1340

Heddens v Esseydric [2007] I.L.Pr. 6, Cass (F)

Hedrich v Standard Bank London Ltd [2007] EWHC 1656 (QB); [2007] P.N.L.R. 31, QBD

Heil v Rankin; *joined cases* Rees v Mabco (102) Ltd (Non-Pecuniary Damages); Schofield v Saunders & Taylor Ltd; Ramsay v Rivers; Kent v Griffiths (Non-Pecuniary Damages); W (A Child) v Northern General Hospital NHS Trust; Annable v Southern Derbyshire HA; Connolly v Tasker [2001] Q.B. 272; [2000] 2 W.L.R. 1173; [2000] 3 All E.R. 138; [2000] I.R.L.R. 334; [2000] P.I.Q.R. Q187; [2000] Lloyd's Rep. Med. 203; (2000) 97(14) L.S.G. 41; (2000) 150 N.L.J. 464; (2000) 144 S.J.L.B. 157; *Times,* March 24, 2000; *Independent,* March 28, 2000, CA (Civ Div) . . . . *Digested, 00/1478*:
Applied, 07/3063: Considered, 00/1529, 00/6165, 01/612, 01/1585, 01/6421:
Followed, 00/1495, 00/1500, 00/1511, 00/1644, 00/1733:
Previous proceedings, 99/1534, 00/4203: Subsequent proceedings, 00/1492

Heilbut Symons & Co v Buckleton [1913] A.C. 30, HL . . . . *Applied, 47-51/1705,*
47-51/4200, 57/3208, 61/7971, 66/10832, 03/2433, 07/2735:
Considered, 65/3520, 70/358: Followed, 00/876

Heintz van Landewyck Sarl v Commission of the European Communities (209/78)
[1980] E.C.R. 3125; [1981] 3 C.M.L.R. 134, ECJ . . . . *Digested,* 82/**1301**:
Applied, 85/1326, 05/555: *Followed,* 02/587, 07/615
Hellard, Re see Pinson Wholesale Ltd, Re
Hellborg v Sweden (47473/99) (2007) 45 E.H.R.R. 3, ECHR . . . . *Digested,* 07/**2204**
Helmet Integrated Systems Ltd v Tunnard [2006] EWCA Civ 1735; [2007] I.R.L.R. 126;
[2007] F.S.R. 16, CA (Civ Div); affirming [2006] F.S.R. 41, PCC . . . . *Digested,* 07/**1324**:
Considered, 07/1342
Hemat v Medical Council [2006] IEHC 187; [2007] E.C.C. 12, HC (Irl) . . . . *Digested,* 07/**654**
Hemmingway v Smith Roddam (A Firm) [2003] EWCA Civ 1342; (2003) 147 S.J.L.B.
1089, CA (Civ Div) *Applied,* 07/350
Hems v Poly Implants Prosthesis (Unreported, August 30, 2006), CC (Nottingham)
[*Ex rel.* Freeth Cartwright LLP Solicitors, Express Buildings, 29 Upper Parliament
Street, Nottingham] . . . . *Digested,* 07/**1063**
Henderson v Scottish Ministers see Somerville v Scottish Ministers
Hendricks v Commissioner of Police of the Metropolis see Commissioner of Police of
the Metropolis v Hendricks
Hendrikman v Magenta Druck & Verlag GmbH (C-78/95) [1997] Q.B. 426; [1997] 2
W.L.R. 349; [1996] All E.R. (EC) 944; [1996] E.C.R. I-4943; [1996] I.L.Pr. 752;
Times, October 17, 1996, ECJ (5th Chamber) . . . . *Digested,* 96/**1100**:
Considered, 06/464, 06/644, 07/507
Hendrix v Raad van Bestuur van het Uitvoeringsinstituut Werknemersverzekeringen
(C-287/05) [2007] 3 C.M.L.R. 46, ECJ (Grand Chamber)
Henry Boot Construction Ltd v Alstom Combined Cycles Ltd [2005] EWCA Civ 814;
[2005] 1 W.L.R. 3850; [2005] 3 All E.R. 832; [2005] 2 C.L.C. 63; [2005]
B.L.R. 437; 101 Con. L.R. 52; (2005) 102(30) L.S.G. 28, CA (Civ Div). . . . . . . *Digested,* 05/**656**:
Applied, 07/2759
Henwood v Barlow Clowes International Ltd (In Liquidation) A2/2007/1757, CA (Civ
Div); reversing [2007] EWHC 1579 (Ch); [2007] B.P.I.R. 1329, Ch D
(Bankruptcy Ct)
Hepburn v Chief Constable of Thames Valley; *sub nom* Chief Constable of Thames
Valley v Hepburn [2002] EWCA Civ 1841; [2002] Po. L.R. 388; (2003) 147
S.J.L.B. 59; *Times,* December 19, 2002, CA (Civ Div) . . . . *Digested,* 03/**3484**:
Distinguished, 07/4191
Hepworth Group Ltd v Stockley [2006] EWHC 3626 (Ch); [2007] 2 All E.R. (Comm)
82, Ch D (Leeds). . . . . *Digested,* 07/**3437**
Herbst v Germany (20027/02) [2007] E.L.R. 363, ECHR
Herczegfalvy v Austria (A/242-B) (1993) 15 E.H.R.R. 437, ECHR . . . . *Digested,* 93/**2154**:
Applied, 03/2958, 07/2197: *Considered,* 01/4431, 03/2158, 05/2823,
06/2860, 06/2861: *Referred to,* 00/4322
Herd v Inland Revenue Commissioners see Inland Revenue Commissioners v Herd
Herefordshire Council v White see White v Herefordshire Council
Herlan Edmunds Engineering (Pty) Ltd, Re see Fourie v Le Roux
Herman v Revenue and Customs Commissioners [2007] S.T.C. (S.C.D.) 571; [2007]
W.T.L.R. 1201; [2007] S.T.I. 1441, Sp Comm . . . . *Digested,* 07/**3991**
Herschel Engineering Ltd v Breen Property Ltd [2000] B.L.R. 272; (2000) 2 T.C.L.R.
473; 70 Con. L.R. 1; (2000) 16 Const. L.J. 366; *Times,* May 10, 2000, QBD
(TCC) . . . . *Digested,* 00/**809**:
Applied, 03/643, 04/598, 07/395
Hertfordshire CC v Department for the Environment, Food and Rural Affairs see R. (on
the application of Hertfordshire CC) v Department for the Environment, Food
and Rural Affairs
Hertsmere BC v Harty see South Buckinghamshire DC v Porter (No.1)
Hertsmere BC v McCarthy & Stone (Developments) Ltd [2007] P.A.D. 77, Planning
Inspector
Hetherington (UK) Ltd v Secretary of State for the Environment [1994] 2 P.L.R. 9 . . . . *Considered,* 07/3266
Heuer v Germany (C-189/94) see Dillenkofer v Germany (C-178/94)
Hewden Tower Cranes Ltd v Wolffkran GmbH [2007] EWHC 857 (TCC); [2007] 2
Lloyd's Rep. 138; [2007] B.L.R. 273; [2007] I.L.Pr. 43, QBD (TCC) . . . . *Digested,* 07/**659**
Hewitt v DS Smith (UK) Ltd (Unreported, March 16, 2007), CC (Redditch) [*Ex rel.*
Stephen Garner, Barrister, No.8 Fountain Court, Steelhouse Lane, Birmingham] *Digested,* 07/**2078**
Hewlett-Packard Development Co LP v Expansys UK Ltd [2005] EWHC 1495 (Ch);
[2007] E.C.C. 9; [2005] E.T.M.R. 111; (2005) 28(8) I.P.D. 28062, Ch D . . . . . *Digested,* 05/**2573**
HEWLETT-PACKARD/Adding and averaging circuit (T571/03) [2006] E.P.O.R. 44, EPO
(Technical Bd App) . . . . *Digested,* 07/**2592**
HG Construction Ltd v Ashwell Homes (East Anglia) Ltd [2007] EWHC 144 (TCC);
[2007] B.L.R. 175; 112 Con. L.R. 128; [2007] C.I.L.L. 2453, QBD (TCC). . . . . . *Digested,* 07/**725**
HH (Ethiopia) v Secretary of State for the Home Department [2007] EWCA Civ 306;
[2007] Imm. A.R. 563, CA (Civ Div). . . . . *Digested,* 07/**2291**
HH (Iraq) v Secretary of State for the Home Department; *sub nom* HH (Rule 23:
Meaning and Extent: Iraq), Re [2007] UKAIT 36; [2007] Imm. A.R. 602, AIT
HH (Rule 23: Meaning and Extent: Iraq), Re see HH (Iraq) v Secretary of State for the
Home Department

HH (Serbia) *v* Secretary of State for the Home Department; *sub nom* HH (Sponsor as
Respresentative: Serbia), Re [2006] UKAIT 63; [2007] Imm. A.R. 108, AIT ...   *Digested, 07/***2372**
HH (Sponsor as Respresentative: Serbia), Re see HH (Serbia) *v* Secretary of State for the
Home Department
HHO Licensing Ltd (In Liquidation), Re; *sub nom* Clements *v* Henry Hadaway
Organisation Ltd [2007] EWHC 2953 (Ch); [2007] B.P.I.R. 1363, Ch D
(Companies Ct)
Hibbert Pownall & Newton (A Firm) *v* Whitehead see Whitehead *v* Searle
HIBT Ltd *v* Revenue and Customs Commissioners [2007] B.V.C. 2280, V&DTr
Hickling *v* Baker [2007] EWCA Civ 287; [2007] 1 W.L.R. 2386; [2007] 4 All E.R.
390; [2007] C.P. Rep. 30; [2007] B.P.I.R. 346; (2007) 104(16) L.S.G. 26;
Times, April 19, 2007, CA (Civ Div) . . . .   *Digested, 07/***2399**
Hicks *v* Chief Constable of South Yorkshire; *sub nom* Hicks *v* Wright; *joined case* Wafer
v Wright [1992] 2 All E.R. 65; [1992] P.I.Q.R. P433; *Times,* March 9, 1992;
Independent, March 11, 1992; *Guardian,* March 11, 1992, HL; affirming [1992] 1
All E.R. 690; [1992] P.I.Q.R. P63; *Independent,* May 16, 1991; *Guardian,* May 8,
1991, CA (Civ Div) . . . .   *Digested, 92/***1554**:
Applied, 96/2115, 07/2919
Hicks *v* Davies (Inspector of Taxes); *sub nom* Davies (Inspector of Taxes) *v* Hicks
[2005] EWHC 847 (Ch); [2005] S.T.C. 850; 78 T.C. 95; [2005] B.T.C. 331;
[2005] S.T.I. 918; *Times,* May 27, 2005, Ch D; affirming [2005] S.T.C. (S.C.D.)
165; [2005] W.T.L.R. 329; [2004] S.T.I. 2544, Sp Comm . . . .   *Digested, 05/***4005**
Hicks *v* Wright see Hicks *v* Chief Constable of South Yorkshire
Hicks Developments Ltd *v* Chaplin [2007] EWHC 141 (Ch); [2007] 16 E.G. 192, Ch D   *Digested, 07/***3354**
High Peak BC *v* High Peak Land Ltd [2007] P.A.D. 51, Planning Inspector
High Quality Lifestyles Ltd *v* Watts [2006] I.R.L.R. 850, EAT . . . .   *Digested, 07/***1331**
High Street Services *v* Bank of Credit and Commerce International see MS Fashions
Ltd *v* Bank of Credit and Commerce International SA (In Liquidation)
High Tech International AG *v* Deripaska [2006] EWHC 3276 (QB); [2007] E.M.L.R. 15,
QBD . . . .   *Digested, 07/***443**
Highland Council *v* Revenue and Customs Commissioners; *sub nom* Highland Council
v VAT and Duties Tribunal [2007] CSIH 36; 2007 S.C. 533; 2007 S.L.T. 529;
[2007] S.T.I. 1588; 2007 G.W.D. 17-312, IH (Ex Div); affirming [2006] B.V.C.
2693; [2006] S.T.I. 1714, V&DTr (Edinburgh) . . . .   *Digested, 07/***5567**
Highland Council *v* VAT and Duties Tribunal see Highland Council *v* Revenue and
Customs Commissioners
HIGHLAND INDUSTRIES/Request for reimbursement of appeal fee (G3/03) [2005]
E.P.O.R. 25, EPO (Enlarged Bd App) . . . .   *Considered, 07/*2605
HIH Casualty & General Insurance Ltd, Re; *sub nom* McMahon *v* McGrath; McGrath *v*
Riddell; *joined cases* FAI General Insurance Co Ltd, Re; World Marine &
General Insurances Pty Ltd, Re; FAI Insurances Ltd, Re [2006] EWCA Civ 732;
[2007] Bus. L.R. 250; [2007] 1 All E.R. 177; [2007] B.C.C. 335; *Times,* July 5,
2006, CA (Civ Div); affirming [2005] EWHC 2125 (Ch); [2006] 2 All E.R. 671,
Ch D (Companies Ct) . . . .   *Digested, 06/***2366**:
Applied, 06/2367
HIH Casualty & General Insurance Ltd *v* JLT Risk Solutions Ltd (formerly Lloyd
Thompson Ltd) [2007] EWCA Civ 710; [2007] 2 All E.R. (Comm) 1106; [2007]
2 Lloyd's Rep. 278; [2007] 2 C.L.C. 62; [2007] Lloyd's Rep. I.R. 717; (2007)
104(30) L.S.G. 35, CA (Civ Div); affirming [2006] EWHC 485 (Comm); [2006]
1 C.L.C. 499; [2006] Lloyd's Rep. I.R. 493; (2006) 103(14) L.S.G. 32, QBD
(Comm) . . . .   *Digested, 07/***2467**
HIH Casualty & General Insurance Ltd *v* New Hampshire Insurance Co [2001] EWCA
Civ 735; [2001] 2 All E.R. (Comm) 39; [2001] 2 Lloyd's Rep. 161; [2001] C.L.C.
1480; [2001] Lloyd's Rep. I.R. 596, CA (Civ Div); affirming [2001] 1 Lloyd's
Rep. 378; [2001] C.L.C. 481, QBD (Comm) . . . .   *Digested, 01/***3840**:
Applied, 03/3908, 04/2245, 06/2673: *Considered,* 07/2748:
Distinguished, 05/2405, 06/2427
Hilali, Re see Hilali *v* Governor of Whitemoor Prison
Hilali *v* Central Court of Criminal Proceedings, Madrid; *sub nom* Hilali *v* Spain [2006]
EWHC 1239 (Admin); [2007] 1 W.L.R. 768; [2006] 4 All E.R. 435; [2006]
Extradition L.R. 154; [2006] A.C.D. 92, QBD (Admin) . . . .   *Digested, 07/***1661**
Hilali *v* Governor of Whitemoor Prison; *sub nom* Hilali, Re [2007] EWHC 939 (Admin);
[2007] 3 W.L.R. 621; [2007] 3 All E.R. 422; *Times,* June 6, 2007, QBD
(Admin) . . . .   *Digested, 07/***1664**
Hilali *v* Spain see Hilali *v* Central Court of Criminal Proceedings, Madrid
Hill *v* Anderton see R. *v* Manchester Stipendiary Magistrate Ex p. Hill
Hill *v* Clifford see Clifford *v* Timms
Hill *v* Haines; *sub nom* Haines *v* Hill [2007] EWCA Civ 1284; [2007] 3 F.C.R. 785;
[2007] B.P.I.R. 1280; [2007] 50 E.G. 109 (C.S.); (2007) 151 S.J.L.B. 1597;
[2007] N.P.C. 132; *Times,* December 12, 2007, CA (Civ Div); reversing [2007]
EWHC 1012 (Ch); [2007] 2 F.L.R. 983; [2007] 2 F.C.R. 513; [2007] B.P.I.R.
727; [2007] Fam. Law 890; [2007] N.P.C. 58; *Times,* May 14, 2007, Ch D . . . .   *Digested, 07/***2454**:
Applied, 07/2408
Hill *v* Morgan see Morgan *v* Hill

Hill v Phillips see Branston & Gothard Ltd, Re
Hill v Spread Trustee Co Ltd; sub nom Nurkowski, Re [2006] EWCA Civ 542; [2007]
  Bus. L.R. 1213; [2007] 1 W.L.R. 2404; [2007] 1 All E.R. 1106; [2006] B.C.C.
  646; [2007] 1 B.C.L.C. 450; [2006] B.P.I.R. 789; [2006] W.T.L.R. 1009; *Times*,
  July 10, 2006, CA (Civ Div); affirming [2005] EWHC 336 (Ch); [2005] B.P.I.R.
  842, Ch D . . . .   *Digested*, 06/**2392**:
                 Distinguished, 07/2442
Hill v Van Der Merwe [2007] EWHC 1613 (Ch); [2007] B.P.I.R. 1562, Ch D (Bristol)
Hills v Chief Constable of Essex [2006] EWHC 2633 (Admin); (2007) 171 J.P. 14,
  QBD (Admin) . . . .   *Digested*, 07/**357**
Hindawi v Secretary of State for the Home Department see R. (on the application of
  Clift) v Secretary of State for the Home Department
Hindawi v Secretary of State for the Home Department see R. (on the application of
  Hindawi) v Secretary of State for the Home Department
Hindle v Birtwistle [1897] 1 Q.B. 192, QBD . . . .   *Applied*, 47-51/6273,
          55/1069, 55/1082, 60/1261, 61/7172: *Considered*, 07/5269:
            Distinguished, 61/3480: *Followed*, 47-51/7877
Hindson v Pipe House Wharf (Swansea) Ltd see Grieves v FT Everard & Sons Ltd
Hinsley v Revenue and Customs Commissioners; *joined case* Milsom v Revenue and
  Customs Commissioners [2007] S.T.C. (S.C.D.) 63; [2007] S.T.I. 197, Sp
  Comm . . . .   *Digested*, 07/**4054**
Hiranand v Harilela (2007-08) 10 I.T.E.L.R. 218, CA (HK); affirming (2005-06) 8
  I.T.E.L.R. 376, CFI (HK)
Hirani v Hirani (1983) 4 F.L.R. 232, CA (Civ Div) . . . .   *Digested*, 83/**1118**:
           Applied, 93/5217, 03/1603, 07/1834
Hirons v Kraft Foods Plc (Unreported, August 29, 2006), CC (Oxford) [*Ex rel.* Richard
  Case, Barrister, 1 Alfred Street, Oxford] . . . .   *Digested*, 07/**3164**
Hirst v United Kingdom (74025/01) (2006) 42 E.H.R.R. 41; 19 B.H.R.C. 546; [2006]
  1 Prison L.R. 220; (2005) 155 N.L.J. 1551; *Times*, October 10, 2005, ECHR
  (Grand Chamber). . . . .   *Digested*, 06/**2150**:
                 Considered, 07/5431
Hiscock v Oxley see Oxley v Hiscock
HITACHI PLANT/Separation apparatus (T444/06) [2007] E.P.O.R. 44, EPO (Technical Bd
  App) . . . .   *Digested*, 07/**2618**
HITACHI/Auction method (T258/03) [2004] E.P.O.R. 55, EPO (Technical Bd App) . .   *Digested*, 05/**2460**:
       Applied, 07/2598: *Considered*, 07/2594: *Followed*, 07/2589
Hitchman v Wilbraham (2007) 151 S.J.L.B. 747, Ch D (Cardiff)
HJ Banks & Co Ltd v Speight (Valuation Officer); *joined case* HJ Banks & Co Ltd v
  Walsh (Valuation Officer) [2007] R.A. 187, Lands Tr
HJ Banks & Co Ltd v Walsh (Valuation Officer) see HJ Banks & Co Ltd v Speight
  (Valuation Officer)
HJ Heinz Co Ltd v Kenrick [2000] I.C.R. 491; [2000] I.R.L.R. 144, EAT . . . .   *Digested*, 00/**2129**:
          Considered, 05/1193, 07/1331: *Followed*, 00/2127
HK v Finland (36065/97) [2007] 1 F.L.R. 633; [2006] 3 F.C.R. 199, ECHR . . . .   *Digested*, 07/**2248**
HK v Secretary of State for the Home Department; *sub nom* HK (Discrimination:
  Refugees Family Policy: Somalia), Re [2006] UKAIT 21; [2006] Imm. A.R. 320,
  AIT . . . .   *Digested*, 07/**2327**
HK (Discrimination: Refugees Family Policy: Somalia), Re see HK v Secretary of State for
  the Home Department
HL v United Kingdom (45508/99); *sub nom* L v United Kingdom (45508/99) (2005)
  40 E.H.R.R. 32; 17 B.H.R.C. 418; (2004) 7 C.C.L. Rep. 498; [2005] Lloyd's
  Rep. Med. 169; (2005) 81 B.M.L.R. 131; [2004] M.H.L.R. 236; *Times*, October
  19, 2004, ECHR . . . .   *Digested*, 05/**2109**:
                 Applied, 07/3913
HM v Switzerland (39187/98) (2004) 38 E.H.R.R. 17; [2002] M.H.L.R. 209, ECHR . .   *Digested*, 04/**1971**:
           Considered, 03/2960, 07/3316
HM Advocate v DS see DS v HM Advocate
HM Advocate v Montgomery (David Shields) see Montgomery v HM Advocate
HM Prison Service v Johnson [2007] I.R.L.R. 951; (2007) 151 S.J.L.B. 1165, EAT . . . .   *Digested*, 07/**1334**
HM's Application for Judicial Review, Re [2007] NICA 2; [2007] N.I. 117, CA (NI)
HN v Poland (77710/01) [2005] 3 F.C.R. 85; (2007) 45 E.H.R.R. 46, ECHR . . . .   *Digested*, 06/**2194**
Hoare v Inland Revenue Commissioners [2002] EWHC 775 (Ch); [2002] B.P.I.R. 986,
  Ch D . . . .   *Digested*, 03/**2351**:
                 Considered, 07/2410
HOB-Vin v Iceland (E4/05) [2006] 2 C.M.L.R. 43, EFTA . . . .   *Digested*, 07/**633**
Hobart v Hobart [2006] EWHC 1784 (Ch); [2007] W.T.L.R. 1213, Ch D
Hobbs v Horsham DC [2006] EWHC 1605 (Admin); [2007] J.P.L. 589; [2006]
  N.P.C. 84, QBD (Admin). . . . .   *Digested*, 07/**3295**
Hobbs v United Kingdom (63684/00); *joined cases* Green v United Kingdom
  (63468/00); Walsh v United Kingdom (63484/00); Richard v United Kingdom
  (63475/00) (2007) 44 E.H.R.R. 54; [2006] S.T.I. 2506; *Times*, November 28,
  2006, ECHR . . . .   *Digested*, 07/**2207**
Hobson (Setting of Minimum Term), Re see Jones (Setting of Minimum Term), Re

Hoddinott *v* Persimmon Homes (Wessex) Ltd [2007] EWCA Civ 1203; (2007) 104(47) L.S.G. 25; *Times*, December 28, 2007, CA (Civ Div)

Hodgetts *v* Chiltern DC; *sub nom* Chiltern DC *v* Hodgetts [1983] 2 A.C. 120; [1983] 2 W.L.R. 577; [1983] 1 All E.R. 1057; (1983) 147 J.P. 372; (1983) 45 P. & C.R. 402; [1983] J.P.L. 377, HL . . . . *Digested*, 83/**3655**:
                Applied, 86/199, 86/952, 05/821: *Considered*, 93/3859, 00/5467, 07/3898:
                                                             Distinguished, 94/4305

Hodgson *v* Toray Textiles Europe Ltd see Toray Textiles Europe Pension Scheme, Re

Hodgson *v* Toray Textiles Europe Ltd see Toray Textiles Europe Pension Scheme, Re

Hoechst AG *v* Inland Revenue Commissioners (C-410/98) see Metallgesellschaft Ltd *v* Inland Revenue Commissioners (C-397/98)

Hoefner *v* Macrotron GmbH (C41/90) [1991] E.C.R. I-1979; [1993] 4 C.M.L.R. 306; (1991) 135 S.J.L.B. 54, ECJ (6th Chamber) . . . . *Applied*, 07/653:
                                                                     Followed, 97/5714

Hoek Loos NV *v* Commission of the European Communities (T-304/02) [2006] E.C.R. II-1887; [2006] 5 C.M.L.R. 8, CFI (5th Chamber) . . . . *Digested*, 07/**608**

HOFFMAN-LA ROCHE/Transfer of opposition (G2/04) [2005] E.P.O.R. 35, EPO (Enlarged Bd App) . . . . *Digested*, 06/**2474**:
                                                                     Considered, 07/2611

Hogan *v* DPP [2007] EWHC 978 (Admin); [2007] 1 W.L.R. 2944; *Times*, February 28, 2007, DC . . . . *Digested*, 07/**907**

Hokkanen *v* Finland (A/299-A); *sub nom* K *v* Finland (19823/92) [1996] 1 F.L.R. 289; [1995] 2 F.C.R. 320; (1995) 19 E.H.R.R. 139; [1996] Fam. Law 22, ECHR (1993) 16 E.H.R.R. CD47, Eur Comm HR . . . . *Digested*, 95/**2660**:
        Applied, 00/3232, 07/2248: *Considered*, 07/2257: *Referred to*, 03/2181

Holbock *v* Finanzamt Salzburg-Land (C-157/05) [2007] S.T.I. 1586, ECJ (4th Chamber)

Holcim (Deutschland) AG (formerly Alsen AG) *v* Commission of the European Communities (C-282/05 P) [2007] 4 C.M.L.R. 26, ECJ (2nd Chamber) . . . . . *Digested*, 07/**1562**

Holden *v* Chief Constable of Lancashire [1987] Q.B. 380; [1986] 3 W.L.R. 1107; [1986] 3 All E.R. 836; (1987) 84 L.S.G. 417; (1986) 130 S.J. 985, CA (Civ Div) . . . . *Digested*, 87/**1144**:
                            Considered, 94/5067: *Followed*, 07/1053

Holder *v* Law Society [2003] EWCA Civ 39; [2003] 1 W.L.R. 1059; [2003] 3 All E.R. 62; (2003) 100(11) L.S.G. 34; (2003) 147 S.J.L.B. 117; *Times*, January 29, 2003, CA (Civ Div); reversing [2002] EWHC 1559 (Ch); *Times*, September 9, 2002, Ch D . . . . *Digested*, 03/**2824**:
                            Applied, 05/2725: *Considered*, 07/2801, 07/2804

Holding *v* Thurrock BC see Thurrock BC *v* Secretary of State for the Environment, Transport and the Regions

Holding and Management (Solitaire) Ltd, Re; *sub nom* Holding and Management (Solitaire) Ltd *v* 1-16 Finland Street RTM Co Ltd [2007] 45 E.G. 162 (C.S.), Lands Tr

Holding and Management (Solitaire) Ltd *v* 1-16 Finland Street RTM Co Ltd see Holding and Management (Solitaire) Ltd, Re

Holin Groep BV cs *v* Staatssecretaris van Financien (C-7/02) see Gemeente Leusden *v* Staatssecretaris van Financien (C-487/01)

Hollicourt (Contracts) Ltd (In Liquidation) *v* Bank of Ireland; *sub nom* Bank of Ireland *v* Hollicourt (Contracts) Ltd; Claughton (Liquidator of Hollicourt (Contracts) Ltd) *v* Bank of Ireland [2001] Ch. 555; [2001] 2 W.L.R. 290; [2001] 1 All E.R. 289; [2001] 1 All E.R. (Comm) 357; [2001] Lloyd's Rep. Bank. 6; [2000] B.C.C. 1210; [2001] 1 B.C.L.C. 233; [2001] B.P.I.R. 47; (2000) 97(45) L.S.G. 41; *Times*, November 1, 2000; *Independent*, October 24, 2000, CA (Civ Div); reversing [2000] 1 W.L.R. 895; [2000] 2 All E.R. 45; [2000] Lloyd's Rep. Bank. 21; [2000] B.C.C. 237; [2000] 1 B.C.L.C. 171; (1999) 96(48) L.S.G. 39; (2000) 144 S.J.L.B. 24; *Times*, November 30, 1999; *Independent*, January 31, 2000, Ch D . . . . *Digested*, 00/**3464**:
                            Distinguished, 00/3465, 07/2419

Hollington *v* F Hewthorn & Co Ltd [1943] K.B. 587, CA; affirming in part [1943] K.B. 27, KBD . . . . *Applied*, 67/759,
        84/1531, 87/1669, 93/2525, 03/509: *Approved*: 66/11738:
Considered, 47-51/6522, 58/957, 67/1608, 67/3246, 69/2418, 70/1018,
        70/1024, 80/2609, 93/3153, 96/1410, 04/192, 06/2926, 07/339:
        Distinguished, 56/2546, 93/3038: *Followed*, 66/7003

Hollins *v* Russell; *joined cases* Sharratt *v* London Central Bus Co Ltd (No.3); Worth *v* McKenna; Pratt *v* Bull; Dunn *v* Ward; Tichband *v* Hurdman [2003] EWCA Civ 718; [2003] 1 W.L.R. 2487; [2003] 4 All E.R. 590; [2003] 3 Costs L.R. 423; (2003) 100(28) L.S.G. 30; (2003) 153 N.L.J. 920; (2003) 147 S.J.L.B. 662; *Times*, June 10, 2003; *Independent*, June 3, 2003, CA (Civ Div) . . . . *Digested*, 03/**334**:
        Applied, 04/2548, 04/2550, 05/377, 05/2705, 06/2737:
                            Considered, 07/2778: *Explained*, 06/376, 06/2735

Hollis *v* Griffin (Unreported, August 9, 2006), CC (Liverpool) [*Ex rel.* Heather Belbin, Barrister, Oriel Chambers, 14 Water Street, Liverpool] . . . . *Digested*, 07/**3125**

Hollis *v* Vabu Pty Ltd 207 C.L.R. 21, HC (Aus) . . . . *Distinguished*, 07/2943

Hollmann v Fazenda Publica (C-443/06) [2007] S.T.I. 2402, ECJ (4th Chamber)

Holman v Howes [2007] EWCA Civ 877; [2007] B.P.I.R. 1085; [2007] W.T.L.R. 1539; (2007-08) 10 I.T.E.L.R. 492; [2007] Fam. Law 987, CA (Civ Div); reversing in part [2005] EWHC 2824 (Ch); [2006] 1 F.L.R. 1003; [2005] 3 F.C.R. 474; [2006] B.P.I.R. 722; [2006] Fam. Law 176, Ch D . . . . *Digested*, 07/**3362**

Holmes-Moorhouse v Richmond upon Thames LBC [2007] EWCA Civ 970; [2007] 3 F.C.R. 736; [2007] N.P.C. 104; *Times*, November 19, 2007, CA (Civ Div) . . . . *Digested*, 07/**2153**

Holt v Edge [2007] EWCA Civ 602; (2007) 97 B.M.L.R. 74; (2007) 151 S.J.L.B. 854, CA (Civ Div); affirming [2006] EWHC 1932 (QB), QBD . . . . *Digested*, 07/**2924**

Holtham v Kelmanson [2006] EWHC 2588 (Ch); [2006] B.P.I.R. 1422; [2007] W.T.L.R. 285; [2006] N.P.C. 112, Ch D . . . . *Digested*, 07/**2404**

Holton v General Medical Council [2006] EWHC 2960 (Admin); (2007) 93 B.M.L.R. 74; [2007] A.C.D. 66, QBD (Admin) . . . . *Digested*, 07/**1952**

Holy Monasteries v Greece (A/301-A) (1995) 20 E.H.R.R. 1, ECHR . . . . *Digested*, 95/**2653**:
Applied, 07/2206: *Considered*, 03/968, 03/2824

Holy Trinity, Bosham, Re [2004] Fam. 125; [2004] 2 W.L.R. 833; [2004] 2 All E.R. 820; *Times*, December 12, 2003, Cons Ct (Chichester) . . . . *Digested*, 04/**943**:
Applied, 07/1084: *Considered*, 05/993

Homburg Houtimport BV v Agrosin Private Ltd (The Starsin); *sub nom* Owners of Cargo Lately Laden on Board the Starsin v Owners of the Starsin; *joined case* Hunter Timber Ltd v Agrosin Private Ltd [2003] UKHL 12; [2004] 1 A.C. 715; [2003] 2 W.L.R. 711; [2003] 2 All E.R. 785; [2003] 1 All E.R. (Comm) 625; [2003] 1 Lloyd's Rep. 571; [2003] 1 C.L.C. 921; 2003 A.M.C. 913; (2003) 100(19) L.S.G. 31; *Times*, March 17, 2003, HL; reversing [2001] EWCA Civ 56; [2001] 1 All E.R. (Comm) 455; [2001] 1 Lloyd's Rep. 437; [2001] C.L.C. 696, CA (Civ Div); reversing in part [1999] 2 All E.R. (Comm) 591; [2000] 1 Lloyd's Rep. 85; [1999] C.L.C. 1769, QBD (Comm) . . . . *Digested*, 03/**3896**:
Applied, 00/4679, 03/3900, 07/2748: *Considered*, 06/2673:
Followed, 04/3480

Home & Colonial Stores Ltd v Colls see Colls v Home & Colonial Stores Ltd
Home Office v Dorgan see Anderton v Clwyd CC
Home Office v Lownds see Lownds v Home Office
Home Office v Y (Kevin Raymond) see Catholic Care (Diocese of Leeds) v Y (Kevin Raymond)
Homepower Stores Ltd, Re see Powerstore (Trading) Ltd, Re
Honda Giken Kogyou Kabushiki Kaisha v KJM Superbikes Ltd [2007] EWCA Civ 313; [2007] C.P. Rep. 28; (2007) 151 S.J.L.B. 431, CA (Civ Div) . . . . *Digested*, 07/**341**

Honeygan-Green v Islington LBC see Islington LBC v Honeygan-Green
Honyvem Informazioni Commerciali Srl v De Zotti (C-465/04) [2006] E.C.R. I-2879, ECJ . . . . *Applied*, 07/68

Hoogkamer v Netherlands (50435/99) see Da Silva v Netherlands (50435/99)
Hooper v Secretary of State for Work and Pensions [2007] EWCA Civ 495; *Times*, June 27, 2007, CA (Civ Div) . . . . *Digested*, 07/**3864**

Hopkins Developments Ltd v First Secretary of State [2006] EWHC 2823 (Admin); [2007] Env. L.R. 14; [2007] 1 P. & C.R. 25; [2007] J.P.L. 1056; [2006] N.P.C. 125, QBD (Admin) . . . . *Digested*, 07/**3236**

Hoppe v Germany (28422/95) [2003] 1 F.L.R. 384; [2003] 1 F.C.R. 176; (2004) 38 E.H.R.R. 15; [2003] Fam. Law 159, ECHR . . . . *Digested*, 03/**2198**:
Applied, 07/2251

Horbury Building Systems Ltd v Hampden Insurance NV [2004] EWCA Civ 418; [2004] 2 C.L.C. 453; [2004] B.L.R. 431; [2007] Lloyd's Rep. I.R. 237; (2004) 148 S.J.L.B. 477, CA (Civ Div); affirming [2003] EWHC 2110 (Comm), QBD (Comm) . . . . *Digested*, 05/**2375**

Horley Town Football Club, Re; *sub nom* Hunt v McLaren [2006] EWHC 2386 (Ch); [2006] W.T.L.R. 1817, Ch D . . . . *Digested*, 07/**4264**

Hormel Foods Corp v Antilles Landscape Investments NV [2005] EWHC 13 (Ch); [2005] E.T.M.R. 54; [2005] R.P.C. 28; (2005) 28(5) I.P.D. 28037; (2005) 102(12) L.S.G. 26; *Times*, February 28, 2005, Ch D . . . . *Digested*, 05/**2505**:
Distinguished, 07/2677

Horn v Sunderland Corp [1941] 2 K.B. 26, CA . . . . *Applied*, 57/487,
65/510, 86/350, 91/453: *Approved*, 67/521: *Considered*, 55/381, 69/433,
78/272, 82/355, 84/341.1, 88/2729, 90/582, 90/587, 99/4357, 07/3385:
Followed, 57/476, 60/455

Horne-Roberts v SmithKline Beecham Plc; *sub nom* MMR/MR Vaccine Litigation; H (A Child) v Merk & Co Inc; H (A Child) v Merck & Co Inc; SmithKline Beecham Plc v Horne-Roberts; H (A Child) v SmithKline Beecham Plc; SmithKline Beecham Plc v H (A Child) [2001] EWCA Civ 2006; [2002] 1 W.L.R. 1662; [2002] C.P. Rep. 20; (2002) 65 B.M.L.R. 79; (2002) 99(8) L.S.G. 35; (2002) 146 S.J.L.B. 19; *Times*, January 10, 2002, CA (Civ Div); affirming [2001] C.P. Rep. 80; [2002] P.I.Q.R. P3, QBD . . . . *Digested*, 02/**507**:
Applied, 04/286, 05/480: *Considered*, 05/315, 07/534: *Followed*, 07/535

Horner v Lancashire CC see R. (on the application of Horner) v Lancashire CC
Horsfold v Bird see Horsford v Bird

Horsford v Bird; *sub nom* Horsfold v Bird [2006] UKPC 3; [2006] 1 E.G.L.R. 75; [2006] 15 E.G. 136; (2006) 22 Const. L.J. 187; (2006) 103(6) L.S.G. 34, PC (Ant) . . . . *Digested*, 06/**1031**: *Considered*, 07/1060

Horsford v Bird (Costs) [2006] UKPC 55; [2007] 2 Costs L.R. 245, PC (Ant) . . . . . .   *Digested*, 07/**378**

Horsforth Riverside LLP v Leeds City Council [2007] P.A.D. 41, Planning Inspector

Horton v Evans [2006] EWHC 2808 (QB); [2007] LS Law Medical 212; (2007) 94 B.M.L.R. 60; [2007] P.N.L.R. 17, QBD . . . .   *Digested*, 07/**2928**

Horton v Sadler [2006] UKHL 27; [2007] 1 A.C. 307; [2006] 2 W.L.R. 1346; [2006] 3 All E.R. 1177; [2006] R.T.R. 27; [2006] P.I.Q.R. P30; (2006) 91 B.M.L.R. 60; (2006) 103(26) L.S.G. 27; (2006) 156 N.L.J. 1024; (2006) 150 S.J.L.B. 808; *Times*, June 19, 2006, HL; reversing [2004] EWCA Civ 936, CA (Civ Div) . . . .   *Digested*, 06/**475**: *Considered*, 07/445, 07/1672

Horton (Setting of Minimum Term), Re; *sub nom* R. v Horton (Gareth Richard) [2006] EWHC 3035 (QB); [2007] M.H.L.R. 35, QBD . . . .   *Digested*, 07/**3696**

Hospice of St Mary of Furness v Howard [2007] I.R.L.R. 944, EAT

Hostick v New Zealand Railway & Locomotive Society Waikato Branch Inc [2007] W.T.L.R. 1563; (2006-07) 9 I.T.E.L.R. 140, HC (NZ) . . . .   *Digested*, 07/**4253**

Hotel Scandic Gasaback AB v Riksskatteverket (C-412/03) [2005] S.T.C. 1311; [2005] E.C.R. I-743; [2005] 1 C.M.L.R. 38; [2005] C.E.C. 335; [2007] B.T.C. 5372; [2007] B.V.C. 391; [2005] S.T.I. 138, ECJ (1st Chamber) . . . .   *Digested*, 05/**4392**

Hounslow LBC v Klusova [2007] EWCA Civ 1127; (2007) 104(45) L.S.G. 29, CA (Civ Div); reversing UKEAT/0325/06/DM, EAT

Hounslow LBC v London and Bath Estates [2007] P.A.D. 20, Planning Inspector

Housden v Conservators of Wimbledon and Putney Commons A3/2007/1173, CA (Civ Div); reversing [2007] EWHC 1171 (Ch); [2007] 1 W.L.R. 2543; *Times*, June 4, 2007, Ch D

House of Donuts International v Office for Harmonisation in the Internal Market (Trade Marks and Designs) (OHIM) (T333/04) [2007] E.T.M.R. 53, CFI . . . .   *Digested*, 07/**2661**

Howard v Savage [2006] EWHC 3693 (Ch); [2007] B.P.I.R. 1097, Ch D

Howard de Walden Estates Ltd v Aggio; *joined case* Earl Cadogan v 26 Cadogan Square Ltd [2007] EWCA Civ 499; [2007] 3 W.L.R. 542; [2007] 3 All E.R. 910; [2007] L. & T.R. 29; [2007] 23 E.G. 165 (C.S.); (2007) 104(23) L.S.G. 29; (2007) 157 N.L.J. 815; [2007] N.P.C. 69, CA (Civ Div) . . . .   *Digested*, 07/**2753**

Howard de Walden Estates Ltd v Maybury Court Freehold Co Ltd see Earl Cadogan v Sportello

Howell v Lees Millais; *sub nom* Howell v Millais [2007] EWCA Civ 720; (2007) 104(29) L.S.G. 24; (2007) 151 S.J.L.B. 922; [2007] N.P.C. 88, CA (Civ Div)

Howell v Millais see Howell v Lees Millais

Howse v Queen, The [2005] UKPC 30, PC (NZ) . . . .   *Considered*, 07/1027

Hoxha v Secretary of State for the Home Department see R. (on the application of Hoxha) v Special Adjudicator

HP Bulmer Ltd v J Bollinger SA (No.2) [1974] Ch. 401; [1974] 3 W.L.R. 202; [1974] 2 All E.R. 1226; [1974] 2 C.M.L.R. 91; [1974] F.S.R. 334; [1975] R.P.C. 321; (1974) 118 S.J. 404, CA (Civ Div); affirming [1974] F.S.R. 263, Ch D . . . .   *Digested*, 74/**1471**: *Applied*, 94/4552, 07/1330: *Considered*, 82/560, 86/1191, 88/88, 95/5047: *Followed*, 91/3927: *Referred to*, 95/4201: *Subsequent proceedings*, 76/1195

HPJ UK Ltd (In Administration), Re [2007] B.C.C. 284, Ch D (Birmingham) . . . .   *Digested*, 07/**2391**

HRH Prince of Wales v Associated Newspapers Ltd; *sub nom* Associated Newspapers Ltd v HRH Prince of Wales [2006] EWCA Civ 1776; [2007] 3 W.L.R. 222; [2007] 2 All E.R. 139; (2007) 104(2) L.S.G. 30; (2007) 157 N.L.J. 106; (2007) 151 S.J.L.B. 63; *Times*, December 28, 2006, CA (Civ Div); affirming [2006] EWHC 522 (Ch); [2006] E.C.D.R. 20; (2006) 156 N.L.J. 512, Ch D . . . .   *Digested*, 07/**2510**

HSBC International Trustee Ltd v Wong Kit Wan; *sub nom* Circle Trust, Re [2007] W.T.L.R. 631; (2006-07) 9 I.T.E.L.R. 676, Grand Ct (CI) . . . .   *Digested*, 07/**4249**

HSBC Trust Co (UK) Ltd (Farmbrough's Executor) v Twiddy [2006] R.V.R. 308; [2006] W.T.L.R. 1533, Lands Tr . . . .   *Digested*, 07/**4109**

HSS Hire Services Group Plc v BMB Builders Merchants Ltd (Costs) [2005] EWCA Civ 626; [2005] 1 W.L.R. 3158; [2005] 3 All E.R. 486; [2006] 2 Costs L.R. 213; *Times*, May 31, 2005, CA (Civ Div) . . . .   *Digested*, 05/**816**: *Applied*, 07/525

Hsu v Commissioner of Police of the Metropolis see Thompson v Commissioner of Police of the Metropolis

Huang v Secretary of State for the Home Department; *joined cases* Abu-Qulbain v Secretary of State for the Home Department; Kashmiri v Secretary of State for the Home Department [2007] UKHL 11; [2007] 2 A.C. 167; [2007] 2 W.L.R. 581; [2007] 4 All E.R. 15; [2007] 1 F.L.R. 2021; [2007] H.R.L.R. 22; [2007] U.K.H.R.R. 759; 24 B.H.R.C. 74; [2007] Imm. A.R. 571; [2007] I.N.L.R. 314; [2007] Fam. Law 587; (2007) 151 S.J.L.B. 435; *Times*, March 22, 2007, HL; reversing in part [2005] EWCA Civ 105; [2006] Q.B. 1; [2005] 3 W.L.R. 488; [2005] 3 All E.R. 435; [2005] H.R.L.R. 15; [2005] U.K.H.R.R. 651; [2005] Imm. A.R. 240; [2005] I.N.L.R. 247; (2005) 102(20) L.S.G. 30; (2005) 149 S.J.L.B. 297; *Times*, March 16, 2005, CA (Civ Div) . . . . *Digested,* 07/**2340**:
Applied, 05/2179, 05/2193, 05/2211, 06/2224, 06/2249, 07/2307, 07/2308, 07/2330, 07/2364: *Considered,* 05/2213, 07/2289, 07/2298: *Explained,* 06/2264

Huckfield, Re see R. v Manchester Crown Court Ex p. DPP
Hudson v Secretary of State for Social Services see Jones v Secretary of State for Social Services
Hudson Contract Services Ltd v Revenue and Customs Commissioners [2007] EWHC 73 (Ch); [2007] S.T.C. 1363; [2007] B.T.C. 150; [2007] S.T.I. 259, Ch D; affirming [2005] S.T.C. (S.C.D.) 740; [2005] S.T.I. 1630, Sp Comm . . . . *Digested,* 07/**3999**
Hudson Contract Services Ltd v Revenue and Customs Commissioners [2007] EWHC 2561 (Ch); [2007] S.T.I. 2652, Ch D
Hudson (Inspector of Taxes) v JDC Services Ltd [2004] EWHC 602 (Ch); [2004] S.T.C. 834; 77 T.C. 134; [2005] B.T.C. 3; [2004] S.T.I. 896; *Times*, April 16, 2004, Ch D . . . . *Digested,* 04/**3710**:
Applied, 05/4017, 06/4138, 06/4209: *Considered,* 07/3997: *Followed,* 05/4036

Hughes v Customs and Excise Commissioners; *sub nom* R v DPP; R. (on the application of Anderson) v Customs and Excise Commissioners; R. (on the application of Hughes) v Customs and Excise Commissioners; *joined cases* Anderson v Customs and Excise Commissioners; R v Crown Prosecution Service [2002] EWCA Civ 734; [2003] 1 W.L.R. 177; [2002] 4 All E.R. 633; (2002) 99(26) L.S.G. 36; (2002) 152 N.L.J. 848; (2002) 146 S.J.L.B. 143; *Times*, May 31, 2002; *Independent*, July 8, 2002, CA (Civ Div) . . . . *Digested,* 02/**907**:
Approved, 07/1014: *Considered,* 04/883, 05/2332
Hughes v Doncaster MBC [1991] 1 A.C. 382; [1991] 2 W.L.R. 16; [1991] 1 All E.R. 295; 89 L.G.R. 257; (1991) 61 P. & C.R. 355; [1991] 05 E.G. 133; [1991] R.V.R. 10; [1990] E.G. 153 (C.S.); (1991) 135 S.J. 18, HL; affirming [1990] 1 W.L.R. 845; [1990] 2 All E.R. 53; (1990) 59 P. & C.R. 365; [1990] 26 E.G. 168; [1990] R.V.R. 15; [1990] J.P.L. 665; (1990) 154 L.G. Rev. 154; [1989] E.G. 152 (C.S.), CA (Civ Div); reversing in part (1988) 55 P. & C.R. 383; [1988] R.V.R. 179, Lands Tr . . . . *Digested,* 91/**453**:
Applied, 07/3228: *Considered,* 93/426: *Followed,* 05/3251
Hughes v First Secretary of State see R. (on the application of Hughes) v Office of the Deputy Prime Minister
Hughes v Grampian Country Food Group Ltd [2007] CSIH 32; 2007 S.L.T. 635; [2007] Eu. L.R. 719; 2007 Rep. L.R. 72; 2007 G.W.D. 18-324; *Times*, June 4, 2007, IH (1 Div); affirming 2006 S.C.L.R. 682; 2006 Rep. L.R. 78; 2006 G.W.D. 14-270, OH . . . . *Digested,* 07/**5272**:
Distinguished, 07/5273

Hughes v Hill see R. v Manchester Stipendiary Magistrate Ex p. Hill
Hughes v Hughes see Hyman v Hyman
Hughes v Lord Advocate; *sub nom* Hughes v Postmaster General [1963] A.C. 837; [1963] 2 W.L.R. 779; [1963] 1 All E.R. 705; 1963 S.C. (H.L.) 31; 1963 S.L.T. 150; (1963) 107 S.J. 232, HL; reversing 1961 S.C. 310; 1962 S.L.T. 90, IH (1 Div) . . . *Digested,* 63/**4056**:
Applied, 64/2500, 67/1197, 67/2675, 70/744, 75/933, 75/2288, 80/1904, 83/3962, 87/2614, 98/3988, 98/6107, 07/2915, 07/5269:
Considered, 69/966, 69/2412, 90/3285, 96/4427, 00/4239, 00/4239, 06/2907: *Distinguished,* 64/2499, 77/363.u, 04/2716: *Followed,* 85/4437
Hughes v Mental Health Tribunal [2007] M.H.L.R. 29, Sh Pr
Hughes v Paxman; *sub nom* Paxman v Hughes; Hughes and Paxman's Patent (EP UK 1048609 B1) [2006] EWCA Civ 818; [2007] R.P.C. 2; *Times*, July 18, 2006, CA (Civ Div); affirming [2005] EWHC 2240; (2006) 29(1) I.P.D. 29006, Ch D (Patents Ct) . . . . *Digested,* 06/**2523**
Hughes v Postmaster General see Hughes v Lord Advocate
Hughes and Paxman's Patent (EP UK 1048609 B1) see Hughes v Paxman
Hugin Cash Registers v Commission of the European Communities (C22/78) see Hugin Kassaregister AB v Commission of the European Communities (C22/78)
Hugin Kassaregister AB v Commission of the European Communities (C22/78); *joined case* Hugin Cash Registers v Commission of the European Communities (C22/78) [1979] E.C.R. 1869; [1979] 3 C.M.L.R. 345, ECJ . . . . *Digested,* 79/**1205**:
Applied, 07/622: *Considered,* 98/716, 98/719
Hugo v Plon SA; *sub nom* Plon SA v Hugo [2007] E.C.D.R. 9, Cass (F); reversing [2005] E.C.D.R. 27, C d'A (Paris) . . . . *Digested,* 07/**2522**

Hui Chi-Ming v Queen, The [1992] 1 A.C. 34; [1991] 3 W.L.R. 495; [1991] 3 All E.R.
　　897; (1992) 94 Cr. App. R. 236; [1992] Crim. L.R. 446; *Times*, September 26,
　　1991; *Independent*, September 19, 1991; *Guardian*, October 9, 1991, PC (HK) . .　　*Digested*, 92/**639**:
　　　　　　　　　　　Applied, 93/917, 05/909, 07/53: *Considered*, 93/2525, 95/1272, 05/733:
　　　　　　　　　　　　　　　　　　　　　　　　　　　　　　　Followed, 95/1238
Huls AG v Commission of the European Communities (C-199/92 P) [1999] E.C.R. I-
　　4287; [1999] 5 C.M.L.R. 1016, ECJ (6th Chamber) . . . .　　*Digested*, 00/**2376**:
　　　　　　　　　　　　　　　　Applied, 06/573, 07/599, 07/644, 07/1545
Humphries v Connor (1864) 17 I.C.L.R. 1 . . . .　　*Considered*, 07/3317
Hung v Chiu (2007-08) 10 I.T.E.L.R. 707, CFI (HK)
Hunt v Carey Canada Inc [1990] 2 S.C.R. 959, Sup Ct (Can) . . . .　　*Applied*, 07/4198
Hunt v McLaren see Horley Town Football Club, Re
Hunt v Ukraine (31111/04) [2006] 3 F.C.R. 756, ECHR. . . . .　　*Digested*, 07/**2253**
Hunte v E Bottomley & Sons Ltd [2007] EWCA Civ 1168; *Times*, November 21, 2007,
　　CA (Civ Div)
Hunter v Canary Wharf Ltd; *sub nom* Hunter v London Docklands Development Corp
　　[1997] A.C. 655; [1997] 2 W.L.R. 684; [1997] 2 All E.R. 426; [1997] C.L.C.
　　1045; 84 B.L.R. 1; 54 Con. L.R. 12; [1997] Env. L.R. 488; [1997] 2 F.L.R. 342;
　　(1998) 30 H.L.R. 409; [1997] Fam. Law 601; [1997] E.G. 59 (C.S.); (1997)
　　94(19) L.S.G. 25; (1997) 147 N.L.J. 634; (1997) 141 S.J.L.B. 108; [1997] N.P.C.
　　64; *Times*, April 25, 1997; *Independent*, May 2, 1997, HL; affirming [1996] 2
　　W.L.R. 348; [1996] 1 All E.R. 482; [1996] C.L.C. 197; 75 B.L.R. 27; 47 Con. L.R.
　　136; [1996] Env. L.R. 138; (1996) 28 H.L.R. 383; [1995] E.G. 153 (C.S.);
　　(1995) 92(39) L.S.G. 28; (1995) 145 N.L.J. 1645; (1995) 139 S.J.L.B. 214;
　　[1995] N.P.C. 155; *Times*, October 13, 1995; *Independent*, October 19, 1995, CA
　　(Civ Div); affirming in part *Independent*, January 23, 1995; *Independent*,
　　December 20, 1994, QBD. . . . .　　*Digested*, 97/**3865**:
　　　　　　　　　　Applied, 01/3800, 07/2961: *Considered*, 99/4067: *Distinguished*, 00/4297:
　　　　　　　　　　　　　　　　　　　　　　　Followed, 98/4040, 99/3681
Hunter v Chief Constable of the West Midlands; *joined cases* McIlkenny v Chief
　　Constable of the West Midlands; Walker v Chief Constable of the West Midlands;
　　Power v Chief Constable of Lancashire [1982] A.C. 529; [1981] 3 W.L.R. 906;
　　[1981] 3 All E.R. 727; (1981) 125 S.J. 829; *Times*, November 26, 1981, HL;
　　affirming [1980] Q.B. 283; [1980] 2 W.L.R. 689; [1980] 2 All E.R. 227; (1980)
　　124 S.J. 83, CA (Civ Div) . . . .　　*Digested*, 82/**2382**:
　　　　　　　　Applied, 83/1128, 89/3073, 90/3542, 93/623, 94/663, 94/3517, 94/4572,
　　　　　　　　　　95/688, 95/2857, 95/3699, 96/4496, 00/2250, 00/4269, 02/3301:
　　　　　　　　　　Considered, 82/650.u, 90/2857, 91/1737, 92/3844, 93/2525, 96/853,
　　　　　　　　　　97/628, 99/4021, 00/597, 01/5, 07/339: *Distinguished*, 88/2610, 93/3084,
　　　　　　　　　　99/313, 03/509, 06/896: *Explained*, 99/485: *Followed*, 96/3912, 96/4490,
　　　　　　　　　　97/1107, 98/4865, 00/332: *Referred to*, 95/3882, 97/3355
Hunter v London Docklands Development Corp see Hunter v Canary Wharf Ltd
Hunter v Murrow; *sub nom* H v M (Abduction: Rights of Custody) [2005] EWCA Civ
　　976; [2005] 2 F.L.R. 1119; [2005] 3 F.C.R. 1; [2005] Fam. Law 762, CA (Civ
　　Div) . . . .　　*Digested*, 05/**1541**:
　　　　　　　　　　　　　　　　　　　　　　　　　　　　Considered, 07/1775
Hunter Timber Ltd v Agrosin Private Ltd see Homburg Houtimport BV v Agrosin Private
　　Ltd (The Starsin)
Huntingford v Hobbs [1993] 1 F.L.R. 736; (1992) 24 H.L.R. 652; [1992] Fam. Law
　　437; [1992] E.G. 38 (C.S.); [1992] N.P.C. 39, CA (Civ Div) . . . .　　*Digested*, 93/**537**:
　　　　　　　　　　　　　　　　　　　　　　　　　　　　Doubted, 07/3367
HUNTSMAN/Polypropylene extrusion coating resins (T829/03) [2007] E.P.O.R. 25, EPO
　　(Technical Bd App) . . . .　　*Digested*, 07/**2559**
Hurley v Taylor (Inspector of Taxes) [1999] S.T.C. 1; 71 T.C. 268; [1998] B.T.C. 479;
　　Times, November 23, 1998; *Independent*, November 2, 1998, CA (Civ Div);
　　reversing [1998] S.T.C. 202; [1998] B.T.C. 32; *Times*, February 10, 1998;
　　Independent, February 16, 1998, Ch D . . . .　　*Digested*, 98/**4668**:
　　　　　　　　　　　　　　　　　　　　　　　　　　　　Applied, 07/4101
Hurst v BDO Stoy Hayward LLP; *joined case* Hurst v Supperstone [2006] EWHC
　　2974 (Ch); [2007] B.P.I.R. 54, Ch D . . . .　　*Digested*, 07/**2936**
Hurst v Bennett (No.1); *sub nom* Debtor (No.303 of 1997), Re [2001] EWCA Civ 182;
　　[2001] 2 B.C.L.C. 290; [2001] B.P.I.R. 287; (2001) 98(17) L.S.G. 38; *Times*,
　　March 15, 2001, CA (Civ Div); affirming [2001] B.P.I.R. 89; *Times*, October 3,
　　2000, Ch D . . . .　　*Digested*, 01/**3780**:
　　　　　　　　　　　　　　　　Applied, 03/462: *Followed*, 07/2452
Hurst v Supperstone see Hurst v BDO Stoy Hayward LLP
Hurst v Supperstone [2007] EWHC 865 (Ch); [2007] B.P.I.R. 1104, Ch D
Hurstanger Ltd v Wilson [2007] EWCA Civ 299; [2007] 1 W.L.R. 2351; [2007] 4 All
　　E.R. 1118; [2007] 2 All E.R. (Comm) 1037; (2007) 104(16) L.S.G. 23; (2007)
　　157 N.L.J. 555; (2007) 151 S.J.L.B. 467; [2007] N.P.C. 41; *Times*, May 11, 2007,
　　CA (Civ Div); reversing in part 5CV02279, CC (Coventry) . . . .　　*Digested*, 07/**765**
Hurter v Switzerland (53146/99) (2007) 44 E.H.R.R. 8, ECHR
Hussain v Rider Holdings Ltd (Unreported, September 7, 2006), CC (Bradford) [*Ex
　　rel*. Andrew Granville Stafford, Barrister, 4 King's Bench Walk, Temple, London] .　　*Digested*, 07/**3153**

Hussain v Salford City Council [2007] R.V.R. 10, Lands Tr . . . .   *Digested,* 07/**3417**

Hussain v United Kingdom; *joined case* Singh v United Kingdom (1996) 22 E.H.R.R. 1; 1 B.H.R.C. 119; *Times,* February 26, 1996, ECHR . . . .   *Digested,* 96/**3135**:
           Applied, 00/4323, 07/2230: *Considered,* 97/3924, 03/2160, 04/3349

Hussain v United Kingdom (8866/04) (2006) 43 E.H.R.R. 22; *Times,* April 5, 2006, ECHR . . . .   *Digested,* 07/**2227**

Hutchison 3G v Tynedale Council [2007] P.A.D. 34, Planning Inspector

Hutchison 3G UK Ltd v Customs and Excise Commissioners (C-369/04) [2007] 3 C.M.L.R. 26; [2007] S.T.I. 1764; *Times,* July 3, 2007, ECJ (Grand Chamber)

Hutchison Telephone (UK) v Ultimate Response [1993] B.C.L.C. 307; *Independent,* October 26, 1992, CA (Civ Div) . . . .   *Digested,* 93/**3161**:
           Applied, 07/416, 07/512: *Considered,* 04/329

Hutten-Czapska v Poland (35014/97) (2007) 45 E.H.R.R. 4; 20 B.H.R.C. 493, ECHR (Grand Chamber) . . . .   *Digested,* 06/**2119**

Hyams v Wilfred East Housing Co-operative Ltd [2007] EWCA Civ 242, CA (Civ Div); affirming [2007] 3 E.G. 126, Lands Tr. . . . .   *Digested,* 07/**2758**

Hyde's Trade Mark Application (Unreported), App Person . . . .   *Considered,* 07/2687

Hydrocarbons Great Britain v Blackclawson International see Hydrocarbons Great Britain Ltd v Cammell Laird Shipbuilders and Automotive Products Ltd (t/a AP Precision Hydraulics)

Hydrocarbons Great Britain Ltd v Cammell Laird Shipbuilders and Automotive Products Ltd (t/a AP Precision Hydraulics); *joined cases* Hydrocarbons Great Britain Ltd v Redman Broughton; Hydrocarbons Great Britain v Blackclawson International 53 B.L.R. 84, CA (Civ Div); reversing 25 Con. L.R. 131, QBD (OR) . . . .   *Digested,* 92/**3574**:
           Considered, 07/492: *Distinguished,* 04/384

Hydrocarbons Great Britain Ltd v Redman Broughton see Hydrocarbons Great Britain Ltd v Cammell Laird Shipbuilders and Automotive Products Ltd (t/a AP Precision Hydraulics)

Hyman v Hyman; *joined case* Hughes v Hughes [1929] A.C. 601, HL; affirming [1929] P. 1, CA . . . .   *Applied,* 47-51/2733,
       47-51/3016, 47-51/3017, 47-51/3033, 52/1058, 55/855, 63/1087, 70/795,
       79/1410, 80/791, 84/1702, 07/3394: *Considered,* 47-51/3060, 67/1290,
       74/1052, 87/1743, 04/1535: *Distinguished,* 56/2748, 99/4635

Hynd v Armstrong [2007] CSIH 16; 2007 S.C. 409; 2007 S.L.T. 299; [2007] I.R.L.R. 338; 2007 G.W.D. 8-145, IH (1 Div) . . . .   *Digested,* 07/**5149**

Hyundai Merchant Marine Co Ltd v Furness Withy (Australia) Pty (The Doric Pride) [2006] EWCA Civ 599; [2006] 2 All E.R. (Comm) 188; [2006] 2 Lloyd's Rep. 175; [2007] 2 C.L.C. 1042, CA (Civ Div); affirming [2005] EWHC 945 (Comm); [2005] 2 Lloyd's Rep. 470; [2005] 1 C.L.C. 780, QBD (Comm) . . . .   *Digested,* 06/**3917**

I, Re; *sub nom* Azam v Iqbal [2007] EWHC 2025 (Admin); [2007] A.C.D. 88, QBD (Admin)

I-21 Germany GmbH v Germany (C-392/04); *joined case* Arcor AG & Co KG (formerly ISIS Multimedia Net GmbH & Co KG) v Germany (C-422/04) [2006] E.C.R. I-8559; [2007] 1 C.M.L.R. 10, ECJ . . . .   *Digested,* 07/**1579**

I/S Fini H v Skatteministeriet (C-32/03) [2005] S.T.C. 903; [2005] E.C.R. I-1599; [2005] 2 C.M.L.R. 20; [2005] C.E.C. 638; [2007] B.T.C. 5396; [2007] B.V.C. 415; [2005] S.T.I. 361, ECJ (3rd Chamber) . . . .   *Digested,* 05/**4380**

IA v Turkey (42571/98) (2007) 45 E.H.R.R. 30, ECHR

IA (Applying Policies: Mauritius), Re see IA (Mauritius) v Secretary of State for the Home Department

IA (Mauritius) v Secretary of State for the Home Department; *sub nom* IA (Applying Policies: Mauritius), Re [2006] UKAIT 82; [2007] I.N.L.R. 328, AIT

IA (Somalia) v Secretary of State for the Home Department [2007] EWCA Civ 323; [2007] Imm. A.R. 685; (2007) 151 S.J.L.B. 574, CA (Civ Div)

IAZ International Belgium SA v Commission of the European Communities (96/82) [1983] E.C.R. 3369; [1984] 3 C.M.L.R. 276, ECJ . . . .   *Digested,* 84/**1377**:
           Applied, 06/578, 07/614

Ibbotson v United Kingdom [1999] Crim. L.R. 153; (1999) 27 E.H.R.R. CD332, Eur Comm HR . . . .   *Applied,* 07/**5429**:
           Considered, 03/866

IBM Corp v Commission of the European Communities (60/81); *sub nom* International Business Machines Corp v Commission of the European Communities (60/81) [1981] E.C.R. 2639; [1981] 3 C.M.L.R. 635, ECJ . . . .   *Digested,* 81/**1266**:
       Applied, 03/576, 05/1426, 07/1586, 07/1588: *Considered,* 03/1431, 06/605:
       Followed, 00/2365, 03/1452, 05/1441

IBM/Document abstracting and retrieving (T22/85) [1990] E.P.O.R. 98, EPO (Technical Bd App) . . . .   *Applied,* 07/2598

IBP Ltd v Commission of the European Communities (T-384/06 R) [2007] 4 C.M.L.R. 24, CFI . . . .   *Digested,* 07/**1549**

ICCO International Corn Co NV v Interbulk see Interbulk Ltd v Aiden Shipping Co (The Vimeira) (No.1)

Ice Media International Ltd (In Liquidation) v Q3 Media Ltd; *sub nom* Q3 Media Ltd, Re;
    Wadsted v Q3 Media Ltd [2006] EWHC 1553 (Ch); [2006] B.P.I.R. 1219;
    (2006) 150 S.J.L.B. 705, Ch D . . . .   *Digested,* 07/**2397**
ICI Plc v Colmer (Inspector of Taxes) (C-264/96) [1999] 1 W.L.R. 108; [1998] All E.R.
    (EC) 585; [1998] S.T.C. 874; [1998] E.C.R. I-4695; [1998] 3 C.M.L.R. 293;
    [1998] C.E.C. 861; [1998] B.T.C. 304; *Times,* August 20, 1998, ECJ . . . .   *Digested,* 98/**4620**:
                    Applied, 06/4154, 07/4145: *Considered,* 01/5212, 02/4208, 03/4148:
                    Followed, 01/2499: *Previous proceedings,* 93/608, 96/1303:
                    Subsequent proceedings, 99/4667
Icopower BV v Secretary of State . . . .   *Applied,* 07/**1518**
IFE Fund SA v Goldman Sachs International [2007] EWCA Civ 811; [2007] 2 Lloyd's
    Rep. 449; [2007] 2 C.L.C. 134; (2007) 104(32) L.S.G. 24, CA (Civ Div);
    affirming [2006] EWHC 2887 (Comm); [2007] 1 Lloyd's Rep. 264; [2006] 2
    C.L.C. 1043, QBD (Comm). . . . .   *Digested,* 07/**4194**
Igen Ltd (formerly Leeds Careers Guidance) v Wong see Wong v Igen Ltd (formerly
    Leeds Careers Guidance)
Iglesias Gil v Spain (56673/00); *sub nom* Gil v Spain (56673/00) [2005] 1 F.L.R. 190;
    [2005] 1 F.C.R. 210; (2005) 40 E.H.R.R. 3; [2005] Fam. Law 20, ECHR . . . . .   *Digested,* 05/**2117**:
                    Applied, 07/**1773**
Ignaccolo-Zenide v Romania (31679/96) (2001) 31 E.H.R.R. 7, ECHR. . . . .   *Digested,* 01/**3550**:
                    Applied, 04/1472, 07/1773: *Considered,* 03/1506, 05/2117, 07/1747, 07/2257
IGT/Computer implemented game process (T1023/06) [2007] E.P.O.R. 36, EPO
    (Technical Bd App) . . . .   *Digested,* 07/**2589**
IHT Internationale Heiztechnik GmbH v Ideal Standard GmbH (C-9/93) [1994] E.C.R.
    I-2789; [1994] 3 C.M.L.R. 857; [1995] F.S.R. 59; *Times,* July 7, 1994; *Financial
    Times,* June 28, 1994, ECJ . . . .   *Digested,* 94/**4870**:
                    Applied, 96/5713, 06/2606, 07/2686: *Considered,* 04/2410:
                    Followed, 01/4029: *Referred to,* 98/3506, 99/3572
Il Ponte Finanziaria SpA v Office for Harmonisation in the Internal Market (Trade Marks
    and Designs) (OHIM) (C-234/06) [2007] Bus. L.R. D121, ECJ
IM (Turkey) v Secretary of State for the Home Department [2007] EWCA Civ 505;
    (2007) 151 S.J.L.B. 674, CA (Civ Div)
Immerzeel v Santam Ltd [2007] Lloyd's Rep. I.R. 106, Sup Ct (SA)
Impact Foiling Ltd v Revenue and Customs Commissioners [2006] S.T.C. (S.C.D.) 764;
    [2006] S.T.I. 2350, Sp Comm . . . .   *Digested,* 07/**4084**
Imperial Chemical Industries (ICI) Ltd v Commission of the European Communities (48/
    69) [1972] E.C.R. 619; [1972] C.M.L.R. 557, ECJ . . . .   *Digested,* 72/**1312**:
                    Applied, 06/602: *Considered,* 00/3704, 05/570, 07/621
Imperial Tobacco Group Ltd, Re (Unreported, February 11, 1969), Ch D . . . .   *Considered,* 07/**2447**
Impexbond v Bank of Credit and Commerce International see MS Fashions Ltd v Bank
    of Credit and Commerce International SA (In Liquidation)
Implementation of Art.5(3) of the Rental Rights Directive, Re (C-53/05) see Commission
    of the European Communities v Portugal (C-53/05)
Impuls Medienmarketing GmbH's Trade Mark Application (I ZR 183/03) [2007] E.T.M.R.
    46, BGH (Ger) . . . .   *Digested,* 07/**2690**
In Health Group SA Public Body & Hospital v Revenue and Customs Commissioners
    [2006] B.V.C. 2718; [2006] V. & D.R. 281; [2006] S.T.I. 2107, V&DTr (London)   *Digested,* 07/**4345**
Inco Europe Ltd v First Choice Distribution [2000] 1 W.L.R. 586; [2000] 2 All E.R.
    109; [2000] 1 All E.R. (Comm) 674; [2000] 1 Lloyd's Rep. 467; [2000] C.L.C.
    1015; [2000] B.L.R. 259; (2000) 2 T.C.L.R. 487; 74 Con. L.R. 55; (2000)
    97(12) L.S.G. 39; (2000) 144 S.J.L.B. 134; [2000] N.P.C. 22; *Times,* March 10,
    2000; *Independent,* March 15, 2000, HL; affirming [1999] 1 W.L.R. 270; [1999]
    1 All E.R. 820; [1999] C.L.C. 165; (1999) 1 T.C.L.R. 169; (1998) 95(41) L.S.G.
    45; (1998) 142 S.J.L.B. 269; *Times,* October 22, 1998; *Independent,* October 12,
    1998, CA (Civ Div) . . . .   *Digested,* 00/**220**:
                    Applied, 02/3792, 02/5549, 03/1962, 07/2810: *Considered,* 05/2742,
                    07/848: *Followed,* 03/5952
Income Tax Commissioner v Hyundai Heavy Industries Co Ltd 10 I.T.L. Rep. 452, Sup
    Ct (Ind)
Income Tax Reductions in the Azores, Re (C-88/03) see Portugal v Commission of the
    European Communities (C-88/03)
Independent Assessor v O'Brien see R. (on the application of O'Brien) v Independent
    Assessor
Independent Committee for the Supervision of Standards of Telephone Information
    Services v Andronikou [2007] EWHC 2307 (Admin); [2007] A.C.D. 103, QBD
    (Admin)
Independent Insurance Co Ltd (In Provisional Liquidation) (No.1), Re [2002] EWHC 1577
    (Ch); [2004] B.C.C. 919; [2002] 2 B.C.L.C. 709; [2003] B.P.I.R. 562, Ch D
    (Companies Ct) . . . .   *Digested,* 03/**2407**:
                    Applied, 07/**2443**
Independent Music Publishers & Labels Association (Impala) v Commission of the
    European Communities (T-464/04) [2006] E.C.R. II-2289; [2006] 5 C.M.L.R.
    19, CFI (3rd Chamber) . . . .   *Digested,* 07/**635**

Independent Petroleum Group Ltd v Seacarriers Count Pte Ltd (The Count) [2006]
EWHC 3222 (Comm); [2007] 1 All E.R. (Comm) 882, QBD (Comm) . . . .   *Digested,* 07/**815**

Independent Water Co Ltd v Water Services Regulation Authority (Costs) [2007] CAT
21; [2007] Comp. A.R. 885, CAT

Independent Water Co Ltd v Water Services Regulation Authority (formerly Director
General of Water Services) [2007] CAT 6; [2007] Comp. A.R. 614, CAT

Independiente Ltd v Music Trading On-Line (HK) Ltd [2007] EWHC 533 (Ch); [2007]
E.M.L.R. 25; [2007] F.S.R. 21; (2007) 30(4) I.P.D. 30028, Ch D . . . .   *Digested,* 07/**2530**

Independiente Ltd v Music Trading On-Line (HK) Ltd [2007] EWCA Civ 111; [2007] 4
All E.R. 736; (2007) 151 S.J.L.B. 159, CA (Civ Div); affirming [2006] EWHC
3081 (Ch); (2006) 103(45) L.S.G. 28, Ch D . . . .   *Digested,* 07/**542**

India v Bow Street Magistrates Court see India v Rajarathinam

India v Rajarathinam; *sub nom* India v Bow Street Magistrates Court [2006] EWHC
2919 (Admin); [2007] 1 W.L.R. 1593; [2006] Extradition L.R. 258, QBD
(Admin) . . . .   *Digested,* 07/**1665**

India v Taylor; *sub nom* Delhi Electric Supply & Traction Co Ltd, Re [1955] A.C. 491;
[1955] 2 W.L.R. 303; [1955] 1 All E.R. 292; 48 R. & I.T. 98; (1955) 34 A.T.C. 10;
[1955] T.R. 9; (1955) 99 S.J. 94, HL; affirming [1954] Ch. 131; [1953] 3
W.L.R. 1085; [1953] 2 All E.R. 1452; 46 R. & I.T. 817; (1953) 32 A.T.C. 413;
[1953] T.R. 385; (1953) 97 S.J. 861, CA; affirming (1953) 32 A.T.C. 341; [1953]
T.R. 325; *Times,* July 31, 1953, Ch D . . . .   *Digested,* 55/**412**:
Applied, 62/416, 71/10889, 75/170, 81/1204, 89/1692: *Considered,* 83/327,
86/1512, 88/408, 97/876, 07/4200

Indicii Salus Ltd (In Receivership) v Chandrasekaran; *sub nom* Indicii Salus Ltd (In
Receivership) v Chandrasekeran [2007] EWHC 406 (Ch); (2007) 30(4) I.P.D.
30027, Ch D

Indicii Salus Ltd (In Receivership) v Chandrasekeran see Indicii Salus Ltd (In
Receivership) v Chandrasekaran

Inertia Partnership LLP, Re [2007] EWHC 539 (Ch); [2007] Bus. L.R. 879; [2007] B.C.C.
656; [2007] 1 B.C.L.C. 739, Ch D . . . .   *Digested,* 07/**2463**

Inex SA v Office for Harmonisation in the Internal Market (Trade Marks and Designs)
(OHIM) (T-153/03) [2006] E.C.R. II-1677; [2006] E.T.M.R. 92, CFI . . . .   *Digested,* 07/**2640**

Ing Re (UK) Ltd v R&V Versicherung AG [2006] EWHC 1544 (Comm); [2006] 2 All
E.R. (Comm) 870; [2007] 1 B.C.L.C. 108; [2006] Lloyd's Rep. I.R. 653, QBD
(Comm) . . . .   *Digested,* 06/**770**

Ingmar GB Ltd v Eaton Leonard Technologies Inc (C-381/98) [2001] All E.R. (EC) 57;
[2001] 1 All E.R. (Comm) 329; [2000] E.C.R. I-9305; [2001] 1 C.M.L.R. 9;
Times, November 16, 2000, ECJ (5th Chamber) . . . .   *Digested,* 00/**115**:
Applied, 07/68: *Previous proceedings,* 98/115:
Subsequent proceedings, 02/65

Ingraham v Glinton [2006] UKPC 40; [2007] 1 W.L.R. 1, PC (Bah) . . . .   *Digested,* 07/**532**

Ingram v Hambleton-Grey (Unreported, April 12, 2006), CC (Kingston on Thames) [*Ex
rel.* Joanna Kerr, Barrister, Lamb Chambers, Lamb Building, Temple, London] . .   *Digested,* 07/**3165**

Inizan v Caisse Primaire d'Assurance Maladie des Hauts de Seine (C-56/01) [2003]
E.C.R. I-12403; [2006] 1 C.M.L.R. 20, ECJ (5th Chamber) . . . .   *Digested,* 06/**1563**:
Applied, 07/1981: *Considered,* 04/1688

Inland Revenue Commissioners v Ainsworth; *sub nom* Ainsworth v Inland Revenue
Commissioners; *joined cases* Inland Revenue Commissioners v Kilic; Inland
Revenue Commissioners v Stringer; Inland Revenue Commissioners v Thwaites
[2005] EWCA Civ 441; [2005] I.C.R. 1149; [2005] I.R.L.R. 465; *Times,* May 16,
2005, CA (Civ Div); reversing UKEAT/0650/03/Tm, UKEAT/0745/03/TM,
UKEAT/0798/03/TM, UKEAT/0901/03/TM, EAT . . . .   *Digested,* 05/**1273**:
Applied, 07/5143: *Cited,* 07/1443: *Considered,* 07/2941

Inland Revenue Commissioners v Ainsworth (Reference to ECJ); *sub nom* Revenue and
Customs Commissioners v Stringer (Reference to ECJ) [2007] 2 C.M.L.R. 20,
HL . . . .   *Digested,* 07/**1443**:
Previous proceedings, 05/1273

Inland Revenue Commissioners v Crossman; *sub nom* Crossman, Re; Paulin, Re; *joined
case* Inland Revenue Commissioners v Mann [1937] A.C. 26, HL; reversing
[1935] 1 K.B. 26, CA . . . .   *Applied,* 53/986,
69/1065, 91/2123: *Considered,* 92/2517, 93/3686, 07/4066:
Distinguished, 82/1574: *Followed,* 91/4440

Inland Revenue Commissioners v Deutsche Morgan Grenfell Group Plc see Deutsche
Morgan Grenfell Group Plc v Inland Revenue Commissioners

Inland Revenue Commissioners v Goldblatt [1972] Ch. 498; [1972] 2 W.L.R. 953;
[1972] 2 All E.R. 202; 47 T.C. 483; (1971) 116 S.J. 332, Ch D . . . .   *Digested,* 72/**392**:
Considered, 07/2445

Inland Revenue Commissioners v Herd; *sub nom* Herd v Inland Revenue
Commissioners [1993] 1 W.L.R. 1090; [1993] 3 All E.R. 56; [1993] S.T.C. 436;
1993 S.C. (H.L.) 35; 1993 S.L.T. 916; 66 T.C. 29; [1993] S.T.I. 1007; (1993)
90(31) L.S.G. 40; (1993) 143 N.L.J. 957; (1993) 137 S.J.L.B. 173; *Times,* June
22, 1993, HL; reversing 1992 S.C. 253; 1992 S.L.T. 766, IH (Ex Div) . . . .   *Digested,* 93/**2294**:
Applied, 05/4102, 07/4072

Inland Revenue Commissioners v John M Whiteford & Son 1962 S.C. 229; 1962 S.L.T.
    269; 40 T.C. 379; (1962) 41 A.T.C. 166; [1962] T.R. 157, IH (1 Div) . . . .   *Digested*, 62/**3466**:
                         Applied, 07/4105
Inland Revenue Commissioners v Kahn see Toshoku Finance UK Plc (In Liquidation), Re
Inland Revenue Commissioners v Kilic see Inland Revenue Commissioners v Ainsworth
Inland Revenue Commissioners v McEntaggart [2004] EWHC 3431 (Ch); [2007]
    B.C.C. 260; [2006] 1 B.C.L.C. 476; [2006] B.P.I.R. 750, Ch D . . . .   *Digested*, 06/**321**
Inland Revenue Commissioners v Mann see Inland Revenue Commissioners v
    Crossman
Inland Revenue Commissioners v National Federation of Self Employed and Small
    Businesses Ltd see R. v Inland Revenue Commissioners Ex p. National
    Federation of Self Employed and Small Businesses Ltd
Inland Revenue Commissioners v Payne 23 T.C. 610; (1941) 110 L.J. K.B. 323 . . . .   *Applied*, 55/1308,
                  81/1384, 07/4100: *Distinguished*, 06/4226: *Doubted*, 47-51/9945
Inland Revenue Commissioners v Spencer-Nairn [1991] S.T.C. 60; 1991 S.L.T. 594, IH
    (1 Div) . . . .   *Digested*, 91/**4441**:
                        Considered, 07/4108
Inland Revenue Commissioners v Stringer see Inland Revenue Commissioners v
    Ainsworth
Inland Revenue Commissioners v Thwaites see Inland Revenue Commissioners v
    Ainsworth
Inland Revenue Commissioners v William Grant & Sons Distillers Ltd see Revenue and
    Customs Commissioners v William Grant & Sons Distillers Ltd (Scotland)
Inland Revenue Commissioners v Willoughby [1997] 1 W.L.R. 1071; [1997] 4 All E.R.
    65; [1997] S.T.C. 995; 70 T.C. 57; [1997] B.T.C. 393; (1997) 94(29) L.S.G. 28;
    (1997) 147 N.L.J. 1062; (1997) 141 S.J.L.B. 176; *Times*, July 16, 1997, HL;
    affirming [1995] S.T.C. 143; (1995) 92(10) L.S.G. 39; (1995) 139 S.J.L.B. 44;
    Times, January 6, 1995; *Independent*, February 13, 1995, CA (Civ Div) . . . .   *Digested*, 97/**2942**:
                    Considered, 96/1301, 07/3993
Inland Revenue Commissioners, Petitioners see Revenue and Customs Commissioners,
    Petitioners
Inntrepreneur Pub Co Ltd v East Crown Ltd; *sub nom* Inntrepreneur Pub Co (GL) v
    East Crown Ltd [2000] 2 Lloyd's Rep. 611; [2000] 3 E.G.L.R. 31; [2000] 41 E.G.
    209; [2000] N.P.C. 93; *Times*, September 5, 2000, Ch D . . . .   *Digested*, 00/**869**:
             Applied, 06/3943, 07/2735: *Followed*, 02/1316
Inntrepreneur Pub Co (CPC) v Crehan see Crehan v Inntrepreneur Pub Co (CPC)
Inntrepreneur Pub Co (GL) v East Crown Ltd see Inntrepreneur Pub Co Ltd v East
    Crown Ltd
InPower Ltd, Re see Drax Holdings Ltd, Re
Institute of Independent Insurance Brokers v Director General of Fair Trading (Costs); *sub*
    nom Association of British Travel Agents Ltd v Director General of Fair Trading
    (Costs) [2002] CAT 2; [2002] Comp. A.R. 141, CCAT. . . . .   *Applied*, 04/500,
                  04/501, 07/393: *Considered*, 06/600
Instituto Nacional de la Seguridad Social (INSS) v Lazaro (C-33/96) see Arjona v
    Instituto Nacional de la Seguridad Social (INSS) (C-31/96)
Instone v Kaur (Unreported, March 21, 2007), CC (Coventry) [*Ex rel*. Stephen Garner,
    Barrister, No. 8 Chambers, Fountain Court, Steelhouse Lane, Birmingham] . . . .   *Digested*, 07/**3100**
Insurance Co of Africa v Scor (UK) Reinsurance Co Ltd [1985] 1 Lloyd's Rep. 312, CA
    (Civ Div); reversing in part [1983] 1 Lloyd's Rep. 541; [1983] Com. L.R. 81,
    QBD (Comm) . . . .   *Digested*, 85/**1803**:
        Applied, 96/3624, 04/2242, 07/2504: *Considered*, 86/366, 86/366, 88/413,
                            94/2697
Intel Corp Inc v CPM United Kingdom Ltd [2007] EWCA Civ 431; [2007] E.T.M.R. 59;
    [2007] R.P.C. 35; (2007) 30(7) I.P.D. 30044, CA (Civ Div) [2006] EWHC
    1878 (Ch); [2006] E.T.M.R. 90, Ch D . . . .   *Digested*, 07/**2666**
Intel Corp (UK) Ltd v Daw see Daw v Intel Corp (UK) Ltd
Intense Investments Ltd v Development Ventures Ltd [2006] EWHC 1628 (TCC), QBD
    (TCC) . . . .   *Applied*, 07/525
Inter-Leisure Ltd v Lamberts [1997] N.P.C. 49, QBD. . . . .   *Applied*, 07/2947:
                        Considered, 01/4536
Interbrew SA v Competition Commission [2001] EWHC Admin 367; [2001]
    U.K.C.L.R. 954; [2001] E.C.C. 40; *Daily Telegraph*, May 29, 2001, QBD
    (Admin) . . . .   *Digested*, 01/**753**:
                        Considered, 07/1506
Interbulk Ltd v Aiden Shipping Co (The Vimeira) (No.1); *joined case* ICCO International
    Corn Co NV v Interbulk [1984] 2 Lloyd's Rep. 66, CA (Civ Div); reversing
    [1983] 2 Lloyd's Rep. 424; [1983] Com. L.R. 142; (1983) 133 N.L.J. 575, QBD
    (Comm) . . . .   *Digested*, 84/**114**:
            Applied, 98/233, 00/225, 06/196: *Considered*, 85/105, 07/250
Intercall Conferencing Services Ltd v Steer [2007] EWHC 519 (QB); (2007) 104(14)
    L.S.G. 24, QBD
InterDigital Technology Corp v Nokia Corp [2007] EWHC 1913 (Pat); (2007) 30(10)
    I.P.D. 30067, Ch D (Patents Ct)

InterDigital Technology Corp v Nokia Corp [2007] EWHC 987 (Pat); (2007) 30(6)
   I.P.D. 30038, Ch D (Patents Ct)
Interfoto Picture Library Ltd v Stiletto Visual Programmes Ltd [1989] Q.B. 433; [1988]
   2 W.L.R. 615; [1988] 1 All E.R. 348; (1988) 7 Tr. L.R. 187; (1988) 85(9) L.S.G.
   45; (1987) 137 N.L.J. 1159; (1988) 132 S.J. 460, CA (Civ Div) . . . .   *Digested,* 88/**430**:
                                     Applied, 00/5989, 01/955: *Considered,* 88/61, 95/4501, 99/1801, 00/876,
                                              00/4710, 06/776: *Distinguished,* 07/233
Intermet FZCO v Ansol Ltd [2007] EWHC 226 (Comm), QBD (Comm) . . . .   *Doubted,* 07/230
International Brands USA Inc v Goldstein; *sub nom* Shruth Ltd (In Liquidation), Re;
   joined case International Brands USA Inc v Haswell [2005] EWHC 1293 (Ch);
   [2007] B.C.C. 960; [2006] 1 B.C.L.C. 294; [2005] B.P.I.R. 1455, Ch D
   (Companies Ct) . . . .   *Digested,* 06/**2393**
International Brands USA Inc v Haswell see International Brands USA Inc v Goldstein
International Business Machines Corp v Commission of the European Communities
   (60/81) see IBM Corp v Commission of the European Communities (60/81)
International Championship Management Ltd, Re see Cohen v Davis
International Finance Corp v DSNL Offshore Ltd [2005] EWHC 1844 (Comm); [2007]
   2 All E.R. (Comm) 305, QBD (Comm) . . . .   *Digested,* 07/**808**
International Hospitals Group Ltd v Kuenyehia see Kuenyehia v International Hospitals
   Group Ltd
International Masters Publishers Ltd v Revenue and Customs Commissioners; *sub nom*
   R. (on the application of International Masters Publishers Ltd) v Revenue and
   Customs Commissioners [2006] EWCA Civ 1455; [2007] S.T.C. 153; [2007]
   B.T.C. 5035; [2006] S.T.I. 2454; (2006) 103(45) L.S.G. 30; (2006) 156 N.L.J.
   1766; *Independent,* November 10, 2006, CA (Civ Div); affirming [2006] EWHC
   127 (Admin); [2006] S.T.C. 1450; [2006] S.T.I. 205; *Times,* January 30, 2006,
   QBD (Admin); affirming (Unreported, April 25, 2005), V&DTr (London) . . . . . .   *Digested,* 07/**4342**
International Transport Workers' Federation v Viking Line ABP (C-438/05), *Times,*
   December 14, 2007, ECJ (Grand Chamber)
Internationaler Hilfsfonds eV v Commission of the European Communities (C-331/05
   P) [2007] 3 C.M.L.R. 31, ECJ (2nd Chamber)
Internet Auction II (I ZR 35/04) [2007] E.T.M.R. 70, BGH (Ger)
Interporc Im- und Export GmbH v Commission of the European Communities (T-92/98)
   [1999] E.C.R. II-3521; [2000] 1 C.M.L.R. 181; [2000] C.E.C. 337; *Times,*
   February 2, 2000, CFI (1st Chamber) . . . .   *Digested,* 00/**2371**:
                                                      Applied, 07/1585
Intersplav v Ukraine (803/02) 9 I.T.L. Rep. 715, ECHR.   *Digested,* 07/**4133**
Investors Compensation Scheme Ltd v Hopkin & Sons see Investors Compensation
   Scheme Ltd v West Bromwich Building Society (No.1)
Investors Compensation Scheme Ltd v West Bromwich Building Society (No.1); *joined*
   cases Investors Compensation Scheme Ltd v Hopkin & Sons; Alford v West
   Bromwich Building Society; Armitage v West Bromwich Building Society [1998]
   1 W.L.R. 896; [1998] 1 All E.R. 98; [1998] 1 B.C.L.C. 531; [1997] C.L.C. 1243;
   [1997] P.N.L.R. 541; (1997) 147 N.L.J. 989; *Times,* June 24, 1997, HL; reversing
   [1998] 1 B.C.L.C. 521; [1997] C.L.C. 348; [1997] P.N.L.R. 166; [1997] N.P.C.
   104; *Times,* November 8, 1996, CA (Civ Div); affirming [1998] 1 B.C.L.C. 493;
   Times, October 10, 1996, Ch D . . . .   *Digested,* 97/**2537**:
                             Applied, 99/852, 99/852, 99/3420, 99/5795, 00/900, 01/375, 01/959,
               01/4272, 01/4950, 01/5508, 02/207, 02/3028, 02/3821, 03/500, 03/530,
               03/671, 03/2460, 03/2723, 04/273, 04/653, 04/670, 04/2215, 04/2223,
               04/3255, 04/4614, 05/288, 05/469, 05/718, 05/2402, 06/203, 06/2411,
           07/1327, 07/2494, 07/3028: *Cited,* 99/2489, 07/1841: *Considered,* 99/2480,
                  00/878, 00/3686, 00/5932, 01/2430, 02/4683, 04/2205, 04/2407,
                        04/4988, 07/1323: *Followed,* 98/807, 00/2173
Investrand BV v Staatssecretaris van Financien (C-435/05) [2007] S.T.I. 340, ECJ
   (4th Chamber)
Inwards v Williamson (Inspector of Taxes) [2003] S.T.C. (S.C.D.) 355; [2003] S.T.I.
   1595, Sp Comm. . . . .   *Digested,* 04/**3701**:
                                                     Applied, 07/4031
Iosub Caras v Romania (7198/04) [2007] 1 F.L.R. 661; [2006] 3 F.C.R. 130; [2007]
   Fam. Law 8, ECHR . . . .   *Digested,* 07/**1747**
Ipourgos Ikonomikon v Georgakis (C-391/04) [2007] All E.R. (EC) 1106; [2007] 2
   B.C.L.C. 692; [2007] 3 C.M.L.R. 4; [2007] C.E.C. 891, ECJ (3rd Chamber) . . .   *Digested,* 07/**585**
Iqbal v Whipps Cross University Hospital NHS Trust; *sub nom* Whipps Cross University
   NHS Trust v Iqbal [2007] EWCA Civ 1190, CA (Civ Div); reversing [2006]
   EWHC 3111 (QB); [2007] P.I.Q.R. Q5; [2007] LS Law Medical 97, QBD . . . . .   *Digested,* 07/**3071**
Iran v Barakat Galleries Ltd [2007] EWCA Civ 1374; [2007] 2 C.L.C. 994, CA (Civ
   Div); reversing [2007] EWHC 705 (QB), QBD
Iran v Berend [2007] EWHC 132 (QB); [2007] 2 All E.R. (Comm) 132; [2007] Bus.
   L.R. D65, QBD . . . .   *Digested,* 07/**677**
Irani v Irani [2006] EWHC 1811 (Ch); [2006] W.T.L.R. 1561, Ch D . . . .   *Digested,* 07/**3955**
Ireland v United Kingdom (A/25) (1979-80) 2 E.H.R.R. 25, ECHR . . . .   *Digested,* 79/**1175**:
                 Applied, 97/2764, 98/3162, 07/2203, 07/2230: *Considered,* 96/3138,
                                 06/2105: *Followed,* 98/3069

Irish Stock Exchange Ltd's Community Trade Mark Application (R 1604/2006-2) [2007] E.T.M.R. 75, OHIM (2nd Bd App)

Irvine v Irvine [2006] EWHC 583 (Ch); [2006] 4 All E.R. 102; [2007] 1 B.C.L.C. 445; [2006] W.T.L.R. 1411; *Times*, April 21, 2006, Ch D . . . . *Digested*, 06/**558**

Irvine v Irvine [2006] EWHC 406 (Ch); [2007] 1 B.C.L.C. 349, Ch D . . . . *Digested*, 07/**578**

Irvine v Talksport Ltd [2002] EWHC 367 (Ch); [2002] 1 W.L.R. 2355; [2002] 2 All E.R. 414; [2002] E.M.L.R. 32; [2002] F.S.R. 60; (2002) 25(6) I.P.D. 25039; (2002) 99(18) L.S.G. 38; (2002) 152 N.L.J. 553; (2002) 146 S.J.L.B. 85, Ch D
. . . . *Digested*, 02/**2783**:
Considered, 07/2674: *Subsequent proceedings*, 03/944

Irving v Revenue and Customs Commissioners C3/2007/0432, CA (Civ Div); affirming [2007] EWHC 147 (Ch); [2007] S.T.C. 1712; [2007] B.T.C. 269; [2007] S.T.I. 339; *Times*, March 8, 2007, Ch D; affirming [2006] S.T.C. (S.C.D.) 241; [2006] S.T.I. 1270, Sp Comm . . . . *Digested*, 07/**4094**

Isaacs v Belfield Furnishings Ltd; *sub nom* Belfield Furnishings Ltd, Re [2006] EWHC 183 (Ch); [2006] 2 B.C.L.C. 705, Ch D (Companies Ct) . . . . *Digested*, 07/**459**

Isaacs v Robertson [1985] A.C. 97; [1984] 3 W.L.R. 705; [1984] 3 All E.R. 140; (1984) 81 L.S.G. 2769; (1984) 134 N.L.J. 745, PC (StV) . . . . *Digested*, 84/**2660**:
Applied, 87/2146, 07/465: *Considered*, 85/2722: *Followed*, 98/3308

Isabelle Lancray SA v Peters und Sickert KG (C-305/88) [1990] E.C.R. I-2725; [1991] I.L.Pr. 99; *Times*, September 19, 1990, ECJ (6th Chamber) . . . . *Digested*, 90/**2096**:
Applied, 07/462: *Considered*, 02/638

Isherwood v Day (Unreported, March 13, 2007), CC (Bradford) [*Ex rel.* Mark Henley, Barrister, Zenith Chambers, 10 Park Square, Leeds] . . . . *Digested*, 07/**1068**

Ishikawajma-Harima Heavy Industries Ltd v Director of Income Tax, Mumbai 9 I.T.L. Rep. 799, Sup Ct (Ind)

Islam v Immigration Appeal Tribunal Ex p. Shah see Islam v Secretary of State for the Home Department

Islam v Secretary of State for the Home Department; *sub nom* R. v Secretary of State for the Home Department Ex p. Shah; Islam v Immigration Appeal Tribunal Ex p. Shah [1999] 2 A.C. 629; [1999] 2 W.L.R. 1015; [1999] 2 All E.R. 545; 6 B.H.R.C. 356; [1999] Imm. A.R. 283; [1999] I.N.L.R. 144; (1999) 96(17) L.S.G. 24; (1999) 143 S.J.L.B. 115; *Times*, March 26, 1999, HL; reversing [1998] 1 W.L.R. 74; [1998] 4 All E.R. 30; 2 B.H.R.C. 590; [1997] Imm. A.R. 584; [1998] I.N.L.R. 97; (1997) 94(36) L.S.G. 43; *Times*, October 13, 1997, CA (Civ Div); reversing [1997] Imm. A.R. 145; *Times*, November 12, 1996; *Independent*, December 2, 1996, QBD. . . . . *Digested*, 99/**3172**:
Applied, 03/2275, 05/2226, 05/2227: *Cited*, 97/2856: *Considered*, 00/3311, 01/3642, 01/3642, 01/3651, 07/2303: *Distinguished*, 00/3293, 00/3315:
Followed, 01/3638

Island Consultants Ltd v Revenue and Customs Commissioners [2007] S.T.C. (S.C.D.) 700; [2007] S.T.I. 1871, Sp Comm

Island Records Ltd v Tring International Plc [1996] 1 W.L.R. 1256; [1995] 3 All E.R. 444; [1995] F.S.R. 560; *Times*, April 28, 1995, Ch D . . . . *Digested*, 95/**849**:
Applied, 07/2530: *Followed*, 97/1031: *Referred to*, 96/1276

Isle of Wight Council v Revenue and Customs Commissioners; *sub nom* Revenue and Customs Commissioners v Isle of Wight Council; *joined cases* South Tyneside MBC v Revenue and Customs Commissioners; West Berkshire Council v Revenue and Customs Commissioners; Mid Suffolk DC v Revenue and Customs Commissioners [2007] EWHC 219 (Ch); [2007] B.T.C. 5240; [2007] B.V.C. 209; [2007] S.T.I. 345, Ch D [2006] B.V.C. 2524; [2006] V. & D.R. 75; [2006] S.T.I. 1367, V&DTr (London) . . . . *Digested*, 07/**4294**

Islington LBC v Honeygan-Green; *sub nom* Honeygan-Green v Islington LBC; B5/2007/1271; B5/2007/0279, CA (Civ Div); reversing [2007] EWHC 1270 (QB); [2007] 4 All E.R. 818; [2007] 39 E.G. 154; (2007) 104(25) L.S.G. 35; (2007) 157 N.L.J. 779; (2007) 151 S.J.L.B. 744; *Times*, June 29, 2007, QBD . . . . *Digested*, 07/**2767**

Islington LBC v Westdeutsche Landesbank Girozentrale see Westdeutsche Landesbank Girozentrale v Islington LBC

Ismail v Barnet LBC see Barnet LBC v Ismail

Isoplus Fernwarmetechnik Vertriebsgesellschaft mbH v Commission of the European Communities (C-202/02 P) see Dansk Rorindustri A/S v Commission of the European Communities (C-189/02 P)

Issa v Turkey (31821/96) (2005) 41 E.H.R.R. 27; 17 B.H.R.C. 473, ECHR . . . . *Digested*, 05/**2065**:
Not applied, 07/2239

Italy v Commission of the European Communities (173/73); *sub nom* Aids to the Textile Industry, Re (173/73) [1974] E.C.R. 709; [1974] 2 C.M.L.R. 593, ECJ . . *Digested*, 75/**1197**:
Applied, 97/2399, 07/651, 07/1646

Italy v Commission of the European Communities (C66/02) [2005] E.C.R. I-10901, ECJ. . . . . *Considered*, 07/650

Italy v Council of the European Union (C-120/99) [2001] E.C.R. I-7997, ECJ (5th Chamber) . . . . *Considered*, 07/107

ITC Innovative Technology Center GmbH v Bundesagentur fur Arbeit (C-208/05) [2007] All E.R. (EC) 611, ECJ (3rd Chamber) . . . . *Digested*, 07/**1627**

Ivanova v Bulgaria (52435/99) 23 B.H.R.C. 208; [2007] E.L.R. 612, ECHR

Ivax Pharmaceuticals UK Ltd v Akzo Nobel BV; *joined case* Arrow Generics Ltd v Akzo Nobel NV [2006] EWHC 1089 (Pat); [2007] R.P.C. 3; (2006) 29(8) I.P.D. 29059, Ch D (Patents Ct) .... *Digested*, 07/**2629**

Ixis Corporate and Investment Bank (formerly CDC Ixis Capital Markets) v Westlb AG [2007] EWHC 1852 (Comm); (2007) 104(36) L.S.G. 30, QBD (Comm)

J, Re see F (Abduction: Unborn Child), Re

J v C see J (Paternity: Welfare of Child), Re

J v C (Void Marriage: Status of Children) [2006] EWCA Civ 551; [2007] Fam. 1; [2006] 3 W.L.R. 876; [2006] 2 F.L.R. 1098; [2006] Fam. Law 742; *Times*, June 1, 2006; *Independent*, May 25, 2006, CA (Civ Div) .... *Digested*, 06/**1719**: *Considered*, 07/1784

J v Crown Prosecution Service see Jennings v CPS

J v E; *sub nom* R (Children) (Confidential Information: Protecting Anonymity), Re; R (Children) (Secure Editing of Documents), Re [2007] EWHC 876 (Fam); [2007] 1 W.L.R. 1654; [2007] 2 F.L.R. 759; [2007] 2 F.C.R. 1; [2007] Fam. Law 703, Fam Div. .... *Digested*, 07/**1816**

J v Newport City Council see MJ (A Child) (Adoption Order or Special Guardianship Order), Re

J v Secretary of State for the Home Department [2006] EWCA Civ 1238; [2007] Imm. A.R. 73, CA (Civ Div) .... *Digested*, 07/**2297**

J v Worcestershire CC see A v Essex CC

J Jarvis & Sons Ltd v Blue Circle Dartford Estates Ltd [2007] EWHC 1262 (TCC); [2007] B.L.R. 439, QBD (TCC) .... *Digested*, 07/**229**

J Sainsbury Ltd v Hitt see Sainsbury's Supermarkets Ltd v Hitt

J Sainsbury Plc v Hitt see Sainsbury's Supermarkets Ltd v Hitt

J Sainsbury Plc v HM Courts Service (South West Region, Devon & Cornwall Area) see Sainsbury's Supermarkets Ltd v HM Courts Service (South West Region, Devon & Cornwall Area)

J Sainsbury Plc v One in a Million Ltd see British Telecommunications Plc v One in a Million Ltd

J Smiths Haulage Ltd, Re [2007] B.C.C. 135, Ch D .... *Digested*, 07/**2390**

J (A Child) v Birmingham Community Sports Ltd (Unreported, April 30, 2007), CC (Wolverhampton) [*Ex rel.* Stephen Garner, Barrister, No. 8 Chambers, Fountain Court, Steelhouse Lane, Birmingham] .... *Digested*, 07/**3190**

J (A Child) v Griffith Jones's Executor (Unreported, November 25, 2005), QBD [*Ex rel.* Andrew Arentsen, 33 Park Place, Cardiff] .... *Digested*, 07/**3080**

J (A Child) v Rushby (Unreported, February 28, 2007), CC (Rotherham) [*Ex rel.* Richard Thyne, Barrister, Paradise Chambers, Sheffield] .... *Digested*, 07/**3084**

J (A Child) (Care Proceedings: Fair Trial), Re; *sub nom* NJ v Essex CC [2006] EWCA Civ 545; [2007] 1 F.L.R. 77; [2006] 2 F.C.R. 107; [2006] Fam. Law 734; *Times*, June 21, 2006, CA (Civ Div). .... *Digested*, 06/**1666**

J (A Child) (Child Returned Abroad: Convention Rights) see J (A Child) (Custody Rights: Jurisdiction), Re

J (A Child) (Custody Rights: Jurisdiction), Re; *sub nom* Jomah v Attar; J (Child Returned Abroad: Human Rights), Re; J (A Child) (Return to Foreign Jurisdiction: Convention Rights), Re; J (A Child) (Child Returned Abroad: Convention Rights) [2005] UKHL 40; [2006] 1 A.C. 80; [2006] 3 W.L.R. 14; [2005] 3 All E.R. 291; [2005] 2 F.L.R. 802; [2005] 2 F.C.R. 381; [2005] Fam. Law 689; (2005) 155 N.L.J. 972; (2005) 149 S.J.L.B. 773; *Times*, June 17, 2005, HL; reversing [2004] EWCA Civ 417; [2004] 2 F.L.R. 85; [2004] 2 F.C.R. 337; [2004] Fam. Law 489; *Times*, April 14, 2004, CA (Civ Div) .... *Digested*, 05/**1569**: *Applied*, 07/1736

J (A Child) (Restrictions on Applications), Re [2007] EWCA Civ 906; [2007] 3 F.C.R. 123; [2007] Fam. Law 1071, CA (Civ Div) .... *Digested*, 07/**1781**

J (A Child) (Return to Foreign Jurisdiction: Convention Rights), Re see J (A Child) (Custody Rights: Jurisdiction), Re

J (A Minor) (Abduction: Custody Rights), Re; *sub nom* C v S (Minors) (Abduction: Illegitimate Child) [1990] 2 A.C. 562; [1990] 3 W.L.R. 492; [1990] 2 All E.R. 961; [1990] 2 F.L.R. 442; [1991] F.C.R. 129; [1991] Fam. Law 57; (1990) 154 J.P.N. 674; (1990) 87(35) L.S.G. 39; (1990) 140 N.L.J. 1191; (1990) 134 S.J. 1039; *Times*, July 31, 1990; *Independent*, August 1, 1990; *Guardian*, July 27, 1990; *Daily Telegraph*, September 18, 1990, HL; affirming [1990] 2 All E.R. 449; (1990) 154 J.P.N. 563, CA (Civ Div) .... *Digested*, 90/**3151**: *Applied*, 94/3155, 94/3156, 94/3280, 94/5446, 95/3438, 97/396, 07/1826: *Cited*, 99/4564: *Considered*, 96/530, 96/534, 96/643, 98/4536, 03/1504, 07/1775: *Followed*, 94/5440, 96/605, 03/1505

J (A Minor) (Prohibited Steps Order: Circumcision), Re; *sub nom* J (A Minor) (Specific Issue Orders: Muslim Upbringing and Circumcision), Re; J (Specific Issue Orders: Child's Religious Upbringing and Circumcision), Re [2000] 1 F.L.R. 571; [2000] 1 F.C.R. 307; (2000) 52 B.M.L.R. 82; [2000] Fam. Law 246; (1999) 96(47) L.S.G. 30; *Times*, December 22, 1999, CA (Civ Div); affirming [1999] 2 F.L.R. 678; [1999] 2 F.C.R. 345; [1999] Fam. Law 543; *Times*, June 1, 1999; *Independent*, June 28, 1999, Fam Div . . . . *Digested*, 00/**2484**:
　　　　　　　　　　　　　Applied, 05/1580, 07/3906: *Followed*, 03/1777

J (A Minor) (Specific Issue Orders: Muslim Upbringing and Circumcision), Re see J (A Minor) (Prohibited Steps Order: Circumcision), Re

J (A Minor) (Wardship: Medical Treatment), Re [1991] Fam. 33; [1991] 2 W.L.R. 140; [1990] 3 All E.R. 930; [1991] 1 F.L.R. 366; [1991] F.C.R. 370; [1990] 2 Med. L.R. 67; (1990) 140 N.L.J. 1533; *Times*, October 23, 1990; *Independent*, October 23, 1990; *Guardian*, October 23, 1990; *Daily Telegraph*, October 23, 1990, CA (Civ Div) . . *Digested*, 91/**2588**:
　　　　　　　　　Applied, 00/3247, 05/1677, 06/1853, 07/1984: *Considered*, 92/2954,
　　　　　　　　　　　　　95/3578, 95/4104, 97/2593, 05/1794, 05/1848, 06/1847

J (Child Returned Abroad: Human Rights), Re see J (A Child) (Custody Rights: Jurisdiction), Re

J (Children), Re; *sub nom* J (Children) (Residence Order: Removal Outside Jurisdiction), Re; J (Children: Leave to Remove: Urgent Case) [2006] EWCA Civ 1897; [2007] 1 F.L.R. 2033; [2007] 2 F.C.R. 149; [2007] Fam. Law 490, CA (Civ Div) . . . . *Digested*, 07/**1795**

J (Children) (Residence Order: Removal Outside Jurisdiction), Re see J (Children), Re

J (Children: Contact), Re, *Times*, August 17, 2007, Fam Div

J (Children: Leave to Remove: Urgent Case) see J (Children), Re

J (Paternity: Welfare of Child), Re; *sub nom* J v C [2006] EWHC 2837 (Fam); [2007] 1 F.L.R. 1064; [2007] 1 F.C.R. 365; [2007] Fam. Law 23, Fam Div . . . . *Digested*, 07/**1785**:
　　　　　　　　　　　　　　　　　　　　　　　　　　Considered, 07/1784

J (Specific Issue Orders: Child's Religious Upbringing and Circumcision), Re see J (A Minor) (Prohibited Steps Order: Circumcision), Re

J&A Developments Ltd v Edina Manufacturing Ltd [2006] N.I. 85; [2007] C.I.L.L. 2417, QBD (NI)

J&H Ritchie Ltd v Lloyd Ltd; *sub nom* JH Ritchie Ltd v Lloyd Ltd [2007] UKHL 9; [2007] Bus. L.R. 944; [2007] 1 W.L.R. 670; [2007] 2 All E.R. 353; [2007] 1 All E.R. (Comm) 987; [2007] 1 Lloyd's Rep. 544; 2007 S.C. (H.L.) 89; 2007 S.L.T. 377; [2007] 1 C.L.C. 208; (2007) 157 N.L.J. 403; (2007) 151 S.J.L.B. 397; 2007 G.W.D. 9-171; *Times*, March 8, 2007, HL; reversing 2005 1 S.C. 155; 2005 S.L.T. 64; 2005 S.C.L.R. 447; 2005 G.W.D. 2-38, IH (Ex Div) . . . . *Digested*, 07/**3568**

J-C (A Child) (Committal Proceedings), Re [2007] EWCA Civ 896; [2007] 3 F.C.R. 135; [2007] Fam. Law 1064, CA (Civ Div) . . . . *Digested*, 07/**1837**

JA v Secretary of State for the Home Department; *sub nom* JA (Practice on Reconsideration: Wani Applied: Ecuador), Re [2006] UKAIT 13; [2006] Imm. A.R. 392, AIT. . . . . *Digested*, 07/**2275**

JA Pye (Oxford) Ltd v United Kingdom (44302/02) 23 B.H.R.C. 405; [2007] R.V.R. 302; [2007] 41 E.G. 200 (C.S.); *Times*, October 1, 2007, ECHR (Grand Chamber)

JA (Practice on Reconsideration: Wani Applied: Ecuador), Re see JA v Secretary of State for the Home Department

Jacklin v Chief Constable of West Yorkshire [2007] EWCA Civ 181; (2007) 151 S.J.L.B. 261, CA (Civ Div)

Jackson v Bell [2001] EWCA Civ 387; [2001] B.P.I.R. 612; [2001] Fam. Law 879, CA (Civ Div) . . . . *Digested*, 01/**3727**:
　　　　　　　　　　　　　　　　　　　　　　　　　Considered, 07/2402

Jackson v Brock Plc see Grieves v FT Everard & Sons Ltd

Jackson v Thakrar [2007] EWHC 626 (TCC); [2007] B.L.R. 241; [2007] B.P.I.R. 367; (2007) 157 N.L.J. 483, QBD (TCC) . . . . *Digested*, 07/**361**

Jackson v Thakrar [2007] EWHC 271 (TCC); 113 Con. L.R. 58; [2007] B.P.I.R. 367; (2007) 157 N.L.J. 331, QBD (TCC) . . . . *Digested*, 07/**811**

Jacob v UIC Insurance Co Ltd; *sub nom* UIC Insurance Co Ltd (In Provisional Liquidation), Re [2006] EWHC 2717 (Ch); [2007] Bus. L.R. 568; [2007] B.C.C. 167; [2007] 2 B.C.L.C. 46; [2007] B.P.I.R. 494, Ch D . . . . *Digested*, 07/**2443**

Jacob v Vockrodt [2007] EWHC 2403 (QB); [2007] B.P.I.R. 1568; [2007] N.P.C. 111, QBD

Jacques v Revenue and Customs Commissioners [2007] S.T.C. (S.C.D.) 166; [2007] S.T.I. 263, Sp Comm. . . . . *Digested*, 07/**4067**

Jacquet v Land Nordrhein-Westfalen (C-65/96) see Land Nordrhein-Westfalen v Uecker (C-64/96)

Jade Palace Ltd v Revenue and Customs Commissioners [2006] S.T.C. (S.C.D.) 419; [2006] S.T.I. 1623, Sp Comm . . . . *Digested*, 07/**4155**:
　　　　　　　　　　　　　　　　　　　　　　　　　Applied, 07/4161

Jaffray v Society of Lloyds [2007] EWCA Civ 586; [2007] C.P. Rep. 36; [2007] 1 C.L.C. 938; (2007) 104(27) L.S.G. 31; (2007) 151 S.J.L.B. 857, CA (Civ Div). . *Digested*, 07/**510**

Jag Communications (Plymouth) Ltd v Revenue and Customs Commissioners [2007] V. & D.R. 251, V&DTr (London)

Jaggard v Sawyer [1995] 1 W.L.R. 269; [1995] 2 All E.R. 189; [1995] 1 E.G.L.R. 146; [1995] 13 E.G. 132; [1994] E.G. 139 (C.S.); [1994] N.P.C. 116; *Independent,* August 22, 1994, CA (Civ Div); affirming [1993] 1 E.G.L.R. 197, CC (Weymouth) . . . . *Digested,* 95/**4142**:
                         Applied, 05/3434, 07/3425: *Cited,* 01/1549: *Considered,* 98/4341, 00/5127,
                                                 04/912, 06/1018, 07/1060

Jaguar Cars Ltd v Controller of Patents, Designs and Trade Marks [2006] IEHC 103; [2006] E.T.M.R. 72, HC (Irl) . . . . *Digested,* 07/**2662**

Jahn v Germany (46720/99) (2006) 42 E.H.R.R. 49, ECHR (Grand Chamber) . . . . . . *Digested,* 06/**2111**:
                                                       Applied, 07/2206

Jain v Secretary of State for the Home Department [2000] Imm. A.R. 76; [2000] I.N.L.R. 71, CA (Civ Div) . . . . *Digested,* 00/**3310**:
                                               Considered, 07/2296

Jain v Trent Strategic HA [2007] EWCA Civ 1186; *Times,* November 30, 2007, CA (Civ Div); reversing [2006] EWHC 3019 (QB), QBD . . . . *Digested,* 07/**2937**

Jalloh v Germany (54810/00) (2007) 44 E.H.R.R. 32; 20 B.H.R.C. 575; [2007] Crim. L.R. 717, ECHR. . . . . *Digested,* 07/**2200**

Jameel v Wall Street Journal Europe SPRL (No.3) [2006] UKHL 44; [2007] 1 A.C. 359; [2007] Bus. L.R. 291; [2006] 3 W.L.R. 642; [2006] 4 All E.R. 1279; [2007] E.M.L.R. 2; [2006] H.R.L.R. 41; 21 B.H.R.C. 471; (2006) 103(41) L.S.G. 36; (2006) 156 N.L.J. 1612; (2006) 150 S.J.L.B. 1392; *Times,* October 12, 2006; *Independent,* October 17, 2006, HL; reversing [2005] EWCA Civ 74; [2005] Q.B. 904; [2005] 2 W.L.R. 1577; [2005] 4 All E.R. 356; [2005] E.M.L.R. 17; [2005] H.R.L.R. 10; (2005) 102(15) L.S.G. 33; *Times,* February 14, 2005; *Independent,* February 9, 2005, CA (Civ Div); affirming [2004] EWHC 37 (QB); [2004] E.M.L.R. 11, QBD . . . . *Digested,* 06/**1050**:
              Applied, 07/1075: *Considered,* 07/2189: *Previous proceedings,* 04/933

James v Greenwich LBC A2/2007/0368, CA (Civ Div); affirming [2007] I.C.R. 577; [2007] I.R.L.R. 168, EAT . . . . *Digested,* 07/**1346**:
                                        Applied, 07/1344: *Considered,* 07/4073

James v Redcats (Brands) Ltd [2007] I.C.R. 1006; [2007] I.R.L.R. 296, EAT . . . . . *Applied,* 07/1345

James v Thomas [2007] EWCA Civ 1212; [2007] 3 F.C.R. 696, CA (Civ Div) . . . . *Digested,* 07/**3361**

James v United Kingdom (8793/79) see James v United Kingdom (A/98)

James v United Kingdom (A/98); *sub nom* Trustees of the Duke of Westminster's Estate v United Kingdom (8793/79); James v United Kingdom (8793/79) (1986) 8 E.H.R.R. 123; [1986] R.V.R. 139, ECHR (1984) 6 E.H.R.R. CD475, Eur Comm HR . . . . *Digested,* 86/**1650**:
             Applied, 03/2171, 05/2027, 06/2187, 06/2193, 07/3977: *Considered,* 96/1118,
                 97/2796, 01/1844, 03/2095, 03/2838, 03/3485, 03/5819, 04/1376,
                 05/3376, 06/2089, 06/2185, 07/2773: *Followed,* 98/4201, 02/3803

James Hay Pension Trustees Ltd v First Secretary of State; *sub nom* First Secretary of State v James Hay Pension Trustees Ltd [2006] EWCA Civ 1387; [2007] 1 P. & C.R. 23; [2007] J.P.L. 643; (2006) 103(43) L.S.G. 27; [2006] N.P.C. 115; *Times,* November 15, 2006, CA (Civ Div); reversing [2005] EWHC 2713 (Admin); [2006] J.P.L. 1004; [2005] N.P.C. 139, QBD (Admin) . . . . *Digested,* 07/**3265**

Jamieson v Commissioner for Internal Revenue [2007] NSWSC 324; 9 I.T.L. Rep. 954, Sup Ct (NSW) . . . . *Digested,* 07/**679**

Janet Reger International Ltd v Tiree Ltd [2006] EWHC 1743 (Ch); [2007] 1 P. & C.R. 24; [2006] 3 E.G.L.R. 131; [2006] 30 E.G. 102 (C.S.), Ch D . . . . *Digested,* 07/**2729**

Janik v Standards Board For England [2007] EWHC 835 (Admin); (2007) 104(14) L.S.G. 22, QBD (Admin)

Janosevic v Sweden (34619/97) (2004) 38 E.H.R.R. 22, ECHR . . . . *Considered,* 07/2226

Januzi v Secretary of State for the Home Department; *joined cases* Hamid v Secretary of State for the Home Department; Gaafar v Secretary of State for the Home Department; Mohammed v Secretary of State for the Home Department [2006] UKHL 5; [2006] 2 A.C. 426; [2006] 2 W.L.R. 397; [2006] 3 All E.R. 305; 21 B.H.R.C. 65; [2006] Imm. A.R. 252; [2006] I.N.L.R. 118; (2006) 103(11) L.S.G. 25; (2006) 150 S.J.L.B. 223; *Times,* February 16, 2006; *Independent,* February 24, 2006, HL; affirming [2003] EWCA Civ 1187; [2003] I.N.L.R. 608, CA (Civ Div) . . . . *Digested,* 06/**2232**

Japan Tobacco Inc v Commission of the European Communities (T-380/00) see Philip Morris International Inc v Commission of the European Communities (T-377/00)

Jardim v Nyatsambo (Unreported, May 15, 2007), CC (Milton Keynes) [*Ex rel.* David McHugh, Barrister, Clerksroom, Tolworth] . . . . *Digested,* 07/**3145**

Jarmain v Secretary of State for the Environment, Transport and the Regions (No.1); *sub nom* R. v Secretary of State for the Environment, Transport and the Regions Ex p. Jarmain [2000] 2 P.L.R. 126; [2000] J.P.L. 1063, CA (Civ Div); affirming [1999] 2 P.L.R. 89; [1999] J.P.L. 1106; [1999] E.G. 41 (C.S.); (1999) 96(12) L.S.G. 35; (1999) 96(15) L.S.G. 30; *Times,* April 13, 1999; *Independent,* April 19, 1999, QBD . . . . *Digested,* 00/**4454**:
                                                     Applied, 07/3232

Jarrah Timber & Wood Paving Corp Ltd v Samuel see Samuel v Jarrah Timber & Wood Paving Corp Ltd

Jarrom v Sellars [2007] EWHC 1366 (Ch); [2007] W.T.L.R. 1219, Ch D
Jarvis v Hampshire CC see Phelps v Hillingdon LBC
Jasmine Trustees Ltd v Wells & Hind (A Firm) [2007] EWHC 38 (Ch); [2007] 3 W.L.R.
    810; [2007] 1 All E.R. 1142; [2007] S.T.C. 660; [2007] Pens. L.R. 71; [2007]
    B.T.C. 185; [2007] W.T.L.R. 489; (2006-07) 9 I.T.E.L.R. 574; [2007] S.T.I. 261;
    Times, February 12, 2007, Ch D ....   Digested, 07/**4258**
Jassi v Gallagher [2006] EWCA Civ 1065; [2007] P.N.L.R. 4; [2006] 31 E.G. 88
    (C.S.); [2006] N.P.C. 91, CA (Civ Div); affirming [2005] EWHC 2962 (Ch);
    [2006] 1 E.G. 99 (C.S.), Ch D ....   Digested, 07/**2945**
Jaura v Ahmed [2002] EWCA Civ 210; Times, March 18, 2002, CA (Civ Div) ....   Digested, 02/**925**:
                    Applied, 07/4359
Javed (Umran) see R. v Saleem (Abdul)
JB Investments Pty Ltd v Valuer General [2007] R.A. 351
JCB Service v Commission of the European Communities (C-167/04 P) [2006] E.C.R.
    I-8935; [2006] 5 C.M.L.R. 23; [2007] C.E.C. 799, ECJ (2nd Chamber) .....   Digested, 07/**615**
JCB Service v Commission of the European Communities (T67/01) [2004] E.C.R. II-
    49; [2004] 4 C.M.L.R. 24, CFI ....   Reversed in part,
                    07/615
JD v East Berkshire Community Health NHS Trust; sub nom MAK v Dewsbury
    Healthcare NHS Trust; D v East Berkshire Community NHS Trust; joined cases K
    v Dewsbury Healthcare NHS Trust; RK v Oldham NHS Trust [2005] UKHL 23;
    [2005] 2 A.C. 373; [2005] 2 W.L.R. 993; [2005] 2 All E.R. 443; [2005] 2
    F.L.R. 284; [2005] 2 F.C.R. 81; [2005] 8 C.C.L. Rep. 185; [2005] Lloyd's Rep.
    Med. 263; (2005) 83 B.M.L.R. 66; [2005] Fam. Law 615; (2005) 155 N.L.J.
    654; Times, April 22, 2005; Independent, April 27, 2005, HL; affirming [2003]
    EWCA Civ 1151; [2004] Q.B. 558; [2004] 2 W.L.R. 58; [2003] 4 All E.R. 796;
    [2003] 2 F.L.R. 1166; [2003] 3 F.C.R. 1; [2003] H.R.L.R. 35; [2003] U.K.H.R.R.
    1200; (2004) 7 C.C.L. Rep. 63; [2003] Lloyd's Rep. Med. 552; (2004) 76
    B.M.L.R. 61; [2003] Fam. Law 816; (2003) 100(36) L.S.G. 37; Times, August
    22, 2003; Independent, October 1, 2003, CA (Civ Div); affirming [2003] Lloyd's
    Rep. Med. 9, CC (Chester) ....   Digested, 05/**2848**:
        Applied, 06/1662: Considered, 06/2887, 07/2916, 07/2937:
        Distinguished, 05/3424: Followed, 07/2934
JD Wetherspoon Plc v Jay Mar Estates [2007] EWHC 856 (TCC); [2007] B.L.R. 285;
    113 Con. L.R. 101; [2007] N.P.C. 53, QBD (TCC) ....   Digested, 07/**252**
JD Wetherspoon Plc v Van De Berg & Co Ltd [2007] EWHC 1044 (Ch); [2007]
    P.N.L.R. 28, Ch D ....   Digested, 07/**471**
JE v DE; sub nom DE, Re [2006] EWHC 3459 (Fam); [2007] 2 F.L.R. 1150; (2007)
    10 C.C.L. Rep. 149; [2007] M.H.L.R. 39, Fam Div ....   Digested, 07/**3913**
Jedamski v Poland (73547/01) (2007) 45 E.H.R.R. 47, ECHR
Jefferey v First Secretary of State; sub nom R. (on the application of Jefferey) v First
    Secretary of State [2007] EWCA Civ 584, CA (Civ Div); affirming [2006]
    EWHC 2920 (Admin); [2007] J.P.L. 907, QBD (Admin) ....   Digested, 07/**3251**
Jenkins v Jones (1866) L.R. 2 Eq. 323, Ct of Chancery ....   Applied, 03/4114,
                    07/3962
Jenkins v Official Receiver [2007] EWHC 1402 (Ch); [2007] B.P.I.R. 740, Ch D .....   Digested, 07/**2417**
Jenner v Ffinch (1879-80) L.R. 5 P.D. 106, PDAD ....   Considered, 07/429
Jennings v CPS; sub nom Crown Prosecution Service v J; J v Crown Prosecution
    Service [2005] EWCA Civ 746; [2006] 1 W.L.R. 182; [2005] 4 All E.R. 391;
    Times, July 12, 2005; Independent, June 30, 2005, CA (Civ Div) ....   Digested, 05/**926**:
                    Applied, 07/3615
Jersey Fishermen's Association Ltd v Guernsey; sub nom Guernsey v Jersey
    Fishermen's Association Ltd [2007] UKPC 30; [2007] Eu. L.R. 670, PC (Gue);
    reversing in part [2005] Eu. L.R. 946, CA (Gue) ....   Digested, 07/**1870**
Jerusalem v Austria (26958/95) (2003) 37 E.H.R.R. 25, ECHR ....   Considered, 07/2177
Jessup v Wetherell [2006] EWHC 2582 (QB); [2007] P.N.L.R. 10; [2007] W.T.L.R.
    515, QBD. ....   Digested, 07/**479**
Jevremovic v Serbia (3150/05) [2007] 2 F.C.R. 671; [2007] Fam. Law 985, ECHR...   Digested, 07/**2219**
Jezierski v Osborne (Valuation Officer) [2007] R.A. 37, Lands Tr...............   Digested, 07/**3349**
JH Ritchie Ltd v Lloyd Ltd see J&H Ritchie Ltd v Lloyd Ltd
Jia v Migrationsverket (C-1/05) [2007] Q.B. 545; [2007] 2 W.L.R. 1005; [2007] All
    E.R. (EC) 575; [2007] 1 C.M.L.R. 41; [2007] C.E.C. 349; [2007] Imm. A.R. 439;
    [2007] I.N.L.R. 336, ECJ..   Digested, 07/**1652**
Jif Lemon case see Reckitt & Colman Products Ltd v Borden Inc (No.3)
Jippes v Minister van Landbouw, Natuurbeheer en Visserij (C-189/01) [2001] E.C.R.
    I-5689; Times, July 19, 2001, ECJ.................................   Digested, 01/**176**:
            Considered, 02/1565, 07/107
JJ, Re see Secretary of State for the Home Department v JJ
JJ v AT see AJ (A Child) (Adoption Order or Special Guardianship Order), Re
JJB Sports Plc v Office of Fair Trading see Argos Ltd v Office of Fair Trading
JJB Sports Plc v Office of Fair Trading; joined case Allsports Ltd v Office of Fair Trading
    [2004] CAT 17; [2005] Comp. A.R. 29, CAT........................   Digested, 05/**570**:
        Followed, 05/2825: Subsequent related litigation, 07/621
JL (Domestic Violence: Evidence and Procedure: India), Re [2006] UKAIT 58, AIT ...   Considered, 07/2353

JL (Sierra Leone) v Secretary of State for the Home Department see HB (Ethiopia) v Secretary of State for the Home Department

JM (Liberia) v Secretary of State for the Home Department; *sub nom* JM (Rule 62(7): Human Rights Unarguable: Liberia), Re [2006] EWCA Civ 1402; [2007] Imm. A.R. 293; [2006] I.N.L.R. 548, CA (Civ Div); reversing [2006] UKAIT 9; [2006] Imm. A.R. 336, AIT . . . . *Digested*, 07/**2286**: *Cited*, 07/2273: *Considered*, 07/2285

JM (Rule 62(7): Human Rights Unarguable: Liberia), Re see JM (Liberia) v Secretary of State for the Home Department

JN (Uganda) v Secretary of State for the Home Department see DK (Serbia) v Secretary of State for the Home Department

JN (Uganda) v Secretary of State for the Home Department [2007] EWCA Civ 802; (2007) 104(32) L.S.G. 26, CA (Civ Div)

Job Centre Coop arl, Re (C-55/96) [1997] E.C.R. I-7119; [1998] 4 C.M.L.R. 708; [1998] C.E.C. 507, ECJ (6th Chamber) . . . . *Digested*, 98/**742**: *Considered*, 07/1627

Jobson v Johnson [1989] 1 W.L.R. 1026; [1989] 1 All E.R. 621; (1988) 4 B.C.C. 488, CA (Civ Div) . . . . *Digested*, 88/**353**: *Considered*, 07/3420

Johansen v Norway (17383/90) (1997) 23 E.H.R.R. 33, ECHR . . . . *Digested*, 97/**2792**: *Applied*, 98/3138: *Considered*, 98/3104, 03/2198, 07/2248: *Distinguished*, 99/2302

John v Associated Newspapers Ltd [2006] EWHC 1611 (QB); [2006] E.M.L.R. 27, QBD . . . . *Digested*, 07/**2887**

John v Germany (Admissibility) (15073/03) (2007) 45 E.H.R.R. SE4, ECHR

John v United States [2006] EWHC 3512 (Admin); [2006] Extradition L.R. 305; [2007] A.C.D. 55, QBD (Admin)

John D Wood & Co (Residential & Agricultural) Ltd v Craze [2007] EWHC 2658 (QB); [2007] 50 E.G. 108 (C.S.); [2007] N.P.C. 130, QBD

John Doyle Construction Ltd v Laing Management (Scotland) Ltd; *sub nom* Laing Management (Scotland) Ltd v John Doyle Construction Ltd 2004 S.C. 713; 2004 S.C.L.R. 872; [2004] B.L.R. 295; (2004) 20 Const. L.J. 477; [2004] C.I.L.L. 2135; 2004 G.W.D. 20-434; *Times*, June 18, 2004, IH (Ex Div); affirming 2004 S.L.T. 678; [2002] B.L.R. 393; [2002] T.C.L.R. 24; 85 Con. L.R. 98; (2003) 19 Const. L.J. 152; 2002 G.W.D. 14-461; *Times*, July 10, 2002, OH . . . . *Digested*, 05/**5071**: *Considered*, 07/254

John F Hunt Demolition Ltd v ASME Engineering Ltd [2007] EWHC 1507 (TCC); [2007] T.C.L.R. 6; 114 Con. L.R. 105; [2007] C.I.L.L. 2496, QBD (TCC) . . . . . . *Digested*, 07/**745**

John Laing & Son v Kingswood Assessment Committee [1949] 1 K.B. 344; [1949] 1 All E.R. 224; 65 T.L.R. 80; (1949) 113 J.P. 111; 47 L.G.R. 64; 42 R. & I.T. 15; (1949) 93 S.J. 26, CA; affirming [1948] 2 K.B. 116; [1948] 1 All E.R. 943; 64 T.L.R. 407, KBD . . . . *Digested*, 47-51/**8292**: *Applied*, 55/2275, 56/7264, 60/2685, 70/2414, 98/4319, 05/3370, 07/3342: *Considered*, 77/2453, 85/2924, 85/2926, 87/3181, 88/3029, 90/3917: *Distinguished*, 75/2776, 99/4333: *Followed*, 99/4335, 01/4821

John Lyon's Free Grammar School v Berman see John Lyon's Free Grammar School v Secchi

John Lyon's Free Grammar School v Secchi; *sub nom* Keepers and Governors of the Possessions, Revenues and Goods of the Free Grammar School of John Lyon v Secchi; Keepers and Governors of the Possessions, Revenues and Goods of the Free Grammar School of John Lyon v Berman; *joined case* John Lyon's Free Grammar School v Berman (2000) 32 H.L.R. 820; [2000] L. & T.R. 308; [1999] 3 E.G.L.R. 49; [1999] 49 E.G. 100; [1999] E.G. 118 (C.S.); [1999] N.P.C. 121; (2000) 79 P. & C.R. D10, CA (Civ Div) . . . . *Digested*, 00/**3910**: *Considered*, 07/2754

John Summers & Sons Ltd v Frost; *sub nom* Frost v John Summers & Sons Ltd [1955] A.C. 740; [1955] 2 W.L.R. 825; [1955] 1 All E.R. 870; 53 L.G.R. 329; (1955) 99 S.J. 257, HL; affirming [1954] 2 Q.B. 21; [1954] 2 W.L.R. 794; [1954] 1 All E.R. 901; 52 L.G.R. 283; (1954) 98 S.J. 250, CA . . . . *Digested*, 55/**1082**: *Applied*, 56/3455, 59/1279, 60/1260, 65/1632, 69/2447, 71/7931: *Considered*, 60/3776, 87/1333, 93/2021, 07/5269

Johnson v Chief Constable of Surrey, *Times*, November 23, 1992, CA (Civ Div) . . . . . . *Digested*, 92/**2817**: *Applied*, 01/4527, 07/482: *Followed*, 96/5677

Johnson v Davies [1999] Ch. 117; [1998] 3 W.L.R. 1299; [1998] 2 All E.R. 649; [1999] B.C.C. 275; [1998] 2 B.C.L.C. 252; [1998] B.P.I.R. 607; (2000) 79 P. & C.R. 14; [1998] L. & T.R. 69; [1998] 3 E.G.L.R. 72; [1998] 49 E.G. 153; (1998) 95(19) L.S.G. 23; (1998) 142 S.J.L.B. 141; [1998] N.P.C. 50; *Times*, March 31, 1998, CA (Civ Div); affirming [1997] 1 W.L.R. 1511; [1997] 1 All E.R. 921; [1997] 1 B.C.L.C. 580; [1997] B.P.I.R. 221; [1997] 1 E.G.L.R. 42; [1997] 19 E.G. 157; (1996) 146 N.L.J. 1814, Ch D . . . . *Digested*, 98/**3351**: *Applied*, 03/2442, 07/2422: *Considered*, 99/3336, 00/3884

Johnson v Gore Wood & Co (No.1); *sub nom* Johnson v Gore Woods & Co [2002] 2
　　A.C. 1; [2001] 2 W.L.R. 72; [2001] 1 All E.R. 481; [2001] C.P.L.R. 49; [2001]
　　B.C.C. 820; [2001] 1 B.C.L.C. 313; [2001] P.N.L.R. 18; (2001) 98(1) L.S.G. 24;
　　(2001) 98(8) L.S.G. 46; (2000) 150 N.L.J. 1889; (2001) 145 S.J.L.B. 29; *Times*,
　　December 22, 2000; *Independent*, February 7, 2001, HL; reversing in part
　　[1999] C.P.L.R. 155; [1999] B.C.C. 474; [1999] Lloyd's Rep. P.N. 91; [1999]
　　P.N.L.R. 426; [1998] N.P.C. 151, CA (Civ Div) . . . . *Digested*, 01/**410**:
　　　　　　　　　　　　　Applied, 99/3313, 01/746, 02/280, 02/281, 02/3286, 02/3310, 03/291,
　　　　　　　　　　　　　　03/470, 03/4600, 04/265, 04/459, 05/520, 05/533, 05/2448, 05/2505,
　　　　　　　　　　　　　06/320, 06/2591, 07/346: *Considered*, 01/675, 01/708, 01/5710, 06/1042,
　　　　　　　　　　　　　07/2677: *Distinguished*, 02/565, 04/2338, 06/562: *Followed*, 01/749,
　　　　　　　　　　　　　　　　　　　　　　　　　　　　　　　04/425, 04/2733, 05/483
Johnson v Gore Woods & Co see Johnson v Gore Wood & Co (No.1)
Johnson v Havering LBC see L v Birmingham City Council
Johnson v Medical Defence Union Ltd [2007] EWCA Civ 262; [2007] 3 C.M.L.R. 9;
　　(2007) 96 B.M.L.R. 99; *Times*, April 10, 2007, CA (Civ Div); reversing in part
　　[2006] EWHC 321 (Ch); [2006] Info. T.L.R. 47; (2006) 89 B.M.L.R. 43; *Times*,
　　April 4, 2006, Ch D . . . . *Digested*, 07/**2383**:
　　　　　　　　　　　　　　　　　　　　　　　　　　　　　　　　Considered, 07/2247
Johnson v Parole Board see R. (on the application of Johnson) v Secretary of State
　　for the Home Department
Johnson v Secretary of State for the Home Department see R. (on the application of
　　Johnson) v Secretary of State for the Home Department
Johnson v Unisys Ltd [2001] UKHL 13; [2003] 1 A.C. 518; [2001] 2 W.L.R. 1076;
　　[2001] 2 All E.R. 801; [2001] I.C.R. 480; [2001] I.R.L.R. 279; [2001] Emp. L.R.
　　469; *Times*, March 23, 2001; *Independent*, March 29, 2001, HL; affirming
　　[1999] 1 All E.R. 854; [1999] I.C.R. 809; [1999] I.R.L.R. 90, CA (Civ Div) . . . . *Digested*, 01/**2253**:
　　　　　　　　　　　　　Applied, 03/1216, 03/1332, 03/1337, 05/1340, 06/1283, 07/1317:
　　　　　　　　　　　　　Considered, 03/1246, 03/1333, 04/1183, 04/1303, 04/1307, 06/1288,
　　　　　　　　　　　　　06/1290, 07/3990: *Distinguished*, 02/5565: *Followed*, 02/1313, 05/1326
Johnston v NEI International Combustion Ltd see Grieves v FT Everard & Sons Ltd
Johnston Publishing (North) Ltd v Revenue and Customs Commissioners [2007]
　　EWHC 512 (Ch); [2007] Bus. L.R. 1172; [2007] S.T.C. 1481; [2007] B.T.C. 405;
　　[2007] S.T.I. 540, Ch D; affirming [2006] S.T.C. (S.C.D.) 779; [2006] S.T.I.
　　2407, Sp Comm. . . . . *Digested*, 07/**4003**
Johor v Tunku Alam Shah ibni Tunku Abdul Rahman [2005] SGHC 156; (2006-07) 9
　　I.T.E.L.R. 1, HC (Sing)
Joint Selling of the Media Rights to the FA Premier League, Re (COMP/C-2/38.173) [2007]
　　C.E.C. 2138, CEC
Jolly v Kine; *sub nom* Kine v Jolly [1907] A.C. 1, HL; affirming [1905] 1 Ch. 480, CA . . *Doubted*, 07/2962
Jomah v Attar see J (A Child) (Custody Rights: Jurisdiction), Re
Jonas v Bamford (Inspector of Taxes) [1973] S.T.C. 519; 51 T.C. 1; [1973] T.R. 225 . . . . *Digested*, 74/**1866**:
　　　　　　　　　　　　Applied, 05/4090, 05/4098, 07/4162: *Considered*, 07/4051
Jones v Associated Tunnelling Co Ltd [1981] I.R.L.R. 477, EAT . . . . *Digested*, 81/**828**:
　　　　　　　　　　　　　　　Applied, 05/1241: *Considered*, 95/1540, 07/1325, 07/3043
Jones v Bennett see Bennett, Re
Jones v Bright Capital Ltd [2006] EWHC 3151 (Ch); [2007] Pens. L.R. 31, Ch D . . . . *Digested*, 07/**3028**
Jones v Chief Constable of South Yorkshire see Alcock v Chief Constable of South
　　Yorkshire
Jones v Cleanthi [2006] EWCA Civ 1712; [2007] 1 W.L.R. 1604; [2007] 3 All E.R.
　　841; [2007] H.L.R. 21; [2007] 1 P. & C.R. 19; [2006] N.P.C. 131, CA (Civ Div);
　　affirming [2005] EWHC 2646 (QB); [2006] 1 All E.R. 1029; [2006] H.L.R. 17;
　　[2006] 1 E.G.L.R. 1; [2006] 12 E.G. 224; [2006] 2 P. & C.R. DG7, QBD . . . . . . *Digested*, 07/**2752**
Jones v Department of Employment [1989] Q.B. 1; [1988] 2 W.L.R. 493; [1988] 1 All
　　E.R. 725; (1988) 85(4) L.S.G. 35; (1987) 137 N.L.J. 1182; (1988) 132 S.J. 128,
　　CA (Civ Div) . . . . *Digested*, 88/**2438**:
　　　　　　　　　　　　　Considered, 07/1755: *Followed*, 89/259, 90/5493, 00/6686
Jones v Garnett (Inspector of Taxes) [2007] UKHL 35; [2007] 1 W.L.R. 2030; [2007]
　　4 All E.R. 857; [2007] S.T.C. 1536; [2007] I.C.R. 1259; [2007] 3 F.C.R. 487; 78
　　T.C. 597; [2007] B.T.C. 476; [2007] W.T.L.R. 1229; [2007] S.T.I. 1899; (2007)
　　157 N.L.J. 1118; (2007) 151 S.J.L.B. 1024; *Times*, August 9, 2007, HL; affirming
　　[2005] EWCA Civ 1553; [2006] 1 W.L.R. 1123; [2006] 2 All E.R. 381; [2006]
　　S.T.C. 283; [2006] I.C.R. 690; [2006] 2 F.C.R. 294; [2006] B.T.C. 24; [2006]
　　W.T.L.R. 67; [2006] S.T.I. 43; (2006) 103(2) L.S.G. 32; (2006) 156 N.L.J. 22;
　　Times, January 3, 2006, CA (Civ Div); reversing [2005] EWHC 849 (Ch);
　　[2005] S.T.C. 1667; [2005] B.T.C. 306; [2005] W.T.L.R. 729; [2005] S.T.I. 892;
　　[2005] S.T.I. 903; *Times*, May 17, 2005, Ch D; affirming [2005] S.T.C. (S.C.D.)
　　9; [2004] W.T.L.R. 1209; [2004] S.T.I. 2263, Sp Comm. . . . . *Digested*, 07/**4100**
Jones v Governing Body of Burdett Coutts School [1999] I.C.R. 38; [1998] I.R.L.R.
　　521; (1998) 95(18) L.S.G. 32; (1998) 142 S.J.L.B. 142; *Times*, April 22, 1998,
　　CA (Civ Div); reversing [1997] I.C.R. 390, EAT . . . . *Digested*, 98/**2128**:
　　　　　　　　　　　　　　　　　　　　　　　　　　　　　　　　Applied, 07/1359

Jones v Herxheimer [1950] 2 K.B. 106; [1950] 1 All E.R. 323; 66 T.L.R. (Pt. 1) 403; (1950) 94 S.J. 97, CA . . . . *Digested*, 47-51/**5419**:
Applied, 47-51/5426, 07/2736: *Considered*, 47-51/5420, 88/2007, 92/2667, 98/122

Jones v Isleworth Crown Court see R. (on the application of Jones) v Isleworth Crown Court

Jones v MBNA International Bank Ltd B2/1998/1560, CA (Civ Div) . . . . *Distinguished*, 07/2832

Jones v Ministry of the Interior Al-Mamlaka Al-Arabiya AS Saudiya see Jones v Saudi Arabia

Jones v Norfolk CC [2006] EWHC 1545 (Admin); [2006] E.L.R. 547, QBD (Admin) . *Digested*, 07/**1263**

Jones v Post Office; *sub nom* Post Office v Jones [2001] EWCA Civ 558; [2001] I.C.R. 805; [2001] I.R.L.R. 384; [2001] Emp. L.R. 527; *Times*, June 5, 2001; *Independent*, April 26, 2001, CA (Civ Div); affirming [2000] I.C.R. 388, EAT . . *Digested*, 01/**2236**:
Applied, 01/6463, 02/1329, 04/1220, 06/1299, 06/1300:
Considered, 04/1215, 05/1227, 06/1136, 07/1331, 07/5115:
Distinguished, 04/1219

Jones v Sandwell MBC see Barber v Somerset CC

Jones v Saudi Arabia; *sub nom* Jones v Ministry of the Interior Al-Mamlaka Al-Arabiya AS Saudiya; *joined case* Mitchell v Al-Dali [2006] UKHL 26; [2007] 1 A.C. 270; [2006] 2 W.L.R. 1424; [2007] 1 All E.R. 113; [2006] H.R.L.R. 32; [2007] U.K.H.R.R. 24; 20 B.H.R.C. 621; (2006) 156 N.L.J. 1025; (2006) 150 S.J.L.B. 811; *Times*, June 15, 2006; *Independent*, June 22, 2006, HL; reversing in part [2004] EWCA Civ 1394; [2005] Q.B. 699; [2005] 2 W.L.R. 808; [2005] U.K.H.R.R. 57; [2005] A.C.D. 50; (2004) 101(44) L.S.G. 31; (2004) 154 N.L.J. 1655; (2004) 148 S.J.L.B. 1286; *Times*, November 1, 2004; *Independent*, November 3, 2004, CA (Civ Div); reversing in part TNS, QBD . . . . *Digested*, 06/**2644**:
Applied, 06/2642

Jones v Secretary of State for Social Services; *sub nom* R. v National Insurance Commissioner Ex p. Lloyd-Jones; R. v National Insurance Commissioner Ex p. Jones; R. v National Insurance Commissioner Ex p. Hudson; *joined case* Hudson v Secretary of State for Social Services [1972] A.C. 944; [1972] 2 W.L.R. 210; [1972] 1 All E.R. 145; (1971) 116 S.J. 57, HL; reversing [1970] 1 Q.B. 477; [1970] 2 W.L.R. 182; [1970] 1 All E.R. 97; 7 K.I.R. 478; (1970) 114 S.J. 10; *Times*, November 15, 1969, CA (Civ Div); affirming [1969] 2 W.L.R. 647; [1969] 2 All E.R. 638 (Note); 6 K.I.R. 123; (1969) 113 S.J. 225, QBD . . . . *Digested*, 72/**2263**:
Distinguished, 07/1672

Jones v Whalley [2006] UKHL 41; [2007] 1 A.C. 63; [2006] 3 W.L.R. 179; [2006] 4 All E.R. 113; [2007] 1 Cr. App. R. 2; [2007] Crim. L.R. 74; (2006) 150 S.J.L.B. 1020; *Times*, July 31, 2006; *Independent*, October 6, 2006, HL; reversing [2005] EWHC 931 (Admin); (2005) 169 J.P. 466; [2006] Crim. L.R. 67; (2005) 169 J.P.N. 679, QBD (Admin) . . . . *Digested*, 06/**973**

Jones v Wright see Alcock v Chief Constable of South Yorkshire

Jones (Setting of Minimum Term), Re; *sub nom* R. v Jones (Neil); R. v Chandi (Amandeep Singh); R. v Multani (Hardeep Singh); R. v Khangura (Sukhjiwan Singh); R. v Dosanjh (Jaswinder Singh); R. v Ashman (Joseph Clifford); R. v Hobson (Mark); *joined cases* Chandi (Setting of Minimum Term), Re; Multani (Setting of Minimum Term), Re; Khangura (Setting of Minimum Term), Re; Dosanjh (Setting of Minimum Term), Re; Ashman (Setting of Minimum Term), Re; Hobson (Setting of Minimum Term), Re [2005] EWCA Crim 3115; [2006] 2 Cr. App. R. (S.) 19; [2006] Crim. L.R. 262, CA (Crim Div) . . . . *Digested*, 06/**3758**:
Considered, 07/3694: *Followed*, 07/3689

Jonesco v Beard [1930] A.C. 298, HL . . . . *Considered*, 57/996, 07/510

Jordan v Lord Chancellor; *sub nom* Jordan's Application for Judicial Review, Re; *joined case* McCaughey v Chief Constable of Northern Ireland [2007] UKHL 14; [2007] 2 A.C. 226; [2007] 2 W.L.R. 754; [2007] N.I. 214; (2007) 151 S.J.L.B. 466, HL (NI); affirming [2004] NICA 29; [2005] N.I. 144, CA (NI) . . . . *Digested*, 07/**4372**:
Considered, 06/4528

Jordan v United Kingdom (24746/94) (2003) 37 E.H.R.R. 2; 11 B.H.R.C. 1; [2001] Inquest L.R. 101; *Times*, May 18, 2001, ECHR . . . . *Digested*, 01/**3575**:
Applied, 02/3779, 04/4066, 06/18, 06/2126, 07/13: *Considered*, 03/2167, 03/4910, 04/37, 07/2234, 07/2980

Jordan v United Kingdom (30280/96) (2001) 31 E.H.R.R. 6; *Times*, March 17, 2000, ECHR . . . . *Digested*, 00/**3214**:
Applied, 07/13: *Considered*, 06/2933

Jordan Grand Prix Ltd v Vodafone Group Plc [2003] EWHC 1956 (Comm); [2003] 2 All E.R. (Comm) 864; [2003] 2 Lloyd's Rep. 874, QBD (Comm) . . . . *Digested*, 04/**659**:
Considered, 07/398

Jordan's Application for Judicial Review, Re see Jordan v Lord Chancellor

Jorgensen (Listing Officer) v Gomperts; *sub nom* R. (on the application of Jorgensen (Listing Officer)) v Gomports [2006] EWHC 1885 (Admin); [2006] R.A. 300; [2006] N.P.C. 93, QBD (Admin) . . . . *Digested*, 07/**2835**

Jouini v Princess Personal Service GmbH (PPS) (C-458/05) [2007] 3 C.M.L.R. 53; [2007] I.R.L.R. 1005, ECJ (4th Chamber)

Joyce v Merton, Sutton and Wandsworth HA [1996] P.I.Q.R. P121; [1996] 7 Med.
 L.R. 1, CA (Civ Div) . . . . *Digested*, 96/**4459**:
 Considered, 96/4454, 07/2917
Joyce v Rigolli [2004] EWCA Civ 79; (2004) 148 S.J.L.B. 234; [2004] 1 P. & C.R.
 DG22, CA (Civ Div). . . . . *Considered*, 07/3365
JP Commodities Ltd v Revenue and Customs Commissioners [2007] EWHC 2474
 (Ch); [2007] S.T.I. 2458, Ch D; affirming [2006] V. & D.R. 526; [2007] S.T.I.
 384, V&DTr (London)
JP Morgan Chase Bank v Springwell Navigation Corp (Application to Strike Out)
 [2006] EWHC 2755 (Comm); [2007] 1 All E.R. (Comm) 549, QBD (Comm). . *Digested*, 07/**335**
JP Morgan Fleming Claverhouse Investment Trust Plc v Revenue and Customs
 Commissioners (C-363/05) [2007] 3 C.M.L.R. 32; [2007] Pens. L.R. 265;
 [2007] S.T.I. 1765, ECJ (3rd Chamber)
JPC v SLW see C v W
JSJ/Re-establishment of rights (T68/05) [2006] E.P.O.R. 59, EPO (Technical Bd App) *Digested*, 07/**2604**
Judd v Kirton (Unreported, July 27, 2007), CC (Ilford) [*Ex rel.* Joanna Kerr, Barrister,
 Lamb Chambers, Temple, London] . . . . *Digested*, 07/**3113**
Judge (Walden's Personal Representative) v Revenue and Customs Commissioners
 [2005] S.T.C. (S.C.D.) 863; [2005] W.T.L.R. 1311; (2006-07) 9 I.T.E.L.R. 21;
 [2005] S.T.I. 1800, Sp Comm . . . . *Digested*, 06/**4242**
Jukes v Etti [2006] EWHC 2493 (QB); [2007] R.T.R. 2, QBD . . . . *Digested*, 07/**2957**
Jurisdiction in a Claim Based on a Prize Draw Notification, Re [2007] I.L.Pr. 15, BGH (Ger)
Jurisdiction in a Direct Action against Motor Insurer, Re (VI ZR 200/05) [2007] I.L.Pr. 40,
 BGH (Ger)
Jussila v Finland (73053/01) (2007) 45 E.H.R.R. 39; 9 I.T.L. Rep. 662, ECHR (Grand
 Chamber) . . . . *Digested*, 07/**2226**
JW Brown & Son v Burnt Fen Internal Drainage Board [2007] R.A. 327, Lands Tr

K, Re; *sub nom* A Local Authority v N [2005] EWHC 2956 (Fam); [2007] 1 F.L.R.
 399; [2007] Fam. Law 211; [2007] Fam. Law 298, Fam Div . . . . *Considered*, 07/1834
K v B see B (Leave to Remove), Re
K v Dewsbury Healthcare NHS Trust see JD v East Berkshire Community Health NHS
 Trust
K v Finland (19823/92) see Hokkanen v Finland (A/299-A)
K v Finland (25702/94) (No.2); *sub nom* T v Finland (25702/94) (No.2) [2001] 2
 F.L.R. 707; [2001] 2 F.C.R. 673; (2003) 36 E.H.R.R. 18; [2001] Fam. Law 733,
 ECHR . . . . *Digested*, 01/**3551**:
 Considered, 07/1774: *Referred to*, 06/2199
K v Hertfordshire CC see R. (on the application of A) v Hertfordshire CC
K v K [2006] EWHC 2685 (Fam); [2007] 1 F.C.R. 355, Fam Div. . . . . *Digested*, 07/**1748**
K v K [2007] EWCA Civ 533; [2007] 2 F.L.R. 996; [2007] 3 F.C.R. 580; [2007]
 Fam. Law 790, CA (Civ Div). . . . . *Digested*, 07/**1740**:
 Doubted, 07/1736
K v K (Financial Relief: Management of Difficult Cases) [2005] EWHC 1070 (Fam);
 [2005] 2 F.L.R. 1137; [2007] 2 F.C.R. 94; [2005] Fam. Law 607, Fam Div . . . . *Digested*, 07/**1687**
K v Lewisham LBC; *sub nom* KW v Lewisham LBC [2006] EWHC 1853 (Admin);
 [2007] E.L.R. 11, QBD (Admin) . . . . *Digested*, 07/**1259**
K v Nottingham University Hospital NHS Trust (Unreported, March 1, 2006), CC
 (Leicester) [*Ex rel.* Wilson Browne, Solicitors, 6 Peacock Lane, Leicester] . . . . . *Digested*, 07/**3207**
K v Secretary of State for the Home Department [2005] EWCA Civ 1627; [2006]
 Imm. A.R. 161, CA (Civ Div) . . . . *Digested*, 07/**2294**
K v Secretary of State for the Home Department; *joined case* Fornah v Secretary of
 State for the Home Department [2006] UKHL 46; [2007] 1 A.C. 412; [2006] 3
 W.L.R. 733; [2007] 1 All E.R. 671; [2006] 3 F.C.R. 381; 23 B.H.R.C. 137;
 [2007] Imm. A.R. 247; [2007] I.N.L.R. 1; (2006) 150 S.J.L.B. 1394; *Times*,
 October 19, 2006; *Independent*, October 20, 2006, HL; reversing [2004]
 EWCA Civ 986; [2004] I.N.L.R. 599, CA (Civ Div) . . . . *Digested*, 06/**2293**:
 Previous proceedings, 05/2226
K v Special Educational Needs and Disability Tribunal see R. (on the application of K) v
 Special Educational Needs and Disability Tribunal (SENDIST)
K v X School see R. (on the application of K) v Special Educational Needs and
 Disability Tribunal (SENDIST)
K & H (Children), Re [2006] EWCA Civ 1898; [2007] 1 F.L.R. 2043; [2007] Fam. Law 485;
 (2007) 151 S.J.L.B. 24, CA (Civ Div) . . . . *Digested*, 07/**1714**
K Ltd v National Westminster Bank Plc [2006] EWCA Civ 1039; [2007] Bus. L.R. 26;
 [2007] 1 W.L.R. 311; [2006] 4 All E.R. 907; [2006] 2 All E.R. (Comm) 655;
 [2006] 2 Lloyd's Rep. 569; [2006] C.P. Rep. 45; (2006) 103(31) L.S.G. 24;
 (2006) 150 S.J.L.B. 982; *Times*, July 27, 2006; *Independent*, July 25, 2006, CA
 (Civ Div) . . . . *Digested*, 06/**260**:
 Applied, 07/1931
K (A Child), Re see S (A Child) v B
K (A Child), Re; *sub nom* K (A Child) (Care Order), Re [2007] EWCA Civ 697; [2007]
 2 F.L.R. 1066; [2007] Fam. Law 797, CA (Civ Div)

K (A Child) (Adoption: Permission to Advertise), Re [2007] EWHC 544 (Fam); [2007] 1
    W.L.R. 2531; [2007] 2 F.L.R. 326; [2007] Fam. Law 681; *Times*, April 20, 2007,
    Fam Div
K (A Child) (Care Order), Re see K (A Child), Re
K (A Child) (Medical Treatment: Declaration), Re; *sub nom* K (A Child) (Withdrawal of
    Treatment), Re [2006] EWHC 1007 (Fam); [2006] 2 F.L.R. 883; [2006] Fam.
    Law 841; (2006) 150 S.J.L.B. 667, Fam Div .... *Digested*, 07/**1984**
K (A Child) (Withdrawal of Treatment), Re see K (A Child) (Medical Treatment: Declaration),
    Re
K (Care: Threshold Criteria), Re see K (Children)
K (Children); *sub nom* K (Care: Threshold Criteria), Re [2005] EWCA Civ 1226;
    [2006] 2 F.L.R. 868; [2006] Fam. Law 626, CA (Civ Div) .... *Digested*, 07/**1733**
K (Children) (Procedure: Family Proceedings Rules), Re [2004] EWCA Civ 1827; [2005] 1
    F.L.R. 764; [2007] 2 F.C.R. 631; [2005] Fam. Law 275; (2005) 149 S.J.L.B. 29, CA
    (Civ Div) .... *Digested*, 05/**1669**:
                                                                           Applied, 07/1793
K (Deceased), Re [2007] EWHC 622 (Ch); [2007] W.T.L.R. 1007; (2006-07) 9 I.T.E.L.R.
    759; *Times*, April 16, 2007, Ch D .... *Digested*, 07/**3957**
K (Order Delay), Re; *sub nom* E LBC v AK [2007] EWHC 2090 (Fam); [2007] Fam.
    Law 1060, Fam Div
KA (Adequacy of Maintenance: Pakistan), Re see KA (Pakistan) v Secretary of State for
    the Home Department
KA (Pakistan) v Secretary of State for the Home Department; *sub nom* KA (Adequacy
    of Maintenance: Pakistan), Re [2006] UKAIT 65; [2007] Imm. A.R. 155, AIT . . *Digested*, 07/**2326**
Kadi v Council of the European Union (T-315/01) [2005] E.C.R. II-3649, CFI .... *Considered*, 07/1645
Kahn v Inland Revenue Commissioners see Toshoku Finance UK Plc (In Liquidation),
    Re
Kahn Scheepvaart BV v Commission of the European Communities (T-398/94) [1996]
    E.C.R. II-477; [1997] 3 C.M.L.R. 63, CFI (3rd Chamber) .... *Applied*, 07/1540
Kaila v Hatfield (Unreported, November 3, 2006), CC (Lincoln) [*Ex rel.* Shabnam Walji,
    Regency Chambers, Cathedral Square, Peterborough] .... *Digested*, 07/**3086**
Kain v Hutton (No.3) [2007] NZCA 199; [2007] W.T.L.R. 1751; (2007-08) 10 I.T.E.L.R.
    287, CA (NZ); reversing in part (2005-06) 8 I.T.E.L.R. 411, HC (NZ)
Kakoulli v Turkey (49429/99) (2007) 45 E.H.R.R. 12, ECHR .... *Digested*, 07/**2237**
Kalashnikov v Russia (47095/99) (2003) 36 E.H.R.R. 34; [2002] Prison L.R. 334,
    ECHR .... *Digested*, 03/**2102**:
                                                   Applied, 07/2201: *Considered*, 04/2047
Kalfelis v Bankhaus Schroder Munchmeyer Hengst & Co (t/a HEMA
    Beteiligungsgesellschaft mbH) (189/87) [1988] E.C.R. 5565; [1989] E.C.C.
    407; *Times*, October 5, 1988, ECJ (5th Chamber) .... *Digested*, 91/**3936**:
                       Applied, 91/5161, 94/5038, 96/5344, 97/898, 03/484, 06/630, 06/640:
                             Considered, 93/450, 98/3466, 99/715, 05/427, 07/657, 07/2584:
                       Distinguished, 96/7098: *Followed*, 94/5036, 96/1085: *Referred to*, 97/3890
Kalhar v Galatola (Unreported, October 9, 2006), CC (Slough) [*Ex rel.* Richard Case,
    Barrister, 1 Alfred Street, Oxford] .... *Digested*, 07/**3140**
Kallang Shipping SA v AXA Assurances Senegal (The Kallang) [2006] EWHC 2825
    (Comm); [2007] 1 Lloyd's Rep. 160, QBD (Comm) .... *Digested*, 07/**3803**
Kalogiannis v Mastorakis [2007] E.C.D.R. 11, Ar Pag (GR)
Kalron Foods Ltd v Revenue and Customs Commissioners [2007] EWHC 695 (Ch);
    [2007] S.T.C. 1101; [2007] B.T.C. 5541; [2007] B.V.C. 509; [2007] S.T.I. 1172;
    (2007) 104(17) L.S.G. 31; (2007) 151 S.J.L.B. 503, Ch D; affirming [2006] S.T.I.
    2582, V&DTr .... *Digested*, 07/**4363**
Kamali v City & Country Properties Ltd; *sub nom* City & Country Properties Ltd v
    Kamali [2006] EWCA Civ 1879; [2007] 1 W.L.R. 1219, CA (Civ Div) .... *Digested*, 07/**516**
Kamer van Koophandel en Fabrieken voor Amsterdam v Inspire Art Ltd (C-167/01)
    [2003] E.C.R. I-10155; [2005] 3 C.M.L.R. 34, ECJ .... *Digested*, 06/**549**:
                                                                           Applied, 07/4145
Kane Constructions Pty Ltd v Sopov [2005] VSC 237; (2007) 23 Const. L.J. 145, Sup
    Ct (Vic)
KANEGAFUCHI/Second medical use (T138/02) [2007] E.P.O.R. 3, EPO (Technical Bd
    App) .... *Digested*, 07/**2609**
Kantor v Leonard Ross & Craig see Yudt v Leonard Ross & Craig (A Firm)
KAO CORP/Absorbent article (T575/05) [2007] E.P.O.R. 42, EPO (Technical Bd App)   *Digested*, 07/**2610**
Kaplan v Austria (45983/99) [2007] 1 F.C.R. 466, ECHR .... *Digested*, 07/**2251**
Kappler v Secretary of State for Trade and Industry [2006] EWHC 3694 (Ch); [2006]
    B.C.C. 845, Ch D (Leeds) .... *Digested*, 07/**565**
Karademirci v Turkey (37101/97) (2007) 44 E.H.R.R. 44, ECHR .... *Digested*, 07/**2188**
Karadzic v Croatia (35030/04) [2006] 1 F.C.R. 36; (2007) 44 E.H.R.R. 45, ECHR ... *Digested*, 07/**2257**
Karagozlu v Commissioner of Police of the Metropolis [2006] EWCA Civ 1691;
    [2007] 1 W.L.R. 1881; [2007] 2 All E.R. 1055; [2006] Po. L.R. 166; (2007) 151
    S.J.L.B. 29; *Times*, December 26, 2006, CA (Civ Div) .... *Digested*, 07/**4192**
Karcheva v Bulgaria (60939/00) [2006] 3 F.C.R. 434, ECHR .... *Digested*, 07/**2225**
Karia (A Bankrupt), Re [2006] B.P.I.R. 1226, Ch D .... *Digested*, 07/**2401**

Karner v Austria (40016/98) [2003] 2 F.L.R. 623; [2004] 2 F.C.R. 563; (2004) 38
E.H.R.R. 24; 14 B.H.R.C. 674; [2003] Fam. Law 724, ECHR . . . . *Digested*, 04/**1983**:
Applied, 07/2233: *Considered*, 05/2118
Kashmiri v Secretary of State for the Home Department see Huang v Secretary of
State for the Home Department
Kassa v Rider Holdings Ltd (Unreported, April 4, 2007), CC (Leeds) [*Ex rel.* Richard
Crane, Barrister, 7 Harrington Street, Liverpool] . . . . *Digested*, 07/**3213**
Kato Kagaku Co Ltd v Revenue and Customs Commissioners [2007] S.T.C. (S.C.D.)
412; [2007] S.T.I. 1181, Sp Comm . . . . *Digested*, 07/**4076**
Kaur v MG Rover Group Ltd [2004] EWCA Civ 1507; [2005] I.C.R. 625; [2005]
I.R.L.R. 40; *Times*, December 6, 2004, CA (Civ Div); reversing [2004] I.R.L.R.
279, QBD . . . . *Digested*, 05/**1216**:
Considered, 07/1396
Kaur v Secretary of State for the Environment (1991) 61 P. & C.R. 249; [1990] J.P.L.
814, QBD. . . . . *Digested*, 91/**3470**:
Considered, 07/3233
Kaur (Pritam) v S Russell & Sons Ltd [1973] Q.B. 336; [1973] 2 W.L.R. 147; [1973] 1
All E.R. 617; (1972) 117 S.J. 91; *Times*, December 19, 1972, CA (Civ Div);
reversing [1972] 3 W.L.R. 663; [1972] 3 All E.R. 305; (1972) 116 S.J. 446,
QBD . . . . *Digested*, 73/**1964**:
Applied, 73/1156, 82/2480, 94/393: *Considered*, 07/477:
Distinguished, 74/1321, 83/1311, 97/2914: *Not followed*, 82/1092
Kay v Commissioner of Police of the Metropolis; *sub nom* R. (on the application of
Kay) v Commissioner of Police of the Metropolis; Commissioner of Police of the
Metropolis v Kay [2007] EWCA Civ 477; [2007] 1 W.L.R. 2915; [2007] 4 All
E.R. 31; (2007) 104(23) L.S.G. 34; *Times*, June 13, 2007, CA (Civ Div); reversing
[2006] EWHC 1536 (Admin); [2006] R.T.R. 39; [2006] Po. L.R. 111; [2006]
A.C.D. 86; (2006) 150 S.J.L.B. 919; *Times*, July 3, 2006, QBD (Admin) . . . . . . *Digested*, 07/**2210**
Kay v Lambeth LBC; *sub nom* Leeds City Council v Price; Lambeth LBC v Kay; *joined
cases* Gorman v Lambeth LBC; Constantine v Lambeth LBC; Barnett v
Lambeth LBC; Cole v Lambeth LBC; Dymny v Lambeth LBC; Price v Leeds City
Council [2006] UKHL 10; [2006] 2 A.C. 465; [2006] 2 W.L.R. 570; [2006] 4
All E.R. 128; [2006] 2 F.C.R. 20; [2006] H.R.L.R. 17; [2006] U.K.H.R.R. 640;
20 B.H.R.C. 33; [2006] H.L.R. 22; [2006] B.L.G.R. 323; [2006] 2 P. & C.R. 25;
[2006] L. & T.R. 8; [2006] 11 E.G. 194 (C.S.); (2006) 150 S.J.L.B. 365;
[2006] N.P.C. 29; *Times*, March 10, 2006; *Independent*, March 14, 2006, HL;
affirming [2004] EWCA Civ 926; [2005] Q.B. 352; [2004] 3 W.L.R. 1396;
[2004] H.L.R. 56; *Times*, July 26, 2004, CA (Civ Div) . . . . *Digested*, 06/**2173**:
Applied, 06/499, 06/2708, 07/2247, 07/2403: *Considered*, 05/3424, 07/855,
07/2242, 07/3867: *Distinguished*, 07/2816: *Previous proceedings*, 05/3424
Kay v United Kingdom (1998) 40 B.M.L.R. 20, Eur Comm HR . . . . *Digested*, 98/**3889**:
Considered, 07/2898: *Previous proceedings*, 90/3101
Kaya v Germany (31753/02) [2007] 2 F.C.R. 527; [2007] Imm. A.R. 802, ECHR
Kayhan v Turkey (8/2005) (2007) 44 E.H.R.R. SE15, UN CEDW
Kazakhstan v Istil Group Inc; *sub nom* Kazakhstan v Istil Group Ltd [2007] EWCA Civ
471; [2007] 2 Lloyd's Rep. 548, CA (Civ Div); affirming [2006] EWHC 448
(Comm); [2006] 2 Lloyd's Rep. 370, QBD (Comm) . . . . *Digested*, 07/**240**
Kazakhstan v Istil Group Inc [2007] EWHC 2729 (Comm); [2007] 2 C.L.C. 870, QBD
(Comm)
Kazakhstan v Istil Group Ltd see Kazakhstan v Istil Group Inc
KE KELIT Kunststoffwerk GmbH v Commission of the European Communities (C-205/
02 P) see Dansk Rorindustri A/S v Commission of the European Communities
(C-189/02 P)
Kearsley v Klarfeld; *sub nom* Kearsley v Klarfield [2005] EWCA Civ 1510; [2006] 2 All
E.R. 303; [2006] C.P. Rep. 20; [2006] R.T.R. 34; [2006] P.I.Q.R. P13; (2006)
103(2) L.S.G. 33; *Independent*, December 16, 2005, CA (Civ Div) . . . . *Digested*, 06/**2909**:
Considered, 07/2954
Kearsley v Klarfield see Kearsley v Klarfeld
Keary Developments Ltd v Tarmac Construction Ltd [1995] 3 All E.R. 534; [1995] 2
B.C.L.C. 395; 73 B.L.R. 115, CA (Civ Div) . . . . *Digested*, 96/**724**:
Applied, 96/692, 96/704, 98/450, 07/416, 07/512: *Considered*, 95/4009,
04/329: *Followed*, 97/563
Keating v Bromley LBC (No.2) see X (Minors) v Bedfordshire CC
Kedem v Leonard Ross & Craig see Yudt v Leonard Ross & Craig (A Firm)
Keech v Sandford 25 E.R. 223; (1726) Sel. Cas. Ch. 61, Ct of Chancery. . . . . *Applied*, 68/**1820**,
72/361, 86/2487, 94/2083, 07/1536: *Distinguished*, 58/3362, 77/2708:
Followed, 66/11052
Keegan v Ireland (16969/90) [1994] 3 F.C.R. 165; (1994) 18 E.H.R.R. 342, ECHR . . . *Digested*, 95/**2659**:
Applied, 97/2819, 01/2541, 02/2527, 07/1787: *Considered*, 96/3296
Keegan v United Kingdom (28867/03) (2007) 44 E.H.R.R. 33; 21 B.H.R.C. 189;
[2006] Po. L.R. 210; *Times*, August 9, 2006, ECHR. . . . . *Digested*, 07/**2243**
Keeley v Fosroc International Ltd [2006] EWCA Civ 1277; [2006] I.R.L.R. 961;
(2006) 103(40) L.S.G. 33; (2006) 150 S.J.L.B. 1328, CA (Civ Div) . . . . *Digested*, 07/**1396**

Keen v Commerzbank AG; *sub nom* Commerzbank AG v Keen [2006] EWCA Civ
1536; [2006] 2 C.L.C. 844; [2007] I.C.R. 623; [2007] I.R.L.R. 132;
Independent, November 23, 2006, CA (Civ Div); reversing [2006] EWHC 785
(Comm), QBD (Comm) .... *Digested,* 07/**1321**
Keen Jewellery Ltd v Revenue and Customs Commissioners [2007] S.T.I. 1704, V&DTr
(London)
Keen Phillips (A Firm) v Field [2006] EWCA Civ 1524; [2007] 1 W.L.R. 686; [2007]
C.P. Rep. 8; *Times*, December 7, 2006, CA (Civ Div) .... *Digested,* 07/**468**
Keen (Graham) v DPP see Knuller (Publishing, Printing and Promotions) Ltd v DPP
Keenan, Re [1998] B.P.I.R. 205, Ch D .... *Digested,* 98/**3277**:
Applied, 07/2412

Keenan v United Kingdom (27229/95) (2001) 33 E.H.R.R. 38; 10 B.H.R.C. 319;
[2001] Inquest L.R. 8; [2001] Prison L.R. 180; *Times*, April 18, 2001, ECHR
(1998) 26 E.H.R.R. CD64, Eur Comm HR .... *Digested,* 01/**3572**:
Applied, 02/3236: *Considered,* 04/37, 04/2685, 07/2238
Keepers and Governors of the Possessions, Revenues and Goods of the Free Grammar
School of John Lyon v Berman see John Lyon's Free Grammar School v Secchi
Keepers and Governors of the Possessions, Revenues and Goods of the Free Grammar
School of John Lyon v Secchi see John Lyon's Free Grammar School v Secchi
Kehoe v Secretary of State for Work and Pensions see R. (on the application of Kehoe)
v Secretary of State for Work and Pensions
Keir v Leeman (1846) 9 L.J. Q.B. 371 .... *Considered,* 07/787
Keisner v Terrus Group Ltd; *joined case* Evolution Trading Group Ltd v Baris (UK) Ltd
[2006] EWHC 2765 (Ch); [2007] 1 B.C.L.C. 303, Ch D (Manchester)....... *Digested,* 07/**587**
Keles v Germany (32231/02) (2007) 44 E.H.R.R. 12, ECHR
Kellar v BBR Graphic Engineers (Yorks) Ltd [2002] B.P.I.R. 544, Ch D .... *Digested,* 03/**2372**:
Considered, 06/2385, 07/2453

Kelly v Churchill Car Insurance see Churchill Car Insurance v Kelly
Kelly-Madden v Manor Surgery [2007] I.C.R. 203; [2007] I.R.L.R. 17, EAT .... *Digested,* 07/**1431**:
Applied, 07/1421: *Considered,* 07/1426
Kemp v Barton (Unreported, October 12, 2006), CC (Stockport) [*Ex rel.* Chris
Middleton, Barrister, Oriel Chambers, 14 Water Street, Liverpool] .... *Digested,* 07/**3115**
Kempf v Staatssecretaris van Justitie (139/85) [1986] E.C.R. 1741; [1987] 1 C.M.L.R.
764, ECJ .... *Digested,* 87/**1565**:
Applied, 07/1631: *Followed,* 96/5389, 96/5390
Kemsley v Foot [1952] A.C. 345; [1952] 1 All E.R. 501; [1952] 1 T.L.R. 532; (1952)
96 S.J. 165, HL; affirming [1951] 2 K.B. 34; [1951] 1 All E.R. 331; [1951] 1 T.L.R.
197, CA .... *Digested,* 52/**2002**:
Applied, 59/1866, 61/4995, 69/2082, 05/982, 07/1071:
Considered, 92/2789: *Followed,* 06/1044
Kendall v Kendall [1977] Fam. 208; [1977] 3 W.L.R. 251; [1977] 3 All E.R. 471; (1977)
7 Fam. Law 145; (1977) 121 S.J. 171, Fam Div .... *Digested,* 77/**853**:
Applied, 07/1809: *Considered,* 79/771
Kennemer Golf & Country Club v Inspecteur Belastingdienst Particulieren/
Ondernemingen Haarlem (C174/00) see Kennemer Golf & Country Club v
Staatssecretaris van Financien (C-174/00)
Kennemer Golf & Country Club v Staatssecretaris van Financien (C-174/00); *sub nom*
Kennemer Golf & Country Club v Inspecteur Belastingdienst Particulieren/
Ondernemingen Haarlem (C174/00) [2002] Q.B. 1252; [2002] 3 W.L.R. 829;
[2002] All E.R. (EC) 480; [2002] S.T.C. 502; [2002] E.C.R. I-3293; [2002] 2
C.M.L.R. 12; [2002] C.E.C. 330; [2002] B.T.C. 5205; [2002] B.V.C. 395; [2002]
S.T.I. 354; *Times*, April 11, 2002, ECJ (5th Chamber) .... *Digested,* 02/**4756**:
Applied, 07/4284, 07/4292: *Considered,* 05/4358: *Followed,* 02/4758
Kennerley v Revenue and Customs Commissioners [2007] S.T.C. (S.C.D.) 188; [2007]
S.T.I. 265, Sp Comm..................................... *Digested,* 07/**4051**
Kenneth Allison Ltd (In Liquidation) v AE Limehouse & Co [1992] 2 A.C. 105; [1991] 3
W.L.R. 671; [1991] 4 All E.R. 500; (1991) 141 N.L.J. 1448; (1991) 135 S.J.L.B.
172; *Times*, October 18, 1991; *Independent*, October 18, 1991; *Financial Times*,
October 20, 1991, HL; reversing [1990] 2 Q.B. 527; [1990] 3 W.L.R. 216;
[1990] 2 All E.R. 723, CA (Civ Div)....................... *Digested,* 92/**3593**:
Applied, 06/350, 07/517: *Considered,* 91/2953
Kenneth (t/a Screw You)'s Community Trade Mark Application (R495/2005-G) [2007]
E.T.M.R. 7, OHIM (1st Bd App) .... *Digested,* 07/**2656**
Kensington and Chelsea RBC v Sager House (Chelsea) Ltd see R. (on the application
of Sager House (Chelsea) Ltd) v First Secretary of State
Kensington and Chelsea RLBC v Danesh see Danesh v Kensington and Chelsea RLBC
Kensington Heights Commercial Co Ltd v Campden Hill Developments Ltd; *sub nom*
Kensington Heights Commercial Property Ltd v Campden Hill Developments Ltd
[2007] EWCA Civ 245; [2007] Ch. 318; [2007] 2 W.L.R. 1040; [2007] 2 All
E.R. 751; [2007] H.L.R. 35; [2007] L. & T.R. 30; [2007] 13 E.G. 255 (C.S.);
(2007) 151 S.J.L.B. 436; [2007] N.P.C. 33; *Times*, April 20, 2007, CA (Civ Div) *Digested,* 07/**2750**
Kensington Heights Commercial Property Ltd v Campden Hill Developments Ltd see
Kensington Heights Commercial Co Ltd v Campden Hill Developments Ltd

Kensington International Ltd v Congo [2006] EWHC 1848 (Comm); [2006] 2 C.L.C.
588, QBD (Comm) . . . . *Digested*, 07/**461**
Kensington International Ltd v Congo [2007] EWCA Civ 1128; [2007] 2 C.L.C. 791;
(2007) 104(45) L.S.G. 31; *Times*, November 30, 2007, CA (Civ Div); affirming
[2007] EWHC 1632 (Comm); [2007] 2 Lloyd's Rep. 382, QBD (Comm) . . . . . *Digested*, 07/**437**
Kent v Griffiths (Non-Pecuniary Damages) see Heil v Rankin
Kent v Kavanagh [2006] EWCA Civ 162; [2007] Ch. 1; [2006] 3 W.L.R. 572; [2006]
2 All E.R. 645; [2006] 2 E.G.L.R. 127; [2006] 10 E.G. 155 (C.S.); [2006] N.P.C.
26; [2006] 2 P. & C.R. DG11; *Times*, March 24, 2006; *Independent*, March 7,
2006, CA (Civ Div) . . . . *Digested*, 06/**3502**:
Applied, 07/3426
Kent CC v B (A Child); *sub nom* B (A Child) (Disclosure), Re [2004] EWHC 411
(Fam); [2004] 2 F.L.R. 142; [2004] 3 F.C.R. 1; [2004] Lloyd's Rep. Med. 303;
[2004] Fam. Law 493; (2004) 154 N.L.J. 498, Fam Div . . . . *Digested*, 04/**1459**:
Applied, 06/445, 07/1711, 07/1732
Kent CC v G see G (A Child) (Interim Care Order: Residential Assessment), Re
Kent Foods Ltd v Revenue and Customs Commissioners [2007] S.T.I. 2704, Sp Comm
Kenyon v Masters (Unreported, July 10, 2006), CC (Birmingham) [*Ex rel*. Stephen
Garner, Barrister, No.8 Chambers, Fountain Court, Steelhouse Lane,
Birmingham] . . . . *Digested*, 07/**3184**
Kenyon-Brown v Desmond Banks & Co (Undue Influence) (No.2) see Royal Bank of
Scotland Plc v Etridge (No.2)
Kerckhaert v Belgium (C-513/04) see Kerckhaert-Morres v Belgium (C-513/04)
Kerckhaert-Morres v Belgium (C-513/04); *sub nom* Kerckhaert v Belgium (C-513/04)
[2007] 1 W.L.R. 1685; [2007] S.T.C. 1349; [2006] E.C.R. I-10967; [2007] 1
C.M.L.R. 32; [2007] C.E.C. 380; [2006] S.T.I. 2508; *Times*, November 29,
2006, ECJ . . . . *Digested*, 07/**4069**
Kerr v Baranow 2007 BCSC 1863; (2007-08) 10 I.T.E.L.R. 763, Sup Ct (BC)
Kersbergen-Lap   v   Raad   van   Bestuur   van   het   Uitvoeringsinstituut
Werknemersverzekeringen (C-154/05) [2006] All E.R. (EC) 973; [2006] E.C.R.
I-6249, ECJ . . . . *Digested*, 07/**1609**
Kershaw Mechanical Services Ltd v Kendrick Construction Ltd [2006] EWHC 727
(TCC); [2006] 4 All E.R. 79; [2006] 2 All E.R. (Comm) 81; 109 Con. L.R. 42;
[2006] C.I.L.L. 2359, QBD (TCC) . . . . *Digested*, 06/**203**
Kessler v Germany (35532/97) see Streletz v Germany (34044/96)
Kew v Bettamix Ltd (formerly Tarmac Roadstone Southern Ltd) [2006] EWCA Civ
1535; [2007] 4 Costs L.R. 527; [2007] P.I.Q.R. P16; (2006) 103(46) L.S.G. 30;
(2006) 150 S.J.L.B. 1534; *Times*, December 4, 2006, CA (Civ Div) . . . . *Digested*, 07/**475**
Keynsham Cemetery, Re [2003] 1 W.L.R. 66; (2002) 99(41) L.S.G. 27; *Times*, October 14,
2002, Cons Ct (Bath & Wells) . . . . *Digested*, 02/**967**:
Applied, 07/1085: *Considered*, 06/2822
Keys v Department of Regional Development [2007] R.V.R. 237, QBD (NI)
Keyte v Wheeler (Unreported, October 5, 2006), CC (Ilford) [*Ex rel*. David McHugh,
Barrister, Clerksroom, DX57508, Tolworth] . . . . *Digested*, 07/**3159**
Khadr v Minister of Justice 2007 FCA 182; 22 B.H.R.C. 573, CA (Can)
Khalid v Barnet and Chase Farm Hospital NHS Trust [2007] EWHC 644 (QB); (2007)
97 B.M.L.R. 82, QBD . . . . *Digested*, 07/**2922**
Khalil v Bishieri [2007] EWCA Civ 837; [2007] 3 F.C.R. 605; [2007] Fam. Law 978;
(2007) 151 S.J.L.B. 987, CA (Civ Div) . . . . *Digested*, 07/**1702**
Khan v Chief Constable of West Yorkshire see Chief Constable of West Yorkshire v
Khan
Khan v Falvey see Khan v RM Falvey & Co
Khan v Heywood and Middleton Primary Care Trust [2006] EWCA Civ 1087; [2007]
I.C.R. 24; [2006] I.R.L.R. 793; (2006) 150 S.J.L.B. 1021; *Times*, August 28,
2006; *Independent*, October 4, 2006, CA (Civ Div); affirming [2006] I.C.R.
543; [2006] I.R.L.R. 345, EAT . . . . *Digested*, 06/**1358**
Khan v Inland Revenue Commissioners see Toshoku Finance UK Plc (In Liquidation),
Re
Khan v London Probation Service see Muschett v Hounslow LBC
Khan v RM Falvey & Co; *sub nom* Khan v Falvey [2002] EWCA Civ 400; [2002]
Lloyd's Rep. P.N. 369; [2002] P.N.L.R. 28; (2002) 99(19) L.S.G. 30; (2002)
146 S.J.L.B. 108; *Times*, April 12, 2002, CA (Civ Div); reversing HQ 9900538,
QBD . . . . *Digested*, 02/**465**:
Applied, 03/431: *Followed*, 07/479
Khangura (Setting of Minimum Term), Re see Jones (Setting of Minimum Term), Re
Khudoyorov v Russia (6847/02) (2007) 45 E.H.R.R. 5, ECHR . . . . *Digested*, 07/**2201**
Kidd (Philip Richard) see R. v Canavan (Darren Anthony)
Kieran Mullin Ltd v Customs and Excise Commissioners [2003] EWHC 4 (Ch); [2003]
S.T.C. 274; [2003] B.T.C. 5455; [2003] B.V.C. 511; [2003] S.T.I. 88, Ch D;
reversing MAN/99/505, V&DTr. . . . . *Digested*, 03/**4591**:
Applied, 04/4017, 07/4344

Kilby v Basildon DC; *sub nom* R. (on the application of Kilby) v Basildon DC [2007]
EWCA Civ 479; [2007] H.L.R. 39; [2007] 22 E.G. 161 (C.S.); (2007) 151
S.J.L.B. 712; [2007] N.P.C. 65, CA (Civ Div); affirming [2006] EWHC 1892
(Admin); [2006] H.L.R. 46; [2006] A.C.D. 94; (2006) 103(37) L.S.G. 34;
Times, August 21, 2006, QBD (Admin) . . . . *Digested*, 07/**2155**

Kilcarne Holdings Ltd v Targetfollow (Birmingham) Ltd [2005] EWCA Civ 1355; [2005]
N.P.C. 132; [2006] 1 P. & C.R. DG20, CA (Civ Div); affirming [2004] EWHC
2547 (Ch); [2005] 2 P. & C.R. 8; [2004] N.P.C. 167, Ch D . . . . *Digested*, 05/**695**:
Applied, 07/3395

Killner v France (1947) 149 E.G. 92, CA; affirming [1946] 2 All E.R. 83; (1946) 175
L.T. 377, KBD . . . . *Digested*,
47-51/**10633**:
Applied, 07/3396: *Considered*, 80/2800

KIMBERLY-CLARK WORLDWIDE/Cellulosic transfer layer (T1354/04) [2007] E.P.O.R. 16,
EPO (Technical Bd App) . . . . *Digested*, 07/**2562**

Kincaid's Application for Judicial Review, Re [2007] NIQB 26; [2007] N.I. 240, QBD (NI)

Kinco Investment Holding Ltd v Commissioner of Rating and Valuation [2007] R.V.R.
156

Kine v Jolly see Jolly v Kine

King v Eaton Ltd (No.2); *sub nom* Eaton Ltd v King 1999 S.L.T. 656; 1998 S.C.L.R.
1017; [1998] I.R.L.R. 686; 1998 G.W.D. 27-1381, IH (2 Div) . . . . *Digested*, 99/**6048**:
Applied, 06/1387: *Considered*, 07/1426: *Followed*, 05/1333

King v Great Britain China Centre [1992] I.C.R. 516; [1991] I.R.L.R. 513; *Times*,
October 30, 1991; *Independent*, October 22, 1991; *Guardian*, October 16, 1991,
CA (Civ Div) . . . . *Digested*, 92/**1959**:
Applied, 97/2239, 97/6011, 98/5810, 98/5817, 01/2296, 02/1413:
Considered, 00/2120, 01/2298, 07/1433: *Followed*, 97/2247, 97/2248:
Superseded, 06/1355

King v Kerrier DC [2006] EWHC 500 (Admin); [2006] R.V.R. 278, QBD (Admin) . . . . *Digested*, 06/**4035**:
Considered, 07/922

King v T Tunnock Ltd 2000 S.C. 424; 2000 S.L.T. 744; [2001] E.C.C. 6; [2000] Eu.
L.R. 531; [2000] I.R.L.R. 569; 2000 G.W.D. 12-408; *Times*, May 12, 2000, IH
(Ex Div); reversing (Unreported, December 24, 1997), Sh Pr; affirming 1996
S.C.L.R. 742, Sh Ct . . . . *Digested*, 00/**5846**:
Applied, 02/65: *Considered*, 06/60: *Distinguished*, 03/79: *Doubted*, 07/68

King v Telegraph Group Ltd [2004] EWCA Civ 613; [2005] 1 W.L.R. 2282; [2004]
C.P. Rep. 35; [2004] 3 Costs L.R. 449; [2004] E.M.L.R. 23; (2004) 101(25)
L.S.G. 27; (2004) 154 N.L.J. 823; (2004) 148 S.J.L.B. 664; *Times*, May 21,
2004, CA (Civ Div); affirming [2003] EWHC 1312 (QB), QBD . . . . *Digested*, 04/**326**:
Applied, 05/354, 06/363, 06/1043, 07/384, 07/389: *Considered*, 06/2739,
07/383, 07/385, 07/398

King v United Kingdom (13881/02) [2005] S.T.C. 438; (2005) 41 E.H.R.R. 2; 76 T.C.
699; [2007] B.T.C. 85; 7 I.T.L. Rep. 339; [2004] S.T.I. 2396; *Times*, November
23, 2004, ECHR. . . . . *Digested*, 05/**2086**

King v United Kingdom (Admissibility) (No.2) (13881/02) [2004] S.T.C. 911; [2007]
B.T.C. 74; 6 I.T.L. Rep. 872; [2004] S.T.I. 1117, ECHR . . . . *Digested*, 04/**1949**:
Applied, 06/4188, 07/4358

King v United Kingdom (Admissibility) (6234/06) (2007) 45 E.H.R.R. SE5, ECHR

King's Prosecutor (Brussels) v Armas see Office of the King's Prosecutor (Brussels) v
Cando Armas

Kingscrest Associates Ltd (t/a Kingscrest Residential Care Homes) v Customs and Excise
Commissioners (C-498/03) [2005] S.T.C. 1547; [2005] E.C.R. I-4427;
[2005] 2 C.M.L.R. 57; [2007] B.T.C. 5560; [2007] B.V.C. 528; [2005] S.T.I.
1019; *Times*, June 9, 2005, ECJ (3rd Chamber) . . . . *Digested*, 06/**4434**:
Applied, 07/4346, 07/4351: *Followed*, 07/4295

Kingsley IT Consulting Ltd v McIntosh [2006] EWHC 1288 (Ch); [2006] B.C.C. 875,
Ch D . . . . *Digested*, 07/**575**

Kingston Upon Hull City Council v Dunnachie (No.1) see Dunnachie v Kingston upon
Hull City Council

Kingstreet Investments Ltd v New Brunswick (Department of Finance) 9 I.T.L. Rep.
591, Sup Ct (Can) . . . . *Digested*, 07/**3439**

Kinlan v Crimmin [2006] EWHC 779 (Ch); [2007] B.C.C. 106; [2007] 2 B.C.L.C. 67,
Ch D (Companies Ct) . . . . *Digested*, 07/**588**

Kinsella v Revenue Commissioners [2006] IEHC 250; 10 I.T.L. Rep. 63, HC (Irl)

Kirklees MBC v Brent LBC [2004] 2 F.L.R. 800, Fam Div . . . . *Digested*, 04/**1455**:
Considered, 07/1791

Kirkman v Euro Exide Corp (CMP Batteries Ltd) [2007] EWCA Civ 66; [2007] C.P.
Rep. 19; (2007) 104(6) L.S.G. 31; (2007) 151 S.J.L.B. 164; *Times*, February 6,
2007, CA (Civ Div) . . . . *Digested*, 07/**338**

Kish Glass Co Ltd v Commission of the European Communities (T-65/96) [2000]
E.C.R. II-1885; [2000] 5 C.M.L.R. 229, CFI (4th Chamber) . . . . *Digested*, 00/**715**:
Affirmed, 02/587: *Applied*, 07/1548

Kitchen v Burwell Reed & Kinghorn Ltd [2005] EWHC 1771 (QB); [2006] 1 Costs
L.R. 82, QBD . . . . *Digested*, 06/**2732**:
Applied, 07/380
Kitfix Swallow Group Ltd v Great Gizmos Ltd [2007] EWHC 2668 (Ch); *Times*,
December 19, 2007, Ch D
Kittel v Belgium (C-439/04); *joined case* Belgium v Recolta Recycling SPRL (C-440/
04) [2006] E.C.R. I-6161; [2006] S.T.I. 1851, ECJ . . . . *Applied*, 07/4317,
07/4318: *Considered*, 07/4312
Kjeldsen v Denmark (A/23); *joined cases* Busk Madsen v Denmark; Pedersen v
Denmark (1979-80) 1 E.H.R.R. 711, ECHR . . . . *Considered*, 06/1848,
06/4009, 07/2975: *Followed*, 97/2787
Klaboe v Canada 2007 TCC 239; 9 I.T.L. Rep. 1099, Tax Ct (Can)
Klamer v Klamer [2007] EWHC 1547 (Fam); [2007] Fam. Law 981, Fam Div
Klass v Germany (A/28) (1979-80) 2 E.H.R.R. 214, ECHR . . . . *Digested*, 80/**1388**:
Applied, 97/2787, 07/2258: *Considered*, 98/3104, 00/3248, 07/2241:
Distinguished, 04/1615
Klein v Rhodos Management Ltd (C73/04) [2005] E.C.R. I-8667; [2006] I.L.Pr. 2,
ECJ (1st Chamber). . . . . *Digested*, 06/**633**:
Considered, 07/666
Klein v Slovakia (72208/01) 21 B.H.R.C. 457, ECHR . . . . *Digested*, 07/**2185**
Kleinwort Benson Ltd v Birmingham City Council see Kleinwort Benson Ltd v Lincoln
City Council
Kleinwort Benson Ltd v Kensington and Chelsea RLBC see Kleinwort Benson Ltd v
Lincoln City Council
Kleinwort Benson Ltd v Lincoln City Council; *joined cases* Kleinwort Benson Ltd v
Birmingham City Council; Kleinwort Benson Ltd v Southwark LBC; Kleinwort
Benson Ltd v Kensington and Chelsea RLBC [1999] 2 A.C. 349; [1998] 3
W.L.R. 1095; [1998] 4 All E.R. 513; [1998] Lloyd's Rep. Bank. 387; [1999]
C.L.C. 332; (1999) 1 L.G.L.R. 148; (1999) 11 Admin. L.R. 130; [1998] R.V.R. 315;
(1998) 148 N.L.J. 1674; (1998) 142 S.J.L.B. 279; [1998] N.P.C. 145; *Times*,
October 30, 1998; *Independent*, November 4, 1998, HL . . . . *Digested*, 98/**2297**:
Applied, 99/2218, 03/4142, 04/383, 07/3973: *Considered*, 99/532, 03/1579,
05/4129, 07/1052: *Not applied*, 04/3173: *Previous proceedings*, 96/425
Kleinwort Benson Ltd v Sandwell BC see Westdeutsche Landesbank Girozentrale v
Islington LBC
Kleinwort Benson Ltd v Southwark LBC see Kleinwort Benson Ltd v Lincoln City
Council
Knauf UK GmbH v British Gypsum Ltd (No.1) [2001] EWCA Civ 1570; [2002] 1 W.L.R.
907; [2002] 2 All E.R. 525; [2001] 2 All E.R. (Comm) 960; [2002] 1 Lloyd's
Rep. 199; [2002] C.L.C. 239; [2002] I.L.Pr. 30; (2001) 145 S.J.L.B. 259; *Times*,
November 15, 2001; *Independent*, November 7, 2001, CA (Civ Div); reversing
[2001] 2 All E.R. (Comm) 332; [2001] C.L.C. 1141, QBD (Comm) . . . . *Digested*, 01/**828**:
Considered, 04/411, 06/507, 06/510, 06/515, 07/244
Knight v Beyond Properties Pty Ltd [2006] EWHC 1242 (Ch); [2007] 1 W.L.R. 625;
[2007] 1 All E.R. 91; [2007] 1 Costs L.R. 5; [2007] F.S.R. 7; (2006) 29(7) I.P.D.
29054; (2006) 103(25) L.S.G. 28; (2006) 156 N.L.J. 989, Ch D . . . . *Digested*, 07/**383**
Knight v Beyond Properties Pty Ltd [2007] EWHC 1251 (Ch); [2007] F.S.R. 34;
(2007) 151 S.J.L.B. 743, Ch D
Knor v Germany (C-190/94) see Dillenkofer v Germany (C-178/94)
Knowles v Superintendent of Prisons of the Commonwealth of the Bahamas see
Knowles v United States
Knowles v United States; *joined case* Knowles v Superintendent of Prisons of the
Commonwealth of the Bahamas [2006] UKPC 38; [2007] 1 W.L.R. 47, PC
(Bah) . . . . *Digested*, 07/**1663**:
Followed, 07/1672
Knowsley Housing Trust v White; *sub nom* White v Knowsley Housing Trust [2007]
EWCA Civ 404; [2007] 1 W.L.R. 2897; [2007] 4 All E.R. 800; [2007] H.L.R. 41;
[2007] L. & T.R. 31; [2007] 30 E.G. 134; [2007] 20 E.G. 294 (C.S.); (2007)
104(20) L.S.G. 27; (2005) 151 S.J.L.B. 611; *Times*, May 15, 2007, CA (Civ Div);
affirming [2007] 2 P. & C.R. DG4, CC (Liverpool) . . . . *Digested*, 07/**2718**
Knox v Gye (1871-72) L.R. 5 H.L. 656, HL . . . . *Considered*, 55/2138,
99/458, 00/513, 07/472
Knuller (Publishing, Printing and Promotions) Ltd v DPP; *sub nom* R. v Knuller
(Publishing, Printing and Promotions) Ltd; *joined cases* Keen (Graham) v DPP;
Stansill (Peter) v DPP; Hall (David) v DPP [1973] A.C. 435; [1972] 3 W.L.R. 143;
[1972] 2 All E.R. 898; (1972) 56 Cr. App. R. 633; [1975] Crim. L.R. 704;
(1972) 116 S.J. 545, HL; affirming in part [1972] 2 Q.B. 179; [1971] 3 W.L.R.
633; [1971] 3 All E.R. 314; (1971) 115 S.J. 772, CA (Crim Div) . . . . *Digested*, 72/**589**:
Applied, 76/524, 06/835: *Considered*, 72/589, 91/966, 95/1268, 96/1490,
07/916
Kobler v Austria (C-224/01) [2004] Q.B. 848; [2004] 2 W.L.R. 976; [2004] All E.R.
(EC) 23; [2003] E.C.R. I-10239; [2003] 3 C.M.L.R. 28; *Times*, October 3, 2003,
ECJ . . . . *Digested*, 04/**1426**:
Considered, 07/1651

Kociukow v District Court of Bialystok III Penal Division [2006] EWHC 56 (Admin); [2006] 1 W.L.R. 3061; [2006] 2 All E.R. 451; [2006] Extradition L.R. 4; [2006] A.C.D. 37, QBD (Admin) . . . .   *Digested,* 06/**1604**: *Distinguished,* 07/1667

Kofoed v Skatteministeriet (C-321/05) [2007] 3 C.M.L.R. 33; [2007] S.T.I. 1793, ECJ (1st Chamber)

KOGAZ rt v Zala Megyei Kozigazgatasi Hivatal Vezetoje (C-283/06); *joined case* OTP Garancia Biztosito rt v Vas Megyei Kozigazgatasi Hivatal (C-312/06) [2007] S.T.I. 2403, ECJ (4th Chamber)

Kohll v Union des Caisses de Maladie (C-158/96) [1998] E.C.R. I-1931; [1998] 2 C.M.L.R. 928, ECJ . . . .   *Considered,* 07/1632

Kohn v Wagschal [2007] EWCA Civ 1022; [2007] 2 C.L.C. 720, CA (Civ Div); affirming [2006] EWHC 3356 (Comm), QBD (Comm)

Kokkinakis v Greece (A/260-A) (1994) 17 E.H.R.R. 397; *Times,* June 11, 1993; *Independent,* June 16, 1993; *Guardian,* June 14, 1993, ECHR . . . .   *Digested,* 94/**2419**: *Applied,* 01/3481: *Considered,* 07/898: *Followed,* 97/2787, 98/3097, 01/3479

Kola v Secretary of State for Work and Pensions; *sub nom* R. (on the application of Kola) v Secretary of State for Work and Pensions; *joined case* Mirzajani v Secretary of State for Work and Pensions [2007] UKHL 54; (2007) 151 S.J.L.B. 1566, HL; reversing [2004] EWCA Civ 638; (2004) 101(26) L.S.G. 28, CA (Civ Div)

Kolden Holdings Ltd v Rodette Commerce Ltd A3/2007/1677, CA (Civ Div); affirming [2007] EWHC 1597 (Comm); [2007] 4 All E.R. 62; [2007] 2 All E.R. (Comm) 737; [2007] 2 C.L.C. 355; [2007] I.L.Pr. 50; (2007) 157 N.L.J. 1010, QBD (Comm) . . . .   *Digested,* 07/**682**

Konami Co Ltd (T928/03) see KUNOMI/Video game (T928/03)

KONICA CORP/Magnetic recording medium (T993/02) [2007] E.P.O.R. 26, EPO (Technical Bd App) . . . .   *Digested,* 07/**2607**

Koninklijke KPN Nederland NV v Benelux-Merkenbureau (C-363/99) [2006] Ch. 1; [2005] 3 W.L.R. 649; [2005] All E.R. (EC) 19; [2004] E.C.R. I-1619; [2005] 2 C.M.L.R. 10; [2005] C.E.C. 216; [2004] E.T.M.R. 57, ECJ (6th Chamber) . . . . .   *Digested,* 05/**2437**: *Applied,* 05/2529, 07/2647, 07/2648: *Considered,* 05/2532

Koninklijke Philips Electronics NV v Remington Consumer Products Ltd (C-299/99); *sub nom* Philips Electronics NV v Remington Consumer Products Ltd (C-299/99) [2003] Ch. 159; [2003] 2 W.L.R. 294; [2002] All E.R. (EC) 634; [2002] E.C.R. I-5475; [2002] 2 C.M.L.R. 52; [2002] C.E.C. 525; [2002] E.T.M.R. 81; [2003] R.P.C. 2; (2002) 25(9) I.P.D. 25060; *Times,* June 20, 2002; *Daily Telegraph,* June 27, 2002, ECJ . . . .   *Digested,* 02/**2903**: *Applied,* 03/2632, 05/2438, 05/2578, 07/1580, 07/2637: *Considered,* 03/2613, 03/2631, 05/2533, 06/2598: *Followed,* 05/2548, 06/2610

KONINKLIJKE PHILIPS ELECTRONICS NV/Medical diagnostic imaging (T9/04) [2007] E.P.O.R. 10, EPO (Technical Bd App) . . . .   *Digested,* 07/**2596**

KONINKLIJKE PHILIPS ELECTRONICS NV/Power adaptive frequency divider (T482/06) [2006] E.P.O.R. 56, EPO (Technical Bd App) . . . .   *Digested,* 07/**2569**

Konkola Copper Mines Plc v Coromin Ltd [2006] EWCA Civ 5; [2006] 1 All E.R. (Comm) 437; [2006] 1 Lloyd's Rep. 410; [2006] 1 C.L.C. 1; [2006] I.L.Pr. 46; [2007] Lloyd's Rep. I.R. 247; [2006] 103(6) L.S.G. 34, CA (Civ Div); affirming [2005] EWHC 898 (Comm); [2005] 2 All E.R. (Comm) 637; [2005] 2 Lloyd's Rep. 555; [2005] 1 C.L.C. 1021; [2005] I.L.Pr. 39; [2006] Lloyd's Rep. I.R. 71, QBD (Comm) . . . .   *Digested,* 06/**515**

Konle v Austria (C-302/97) [1999] E.C.R. I-3099; [2000] 2 C.M.L.R. 963, ECJ . . . .   *Digested,* 00/**2383**: *Applied,* 04/3258, 07/1602: *Followed,* 06/3504

Konrad v Germany (Admissibility) (35504/03) [2007] E.L.R. 435; (2007) 44 E.H.R.R. SE8, ECHR

Konstatinov v Netherlands (16351/03) [2007] 2 F.C.R. 194, ECHR . . . .   *Digested,* 07/**2259**

Konsumentombudsmannen (KO) v Gourmet International Products AB (C-405/98) [2001] All E.R. (EC) 308; [2001] E.C.R. I-1795; [2001] 2 C.M.L.R. 31; [2001] C.E.C. 98, ECJ (6th Chamber) . . . .   *Digested,* 01/**2486**: *Considered,* 07/1604

Koonmen v Bender [2007] W.T.L.R. 293; (2003-04) 6 I.T.E.L.R. 568, CA (Jer) (2002-03) 5 I.T.E.L.R. 247, Royal Ct (Jer) . . . .   *Digested,* 07/**683**

Korab-Karpinski v Lucas-Gardiner see Zielinski (Deceased), Re

Korea National Insurance Corp v Allianz Global Corporate and Specialty AG (formerly Allianz Marine and Aviation Versicherungs AG) (London Branch) [2007] EWCA Civ 1066; [2007] 2 C.L.C. 748, CA (Civ Div); affirming [2007] EWHC 1744 (Comm), QBD (Comm)

Korner v Inland Revenue Commissioners [1969] 1 W.L.R. 554; [1969] 1 All E.R. 679; 1969 S.C. (H.L.) 13; 1969 S.L.T. 109; 45 T.C. 287; (1969) 48 A.T.C. 29; [1968] T.R. 249; [1969] T.R. 33; (1969) 113 S.J. 245, HL; affirming 1969 S.L.T. 37; 1968 S.L.T. (Notes) 82, IH (1 Div) . . . .   *Digested,* 69/**4000**: *Applied,* 03/4256, 07/4105

Kosmar Villa Holidays Plc v Trustees of Syndicate 1243 A3/2007/0888, CA (Civ Div);
  reversing [2007] EWHC 458 (Comm); [2007] 2 All E.R. (Comm) 217; [2007] 1
  C.L.C. 642, QBD (Comm) . . . . *Digested*, 07/**2470**
Kosteski v Macedonia (55170/00) (2007) 45 E.H.R.R. 31, ECHR
Kostic v Chaplin [2007] EWHC 2298 (Ch); (2007-08) 10 I.T.E.L.R. 364, Ch D . . . . . . *Digested*, 07/**3958**
Kotak Mahindra Primus Ltd v Deputy Director of Income Tax 9 I.T.L. Rep. 615, ITAT (Ind)
Kotrie v Globe Equities Ltd see Globe Equities Ltd v Globe Legal Services Ltd
Koufos v C Czarnikow Ltd (The Heron II); *sub nom* C Czarnikow Ltd v Koufos (The
  Heron II) [1969] 1 A.C. 350; [1967] 3 W.L.R. 1491; [1967] 3 All E.R. 686;
  [1967] 2 Lloyd's Rep. 457; (1967) 111 S.J. 848, HL; affirming [1966] 2 Q.B. 695;
  [1966] 2 W.L.R. 1397; [1966] 2 All E.R. 593; [1966] 1 Lloyd's Rep. 595, CA;
  reversing [1966] 1 Lloyd's Rep. 259; (1966) 110 S.J. 287, QBD (Comm) . . . . . *Digested*, 67/**3623**:
            Applied, 70/924, 77/2881, 78/2821, 85/198, 88/1165, 96/3566, 97/6093,
                99/5790, 03/3919, 07/1064: *Approved*, 66/3146: *Considered*, 67/3623,
                            68/1013, 69/3226, 72/990, 75/2324, 94/5413, 07/5015
KP (Sri Lanka) v Secretary of State for the Home Department [2007] EWCA Civ 62;
  (2007) 151 S.J.L.B. 125, CA (Civ Div)
KPMG v Network Rail Infrastructure Ltd [2007] EWCA Civ 363; [2007] Bus. L.R.
  1336; [2007] L. & T.R. 32; (2007) 151 S.J.L.B. 611; [2007] N.P.C. 51, CA (Civ
  Div); affirming [2006] EWHC 67 (Ch); [2006] 2 P. & C.R. 7; [2006] 6 E.G. 171
  (C.S.); [2006] N.P.C. 11, Ch D . . . . *Digested*, 07/**2748**
KR v Bryn Alyn Community (Holdings) Ltd (In Liquidation); *sub nom* Various
  Claimants v BACHL; Various Claimants v Bryn Alyn Community (Holdings) Ltd
  (In Liquidation) [2003] EWCA Civ 85; [2003] Q.B. 1441; [2003] 3 W.L.R. 107;
  [2004] 2 All E.R. 716; [2003] 1 F.L.R. 1203; [2003] 1 F.C.R. 385; [2003]
  Lloyd's Rep. Med. 175; [2003] Fam. Law 482; *Times*, February 17, 2003, CA
  (Civ Div); affirming HQ/99/01473, QBD . . . . *Digested*, 03/**432**:
            Applied, 05/2859: *Considered*, 07/5096: *Doubted*, 07/473, 07/483:
                                                                    Followed, 06/476
KR v Royal & Sun Alliance Plc [2006] EWCA Civ 1454; [2007] Bus. L.R. 139; [2007]
  1 All E.R. (Comm) 161; [2007] B.C.C. 522; [2007] Lloyd's Rep. I.R. 368;
  [2007] P.I.Q.R. P14; (2006) 150 S.J.L.B. 1467; *Times*, November 8, 2006, CA
  (Civ Div); reversing [2006] EWHC 48 (QB); [2006] Lloyd's Rep. I.R. 327,
  QBD . . . . *Digested*, 07/**2485**
KR (Iraq) v Secretary of State for the Home Department [2007] EWCA Civ 514;
  [2007] I.N.L.R. 373, CA (Civ Div)
Kranemann v Land Nordrhein-Westfalen (C-109/04) [2005] E.C.R. I-2421; [2005] 2
  C.M.L.R. 15; [2005] C.E.C. 707, ECJ (1st Chamber). . . . . *Digested*, 05/**1461**:
                                                                    Considered, 07/1629
Krasniqi v Secretary of State for the Home Department [2006] EWCA Civ 391; *Times*,
  April 20, 2006, CA (Civ Div) . . . . *Digested*, 06/**2251**:
                                                                    Applied, 07/2368
Krasulya v Russia (12365/03) (2007) 45 E.H.R.R. 40, ECHR
Krasuski v Poland (61444/00) (2007) 44 E.H.R.R. 10, ECHR
Kraus v Penna Plc [2004] I.R.L.R. 260, EAT . . . . *Digested*, 04/**1274**:
                                                    Applied, 06/1401: *Not followed*, 07/1441
Krenz v Germany (44801/98) see Streletz v Germany (34044/96)
Kretzinger v Hauptzollamt Augsburg (C-288/05) [2007] E.C.R. I-6441; [2007] 3
  C.M.L.R. 43, ECJ (2nd Chamber)
Kretztechnik AG v Finanzamt Linz (C-465/03) [2005] 1 W.L.R. 3755; [2005] S.T.C.
  1118; [2005] E.C.R. I-4357; [2005] 2 C.M.L.R. 46; [2005] B.T.C. 5823; [2006]
  B.V.C. 66; [2005] S.T.I. 1020; *Times*, June 21, 2005, ECJ (1st Chamber) . . . . . . *Digested*, 05/**4363**:
                                                    Considered, 05/4371, 06/4471, 07/4314
Krippendorf v General Medical Council [2001] 1 W.L.R. 1054; [2001] Lloyd's Rep.
  Med. 9; (2001) 59 B.M.L.R. 81; (2001) 145 S.J.L.B. 5; *Times*, November 29,
  2000, PC (UK) . . . . *Digested*, 01/**2927**:
                                                    Considered, 03/1721, 07/1952
Krohn & Co Import-Export GmbH & Co KG v Commission of the European Communities
  (175/84) [1986] E.C.R. 753; [1987] 1 C.M.L.R. 745, ECJ . . . . *Digested*, 87/**1451**:
                                                                    Applied, 07/552
Kroon v Netherlands (A/297-C) [1995] 2 F.C.R. 28; (1995) 19 E.H.R.R. 263, ECHR . . *Applied*, 01/**2541**,
            06/1685, 07/1787: *Considered*, 06/2193, 06/2199, 07/2254
Kudla v Poland (30210/96) (2002) 35 E.H.R.R. 11; 10 B.H.R.C. 269; [2000] Prison
  L.R. 380, ECHR . . . . *Digested*, 01/**3543**:
            Applied, 06/2127, 07/2198, 07/2227, 07/2230, 07/2231
Kuenyehia v International Hospitals Group Ltd; *sub nom* International Hospitals Group
  Ltd v Kuenyehia; Ashiagbor (Deceased), Re [2007] EWCA Civ 274; (2007) 151
  S.J.L.B. 331, CA (Civ Div); reversing [2006] EWHC 3503 (QB), QBD
Kufaan Publishing Ltd v Al-Warrak Bookshop Ltd see Kufaan Publishing Ltd v Al-Warrak
  Publishing Ltd
Kufaan Publishing Ltd v Al-Warrak Publishing Ltd; *joined cases* Kufaan Publishing Ltd v
  Al-Warrak Bookshop Ltd; Kufaan Publishing Ltd v Shubber; CHANI 1998/
  1431/A3, FC2 1999/5294/A3, FC2 2000/5419/A3, CA (Civ Div) . . . . *Applied*, 07/416,
                                                                    07/512

Kufaan Publishing Ltd v Shubber see Kufaan Publishing Ltd v Al-Warrak Publishing Ltd
Kuhne & Heitz NV v Productschap voor Pluimvee en Eieren (C-453/00) [2004] E.C.R.
    I-837; [2006] 2 C.M.L.R. 17, ECJ . . . .   *Applied,* 07/1640:
                                                   Distinguished, 07/1579
Kuijer v Council of the European Union (T-188/98) [2000] E.C.R. II-1959; [2000] 2
    C.M.L.R. 400; *Times,* April 14, 2000, CFI (4th Chamber) . . . .   *Digested,* 00/**2392**:
                                          Applied, 05/1425, 07/1585
Kuijer v Council of the European Union (T-211/00) [2002] 1 W.L.R. 1941; [2003] All
    E.R. (EC) 276; [2002] E.C.R. II-485; [2002] 1 C.M.L.R. 42; [2002] C.E.C. 238,
    CFI (4th Chamber). . . . .   *Digested,* 02/**1546**:
                                          Applied, 06/1523, 07/1539
Kuijper v Netherlands (Admissibility) (64848/01) (2005) 41 E.H.R.R. SE16, ECHR . . .   *Applied,* 07/2246
KUNOMI/Video game (T928/03); *sub nom* Konami Co Ltd (T928/03) [2006] E.P.O.R.
    53; (2006) 29(9) I.P.D. 29071, EPO (Technical Bd App) . . . .   *Digested,* 07/**2588**:
                                          Followed, 07/2589
Kurdistan Workers Party (PKK) v Council of the European Union (C-229/05 P); *sub
    nom* Ocalan v Council of the European Union (C-229/05 P) [2007] All E.R.
    (EC) 875, ECJ
Kurt v Turkey (37038/97) (2007) 44 E.H.R.R. 36, ECHR.   *Digested,* 07/**2255**
Kustom Musical Amplification Inc v Office for Harmonisation in the Internal Market
    (Trade Marks and Designs) (OHIM) (T-317/05) [2007] E.T.M.R. 72, CFI (3rd
    Chamber)
Kuwait Petroleum (GB) Ltd v Customs and Excise Commissioners (C-48/97) [1999]
    All E.R. (EC) 450; [1999] S.T.C. 488; [1999] E.C.R. I-2323; [1999] 2 C.M.L.R.
    651; [1999] C.E.C. 201; [1999] B.T.C. 5203; [1999] B.V.C. 250; *Times,* May 14,
    1999, ECJ . . . .   *Digested,* 99/**4967**:
                     Considered, 04/3981, 07/4290: *Distinguished,* 07/4323
Kuzel v Roche Products Ltd A2/2007/0630, CA (Civ Div); reversing in part [2007]
    I.C.R. 945; [2007] I.R.L.R. 309; *Times,* April 9, 2007, EAT . . . .   *Digested,* 07/**1433**
KVS International BV v Minister van Landbouw, Natuurbeheer en Visserij (C-301/98)
    [2000] E.C.R. I-3583, ECJ . . . .   *Applied,* 07/2519
KVZ Retec GmbH v Austria (C-176/05) [2007] Env. L.R. D14, ECJ
KW v Lewisham LBC see K v Lewisham LBC
Kwekerij Gebroeders van der Kooy BV v Commission of the European Communities (67/
    85) [1988] E.C.R. 219; [1989] 2 C.M.L.R. 804, ECJ . . . .   *Digested,* 90/**2221**:
                           Considered, 07/1540: *Distinguished,* 07/1564
Kwesi Armah, Re see Armah v Ghana (No.1)
Kyi v Secretary of State for the Home Department [2006] EWCA Civ 1336; [2007]
    Imm. A.R. 220; [2007] I.N.L.R. 254, CA (Crim Div).   *Digested,* 07/**2352**
Kyle Bay Ltd (t/a Astons Nightclub) v Underwriters [2007] EWCA Civ 57; [2007] 1
    C.L.C. 164; [2007] Lloyd's Rep. I.R. 460, CA (Civ Div); affirming [2006] EWHC
    607 (Comm); [2006] Lloyd's Rep. I.R. 718; *Times,* May 29, 2006, QBD
    (Comm) . . . .   *Digested,* 07/**2468**
Kyprianou v Cyprus (73797/01) (2007) 44 E.H.R.R. 27, ECHR
Kyrgystan v Finrep GmbH see Kyrgyz Republic Ministry of Transport Department of
    Civil Aviation v Finrep GmbH
Kyrgyz Republic Ministry of Transport Department of Civil Aviation v Finrep GmbH; *sub
    nom* Kyrgystan v Finrep GmbH [2006] EWHC 1722 (Comm); [2006] 2 C.L.C.
    402; [2007] Bus. L.R. D17, QBD (Comm) . . . .   *Digested,* 07/**244**

L v A Local Authority see W (A Child), Re
L v Birmingham City Council; *sub nom* R. (on the application of Johnson) v Havering
    LBC; Johnson v Havering LBC; *joined case* YL v Birmingham City Council
    [2007] UKHL 27; [2007] 3 W.L.R. 112; [2007] 3 All E.R. 957; [2007] H.R.L.R.
    32; [2007] H.L.R. 44; (2007) 10 C.C.L. Rep. 505; [2007] LS Law Medical 472;
    (2007) 96 B.M.L.R. 1; (2007) 104(27) L.S.G. 29; (2007) 157 N.L.J. 938;
    (2007) 151 S.J.L.B. 860; [2007] N.P.C. 75; *Times,* June 21, 2007, HL; affirming
    [2007] EWCA Civ 26; [2007] 2 W.L.R. 1097; [2007] H.R.L.R. 15; [2007]
    U.K.H.R.R. 645; [2007] B.L.G.R. 241; (2007) 10 C.C.L. Rep. 7; (2007) 95
    B.M.L.R. 33; [2007] M.H.L.R. 69; (2007) 151 S.J.L.B. 199; [2007] N.P.C. 12;
    Times, February 2, 2007, CA (Civ Div); affirming [2006] EWHC 1714 (Admin);
    [2006] B.L.G.R. 631; (2006) 9 C.C.L. Rep. 503; [2006] Lloyd's Rep. Med. 447;
    [2006] A.C.D. 95, QBD (Admin) . . . .   *Digested,* 07/**3912**:
                                          Applied, 07/2300
L v Crown Prosecution Service; *sub nom* L v DPP [2007] EWHC 1843 (Admin);
    (2007) 171 J.P. 635; *Times,* October 8, 2007, DC . . . .   *Digested,* 07/**1028**
L v DPP see L v Crown Prosecution Service
L v J see R. (on the application of L (A Child)) v J School Governors
L v L [2007] EWHC 140 (QB); [2007] 2 F.L.R. 171; [2007] Fam. Law 692, QBD . . . . .   *Digested,* 07/**331**
L v M Ltd [2006] EWHC 3395 (Ch); [2007] Pens. L.R. 11, Ch D . . . .   *Digested,* 07/**3025**
L v Pembrokeshire CC see Lawrence v Pembrokeshire CC
L v Portsmouth City Council (Unreported, October 9, 2006), QBD (Winchester) [*Ex
    rel.* Frank Moat, Barrister, 3 Pump Court, Temple, London] . . . .   *Digested,* 07/**3082**

L v Reading BC see B v Reading BC

L v Reading BC [2006] EWHC 2449 (QB); [2007] B.L.G.R. 576, QBD . . . .   *Digested*, 07/**2916**

L v United Kingdom (45508/99) see HL v United Kingdom (45508/99)

L Minors, Re see L (Minors) (Wardship: Jurisdiction), Re

L (A Child), Re see R. (on the application of L (A Child)) v J School Governors

L (A Child), Re; *sub nom* L (A Child) (Special Guardianship: Surname), Re; E (A Child),
Re [2007] EWCA Civ 196; [2007] 2 F.L.R. 50; [2007] 1 F.C.R. 804; [2007]
Fam. Law 498; *Times*, April 11, 2007, CA (Civ Div) . . . .   *Digested*, 07/**1796**

L (A Child), Re; *sub nom* CT v Bristol City Council; *joined case* H (A Child), Re [2007]
EWCA Civ 213; [2007] 1 F.L.R. 1370; [2007] 3 F.C.R. 259; [2007] Fam. Law
584, CA (Civ Div) . . . .   *Digested*, 07/**1751**

L (A Child) v Birmingham Children's Hospital NHS Trust (Unreported, May 17, 2007),
CC (Birmingham) [*Ex rel.* Stephen Garner, Barrister, No.8 Chambers, Fountain
Court, Steelhouse Lane, Birmingham] . . . .   *Digested*, 07/**3193**

L (A Child) v Royal Wolverhampton NHS Trust (Unreported, May 2, 2006), CC
(Birmingham) [*Ex rel.* Stephen Garner, Barrister, No.8 Chambers, Fountain
Court, Steelhouse Lane, Birmingham] . . . .   *Digested*, 07/**3217**

L (A Child) (Care: Threshold Criteria), Re [2007] 1 F.L.R. 1050; [2007] Fam. Law 297, Fam
Div

L (A Child) (Medical Treatment: Benefit), Re [2004] EWHC 2713 (Fam); [2005] 1 F.L.R.
491; [2005] Fam. Law 211, Fam Div . . . .   *Digested*, 05/**1677**:
Applied, 05/1794, 06/1852, 07/1984

L (A Child) (Special Guardianship: Surname), Re see L (A Child), Re

L (Care Order: Immigration Powers to Remove), Re [2007] EWHC 158 (Fam); [2007] 2
F.L.R. 789; [2007] Fam. Law 486, Fam Div

L (Children) (Care proceedings: Significant Harm), Re see L (Children) (Care Proceedings:
Threshold Criteria), Re

L (Children) (Care Proceedings: Threshold Criteria), Re; *sub nom* L (Children) (Care
proceedings: Significant Harm), Re [2006] EWCA Civ 1282; [2007] 1 F.L.R.
1068; [2006] 3 F.C.R. 301; [2007] Fam. Law 17; (2006) 103(36) L.S.G. 36;
(2006) 150 S.J.L.B. 1152, CA (Civ Div) . . . .   *Digested*, 07/**1716**

L (Minors) (Wardship: Jurisdiction), Re; *sub nom* L Minors, Re [1974] 1 W.L.R. 250;
[1974] 1 All E.R. 913; (1973) 4 Fam. Law 94; (1973) 118 S.J. 22; *Times*,
November 9, 1973, CA (Civ Div) . . . .   *Digested*, 74/**2417**:
Applied, 74/170.u, 77/1962, 89/2454, 92/3046, 95/3443, 95/3445:
Considered, 75/2202, 76/1772, 81/1776, 82/467.u, 07/1736:
Distinguished, 77/345.u

L (Residence: Jurisdiction), Re see V v V

L-K v K (Brussels II Revised: Maintenance Pending Suit) [2006] EWHC 153 (Fam);
[2006] 2 F.L.R. 1113; [2006] Fam. Law 635, Fam Div . . . .   *Digested*, 07/**1701**

L-K v K (No.2) [2006] EWHC 3280 (Fam); [2007] 2 F.L.R. 729; [2007] Fam. Law
693, Fam Div

L-K v K (No.3) [2006] EWHC 3281 (Fam); [2007] 2 F.L.R. 741; [2007] Fam. Law
800, Fam Div

L'Oreal SA v Bellure NV [2007] EWCA Civ 968, CA (Civ Div) [2006] EWHC 2355
(Ch); [2007] E.T.M.R. 1; [2007] R.P.C. 14; (2006) 29(10) I.P.D. 29074, Ch D . .   *Digested*, 07/**2674**

La Caisse Regional du Credit v Ashdown see La Caisse Regional du Credit Agricole
Nord de France v Ashdown

La Caisse Regional du Credit Agricole Nord de France v Ashdown; *sub nom* La Caisse
Regional du Credit v Ashdown [2007] EWCA Civ 574, CA (Civ Div); reversing
[2007] EWHC 528 (QB); [2007] I.L.Pr. 23, QBD

La Cascina Soc Coop Arl v Ministero della Difesa (C-226/04) [2006] E.C.R. I-1347;
[2006] 2 C.M.L.R. 40, ECJ (1st Chamber) . . . .   *Digested*, 07/**3326**

La Torre (Antonio) v HM Advocate [2006] HCJAC 56; 2006 S.L.T. 989; 2006
S.C.C.R. 503; [2007] Eu. L.R. 70; 2006 G.W.D. 31-667, HCJ . . . .   *Digested*, 06/**5339**:
Considered, 07/517C

Labita v Italy (26772/95) [2000] Prison L.R. 337, ECHR (Grand Chamber) . . . .   *Considered*, 04/1981
06/2162, 07/226

Laboratoires Boiron SA v Agence Centrale des Organismes de Securite Sociale
(ACOSS) (C-526/04) see Laboratoires Boiron SA v Union de Recouvrement
des Cotisations de Securite Sociale et d'Allocations Familiales (URSSAF) de
Lyon (C-526/04)

Laboratoires Boiron SA v Union de Recouvrement des Cotisations de Securite Sociale
et d'Allocations Familiales (URSSAF) de Lyon (C-526/04); *sub nom*
Laboratoires Boiron SA v Agence Centrale des Organismes de Securite Sociale
(ACOSS) (C-526/04) [2006] E.C.R. I-7529; [2006] 3 C.M.L.R. 50; [2007]
C.E.C. 77, ECJ (2nd Chamber) . . . .   *Digested*, 07

Laboratoires Pharmaceutiques Bergaderm SA v Commission of the European
Communities (C-352/98 P) [2000] E.C.R. I-5291, ECJ . . . .   *Applied*, 03
07/1562: *Considered*, 05

Labour Party v Ahsan see Carter v Ahsan (No.1)

LABRONIX CONCEPT INC/Auxiliary game (T717/05) [2007] E.P.O.R. 35, EPO (Technical
Bd App)

Laceys (Wholesale) Footwear Ltd v Bowler International Freight Ltd [1997] 2 Lloyd's
Rep. 369; *Times*, May 12, 1997, CA (Civ Div) . . . . *Digested*, 97/**4287**:
Applied, 98/4807, 05/3455: *Considered*, 07/4215
Ladbroke Group Plc v Bristol City Council [1988] 23 E.G. 125; [1988] E.G. 8 (C.S.),
CA (Civ Div); reversing (1987) 283 E.G. 1071, QBD . . . . *Digested*, 88/**2072**:
Applied, 07/2748

Ladbroke Group Plc v One in a Million Ltd see British Telecommunications Plc v One in
a Million Ltd
Ladbrokes v Wokingham DC [2007] P.A.D. 32, Planning Inspector
Ladbrokes Ltd v Norway (E-3/06) [2007] 3 C.M.L.R. 12, EFTA
Ladd v Marshall [1954] 1 W.L.R. 1489; [1954] 3 All E.R. 745; (1954) 98 S.J. 870, CA . *Digested*, 54/**2507**:
Applied, 61/6769, 67/3202, 68/1544, 68/1545, 69/572, 71/3489, 73/2097,
79/318.u, 84/1737, 88/2128, 91/2927, 91/2928, 92/604,
92/3384.A, 93/1855, 95/504, 95/3922, 96/654, 96/656, 96/5321,
97/2869, 98/3200, 00/302, 01/632, 01/633, 02/309, 02/2859, 03/274,
03/943, 03/2235, 04/255, 05/2208, 05/2224, 05/2494, 06/310,
06/314, 06/441, 07/3364: *Considered*, 63/1013, 67/1339,
74/113.u, 74/163.u, 74/199.u, 74/226.u, 74/227.u, 74/252.u, 75/230.u, 75/
374.u, 79/355.u, 82/2382, 83/2702, 83/3016, 85/1256, 86/1853, 86/2017,
87/2494, 90/1552, 91/471, 94/2623, 94/3746, 95/3442, 95/3532, 96/680,
96/2994, 96/3242, 96/5722, 97/2865, 97/4903, 98/322, 00/305, 00/306,
00/562, 00/3292, 01/634, 01/3621, 02/270, 02/271, 02/506, 03/2242,
03/2597, 04/2030, 05/290, 05/464, 07/3387: *Distinguished*, 61/2556,
61/6677, 63/603, 90/3542, 92/2059, 96/756, 97/3366, 99/3546:
Followed, 59/2147, 83/2860, 92/3290, 97/458: *Not applied*, 97/3000,
00/3710: *Referred to*, 76/470.u, 99/3153, 99/3256, 99/4014
Laddingford Enclosures Ltd v Forsyth see Ruxley Electronics & Construction Ltd v
Forsyth
Lady Fox's Executors v Inland Revenue Commissioners see Gray v Inland Revenue
Commissioners
Lafayette Electronics Europe Ltd, Re [2006] EWHC 1005 (Ch); [2007] B.C.C. 890, Ch D
Lafayette Electronics Europe Ltd, Re [2006] EWHC 1006 (Ch); [2007] B.C.C. 890, Ch D
Lagden v O'Connor; *sub nom* Clark v Tull (t/a Ardington Electrical Services); *joined
cases* Clark v Ardington Electrical Services; Dennard v Plant; Sen v Steelform
Engineering Co Ltd; Burdis v Livsey [2003] UKHL 64; [2004] 1 A.C. 1067;
[2003] 3 W.L.R. 1571; [2004] 1 All E.R. 277; [2004] R.T.R. 24; [2004] Lloyd's
Rep. I.R. 315; (2003) 153 N.L.J. 1869; (2003) 147 S.J.L.B. 1430; *Times*,
December 5, 2003, HL; affirming [2002] EWCA Civ 510; [2003] Q.B. 36;
[2002] 3 W.L.R. 762; [2003] R.T.R. 3; [2002] Lloyd's Rep. I.R. 524, CA (Civ
Div); reversing in part [2002] Lloyd's Rep. I.R. 138, CC (Oxford) . . . . *Digested*, 04/**630**:
Applied, 06/5246, 07/1066: *Cited*, 02/687: *Considered*, 07/767, 07/2497:
Followed, 06/1033

Lagergren v Denmark (Admissibility) (18668/03) (2007) 44 E.H.R.R. SE10, ECHR
Lagesse v DPP of Mauritius [1990] M.R. 194 . . . . *Doubted*, 07/55
Lahey v Pirelli Tyres Ltd [2007] EWCA Civ 91; [2007] 1 W.L.R. 998; [2007] C.P. Rep.
21; [2007] 3 Costs L.R. 462; [2007] P.I.Q.R. P20; (2007) 104(9) L.S.G. 30;
(2007) 157 N.L.J. 294; *Times*, February 19, 2007, CA (Civ Div) . . . . *Digested*, 07/**403**
Laing v Laing [2005] EWHC 3152 (Fam); [2007] 2 F.L.R. 199, Fam Div
Laing v Manchester City Council [2006] I.C.R. 1519; [2006] I.R.L.R. 748, EAT . . . . . . *Digested*, 06/**1349**:
Approved, 07/1401

Laing v Taylor Walton (A Firm); *sub nom* Taylor Walton (A Firm) v Laing [2007] EWCA
Civ 1146; [2007] 47 E.G. 169 (C.S.); (2007) 104(46) L.S.G. 27, CA (Civ Div);
reversing [2007] EWHC 196 (QB); [2007] 9 E.G. 202 (C.S.), QBD
Laing Management (Scotland) Ltd v John Doyle Construction Ltd see John Doyle
Construction Ltd v Laing Management (Scotland) Ltd
Laino v Italy (33158/96) (Unreported, February 18, 1999), ECHR . . . . *Applied*, 07/2220:
Considered, 07/2221: *Distinguished*, 06/2139
Lake v British Transport Police [2007] EWCA Civ 424; [2007] I.C.R. 1293, CA (Civ
Div); affirming [2007] I.C.R. 47, EAT . . . . *Digested*, 07/**1439**
Lake v Lake [1955] P. 336; [1955] 3 W.L.R. 145; [1955] 2 All E.R. 538; (1955) 99
S.J. 432, CA . . . . *Digested*, 55/**773**:
Applied, 01/686, 07/4303: *Considered*, 84/388, 07/3897:
Distinguished, 98/3670
Lake v Lake [2006] EWCA Civ 1250; [2007] 1 F.L.R. 427; [2006] Fam. Law 1035;
Times, August 16, 2006, CA (Civ Div) . . . . *Digested*, 06/**1717**
Lalani v Crump Holdings Ltd [2007] EWHC 47 (Ch); [2007] 8 E.G. 136 (C.S.), Ch D
Lama v Hope [2006] NZCA 117; [2007] W.T.L.R. 1551; (2006-07) 9 I.T.E.L.R. 438,
CA (NZ); reversing (2005-06) 8 I.T.E.L.R. 49, HC (NZ) . . . . *Digested*, 07/**4260**
Lambert v Cardiff CC [2007] EWHC 869 (QB); [2007] 3 F.C.R. 148; (2007) 97
B.M.L.R. 101, QBD . . . . *Digested*, 07/**1778**
Lambeth LBC v A see R. (on the application of Lindsay) v Lambeth LBC
Lambeth LBC v Corlett [2007] I.C.R. 88, EAT . . . . *Digested*, 07/**1350**
Lambeth LBC v Howard [2001] EWCA Civ 468; (2001) 33 H.L.R. 58, CA (Civ Div) . . *Digested*, 01/**4200**:
Applied, 05/298: *Considered*, 07/497

Lambeth LBC v Ireneschild see R. (on the application of Ireneschild) v Lambeth LBC
Lambeth LBC v Kay see Kay v Lambeth LBC
Lambeth LBC v Lindsay see R. (on the application of Lindsay) v Lambeth LBC
Lambeth LBC v Onayomake see Southwark LBC v Onayomake
Lambeth LBC v S [2006] EWHC 326 (Fam); [2007] 1 F.L.R. 152; [2006] Fam. Law
   843, Fam Div . . . . *Digested,* 07/**1731**
Lambeth LBC v Simon [2007] B.P.I.R. 1629, Ch D
Lambretta Clothing Co Ltd v Next Retail Plc see Lambretta Clothing Co Ltd v Teddy
   Smith (UK) Ltd
Lambretta Clothing Co Ltd v Teddy Smith (UK) Ltd; *joined case* Lambretta Clothing Co
   Ltd v Next Retail Plc [2004] EWCA Civ 886; [2005] R.P.C. 6; (2004) 148
   S.J.L.B. 911; *Times,* September 28, 2004, CA (Civ Div); affirming [2003] EWHC
   1204 (Ch); [2003] R.P.C. 41, Ch D . . . . *Digested,* 04/**2262**:
                                                  Applied, 05/2590: *Considered,* 07/2517
Lamont v Burton [2007] EWCA Civ 429; [2007] 1 W.L.R. 2814; [2007] 3 All E.R.
   173; [2007] C.P. Rep. 33; [2007] 4 Costs L.R. 574; [2007] P.I.Q.R. Q8; (2007)
   104(21) L.S.G. 26; (2007) 157 N.L.J. 706; (2007) 151 S.J.L.B. 670; *Times,*
   June 7, 2007, CA (Civ Div) . . . . *Digested,* 07/**418**
Lancashire Fires Ltd v SA Lyons & Co Ltd [1997] I.R.L.R. 113; [1996] F.S.R. 629;
   (1996) 19(8) I.P.D. 19068, CA (Civ Div); reversing (1996) 19(5) I.P.D. 19032,
   Ch D . . . . *Digested,* 96/**2519**:
                                  Considered, 07/1342: *Explained,* 05/2416
Lancaster-Thomas v Teignbridge DC [2007] R.V.R. 241, Lands Tr
Lancecrest Ltd v Asiwaju [2005] EWCA Civ 117; [2005] L. & T.R. 22; [2005] 1
   E.G.L.R. 40; [2005] 16 E.G. 146; [2005] N.P.C. 21, CA (Civ Div) . . . . *Digested,* 05/**2679**:
                                Applied, 07/2728
Land v Land (Deceased); *sub nom* Land, In the Estate of [2006] EWHC 2069 (Ch);
   [2007] 1 W.L.R. 1009; [2007] 1 All E.R. 324; [2006] W.T.L.R. 1447, Ch D
   (Birmingham) . . . . *Digested,* 06/**4075**
Land Brandenburg v Sass (C-284/02) [2004] E.C.R. I-11143; [2005] 1 C.M.L.R. 27;
   [2005] C.E.C. 3; [2005] I.R.L.R. 147, ECJ (1st Chamber) . . . . *Digested,* 05/**1266**:
                                  Applied, 07/1405
Land Nordrhein-Westfalen v Uecker (C-64/96); *sub nom* Uecker v Land Nordrhein-
   Westfalen (C-64/96); *joined case* Jacquet v Land Nordrhein-Westfalen (C-65/
   96) [1997] E.C.R. I-3171; [1997] 3 C.M.L.R. 963; [1997] I.C.R. 1025; [1998]
   I.N.L.R. 300; *Times,* August 11, 1997, ECJ (3rd Chamber) . . . . *Digested,* 97/**2219**:
                               Considered, 07/1608
Land Oberosterreich v CEZ AS (C-343/04) [2006] 2 All E.R. (Comm) 665; [2006]
   E.C.R. I-4557; [2006] I.L.Pr. 25, ECJ (1st Chamber) . . . . *Digested,* 07/**666**
Land Oberosterreich v Commission of the European Communities (C-439/05); *joined*
   case Land Oberosterreich v Commission of the European Communities (C-454/
   05) [2007] 3 C.M.L.R. 52, ECJ (3rd Chamber)
Land Oberosterreich v Commission of the European Communities (C-454/05) see
   Land Oberosterreich v Commission of the European Communities (C-439/05)
Land Securities Group Plc v Scottish Ministers [2006] UKHL 48; 2007 S.C. (H.L.) 57;
   2006 S.L.T. 1019; 2006 S.C.L.R. 908; [2007] J.P.L. 710; [2006] 45 E.G. 190
   (C.S.); (2006) 103(43) L.S.G. 30; (2006) 150 S.J.L.B. 1429; [2006] N.P.C. 113;
   2006 G.W.D. 35-723, HL . . . . *Digested,* 07/**5466**
Land, In the Estate of see Land v Land (Deceased)
Landeshauptstadt Kiel v Jaeger (C-151/02) [2004] All E.R. (EC) 604; [2003] E.C.R. I-
   8389; [2003] 3 C.M.L.R. 16; [2004] I.C.R. 1528; [2003] I.R.L.R. 804; (2004)
   75 B.M.L.R. 201; *Times,* September 26, 2003, ECJ . . . . *Digested,* 04/**1316**:
                                  Applied, 06/1405, 07/1393
Landis & Gyr Ltd v Scaleo Chip ET [2007] EWHC 1880 (QB); [2007] I.L.Pr. 53, QBD
   (Leeds) . . . . *Digested,* 07/**501**
Landlord Protect Ltd v Dolman [2007] 18 E.G. 154, CC (Central London) . . . . *Digested,* 07/**2751**
Landmatters Co-operative v South Hams DC [2007] P.A.D. 87, Planning Inspector
Landor & Hawa International Ltd v Azure Designs Ltd [2006] EWCA Civ 1285; [2006]
   E.C.D.R. 31; [2007] F.S.R. 9; (2007) 30(1) I.P.D. 30003, CA (Civ Div);
   affirming [2006] F.S.R. 22, PCC . . . . *Digested,* 07/**2538**
Lane v Lane 1985-86 Jer. L.R. 48 . . . . *Considered,* 03/4471,
                                                07/4244
Lane v Woolway (Valuation Officer) [2006] R.A. 410, Lands Tr . . . . *Digested,* 07/**3342**
Langborger v Sweden (11179/84) see Langborger v Sweden (A/155)
Langborger v Sweden (A/155); *sub nom* Langborger v Sweden (11179/84) (1990) 12
   E.H.R.R. 416, ECHR (1990) 12 E.H.R.R. CD120, Eur Comm HR . . . . *Considered,* 07/**2798**
Langley v Bexley LBC [2007] P.A.D. 62, Planning Inspector
Langley v Bradford MDC see M v Secretary of State for Work and Pensions
Langley v Burlo see Burlo v Langley
Langley v Burso see Burlo v Langley
Langridge v Evans see CIPC (Ocean View) Ltd Partnership v Churchill International
   Property Corp
Langroudi v Commissioner of Internal Revenue 10 I.T.L. Rep. 102, US Court

Lankhorst-Hohorst GmbH *v* Finanzamt Steinfurt (C-324/00) [2003] S.T.C. 607; [2002] E.C.R. I-11779; [2003] 2 C.M.L.R. 22; [2003] B.T.C. 254; 5 I.T.L. Rep. 467; [2002] S.T.I. 1807; *Times*, December 27, 2002, ECJ (5th Chamber) . . . . .   *Digested*, 03/**4181**:   *Applied*, 07/1614

Larkstore Ltd *v* Technotrade Ltd see Offer-Hoar *v* Larkstore Ltd

Laserdisken ApS *v* Kulturministeriet (C479/04) [2007] All E.R. (EC) 549; [2006] E.C.R. I-8089; [2007] 1 C.M.L.R. 6; [2007] C.E.C. 32; [2006] E.C.D.R. 30, ECJ. . . . .   *Digested*, 07/**2516**

Lasertec Gesellschaft fur Stanzformen mbH *v* Finanzamt Emmendingen (C-492/04) [2007] 3 C.M.L.R. 5, ECJ . . . .   *Digested*, 07/**1617**

Latimer *v* Carney [2006] EWCA Civ 1417; [2007] 1 P. & C.R. 13; [2007] L. & T.R. 5; [2006] 3 E.G.L.R. 13; [2006] 50 E.G. 86; [2006] 45 E.G. 191 (C.S.); (2006) 103(44) L.S.G. 31; [2006] N.P.C. 117, CA (Civ Div) . . . .   *Digested*, 07/**2736**

Latimer Management Consultants Ltd *v* Ellingham Investments Ltd [2006] EWHC 3662 (Ch); [2007] 1 W.L.R. 2569; [2007] 3 All E.R. 485, Ch D . . . .   *Digested*, 07/**387**

Latour Trust Co Ltd and Latour Trustees (Jersey) Ltd's Representation, Re see Rabaiotti1989 Settlement, Re

Lauder *v* Lauder [2007] EWHC 1227 (Fam); [2007] 2 F.L.R. 802, Fam Div . . . .   *Digested*, 07/**1706**:   *Applying*, 06/1629, 06/1629

Lauri *v* Renad [1892] 3 Ch. 402, CA . . . .   *Considered*, 79/52:   *Distinguished*, 07/2527

Lavalife Inc's Trade Mark Application [2007] E.T.M.R. 45, OHIM (2nd Bd App)

Lavin *v* Albert see Albert *v* Lavin

Law Debenture Trust Corp Plc *v* Elektrim Finance NV [2006] EWHC 1305; [2007] 1 P. & C.R. DG6, Ch D

Law on Licensing System of Performing Artists Agents, Re (C-255/04) see Commission of the European Communities *v* France (C-255/04)

Law Society *v* Adcock [2006] EWHC 3212 (Admin); [2007] 1 W.L.R. 1096; [2007] A.C.D. 63; (2007) 104(3) L.S.G. 29; (2007) 157 N.L.J. 66; *Times*, January 16, 2007, QBD (Admin) . . . .   *Digested*, 07/**2802**

Law Society *v* Earp (Official Receiver) see Law Society *v* Shah

Law Society *v* Sephton & Co [2006] UKHL 22; [2006] 2 A.C. 543; [2006] 2 W.L.R. 1091; [2006] 3 All E.R. 401; [2006] P.N.L.R. 31; (2006) 156 N.L.J. 844; (2006) 150 S.J.L.B. 669; [2006] N.P.C. 56; *Times*, May 11, 2006, HL; affirming [2004] EWCA Civ 1627; [2005] Q.B. 1013; [2005] 3 W.L.R. 212; [2005] P.N.L.R. 21; (2005) 102(5) L.S.G. 29; (2005) 149 S.J.L.B. 56; *Times*, January 11, 2005, CA (Civ Div); reversing in part [2004] EWHC 544 (Ch); [2004] P.N.L.R. 27, Ch D . . . .   *Digested*, 06/**474**:   *Considered*, 07/2490: *Followed*, 07/479

Law Society *v* Shah; *sub nom* Aziz, Re; Law Society *v* Earp (Official Receiver) [2007] EWHC 2841 (Ch); [2007] B.P.I.R. 1595; *Times*, December 20, 2007, Ch D

Lawntown Ltd *v* Camenzuli [2007] EWCA Civ 949; [2007] 42 E.G. 295 (C.S.); (2007) 104(41) L.S.G. 26; [2007] N.P.C. 103; *Times*, November 14, 2007, CA (Civ Div)

Lawrence *v* Grenada [2007] UKPC 18; [2007] 1 W.L.R. 1474, PC (Gren) . . . .   *Digested*, 07/**715**

Lawrence *v* Pembrokeshire CC; *sub nom* L *v* Pembrokeshire CC; SL *v* Pembrokeshire CC [2007] EWCA Civ 446; [2007] 1 W.L.R. 2991; [2007] 2 F.L.R. 705; [2007] 2 F.C.R. 329; [2007] H.R.L.R. 30; (2007) 10 C.C.L. Rep. 367; (2007) 96 B.M.L.R. 158; [2007] Fam. Law 804; (2007) 104(22) L.S.G. 24; *Times*, May 29, 2007, CA (Civ Div); affirming [2006] EWHC 1029 (QB); [2006] 2 F.C.R. 363; (2007) 10 C.C.L. Rep. 319; [2007] P.I.Q.R. P1; [2006] Lloyd's Rep. Med. 383; (2006) 150 S.J.L.B. 670, QBD . . . .   *Digested*, 07/**2934**

Lawrence *v* Prison Service [2007] I.R.L.R. 468, EAT . . . .   *Digested*, 07/**1375**

Lawrie-Blum *v* Land Baden-Wurttemberg (C-66/85) [1986] E.C.R. 2121; [1987] 3 C.M.L.R. 389; [1987] I.C.R. 483, ECJ . . . .   *Digested*, 87/**1569**:   *Applied*, 91/3958, 00/2389, 05/3856, 07/1631: *Distinguished*, 07/1386

Lawson *v* Serco Ltd; *sub nom* Serco Ltd *v* Lawson; *joined cases* Crofts *v* Veta Ltd; Botham *v* Ministry of Defence [2006] UKHL 3; [2006] 1 All E.R. 823; [2006] I.C.R. 250; [2006] I.R.L.R. 289; (2006) 103(6) L.S.G. 36; (2006) 156 N.L.J. 184; (2006) 150 S.J.L.B. 131; *Times*, January 27, 2006, HL; reversing [2004] EWCA Civ 12; [2004] 2 All E.R. 200; [2004] I.C.R. 204; [2004] I.R.L.R. 206; (2004) 148 S.J.L.B. 148; *Times*, January 30, 2004, CA (Civ Div); reversing EAT/ 0018/02TM, EAT . . . .   *Digested*, 06/**1390**:   *Applied*, 05/1210, 05/1329, 07/1355: *Not followed*, 03/1264

Lawson (Inspector of Taxes) *v* Johnson Matthey [1992] 2 A.C. 324; [1992] 2 W.L.R. 826; [1992] 2 All E.R. 947; [1992] S.T.C. 466; 65 T.C. 39; [1992] S.T.I. 529; (1992) 136 S.J.L.B. 164; *Times*, May 18, 1992; *Independent*, May 19, 1992; *Financial Times*, May 20, 1992, HL; reversing [1991] 1 W.L.R. 558; [1991] S.T.C. 259; (1991) 135 S.J.L.B. 509; *Times*, April 11, 1991; *Financial Times*, April 19, 1991, CA (Civ Div); affirming [1990] 1 W.L.R. 414; [1990] S.T.C. 149; (1990) 87(4) L.S.G. 34; (1990) 134 S.J. 758, Ch D . . . .   *Digested*, 92/**610**:   *Distinguished*, 95/893, 07/4076

Lay v Drexler [2007] EWCA Civ 464; [2007] Bus. L.R. 1357; [2007] 5 Costs L.R.
695; [2007] L. & T.R. 33; [2007] 31 E.G. 82; [2007] 22 E.G. 160 (C.S.); [2007]
N.P.C. 66; [2007] 2 P. & C.R. DG13; *Times*, June 20, 2007, CA (Civ Div) . . . . *Digested*, 07/**2722**

Layland v Creative Print & Design Ltd (Unreported, December 2, 2005), CC (Cardiff)
[*Ex rel.* AndrewArentsen, Barrister, 33 Park Place, Cardiff] . . . . *Digested*, 07/**3186**

LB Europe Ltd v Smurfit Bag in Box SA [2006] EWHC 2936 (Pat); (2007) 30(1) I.P.D.
30007, Ch D (Patents Ct)

LCP Retail Ltd v Segal [2006] EWHC 2087 (Ch); [2007] B.C.C. 584; (2006) 103(35)
L.S.G. 32; [2007] 1 P. & C.R. DG8, Ch D (Companies Ct)

Le Compte v Belgium (A/43); *joined cases* Van Leuven v Belgium (A/43); De Meyere
v Belgium (A/43) [1982] E.C.C. 240; (1982) 4 E.H.R.R. 1, ECHR; *reversing*
[1980] E.C.C. 294, Eur Comm HR . . . . *Applied*, 97/2811,
98/3120, 98/3156, 00/2212, 05/2734: *Considered*, 07/1951

Leachinsky v Christie see Christie v Leachinsky

Lead Technical Services Ltd v CMS Medical Ltd [2007] EWCA Civ 316; [2007] B.L.R.
251; 116 Con. L.R. 192; (2007) 23 Const. L.J. 547, CA (Civ Div)

Leakey v National Trust for Places of Historic Interest or Natural Beauty [1980] Q.B.
485; [1980] 2 W.L.R. 65; [1980] 1 All E.R. 17; 78 L.G.R. 100; (1979) 123 S.J.
606, CA (Civ Div); *affirming* [1978] Q.B. 849; [1978] 2 W.L.R. 774; [1978] 3 All
E.R. 234; 76 L.G.R. 488; (1978) 122 S.J. 231, QBD . . . . *Digested*, 80/**2006**:
Applied, 81/2005, 83/2739, 85/2499.a, 87/2752, 97/4863, 00/5121,
01/4482, 01/4547, 03/2966, 04/2756: *Considered*, 82/667, 82/2267,
83/2741, 92/3223, 00/4287, 01/1544, 07/2961: *Distinguished*, 04/2763:
Followed, 88/2034

Leander v Sweden (9248/81) see Leander v Sweden (A/116)

Leander v Sweden (A/116); *sub nom* Leander v Sweden (9248/81) (1987) 9 E.H.R.R.
433; *Times*, April 25, 1987, ECHR (1985) 7 E.H.R.R. CD557, Eur Comm HR . . . *Digested*, 87/**1919**:
Applied, 98/3096, 02/57, 02/1835, 07/2249, 07/2258: *Considered*, 00/3248

LearningTrust v MP [2007] EWHC 1634 (Admin); [2007] E.L.R. 658, QBD (Admin)

Leatham v Hillingdon LBC [2006] EWHC 2283 (QB); [2007] B.L.G.R. 45, QBD . . . . . *Digested*, 07/**2869**

Leavis v Leavis [1921] P. 299, PDAD . . . . *Applied*, 57/1086,
07/241

Lecarpentier v France (67847/01) (Unreported, February 14, 2006), ECHR . . . . *Distinguished*, 07/2636

Lechouritou v Dimosio tis Omospondiakis Dimokratias tis Germanias (C-292/05) see
Lechouritou v Germany (C-292/05)

Lechouritou v Germany (C-292/05); *sub nom* Lechouritou v Dimosio tis
Omospondiakis Dimokratias tis Germanias (C-292/05) [2007] All E.R. (EC)
1177; [2007] 2 All E.R. (Comm) 57; [2007] I.L.Pr. 14, ECJ (2nd Chamber) . . . . *Digested*, 07/**688**

Ledger-Beadell v Peach [2006] EWHC 2940 (Ch); [2007] 2 F.L.R. 210; [2007] Fam.
Law 595; [2006] 48 E.G. 230 (C.S.), Ch D . . . . *Digested*, 07/**3393**

Lee vAccent Foundation Ltd see Accent Foundation Ltd v Lee

Lee v Forshaw (Unreported, March 26, 1999), CA . . . . *Distinguished*, 07/2956

Lee v Herbert-Smith [2000] R.V.R. 227, LandsTr . . . . *Digested*, 00/**3895**:
Considered, 07/3228

Lee v Lee's Air Farming Ltd [1961] A.C. 12; [1960] 3 W.L.R. 758; [1960] 3 All E.R.
420; (1960) 104 S.J. 869, PC (NZ); *reversing* [1959] N.Z.L.R. 393, CA (NZ) . . *Digested*, 60/**3342**:
Applied, 69/3508, 03/2506, 07/1348: *Considered*, 98/2188:
Distinguished, 97/2251

Lee v Leeds City Council see Ratcliffe v Sandwell MBC

Leeds City Council v Channel FourTelevision Corp [2005] EWHC 3522 (Fam); [2007]
1 F.L.R. 678; [2007] Fam. Law 24, Fam Div

Leeds City Council v G see Leeds City Council v RG

Leeds City Council v Price see Kay v Lambeth LBC

Leeds City Council v RG; *sub nom* Leeds City Council v G [2007] EWHC 1612
(Admin); [2007] 1 W.L.R. 3025; [2007] 4 All E.R. 652; (2007) 171 J.P. 581;
Times, September 11, 2007, QBD (Admin) . . . . *Digested*, 07/**358**

Leeds Industrial Cooperative Society v Slack (No.2); *sub nom* Slack v Leeds Industrial
Cooperative Society Ltd [1924] 2 Ch. 475, CA . . . . *Applied*, 07/2962

Leeds Shipping Co v Societe Francaise Bunge SA (The Eastern City) [1958] 2 Lloyd's
Rep. 127, CA; *affirming* [1957] 2 Lloyd's Rep. 153; *Times*, July 17, 1957, QBD
(Comm) . . . . *Digested*, 58/**3144**:
Applied, 77/2760, 95/4517: *Approved*, 79/2445: *Considered*, 69/3301,
78/2723, 07/3817

Leeds United Association Football Club Ltd, Re; *sub nom* Leeds United Association
Football Club Ltd (In Administration), Re [2007] EWHC 1761 (Ch); [2007] Bus.
L.R. 1560; [2007] I.C.R. 1688; *Times*, September 4, 2007, Ch D (Leeds)

Leeds United Association Football Club Ltd (In Administration), Re see Leeds United
Association Football Club Ltd, Re

Leek v Donkersley see GKN Bolts & Nuts Ltd (Automotive Division) Birmingham
Works Sports & Social Club, Re

Lees (HJ) & Son (London)'s Application, Re (1955) 72 R.P.C. 75 . . . . *Digested*, 55/**2786**:
Considered, 07/2662

Leeson v Marsden see Collier vWilliams

Legal & General Assurance Co Ltd v Kirk [2001] EWCA Civ 1803; [2002] I.R.L.R. 124;
[2002] Emp. L.R. 585, CA (Civ Div) . . . .   *Digested*, 02/**3277**:
Applied, 07/1944

Legal & General Assurance Society Ltd v Expeditors International (UK) Ltd [2007]
EWCA Civ 7; [2007] 2 P. & C.R. 10; [2007] L. & T.R. 16; [2007] 5 E.G. 307
(C.S.); (2007) 104(6) L.S.G. 32; (2007) 151 S.J.L.B. 163; [2007] N.P.C. 10, CA
(Civ Div); affirming [2006] EWHC 1008 (Ch); [2007] 1 P. & C.R. 5; [2006] L.
& T.R. 22; [2006] 18 E.G. 151 (C.S.); (2006) 150 S.J.L.B. 573, Ch D . . . .   *Digested*, 07/**2720**

Legal & General Assurance Society Ltd v Revenue and Customs Commissioners [2006]
EWHC 1770 (Ch); [2006] S.T.C. 1763; 78 T.C. 321; [2006] B.T.C. 713; 8 I.T.L.
Rep. 1124; [2006] S.T.I. 1884; *Independent*, July 20, 2006, Ch D . . . .   *Digested*, 06/**4160**:
Previous proceedings, 05/4027, 06/4150

Legal Protection of Biotechnological Inventions, Re (C-377/98) see Netherlands v
European Parliament (C-377/98)

Lego Juris A/S v Mega Brands Inc (R 856/2004-G) [2007] E.T.M.R. 11, OHIM (1st Bd
App) . . . .   *Digested*, 07/**2637**

Leicestershire CC v UNISON; *sub nom* UNISON v Leicestershire CC [2006] EWCA Civ
825; [2006] I.R.L.R. 810; [2007] B.L.G.R. 208, CA (Civ Div); reversing in part
[2005] I.R.L.R. 920; (2005) 102(42) L.S.G. 24, EAT

Leigh v Michelin Tyre Plc [2003] EWCA Civ 1766; [2004] 1 W.L.R. 846; [2004] 2 All
E.R. 175; [2004] C.P. Rep. 20; [2004] 1 Costs L.R. 148; *Times*, December 16,
2003; *Independent*, December 18, 2003, CA (Civ Div) . . . .   *Digested*, 04/**302**:
Applied, 06/345: *Considered*, 06/365, 07/385

Leighton Contractors (Asia) Ltd v Stelux Holdings Ltd (2007) 23 Const. L.J. 70, CFI
(HK)

Leisure Employment Services Ltd v Revenue and Customs Commissioners see Revenue
and Customs Commissioners v Leisure Employment Services Ltd

Lemage v Goodban (1865-69) L.R. 1 P. & D. 57; (1865) 12 Jur. N.S. 32, Ct of
Probate . . . .   *Considered*, 07/429

Leman-Klammers v Klammers [2007] EWCA Civ 919; [2007] Fam. Law 1068; (2007)
151 S.J.L.B. 986; *Times*, October 4, 2007, CA (Civ Div)

Lennartz v Finanzamt Munchen III (C97/90) [1995] S.T.C. 514; [1991] E.C.R. I-3795;
[1993] 3 C.M.L.R. 689; [1991] S.T.I. 700, ECJ (6th Chamber) . . . .   *Digested*, 95/**5057**:
Applied, 03/4272, 03/4563, 06/4506: *Considered*, 07/4309:
Distinguished, 96/5860, 03/4553: *Followed*, 05/4364, 05/4365

Lenz v Finanzlandesdirektion fur Tirol (C-315/02) [2004] E.C.R. I-7063; [2004] 3
C.M.L.R. 13; [2007] B.T.C. 131, ECJ (1st Chamber) . . . .   *Digested*, 07/**1601**:
Considered, 07/3974

Lenzing AG v United Kingdom (Admissibility) (38817/97) (Unreported, September 9,
1998), Eur Comm HR . . . .   *Applied*, 07/2636

Leogem Ltd v Revenue and Customs Commissioners [2007] S.T.I. 372, V&DTr

Leon v Leon [1967] P. 275; [1966] 3 W.L.R. 1164; [1966] 3 All E.R. 820; (1966) 110
S.J. 546, PDAD . . . .   *Digested*, 67/**555**:
Applied, 07/1735

Leppington v Belfast Corp. . . . .   *Considered*, 07/4518

Les Laboratoires Servier v Apotex Inc; *joined case* Lupin (Europe) Ltd v Les
Laboratoires Servier [2006] EWHC 3443 (Pat); (2007) 30(2) I.P.D. 30015,
Ch D (Patents Ct)

Les Laboratoires Servier v Apotex Inc [2007] EWHC 591 (Pat); (2007) 30(4) I.P.D.
30030, Ch D (Patents Ct)

Les Laboratoires Servier v Apotex Inc [2007] EWCA Civ 783; (2007) 30(10) I.P.D.
30060, CA (Civ Div)

Les Laboratoires Servier v KRKA Polska Sp ZoO [2006] EWHC 2453 (Pat); (2007)
30(1) I.P.D. 30006, Ch D (Patents Ct)

Lesotho Highlands Development Authority v Impregilo SpA [2005] UKHL 43; [2006]
1 A.C. 221; [2005] 3 W.L.R. 129; [2005] 3 All E.R. 789; [2005] 2 All E.R.
(Comm) 265; [2005] 2 Lloyd's Rep. 310; [2005] 2 C.L.C. 1; [2005] B.L.R. 351;
101 Con. L.R. 1; (2005) 27 E.G. 220 (C.S.); (2005) 155 N.L.J. 1046; *Times*,
July 6, 2005, HL; reversing [2003] EWCA Civ 1159; [2004] 1 All E.R. (Comm)
97; [2003] 2 Lloyd's Rep. 497; [2003] B.L.R. 347; (2003) 100(39) L.S.G. 37;
(2003) 153 N.L.J. 1239; *Times*, September 15, 2003, CA (Civ Div); affirming
[2002] EWHC 2435 (Comm); [2003] 1 All E.R. (Comm) 22; [2003] B.L.R. 98;
Times, December 6, 2002, QBD (Comm) . . . .   *Digested*, 05/**207**:
Applied, 07/250, 07/253: *Distinguished*, 06/203

Letang v Cooper [1965] 1 Q.B. 232; [1964] 3 W.L.R. 573; [1964] 2 All E.R. 929;
[1964] 2 Lloyd's Rep. 339; (1964) 108 S.J. 519, CA; reversing [1964] 2 Q.B.
53; [1964] 2 W.L.R. 642; [1964] 1 All E.R. 669; [1964] 1 Lloyd's Rep. 188;
(1964) 108 S.J. 180, QBD . . . .   *Digested*, 64/**3499**:
Applied, 68/2253, 92/4436, 93/2608, 00/2130, 04/271:
Considered, 86/3464, 97/3592, 99/3944, 01/5354, 06/476:
Followed, 07/2633

Letterstedt v Broers; *sub nom* Vicomtesse Montmort v Broers (1883-84) L.R. 9 App.
Cas. 371; [1881-85] All E.R. Rep. 882, PC (Cape) . . . .   *Applied*, 07/3956:
Considered, 85/3131

Level Properties Ltd v Balls Brothers Ltd [2007] EWHC 744 (Ch); [2007] 23 E.G. 166;
[2007] 15 E.G. 146 (C.S.), Ch D . . . . *Digested*, 07/**2756**
Lever Bros Ltd v Bell see Bell v Lever Brothers Ltd
Levi Strauss & Co v Casucci SpA (C-145/05) [2006] E.C.R. I-3703; [2006] E.T.M.R.
71; [2007] F.S.R. 8, ECJ (3rd Chamber) . . . . *Digested*, 07/**2667**
Levi Strauss & Co v Costco Wholesale UK Ltd (C-416/99) see Zino Davidoff SA v A&G
Imports Ltd (C-414/99)
Levi Strauss & Co v Tesco Stores Ltd (C-415/99) see Zino Davidoff SA v A&G Imports
Ltd (C-414/99)
Levin v Beatt [2005] EWHC 828 (Ch); [2007] W.T.L.R. 1029, Ch D . . . . *Digested*, 07/**3424**
Levob Verzekeringen BV v Staatssecretaris van Financien (C-41/04) [2006] S.T.C. 766;
[2005] E.C.R. I-9433; [2006] 2 C.M.L.R. 8; [2006] C.E.C. 424; [2007] B.T.C.
5186; [2007] B.V.C. 155; [2005] S.T.I. 1777, ECJ (1st Chamber) . . . . *Digested*, 06/**4501**:
Applied, 07/4332, 07/4341
Levy v ABN AMRO Bank NV see Norglen Ltd (In Liquidation) v Reeds Rains
Prudential Ltd
Levy to Income on Investments, Re (C-334/02) see Commission of the European
Communities v France (C-334/02)
Lewen v Denda (C-333/97) [2000] All E.R. (EC) 261; [1999] E.C.R. I-7243; [2000]
2 C.M.L.R. 38; [2000] C.E.C. 415; [2000] I.C.R. 648; [2000] I.R.L.R. 67; *Times*,
November 16, 1999, ECJ (6th Chamber) . . . . *Digested*, 99/**2065**:
Applied, 07/1405
Lewis v Cox [1985] Q.B. 509; [1984] 3 W.L.R. 875; [1984] 3 All E.R. 672; (1985) 80
Cr. App. R. 1; (1984) 148 J.P. 601; [1984] Crim. L.R. 756; (1984) 81 L.S.G.
2538; (1984) 128 S.J. 596, DC . . . . *Digested*, 84/**676**:
Applied, 07/873: *Considered*, 86/659
Lewis v Gibson [2005] EWCA Civ 587; [2005] 2 F.C.R. 241; (2005) 8 C.C.L. Rep.
399; (2006) 87 B.M.L.R. 93; [2005] M.H.L.R. 309, CA (Civ Div) . . . . *Digested*, 05/**2819**:
Considered, 07/2897
Lewis v Havering LBC [2006] EWCA Civ 1793; [2007] H.L.R. 20; (2006) 150
S.J.L.B. 1569, CA (Civ Div)
Lewis v Motorworld Garages Ltd [1986] I.C.R. 157; [1985] I.R.L.R. 465, CA (Civ Div)   *Digested*, 86/**1261**:
Applied, 00/2132, 05/1209, 07/1317
Lewis v Pensions Ombudsman; *sub nom* Nortel Networks UK Pension Plan, Re
[2005] EWHC 103 (Ch); [2005] O.P.L.R. 41; [2005] Pens. L.R. 195, Ch D   . . . *Considered*, 07/3027
Lewis v Vincent see Allen (Deceased), Re
Lewisham Hospital NHS Trust v Hamuth see University Hospital Lewisham NHS Trust v
Hamuth
Lewisham LBC v Malcolm see Malcolm v Lewisham LBC
LG Philips LCD Co Ltd v Tatung (UK) Ltd [2006] EWCA Civ 1774; [2007] R.P.C. 21;
(2007) 30(3) I.P.D. 30016, CA (Civ Div) . . . . *Digested*, 07/**2549**
LH v Secretary of State for the Home Department; *sub nom* LH (Truly Exceptional:
Ekinci Applied: Jamaica), Re [2006] UKAIT 19; [2006] Imm. A.R. 306, AIT . . . *Digested*, 07/**2364**
LH Charles & Co, Re [1935] W.N. 15 . . . . *Considered*, 82/328,
92/410, 07/2396: *Distinguished*, 47-51/1258
LH (Truly Exceptional: Ekinci Applied: Jamaica), Re see LH v Secretary of State for the
Home Department
Lia Oil SA v ERG Petroli SpA [2007] EWHC 505 (Comm); [2007] 2 Lloyd's Rep. 509,
QBD (Comm) . . . . *Digested*, 07/**3813**
Libertel Groep BV v Benelux-Merkenbureau (C-104/01) [2004] Ch. 83; [2004] 2
W.L.R. 1081; [2003] E.C.R. I-3793; [2005] 2 C.M.L.R. 45; [2003] E.T.M.R. 63;
[2004] F.S.R. 4; *Times*, May 12, 2003, ECJ . . . . *Digested*, 04/**2362**:
Applied, 04/2370, 05/2529, 05/2533: *Considered*, 05/2532, 07/2673:
Followed, 05/2553
Licensing of Debt Collection Services, Re (C-134/05) see Commission of the European
Communities v Italy (C-134/05)
Lidl Belgium GmbH & Co KG v Etablissementen Franz Colruyt NV (C-356/04) [2007]
Bus. L.R. 492; [2006] E.C.R. I-8501; [2007] 1 C.M.L.R. 9; [2007] C.E.C. 3;
[2007] E.T.M.R. 28, ECJ . . . . *Digested*, 07/**1570**:
Applied, 07/1571
Lidsey Landfill Ltd v West Sussex CC [2007] P.A.D. 46, Planning Inspector
LIFFE Administration & Management v Pinkava; *sub nom* Pinkava v LIFFE
Administration & Management [2007] EWCA Civ 217; [2007] Bus. L.R. 1369;
[2007] 4 All E.R. 981; [2007] I.C.R. 1489; [2007] R.P.C. 30, CA (Civ Div);
affirming [2006] EWHC 595 (Pat), Ch D (Patents Ct) . . . . *Digested*, 07/**2556**
Liles v Kalloo (Unreported, May 18, 2006), CC (Wigan) [*Ex rel.* Ian Skeate, Barrister,
St Johns Building, 24a-28 St John Street, Manchester] . . . . *Digested*, 07/**3072**
Limburgse Vinyl Maatschappij NV (LVM) v Commission of the European Communities
(C-238/99 P); *joined case* DSM Kunststoffen BV v Commission of the European
Communities (C-244/99 P) [2002] E.C.R. I-8375; [2003] 4 C.M.L.R. 10, ECJ   *Digested*, 03/**554**:
Applied, 07/604, 07/614, 07/1545: *Followed*, 05/553, 07/611
Lime Avenue Sales & Services Ltd v Revenue and Customs Commissioners [2007] V. &
D.R. 55; [2007] S.T.I. 2241, V&DTr (London)

Limit No.2 Ltd v Axa Versicherung AG (formerly Albingia Versicherung AG) [2007] EWHC 2321 (Comm); [2007] 2 C.L.C. 610, QBD (Comm)

Limitgood Ltd v Revenue and Customs Commissioners; *sub nom* Revenue and Customs Commissioners v Limitgood Ltd; Revenue and Customs Commissioners v Prizedome Ltd; *joined case* Prizedome Ltd v Revenue and Customs Commissioners; CH/2007/APP/0412, Ch D; reversing [2007] S.T.C. (S.C.D.) 635; [2007] S.T.I. 1693, Sp Comm . . . . *Digested*, 07/**4004**

Lincolnshire CC v Fire Brigades Union see Bull v Nottinghamshire and City of Nottingham Fire and Rescue Authority

Lindqvist v Aklagarkammaren i Jonkoping (C-101/01) see Criminal Proceedings against Lindqvist (C-101/01)

Lindsay v Inland Revenue Commissioners 1953 S.L.T. (Notes) 14; 46 R. & I.T. 146; 34 T.C. 289; (1953) 32 A.T.C. 1; [1953] T.R. 5, IH (1 Div) . . . . *Digested*, 53/**4272**:
Applied, 07/4105

Lindsay v United Kingdom (11089/84) (1987) 9 E.H.R.R. CD555, Eur Comm HR . . . . *Applied*, 07/2205

Lindsay v Wood [2006] EWHC 2895 (QB); [2006] M.H.L.R. 341; *Times*, December 8, 2006, QBD . . . . *Digested*, 07/**484**

Liquidator of West Mercia Safetywear Ltd v Dodd; *sub nom* West Mercia Safetywear Ltd (In Liquidation) v Dodd (1988) 4 B.C.C. 30; [1988] B.C.L.C. 250; [1988] P.C.C. 212, CA (Civ Div) . . . . *Digested*, 88/**308**:
Applied, 03/521, 07/2429

Liskojarvi v Oy Liikenne AB (C-172/99) see Oy Liikenne AB v Liskojarvi (C-172/99)

Lister v Hesley Hall Ltd [2001] UKHL 22; [2002] 1 A.C. 215; [2001] 2 W.L.R. 1311; [2001] 2 All E.R. 769; [2001] I.C.R. 665; [2001] I.R.L.R. 472; [2001] Emp. L.R. 819; [2001] 2 F.L.R. 307; [2001] 2 F.C.R. 97; (2001) 3 L.G.L.R. 49; [2001] E.L.R. 422; [2001] Fam. Law 595; (2001) 98(24) L.S.G. 45; (2001) 151 N.L.J. 728; (2001) 145 S.J.L.B. 126; [2001] N.P.C. 89; *Times*, May 10, 2001; *Independent*, June 11, 2001; *Daily Telegraph*, May 8, 2001, HL; reversing *Times*, October 13, 1999; *Independent*, November 22, 1999, CA (Civ Div) . . . . *Digested*, 01/**5359**:
Applied, 02/1531, 03/432, 03/3033, 03/3046, 04/655, 05/4199, 05/4200, 06/1337, 07/4201: *Cited*, 02/5360, 03/2975: *Considered*, 05/5573, 06/476, 06/5592, 07/5427

Lithuania v Barcys; *sub nom* District Court of Vilnius City v Barcys [2007] EWHC 615 (Admin); [2007] 1 W.L.R. 3249, QBD (Admin)

Little Olympian Each Ways Ltd (No.1), Re [1994] 2 B.C.L.C. 420, Ch D . . . . *Applied*, 07/459

Littlewood v Rolfe [1981] 2 All E.R. 51; (1982) 43 P. & C.R. 262; (1980) 258 E.G. 168, DC. . . . . *Digested*, 82/**33**:
Considered, 07/2714: *Followed*, 85/40

Littlewoods Organisation Ltd v Harris [1977] 1 W.L.R. 1472; [1978] 1 All E.R. 1026; (1977) 121 S.J. 727, CA (Civ Div) . . . . *Digested*, 78/**2941**:
Considered, 97/2256, 07/1328: *Distinguished*, 00/2200

Liverpool City Council v Irwin [1977] A.C. 239; [1976] 2 W.L.R. 562; [1976] 2 All E.R. 39; (1984) 13 H.L.R. 38; 74 L.G.R. 392; (1976) 32 P. & C.R. 43; (1976) 238 E.G. 879; [1976] J.P.L. 427; (1976) 120 S.J. 267, HL; affirming in part [1976] Q.B. 319; [1975] 3 W.L.R. 663; [1975] 3 All E.R. 658; 74 L.G.R. 21; (1976) 31 P. & C.R. 34; (1975) 119 S.J. 612, CA (Civ Div). . . . . *Digested*, 76/**1532**:
Applied, 81/1574, 82/1015, 84/1024, 86/1152, 90/2822, 90/4101, 96/5856, 06/2446: *Considered*, 76/2766, 80/17, 80/105, 83/2064, 84/411, 85/388, 85/1929, 88/2082, 92/2758, 93/550, 93/2462, 94/2367, 95/2994, 96/2525, 07/3568: *Distinguished*, 85/1993: *Followed*, 80/357, 80/1626

Living in Radiance's Application for Registration as a Charity [2007] W.T.L.R. 683, Charity Comm . . . . *Digested*, 07/**323**

Livingstone v Adjudication Panel for England [2006] EWHC 2533 (Admin); [2006] H.R.L.R. 45; [2006] B.L.G.R. 799; [2007] A.C.D. 22; (2006) 156 N.L.J. 1650; *Times*, November 9, 2006, QBD (Admin) . . . . *Digested*, 06/**2833**

Lizarraga v Spain (62543/00) (2007) 45 E.H.R.R. 45, ECHR

LK v Secretary of State for the Home Department see AA v Secretary of State for the Home Department

LK (AA Applied: Zimbabwe), Re see AA v Secretary of State for the Home Department

Lloyd v Sutcliffe; *sub nom* Sutcliffe v Lloyd [2007] EWCA Civ 153; [2007] 22 E.G. 162; [2007] 10 E.G. 183 (C.S.); [2007] N.P.C. 23, CA (Civ Div) . . . . *Digested*, 07/**1537**

Lloyd Schuhfabrik Meyer & Co GmbH v Klijsen Handel BV (C-342/97) [1999] All E.R. (EC) 587; [1999] E.C.R. I-3819; [1999] 2 C.M.L.R. 1343; [1999] C.E.C. 285; [1999] E.T.M.R. 690; [2000] F.S.R. 77; (1999) 22(11) I.P.D. 22111; *Times*, June 30, 1999, ECJ . . . . *Digested*, 99/**3538**:
Applied, 01/4056, 01/5881, 04/2375, 07/1560, 07/2639, 07/2641: *Considered*, 04/2380, 05/2509, 05/2514, 06/2546, 06/2557, 06/2585, 07/2640: *Followed*, 00/3773

Lloyd-Briden v Worthing College [2007] 3 C.M.L.R. 27, EAT . . . . *Digested*, 07/**1420**

Lloyds Bank Plc v Rogers (No.1), *Times*, March 24, 1997, CA (Civ Div); affirming *Times*, April 11, 1996, QBD . . . . *Digested*, 97/**687**:
Applied, 07/350

Lloyds Bank Plc v Rosset [1991] 1 A.C. 107; [1990] 2 W.L.R. 867; [1990] 1 All E.R. 1111; [1990] 2 F.L.R. 155; (1990) 22 H.L.R. 349; (1990) 60 P. & C.R. 311; (1990) 140 N.L.J. 478, HL; reversing [1989] Ch. 350; [1988] 3 W.L.R. 1301; [1988] 3 All E.R. 915; [1989] 1 F.L.R. 51; (1989) 57 P. & C.R. 62; [1988] Fam. Law 472; (1989) 86(1) L.S.G. 39; (1988) 138 N.L.J. Rep. 149; (1988) 132 S.J. 1698; *Times*, May 23, 1988; *Independent*, June 3, 1988; *Guardian*, June 9, 1988; *Daily Telegraph*, June 9, 1988, CA (Civ Div) . . . . *Digested*, 90/**706**:
Applied, 92/2034, 96/4993, 01/5503, 02/1670, 02/1684, 02/3823, 02/4317, 03/3592, 03/4479, 04/3233, 04/3948, 05/3379, 07/3363, 07/3392: *Approved*, 90/707, 90/707: *Considered*, 89/467, 92/2031, 96/4950, 96/4995, 97/4937: *Distinguished*, 02/4342: *Followed*, 95/2187, 96/4943

Lloyds Investment (Scandinavia) Ltd v Ager-Hanssen [2003] EWHC 1740 (Ch), Ch D   *Applied*, 05/420, 07/387

LM v Medway Council; *sub nom* M (A Child) (Care Proceedings: Witness Summons), Re [2007] EWCA Civ 9; [2007] 1 F.L.R. 1698; [2007] 1 F.C.R. 253; [2007] Fam. Law 491; (2007) 157 N.L.J. 142; (2007) 151 S.J.L.B. 124, CA (Civ Div) . . *Digested*, 07/**1727**

LM (A Child), Re see LM (Reporting Restrictions: Coroner's Inquest), Re

LM (Reporting Restrictions: Coroner's Inquest), Re; *sub nom* LM (A Child), Re [2007] EWHC 1902 (Fam); [2007] C.P. Rep. 48; [2007] 3 F.C.R. 44; [2007] Fam. Law 1074; *Times*, November 20, 2007, Fam Div . . . . *Digested*, 07/**1806**

Loade v DPP [1990] 1 Q.B. 1052; [1989] 3 W.L.R. 1281; [1990] 1 All E.R. 36; (1990) 90 Cr. App. R. 162; (1989) 153 J.P. 674; [1989] Crim. L.R. 808; [1990] C.O.D. 58; (1989) 153 J.P.N. 739; (1989) 133 S.J. 1061, QBD . . . . *Digested*, 90/**856**:
Approved, 07/989: *Considered*, 92/3536, 94/944

Locabail (UK) Ltd v Bayfield Properties Ltd (Leave to Appeal); *joined cases* R. v Bristol Betting and Gaming Licensing Committee Ex p. O'Callaghan; Williams v Inspector of Taxes; Timmins v Gormley; Locabail (UK) Ltd v Waldorf Investment Corp (Leave to Appeal) [2000] Q.B. 451; [2000] 2 W.L.R. 870; [2000] 1 All E.R. 65; [2000] I.R.L.R. 96; [2000] H.R.L.R. 290; [2000] U.K.H.R.R. 300; 7 B.H.R.C. 583; (1999) 149 N.L.J. 1793; [1999] N.P.C. 143; *Times*, November 19, 1999; *Independent*, November 23, 1999, CA (Civ Div) . . . . *Digested*, 99/**38**:
Applied, 00/52, 00/53, 01/13, 01/2268, 04/30, 05/890, 06/19, 06/30, 06/2803, 06/5206, 07/31, 07/1351: *Considered*, 00/4140, 00/6092, 01/334, 02/4828, 03/5169, 06/961, 06/2755, 07/2558

Locabail (UK) Ltd v Waldorf Investment Corp (Leave to Appeal) see Locabail (UK) Ltd v Bayfield Properties Ltd (Leave to Appeal)

Lodwick v Southwark LBC [2004] EWCA Civ 306; [2004] I.C.R. 884; [2004] I.R.L.R. 554; (2004) 148 S.J.L.B. 385; *Times*, April 9, 2004, CA (Civ Div) . . . . *Applied*, 07/1343: *Considered*, 05/1220

Loftus (Deceased), Re see Green v Gaul

Logan Salton v Durham CC [1989] I.R.L.R. 99, EAT. . . . . *Digested*, 90/**1961**: *Considered*, 07/1435

Logstor Ror (Deutschland) GmbH v Commission of the European Communities (T-16/99) [2002] E.C.R. II-1633, CFI . . . . *Applied*, 07/1546: *Preliminary ruling given*, 06/574

Lomax Leisure Ltd (In Liquidation) v Miller [2007] EWHC 2508 (Ch); [2007] B.P.I.R. 1615, Ch D

Lommers v Minister van Landbouw, Natuurbeheer en Visserij (C-476/99) [2002] E.C.R. I-2891; [2004] 2 C.M.L.R. 49; [2002] I.R.L.R. 430, ECJ. . . . . *Considered*, 07/1399

London and Quadrant Housing Trust v Ansell [2007] EWCA Civ 326; [2007] H.L.R. 37; [2007] 17 E.G. 173 (C.S.); (2007) 104(18) L.S.G. 27; [2007] N.P.C. 45; *Times*, April 25, 2007, CA (Civ Div) . . . . *Digested*, 07/**2769**

London & Thames Haven Oil Wharves Ltd v Attwooll (Inspector of Taxes) [1967] Ch. 772; [1967] 2 W.L.R. 743; [1967] 2 All E.R. 124; [1967] 1 Lloyd's Rep. 204; 43 T.C. 491; (1966) 45 A.T.C. 148; [1966] T.R. 411; (1966) 110 S.J. 979; *Times*, December 17, 1966, CA; reversing [1966] 3 W.L.R. 325; [1966] 3 All E.R. 145; [1966] 2 Lloyd's Rep. 28; (1966) 45 A.T.C. 148; [1966] T.R. 129; (1966) 110 S.J. 351, Ch D . . . . *Digested*, 67/**1943**:
Applied, 67/1945, 76/1561, 77/3321, 79/1461, 80/1504, 90/763: *Considered*, 96/3377: *Followed*, 95/2761, 07/4061

London Association for the Protection of Trade v Greenlands Ltd; *sub nom* Greenlands Ltd v Wilmshurst [1916] 2 A.C. 15, HL; reversing [1913] 3 K.B. 507, CA . . . . . . *Applied*, 95/3133, 07/1074: *Approved*, 79/385

London Fire and Civil Defence Authority v Betty [1994] I.R.L.R. 384, EAT . . . . *Digested*, 95/**2090**: *Considered*, 07/1430: *Distinguished*, 01/2345

London Life Association, Re, *Independent*, February 27, 1989, Ch D . . . . *Applied*, 05/2362: *Considered*, 07/2481: *Followed*, 98/3370: *Referred to*, 95/2924

London Life Linked Assurances Ltd, Re see Pearl Assurance (Unit Linked Pensions) Ltd, Re

London Metallurgical Co, Re [1895] 1 Ch. 758, Ch D . . . . *Applied*, 07/2440: *Considered*, 85/158, 01/507: *Followed*, 90/517

London Recruitment Services Ltd v Revenue and Customs Commissioners [2006] S.T.C. (S.C.D.) 502; [2006] S.T.I. 1820, Sp Comm . . . . *Digested*, 07/**4063**

London Underground Ltd *v* Citylink Telecommunications Ltd [2007] EWHC 1749 (TCC); [2007] 2 All E.R. (Comm) 694; [2007] B.L.R. 391; 114 Con. L.R. 1, QBD (TCC) . . . . *Digested*, 07/**254**

Long Beach Ltd *v* Global Witness Ltd [2007] EWHC 1980 (QB); (2007) 104(34) L.S.G. 28, QBD

Longborough Festival Opera *v* Revenue and Customs Commissioners (Leave to Appeal) see Bournemouth Symphony Orchestra *v* Revenue and Customs Commissioners

Lonrho Plc *v* Al-Fayed (No.1); *sub nom* Lonrho Plc *v* Fayed [1992] 1 A.C. 448; [1991] 3 W.L.R. 188; [1991] 3 All E.R. 303; [1991] B.C.C. 641; [1991] B.C.L.C. 779; (1991) 141 N.L.J. 927; (1991) 135 S.J.L.B. 68; *Times*, July 3, 1991; *Independent*, July 3, 1991; *Financial Times*, July 3, 1991; *Guardian*, June 28, 1991, HL; affirming [1990] 2 Q.B. 479; [1989] 3 W.L.R. 631; [1989] 2 All E.R. 65; (1989) 5 B.C.C. 411; [1989] B.C.L.C. 485; [1989] P.C.C. 215; (1989) 139 N.L.J. 539, CA (Civ Div); reversing [1990] 1 Q.B. 490; [1989] 2 W.L.R. 356; (1988) 4 B.C.C. 688; [1989] B.C.L.C. 75; [1989] P.C.C. 173; (1989) 86(10) L.S.G. 43; (1988) 138 N.L.J. Rep. 225; (1989) 133 S.J. 220; *Independent*, July 19, 1988, QBD . . . . *Digested*, 92/**4130**:
Applied, 92/2, 03/4357, 05/2812, 06/2435: *Considered*, 98/4069, 07/4298:
Followed, 94/4040

Lonrho Plc *v* Fayed see Lonrho Plc *v* Al-Fayed (No.1)

Lonsdale (t/a Lonsdale Agencies) *v* Howard & Hallam Ltd [2007] UKHL 32; [2007] 1 W.L.R. 2055; [2007] 4 All E.R. 1; [2007] 2 All E.R. (Comm) 621; [2007] 2 C.L.C. 1; [2007] Eu. L.R. 799; [2007] I.C.R. 1338; [2007] I.R.L.R. 825; (2007) 151 S.J.L.B. 922; *Times*, July 10, 2007, HL; affirming [2006] EWCA Civ 63; [2006] 1 W.L.R. 1281; [2006] 1 Lloyd's Rep. 760; [2006] 1 C.L.C. 219; [2006] Eu. L.R. 804; [2006] I.C.R. 584; [2006] I.R.L.R. 481; (2006) 103(9) L.S.G. 30; *Times*, February 21, 2006, CA (Civ Div) . . . . *Digested*, 07/**68**

Loosemore *v* Tiverton and North Devon Railway Co see Tiverton and North Devon Railway Co *v* Loosemore

Lopez Ostra *v* Spain (A/303-C) (1995) 20 E.H.R.R. 277, ECHR . . . . *Digested*, 96/**3118**:
Applied, 98/3096, 07/2256: *Considered*, 98/3154, 01/5378, 02/3714, 04/4294

Lord Chancellor *v* Frieze [2007] EWHC 1490 (QB); [2007] 5 Costs L.R. 684, QBD

Lord Chancellor *v* Haggan [2007] EWHC 1212 (QB); [2007] 5 Costs L.R. 722; (2007) 104(24) L.S.G. 28, QBD

Lord Fisher DSC *v* Customs and Excise Commissioners see Customs and Excise Commissioners *v* Lord Fisher

Lord Napier and Ettrick *v* Hunter see Lord Napier and Ettrick *v* RF Kershaw Ltd (No.1)

Lord Napier and Ettrick *v* RF Kershaw Ltd (No.1); *joined case* Lord Napier and Ettrick *v* Hunter [1993] A.C. 713; [1993] 2 W.L.R. 42; [1993] 1 All E.R. 385; [1993] 1 Lloyd's Rep. 197; (1993) 137 S.J.L.B. 44; *Times*, December 16, 1992; *Independent*, December 11, 1992, HL; reversing [1993] 1 Lloyd's Rep. 10; *Times*, July 17, 1992; *Financial Times*, July 22, 1992, CA (Civ Div); reversing in part (Unreported, May 14, 1992), Ch D . . . . *Digested*, 93/**2422**:
Applied, 99/3431: *Cited*, 99/3404: *Considered*, 96/3591, 07/2441, 07/2488:
Followed, 96/3592, 00/3514

Lord Redesdale *v* Northumberland National Park Authority [2007] P.A.D. 23, Planning Inspector

Lord Saville of Newdigate *v* Widgery Soldiers see R. (on the application of A) *v* Lord Saville of Newdigate (Bloody Sunday Inquiry)

Lorse *v* Netherlands (52750/99) (2003) 37 E.H.R.R. 3; [2003] Prison L.R. 407, ECHR . . . . *Digested*, 03/**2105**:
Followed, 07/2170

Lotus & Delta *v* Culverwell (1976) 239 E.G. 287; [1976] R.A. 141, Lands Tr . . . . *Digested*, 76/**2260.9**:
Applied, 03/3497, 06/3445: *Considered*, 07/3371

Lough *v* First Secretary of State [2004] EWCA Civ 905; [2004] 1 W.L.R. 2557; [2005] 1 P. & C.R. 5; [2005] J.P.L. 208; [2004] 31 E.G. 92 (C.S.); (2004) 148 S.J.L.B. 879; [2004] N.P.C. 115; *Times*, July 29, 2004, CA (Civ Div); affirming [2004] EWHC 23 (Admin); [2004] 3 P.L.R. 38, QBD (Admin) . . . . *Digested*, 04/**3042**:
Applied, 05/2027, 05/3295, 06/1482: *Considered*, 07/2879

Louloudakis *v* Elliniko Dimosio (C-262/99) see Louloudakis *v* Greece (C-262/99)

Louloudakis *v* Greece (C-262/99); *sub nom* Louloudakis *v* Elliniko Dimosio (C-262/99) [2001] E.C.R. I-5547; [2003] 2 C.M.L.R. 3, ECJ (6th Chamber) . . . . *Applied*, 03/910, 04/4001, 07/1575

Lovelock *v* First Secretary of State; *sub nom* R. (on the application of Lovelock) *v* First Secretary of State [2006] EWHC 2423 (Admin); [2007] J.P.L. 600; (2006) 150 S.J.L.B. 1254, QBD (Admin)

Lowe *v* Associated Newspapers Ltd [2006] EWHC 320 (QB); [2007] Q.B. 580; [2007] 2 W.L.R. 595; [2006] 3 All E.R. 357; [2006] E.M.L.R. 17; *Times*, March 29, 2006, QBD . . . . *Digested*, 06/**1044**

Lowe v Guise [2002] EWCA Civ 197; [2002] Q.B. 1369; [2002] 3 W.L.R. 562; [2002] 3 All E.R. 454; [2002] P.I.Q.R. Q9; (2002) 99(15) L.S.G. 33; (2002) 146 S.J.L.B. 74; *Times*, March 25, 2002; *Daily Telegraph*, March 7, 2002, CA (Civ Div) . . . . *Digested*, 02/**3411**:
　　　　　　　　　　　　　　　　　　　　　　　　　　　　　　　　Applied, 07/3072
Lowe v Peters see Lowe v Walker
Lowe v Walker; *sub nom* Lowe v Peters 20 T.C. 25, CA (Civ Div) . . . . *Considered*, 07/4094
Lownds v Home Office; *sub nom* Home Office v Lownds; Lownds v Secretary of State for the Home Department [2002] EWCA Civ 365; [2002] 1 W.L.R. 2450; [2002] 4 All E.R. 775; [2002] C.P. Rep. 43; [2002] C.P.L.R. 328; [2002] 2 Costs L.R. 279; (2002) 99(19) L.S.G. 28; (2002) 146 S.J.L.B. 86; *Times*, April 5, 2002, CA (Civ Div) . . . . *Digested*, 02/**333**:
　　　　Applied, 03/259, 03/347, 04/293, 04/301, 04/303, 04/316, 04/320, 05/331,
　　　　　　　　05/372, 06/371, 06/2421: *Considered*, 04/319, 06/556, 07/389
Lownds v Secretary of State for the Home Department see Lownds v Home Office
Lowther Estate Trust v Lake District National Park Authority [2007] P.A.D. 3, Planning Inspector
Loyalty Management UK Ltd v Revenue and Customs Commissioners see Revenue and Customs Commissioners v Loyalty Management UK Ltd
LR af 1998 A/S v Commission of the European Communities (C-206/02 P) see Dansk Rorindustri A/S v Commission of the European Communities (C-189/02 P)
LR AF 1998 (Deutschland) GmbH v Commission of the European Communities (C-208/02 P) see Dansk Rorindustri A/S v Commission of the European Communities (C-189/02 P)
LTJ Diffusion SA v Sadas Vertbaudet SA (C-291/00) [2003] E.C.R. I-2799; [2003] C.E.C. 283; [2003] E.T.M.R. 83; [2003] F.S.R. 34; *Times*, March 26, 2003, ECJ . . . . *Digested*, 03/**2611**:
　　　　　　　　Applied, 04/2394, 04/2402, 07/2663: *Considered*, 02/2907
Lucas v Ministry of Defence see Saggar v Ministry of Defence
LUCKY STRIKE Trade Mark, Re [2007] E.C.C. 18, OGH (A)
Ludwig v Finanzamt Luckenwalde (C-453/05) [2007] 3 C.M.L.R. 23; [2007] S.T.I. 1738, ECJ (1st Chamber)
Luke v Stoke on Trent City Council [2007] EWCA Civ 761; [2007] I.C.R. 1678; [2007] I.R.L.R. 777, CA (Civ Div); affirming [2007] I.R.L.R. 305, EAT . . . . *Digested*, 07/**1325**
Lukhat v Grote (Unreported, April 13, 2006), CC (Bolton) [*Ex rel.* Chris Middleton, Barrister, Oriel Chambers, 14 Water Street, Liverpool] . . . . *Digested*, 07/**3134**
Lumley v Gye 118 E.R. 749; (1853) 2 El. & Bl. 216, QB . . . . *Applied*, 52/**3507**,
　　　　　64/3702, 69/3574, 07/4190: *Cited*, 99/280: *Considered*, 88/503, 93/3788,
　　　　　　　　　　　　　　　　　　　　　　　　　　　　　　　　95/2192
Lunan Group Ltd v Edwin Co Ltd; *sub nom* FIORELLI Trade Mark [2006] EWHC 3284 (Ch); [2007] R.P.C. 18; [2007] Bus. L.R. D82, Ch D
Lune Metal Products Ltd (In Administration), Re [2006] EWCA Civ 1720; [2007] Bus. L.R. 589; [2007] B.C.C. 217; [2007] 2 B.C.L.C. 746; *Times*, December 27, 2006, CA (Civ Div) . . . . *Digested*, 07/**2392**
Lunn v Dillingham (Unreported, November 20, 2006), Ch D (Leeds) [*Ex rel.* William Hanbury, Barrister, Zenith Chambers, 10 Park Square, Leeds] . . . . *Digested*, 07/**1060**
Lunn Poly Ltd v Liverpool & Lancashire Properties Ltd [2006] EWCA Civ 430; [2007] L. & T.R. 6; [2006] 2 E.G.L.R. 29; [2006] 25 E.G. 210; [2006] 12 E.G. 222 (C.S.); *Times*, April 18, 2006, CA (Civ Div) . . . . *Digested*, 06/**1019**
LuP GmbH v Finanzamt Bochum-Mitte (C-106/05) [2006] S.T.I. 1620, ECJ (3rd Chamber) . . . . *Applied*, 07/4345
Lupin (Europe) Ltd v Les Laboratories Servier see Les Laboratoires Servier v Apotex Inc
Luxembourg v Lakebrink (C-182/06) [2007] S.T.I. 1861, ECJ
Luxembourg v Vermietungsgesellschaft Objekt Kirchberg Sarl (C-269/03) [2005] S.T.C. 1345; [2004] E.C.R. I-8067; [2004] 3 C.M.L.R. 49; [2007] B.T.C. 5174; [2007] BV.C. 143; [2004] S.T.I. 2070, ECJ (1st Chamber) . . . . *Digested*, 05/**4384**
Luxembourg Brewers Cartel, Re (T49/02) see Brasserie Nationale SA v Commission of the European Communities (T49/02)
Luxim Corp v Ceravision Ltd [2007] EWHC 1624 (Ch); [2007] Bus. L.R. 1534; [2007] R.P.C. 33; (2007) 30(9) I.P.D. 30057, Ch D (Patents Ct)
Lykourezos v Greece (33554/03) 21 B.H.R.C. 593, ECHR . . . . *Digested*, 07/**2228**
Lymington Marina Ltd v Macnamara [2007] EWCA Civ 151; [2007] 2 All E.R. (Comm) 825; [2007] N.P.C. 27; [2007] Bus. L.R. D29, CA (Civ Div); affirming [2006] EWHC 704 (Ch); [2006] 2 All E.R. (Comm) 200; [2006] N.P.C. 43, Ch D . . . *Digested*, 06/**763**
Lynch v Moran [2006] IESC 31; 21 B.H.R.C. 1, Sup Ct (Irl)
Lyndendown Ltd v Vitamol Ltd [2007] EWCA Civ 826; [2007] 47 E.G. 170; [2007] 29 E.G. 142 (C.S.), CA (Civ Div)
Lyon's Personal Representatives v Revenue and Customs Commissioners [2007] S.T.C. (S.C.D.) 675; [2007] W.T.L.R. 1257; [2007] S.T.I. 1816, Sp Comm
Lyons v Gardner [2007] EWCA Civ 259; (2007) 151 S.J.L.B. 299; [2007] Env. L.R. D13, CA (Civ Div)
Lyyski v Umea Universitat (C-40/05) [2007] 2 C.M.L.R. 3; [2007] C.E.C. 412, ECJ (3rd Chamber) . . . . *Digested*, 07/**1630**

M *v* DPP [2007] EWHC 1032 (Admin); (2007) 171 J.P. 457; (2007) 171 J.P.N. 769, DC

M *v* H [2007] I.L.Pr. 37, OL (DK)

M *v* HM Treasury; *sub nom* R. (on the application of M) *v* HM Treasury; *joined cases* MM *v* HM Treasury; A *v* HM Treasury [2007] EWCA Civ 173, CA (Civ Div); affirming [2006] EWHC 2328 (Admin); [2007] A.C.D. 34; (2006) 103(39) L.S.G. 33, QBD (Admin)

M *v* Inner London Crown Court see R. (on the application of M) *v* Inner London Crown Court

M *v* Islington LBC see R. (on the application of M) *v* Islington LBC

M *v* M [2007] EWHC 1404 (Fam); [2007] 2 F.L.R. 1010; [2007] Fam. Law 887, Fam Div

M *v* M [2007] EWHC 2047 (Fam); [2007] 2 F.L.R. 1018; [2007] Fam. Law 1069, Fam Div

M *v* M (Short Marriage: Clean Break) see Miller *v* Miller

M *v* M (Specific Issue: Choice of School) [2005] EWHC 2769 (Fam); [2007] 1 F.L.R. 251; [2006] Fam. Law 1024, Fam Div

M *v* M (Stay of Proceedings: Return of Children) [2005] EWHC 1159 (Fam); [2006] 1 F.L.R. 138; [2005] Fam. Law 853, Fam Div. . . . . *Applied,* 07/**1790**

M *v* Newlands Manor School see Mountford *v* Newlands School

M *v* Secretary of State for Work and Pensions; *sub nom* Secretary of State for Work and Pensions *v* M; *joined case* Langley *v* Bradford MDC [2006] UKHL 11; [2006] 2 A.C. 91; [2006] 2 W.L.R. 637; [2006] 4 All E.R. 929; [2006] 2 F.L.R. 56; [2006] 1 F.C.R. 497; [2006] H.R.L.R. 19; [2006] U.K.H.R.R. 799; 21 B.H.R.C. 254; [2006] Fam. Law 524; (2006) 150 S.J.L.B. 363; *Times,* March 14, 2006, HL; reversing [2004] EWCA Civ 1343; [2006] Q.B. 380; [2005] 2 W.L.R. 740; [2005] 1 F.L.R. 498; [2004] 3 F.C.R. 507; [2005] A.C.D. 58; (2004) 101(45) L.S.G. 31; (2004) 148 S.J.L.B. 1244; *Times,* November 11, 2004, CA (Civ Div) . . . . *Digested,* 06/**1649**: *Applied,* 06/**1714**, 07/**3875**: *Considered,* 06/**1706**

M *v* Serbia (39177/05) [2007] 1 F.C.R. 760, ECHR . . . . *Digested,* 07/**2223**

M *v* South Africa 23 B.H.R.C. 697, Const Ct (SA)

M *v* W (Declaration of Parentage) [2006] EWHC 2341 (Fam); [2007] 2 F.L.R. 270; [2007] Fam. Law 397, Fam Div

M *v* Warwickshire CC see Warwickshire CC *v* M

M and R (Minors) (Child Abuse: Expert Evidence), Re; *sub nom* M and R (Minors) (Expert Opinion: Evidence), Re [1996] 4 All E.R. 239; [1996] 2 F.L.R. 195; [1996] 2 F.C.R. 617; [1996] Fam. Law 541; *Times,* July 1, 1996, CA (Civ Div) . . *Digested,* 96/**490**: *Applied,* 02/**1636**, 03/**2055**: *Considered,* 99/**3440**: *Referred to,* 07/**1754**

M and R (Minors) (Expert Opinion: Evidence), Re see M and R (Minors) (Child Abuse: Expert Evidence), Re

M (A Child) *v* Arethusa Venture Centre (Unreported, March 3, 2006), CC (Croydon) [*Ex rel.* Matthew Gullick, Barrister, 3 Paper Buildings, Temple, London] . . . . *Digested,* 07/**3166**

M (A Child) *v* Brown (Unreported, October 18, 2006), CC (Birmingham) [*Ex rel.* Stephen Garner, Barrister, No.8 Chambers, Fountain Court, Steelhouse Lane, Birmingham] . . . . *Digested,* 07/**3178**

M (A Child) *v* Chana (Unreported, February 20, 2007), CC (Birmingham) [*Ex rel.* Stephen Garner, Barrister, No.8 Chambers, Fountain Court, Steelhouse Lane, Birmingham] . . . . *Digested,* 07/**3089**

M (A Child) *v* JJB Sports (Unreported, September 20, 2006), CC (Coventry) [*Ex rel.* Stephen Garner, Barrister, No.8 Fountain Court, Steelhouse Lane, Birmingham] . . . . *Digested,* 07/**3090**

M (A Child) *v* Salford City Council (Unreported, February 28, 2006), CC (Salford) [*Ex rel.* Simon Plaut, Barrister, Park Lane Chambers, 19 Westgate, Leeds] . . . . *Digested,* 07/**3192**

M (A Child) *v* Savill (Unreported, May 26, 2006), CC (Edmonton) [*Ex rel.* Joanna Kerr, Barrister, Lamb Chambers, Temple, London] . . . . *Digested,* 07/**3128**

M (A Child) *v* WM Morrisons Supermarkets Plc (Unreported, March 7, 2007), CC (Manchester) [*Ex rel.* Elahe Youshani, Barrister, St James's Chambers, 68 Quay Street, Manchester] . . . . *Digested,* 07/**3202**

M (A Child) (Abduction: Brussels II Revised), Re; *sub nom* V *v* M; Vigreux *v* Michel [2006] EWCA Civ 630; [2006] 2 F.L.R. 1180; [2007] 3 F.C.R. 196; [2006] Fam. Law 728; (2006) 103(22) L.S.G. 26; (2006) 150 S.J.L.B. 666; *Times,* July 3, 2006, *Independent,* May 24, 2006, CA (Civ Div). . . . . *Digested,* 06/**1643**: *Doubted,* 07/**1736**

M (A Child) (Abduction: Child's Objections), Re [2007] EWCA Civ 260; [2007] 2 F.L.R. 72; [2007] 3 F.C.R. 631; [2007] Fam. Law 678; (2007) 151 S.J.L.B. 434, CA (Civ Div) *Doubted,* 07/**1736**

M (A Child) (Care Proceedings: Best Evidence), Re; *sub nom* MM (A Child), Re [2007] EWCA Civ 589; [2007] 2 F.L.R. 1006; [2007] 2 F.C.R. 797; [2007] Fam. Law 893, CA (Civ Div) . . . . *Digested,* 07/**1780**

M (A Child) (Care Proceedings: Witness Summons), Re see LM *v* Medway Council

M (A Child) (Residence Order), Re [2007] EWCA Civ 954; (2007) 104(35) L.S.G. 34; (2007) 151 S.J.L.B. 1129, CA (Civ Div)

M (A Child) (Supervised Contact), Re [2006] EWCA Civ 499, CA (Civ Div) . . . . *Considered,* 07/**1740**

M (A Minor) v Newham LBC see X (Minors) v Bedfordshire CC
M (A Minor) (Abduction: Habitual Residence), Re [1996] 1F.L.R.887; [1996] 2 F.C.R.333;
    [1996] Fam. Law 402; *Times*, January 3, 1996; *Independent*, January 29, 1996,
    CA (Civ Div) . . . . *Digested*, 96/**643**:
                                     Applied, 98/2382: *Considered*, 07/1750
M (Child Abduction: Delay), Re, *Times*, August 28, 2007, CA (Civ Div)
M (Children) (Abduction), Re; *sub nom* MM v VM [2007] UKHL 55; [2007] 3 W.L.R.
    975; (2007) 151 S.J.L.B. 1595; *Times*, December 6, 2007, HL; reversing [2007]
    EWCA Civ 992; [2007] 3 F.C.R. 564, CA (Civ Div); affirming [2007] EWHC
    1820 (Fam); [2007] Fam. Law 888, Fam Div . . . . *Digested*, 07/**1736**
M (Children) (Interim Care Order: Removal), Re [2005] EWCA Civ 1594; [2006] 1 F.C.R.
    303; [2006] Fam. Law 258; (2005) 149 S.J.L.B. 1355; *Times*, November 11, 2005,
    CA (Civ Div) . . . . *Digested*, 06/**1657**:
                                          Applied, 07/1714
M (Children) (Interviewing Children), Re [2007] EWCA Civ 1150; (2007) 151 S.J.L.B.1401,
    CA (Civ Div)
M (Children) (Placement Order), Re see Warwickshire CC v M
M (Minors) (Residence Order: Jurisdiction), Re [1993] 1 F.L.R. 495; [1993] 1 F.C.R. 718;
    [1993] Fam. Law 285; *Times*, November 6, 1992, CA (Civ Div) . . . . *Digested*, 93/**2866**:
                         Considered, 07/1737: *Distinguished*, 96/485
M&M (Land) Ltd v Secretary of State for Communities and Local Government [2007]
    EWHC 489 (Admin); [2007] 2 P. & C.R. 18; [2007] J.P.L.1474, QBD (Admin)
M-H (A Child), Re; *sub nom* M-H (A Child) (Care Order), Re [2006] EWCA Civ 1864;
    [2007] 1 F.L.R. 1715; [2007] 3 F.C.R. 319; [2007] Fam. Law 487; (2007) 151
    S.J.L.B. 62, CA (Civ Div) . . . . *Digested*, 07/**1712**
M-H (A Child) (Care Order), Re see M-H (A Child), Re
M-K (A Child) (Relocation Outside the Jurisdiction), Re [2006] EWCA Civ 1013; [2007] 1
    F.L.R. 432; [2006] 2 F.C.R. 671; [2006] Fam. Law 1034, CA (Civ Div) . . . . . . *Digested*, 06/**1689**
M-T v T see NMT v MOT
MA (Pakistan) v Secretary of State for the Home Department; *sub nom* MA (Seven
    Year Child Concession: Pakistan), Re; *joined cases* MA (Sudan) v Secretary of
    State for the Home Department; AM (Serbia) v Secretary of State for the Home
    Department [2007] EWCA Civ 16; [2007] I.N.L.R. 211; (2007) 104(6) L.S.G.
    30; (2007) 151 S.J.L.B. 161; *Times*, February 19, 2007, CA (Civ Div); reversing
    [2005] UKIAT 90; [2005] Imm. A.R. 338, IAT . . . . *Digested*, 07/**2285**
MA (Seven Year Child Concession: Pakistan), Re see MA (Pakistan) v Secretary of State
    for the Home Department
MA (Sudan) v Secretary of State for the Home Department see MA (Pakistan) v
    Secretary of State for the Home Department
McAdie v Royal Bank of Scotland Plc see Royal Bank of Scotland Plc v McAdie
McAlister v Stevenson see Donoghue v Stevenson
Macalister v Young see General Assembly of Free Church of Scotland v Lord Overtoun
McAllister v General Medical Council [1993] A.C. 388; [1993] 2 W.L.R. 308; [1993]
    1 All E.R. 982; 1993 S.C. 388; [1993] 4 Med. L.R. 29; (1993) 137 S.J.L.B. 12,
    PC (UK) . . . . *Digested*, 93/**2704**:
                              Considered, 03/1721, 07/1949
McArthur v Bury MBC . . . . *Followed*, 07/3496
McAuley v Bristol City Council [1992] Q.B. 134; [1991] 3 W.L.R. 968; [1992] 1 All
    E.R. 749; (1991) 23 H.L.R. 586; 89 L.G.R. 931; [1991] 2 E.G.L.R. 64; [1991] 45
    E.G. 155; [1991] E.G. 70 (C.S.); [1991] N.P.C. 81, CA (Civ Div) . . . . *Digested*, 92/**2674**:
                                     Distinguished, 07/2738
McAuley Catholic High School v C [2003] EWHC 3045 (Admin); [2004] 2 All E.R.
    436; [2004] I.C.R. 1563; [2004] E.L.R. 89; [2004] A.C.D. 24, QBD (Admin) . *Digested*, 04/**1077**:
                              Considered, 07/5115
McBride v United Kingdom (Admissibility) (1396/06) (2006) 43 E.H.R.R. SE10,
    ECHR . . . . *Considered*, 07/2234
McBride (Setting of Minimum Term), Re [2007] EWHC 698 (QB); (2007) 151 S.J.L.B. 507,
    QBD
McCabe v Cornwall CC see Eastwood v Magnox Electric Plc
McCafferty v Metropolitan Police District Receiver [1977] 1 W.L.R. 1073; [1977] 2 All
    E.R. 756; [1977] I.C.R. 799; (1977) 121 S.J. 678, CA (Civ Div) . . . . *Digested*, 77/**999**:
           Applied, 83/2218, 97/656: *Considered*, 86/3142, 03/432, 07/483:
                             Referred to, 90/2961, 97/651, 00/528
McCann v United Kingdom (A/324) (1996) 21 E.H.R.R. 97; *Times*, October 9, 1995;
    Independent, October 6, 1995, ECHR . . . . *Digested*, 95/**2665**:
            Applied, 98/3157, 99/3144, 06/2170, 07/2237: *Considered*, 02/2493, 04/37,
                                        06/15
McCartan Turkington Breen v Times Newspapers Ltd; *sub nom* Turkington v Times
    Newspapers Ltd [2001] 2 A.C. 277; [2000] 3 W.L.R. 1670; [2000] 4 All E.R.
    913; [2000] N.I. 410; [2001] E.M.L.R. 1; [2001] U.K.H.R.R. 184; 9 B.H.R.C. 497;
    (2000) 97(47) L.S.G. 40; (2000) 150 N.L.J. 1657; (2000) 144 S.J.L.B. 287;
    Times, November 3, 2000; *Independent*, November 7, 2000, HL (NI); reversing
    [1998] N.I. 358; *Times*, November 4, 1998, CA (NI) . . . . *Digested*, 00/**5491**:
                             Considered, 07/1070, 07/2217

McCarthy v McCarthy & Stone Plc [2007] EWCA Civ 664, CA (Civ Div); affirming
   [2006] EWHC 1851 (Ch); [2006] 4 All E.R. 1127, Ch D . . . .   *Digested*, 07/**583**

McCartney v United Kingdom (34575/04) see Brecknell v United Kingdom (32457/
   04)

McCaughey v Chief Constable of Northern Ireland see Jordan v Lord Chancellor

McClintock v Department of Constitutional Affairs, *Times*, December 5, 2007, EAT . . .   *Digested*, 07/**1400**

McConnell Dowell Constructors (Aust) Pty Ltd v National Grid Gas Plc (formerly
   Transco Plc) [2006] EWHC 2551 (TCC); [2007] B.L.R. 92, QBD (TCC) . . . . .   *Digested*, 07/**731**

McCormack v Walker (Unreported, December 6, 2006), CC (Rotherham) [*Ex rel.*
   Nicholas J H Preston, Barrister, Clerksroom, 218 Strand, London] . . . .   *Digested*, 07/**3212**

McCoubrey v Ministry of Defence [2007] EWCA Civ 17; [2007] 1 W.L.R. 1544;
   [2007] LS Law Medical 150; (2007) 151 S.J.L.B. 159; *Times*, January 26, 2007,
   CA (Civ Div) . . . .   *Digested*, 07/**483**

McDonagh v Thom (t/a Royal Hotel Dungannon) [2007] NICA 3; [2007] N.I. 138, CA
   (NI)

MacDonald v Advocate General for Scotland see Advocate General for Scotland v
   MacDonald

McDonald v Coys of Kensington Holdings Ltd see Cressman v Coys of Kensington
   (Sales) Ltd

MacDonald v Ministry of Defence see Advocate General for Scotland v MacDonald

MacDonald (Inspector of Taxes) v Dextra Accessories Ltd see Dextra Accessories Ltd v
   MacDonald (Inspector of Taxes)

McEwan v DPP [2007] EWHC 740 (Admin); (2007) 171 J.P. 308; (2007) 171 J.P.N.
   642, DC

McFadden v United Kingdom (11365/85) see Brogan v United Kingdom (A/145-B)

MacFarlane v Glasgow City Council [2001] I.R.L.R. 7, EAT. . . . .   *Digested*, 01/**6468**:
                               Applied, 03/4030, 07/1345: *Considered*, 05/1325

McFarlane v McFarlane see Miller v Miller

McFarlane v Tayside Health Board [2000] 2 A.C. 59; [1999] 3 W.L.R. 1301; [1999] 4
   All E.R. 961; 2000 S.C. (H.L.) 1; 2000 S.L.T. 154; 2000 S.C.L.R. 105; [2000] 1
   F.C.R. 102; [2000] P.I.Q.R. Q101; [2000] Lloyd's Rep. Med. 1; (2000) 52
   B.M.L.R. 1; (1999) 149 N.L.J. 1868; 1999 G.W.D. 39-1888; *Times*, November 26,
   1999; *Independent*, December 3, 1999, HL; reversing in part 1998 S.C. 389;
   1998 S.L.T. 307; 1998 S.C.L.R. 126; (1998) 44 B.M.L.R. 140; 1998 G.W.D. 4-
   180; *Times*, May 8, 1998, IH (2 Div); reversing 1997 S.L.T. 211; 1996 Rep. L.R.
   159; *Times*, November 11, 1996, OH . . . .   *Digested*, 00/**6162**:
            Applied, 01/4462, 01/6412, 02/1683, 04/378: *Cited*, 00/2777:
                Considered, 00/4200, 01/4463, 02/927, 04/925, 07/3063:
            Distinguished, 01/1508, 01/4464: *Followed*, 01/1509, 03/3120, 03/3129:
                                   Not followed, 98/6115

McGavin v McIntyre Bros see McIntyre Bros v McGavin

McGhee v National Coal Board [1973] 1 W.L.R. 1; [1972] 3 All E.R. 1008; 1973 S.C.
   (H.L.) 37; 1973 S.L.T. 14; 13 K.I.R. 471; (1972) 116 S.J. 967, HL; reversing 1972
   S.L.T. (Notes) 61, IH (1 Div). . . . .   *Digested*, 73/**3841**:
        Applied, 83/2548, 92/1552, 94/3399, 99/3987, 00/4187, 02/2225,
            06/2866, 07/5100: *Considered*, 85/2319, 87/2604, 96/4426, 00/5114,
            04/2693, 06/2867: *Distinguished*, 87/4758, 88/2415, 90/5497, 98/1501:
                                   Followed, 04/2714

McGhie v British Telecommunications Plc [2005] EWCA Civ 48; (2005) 149 S.J.L.B.
   114, CA (Civ Div) . . . .   *Considered*, 07/**475**

McGlinchey v United Kingdom (50390/99) (2003) 37 E.H.R.R. 41; [2003] Lloyd's
   Rep. Med. 264; (2003) 72 B.M.L.R. 168; [2003] Prison L.R. 314; [2007]
   Inquest L.R. 191; *Times*, May 1, 2003, ECHR . . . .   *Digested*, 03/**2104**

McGlinn v Waltham Contractors Ltd [2006] EWHC 2322 (TCC); [2006] B.L.R. 489;
   108 Con. L.R. 43, QBD (TCC) . . . .   *Digested*, 07/**344**

McGlinn v Waltham Contractors Ltd [2007] EWHC 149 (TCC); 111 Con. L.R. 1; [2007]
   C.I.L.L. 2441; *Times*, March 20, 2007, QBD (TCC)

McGlinn v Waltham Contractors Ltd [2007] EWHC 698 (TCC); 112 Con. L.R. 148,
   QBD (TCC)

McGlinn v Waltham Contractors Ltd (Costs) [2007] EWHC 294 (TCC); [2007] B.L.R.
   188, QBD (TCC) . . . .   *Digested*, 07/**386**

McGlynn v Mental Health Tribunal for Scotland [2007] M.H.L.R. 16; 2006 G.W.D. 13-
   248, Sh Pr

McGrath v Riddell see HIH Casualty & General Insurance Ltd, Re

McGrath v United Kingdom (34651/04) see Brecknell v United Kingdom (32457/04)

McGrath (An Infant), Re; *sub nom* McGrath (Infants), Re [1893] 1 Ch. 143, CA;
   affirming [1892] 2 Ch. 496, Ch D . . . .   *Considered*, 07/3911

McGrath (Infants), Re see McGrath (An Infant), Re

McHugh v Gray [2006] EWHC 1968 (QB); [2006] Lloyd's Rep. Med. 519; (2006)
   150 S.J.L.B. 1051, QBD . . . .   *Digested*, 07/**478**

McIlkenny v Chief Constable of the West Midlands see Hunter v Chief Constable of
   the West Midlands

McIntyre *v* Harland & Wolff Plc; *sub nom* Harland & Wolff Plc *v* McIntyre [2006]
   EWCA Civ 287; [2006] 1 W.L.R. 2577; [2007] 2 All E.R. 24; [2006] I.C.R. 1222;
   [2006] P.I.Q.R. Q8; (2006) 103(15) L.S.G. 23, CA (Civ Div) . . . .   *Digested*, 06/**1021**:
                                                        Applied, 07/1056

McIntyre Bros *v* McGavin; *sub nom* McGavin *v* McIntyre Bros [1893] A.C. 268;
   (1893) 20 R. (H.L.) 49; (1893) 1 S.L.T.110, HL . . . .   *Applied*, 07/363:
                                                        Considered, 59/77

McKay *v* United Kingdom (543/03) (2007) 44 E.H.R.R. 41; *Times*, October 30, 2006,
   ECHR . . . .   *Digested*, 07/**2231**

McKennitt *v* Ash; *sub nom* Ash *v* McKennitt [2006] EWCA Civ 1714; [2007] 3 W.L.R.
   194; [2007] E.M.L.R. 4; (2007) 151 S.J.L.B. 27; *Times*, December 20, 2006,
   CA (Civ Div); affirming [2005] EWHC 3003 (QB); [2006] E.M.L.R.10, QBD. .   *Digested*, 07/**2250**:
                                        Applied, 07/2247, 07/2893

McKerr, Re see McKerr's Application for Judicial Review, Re
McKerr's Application for Judicial Review, Re; *sub nom* McKerr, Re [2004] UKHL 12;
   [2004] 1 W.L.R. 807; [2004] 2 All E.R. 409; [2004] N.I. 212; [2004] H.R.L.R.
   26; [2004] U.K.H.R.R. 385; 17 B.H.R.C. 68; [2004] Lloyd's Rep. Med. 263;
   [2004] Inquest L.R. 35; (2004) 101(13) L.S.G. 33; (2004) 148 S.J.L.B. 355;
   Times, March 12, 2004, HL (NI); reversing [2003] NICA 1; [2003] N.I. 117, CA
   (NI) . . . .   *Digested*, 04/**1976**:
           Applied, 06/17, 06/2932, 06/4528: *Considered*, 05/17: *Followed*, 07/27

McKinnon *v* United States [2007] EWHC 762 (Admin); (2007) 157 N.L.J. 554; *Times*,
   April 19, 2007, DC . . . .   *Digested*, 07/**1667**

McKnight *v* Ice Skating Queensland Inc [2007] QSC 273; (2007-08) 10 I.T.E.L.R.
   570, Sup Ct (Qld)

McLaughlin *v* Governor of the Cayman Islands [2007] UKPC 50; [2007] 1 W.L.R.
   2839; *Times*, July 27, 2007, PC (CI)

McLean *v* Rainbow Homeloans Ltd [2007] I.R.L.R. 14, EAT (SC) . . . .   *Digested*, 07/**5150**

MacLean *v* Revenue and Customs Commissioners [2007] S.T.C. (S.C.D.) 350; [2007]
   S.T.I. 1058, Sp Comm

McLellan *v* Bracknell Forest BC see R. (on the application of McLellan) *v* Bracknell
   Forest BC

McLeod *v* United Kingdom (24755/94) [1998] 2 F.L.R. 1048; [1999] 1 F.C.R. 193;
   (1999) 27 E.H.R.R. 493; 5 B.H.R.C. 364; [1999] Crim. L.R. 155; [1998] H.R.C.D.
   878; [1998] Fam. Law 734; *Times*, October 1, 1998, ECHR (1996) 22 E.H.R.R.
   CD158, Eur Comm HR . . . .   *Digested*, 98/**3103**:
                                                      Applied, 07/2243

McLoughlin *v* Revenue and Customs Commissioners [2006] S.T.C. (S.C.D.) 467;
   [2006] S.T.I. 1630, Sp Comm . . . .   *Digested*, 07/**4070**

McMahon *v* McGrath see HIH Casualty & General Insurance Ltd, Re
McManus *v* Sharif see Cranfield *v* Bridgegrove Ltd
McMenemy *v* Capita Business Services Ltd 2007 S.C. 492; 2007 S.L.T. 428; [2007]
   I.R.L.R. 400; 2007 G.W.D. 13-267, IH (Ex Div); affirming [2006] I.R.L.R. 761;
   (2006) 150 S.J.L.B. 665, EAT (SC) . . . .   *Digested*, 07/**5145**

McMichael *v* United Kingdom (16424/90) see McMichael *v* United Kingdom (A/308)
McMichael *v* United Kingdom (A/308); *sub nom* McMichael *v* United Kingdom
   (16424/90) [1995] 2 F.C.R. 718; (1995) 20 E.H.R.R. 205; [1995] Fam. Law
   478; *Times*, March 2, 1995, ECHR (1993) 15 E.H.R.R. CD80, Eur Comm HR . . .   *Applied*, 97/2803,
           99/6065: *Considered*, 07/2248: *Distinguished*, 99/6064:
                                                 Referred to, 02/2409

McNerny *v* Lambeth LBC (1989) 21 H.L.R. 188; [1989] 19 E.G. 77; (1990) 154 L.G.
   Rev. 272; [1988] E.G. 169 (C.S.); (1989) 139 N.L.J. 114; *Independent*, December
   23, 1988, CA (Civ Div) . . . .   *Digested*, 90/**2871**:
                                     Considered, 93/3796, 07/2738

McPhail *v* Doulton see Baden's Deed Trusts (No.1), Re
McQueen *v* Revenue and Customs Commissioners [2007] S.T.C. (S.C.D.) 457;
   [2007] S.T.I. 1188, Sp Comm
McQUEEN CLOTHING CO Trade Mark see Croom's Trade Mark Application
Macrossan *v* Comptroller General of Patents, Designs and Trade Marks see
   Macrossan's Patent Application (No.0314464.9)
Macrossan's Patent Application (No.0314464.9) see Aerotel Ltd *v* Telco Holdings Ltd
Macrossan's Patent Application (No.0314464.9); *sub nom* Macrossan *v* Comptroller
   General of Patents, Designs and Trade Marks [2006] EWHC 705 (Pat); (2006)
   29(5) I.P.D. 29043, Ch D (Patents Ct) . . . .   *Digested*, 07/**2632**:
                             Subsequent related litigation, 07/2615

McShane *v* Hanson Brick (Unreported, September 20, 2006), CC (Peterborough) [*Ex
   rel.* Jeffrey Deegan, Barrister, Fenners Chambers, 3 Madingley Road,
   Cambridge] . . . .   *Digested*, 07/**3172**

Macedonian Orthodox Community Church St Petka Inc, Re [2006] NSWSC1247; [2007]
   W.T.L.R. 1429, Sup Ct (NSW)
Machin *v* Devon CC [2007] R.V.R. 81, Lands Tr . . . .   *Digested*, 07/**3246**
Mackova *v* Slovakia (51543/99) (Unreported, March 29, 2005), ECHR . . . .   *Applied*, 07/2218

Maco Door and Window Hardware (UK) Ltd v Revenue and Customs Commissioners; *sub nom* Revenue and Customs Commissioners v Maco Door & Window Hardware (UK) Ltd [2007] EWCA Civ 545; [2007] Bus. L.R. 1686; [2007] S.T.C. 1442; [2007] B.T.C. 607; [2007] S.T.I. 1773; (2007) 151 S.J.L.B. 861; [2007] N.P.C. 73, CA (Civ Div); reversing [2006] EWHC 1832 (Ch); [2007] S.T.C. 721; [2006] B.T.C. 829; [2006] S.T.I. 1919; *Times*, August 11, 2006, Ch D; reversing [2006] S.T.C. (S.C.D.) 1; [2005] S.T.I. 1996, Sp Comm . . . .   *Digested*, 06/**4158**

Macovei v Moldova (19253/03) (2007) 45 E.H.R.R. 48, ECHR

Macrino v Meloni (C-202/04) see Cipolla v Fazari (C-94/04)

Madan v Secretary of State for the Home Department; *sub nom* R. (on the application of Madan) v Secretary of State for the Home Department; *joined case* R. (on the application of Kapoor) v Secretary of State for the Home Department [2007] EWCA Civ 770; [2007] 1 W.L.R. 2891; [2007] I.N.L.R. 531; (2007) 151 S.J.L.B. 1023; *Times*, August 27, 2007, CA (Civ Div) . . . .   *Digested*, 07/**56**

Madarassy v Nomura International Plc [2007] EWCA Civ 33; [2007] I.C.R. 867; [2007] I.R.L.R. 246, CA (Civ Div); affirming UKEAT/0326/31/ILB, EAT . . . . . .   *Digested*, 07/**1401**:
              Applied, 07/1184

Madaus AG v Office for Harmonisation in the Internal Market (Trade Marks and Designs) (OHIM) (T-202/04) [2006] E.C.R. II-1115; [2006] E.T.M.R. 76, CFI (1st Chamber) . . . .   *Digested*, 07/**2658**

Madeley v Revenue and Customs Commissioners [2006] S.T.C. (S.C.D.) 513; [2006] S.T.I. 1823, Sp Comm . . . .   *Digested*, 07/**4052**

Madgett (t/a Howden Court Hotel) v Customs and Excise Commissioners (C-308/96); *sub nom* Customs and Excise Commissioners v Madgett (t/a Howden Court Hotel) (C-308/96) [1998] S.T.C. 1189; [1998] E.C.R. I-6229; [1999] 2 C.M.L.R. 392; [1998] C.E.C. 1004; [1998] B.T.C. 5440; [1998] B.V.C. 458, ECJ (5th Chamber) . . . .   *Digested*, 99/**5002**:
     Applied, 03/4537, 07/4352: *Considered*, 06/4424: *Explained*, 04/3968:
              Followed, 05/4406

Madgett (t/a Howden Court Hotel) v Revenue and Customs Commissioners [2007] B.V.C. 2090; [2006] V. & D.R. 213; [2006] S.T.I. 2578, V&DTr (London) . . . . . .   *Digested*, 07/**4331**

Madson Estate v Saylor 2007 SCC 18; [2007] W.T.L.R. 1579; (2006-07) 9 I.T.E.L.R. 903, Sup Ct (Can)

Maersk Olie & Gas A/S v Firma M de Haan & W de Boer [2007] I.L.Pr. 5, HR (DK)

Mag Instrument Inc v Office for Harmonisation in the Internal Market (Trade Marks and Designs) (OHIM) (T-88/00) see Mag Instrument Inc v Office for Harmonisation in the Internal Market (Trade Marks and Designs) (OHIM) (C-136/02 P)

Mag Instrument Inc v Office for Harmonisation in the Internal Market (Trade Marks and Designs) (OHIM) (C-136/02 P); *sub nom* Mag Instrument Inc v Office for Harmonisation in the Internal Market (Trade Marks and Designs) (OHIM) (T-88/00) [2004] E.C.R. I-9165; [2005] E.T.M.R. 46, ECJ (2nd Chamber) . . . .   *Digested*, 05/**2556**:
        Applied, 07/2660: *Previous proceedings*, 02/2879

Magajane v Chairperson, North West Gambling Board 22 B.H.R.C. 251, Const Ct (SA)

Maggs v Anstey [2007] EWHC 515 (QB); (2007) 151 S.J.L.B. 506, QBD

Maggs (t/a BM Builders) v Marsh [2006] EWCA Civ 1058; [2006] B.L.R. 395; [2006] C.I.L.L. 2369; (2006) 150 S.J.L.B. 918, CA (Civ Div) . . . .   *Digested*, 07/**785**

Magill v Porter see Porter v Magill

Magill v Weeks see Porter v Magill

Maharaj v Teaching Service Commission [2006] UKPC 36, PC (Trin) . . . .   *Digested*, 07/**47**

Mahme Trust Reg v Lloyds TSB Bank Plc [2006] EWHC 1321 (Ch), Ch D . . . .   *Followed*, 07/**2944**

Mahmood v GMC; *sub nom* R. (on the application of Mahmood) v General Medical Council [2007] EWHC 474 (Admin); (2007) 95 B.M.L.R. 229, QBD (Admin)

Mahmood (Amjad) v Secretary of State for the Home Department see R. (on the application of Mahmood (Amjad)) v Secretary of State for the Home Department

Mahmud v Bank of Credit and Commerce International SA (In Liquidation) see Malik v Bank of Credit and Commerce International SA (In Liquidation)

Mainstream Properties Ltd v Young see OBG Ltd v Allan

Mainstream Properties Ltd v Young [2005] EWCA Civ 861; [2005] I.R.L.R. 964; (2005) 102(30) L.S.G. 31; *Times*, July 28, 2005, CA (Civ Div) . . . .   *Digested*, 05/**4188**:
              Affirmed, 07/4190

Majorowski v Guy's and St Thomas's NHS Trust see Majrowski v Guy's and St Thomas's NHS Trust

Majorstake Ltd v Curtis [2006] EWCA Civ 1171; [2007] Ch. 300; [2006] 3 W.L.R. 1114; [2006] 4 All E.R. 1326; [2006] B.L.R. 461; [2007] H.L.R. 16; [2007] L. & T.R. 7; [2006] 3 E.G.L.R. 50; [2006] 37 E.G. 194; (2006) 103(33) L.S.G. 25; [2007] 1 P. & C.R. DG9, CA (Civ Div); reversing CHY0428, CC (Central London) . . . .   *Digested*, 06/**2692**

Majrowski v Guy's and St Thomas's NHS Trust; *sub nom* Majorowski v Guy's and St Thomas's NHS Trust [2006] UKHL 34; [2007] 1 A.C. 224; [2006] 3 W.L.R. 125; [2006] 4 All E.R. 395; [2006] I.C.R. 1199; [2006] I.R.L.R. 695; (2006) 91 B.M.L.R. 85; (2006) 156 N.L.J. 1173; (2006) 150 S.J.L.B. 986; *Times*, July 13, 2006; *Independent*, July 14, 2006, HL; affirming [2005] EWCA Civ 251; [2005] Q.B. 848; [2005] 2 W.L.R. 1503; [2005] I.C.R. 977; [2005] I.R.L.R. 340; (2005) 149 S.J.L.B. 358; *Times*, March 21, 2005; *Independent*, April 8, 2005, CA (Civ Div) . . . . *Digested, 06/***1337**:
Applied, 06/2916, 07/1377, 07/1437: *Considered,* 07/1828

MAK v Dewsbury Healthcare NHS Trust see JD v East Berkshire Community Health NHS Trust

Makaratzis v Greece (50385/99) (2005) 41 E.H.R.R. 49, ECHR . . . . *Applied,* 07/2237

Makepeace v Evans Bros (Reading) [2000] B.L.R. 287; [2001] I.C.R. 241; (2000) 97(23) L.S.G. 42; *Times*, June 13, 2000, CA (Civ Div) . . . . *Digested, 00/***4206**:
Considered, 07/2935: *Distinguished,* 03/2986

Makers UK Ltd v Office of Fair Trading; *joined case* Prater Ltd v Office of Fair Trading [2006] CAT 13; [2006] Comp. A.R. 579, CAT . . . . *Digested, 07/***624**

Makers UK Ltd v Office of Fair Trading [2007] CAT 11; [2007] Comp. A.R. 699, CAT

Makri v Greece (Admissibility) (5977/03) (Unreported, March 24, 2005), ECHR . . . . . *Applied,* 07/2233

Malcolm v DPP [2007] EWHC 363 (Admin); [2007] 1 W.L.R. 1230; [2007] 3 All E.R. 578; [2007] 2 Cr. App. R. 1; (2007) 171 J.P. 293; [2007] R.T.R. 27; [2007] Crim. L.R. 894; (2007) 171 J.P.N. 611; *Times*, April 4, 2007, DC . . . . *Digested, 07/***944**

Malcolm v Lewisham LBC; *sub nom* Lewisham LBC v Malcolm [2007] EWCA Civ 763; [2007] 32 E.G. 88 (C.S.); [2007] N.P.C. 94; *Times*, August 28, 2007, CA (Civ Div)

Malik v Bank of Credit and Commerce International SA (In Liquidation); *sub nom* BCCI SA, Re; Mahmud v Bank of Credit and Commerce International SA (In Liquidation) [1998] A.C. 20; [1997] 3 W.L.R. 95; [1997] 3 All E.R. 1; [1997] I.C.R. 606; [1997] I.R.L.R. 462; (1997) 94(25) L.S.G. 33; (1997) 147 N.L.J. 917; *Times*, June 13, 1997; *Independent*, June 20, 1997, HL; reversing [1995] 3 All E.R. 545; [1996] I.C.R. 406; [1995] I.R.L.R. 375; (1995) 145 N.L.J. 593; *Times*, April 12, 1995; *Independent*, March 17, 1995, CA (Civ Div); affirming [1994] I.R.L.R. 282; *Times*, February 23, 1994; *Independent*, March 21, 1994, Ch D . . . *Digested, 97/***2192**:
Applied, 99/2010, 01/2305, 03/1216, 04/1193, 04/1196, 04/2215, 05/1209:
Considered, 96/2673, 98/2106, 99/2030, 99/2149, 01/2253, 03/1246,
07/1320: *Explained,* 99/2111

Malik v Central Criminal Court see R. (on the application of Malik) v Central Criminal Court

Malisiewicz-Gasior v Poland (43797/98) (2007) 45 E.H.R.R. 21, ECHR

Malkins Nominees Ltd v Societe Financiere Mirelis SA (Damages) [2006] EWHC 2132 (Ch); [2007] 1 P. & C.R. DG16, Ch D

Mall Corporate Events Ltd, Re see Cohen v Davis

Maloco v Littlewoods Organisation Ltd; *joined case* Smith v Littlewoods Organisation Ltd [1987] A.C. 241; [1987] 2 W.L.R. 480; [1987] 1 All E.R. 710; 1987 S.C. (H.L.) 37; 1987 S.L.T. 425; 1987 S.C.L.R. 489; (1987) 84 L.S.G. 905; (1987) 137 N.L.J. 149; (1987) 131 S.J. 226, HL; affirming 1986 S.L.T. 272, IH (1 Div); reversing 1982 S.L.T. 267, OH . . . . *Digested, 87/***4737**:
Applied, 95/3668, 04/2711: *Considered,* 88/2019, 93/2934, 94/3365,
96/1162, 98/4037: *Distinguished,* 90/250, 96/3699: *Followed,* 07/5419:
Not followed, 85/4437

Malone v United Kingdom (8691/79) see Malone v United Kingdom (A/82)

Malone v United Kingdom (A/82); *sub nom* Malone v United Kingdom (8691/79) (1985) 7 E.H.R.R. 14, ECHR (1983) 5 E.H.R.R. 385, Eur Comm HR . . . . *Applied,* 98/3106,
00/3252, 07/2241: *Considered,* 00/921, 01/3576: *Distinguished,* 95/941

Man Nutzfahrzeuge AG v Ernst & Young see Man Nutzfahrzeuge AG v Freightliner Ltd

Man Nutzfahrzeuge AG v Freightliner Ltd; *sub nom* Man Nutzfahrzeuge AG v Ernst & Young [2007] EWCA Civ 910; [2007] B.C.C. 986; [2007] 2 C.L.C. 455; (2007) 104(37) L.S.G. 35; (2007) 151 S.J.L.B. 1229, CA (Civ Div); affirming [2005] EWHC 2347 (Comm), QBD (Comm)

MAN/Provision of product specific data (T1242/04) [2007] E.P.O.R. 45, EPO (Technical Bd App) . . . . *Applied,* 07/2630

MAN/Transfer of Opposition (G04/88) [1990] E.P.O.R. 1, EPO (Enlarged Bd App) . . . *Applied,* 07/2611

Manches LLP v Freer [2006] EWHC 991; (2007) 151 S.J.L.B. 24, QBD

Manchester City Council v Falcon Outdoor (North) Ltd [2007] P.A.D. 52, Planning Inspector

Manchester City Council v Romano; *joined case* Manchester City Council v Samari [2004] EWCA Civ 834; [2005] 1 W.L.R. 2775; [2005] 4 All E.R. 21; [2004] H.L.R. 47; [2005] B.L.G.R. 282; (2005) 83 B.M.L.R. 175; [2005] L. & T.R. 13; (2004) 101(27) L.S.G. 32; (2004) 148 S.J.L.B. 824; [2004] N.P.C. 106; *Times*, July 27, 2004, CA (Civ Div) . . . . *Digested, 04/***2532**:
Distinguished, 07/2716, 07/2765

Manchester City Council v Samari see Manchester City Council v Romano

Mandrake Associates Ltd v Balanus Ltd; *sub nom* Mandrake Holdings Ltd (aka Plusnet Ltd) v Balanus Ltd (formerly Countrywide Assured Group Plc) [2006] EWCA Civ 1716; [2007] Pens. L.R. 43, CA (Civ Div); affirming [2006] EWHC 354 (Ch), Ch D . . . . *Digested,* 07/**805**

Mandrake Holdings Ltd (aka Plusnet Ltd) v Balanus Ltd (formerly Countrywide Assured Group Plc) see Mandrake Associates Ltd v Balanus Ltd

Manfredi v Lloyd Adriatico Assicurazioni SpA (C-295/04); *joined cases* Cannito v Fondiaria Sai SpA (C-296/04); Tricarico v Assitalia SpA (C-297/04); Murgulo v Assitalia SpA (C-298/04) [2007] Bus. L.R. 188; [2007] All E.R. (EC) 27; [2006] E.C.R. I-6619; [2007] R.T.R. 7; [2006] 5 C.M.L.R. 17, ECJ (3rd Chamber) . . . . *Digested,* 07/**622**: *Applied,* 07/626

Mango Personnel Ltd v Revenue and Customs Commissioners [2007] S.T.I. 379, V&DTr (London)

Mangold v Helm (C-144/04) [2006] All E.R. (EC) 383; [2005] E.C.R. I-9981; [2006] 1 C.M.L.R. 43; [2006] C.E.C. 372; [2006] I.R.L.R. 143, ECJ . . . . *Considered,* 07/1332, 07/1399, 07/1420, 07/1583

Manley v Commissioner of Police of the Metropolis [2006] EWCA Civ 879; [2006] Po. L.R. 117; (2006) 150 S.J.L.B. 889, CA (Civ Div) . . . . *Digested,* 07/**1051**

Mann v Brodie (1884-85) L.R. 10 App. Cas. 378, HL . . . . *Considered,* 07/3421

Mann v Davies (Unreported, November 15, 2006), CC (Pontefract) [*Ex rel.* Roger Quickfall, Barrister, Park Lane Chambers, 19 Westgate, Leeds] . . . . *Digested,* 07/**4199**

Mannai Investment Co Ltd v Eagle Star Life Assurance Co Ltd [1997] A.C. 749; [1997] 2 W.L.R. 945; [1997] 3 All E.R. 352; [1997] C.L.C. 1124; [1997] 1 E.G.L.R. 57; [1997] 24 E.G. 122; [1997] 25 E.G. 138; (1997) 16 Tr. L.R. 432; [1997] E.G. 82 (C.S.); (1997) 94(30) L.S.G. 30; (1997) 147 N.L.J. 846; (1997) 141 S.J.L.B. 130; [1997] N.P.C. 81; *Times,* May 26, 1997, HL; reversing [1995] 1 W.L.R. 1508; [1996] 1 All E.R. 55; (1996) 71 P. & C.R. 129; [1996] 1 E.G.L.R. 69; [1996] 06 E.G. 140; [1995] E.G. 124 (C.S.); (1995) 139 S.J.L.B. 179; [1995] N.P.C. 117; *Times,* July 19, 1995, CA (Civ Div) . . . . *Digested,* 97/**3256**: *Applied,* 98/3598, 00/5612, 01/4156, 01/4182, 02/3008, 03/2723, 04/670, 04/2243, 04/2497, 05/523, 05/2646, 06/284, 07/2728: *Considered,* 03/2758, 05/475, 07/2754: *Distinguished,* 98/3033, 98/3608, 00/3910, 04/2488: *Explained,* 06/2703: *Followed,* 98/3614, 00/3885, 00/4421

Manninen, Re (C-319/02) see Proceedings brought by Manninen (C-319/02)

Manninen v Finland (C-319/02) see Proceedings brought by Manninen (C-319/02)

Manning v AIG Europe UK Ltd; *sub nom* SSSL Realisations (2002) Ltd (formerly Save Service Stations Ltd) (In Liquidation), Re; Save Group Plc (In Liquidation), Re; Squires v AIG Europe UK Ltd; *joined case* Robinson v AIG Europe UK Ltd [2006] EWCA Civ 7; [2006] Ch. 610; [2006] 2 W.L.R. 1369; [2006] B.C.C. 233; [2007] 1 B.C.L.C. 29; [2006] B.P.I.R. 457; [2006] W.T.L.R. 705; *Times,* January 20, 2006, CA (Civ Div); affirming [2004] EWHC 1760 (Ch); [2005] 1 B.C.L.C. 1; [2004] B.P.I.R. 1334, Ch D (Companies Ct) . . . . *Digested,* 06/**2359**

Mansfield DC v Langridge B5/2007/2500, CA (Civ Div); reversing [2007] EWHC 3152 (QB); (2007) 104(39) L.S.G. 31, QBD

Mansworth (Inspector of Taxes) v Jelley [2002] EWCA Civ 1829; [2003] S.T.C. 53; 75 T.C. 1; [2003] B.T.C. 3; [2002] S.T.I. 1808; (2003) 100(10) L.S.G. 29; *Times,* December 20, 2002, CA (Civ Div); affirming [2002] EWHC 442 (Ch); [2002] S.T.C. 1013; [2002] B.T.C. 270; [2002] S.T.I. 353; (2002) 99(18) L.S.G. 37; *Times,* April 24, 2002, Ch D . . . . *Digested,* 03/**4161**: *Considered,* 07/3990

MANTIS WILDLIFE/Wide angle (T1033/04) [2007] E.P.O.R. 22, EPO (Technical Bd App)   *Digested,* 07/**2572**

Mantovanelli v France (1997) 24 E.H.R.R. 370, ECHR. . . . . *Digested,* 98/**3126**: *Applied,* 03/1522: *Distinguished,* 07/2213

Marangopoulos Foundation for Human Rights (MFHR) v Greece (30/2005) (2007) 45 E.H.R.R. SE11, ECHR

Maranowska v Richardson [2007] EWHC 1264 (QB); (2007) 151 S.J.L.B. 745, QBD

Marca Mode CV v Adidas AG (C-425/98) [2000] All E.R. (EC) 694; [2000] E.C.R. I-4861; [2000] 2 C.M.L.R. 1061; [2000] C.E.C. 395; [2000] E.T.M.R. 723, ECJ (6th Chamber) . . . . *Digested,* 00/**3701**: *Applied,* 07/2641

Marcan Shipping (London) Ltd v Kefalas [2007] EWCA Civ 463; [2007] 1 W.L.R. 1864; [2007] 3 All E.R. 365; [2007] C.P. Rep. 41; [2007] 1 C.L.C. 785; (2007) 104(22) L.S.G. 23, CA (Civ Div)

Marcic v Thames Water Utilities Ltd; *sub nom* Thames Water Utilities Ltd v Marcic
[2003] UKHL 66; [2004] 2 A.C. 42; [2003] 3 W.L.R. 1603; [2004] 1 All E.R.
135; [2004] B.L.R. 1; 91 Con. L.R. 1; [2004] Env. L.R. 25; [2004] H.R.L.R. 10;
[2004] U.K.H.R.R. 253; [2003] 50 E.G. 95 (C.S.); (2004) 101 (4) L.S.G. 32;
(2003) 153 N.L.J. 1869; (2003) 147 S.J.L.B. 1429; [2003] N.P.C. 150; *Times,*
December 5, 2003; *Independent,* December 9, 2003, HL; reversing [2002]
EWCA Civ 64; [2002] Q.B. 929; [2002] 2 W.L.R. 932; [2002] 2 All E.R. 55;
[2002] B.L.R. 174; [2002] T.C.L.R. 15; 81 Con. L.R. 193; [2002] Env. L.R. 32;
[2003] E.H.L.R. 2; [2002] H.R.L.R. 22; [2002] U.K.H.R.R. 1041; (2002) 18
Const. L.J. 152; [2002] 7 E.G. 122 (C.S.); (2002) 99 (12) L.S.G. 34; (2002) 146
S.J.L.B. 51; [2002] N.P.C. 20; *Times,* February 14, 2002; *Independent,* February
12, 2002, CA (Civ Div); reversing in part [2001] 3 All E.R. 698; (2001) 3
T.C.L.R. 28; 77 Con. L.R. 42; [2002] Env. L.R. 6; [2001] H.R.L.R. 52; [2001] 3
E.G.L.R. 111; [2001] N.P.C. 95; [2001] E.H.L.R. Dig. 6; *Independent,* July 9,
2001, QBD (TCC) . . . . *Digested,* 04/**2763**:
　　　　　　　　　Applied, 03/3038, 05/2893, 07/2961: *Considered,* 06/1482, 07/3990,
　　　　　　　　　07/4276: *Distinguished,* 04/1373, 04/2756, 06/4417, 07/3973:
　　　　　　　　　　　　　　　　　　　　　　　Previous proceedings, 01/1525
Marckx v Belgium (A/31) (1979-80) 2 E.H.R.R. 330, ECHR . . . . *Applied,* 00/6142,
　　　　　　　　　02/3079, 05/2126, 07/2221: *Followed,* 02/1700
Marconi Communications International Ltd v PT Pan Indonesia Bank TBK [2005]
EWCA Civ 422; [2005] 2 All E.R. (Comm) 325; [2007] 2 Lloyd's Rep. 72;
Times, May 18, 2005, CA (Civ Div); affirming [2004] EWHC 129 (Comm);
[2004] 1 Lloyd's Rep. 594; [2004] 2 C.L.C. 570, QBD (Comm) . . . . *Digested,* 05/**628**
Marcos Roman Parra v Commission of the European Communities (T-117/01) [2002]
E.C.R. IA-27, CFI . . . . *Applied,* 07/1645
Maredelanto Compania Naviera SA v Bergbau-Handel GmbH (The Mihalis Angelos)
[1971] 1 Q.B. 164; [1970] 3 W.L.R. 601; [1970] 3 All E.R. 125; [1970] 2 Lloyd's
Rep. 43; (1970) 114 S.J. 548, CA (Civ Div); reversing [1970] 2 W.L.R. 907;
[1970] 1 All E.R. 673; [1970] 1 Lloyd's Rep. 118, QBD (Comm) . . . . *Digested,* 70/**357**:
　　　　　　　　　Considered, 71/1838, 76/2547, 07/3816: *Followed,* 98/811, 00/4702
Maridive & Oil Services SAE v CNA Insurance Co (Europe) Ltd [2002] EWCA Civ 369;
[2002] 1 All E.R. (Comm) 653; [2002] 2 Lloyd's Rep. 9; [2002] C.P. Rep. 45;
[2002] C.L.C. 972, CA (Civ Div) . . . . *Digested,* 02/**486**:
　　　　　　　　　　　　　　　　　　　　　　　Applied, 07/2920
Marina Offshore Pte Ltd v China Insurance Co (Singapore) Pte Ltd [2006] SGCA 28;
[2007] 1 Lloyd's Rep. 66; [2007] Lloyd's Rep. I.R. 383, CA (Sing) . . . . *Digested,* 07/**2491**
Marine Contractors Inc v Shell Petroleum Development Co of Nigeria Ltd [1984] 2
Lloyd's Rep. 77; 27 B.L.R. 127; (1984) 81 L.S.G. 1044, CA (Civ Div); affirming
[1983] Com. L.R. 251, QBD . . . . *Digested,* 84/**105**:
　　　　　　　　　　　　　　Applied, 00/217: *Considered,* 07/233
Marinovich v General Medical Council [2002] UKPC 36, PC (UK) . . . . *Applied,* 07/1943
Marios Chippery, Re see Georgiou (t/a Marios Chippery) v Customs and Excise
Commissioners
Marius Pedersen A/S v KODA [2007] E.C.D.R. 15, HR (DK)
Mark One (Oxford Street) Plc, Re [1999] 1 W.L.R. 1445; [1999] 1 All E.R. 608; [1998] B.C.C.
984; [2000] 1 B.C.L.C. 462, Ch D (Companies Ct) . . . . *Digested,* 99/**3349**:
　　　　　　　　　Applied, 07/2392: *Considered,* 01/3708, 02/2651, 07/2395
Markel International Co Ltd v Craft (The Norseman) [2006] EWHC 3150 (Comm);
[2007] Lloyd's Rep. I.R. 403, QBD (Comm)
Markem Corp v Zipher Ltd; *joined case* Markem Technologies Ltd v Buckby [2005]
EWCA Civ 267; [2005] R.P.C. 31; (2005) 28(6) I.P.D. 28042, CA (Civ Div);
reversing (2005) 28(5) I.P.D. 28041, Ch D (Patents Ct) . . . . *Digested,* 05/**2448**:
　　　　　　　　　Applied, 06/2522: *Overruled,* 07/2557: *Previous proceedings,* 04/363,
　　　　　　　　　　　　　　　　　　　　　　　　04/2283, 05/2447
Markem Technologies Ltd v Buckby see Markem Corp v Zipher Ltd
Market Tools Inc v Optimus Telecomunicacoes SA (R 253/2006-2) [2007] E.T.M.R. 74,
OHIM (2nd Bd App)
Marketing Services Worldwide (UK) Ltd, Re see Alpha Club (UK) Ltd, Re
Markham v Karsten [2007] EWHC 1509 (Ch); [2007] B.P.I.R. 1109; (2007-08) 10
I.T.E.L.R. 475, Ch D . . . . *Digested,* 07/**2415**
Markinson v Information Commissioner [2007] R.V.R. 94, IT. . . . . *Digested,* 07/**1485**
Markovic v Italy (1398/03) (2007) 44 E.H.R.R. 52; 22 B.H.R.C. 641, ECHR . . . . *Digested,* 07/**2212**
Marks & Spencer Plc v Halsey (Inspector of Taxes) (C-446/03) [2006] Ch. 184;
[2006] 2 W.L.R. 250; [2006] All E.R. (EC) 255; [2006] S.T.C. 237; [2005]
E.C.R. I-10837; [2006] 1 C.M.L.R. 18; [2006] C.E.C. 299; [2006] B.T.C. 318; 8
I.T.L. Rep. 358; [2006] S.T.I. 41; *Times,* December 15, 2005, ECJ . . . . *Digested,* 06/**4157**:
　　　　　　　　　Considered, 06/4123, 07/3971: *Subsequent proceedings,* 06/4156

Marks & Spencer Plc *v* Halsey (Inspector of Taxes); *sub nom* Halsey (Inspector of Taxes) *v* Marks & Spencer Plc [2007] EWCA Civ 117; [2007] 2 C.M.L.R. 21; [2007] Eu. L.R. 577; [2007] B.T.C. 204; 9 I.T.L. Rep. 739; [2007] S.T.I. 410; (2007) 151 S.J.L.B. 300; *Times*, February 22, 2007, CA (Civ Div); affirming in part [2006] EWHC 811 (Ch); [2006] S.T.C. 1235; [2006] 3 C.M.L.R. 8; [2006] B.T.C. 346; 8 I.T.L. Rep. 1012; [2006] S.T.I. 1352, Ch D; reversing in part [2003] Eu. L.R. 46; [2003] S.T.C. (S.C.D.) 70; 5 I.T.L. Rep. 536; [2003] S.T.I. 68, Sp Comm . . . . *Digested,* 06/**4156**:
Previous proceedings, 06/4157: *Subsequent proceedings,* 06/4157
Marks & Spencer Plc *v* One in a Million Ltd see British Telecommunications Plc *v* One in a Million Ltd
Marlborough (West End) Ltd *v* Wilks Head & Eve (Unreported, December 20, 1996) . . *Considered,* 07/2757:
Followed, 05/3434
Marleasing SA *v* La Comercial Internacional de Alimentacion SA (C-106/89) [1990] E.C.R. I-4135; [1993] B.C.C. 421; [1992] 1 C.M.L.R. 305, ECJ (6th Chamber) . *Applied,* 97/2383, 00/5520, 02/4402, 07/27, 07/1370: *Considered,* 03/2647, 05/4411, 06/4484, 07/2496: *Distinguished,* 95/2938
Marsh *v* DPP; *sub nom* R. (on the application of Marsh) *v* DPP [2006] EWHC 1525 (Admin); [2007] Crim. L.R. 162, QBD (Admin)
Marsh *v* Revenue and Customs Commissioners [2007] S.T.I. 1701, V&DTr (London)
Marshall *v* London Passenger Transport Board [1936] 3 All E.R. 83, CA . . . . *Considered,* 07/369:
Distinguished, 47-51/1492, 47-51/6868, 47-51/7936, 53/1992, 53/2877, 62/2489
Marshall *v* Maggs see Collier *v* Williams
Marshall Motor Group Ltd *v* Revenue and Customs Commissioners [2007] S.T.I. 372, V&DTr
Marshall (Inspector of Taxes) *v* Kerr [1995] 1 A.C. 148; [1994] 3 W.L.R. 299; [1994] 3 All E.R. 106; [1994] S.T.C. 638; 67 T.C. 81; (1994) 91(30) L.S.G. 32; (1994) 138 S.J.L.B. 155; *Times*, July 5, 1994; *Independent*, July 18, 1994, HL; reversing [1993] S.T.C. 360; 67 T.C. 73; [1993] S.T.I. 353; (1993) 90(14) L.S.G. 45; *Times*, March 8, 1993; *Independent*, April 26, 1993, CA (Civ Div); reversing [1991] S.T.C. 686; 67 T.C. 56; (1992) 89(3) L.S.G. 33; *Times*, November 13, 1991; *Independent*, December 2, 1991, Ch D . . . . *Digested,* 94/**359**:
Applied, 06/4117: *Considered,* 96/438, 99/4704, 07/3988:
Followed, 04/2733: *Referred to,* 95/529
Marston Thompson & Evershed Plc *v* Benn [2007] W.T.L.R. 315, Ch D . . . . *Digested,* 98/**4875**
Martin *v* Childs [2002] EWCA Civ 283, CA (Civ Div) . . . . *Considered,* 07/3400
Martin *v* Lancehawk Ltd (t/a European Telecom Solutions) UKEAT/0525/ILB, EAT . . . *Applied,* 07/1402:
Approved, 05/1221
Martin *v* Medina Housing Association Ltd [2006] EWCA Civ 367; [2007] 1 W.L.R. 1965; [2007] 1 All E.R. 813; [2006] H.L.R. 40; [2006] 15 E.G. 134 (C.S.); [2006] N.P.C. 42; *Times*, April 20, 2006, CA (Civ Div) . . . . *Digested,* 06/**2070**
Martin *v* United Kingdom (40426/98) (2007) 44 E.H.R.R. 31; *Times*, November 27, 2006, ECHR . . . . *Digested,* 07/**2216**
Martin-Sklan *v* White [2006] EWHC 3313 (Ch); [2007] B.P.I.R. 76, Ch D
Martine *v* South East Kent HA, *Times*, March 8, 1993, CA (Civ Div) . . . . *Digested,* 93/**2947**:
Applied, 07/2937
Martinie *v* France (58675/00) (2007) 45 E.H.R.R. 15, ECHR (Grand Chamber)
Maryland Estates Ltd *v* Bar-Joseph see Maryland Estates Ltd *v* Joseph
Maryland Estates Ltd *v* Joseph; *sub nom* Maryland Estates Ltd *v* Bar-Joseph [1999] 1 W.L.R. 83; [1998] 3 All E.R. 193; (1999) 31 H.L.R. 269; (1999) 77 P. & C.R. 150; [1998] L. & T.R. 105; [1998] 2 E.G.L.R. 47; [1998] 27 E.G. 142; [1998] E.G. 66 (C.S.); (1998) 95(17) L.S.G. 33; (1998) 95(21) L.S.G. 36; (1998) 142 S.J.L.B. 157; [1998] N.P.C. 70; *Times*, May 6, 1998; *Independent*, May 1, 1998, CA (Civ Div); affirming [1997] 2 E.G.L.R. 96; [1997] 46 E.G. 155; (1997) 147 N.L.J. 1386, CC (Central London) . . . . *Digested,* 98/**3634**:
Considered, 07/2725: *Distinguished,* 04/2500
Masdar (UK) Ltd *v* Commission of the European Communities (T-333/03) [2007] 2 All E.R. (Comm) 261, CFI
Mashreqbank psc *v* Deputy Director of Income Tax 9 I.T.L. Rep. 1062, ITAT (Ind)
Maslov *v* Austria (1638/03) [2007] 1 F.C.R. 707, ECHR . . . . *Digested,* 07/**2262**
Masri *v* Consolidated Contractors International Co SAL [2007] EWCA Civ 688; [2007] 2 C.L.C. 49, CA (Civ Div); reversing [2006] EWHC 1931 (Comm), QBD (Comm)
Massachusetts Institute of Technology, Re (C-431/04) see Proceedings brought by Massachusetts Institute of Technology (C-431/04)
Massey *v* UNIFI see UNIFI *v* Massey
Mast Electrical Services *v* Kendall Cross Holdings Ltd [2007] EWHC 1296 (TCC); [2007] N.P.C. 70, QBD (TCC)
Mastercard UK Members Forum Ltd *v* Office of Fair Trading (Costs) [2006] CAT 15; [2006] Comp. A.R. 607, CAT . . . . *Digested,* 07/**393**
Mastercard UK Members Forum Ltd *v* Office of Fair Trading (Nature of Decision) [2006] CAT 10; [2006] Comp. A.R. 585, CAT . . . . *Digested,* 07/**601**

Mastercard UK Members Forum Ltd v Office of Fair Trading (Setting Aside Decision)
[2006] CAT 14; [2006] Comp. A.R. 595, CAT . . . . *Digested*, 07/**613**
Mastercigars Direct Ltd v Hunters & Frankau Ltd; *joined case* Corporacion Habanos SA
v Mastercigars Direct Ltd [2007] EWCA Civ 176; [2007] E.T.M.R. 44; [2007]
R.P.C. 24; (2007) 30(4) I.P.D. 30026; (2007) 104(12) L.S.G. 32, CA (Civ Div);
reversing [2006] EWHC 410 (Ch); [2006] R.P.C. 32, Ch D . . . . *Digested*, 06/**2581**
Mastercigars Direct Ltd v Withers LLP [2007] EWHC 2733 (Ch); (2007) 157 N.L.J.
1731, Ch D
Masterfoods v Wilson [2007] I.C.R. 370, EAT . . . . *Digested*, 07/**1422**
Masterman-Lister v Brutton & Co see Masterman-Lister v Jewell
Masterman-Lister v Jewell; *joined case* Masterman-Lister v Brutton & Co [2002]
EWCA Civ 1889; [2003] 1 W.L.R. 1511; [2003] 3 All E.R. 162; [2003] C.P. Rep.
29; (2004) 7 C.C.L. Rep. 5; [2003] P.I.Q.R. P20; [2003] Lloyd's Rep. Med.
244; (2003) 73 B.M.L.R. 1; [2003] M.H.L.R. 166; [2003] W.T.L.R. 259; (2003)
147 S.J.L.B. 60; *Times*, December 28, 2002, CA (Civ Div); affirming [2002]
EWHC 417 (QB); [2002] Lloyd's Rep. Med. 239; [2002] M.H.L.R. 161; [2002]
W.T.L.R. 563, QBD . . . . *Digested*, 03/**311**:
Applied, 06/482, 06/483: *Considered*, 03/4492, 07/484: *Followed*, 05/473
Masterman's Application see Masterman's Design
Masterman's Design; *sub nom* Masterman's Application [1991] R.P.C. 89; *Times*,
December 19, 1990, RDAT . . . . *Digested*, 92/**3312**:
Applied, 02/2920: *Considered*, 07/2681
Matalan Retail Ltd v Renfrewshire Valuation Joint Board Assessor [2007] CSIH 40;
2007 S.C. 663; [2007] R.A. 339; 2007 G.W.D. 18-329, LVAC
Matalulu v DPP of Fiji [2003] 4 L.R.C. 712. . . . . *Applied*, 07/55
Mateos v Instituto Nacional de la Seguridad Social (INSS) (C-32/96) see Arjona v
Instituto Nacional de la Seguridad Social (INSS) (C-31/96)
Matratzen Concord GmbH v Office for Harmonisation in the Internal Market (Trade
Marks and Designs) (OHIM) (C-3/03 P) [2004] E.C.R. I-3657, ECJ . . . . *Applied*, 07/1560:
Considered, 06/2585
MATSUSHITA/Transmission system (T679/04) [2007] E.P.O.R. 18, EPO (Technical Bd
App)
Mattenklott v Germany (Admissibility) (41092/06) (2007) 44 E.H.R.R. SE12, ECHR
Mattern v Ministre du Travail et de l'Emploi (C-10/05) [2006] E.C.R. I-3145; [2006] 2
C.M.L.R. 42; [2006] Imm. A.R. 471, ECJ (1st Chamber) . . . . *Digested*, 07/**1629**
Matthews v Associated Portland Cement Manufacturers (1978) Ltd see Fairchild v
Glenhaven Funeral Services Ltd (t/a GH Dovener & Son)
Matthews v British Uralite Plc see Fairchild v Glenhaven Funeral Services Ltd (t/a GH
Dovener & Son)
Matthews v Metal Improvements Co Inc [2007] EWCA Civ 215; [2007] C.P. Rep. 27;
(2007) 151 S.J.L.B. 396, CA (Civ Div)
Matthews v United Kingdom (24833/94) (1999) 28 E.H.R.R. 361; 5 B.H.R.C. 686;
Times, March 3, 1999, ECHR (1996) 22 E.H.R.R. CD175, Eur Comm HR . . . . . . *Digested*, 99/**3103**:
Considered, 07/1553
Mattu v University Hospitals Coventry and Warwickshire NHS Trust [2006] EWHC
1774 (QB); [2007] LS Law Medical 122, QBD. . . . . *Digested*, 07/**458**
Maund v Penwith DC [1984] I.C.R. 143; [1984] I.R.L.R. 24; (1984) 134 N.L.J. 147,
CA (Civ Div); affirming [1982] I.C.R. 732, EAT . . . . *Digested*, 84/**1300**:
Applied, 07/1433
Mauri v Ministero della Giustizia (C250/03 R) [2005] E.C.R. I-1267; [2005] 4
C.M.L.R. 11, ECJ (2nd Chamber) . . . . *Digested*, 05/**1429**:
Applied, 07/617
Maurice v France (11810/03) [2005] 3 F.C.R. 365; (2006) 42 E.H.R.R. 42, ECHR
(Grand Chamber) . . . . *Distinguished*, 07/2636
Maurice v Hollow-Ware Products Ltd; *sub nom* Maurice v Holloware Products [2005]
EWHC 815 (Ch); [2005] 2 E.G.L.R. 71; [2005] 26 E.G. 132; (2005) 102(19)
L.S.G. 34; *Times*, March 31, 2005, Ch D . . . . *Digested*, 05/**2666**:
Overruled, 07/2753
Maurice v Holloware Products see Maurice v Hollow-Ware Products Ltd
Maurice Investments Ltd v Lincoln Insurance Services Ltd [2006] EWHC 376 (Ch);
[2007] 1 P. & C.R. 14, Ch D . . . . *Digested*, 07/**2728**
Mauritius v Hurnam; *sub nom* DPP of Mauritius v Hurnam [2007] UKPC 24; [2007] 1
W.L.R. 1582, PC (Mau) . . . . *Digested*, 07/**873**
Mauritius v Khoyratty [2006] UKPC 13; [2007] 1 A.C. 80; [2006] 2 W.L.R. 1330, PC
(Mau) . . . . *Digested*, 06/**656**:
MAX-PLANCK/BDP1 phosphatase (T870/04) [2006] E.P.O.R. 14, EPO (Legal Bd App) *Digested*, 06/**2482**:
Considered, 07/2583
Maybeck LLP v Revenue and Customs Commissioners [2007] S.T.I. 382, V&DTr
(Manchester)
Mayeka v Belgium (13178/03) [2007] 1 F.L.R. 1726; [2006] 3 F.C.R. 637; [2007]
Fam. Law 982, ECHR. . . . . *Digested*, 07/**2202**
Mayer Parry Recycling Ltd v Environment Agency [1999] 1 C.M.L.R. 963; [1999] Env.
L.R. 489; (1999) 96(6) L.S.G. 32; *Times*, December 3, 1998, Ch D . . . . *Digested*, 99/**2207**:
Considered, 01/573, 02/1520, 05/1362, 07/1518: *Not applied*, 01/2413

Mayflower Theatre Trust Ltd *v* Revenue and Customs Commissioners [2007] EWCA Civ 116; [2007] S.T.C. 880; [2007] B.T.C. 5221; [2007] B.V.C. 190; [2007] S.T.I. 413; (2007) 104(10) L.S.G. 30; (2007) 151 S.J.L.B. 294; [2007] N.P.C. 24, CA (Civ Div); affirming [2006] EWHC 706 (Ch); [2006] S.T.C. 1607; [2007] B.T.C. 5018; [2007] B.V.C. 41; [2006] S.T.I. 1150, Ch D; reversing [2006] B.V.C. 2199; [2006] S.T.I. 279, V&DTr (London) . . . . *Digested,* 06/**4494**
Mayhew-Lewis *v* Westminster Scaffolding Group Plc see Norglen Ltd (In Liquidation) *v* Reeds Rains Prudential Ltd
Maynards Confectionery BV *v* Societe des Produits Nestle SA [2007] E.T.M.R. 40, PO (Irl)
Mayr-melnhof Kartongesellschaft mbh *v* Commission of the European Communities (T347/94) [1998] E.C.R. II-1751, CFI . . . . *Applied,* 07/599:
Followed, 01/768, 05/554, 07/610
MB, Re see Secretary of State for the Home Department *v* MB
MB *v* DPP see Bucknell *v* DPP
MB *v* KB; *sub nom* B *v* B [2007] EWHC 789 (Fam); [2007] 2 F.L.R. 586; [2007] Fam. Law 801, Fam Div . . . . *Digested,* 07/**1685**
MB (Bangladesh) *v* Secretary of State for the Home Department; *sub nom* MB (Para 317: In Country Applications: Bangladesh), Re [2006] UKAIT 91; [2007] Imm. A.R. 389; [2007] I.N.L.R. 507, AIT . . . . *Digested,* 07/**2350**
MB (Libya) *v* Secretary of State for the Home Department see FP (Iran) *v* Secretary of State for the Home Department
MB (Para 317: In Country Applications: Bangladesh), Re see MB (Bangladesh) *v* Secretary of State for the Home Department
Mbasogo *v* Logo Ltd (No.1) [2006] EWCA Civ 1370; [2007] Q.B. 846; [2007] 2 W.L.R. 1062; *Times,* October 27, 2006; *Independent,* October 26, 2006, CA (Civ Div); affirming [2005] EWHC 2034 (QB); (2005) 102(39) L.S.G. 32, QBD . . . *Digested,* 07/**4200**:
Considered, 07/4298
MBNA Europe Bank Ltd *v* Revenue and Customs Commissioners [2006] EWHC 2326 (Ch); [2006] S.T.C. 2089; [2006] B.T.C. 5808; [2007] B.V.C. 3; [2006] S.T.I. 2234; (2006) 103(39) L.S.G. 34; (2006) 150 S.J.L.B. 1293, Ch D; reversing in part [2006] B.V.C. 2395; [2006] S.T.I. 1362, V&DTr . . . . *Digested,* 07/**4333**:
Distinguished, 06/4454
MCAA, Re (COMP/E-1/.37.773) [2007] C.E.C. 2003, CEC
MD (Iran) *v* Secretary of State for the Home Department see BR (Iran) *v* Secretary of State for the Home Department
MDA Investment Management Ltd (No.2), Re; *sub nom* Whalley *v* Doney (No.2) [2004] EWHC 42 (Ch); [2005] B.C.C. 783, Ch D . . . . *Digested,* 05/**531**:
Applied, 07/2429
Mea Corp, Re see Secretary of State for Trade and Industry *v* Aviss
Mead Corp *v* Riverwood Multiple Packaging Division of Riverwood International Corp [1997] F.S.R. 484; (1997) 20(8) I.P.D. 20072; *Times,* March 28, 1997, Ch D . . *Digested,* 97/**3899**:
Applied, 07/2548: *Followed,* 00/3682: *Referred to,* 99/3493
Meadow *v* General Medical Council; *sub nom* General Medical Council *v* Meadow [2006] EWCA Civ 1390; [2007] Q.B. 462; [2007] 2 W.L.R. 286; [2007] 1 All E.R. 1; [2007] I.C.R. 701; [2007] 1 F.L.R. 1398; [2006] 3 F.C.R. 447; [2007] LS Law Medical 1; (2006) 92 B.M.L.R. 51; [2007] Fam. Law 214; [2006] 44 E.G. 196 (C.S.); (2006) 103(43) L.S.G. 28; (2006) 156 N.L.J. 1686; *Times,* October 31, 2006; *Independent,* October 31, 2006, CA (Civ Div); reversing in part [2006] EWHC 146 (Admin); [2006] 1 W.L.R. 1452; [2006] 2 All E.R. 329; [2006] 1 F.L.R. 1161; [2006] 2 F.C.R. 777; [2006] Lloyd's Rep. Med. 233; (2006) 89 B.M.L.R. 143; [2006] A.C.D. 43; [2006] Fam. Law 354; [2006] 9 E.G. 182 (C.S.); (2006) 156 N.L.J. 328; [2006] N.P.C. 19; *Times,* February 22, 2006; *Independent,* February 22, 2006, QBD (Admin) . . . . *Digested,* 07/**340**
Mears *v* RG Carter Ltd see Grieves *v* FT Everard & Sons Ltd
Meca-Medina *v* Commission of the European Communities (C-519/04 P) [2006] All E.R. (EC) 1057; [2006] E.C.R. I-6991; [2006] 5 C.M.L.R. 18, ECJ (3rd Chamber) . . . . *Digested,* 07/**623**:
Previous proceedings, 05/3963
Meca-Medina *v* Commission of the European Communities (T313/02) [2004] E.C.R. II-3291; [2004] 3 C.M.L.R. 60; [2005] C.E.C. 176; *Times,* October 25, 2004, CFI (4th Chamber) . . . . *Digested,* 05/**3963**:
Considered, 06/2459: *Subsequent proceedings,* 07/623
MEDI-PHYSICS/Treatment by surgery (T992/03) [2007] E.P.O.R. 32, EPO (Technical Bd App)
Medical Defence Union Ltd *v* Department of Trade [1980] Ch. 82; [1979] 2 W.L.R. 686; [1979] 2 All E.R. 421; [1979] 1 Lloyd's Rep. 499; [1979] E.C.C. 101; (1979) 123 S.J. 338, Ch D . . . . *Digested,* 79/**1505**:
Considered, 07/1976: *Distinguished,* 99/3411
Medical House Plc *v* Revenue and Customs Commissioners [2007] 2 C.M.L.R. 8; [2007] S.T.I. 378, V&DTr (Manchester) . . . . *Digested,* 07/**4314**
Medicaments and Related Classes of Goods (No.2), Re see Director General of Fair Trading *v* Proprietary Association of Great Britain

Medina Property Ltd v Windsor and Maidenhead RLBC [2007] P.A.D. 59, Planning Inspector

Medipac-Kazantzidis AE v Venizelio-Pananio (PESY KRITIS) (C-6/05) [2007] 3 C.M.L.R. 16, ECJ (1st Chamber)

Medway Oil and Storage Co Ltd v Continental Contractors Ltd; sub nom Continental Contractors Ltd v Medway Oil and Storage Co Ltd [1929] A.C. 88, HL; reversing [1928] 1 K.B. 238, CA . . . . *Applied*, 80/1659,
07/388: *Considered*, 87/2963, 95/4009

Meek v Birmingham DC [1987] I.R.L.R. 250, CA (Civ Div) . . . . *Digested*, 87/**1399**:
Applied, 03/1224, 06/1384, 06/4090, 07/1424: *Followed*, 05/1333

Megantic Services Ltd v Revenue and Customs Commissioners [2006] EWHC 3232 (Admin); [2007] B.T.C. 5653; [2007] B.V.C. 621, QBD (Admin) . . . . *Digested*, 07/**4312**

Megaro v Di Popolo Hotels Ltd [2007] EWCA Civ 309; [2007] 2 P. & C.R. 28, CA (Civ Div)

Meilicke v Finanzamt Bonn-Innenstadt (C-292/04) [2007] 2 C.M.L.R. 19; [2007] C.E.C. 689; 9 I.T.L. Rep. 834; [2007] S.T.I. 484, ECJ . . . . *Digested*, 07/**1600**

Mellors v Gibson see Gibson's Settlement Trusts, Re

Melnychuk v Ukraine (Admissibility) (28743/03) (Unreported, July 5, 2005), ECHR . . *Applied*, 07/2636

Melville Dundas Ltd (In Receivership) v George Wimpey UK Ltd [2007] UKHL 18; [2007] Bus. L.R. 1182; [2007] 1 W.L.R. 1136; [2007] 3 All E.R. 889; 2007 S.C. (H.L.) 116; 2007 S.L.T. 413; 2007 S.C.L.R. 429; [2007] B.L.R. 257; 112 Con. L.R. 1; [2007] C.I.L.L. 2469; (2007) 104(19) L.S.G. 25; (2007) 151 S.J.L.B. 571; 2007 G.W.D. 14-276; *Times*, May 8, 2007, HL; reversing 2006 S.C. 310; 2006 S.L.T. 95; 2006 S.C.L.R. 356; [2006] B.L.R. 164; 2006 G.W.D. 2-26, IH (Ex Div); reversing 2005 S.L.T. 24; 2005 S.C.L.R. 116, OH . . . . *Digested*, 06/**5149**

Melwood Units Pty v Commissioner of Main Roads [1979] A.C. 426; [1978] 3 W.L.R. 520; [1977] 1 All E.R. 161; (1979) 38 P. & C.R. 195; (1978) 122 S.J. 434, PC (Aus) . . . . *Digested*, 78/**269**:
Applied, 07/3389: *Considered*, 83/806

Meman v CIT (International Taxation) Mumbai; *joined case* Bhatia v CIT (International Taxation) Mumbai 9 I.T.L. Rep. 139, Advance Rulings (Ind)

Member of Executive Council for Education v Pillay 23 B.H.R.C. 475, Const Ct (SA)

Memory Corp Plc v Sidhu (No.1); sub nom Sidhu v Memory Corp Plc (No.1) [2000] 1 W.L.R. 1443; [2000] C.P.L.R. 171; [2000] F.S.R. 921; *Times*, February 15, 2000, CA (Civ Div); affirming (1999) 96(24) L.S.G. 38; *Times*, May 31, 1999, Ch D . . *Digested*, 00/**488**:
Applied, 07/465: *Considered*, 01/764, 06/446

Mendoza v Ghaidan see Ghaidan v Godin-Mendoza

Menesheva v Russia (59261/00) (2007) 44 E.H.R.R. 56, ECHR . . . . *Digested*, 07/**2203**

Mental Health Review Tribunal v Hempstock (1998) 39 B.M.L.R. 123; [1997] C.O.D. 443, QBD . . . . *Digested*, 98/**3894**:
Applied, 07/2909

Mentese v Turkey (36217/97) (2007) 44 E.H.R.R. 6, ECHR

MEPC Holdings Ltd v Taylor (Inspector of Taxes) see Taylor (Inspector of Taxes) v MEPC Holdings Ltd

Mercantile Group (Europe) AG v Aiyela [1994] Q.B. 366; [1993] 3 W.L.R. 1116; [1994] 1 All E.R. 110; *Times*, August 4, 1993; *Independent*, August 12, 1993, CA (Civ Div); affirming [1993] F.S.R. 745, QBD (Comm) . . . . *Digested*, 94/**3738**:
Applied, 01/45, 03/414, 07/456

Mercedes Contract Repairer, Re (KZR 26/04) [2007] E.C.C. 11, BGH (Ger) . . . . *Digested*, 07/**632**

Merck Genericos Produtos Farmaceuticos Lda v Merck & Co Inc (C-431/05) [2007] 3 C.M.L.R. 49, ECJ (Grand Chamber)

Meretz Investments NV v ACP Ltd [2007] EWCA Civ 1303, CA (Civ Div); affirming in part [2006] EWHC 74 (Ch); [2007] Ch. 197; [2007] 2 W.L.R. 403; [2006] 3 All E.R. 1029; [2006] 2 P. & C.R. 23; [2006] 6 E.G. 170 (C.S.); *Times*, April 27, 2006, Ch D . . . . *Digested*, 06/**3491**

Meridian Global Funds Management Asia Ltd v Securities Commission [1995] 2 A.C. 500; [1995] 3 W.L.R. 413; [1995] 3 All E.R. 918; [1995] B.C.C. 942; [1995] 2 B.C.L.C. 116; (1995) 92(28) L.S.G. 39; (1995) 139 S.J.L.B. 152; *Times*, June 29, 1995, PC (NZ) . . . . *Digested*, 96/**969**:
Applied, 04/456, 07/439, 07/2485: *Considered*, 00/980, 05/2307

Merit v Ukraine (6656/01) (Unreported, March 30, 2004), ECHR. . . . . *Followed*, 07/2197

Merkur Island Shipping Corp v Laughton (The Hoegh Anapa) [1983] 2 A.C. 570; [1983] 2 W.L.R. 778; [1983] 2 All E.R. 189; [1983] 2 Lloyd's Rep. 1; [1983] I.C.R. 490; [1983] I.R.L.R. 218; (1983) 133 N.L.J. 577; (1983) 127 S.J. 306, HL; affirming [1983] 2 W.L.R. 45; [1982] 1 All E.R. 334; [1983] 1 Lloyd's Rep. 154; [1983] I.C.R. 178; [1982] I.R.L.R. 26; (1983) 80 L.S.G. 213; (1983) 133 N.L.J. 186; (1982) 126 S.J. 745; *Times*, November 5, 1982, CA (Civ Div) . . . . . *Digested*, 83/**3794**:
Applied, 84/3553, 85/3384, 87/3769: *Considered*, 87/3759, 89/3519, 05/4189: *Overruled in part*, 07/4190

Merrill Lynch Inc's Patent Application [1989] R.P.C. 561; *Times*, April 27, 1989; *Daily Telegraph*, April 28, 1989, CA (Civ Div); affirming [1988] R.P.C. 1, Ch D (Patents Ct) . . . . *Digested*, 89/**2798**:
Applied, 95/3777: *Cited*, 03/2519: *Considered*, 92/3279, 06/2521, 06/2528: *Followed*, 05/2446, 07/2615: *Referred to*, 02/2846

Merrill Lynch International Bank Ltd (formerly Merrill Lynch Capital Markets Bank Ltd) *v* Winterthur Swiss Insurance Co [2007] EWHC 893 (Comm); [2007] 2 All E.R. (Comm) 846; [2007] 1 C.L.C. 671; [2007] Lloyd's Rep. I.R. 532, QBD (Comm)   *Digested,* 07/**2487**

Mersey Care NHS Trust *v* Ackroyd (No.2); *sub nom* Ackroyd *v* Mersey Care NHS Trust (No.2) [2007] EWCA Civ 101; [2007] H.R.L.R. 19; (2007) 94 B.M.L.R. 84; (2007) 104(10) L.S.G. 31; (2007) 151 S.J.L.B. 298; *Times,* February 26, 2007, CA (Civ Div); affirming [2006] EWHC 107 (QB); [2006] E.M.L.R. 12; (2006) 88 B.M.L.R. 1; (2006) 103(12) L.S.G. 30; *Times,* February 9, 2006, QBD   *Digested,* 07/**486**: *Applied,* 07/25

Merstham Manor Ltd *v* Coulsdon and Purley Urban DC [1937] 2 K.B. 77, KBD   *Considered,* 47-51/9808, 07/3421

Messe Munchen GmbH *v* Office for Harmonisation in the Internal Market (Trade Marks and Designs) (OHIM) (T-32/00) [2000] E.C.R. II-3829; [2001] C.E.C. 3; [2001] E.T.M.R.13; (2001) 24(1) I.P.D. 24002, CFI (4th Chamber)   *Digested,* 01/**3993**: *Applied,* 04/2367, 05/2505, 07/2641

Messenger Leisure Developments Ltd *v* Customs and Excise Commissioners; *sub nom* Messenger Leisure Developments Ltd *v* Revenue and Customs Commissioners [2005] EWCA Civ 648; [2005] S.T.C. 1078; [2005] B.T.C. 5332; [2005] B.V.C. 363; [2005] S.T.I. 1022; *Times,* June 14, 2005; *Independent,* June 9, 2005, CA (Civ Div); affirming [2004] EWHC 1761 (Ch); [2004] S.T.C. 1563; [2004] B.T.C. 5785; [2004] B.V.C. 844; [2004] S.T.I. 1725, Ch D; affirming [2004] B.V.C. 2003; [2003] S.T.I. 2204, V&DTr   *Digested,* 05/**4358**: *Considered,* 07/4292

Messenger Leisure Developments Ltd *v* Revenue and Customs Commissioners see Messenger Leisure Developments Ltd *v* Customs and Excise Commissioners

Messier Dowty Ltd *v* Sabena SA [2000] 1 W.L.R. 2040; [2001] 1 All E.R. 275; [2000] 1 All E.R. (Comm) 833; [2000] 1 Lloyd's Rep. 428; [2000] C.P. Rep. 72; [2000] C.L.C. 889; [2001] I.L.Pr. 5; (2000) 97(10) L.S.G. 36; (2000) 144 S.J.L.B. 124; *Times,* March 14, 2000; *Independent,* February 29, 2000, CA (Civ Div)   *Digested,* 00/**778**: *Considered,* 05/434, 07/2555: *Distinguished,* 06/631: *Followed,* 01/543, 04/566

Metallgesellschaft Ltd *v* Inland Revenue Commissioners (C-397/98); *joined case* Hoechst AG *v* Inland Revenue Commissioners (C-410/98) [2001] Ch. 620; [2001] 2 W.L.R. 1497; [2001] All E.R. (EC) 496; [2001] S.T.C. 452; [2001] E.C.R. I-1727; [2001] 2 C.M.L.R. 32; [2001] B.T.C. 99; 3 I.T.L. Rep. 385; [2001] S.T.I. 498; *Times,* March 20, 2001, ECJ (5th Chamber)   *Digested,* 01/**5173**: *Considered,* 03/4141, 03/4142, 04/3681, 04/3682, 05/3984, 05/4056, 05/4129, 05/4387, 06/4123, 07/3973, 07/3974, 07/4359: *Followed,* 04/3721

Metalloy Supplies Ltd (In Liquidation) *v* MA (UK) Ltd [1997] 1 W.L.R. 1613; [1997] 1 All E.R. 418; [1997] B.C.C. 165; [1997] 1 B.C.L.C. 165; [1998] 1 Costs L.R. 85; *Times,* December 12, 1996; *Independent,* October 21, 1996, CA (Civ Div)   *Digested,* 96/**3464**: *Considered,* 04/328: *Distinguished,* 07/404: *Followed,* 03/339

Metropol Treuhand Wirtschaftstreuhand GmbH *v* Finanzlandesdirektion fur Steiermark (C-409/99); *joined case* Stadler *v* Finanzlandesdirektion fur Vorarlberg (C-409/99) [2002] E.C.R. I-81; [2004] B.T.C. 5364; [2004] B.V.C. 424, ECJ (5th Chamber)   *Digested,* 04/**3989**: *Applied,* 07/4304: *Followed,* 05/4365

Metropole (Folkstone) Ltd *v* Revenue and Customs Commissioners [2007] S.T.I. 387, V&DTr (London)

Metropolis Motorcycles Ltd, Re see Hale *v* Waldock

Metropolitan Church of Bessarabia *v* Moldova (45701/99) (2002) 35 E.H.R.R. 13, ECHR   *Digested,* 03/**2101**: *Applied,* 07/2192

Metsa-Serla Sales Oy *v* Commission of the European Communities (C298/98) [2000] E.C.R. I-10157, ECJ   *Followed,* 07/610

Metso Paper Automation Oy *v* Office for Harmonisation in the Internal Market (Trade Marks and Designs) (OHIM) (T-19/04) [2005] E.C.R. II-2383; [2007] E.T.M.R. 2, CFI (4th Chamber)

Meux's Brewery Co *v* City of London Electric Lighting Co see Shelfer *v* City of London Electric Lighting Co (No.1)

Meyrick Estate Management Ltd *v* Secretary of State for the Environment, Food and Rural Affairs [2007] EWCA Civ 53; [2007] Env. L.R. 26; [2007] J.P.L. 1187; [2007] A.C.D. 62; (2007) 104(7) L.S.G. 25; (2007) 151 S.J.L.B. 200; [2007] N.P.C. 13; *Times,* February 15, 2007, CA (Civ Div); affirming [2005] EWHC 2618 (Admin); [2006] J.P.L. 1049; [2005] 45 E.G. 169 (C.S.); [2005] N.P.C. 137; [2006] Env. L.R. D6, QBD (Admin)   *Digested,* 07/**1514**: *Applied,* 06/3287

Mezey *v* South West London and St George's Mental Health NHS Trust [2006] EWHC 3473 (QB); [2007] I.R.L.R. 237; [2007] LS Law Medical 525, QBD   *Digested,* 07/**1379**

Mezey *v* South West London and St George's Mental Health NHS Trust [2007] EWHC 62 (QB); [2007] I.R.L.R. 237, QBD   *Digested,* 07/**1381**

Mezey v South West London and St George's Mental Health NHS Trust (Permission to
    Appeal) [2007] EWCA Civ 106; [2007] I.R.L.R. 244; (2007) 94 B.M.L.R. 25,
    CA (Civ Div) . . . .   *Digested*, 07/**1380**
MG v Secretary of State for the Home Department see MM v Secretary of State for
    the Home Department
MG v Secretary of State for the Home Department; *sub nom* MG and VC (EEA
    Regulations 2006: Conducive Deportation: Ireland), Re; *joined case* VC v
    Secretary of State for the Home Department [2006] UKAIT 53; [2006] Imm.
    A.R. 619, AIT . . . .   *Digested*, 07/**2320**
MG and VC (EEA Regulations 2006: Conducive Deportation: Ireland), Re see MG v
    Secretary of State for the Home Department
MG Rover Beluxl SA/NV (In Administration), Re [2006] EWHC 1296 (Ch); [2007] B.C.C.
    446, Ch D . . . .   *Digested*, 07/**2389**
MHC Consulting Services Ltd v Tansell; *sub nom* Abbey Life Assurance Co Ltd v Tansell
    [2000] I.C.R. 789; [2000] I.R.L.R. 387; (2000) 97(19) L.S.G. 43; (2000) 150
    N.L.J. 651; (2000) 144 S.J.L.B. 205; *Times*, April 19, 2000; *Independent*, May
    22, 2000, CA (Civ Div); affirming [1999] I.C.R. 1211; [1999] I.R.L.R. 677, EAT .   *Digested*, 00/**2119**:
                                                                                            Applied, 07/**1344**
Miah v Birmingham and the Black Country Strategic HA [2007] EWCA Civ 290;
    (2007) 96 B.M.L.R. 54, CA (Civ Div) . . . .   *Digested*, 07/**2925**
Mibanga v Secretary of State for the Home Department [2005] EWCA Civ 367;
    [2005] I.N.L.R. 377, CA (Civ Div) . . . .   *Digested*, 05/**2187**:
                                                             Applied, 06/**1966**: *Distinguished*, 07/337
Microsoft Corp v Commission of the European Communities (T-201/04) [2007] 5
    C.M.L.R. 11, CFI
Microsoft Corp v McDonald (t/a Bizads) [2006] EWHC 3410 (Ch); [2007] Bus. L.R.
    548; [2007] Info. T.L.R. 300; *Times*, January 26, 2007, Ch D . . . .   *Digested*, 07/**2691**
Microsoft Corp v Raval [2007] F.S.R. 11, HC (Ind)
Microsoft Corp's Community Design [2006] E.C.D.R. 29, OHIM (Cancellation Div). . .   *Digested*, 07/**2531**
MICROSOFT/Clipboard formats I (T424/03) [2006] E.P.O.R. 39, EPO (Technical Bd App)   *Digested*, 07/**2594**
Mid Staffordshire General Hospitals NHS Trust v Cambridge [2003] I.R.L.R. 566, EAT.   *Digested*, 04/**1218**:
                                                             Considered, 07/**1334**: *Not applied*, 06/1297
Mid Suffolk DC v Clarke [2006] EWCA Civ 71; [2007] 1 W.L.R. 980; [2006] Env. L.R.
    38; [2006] 8 E.G. 174 (C.S.); [2006] N.P.C. 15; *Times*, March 10, 2006, CA
    (Civ Div) . . . .   *Digested*, 06/**523**
Mid Suffolk DC v Revenue and Customs Commissioners see Isle of Wight Council v
    Revenue and Customs Commissioners
Mid Sussex DC v Hire 2000 Ltd [2007] P.A.D. 29, Planning Inspector
Middlesbrough BC v Surtees [2007] I.R.L.R. 981, EAT.   *Digested*, 07/**1363**
Middlesbrough BC v Surtees [2007] I.C.R. 1644; [2007] I.R.L.R. 869, EAT . . . .   *Digested*, 07/**1364**
Midhage v 60 Coolhurst Road Ltd [2007] 36 E.G. 302, Lands Tr
Midland Bank Plc v Wallace see Royal Bank of Scotland Plc v Etridge (No.2)
Midland Expressway Ltd v Carillion Construction Ltd (No.1) [2006] EWCA Civ 936;
    107 Con. L.R. 235; (2007) 23 Const. L.J. 75, CA (Civ Div); affirming [2005]
    EWHC 2810 (TCC); 106 Con. L.R. 49, QBD (TCC) . . . .   *Digested*, 06/**681**
Midland Marts Ltd v Hobday [1989] 1 W.L.R. 1143; [1989] 3 All E.R. 246; (1989)
    86(27) L.S.G. 41; (1989) 133 S.J. 1109; *Times*, April 25, 1989, Ch D . . . .   *Digested*, 89/**2927**:
                                                             Applied, 05/**2421**, 07/**2530**: *Considered*, 00/494
Midlands Co-operative Society Ltd v Revenue and Customs Commissioners A3/2007/
    1496, CA (Civ Div); affirming [2007] EWHC 1432 (Ch); [2007] B.T.C. 5685;
    [2007] B.V.C. 653; [2007] S.T.I. 1767; *Times*, June 29, 2007, Ch D; reversing
    [2005] S.T.I. 1737, V&DTr . . . .   *Digested*, 07/**4321**
Miftari v Secretary of State for the Home Department [2005] EWCA Civ 481, CA (Civ
    Div). . . . .   *Applied*, 05/**2213**,
                                                             06/**2278**: *Considered*, 07/**2342**
Mighell v Reading see White (Brian) v White
Migotti v Colvill (1878-79) L.R. 4 C.P.D. 233, CA. . . . .   *Applied*, 07/**2354**
Mikulic v Croatia (53176/99) [2002] 1 F.C.R. 720; 11 B.H.R.C. 689, ECHR . . . .   *Digested*, 02/**2527**:
                                                             Applied, 07/**2225**: *Considered*, 06/**1685**, 07/2219
MIL (Investments) SA v Canada 2007 FCA 236; 9 I.T.L. Rep. 1111, CA (Can); affirming
    2006 TCC 460; 9 I.T.L. Rep. 25, Tax Ct (Can)
Milatova v Czech Republic (61811/00) (2007) 45 E.H.R.R. 18, ECHR
Miles v National Assembly for Wales [2007] EWHC 10 (Admin); [2007] J.P.L. 1235,
    QBD (Admin) . . . .   *Digested*, 07/**3227**
Miles v Wakefield MDC [1987] A.C. 539; [1987] 2 W.L.R. 795; [1987] 1 All E.R. 1089;
    [1987] I.C.R. 368; [1987] I.R.L.R. 193; [1987] 1 F.T.L.R. 533; 85 L.G.R. 649;
    (1987) 84 L.S.G. 1239; (1987) 137 N.L.J. 266; (1987) 131 S.J. 408, HL;
    reversing [1985] 1 W.L.R. 822; [1985] 1 All E.R. 905; [1985] I.C.R. 363; [1985]
    I.R.L.R. 108; 84 L.G.R. 335; (1985) 82 L.S.G. 1166; (1985) 129 S.J. 299, CA
    (Civ Div); reversing [1984] I.C.R. 332; 83 L.G.R. 395; *Times*, November 22,
    1983, QBD . . . .   *Digested*, 87/**1380**:
                                                             Applied, 84/1191, 07/**1436**: *Considered*, 96/2638, 96/2673
Millam v Print Factory (London) 1991 Ltd see Print Factory (London) 1991 Ltd v
    Millam

Millar v Bassey [1994] E.M.L.R. 44; *Independent*, August 26, 1993, CA (Civ Div) . . . .   *Digested*, 93/**3791**:
                                                                                                                Overruled, 07/4190

Millbanks v Home Office see O'Reilly v Mackman
Millbanks v Secretary of State for the Home Department see O'Reilly v Mackman
Millbrook Furnishing Industries v McIntosh [1981] I.R.L.R. 309, EAT. . . . .   *Applied*, 07/1325:
                                                                                                                Considered, 84/1194

Millennium College UK Ltd's Application for Registration as a Charity (Unreported, April 27,
    2004), Charity Comm . . . .   *Applied*, 07/323
MILLENNIUM PETROCHEMICALS/Pre-treatment of palladium-gold catalysts (T990/01)
    [2007] E.P.O.R. 12, EPO (Technical Bd App) . . . .   *Digested*, 07/**2570**
Miller v Garton Shires (formerly Gartons) [2006] EWCA Civ 1386; [2007] C.P. Rep. 9;
    [2007] R.T.R. 24; [2007] P.N.L.R. 11, CA (Civ Div) . . . .   *Digested*, 07/**538**
Miller v Hales [2006] EWHC 1529 (QB); [2007] Lloyd's Rep. I.R. 54, QBD . . . .   *Digested*, 07/**3526**
Miller v Hales (Costs) [2006] EWHC 1717 (QB); [2007] 4 Costs L.R. 521, QBD . . . . .   *Digested*, 07/**401**
Miller v Jackson [1977] Q.B. 966; [1977] 3 W.L.R. 20; [1977] 3 All E.R. 338, CA (Civ
    Div). . . . .   *Digested*, 77/**2146**:
                                            Applied, 07/1531: *Considered*, 80/2007, 84/2651, 95/3766
Miller v Miller; *sub nom* M v M (Short Marriage: Clean Break); *joined case* McFarlane
    v McFarlane [2006] UKHL 24; [2006] 2 A.C. 618; [2006] 2 W.L.R. 1283;
    [2006] 3 All E.R. 1; [2006] 1 F.L.R. 1186; [2006] 2 F.C.R. 213; [2006] Fam.
    Law 629; (2006) 103(23) L.S.G. 28; (2006) 156 N.L.J. 916; (2006) 150
    S.J.L.B. 704; *Times*, May 25, 2006; *Independent*, May 26, 2006, HL; affirming
    [2005] EWCA Civ 984; [2006] 1 F.L.R. 151; [2005] 2 F.C.R. 713; [2005] Fam.
    Law 766; (2005) 102(33) L.S.G. 24, CA (Civ Div); affirming [2005] EWHC
    528 (Fam); [2005] 2 F.L.R. 533; [2005] Fam. Law 537, Fam Div . . . .   *Digested*, 06/**1629**:
                            Applied, 06/4090, 07/1695, 07/1700: *Cited*, 07/1694: *Considered*, 06/1627,
                            07/1691, 07/1697, 07/1704: *Distinguished*, 06/1717: *Followed*, 07/1706:
                                                                                            Previous proceedings, 04/1523
Miller v South of Scotland Electricity Board 1958 S.C. (H.L.) 20; 1958 S.L.T. 229, HL;
    reversing (Unreported, June 21, 1957), IH (1 Div); affirming 1957 S.L.T. (Notes)
    19, OH . . . .   *Digested*, 58/**3967**:
                                    Applied, 63/330, 07/5269: *Considered*, 61/9848, 63/4056, 90/5608:
                                                                Distinguished, 85/4448: *Followed*, 93/5668
Miller-Mead v Minister of Housing and Local Government [1963] 2 Q.B. 196; [1963]
    2 W.L.R. 225; [1963] 1 All E.R. 459; (1963) 127 J.P. 122; 61 L.G.R. 152; (1963)
    14 P. & C.R. 266; [1963] J.P.L. 151; (1962) 106 S.J. 1052, CA; reversing in part
    [1962] 2 Q.B. 555; [1962] 3 W.L.R. 654; [1962] 3 All E.R. 99; (1962) 126 J.P.
    457; 60 L.G.R. 340; (1962) 13 P. & C.R. 425; (1962) 106 S.J. 492, QBD . . . . .   *Digested*, 63/**3406**:
                            Applied, 64/3580, 64/3584, 65/3828, 66/11738, 66/11846, 68/3830,
                            71/11427, 74/3740, 76/2696, 76/2697, 78/2877, 86/3266, 87/3604,
                            91/3470, 99/4249, 02/3675, 07/3233: *Considered*, 69/3453, 69/3470,
                            70/2775, 79/2625, 86/3268, 90/4360, 90/4367, 91/3520, 94/2219,
                            95/4867, 96/4798: *Distinguished*, 63/3358: *Followed*, 94/4439:
                                                                                            Not followed, 98/4183

Mills v Birchall see Dolphin Quays Developments Ltd v Mills
Milsom v Revenue and Customs Commissioners see Hinsley v Revenue and Customs
    Commissioners
Milton v Crown Prosecution Service; *sub nom* Milton v DPP [2007] EWHC 532
    (Admin); [2007] 4 All E.R. 1026; (2007) 171 J.P. 669; [2007] R.T.R. 43, QBD
    (Admin) . . . .   *Digested*, 07/**3451**
Milton v DPP see Milton v Crown Prosecution Service
Mincher v Leaper (Unreported, September 25, 2006), CC (Leeds) [*Ex rel.* Weightmans
    Solicitors, India Buildings, Water Street, Liverpool] . . . .   *Digested*, 07/**3485**
Minister for Immigration and Multicultural and Indigenous Affairs v QAAH of 2004 23
    B.H.R.C. 94, HC (Aus)
Minister for Social Security v Greenham Ready Mixed Concrete Ltd see Ready Mixed
    Concrete (South East) Ltd v Minister of Pensions and National Insurance
Minister for Social Security v Ready Mixed Concrete (South East) Ltd see Ready
    Mixed Concrete (South East) Ltd v Minister of Pensions and National
    Insurance
Ministero dell'Economia e delle Finanze v FCE Bank Plc (C-210/04) [2007] S.T.C. 165;
    [2006] E.C.R. I-2803; [2006] S.T.I. 1141, ECJ (2nd Chamber) . . . .   *Digested*, 07/**4284**
Ministero delle Finanze - Ufficio IVA di Milano v CO.GE.P. Srl (C-174/06) [2007] S.T.I.
    2519, ECJ (2nd Chamber)
Ministre de l'Economie, des Finances et de l'Industrie v Societe Bank of Scotland 9 I.T.L.
    Rep. 683, CE (F) . . . .   *Digested*, 07/**4168**
Ministry of Defence v Gandiya see Saggar v Ministry of Defence
Ministry of Defence v Thames Water Utilities Ltd; *sub nom* Thames Water Utilities Ltd v
    Ministry of Defence [2006] EWCA Civ 1620; [2007] Env. L.R. 15; (2006) 150
    S.J.L.B. 1608, CA (Civ Div); reversing [2006] EWHC 66 (TCC); [2006] Env.
    L.R. 37, QBD (TCC) . . . .   *Digested*, 07/**4276**
Ministry of Defence and Support of the Armed Forces for Iran v Faz Aviation (formerly FN
    Aviation Ltd) [2007] EWHC 1042 (Comm); [2007] I.L.Pr. 42, QBD (Comm) . .   *Digested*, 07/**441**
Minto v Revenue and Customs Commissioners [2007] S.T.I. 2124, Sp Comm

Mir v Marshall (Unreported, December 7, 2006), CC (Manchester) [*Ex rel.* Chris Middleton, Barrister, Oriel Chambers, 14 Water Street, Liverpool] . . . .   *Digested*, 07/**3117**

Mirant Asia-Pacific Construction (Hong Kong) Ltd v Ove Arup & Partners International Ltd [2007] EWHC 918 (TCC); [2007] C.I.L.L. 2480, QBD (TCC)

Mirimskaya v Evans [2007] EWHC 2073 (TCC); 114 Con. L.R. 144; (2007) 151 S.J.L.B. 1226, QBD (TCC)   *Digested*, 07/**754**

Mirror Group Newspapers Plc v Maxwell (No.1) [1998] B.C.C. 324; [1998] 1 B.C.L.C. 638; *Times*, July 15, 1997, Ch D . . . .   *Digested*, 97/**3072**:
                    Applied, 07/2443: *Considered*, 05/352: *Subsequent related litigation*, 99/3287

Mirvahedy v Henley [2003] UKHL 16; [2003] 2 A.C. 491; [2003] 2 W.L.R. 882; [2003] 2 All E.R. 401; [2003] R.T.R. 26; [2003] P.I.Q.R. P25; (2003) 100(19) L.S.G. 31; (2003) 153 N.L.J. 483; (2003) 147 S.J.L.B. 352; [2003] N.P.C. 38; *Times*, March 24, 2003, HL; affirming [2001] EWCA Civ 1749; [2002] Q.B. 769; [2002] 2 W.L.R. 566; [2002] P.I.Q.R. P19; (2002) 99(3) L.S.G. 25; (2002) 146 S.J.L.B. 12; *Times*, December 11, 2001; *Daily Telegraph*, November 27, 2001, CA (Civ Div) . . . .   *Digested*, 03/**178**:
                   Applied, 04/169: *Cited*, 03/59: *Considered*, 07/203: *Followed*, 05/189

Mirzajani v Secretary of State for Work and Pensions see Kola v Secretary of State for Work and Pensions

Mishcon de Reya (A Firm) v Barrett [2006] EWHC 952 (Ch); [2007] 1 B.C.L.C. 153, Ch D . . . .   *Digested*, 07/**2951**

Miss World Ltd v Channel 4 Television Corp [2007] EWHC 982 (Pat); [2007] E.T.M.R. 66; [2007] F.S.R. 30; (2007) 30(6) I.P.D. 30042, Ch D (Patents Ct)

Mitchell v Al-Dali see Jones v Saudi Arabia

Mitchell v Cantrill (1888) L.R. 37 Ch. D. 56, CA . . . .   *Considered*, 07/2757

Mitchell v DPP of Grenada [1986] A.C. 73; [1985] 3 W.L.R. 724; (1985) 129 S.J. 716, PC (Gren) . . . .   *Digested*, 85/**2764**:
                                         Applied, 07/3625

Mitchell v Gard 164 E.R. 1280; (1863) 3 Sw. & Tr. 275, Ct of Probate. . . . .   *Considered*, 07/429

Mitchell v Waverley BC [2007] P.A.D. 2, Planning Inspector

MITSUBISHI HEAVY INDUSTRIES/Possible reasons for exclusion (J15/04) [2006] E.P.O.R. 46, EPO (Legal Bd App) . . . .   *Digested*, 07/**2582**

MITSUI CHEMICALS/Withdrawal of application (J25/03) [2006] E.P.O.R. 45, EPO (Legal Bd App) . . . .   *Applied*, 07/2574

Mizzi v Malta (26111/02) [2006] 1 F.L.R. 1048; [2006] 1 F.C.R. 256, ECHR . . . .   *Digested*, 06/**2193**:
                                         Considered, 07/1787

MJ Harrington Syndicate 2000 v Axa Oyak Sigorta AS [2006] EWHC 1112 (Comm); [2007] Lloyd's Rep. I.R. 60, QBD (Comm) . . . .   *Digested*, 07/**2503**

MJ (A Child) (Adoption Order or Special Guardianship Order), Re; *sub nom* J v Newport City Council [2007] EWCA Civ 56; [2007] 1 F.L.R. 691; [2007] 1 F.C.R. 329; [2007] Fam. Law 389; (2007) 104(8) L.S.G. 38, CA (Civ Div) . . . .   *Digested*, 07/**1800**

MK (Adequacy of Maintenance: Disabled Sponsor: Somalia) see MK (Somalia) v Secretary of State for the Home Department

MK (Somalia) v Secretary of State for the Home Department; *sub nom* MK (Adequacy of Maintenance: Disabled Sponsor: Somalia) [2007] EWCA Civ 1521, CA (Civ Div); reversing [2007] UKAIT 28; [2007] Imm. A.R. 557, AIT

MKG-Kraftfahrzeuge-Factory GmbH v Finanzamt Gross-Gerau (C-305/01) see Finanzamt Gross-Gerau v MKG-Kraftfahrzeuge-Factoring GmbH (C-305/01)

ML and AL (Children) (Contact Order: Brussels II Regulation), Re (No.1) [2006] EWHC 2385 (Fam); [2007] 1 F.C.R. 475, Fam Div . . . .   *Digested*, 07/**1772**

ML and AL (Children) (Contact Order: Brussels II Regulation), Re (No.2) [2006] EWHC 3631 (Fam); [2007] 1 F.C.R. 496, Fam Div . . . .   *Digested*, 07/**1768**

ML (Mauritius) v Secretary of State for the Home Department; *sub nom* ML (Student: Satisfactory Progress: Zhou Explained: Mauritius), Re [2007] UKAIT 61; [2007] Imm. A.R. 773, AIT

ML (Student: Satisfactory Progress: Zhou Explained: Mauritius), Re see ML (Mauritius) v Secretary of State for the Home Department

MM v HM Treasury see M v HM Treasury

MM v Secretary of State for the Home Department; *sub nom* MM (Out of Time Appeals: Burundi), Re; *joined cases* CN v Secretary of State for the Home Department; MG v Secretary of State for the Home Department [2004] UKIAT 182; [2004] Imm. A.R. 515; [2004] I.N.L.R. 482, IAT . . . .   *Digested*, 05/**322**:
                                         Considered, 07/2284

MM v VM see M (Children) (Abduction), Re

MM (A Child), Re see M (A Child) (Care Proceedings: Best Evidence), Re

MM (Out of Time Appeals: Burundi), Re see MM v Secretary of State for the Home Department

MMO2 Plc v Revenue and Customs Commissioners [2006] V. & D.R. 108; [2006] S.T.I. 1708, V&D Tr (London) . . . .   *Digested*, 07/**4159**

MMR/MR Vaccine Litigation see Horne-Roberts v SmithKline Beecham Plc

MN (India) v Secretary of State for the Home Department; *sub nom* MN (Non-recognised Adoptions: Unlawful Discrimination: India), Re; C5/2007/1290, CA (Civ Div); affirming [2007] UKAIT 15; [2007] Imm. A.R. 515, AIT

MN (Non-recognised Adoptions: Unlawful Discrimination: India), Re see MN (India) *v* Secretary of State for the Home Department

Mobile Export 365 Ltd *v* Revenue and Customs Commissioners [2007] EWHC 1737 (Ch); [2007] S.T.C. 1794; [2007] S.T.I. 1900, Ch D .... *Digested,* 07/**4319**

Mobilx Ltd *v* Revenue and Customs Commissioners (Unreported, October 6, 2006), V&DTr (Manchester) .... *Doubted,* 07/4303

Mobistar SA *v* Commune de Fleron (C-544/03); *joined case* Belgacom Mobile SA *v* Commune de Schaerbeek (C-545/03) [2005] E.C.R. I-7723; [2005] 3 C.M.L.R. 46, ECJ (1st Chamber) .... *Digested,* 06/**4322**: *Applied,* 07/3977

Modern Engineering (Bristol) Ltd *v* Gilbert Ash (Northern) Ltd see Gilbert Ash (Northern) Ltd *v* Modern Engineering (Bristol) Ltd

Modling Waste Disposal Contract, Re (C-29/04) see Commission of the European Communities *v* Austria (C-29/04)

Mohamed *v* Hammersmith and Fulham LBC; *sub nom* Surdonja *v* Ealing LBC; Mohammed *v* Hammersmith and Fulham LBC; *joined case* Ealing LBC *v* Surdonja [2001] UKHL 57; [2002] 1 A.C. 547; [2001] 3 W.L.R. 1339; [2002] 1 All E.R. 176; [2002] 1 F.C.R. 183; [2002] H.L.R. 7; (2001) 98(45) L.S.G. 26; (2001) 151 N.L.J. 1664; (2001) 145 S.J.L.B. 253; [2001] N.P.C. 154; *Times,* November 2, 2001; *Independent,* November 8, 2001; *Daily Telegraph,* November 6, 2001, HL; affirming [2001] Q.B. 97; [2000] 3 W.L.R. 481; [2000] 2 All E.R. 597; (2000) 32 H.L.R. 481; [2000] N.P.C. 5; *Times,* February 11, 2000, CA (Civ Div) .... *Digested,* 01/**3419**: *Applied,* 05/2008, 07/3910: *Considered,* 03/2050: *Distinguished,* 06/2045

Mohammed *v* Hammersmith and Fulham LBC see Mohamed *v* Hammersmith and Fulham LBC

Mohammed *v* Secretary of State for the Home Department see Januzi *v* Secretary of State for the Home Department

Mohammed *v* Walker (Valuation Officer) [2006] R.A. 311, Lands Tr .... *Digested,* 07/**3348**

Mohan *v* Director of Income Tax (International Taxation) 10 I.T.L. Rep. 151, Advance Rulings (Ind)

Mohanaei *v* Mohanaei [2007] EWCA Civ 1051; (2007) 151 S.J.L.B. 1299, CA (Civ Div) CHY05120, CC (Central London)

Mohit *v* DPP of Mauritius [2006] UKPC 20; [2006] 1 W.L.R. 3343, PC (Mau) ...... *Digested,* 07/**55**

Mohunram *v* National Director of Public Prosecutions 23 B.H.R.C. 356, Const Ct (SA)

Moir *v* Wallersteiner (No.2) see Wallersteiner *v* Moir (No.2)

Moldovan *v* Romania (41138/98) (2007) 44 E.H.R.R. 16, ECHR

Molenaar *v* Allgemeine Ortskrankenkasse Baden-Wurttemberg (C-160/96) [1998] E.C.R. I-843, ECJ .... *Applied,* 05/3859, 06/1572: *Followed,* 07/3854

Molins Plc *v* GD SpA [2000] 1 W.L.R. 1741; [2000] 2 Lloyd's Rep. 234; [2000] C.P. Rep. 54; [2000] C.L.C. 1027; [2001] I.L.Pr. 14; [2000] F.S.R. 893; *Times,* March 29, 2000; *Independent,* March 23, 2000, CA (Civ Div); reversing [2001] I.L.Pr. 1; (2000) 23(4) I.P.D. 23027; (2000) 97(8) L.S.G. 35; *Times,* March 1, 2000, Ch D (Patents Ct) .... *Digested,* 00/**567**: *Applied,* 07/433: *Considered,* 06/510: *Distinguished,* 04/579: *Followed,* 05/468

Molnlycke AB *v* Procter & Gamble Ltd (No.5) [1994] R.P.C. 49, CA (Civ Div); affirming [1992] F.S.R. 549, Ch D (Patents Ct) .... *Digested,* 95/**3778**: *Applied,* 96/4568, 99/3471, 04/2346, 06/2530, 07/2622: *Considered,* 99/3495: *Followed,* 95/3777, 97/3901, 04/2280

Monavon Construction Ltd *v* Davenport [2006] EWHC 1094 (TCC); 108 Con. L.R. 15, QBD (TCC) .... *Digested,* 07/**738**

Moncrieff *v* Jamieson [2007] UKHL 42; [2007] 1 W.L.R. 2620; 2007 S.L.T. 989; 2007 S.C.L.R. 790; [2007] 43 E.G. 200 (C.S.); (2007) 151 S.J.L.B. 1368; [2007] N.P.C. 106; 2007 G.W.D. 33-564, HL; affirming 2005 1 S.C. 281; 2005 S.L.T. 225; 2005 S.C.L.R. 463; 2005 G.W.D. 5-66, IH (Ex Div); affirming 2004 S.C.L.R. 135, Sh Ct (Grampian) .... *Digested,* 07/**5277**

Moncure *v* Cahusac [2006] UKPC 54; [2007] 2 P. & C.R. DG7, PC (Jam)

Mond *v* Smurthwaite see Smurthwaite *v* Simpson-Smith

Mongan *v* Department for Social Development [2005] NICA 16; [2006] N.I. 43, CA (NI) .... *Applied,* 07/3864

Mongiardi *v* IBC Vehicles see Burrows *v* Vauxhall Motors Ltd

Monopoly on Hydropower Resources, Re (E-2/06) see EFTA Surveillance Authority *v* Norway (E-2/06)

Monro *v* Revenue and Customs Commissioners A3/2007/0392, CA (Civ Div); affirming [2007] EWHC 114 (Ch); [2007] S.T.C. 1182; [2007] B.T.C. 325; [2007] S.T.I. 290, Ch D .... *Digested,* 07/**3990**

Monsanto Plc *v* Farris (Valuation Officer) [1999] 1 E.G.L.R. 199; [1998] R.A. 107, Lands Tr .... *Digested,* 98/**4314**: *Considered,* 07/3345

Monsanto Technology LLC *v* Cargill International SA [2006] EWHC 2864 (Ch); (2007) 30(3) I.P.D. 30018, Ch D

Monsanto Technology LLC v Cargill International SA; *sub nom* Monsanto Technology
   LLC v Cargill Plc [2007] EWHC 1204 (Pat); (2007) 30(6) I.P.D. 30041, Ch D
   (Patents Ct)
Monsanto Technology LLC v Cargill Plc see Monsanto Technology LLC v Cargill
   International SA
Montecatini SpA v Commission of the European Communities (C-235/92 P) [1999]
   E.C.R. I-4539; [2001] 4 C.M.L.R. 18, ECJ (6th Chamber) . . . . *Digested,* 01/**2463**:
                                                         Applied, 06/573, 07/614, 07/644
Montex Holdings Ltd v Controller of Patents, Designs and Trade Marks [2001] IESC 29;
   [2002] E.T.M.R. 24, Sup Ct (Irl); affirming [2000] E.T.M.R. 658, HC (Irl) . . . . . *Digested,* 00/**3781**:
                                       Applied, 07/2662: *Considered,* 07/2663
Montex Holdings Ltd v Diesel SpA (C-281/05) [2006] E.C.R. I-10881; [2007] E.T.M.R.
   13, ECJ (2nd Chamber) . . . . *Digested,* 07/**2638**
Montgomery v HM Advocate; *sub nom* HM Advocate v Montgomery (David Shields);
   joined case Coulter v HM Advocate [2003] 1 A.C. 641; [2001] 2 W.L.R. 779;
   2001 S.C. (P.C.) 1; 2001 S.L.T. 37; 2000 S.C.C.R. 1044; [2001] U.K.H.R.R. 124; 9
   B.H.R.C. 641; 2000 G.W.D. 40-1487; *Times,* December 6, 2000, PC (Sc) . . . . . *Digested,* 01/**6371**:
                                        Applied, 04/1629: *Considered,* 06/5552, 07/923:
                                               Previous proceedings, 00/6068
Moody v Anderton see R. v Manchester Stipendiary Magistrate Ex p. Hill
Moody v United Kingdom (22613/93) (1995) 19 E.H.R.R. CD90, Eur Comm HR . . . . *Applied,* 07/2227
Moon v Garrett [2006] EWCA Civ 1121; [2006] C.P. Rep. 46; [2006] B.L.R. 402;
   [2007] 1 Costs L.R. 41; [2007] I.C.R. 95; [2007] P.I.Q.R. P3; *Times,* September
   1, 2006, CA (Civ Div). . . . . *Digested,* 06/**366**
Moore v Canadian Lawyers Insurance Association (Unreported), Sup Ct (NS) . . . . . . *Considered,* 07/2488
Moore v Clench (1875-76) L.R. 1 Ch. D. 447, Ch D . . . . *Applied,* 07/4243
Moore v Gadd see Farmizer (Products) Ltd, Re
Moore v Moore [2007] EWCA Civ 361; [2007] I.L.Pr. 36; [2007] 2 F.L.R. 339;
   [2007] 2 F.C.R. 353; [2007] Fam. Law 698; (2007) 151 S.J.L.B. 573; *Times,*
   April 25, 2007, CA (Civ Div) . . . . *Digested,* 07/**1697**
Moore v Secretary of State for Transport [2007] EWHC 879 (QB); [2007] Eu. L.R.
   645; [2007] Lloyd's Rep. I.R. 469; [2007] P.I.Q.R. P24, QBD . . . . *Digested,* 07/**2469**
Morelle v Wakeling [1955] 2 Q.B. 379; [1955] 2 W.L.R. 672; [1955] 1 All E.R. 708;
   (1955) 99 S.J. 218, CA . . . . *Digested,* 55/**351**:
            Applied, 85/471, 90/3733: *Considered,* 56/4757, 70/379, 86/2717, 07/4518
Morgan v Brith Gof Cyf [2001] I.C.R. 978, EAT . . . . *Digested,* 01/**2270**:
                                                    Considered, 07/1352
Morgan v Hill; *sub nom* Hill v Morgan [2006] EWCA Civ 1602; [2007] 1 W.L.R. 855;
   [2007] 1 F.L.R. 1480; [2006] 3 F.C.R. 620; [2007] Fam. Law 112; (2006) 150
   S.J.L.B. 1605; *Times,* December 8, 2006; *Independent,* November 30, 2006, CA
   (Civ Div) . . . . *Digested,* 07/**1830**
Morgan Est (Scotland) Ltd v Hanson Concrete Products Ltd [2005] EWCA Civ 134;
   [2005] 1 W.L.R. 2557; [2005] 3 All E.R. 135; [2005] C.P. Rep. 23; [2005]
   B.L.R. 218; (2005) 102(17) L.S.G. 32; *Times,* February 28, 2005, CA (Civ Div);
   affirming [2004] EWHC 1778 (TCC), QBD (TCC) . . . . *Digested,* 05/**315**:
                          Applied, 06/197: *Considered,* 07/490: *Doubted,* 07/534
Morgan Stanley & Co Inc v Director of Income Tax (International Taxation), Mumbai see
   Director of Income Tax (International Taxation), Mumbai v Morgan Stanley & Co
   Inc
Morganash Ltd v Revenue and Customs Commissioners [2007] B.V.C. 2184; [2006]
   S.T.I. 2587, V&DTr (Manchester)
Morgans v Alpha Plus Security Ltd [2005] 4 All E.R. 655; [2005] I.C.R. 525; [2005]
   I.R.L.R. 234, EAT . . . . *Digested,* 05/**1322**:
                  Applied, 07/1317: *Distinguished,* 06/1385: *Followed,* 06/1388
Morina v Secretary of State for Work and Pensions see Secretary of State for Work
   and Pensions v Morina
Morley Fund Management v Northampton BC [2007] P.A.D. 25, Planning Inspector
Morrell v Workers Savings & Loan Bank [2007] UKPC 3; [2007] Bus. L.R. D57, PC
   (Jam)
Morris v Revenue and Customs Commissioners [2006] V. & D.R. 263, V&DTr
   (London). . . . . *Digested,* 07/**4358**
Morris v Revenue and Customs Commissioners [2007] EWHC 1181 (Ch); [2007]
   B.T.C. 448, Ch D
Morris v Roberts (Inspector of Taxes) (Wasted Costs Order) [2005] EWHC 1040
   (Ch); [2006] S.T.C. 135; [2005] P.N.L.R. 41; 77 T.C. 204; [2007] B.T.C. 432;
   [2005] S.T.I. 1014, Ch D . . . . *Digested,* 05/**496**
Morshead Mansions Ltd v Mactra Properties Ltd [2006] EWCA Civ 492; [2007] 2
   B.C.L.C. 88, CA (Civ Div). . . . . *Digested,* 07/**2760**
Morton-Norwich Products Inc v Customs and Excise Commissioners see Norwich
   Pharmacal Co v Customs and Excise Commissioners
Mosaic Homes v Hackney LBC [2007] P.A.D. 36, Planning Inspector
Moscow Branch of the Salvation Army v Russia (72881/01) (2007) 44 E.H.R.R. 46; 23
   B.H.R.C. 183, ECHR . . . . *Digested,* 07/**2192**

Moser v Austria (12643/02) [2007] 1 F.L.R. 702; [2006] 3 F.C.R. 107; [2007] Fam.
Law 20, ECHR . . . . *Digested,* 07/**1774**
Moses-Taiga v Taiga; *sub nom* Taiga v Taiga [2005] EWCA Civ 1013; [2006] 1 F.L.R.
1074; [2006] Fam. Law 266, CA (Civ Div) . . . . *Digested,* 06/**1632**:
Applied, 07/1701, 07/1707
Moss v McLachlan (1985) 149 J.P. 167; [1985] I.R.L.R. 76; (1985) 149 J.P.N. 149;
Times, November 29, 1984, DC. . . . . *Digested,* 85/**647**:
Applied, 04/3144: *Approved,* 05/3341: *Distinguished,* 07/3317
Mostaza Claro v Centro Movil Milenium SL (C-168/05) [2007] Bus. L.R. 60; [2006]
E.C.R. I-10421; [2007] 1 C.M.L.R. 22; [2007] C.E.C. 290, ECJ (1st Chamber) . *Digested,* 07/**256**
Mote v Secretary of State for Work and Pensions [2007] EWCA Civ 1324; *Times,*
December 28, 2007, CA (Civ Div)
Motis Exports Ltd v Dampskibsselskabet AF 1912 A/S (No.1); *sub nom*
Dampskibsselskabet AF 1912 A/S v Motis Exports Ltd [2000] 1 All E.R. (Comm)
91; [2000] 1 Lloyd's Rep. 211; [2000] C.L.C. 515; (2000) 97(3) L.S.G. 37;
Times, January 26, 2000, CA (Civ Div); affirming [1999] 1 All E.R. (Comm) 571;
[1999] 1 Lloyd's Rep. 837; [1999] C.L.C. 914; *Times,* March 31, 1999, QBD
(Comm) . . . . *Digested,* 00/**4680**:
Applied, 07/3800: *Considered,* 02/4096
Moto Hospitality Ltd v Secretary of State for Transport [2007] EWCA Civ 764; [2007]
R.V.R. 247; (2007) 157 S.J.L.B. 1426; [2007] N.P.C. 95, CA (Civ Div);
affirming [2006] R.V.R. 280, Lands Tr
Motor Insurers Bureau v Phillips see Phillips v Rafiq
Motor Vehicle Transfer Licences, Re (C-54/05) see Commission of the European
Communities v Finland (C-54/05)
Motorola Credit Corp v Uzan (No.6) [2003] EWCA Civ 752; [2004] 1 W.L.R. 113;
[2003] C.P. Rep. 56; [2003] 2 C.L.C. 1026; (2003) 100(32) L.S.G. 34; (2003)
147 S.J.L.B. 752; *Times,* June 19, 2003; *Independent,* July 23, 2003, CA (Civ
Div). . . . . *Digested,* 03/**413**:
Applied, 07/457: *Considered,* 04/259, 06/386
Motorola Ltd v Revenue and Customs Commissioners [2006] V. & D.R. 136, V&D Tr
(London). . . . . *Digested,* 07/**1033**
Mott MacDonald Ltd v London & Regional Properties Ltd [2007] EWHC 1055 (TCC);
113 Con. L.R. 33; [2007] C.I.L.L. 2481, QBD (TCC) . . . . *Digested,* 07/**730**
Mount Cook Land Ltd v Westminster City Council see R. (on the application of Mount
Cook Land Ltd) v Westminster City Council
Mountford v Newlands School; *sub nom* M v Newlands Manor School [2007] EWCA
Civ 21; [2007] E.L.R. 256; (2007) 151 S.J.L.B. 164, CA (Civ Div) . . . . *Digested,* 07/**2938**
Mouvement contre le Racisme, l'Antisemitisme et la Xenophobie ASBL (MRAX) v Belgium
(C-459/99) [2003] 1 W.L.R. 1073; [2002] E.C.R. I-6591; [2002] 3 C.M.L.R.
25, ECJ . . . . *Digested,* 03/**1446**:
Applied, 05/1480, 07/1559
MR Dean & Sons (Edgware) Ltd v First Secretary of State; *sub nom* First Secretary of
State v Sainsbury's Supermarkets Ltd; *joined case* Sainsbury Supermarkets Ltd v
First Secretary of State [2007] EWCA Civ 1083; [2007] N.P.C. 119, CA (Civ
Div); reversing [2007] EWHC 1 (Admin); [2007] 2 P. & C.R. 6; [2007] J.P.L.
1042; [2007] N.P.C. 6, QBD (Admin) . . . . *Digested,* 07/**3282**
MS Fashions Ltd v Bank of Credit and Commerce International SA (In Liquidation); *sub
nom* MS Fashions Ltd v Bank of Credit and Commerce International SA (No.2);
joined cases High Street Services v Bank of Credit and Commerce
International; Impexbond v Bank of Credit and Commerce International [1993]
Ch. 425; [1993] 3 W.L.R. 220; [1993] 3 All E.R. 769; [1993] B.C.C. 360; [1993]
B.C.L.C. 1200; (1993) 137 S.J.L.B. 132; *Times,* March 26, 1993; *Independent,*
April 6, 1993, CA (Civ Div); affirming [1993] B.C.C. 70; *Times,* December 24,
1992; *Independent,* January 6, 1993, Ch D . . . . *Digested,* 93/**2391**:
Applied, 07/2451: *Considered,* 95/2868: *Distinguished,* 97/3047
MS Fashions Ltd v Bank of Credit and Commerce International SA (No.2) see MS
Fashions Ltd v Bank of Credit and Commerce International SA (In Liquidation)
MS (Ivory Coast) v Secretary of State for the Home Department [2007] EWCA Civ
133; [2007] Imm. A.R. 538; [2007] I.N.L.R. 513; (2007) 104(10) L.S.G. 28;
Times, March 27, 2007, CA (Civ Div) . . . . *Digested,* 07/**2277**
MS (Somalia) v Secretary of State for the Home Department see DK (Serbia) v
Secretary of State for the Home Department
MSD (Darlington) Ltd v Revenue and Customs Commissioners [2007] S.T.I. 382,
V&D Tr (Manchester)
MT (Algeria) v Secretary of State for the Home Department; *joined cases* RB (Algeria)
v Secretary of State for the Home Department; U (Algeria) v Secretary of State
for the Home Department [2007] EWCA Civ 808; [2007] H.R.L.R. 41; [2007]
U.K.H.R.R. 1267; *Times,* August 3, 2007, CA (Civ Div) . . . . *Digested,* 07/**2318**
Mubarak v Mubarik [2006] EWHC 1260 (Fam); [2007] 1 W.L.R. 271; [2007] 1 F.L.R.
722; [2007] Fam. Law 13, Fam Div. . . . . *Digested,* 07/**1698**
Mubarak v Mubarik [2007] EWHC 220 (Fam); [2007] 2 F.L.R. 364; [2007] Fam.
Law 793, Fam Div

Mucelli *v* Albania [2007] EWHC 2632 (Admin); (2007) 157 N.L.J. 1659, QBD (Admin)

Muhid (Abdul) see R. *v* Saleem (Abdul)

Muhlens GmbH & Co KG *v* Office for Harmonisation in the Internal Market (Trade Marks and Designs) (OHIM) (C-206/04 P) [2006] E.C.R. I-2717; [2006] E.T.M.R. 57, ECJ . . . . *Digested*, 06/**2557**:
Applied, 07/1560: *Previous proceedings*, 05/2510

Mukarkar *v* Secretary of State for the Home Department [2006] EWCA Civ 1045; [2007] Imm. A.R. 57; [2006] I.N.L.R. 486; *Times*, August 16, 2006; *Independent*, October 3, 2006, CA (Civ Div) . . . . *Digested*, 06/**2286**

Mulheir *v* Gannon (p/a Claffey Gannon Solicitors) [2006] IEHC 274; [2007] P.N.L.R. 13, HC (Irl)

Muller-Faure *v* Onderlinge Waarborgmaatschappij OZ Zorgverzekeringen UA (C-385/99); *joined case* Van Riet *v* Onderlinge Waarborgmaatschappij OZ Zorgverzekeringen UA (C-385/99) [2004] Q.B. 1081; [2004] 3 W.L.R. 374; [2005] All E.R. (EC) 62; [2003] E.C.R. I-4509; [2004] 2 C.M.L.R. 33; (2004) 80 B.M.L.R. 68, ECJ . . . . *Digested*, 05/**1849**:
Applied, 07/1981: *Considered*, 03/1799, 04/1688, 07/1632

Multani *v* Commission Scolaire Marguerite-Bourgeoys 2006 SCC 6; 23 B.H.R.C. 435, Sup Ct (Can)

Multani (Setting of Minimum Term), Re see Jones (Setting of Minimum Term), Re

Multiple Claimants *v* Sanifo-Synthelabo Ltd [2007] EWHC 1860 (QB); (2007) 98 B.M.L.R. 192, QBD . . . . *Digested*, 07/**505**

Multiplex Constructions (UK) Ltd *v* Cleveland Bridge UK Ltd [2007] EWCA Civ 1372, CA (Civ Div); reversing in part [2007] EWHC 145 (TCC); 111 Con. L.R. 48, QBD (TCC) . . . . *Digested*, 07/**741**

Multiplex Constructions (UK) Ltd *v* Cleveland Bridge UK Ltd [2007] EWHC 659 (TCC); (2007) 23 Const. L.J. 299, QBD (TCC) . . . . *Digested*, 07/**414**

Multiplex Constructions (UK) Ltd *v* Honeywell Control Systems Ltd [2007] EWHC 236 (TCC); [2007] B.L.R. 167; [2007] Bus. L.R. D13, QBD (TCC) . . . . *Digested*, 07/**495**

Multiplex Constructions (UK) Ltd *v* Honeywell Control Systems Ltd (No.2) [2007] EWHC 447 (TCC); [2007] B.L.R. 195; 111 Con. L.R. 78; [2007] C.I.L.L. 2458; [2007] Bus. L.R. D109, QBD (TCC) . . . . *Digested*, 07/**816**

Multiplex Constructions (UK) Ltd *v* Mott MacDonald Ltd [2007] EWHC 20 (TCC); 110 Con. L.R. 63; [2007] C.I.L.L. 2446, QBD (TCC) . . . . *Digested*, 07/**729**

Multiplex Constructions (UK) Ltd *v* West India Quay Development Co (Eastern) Ltd [2006] EWHC 1569 (TCC); 111 Con. L.R. 33, QBD (TCC) . . . . *Digested*, 07/**728**

Muman *v* Nagasena [2000] 1 W.L.R. 299; [1999] 4 All E.R. 178, CA (Civ Div) . . . . . . *Digested*, 00/**296**:
Considered, 04/941, 07/321

Municipal Mutual Insurance Ltd *v* Sea Insurance Co Ltd [1998] C.L.C. 957; [1998] Lloyd's Rep. I.R. 421, CA (Civ Div); reversing in part [1996] L.R.L.R. 265; [1996] C.L.C. 1515; *Lloyd's List*, June 11, 1996, QBD (Comm) . . . . *Digested*, 98/**3401**:
Applied, 99/3426, 07/2504: *Considered*, 03/2454

Munroe *v* DPP (1988) 152 J.P. 657; [1988] Crim. L.R. 823; [1989] C.O.D. 182; (1988) 152 J.P.N. 834, QBD . . . . *Digested*, 89/**612**:
Considered, 07/989

Murgulo *v* Assitalia SpA (C-298/04) see Manfredi *v* Lloyd Adriatico Assicurazioni SpA (C-295/04)

Murphy *v* An Bord Telecom Eireann (157/86) [1988] E.C.R. 673; [1988] 1 C.M.L.R. 879; [1988] I.C.R. 445; [1988] I.R.L.R. 267, ECJ . . . . *Digested*, 88/**1275**:
Applied, 07/1366

Murphy *v* Gooch [2007] EWCA Civ 603; [2007] 2 F.L.R. 934; [2007] 3 F.C.R. 96; [2007] B.P.I.R. 1123; (2007-08) 10 I.T.E.L.R. 300; [2007] Fam. Law 905; (2007) 151 S.J.L.B. 896; [2007] N.P.C. 78, CA (Civ Div) . . . . *Digested*, 07/**3366**

Murphy *v* Staples UK Ltd see Cranfield *v* Bridgegrove Ltd

Murray *v* Big Pictures (UK) Ltd see Murray *v* Express Newspapers Plc

Murray *v* Express Newspapers Plc; *sub nom* Murray *v* Big Pictures (UK) Ltd; A3/2007/2236, CA (Civ Div); reversing [2007] EWHC 1908 (Ch); [2007] E.C.D.R. 20; [2007] E.M.L.R. 22; [2007] 3 F.C.R. 331; [2007] H.R.L.R. 44; [2007] U.K.H.R.R. 1322; [2007] Fam. Law 1073; (2007) 157 N.L.J. 1199; *Times*, October 4, 2007, Ch D . . . . *Digested*, 07/**2247**

Murray *v* Ministry of Defence [1988] 1 W.L.R. 692; [1988] 2 All E.R. 521; (1989) 153 J.P.N. 200; (1988) 138 N.L.J. Rep. 164; (1988) 132 S.J. 852, HL (NI); affirming [1985] 12 N.I.J.B. 1, CA (NI) . . . . *Digested*, 88/**2655**:
Applied, 07/4191: *Complaint dismissed*, 95/2662: *Distinguished*, 03/3484

Murray Clayton *v* Rafidair Bank see United Trading Corp SA *v* Allied Arab Bank Ltd

Mursel Eren *v* Turkey (60856/00) (2007) 44 E.H.R.R. 28; [2006] E.L.R. 155, ECHR . . *Digested*, 06/**1239**

Musawi *v* RE International (UK) Ltd [2007] EWHC 2981 (Ch); [2007] N.P.C. 137, Ch D

Muscat *v* Cable & Wireless Plc see Cable & Wireless Plc *v* Muscat

Muschett *v* Hounslow LBC; *joined cases* Khan *v* London Probation Service; Ogbuneke *v* Minster Lodge; Tallington Lakes Ltd *v* Reilly (2007) 151 S.J.L.B. 1262, EAT

Museum Admission Rates, Re (C-388/01) see Commission of the European Communities v Italy (C-388/01)

Musique Diffusion Francaise SA v Commission of the European Communities (100/80); *joined cases* Pioneer High Fidelity (GB) Ltd v Commission of the European Communities (103/80); Pioneer Electronic (Europe) NV v Commission of the European Communities (102/80); C Melchers & Co v Commission of the European Communities (101/80) [1983] E.C.R. 1825; [1983] 3 C.M.L.R. 221, ECJ . . . . *Digested*, 83/**1576**:
Applied, 85/1326, 07/603, 07/606, 07/1546: *Considered*, 02/579:
Followed, 06/596

Musisi v Secretary of State for the Home Department see Bugdaycay v Secretary of State for the Home Department

My Fotostop Ltd (In Administration) v Fotostop Group Ltd [2006] EWHC 2729 (Ch); [2007] F.S.R. 17, Ch D . . . . *Digested*, 07/**789**

Myatt v National Coal Board; *joined case* Garrett v Halton BC [2006] EWCA Civ 1017; [2007] 1 W.L.R. 554; [2007] 1 All E.R. 147; [2006] 5 Costs L.R. 798; (2006) 103(31) L.S.G. 26; (2006) 150 S.J.L.B. 1190; *Times*, July 25, 2006; *Independent*, July 26, 2006, CA (Civ Div); affirming (Unreported, August 12, 2005), Sup Ct Costs Office . . . . *Digested*, 06/**2735**:
Cited, 07/428

Myatt v National Coal Board [2007] EWCA Civ 307; [2007] 1 W.L.R. 1559; [2007] 4 All E.R. 1094; [2007] 4 Costs L.R. 564; [2007] P.N.L.R. 25; *Times*, March 27, 2007, CA (Civ Div) . . . . *Digested*, 07/**428**

MyTravel Group Plc v Customs and Excise Commissioners (C-291/03) [2005] S.T.C. 1617; [2005] E.C.R. I-8477; [2006] 1 C.M.L.R. 13; [2005] C.E.C. 782; [2005] S.T.I. 1679, ECJ (3rd Chamber) . . . . *Digested*, 07/**4352**:
Applied, 07/4331

N v Chief Constable of Merseyside [2006] EWHC 3041 (QB); [2006] Po. L.R. 160, QBD . . . . *Digested*, 07/**4201**

N v DPP [2007] EWHC 883 (Admin); (2007) 171 J.P. 393; (2007) 171 J.P.N. 707, QBD (Admin) . . . . *Digested*, 07/**3770**

N v Inspecteur van de Belastingdienst Oost/Kantoor Almelo (C-470/04) [2006] E.C.R. I-7409; [2006] 3 C.M.L.R. 49; [2007] C.E.C. 98; [2006] S.T.I. 2180, ECJ (2nd Chamber) . . . . *Digested*, 07/**1624**

N v N [2006] EWHC 3269 (Fam); [2007] 1 F.C.R. 749; [2007] Fam. Law 294, Fam Div . . . . *Digested*, 07/**1705**

N v Secretary of State for the Home Department [2006] EWCA Civ 299, CA (Civ Div) . . . . *Digested*, 07/**2321**

N (A Child), Re [2006] EWCA Civ 357; [2006] 2 F.L.R. 1124; [2006] Fam. Law 737, CA (Civ Div) . . . . *Digested*, 07/**1789**

N (A Child), Re; *sub nom* N (A Child) (Jurisdiction), Re [2007] Fam. Law 901, Fam Div

N (A Child) v Davies (Unreported, March 26, 2007), CC (Leicester) [*Ex rel.* Shabnam Walji, Barrister, Regency Chambers, Cathedral Square, Peterborough] . . . . *Digested*, 07/**3187**

N (A Child) v Entry Clearance Officer see N (A Child) v Immigration Appeal Tribunal

N (A Child) v Immigration Appeal Tribunal; *sub nom* N (A Child) v Entry Clearance Officer; N (A Child) v Immigration Officer [2001] I.N.L.R. 26; (2000) 97(36) L.S.G. 41; *Times*, September 6, 2000, CA (Civ Div) . . . . *Digested*, 00/**3356**:
Considered, 07/2325

N (A Child) v Immigration Officer see N (A Child) v Immigration Appeal Tribunal

N (A Child) v Naduva (Unreported, August 1, 2006), CC (Portsmouth) [*Ex rel.* Richard Wheeler, Barrister, 3 Paper Buildings, 4 St Peters Street, Winchester] . . . . *Digested*, 07/**3088**

N (A Child) v Newham LBC (Unreported, March 7, 2007), CC (Central London) [*Ex rel.* John Gallagher, Barrister, Hardwicke Building, New Square, Lincoln's Inn, London] . . . . *Digested*, 07/**2931**

N (A Child) (Jurisdiction), Re see N (A Child), Re

N (Children), Re [2006] EWCA Civ 1562; [2007] Fam. Law 121, CA (Civ Div)

N (Jurisdiction), Re [2007] EWHC 1274 (Fam); [2007] 2 F.L.R. 1196, Fam Div

N (Minors) (Child Abduction), Re [1991] 1 F.L.R. 413; [1991] F.C.R. 765; [1991] Fam. Law 367, Fam Div . . . . *Digested*, 91/**2530**:
Applied, 96/536, 00/2441: *Considered*, 07/1746: *Followed*, 02/5606:
Referred to, 94/5440

NA v MA see A v A

NA v Turkey (37451/97) (2007) 45 E.H.R.R. 9, ECHR . . . . *Digested*, 07/**2206**

Nachi Europe GmbH v Hauptzollamt Krefeld (C-239/99) [2001] E.C.R. I-1197, ECJ . . *Applied*, 07/1644

Nachova v Bulgaria (43577/98) (2004) 39 E.H.R.R. 37, ECHR . . . . *Digested*, 05/**2112**:
Applied, 07/2237: *Subsequent proceedings*, 06/2168

Nadanasikamani v Secretary of State for the Home Department [2005] EWCA Civ 1666, CA (Civ Div) . . . . *Applied*, 07/2290

Nadarajah v Secretary of State for the Home Department see R. (on the application of Nadarajah) v Secretary of State for the Home Department

Nadasdi v Vam- es Penzugyorseg Eszak-Alfoldi Regionalis Parancsnoksaga (C-290/
  05) [2006] E.C.R. I-10115; [2007] 1 C.M.L.R. 21, ECJ (1st Chamber). . . . .   *Digested*, 07/**1044**:
                                                      Applied, 07/1607
Nagarajan v London Regional Transport; *sub nom* Swiggs v Nagarajan (No.2); *joined*
  case Nagarajan v Swiggs (No.2) [2000] 1 A.C. 501; [1999] 3 W.L.R. 425;
  [1999] 4 All E.R. 65; [1999] I.C.R. 877; [1999] I.R.L.R. 572; (1999) 96(31)
  L.S.G. 36; (1999) 149 N.L.J. 1109; (1999) 143 S.J.L.B. 219; *Times*, July 19, 1999;
  Independent, October 11, 1999, HL; reversing [1998] I.R.L.R. 73, CA (Civ Div) .   *Digested*, 99/**2093**:
                              Applied, 02/1332, 02/1415, 05/1290, 05/2162, 06/1368, 07/1402:
                               Cited, 07/1404: *Considered*, 01/2301, 07/266: *Followed*, 03/1354
Nagarajan v Swiggs (No.2) see Nagarajan v London Regional Transport
Nageh v Giddings [2006] EWHC 3240 (TCC); [2007] C.I.L.L. 2420, QBD (TCC)
Nagra v OT Computers Ltd see OT Computers Ltd (In Administration), Re
Nakajima All Precision Co Ltd v Council of the European Communities (C-69/89)
  [1991] E.C.R. I-2069, ECJ . . . .   *Applied*, 02/2983,
                           07/1584: *Considered*, 00/2366: *Distinguished*, 06/1535
Nakajima All Precision Co Ltd v Council of the European Communities (C-69/89 R)
  [1989] E.C.R. 1689, ECJ . . . .   *Applied*, 07/1584:
                      Considered, 02/2983, 06/1535: *Followed*, 00/2346, 00/2366
Nakhmanovich v Russia (55669/00) (2007) 45 E.H.R.R. 41, ECHR
Nanning v Germany (39741/02) [2007] 2 F.C.R. 543, ECHR
Napp Pharmaceutical Holdings Ltd v Director General of Fair Trading (No.4) [2002]
  CAT 1; [2002] Comp. A.R. 13; [2002] E.C.C. 13; (2002) 64 B.M.L.R. 165,
  CCAT . . . .   *Digested*, 02/**597**:
                    Applied, 04/542, 05/570: *Approved*, 07/621: *Followed*, 05/572
Nason v Revenue and Customs Commissioners [2007] Pens. L.R. 67; [2007] S.T.C.
  (S.C.D.) 125; [2007] S.T.I. 200, Sp Comm. . . . .   *Digested*, 07/**4095**
Nasseri v Secretary of State for the Home Department; *sub nom* R. (on the application
  of Nasseri) v Secretary of State for the Home Department; C4/2007/1785, CA
  (Civ Div); reversing [2007] EWHC 1548 (Admin); [2007] H.R.L.R. 36; [2007]
  U.K.H.R.R. 1008; *Times*, August 3, 2007, QBD (Admin) . . . .   *Digested*, 07/**2306**
Nastou v Greece (16163/02) (Unreported, July 15, 2005), ECHR . . . .   *Applied*, 07/2206
National Assembly for Wales v Condron see R. (on the application of Condron) v
  National Assembly for Wales
National Bank Ltd, Re [1966] 1 W.L.R. 819; [1966] 1 All E.R. 1006; (1966) 110 S.J. 226, Ch D
  . . . .   *Digested*, 66/**1305**:
              Applied, 00/683, 02/2715, 05/2334: *Considered*, 00/684, 07/2447
National Basketball Association v Athletic Union of Constantinople (AEK) (Application
  to Strike Out) see Athletic Union of Constantinople (AEK) v National Basketball
  Association (Application to Strike Out)
National Galleries of Scotland v Revenue and Customs Commissioners [2007] V. &
  D.R. 234, V&DTr (Edinburgh)
National Greyhound Racing Club Ltd v Flaherty see Flaherty v National Greyhound
  Racing Club Ltd
National Grid Co Plc v M25 Group Ltd (No.1) [1999] 1 E.G.L.R. 65; [1999] 08 E.G.
  169; [1999] E.G. 2 (C.S.), CA (Civ Div); reversing [1998] 2 E.G.L.R. 85; [1998]
  32 E.G. 90; [1998] N.P.C. 172, Ch D . . . .   *Digested*, 99/**3727**:
                                                 Applied, 07/2756
National Pensions Office v Jonkman (C-231/06); *joined cases* Permesaen v National
  Pensions Office (C-233/06); National Pensions Office v Vercheval (C-232/06)
  [2007] 3 C.M.L.R. 25; [2007] Pens. L.R. 225, ECJ (1st Chamber)
National Pensions Office v Vercheval (C-232/06) see National Pensions Office v
  Jonkman (C-231/06)
National Power Plc, Re (C-151/97 P (I)); *sub nom* British Coal Corp v Commission of
  the European Communities (T-367/94); *joined case* PowerGen Plc, Re (C-157/
  97 P (I)) [1997] All E.R. (E.C.) 673; [1997] E.C.R. I-3491; [1998] 4 C.M.L.R.
  502, ECJ. . . . .   *Digested*, 98/**2306**:
                     Considered, 07/2799: *Followed*, 01/2472, 05/576, 05/577
National Provincial Bank v Barwell see Palmer, Re
National Union of Flint Glassworkers, Re [2006] B.C.C. 828, Ch D . . . .   *Digested*, 07/**596**
National Westminster Bank Plc v Ashe see Ashe v National Westminster Bank Plc
National Westminster Bank Plc v Gill see Royal Bank of Scotland Plc v Etridge (No.2)
National Westminster Bank Plc v Kotonou (Costs); *joined case* Angelikotonou v National
  Westminster Bank Plc [2007] EWCA Civ 223; [2007] C.P. Rep. 22, CA (Civ
  Div); affirming [2006] EWHC 1785 (Ch); (2006) 150 S.J.L.B. 1288, Ch D . . . .   *Digested*, 07/**400**
National Westminster Bank Plc v Rabobank Nederland (Application to Strike Out)
  [2006] EWHC 2959 (Comm); [2007] 1 All E.R. (Comm) 975, QBD (Comm) . .   *Digested*, 07/**533**
Navicon SA v Administracion del Estado (C-97/06) [2007] S.T.I. 2405, ECJ (4th
  Chamber)
Navitaire Inc v EasyJet Airline Co Ltd (No.3) [2004] EWHC 1725 (Ch); [2005] E.C.C.
  30; [2005] E.C.D.R. 17; [2005] Info. T.L.R. 1; [2006] R.P.C. 3, Ch D . . . .   *Digested*, 05/**2427**:
                                                      Applied, 07/2514
Nazar v Pendle BC [2007] R.V.R. 344, Lands Tr

NB (France) v Secretary of State for the Home Department; *sub nom* NB (Right of Permanent Residence: France), Re [2007] UKAIT 39; [2007] Imm. A.R. 609, AIT

NB (Right of Permanent Residence: France), Re see NB (France) v Secretary of State for the Home Department

NBH Ltd v Hoare [2006] EWHC 73 (Ch); [2006] 2 B.C.L.C. 649, Ch D . . . .   *Digested*, 07/**572**

Nearfield Ltd v Lincoln Nominees Ltd [2006] EWHC 2421 (Ch); [2007] 1 All E.R. (Comm) 441, Ch D   *Digested*, 07/**784**

Neath Port Talbot CBC v Ware see R. (on the application of Ware) v Neath Port Talbot CBC

Neath Rugby Ltd, Re see Cuddy v Hawkes

Neath Rugby Ltd, Re see Hawkes v Cuddy

NEC Semi Conductors Ltd v Revenue and Customs Commissioners see Boake Allen Ltd v Revenue and Customs Commissioners

Neck v Taylor [1893] 1 Q.B. 560, CA . . . .   *Applied*, 07/**512**

Nederlandsche Banden Industrie Michelin NV v Commission of the European Communities (322/81) [1983] E.C.R. 3461; [1985] 1 C.M.L.R. 282; [1985] F.S.R. 250, ECJ . . . .   *Digested*, 85/**1319**:
Applied, 02/597, 07/1547, 07/1548: *Considered*, 05/571, 05/575, 06/605:
Followed, 00/715

Nederlandse Federatieve Vereniging voor de Groothandel op Elektrotechnisch Gebied v Commission of the European Communities (C-105/04 P) [2006] E.C.R. I-8725; [2006] 5 C.M.L.R. 22, ECJ (1st Chamber) . . . .   *Digested*, 07/**611**

Nederlandse Federatieve Vereniging voor de Groothandel op Elektrotechnisch Gebied v Commission of the European Communities (T5/00) [2003] E.C.R. II-5761; [2004] 5 C.M.L.R. 20, CFI (1st Chamber) . . . .   *Reversed in part*, 07/611

Nee v Jackson (Unreported, May 25, 2006), CC (Coventry) [*Ex rel.* Nicholas Preston, Barrister, Clerksroom 199 Strand, London WC2] . . . .   *Digested*, 07/**3215**

Needham v Panesar (Unreported, December 13, 2006), CC (Chester) [*Ex rel.* Chris Middleton, Barrister, Oriel Chambers, 14 Water Street, Liverpool] . . . .   *Digested*, 07/**3147**

Neil Martin Ltd v Revenue and Customs Commissioners [2007] EWCA Civ 1041; [2007] S.T.C. 1802; [2007] B.T.C. 662; [2007] S.T.I. 2459; (2007) 151 S.J.L.B. 1403, CA (Civ Div); reversing [2006] EWHC 2425 (Ch); [2007] S.T.C. 823; [2007] B.T.C. 3; [2006] S.T.I. 2260; *Times*, October 13, 2006, Ch D . . . .   *Digested*, 07/**4144**

Neill's Application for Judicial Review, Re [2006] NICA 5; [2006] N.I. 278, CA (NI) . .   *Digested*, 07/**4646**

Neilson v Poole (1969) 20 P. & C.R. 909, Ch D . . . .   *Digested*, 69/**178**:
Applied, 04/3261: *Considered*, 07/3365: *Distinguished*, 73/955:
Followed, 07/3364

Nelidow Santis v Secretary of State for the Home Department see Bugdaycay v Secretary of State for the Home Department

Nelson v Clearsprings (Management) Ltd [2006] EWCA Civ 1252; [2007] 1 W.L.R. 962; [2007] 2 All E.R. 407; [2007] C.P. Rep. 2; [2007] H.L.R. 14; (2006) 103(39) L.S.G. 32; (2006) 156 N.L.J. 1525; (2006) 150 S.J.L.B. 1250; [2006] N.P.C. 103; *Times*, October 5, 2006, CA (Civ Div) . . . .   *Digested*, 07/**370**

Nelson v Greening & Sykes (Builders) Ltd [2007] EWCA Civ 1358; (2007-08) 10 I.T.E.L.R. 689, CA (Civ Div)

Nelson v Hannam [1943] Ch. 59, CA . . . .   *Applied*, 55/**1494**, 07/304

Nemec v Caisse Regionale d'Assurance Maladie du Nord-Est (C-205/05) [2007] 1 C.M.L.R. 29; [2007] C.E.C. 542, ECJ (2nd Chamber) . . . .   *Digested*, 07/**1626**

Nesbitt v Holt [2007] EWCA Civ 249; [2007] P.N.L.R. 24; (2007) 151 S.J.L.B. 430, CA (Civ Div) . . . .   *Digested*, 07/**345**

Nesbitt v Secretary of State for Trade and Industry [2007] I.R.L.R. 847, EAT . . . .   *Digested*, 07/**1348**

Nesheim v Kosa [2006] EWHC 2710 (Ch); [2007] W.T.L.R. 149, Ch D

Nessa v Chief Adjudication Officer [1999] 1 W.L.R. 1937; [1999] 4 All E.R. 677; [1999] 2 F.L.R. 1116; [1999] 3 F.C.R. 538; [2000] Fam. Law 28; (1999) 96(42) L.S.G. 42; (1999) 149 N.L.J. 1619; (1999) 143 S.J.L.B. 250; *Times*, October 27, 1999; *Independent*, October 27, 1999, HL; affirming [1998] 2 All E.R. 728; [1998] 1 F.L.R. 879; [1998] 2 F.C.R. 461; [1998] Fam. Law 329; (1998) 142 S.J.L.B. 78; *Times*, February 11, 1998, CA (Civ Div) . . . .   *Digested*, 99/**4564**:
Applied, 02/4208: *Considered*, 06/4008, 07/1737

Neste Oy v Lloyds Bank Plc (The Tiiskeri, The Nestegas and The Enskeri) [1983] 2 Lloyd's Rep. 658; [1983] Com. L.R. 145; (1983) 133 N.L.J. 597, QBD (Comm)   *Digested*, 83/**201**:
Applied, 97/5578, 00/3433, 07/2388: *Considered*, 92/489, 93/73

Nestorway Ltd (t/a Electrographic International) v Ambaflex BV [2006] IEHC 235; [2007] I.L.Pr. 48, HC (Irl)

Netherlands v Commission of the European Communities (C-174/98 P); *joined case* Van der Wal v Commission of the European Communities (C-189/98 P) [2000] E.C.R. I-1; [2002] 1 C.M.L.R. 16; *Times*, February 22, 2000, ECJ . . . .   *Digested*, 00/**2395**:
Applied, 07/1585: *Followed*, 02/1547

Netherlands *v* European Parliament (C-377/98); *sub nom* Legal Protection of Biotechnological Inventions, Re (C-377/98) [2002] All E.R. (EC) 97; [2001] E.C.R. I-7079; [2001] 3 C.M.L.R. 49; [2002] F.S.R. 36; (2002) 68 B.M.L.R. 1, ECJ . . . . *Digested,* 02/**2792**:
                                      Applied, 07/**1556**: *Considered,* 03/1455

Netherlands Antilles *v* Council of the European Union (C-452/98) [2001] E.C.R. I-8973, ECJ . . . . *Applied,* 07/**1591**:
                                              Followed, 07/**1647**

Neumeister *v* Austria (No.1) (A/8) (1979-80) 1 E.H.R.R. 91, ECHR . . . . *Digested,* 80/**1383**:
                                              Considered, 07/**2232**

Neville *v* Cowdray Trust Ltd [2006] EWCA Civ 709; [2006] 1 W.L.R. 2097; [2007] H.L.R. 9; [2007] 2 P. & C.R. 23; [2006] 3 E.G.L.R. 47; [2006] 35 E.G. 144, CA (Civ Div) . . . . *Digested,* 06/**2694**

Neville *v* Gardner Merchant Ltd; *sub nom* Neville (Westminster City Council) *v* Gardner Merchant Ltd (1983) 5 Cr. App. R. (S.) 349; 83 L.G.R. 577; (1984) 148 J.P.N. 238, DC. . . . . *Digested,* 84/**2096**:
                      Considered, 06/920, 07/961: *Followed,* 96/1568

Neville *v* Wilson [1997] Ch. 144; [1996] 3 W.L.R. 460; [1996] 3 All E.R. 171; [1996] 2 B.C.L.C. 310; *Times,* April 4, 1996, CA (Civ Div) . . . . *Digested,* 96/**5781**:
                                              Considered, 07/**3358**

Neville Estates Ltd *v* Madden [1962] Ch. 832; [1961] 3 W.L.R. 999; [1961] 3 All E.R. 769; (1961) 105 S.J. 806, Ch D . . . . *Digested,* 61/**1002**:
         Applied, 71/12147, 07/**4264**: *Considered,* 87/3759: *Distinguished,* 68/365:
                                              Followed, 99/3561

Neville (Administrator of Unigreg Ltd) *v* Krikorian [2006] EWCA Civ 943; [2006] B.C.C. 937; [2007] 1 B.C.L.C. 1; *Times,* July 21, 2006; *Independent,* July 11, 2006, CA (Civ Div) . . . . *Digested,* 06/**544**

Neville (Westminster City Council) *v* Gardner Merchant Ltd see Neville *v* Gardner Merchant Ltd

Nevmerzhitsky *v* Ukraine (54825/00) (2006) 43 E.H.R.R. 32; 19 B.H.R.C. 177; [2006] 1 Prison L.R. 119, ECHR . . . . *Digested,* 07/**2197**

New Cotton Support Scheme, Re (C-310/04) see Spain *v* Council of the European Union (C-310/04)

New Fashions (London) Ltd *v* Revenue and Customs Commissioners [2005] EWHC 1628 (Ch); [2006] S.T.C. 175; [2007] B.T.C. 694; [2005] S.T.I. 1317, Ch D . . . . *Digested,* 06/**4189**

New Hampshire Insurance Co Ltd *v* Philips Electronics North America Corp (No.1) [1998] C.L.C. 1062; [1998] I.L.Pr. 256; [1999] Lloyd's Rep. I.R. 58, CA (Civ Div). . . . . *Digested,* 97/**890**:
          Applied, 06/637: *Considered,* 98/777, 07/2492: *Followed,* 00/3516

New ISG Ltd *v* Vernon [2007] EWHC 2665 (Ch); *Times,* December 12, 2007, Ch D . . . *Digested,* 07/**1418**

New Islington and Hackney Housing Association Ltd *v* Pollard Thomas and Edwards Ltd [2001] B.L.R. 74; (2001) 3 T.C.L.R. 25; 85 Con. L.R. 194; [2001] Lloyd's Rep. P.N. 243; [2001] P.N.L.R. 20; (2001) 17 Const. L.J. 55, QBD (TCC) . . . . *Digested,* 01/**4511**:
                                              Applied, 07/481

New Sombrero Phosphate Co *v* Erlanger see Erlanger *v* New Sombrero Phosphate Co

New Testament Church of God *v* Stewart [2007] EWCA Civ 1004; *Times,* November 20, 2007, CA (Civ Div); affirming [2007] I.R.L.R. 178, EAT . . . . *Digested,* 07/**1326**

New York City *v* Permanent Mission of India to the United Nations 10 I.T.L. Rep. 557, US Court

Newcastle City Council *v* Z; *sub nom* S (A Child), Re [2005] EWHC 1490 (Fam); [2007] 1 F.L.R. 861; [2007] Fam. Law 10, Fam Div . . . . *Digested,* 07/**3906**

Newcastle United Plc *v* Revenue and Customs Commissioners [2007] EWHC 612 (Ch); [2007] S.T.C. 1330; [2007] B.T.C. 5481; [2007] B.V.C. 449; [2007] S.T.I. 1050, Ch D; reversing [2007] B.V.C. 2049, V&DTr (Manchester) . . . . *Digested,* 07/**4350**

Newham LBC *v* Unknown [2006] R.V.R. 231, Lands Tr . . . . *Digested,* 07/**3388**

Newlands (Seaford) Educational Trust (In Administration), Re see Chittenden *v* Pepper

Newman (t/a Newman Associates) *v* Wenden Properties Ltd [2007] EWHC 336 (TCC); 114 Con. L.R. 95; [2007] C.I.L.L. 2474, QBD (TCC) . . . . *Digested,* 07/**416**

News Datacom Ltd *v* Atkinson (Inspector of Taxes) [2006] S.T.C. (S.C.D.) 732; [2006] S.T.I. 2346, Sp Comm. . . . . *Digested,* 07/**4006**

Newspaper Advertising, Re (4 Ob 164/06 F) [2007] E.C.C. 26, OGH (A)

Newton-Dunn *v* Myers (Unreported, July 19, 2007), CC (Central London) [*Ex rel.* Adam Dawson, Barrister, 9 Gough Square, London] . . . . *Digested,* 07/**3094**

Nexen Energy Marketing London Ltd *v* Revenue and Customs Commissioners [2007] S.T.I. 1700, V&DTr (London)

NGK INSULATORS LTD/Processing method (T211/06) [2007] E.P.O.R. 40, EPO (Technical Bd App) . . . . *Digested,* 07/**2621**

Nguyen *v* Netherlands (Communication No.3/2004) (2007) 45 E.H.R.R. SE9, UN CEDW

NHS Trust A v M; *joined case* NHS Trust B v H [2001] Fam. 348; [2001] 2 W.L.R. 942; [2001] 1 All E.R. 801; [2001] 2 F.L.R. 367; [2001] 1 F.C.R. 406; [2001] H.R.L.R. 12; [2001] Lloyd's Rep. Med. 28; (2001) 58 B.M.L.R. 87; [2001] Fam. Law 501; *Times,* November 29, 2000; *Daily Telegraph,* October 31, 2000, Fam Div . . . . *Digested,* 01/**3571**:
Applied, 07/1986: *Considered,* 04/1692: *Followed,* 02/1888

NHS Trust v A (A Child) [2007] EWHC 1696 (Fam); (2007) 10 C.C.L. Rep. 677; (2007) 98 B.M.L.R. 141, Fam Div . . . . *Digested,* 07/**1980**

NHS Trust B v H see NHS Trust A v M

Niazi Services Ltd v Van der Loo [2004] EWCA Civ 53; [2004] 1 W.L.R. 1254; [2004] H.L.R. 34; [2004] 1 E.G.L.R. 62; [2004] 17 E.G. 130; [2004] 8 E.G. 134 (C.S.); (2004) 148 S.J.L.B. 232; [2004] N.P.C. 18; [2004] 1 P. & C.R. DG23, CA (Civ Div) . . . . *Digested,* 04/**2529**:
Applied, 07/2747

Nichia Corp v Argos Ltd [2007] EWCA Civ 741; [2007] Bus. L.R. 1753; [2007] F.S.R. 38; (2007) 30(8) I.P.D. 30050, CA (Civ Div) . . . . *Digested,* 07/**2622**

Nicholds v Security Industry Authority; *sub nom* R. (on the application of Thorpe) v Security Industry Authority; R. (on the application of Hancock) v Security Industry Authority; R. (on the application of Nicholds) v Security Industry Authority; *joined cases* Thorpe v Security Industry Authority; Hancock v Security Industry Authority [2006] EWHC 1792 (Admin); [2007] 1 W.L.R. 2067; [2007] I.C.R. 1076, QBD (Admin). . . . . *Digested,* 07/**2815**:
Applied, 07/1944

Nicholls v Hudson [2006] EWHC 3006 (Ch); [2007] W.T.L.R. 341; (2006) 150 S.J.L.B. 1333, Ch D

Nicholls v Lan [2006] EWHC 1255 (Ch); [2007] 1 F.L.R. 744; [2006] B.P.I.R. 1243; [2006] Fam. Law 1020; *Times,* August 4, 2006, Ch D . . . . *Digested,* 07/**2402**

Nicholson v Goff [2007] 13 E.G. 256, Lands Tr

Nickerson v Barroughclough [1981] Ch. 426; [1981] 2 W.L.R. 773; [1981] 2 All E.R. 369; (1981) 41 P. & C.R. 225; (1981) 125 S.J. 185, CA (Civ Div); reversing [1980] Ch. 325; [1979] 3 W.L.R. 562; [1979] 3 All E.R. 312; (1980) 39 P. & C.R. 144; (1979) 252 E.G. 487; (1980) 130 N.L.J. 205; (1979) 123 S.J. 736, Ch D . . . . *Digested,* 81/**745**:
Considered, 07/3399: *Followed,* 97/4264

Niderost-Huber v Switzerland (18990/91) (1998) 25 E.H.R.R. 709, ECHR . . . . *Digested,* 98/**3125**:
Applied, 98/3126: *Considered,* 07/1774

Niemietz v Germany (A/251-B) (1993) 16 E.H.R.R. 97, ECHR. . . . . *Digested,* 93/**2157**:
Applied, 98/3154: *Considered,* 00/3248, 04/1304, 05/2116, 07/204

Night Flight Restrictions, Re (C-422/05) see Commission of the European Communities v Belgium (C-422/05)

Nikken Kosakusho Works v Pioneer Trading Co [2005] EWCA Civ 906; [2006] F.S.R. 4, CA (Civ Div); affirming [2004] EWHC 2426 (Ch), Ch D . . . . *Digested,* 06/**2531**:
Considered, 07/2613, 07/2633

Nikonovs v Governor of Brixton Prison see R. (on the application of Nikonovs) v Brixton Prison Governor

Nikowitz v Austria [2007] E.M.L.R. 8, ECHR . . . . *Digested,* 07/**2186**

Nippon Carbon Co Ltd v Commission of the European Communities (T-244/01) see Tokai Carbon Co Ltd v Commission of the European Communities (T-236/01)

Niru Battery Manufacturing Co v Milestone Trading Ltd (No.1) [2003] EWCA Civ 1446; [2004] Q.B. 985; [2004] 2 W.L.R. 1415; [2004] 1 All E.R. (Comm) 193; [2004] 1 Lloyd's Rep. 344; [2004] 1 C.L.C. 647; [2004] W.T.L.R. 377; (2003) 100(44) L.S.G. 33; *Times,* October 30, 2003, CA (Civ Div); affirming [2002] EWHC 1425 (Comm); [2002] 2 All E.R. (Comm) 705, QBD (Comm) . . . . *Digested,* 03/**257**:
Applied, 06/4331, 06/4380, 07/4237: *Considered,* 03/3610

Niru Battery Manufacturing Co v Milestone Trading Ltd (No.2) [2004] EWCA Civ 487; [2004] 2 All E.R. (Comm) 289; [2004] 2 Lloyd's Rep. 319; [2004] 1 C.L.C. 882; (2004) 148 S.J.L.B. 538, CA (Civ Div); affirming [2003] EWHC 1032 (Comm); [2003] 2 All E.R. (Comm) 365, QBD (Comm) . . . . *Digested,* 04/**3267**:
Applied, 07/4248: *Considered,* 07/2500

Nissan Motor Manufacturing (UK) Ltd v Revenue and Customs Commissioners [2007] V. & D.R. 1, V&DTr (Manchester)

NJ v Essex CC see J (A Child) (Care Proceedings: Fair Trial), Re

NM (No Retrospective Cancellation of Leave: Zimbabwe), Re see NM (Zimbabwe) v Secretary of State for the Home Department

NM (Zimbabwe) v Secretary of State for the Home Department; *sub nom* NM (No Retrospective Cancellation of Leave: Zimbabwe), Re [2007] UKAIT 2; [2007] I.N.L.R. 391, AIT

NMH Stahlwerke GmbH v Commission of the European Communities (T-134/94 R) [1996] E.C.R. II-537; [1997] 5 C.M.L.R. 227, CFI (2nd Chamber) . . . . *Applied,* 07/1551

NMMT v MOT see NMT v MOT

NMT v MOT; *sub nom* NMMT v MOT; T v T; M-T v T [2006] EWHC 2494 (Fam); [2007] 2 F.L.R. 925; [2007] Fam. Law 1066, Fam Div

Noble Assurance Co v Gerling-Konzern General Insurance Co [2007] EWHC 253 (Comm); [2007] 1 C.L.C. 85, QBD (Comm) . . . . *Digested,* 07/**355**:
Applied, 07/353

Noblebright Ltd v Sirius International Corp [2007] Lloyd's Rep. I.R. 584, QBD (Manchester) . . . . *Digested,* 07/**2483**

Nokia Corp v InterDigital Technology Corp [2005] EWCA Civ 614, CA (Civ Div); affirming [2004] EWHC 2920 (Pat); (2005) 28(5) I.P.D. 28039, Ch D (Patents Ct) . . . . *Considered,* 07/2555

Nokia Corp v InterDigital Technology Corp [2007] EWHC 1076 (Pat); (2007) 30(6) I.P.D. 30040, Ch D (Patents Ct)

Nokia Corp v InterDigital Technology Corp (Application to Set Aside) [2006] EWCA Civ 1618; [2007] F.S.R. 23; (2007) 30(2) I.P.D. 30010, CA (Civ Div); affirming [2006] EWHC 802 (Pat); (2006) 29(7) I.P.D. 29053, Ch D (Patents Ct) . . . . . *Digested,* 07/**2555**

Nokia Corp v InterDigital Techology Corp [2007] EWHC 1041 (Pat); (2007) 30(6) I.P.D. 30039, Ch D (Patents Ct)

Nokia Corp v Wardell (C-316/05) [2007] 1 C.M.L.R. 37; [2007] C.E.C. 393; [2007] E.T.M.R. 20; [2007] Bus. L.R. D16, ECJ (1st Chamber) . . . . *Digested,* 07/**2652**

Nolan v Pearson (Unreported, May 23, 2006), CC (Liverpool) [*Ex rel.* Chris Middleton, Barrister, Oriel Chambers, 14 Water Street, Liverpool] . . . . *Digested,* 07/**3119**

Nomura International Plc v Granada Group Ltd [2007] EWHC 642 (Comm); [2007] 2 All E.R. (Comm) 878; [2007] 1 C.L.C. 479, QBD (Comm) . . . . *Digested,* 07/**369**

Norbrook Laboratories Ltd v Tank [2006] EWHC 1055 (Comm); [2006] 2 Lloyd's Rep. 485; [2006] B.L.R. 412, QBD (Comm) . . . . *Digested,* 07/**251**

Norfolk CC v Knights; *sub nom* Caister on Sea Joint Burial Committee, Re [1958] 1 W.L.R. 309; [1958] 1 All E.R. 394 (Note); (1958) 122 J.P. 115; (1958) 102 S.J. 197, Cons Ct . . . . *Digested,* 58/**1110**:
Considered, 07/1084

Norfolk CC v Webster see Webster (A Child), Re

Norfolk CC v Webster see Webster (A Child), Re

Norglen Ltd (In Liquidation) v Reeds Rains Prudential Ltd; *joined cases* Mayhew-Lewis v Westminster Scaffolding Group Plc; Levy v ABN AMRO Bank NV; Circuit Systems Ltd (In Liquidation) v Zuken-Redac (UK) Ltd [1999] 2 A.C. 1; [1997] 3 W.L.R. 1177; [1998] 1 All E.R. 218; [1998] B.C.C. 44; [1998] 1 B.C.L.C. 176; 87 B.L.R. 1; (1997) 94(48) L.S.G. 29; (1997) 147 N.L.J. 1773; (1998) 142 S.J.L.B. 26; (1998) 75 P. & C.R. D21; *Times,* December 1, 1997, HL; affirming [1996] 1 W.L.R. 864; [1996] 1 All E.R. 945; [1996] B.C.C. 532; [1996] 1 B.C.L.C. 690; *Times,* December 6, 1995; *Independent,* January 12, 1996, CA (Civ Div); reversing [1994] E.G. 21 (C.S.), Ch D . . . . *Digested,* 98/**375**:
Applied, 02/363, 07/4301: *Considered,* 06/323: *Distinguished,* 03/339:
Followed, 96/682, 98/401, 99/3312: *Subsequent related litigation,* 96/682

Norman v Secretary of State for the Home Department see Bugdaycay v Secretary of State for the Home Department

Norris v First Secretary of State [2006] EWCA Civ 12; [2007] 1 P. & C.R. 3; [2006] J.P.L. 1574; [2006] A.C.D. 39; [2006] 4 E.G. 167 (C.S.); [2006] N.P.C. 5, CA (Civ Div); affirming [2005] EWHC 890 (Admin), QBD (Admin) . . . . *Digested,* 06/**3344**

Norris v United States [2007] EWHC 71 (Admin); [2007] 1 W.L.R. 1730; [2007] 2 All E.R. 29; [2007] U.K.C.L.R. 1487; (2007) 157 N.L.J. 179; *Times,* February 7, 2007, QBD (Admin); affirming [2005] U.K.C.L.R. 1205, MC . . . . *Digested,* 07/**1670**:
Distinguished, 07/1659

Nortel Networks UK Pension Plan, Re see Lewis v Pensions Ombudsman

North v North [2007] EWCA Civ 760; [2007] 2 F.C.R. 601; (2007) 151 S.J.L.B. 1022; *Times,* August 17, 2007, CA (Civ Div)

North & South Trust Co v Berkeley; *sub nom* Berkeley v North & South Trust Co [1971] 1 W.L.R. 470; [1971] 1 All E.R. 980; [1970] 2 Lloyd's Rep. 467; (1970) 115 S.J. 244, QBD (Comm) . . . . *Digested,* 71/**111**:
Applied, 05/2355: *Considered,* 07/2467: *Distinguished,* 93/72

North Norfolk DC v MMO2 Airwave Ltd [2007] P.A.D. 90, Planning Inspector

North Range Shipping Ltd v Seatrans Shipping Corp (The Western Triumph) [2002] EWCA Civ 405; [2002] 1 W.L.R. 2397; [2002] 4 All E.R. 390; [2002] 2 All E.R. (Comm) 193; [2002] 2 Lloyd's Rep. 1; [2002] C.L.C. 992; (2002) 99(20) L.S.G. 31; *Times,* April 18, 2002; *Daily Telegraph,* May 13, 2002, CA (Civ Div) . . *Digested,* 02/**208**:
Applied, 04/181: *Considered,* 07/240: *Distinguished,* 07/249:
Followed, 06/204

North Somerset Council v Vanderplank [2007] P.A.D. 10, Planning Inspector

North Star Shipping Ltd v Sphere Drake Insurance Plc [2006] EWCA Civ 378; [2006] 2 All E.R. (Comm) 65; [2006] 2 Lloyd's Rep. 183; [2006] 1 C.L.C. 606; [2006] Lloyd's Rep. I.R. 519, CA (Civ Div); affirming [2005] EWHC 665 (Comm); [2005] 2 Lloyd's Rep. 76; [2005] 2 C.L.C. 238, QBD (Comm) . . . . . *Digested,* 06/**2424**:
Considered, 07/2484

North Warwickshire BC v TNT Logistics UK Ltd [2007] P.A.D. 16, Planning Inspector

North Wiltshire DC *v* Secretary of State for the Environment (1993) 65 P. & C.R. 137;
   [1992] 3 P.L.R. 113; [1992] J.P.L. 955; [1992] E.G. 65 (C.S.); [1992] N.P.C. 57;
   Times, April 21, 1992, CA (Civ Div); affirming . . . .   *Digested,* 93/**3930**:
                        Applied, 00/4519: *Considered,* 94/4464, 95/4875, 95/4875, 07/3276,
                                                          07/3283: *Distinguished,* 96/4702

NorthYorkshire CC *v* B [2007] Fam. Law 895, Fam Div
NorthYorkshire CC *v* Ratcliffe see Ratcliffe *v* NorthYorkshire CC
Northern Foods Plc *v* Department for the Environment, Food and Rural Affairs; *sub
   nom* R. (on the application of Northern Foods Plc) *v* Department for the
   Environment, Food and Rural Affairs [2005] EWHC 2971 (Admin); [2007] 1 All
   E.R. 216; [2006] Eu. L.R. 643; [2006] E.T.M.R. 31; [2006] F.S.R. 29; (2006)
   103(5) L.S.G. 31; *Times,* January 9, 2006, QBD (Admin) . . . .   *Digested,* 06/**2609**
Northern Light Music Ltd *v* Comptroller General of the UK Intellectual Property Office
   [2007] EWHC 1966 (Ch); (2007) 30(9) I.P.D. 30056, Ch D
Northern Sydney and Central Coast Area Health Service *v* Attorney General (New South
   Wales) [2007] NSWSC 881; (2007-08) 10 I.T.E.L.R. 351, Sup Ct (NSW)
Northstar Land Ltd *v* Brooks [2006] EWCA Civ 756; [2006] 2 E.G.L.R. 67; [2006] 32
   E.G. 80; [2006] 25 E.G. 208 (C.S.); [2007] 1 P. & C.R. DG1; *Times,* July 17,
   2006, CA (Civ Div); affirming [2005] EWHC 1919 (Ch), Ch D . . . .   *Digested,* 06/**3468**
Northstar Systems Ltd *v* Fielding (Costs) see Ultraframe (UK) Ltd *v* Fielding (Costs)
Northstar Systems Ltd (In Liquidation) *v* Fielding see Ultraframe (UK) Ltd *v* Fielding
Northumberland CC *v* Thompson (2007) 104(38) L.S.G. 35, EAT
Norton Tool Co Ltd *v* Tewson [1973] 1 W.L.R. 45; [1973] 1 All E.R. 183; [1972] I.C.R.
   501; [1972] I.R.L.R. 86; (1972) 13 K.I.R. 328; [1973] I.T.R. 23; (1973) 117 S.J.
   33, NIRC . . . .   *Digested,* 73/**1136**:
                        Applied, 73/1137, 74/1305, 74/1312, 74/1346, 75/1145, 75/1165, 76/963,
                                          76/965, 84/1289, 03/1333, 05/1331: *Approved,* 04/1303:
                                 Considered, 73/1143, 81/935, 97/2190, 98/2238: *Followed,* 74/1287,
                            74/1290, 76/960, 87/1388: *Not followed,* 06/1388: *Referred to,* 88/1336,
                                                                                              07/1425
Norvill *v* Chapman (1995) 133 A.L.R. 226, Fed Ct (Aus) (Full Ct) . . . .   *Distinguished,* 07/3295
Norwich City Council *v* Colliers CRE [2007] P.A.D. 85, Planning Inspector
Norwich City Council *v* Harvey (Paul Clarke) [1989] 1 W.L.R. 828; [1989] 1 All E.R.
   1180; 45 B.L.R. 14; (1989) 5 Const. L.J. 154; (1989) 86(25) L.S.G. 45; (1989)
   139 N.L.J. 40; (1989) 133 S.J. 694; *Times,* January 11, 1989; *Independent,*
   January 16, 1989; *Independent,* January 6, 1989, CA (Civ Div); affirming 39
   B.L.R. 75; (1988) 4 Const. L.J. 217, QBD . . . .   *Digested,* 89/**2587**:
                        Applied, 97/5721: *Considered,* 90/4724, 90/4724, 93/2997, 07/745
Norwich Pharmacal Co *v* Customs and Excise Commissioners; *sub nom* Morton-
   Norwich Products Inc *v* Customs and Excise Commissioners [1974] A.C. 133;
   [1973] 3 W.L.R. 164; [1973] 2 All E.R. 943; [1973] F.S.R. 365; [1974] R.P.C.
   101; (1973) 117 S.J. 567, HL; reversing [1972] 3 W.L.R. 870; [1972] 3 All E.R.
   813; [1972] F.S.R. 405; [1972] R.P.C. 743; (1972) 116 S.J. 823, CA (Civ Div);
   reversing [1972] Ch. 566; [1972] 2 W.L.R. 864; [1972] 1 All E.R. 972; [1972]
   F.S.R. 1; (1971) 116 S.J. 315, Ch D . . . .   *Digested,* 73/**2643**:
                        Applied, 74/2936, 80/2132, 80/2136, 88/2832, 90/3660, 93/3348,
                            98/3508, 98/4872, 02/338, 02/425, 03/407, 03/424, 06/2096, 07/461:
                            Considered, 81/2115, 84/2596, 84/2625, 86/1501, 86/1503, 90/3581,
                            91/781, 92/3476, 93/3211, 95/4130, 96/553, 96/769, 97/2205, 98/332,
                                 99/3444, 02/1884, 03/282: *Followed,* 94/3552, 94/3738, 96/764,
                                                          00/5532: *Referred to,* 99/319, 01/4413
Norwich Union Insurance Ltd *v* Meisels [2006] EWHC 2811 (QB); [2007] 1 All E.R.
   (Comm) 1138; [2007] Lloyd's Rep. I.R. 69, QBD . . . .   *Digested,* 07/**2484**
Notting Hill Housing Trust *v* Roomus [2006] EWCA Civ 407; [2006] 1 W.L.R. 1375;
   [2007] H.L.R. 2; [2006] L. & T.R. 23, CA (Civ Div) . . . .   *Digested,* 06/**2703**:
                                                                          Considered, 07/2766
Nottinghamshire CC *v* Woolworths Plc [2007] F.S.R. 19, MC . . . .   *Digested,* 07/**2688**
Nova Productions Ltd *v* Bell Fruit Games Ltd see Nova Productions Ltd *v* Mazooma
   Games Ltd
Nova Productions Ltd *v* Bell Fruit Games Ltd (Application for Preliminary Reference)
   see Nova Productions Ltd *v* Mazooma Games Ltd (Application for Preliminary
   Reference)
Nova Productions Ltd *v* Mazooma Games Ltd; *joined case* Nova Productions Ltd *v* Bell
   Fruit Games Ltd [2007] EWCA Civ 219; [2007] Bus. L.R. 1032; [2007] E.C.C.
   21; [2007] E.C.D.R. 6; [2007] E.M.L.R. 14; [2007] Info. T.L.R. 15; [2007] R.P.C.
   25; (2007) 30(5) I.P.D. 30032; *Times,* April 5, 2007, CA (Civ Div); affirming
   [2006] EWHC 24 (Ch); [2006] E.M.L.R. 14; [2006] R.P.C. 14; (2006) 29(3)
   I.P.D. 29023; (2006) 103(8) L.S.G. 24, Ch D . . . .   *Digested,* 07/**2514**
Nova Productions Ltd *v* Mazooma Games Ltd (Application for Preliminary Reference);
   joined case Nova Productions Ltd *v* Bell Fruit Games Ltd (Application for
   Preliminary Reference) [2006] EWCA Civ 1044; [2006] Eu. L.R. 1255; (2006)
   29(10) I.P.D. 29073, CA (Civ Div) . . . .   *Digested,* 07/**2528**

Novartis AG v Ivax Pharmaceuticals UK Ltd [2007] EWCA Civ 971; (2007) 30(10)
I.P.D. 30061, CA (Civ Div); affirming [2006] EWHC 2506 (Pat), Ch D (Patents
Ct)
NOVELL/Virtual machine (T856/05) [2007] E.P.O.R. 57, EPO (Technical Bd App)
NOVO NORDISK/NIDDM co-administration regimen (T137/04) [2007] E.P.O.R. 5, EPO
(Technical Bd App) . . . .   *Digested*, 07/**2599**
Novoselov v Russia (66460/01) (2007) 44 E.H.R.R. 11, ECHR
NPI Ltd, Re see Pearl Assurance (Unit Linked Pensions) Ltd, Re
Npower Renewables v Maldon DC [2007] P.A.D. 92, Planning Inspector
NS v MI [2006] EWHC 1646 (Fam); [2007] 1 F.L.R. 444; [2007] 2 F.C.R. 748;
[2006] Fam. Law 839, Fam Div . . . .   *Digested*, 07/**1834**
NSM Music Ltd v Leefe [2006] I.C.R. 450, EAT . . . .   *Digested*, 06/**1322**:
                                                                                                  Applied, 07/1382

Nugent v Benfield Greig Group Plc; *sub nom* Benfield Greig Group Plc, Re [2001]
EWCA Civ 397; [2002] B.C.C. 256; [2002] 1 B.C.L.C. 65; [2002] W.T.L.R. 769,
CA (Civ Div); reversing [2001] B.C.C. 92; [2000] 2 B.C.L.C. 488, Ch D
(Companies Ct) . . . .   *Digested*, 01/**745**:
                                                                                                  Considered, 07/459
Nunes v Davies Laing & Dick Ltd (1986) 51 P. & C.R. 310; [1986] 1 E.G.L.R. 106;
(1985) 277 E.G. 416, Ch D . . . .   *Digested*, 86/**1923**:
                        Applied, 90/651, 05/2679, 07/2728: *Considered*, 86/1917, 88/2067, 89/2159,
                                                        90/118, 90/2862, 92/106, 92/2733, 93/2536, 93/2536:
                                                                                                  Distinguished, 89/2181
Nurkowski, Re see Hill v Spread Trustee Co Ltd
Nuutinen v Finland (32842/96) (2002) 34 E.H.R.R. 15, ECHR . . . .   *Digested*, 02/**2459**:
                                                      Applied, 04/1472, 07/2251: *Considered*, 07/1747
Nykredit Mortgage Bank Plc v Edward Erdman Group Ltd see South Australia Asset
Management Corp v York Montague Ltd

O v Lewisham LBC [2007] EWHC 2130 (Admin); [2007] E.L.R. 633; (2007) 104(37)
L.S.G. 38, QBD (Admin)
O v Wandsworth LBC see R. v Wandsworth LBC Ex p. O
O Sang Ng v DPP [2007] EWHC 36 (Admin); [2007] R.T.R. 35; *Times*, February 7,
2007, QBD (Admin) . . . .   *Digested*, 07/**882**
O (Children) (Contact: Permission to Appeal), Re; *joined case* B (A Child) (Contact:
Permission to Appeal), Re [2006] EWCA Civ 1199; [2007] 1 F.L.R. 530; [2007]
Fam. Law 19; *Times*, October 6, 2006, CA (Civ Div) . . . .   *Digested*, 06/**1682**:
                                                                          Previous proceedings, 05/1646
O (Writ of Habeas Corpus), Re see R. (on the application of O) v Harrow Crown Court
O'Brien v Chief Constable of South Wales [2005] UKHL 26; [2005] 2 A.C. 534;
[2005] 2 W.L.R. 1038; [2005] 2 All E.R. 931; *Times*, April 29, 2005;
Independent, May 4, 2005, HL; affirming [2003] EWCA Civ 1085; [2004] C.P.
Rep. 5; [2004] Po. L.R. 21; (2003) 100(37) L.S.G. 32; *Times*, August 22, 2003,
CA (Civ Div) . . . .   *Digested*, 05/**302**:
                                                                                                  Applied, 07/493
O'Brien v Clark (Valuation Officer) [2006] R.A. 403, Lands Tr . . . .   *Digested*, 07/**3346**
O'Brien v Clark (Valuation Officer) (Permission to Appeal) [2006] EWCA Civ 1612;
[2007] R.V.R. 4, CA (Civ Div) . . . .   *Digested*, 07/**3347**
O'Brien v Clark (Valuation Officer) [2007] R.A. 17, Lands Tr . . . .   *Digested*, 07/**3341**
O'Brien v Independent Assessor see R. (on the application of O'Brien) v Independent
Assessor
O'Brien v Seagrave see Seagrave (Deceased), Re
O'Byrne v Aventis Pasteur MSD Ltd; *sub nom* O'Byrne v Aventis Pasteur SA [2007]
EWCA Civ 966; (2007) 98 B.M.L.R. 160; (2007) 104(41) L.S.G. 27; *Times*,
November 19, 2007, CA (Civ Div); affirming [2006] EWHC 2562 (QB); [2007]
1 W.L.R. 757; (2006) 92 B.M.L.R. 130; *Times*, November 21, 2006, QBD . . . . .   *Digested*, 07/**535**
O'Byrne v Aventis Pasteur SA see O'Byrne v Aventis Pasteur MSD Ltd
O'Connor v Haq (Unreported, January 4, 2007), CC (Brighton) [*Ex rel.* Richard
Wheeler, Barrister, 3 Paper Buildings, 4 St Peters Street, Winchester] . . . .   *Digested*, 07/**3174**
O'Connor v Kensington and Chelsea RLBC [2004] EWCA Civ 394; [2004] H.L.R. 37,
CA (Civ Div) . . . .   *Digested*, 04/**1900**:
                                                                                                  Applied, 07/2135
O'Connor v Wiltshire CC [2007] EWCA Civ 426; [2007] B.L.G.R. 865; [2007] R.V.R.
179; [2007] N.P.C. 57; *Times*, May 28, 2007, CA (Civ Div); reversing [2006] 2
E.G.L.R. 81; [2006] 18 E.G. 152, Lands Tr . . . .   *Digested*, 07/**3463**
O'Dowd v United Kingdom (34622/04) see Brecknell v United Kingdom (32457/04)
O'Halloran v United Kingdom (15809/02); *joined case* Francis v United Kingdom
(25624/02) [2007] Crim. L.R. 897; *Times*, July 13, 2007, ECHR (Grand
Chamber)
O'Hanlon v Revenue and Customs Commissioners [2007] EWCA Civ 283; [2007]
I.C.R. 1359; [2007] I.R.L.R. 404; *Times*, April 20, 2007, CA (Civ Div); affirming
[2006] I.C.R. 1579; [2006] I.R.L.R. 840, EAT . . . .   *Digested*, 07/**1336**

O'Kelly *v* Harvey (1883) L.R. 14 Ir. 105 . . . .   *Applied*, 07/3316:
                                                                                                        Considered, 07/3317

O'Neill *v* Phillips; *sub nom* Company (No.000709 of 1992), Re; Pectel Ltd, Re [1999]
    1 W.L.R. 1092; [1999] 2 All E.R. 961; [1999] B.C.C. 600; [1999] 2 B.C.L.C. 1;
    (1999) 96(23) L.S.G. 33; (1999) 149 N.L.J. 805; *Times*, May 21, 1999, HL;
    affirming [1998] B.C.C. 405; [1997] 2 B.C.L.C. 739, CA (Civ Div) . . . .   *Digested*, 99/**634**:
                                                Applied, 00/691, 01/747, 02/5375, 05/39, 06/565, 07/563:
                                        Considered, 04/477, 04/478, 06/553, 06/567: *Distinguished*, 03/545,
                                                                                                        03/545

O'Reilly *v* Mackman; *joined cases* Millbanks *v* Secretary of State for the Home
    Department; Derbyshire *v* Mackman; Dougan *v* Mackman; Millbanks *v* Home
    Office [1983] 2 A.C. 237; [1982] 3 W.L.R. 1096; [1982] 3 All E.R. 1124; (1982)
    126 S.J. 820, HL; affirming [1982] 3 W.L.R. 604; [1982] 3 All E.R. 680;
    (1982) 79 L.S.G. 1176; (1982) 126 S.J. 578, CA (Civ Div); reversing (1982) 126
    S.J. 312; *Times*, March 16, 1982, QBD . . . .   *Digested*, 82/**2603**:
                        Applied, 82/1465, 82/2527, 84/14, 84/447, 85/12, 85/2230, 86/324,
                        88/2976: *Considered*, 83/2943, 84/1344, 85/1702, 86/2017, 86/2662,
                        87/12, 87/20, 87/2378, 87/3052, 87/3162, 88/24, 88/2226, 88/3432, 89/35,
                        90/3908, 94/8, 94/43, 95/137, 95/835, 95/3252, 95/3907, 97/490, 00/44,
                        01/4715, 07/51: *Distinguished*, 83/3679, 85/9, 85/2722, 92/79, 92/2740:
                                                Doubted, 00/2001: *Followed*, 83/24, 87/2460

O2 *v* Chester-le-Street DC [2007] P.A.D. 28, Planning Inspector
O2 Holdings Ltd (formerly O2 Ltd) *v* Hutchison 3G Ltd [2006] EWCA Civ 1656; [2007]
    2 C.M.L.R. 15; [2007] E.C.C. 14; [2007] E.T.M.R. 19; [2007] R.P.C. 16, CA (Civ
    Div) [2006] EWHC 534 (Ch); [2006] E.T.M.R. 55; [2006] R.P.C. 29; (2006)
    29(7) I.P.D. 29051, Ch D . . . .   *Digested*, 07/**2671**
O2 (Germany) GmbH & Co OHG *v* Commission of the European Communities (T-328/
    03) [2006] E.C.R. II-1231; [2006] 5 C.M.L.R. 5, CFI (4th Chamber) . . . .   *Digested*, 07/**618**
OA (Nigeria) *v* Secretary of State for the Home Department; *sub nom* OA (Prisoner -
    Not a Qualified Worker: Nigeria), Re [2006] UKAIT 66; [2007] Imm. A.R. 96,
    AIT . . . .   *Digested*, 07/**1631**
OA (Prisoner - Not a Qualified Worker: Nigeria), Re see OA (Nigeria) *v* Secretary of State
    for the Home Department
Oakfern Properties Ltd *v* Ruddy; *sub nom* Ruddy *v* Oakfern Properties Ltd [2006]
    EWCA Civ 1389; [2007] Ch. 335; [2007] 3 W.L.R. 524; [2007] 1 All E.R. 337;
    [2007] L. & T.R. 9; [2006] 3 E.G.L.R. 30; [2006] 49 E.G. 96; (2006) 103(43)
    L.S.G. 31; [2006] N.P.C. 114; [2007] 2 P. & C.R. DG2; *Independent*, November
    3, 2006, CA (Civ Div) . . . .   *Digested*, 06/**2709**
Oakley *v* Osiris Trustees Ltd (2007-08) 10 I.T.E.L.R. 789, PC (IoM)
Oakley Inc *v* Animal Ltd [2005] EWCA Civ 1191; [2006] Ch. 337; [2006] 2 W.L.R.
    294; [2006] 1 C.M.L.R. 22; [2006] Eu. L.R. 323; [2006] E.C.D.R. 7; [2006]
    R.P.C. 9; (2006) 29(2) I.P.D. 29010; *Times*, November 7, 2005, CA (Civ Div);
    reversing [2005] EWHC 419 (Pat); [2005] Eu. L.R. 713, Ch D (Patents Ct) . . .   *Digested*, 06/**2460**:
                                                                                                        Applied, 07/69
OAO Northern Shipping Co *v* Remolcadores de Marin SL (The Remmar) [2007] EWHC
    1821 (Comm); [2007] 2 Lloyd's Rep. 302, QBD (Comm) . . . .   *Digested*, 07/**250**
OAO Plodovaya Kompaniya *v* Russia (1641/02) [2007] E.T.M.R. 55, ECHR . . . .   *Digested*, 07/**2209**
OB (Iraq) *v* Secretary of State for the Home Department [2007] EWCA Civ 585;
    (2007) 151 S.J.L.B. 810, CA (Civ Div)
Obermeier *v* Austria (11761/85) see Obermeier *v* Austria (A/179)
Obermeier *v* Austria (A/179); *sub nom* Obermeier *v* Austria (11761/85) (1991) 13
    E.H.R.R. 290, ECHR (1989) 11 E.H.R.R. CD57, Eur Comm HR . . . .   *Applied*, 07/**2214**
OBG Ltd *v* Allan; *sub nom* OBG Ltd *v* Allen; *joined cases* Douglas *v* Hello! Ltd;
    Mainstream Properties Ltd *v* Young [2007] UKHL 21; [2007] 2 W.L.R. 920;
    [2007] Bus. L.R. 1600; [2007] 4 All E.R. 545; [2007] I.R.L.R. 608; [2007]
    E.M.L.R. 12; [2007] B.P.I.R. 746; (2007) 30(6) I.P.D. 30037; [2007] 19 E.G. 165
    (C.S.); (2007) 151 S.J.L.B. 674; [2007] N.P.C. 54; *Times*, May 3, 2007; *Times*,
    May 4, 2007, HL; affirming [2005] EWCA Civ 106; [2005] Q.B. 762; [2005] 2
    W.L.R. 1174; [2005] 2 All E.R. 602; [2005] 1 All E.R. (Comm) 639; [2005] 1
    B.C.L.C. 711; [2005] B.L.R. 245; [2005] B.P.I.R. 928; [2005] P.N.L.R. 27;
    (2005) 102(14) L.S.G. 27; *Times*, February 24, 2005; *Independent*, February 18,
    2005, CA (Civ Div) . . . .   *Digested*, 07/**4190**
OBG Ltd *v* Allen see OBG Ltd *v* Allan
Ocalan *v* Council of the European Union (C-229/05 P) see Kurdistan Workers Party
    (PKK) *v* Council of the European Union (C-229/05 P)
Ocampo *v* Secretary of State for the Home Department see GO (Colombia) *v*
    Secretary of State for the Home Department
Oce van der Grinten NV *v* Inland Revenue Commissioners (C-58/01) [2003] S.T.C.
    1248; [2003] E.C.R. I-9809; [2003] 3 C.M.L.R. 30; [2003] B.T.C. 535; 6 I.T.L.
    Rep. 137; [2003] S.T.I. 1664, ECJ (5th Chamber) . . . .   *Digested*, 03/**4333**:
                                                                Applied, 06/4255: *Considered*, 07/3974

Oceano Grupo Editorial SA v Quintero (C-240/98); *joined cases* Salvat Editores SA v
    Feliu (C-244/98); Salvat Editores SA v Berroane (C-243/98); Salvat Editores
    SA v Badillo (C-242/98); Salvat Editores SA v Prades (C-241/98) [2000]
    E.C.R. I-4941; [2002] 1 C.M.L.R. 43, ECJ . . . .   *Digested,* 02/**693**:
                                                                Followed, 07/256
Oceanografia SA de CV v DSND Subsea AS (The Botnica) [2006] EWHC 1360;
    [2007] 1 All E.R. (Comm) 28; [2007] 1 Lloyd's Rep. 37, QBD (Comm)
ODC Enterprises Ltd v Tommy Hilfiger Licensing Inc [2006] E.T.M.R. 78, PO (Irl) . . . . .   *Digested,* 07/**2663**
Odey v Barber [2006] EWHC 3109 (Ch); [2007] 3 All E.R. 543, Ch D (Bristol)
Odhams Leisure Group Ltd v Customs and Excise Commissioners [1992] S.T.C. 332;
    Independent, March 16, 1992, QBD. . . . .   *Digested,* 92/**4562**:
                                              Considered, 07/4322
Odievre v France (42326/98) [2003] 1 F.C.R. 621; (2004) 38 E.H.R.R. 43; 14
    B.H.R.C. 526, ECHR . . . .   *Digested,* 03/**2180**:
                         Applied, 07/2260: *Considered,* 06/2174
Offer-Hoar v Larkstore Ltd; *sub nom* Larkstore Ltd v Technotrade Ltd; Technotrade Ltd
    v Larkstore Ltd [2006] EWCA Civ 1079; [2006] 1 W.L.R. 2926; [2007] 1 All
    E.R. (Comm) 104; [2006] B.L.R. 345; 109 Con. L.R. 92; [2006] P.N.L.R. 37;
    [2006] 3 E.G.L.R. 5; [2006] 42 E.G. 246; [2006] C.I.L.L. 2389; [2006] 31 E.G.
    89 (C.S.); (2006) 103(32) L.S.G. 20; [2006] N.P.C. 96, CA (Civ Div);
    affirming [2005] EWHC 2742 (TCC); [2006] P.N.L.R. 17; [2005] 50 E.G. 90
    (C.S.), QBD (TCC) . . . .   *Digested,* 06/**751**:
                                                      Applied, 07/2719
Office des Poursuites et des Faillites de Nyon (OPF) v Dumartheray [2007] I.L.Pr. 29,
    Cass (F) . . . .   *Digested,* 07/**675**
Office for Harmonisation in the Internal Market (Trade Marks and Designs) (OHIM) v
    Celltech R&D Ltd (C-273/05 P) [2007] E.T.M.R. 52, ECJ . . . .   *Digested,* 07/**2648**
Office for Harmonisation in the Internal Market (Trade Marks and Designs) (OHIM) v Kaul
    GmbH (C-29/05) [2007] E.T.M.R. 37, ECJ. . . . .   *Digested,* 07/**2655**
Office of Fair Trading v Lloyds TSB Bank Plc [2007] UKHL 48; [2007] 3 W.L.R. 733;
    (2007) 104(44) L.S.G. 31; (2007) 157 N.L.J. 1614; (2007) 151 S.J.L.B. 1432;
    Times, November 12, 2007, HL; affirming [2006] EWCA Civ 268; [2007] Q.B. 1;
    [2006] 3 W.L.R. 452; [2006] 2 All E.R. 821; [2006] 1 All E.R. (Comm) 629;
    (2006) 103(14) L.S.G. 28; (2006) 156 N.L.J. 553; *Times,* April 7, 2006, CA (Civ
    Div) [2004] EWHC 2600 (Comm); [2005] 1 All E.R. 843; [2005] 1 All E.R.
    (Comm) 354; [2005] E.C.C. 27; (2004) 154 N.L.J. 1728, QBD (Comm) . . . . .   *Digested,* 06/**699**
Office of the King's Prosecutor (Brussels) v Cando Armas; *sub nom* King's Prosecutor
    (Brussels) v Armas [2005] UKHL 67; [2006] 2 A.C. 1; [2005] 3 W.L.R. 1079;
    [2006] 1 All E.R. 647; [2005] Extradition L.R. 139; (2005) 155 N.L.J. 1809;
    Times, November 18, 2005; *Independent,* November 22, 2005, HL; affirming
    [2004] EWHC 2019 (Admin); [2005] 1 W.L.R. 1389; [2005] 2 All E.R. 181;
    [2005] Extradition L.R. 22; (2004) 154 N.L.J. 1498; *Times,* October 8, 2004,
    QBD (Admin) . . . .   *Digested,* 06/**1594**:
                   Applied, 06/1596, 07/1657: *Considered,* 06/1600, 07/5169:
                                                Followed, 07/1670
Officer L, Re [2007] UKHL 36; [2007] 1 W.L.R. 2135; [2007] 4 All E.R. 965; [2007] N.I.
    277; [2007] H.R.L.R. 42; [2007] U.K.H.R.R. 1023; (2007) 157 N.L.J. 1274; (2007)
    151 S.J.L.B. 1061; *Times,* August 1, 2007, HL; reversing [2007] NICA 8, CA (NI);
    affirming [2006] NIQB 75; [2006] Inquest L.R. 211, QBD (NI). . . . .   *Digested,* 07/**544**
Officer van Justitie v Van Bennekom (C-227/82); *sub nom* Criminal Proceedings
    against van Bennekom (C-227/82) [1983] E.C.R. 3883; [1985] 2 C.M.L.R.
    692, ECJ (5th Chamber) . . . .   *Digested,* 85/**1457**:
                                                      Followed, 07/1606
Official Receiver v Doganci [2007] B.P.I.R. 87, Ch D . . . .   *Digested,* 07/**2416**
Official Receiver v Doshi see Smart-Tel (UK) Ltd, Re
Official Receiver v Eichler [2007] B.P.I.R. 1636, Ch D
Official Receiver v Hollens [2007] EWHC 754 (Ch); [2007] Bus. L.R. 1402; [2007] 3
    All E.R. 767; [2007] B.P.I.R. 830, Ch D . . . .   *Digested,* 07/**2964**
Official Receiver v Merchant [2006] B.P.I.R. 1525, Ch D . . . .   *Digested,* 07/**2400**
Official Receiver v Pyman [2007] EWHC 2002 (Ch); [2007] B.P.I.R. 1150, Ch D
Official Receiver v Randhawa see Randhawa v Official Receiver
Officier van Justitie v Kramer (3/76); *joined cases* Officier van Justitie v Van Den Berg
    (4/76); Officier van Justitie v Kramer en Bais & Co (6/76) [1976] E.C.R. 1279;
    [1976] 2 C.M.L.R. 440, ECJ. . . . .   *Digested,* 76/**1056**:
                                                      Applied, 07/1870
Officier van Justitie v Kramer en Bais & Co (6/76) see Officier van Justitie v Kramer (3/
    76)
Officier van Justitie v Van Den Berg (4/76) see Officier van Justitie v Kramer (3/76)
Ogbuneke v Minster Lodge see Muschett v Hounslow LBC
Ognyanova v Bulgaria (46317/99) (2007) 44 E.H.R.R. 7, ECHR . . . .   *Digested,* 07/**2236**
Ogunrinde v Law Society [2007] EWHC 1972 (Ch); (2007) 151 S.J.L.B. 745, Ch D
Okonedo v Kirby [2006] EWCA Civ 1055; [2006] R.V.R. 294, CA (Civ Div) . . . .   *Digested,* 07/**2773**
Olafsson v Gissurarson B1/2007/0207, CA (Civ Div); affirming [2006] EWHC 3214
    (QB); [2007] 1 Lloyd's Rep. 188, QBD . . . .   *Digested,* 07/**371**

Olafsson v Gissurarson [2006] EWHC 3162 (QB); [2007] 2 All E.R. 88; [2007] 1 All
E.R. (Comm) 776; [2007] 1 Lloyd's Rep. 182; (2007) 157 N.L.J. 30; *Times*,
December 22, 2006, QBD . . . . *Digested*, 07/**522**
Olchfa Comprehensive School Governors v E [2006] EWHC 1468 (Admin); [2006]
E.L.R. 503, QBD (Admin). . . . . *Digested*, 07/**1182**
Old Pinfold House, 16 The Green, Barby, Rugby, Warwickshire, CV23 8TS, Re see Vince's
Application, Re
Oldham MBC v GW [2007] EWHC 136 (Fam); [2007] 2 F.L.R. 597; (2007) 97
B.M.L.R. 146; [2007] Fam. Law 582, Fam Div (Manchester) . . . . *Digested*, 07/**1729**:
Applied, 07/1711

Oliver v RSN Ltd [2007] EWHC 320 (Ch); [2007] 10 E.G. 182 (C.S.), Ch D
Oliver v Secretary of State for the Environment see Thrasyvoulou v Secretary of State
for the Environment
Ollinger v Austria (76900/01) 22 B.H.R.C. 25, ECHR . . . . *Digested*, 07/**2177**
Olsson v Sweden (A/250) (1994) 17 E.H.R.R. 134, ECHR . . . . *Digested*, 94/**2426**:
Applied, 07/2248: *Considered*, 07/2253
Olupitan v Director of the Assets Recovery Agency see Director of the Assets
Recovery Agency v Olupitan
OM v Secretary of State for the Home Department; *sub nom* OM (Children:
Settlement: Cross Border Movement: Jamaica), Re [2005] UKIAT 177; [2006]
Imm. A.R. 200, IAT. . . . . *Distinguished*, 07/2332
OM (Children: Settlement: Cross Border Movement: Jamaica), Re see OM v Secretary of
State for the Home Department
Omar v Birmingham City Council [2007] EWCA Civ 610; [2007] H.L.R. 43; (2007)
104(25) L.S.G. 36; (2007) 151 S.J.L.B. 809; *Times*, June 12, 2007, CA (Civ
Div). . . . . *Digested*, 07/**2140**
Omar Parks Ltd v Elkington; *joined case* Ron Grundy (Melbourne) Ltd v Bonehevo
[1992] 1 W.L.R. 1270; [1993] 1 All E.R. 282; (1992) 24 H.L.R. 690; (1993) 65 P.
& C.R. 26; [1992] 42 E.G. 108; [1992] E.G. 98 (C.S.); (1992) 136 S.J.L.B. 229;
[1992] N.P.C. 96; *Times*, July 23, 1992, CA (Civ Div) . . . . *Digested*, 93/**3914**:
Considered, 07/4003
Omega SA v Omega Engineering Inc [2003] EWHC 1334 (Ch); [2003] F.S.R. 49,
Ch D . . . . *Digested*, 03/**2654**:
Applied, 07/2684
Omega Spielhallen- und Automatenaufstellungs GmbH v Bundesstadt Bonn (C-36/02)
[2004] E.C.R. I-9609; [2005] 1 C.M.L.R. 5; [2005] C.E.C. 391; *Times*, October
20, 2004, ECJ (1st Chamber) . . . . *Digested*, 05/**1467**:
Applied, 07/4145: *Considered*, 05/190, 07/204
Omilaju v Waltham Forest LBC (No.2); *sub nom* Waltham Forest LBC v Omilaju (No.2)
[2004] EWCA Civ 1493; [2005] 1 All E.R. 75; [2005] I.C.R. 481; [2005]
I.R.L.R. 35; (2004) 148 S.J.L.B. 1370; *Times*, November 26, 2004, CA (Civ Div);
reversing [2004] 3 All E.R. 129, EAT . . . . *Digested*, 05/**1209**:
Applied, 07/1317: *Considered*, 06/1321, 07/1319
Omokwe v HFC Bank Ltd [2007] B.P.I.R. 1157, HC . . . . *Digested*, 07/**2414**
Optare Group Ltd v Transport and General Workers Union [2007] I.R.L.R. 931; (2007)
104(30) L.S.G. 34, EAT . . . . *Digested*, 07/**1398**
Optical Express Ltd v Williams [2007] I.R.L.R. 928, EAT. *Digested*, 07/**1397**
Optical Storage A/S v Norddahl [2007] I.L.Pr. 11, OL (DK) . . . . *Digested*, 07/**670**
Optigen Ltd v Customs and Excise Commissioners; *joined case* Fulcrum Trading Co
(UK) Ltd (In Liquidation) v Customs and Excise Commissioners [2003] B.V.C.
2518; [2003] S.T.I. 1513, V&DTr. . . . . *Referred to*, 07/4302
Optigen Ltd v Customs and Excise Commissioners (C-354/03); *joined cases* Bond
House Systems Ltd v Customs and Excise Commissioners (C-484/03); Fulcrum
Electronics Ltd v Customs and Excise Commissioners (C-355/03) [2006] Ch.
218; [2006] 2 W.L.R. 456; [2006] S.T.C. 419; [2006] E.C.R. I-483; [2006] 2
C.M.L.R. 18; [2006] C.E.C. 509; [2006] B.T.C. 5050; [2006] B.V.C. 119; [2006]
S.T.I. 162; *Times*, January 17, 2006, ECJ (3rd Chamber) . . . . *Digested*, 06/**4456**:
Applied, 07/4318: *Considered*, 06/4464, 07/4302, 07/4311, 07/4315:
Followed, 06/4467: *Referred to*, 07/4302
Optos Plc v Revenue and Customs Commissioners [2006] S.T.C. (S.C.D.) 687; [2006]
S.T.I. 2236, Sp Comm. . . . . *Digested*, 07/**4031**
Orams v Apostolides [2006] EWHC 2226 (QB); [2007] 1 W.L.R. 241; [2007] 1 All
E.R. (Comm) 1; (2006) 103(38) L.S.G. 34; (2006) 156 N.L.J. 1441; (2006) 150
S.J.L.B. 1188; *Times*, September 22, 2006, QBD . . . . *Digested*, 06/**644**
Ordre des Barreaux Francophones et Germanophone v Conseil des Ministres (C-305/
05) [2007] All E.R. (EC) 953; [2007] 3 C.M.L.R. 28; *Times*, July 2, 2007, ECJ
(Grand Chamber)
Organisation des Modjahedines du Peuple d'Iran v Council of the European Union (T-
228/02) [2007] All E.R. (EC) 447; [2007] 1 C.M.L.R. 34, CFI (2nd Chamber) . *Digested*, 07/**1645**
Oriel Support Ltd v Revenue and Customs Commissioners [2007] S.T.I. 2463, Sp
Comm
Oriel Support Ltd v Revenue and Customs Commissioners (Costs) [2007] S.T.C.
(S.C.D.) 670; [2007] S.T.I. 1797, Sp Comm
Oriental Bank Corp Ex p. Guillemin, Re (1885) L.R. 28 Ch. D. 634, Ch D . . . . *Considered*, 07/2390

Orkem SA (formerly CdF Chimie SA) v Commission of the European Communities (C374/87); *joined case* Solvay et Cie SA v Commission of the European Communities (C27/88) [1989] E.C.R. 3283; [1991] 4 C.M.L.R. 502; *Times,* November 15, 1989; *Independent,* December 4, 1989, ECJ . . . . *Digested,* 90/**2069**:
                                  Applied, 07/609, 07/610: *Considered,* 00/2300, 03/1707: *Followed,* 01/768:
                                                   Referred to, 00/2377
Orton v Collins [2007] EWHC 803 (Ch); [2007] 1 W.L.R. 2953; [2007] 3 All E.R. 863; (2007) 151 S.J.L.B. 608; [2007] N.P.C. 49, Ch D . . . . *Digested,* 07/**488**
Osborn v Cole [1999] B.P.I.R. 251, Ch D . . . . *Digested,* 99/**382**:
                                          Applied, 07/2444: *Approved,* 07/2409
Osborne's Big Man Shop v Revenue and Customs Commissioners [2006] EWHC 3172 (Ch); [2007] S.T.C. 586; [2006] S.T.I. 324, Ch D . . . . *Digested,* 07/**4293**
Osea Road Campsites Ltd, Re see Bamber v Eaton
Osei v Southwark LBC [2007] EWCA Civ 787; [2007] N.P.C. 98, CA (Civ Div)
Osman v United Kingdom (23452/94) [1999] 1 F.L.R. 193; (2000) 29 E.H.R.R. 245; 5 B.H.R.C. 293; (1999) 1 L.G.L.R. 431; (1999) 11 Admin. L.R. 200; [2000] Inquest L.R. 101; [1999] Crim. L.R. 82; [1998] H.R.C.D. 966; [1999] Fam. Law 86; (1999) 163 J.P.N. 297; *Times,* November 5, 1998, ECHR (1996) 22 E.H.R.R. CD137, Eur Comm HR . . . . *Digested,* 98/**3102**:
                    Applied, 01/3476, 01/3571, 02/38, 02/2489, 02/3236, 03/2238, 04/13,
                    06/2171, 07/544: *Considered,* 99/3966, 99/3982, 00/3170, 00/3239,
                    01/3459, 04/2039, 06/989, 06/1607, 06/4806, 07/2238, 07/2980:
                                             Distinguished, 01/82
Osorio v Secretary of State for the Home Department see Saad v Secretary of State for the Home Department
Ospelt v Schlossle Weissenberg Familienstiftung (C-452/01) see Ospelt v Unabhangiger Verwaltungssenat des Landes Vorarlberg (C-452/01)
Ospelt v Unabhangiger Verwaltungssenat des Landes Vorarlberg (C-452/01); *sub nom* Ospelt v Schlossle Weissenberg Familienstiftung (C-452/01) [2003] E.C.R. I-9743; [2005] 3 C.M.L.R. 40; [2003] N.P.C. 109, ECJ . . . . *Digested,* 06/**3504**:
                                                    Applied, 07/1602
OSS Group Ltd v Environment Agency; *sub nom* R. (on the application of OSS Group Ltd) v Environment Agency; Solvent Resource Management Ltd v Environment Agency [2007] EWCA Civ 611; [2007] Bus. L.R. 1732; [2007] 3 C.M.L.R. 30; [2007] J.P.L. 1597; (2007) 104(28) L.S.G. 26; (2007) 151 S.J.L.B. 892; [2007] N.P.C. 80; *Times,* July 6, 2007, CA (Civ Div); affirming [2006] EWHC 3023 (Admin); [2007] Env. L.R. 19; [2007] A.C.D. 43; [2006] 49 E.G. 95 (C.S.); [2006] N.P.C. 128, QBD (Admin) . . . . *Digested,* 07/**1518**
Osseily v Westminster City Council [2007] EWCA Civ 1108; (2007) 151 S.J.L.B. 1298, CA (Civ Div)
Osterreichische Postsparkasse AG v Commission of the European Communities (T-213/01) [2006] E.C.R. II-1601; [2007] 4 C.M.L.R. 14, CFI (5th Chamber) . . . . *Digested,* 07/**1551**
Ostrovar v Moldova (35207/03) (2007) 44 E.H.R.R. 19; [2006] 1 Prison L.R. 99, ECHR
Osunta v Germany [2007] EWHC 1562 (Admin); [2007] 4 All E.R. 1038, DC . . . . . . *Digested,* 07/**1660**
OT Africa Line Ltd v Magic Sportswear Corp 2006 FCA 284; [2007] 1 Lloyd's Rep. 85, CA (Can) . . . . *Digested,* 07/**685**
OT Computers Ltd (In Administration), Re; *sub nom* First National Tricity Finance Ltd v Ellis; First National Tricity Finance Ltd v OT Computers Ltd (In Administration); Nagra v OT Computers Ltd [2004] EWCA Civ 653; [2004] Ch. 317; [2004] 3 W.L.R. 886; [2004] 2 All E.R. (Comm) 331; [2004] 2 B.C.L.C. 682; [2004] 2 C.L.C. 863; [2004] B.P.I.R. 932; [2004] Lloyd's Rep. I.R. 669; *Times,* May 31, 2004, CA (Civ Div); reversing [2003] EWHC 2490 (Ch); [2004] 1 All E.R. (Comm) 320; [2004] B.P.I.R. 195, Ch D . . . . *Digested,* 04/**2217**:
                                                    Applied, 07/511
OT Computers Ltd (In Administration) v First National Tricity Finance Ltd [2003] EWHC 1010 (Ch); [2007] W.T.L.R. 165; (2003-04) 6 I.T.E.L.R. 117, Ch D
OTP Garancia Biztosito rt v Vas Megyei Kozigazgatasi Hivatal (C-312/06) see KOGAZ rt v Zala Megyei Kozigazgatasi Hivatal Vezetoje (C-283/06)
Oulane v Minister voor Vreemdelingenzaken en Integratie (C-215/03) [2005] Q.B. 1055; [2005] 3 W.L.R. 543; [2005] E.C.R. I-1215; *Times,* February 21, 2005, ECJ . . . . *Digested,* 06/**1576**:
                                       Applied, 07/1611: *Considered,* 07/1652
Ouranio Toxo v Greece (74989/01) (2007) 45 E.H.R.R. 8, ECHR
Outokumpu Oy (C-213/96) [1998] E.C.R. I-1777, ECJ . . . . *Applied,* 07/1607
Oval 1742 Ltd (In Creditors Voluntary Liquidation), Re; *sub nom* Customs and Excise Commissioners v Royal Bank of Scotland Plc [2007] EWCA Civ 1262, CA (Civ Div); affirming [2006] EWHC 2813 (Ch); [2007] Bus. L.R. 474; [2007] B.C.C. 567; [2007] 2 B.C.L.C. 714, Ch D . . . . *Digested,* 07/**2445**
Owers v Bailey (2006) 103(39) L.S.G. 34; (2006) 150 S.J.L.B. 1292; [2007] 1 P. & C.R. DG17, Ch D . . . . *Considered,* 07/1060
Owners and/or Demise Charterers of the Tug Sea Tractor v Owners of the Tramp [2007] EWHC 31 (Admlty); [2007] 2 Lloyd's Rep. 363, QBD (Admlty) . . . . *Digested,* 07/**3810**

Owners of Cargo Lately Laden on Board the Rewia v Caribbean Liners (Caribtainer) Ltd
[1991] 2 Lloyd's Rep. 325; [1993] I.L.Pr. 507; *Financial Times*, July 12, 1991,
CA (Civ Div); reversing [1991] 1 Lloyd's Rep. 69; *Lloyd's List*, September 21,
1990, QBD (Admlty) . . . . *Digested*, 92/**3917**:
Applied, 03/484, 07/441

Owners of Cargo Lately Laden on Board the Starsin v Owners of the Starsin see
Homburg Houtimport BV v Agrosin Private Ltd (The Starsin)

Owners of the Bow Spring v Owners of the Manzanillo II [2004] EWCA Civ 1007;
[2005] 1 W.L.R. 144; [2004] 4 All E.R. 899; [2005] 1 All E.R. (Comm) 53;
[2005] 1 Lloyd's Rep. 1; [2005] 1 C.L.C. 394; *Times*, August 19, 2004;
Independent, October 8, 2004, CA (Civ Div); affirming [2003] EWHC 1802
(Admlty); [2004] 1 Lloyd's Rep. 647, QBD (Admlty) . . . . *Digested*, 04/**3495**:
Applied, 07/2625: *Considered*, 05/3794

Owners of the P Caland v Glamorgan Steamship Co Ltd (The P Caland) [1893] A.C.
207, HL; affirming [1892] P. 191, CA; affirming [1891] P. 313, PDAD . . . . *Applied*, 07/363:
Considered, 59/77, 76/2558

Owners of the Sardinia Sulcis v Owners of the Al Tawwab [1991] 1 Lloyd's Rep. 201;
Times, November 21, 1990; *Independent*, December 3, 1990; *Financial Times*,
November 13, 1990, CA (Civ Div) . . . . *Digested*, 91/**3204**:
Applied, 99/494, 05/89, 06/197, 07/534: *Followed*, 96/890:
Not followed, 05/315

Owners of the Steamship Mediana v Owners of the Lightship Comet [1900] A.C. 113,
HL; affirming [1899] P. 127, CA. . . . . *Applied*, 47-51/2554,
03/943, 05/4193: *Considered*, 52/893, 78/44.u, 07/2497

Oxford Architects Partnership v Cheltenham Ladies College [2006] EWHC 3156
(TCC); [2007] B.L.R. 293; [2007] P.N.L.R. 18; [2007] Bus. L.R. D25, QBD
(TCC) . . . . *Digested*, 07/**481**

Oxford City Council v Secretary of State for Communities and Local Government
[2007] EWHC 769 (Admin); [2007] 2 P. & C.R. 29; [2007] N.P.C. 42, QBD
(Admin) . . . . *Digested*, 07/**3283**

Oxfordshire CC v B; *sub nom* R. (on the application of GB) v Oxfordshire CC;
Oxfordshire CC v GB [2001] EWCA Civ 1358; [2002] B.L.G.R. 279; [2002]
E.L.R. 8, CA (Civ Div); reversing in part [2001] EWHC Admin 378; [2001]
E.L.R. 797, QBD (Admin) . . . . *Digested*, 02/**1165**:
Considered, 07/5121

Oxfordshire CC v GB see Oxfordshire CC v B

Oxfordshire CC v Oxford City Council [2006] UKHL 25; [2006] 2 A.C. 674; [2006] 2
W.L.R. 1235; [2006] 4 All E.R. 817; [2006] B.L.G.R. 713; [2006] 2 E.G.L.R.
95; [2006] 22 E.G. 177 (C.S.); (2006) 103(23) L.S.G. 30; (2006) 150 S.J.L.B.
706; [2006] N.P.C. 62; *Times*, May 31, 2006, HL; reversing in part [2005]
EWCA Civ 175; [2006] Ch. 43; [2005] 3 W.L.R. 1043; [2005] 3 All E.R. 961;
[2005] B.L.G.R. 664; [2005] 2 P. & C.R. 28; [2005] 2 P.L.R. 75; [2005] 2
E.G.L.R. 91; [2005] 9 E.G. 189 (C.S.); (2005) 149 S.J.L.B. 267; [2005] N.P.C.
28; *Independent*, March 2, 2005, CA (Civ Div); reversing in part [2004] EWHC
12 (Ch); [2004] Ch. 253; [2004] 2 W.L.R. 1291; [2004] 2 P. & C.R. 19;
[2004] 2 P.L.R. 65; [2004] 1 E.G.L.R. 105; [2004] 6 E.G. 144 (C.S.); (2004)
101(6) L.S.G. 32; [2004] N.P.C. 6; *Times*, January 30, 2004, Ch D . . . . *Digested*, 06/**3456**:
Considered, 04/3262, 07/3422

Oxley v Hiscock; *sub nom* Hiscock v Oxley [2004] EWCA Civ 546; [2005] Fam. 211;
[2004] 3 W.L.R. 715; [2004] 3 All E.R. 703; [2004] 2 F.L.R. 669; [2004] 2
F.C.R. 295; [2004] W.T.L.R. 709; (2003-04) 6 I.T.E.L.R. 1091; [2004] Fam. Law
569; [2004] 20 E.G. 166 (C.S.); (2004) 101(21) L.S.G. 35; (2004) 148
S.J.L.B. 571; [2004] N.P.C. 70; [2004] 2 P. & C.R. DG14; *Times*, July 14, 2004,
CA (Civ Div) . . . . *Digested*, 04/**3196**:
Applied, 05/3379, 05/3380, 05/3391, 07/3367, 07/3393:
Considered, 05/3378, 06/4378

Oy Liikenne AB v Liskojarvi (C-172/99); *sub nom* Liskojarvi v Oy Liikenne AB (C-172/
99) [2001] All E.R. (EC) 544; [2001] E.C.R. I-745; [2001] 3 C.M.L.R. 37;
[2002] I.C.R. 155; [2001] I.R.L.R. 171; [2001] Emp. L.R. 235; *Times*, February
27, 2001, ECJ (6th Chamber) . . . . *Digested*, 01/**2335**:
Considered, 07/1415: *Explained*, 03/1328

Oyarce v Cheshire CC A2/2007/1532, CA (Civ Div); affirming [2007] I.C.R. 1693,
EAT. . . . . *Digested*, 07/**1391**

Oysterfleet Hotel Plc v Secretary of State for Communities and Local Government
(2007) 104(39) L.S.G. 32, QBD (Admin)

Ozturk v Secretary of State for the Home Department see R. (on the application of
Ozturk) v Secretary of State for the Home Department

P, Re see C (A Child), Re

P v E see P v G (Family Provision: Relevance of Divorce Provision)

P v G (Family Provision: Relevance of Divorce Provision); *sub nom* P v E [2004]
EWHC 2944 (Fam); [2006] 1 F.L.R. 431; [2007] W.T.L.R. 691; [2006] Fam.
Law 178, Fam Div. . . . . *Digested*, 06/**4091**

P v P see Pettitt v Pettitt
P v P see P (Children), Re
P v P; *sub nom* Patel v Patel [2007] EWCA Civ 384; (2007) 104(17) L.S.G. 30;
　(2007) 151 S.J.L.B. 502, CA (Civ Div)
P v P (Removal of Child to New Zealand) see Payne v Payne
P v Schools Adjudicator [2006] EWHC 1934 (Admin); [2007] B.L.G.R. 346, QBD
　(Admin) . . . .　*Digested*, 07/**1157**
P v South Gloucestershire Council see C (A Child), Re
P vTsee P (A Child) (Financial Provision), Re
P v United Kingdom (35974/97) see B v United Kingdom (36337/97)
P v United Kingdom (56547/00) [2002] 2 F.L.R. 631; [2002] 3 F.C.R. 1; (2002) 35
　E.H.R.R. 31; 12 B.H.R.C. 615; [2002] Fam. Law 811; *Times*, August 16, 2002,
　ECHR . . . .　*Digested*, 02/**2525**:
　　　　　　　　　　　　　　　Considered, 03/1523, 04/1477, 07/1774
P (A Child), Re [2006] EWCA Civ 1792; [2007] 1 F.L.R. 1820; [2007] Fam. Law 299, CA
　(Civ Div) . . . .　*Digested*, 07/**376**
P (A Child) v Allison (Unreported, March 17, 2006), CC (Croydon) [*Ex rel.* Tim Sharpe,
　1 Temple Gardens,Temple, London] . . . .　*Digested*, 07/**3135**
P (A Child) v Bevies (Unreported, September 19, 2006), CC (Aldershot & Farnham)
　[*Ex rel.* Richard Wheeler, Barrister, 3 Paper Buildings, 4 St Peters Street,
　Winchester] . . . .　*Digested*, 07/**3180**
P (A Child) v BHS Ltd (Unreported, January 24, 2007), CC (Coventry) [*Ex rel.* Stephen
　Garner, Barrister, 8 Fountain Court, Steelhouse Lane, Birmingham] . . . .　*Digested*, 07/**3091**
P (A Child) (Adoption: Leave Proceedings), Re see P (A Child) (Adoption Order: Leave to
　Oppose Making of Adoption Order), Re
P (A Child) (Adoption Order: Leave to Oppose Making of Adoption Order), Re; *sub nom* P
　(A Child) (Adoption Proceedings), Re; P (A Child) (Adoption: Leave
　Proceedings), Re [2007] EWCA Civ 616; [2007] 1 W.L.R. 2556; [2007] 2 F.L.R.
　1069; [2007] 2 F.C.R. 407; [2007] Fam. Law 889; (2007) 151 S.J.L.B. 894;
　Times, June 29, 2007, CA (Civ Div) . . . .　*Digested*, 07/**1684**:
　　　　　　　　　　　　　　　　　　　　　　　Explained, 07/1679
P (A Child) (Adoption Proceedings), Re see P (A Child) (Adoption Order: Leave to Oppose
　Making of Adoption Order), Re
P (A Child) (Adoption: Unmarried Couples), Re [2007] NICA 20; [2007] N.I. 251, CA (NI)
P (A Child) (Financial Provision), Re; *sub nom* P vT [2003] EWCA Civ 837; [2003] 2
　F.L.R. 865; [2003] 2 F.C.R. 481; [2003] Fam. Law 717; (2003) 100(33) L.S.G.
　27; *Times*, July 24, 2003; *Independent*, July 3, 2003, CA (Civ Div); reversing
　[2003] Fam. Law 303; *Independent*, December 11, 2002, Fam Div . . . .　*Digested*, 03/**1577**:
　　　　　　Applied, 05/1666: *Considered*, 07/1688: *Distinguished*, 05/1652
P (A Minor) (Care Proceedings: Witness Summons), Re see P (A Minor) (Witness
　Summons), Re
P (A Minor) (Residence Order: Child's Welfare), Re; *sub nom* P (Section 91(14)
　Guidelines: Residence and Religious Heritage), Re [2000] Fam. 15; [1999] 3
　W.L.R. 1164; [1999] 3 All E.R. 734; [1999] 2 F.L.R. 573; [1999] 2 F.C.R. 289;
　[1999] Fam. Law 531; (1999) 163 J.P.N. 712; (1999) 96(21) L.S.G. 38; (1999)
　149 N.L.J. 719; (1999) 143 S.J.L.B. 141; *Times*, May 11, 1999, CA (Civ Div) . . . .　*Digested*, 99/**2389**:
　　　　　　Applied, 05/1587, 06/1681: *Considered*, 02/1664, 03/47: *Followed*, 07/1782
P (A Minor) (Witness Summons), Re; *sub nom* P (A Minor) (Care Proceedings: Witness
　Summons), Re [1997] 2 F.L.R. 447; [1997] 3 F.C.R. 322; [1997] Fam. Law
　652; *Times*, April 18, 1997, CA (Civ Div) . . . .　*Digested*, 97/**384**:
　　　　　　　　　　　　　　　　　　　　　　　Applied, 07/1727
P (Children), Re; *sub nom* P v P [2006] EWHC 2410 (Fam); [2007] 2 F.L.R. 439;
　[2007] Fam. Law 599, Fam Div
P (Children) (Care Proceedings: Split Hearing), Re; *sub nom* AP v Vale of Glamorgan CC
　[2007] EWCA Civ 1265; (2007) 151 S.J.L.B. 1596, CA (Civ Div)
P (Section 91(14) Guidelines: Residence and Religious Heritage), Re see P (A Minor)
　(Residence Order: Child's Welfare), Re
P&O Nedlloyd BV v Arab Metals Co (No.2) see P&O Nedlloyd BV v Arab Metals Co
　(The UB Tiger)
P&O Nedlloyd BV v Arab Metals Co (The UB Tiger); *sub nom* P&O Nedlloyd BV v Arab
　Metals Co (No.2) [2006] EWCA Civ 1717; [2007] 1 W.L.R. 2288; [2007] 2 All
　E.R. (Comm) 401; [2007] 2 Lloyd's Rep. 231; [2006] 2 C.L.C. 985; 116 Con.
　L.R. 200; *Times*, January 15, 2007, CA (Civ Div); affirming [2006] EWHC 2433
　(Comm), QBD (Comm) . . . .　*Digested*, 07/**472**
P&O Nedlloyd BV v Arab Metals Co (The UB Tiger) [2006] EWCA Civ 1300; [2007] 1
　W.L.R. 2483; [2007] 2 Lloyd's Rep. 148, CA (Civ Div); reversing [2005]
　EWHC 1276 (Comm); [2005] 1 W.L.R. 3733; [2006] 1 Lloyd's Rep. 111; *Times*,
　August 3, 2005, QBD (Comm) . . . .　*Digested*, 05/**314**
P&S Amusements Ltd v Valley House Leisure Ltd [2006] EWHC 1510 (Ch); [2006]
　U.K.C.L.R. 876, Ch D . . . .　*Digested*, 07/**2723**
P&S Amusements Ltd v Valley House Leisure Ltd [2006] EWHC 99 (Ch); [2006]
　U.K.C.L.R. 855; [2006] 2 P. & C.R. DG6, Ch D . . . .　*Digested*, 07/**2724**
P-B (A Child) (Placement Order), Re [2006] EWCA Civ 1016; [2007] 1 F.L.R. 1106; [2007]
　3 F.C.R. 308; [2007] Fam. Law 9, CA (Civ Div)

P4 Ltd v Unite Integrated Solutions Plc [2006] EWHC 2924 (TCC); [2007] B.L.R. 1;
    [2007] C.I.L.L. 2422, QBD (TCC) . . . .   *Digested*, 07/**406**
Pabari v Secretary of State for Work and Pensions [2004] EWCA Civ 1480; [2005] 1
    All E.R. 287; *Independent*, November 17, 2004, CA (Civ Div) . . . .   *Digested*, 05/**1555**:
                                                           Considered, 07/3294

Pacol Ltd v Joint Stock Co Rossakhar [1999] 2 All E.R. (Comm) 778; [2000] 1 Lloyd's
    Rep. 109; [2000] C.L.C. 315, QBD (Comm) . . . .   *Digested*, 00/**225**:
                                                           Applied, 07/250

Page v Sheerness Steel Co Plc see Wells v Wells
Page v Smith [1996] A.C. 155; [1995] 2 W.L.R. 644; [1995] 2 All E.R. 736; [1995] 2
    Lloyd's Rep. 95; [1995] R.T.R. 210; [1995] P.I.Q.R. P329; (1995) 92(23) L.S.G.
    33; (1995) 145 N.L.J. 723; (1995) 139 S.J.L.B. 173; *Times*, May 12, 1995;
    Independent, May 12, 1995; *Lloyd's List*, May 25, 1995, HL; reversing [1994] 4
    All E.R. 522; [1994] R.T.R. 293; [1995] P.I.Q.R. P58; (1994) 144 N.L.J. 756;
    Times, May 4, 1994, CA (Civ Div); reversing [1993] P.I.Q.R. Q55, QBD . . . . . .   *Digested*, 95/**3682**:
                      Applied, 99/3978, 00/6582, 04/4901: *Considered*, 96/4426, 96/4478,
                         96/4862, 98/3954, 98/3981, 99/4059, 00/4220, 00/6598, 02/3275,
                   02/3307, 04/1277, 06/2877: *Distinguished*, 07/2919: *Followed*, 99/3980
Pal (t/a Tapas Bar Cerveceria) v Revenue and Customs Commissioners; *sub nom*
    Revenue and Customs Commissioners v Pal (t/a Tapas Bar Cerveceria) [2006]
    EWHC 2016 (Ch); [2007] B.T.C. 5967; [2006] S.T.I. 2074; *Times*, August 29,
    2006, Ch D; reversing in part VADT19463,V&DTr (London) . . . .   *Digested*, 07/**4285**
Palacios de la Villa v Cortefiel Servicios SA (C-411/05) [2007] I.R.L.R. 989; [2007]
    Pens. L.R. 411; *Times*, October 23, 2007, ECJ (Grand Chamber) . . . .   *Digested*, 07/**1583**:
                                                           Considered, 07/1420

Palfrey v Wilson [2007] EWCA Civ 94; [2007] N.P.C. 18; *Times*, March 5, 2007, CA
    (Civ Div)
Palin Granit Oy v Lounais-Suomen Ymparistokeskus (C-9/00); *sub nom* Palin Granit
    Oy's Application, Re (C-9/00); Palin Granit Oy v Vehmassalon
    Kansanterveystyon Kuntayhtyman Hallitus (C-9/00) [2002] 1 W.L.R. 2644;
    [2003] All E.R. (EC) 366; [2002] E.C.R. I-3533; [2002] 2 C.M.L.R. 24; [2002]
    Env. L.R. 35, ECJ (6th Chamber) . . . .   *Digested*, 02/**1521**:
                             Considered, 04/1350, 07/1518: *Followed*, 05/1414
Palin Granit Oy v Vehmassalon Kansanterveystyon Kuntayhtyman Hallitus (C-9/00) see
    Palin Granit Oy v Lounais-Suomen Ymparistokeskus (C-9/00)
Palin Granit Oy's Application, Re (C-9/00) see Palin Granit Oy v Lounais-Suomen
    Ymparistokeskus (C-9/00)
Palmaz v Boston Scientific BV; *sub nom* Boston Scientific Ltd v Palmaz; Palmaz's
    European Patents (UK), Re; *joined case* Expandable Grafts Partnership v Boston
    Scientific BV [2000] R.P.C. 631; (2000) 23(6) I.P.D. 23043, CA (Civ Div);
    affirming [1999] R.P.C. 47; (1998) 21(9) I.P.D. 21093, Ch D (Patents Ct) . . . . .   *Digested*, 00/**3649**:
                                                  Applied, 07/2549: *Referred to*, 99/3466
Palmaz's European Patents (UK), Re see Palmaz v Boston Scientific BV
Palmer, Re; *joined case* National Provincial Bank v Barwell [1945] Ch. 8, CA; affirming
    [1944] Ch. 374, Ch D . . . .   *Considered*, 07/3962
Palmer v East and North Hertfordshire NHS Trust [2006] EWHC 1997 (QB); [2006]
    Lloyd's Rep. Med. 472, QBD . . . .   *Digested*, 07/**793**
Palmer v Marks and Spencer Plc [2001] EWCA Civ 1528, CA (Civ Div) . . . .   *Applied*, 07/2081
Palmer v Revenue and Customs Commissioners [2006] CSIH 8; 2006 S.C. 464;
    2006 S.L.T. 259; 77 T.C. 738; [2007] B.T.C. 126; [2006] S.T.I. 580; 2006 G.W.D.
    6-117, IH (Ex Div) . . . .   *Digested*, 06/**5703**
Pan United Marine Ltd v Chief Assessor, Singapore [2007] SGHC 21; [2007] R.A. 314,
    HC (Sing)
Papadimitriou, Petitioner [2004] W.T.L.R. 1141, HC (IoM) . . . .   *Digested*, 05/**4306**:
                                                           Considered, 07/4249

Pape v Minister van Landbouw, Natuurbeheer en Visserij (C-175/02) [2007] S.T.C.
    715; [2005] E.C.R. I-127; [2005] S.T.I. 136, ECJ (1st Chamber)
Parade Park Hotel v Revenue and Customs Commissioners [2007] S.T.C. (S.C.D.) 430;
    [2007] S.T.I. 1183, Sp Comm . . . .   *Digested*, 07/**4132**
Paragon Finance Plc v DB Thakerar & Co; *joined case* Paragon Finance Plc v Thimbleby
    & Co [1999] 1 All E.R. 400; (1998) 95(35) L.S.G. 36; (1998) 142 S.J.L.B.
    243; *Times*, August 7, 1998, CA (Civ Div) . . . .   *Digested*, 98/**536**:
                        Applied, 00/513, 00/1452, 03/519, 04/3800, 06/470, 06/543, 06/561, 07/476,
                   07/491: *Considered*, 98/383, 99/501, 00/520, 01/626, 01/5505, 07/4258:
                                                           Followed, 99/458
Paragon Finance Plc v Thimbleby & Co see Paragon Finance Plc v DB Thakerar & Co
Paramount Airways Ltd (No.2), Re; *sub nom* Powdrill v Hambros Bank (Jersey) Ltd
    [1993] Ch. 223; [1992] 3 W.L.R. 690; [1992] 3 All E.R. 1; [1992] B.C.C. 416;
    [1992] B.C.L.C. 710; (1992) 89(14) L.S.G. 31; (1992) 136 S.J.L.B. 97; [1992]
    N.P.C. 27; *Times*, March 5, 1992; *Financial Times*, March 10, 1992, CA (Civ Div);
    reversing [1992] Ch. 160; [1991] 3 W.L.R. 318; [1991] 4 All E.R. 267; [1991]
    B.C.C. 559; [1991] B.C.L.C. 767; (1991) 135 S.J.L.B. 76; [1991] N.P.C. 75; *Times*,
    June 20, 1991, Ch D (Companies Ct) . . . .   *Digested*, 92/**2528**:
                                                   Applied, 07/2407: *Considered*, 98/529

Parish v Reddin (Unreported, August 23, 2006), CC (Birkenhead) [*Ex rel.* Horwich
    Farrelly Solicitors, National House, 36 St Ann Street, Manchester] . . . .   *Digested,* 07/**408**
Parker v Levy (t/a Essex Marinas) (2007) 151 S.J.L.B. 1166, QBD
Parker v TUI UK Ltd (t/a Austravel) (Unreported, October 30, 2006), CC (Central
    London) [*Ex rel.* Jack Harding, Barrister, 1 Chancery Lane, London] . . . .   *Digested,* 07/**297**
Parkes v Secretary of State for the Environment [1978] 1 W.L.R. 1308; [1979] 1 All
    E.R. 211; 77 L.G.R. 39; (1978) 36 P. & C.R. 387; (1978) 248 E.G. 595; [1979]
    J.P.L. 33; (1978) 122 S.J. 349, CA (Civ Div); reversing [1978] J.P.L. 316, HC . .   *Digested,* 78/**2870**:
                   Considered, 03/3388, 07/3263: *Distinguished,* 83/3722
Parking Brixen GmbH v Gemeinde Brixen (C-458/03) [2006] All E.R. (EC) 779;
    [2005] E.C.R. I-8612; [2006] 1 C.M.L.R. 3; [2006] C.E.C. 144, ECJ (1st
    Chamber) . . . .   *Digested,* 06/**3418**:
                                               Followed, 07/3325
Parrott v Parkin (The Up Yaws) [2007] EWHC 210 (Admlty); [2007] 1 Lloyd's Rep.
    719; [2007] 2 F.L.R. 444; [2007] 3 F.C.R. 515; [2007] Fam. Law 597, QBD
    (Admlty) . . . .   *Digested,* 07/**3363**
Parry v Department for Work and Pensions see Parry v Halton Magistrates Court
Parry v Halton Magistrates Court; *sub nom* Parry v Department for Work and Pensions
    [2005] EWHC 1486 (Admin), QBD (Admin) . . . .   *Applied,* 07/3898
Partidul Comunistilor (Nepeceristi) v Romania (46626/99) (2007) 44 E.H.R.R. 17,
    ECHR
Pascoe v First Secretary of State [2006] EWHC 2356 (Admin); [2007] 1 W.L.R. 885;
    [2006] 4 All E.R. 1240; [2007] J.P.L. 607; [2007] A.C.D. 36; [2006] N.P.C.
    104; *Times,* October 4, 2006, QBD (Admin) . . . .   *Digested,* 06/**3287**
Pascoe v Hallen & Medway [1975] I.R.L.R. 116, IT . . . .   *Digested,* 75/**1171.46**:
                                           Considered, 07/1435
Patak (Spices) Ltd's Community Trade Mark Application (R746/2005-4) [2007] E.T.M.R.
    3, OHIM (4th Bd App) . . . .   *Digested,* 07/**2644**
Patch v Revenue and Customs Commissioners [2007] S.T.C. (S.C.D.) 453; [2007]
    W.T.L.R. 1825; [2007] S.T.I. 1186, Sp Comm . . . .   *Digested,* 07/**4111**
Patel v Keogh (Unreported, January 23, 2007), CC (Liverpool) [*Ex rel.* Tom Gosling,
    Barrister, Oriel Chambers, 14 Water Street, Liverpool] . . . .   *Digested,* 07/**3168**
Patel v Patel see P v P
Paterson v Commissioner of Police of the Metropolis [2007] I.C.R. 1522; [2007]
    I.R.L.R. 763; *Times,* August 22, 2007, EAT. . . . .   *Digested,* 07/**1332**
Paterson v Kent 2007 S.L.T. (Sh Ct) 8; [2007] M.H.L.R. 20; 2006 G.W.D. 24-541, Sh
    Pr . . . .   *Digested,* 07/**5412**
Patrick v Royal London Mutual Insurance Society Ltd see Ronson International Ltd v
    Patrick
Pattni v Ali; *sub nom* Ali v Pattni [2006] UKPC 51; [2007] 2 A.C. 85; [2007] 2 W.L.R.
    102; [2007] 2 All E.R. (Comm) 427, PC (IoM) . . . .   *Digested,* 07/**448**
Pattrick v Marley Estates Management [2007] EWCA Civ 1176; [2007] N.P.C. 122, CA
    (Civ Div)
Paul v Deputy Coroner of the Queen's Household and Assistant Deputy Coroner for
    Surrey; *sub nom* R. (on the application of Paul) v Deputy Coroner of the Queen's
    Household and Assistant Deputy Coroner for Surrey; R. (on the application of
    Al-Fayed) v Deputy Coroner of the Queen's Household and Assistant Deputy
    Coroner for Surrey; *joined case* Al-Fayed v Deputy Coroner of the Queen's
    Household and Assistant Deputy Coroner for Surrey [2007] EWHC 408
    (Admin); [2007] 3 W.L.R. 503; [2007] 2 All E.R. 509; (2007) 95 B.M.L.R. 137;
    (2007) 157 N.L.J. 366, QBD (Admin). . . . .   *Digested,* 07/**26**
Paul v Germany (C-222/02) [2004] E.C.R. I-9425; [2006] 2 C.M.L.R. 62, ECJ . . . . .   *Applied,* 07/2490
Paulik v Slovakia (10699/05) [2007] 1 F.L.R. 1090; [2006] 3 F.C.R. 323; [2007]
    Fam. Law 22, ECHR. . . . .   *Digested,* 07/**2254**
Paulin, Re see Inland Revenue Commissioners v Crossman
Pavlou (A Bankrupt), Re [1993] 1 W.L.R.1046; [1993] 3 All E.R. 955; [1993] Fam. Law 629,
    Ch D . . . .   *Digested,* 93/**1920**:
           Applied, 03/3542, 07/3432: *Considered,* 03/3604, 06/4391
Paxman v Hughes see Hughes v Paxman
Payne v Caerphilly CBC see Payne v National Assembly for Wales
Payne v National Assembly for Wales; *joined case* Payne v Caerphilly CBC [2006]
    EWHC 597 (Admin); [2007] 1 P. & C.R. 4; [2007] J.P.L. 117, QBD (Admin) . . .   *Digested,* 07/**3233**
Payne v Payne; *sub nom* P v P (Removal of Child to New Zealand) [2001] EWCA Civ
    166; [2001] Fam. 473; [2001] 2 W.L.R. 1826; [2001] 1 F.L.R. 1052; [2001] 1
    F.C.R. 425; [2001] H.R.L.R. 28; [2001] U.K.H.R.R. 484; (2001) 165 J.P.N. 466;
    (2001) 98(10) L.S.G. 41; (2001) 145 S.J.L.B. 61; *Times,* March 9, 2001;
    Independent, February 22, 2001; *Daily Telegraph,* February 27, 2001, CA (Civ
    Div). . . . .   *Digested,* 01/**2596**:
        Applied, 01/2597, 03/1545, 05/1590, 06/1626, 06/1688, 06/5363, 07/1794:
        Considered, 05/1572, 05/1574, 05/1635, 07/1795: *Distinguished,* 05/1575:
                                             Followed, 06/1691
PB v Haringey LBC see R. (on the application of B) v Haringey LBC

PBS PARTNERSHIP/Controlling pension benefits systems (T931/95) [2002] E.P.O.R. 52,
   EPO (Technical Bd App) . . . . *Digested,* 03/**2515**:
                              Applied, 07/2598: *Distinguished,* 05/2460: *Followed,* 04/2329
PE (Nigeria) v Secretary of State for the Home Department see DK (Serbia) v
   Secretary of State for the Home Department
Peaceform Ltd v Cussens [2006] EWHC 2657 (Ch); [2006] 3 E.G.L.R. 67; [2006] 47
   E.G. 182; [2006] 43 E.G. 178 (C.S.); [2006] N.P.C. 116; [2007] 2 P. & C.R.
   DG1, Ch D . . . . *Digested,* 07/**2754**
Peacock AG v Hauptzollamt Paderborn (C-339/98) [2000] E.C.R. I-8947, ECJ . . . . .   *Considered,* 07/1033
Pearce v Mayfield Secondary School Governing Body see Advocate General for
   Scotland v MacDonald
Pearce v Pearce [2003] EWCA Civ 1054; [2004] 1 W.L.R. 68; [2003] 2 F.L.R. 1144;
   [2003] 3 F.C.R. 178; [2003] Fam. Law 723; (2003) 100(36) L.S.G. 39; *Times,*
   September 1, 2003, CA (Civ Div) . . . . *Digested,* 03/**1595**:
                                         Applied, 04/1513: *Considered,* 07/1706
Pearce v Pearce 52 E.R. 1103; (1856) 22 Beav. 248, Ct of Chancery . . . .   *Considered,* 07/4258
Pearl Assurance (Unit Funds) Ltd, Re see Pearl Assurance (Unit Linked Pensions) Ltd, Re
Pearl Assurance (Unit Linked Pensions) Ltd, Re; *sub nom* Pearl Assurance (Unit Funds)
   Ltd, Re; London Life Linked Assurances Ltd, Re; NPI Ltd, Re [2006] EWHC
   2291 (Ch); (2006) 103(38) L.S.G. 33; (2006) 150 S.J.L.B. 1250; [2007] Bus.
   L.R. D10, Ch D (Companies Ct) . . . . *Digested,* 07/**2472**
Pearson v HM Coroner for Inner London North [2005] EWHC 833 (Admin); [2005]
   U.K.H.R.R. 896; [2005] Inquest L.R. 18, QBD (Admin) . . . . *Digested,* 06/**17**:
                                        Applied, 07/27: *Distinguished,* 05/17
Pearson Education Ltd v Charter Partnership Ltd [2007] EWCA Civ 130; [2007] B.L.R.
   324; [2007] 21 E.G. 132; [2007] 9 E.G. 203 (C.S.); (2007) 104(10) L.S.G. 31;
   (2007) 151 S.J.L.B. 300; *Times,* March 7, 2007, CA (Civ Div); affirming [2005]
   EWHC 2021 (TCC); [2006] P.N.L.R. 14, QBD (TCC) . . . .   *Digested,* 07/**2915**
Pearson (Deceased), Re; *sub nom* Robin Hood Cemetery, Solihull, Re *Times,* January
   10, 2007, Cons Ct (Birmingham)
Peck v United Kingdom (44647/98) [2003] E.M.L.R. 15; (2003) 36 E.H.R.R. 41; 13
   B.H.R.C. 669; [2003] Info. T.L.R. 221; *Times,* February 3, 2003, ECHR . . . .   *Digested,* 03/**2194**:
                                   Considered, 03/4363: *Disapproved,* 07/204
Pecore v Pecore 2007 SCC 17; [2007] W.T.L.R. 1591; (2006-07) 9 I.T.E.L.R. 873, Sup
   Ct (Can)
Pectel Ltd, Re see O'Neill v Phillips
Pedersen v Denmark see Kjeldsen v Denmark (A/23)
Peer International Corp v Termidor Music Publishers Ltd [2006] EWHC 2883 (Ch);
   [2007] E.C.D.R. 1, Ch D . . . .   *Digested,* 07/**2524**
Peerbooms v Stichting CZ Groep Zorgverzekeringen (C-157/99) see Geraets-Smits v
   Stichting Ziekenfonds VGZ (C-157/99)
Peers v Greece (28524/95) (2001) 33 E.H.R.R. 51; 10 B.H.R.C. 364; [2001] Prison
   L.R. 245, ECHR . . . .   *Digested,* 01/**3582**:
                                                                    Applied, 07/2201
Pell v Addison . . . .   *Followed,* 07/1082
Pembrokeshire Coast National Park Authority v Lorch [2007] P.A.D. 67, Planning
   Inspector
Pendleton v Stone & Webster Engineering Ltd see Fairchild v Glenhaven Funeral
   Services Ltd (t/a GH Dovener & Son)
Pengelly v Pengelly [2007] W.T.L.R. 1619, Ch D
Peninsular & Oriental Steam Navigation Co, Re [2006] EWHC 3279 (Ch); [2007] Bus. L.R.
   554, Ch D . . . .   *Digested,* 07/**2447**
Penk v Wright see Alcock v Chief Constable of South Yorkshire
Penn v Bristol and West Building Society; *sub nom* Brill & Co v Penn [1997] 1 W.L.R.
   1356; [1997] 3 All E.R. 470; [1997] 3 F.C.R. 789; [1997] P.N.L.R. 607; (1997)
   74 P. & C.R. 210; [1997] E.G. 54 (C.S.); (1997) 94(18) L.S.G. 32; (1997) 141
   S.J.L.B. 105; [1997] N.P.C. 58; *Times,* April 24, 1997, CA (Civ Div); affirming
   [1995] 2 F.L.R. 938; [1996] 2 F.C.R. 729; [1996] Fam. Law 28; (1995) 92(27)
   L.S.G. 31; (1995) 139 S.J.L.B. 164; *Times,* June 19, 1995, Ch D . . . .   *Digested,* 97/**1023**:
                                   Applied, 98/4027, 99/4379, 07/3396: *Followed,* 99/4036
Pennington v Crossley & Sons (1897) 13 T.L.R. 513 . . . .   *Considered,* 07/3420:
                                                                    Distinguished, 79/50
Pennington v Surrey CC [2006] EWCA Civ 1493; [2007] P.I.Q.R. P11; (2006)
   103(45) L.S.G. 28, CA (Civ Div) . . . .   *Digested,* 07/**2080**
Pennwell Publishing (UK) Ltd v Ornstien [2007] EWHC 1570 (QB); [2007] I.R.L.R.
   700, QBD . . . .   *Digested,* 07/**1342**
Pennywise Trust, Re see Toland Trust, Re
Pensioner's Pledge of Securities, Re [2007] E.C.C. 4, BGH (Ger)

Pepper (Inspector of Taxes) v Hart [1993] A.C. 593; [1992] 3 W.L.R. 1032; [1993] 1 All
E.R. 42; [1992] S.T.C. 898; [1993] I.C.R. 291; [1993] I.R.L.R. 33; [1993] R.V.R.
127; (1993) 143 N.L.J. 17; [1992] N.P.C. 154; *Times*, November 30, 1992;
Independent, November 26, 1992, HL; reversing [1991] Ch. 203; [1991] 2
W.L.R. 483; [1990] S.T.C. 786; [1991] I.C.R. 681; [1991] I.R.L.R. 125; (1990)
134 S.J. 1478; *Times*, November 15, 1990; *Financial Times*, November 16, 1990;
Guardian, November 21, 1990; *Daily Telegraph*, November 19, 1990, CA (Civ Div);
affirming [1990] 1 W.L.R. 204; [1990] S.T.C. 6; (1989) 86(46) L.S.G. 41, Ch D
. . . . *Digested*, 93/**459**:
Applied, 93/3714, 94/2514, 98/321, 98/966, 01/4489, 03/3600, 05/4063:
Cited, 00/5239: *Considered*, 93/426, 93/1866, 93/2260, 93/3860, 94/3413,
94/3900, 96/1297, 96/1606, 96/3928, 01/5174, 04/628, 05/2742, 06/635,
07/3064: *Distinguished*, 95/181, 95/2520, 97/4657, 00/2122, 01/4284:
Followed, 96/4190: *Not applied*, 01/4206: *Referred to*, 93/486, 94/353,
94/2723, 94/2729, 94/5459, 94/5899, 95/522, 95/861

Perceval v Elms (Unreported, December 1, 2006), CC (Salford) [*Ex rel.* Chris
Middleton, Barrister, Oriel Chambers, 14 Water Street, Liverpool] . . . . *Digested*, 07/**3148**
Perceval-Price v Department of Economic Development [2000] N.I. 141; [2000]
I.R.L.R. 380; *Times*, April 28, 2000, CA (NI) . . . . *Digested*, 00/**5520**:
Considered, 07/1386

Percy v Church of Scotland Board of National Mission [2005] UKHL 73; [2006] 2
A.C. 28; [2006] 2 W.L.R. 353; [2006] 4 All E.R. 1354; 2006 S.C. (H.L.) 1; 2006
S.L.T. 11; [2006] I.C.R. 134; [2006] I.R.L.R. 195; (2006) 150 S.J.L.B. 30; *Times*,
December 16, 2005; *Independent*, December 20, 2005, HL; reversing 2001
S.C. 757; 2001 S.L.T. 497; 2001 G.W.D. 12-434, IH (1 Div) . . . . *Digested*, 06/**5318**:
Explained, 07/1326

Pereira v Inner South London Coroner [2007] EWHC 1723 (Admin); [2007] 1 W.L.R.
3256; *Times*, June 22, 2007, DC . . . . *Digested*, 07/**12**
Performing Rights Society v Thompson (Unreported, December 8, 2006), CC (Thanet)
[*Ex rel.* Mathew Gullick, 3 Paper Buildings, Temple, London EC4Y 7EU] . . . . . . *Digested*, 07/**425**
Permanent Mission of India to the United Nations v City of New York 9 I.T.L. Rep. 1114,
US Court
Permesaen v National Pensions Office (C-233/06) see National Pensions Office v
Jonkman (C-231/06)
Peros v Brain (Listing Officer) [2007] R.A. 407, VT
Peroxidos Organicos SA v Commission of the European Communities (T-120/04)
[2007] 4 C.M.L.R. 4, CFI (3rd Chamber)
Perrin v Northampton BC [2007] EWCA Civ 1353; [2007] N.P.C. 139, CA (Civ Div);
reversing [2006] EWHC 2331 (TCC); [2007] 1 All E.R. 929; [2006] B.L.R. 504;
[2007] Env. L.R. 12; [2007] B.L.G.R. 19; [2007] 1 P. & C.R. 28; [2006] 3
E.G.L.R. 71; [2006] 48 E.G. 232; [2007] J.P.L. 723; [2006] 41 E.G. 224 (C.S.),
QBD (TCC) . . . . *Digested*, 07/**3294**
Persad v Trinidad and Tobago; *sub nom* Persaud v Trinidad and Tobago [2007] UKPC
51; [2007] 1 W.L.R. 2379; *Times*, August 7, 2007, PC (Trin) . . . . *Digested*, 07/**842**
Persaud v Trinidad and Tobago see Persad v Trinidad and Tobago
Peter Acatos No.2 Settlement, Re see Stuart-Hutcheson v Spread Trustee Co Ltd
Peter Clay Discretionary Trust Trustees v Revenue and Customs Commissioners; *sub nom*
Revenue and Customs Commissioners v Peter Clay Discretionary Trust Trustees
[2007] EWHC 2661 (Ch); [2007] B.T.C. 724; (2007-08) 10 I.T.E.L.R. 654;
[2007] S.T.I. 2654, Ch D; affirming [2007] S.T.C. (S.C.D.) 362; [2007] W.T.L.R.
643; (2006-07) 9 I.T.E.L.R. 738; [2007] S.T.I. 1060, Sp Comm . . . . *Digested*, 07/**4241**
Peters v Revenue and Customs Commissioners [2007] S.T.I. 380, V&DTr (Manchester)
Petroleo Brasileiro SA Petrobras v Petromec Inc (No.4) see Petromec Inc v Petroleo
Brasileiro SA Petrobras (No.4)
Petrolite Holdings Inc v Dyno Oil Field Chemicals UK Ltd (No.1) [1998] F.S.R. 190;
(1998) 21 (2) I.P.D. 21014, Ch D . . . . *Digested*, 98/**3461**:
Distinguished, 07/2633
Petromec Inc v Petroleo Brasiliero SA Petrobras (No.4); *sub nom* Petroleo Brasileiro SA
Petrobras v Petromec Inc (No.4) [2006] EWCA Civ 1038; [2007] 2 Costs L.R.
212; (2006) 103(31) L.S.G. 25, CA (Civ Div); affirming [2005] EWHC 2430
(Comm), QBD (Comm) . . . . *Digested*, 07/**404**:
Considered, 07/387, 07/421
Petromec Inc v Petroleo Brasiliero SA Petrobras [2006] EWHC 1443 (Comm); [2007]
1 Lloyd's Rep. 629, QBD (Comm) . . . . *Digested*, 07/**4189**
Petrotrade Inc v Texaco Ltd [2002] 1 W.L.R. 947 (Note); [2001] 4 All E.R. 853; [2001]
C.P. Rep. 29; [2000] C.L.C. 1341; [2002] 1 Costs L.R. 60; *Times*, June 14,
2000; *Independent*, July 10, 2000, CA (Civ Div); affirming 1998 Folio 1348,
QBD (Comm) . . . . *Digested*, 00/**539**:
Applied, 01/484, 02/346, 02/349, 02/356: *Considered*, 02/347, 05/369,
07/343
Pettit v Novakovic; *sub nom* Pettit (Trustee in Bankruptcy of Thrussell) v Novakovic
[2007] B.C.C. 462; [2007] B.P.I.R. 1643, Ch D (Birmingham) . . . . *Digested*, 07/**2419**
Pettit (Trustee in Bankruptcy of Thrussell) v Novakovic see Pettit v Novakovic

Pettitt *v* Pettitt; *sub nom* P *v* P [1970] A.C. 777; [1969] 2 W.L.R. 966; [1969] 2 All
E.R. 385; (1969) 20 P. & C.R. 991; (1969) 113 S.J. 344, HL; reversing [1968] 1
W.L.R. 443; [1968] 1 All E.R. 1053; (1968) 19 P. & C.R. 245; (1968) 112 S.J.
111, CA (Civ Div) . . . . *Digested*, 69/**1639**:
Applied, 69/517, 69/1647, 70/1228, 70/1234, 71/5441, 72/1684, 72/1691,
75/1609, 78/1785, 84/1676, 96/5546: *Considered*, 70/820, 70/1241,
70/1243, 71/5476, 84/1675, 84/1677, 86/1857, 86/3034, 86/3551, 92/2031,
95/2187, 07/3367: *Distinguished*, 68/1827, 69/1651: *Followed*, 69/3277,
86/3037

Pexum Ltd *v* Revenue and Customs Commissioners [2007] S.T.I. 1699, V&DTr
(Manchester)

Pfeiffer *v* Deutsches Rotes Kreuz Kreisverband Waldshut eV (C-397/01) [2004] E.C.R.
I-8835; [2005] 1 C.M.L.R. 44; [2005] I.C.R. 1307; [2005] I.R.L.R. 137, ECJ . . *Digested*, 05/**1275**:
Applied, 05/358, 07/1330, 07/1370

Phaik Seang Tan *v* Sitkowski; *sub nom* Tan *v* Sitkowski [2007] EWCA Civ 30; [2007] 1
W.L.R. 1628; [2007] L. & T.R. 17; [2007] 6 E.G. 165 (C.S.); (2007) 104(7)
L.S.G. 25; [2007] N.P.C. 14; *Times*, February 15, 2007, CA (Civ Div) . . . . *Digested*, 07/**2771**

Pharos SA *v* Commission of the European Communities (C-151/98 P (R)) [1998]
E.C.R. I-5441, ECJ. . . . . *Considered*, 07/**2799**:
Followed, 05/576, 05/577

Phelps *v* Hillingdon LBC; *sub nom* G (A Child), Re; *joined cases* Jarvis *v* Hampshire
CC; G (A Child) *v* Bromley LBC; Anderton *v* Clwyd CC [2001] 2 A.C. 619;
[2000] 3 W.L.R. 776; [2000] 4 All E.R. 504; [2000] 3 F.C.R. 102; (2001) 3
L.G.L.R. 5; [2000] B.L.G.R. 651; [2000] Ed. C.R. 700; [2000] E.L.R. 499;
(2000) 3 C.C.L. Rep. 156; (2000) 56 B.M.L.R. 1; (2000) 150 N.L.J. 1198;
(2000) 144 S.J.L.B. 241; *Times*, July 28, 2000; *Independent*, November 13,
2000, HL; reversing [1999] 1 W.L.R. 500; [1999] 1 All E.R. 421; [1999] 1 F.C.R.
440; (1999) 1 L.G.L.R. 246; [1999] B.L.G.R. 103; [1999] Ed. C.R. 368; [1998]
E.L.R. 587; (1999) 46 B.M.L.R. 100; (1998) 95(45) L.S.G. 41; (1998) 148 N.L.J.
1710; (1999) 143 S.J.L.B. 11; *Times*, November 9, 1998, CA (Civ Div); reversing
[1997] 3 F.C.R. 621; (1997) 9 Admin. L.R. 657; [1998] Ed. C.R. 47; [1998]
E.L.R. 38; (1998) 39 B.M.L.R. 51; (1997) 94(39) L.S.G. 39; (1997) 147 N.L.J.
1421; (1997) 141 S.J.L.B. 214; *Times*, October 10, 1997, QBD . . . . *Digested*, 00/**1947**:
Applied, 99/1889, 99/4010, 01/4540, 03/2972, 05/1042, 05/1140, 05/2845,
05/2861, 06/1014: *Considered*, 99/3966, 99/3968, 04/996, 04/1818,
04/2719, 05/2891, 07/3076: *Distinguished*, 99/3967: *Explained*, 03/1118:
Followed, 05/2871

Phelps *v* Spon Smith & Co (Preliminary Issues) [2001] B.P.I.R. 326, Ch D . . . . *Digested*, 01/**2430**:
Considered, 07/2920: *Previous proceedings*, 00/586

Phelps *v* Stewarts (A Firm) [2007] EWHC 1561 (Ch); [2007] P.N.L.R. 32; [2007]
W.T.L.R. 1267; [2007] N.P.C. 86, Ch D . . . . *Digested*, 07/**2803**

Philadelphia National Bank *v* Price (1938) 60 Ll. L. Rep. 257, CA; affirming (1937) 58
Ll. L. Rep. 238, KBD . . . . *Applied*, 07/2506

Philip Morris Holland BV *v* Commission of the European Communities (730/79) [1980]
E.C.R. 2671; [1981] 2 C.M.L.R. 321, ECJ . . . . *Digested*, 81/**1168**:
Applied, 07/1649

Philip Morris International Inc *v* Commission of the European Communities (T-377/00);
joined cases Japan Tobacco Inc *v* Commission of the European Communities
(T-380/00); RJ Reynolds Tobacco Holdings Inc *v* Commission of the European
Communities (T-379/00) [2003] All E.R. (EC) 1008; [2003] E.C.R. II-1; [2003]
1 C.M.L.R. 21; *Times*, January 27, 2003, CFI (2nd Chamber). . . . . *Digested*, 03/**1431**:
Subsequent proceedings, 07/1587

Philips Electronics NV *v* Remington Consumer Products Ltd (C-299/99) see
Koninklijke Philips Electronics NV *v* Remington Consumer Products Ltd (C-299/
99)

PHILIPS/High intensity discharge lamp (T671/06) [2007] E.P.O.R. 53, EPO (Technical Bd
App)

Phillips *v* Barlow (Unreported, August 2, 2006), CC (Cardiff) [*Ex rel.* Mark Roberts,
Barrister, 7 Harrington Street, Liverpool] . . . . *Digested*, 07/**409**

Phillips *v* Magill see Porter *v* Magill

Phillips *v* Peace [1996] 2 F.L.R. 230; [1996] 2 F.C.R. 237; [1996] Fam. Law 603,
Fam Div. . . . . *Digested*, 96/**2854**:
Approved, 07/1767

Phillips *v* Rafiq; *sub nom* Motor Insurers Bureau *v* Phillips; Phillips (Deceased), Re
[2007] EWCA Civ 74; [2007] 1 W.L.R. 1351; [2007] 3 All E.R. 382; [2007] 2 All
E.R. (Comm) 484; [2007] R.T.R. 33; [2007] Lloyd's Rep. I.R. 413; [2007]
P.I.Q.R. P21; (2007) 151 S.J.L.B. 263; *Times*, February 21, 2007, CA (Civ Div);
affirming [2006] EWHC 1461 (QB); [2007] R.T.R. 3; [2006] Lloyd's Rep. I.R.
809, QBD . . . . *Digested*, 07/**2494**

Phillips *v* Symes [2005] EWHC 2867 (Ch); [2006] B.P.I.R. 1430, Ch D . . . . *Digested*, 07/**2406**

Phillips *v* Whatley see Phillips & Co *v* Whatley

Phillips & Co *v* Whatley; *joined case* Phillips *v* Whatley [2007] UKPC 28; [2007]
P.N.L.R. 27; (2007) 104(20) L.S.G. 28; (2007) 151 S.J.L.B. 612, PC (Gib) . . . . *Digested*, 07/**1058**

Phillips (Deceased), Re see Phillips *v* Rafiq

Phillips (Liquidator of AJ Bekhor & Co) v Brewin Dolphin Bell Lawrie Ltd (formerly
   Brewin Dolphin & Co Ltd) [2001] UKHL 2; [2001] 1 W.L.R. 143; [2001] 1 All
   E.R. 673; [2001] B.C.C. 864; [2001] 1 B.C.L.C. 145; [2001] B.P.I.R. 119; (2001)
   98(12) L.S.G. 43; (2001) 145 S.J.L.B. 32; *Times*, January 23, 2001, HL;
   affirming [1999] 1 W.L.R. 2052; [1999] 2 All E.R. 844; [1999] B.C.C. 557;
   [1999] 1 B.C.L.C 714; [1999] B.P.I.R. 797; *Times*, March 30, 1999, CA (Civ Div);
   affirming [1998] 1 B.C.L.C. 700, Ch D . . . . *Digested*, 01/**3753**:
                         Applied, 02/2669: *Considered*, 03/2437, 07/2425, 07/2430
Phipps v Boardman see Boardman v Phipps
Phizackerley v Revenue and Customs Commissioners [2007] S.T.C. (S.C.D.) 328;
   [2007] W.T.L.R. 745; [2007] S.T.I. 559, Sp Comm. *Digested*, 07/**4112**
Phoenix Venture Holdings Ltd v Independent Trustee Services Ltd [2005] EWHC 1379
   (Ch); [2005] Pens. L.R. 379, Ch D (Companies Ct) . . . . *Digested*, 05/**2997**:
                                              Considered, 07/3025
Phones 4U Ltd v Phone4U.co.uk Internet Ltd [2006] EWCA Civ 244; [2007] R.P.C. 5;
   (2006) 103(23) L.S.G. 32; (2006) 150 S.J.L.B. 668, CA (Civ Div); reversing
   in part [2005] EWHC 334 (Ch), Ch D . . . . *Digested*, 07/**2545**
Phonographic Performance Ltd v AEI Rediffusion Music Ltd (Costs) see AEI Rediffusion
   Music Ltd v Phonographic Performance Ltd (Costs)
Pick (Virdi's Trustee) v Goel see Goel v Pick
Pickering v Lynch see Premier Electronics (GB) Ltd, Re
Pickersgill v Riley [2004] UKPC 14; [2004] Lloyd's Rep. I.R. 795; [2004] P.N.L.R. 31;
   [2004] 14 E.G. 140 (C.S.); (2004) 101(12) L.S.G. 37; (2004) 148 S.J.L.B. 295;
   Times, March 2, 2004, PC (Jer) . . . . *Digested*, 04/**2732**:
                                              Considered, 07/2950
Pickett v British Rail Engineering Ltd; *sub nom* Ralph Henry Pickett (Deceased), Re
   [1980] A.C. 136; [1978] 3 W.L.R. 955; [1979] 1 All E.R. 774; [1979] 1 Lloyd's
   Rep. 519; (1978) 122 S.J. 778, HL; reversing (1977) 121 S.J. 814, CA (Civ Div) . *Digested*, 79/**656**:
               Applied, 79/2367, 81/581, 82/771, 82/791, 84/1030, 85/1036, 89/2195,
               07/3071: *Considered*, 79/663, 79/669, 79/2150, 80/633, 82/772, 82/774,
                         83/976: *Distinguished*, 84/1042: *Followed*, 96/2126
Pierce v Doncaster MBC [2007] EWHC 2968 (QB); *Times*, December 27, 2007, QBD
Pierce Design International Ltd v Johnston [2007] EWHC 1691 (TCC); [2007] B.L.R.
   381; 115 Con. L.R. 110; [2007] C.I.L.L. 2507, QBD (TCC). . . . . *Digested*, 07/**744**
Pierhead Purchasing Ltd v Revenue and Customs Commissioners [2007] V. & D.R.
   102, V&DTr (London)
Piersack v Belgium (A/53) (1983) 5 E.H.R.R. 169, ECHR . . . . *Applied*, 97/2811,
                         00/6092, 07/2558: *Considered*, 98/3090
Piglowska v Piglowski [1999] 1 W.L.R. 1360; [1999] 3 All E.R. 632; [1999] 2 F.L.R.
   763; [1999] 2 F.C.R. 481; [1999] Fam. Law 617; (1999) 96(27) L.S.G. 34;
   (1999) 143 S.J.L.B. 190; *Times*, June 25, 1999, HL; reversing (Unreported,
   November 3, 1997), CA (Civ Div) . . . . *Digested*, 99/**2421**:
                         Applied, 06/1633, 07/1766: *Considered*, 00/2489, 01/2632, 01/4450
Pilkington UK Ltd v CGU Insurance Plc [2004] EWCA Civ 23; [2005] 1 All E.R.
   (Comm) 283; [2004] 1 C.L.C. 1059; [2004] B.L.R. 97; [2004] T.C.L.R. 5;
   [2004] Lloyd's Rep. I.R. 891; [2004] N.P.C. 10, CA (Civ Div) . . . . *Digested*, 05/**2378**:
                                              Considered, 07/2482
Pinkava v LIFFE Administration & Management see LIFFE Administration &
   Management v Pinkava
Pinochet Ugarte (No.2), Re see R. v Bow Street Metropolitan Stipendiary Magistrate Ex
   p. Pinochet Ugarte (No.2)
Pinson Wholesale Ltd, Re; *sub nom* Hellard, Re [2007] B.P.I.R. 1322, Ch D
   (Birmingham)
Pinto v Brixton Prison Governor [2004] EWHC 2986 (QB); [2005] Extradition L.R.
   35, QBD . . . . *Considered*, 07/1664
Pioneer Electronic (Europe) NV v Commission of the European Communities (102/80)
   see Musique Diffusion Francaise SA v Commission of the European
   Communities (100/80)
Pioneer High Fidelity (GB) Ltd v Commission of the European Communities (103/80)
   see Musique Diffusion Francaise SA v Commission of the European
   Communities (100/80)
Pioneer Shipping Ltd v BTP Tioxide Ltd (The Nema) (No.2); *sub nom* BTP Tioxide Ltd
   v Pioneer Shipping Ltd; *joined case* BTP Tioxide Ltd v Armada Marine SA
   [1982] A.C. 724; [1981] 3 W.L.R. 292; [1981] 2 All E.R. 1030; [1981] 2 Lloyd's
   Rep. 239; [1981] Com. L.R. 197; (1981) 125 S.J. 542, HL; affirming [1980]
   Q.B. 547; [1980] 3 W.L.R. 326; [1980] 3 All E.R. 117; [1980] 2 Lloyd's Rep.
   339; [1980] E.C.C. 467, CA (Civ Div); reversing [1980] 2 Lloyd's Rep. 83, QBD
   (Comm) . . . . *Digested*, 81/**76**:
         Applied, 82/82, 82/84, 82/85, 82/138, 85/113, 87/146: *Cited*, 84/96, 84/127,
               84/243, 89/114, 90/193, 90/2850, 92/164, 92/2745: *Considered*, 82/83,
               82/89, 82/115, 82/2856, 83/112, 83/131, 86/91, 86/92, 86/1907, 90/202,
               90/206, 91/201, 91/203, 92/2734, 93/163, 07/254: *Distinguished*, 83/111,
               89/104: *Followed*, 82/86, 82/87: *Not applied*, 86/1926: *Referred to*, 82/88,
                         83/125, 87/2216

Piper v JRI (Manufacturing) Ltd [2006] EWCA Civ 1344; (2006) 92 B.M.L.R. 141; (2006) 150 S.J.L.B. 1391, CA (Civ Div) . . . . *Digested*, 07/**777**

Piper-Heidsieck SA Co v Champagne Vranken Co [2007] E.T.M.R. 65, Trib Gde Inst (Paris)

Pippig Augenoptik GmbH & Co KG v Hartlauer Handelsgesellschaft mbH (C-44/01) [2004] All E.R. (EC) 1156; [2003] E.C.R. I-3095; [2004] 1 C.M.L.R. 39; [2004] E.T.M.R. 5, ECJ . . . . *Digested*, 04/**504**:
Applied, 07/1571: *Considered*, 06/2615, 07/1570, 07/2671

Pirelli Cable Holding NV v Inland Revenue Commissioners; *joined cases* Pirelli Tyre Holding NV v Inland Revenue Commissioners; Pirelli SpA v Inland Revenue Commissioners; Pirelli General Plc v Inland Revenue Commissioners; Pirelli Plc v Inland Revenue Commissioners [2006] UKHL 4; [2006] 1 W.L.R. 400; [2006] 2 All E.R. 81; [2006] S.T.C. 548; [2006] Eu. L.R. 827; 77 T.C. 409; [2006] B.T.C. 181; 8 I.T.L. Rep. 872; [2006] S.T.I. 381; (2006) 103(9) L.S.G. 32; (2006) 150 S.J.L.B. 226; *Times*, February 13, 2006, HL; reversing [2003] EWCA Civ 1849; [2004] S.T.C. 130; [2004] Eu. L.R. 459; [2004] B.T.C. 50; 6 I.T.L. Rep. 503; [2004] S.T.I. 49, CA (Civ Div); affirming [2003] EWHC 32 (Ch); [2003] S.T.C. 250; [2003] 2 C.M.L.R. 23; [2003] Eu. L.R. 166; [2003] B.T.C. 218; 5 I.T.L. Rep. 930; [2003] S.T.I. 103; (2003) 100(11) L.S.G. 34; *Times*, January 29, 2003, Ch D . . . . *Digested*, 06/**4255**:
Applied, 07/3972: *Considered*, 06/4163

Pirelli Cable Holding NV v Revenue and Customs Commissioners A3/2007/0875, CA (Civ Div); affirming [2007] EWHC 583 (Ch); [2007] B.T.C. 362; [2007] S.T.I. 1047, Ch D . . . . *Digested*, 07/**3975**

Pirelli General Cable Works Ltd v Oscar Faber & Partners [1983] 2 A.C. 1; [1983] 2 W.L.R. 6; [1983] 1 All E.R. 65; (1983) 265 E.G. 979; *Times*, December 11, 1982, HL; reversing (1982) 262 E.G. 879, CA (Civ Div) . . . . *Digested*, 83/**2216**:
Applied, 83/2215, 84/212, 84/2675, 85/208, 85/212, 87/2330, 88/2158, 96/1156, 01/4511, 01/4907, 05/436, 07/481: *Considered*, 85/189, 88/2418, 89/2585, 89/3516, 91/2660, 93/2997: *Disapproved*, 96/4438: *Distinguished*, 86/1993, 87/2321, 92/3219: *Followed*, 88/2154, 94/6161: *Not followed*, 85/2303: *Referred to*, 84/240

Pirelli General Plc v Inland Revenue Commissioners see Pirelli Cable Holding NV v Inland Revenue Commissioners

Pirelli Plc v Inland Revenue Commissioners see Pirelli Cable Holding NV v Inland Revenue Commissioners

Pirelli SpA v Inland Revenue Commissioners see Pirelli Cable Holding NV v Inland Revenue Commissioners

Pirelli Tyre Holding NV v Inland Revenue Commissioners see Pirelli Cable Holding NV v Inland Revenue Commissioners

Pithouse v Surrey CC (Unreported, October 17, 2006), CC (Macclesfield) [*Ex rel.* Jack Harding, Barrister, 1 Chancery Lane, London] . . . . *Digested*, 07/**503**

PITNEY BOWES/Undeliverable mail (T388/04) [2007] E.P.O.R. 31, EPO (Technical Bd App)

Pittalis v Grant [1989] Q.B. 605; [1989] 3 W.L.R. 139; [1989] 2 All E.R. 622; (1989) 21 H.L.R. 368; [1989] 28 E.G. 126; [1989] E.G. 37 (C.S.); (1989) 139 N.L.J. 578; (1989) 133 S.J. 752, CA (Civ Div) . . . . *Digested*, 89/**2890**:
Applied, 92/2755: *Considered*, 92/1553, 95/3082, 97/3332, 07/3989: *Distinguished*, 92/4507: *Not followed*, 97/3334

Pitts v Earl Cadogan [2007] R.V.R. 269, Lands Tr

Pitts v Earl Cadogan; *joined case* Earl Cadogan v Atlantic Telecasters Ltd [2007] EWCA Civ 1280, CA (Civ Div); affirming [2007] 42 E.G. 296; [2007] R.V.R. 272, Lands Tr

Pitts v Jones [2007] EWCA Civ 1301; [2007] 2 C.L.C. 947; (2007) 151 S.J.L.B. 1594; *Times*, December 19, 2007, CA (Civ Div)

Plantiflor Ltd v Customs and Excise Commissioners see Customs and Excise Commissioners v Plantiflor Ltd

Planzer Luxembourg Sarl v Bundeszentralamt fur Steuern (C-73/06) [2007] S.T.I. 1768, ECJ (4th Chamber)

Plattform Arzte fur das Leben v Austria (A/139) (1991) 13 E.H.R.R. 204; *Times*, June 30, 1988, ECHR . . . . *Digested*, 88/**1807**:
Applied, 97/2787: *Considered*, 07/2177: *Referred to*, 97/2774

Plaumann & Co v Commission of the European Economic Community (25/62) [1963] E.C.R. 95; [1964] C.M.L.R. 29, ECJ . . . . *Digested*, 64/**1440**:
Applied, 65/1518, 98/735, 98/2311, 05/1470, 07/1564: *Considered*, 02/1588: *Followed*, 02/1543

PLAYERS Trade Mark [1965] R.P.C. 363 . . . . *Digested*, 65/**3949**:
Considered, 07/2662

Plon SA v Hugo see Hugo v Plon SA

Pluck v Pluck [2007] EWCA Civ 1250; (2007) 151 S.J.L.B. 1401, CA (Civ Div)

Plummer v Inland Revenue Commissioners [1988] 1 W.L.R. 292; [1988] 1 All E.R. 97; [1987] S.T.C. 698; 60 T.C. 452; (1988) 132 S.J. 54, Ch D . . . . *Digested*, 88/**398**:
Considered, 07/4068

Plymouth and South West Co-operative Society Ltd *v* Architecture, Structure & Management Ltd [2006] EWHC 3252 (TCC); 111 Con. L.R. 189; [2007] Lloyd's Rep. I.R. 596, QBD (TCC) . . . . *Digested,* 07/**749**
Podkolzina *v* Latvia (Admissibility) (46726/99) (Unreported, April 9, 2000), ECHR . . . *Applied,* 07/2263
Point Solutions Ltd *v* Focus Business Solutions Ltd [2007] EWCA Civ 14; (2007) 151 S.J.L.B. 162, CA (Civ Div); affirming [2005] EWHC 3096 (Ch); [2006] F.S.R. 31, Ch D . . . . *Digested,* 06/**2443**
Pointon York Group Plc *v* Poulton [2006] EWCA Civ 1001; [2007] 1 P. & C.R. 6; [2007] L. & T.R. 8; [2006] 3 E.G.L.R. 37; [2006] 38 E.G. 192; [2006] 29 E.G. 133 (C.S.); [2006] N.P.C. 86, CA (Civ Div) . . . . *Digested,* 06/**2675**
Polanski *v* Conde Nast Publications Ltd [2005] UKHL 10; [2005] 1 W.L.R. 637; [2005] 1 All E.R. 945; [2005] C.P. Rep. 22; [2005] E.M.L.R. 14; [2005] H.R.L.R. 11; [2005] U.K.H.R.R. 277; (2005) 102(10) L.S.G. 29; (2005) 155 N.L.J. 245; *Times,* February 11, 2005; *Independent,* February 16, 2005, HL; reversing [2003] EWCA Civ 1573; [2004] 1 W.L.R. 387; [2004] 1 All E.R. 1220; [2004] C.P. Rep. 13; [2004] E.M.L.R. 7; [2004] U.K.H.R.R. 278; (2003) 100(46) L.S.G. 24; (2003) 153 N.L.J. 1760; (2003) 147 S.J.L.B. 1363; *Times,* November 18, 2003, CA (Civ Div) . . . . *Digested,* 05/**303**:
                                                                                     Applied, 07/344
Polar Park Enterprises Inc *v* Allason see Polarpark Enterprises Inc *v* Allason
Polarpark Enterprises Inc *v* Allason; *sub nom* Polar Park Enterprises Inc *v* Allason [2007] EWHC 1088 (Ch); [2007] 33 E.G. 92; [2007] W.T.L.R. 1829; *Times,* June 26, 2007, Ch D . . . . *Digested,* 07/**2761**
Police Service of Northern Ireland *v* McCaughey [2005] NICA 1; [2005] N.I. 344; [2005] Inquest L.R. 3, CA (NI) . . . . *Digested,* 06/**4528**:
                                                          Reversed in part, 07/4372
Pollard *v* Chief Constable of West Yorkshire [1999] P.I.Q.R. P219, CA (Civ Div) . . . . . . *Digested,* 98/**4257**:
                                                          Distinguished, 07/4191
Pollard *v* Pollard (2007) 151 S.J.L.B. 1260, Ch D (Bristol)
Polo Farm Sports Club *v* Revenue and Customs Commissioners [2007] V. & D.R. 44; [2007] S.T.I. 1705, V&DTr (London)
Polo/Lauren Co LP *v* PT Dwidua Langgeng Pratama International Freight Forwarders (C-383/98) [2000] E.C.R. I-2519; [2000] E.T.M.R. 535; *Times,* April 14, 2000, ECJ (1st Chamber) . . . . *Digested,* 00/**2341**:
                                      Applied, 04/1394: *Considered,* 07/2638
Ponente Carni *v* Amministrazione delle Finanze dello Stato (C-71/91) [1993] E.C.R. I-1915, ECJ . . . . *Digested,* 93/**4405**:
                                                                                     Applied, 07/3985
Poole *v* HM Treasury [2007] EWCA Civ 1021; [2007] 2 C.L.C. 727; (2007) 104(43) L.S.G. 32; *Times,* December 24, 2007, CA (Civ Div); affirming [2006] EWHC 2731 (Comm); [2007] 1 All E.R. (Comm) 255; [2006] 2 C.L.C. 865; [2007] Eu. L.R. 305; [2007] Lloyd's Rep. I.R. 114; *Times,* December 1, 2006, QBD (Comm)   *Digested,* 07/**2490**
Pope Ex p. Dicksee, Re [1908] 2 K.B. 169, CA . . . . *Applied,* 75/176,
                                                                                     82/205, 07/2454
Popeley *v* Popeley see Popely *v* Popely
Popely *v* Popely; *sub nom* Popeley *v* Popeley [2004] EWCA Civ 463; [2004] B.P.I.R. 778; (2004) 101(19) L.S.G. 29; (2004) 148 S.J.L.B. 569; *Times,* May 14, 2004; *Independent,* May 5, 2004, CA (Civ Div); affirming [2003] EWHC 2028 (Ch); [2003] B.P.I.R. 1398; (2003) 100(37) L.S.G. 33; *Times,* September 15, 2003, Ch D . . . . *Digested,* 04/**2180**:
                                      Considered, 07/2452, 07/2453
Porter *v* Magill; *sub nom* Magill *v* Porter; Magill *v* Weeks; *joined cases* Phillips *v* Magill; England *v* Magill; Hartley *v* Magill; Weeks *v* Magill [2001] UKHL 67; [2002] 2 A.C. 357; [2002] 2 W.L.R. 37; [2002] 1 All E.R. 465; [2002] H.R.L.R. 16; [2002] H.L.R. 16; [2002] B.L.G.R. 51; (2001) 151 N.L.J. 1886; [2001] N.P.C. 184; *Times,* December 14, 2001; *Independent,* February 4, 2002; *Daily Telegraph,* December 20, 2001, HL; reversing [2000] 2 W.L.R. 1420; (1999) 31 H.L.R. 823; (1999) 1 L.G.L.R. 523; [1999] B.L.G.R. 375; (1999) 11 Admin. L.R. 661; (1999) 163 J.P.N. 1025; (1999) 96(21) L.S.G. 39; (1999) 143 S.J.L.B. 147; *Times,* May 6, 1999, CA (Civ Div); reversing (1998) 30 H.L.R. 997, QBD . . . . .   *Digested,* 02/**3185**:
                        Applied, 03/319, 03/1251, 03/1261, 04/30, 04/2652, 05/13, 05/894,
                        05/2153, 05/2908, 05/3279, 06/207, 06/967, 06/2755, 06/3339, 06/3987,
                        07/31, 07/1343, 07/1428, 07/3252, 07/3264: *Considered,* 02/294, 02/451,
                        05/646: *Followed,* 03/5397, 04/1904, 04/4467:
                                                          Subsequent proceedings, 02/3161
Porto Segura Companhia de Seguros *v* Belcan SA (The Federal Danube) [1997] 3 S.C.R. 1278, Sup Ct (Can) . . . . *Applied,* 07/2625
Portsmouth NHS Trust *v* Wyatt; *sub nom* Wyatt (A Child) (Medical Treatment: Continuation of Order), Re [2005] EWCA Civ 1181; [2005] 1 W.L.R. 3995; [2006] 1 F.L.R. 554; [2005] 3 F.C.R. 263; (2006) 9 C.C.L. Rep. 131; [2005] Lloyd's Rep. Med. 474; (2005) 86 B.M.L.R. 173; [2006] Fam. Law 13, CA (Civ Div); affirming [2005] EWHC 693 (Fam); [2005] 2 F.L.R. 480; [2005] Fam. Law 614, Fam Div . . . . *Digested,* 05/**1794**:
                        Applied, 06/1847, 07/1984: *Previous proceedings,* 05/1848

Portugaia Construcoes Lda v Urlaubs- und Lohnausgleichskasse der Bauwirtschaft (C-70/98) see Finalarte Sociedade de Construcao Civil Lda v Urlaubs- und Lohnausgleichskasse der Bauwirtschaft (C-49/98)

Portugal v Commission of the European Communities (C-88/03); *sub nom* Income Tax Reductions in the Azores, Re (C-88/03) [2007] S.T.C. 1032; [2006] E.C.R. I-7115; [2006] 3 C.M.L.R. 45; [2006] S.T.I. 2179, ECJ . . . .   *Digested*, 07/**651**

Poseidon Chartering BV v Marianne Zeeschip Vof (C-3/04) [2007] Bus. L.R. 446; [2006] 2 Lloyd's Rep. 105; [2006] E.C.R. I-2505, ECJ . . . .   *Digested*, 07/**67**

Post Office v Howell [2000] I.C.R. 913; [2000] I.R.L.R. 224; *Times*, November 11, 1999, EAT . . . .   *Digested*, 99/**2050**:
                         Applied, 01/2270: *Considered*, 07/1352

Post Office v Jones see Jones v Post Office

Postlethwaite's Executors v Revenue and Customs Commissioners; *sub nom* Aspinall v Revenue and Customs Commissioners [2007] S.T.C. (S.C.D.) 83; [2007] W.T.L.R. 353; [2007] S.T.I. 346, Sp Comm . . . .   *Digested*, 07/**4108**

Potter v Hillingdon LBC see R. (on the application of Hall) v First Secretary of State

Potter v Scottish Ministers see Potter v Scottish Prison Service

Potter v Scottish Prison Service; *sub nom* Potter v Scottish Ministers [2007] CSIH 67; 2007 S.L.T. 1019; [2007] U.K.H.R.R. 1361; 2007 G.W.D. 28-500, IH (1 Div); reversing [2007] CSOH 56; 2007 S.L.T. 363; 2007 G.W.D. 10-196; *Times*, April 4, 2007, OH . . . .   *Digested*, 07/**5434**

Poulton v Adjustable Cover & Boiler Block Co [1908] 2 Ch. 430, CA . . . .   *Applied*, 04/2338:
                                     Considered, 07/2606

Pountney v Griffiths; *sub nom* R. v Bracknell Justices Ex p. Griffiths [1976] A.C. 314; [1975] 3 W.L.R. 140; [1975] 2 All E.R. 881; [1975] Crim. L.R. 702; (1975) 119 S.J. 493, HL; affirming [1975] 2 W.L.R. 291; [1975] 1 All E.R. 900; (1975) 119 S.J. 114, DC . . . .   *Digested*, 75/**2128**:
       Applied, 07/2908: *Considered*, 75/2128, 81/175.u, 05/2826

Pour v Westminster City Council see Feld v Barnet LBC

Powdrill v Hambros Bank (Jersey) Ltd see Paramount Airways Ltd (No.2), Re

Powell v Benney [2007] EWCA Civ 1283; (2007) 151 S.J.L.B. 1598, CA (Civ Div)

Powell v Boladz; *sub nom* Powell v Boladz [1998] Lloyd's Rep. Med. 116; (1998) 39 B.M.L.R. 35, CA (Civ Div) . . . .   *Considered*, 06/**2885**:
                                      Followed, 07/4298

Powell v Boladz see Powell v Boladz

Powell v Smith (Unreported, March 27, 2007), CC (Liverpool) [*Ex rel.* Andrew Arentsen Barrister, 33 Park Place, Cardiff] . . . .   *Digested*, 07/**3102**

Powell v United Kingdom (9310/81) see Powell v United Kingdom (A/172)

Powell v United Kingdom (A/172); *sub nom* Powell v United Kingdom (9310/81) (1990) 12 E.H.R.R. 355; *Times*, February 22, 1990, ECHR (1990) 12 E.H.R.R. CD288, Eur Comm HR . . . .   *Digested*, 90/**2525**:
                                      Applied, 07/2256

Power v Chief Constable of Lancashire see Hunter v Chief Constable of the West Midlands

Power v Regent Security Services Ltd; *sub nom* Regent Security Services Ltd v Power [2007] EWCA Civ 1188; (2007) 104(47) L.S.G. 26, CA (Civ Div); affirming [2007] 4 All E.R. 354; [2007] I.C.R. 970; [2007] I.R.L.R. 226, EAT . .   *Digested*, 07/**1414**

PowerGen Plc, Re (C-157/97 P (I)) see National Power Plc, Re (C-151/97 P (I))

Powerhouse Retail Ltd v Burroughs; *sub nom* Fletcher v Midland Bank Plc (No.3); Preston v Wolverhampton Healthcare NHS Trust (No.3) [2006] UKHL 13; [2006] 3 All E.R. 193; [2007] 2 C.M.L.R. 38; [2006] I.C.R. 606; [2006] I.R.L.R. 381; [2006] Pens. L.R. 113; (2006) 103(12) L.S.G. 29; (2006) 150 S.J.L.B. 364; *Times*, March 13, 2006, HL; affirming [2004] EWCA Civ 1281; [2005] I.C.R. 222; [2004] I.R.L.R. 979; [2004] O.P.L.R. 363; [2004] Pens. L.R. 377; (2004) 148 S.J.L.B. 1212; *Times*, October 27, 2004; *Independent*, October 14, 2004, CA (Civ Div) . . . .   *Digested*, 06/**1327**:
                                Previous proceedings, 04/1256

Powerstore (Trading) Ltd, Re; *joined case* Homepower Stores Ltd, Re [1997] 1 W.L.R. 1280; [1998] 1 All E.R. 121; [1998] B.C.C. 305; [1998] 1 B.C.L.C. 90; (1997) 94(24) L.S.G. 31; (1997) 141 S.J.L.B. 137; *Times*, May 19, 1997, Ch D (Companies Ct) . . . .   *Digested*, 97/**3051**:
       Applied, 07/2392: *Cited*, 02/2651: *Considered*, 98/3346, 99/3361, 01/3708,
                          03/2391, 04/2112, 07/2395: *Not followed*, 99/3349

Powys CC v Maidenhead & Malamar Homes Ltd [2007] P.A.D. 70, Planning Inspector

Pozzoli SpA v BDMO SA [2007] EWCA Civ 588; [2007] F.S.R. 37; (2007) 30(8) I.P.D. 30051; [2007] Bus. L.R. D117, CA (Civ Div); affirming [2006] EWHC 1398 (Ch); (2006) 29(7) I.P.D. 29056, Ch D (Patents Ct) . . . .   *Digested*, 07/**2634**

PPG Industries Ohio Inc v Saint-Gobain Glass France (G1/03) see PPG/Disclaimer (G1/03)

PPG/Disclaimer (G1/03); *sub nom* Genetic Systems/Disclaimer (G2/03); PPG Industries Ohio Inc v Saint-Gobain Glass France (G1/03); Genetic Systems v Roche Diagnostics GmbH (G2/03) [2004] E.P.O.R. 33, EPO (Enlarged Bd App) . . . .   *Applied*, 05/2466,
                            05/2468, 06/2489, 07/2564, 07/2570

Practice Direction (CA (Crim Div): Criminal Appeals: Forms) [2007] 1 W.L.R. 2607, CA
(Crim Div)
Practice Direction (CA (Crim Div): Criminal Proceedings: Consolidation); *sub nom*
Practice Statement (CA (Crim Div): Consolidated Criminal Practice Direction)
[2002] 1 W.L.R. 2870; [2002] 3 All E.R. 904; [2002] 2 Cr. App. R. 35, CA
(Crim Div) . . . . *Digested*, 02/**899**:
Cited, 04/856, 05/3678, 06/3888, 07/1010: *Considered*, 05/913:
Followed, 03/3780: *Superseded in part*, 03/899, 04/877, 04/879, 05/914,
05/3708, 05/3710, 06/971
Practice Direction (CA (Crim Div): Criminal Proceedings: Consolidation) (2007) 151
S.J.L.B. 609, Sup Ct
Practice Direction (Ch D: Validation Orders: Insolvency Act 1986 ss127 and 284); *sub nom*
Practice Note (Validation Orders: Insolvency Act 1986 ss127 and 284) [2007]
B.C.C. 91; [2007] B.P.I.R. 94, Ch D . . . . *Digested*, 07/**2458**
Practice Direction (Crown Ct: Guidance to Jurors); *sub nom* Consolidated Criminal
Practice Direction (Amendment No.4) (Guidance to Jurors) [2004] 1 W.L.R.
665; [2004] 2 Cr. App. R. 1; *Times*, February 27, 2004, CA (Crim Div) . . . . *Digested*, 04/**856**:
Cited, 07/1000: *Considered*, 05/849
Practice Direction (EAT: Appeal Procedure) [2003] I.C.R. 122; [2003] I.R.L.R. 65, EAT *Digested*, 03/**1291**:
Cited, 05/1242: *Considered*, 07/1343: *Superseded*, 05/1285
Practice Direction (Fam Div: Applications for Reporting Restriction Orders) [2005] 2 F.L.R.
120, Fam Div . . . . *Digested*, 05/**1683**:
Cited, 07/1711
Practice Direction (Fam Div: Children Act 1989: Risk Assessments under s.16A) see
Practice Direction (Fam Div: Children: Risk Assessments)
Practice Direction (Fam Div: Children: Risk Assessments); *sub nom* Practice Direction
(Fam Div: Children Act 1989: Risk Assessments under s.16A) [2007] 1 W.L.R.
2521; [2007] 2 F.L.R. 625; [2007] 3 F.C.R. 784, Fam Div
Practice Direction (Fam Div: Family Assistance Orders: Consultation) see Practice
Direction (Fam Div: Family Proceedings: Family Assistance Orders)
Practice Direction (Fam Div: Family Proceedings: Court Bundles) [2000] 1 W.L.R. 737;
[2000] 2 All E.R. 287; [2000] 1 F.L.R. 537; [2000] 1 F.C.R. 521; (2000) 144 S.J.L.B.
74; *Times*, March 22, 2000, Fam Div . . . . *Digested*, 00/**2550**:
Cited, 00/2553, 00/2554: *Superseded*, 07/1819: *Superseded in part*, 04/1536
Practice Direction (Fam Div: Family Proceedings: Court Bundles) [2006] 1 W.L.R. 2843;
[2006] 2 F.L.R. 199; [2006] 2 F.C.R. 834, Fam Div . . . . *Digested*, 07/**1819**
Practice Direction (Fam Div: Family Proceedings: Family Assistance Orders); *sub nom*
Practice Direction (Fam Div: Family Assistance Orders: Consultation) [2007] 1
W.L.R. 2522; [2007] 2 F.L.R. 626, Fam Div
Practice Direction (Fam Div: Guide to Vacation Business) [2006] 2 F.L.R. 486; [2006] 2
F.C.R. 840, Fam Div . . . . *Digested*, 07/**1818**
Practice Direction (IAT: Appeal and Immigration Tribunal); *sub nom* Practice Direction
(IAT: Asylum and Immigration Tribunal) [2005] Imm. A.R. 1; [2005] I.N.L.R. 357,
IAT . . . . *Digested*, 05/**2225**:
Cited, 06/2241: *Considered*, 07/2275
Practice Direction (IAT: Asylum and Immigration Tribunal) see Practice Direction (IAT:
Appeal and Immigration Tribunal)
Practice Direction (Lands Tr: Practice Directions) [2006] R.V.R. 221, Lands Tr . . . . *Digested*, 07/**3416**:
Considered, 07/413
Practice Direction (QBD: Admiralty: Assessors' Remuneration) [2007] 1 W.L.R. 2508,
QBD
Practice Direction (QBD (Admlty): Remuneration of Nautical and Other Assessors) [2007]
2 All E.R. (Comm) 364, QBD (Admlty)
Practice Direction (Sup Ct: Crime: Costs in Criminal Proceedings); *sub nom* Practice
Direction (Sup Ct: Crime: Defence Costs); Practice Note (Sup Ct: Criminal Law:
Costs) [1999] 1 W.L.R. 1832; [1999] 4 All E.R. 436; [2000] 1 Cr. App. R. 60;
[2000] 1 Cr. App. R. 76; *Times*, October 6, 1999, Sup Ct. . . . . *Digested*, 99/**1040**:
Cited, 07/2227
Practice Direction (Sup Ct: Crime: Defence Costs) see Practice Direction (Sup Ct: Crime:
Costs in Criminal Proceedings)
Practice Note (CA (Civ Div): Asylum and Immigration Cases) see Practice Note (CA (Civ
Div): Asylum Seeker Anonymisation)
Practice Note (CA (Civ Div): Asylum Seeker Anonymisation); *sub nom* Practice Note (CA
(Civ Div): Asylum and Immigration Cases) [2006] 1 W.L.R. 2461; [2006] 4 All
E.R. 928; *Times*, August 24, 2006, CA (Civ Div) . . . . *Digested*, 07/**2270**
Practice Note (Official Solicitor, CAFCASS and National Assembly for Wales: Urgent and
Out of Hours Cases in the Family Division) [2006] 2 F.L.R. 354, Fam Div. . . . . *Digested*, 07/**1801**
Practice Note (Official Solicitor: Declaratory Proceedings: Medical and Welfare Decisions
for Adults who Lack Capacity) [2006] 2 F.L.R. 373, Fam Div. . . . . *Digested*, 07/**3943**
Practice Note (Official Solicitor: Declaratory Proceedings: Medical and Welfare
Proceedings for Adults Who Lack Capacity) [2001] 2 F.L.R. 158; [2001] 2 F.C.R.
569 . . . . *Digested*, 01/**2662**:
Considered, 02/1712: *Superseded*, 07/3943

Practice Note (Official Solicitor: Deputy Director of Legal Services: CAFCASS: Applications for Reporting Restriction Orders) [2005] 2 F.L.R. 111, Fam Div . . .   *Digested*, 05/**1685**: *Cited*, 07/1711

Practice Note (PO: Patents Act 1977: Patentable Subject Matter) [2007] Bus. L.R. 672; [2007] R.P.C. 8, PO . . . .   *Digested*, 07/**2635**

Practice Note (Sup Ct: Criminal Law: Costs) see Practice Direction (Sup Ct: Crime: Costs in Criminal Proceedings)

Practice Note (Validation Orders: Insolvency Act 1986 ss127 and 284) see Practice Direction (Ch D: Validation Orders: Insolvency Act 1986 ss127 and 284)

Practice Statement (CA (Crim Div): Consolidated Criminal Practice Direction) see Practice Direction (CA (Crim Div): Criminal Proceedings: Consolidation)

Practice Statement (QBD (Admin Ct): Judicial Review: Costs) [2004] 1 W.L.R. 1760; [2004] 2 All E.R. 994; *Times*, May 20, 2004, QBD (Admin) . . . .   *Digested*, 04/**368**: *Cited*, 07/402

Prater *v* Cornwall CC see Cornwall CC *v* Prater

Prater Ltd *v* Office of Fair Trading see Makers UK Ltd *v* Office of Fair Trading

Prater Ltd *v* Office of Fair Trading (Time Limits) [2006] CAT 11; [2006] Comp. A.R. 624, CAT . . . .   *Digested*, 07/**359**

Pratt *v* Bull see Hollins *v* Russell

Prazic *v* Prazic [2006] EWCA Civ 497; [2007] I.L.Pr. 31; [2006] 2 F.L.R. 1125; [2007] 1 F.C.R. 503; [2006] Fam. Law 745, CA (Civ Div) . . . .   *Digested*, 07/**1710**

Prebble *v* Dunn (Unreported, November 14, 2006), CC (Uxbridge) [*Ex rel.* Elliot Gold, Barrister, 5 Essex Court, Temple, London] . . . .   *Digested*, 07/**3203**

PRECO INDUSTRIES/Die stamping press (T561/01) [2007] E.P.O.R. 23, EPO (Technical Bd App) . . . .   *Digested*, 07/**2611**

Preece *v* Caerphilly CC (Unreported, February 16, 2007), CC (Blackwood) [*Ex rel.* Andrew Arentson, Barrister, 33 Park Place, Cardiff] . . . .   *Digested*, 07/**3185**

Preece *v* Caerphilly CC (2007) 104(34) L.S.G. 29, CC (Cardiff)

Prekons Insaat Sanayi AS *v* Rowlands Castle Contracting Group Ltd [2006] EWHC 1367 (Comm); [2007] 1 Lloyd's Rep. 98, QBD (Comm) . . . .   *Digested*, 07/**238**

Preloznik *v* Slovakia (54330/00) [2007] 1 F.C.R. 167, ECHR. . . . .   *Digested*, 07/**2218**

Premier Electronics (GB) Ltd, Re; *sub nom* Pickering *v* Lynch [2002] B.C.C. 911; [2002] 2 B.C.L.C. 634; *Times*, February 27, 2001, Ch D . . . .   *Digested*, 01/**726**: *Applied*, 07/456

Premier Foods (Holdings Ltd) *v* Revenue and Customs Commissioners see Revenue and Customs Commissioners *v* Premier Foods Ltd

Premium Nafta Products Ltd *v* Fili Shipping Co Ltd see Fiona Trust & Holding Corp *v* Privalov

Prescott *v* Dunwoody Sports Marketing [2007] EWCA Civ 461; [2007] 1 W.L.R. 2343; [2007] C.P. Rep. 34; *Times*, May 25, 2007, CA (Civ Div) . . . .   *Digested*, 07/**537**

Presentation Social Investment Agency *v* Haringey LBC [2007] P.A.D. 4, Planning Inspector

President of the Methodist Conference *v* Parfitt [1984] Q.B. 368; [1984] 2 W.L.R. 84; [1983] 3 All E.R. 747; [1984] I.C.R. 176; [1984] I.R.L.R. 141, CA (Civ Div) reversing *Times*, November 18, 1982, EAT . . . .   *Digested*, 84/**1241**: *Applied*, 90/1863, 92/2003: *Considered*, 95/2078, 96/2652, 06/5318, 07/1326: *Distinguished*, 85/1299: *Followed*, 86/1172

Pressos Compania Naviera SA *v* Belgium (A/332) (1996) 21 E.H.R.R. 301, ECHR . . . .   *Digested*, 96/**5325**: *Considered*, 06/2120: *Distinguished*, 07/2636

Preston *v* Wolverhampton Healthcare NHS Trust (No.2); *joined case* Fletcher *v* Midland Bank Plc (No.2) [2001] UKHL 5; [2001] 2 A.C. 455; [2001] 2 W.L.R. 448; [2001] 3 All E.R. 947; [2001] 1 C.M.L.R. 46; [2001] I.C.R. 217; [2001] I.R.L.R. 237; [2001] Emp. L.R. 256; [2001] O.P.L.R. 1; [2001] Pens. L.R. 39; (2001) 98(10) L.S.G. 41; (2001) 145 S.J.L.B. 55; *Times*, February 9, 2001, HL . . . . . .   *Digested*, 01/**2279**: *Applied*, 05/1263, 06/1326, 07/2496: *Previous proceedings*, 00/2162: *Subsequent proceedings*, 03/3095

Preston *v* Wolverhampton Healthcare NHS Trust (No.3) see Powerhouse Retail Ltd *v* Burroughs

Preston *v* Wolverhampton Healthcare NHS Trust (No.3); *joined case* Fletcher *v* Midland Bank Plc (No.3) [2004] I.C.R. 993; [2004] I.R.L.R. 96; [2004] O.P.L.R. 33; [2004] Pens. L.R. 97, EAT; reversing in part [2002] O.P.L.R. 323; [2002] Pens. L.R. 389, ET . . . .   *Digested*, 04/**1256**: *Applied*, 05/1263, 06/1326, 07/1359: *Reversed in part*, 05/1217

Pret a Manger (Europe) Ltd *v* Revenue and Customs Commissioners [2007] B.V.C. 2172, V&DTr

Pretty *v* United Kingdom (2346/02); *sub nom* R. (on the application of Pretty) *v* DPP (2346/02) [2002] 2 F.L.R. 45; [2002] 2 F.C.R. 97; (2002) 35 E.H.R.R. 1; 12 B.H.R.C. 149; (2002) 66 B.M.L.R. 147; [2002] Fam. Law 588; (2002) 152 N.L.J. 707, ECHR . . . .   *Digested*, 02/**2528**: *Applied*, 04/2027, 06/2188, 06/3651: *Considered*, 03/4070, 06/844, 06/2217, 07/2260: *Distinguished*, 07/204: *Referred to*, 04/2026

Price *v* Craig; *sub nom* Craig (Deceased), Re [2006] EWHC 2561 (Ch); [2006] W.T.L.R. 1873; (2006-07) 9 I.T.E.L.R. 393, Ch D . . . .   *Digested*, 07/**3964**

Price *v* Leeds City Council see Kay *v* Lambeth LBC

Price v William-Wynn [2006] EWHC 788 (Ch); [2006] W.T.L.R. 1633, Ch D . . . .   *Digested,* 07/**4256**
Price's Estate, Re (2007-08) 10 I.T.E.L.R. 920, US Court
Primlake Ltd (In Liquidation) v Matthews Associates [2006] EWHC 1227 (Ch); [2007]
   1 B.C.L.C. 666, Ch D . . . .   *Digested,* 07/**3438**
Primlaks (UK) Ltd, Re [1990] B.C.L.C. 234 . . . .   *Digested,* 90/**501**:
                                        Considered, 07/2422
Prince Radu of Hohenzollern v Houston [2006] EWCA Civ 1575; [2007] C.P. Rep. 11;
   [2007] 5 Costs L.R. 671; (2006) 156 N.L.J. 1847; (2006) 150 S.J.L.B. 1567;
   Times, January 1, 2007, CA (Civ Div); reversing [2006] EWHC 231 (QB), QBD   *Digested,* 07/**513**
Princes House Ltd v Distinctive Clubs Ltd [2007] EWCA Civ 374; [2007] L. & T.R. 34;
   [2007] 27 E.G. 304; [2007] 14 E.G. 104 (C.S.), CA (Civ Div); affirming [2007]
   1 P. & C.R. DG20, Ch D . . . .   *Digested,* 07/**2731**
Principe SpA v Principles Retail Ltd [2007] E.T.M.R. 56, PO (Irl)
Print Factory (London) 1991 Ltd v Millam; *sub nom* Millam v Print Factory (London)
   1991 Ltd [2007] EWCA Civ 322; [2007] I.C.R. 1331; [2007] I.R.L.R. 526;
   (2007) 104(18) L.S.G. 28, CA (Civ Div); reversing [2006] I.R.L.R. 923, EAT . .   *Digested,* 07/**1419**
Prior (Inspector of Taxes) v Saunders [1993] S.T.C. 562; 66 T.C. 210, Ch D . . . .   *Digested,* 94/**2523**:
                                          Applied, 07/4055
Prison Charities, Re (1873) L.R. 16 Eq. 129, Ct of Chancery.   *Considered,* 07/318
Prison Service v Barua [2007] I.C.R. 671; [2007] I.R.L.R. 4, EAT . . . .   *Digested,* 07/**1409**
Pritchard (A Bankrupt), Re; *sub nom* Williams v Pritchard [2007] B.P.I.R. 1385, Ch D
Prizedome Ltd v Revenue and Customs Commissioners see Limitgood Ltd v Revenue
   and Customs Commissioners
Probstmeier v Germany (20950/92) (Unreported, July 1, 1997), ECHR . . . .   *Applied,* 07/2219
Proceedings brought by Manninen (C-319/02); *sub nom* Manninen, Re (C-319/02);
   Manninen v Finland (C-319/02) [2005] Ch. 236; [2005] 2 W.L.R. 670; [2005]
   All E.R. (EC) 465; [2004] S.T.C. 1444; [2004] E.C.R. I-7477; [2004] 3
   C.M.L.R. 40; [2005] C.E.C. 507; [2007] B.T.C. 163; 7 I.T.L. Rep. 119; [2004]
   S.T.I. 2068, ECJ . . . .   *Digested,* 05/**4028**:
                         Applied, 07/1600: *Considered,* 07/3974
Proceedings brought by Massachusetts Institute of Technology (C-431/04); *sub nom*
   Massachusetts Institute of Technology, Re (C-431/04) [2006] E.C.R. I-4089;
   [2006] R.P.C. 34, ECJ (2nd Chamber) . . . .   *Digested,* 07/**2539**
Proceedings brought by Oy AA (C-231/05) [2007] All E.R. (EC) 1079; [2007] S.T.I. 1863,
   ECJ (Grand Chamber)
Proceedings brought by Turpeinen (C-520/04) [2006] E.C.R. I-10685; [2007] 1 C.M.L.R.
   28; [2007] C.E.C. 480; [2006] S.T.I. 2458, ECJ (1st Chamber) . . . .   *Digested,* 07/**1610**
Proceedings brought by Voigt (C-83/05); *sub nom* Voight v Regierungsprasidium
   Karlsruhe-Bretten (C-83/05) [2006] E.C.R. I-6799; [2006] R.T.R. 36, ECJ (6th
   Chamber) . . . .   *Digested,* 07/**3488**
Procter & Gamble Co v Office for Harmonisation in the Internal Market (Trade Marks
   and Designs) (OHIM) (T-122/99); *sub nom* Procter & Gamble Co's Community
   Trade Mark Application (Shaped Soap) [2000] E.C.R. II-265; [2000] 2
   C.M.L.R. 303; [2000] C.E.C. 107; [2000] E.T.M.R. 580; (2000) 23(6) I.P.D.
   23042, CFI (2nd Chamber); reversing in part [1999] E.T.M.R. 776, OHIM (3rd
   Bd App) . . . .   *Digested,* 00/**3788**:
                 Applied, 01/4004, 07/2641: *Considered,* 00/3754
Procter & Gamble Co v Reckitt Benckiser (UK) Ltd [2006] EWHC 2872 (Pat); (2007)
   30(3) I.P.D. 30023, Ch D (Patents Ct)
Procter & Gamble Co v Reckitt Benckiser (UK) Ltd [2007] EWCA Civ 936; (2007)
   104(41) L.S.G. 28; *Times,* October 17, 2007, CA (Civ Div); reversing in part
   [2006] EWHC 3154 (Ch); [2007] E.C.D.R. 4; [2007] F.S.R. 13, Ch D (Patents
   Ct) . . . .   *Digested,* 07/**2535**
Procter & Gamble Co's Community Trade Mark Application (Shaped Soap) see Procter &
   Gamble Co v Office for Harmonisation in the Internal Market (Trade Marks and
   Designs) (OHIM) (T-122/99)
Procter & Gamble (UK) v Revenue and Customs Commissioners [2007] S.T.I. 2251,
   V&D Tr (London)
Procureur du Roi v Dassonville (8/74); *sub nom* Dassonville v Commission of the
   European Communities (8/74) [1974] E.C.R. 837; [1974] 2 C.M.L.R. 436;
   [1975] F.S.R. 191, ECJ . . . .   *Digested,* 75/**1285**:
             Applied, 98/728, 05/1450, 06/1554, 06/1557, 07/1650:
     Considered, 94/4885: *Distinguished,* 06/1561: *Followed,* 80/1193.a, 96/4865,
                               01/2489, 01/2508
Professional Trustees v Infant Prospecive Beneficiary [2007] EWHC 1922 (Ch); [2007]
   W.T.L.R. 1631, Ch D
Proform Sports Management Ltd v Proactive Sports Management Ltd [2006] EWHC
   2903 (Ch); [2007] Bus. L.R. 93; [2007] 1 All E.R. 542; [2007] 1 All E.R.
   (Comm) 356; (2006) 156 N.L.J. 1723; *Times,* November 13, 2006, Ch D
   (Manchester) . . . .   *Digested,* 07/**4197**
Prohibition of Marketing of Enriched Foods, Re (C-192/01) see Commission of the
   European Communities v Denmark (C-192/01)
Project v Hutt (2006) 150 S.J.L.B. 702, EAT (SC) . . . .   *Applied,* 07/467
Project Management Institute v Latif [2007] I.R.L.R. 579, EAT . . . .   *Applied,* 07/1334

ProLife Alliance v BBC see R. (on the application of ProLife Alliance) v BBC
Prosecution Right of Appeal (No.23 of 2007), Re see R. v R
PRP Architects v Reid [2006] EWCA Civ 1119; [2007] I.C.R. 78; [2007] P.I.Q.R. P4;
  (2006) 103(33) L.S.G. 24; [2006] N.P.C. 95, CA (Civ Div) . . . .   *Digested*, 07/**2082**
Prudential Assurance Co Ltd v Ayres A3/2007/0899, CA (Civ Div); reversing [2007]
  EWHC 775 (Ch); [2007] 3 All E.R. 946; [2007] L. & T.R. 35; [2007] 28 E.G.
  122; [2007] 16 E.G. 190 (C.S.); (2007) 151 S.J.L.B. 504, Ch D . . . .   *Digested*, 07/**2746**
Prudential Assurance Co Ltd v Newman Industries Ltd (No.2) [1982] Ch. 204; [1982]
  2 W.L.R. 31; [1982] 1 All E.R. 354, CA (Civ Div); reversing in part [1981] Ch.
  257; [1980] 3 W.L.R. 543; [1980] 2 All E.R. 841, Ch D . . . .   *Digested*, 82/**331**:
                    Applied, 98/691, 99/4025, 00/4257, 01/964: *Cited*, 00/5268:
                    Considered, 82/330, 83/3611, 96/1213, 00/371, 02/566, 07/435:
                                    Followed, 96/682: *Referred to*, 95/3755
Prudential Assurance Co Ltd v PRG Powerhouse Ltd [2007] EWHC 1002 (Ch); [2007]
  Bus. L.R. 1771; [2007] B.C.C. 500; [2007] B.P.I.R. 839; [2007] 19 E.G. 164
  (C.S.); (2007) 104(20) L.S.G. 30, Ch D . . . .   *Digested*, 07/**2422**
Prudential Assurance Co Ltd v Revenue and Customs Commissioners [2006] V. & D.R.
  301; [2006] S.T.I. 2109, V&DTr (London) . . . .   *Digested*, 07/**4361**
Prudential Plc v Revenue and Customs Commissioners [2007] S.T.I. 2412, Sp Comm
PS v Secretary of State for the Home Department; *sub nom* PS (LTTE: Internal Flight:
  Sufficiency of Protection) Sri Lankan, Re [2004] UKIAT 297, IAT . . . .   *Applied*, 07/2290
PS (Incapacitated or Vulnerable Adult), Re see Sunderland City Council v P
PS (LTTE: Internal Flight: Sufficiency of Protection) Sri Lankan, Re see PS v Secretary of
  State for the Home Department
PT Indah Kiat Pulp & Paper Tbk v US Bank National Association 10 I.T.L. Rep. 1
Public Trustee v Baron Newborough see Wynn's Will Trusts, Re (No.1)
Pugh v Savage [1970] 2 Q.B. 373; [1970] 2 W.L.R. 634; [1970] 2 All E.R. 353;
  (1970) 21 P. & C.R. 242; (1970) 114 S.J. 109, CA (Civ Div). . . . .   *Digested*, 70/**827**:
                    Applied, 73/953, 07/3428: *Distinguished*, 74/1081
Pulleng v Curran (1982) 44 P. & C.R. 58, CA (Civ Div) . . . .   *Digested*, 82/**1740**:
                    Applied, 89/2154, 89/2171, 07/2771: *Considered*, 89/2156, 89/2169
Pullum v Crown Prosecution Service [2000] C.O.D. 206, DC. . . . .   *Applied*, 07/1016
Purnell v Business F1 Magazine Ltd [2007] EWCA Civ 744; (2007) 104(18) L.S.G.
  29, CA (Civ Div)
Purple International Plc v Revenue and Customs Commissioners [2007] B.V.C. 2208;
  [2006] S.T.I. 2589, V&DTr (London)
Purver v Winchester and Eastleigh Healthcare NHS Trust [2007] EWHC 34 (QB);
  [2007] LS Law Medical 193, QBD . . . .   *Digested*, 07/**3060**
Pusa v Osuuspankkien Keskinainen Vakuutusyhtio (C-224/02) [2004] All E.R. (EC)
  797; [2004] S.T.C. 1066; [2004] E.C.R. I-5763; [2004] 2 C.M.L.R. 23; [2004]
  S.T.I. 1167, ECJ (5th Chamber) . . . .   *Digested*, 05/**3002**:
                    Applied, 07/1610: *Considered*, 07/1625
Putans v Tower Hamlets LBC [2006] EWHC 1634 (Ch); [2007] H.L.R. 10, Ch D . . . . .   *Digested*, 07/**2141**

Q3 Media Ltd, Re see Ice Media International Ltd (In Liquidation) v Q3 Media Ltd
Qazi v Harrow LBC; *sub nom* Harrow LBC v Qazi; Harrow LBC v Quazi [2003] UKHL
  43; [2004] 1 A.C. 983; [2003] 3 W.L.R. 792; [2003] 4 All E.R. 461; [2003] 2
  F.L.R. 973; [2003] 3 F.C.R. 43; [2003] H.R.L.R. 40; [2003] U.K.H.R.R. 974;
  [2003] H.L.R. 75; [2004] 1 P. & C.R. 19; [2004] L. & T.R. 9; [2003] 3 E.G.L.R.
  109; [2003] Fam. Law 875; (2003) 100(38) L.S.G. 34; (2003) 147 S.J.L.B.
  937; [2003] N.P.C. 101; *Times*, August 1, 2003; *Independent*, October 3, 2003,
  HL; reversing [2001] EWCA Civ 1834; [2002] U.K.H.R.R. 316; [2002] H.L.R.
  14; [2002] L. & T.R. 23; *Independent*, January 14, 2002, CA (Civ Div) . . . .   *Digested*, 03/**2786**:
                    Applied, 02/3060, 04/2519, 04/3042, 05/190, 07/2766:
                    Considered, 06/2352, 07/2242: *Doubted*, 06/2173: *Followed*, 05/3424
Quark Fishing Ltd v United Kingdom (Admissibility) (15305/06) 22 B.H.R.C. 568;
  (2007) 44 E.H.R.R. SE4, ECHR
Quazi v Quazi [1980] A.C. 744; [1979] 3 W.L.R. 833; [1979] 3 All E.R. 897; (1979)
  10 Fam. Law 148; (1979) 123 S.J. 824, HL; reversing [1979] 3 W.L.R. 402;
  [1979] 3 All E.R. 424; (1979) 9 Fam. Law 219; (1979) 123 S.J. 674, CA (Civ
  Div); reversing (1978) 8 Fam. Law 203, QBD . . . .   *Digested*, 79/**772**:
                    Applied, 81/725, 84/1147, 07/1809: *Considered*, 80/88u, 80/798, 81/732,
                    83/1128, 85/1080, 86/1111, 96/3312: *Followed*, 82/954
Queens Moat Houses Plc, Re see Secretary of State for Trade and Industry v Bairstow
Queensway Systems Ltd v Walker [2006] EWHC 2496 (Ch); [2007] 2 B.C.L.C. 577,
  Ch D (Companies Ct)
Quelle AG v Office for Harmonisation in the Internal Market (Trade Marks and Designs)
  (OHIM) (T-88/05) [2007] E.T.M.R. 62, CFI
Quest 4 Finance Ltd v Maxfield [2007] EWHC 2313 (QB); [2007] 2 C.L.C. 706, QBD
QUEST INTERNATIONAL/Odour selection (T619/02) [2006] E.P.O.R. 52, EPO (Technical
  Bd App) . . . .   *Digested*, 07/**2598**
Quest Trading Co Ltd (In Liquidation) v Revenue and Customs Commissioners [2006] V.
  & D.R. 202; [2007] S.T.I. 386, V&DTr (London). . . . .   *Digested*, 07/**4301**

Questore di Verona v Zenatti (C-67/98) [1999] E.C.R. I-7289; [2000] 1 C.M.L.R. 201,
  ECJ . . . .   *Digested*, 00/**2397**:
             Applied, 06/1568, 07/1619: *Considered*, 05/1467: *Followed*, 02/1581,
                                            02/1581
Qufaj Co SHPK v Albania (54268/00) (2006) 43 E.H.R.R. 28, ECHR . . . .   *Considered*, 07/1773
Quick v Taff Ely BC [1986] Q.B. 809; [1985] 3 W.L.R. 981; [1985] 3 All E.R. 321;
  (1986) 18 H.L.R. 66; [1985] 2 E.G.L.R. 50; (1985) 276 E.G. 452, CA (Civ
  Div) . . . .   *Digested*, 85/**1610**:
             Applied, 87/2141, 98/2987: *Considered*, 91/2228, 93/2462, 95/3062,
            02/3059, 02/3066, 07/2738: *Distinguished*, 98/3628: *Followed*, 01/4203:
                                          Referred to, 87/2140
Quietfield Ltd v Vascroft Construction Ltd see Quietfield Ltd v Vascroft Contractors Ltd
Quietfield Ltd v Vascroft Contractors Ltd; *sub nom* Quietfield Ltd v Vascroft
  Construction Ltd [2006] EWCA Civ 1737; [2007] B.L.R. 67; 114 Con. L.R. 81;
  [2007] C.I.L.L. 2425; [2007] Bus. L.R. D1, CA (Civ Div); affirming [2006]
  EWHC 174 (TCC); 109 Con. L.R. 29; [2006] C.I.L.L. 2329, QBD (TCC) . . . . . .   *Digested*, 07/**723**
Quinn v George Clark & Nem Ltd see Grieves v FT Everard & Sons Ltd
Quinn v Leathem [1901] A.C. 495, HL (UK-Irl); affirming [1899] 2 I.R. 667, CA (UK-
  Irl) . . . .   *Applied*, 47-51/1721,
            04/364: *Considered*, 47-51/2157, 52/3507, 74/3704, 07/4190

R v Crown Prosecution Service see Hughes v Customs and Excise Commissioners
R v DPP see Hughes v Customs and Excise Commissioners
R v DPP; *joined case* B v DPP [2007] EWHC 739 (Admin); (2007) 171 J.P. 404;
  (2007) 171 J.P.N. 738; *Times*, March 27, 2007, QBD (Admin) . . . .   *Digested*, 07/**912**
R v Holden (Inspector of Taxes) see Wood v Holden (Inspector of Taxes)
R v R see TR v MR
R v Secretary of State for the Home Department see E v Secretary of State for the
  Home Department
R v Switzerland (10881/84) (Unreported, March 4, 1987), Eur Comm HR . . . .   *Considered*, 07/236
R v United Kingdom (A/121); *sub nom* A v United Kingdom (1988) 10 E.H.R.R. 74,
  ECHR (1985) 7 E.H.R.R. CD147, Eur Comm HR . . . .   *Distinguished*, 07/1717
R v United Kingdom (Admissibility) (33506/05) (2007) 44 E.H.R.R. SE17, ECHR
R Twining & Co Ltd v Revenue and Customs Commissioners [2007] S.T.I. 2255, V&DTr
  (London)
R (A Child), Re; *sub nom* R (Care: Rehabilitation in Context of Domestic Violence), Re
  [2006] EWCA Civ 1638; [2007] 1 F.L.R. 1830; [2007] Fam. Law 210; (2006)
  103(46) L.S.G. 29; (2006) 150 S.J.L.B. 1533, CA (Civ Div)
R (A Child) (Adoption: Contact Orders), Re [2005] EWCA Civ 1128; [2006] 1 F.L.R. 373;
  [2007] 1 F.C.R. 149; [2006] Fam. Law 9; *Times*, September 15, 2005, CA (Civ
  Div) . . . .   *Digested*, 06/**1669**
R (A Child) (Adoption: Disclosure), Re see R (A Child) (Adoption: Duty to Investigate), Re
R (A Child) (Adoption: Duty to Investigate), Re; *sub nom* Z CC v R; R (A Child)
  (Adoption: Disclosure), Re [2001] 1 F.L.R. 365; [2001] 1 F.C.R. 238; [2001]
  Fam. Law 8; *Times*, February 13, 2001, Fam Div . . . .   *Digested*, 01/**2534**:
                                             Considered, 07/1723
R (A Child) (Special Guardianship Order), Re; *sub nom* Birmingham City Council v R
  [2006] EWCA Civ 1748; [2007] Fam. 41; [2007] 2 W.L.R. 1130; [2007] 1 F.L.R.
  564; [2007] 1 F.C.R. 121; *Times*, December 29, 2006, CA (Civ Div) . . . .   *Digested*, 07/**1798**
R (Abduction: Habitual Residence), Re [2003] EWHC 1968 (Fam); [2004] 1 F.L.R. 216;
  [2004] Fam. Law 8, Fam Div . . . .   *Digested*, 04/**1471**:
                                          Distinguished, 07/1738
R (B by her Litigation Friend MB) v Lambeth LBC see R. (on the application of B) v
  Lambeth LBC
R (Care: Rehabilitation in Context of Domestic Violence), Re see R (A Child), Re
R (Children) (Care Proceedings: Maternal Grandmother's Applications), Re; *sub nom* G v
  A Local Authority [2007] EWCA Civ 139; [2007] 1 F.C.R. 439; (2007) 151
  S.J.L.B. 334, CA (Civ Div) . . . .   *Digested*, 07/**1726**
R (Children) (Confidential Information: Protecting Anonymity), Re see J v E
R (Children) (Secure Editing of Documents), Re see J v E
R (Minors) (Wardship: Jurisdiction), Re (1981) 2 F.L.R. 416, CA (Civ Div) . . . .   *Applied*, 07/**1736**
R (on the application of Davey) Aylesbury Vale DC see Davey v Aylesbury Vale DC
R&H Electric Ltd v Haden Bill Electrical Ltd; *sub nom* Haden Bill Electrical Ltd, Re
  [1995] B.C.C. 958; [1995] 2 B.C.L.C. 280, Ch D (Companies Ct) . . . .   *Digested*, 96/**1025**:
                              Approved, 07/592: *Followed*, 97/841
R+V Versicherung AG v Risk Insurance & Reinsurance Solutions SA [2007] EWHC 79
  (Comm); *Times*, February 26, 2007, QBD (Comm) . . . .   *Digested*, 07/**464**
R+V Versicherung AG v Risk Insurance & Reinsurance Solutions SA (No.3) [2006]
  EWHC 42 (Comm), QBD (Comm) . . . .   *Approved*, 07/1059
R. v A [2006] EWCA Crim 1803; [2007] 1 Cr. App. R. (S.) 60; [2006] Crim. L.R.
  1080, CA (Crim Div) . . . .   *Digested*, 07/**3667**
R. v A [2007] EWCA Crim 245; [2007] 2 Cr. App. R. (S.) 62, CA (Crim Div)

R. v A (Informer: Reduction of Sentence); *joined case* R. v B (Informer: Reduction of Sentence) [1999] 1 Cr. App. R. (S.) 52; [1998] Crim. L.R. 757; *Times*, May 1, 1998, CA (Crim Div) . . . . *Digested*, 98/**1267**:
Considered, 02/3992: *Distinguished*, 07/3667: *Followed*, 03/3685

R. v A (Prosecutor's Appeal) see R. v C
R. v AB see R. v IK
R. v Abdi (Hassan) see R. v Lang (Stephen Howard)
R. v Abdi (Liban) [2007] EWCA Crim 1913; [2007] I.N.L.R. 442; [2007] Crim. L.R. 992, CA (Crim Div)
R. v Abdroikof (Nurlon) see R. v Abdroikov (Nurlon)
R. v Abdroikov (Nurlon); *sub nom* R. v Abdroikof (Nurlon); *joined cases* R. v Green (Richard John); R. v Williamson (Kenneth Joseph) [2007] UKHL 37; [2007] 1 W.L.R. 2679; (2007) 151 S.J.L.B. 1365; *Times*, November 8, 2007, HL; affirming in part [2005] EWCA Crim 1986; [2005] 1 W.L.R. 3538; [2005] 4 All E.R. 869; [2006] 1 Cr. App. R. 1; [2006] Crim. L.R. 245; *Times*, August 18, 2005, CA (Crim Div) . . . . *Digested*, 05/**894**
R. v Abdullahi (Osmund Mohammed) [2006] EWCA Crim 2060; [2007] 1 W.L.R. 225; [2007] 1 Cr. App. R. 14; [2007] Crim. L.R. 184; *Times*, August 24, 2006, CA (Crim Div) . . . . *Digested*, 07/**861**
R. v Abery (Lee Alan) see R. v Richardson (Jack Virgil)
R. v Ablewhite (Jonathan Charles); *joined cases* R. v Whitburn (Kerry Deanian); R. v Smith (John) [2007] EWCA Crim 832; [2007] 2 Cr. App. R. (S.) 93, CA (Crim Div) . . . . *Digested*, 07/**3678**
R. v Abu Hamza [2006] EWCA Crim 2918; [2007] Q.B. 659; [2007] 2 W.L.R. 226; [2007] 3 All E.R. 451; [2007] 1 Cr. App. R. 27; [2007] Crim. L.R. 320; *Times*, November 30, 2006, CA (Crim Div) . . . . *Digested*, 07/**923**
R. v AD see R. v D
R. v Adams (Andrew) [2007] EWCA Crim 1; [2007] 1 Cr. App. R. 34; [2007] Crim. L.R. 559; (2007) 151 S.J.L.B. 123; *Times*, January 30, 2007, CA (Crim Div) . . . *Digested*, 07/**1000**
R. v Adams (Ishmael) [2007] EWCA Crim 3025; *Times*, December 14, 2007, CA (Crim Div)
R. v Adaway (Glen) [2004] EWCA Crim 2831; (2004) 168 J.P. 645; (2004) 168 J.P.N. 956; *Times*, November 22, 2004, CA (Crim Div) . . . . *Digested*, 05/**936**:
Considered, 07/3314

R. v Adderson (Lee) see R. v Lawson (Michael David)
R. v Adebayo (Adekunle) [2007] EWCA Crim 878, CA (Crim Div) . . . . *Digested*, 07/**3716**
R. v Adenusi (Oladele) [2006] EWCA Crim 1059; (2007) 171 J.P. 169; [2006] Crim. L.R. 929; (2007) 171 J.P.N. 428; (2007) 171 J.P.N. 514, CA (Crim Div)
R. v Adjei (Francis) see R. v Gyima (Edward)
R. v Afonso (Americo Practicio); *joined cases* R. v Andrews (Douglas); R. v Sajid (Mohammed) [2004] EWCA Crim 2342; [2005] 1 Cr. App. R. (S.) 99; [2005] Crim. L.R. 73; (2004) 148 S.J.L.B. 1120; *Times*, October 14, 2004, CA (Crim Div) . . . . *Digested*, 04/**3454**:
Applied, 06/3703: *Considered*, 05/3700, 05/3748, 05/3751, 06/3695,
06/3704, 07/3633: *Distinguished*, 05/3752, 07/3632

R. v Afzal (Mohammed) [2005] EWCA Crim 384, CA (Crim Div) . . . . *Applied*, 07/**3775**:
Considered, 06/3813

R. v Ahmad (Bakhtiar) see R. v Vernett-Showers (Michael)
R. v Ahmati (Agron) (Order for Costs) [2006] EWCA Crim 1826; [2007] P.N.L.R. 3, CA (Crim Div) . . . . *Digested*, 07/**962**
R. v Ahmed (Mumtaz) see R. v Vernett-Showers (Michael)
R. v Ahmed (Nisar) see R. v Vernett-Showers (Michael)
R. v Ahmed (Rizwan) see R. v Vernett-Showers (Michael)
R. v Ainsworth (Costs) [2007] 5 Costs L.R. 865, Sup Ct Costs Office
R. v Ainsworth (Dale) [2006] EWCA Crim 2311; *Times*, September 13, 2006, CA (Crim Div) . . . . *Digested*, 07/**3689**
R. v Akhtar (Abdul Quayyum); *sub nom* R. v Aktar (Abdul Quayyum); 98/5071/W2, CA (Crim Div) . . . . *Considered*, 07/932
R. v Akram (Kamer) see R. v Rahman (Islamur)
R. v Aktar (Abdul Quayyum) see R. v Akhtar (Abdul Quayyum)
R. v Alays (Costs) see R. v Alyas (Mohammed) (Costs)
R. v Alford (John James) see R. v Shannon (John James)
R. v Ali (Abdi Aziz) [2006] EWCA Crim 2906, CA (Crim Div) . . . . *Considered*, 07/994
R. v Ali (Liaquat) see R. v Rahman (Islamur)
R. v Ali (Liaquat); *joined cases* R. v Hussein (Akhtar); R. v Khan (Mohsan); R. v Bhatti (Shahid) [2005] EWCA Crim 87; [2006] Q.B. 322; [2006] 2 W.L.R. 316; [2006] 1 Cr. App. R. 8; [2005] Crim. L.R. 864; (2005) 149 S.J.L.B. 770, CA (Crim Div) . . . . *Digested*, 06/**834**:
Considered, 07/871

R. v Ali (Sajid Pasha) see R. v Graham (Hemamali Krishna)
R. v Ali (Shaukat) see R. v Mahmood (Zahid)
R. v Ali (Soran) [2006] EWCA Crim 3084, CA (Crim Div) . . . . *Considered*, 07/994

R. v Allen (William) [2001] EWCA Crim 302; [2001] 2 Cr. App. R. (S.) 76, CA (Crim Div) . . . . *Digested*, 01/**1305**:
Considered, 07/3575

R. v Alleyne (Carl Anthony) see R. v Jordan (Andrew James)

R. v Allsopp (Michael Nevin); *joined cases* R. v Kelly (Anthony Joseph); R. v Wolf (Karl Christian); R. v West (Melvin) [2005] EWCA Crim 703; (2005) 149 S.J.L.B. 388, CA (Crim Div) . . . . *Considered*, 07/3757

R. v Alyas (Mohammed) (Costs); *sub nom* R. v Alays (Costs) [2007] 2 Costs L.R. 321, Sup Ct Costs Office

R. v Amber Valley DC Ex p. Jackson [1985] 1 W.L.R. 298; [1984] 3 All E.R. 501; (1985) 50 P. & C.R. 136, QBD . . . . *Digested*, 84/**3481**:
Considered, 95/3252: *Followed*, 07/2867

R. v Amies (Marie Mandy) see Attorney General's Reference (No.100 of 2006), Re

R. v Amin (Anjum Nisa) see R. v Rahman (Islamur)

R. v Anderson (Lascelles Fitzalbert); *joined case* R. v Morris (Emmanuel) [1966] 2 Q.B. 110; [1966] 2 W.L.R. 1195; [1966] 2 All E.R. 644; (1966) 50 Cr. App. R. 216; (1966) 130 J.P. 318; (1966) 110 S.J. 369, CCA . . . . *Digested*, 66/**2603**:
Applied, 69/804, 81/1879, 84/667, 87/801, 89/846, 00/5468:
Considered, 77/485, 95/1067, 95/1271, 95/1272, 07/877:
Distinguished, 77/591, 95/2634

R. v Andre (Lyla) see R. v Burton (Evelyn)

R. v Andrews (Barrie Lee) [2006] EWCA Crim 2228; [2007] 1 Cr. App. R. (S.) 81; [2007] Crim. L.R. 87, CA (Crim Div) . . . . *Digested*, 07/**946**

R. v Andrews (Douglas) see R. v Afonso (Americo Practicio)

R. v Andrews (Paul) (1986) 82 Cr. App. R. 148; [1986] Crim. L.R. 124; (1985) 135 N.L.J. 1163; (1985) 129 S.J. 869, CA (Crim Div) . . . . *Digested*, 86/**943**:
Applied, 01/1144: *Considered*, 96/2076, 07/992

R. v Angel (Robert Charles) [1968] 1 W.L.R. 669; [1968] 2 All E.R. 607 (Note); (1968) 52 Cr. App. R. 280; (1968) 112 S.J. 310, CA (Crim Div) . . . . *Digested*, 68/**892**:
Applied, 07/2908: *Considered*, 05/2826

R. v Annable (Martin William) see R. v Cuthbertson (Brian George)

R. v Annesley (Kevin) [1976] 1 W.L.R. 106; [1976] 1 All E.R. 589; (1976) 62 Cr. App. R. 113; [1976] R.T.R. 150; [1976] Crim. L.R. 201; (1975) 120 S.J. 27; *Times*, November 25, 1975, CA (Crim Div) . . . . *Digested*, 76/**575**:
Applied, 07/3735: *Considered*, 07/966

R. v Aranguren (Jose de Jesus); *joined cases* R. v Aroyewumi (Bisi); R. v Bioshogun (Nimota); R. v Littlefield (John); R. v Gould (Robert Sidney) (1994) 99 Cr. App. R. 347; (1995) 16 Cr. App. R. (S.) 211; [1994] Crim. L.R. 695; (1994) 144 N.L.J. 864; *Times*, June 23, 1994; *Independent*, June 30, 1994, CA (Crim Div) . *Digested*, 95/**1364**:
Considered, 96/1872, 96/1875, 96/1879, 98/1191, 99/1124, 99/1129, 00/1211, 00/1233, 03/3695, 05/3591, 05/3598, 05/3754, 07/3757:
Distinguished, 96/1873: *Followed*, 97/1522, 04/3343, 05/3589

R. v Archbold (Ronald) [2007] EWCA Crim 2137; (2007) 171 J.P. 664, CA (Crim Div) . *Digested*, 07/**998**

R. v Archer (Daniel John) [2007] EWCA Crim 536; [2007] 2 Cr. App. R. (S.) 71; [2007] Crim. L.R. 484, CA (Crim Div)

R. v Ardener (Tony) [2006] EWCA Crim 2103; [2007] 1 Cr. App. R. (S.) 92, CA (Crim Div) . . . . *Digested*, 07/**3587**:
Considered, 07/3586, 07/3605

R. v Armitage (Lewis) see R. v Lang (Stephen Howard)

R. v Aroyewumi (Bisi) see R. v Aranguren (Jose de Jesus)

R. v Artan (Abdekhader) see Attorney General's Reference (Nos.24, 25, 26, 27, 28 and 29 of 2006), Re

R. v Ashman (Joseph Clifford) see Jones (Setting of Minimum Term), Re

R. v Ashton (John); *joined cases* R. v O'Reilly (Darren); R. v Draz (Omar) [2006] EWCA Crim 794; [2007] 1 W.L.R. 181; [2006] 2 Cr. App. R. 15; [2006] Crim. L.R. 1004; *Times*, April 18, 2006, CA (Crim Div) . . . . *Digested*, 06/**950**:
Considered, 07/1017

R. v Atkinson (Clayton Clar) [2006] EWCA Crim 1424; (2006) 170 J.P. 605; (2007) 171 J.P.N. 85, CA (Crim Div) . . . . *Digested*, 06/**793**

R. v Attorney General of Northern Ireland Ex p. Breslin see R. v Attorney General of Northern Ireland Ex p. Devine

R. v Attorney General of Northern Ireland Ex p. Devine; *joined case* R. v Attorney General of Northern Ireland Ex p. Breslin [1992] 1 W.L.R. 262; [1992] 1 All E.R. 609; (1992) 136 S.J.L.B. 82; *Times*, February 11, 1992; *Guardian*, February 19, 1992, HL . . . . *Digested*, 92/**594**:
Considered, 07/11

R. v Austin (Costs) [2006] 5 Costs L.R. 857, Sup Ct Costs Office . . . . *Digested*, 07/**956**

R. *v* Avis (Tony); *joined cases* R. *v* Thomas (Richard Bartgerald); R. *v* Torrington (Richard Edward); R. *v* Marquez (Shaun); R. *v* Goldsmith (Harold Egan) [1998] 1 Cr. App. R. 420; [1998] 2 Cr. App. R. (S.) 178; [1998] Crim. L.R. 428; *Times,* December 19, 1997, CA (Crim Div) . . . . *Digested,* 98/**1214**:
Applied, 01/1299, 01/1308, 02/3873, 04/876, 04/3350, 04/3409, 06/3719:
Considered, 99/1158, 99/1160, 99/1161, 99/1162, 99/1164, 99/1165, 00/1242, 00/1244, 00/1245, 00/1247, 00/1250, 00/1252, 00/1253, 01/1298, 01/1304, 01/1312, 01/1313, 02/3941, 02/3947, 02/3948, 02/4057, 04/3411, 05/3690, 05/3692, 05/3696, 05/3759, 06/3716, 06/3718, 07/3649:
Followed, 99/1168, 05/3675: *Referred to,* 99/1110

R. *v* Awofadeju (Moses) see R. *v* Odewale (Ayodele)
R. *v* Axhami (Tasim) see R. *v* Kizlaite (Vilma)
R. *v* Aziz (Abdul) [1996] 1 Cr. App. R. (S.) 265, CA (Crim Div) . . . . *Digested,* 96/**2080**:
Applied, 07/3597: *Considered,* 98/1389, 00/1433

R. *v* B see R. *v* M
R. *v* B see R. *v* G
R. *v* B see R. *v* M
R. *v* B see R. *v* Harries (Michael John)
R. *v* B; *sub nom* B, Re [2006] EWCA Crim 2692; [2007] E.M.L.R. 5; [2007] H.R.L.R. 1; [2007] U.K.H.R.R. 577; *Times,* November 6, 2006, CA (Crim Div) . . . .   *Digested,* 07/**1018**
R. *v* B [2006] EWCA Crim 2945; [2007] 1 W.L.R. 1567; [2007] 1 Cr. App. R. 29; (2006) 150 S.J.L.B. 1392, CA (Crim Div) . . . .   *Digested,* 07/**920**
R. *v* B (Caroline) [2001] 1 Cr. App. R. (S.) 74; *Times,* July 4, 2000, CA (Crim Div) . . . .   *Digested,* 00/**1285**:
Considered, 07/3746
R. *v* B (Christopher) see Attorney General's Reference (No.39 of 2006), Re
R. *v* B (Informer: Reduction of Sentence) see R. *v* A (Informer: Reduction of Sentence)
R. *v* B (Ivan Leon) see Attorney General's Reference (Nos.24, 25, 26, 27, 28 and 41 of 2006), Re
R. *v* B (Lee James) (A Juvenile) [2001] 1 Cr. App. R. (S.) 89; [2000] Crim. L.R. 870, CA (Crim Div) . . . .   *Digested,* 01/**1475**:
Applied, 07/3789
R. *v* B (Sharon Kristine) (1994) 15 Cr. App. R. (S.) 815, CA (Crim Div) . . . .   *Digested,* 95/**1405**:
Considered, 00/1278, 07/3607
R. *v* B CC Ex p. P [1991] 1 W.L.R. 221; [1991] 2 All E.R. 65; [1991] 1 F.L.R. 470; [1991] Fam. Law 313, CA (Civ Div) . . . .   *Digested,* 91/**2517**:
Applied, 07/1727: *Considered,* 97/1389: *Followed,* 97/384
R. *v* B School Governors Ex p. W see R. (on the application of L (A Child)) *v* J School Governors
R. *v* Bailey (Gareth Scott) see R. *v* Rigby (Carl)
R. *v* Bailey (James Christopher) [2007] EWCA Crim 778; [2007] 2 Cr. App. R. (S.) 90, CA (Crim Div)
R. *v* Bailey (Suzanne) [2007] EWCA Crim 2873; (2007) 104(46) L.S.G. 28, CA (Crim Div)
R. *v* Baillie (Keith Noel Adrian) see R. *v* Bentham (John Preston)
R. *v* Bakewell (Russell Joseph) [2006] EWCA Crim 2; [2006] 2 Cr. App. R. (S.) 42; [2006] Crim. L.R. 453, CA (Crim Div) . . . .   *Digested,* 06/**910**:
Considered, 07/2413: *Followed,* 06/3676
R. *v* Baldrey (Danny) see R. *v* C
R. *v* Baldwin (Leslie) see R. *v* Oliver (Mark David)
R. *v* Balfour Beatty Rail Infrastructure Services Ltd [2006] EWCA Crim 1586; [2007] Bus. L.R. 77; [2007] 1 Cr. App. R. (S.) 65; [2007] I.C.R. 354; (2006) 150 S.J.L.B. 922; *Times,* July 18, 2006, CA (Crim Div) . . . .   *Digested,* 06/**3713**
R. *v* Ballantyne (John) see R. *v* McGinlay (Alexander)
R. *v* Ballard (Arthur William) [2007] EWCA Crim 751; [2007] 2 Cr. App. R. (S.) 94, CA (Crim Div)
R. *v* Banks (Joel) see Attorney General's Reference (Nos.24, 25, 26, 27, 28 and 29 of 2006), Re
R. *v* Banks-Nash (Billy) [2006] EWCA Crim 1211; [2007] 1 Cr. App. R. (S.) 18, CA (Crim Div) . . . .   *Considered,* 07/3638
R. *v* Banton (Sheila) [2007] EWCA Crim 1847, CA (Crim Div) . . . .   *Considered,* 07/994
R. *v* Barber (David Stuart) [2005] EWCA Crim 2217; [2006] 1 Cr. App. R. (S.) 90, CA (Crim Div) . . . .   *Digested,* 06/**3715**:
Considered, 07/3791
R. *v* Barber (Kenneth Leslie) see R. *v* Pepper (Jeremy Paul)

R. v Barnet LBC Ex p. Shah (Nilish); *joined cases* Akbarali v Brent LBC; Abdullah v
　　Shropshire CC; Shabpar v Barnet LBC; Shah (Jitendra) v Barnet LBC; Ablack v
　　Inner London Education Authority; R. v Shropshire CC Ex p. Abdullah [1983] 2
　　A.C. 309; [1983] 2 W.L.R. 16; [1983] 1 All E.R. 226; 81 L.G.R. 305; (1983) 133
　　N.L.J. 61; (1983) 127 S.J. 36, HL; reversing [1982] Q.B. 688; [1982] 2 W.L.R.
　　474; [1982] 1 All E.R. 698; 80 L.G.R. 571; *Times*, November 12, 1981, CA (Civ
　　Div); affirming [1981] 2 W.L.R. 86; [1980] 3 All E.R. 679; 79 L.G.R. 210; (1981)
　　125 S.J. 64, QBD . . . . *Digested*, 83/**1157**:
　　　　　　　　　Applied, 80/853, 84/3033, 85/1074, 85/1737, 86/703, 86/1692, 87/3489,
　　　　　　　　　　　　　98/3007, 01/2612, 01/2617, 03/1127, 03/1556, 05/1627, 07/3910:
　　　　　　　　Considered, 82/973, 84/1173, 84/1645, 85/1107, 85/1108, 85/1127, 85/1771,
　　　　　　　　　　　　　85/2165, 86/1136, 86/1703, 91/2372, 95/3206, 99/4564, 00/2778:
　　　　　　　　Distinguished, 83/1800, 04/1885: *Followed*, 87/1928: *Referred to*, 91/2373
R. v Barot (Dhiren) [2007] EWCA Crim 1119; [2007] Crim. L.R. 741; *Times*, May 23,
　　2007, CA (Crim Div) . . . . *Digested*, 07/**3691**
R. v Barrass (Ian Phillip) [2006] EWCA Crim 2744; [2007] 2 Cr. App. R. (S.) 1, CA
　　(Crim Div) . . . . *Digested*, 07/**3740**
R. v Barrick (John) (1985) 81 Cr. App. R. 78; (1985) 7 Cr. App. R. (S.) 142; (1985)
　　149 J.P. 705; (1985) 129 S.J. 416, CA (Crim Div) . . . . *Digested*, 85/**765**:
　　　　　　　　　Applied, 86/884, 86/885, 86/889, 03/3870, 07/3760: *Cited*, 88/999,
　　　　　　　　　88/1001, 89/1123, 90/1429, 91/1228, 91/1230, 92/1442, 93/1294, 94/1366:
　　　　　　　　　Considered, 87/948, 87/1013, 87/1015, 87/1056, 87/1057, 87/1061, 87/1062,
　　　　　　　　　87/1063, 88/925, 88/1002, 88/1713, 89/1046, 89/1121, 91/1173, 91/1225,
　　　　　　　　　92/1167, 95/1385, 96/1752, 97/1549, 98/1316, 98/1391, 98/1392, 99/1174,
　　　　　　　　　99/1277, 99/1359, 99/1362, 00/1436, 03/3670, 05/3611:
　　　　　　　　　Distinguished, 87/1058, 03/3811: *Followed*, 04/3353: *Referred to*, 87/1055,
　　　　　　　　　　　　　　　　　　　　　　　　　　　　　　　　87/1064
R. v Bartle Ex p. Pinochet Ugarte (No.2) see R. v Bow Street Metropolitan Stipendiary
　　Magistrate Ex p. Pinochet Ugarte (No.2)
R. v Bartley (Anthony Michael) see R. v C
R. v Basra (Gurmail Singh) (1989) 11 Cr. App. R. (S.) 527, CA (Crim Div) . . . . *Digested*, 91/**1060**:
　　　　　　　　　　　　　　　　　　　　Cited, 92/1210: *Considered*, 07/3616
R. v Bate (Dean) see Attorney General's Reference (Nos.32, 33 and 34 of 2007), Re
R. v Bates (Mark Ian) [2006] EWCA Crim 1015; [2007] 1 Cr. App. R. (S.) 2, CA (Crim
　　Div) . . . . *Digested*, 07/**3612**
R. v Beard (Gary Colin) see Attorney General's Reference (Nos.120 and 121 of 2004),
　　Re
R. v Beardmore (Ronald Lionel) [2006] EWCA Crim 1684; [2007] 1 Cr. App. R. (S.)
　　47, CA (Crim Div) . . . . *Digested*, 07/**3698**
R. v Beatty (David William) [2006] EWCA Crim 2359; (2006) 92 B.M.L.R. 22;
　　[2006] M.H.L.R. 333, CA (Crim Div) . . . . *Digested*, 07/**3626**
R. v Bebbington (Shaun Anthony) see R. v Boness (Dean)
R. v Beckford (Ian Anthony) [1996] 1 Cr. App. R. 94; (1995) 159 J.P. 305; [1995]
　　R.T.R. 251; [1995] Crim. L.R. 712; *Times*, January 27, 1995, CA (Crim Div) . . . . *Digested*, 95/**1109**:
　　　　　　　　　　　　Considered, 97/1172, 97/1256, 98/1079, 02/911, 07/1011
R. v Beedall (Lee James) [2007] EWCA Crim 23; [2007] Crim. L.R. 910, CA (Crim
　　Div)
R. v Beedie (Thomas Sim) [1998] Q.B. 356; [1997] 3 W.L.R. 758; [1997] 2 Cr. App.
　　R. 167; (1997) 161 J.P. 313; [1997] Crim. L.R. 747; (1997) 161 J.P.N. 531; (1997)
　　94(15) L.S.G. 26; (1997) 141 S.J.L.B. 83; *Times*, March 14, 1997; *Independent*,
　　April 21, 1997, CA (Crim Div) . . . . *Digested*, 97/**1317**:
　　　　　　　　　　　　　　　　　　　　　　　　　　　Distinguished, 07/1022
R. v Beg (Mohammed Akram) see R. v Vernett-Showers (Michael)
R. v Bennett (Adam) see Attorney General's Reference (No.134 of 2006), Re
R. v Bentham (John Preston); *joined cases* R. v Baillie (Keith Noel Adrian); R. v
　　Simpson (Ronald Walker) [1973] Q.B. 357; [1972] 3 W.L.R. 398; [1972] 3 All
　　E.R. 271; (1972) 56 Cr. App. R. 618; [1972] Crim. L.R. 640; (1972) 116 S.J. 398,
　　CA (Crim Div) . . . . *Digested*, 72/**1553**:
　　　　　　　　　　　　　　　　　　　　　　　　　　　　　　Applied, 07/904
R. v Bentley (David Colin) [2006] EWCA Crim 1535; [2007] 1 Cr. App. R. (S.) 44, CA
　　(Crim Div) . . . . *Digested*, 07/**3631**
R. v Benton (Robert) see R. v Cain (Alan John)
R. v Bernard 175 E.R. 709; (1858) 1 F. & F. 240; (1858) 8 St. Tr. (N.S.) 887, QB . . . . . . *Considered*, 57/697,
　　　　　　　　　　　　　　　　　　　　　　　　　　　　　　　07/923
R. v Bernard (Basil Mortimer) [1997] 1 Cr. App. R. (S.) 135; (1997) 33 B.M.L.R. 23;
　　[1996] Crim. L.R. 673; (1996) 140 S.J.L.B. 148; *Times*, July 2, 1996, CA (Crim
　　Div) . . . . *Digested*, 96/**1877**:
　　　　　　　　　Applied, 07/3664: *Approved*, 97/1657: *Considered*, 98/1322,
R. v Berryman (Exekiel Levi) [2006] EWCA Crim 1065; [2007] 1 Cr. App. R. (S.) 13,
　　CA (Crim Div)
R. v Bexley LBC Ex p. B (Care Hours Provision) (2000) 3 C.C.L. Rep. 15, QBD [*Ex rel.*
　　Timothy Jones, Barrister, 7 Fountain Court, Birmingham] . . . . *Digested*, 95/**3225**:
　　　　　　　　　　　　　　　　　　　　　　　　　　　　　　Applied, 07/2165
R. v Bhatti (Shahid) see R. v Ali (Liaquat)

R. v Bilinski (Edward) (1988) 86 Cr. App. R. 146; (1987) 9 Cr. App. R. (S.) 360;
[1987] Crim. L.R. 782, CA (Crim Div) . . . . *Digested*, 88/**930**:
Applied, 90/1300, 91/1094: *Approved*, 90/1289: *Cited*, 90/1288, 93/1123,
93/1127, 93/1128, 93/1131, 94/1403: *Considered*, 89/948, 89/949, 90/1268,
90/1284, 90/1290, 90/1291, 90/1310, 91/1093, 91/1097, 91/1098, 92/1247,
95/1363, 95/1364, 00/1223, 02/3921, 03/3695, 07/3757:
Followed, 03/3691: *Referred to*, 95/1367

R. v Billam (Keith) [1986] 1 W.L.R. 349; [1986] 1 All E.R. 985; (1986) 82 Cr. App. R.
347; (1986) 8 Cr. App. R. (S.) 48; [1986] Crim. L.R. 347, CA (Crim Div) . . . . . *Digested*, 86/**868**:
Applied, 91/1192, 92/1376, 92/1379, 93/1265, 96/1976, 96/1992, 96/2052,
99/1314, 00/1333, 03/3827, 03/3833, 04/3424, 05/3718, 07/3725:
Cited, 94/1411: *Considered*, 87/1032, 88/867, 88/868, 88/975, 88/976,
88/980, 88/1007, 89/935, 89/937, 89/1099, 89/1102, 90/1203, 90/1204,
90/1213, 90/1394, 90/1395, 90/1398, 91/1191, 91/1195, 92/1153, 93/1258,
93/1262, 93/1263, 94/1181, 94/1183, 94/1333, 94/1335, 94/1337, 94/1338,
94/1340, 94/3838, 95/1426, 95/1456, 95/1459, 95/1462, 95/1463,
96/1939, 96/2039, 96/2044, 96/2045, 96/2047, 96/2048, 96/2051,
97/1432, 97/1452, 97/1454, 98/1143, 98/1286, 98/1292, 98/1339, 98/1343,
98/1346, 98/1347, 98/1349, 98/1351, 98/1352, 98/1354, 99/869, 99/1298,
99/1304, 99/1306, 99/1311, 00/1311, 00/1392, 00/1395, 00/1401, 00/1402,
01/1455, 01/1463, 02/4054, 03/3834, 04/3422: *Followed*, 97/1645,
99/1297, 99/1312: *Referred to*, 89/1105, 89/1213, 90/1220, 90/1392,
90/1487, 91/1194, 91/1196, 92/1163, 92/1375, 92/1377, 93/1014, 93/1214,
93/1257, 93/1260, 93/1261, 93/1264, 94/1307, 97/1646, 97/1648

R. v Bioshogun (Nimota) see R. v Aranguren (Jose de Jesus)

R. v Birch (Kevin) [2006] EWCA Crim 2240, CA (Crim Div) . . . . *Considered*, 07/3789

R. v Birmingham (Gareth) see R. v Foster (Mark)

R. v Bishop (Costs) [2007] 3 Costs L.R. 506, Sup Ct Costs Office

R. v Black (Joseph Christopher); *joined case* R. v Gowan (Lloyd) [2006] EWCA Crim
2306; (2006) 103(37) L.S.G. 30; (2006) 150 S.J.L.B. 1255, CA (Crim Div). . . *Digested*, 07/**3792**

R. v Blackburn (Derek Stephen) see R. v P

R. v Blackfriars Crown Court Ex p. Sunworld Ltd see Sunworld Ltd v Hammersmith
and Fulham LBC

R. v Blenman (David) see R. v Case (Darren Lee)

R. v Bolkis (William) (1934) 24 Cr. App. R. 19, CCA . . . . *Applied*, 82/2772,
07/1006

R. v Bolton MBC Ex p. Kirkman [1998] Env. L.R. 719; [1998] J.P.L. 787; [1998] N.P.C.
80, CA (Civ Div); affirming [1998] Env. L.R. 560; (1998) 76 P. & C.R. 548;
[1998] C.O.D. 290; [1997] N.P.C. 188, QBD . . . . *Digested*, 98/**4236**:
Applied, 07/3236: *Considered*, 00/2278

R. v Bombatu (Eugene) see R. v Soule Ali (Adamou)

R. v Bonbatu (Eugene) see R. v Soule Ali (Adamou)

R. v Boness (Dean); *joined case* R. v Bebbington (Shaun Anthony) [2005] EWCA
Crim 2395; [2006] 1 Cr. App. R. (S.) 120; (2005) 169 J.P. 621; [2006] Crim.
L.R. 160; [2006] A.C.D. 5; (2005) 169 J.P.N. 937; *Times*, October 24, 2005, CA
(Crim Div) . . . . *Digested*, 06/**3643**:
Applied, 06/327, 06/328, 06/3639, 07/3770: *Considered*, 06/3644, 07/3738:
Followed, 07/357

R. v Bossom (Graeme); *joined case* R. v Joy (Paul) [2006] EWCA Crim 1489; [2006]
4 All E.R. 995; [2006] Eu. L.R. 1131, CA (Crim Div); affirming [2005] Eu. L.R.
765, Crown Ct (Lewes) . . . . *Digested*, 07/**1865**

R. v Botchett (Darren) see Attorney General's Reference (Nos.90 and 91 of 2006), Re

R. v Bothwell (Deborah) [2006] NICA 35; [2007] N.I. 58, CA (NI)

R. v Bott (Christine) see R. v Cuthbertson (Brian George)

R. v Bouchereau (Pierre Roger) (30/77) [1978] Q.B. 732; [1978] 2 W.L.R. 250;
[1981] 2 All E.R. 924; [1977] E.C.R. 1999; (1978) 66 Cr. App. R. 202; [1977] 2
C.M.L.R. 800; (1978) 122 S.J. 79, ECJ . . . . *Digested*, 78/**629**:
Applied, 87/1938, 89/1108, 00/3345, 06/3723, 07/1559:
Considered, 83/1895, 93/5141, 97/2902: *Followed*, 05/1462:
Referred to, 83/806, 90/1405, 93/1108

R. v Bouhaddaou (Yousef) [2006] EWCA Crim 3190; [2007] 2 Cr. App. R. (S.) 23;
[2007] Crim. L.R. 305; *Times*, December 15, 2006, CA (Crim Div) . . . . *Digested*, 07/**3697**

R. v Bourgass (Kamel) [2006] EWCA Crim 3397; [2007] 2 Cr. App. R. (S.) 40, CA
(Crim Div) . . . . *Digested*, 07/**853**

R. v Bow Street Metropolitan Stipendiary Magistrate Ex p. Pinochet Ugarte (No.2);
sub nom R. v Bartle Ex p. Pinochet Ugarte (No.2); R. v Evans Ex p. Pinochet
Ugarte (No.2); Pinochet Ugarte (No.2), Re [2000] 1 A.C. 119; [1999] 2 W.L.R.
272; [1999] 1 All E.R. 577; 6 B.H.R.C. 1; (1999) 11 Admin. L.R. 57; (1999) 96(6)
L.S.G. 33; (1999) 149 N.L.J. 88; *Times*, January 18, 1999; *Independent*,
January 19, 1999, HL . . . . *Digested*, 99/**39**:
Applied, 99/38, 04/30, 06/19, 06/2755: *Considered*, 00/4140, 00/6092,
01/6705, 05/13: *Distinguished*, 07/248

R. *v* Bowden (Jonathan) [2001] Q.B. 88; [2000] 2 W.L.R. 1083; [2000] 2 All E.R.
418; [2000] 1 Cr. App. R. 438; [2000] 2 Cr. App. R. (S.) 26; [2000] Crim. L.R.
381; (1999) 96(47) L.S.G. 29; (2000) 144 S.J.L.B. 5; *Times*, November 19,
1999; *Independent*, November 26, 1999, CA (Crim Div)............... *Digested*, 99/**947**:
                                 Applied, 00/993, 01/1450: *Followed*, 00/6039, 02/819, 07/5036
R. *v* Bowe (Forrester) see Bowe *v* Queen, The
R. *v* Bowker (Anthony) [2007] EWCA Crim 1608; [2007] Crim. L.R. 904, CA (Crim
Div)
R. *v* Bowles (Costs) [2007] 3 Costs L.R. 514, Sup Ct Costs Office
R. *v* Bowman (Maximus John) [2005] EWCA Crim 3612; [2006] 2 Cr. App. R. (S.)
40, CA (Crim Div) .... *Digested*, 07/**3739**
R. *v* Bowman (Thomas Damien) (Costs) [2006] EWCA Crim 1077; [2007] 1 Costs
L.R. 1, CA (Crim Div)
R. *v* Bowser (Clive Thomas) [2006] EWCA Crim 1314; [2007] 1 Cr. App. R. (S.) 21,
CA (Crim Div) .... *Digested*, 07/**3579**
R. *v* Boyle (Jason) [2007] EWCA Crim 98; [2007] 2 Cr. App. R. (S.) 46, CA (Crim
Div) .... *Digested*, 07/**3732**
R. *v* Brack (Joseph James) see R. *v* Brack (Joseph William)
R. *v* Brack (Joseph William); *joined case* R. *v* Brack (Joseph James) [2007] EWCA
Crim 1205; (2007) 104(19) L.S.G. 26, CA (Crim Div)
R. *v* Bracknell Justices Ex p. Griffiths see Pountney *v* Griffiths
R. *v* Bradstock (Oliver) see Attorney General's Reference (No.7 of 2007), Re
R. *v* Brady (Carl Jason); *joined case* R. *v* Paton (James Daniel) [2006] EWCA Crim
2780; [2007] 1 Cr. App. R. (S.) 117, CA (Crim Div)
R. *v* Brady (Philip) [2006] EWCA Crim 2413; [2007] Crim. L.R. 564, CA (Crim Div)
R. *v* Bramich (David) see R. *v* Graham (Hemamali Krishna)
R. *v* Branton-Speak (Cory) [2006] EWCA Crim 1745; [2007] 1 Cr. App. R. (S.) 55,
CA (Crim Div) .... *Digested*, 07/**3630**
R. *v* Bravard (Jacques) see R. *v* May (Raymond George)
R. *v* Braxton (Curtis) (Application for Leave to Appeal) [2004] EWCA Crim 1374;
[2005] 1 Cr. App. R. (S.) 36, CA (Crim Div) .... *Digested*, 05/**3528**:
                   Applied, 06/3639: *Considered*, 06/3642, 06/3644, 07/3738
R. *v* Bree (Benjamin) [2007] EWCA Crim 804; [2007] 3 W.L.R. 600; [2007] 2 All
E.R. 676; [2007] 2 Cr. App. R. 13; [2007] Crim. L.R. 900; (2007) 104(15)
L.S.G. 23; (2007) 151 S.J.L.B. 432; *Times*, May 7, 2007, CA (Crim Div) ...... *Digested*, 07/**919**
R. *v* Breitkopf (Joseph Eduarde) [2006] EWCA Crim 1512; [2007] 1 Cr. App. R. (S.)
42, CA (Crim Div) .... *Digested*, 07/**3747**
R. *v* Brennan (Gary Thomas) [2007] EWCA Crim 161; [2007] 2 Cr. App. R. (S.) 50,
CA (Crim Div) .... *Digested*, 07/**3601**
R. *v* Brent LBC Ex p. Blatt (1992) 24 H.L.R. 319; [1991] N.P.C. 134; *Independent*,
January 20, 1992, DC. .... *Digested*, 92/**2330**:
                                            Considered, 06/2720, 07/2155
R. *v* Brent LBC Ex p. Gunning 84 L.G.R. 168; *Times*, April 30, 1985, QBD .... *Digested*, 86/**1127**:
                   Considered, 91/94, 93/3679, 95/30, 96/2483, 96/2487, 07/2048
R. *v* Brent LBC Ex p. O'Malley see R. *v* Secretary of State for the Environment,
Transport and the Regions Ex p. Walters
R. *v* Bretscher (Gordon Maxwell) see R. *v* Townsend (Philip Henry)
R. *v* Brewer (Peter) (Costs) [2007] 4 Costs L.R. 662, Sup Ct Costs Office
R. *v* Briggs (Adam Daniel) [2007] EWCA Crim 452; [2007] 2 Cr. App. R. (S.) 67, CA
(Crim Div) .... *Digested*, 07/**3780**
R. *v* Brima (Jimmy) [2006] EWCA Crim 408; [2007] 1 Cr. App. R. 24, CA (Crim Div) . *Digested*, 07/**838**
R. *v* Bristol Betting and Gaming Licensing Committee Ex p. O'Callaghan see Locabail
(UK) Ltd *v* Bayfield Properties Ltd (Leave to Appeal)
R. *v* Bristol City Council Ex p. DL Barrett & Sons (2001) 3 L.G.L.R. 11, QBD .... *Digested*, 01/**4405**:
                                             Applied, 07/1197
R. *v* Britton (Stephen Kade) [2006] EWCA Crim 2875; [2007] 1 Cr. App. R. (S.) 121,
CA (Crim Div) .... *Digested*, 07/**3774**
R. *v* Brixton Prison Governor Ex p. Atkinson see Atkinson *v* United States
R. *v* Brizzalari (Michael) [2004] EWCA Crim 310; *Times*, March 3, 2004, CA (Crim
Div) .... *Digested*, 04/**824**:
                                            Considered, 07/3575
R. *v* Broad (Wayne Malcolm) see R. *v* C
R. *v* Bromley LBC Ex p. Baker see R. (on the application of Barker) *v* Bromley LBC
R. *v* Bromley LBC Ex p. Barker see R. (on the application of Barker) *v* Bromley LBC
R. *v* Brough (Philip Ian) [1997] 1 Cr. App. R. (S.) 55, CA (Crim Div) .... *Digested*, 97/**1457**:
                                            Considered, 07/3743
R. *v* Broughton (Thomas Michael) [2007] EWCA Crim 566; [2007] 2 Cr. App. R. (S.)
72, CA (Crim Div) .... *Digested*, 07/**3586**
R. *v* Brown (Alan) see R. *v* Lambert (John Ritchie)
R. *v* Brown (Clinton George) (1994) 15 Cr. App. R. (S.) 337, CA (Crim Div) .... *Considered*, 07/3643
R. *v* Brown (Craig William); *joined case* R. *v* Butterworth (James Thomas) [2006]
EWCA Crim 1996; [2007] 1 Cr. App. R. (S.) 77; [2006] Crim. L.R. 1082, CA
(Crim Div) .... *Digested*, 07/**3640**:
                                  Applied, 07/3641: *Considered*, 07/3639

R. *v* Brown (Darren Junior) see R. *v* Hart (Clifford)
R. *v* Brown (Deland Anthony) see Attorney General's Reference (Nos.143 and 144 of 2006), Re
R. *v* Brown (Kevin) (1984) 1 B.C.C. 98970; (1984) 79 Cr. App. R. 115; [1984] Crim. L.R.167, CA (Crim Div) . . . . *Digested*, 84/**624**:
Applied, 95/1091, 97/1179, 01/1149: *Considered*, 86/667, 88/659, 88/786, 88/864, 92/785, 94/1040, 94/1137, 95/1063, 96/1633, 96/1674, 97/1187: *Distinguished*, 86/606, 99/1059, 05/793: *Followed*, 07/990
R. *v* Brown (Kirsty Elizabeth) [2007] EWCA Crim 2632; *Times*, November 16, 2007, CMAC . . . . *Digested*, 07/**270**
R. *v* Browning (Paul Christopher) [2001] EWCA Crim 1831; [2002] 1 Cr. App. R. (S.) 88, CA (Crim Div) . . . . *Considered*, 07/3592
R. *v* Bryan (Alsent) see Bryan (Setting of Minimum Term), Re
R. *v* Bryan (Leslie) see Bryan (Setting of Minimum Term), Re
R. *v* Bryan (Paul Barry) see R. *v* Czyzewski (Jozef Eugene) (Appeal against Sentence)
R. *v* Bullen (David Frederick) see R. *v* Soneji (Kamlesh Kumar)
R. *v* Bulmer (Ralph Henry) (1989) 11 Cr. App. R. (S.) 586, CA (Crim Div) . . . . *Digested*, 91/**1233**:
Considered, 07/3743: *Referred to*, 97/1457
R. *v* Burch (David William) see Attorney General's Reference (Nos.88, 89, 90 and 91 of 2006), Re
R. *v* Burt (Scott-Rab John) see R. *v* S
R. *v* Burton (Evelyn); *joined case* R. *v* Andre (Lyla) [2001] EWCA Crim 1206; [2002] 1 Cr. App. R. (S.) 24; [2001] Crim. L.R. 660, CA (Crim Div) . . . . *Digested*, 02/**3952**:
Distinguished, 07/3684
R. *v* Butterworth (James Thomas) see R. *v* Brown (Craig William)
R. *v* Byatt (Alan) [2006] EWCA Crim 904; [2006] 2 Cr. App. R. (S.) 116, CA (Crim Div) . . . . *Digested*, 07/**3615**
R. *v* Byfield (Wayne Leonard) see Attorney General's Reference (Nos.117 and 118 of 2005), Re
R. *v* Byrne (Alan) see Attorney General's Reference (Nos.19, 20 and 21 of 2001), Re
R. *v* C see R. *v* Corran (Ben)
R. *v* C see R. *v* H
R. *v* C see Attorney General's Reference (Nos.66 and 67 of 2006), Re
R. *v* C; *sub nom* R. *v* A (Prosecutor's Appeal) [2005] EWCA Crim 3533; [2006] 1 Cr. App. R. 28; *Times*, January 5, 2006, CA (Crim Div) . . . . *Digested*, 06/**881**:
Applied, 06/3889: *Considered*, 07/848
R. *v* C [2006] EWCA Crim 2132; [2007] Crim. L.R. 235; *Times*, August 17, 2006, CA (Crim Div) . . . . *Digested*, 07/**1017**
R. *v* C [2006] EWCA Crim 1079; [2006] 1 W.L.R. 2994; [2006] 3 All E.R. 689; [2006] 2 Cr. App. R. 28; (2007) 171 J.P. 108; [2006] Crim. L.R. 1058; (2007) 171 J.P.N. 344; *Times*, May 24, 2006, CA (Crim Div) . . . . *Digested*, 06/**800**
R. *v* C [2007] EWCA Crim 2581; (2007) 104(45) L.S.G. 31; *Times*, December 6, 2007, CA (Crim Div) . . . . *Digested*, 07/**848**
R. *v* C; *joined cases* R. *v* Broad (Wayne Malcolm); R. *v* Price (Robert William); R. *v* Baldrey (Danny); R. *v* Bartley (Anthony Michael) [2007] EWCA Crim 680; [2007] 3 All E.R. 735; [2007] 2 Cr. App. R. (S.) 98; [2007] Crim. L.R. 581; *Times*, May 9, 2007, CA (Crim Div) . . . . *Digested*, 07/**3639**
R. *v* C [2007] EWCA Crim 854; (2007) 151 S.J.L.B. 572, CA (Crim Div)
R. *v* C (Angela Heidi) [2006] EWCA Crim 1781; [2007] 1 Cr. App. R. (S.) 61, CA (Crim Div) . . . . *Digested*, 07/**3607**
R. *v* C (Craig) (A Juvenile) see Attorney General's Reference (Nos.19, 20 and 21 of 2001), Re
R. *v* C (James) see R. *v* R (Amer)
R. *v* C (Patrick Stuart) [2006] EWCA Crim 1618; [2007] 1 Cr. App. R. (S.) 51, CA (Crim Div) . . . . *Digested*, 07/**3777**
R. *v* Cadman (John Richard) see Cadman (Setting of Minimum Term), Re
R. *v* Cain (Alan John); *joined cases* R. *v* Hodson (Phillip); R. *v* Liversidge (Ian John); R. *v* Benton (Robert) [2006] EWCA Crim 3233; [2007] 2 Cr. App. R. (S.) 25; [2007] Crim. L.R. 310; *Times*, December 26, 2006, CA (Crim Div) . . . . *Digested*, 07/**3736**
R. *v* Cain (Douglas Roy) [1985] A.C. 46; [1984] 3 W.L.R. 393; [1984] 2 All E.R. 737; (1984) 79 Cr. App. R. 298; (1985) 149 J.P. 73; [1984] Crim. L.R. 679; (1984) 81 L.S.G. 2693; (1984) 134 N.L.J. 886; (1984) 128 S.J. 530, HL; affirming (1983) 5 Cr. App. R. (S.) 272; (1983) 147 J.P.N. 833, CA (Crim Div) . . . . *Digested*, 84/**557**:
Applied, 07/967: *Considered*, 86/832, 88/894, 93/833: *Distinguished*, 92/717
R. *v* Caines (Timothy Carlton) see Caines (Setting of Minimum Term), Re
R. *v* Caley-Knowles (Edward); *joined case* R. *v* Jones (Iorwerth) [2006] EWCA Crim 1611; [2006] 1 W.L.R. 3181; [2007] 1 Cr. App. R. 13; [2007] Crim. L.R. 61; *Times*, October 4, 2006, CA (Crim Div) . . . . *Digested*, 06/**963**
R. *v* Cambray (Paul) [2006] EWCA Crim 1708; [2007] R.T.R. 10, CA (Crim Div) . . . . . *Digested*, 07/**862**
R. *v* Campbell (Kenneth George) [2007] EWCA Crim 1472; [2007] 1 W.L.R. 2798; [2007] 2 Cr. App. R. 28; (2007) 171 J.P. 525; (2007) 104(28) L.S.G. 28; *Times*, July 4, 2007, CA (Crim Div) . . . . *Digested*, 07/**995**

R. *v* Campbell (Marvin) (Leave to Appeal) [2006] EWCA Crim 1305; (2006) 150
    S.J.L.B. 1327; *Times,* May 30, 2006, CA (Crim Div) . . . . *Digested,* 07/**837**
R. *v* Campbell (Shantelle Jamie) see R. *v* Peters (Benjamin)
R. *v* Canavan (Darren Anthony); *joined cases* Kidd (Philip Richard); R. *v* Shaw
    (Dennis) [1998] 1 W.L.R. 604; [1998] 1 All E.R. 42; [1998] 1 Cr. App. R. 79;
    [1998] 1 Cr. App. R. (S.) 243; (1997) 161 J.P. 709; [1997] Crim. L.R. 766; (1997)
    161 J.P.N. 838; (1997) 94(35) L.S.G. 33; (1997) 147 N.L.J. 1457; (1997) 141
    S.J.L.B. 169; *Times,* July 21, 1997, CA (Crim Div) . . . . *Digested,* 97/**1492**:
                  Applied, 04/3376, 05/3742, 07/3723: *Considered,* 98/1387, 99/1351,
                                 99/1352, 07/3606: *Distinguished,* 03/3826
R. *v* Carasco (Charles) see R. *v* Lang (Stephen Howard)
R. *v* Cardiff CC Ex p. Sears Group Properties Ltd [1998] 3 P.L.R. 55; [1998] P.L.C.R.
    262; (1998) 95(17) L.S.G. 29; [1998] N.P.C. 46; *Times,* April 29, 1998, QBD . . *Digested,* 98/**4202**:
                                 Considered, 07/2305
R. *v* Carp (Anthony Mark) see R. *v* Highton (Edward Paul)
R. *v* Carpenter (Agnes Jane) see Carpenter (Setting of Minimum Term), Re
R. *v* Carr (Craig Edward) see R. *v* S
R. *v* Carragher (James Redmond) [2006] EWCA Crim 1306; [2007] 1 Cr. App. R. (S.)
    25, CA (Crim Div) . . . . *Digested,* 07/**3575**
R. *v* Carson (Nicholas Craig) (1991) 92 Cr. App. R. 236; (1990) 154 J.P. 794; [1990]
    Crim. L.R. 729; (1990) 154 J.P.N. 489, CA (Crim Div) . . . . *Digested,* 91/**775**:
                                 Applied, 07/1004
R. *v* Carter (Jahroy) [1997] 1 Cr. App. R. (S.) 434, CA (Crim Div) . . . . *Digested,* 97/**1459**:
                   Considered, 00/1429, 00/1430, 07/3743
R. *v* Carter (Stephen) see Attorney General's Reference (No.145 of 2006), Re
R. *v* Carty (Donnel Marcus) see Attorney General's Reference (Nos.143 and 144 of
    2006), Re
R. *v* Case (Darren Lee); *sub nom* R. *v* Blenman (David); R. *v* Sargent (Reece) [2006]
    EWCA Crim 1746; [2007] 1 Cr. App. R. (S.) 57, CA (Crim Div) . . . . *Digested,* 07/**3781**
R. *v* Caswell (Richard) [2006] EWCA Crim 1398; [2007] 1 Cr. App. R. (S.) 10, CA
    (Crim Div)
R. *v* Cemex Cement Ltd [2007] EWCA Crim 1759; (2007) 151 S.J.L.B. 985; [2007]
    N.P.C. 100, CA (Crim Div). . . . . *Digested,* 07/**986**
R. *v* Central London County Court Ex p. London [1999] Q.B. 1260; [1999] 3 W.L.R. 1;
    [1999] 3 All E.R. 991; [2000] C.P. Rep. 75; [1999] 2 F.L.R. 161; (1999) 2
    C.C.L. Rep. 256; [1999] C.O.D. 196; [1999] Fam. Law 452; (1999) 96(15)
    L.S.G. 30; *Times,* March 23, 1999; *Independent,* March 18, 1999, CA (Civ Div) . *Digested,* 99/**3937**:
                                   Considered, 07/2897
R. *v* Cervi (John Matthew) [2007] EWCA Crim 213; [2007] 2 Cr. App. R. (S.) 60, CA
    (Crim Div) . . . . *Digested,* 07/**3724**
R. *v* CF; *sub nom* R. *v* CPS (Leicester); R. *v* F [2006] EWCA Crim 3323; [2007] 1
    W.L.R. 1021; [2007] 1 Cr. App. R. 36; [2007] Crim. L.R. 574; (2007) 151 S.J.L.B.
    61; *Times,* January 17, 2007, CA (Crim Div) . . . . *Digested,* 07/**865**
R. *v* Chal (Amolak Singh) [2007] EWCA Crim 2647; (2007) 151 S.J.L.B. 1296; *Times,*
    October 26, 2007, CA (Crim Div)
R. *v* Chandi (Amandeep Singh) see Jones (Setting of Minimum Term), Re
R. *v* Chapple (Ronald) (Costs) [2007] 2 Costs L.R. 310, Sup Ct Costs Office
R. *v* Charge (Warren James) see R. *v* Hobbs (Stephen Paul)
R. *v* Charnley (Kenneth Desmond) [2007] EWCA Crim 1354; [2007] 2 Cr. App. R. 33;
    [2007] Crim. L.R. 984, CA (Crim Div) . . . . *Digested,* 07/**992**
R. *v* Cheetham (Oliver Lewis) [2006] EWCA Crim 2644; [2007] 1 Cr. App. R. (S.)
    116, CA (Crim Div)
R. *v* Chen (Costs) (No.1) see R. *v* Cheng (Costs) (No.1)
R. *v* Chen (Costs) (No.2) see R. *v* Cheng (Costs) (No.2)
R. *v* Cheng (Costs) (No.1); *joined case* R. *v* Chen (Costs) (No.1) [2007] 4 Costs L.R.
    626, Sup Ct Costs Office
R. *v* Cheng (Costs) (No.2); *joined cases* R. *v* Miah (Costs) (No.2); R. *v* Chen (Costs)
    (No.2) [2007] 4 Costs L.R. 634, Sup Ct Costs Office
R. *v* Chief Constable of Greater Manchester Ex p. Lainton [2000] I.C.R. 1324; [2000]
    P.o. L.R. 67; (2000) 97(16) L.S.G. 40; (2000) 144 S.J.L.B. 203; *Times,* April 4,
    2000, CA (Civ Div); reversing *Times,* July 13, 1999; *Independent,* June 28, 1999,
    QBD . . . . *Digested,* 00/**4545**:
                                   Considered, 07/2811
R. *v* Chief Constable of Kent Ex p. L; *joined case* R. *v* DPP Ex p. B [1993] 1 All E.R.
    756; (1991) 93 Cr. App. R. 416; [1991] Crim. L.R. 841; [1991] C.O.D. 446; (1991)
    155 J.P.N. 636; (1992) 136 S.J.L.B. 136; *Times,* April 17, 1991; *Independent,*
    April 30, 1991; *Daily Telegraph,* April 22, 1991, DC . . . . *Digested,* 92/**1028**:
                 Applied, 04/893: *Considered,* 95/122, 07/3314
R. *v* Chief National Insurance Commissioner Ex p. Connor [1981] Q.B. 758; [1981] 2
    W.L.R. 412; [1981] 1 All E.R. 769; [1980] Crim. L.R. 579; (1980) 124 S.J. 478,
    QBD . . . . *Digested,* 81/**2619**:
            Applied, 90/96, 91/2484, 07/3026: *Considered,* 96/2852, 01/4702:
                                 Followed, 80/55
R. *v* Chirila (Adina Ramova) see R. *v* Chirila (Remus Tenistocle)

R. v Chirila (Remus Tenistocle); *joined cases* R. v Monteanu (Adrian); R. v Chirila (Adina Ramova) [2004] EWCA Crim 2200; [2005] 1 Cr. App. R. (S.) 93, CA (Crim Div) . . . .   *Digested*, 05/**3614**:
                                                        Considered, 07/3618

R. v Choi (Ching) (Unreported, May 7, 1999), CA (Crim Div) . . . .   *Considered*, 07/916

R. v Chopra (Manoj Kumar) [2006] EWCA Crim 2133; [2007] 1 Cr. App. R. 16; [2007] Crim. L.R. 380, CA (Crim Div) . . . .   *Digested*, 07/**823**

R. v Christian (Stevens Raymond) see Christian v Queen, The

R. v Chute (Patrick Joseph) [2003] EWCA Crim 177; [2003] 2 Cr. App. R. (S.) 74; [2003] Crim. L.R. 295; *Times*, February 13, 2003, CA (Crim Div) . . . .   *Digested*, 03/**3785**:
                                                       Applied, 07/946

R. v Clark (Trevor) [1998] 2 Cr. App. R. 137; [1998] 2 Cr. App. R. (S.) 95; [1998] Crim. L.R. 227; (1998) 95(2) L.S.G. 22; (1998) 142 S.J.L.B. 27; *Times*, December 4, 1997, CA (Crim Div) . . . .   *Digested*, 98/**1392**:
              Applied, 00/1237, 01/1491, 03/3870, 04/858, 04/3318, 07/3760:
                     Considered, 98/1316, 98/1394, 99/1121, 99/1174, 99/1277, 99/1359,
                        99/1362, 99/1364, 00/1436, 02/4038, 02/4039, 05/3611, 06/3742, 07/3761:
                         Distinguished, 03/3811, 07/3618: *Followed*, 04/3353

R. v Clarke (Jason) see R. v Hart (Clifford)

R. v Clarke (Martin Paul) [2007] EWCA Crim 2532; *Times*, October 29, 2007, CA (Crim Div) . . . .   *Digested*, 07/**969**

R. v Clemow (William Alfred) see Attorney General's Reference (Nos.42, 43 and 44 of 2006), Re

R. v Clifton Steel Ltd [2007] EWCA Crim 1537; (2007) 151 S.J.L.B. 808, CA (Crim Div). . . . .   *Considered*, 07/986

R. v Cluff (Allan Keith) see Attorney General's Reference (No.34 of 2006), Re

R. v Coates (Phillip) [2007] EWCA Crim 1471; [2007] Crim. L.R. 887, CMAC . . . .   *Digested*, 07/**854**

R. v Cole (Konrad); *joined case* R. v Keet (Rocky) [2007] EWCA Crim 1924; [2007] 1 W.L.R. 2716; *Times*, October 2, 2007, CA (Crim Div)

R. v Coleman (Anthony Neville) (1992) 95 Cr. App. R. 159; (1992) 13 Cr. App. R. (S.) 508; [1992] Crim. L.R. 315; *Times*, December 10, 1991, CA (Crim Div) . . . .   *Digested*, 93/**1224**:
             Applied, 06/3764: *Cited*, 01/1427: *Considered*, 97/1554, 99/1261, 00/1362,
                     04/3470, 05/3662, 05/3667, 06/3744, 07/3782: *Referred to*, 94/1306,
                                                          95/1434, 97/1620

R. v Coles (Lyndon) see R. v Maxwell (Andrew Robert)

R. v Coles (Robert) see R. v Maxwell (Andrew Robert)

R. v Collier (Edward) see R. v Lang (Stephen Howard)

R. v Commissioner for Local Administration Ex p. Croydon LBC [1989] 1 All E.R. 1033; 87 L.G.R. 221; [1989] C.O.D. 226; (1989) 153 L.G. Rev. 131; *Times*, June 9, 1988; *Independent*, June 9, 1988; *Guardian*, June 17, 1988, QBD . . . .   *Digested*, 89/**2328**:
             Applied, 95/1911: *Considered*, 92/1858, 97/2108, 98/1915, 00/1921, 05/402,
                                           07/1267: *Referred to*, 92/1852

R. v Commissioner of Police of the Metropolis Ex p. Blackburn (No.1) [1968] 2 Q.B. 118; [1968] 2 W.L.R. 893; [1968] 1 All E.R. 763; (1968) 112 S.J. 112, CA (Civ Div). . . . .   *Digested*, 68/**1703**:
             Applied, 73/2580, 90/68: *Considered*, 87/2857, 90/28, 92/1028, 02/1415,
                                            07/3314: *Followed*, 01/1072

R. v Commissioner of Police of the Metropolis Ex p. Thompson [1997] 1 W.L.R. 1519; [1997] 2 Cr. App. R. 49; [1997] C.O.D. 313, QBD . . . .   *Digested*, 97/**1274**:
                         Applied, 04/366: *Considered*, 98/1004, 07/3314

R. v Committee of the Judicial Committee of the Privy Council acting for the Visitor of the University of London Ex p. Vijayatunga see R. v HM Queen in Council Ex p. Vijayatunga

R. v Connolly (Mark Anthony); *joined case* R. v Kennett (Roy Patrick) [2007] EWCA Crim 790; [2007] 2 Cr. App. R. (S.) 82, CA (Crim Div) . . . .   *Digested*, 07/**990**

R. v Connor (Ben) see R. v Mirza (Shabbir Ali)

R. v Connors (John) [2005] EWCA Crim 3555; [2006] 2 Cr. App. R. (S.) 31, CA (Crim Div) . . . .   *Digested*, 07/**3704**

R. v Considine (Lawrence Philip); *joined case* R. v Davis (Jay) [2007] EWCA Crim 1166; [2007] 3 All E.R. 621; [2007] Crim. L.R. 824, CA (Crim Div). . . . .   *Digested*, 07/**3723**

R. v Cook (Gary) [2006] EWCA Crim 780; [2006] 2 Cr. App. R. (S.) 106, CA (Crim Div). . . . .   *Digested*, 07/**3583**

R. v Cook (Neil Terence) see R. v Cooksley (Robert Charles)

R. v Cook Ex p. DPP [2001] Crim. L.R. 321, QBD . . . .   *Considered*, 07/944

R. v Cooksley (Robert Charles); *sub nom* Attorney General's Reference (No.152 of 2002), Re; *joined cases* R. v Stride (Ian Paul); R. v Cook (Neil Terence); R. v Crump (Richard James) [2003] EWCA Crim 996; [2003] 3 All E.R. 40; [2003] 2 Cr. App. R. 18; [2004] 1 Cr. App. R. (S.) 1; [2003] R.T.R. 32; (2003) 100(23) L.S.G. 36; *Times*, April 8, 2003; *Independent*, June 30, 2003, CA (Crim Div) . . 　*Digested*, 04/**3333**:
　　　　　　　　　　　　　Applied, 04/3295, 04/3296, 04/3298, 05/3547, 05/3550, 06/3811,
　　　　　　　　　　06/3814, 06/3820, 06/3874, 06/3875, 06/3876, 07/862, 07/3588, 07/3595,
　　　　　　　　　　07/3775: *Considered*, 04/3294, 04/3297, 04/3467, 05/3546, 05/3549,
　　　　　　　　　　05/3551, 05/3552, 05/3553, 05/3581, 05/3766, 05/5657, 06/3805,
　　　　　　　　　　06/3806, 06/3807, 06/3808, 06/3809, 06/3810, 06/3812, 06/3813,
　　　　　　　　　　06/3815, 06/3873, 06/3877, 06/5669, 07/3589, 07/3590, 07/3591,
　　　　　　　　　　07/3592, 07/3594, 07/5512: *Followed*, 04/4371, 05/3548, 07/3593
R. v Cornfield (Mark) [2006] EWCA Crim 2909; [2007] 1 Cr. App. R. (S.) 124, CA (Crim Div) . . . . 　*Digested*, 07/**3614**
R. v Coroner for Exeter and East Devon Ex p. Palmer FC3 97/7452/D, CA (Civ Div) . . 　*Applied*, 07/29
R. v Corran (Ben); *joined cases* R. v C; R. v Heard (Kevin Phillip); R. v Williams (Anthony Michael) [2005] EWCA Crim 192; [2005] 2 Cr. App. R. (S.) 73; [2005] Crim. L.R. 404; *Times*, March 8, 2005, CA (Crim Div) . . . . 　*Digested*, 05/**3734**:
　　　　　　　　Applied, 06/830: *Approved*, 05/3776: *Considered*, 06/3668, 06/3893,
　　　　　　　　06/3894, 06/3905, 07/3740, 07/3744: *Distinguished*, 06/3850
R. v Corry (Peter Thomas) see R. v Steele (Michael)
R. v Cort (Peter Laurence) [2003] EWCA Crim 2149; [2004] Q.B. 388; [2003] 3 W.L.R. 1300; [2004] 4 All E.R. 137; [2004] 1 Cr. App. R. 18; (2003) 167 J.P. 504; (2003) 167 J.P.N. 692; (2003) 100(35) L.S.G. 35; (2003) 147 S.J.L.B. 872; *Times*, July 23, 2003, CA (Crim Div) . . . . 　*Digested*, 03/**793**:
　　　　　　　　　　　　　　　　　　　　　　　　　Considered, 07/888
R. v Cory (Rodney Phillip) see R. v Norman (Shane Martin)
R. v Cotterill (James Michael) [2007] EWCA Crim 526; [2007] 2 Cr. App. R. (S.) 64, CA (Crim Div) . . . . 　*Digested*, 07/**3653**
R. v Cottrell (Steven); *joined case* R. v Fletcher (Joseph) [2007] EWCA Crim 2016; [2007] 1 W.L.R. 3262; *Times*, September 5, 2007, CA (Crim Div) . . . . 　*Digested*, 07/**970**
R. v Courtney (William) [2007] NICA 6; [2007] N.I. 178, CA (Crim Div) (NI)
R. v Coutts (Graham) (Costs) [2007] 5 Costs L.R. 878, Sup Ct Costs Office
R. v Coutts (Graham James) [2006] UKHL 39; [2006] 1 W.L.R. 2154; [2006] 4 All E.R. 353; [2007] 1 Cr. App. R. 6; [2006] Crim. L.R. 1065; (2006) 156 N.L.J. 1213; (2006) 150 S.J.L.B. 984; *Times*, July 24, 2006; *Independent*, July 21, 2006, HL; reversing [2005] EWCA Crim 52; [2005] 1 W.L.R. 1605; [2005] 1 Cr. App. R. 31; [2005] Crim. L.R. 784; (2005) 102(9) L.S.G. 28; *Times*, January 26, 2005, CA (Crim Div) . . . . 　*Digested*, 06/**986**:
　　　　　　　　　　　　　　　　　　　　　Considered, 07/923, 07/994
R. v Cowley (Mark Antony) [2007] EWCA Crim 588; [2007] 2 Cr. App. R. (S.) 79, CA (Crim Div) . . . . 　*Digested*, 07/**3745**
R. v Coyne (Timothy Malcolm) see R. v S
R. v CPS [2005] EWCA Crim 2342, CA (Crim Div) . . . . 　*Followed*, 07/981
R. v CPS (Leicester) see R. v CF
R v Crane (Sara) see R. v Last (Emma)
R v Cranfield University Senate Ex p. Bashir [1999] Ed. C.R. 772; [1999] E.L.R. 317, CA (Civ Div) . . . . 　*Digested*, 99/**1934**:
　　　　　　　　　　　　　　　　　　　　　　　　　　Applied, 07/1281
R. v Crimp (Justin James) (1995) 16 Cr. App. R. (S.) 346, CA (Crim Div) . . . . 　*Cited*, 01/1427:
　　　　　　　　　　　　　　　　　　　　　　　Considered, 07/3797
R. v Croxson (Matthew Louis) see R. v Johnstone (Robert Alexander)
R. v Croydon Crown Court Ex p. Cox [1997] 1 Cr. App. R. 20; [1997] Crim. L.R. 52, QBD . . . . 　*Digested*, 96/**1552**:
　　　　　　　　　　　　　　　　　　　　　　　Considered, 07/940
R. v Croydon Justices Ex p. Dean [1993] Q.B. 769; [1993] 3 W.L.R. 198; [1993] 3 All E.R. 129; (1994) 98 Cr. App. R. 76; (1993) 157 J.P. 975; [1993] Crim. L.R. 759; [1993] C.O.D. 290; (1993) 157 J.P.N. 457; (1993) 143 N.L.J. 508; *Times*, March 15, 1993; *Independent*, March 9, 1993; *Guardian*, March 5, 1993, DC . . . 　*Digested*, 94/**663**:
　　　　　　　Applied, 97/1255, 06/973: *Considered*, 96/1655, 98/1079, 07/923
R. v Crucefix (Costs) [2007] 5 Costs L.R. 770, Sup Ct Costs Office
R. v Crump (Richard James) see R. v Cooksley (Robert Charles)
R. v Crump (Robert John) see R. v Marshall (Jay David)
R. v Cullen (Dean James) [2007] EWCA Crim 358; [2007] 2 Cr. App. R. (S.) 65, CA (Crim Div)
R. v Cumming (Donna Marie) [2006] EWCA Crim 3223; [2007] 2 Cr. App. R. (S.) 20, CA (Crim Div) . . . . 　*Digested*, 07/**3686**
R. v Cunningham (Alec) [2007] EWCA Crim 524; [2007] 2 Cr. App. R. (S.) 61, CA (Crim Div) . . . . 　*Digested*, 07/**3709**
R. v Cunningham (Paul Todd) [2006] EWCA Crim 1092; [2007] 1 Cr. App. R. (S.) 14, CA (Crim Div) . . . . 　*Digested*, 07/**3675**
R. v Currie (Paul Alan) [2007] EWCA Crim 926; [2007] 2 Cr. App. R. 18; [2007] R.T.R. 37; (2007) 151 S.J.L.B. 609, CA (Crim Div) . . . . 　*Digested*, 07/**1006**

R. v Curtis (David) [2007] EWCA Crim 136; [2007] 2 Cr. App. R. (S.) 52, CA (Crim
Div). . . . . *Digested,* 07/**3584**
R. v Customs and Excise Commissioners Ex p. EMU Tabac Sarl (C-296/95) [1998]
Q.B. 791; [1998] 3 W.L.R. 298; [1998] All E.R. (EC) 402; [1998] E.C.R. I-1605;
[1998] 2 C.M.L.R. 1205; [1998] C.E.C. 558; *Times,* April 9, 1998, ECJ . . . . *Digested,* 98/**4643**:
Considered, 03/926: *Followed,* 00/2349, 07/1034
R. v Customs and Excise Commissioners Ex p. Faroe Seafood Co Ltd (C-153/94);
joined case R. v Customs and Excise Commissioners Ex p. Smith (t/a Arthur
Smith) (C-204/94) [1996] All E.R. (E.C.) 606; [1996] E.C.R. I-2465; [1996] 2
C.M.L.R. 821, ECJ (5th Chamber) . . . . *Digested,* 96/**5576**:
Applied, 07/1031: *Considered,* 04/906: *Followed,* 00/4953
R. v Customs and Excise Commissioners Ex p. Smith (t/a Arthur Smith) (C-204/94)
see R. v Customs and Excise Commissioners Ex p. Faroe Seafood Co Ltd (C-
153/94)
R. v Cuthbertson (Brian George); *joined cases* R. v Todd (Henry Barclay); R. v Todd
(David Brown); R. v Kemp (Richard); R. v Bott (Christine); R. v Solomon
(David); R. v McCoy (Keith Thomas); R. v Munro (Andrew); R. v Fielding (Nigel);
R. v Hughes (Alston Frederick); R. v Annable (Martin William); R. v Robertson
(David John); R. v McDonnell (John Patrick); R. v Lochhead (William Stewart);
R. v Spenceley (Russell Stephen) [1981] A.C. 470; [1980] 3 W.L.R. 89; [1980]
2 All E.R. 401; (1980) 71 Cr. App. R. 148; [1980] Crim. L.R. 583; (1980) 124
S.J. 443, HL; reversing (1979) 69 Cr. App. R. 330; (1979) 1 Cr. App. R. (S.) 218;
[1979] Crim. L.R. 665; [1979] Crim. L.R. 794, CA (Crim Div) . . . . *Digested,* 80/**526**:
Applied, 84/541, 86/808, 86/2866, 87/945: *Considered,* 86/603, 86/604,
86/829, 91/923, 07/3721: *Distinguished,* 83/607: *Followed,* 82/692
R. v Czyzewski (Jozef Eugene) (Appeal against Sentence); *joined cases* R. v Bryan
(Paul Barry); R. v Mitchell (John); R. v Diafi (Karim Djamel); R. v Ward (Brian)
[2003] EWCA Crim 2139; [2004] 3 All E.R. 135; [2004] 1 Cr. App. R. (S.) 49;
(2003) 167 J.P. 409; *Times,* July 25, 2003, CA (Crim Div) . . . . *Digested,* 03/**3719**:
Considered, 06/3650, 07/3598: *Distinguished,* 07/3597
R. v D see R. v Gordon (Gavin Stephen)
R. v D see R. v Reynolds (Michael Edwin)
R. v D see R. v Lang (Stephen Howard)
R. v D [2006] EWCA Crim 1354; [2007] 1 W.L.R. 1657; [2007] 1 All E.R. 593;
[2007] 1 Cr. App. R. 8; [2007] Crim. L.R. 390; *Times,* September 14, 2006, CA
(Crim Div) . . . . *Digested,* 06/**977**
R. v D; *joined cases* R. v Potter; R. v Heppenstall [2007] EWCA Crim 2485; (2007)
151 S.J.L.B. 1399, CA (Crim Div)
R. v D; *sub nom* R. v AD [2007] EWCA Crim 1009; (2007) 104(21) L.S.G. 26; *Times,*
May 18, 2007, CA (Crim Div) . . . . *Digested,* 07/**952**
R. v D (Anthony); *joined case* R. v S (Joe) [2006] EWCA Crim 1694; [2007] 1 Cr.
App. R. (S.) 67, CA (Crim Div) . . . . *Digested,* 07/**3785**
R. v D (Ian Malcolm) [1984] A.C. 778; [1984] 3 W.L.R. 186; [1984] 2 All E.R. 449;
(1984) 79 Cr. App. R. 313; [1984] Crim. L.R. 558; [1984] Fam. Law 311; (1984)
81 L.S.G. 2458, HL; reversing [1984] 2 W.L.R. 112; [1984] 1 All E.R. 574;
(1984) 78 Cr. App. R. 219; [1984] Crim. L.R. 103; (1983) 80 L.S.G. 2998;
(1984) 128 S.J. 63, CA (Crim Div) . . . . *Digested,* 84/**651**:
Applied, 07/888: *Considered,* 86/599, 87/790, 03/793
R. v D (Mark Gordon) [2007] Crim. L.R. 240, CC (Lewes)
R. v Da Hua Weng; *joined case* R. v Guo Xing Wang [2005] EWCA Crim 2248;
[2006] 1 Cr. App. R. (S.) 97, CA (Crim Div) . . . . *Digested,* 06/**3738**:
Considered, 07/2323
R. v Da Silva (Hilda Gondwe) [2006] EWCA Crim 1654; [2007] 1 W.L.R. 303;
[2006] 4 All E.R. 900; [2006] 2 Cr. App. R. 35; [2007] Crim. L.R. 77; *Times,*
August 4, 2006, CA (Crim Div) . . . . *Digested,* 06/**884**:
Applied, 06/260
R. v Danga (Harbeer Singh) [1992] Q.B. 476; [1992] 2 W.L.R. 277; [1992] 1 All E.R.
624; (1992) 94 Cr. App. R. 252; (1992) 13 Cr. App. R. (S.) 408; (1992) 156 J.P.
382; [1992] Crim. L.R. 219; (1992) 156 J.P.N. 382; *Times,* November 1, 1991,
CA (Crim Div) . . . . *Digested,* 92/**1450**:
Applied, 96/1941, 00/1317, 02/4047, 03/3751, 07/967: *Cited,* 95/1501
R. v Daniels (Antonio Eval) see R. v Powell (Anthony Glassford)
R. v Dartford Justices Ex p. Dhesi see R. v Manchester Stipendiary Magistrate Ex p.
Hill
R. v Dass (Rajesh Kumar) see Dass (Setting of Minimum Term), Re
R. v Davies (Anita Elizabeth) [2006] EWCA Crim 2643; [2007] 2 All E.R. 1070;
(2006) 150 S.J.L.B. 1288, CA (Crim Div)
R. v Davies (Benjamin) (Costs) [2007] 1 Costs L.R. 116, Sup Ct Costs Office
R. v Davies (Trono) see Bowe v Queen, The
R. v Davis (Aaron Christopher) see Attorney General's Reference (Nos.42, 43 and 44
of 2006), Re

R. v Davis (Iain); *joined cases* R. v Simms (Rodrigo Fernando); R. v Ellis (Marcus Junior); R. v Gregory (Michael); R. v Martin (Nathan) [2006] EWCA Crim 1155; [2006] 1 W.L.R. 3130; [2006] 4 All E.R. 648; [2006] 2 Cr. App. R. 32; [2007] Crim. L.R. 70; *Times*, June 1, 2006, CA (Crim Div) . . . . *Digested*, 06/**989**
R. v Davis (Jay) see R. v Considine (Lawrence Philip)
R. v Dawson (Russell Leslie) [2007] EWCA Crim 822; (2007) 151 S.J.L.B. 432, CA (Crim Div)
R. v Dearsley (Simon Robert) see R. v Townsend (Philip Henry)
R. v Degane (Behnam) [2006] EWCA Crim 1630; [2007] 1 Cr. App. R. (S.) 46, CA (Crim Div) . . . . *Digested*, 07/**3634**
R. v Delaney (Terry) [2006] EWCA Crim 2242; [2007] 1 Cr. App. R. (S.) 93, CA (Crim Div) . . . . *Digested*, 07/**3599**
R. v Delay (Timothy) [2006] EWCA Crim 1110; (2006) 170 J.P. 581; (2006) 170 J.P.N. 997, CA (Crim Div) . . . . *Digested*, 07/**840**
R. v Delgado-Fernandez (Elisabeth) see Attorney General's Reference (Nos.129 and 132 of 2006), Re
R. v Demarku (Agron) [2006] EWCA Crim 2049; [2007] 1 Cr. App. R. (S.) 83, CA (Crim Div) . . . . *Digested*, 07/**3764**
R. v Demers (Rejean) 2004 SCC 46; 19 B.H.R.C. 247, Sup Ct (Can) . . . . *Digested*, 07/**1008**
R. v Denton (Vincent) see R. v S
R. v Derby Magistrates Court Ex p. B [1996] A.C. 487; [1995] 3 W.L.R. 681; [1995] 4 All E.R. 526; [1996] 1 Cr. App. R. 385; (1995) 159 J.P. 785; [1996] 1 F.L.R. 513; [1996] Fam. Law 210; (1995) 159 J.P.N. 778; (1995) 145 N.L.J. 1575; [1995] 139 S.J.L.B. 219; *Times*, October 25, 1995; *Independent*, October 27, 1995, HL; reversing *Times*, October 31, 1994, DC . . . . *Digested*, 96/**1402**:
Applied, 97/1143, 02/4504, 03/451, 03/2822, 04/719: *Considered*, 99/335, 07/999: *Followed*, 00/2465
R. v Derekis (Theresa Anne) [2004] EWCA Crim 2729; [2005] 2 Cr. App. R. (S.) 1, CA (Crim Div) . . . . *Digested*, 05/**3664**:
Considered, 07/3707
R. v Devani (Maya) [2007] EWCA Crim 1926, CA (Crim Div) . . . . *Digested*, 07/**851**
R. v Devon CC Ex p. Baker; *joined cases* R. v Durham CC Ex p. Curtis; R. v Devon CC Ex p. Ruxton [1995] 1 All E.R. 73; 91 L.G.R. 479; (1994) 6 Admin. L.R. 113; [1993] C.O.D. 253; *Times*, January 21, 1993; *Independent*, February 22, 1993, CA (Civ Div); affirming [1993] C.O.D. 138; *Times*, October 20, 1992, QBD. . . . . *Digested*, 95/**88**:
Applied, 95/3252, 96/5526, 03/4083: *Considered*, 95/68, 01/6790, 07/45: *Followed*, 97/4713: *Referred to*, 98/3001
R. v Devon CC Ex p. Ruxton see R. v Devon CC Ex p. Baker
R. v Dhillon (Pritpal Sineh) [2005] EWCA Crim 2996; [2006] 1 W.L.R. 1535; [2006] 1 Cr. App. R. 15; *Times*, November 29, 2005, CA (Crim Div) . . . . *Digested*, 06/**849**:
Considered, 07/886
R. v Diafi (Karim Djamel) see R. v Czyzewski (Jozef Eugene) (Appeal against Sentence)
R. v Dica (Mohammed) [2004] EWCA Crim 1103; [2004] Q.B. 1257; [2004] 3 W.L.R. 213; [2004] 3 All E.R. 593; [2004] 2 Cr. App. R. 28; (2004) 77 B.M.L.R. 243; (2004) 101(21) L.S.G. 35; (2004) 148 S.J.L.B. 570; *Times*, May 11, 2004, CA (Crim Div) . . . . *Digested*, 04/**749**:
Applied, 05/766: *Considered*, 05/795, 07/920
R. v Djahit (Turkesh) [1999] 2 Cr. App. R. (S.) 142, CA (Crim Div) . . . . *Digested*, 99/**1137**:
Applied, 01/1282, 07/3719: *Considered*, 00/1225, 02/3928, 03/3695, 04/3412, 04/3450, 04/3452, 05/3590, 05/3707, 05/3748, 05/3751, 05/3753, 06/3695, 06/3700, 07/3633, 07/3757: *Distinguished*, 04/3454
R. v Docherty (Michael) [1999] 1 Cr. App. R. 274, CA (Crim Div) . . . . *Digested*, 99/**1016**:
Considered, 07/1025
R. v Doe (Nelson) see Attorney General's Reference (No.59 of 2006), Re
R. v Doherty (Michael Patrick) [2006] EWCA Crim 2716; (2007) 171 J.P. 79; (2007) 171 J.P.N. 346, CA (Crim Div) . . . . *Digested*, 07/**858**
R. v Donohoe (Mark Edward) [2006] EWCA Crim 2200; [2007] 1 Cr. App. R. (S.) 88; [2007] Crim. L.R. 90; *Times*, October 20, 2006, CA (Crim Div) . . . . *Digested*, 06/**912**
R. v Donohue (Ryan) see Attorney General's Reference (No.78 of 2006), Re
R. v Dorset CC Ex p. Goddard [1995] E.L.R. 109; *Times*, December 30, 1994, QBD . . . *Digested*, 95/**1935**:
Applied, 07/1258: *Distinguished*, 96/2480
R. v Dosanjh (Jaswinder Singh) see Jones (Setting of Minimum Term), Re
R. v Doughan (Christopher John) [2007] EWCA Crim 598; (2007) 171 J.P. 397; (2007) 171 J.P.N. 722; (2007) 151 S.J.L.B. 295, CA (Crim Div) . . . . *Digested*, 07/**938**
R. v Douglas (Aaron) [2006] EWCA Crim 1776; [2007] 1 Cr. App. R. (S.) 58, CA (Crim Div) . . . . *Digested*, 07/**3674**
R. v Dowd (Jeffrey); *joined case* R. v Huskins (Malcom) [2000] 1 Cr. App. R. (S.) 349, CA (Crim Div) . . . . *Digested*, 00/**1378**:
Applied, 06/3790: *Considered*, 03/3818, 07/3713
R. v DPP Ex p. B see R. v Chief Constable of Kent Ex p. L
R. v DPP Ex p. Boukemiche (Farid) see R. v DPP Ex p. Kebilene
R. v DPP Ex p. Kebelene see R. v DPP Ex p. Kebilene

R. v DPP Ex p. Kebilene; *sub nom* R. v DPP Ex p. Kebelene; *joined cases* R. v DPP Ex p. Boukemiche (Farid); R. v DPP Ex p. Souidi (Sofiane); R. v DPP Ex p. Rechachi (Fatah) [2000] 2 A.C. 326; [1999] 3 W.L.R. 972; [1999] 4 All E.R. 801; [2000] 1 Cr. App. R. 275; [2000] H.R.L.R. 93; [2000] U.K.H.R.R. 176; (2000) 2 L.G.L.R. 697; (1999) 11 Admin. L.R. 1026; [2000] Crim. L.R. 486; (1999) 96(43) L.S.G. 32; *Times*, November 2, 1999, HL; reversing [1999] 3 W.L.R. 175; (1999) 11 Admin. L.R. 785; [1999] Crim. L.R. 994; [1999] C.O.D. 207; *Times*, March 31, 1999, QBD . . . . *Digested*, 99/**1045**:
Applied, 00/921, 00/5473, 01/564, 01/5291, 01/5879, 02/3079, 03/1938, 03/2171, 04/2088, 07/53: *Cited*, 00/3230: *Considered*, 99/881, 02/795, 02/849, 02/5866, 03/761, 03/2676

R. v DPP Ex p. Manning [2001] Q.B. 330; [2000] 3 W.L.R. 463; [2001] H.R.L.R. 3; [2000] Inquest L.R. 133; [2000] Po. L.R. 172; *Times*, May 19, 2000; *Independent*, June 6, 2000, QBD (Admin) . . . . *Digested*, 00/**1096**:
Considered, 07/980

R. v DPP Ex p. Rechachi (Fatah) see R. v DPP Ex p. Kebilene
R. v DPP Ex p. Souidi (Sofiane) see R. v DPP Ex p. Kebilene
R. v Draz (Omar) see R. v Ashton (John)
R. v Drewett (Mark Clive) [2006] EWCA Crim 1140; [2007] 1 Cr. App. R. (S.) 32; [2006] Crim. L.R. 770, CA (Crim Div). . . . . *Digested*, 07/**3627**
R. v Dryden-Hall (Julie Ann) [1997] 2 Cr. App. R. (S.) 235, CA (Crim Div) . . . . *Digested*, 97/**1429**:
Considered, 07/3601

R. v Duff (Jonathan Michael) [2002] EWCA Crim 2117; [2003] 1 Cr. App. R. (S.) 88, CA (Crim Div) . . . . *Digested*, 03/**3705**:
Considered, 07/3685

R. v Duncan (Alexander Robert) [2005] EWCA Crim 3594; [2006] 2 Cr. App. R. (S.) 28; [2006] Crim. L.R. 450, CA (Crim Div) . . . . *Digested*, 07/**3658**
R. v Duncan (Andrew Peter Francis) [2006] EWCA Crim 2647; [2007] 1 Cr. App. R. (S.) 103, CA (Crim Div)
R. v Duncan (Christopher) [2006] EWCA Crim 1576; [2007] 1 Cr. App. R. (S.) 26, CA (Crim Div) . . . . *Digested*, 07/**3693**
R. v Dunn (Simon Anthony) [2006] EWCA Crim 1175; [2007] 1 Cr. App. R. (S.) 17, CA (Crim Div)
R. v Dunraven School Governors Ex p. B (A Child) [2000] B.L.G.R. 494; [2000] Ed. C.R. 291; [2000] E.L.R. 156; (2000) 97(4) L.S.G. 32; (2000) 144 S.J.L.B. 51; *Times*, February 3, 2000, CA (Civ Div); reversing *Times*, November 10, 1999, QBD . . . . *Digested*, 00/**1925**:
Applied, 01/1975, 03/1058: *Considered*, 05/1071, 07/1143: *Distinguished*, 03/1055, 04/1065

R. v Durham CC Ex p. Curtis see R. v Devon CC Ex p. Baker
R. v Durham CC Ex p. Lowther see R. (on the application of Lowther) v Durham CC
R. v E see R. v P
R. v Eagles (Andrew James) [2006] EWCA Crim 2368; [2007] 1 Cr. App. R. (S.) 99; [2007] Crim. L.R. 94, CA (Crim Div). . . . . *Digested*, 07/**3771**
R. v East London and the City Mental Health NHS Trust Ex p. von Brandenburg see R. (on the application of von Brandenburg) v East London and the City Mental Health NHS Trust
R. v East Sussex CC Ex p. Reprotech (Pebsham) Ltd see R. (on the application of Reprotech (Pebsham) Ltd) v East Sussex CC
R. v Easterbrook (Ronald Leonard) (1990-91) 12 Cr. App. R. (S.) 331; [1991] Crim. L.R. 72, CA (Crim Div) . . . . *Digested*, 92/**1328**:
Considered, 07/3616

R. v Eastlake (Nicky) [2007] EWCA Crim 603; (2007) 151 S.J.L.B. 258, CA (Crim Div). . . . . *Digested*, 07/**828**
R. v Edmonton Justices Ex p. Hughes see R. v Manchester Stipendiary Magistrate Ex p. Hill
R. v Edmunson (James Hamilton) [2007] EWCA Crim 382; [2007] 2 Cr. App. R. (S.) 63, CA (Crim Div) . . . . *Digested*, 07/**3726**
R. v Edwards (Frederick) [2006] EWCA Crim 3362; [2007] 1 Cr. App. R. (S.) 106, CA (Crim Div) . . . . *Digested*, 07/**3660**
R. v Edwards (Glyn) [2004] EWCA Crim 2923; [2005] 2 Cr. App. R. (S.) 29; (2004) 148 S.J.L.B. 1433, CA (Crim Div) . . . . *Digested*, 05/**794**:
Considered, 07/2413

R. v Edwards (Kyle Frederick) see R. v Lang (Stephen Howard)
R. v Edwards (Michelle Marie) [2006] EWCA Crim 2833; [2007] 1 Cr. App. R. (S.) 111, CA (Crim Div)
R. v Edwards (Simon) (Guilty Plea) (1994) 15 Cr. App. R. (S.) 442, CA (Crim Div) . . . *Considered*, 07/3798
R. v Egan (Jason) see R. v Norman (Shane Martin)
R. v Eley (Charles Thomas) see R. v Johnstone (Robert Alexander)
R. v Elfes (Julian Charles) [2006] EWCA Crim 2799; [2007] 1 Cr. App. R. (S.) 118, CA (Crim Div)
R. v Elliott (Gregory) [2007] EWCA Crim 1002; [2007] 2 Cr. App. R. (S.) 68, CA (Crim Div) . . . . *Digested*, 07/**3722**
R. v Ellis (Marcus Junior) see R. v Davis (Iain)

R. v Embaye (Senait Tekie) see R. v Navabi (Fraydon)
R. v Enfield LBC Ex p. TF Unwin (Roydon) 46 B.L.R. 1; (1989) 1 Admin. L.R. 51;
    [1989] C.O.D. 466; (1989) 153 L.G. Rev. 890, DC. . . . .   *Digested*, 90/**59**:
                             Considered, 94/43: *Followed*, 01/4405, 07/1197
R. v English (Philip) see R. v Powell (Anthony Glassford)
R. v Ennis-Simpson (Michael) see R. v Myers (Dean Earl)
R. v Environment Agency Ex p. Castle Cement Ltd see Castle Cement Ltd v
    Environment Agency
R. v Environment Agency Ex p. Gibson (No.2); *joined cases* R. v Environment Agency
    Ex p. Leam (No.2); R. v Environment Agency Ex p. Sellers (No.2) [1999] Env.
    L.R. 73, QBD . . . .   *Digested*, 99/**2190**:
                                      Considered, 07/1506
R. v Environment Agency Ex p. Leam (No.2) see R. v Environment Agency Ex p.
    Gibson (No.2)
R. v Environment Agency Ex p. Sellers (No.2) see R. v Environment Agency Ex p.
    Gibson (No.2)
R. v Esimu (Godfrey) [2007] EWCA Crim 1380; (2007) 171 J.P. 452; (2007) 171
    J.P.N. 799, CA (Crim Div). . . . .   *Digested*, 07/**843**
R v Evans (Ann Marie) [2006] EWCA Crim 2040; [2007] 1 Cr. App. R. (S.) 89, CA
    (Crim Div)
R. v Evans Ex p. Pinochet Ugarte (No.2) see R. v Bow Street Metropolitan Stipendiary
    Magistrate Ex p. Pinochet Ugarte (No.2)
R. v F see R. v CF
R. v F see R. v W
R. v F see Attorney General's Reference (Nos.74 and 83 of 2007), Re
R. v F see Attorney General's Reference (Nos.74 and 83 of 2007), Re
R. v F [2007] EWCA Crim 243; [2007] Q.B. 960; [2007] 3 W.L.R. 164; [2007] 2 All
    E.R. 193; [2007] 2 Cr. App. R. 3; *Times*, February 20, 2007, CA (Crim Div) . . . .   *Digested*, 07/**925**
R. v F (Jacqueline Ann) (1992) 13 Cr. App. R. (S.) 358, CA (Crim Div) . . . .   *Digested*, 93/**1185**:
                                      Considered, 07/3607
R. v F (Nathan Leon) see Attorney General's Reference (Nos.24, 25, 26, 27, 28 and 41
    of 2006), Re
R. v F Howe & Son (Engineers) Ltd [1999] 2 All E.R. 249; [1999] 2 Cr. App. R. (S.)
    37; (1999) 163 J.P. 359; [1999] I.R.L.R. 434; [1999] Crim. L.R. 238; (1999)
    163 J.P.N. 693; (1998) 95(46) L.S.G. 34; *Times*, November 27, 1998;
    Independent, November 13, 1998, CA (Crim Div).   *Digested*, 98/**2839**:
                    Applied, 99/2860, 01/3296, 03/1922, 03/1923, 06/3713, 07/986:
               Considered, 00/2968, 01/1348, 01/1350, 02/3968, 03/3715, 05/1945,
                      05/3630, 06/1971, 06/3712, 07/3655: *Followed*, 99/2858
R. v Fairhurst (Elivra Catrina) [2007] EWCA Crim 25; [2007] 2 Cr. App. R. (S.) 41, CA
    (Crim Div) . . . .   *Digested*, 07/**3746**
R. v Faraj (Shwan) [2007] EWCA Crim 1033; [2007] 2 Cr. App. R. 25; (2007)
    104(21) L.S.G. 25, CA (Crim Div). . . . .   *Digested*, 07/**887**
R. v Farish (Michael John) see Attorney General's Reference (No.6 of 2006), Re
R. v Farrar (Stuart) [2006] EWCA Crim 3261; [2007] 2 Cr. App. R. (S.) 35; [2007]
    Crim. L.R. 308, CA (Crim Div) . . . .   *Digested*, 07/**3606**:
                                      Explained, 07/3723
R. v Farrell (1862) 9 Cox C.C. 446. . . . .   *Applied*, 63/737,
                                      07/917
R. v Farrell (David); *joined case* R. v Hough Green Garage Ltd [2007] EWCA Crim
    1896; (2007) 151 S.J.L.B. 1130, CA (Crim Div)
R. v Farrell (Trevor) (Costs) [2007] 3 Costs L.R. 495, Sup Ct Costs Office
R. v Farrow (Andrew) see Attorney General's Reference (No.48 of 2006), Re
R. v Faversham and Sittingbourne Justices Ex p. Stickings (1996) 160 J.P. 801; [1996]
    C.O.D. 439; (1996) 160 J.P.N. 811; *Times*, May 9, 1996, DC . . . .   *Digested*, 96/**73**:
                                      Considered, 07/1011
R. v Fawcett (Kenneth John) (1983) 5 Cr. App. R. (S.) 158, CA (Crim Div) . . . .   *Digested*, 84/**836**:
                     Applied, 00/1335, 03/3818, 07/3785: *Cited*, 93/1025, 96/1866:
               Considered, 96/1926, 97/1511, 98/1172, 04/785, 05/3764, 06/3713,
                              06/3782: *Followed*, 01/1385
R. v Featherstone (Robert Clifford) [2007] EWCA Crim 208; [2007] 2 Cr. App. R.
    (S.) 57, CA (Crim Div) . . . .   *Digested*, 07/**3595**
R. v Feihn (Steven) see R. v Lang (Stephen Howard)
R. v Fenton (Lee) see R. v Wheatley (Jason)
R. v Fenton (Steven) [2006] EWCA Crim 2156; [2007] 1 Cr. App. R. (S.) 97, CA
    (Crim Div) . . . .   *Digested*, 07/**3738**:
                                        Considered, 07/3726
R. v Fergus (Ivan) (1994) 98 Cr. App. R. 313; (1993) 157 J.P.N. 699; *Times*, June 30,
    1993; *Independent*, June 29, 1993, CA (Crim Div) . . . .   *Digested*, 95/**1131**:
                                        Considered, 07/996

R. *v* FG (Autrefois Acquit) [2001] EWCA Crim 1215; [2001] 1 W.L.R. 1727; [2001] 2 Cr. App. R. 31; (2001) 165 J.P. 513; [2001] Crim. L.R. 898; (2001) 165 J.P.N. 585; (2001) 98(24) L.S.G. 43; (2001) 145 S.J.L.B. 126; *Times*, May 25, 2001, CA (Crim Div)   *Digested*, 01/**1061**: *Applied*, 07/984

R. *v* Field (Jason) see Attorney General's Reference (Nos.19, 20 and 21 of 2001), Re

R. *v* Fieldhouse (Paul Michael); *joined case* R. *v* Watts (Dale) [2001] 1 Cr. App. R. (S.) 104; (2001) 165 J.P. 77; [2000] Crim. L.R. 1020, CA (Crim Div)   *Digested*, 01/**1224**: *Applied*, 07/3789

R. *v* Fielding (Michael) [2006] EWCA Crim 3183; [2007] 2 Cr. App. R. (S.) 22, CA (Crim Div)   *Digested*, 07/**3763**

R. *v* Fielding (Nigel) see R. *v* Cuthbertson (Brian George)

R. *v* Finch (Andrew George) [2006] EWCA Crim 1331; [2007] Crim. L.R. 481, CA (Crim Div)

R. *v* Finch (David) see Attorney General's Reference (No.58 of 2006), Re

R. *v* Finch (David Barry) [2007] EWCA Crim 36; [2007] 1 W.L.R. 1645; [2007] 1 Cr. App. R. 33; *Times*, January 22, 2007, CA (Crim Div)   *Digested*, 07/**819**

R. *v* Finlay (Paul Anthony) [2003] EWCA Crim 3868, CA (Crim Div)   *Considered*, 05/803: *Overruled*, 07/899

R. *v* Flattery (John) (1876-77) L.R. 2 Q.B.D. 410; (1887) 13 Cox C.C. 388, Crown Cases Reserved   *Considered*, 07/921

R. *v* Fletcher (Clare) [2005] EWCA Crim 3284; [2006] 2 Cr. App. R. (S.) 24, CA (Crim Div)   *Digested*, 07/**3711**

R. *v* Fletcher (Joseph) see R. *v* Cottrell (Steven)

R. *v* Ford (Kevin) [2005] EWCA Crim 1358; [2006] 1 Cr. App. R. (S.) 36; [2005] Crim. L.R. 807, CA (Crim Div)   *Digested*, 06/**3774**: *Applied*, 07/993

R. *v* Foster (Mark); *joined cases* R. *v* Birmingham (Gareth); R. *v* Kempster (Mark); R. *v* Newman (Lee) [2007] EWCA Crim 2869; (2007) 151 S.J.L.B. 1594; *Times*, December 10, 2007, CA (Civ Div)   *Digested*, 07/**994**

R. *v* Fowles (Herbert) see R. *v* May (Raymond George)

R. *v* Frank (Timothy Aaron) [2005] EWCA Crim 3481; [2006] 2 Cr. App. R. (S.) 37, CA (Crim Div)   *Digested*, 07/**3734**

R. *v* Frazer (John William) [2006] EWCA Crim 1977; [2007] 1 Cr. App. R. (S.) 69; [2006] Crim. L.R. 1007, CA (Crim Div)

R. *v* French (Tanya) see Attorney General's Reference (Nos.14 and 15 of 2006), Re

R. *v* Fulton (Robert William) [2006] EWCA Crim 960; [2007] 1 Cr. App. R. (S.) 5, CA (Crim Div)   *Digested*, 07/**3751**

R. *v* Furby (Andrew) [2005] EWCA Crim 3147; [2006] 2 Cr. App. R. (S.) 8; [2006] Crim. L.R. 259, CA (Crim Div)   *Digested*, 06/**3764**: *Considered*, 06/3744, 07/3675, 07/3782

R. *v* G see R. *v* Pepper (Jeremy Paul)

R. *v* G see R. *v* McNee (Michael)

R. *v* G; *joined case* R. *v* B [2004] EWCA Crim 1368; [2004] 1 W.L.R. 2932; [2004] 2 Cr. App. R. 37; (2004) 101(25) L.S.G. 27; (2004) 148 S.J.L.B. 696; *Times*, June 8, 2004, CA (Crim Div)   *Digested*, 04/**872**: *Applied*, 07/935

R. *v* G [2006] EWCA Crim 3294; [2007] 2 Cr. App. R. (S.) 27, CA (Crim Div)   *Digested*, 07/**3605**

R. *v* G [2006] EWCA Crim 3277; [2007] 2 Cr. App. R. (S.) 32, CA (Crim Div)   *Digested*, 07/**3788**

R. *v* G [2006] EWCA Crim 821; [2006] 1 W.L.R. 2052; [2006] 2 Cr. App. R. 17; [2006] H.R.L.R. 28; [2006] Crim. L.R. 930; *Times*, May 9, 2006, CA (Crim Div)   *Digested*, 06/**830**: *Considered*, 07/258

R. *v* G (Entrapment) see Attorney General's Reference (No.3 of 2000), Re

R. *v* G (Martine) [2006] EWCA Crim 3097; [2007] 2 Cr. App. R. (S.) 14, CA (Crim Div)   *Digested*, 07/**3603**

R. *v* G (Richard) see Attorney General's Reference (No.15 of 2000), Re

R. *v* Gabriel (Janis) [2006] EWCA Crim 229; [2007] 1 W.L.R. 2272; [2007] 2 Cr. App. R. 11; [2006] Crim. L.R. 852, CA (Crim Div)   *Distinguished*, 07/909

R. *v* Galbraith (George Charles) [1981] 1 W.L.R. 1039; [1981] 2 All E.R. 1060; (1981) 73 Cr. App. R. 124; [1981] Crim. L.R. 648; (1981) 125 S.J. 442, CA (Crim Div) .   *Digested*, 81/**513**: *Applied*, 89/849, 90/1175, 93/725, 93/1869, 96/1420, 97/1339, 02/743, 03/959, 04/928: *Cited*, 00/1022: *Considered*, 88/651, 89/769, 90/1043, 95/1060, 95/1128, 96/1635, 07/13, 07/1004: *Distinguished*, 07/29: *Followed*, 96/1393, 97/1164, 01/1821

R. *v* Ganley (Stephen) [2001] 1 Cr. App. R. (S.) 17; *Times*, June 7, 2000; *Independent*, May 9, 2000, CA (Crim Div)   *Digested*, 00/**1319**: *Applied*, 07/3789: *Considered*, 01/1475

R. *v* Gant (Jade Frances) [2007] EWCA Crim 901; [2007] 2 Cr. App. R. (S.) 100, CA (Crim Div)

R. *v* Garvey (Wayne) see Attorney General's Reference (No.104 of 2004), Re

R. *v* Gateshead Justices Ex p. Ives see R. *v* Manchester Stipendiary Magistrate Ex p. Hill

R. *v* Gay (Alan Thomas) see Attorney General's Reference (No.25 of 2004), Re

R. *v* Gaynor (David Anthony) see R. *v* Szypusz (Simeon)
R. *v* Gazzard (Royston John) see R. *v* RG
R. *v* Gbedje (Nanguy Ruddy); *joined case* R. *v* Owoola (Donga James) [2007] EWCA
     Crim 730; [2007] 2 Cr. App. R. (S.) 89, CA (Crim Div)
R. *v* GC see Attorney General's Reference (No.4 of 2000), Re
R. *v* Geddes (Daniel Peter) see Attorney General's Reference (No.87 of 2006), Re
R. *v* George (Barry) [2007] EWCA Crim 2722; (2007) 151 S.J.L.B. 1498, CA (Crim
     Div)
R. *v* George (Christabelle) see R. *v* Hart (Clifford)
R. *v* Ghafoor (Imran Hussain) [2002] EWCA Crim 1857; [2003] 1 Cr. App. R. (S.) 84;
     (2002) 166 J.P. 601; [2002] Crim. L.R. 739; (2002) 166 J.P.N. 744, CA (Crim
     Div) . . . . *Digested, 02/***4047***:*
                 Applied, 04/3380: Considered, 05/3765, 06/3890: Followed, 07/3774
R. *v* Giga (Zulfikar Ali) [2007] EWCA Crim 345; [2007] Crim. L.R. 571, CA (Crim Div)
R. *v* Gill (Steven) (Costs) [2006] 5 Costs L.R. 837, Sup Ct Costs Office . . . . *Digested, 07/***954***
R. *v* Gilliatt (Paul William) [2006] EWCA Crim 2020; [2007] 1 Cr. App. R. (S.) 78, CA
     (Crim Div) . . . . *Digested, 07/***3707***
R. *v* Gittins (Marvin); *joined case* R. *v* Khan (Safdar) [2007] EWCA Crim 806; [2007]
     4 Costs L.R. 549, CA (Crim Div)
R. *v* Glanville (Peter) see Attorney General's Reference (Nos.24, 25, 26, 27, 28 and 29
     of 2006), Re
R. *v* Glave (Heathcliffe) see R. *v* Lang (Stephen Howard)
R. *v* Gleeson (John Vincent) [2003] EWCA Crim 3357; [2004] 1 Cr. App. R. 29;
     [2004] Crim. L.R. 579; (2003) 100(42) L.S.G. 31; *Times,* October 30, 2003, CA
     (Crim Div) . . . . *Digested, 04/***847***:*
                                                     Considered, 07/988
R. *v* Glover (Ian Robert) see Attorney General's Reference (No.112 of 2006), Re
R. *v* Gokal (Abbas Kassimali) (Unreported, March 11, 1999), CA (Crim Div) . . . . *Considered, 07/3652*
R. *v* Golding (Jamie) [2007] EWCA Crim 118; [2007] 2 Cr. App. R. (S.) 49, CA (Crim
     Div) . . . . *Digested, 07/***3638***
R. *v* Golding (Ronald Lonford) [2006] EWCA Crim 1965; [2007] 1 Cr. App. R. (S.)
     79; [2006] M.H.L.R. 272; [2007] Crim. L.R. 170, CA (Crim Div) . . . . *Digested, 07/***3585***
R. *v* Goldman (Terence) [2001] EWCA Crim 1684; [2001] Crim. L.R. 822, CA (Crim
     Div) . . . . *Considered, 07/1017*
R. *v* Goldsmith (Harold Egan) see R. *v* Avis (Tony)
R. *v* Goluchowski (Pawel) [2006] EWCA Crim 1972, CA (Crim Div) . . . . *Digested, 07/***904***
R. *v* Gonzalez (Carmen Janeth) see R. *v* Sarmiento (Danielle)
R. *v* Goodman (Aaron Leonard) see Goodman (Setting of Minimum Term), Re
R. *v* Goodwin (William) [1944] K.B. 518; [1997] Costs L.R. (Core Vol.) 425; (1945)
     30 Cr. App. R. 20, CCA . . . . *Applied, 07/1028*
R. *v* Goodyear (Karl) [2005] EWCA Crim 888; [2005] 1 W.L.R. 2532; [2005] 3 All
     E.R. 117; [2005] 2 Cr. App. R. 20; [2006] 1 Cr. App. R. (S.) 6; [2005] Crim. L.R.
     659; *Times,* April 21, 2005, CA (Crim Div) . . . . *Digested, 05/***893***:*
                Applied, 06/1971, 07/3666: Considered, 07/3678: Followed, 06/3867
R. *v* Gordon (Gavin Stephen); *joined case* R. *v* D; R. *v* McManus (Kevin Peter); R. *v*
     Shaukat (Mirza Hamayou); R. *v* Pusey (Lloyd Aaron); R. *v* Taylor (Mark William)
     [2007] EWCA Crim 165; [2007] 1 W.L.R. 2117; [2007] 2 All E.R. 768; [2007] 2
     Cr. App. R. (S.) 66; [2007] Crim. L.R. 402; (2007) 151 S.J.L.B. 264; *Times,*
     February 13, 2007, CA (Crim Div) . . . . *Digested, 07/***3735***:*
                                                    Applied, 07/966
R. *v* Gordon (Tyrone Leslie) see R. *v* Johnson (Paul Anthony)
R. *v* Gould (Robert Sidney) see R. *v* Aranguren (Jose de Jesus)
R. *v* Governor of Brixton Prison Ex p. Armah (No.1) see Armah *v* Ghana (No.1)
R. *v* Governor of Whitemoor Prison Ex p. Main see R. *v* Secretary of State for the
     Home Department Ex p. Simms
R. *v* Gowan (Jason) [2007] EWCA Crim 1360; [2007] Crim. L.R. 812, CA (Crim Div) . *Digested, 07/***939***
R. *v* Gowan (Lloyd) see R. *v* Black (Joseph Christopher)
R. *v* Graham (Garry Allan) see R. *v* Graham (Hemamali Krishna)
R. *v* Graham (Hemamali Krishna); *joined cases* R. *v* Bramich (David); R. *v* Price (Paul
     Graham); R. *v* Graham (Garry Allan); R. *v* Marsh (Terence Colin); R. *v* Ali (Sajid
     Pasha); R. *v* Kansal (Rupe Lal) [1997] 1 Cr. App. R. 302; [1997] Crim. L.R. 340;
     (1996) 93(44) L.S.G. 29; (1996) 140 S.J.L.B. 253; *Times,* October 28, 1996;
     Independent, October 30, 1996, CA (Crim Div) . . . . *Digested, 96/***1532***:*
                     Applied, 97/1228, 98/892, 02/809: Approved, 00/5480:
                     Considered, 97/1224, 97/1226, 97/1227, 97/1249, 07/971:
           Distinguished, 07/869: Followed, 97/1126: Referred to, 97/1225, 97/1229,
                                        97/1230, 97/1231, 97/1304
R. *v* Gray (Benedict Matthew) [2005] EWCA Crim 1238; [2006] 1 Cr. App. R. (S.) 21,
     CA (Crim Div) . . . . *Digested, 06/***3814***:*
                                     Applied, 07/3775: Followed, 06/3812
R. *v* Gray (Robert Lee) [2007] EWCA Crim 979; [2007] 2 Cr. App. R. (S.) 78, CA
     (Crim Div) . . . . *Digested, 07/***3679***

R. v Grays Justices Ex p. Low [1990] 1 Q.B. 54; [1989] 2 W.L.R. 948; [1988] 3 All
  E.R. 834; (1989) 88 Cr. App. R. 291; (1988) 152 J.P. 627; [1989] Crim. L.R. 69;
  (1988) 152 J.P.N. 687; (1988) 138 N.L.J. Rep. 159; *Independent*, May 20,
  1988, DC. . . . .   *Digested*, 89/**723**:
                                                                                                     Applied, 07/53
R. v Green (Ashley) see Attorney General's Reference (No.35 of 2006), Re
R. v Green (Mark) [2007] EWCA Crim 1248; [2007] 3 All E.R. 751; *Times*, June 15,
  2007, CA (Crim Div) . . . .   *Digested*, 07/**949**
R. v Green (Peter Donovan) [2002] EWCA Crim 1501, CA (Crim Div) . . . .   *Applied*, 04/3278:
                                                                                                     Considered, 07/921
R. v Green (Richard John) see R. v Abdroikov (Nurlon)
R. v Gregory (Michael) see R. v Davis (Iain)
R. v Gregson (Kathleen Mary) (1993) 14 Cr. App. R. (S.) 85, CA (Crim Div) . . . .   *Digested*, 93/**1242**:
                                            Cited, 94/1324: *Considered*, 94/1322, 98/1325, 07/3712
R. v Griffiths (Philip); *joined case* R. v Pattison (Leslie Dennis) [2006] EWCA Crim
  2155; [2007] 1 Cr. App. R. (S.) 95, CA (Crim Div) . . . .   *Digested*, 07/**3685**
R. v Grindy (Brian) [2006] NICA 10; [2006] N.I. 290, CA (Crim Div) (NI) . . . .   *Digested*, 07/**4477**
R. v Guang Jie Li see Attorney General's Reference (No.54 of 2006), Re
R. v Guider (James Keith) [2006] EWCA Crim 2275; (2006) 150 S.J.L.B. 1153, CA
  (Crim Div) . . . .   *Digested*, 07/**3593**
R. v Guidera (Michael) see R. v Lang (Stephen Howard)
R. v Gunner (James) see Attorney General's Reference (No.147 of 2006), Re
R. v Guo Xing Wang see R. v Da Hua Weng
R. v Gyima (Edward); *joined case* R. v Adjei (Francis) [2007] EWCA Crim 429;
  [2007] Crim. L.R. 890, CA (Crim Div)
R. v H see R. v S
R. v H see Attorney General's Reference (No.126 of 2006), Re
R. v H; *joined case* R. v C [2004] UKHL 3; [2004] 2 A.C. 134; [2004] 2 W.L.R. 335;
  [2004] 1 All E.R. 1269; [2004] 2 Cr. App. R. 10; [2004] H.R.L.R. 20; 16
  B.H.R.C. 332; (2004) 101(8) L.S.G. 29; (2004) 148 S.J.L.B. 183; *Times*,
  February 6, 2004; *Independent*, February 10, 2004; affirming [2003] EWCA
  Crim 2847; [2003] 1 W.L.R. 3006; [2004] 1 Cr. App. R. 17; (2003) 100(43)
  L.S.G. 31; *Times*, October 24, 2003; *Independent*, November 14, 2003, CA (Crim
  Div) . . . .   *Digested*, 04/**798**:
                                  Applied, 05/840: *Considered*, 07/1025: *Followed*, 05/875
R. v H; *joined case* R. v P [2006] EWCA Crim 2385, CA (Crim Div) . . . .   *Considered*, 07/3598
R. v H; *joined cases* R. v Lovegrove (David Lee); R. v Stevens (Cyril John) [2006]
  EWCA Crim 255; [2006] 2 Cr. App. R. (S.) 68; (2006) 170 J.P. 362; [2006]
  Crim. L.R. 569; (2006) 170 J.P.N. 595; (2006) 150 S.J.L.B. 167; *Times*,
  February 24, 2006, CA (Crim Div) . . . .   *Digested*, 06/**3639**:
                                                                                                     Considered, 07/3738
R. v H (Interlocutory Application: Disclosure) [2007] UKHL 7; [2007] 2 A.C. 270;
  [2007] 2 W.L.R. 364; [2007] 3 All E.R. 269; [2007] 2 Cr. App. R. 6; [2007]
  Crim. L.R. 731; (2007) 151 S.J.L.B. 332; *Times*, March 2, 2007, HL; affirming
  [2006] EWCA Crim 1975; [2007] 1 Cr. App. R. 21; *Times*, August 1, 2006, CA
  (Crim Div) . . . .   *Digested*, 07/**981**
R. v H (Tyrone) [2002] EWCA Crim 2988, CA (Crim Div) . . . .   *Applied*, 07/1023
R. v Hadley (Paul) see R. v Suchedina (Hasnain)
R. v Hall (Andrew Mark) [2007] EWCA Crim 195; [2007] 2 Cr. App. R. (S.) 42, CA
  (Crim Div) . . . .   *Digested*, 07/**3710**
R. v Hall-Chung (Teon) [2007] EWCA Crim 3429; (2007) 151 S.J.L.B. 1020, CA
  (Crim Div)
R. v Hallam (Sam) [2007] EWCA Crim 966; (2007) 151 S.J.L.B. 433, CA (Crim Div)
R. v Hamar (Laszlo); *sub nom* R. v LH (A Juvenile) (Manslaughter: Sentencing)
  [2001] EWCA Crim 114; [2001] 2 Cr. App. R. (S.) 61, CA (Crim Div). . . . .   *Digested*, 01/**1391**:
                                                                                                     Considered, 07/3797
R. v Hamilton (Gerald Anthony) see R. v Johnson (Paul Anthony)
R. v Hamilton (Simon Austin) [2007] EWCA Crim 2062; (2007) 104(34) L.S.G. 28;
  (2007) 157 N.L.J. 1234; *Times*, October 16, 2007, CA (Crim Div) . . . .   *Digested*, 07/**916**
R. v Hammersmith and Fulham LBC Ex p. Beddowes [1987] Q.B. 1050; [1987] 2
  W.L.R. 263; [1987] 1 All E.R. 369; (1986) 18 H.L.R. 458; 85 L.G.R. 270; [1987]
  R.V.R. 189; (1986) 83 L.S.G. 3001; (1986) 130 S.J. 696, CA (Civ Div) . . . .   *Digested*, 87/**1867**:
                                                                                                     Distinguished, 07/2155
R. v Hammersmith and Fulham LBC Ex p. M; *joined cases* R. v Lambeth LBC Ex p. P;
  R. v Westminster City Council Ex p. A; R. v Lambeth LBC Ex p. X (1998) 30
  H.L.R. 10; (1997) 9 Admin. L.R. 504; (1997-98) 1 C.C.L. Rep. 85; *Times*,
  February 19, 1997; *Independent*, February 27, 1997, CA (Civ Div); affirming
  (1997-98) 1 C.C.L. Rep. 69; [1997] C.O.D. 140; (1996) 93(42) L.S.G. 28;
  (1996) 140 S.J.L.B. 222; *Times*, October 10, 1996; *Independent*, October 16,
  1996, QBD . . . .   *Digested*, 97/**2885**:
                                  Applied, 98/3007, 00/4147, 06/2216: *Considered*, 97/4720, 99/4621,
                                  02/4288, 04/2020, 04/2020, 07/2312: *Followed*, 97/3429, 03/4068:
                                                                                     Referred to, 97/2884, 98/4571
R. v Hanson (Brian) see R. v Thompson (Glyn)

R. v Harding (Paul William) see Attorney General's Reference (Nos.68 and 92 of 2007), Re

R. v Hardison (Casey) [2006] EWCA Crim 1502; [2007] 1 Cr. App. R. (S.) 37, CA (Crim Div) . . . . *Digested*, 07/**3721**

R. v Hardwick (Glenys Margaret) [2006] EWCA Crim 969; [2007] 1 Cr. App. R. (S.) 11, CA (Crim Div)

R. v Hardwicke (Joseph Philip); *joined case* R. v Thwaites (Stefan Peter) [2001] Crim. L.R. 220; *Times*, November 16, 2000, CA (Crim Div) . . . . *Digested*, 00/**917**: *Applied*, 07/1953

R. v Hardy (James Andrew) see Attorney General's Reference (No.1 of 2007), Re

R. v Hargreaves (Stephen Lee) see R. v S

R. v Harper (Costs) [2007] 5 Costs L.R. 862, Sup Ct Costs Office

R. v Harper (Roger) see R. v Welcher (Anthony Frederick)

R. v Harries (Gavin Wade) [2007] EWCA Crim 820; *Times*, March 26, 2007, CA (Crim Div) . . . . *Digested*, 07/**997**

R. v Harries (Michael John); *joined cases* R. v S (Robert Michael); R. v B; R. v S; R. v Kai Ho Fan [2007] EWCA Crim 1622; [2007] Crim. L.R. 820; *Times*, July 9, 2007, CA (Crim Div) . . . . *Digested*, 07/**3624**

R. v Harris (Christopher) see R. v O'Brien (Karl)

R. v Harris (Joseph) [2006] EWCA Crim 3303; [2007] 2 Cr. App. R. (S.) 37, CA (Crim Div) . . . . *Digested*, 07/**3577**

R. v Harris (Melvin Sidney) [2006] EWCA Crim 1864; [2007] 1 Cr. App. R. (S.) 64, CA (Crim Div) . . . . *Digested*, 07/**3637**

R. v Harrison (Richard James) see R. v Johnstone (Robert Alexander)

R. v Harrison (Thomas Robert) [2006] EWCA Crim 18, CA (Civ Div) . . . . *Distinguished*, 07/3710

R. v Hart (Clifford); *joined cases* R. v George (Christabelle); R. v Clarke (Jason); R. v Brown (Darren Junior) [2006] EWCA Crim 3239; [2007] 1 Cr. App. R. 31; [2007] 2 Cr. App. R. (S.) 34; [2007] Crim. L.R. 313; *Times*, February 16, 2007, CA (Crim Div) . . . . *Digested*, 07/**968**

R. v Hart (Stanley) see R. v Jackson (Dennis James)

R. v Hartley (Stewart Joseph) [2006] EWCA Crim 3006; [2007] 2 Cr. App. R. (S.) 13, CA (Crim Div). . . . . *Digested*, 07/**3744**

R. v Hartrey (Michael Patrick) see R. v Oliver (Mark David)

R. v Harvey (Calvin David) see Attorney General's Reference (No.47 of 2000), Re

R. v Hastings and Rother Magistrates Court Ex p. Anscombe (1998) 162 J.P. 340; [1998] Crim. L.R. 812; (1998) 162 J.P.N. 387, QBD [*Ex rel.* Lisa Hatch, Pupil Barrister, 4 King's Bench Walk, Temple, London] . . . . *Digested*, 98/**1149**: *Considered*, 07/950

R. v Hathaway (Scott) see Attorney General's Reference (Nos.104, 105 and 106 of 2006), Re

R. v Hatton (Christoher) see Attorney General's Reference (No.196 of 2006), Re

R. v Havell (Darren); *joined case* R. v Miller (Gordon) [2006] EWCA Crim 735; [2006] 2 Cr. App. R. (S.) 97, CA (Crim Div) . . . . *Digested*, 07/**3582**

R. v Hawkes (John Clayton) see Attorney General's Reference (Nos.68 and 92 of 2007), Re

R. v Hayes (Andrew Michael) see R. v Liddle (Mark) (Appeal against Sentence)

R. v Hayward (John Victor) (No.2) see R. v Jones (Anthony William)

R. v Haywood (John Victor) see R. v Jones (Anthony William)

R. v Heard (Kevin Phillip) see R. v Corran (Ben)

R. v Heard (Lee) [2007] EWCA Crim 125; [2007] 3 W.L.R. 475; [2007] 3 All E.R. 306; [2007] 1 Cr. App. R. 37; [2007] Crim. L.R. 654; (2007) 104(9) L.S.G. 32; (2007) 151 S.J.L.B. 259; *Times*, March 6, 2007, CA (Crim Div). . . . . *Digested*, 07/**876**

R. v Hedworth (Peter John) [1997] 1 Cr. App. R. 421, CA (Crim Div). . . . . *Digested*, 96/**1611**: *Applied*, 98/990, 04/855, 07/981

R. v Held (Deborah) [2006] EWCA Crim 2174; [2007] 1 Cr. App. R. (S.) 24, CA (Crim Div) . . . . *Digested*, 07/**3741**

R. v Hendy-Freegard (Costs) [2007] 5 Costs L.R. 776, Sup Ct Costs Office

R. v Hendy-Freegard (Robert) [2007] EWCA Crim 1236; [2007] 3 W.L.R. 488; [2007] 2 Cr. App. R. 27; [2007] Crim. L.R. 986; (2007) 151 S.J.L.B. 708; *Times*, May 30, 2007, CA (Crim Div) . . . . *Digested*, 07/**888**

R. v Heppenstall see R. v D

R. v Herbert (Stephen Ronald) see Attorney General's Reference (Nos.120 and 121 of 2004), Re

R. v Herbert (William Andrew) see Attorney General's Reference (No.142 of 2006), Re

R. v Hesketh (Christopher John) [2006] EWCA Crim 2596; (2006) 150 S.J.L.B. 1468, CA (Crim Div) . . . . *Digested*, 07/**3613**

R. v Hibbert (Glen Raymond) [2001] EWCA Crim 2847; [2002] 2 Cr. App. R. (S.) 29, CA (Crim Div) . . . . *Considered*, 07/3643

R. v Hickson (Jeffrey) [2001] EWCA Crim 1595; [2002] 1 Cr. App. R. (S.) 71, CA (Crim Div) . . . . *Digested*, 02/**3923**: *Considered*, 03/3704, 07/3679

R. v Highton (Edward Paul); *joined cases* R. v Carp (Anthony Mark); R. v Van Nguyen (Dong) [2005] EWCA Crim 1985; [2005] 1 W.L.R. 3472; [2006] 1 Cr. App. R. 7; [2006] Crim. L.R. 52; *Times*, September 2, 2005; *Times*, August 9, 2005, CA (Crim Div) . . . .   *Digested*, 05/**726**:
                                    Applied, 07/995: *Considered*, 06/780

R. v Hill (Costs) [2007] 5 Costs L.R. 788, Sup Ct Costs Office

R. v Hindawi (Nezar Nawat) (1988) 10 Cr. App. R. (S.) 104, CA (Crim Div) . . . .   *Digested*, 90/**1201**:
                                    Considered, 07/3691

R. v Hipwell (James) [2006] EWCA Crim 736; [2006] 2 Cr. App. R. (S.) 98, CA (Crim Div) . . . .   *Digested*, 07/**3645**

R. v HM Coroner for Exeter and East Devon Ex p. Palmer [2000] Inquest L.R. 78, CA (Civ Div) . . . .   *Considered*, 07/13

R. v HM Coroner for Inner London South District Ex p. Douglas-Williams [1999] 1 All E.R. 344; (1998) 162 J.P. 751; [2003] Lloyd's Rep. Med. 317; [1998] C.O.D. 358; *Times*, September 4, 1998, CA (Civ Div) . . . .   *Digested*, 98/**42**:
                       Applied, 01/25, 04/36: *Considered*, 07/13

R. v HM Coroner for North Humberside and Scunthorpe Ex p. Jamieson [1995] Q.B. 1; [1994] 3 W.L.R. 82; [1994] 3 All E.R. 972; (1994) 158 J.P. 1011; [1994] 5 Med. L.R. 217; [1994] C.O.D. 455; *Times*, April 28, 1994; *Independent*, April 27, 1994, CA (Civ Div); affirming [1994] C.O.D. 173; *Times*, July 23, 1993; *Independent*, October 18, 1993; *Independent*, October 4, 1993; *Guardian*, July 12, 1993, QBD . . . .   *Digested*, 94/**631**:
         Applied, 00/50, 01/26, 02/26, 03/13, 04/36, 06/16, 06/17, 07/27:
       Considered, 95/872, 95/873, 96/42, 96/44, 96/49, 97/39, 00/49, 01/27,
                     02/25, 04/12, 04/38, 05/17, 06/4528: *Disapproved*, 04/37

R. v HM Coroner for Southwark Ex p. Hicks [1987] 1 W.L.R. 1624; [1987] 2 All E.R. 140; (1987) 151 J.P. 441; (1987) 131 S.J. 1590, QBD . . . .   *Digested*, 87/**533**:
       Applied, 91/582, 07/11: *Considered*, 92/593, 93/593, 93/597, 94/633,
                                94/637, 94/638, 97/39

R. v HM Coroner for West Yorkshire Ex p. Sacker see R. (on the application of Sacker) v HM Coroner for West Yorkshire

R. v HM Coroner for Western Somerset Ex p. Middleton see R. (on the application of Middleton) v HM Coroner for Western Somerset

R. v HM Queen in Council Ex p. Vijayatunga; *sub nom* R. v University of London Ex p. Vijayatunga; R. v Committee of the Judicial Committee of the Privy Council acting for the Visitor of the University of London Ex p. Vijayatunga [1990] 2 Q.B. 444; [1989] 3 W.L.R. 13; [1989] 2 All E.R. 843; [1989] C.O.D. 440; (1989) 133 S.J. 818; *Times*, March 30, 1989; *Independent*, March 16, 1989; *Guardian*, April 4, 1989; *Daily Telegraph*, April 13, 1989, CA (Civ Div); affirming [1988] Q.B. 322; [1988] 2 W.L.R. 106; [1987] 3 All E.R. 204; (1988) 132 S.J. 52, QBD . . .   *Digested*, 89/**1383**:
                Applied, 99/1934, 07/1281: *Considered*, 97/3365

R. v Ho (Toon Chin) see R. v Johnstone (Robert Alexander)

R. v Hobbs (Darren Wayne) see R. v Hobbs (Stephen Paul)

R. v Hobbs (John William) see R. v Hobbs (Stephen Paul)

R. v Hobbs (Stephen Paul); *joined cases* R. v Hobbs (John William); R. v Hobbs (Darren Wayne); R. v Charge (Warren James) [2002] EWCA Crim 387; [2002] 2 Cr. App. R. 22; [2002] 2 Cr. App. R. (S.) 93; [2002] Crim. L.R. 414, CA (Crim Div) . . . .   *Digested*, 02/**3901**:
                                    Considered, 07/3624

R. v Hobson (Mark) see Jones (Setting of Minimum Term), Re

R. v Hodgson (Rowland Jack) (1968) 52 Cr. App. R. 113; [1968] Crim. L.R. 46, CA (Crim Div) . . . .   *Digested*, 68/**848**:
       Applied, 88/977, 96/1987, 96/2049, 97/1645, 00/1346, 02/3878, 07/3777:
        Approved, 90/1350, 99/1250: *Considered*, 85/813, 86/838, 90/1351, 91/1161,
          92/1329, 93/1211, 94/1297, 96/1912, 96/1985, 96/1986, 96/1989, 98/1233,
                 98/1346, 99/1251, 06/3898: *Followed*, 96/2050

R. v Hodson (Phillip) see R. v Cain (Alan John)

R. v Hogan (Simon) [2006] EWCA Crim 2691; [2007] 1 Cr. App. R. (S.) 110, CA (Crim Div)

R. v Hogg (Brian Maurice) [2007] EWCA Crim 1357; [2007] Crim. L.R. 990, CA (Crim Div)

R. v Holbrook (Lee David) see R. v Last (Emma)

R. v Holder (Keiffer) see Attorney General's Reference (Nos.24, 25, 26, 27, 28 and 29 of 2006), Re

R. v Hollywood (Paul) (1990-91) 12 Cr. App. R. (S.) 325; (1990) 154 J.P. 705; [1990] Crim. L.R. 817; (1990) 154 J.P.N. 506; *Times*, June 28, 1990; *Independent*, July 9, 1990; *Daily Telegraph*, August 20, 1990, CA (Crim Div) . . .   *Digested*, 92/**1296**:
                                    Considered, 07/967

R. v Holman (Jean-Paul) [2006] EWCA Crim 1638; [2007] 1 Cr. App. R. (S.) 52, CA (Crim Div) . . . .   *Digested*, 07/**3643**

R. v Honore (James) see R. v Reynolds (Michael Edwin)

R. v Hoque (Abdul) see Attorney General's Reference (Nos.108, 109, 110 and 111 of 2006), Re

R. v Horseferry Road Magistrates Court Ex p. Bennett (No.1); *sub nom* Bennett v Horseferry Road Magistrates Court [1994] 1 A.C. 42; [1993] 3 W.L.R. 90; [1993] 3 All E.R. 138; (1994) 98 Cr. App. R. 114; [1994] C.O.D. 123; (1993) 157 J.P.N. 506; (1993) 143 N.L.J. 955; (1993) 137 S.J.L.B. 159; *Times*, June 25, 1993; *Independent*, July 1, 1993, HL; reversing [1993] 2 All E.R. 474; (1993) 97 Cr. App. R. 29; (1993) 157 J.P. 713; [1993] C.O.D. 22; (1993) 157 J.P.N. 189; (1993) 137 S.J.L.B. 159; *Times*, September 1, 1992; *Independent*, September 14, 1992, QBD . . . . *Digested*, 93/**1867**:
Applied, 94/658, 98/984, 99/5205, 07/53, 07/1007: *Considered*, 94/662, 95/906, 95/2287, 95/5744, 96/1541, 96/1599, 97/1256, 97/1257, 97/1375, 99/485, 99/881, 99/5215, 05/3343, 06/973, 06/2200: *Distinguished*, 94/2137, 98/260, 98/2353, 02/1593

R. v Horseferry Road Magistrates Court Ex p. K [1997] Q.B. 23; [1996] 3 W.L.R. 68; [1996] 3 All E.R. 719; [1996] 2 Cr. App. R. 574; (1996) 160 J.P. 441; (1997) 33 B.M.L.R. 28; [1997] Crim. L.R. 129; (1996) 160 J.P.N. 482; (1996) 93(11) L.S.G. 29; (1996) 140 S.J.L.B. 64; *Times*, February 22, 1996, QBD . . . . *Digested*, 96/**1642**:
Applied, 07/934: *Approved*, 97/1199

R. v Horton (Gareth Richard) see Horton (Setting of Minimum Term), Re

R. v Hosier (Kevin James) see R. v Suchedina (Hasnain)

R. v Hough (Charlotte Helen) (1984) 6 Cr. App. R. (S.) 406; [1985] Crim. L.R. 248, CA (Crim Div) . . . . *Digested*, 85/**758**:
Considered, 93/1001: *Distinguished*, 07/3686

R. v Hough Green Garage Ltd see R. v Farrell (David)

R. v Houghton (Andrew) [1982] Crim. L.R. 112, CA (Crim Div) . . . . *Digested*, 82/**640**:
Considered, 07/904

R. v Howden (Matthew) [2006] EWCA Crim 1691; [2007] 1 Cr. App. R. (S.) 31, CA (Crim Div) . . . . *Digested*, 07/**967**

R. v Howe (Paul Alfred) [2006] EWCA Crim 3147; [2007] 2 Cr. App. R. (S.) 11; [2007] Crim. L.R. 395, CA (Crim Div) . . . . *Digested*, 07/**3665**:
Applied, 07/3624

R. v Howell (Ian Lloyd) [2006] EWCA Crim 860; [2006] 2 Cr. App. R. (S.) 115; [2006] Crim. L.R. 763, CA (Crim Div) . . . . *Digested*, 06/**3682**:
Considered, 07/3735

R. v HTM Ltd [2006] EWCA Crim 1156; [2007] 2 All E.R. 665; [2006] I.C.R. 1383, CA (Crim Div) . . . . *Digested*, 06/**1970**

R. v Huggins (Raffael) [2007] EWCA Crim 732; [2007] 2 Cr. App. R. 8; [2007] Crim. L.R. 798; *Times*, January 23, 2007, CA (Crim Div)

R. v Hughes (Alston Frederick) see R. v Cuthbertson (Brian George)

R. v Hulme (Mark Simon) [2006] EWCA Crim 2899; [2007] 1 Cr. App. R. 26; [2007] Crim. L.R. 407, CA (Crim Div). . . . . *Digested*, 07/**857**

R. v Humble (John Samuel) [2006] EWCA Crim 2775; [2007] 1 Cr. App. R. (S.) 113, CA (Crim Div)

R. v Hurley (Joseph Robert) [1998] 1 Cr. App. R. (S.) 299; [1997] Crim. L.R. 840; *Times*, October 3, 1997; *Times*, August 5, 1997, CA (Crim Div) . . . . *Digested*, 97/**1508**:
Considered, 07/3721

R. v Huskins (Malcom) see R. v Dowd (Jeffrey)

R. v Hussain (Basharat) [2006] EWCA Crim 1350; [2007] 1 Cr. App. R. (S.) 8, CA (Crim Div) . . . . *Digested*, 07/**3578**

R. v Hussain (Ghulam) see Attorney General's Reference (No.111 of 2006), Re

R. v Hussain (Imtiaz) see Attorney General's Reference (No.36 of 2006), Re

R. v Hussain (Jameed) see R. v Norman (Shane Martin)

R. v Hussein (Akhtar) see R. v Ali (Liaquat)

R. v I see R. v M

R. v I see R. v M

R. v I [2007] EWCA Crim 923; [2007] 2 Cr. App. R. 24; (2007) 151 S.J.L.B. 160, CA (Crim Div) . . . . *Digested*, 07/**850**

R. v Igbanoi (Ambrose Otsemobor) see R. v Norman (Shane Martin)

R. v IK see R. v K

R. v IK; *joined cases* R. v AB; R. v KA [2007] EWCA Crim 971; [2007] 2 Cr. App. R. 15; [2007] Crim. L.R. 882; *Times*, May 16, 2007, CA (Crim Div) . . . . *Digested*, 07/**1022**

R. v Immigration Appeal Tribunal Ex p. Jeyeanthan see R. v Secretary of State for the Home Department Ex p. Jeyeanthan

R. v Immigration Appeal Tribunal Ex p. Kwok On Tong [1981] Imm. A.R. 214; *Times*, December 8, 1981, QBD . . . . *Digested*, 83/**1881**:
Applied, 07/2337: *Considered*, 95/2733: *Distinguished*, 89/1946: *Followed*, 91/2058

R. v Immigration Appeal Tribunal Ex p. Rajendrakumar see R. v Secretary of State for the Home Department Ex p. Ravichandran (No.1)

R. v Immigration Appeal Tribunal Ex p. Sandralingam (No.1) see R. v Secretary of State for the Home Department Ex p. Ravichandran (No.1)

R. v Immigration Appellate Authority Ex p. Secretary of State for the Home Department see R. v Special Adjudicator Ex p. Secretary of State for the Home Department

R. *v* Imran (Mohammed) [2006] EWCA Crim 754; [2006] 2 Cr. App. R. (S.) 93, CA
   (Crim Div) . . . .   *Digested,* 07/**3688**
R. *v* Inaam (Mohammed) [2006] EWCA Crim 1073; [2007] 1 Cr. App. R. (S.) 7, CA
   (Crim Div)
R. *v* Ings (Luke David) [2006] EWCA Crim 2811; [2007] 2 Cr. App. R. (S.) 2, CA
   (Crim Div) . . . .   *Digested,* 07/**3778**
R. *v* Inland Revenue Commissioners Ex p. Matteson's Walls Ltd see R. *v* Inland
   Revenue Commissioners Ex p. Unilever Plc
R. *v* Inland Revenue Commissioners Ex p. MFK Underwriting Agencies see R. *v* Inland
   Revenue Commissioners Ex p. MFK Underwriting Agents Ltd
R. *v* Inland Revenue Commissioners Ex p. MFK Underwriting Agents Ltd; *sub nom* R.
   v Inland Revenue Commissioners Ex p. MFK Underwriting Agencies [1990] 1
   W.L.R. 1545; [1990] 1 All E.R. 91; [1990] S.T.C. 873; 62 T.C. 607; [1990] C.O.D.
   143; (1989) 139 N.L.J. 1343; *Times,* July 17, 1989; *Independent,* August 7,
   1989; *Independent,* August 4, 1989; *Financial Times,* July 19, 1989; *Guardian,*
   July 20, 1989, QBD . . . .   *Digested,* 90/**2651**:
                          Applied, 93/32, 94/651, 96/249, 06/3526, 06/4198, 06/4215, 07/4324:
                          Considered, 93/2254, 94/2569, 97/4107, 00/5365: *Followed,* 02/46,
                                                                                   02/1701
R. *v* Inland Revenue Commissioners Ex p. Morgan Grenfell & Co Ltd see R. (on the
   application of Morgan Grenfell & Co Ltd) *v* Special Commissioners of Income
   Tax
R. *v* Inland Revenue Commissioners Ex p. National Federation of Self Employed and
   Small Businesses Ltd; *sub nom* Inland Revenue Commissioners *v* National
   Federation of Self Employed and Small Businesses Ltd [1982] A.C. 617; [1981]
   2 W.L.R. 722; [1981] 2 All E.R. 93; [1981] S.T.C. 260; 55 T.C. 133; (1981) 125
   S.J. 325, HL; reversing [1980] Q.B. 407; [1980] 2 W.L.R. 579; [1980] 2 All E.R.
   378; [1980] S.T.C. 261; [1980] T.R. 49; (1980) 124 S.J. 189, CA (Civ Div) . . . .   *Digested,* 81/**1433**:
                          Applied, 83/1981, 85/1782, 87/679, 90/2635, 91/3641, 03/2230:
                          Considered, 85/1479, 86/324, 87/28, 87/274, 89/12, 90/20, 91/53, 95/139,
                                     95/140, 95/142, 95/143, 97/2785, 00/5436, 04/3695, 07/3967:
                                                                          Distinguished, 87/5156
R. *v* Inland Revenue Commissioners Ex p. Unilever Plc; *joined case* R. *v* Inland
   Revenue Commissioners Ex p. Matteson's Walls Ltd [1996] S.T.C. 681; 68 T.C.
   205; [1996] C.O.D. 421, CA (Civ Div); affirming [1994] S.T.C. 841; [1994] S.T.I.
   1023; *Independent,* September 12, 1994, QBD. . . . .   *Digested,* 95/**895**:
                          Applied, 00/4072: *Considered,* 01/5605, 06/4198, 07/45:
                                                            Distinguished, 04/3786, 05/4121
R. *v* Inner London Education Authority Ex p. Ali (1990) 2 Admin. L.R. 822; [1990]
   C.O.D. 317; (1990) 154 L.G. Rev. 852; *Times,* February 21, 1990; *Independent,*
   February 15, 1990; *Guardian,* March 6, 1990; *Daily Telegraph,* February 22, 1990,
   QBD . . . .   *Digested,* 91/**1541**:
                          Applied, 99/1887, 07/1186: *Considered,* 94/35, 95/67, 95/3252
R. *v* Intervention Board for Agricultural Produce Ex p. Accrington Beef Co Ltd (C-241/
   95) [1996] E.C.R. I-6699; [1997] 1 C.M.L.R. 675, ECJ (1st Chamber) . . . .   *Considered,* 07/1644
R. *v* Iqbal (Javed) see R. *v* Mahmood (Zahid)
R. *v* Isa (Mustapha Abdi) [2005] EWCA Crim 3330; [2006] 2 Cr. App. R. (S.) 29;
   [2006] Crim. L.R. 356, CA (Crim Div) . . . .   *Digested,* 07/**3623**:
                                              Applied, 07/3742: *Considered,* 07/3622
R. *v* Isichei (Marvin) [2006] EWCA Crim 1815; (2006) 170 J.P. 753; (2007) 171 J.P.N.
   235, CA (Crim Div)
R. *v* Islam (Mohammed Saiful) [2006] EWCA Crim 1523; [2007] 1 Cr. App. R. (S.)
   43, CA (Crim Div) . . . .   *Digested,* 07/**3729**
R. *v* Islington LBC Ex p. Batantu see R. (on the application of Batantu) *v* Islington LBC
R. *v* Islington LBC Ex p. Reilly (1999) 31 H.L.R. 651, QBD . . . .   *Digested,* 98/**3032**:
                                              Applied, 00/3152: *Considered,* 07/2152
R. *v* Ismailaj (Vullnet) see R. *v* Roci (Lorenc)
R. *v* J; *sub nom* R. *v* MJ [2004] UKHL 42; [2005] 1 A.C. 562; [2004] 3 W.L.R. 1019;
   [2005] 1 All E.R. 1; [2005] 1 Cr. App. R. 19; (2004) 101 (40) L.S.G. 28; (2004)
   148 S.J.L.B. 1216; *Times,* October 15, 2004; *Independent,* October 20, 2004,
   HL; reversing [2002] EWCA Crim 2983; [2003] 1 W.L.R. 1590; [2003] 1 All
   E.R. 518; [2003] 2 Cr. App. R. 8; (2003) 167 J.P. 108; [2003] Crim. L.R. 391;
   (2003) 167 J.P.N. 191; *Times,* February 7, 2003, CA (Crim Div) . . . .   *Digested,* 05/**921**:
                          Considered, 03/3864, 06/5231, 07/970: *Distinguished,* 06/831
R. *v* J (Dennis Jerome) see Attorney General's Reference (Nos. 24, 25, 26, 27, 28 and
   41 of 2006), Re
R. *v* J (Rodney Clive) see Attorney General's Reference (No. 39 of 2006), Re
R. *v* J (SJ) see Attorney General's Reference (No. 49 of 2006), Re
R. *v* J (Unreasonable Delay) see Attorney General's Reference (No. 2 of 2001), Re
R. *v* J School Governors Ex p. L see R. (on the application of L (A Child)) *v* J School
   Governors

R. *v* Jackson (Dennis James); *joined case* R. *v* Hart (Stanley) [1970] 1 Q.B. 647; [1969] 2 W.L.R. 1339; [1969] 2 All E.R. 453; (1969) 53 Cr. App. R. 341; (1969) 133 J.P. 358; [1970] R.T.R. 165; (1969) 113 S.J. 310, CA (Crim Div) . . . .   *Digested,* 69/**3177**:
                       Considered, 70/1099, 01/1265, 07/882: *Referred to,* 88/4841

R. *v* Jackson (Robert Valentine) [2006] EWCA Crim 2380; [2007] 1 W.L.R. 1035; [2007] 1 Cr. App. R. 28; *Times,* November 3, 2006, CMAC . . . .   *Digested,* 07/**258**

R. *v* Jales (Brian); *joined case* R. *v* Lawrence (Raymond Francis) [2007] EWCA Crim 393; [2007] Crim. L.R. 800; (2007) 151 S.J.L.B. 194, CA (Crim Div)

R. *v* Jarvis (Marcus Lee) [2002] EWCA Crim 885; [2002] 2 Cr. App. R. (S.) 123, CA (Crim Div) . . . .   *Digested,* 03/**3709**:
                                               Considered, 07/3638

R. *v* Jayson (Mike) see R. *v* Smith (Graham Westgarth)

R. *v* JCR (A Juvenile) [2001] EWCA Crim 1371; [2002] 1 Cr. App. R. (S.) 54, CA (Crim Div) . . . .   *Considered,* 07/3798

R. *v* Jesson (Anthony Wayne) [2007] EWCA Crim 1399; [2007] Crim. L.R. 810, CA (Crim Div)

R. *v* Jesus (Lucas) see Attorney General's Reference (Nos.118 and 119 of 2006), Re

R. *v* Jewell (Ian John) see R. *v* Stillwell (Kenneth Michael)

R. *v* Jheeta (Harvinder Singh) [2007] EWCA Crim 1699; [2007] 2 Cr. App. R. 34, CA (Crim Div) . . . .   *Digested,* 07/**921**

R. *v* JM see Attorney General's Reference (Nos.108, 109, 110 and 111 of 2006), Re

R. *v* Johnson (Costs) [2006] 5 Costs L.R. 852, Sup Ct Costs Office. . . . .   *Digested,* 07/**955**

R. *v* Johnson (Craig) (Costs) [2007] 2 Costs L.R. 316, Sup Ct Costs Office

R. *v* Johnson (Dean) [2007] EWCA Crim 1978; (2007) 104(37) L.S.G. 35; (2007) 151 S.J.L.B. 1262, CA (Crim Div)

R. *v* Johnson (Derek John) see R. *v* Lawson (Michael David)

R. *v* Johnson (Jason Everton) [2007] EWCA Crim 1651; (2007) 171 J.P. 574, CA (Crim Div) . . . .   *Digested,* 07/**831**

R. *v* Johnson (Paul Anthony); *sub nom* R. *v* Jones (Andrew); *joined cases* R. *v* Hamilton (Gerald Anthony); R. *v* Gordon (Tyrone Leslie); Attorney General's Reference (No.64 of 2006), Re [2006] EWCA Crim 2486; [2007] 1 W.L.R. 585; [2007] 1 All E.R. 1237; [2007] 1 Cr. App. R. (S.) 112; (2007) 171 J.P. 172; [2007] Crim. L.R. 177; (2007) 171 J.P.N. 410; *Times,* November 2, 2006, CA (Crim Div) . . . .   *Digested,* 07/**3622**:
                       Considered, 07/3673, 07/3708, 07/3723, 07/3730

R. *v* Johnson (William James) [2005] EWCA Crim 3602; [2006] 2 Cr. App. R. (S.) 23, CA (Crim Div) . . . .   *Digested,* 07/**3713**

R. *v* Johnstone (Robert Alexander); *joined cases* R. *v* Harrison (Richard James); R. *v* Mayron Multimedia Ltd; R. *v* Eley (Charles Thomas); R. *v* Ho (Toon Chin); R. *v* Croxson (Matthew Louis) [2003] UKHL 28; [2003] 1 W.L.R. 1736; [2003] 3 All E.R. 884; [2003] 2 Cr. App. R. 33; (2003) 167 J.P. 281; [2004] E.T.M.R. 2; [2003] H.R.L.R. 25; [2003] U.K.H.R.R. 1239; [2003] F.S.R. 42; [2004] Crim. L.R. 244; (2003) 167 J.P.N. 453; (2003) 100(26) L.S.G. 36; (2003) 147 S.J.L.B. 625; *Times,* May 29, 2003; *Independent,* June 5, 2003, HL; affirming [2002] EWCA Crim 194; [2003] E.T.M.R. 1; [2002] F.S.R. 56; (2002) 99(13) L.S.G. 25; (2002) 146 S.J.L.B. 60; *Times,* March 12, 2002, CA (Crim Div) . . . .   *Digested,* 03/**2644**:
                       Considered, 04/707, 04/800, 06/2546: *Distinguished,* 07/5324:
                                               Doubted, 03/814

R. *v* Jones (Andrew) see R. *v* Johnson (Paul Anthony)

R. *v* Jones (Anthony William); *sub nom* R. *v* Haywood (John Victor); *joined cases* R. *v* Purvis (Paul Nigel); R. *v* Hayward (John Victor) (No.2) [2002] UKHL 5; [2003] 1 A.C. 1; [2002] 2 W.L.R. 524; [2002] 2 All E.R. 113; [2002] 2 Cr. App. R. 9; (2002) 166 J.P. 333; [2002] H.R.L.R. 23; (2002) 166 J.P.N. 431; (2002) 99(13) L.S.G. 26; (2002) 146 S.J.L.B. 61; *Times,* February 21, 2002; *Independent,* February 27, 2002, HL; affirming [2001] EWCA Crim 168; [2001] Q.B. 862; [2001] 3 W.L.R. 125; [2001] 2 Cr. App. R. 11; (2001) 165 J.P. 281; [2001] Crim. L.R. 502; (2001) 165 J.P.N. 665; (2001) 98(9) L.S.G. 38; (2001) 145 S.J.L.B. 53; *Times,* February 14, 2001; *Independent,* February 8, 2001, CA (Crim Div) . . . .   *Digested,* 02/**913**:
               Applied, 07/963: *Considered,* 05/1488, 05/1488: *Followed,* 04/877, 06/1606

R. *v* Jones (Barry John); *joined cases* R. *v* Lawes (Paul Desmond); R. *v* Richards (Natalie); R. *v* Jones (Samantha Jane) [2006] EWCA Crim 2061; [2007] 1 W.L.R. 7; [2007] 1 Cr. App. R. (S.) 71; *Times,* August 8, 2006, CA (Crim Div) . .   *Digested,* 07/**951**

R. *v* Jones (Ian Anthony) [2007] EWCA Crim 1118; [2007] 3 W.L.R. 907; [2007] 4 All E.R. 112; [2007] 2 Cr. App. R. 21; [2007] Crim. L.R. 979; (2007) 104(22) L.S.G. 24; *Times,* June 8, 2007, CA (Crim Div). . . . .   *Digested,* 07/**849**

R. *v* Jones (Iorwerth) see R. *v* Caley-Knowles (Edward)

R. *v* Jones (John Ivor) (Costs) [2007] 5 Costs L.R. 873, Sup Ct Costs Office

R. *v* Jones (Kate Elizabeth) see Attorney General's Reference (No.130 of 2006), Re

R. *v* Jones (Margaret); *joined cases* Swain *v* DPP; Ayliffe *v* DPP; R. *v* Richards (Josh);
    R. *v* Pritchard (Philip); R. *v* Olditch (Toby); R. *v* Milling (Arthur Paul) [2006]
    UKHL 16; [2007] 1 A.C. 136; [2006] 2 W.L.R. 772; [2006] 2 All E.R. 741;
    [2006] 2 Cr. App. R. 9; [2007] Crim. L.R. 66; [2006] A.C.D. 52; (2006) 170
    J.P.N. 263; (2006) 103(15) L.S.G. 20; (2006) 156 N.L.J. 600; *Times,* March 30,
    2006, HL; affirming [2004] EWCA Crim 1981; [2005] Q.B. 259; [2004] 3
    W.L.R. 1362; [2004] 4 All E.R. 955; [2005] 1 Cr. App. R. 12; [2005] Crim. L.R.
    122; [2005] A.C.D. 5; (2004) 148 S.J.L.B. 1149; *Times,* July 30, 2004, CA
    (Crim Div); affirming in part (Unreported, May 12, 2004), Crown Ct (Bristol) . .   *Digested,* 06/**835**:
                                                        Applied, 05/754, 06/2622, 07/2234
R. *v* Jones (Neil) see Jones (Setting of Minimum Term), Re
R. *v* Jones (Peter) see R. *v* Lawson (Michael David)
R. *v* Jones (Robert Edward Wynyard) (No.2) [1972] 1 W.L.R. 887; [1972] 2 All E.R.
    731; (1972) 56 Cr. App. R. 413; [1972] Crim. L.R. 593; (1972) 116 S.J. 483, CA
    (Crim Div) . . . .   *Digested,* 72/**759**:
                                            Applied, 07/935: *Considered,* 86/937: *Explained,* 82/733
R. *v* Jones (Samantha Jane) see R. *v* Jones (Barry John)
R. *v* Jordan (Andrew James); *joined cases* R. *v* Alleyne (Carl Anthony); R. *v* Redfern
    (David Christopher) [2004] EWCA Crim 3291; [2005] 2 Cr. App. R. (S.) 44;
    [2005] Crim. L.R. 312, CA (Crim Div) . . . .   *Digested,* 05/**3690**:
                                        Applied, 07/3649: *Considered,* 05/3694, 06/3714, 06/3715, 06/3716
R. *v* Jordan (Nicholas James) [2006] EWCA Crim 3311; [2007] 2 Cr. App. R. (S.) 33,
    CA (Crim Div)
R. *v* Jordan (River) see R. *v* Jordon (River)
R. *v* Jordon (River); *sub nom* R. *v* Jordan (River) [1998] 2 Cr. App. R. (S.) 83; [1998]
    Crim. L.R. 353, DC. . . . .   *Digested,* 98/**1147**:
                                                        Applied, 01/1488, 03/3785, 07/946
R. *v* Joy (Paul) see R. *v* Bossom (Graeme)
R. *v* Juhel (Abdul) see Attorney General's Reference (Nos.108, 109, 110 and 111 of
    2006), Re
R. *v* Juma (Salum Sayid) [2007] EWCA Crim 936, CA (Crim Div). . . . .   *Digested,* 07/**3717**
R. *v* K [2002] EWCA Crim 927; [2003] 1 Cr. App. R. (S.) 6, CA (Crim Div) . . . .   *Digested,* 03/**3685**:
                                                                            Distinguished, 07/3667
R. *v* K; *sub nom* R. *v* K (I); R. *v* IK [2007] EWCA Crim 491; [2007] 1 W.L.R. 2262;
    [2007] 2 Cr. App. R. 10; [2007] W.T.L.R. 817; [2007] Crim. L.R. 645; [2007]
    S.T.I. 1771; (2007) 151 S.J.L.B. 399; *Times,* March 28, 2007, CA (Crim Div) . . . .   *Digested,* 07/**909**
R. *v* K; *joined cases* R. *v* S; R. *v* X [2007] EWCA Crim 1888; [2007] 1 W.L.R. 3190,
    CA (Crim Div) . . . .   *Digested,* 07/**869**
R. *v* K (I) see R. *v* K
R. *v* K (John) [2007] EWCA Crim 1339; (2007) 104(26) L.S.G. 32, CA (Crim Div)
R. *v* KA see R. *v* IK
R. *v* Kai Ho Fan see R. *v* Harries (Michael John)
R. *v* Kansal (Rupe Lal) see R. *v* Graham (Hemamali Krishna)
R. *v* Karakaya (Adem) [2005] EWCA Crim 346; [2005] 2 Cr. App. R. 5; [2005] Crim.
    L.R. 574; *Times,* February 28, 2005, CA (Crim Div) . . . .   *Digested,* 05/**832**:
                                                                            Distinguished, 07/991
R. *v* Karim (Shahid) see R. *v* Mahmood (Zahid)
R. *v* Kassim (Ghazi Ahmed) [2005] EWCA Crim 1020; [2006] 1 Cr. App. R. (S.) 4,
    CA (Crim Div) . . . .   *Considered,* 07/3715
R. *v* Kayani (Costs) [2007] 3 Costs L.R. 490, Sup Ct Costs Office
R. *v* Keating (Stephen James) see R. *v* McInerney (William Patrick)
R. *v* Keet (Rocky) see R. *v* Cole (Konrad)
R. *v* Kelly (Anthony Joseph) see R. *v* Allsopp (Michael Nevin)
R. *v* Kemp (Richard) see R. *v* Cuthbertson (Brian George)
R. *v* Kempster (Mark) see R. *v* Foster (Mark)
R. *v* Kennedy (Simon) [2007] UKHL 38; [2007] 3 W.L.R. 612; [2007] 4 All E.R.
    1083; (2007) 104(42) L.S.G. 33; (2007) 151 S.J.L.B. 1365; *Times,* October 19,
    2007, HL; reversing [2005] EWCA Crim 685; [2005] 1 W.L.R. 2159; [2005] 2
    Cr. App. R. 23; *Times,* April 6, 2005, CA (Crim Div) . . . .   *Digested,* 07/**899**
R. *v* Kennett (Roy Patrick) see R. *v* Connolly (Mark Anthony)
R. *v* Keogh (David) [2007] EWCA Crim 528; [2007] 1 W.L.R. 1500; [2007] 3 All E.R.
    789; [2007] 2 Cr. App. R. 9; [2007] H.R.L.R. 21; (2007) 104(12) L.S.G. 35;
    (2007) 151 S.J.L.B. 397, CA (Crim Div). . . . .   *Digested,* 07/**847**
R. *v* Kerr (Andrew John) see R. *v* Ranson (Raymond)
R. *v* Keyte (David Andrew) [1998] 2 Cr. App. R. (S.) 165, CA (Crim Div) . . . .   *Digested,* 98/**1332**:
                                                            Considered, 06/3772, 07/3715
R. *v* Khan (Fahad Tariq); *joined case* R. *v* Khan (Zayn) [2007] EWCA Crim 929;
    [2007] 2 Cr. App. R. (S.) 95, CA (Crim Div)
R. *v* Khan (Mohammed Kurshid) see R. *v* Vernett-Showers (Michael)
R. *v* Khan (Mohsan) see R. *v* Ali (Liaquat)
R. *v* Khan (Safdar) see R. *v* Gittins (Marvin)
R. *v* Khan (Zayn) see R. *v* Khan (Fahad Tariq)
R. *v* Khangura (Sukhjiwan Singh) see Jones (Setting of Minimum Term), Re

R. v Khelifi (Ali) [2006] EWCA Crim 770; [2006] 2 Cr. App. R. (S.) 100; [2006]
M.H.L.R. 257, CA (Crim Div) . . . . *Digested*, 07/**3617**
R. v Kingston upon Thames Justices Ex p. Martin [1994] Imm. A.R. 172; *Times*,
December 10, 1993, QBD . . . . *Digested*, 94/**3519**:
Applied, 96/3184, 01/3597, 07/936: *Considered*, 96/670
R. v Kitchener (Marvine Wayne) see Attorney General's Reference (No.19 of 1999), Re
R. v Kizlaite (Vilma); *joined case* R. v Axhami (Tasim) [2006] EWCA Crim 1492;
[2007] 1 Cr. App. R. (S.) 30, CA (Crim Div). . . . . *Digested*, 07/**3796**
R. v Klair (Jaspal) (1995) 16 Cr. App. R. (S.) 660, CA (Crim Div) . . . . *Digested*, 96/**1996**:
Considered, 99/1110, 07/3780
R. v Knight (Anthony Lee) [2007] EWCA Crim 606; [2007] 2 Cr. App. R. (S.) 76, CA
(Crim Div) . . . . *Digested*, 07/**3661**
R. v Knight (Colin Charles) (1984) 6 Cr. App. R. (S.) 31; [1984] Crim. L.R. 304, CA
(Crim Div) . . . . *Digested*, 85/**826**:
Considered, 90/1492, 91/1181, 07/3709
R. v Knuller (Publishing, Printing and Promotions) Ltd see Knuller (Publishing, Printing
and Promotions) Ltd v DPP
R. v Kolawole (David Oladotun) [2004] EWCA Crim 3047; [2005] 2 Cr. App. R. (S.)
14; [2005] Crim. L.R. 245; (2004) 148 S.J.L.B. 1370; *Times*, November 16,
2004, CA (Crim Div) . . . . *Digested*, 05/**3610**:
Considered, 06/3724, 07/3717: *Distinguished*, 07/3644: *Followed*, 07/3716
R. v Kordasinski (Leszek) [2006] EWCA Crim 2984; [2007] 1 Cr. App. R. 17; (2007)
171 J.P. 206; [2007] Crim. L.R. 794; (2007) 171 J.P.N. 479; (2006) 103(46)
L.S.G. 34; *Times*, November 16, 2006, CA (Crim Div). . . . . *Digested*, 07/**826**
R. v Krivec (Danielle) see Attorney General's Reference (No.8 of 2007), Re
R. v Kulah (Mustafa Nour) [2007] EWCA Crim 1701; [2007] Crim. L.R. 907; *Times*,
August 6, 2007, CA (Crim Div) . . . . *Digested*, 07/**3666**
R. v L see R. v Reynolds (Michael Edwin)
R. v L see Attorney General's Reference (No.113 of 2006), Re
R. v L (Abraham) see R. v R (Amer)
R. v L (Indecent Assault: Sentencing) [1999] 1 Cr. App. R. 117; [1999] 1 Cr. App. R.
(S.) 19; (1998) 95(26) L.S.G. 31; (1998) 142 S.J.L.B. 156; *Times*, April 28, 1998;
Independent, April 28, 1998, CA (Crim Div) . . . . *Digested*, 98/**1257**:
Applied, 99/1196: *Considered*, 99/1194, 99/1199, 99/1203, 99/1302,
00/1288, 01/1354, 05/3637, 07/3664: *Followed*, 99/1207, 01/1484
R. v Lackenby (Ian Stuart) see R. v Millberry (William Christopher)
R. v Lamb (Christopher) [2005] EWCA Crim 3000; [2006] 2 Cr. App. R. (S.) 11;
[2006] Crim. L.R. 256; *Times*, December 1, 2005, CA (Crim Div) . . . . *Digested*, 06/**3642**:
Applied, 06/3639: *Considered*, 07/3738
R. v Lambert (John Ritchie); *joined cases* R. v McGrath (Lee James); R. v Brown
(Alan) [2006] EWCA Crim 827; [2006] 2 Cr. App. R. (S.) 107; [2006] Crim.
L.R. 995, CA (Crim Div) . . . . *Digested*, 07/**3720**
R. v Lambeth LBC Ex p. Ly (1987) 19 H.L.R. 51, QBD . . . . *Digested*, 87/**1875**:
Considered, 07/2153: *Distinguished*, 98/2998
R. v Lambeth LBC Ex p. P see R. v Hammersmith and Fulham LBC Ex p. M
R. v Lambeth LBC Ex p. X see R. v Hammersmith and Fulham LBC Ex p. M
R. v Lamont (Martin) see R. v Pepper (Jeremy Paul)
R. v Lang (Stephen Howard); *joined cases* R. v D; R. v Edwards (Kyle Frederick); R. v
Guidera (Michael); R. v Sheppard (James); R. v Collier (Edward); R. v Glave
(Heathcliffe); R. v Armitage (Lewis); R. v Smith (Gary); R. v Wright (Robert); R. v
Feihn (Steven); R. v Carasco (Charles); R. v Winters (Keith); R. v Abdi (Hassan)
[2005] EWCA Crim 2864; [2006] 1 W.L.R. 410; [2006] 2 All E.R. 410;
[2006] 2 Cr. App. R. (S.) 3; [2006] Crim. L.R. 174; *Times*, November 10, 2005,
CA (Crim Div) . . . . *Digested*, 06/**3836**:
Applied, 06/3669, 06/3681, 06/3719, 06/3872, 06/3886, 06/3902,
07/3623, 07/3640, 07/3656, 07/3658, 07/3663, 07/3675, 07/3742, 07/3788:
Considered, 06/993, 06/3709, 06/3755, 06/3756, 06/3829, 06/3830,
06/3883, 06/3890, 07/3622, 07/3657, 07/3662, 07/3729, 07/3751:
Followed, 06/3749
R. v Langham (Christopher) [2007] EWCA Crim 3004; (2007) 104(46) L.S.G. 27,
CA (Crim Div)
R. v Larsh (Costs) [2007] 5 Costs L.R. 783, Sup Ct Costs Office
R. v Last (Emma); *joined cases* R. v Holbrook (Lee David); R. v Quillan (James
Angus); R. v Quillan (Edward Steven); R. v Crane (Sara) [2005] EWCA Crim
106; [2005] 2 Cr. App. R. (S.) 64; [2005] Crim. L.R. 407; (2005) 149 S.J.L.B.
147; *Times*, January 31, 2005, CA (Crim Div) . . . . *Digested*, 05/**3680**:
Applied, 05/3682, 05/3735: *Considered*, 06/3779, 07/3693, 07/3694
R. v Latham (Craig) see Attorney General's Reference (No.72 of 2006), Re
R. v Latham (Daniel George) see Attorney General's Reference (No.33 of 1996), Re

R. v Latif (Khalid); *joined case* R. v Shahzad (Mohammed Khalid) [1996] 1 W.L.R. 104; [1996] 1 All E.R. 353; [1996] 2 Cr. App. R. 92; [1996] Crim. L.R. 414; (1996) 93(5) L.S.G. 30; (1996) 146 N.L.J. 121; (1996) 140 S.J.L.B. 39; *Times*, January 23, 1996; *Independent*, January 23, 1996, HL; affirming [1995] 1 Cr. App. R. 270; (1994) 15 Cr. App. R. (S.) 864; [1994] Crim. L.R. 750; (1994) 91(18) L.S.G. 37; (1994) 138 S.J.L.B. 85; *Times*, March 17, 1994, CA (Crim Div). . . . . *Digested*, 96/**1432**:
Applied, 07/2808: *Considered*, 96/1599, 97/1503, 99/1129, 06/2200:
Distinguished, 00/917: *Followed*, 00/1086, 01/992
R. v Lawes (Paul Desmond) see R. v Jones (Barry John)
R. v Lawrence (Costs) [2007] 1 Costs L.R. 138, Sup Ct Costs Office
R. v Lawrence (Raymond Francis) see R. v Jales (Brian)
R. v Lawrence (Steven) see R. v May (Raymond George)
R. v Lawson (Jonathan Eric) [2006] EWCA Crim 2572; [2007] 1 W.L.R. 1191; [2007] 1 Cr. App. R. 11; (2007) 171 J.P. 43; [2007] Crim. L.R. 232; (2007) 171 J.P.N. 323; (2006) 150 S.J.L.B. 1152, CA (Crim Div). *Digested*, 07/**822**
R. v Lawson (Karen) (aka Mark) [2005] EWCA Crim 3583; [2006] 2 Cr. App. R. (S.) 30, CA (Crim Div) . . . . *Digested*, 07/**3581**
R. v Lawson (Michael David); *sub nom* R. v Roberts (Darren); R. v Jones (Peter); R. v Johnson (Derek John); R. v Adderson (Lee) [2005] EWCA Crim 84; [2007] 1 Cr. App. R. 20; *Times*, November 6, 2006, CA (Crim Div) . . . . *Digested*, 07/**1025**
R. v Lawton (Jamie) see R. v Johnson (Paul Anthony)
R. v Lay (Andrew) (No.2) [2006] EWCA Crim 2924; [2007] 2 Cr. App. R. (S.) 4, CA (Crim Div) . . . . *Digested*, 07/**3641**
R. v Lazarus (Tony Jason) [2004] EWCA Crim 2297; [2005] 1 Cr. App. R. (S.) 98; [2005] Crim. L.R. 64, CA (Crim Div) . . . . *Digested*, 05/**843**:
Applied, 06/3674, 07/949
R. v Leaf (Ian Andrew) [2007] EWCA Crim 802; (2007) 104(17) L.S.G. 30, CA (Crim Div). . . . . *Digested*, 07/**3652**
R. v Lee (Darrell Anthony) [2006] EWCA Crim 2502; [2007] 1 Cr. App. R. (S.) 102, CA (Crim Div). . . . . *Digested*, 07/**3772**
R. v Leeds Justices Ex p. Hanson see R. v Manchester Stipendiary Magistrate Ex p. Hill
R. v Lees-Wolfenden (Danielle Jayne) [2006] EWCA Crim 3068; [2007] 1 Cr. App. R. (S.) 119; [2007] Crim. L.R. 393, CA (Crim Div) . . . . *Digested*, 07/**3758**
R. v Lehaney (Francis Glen) see R. v Suchedina (Hasnain)
R. v Leicester City Council Ex p. Bhikha see R. v Wandsworth LBC Ex p. O
R. v Levey (Stephen) [2006] EWCA Crim 1902; [2006] 1 W.L.R. 3092; [2007] 1 Cr. App. R. 1; [2007] 1 F.L.R. 462; [2006] 2 F.C.R. 724; [2007] Crim. L.R. 472; [2006] Fam. Law 1021; *Times*, August 24, 2006, CA (Crim Div). . . . . *Digested*, 06/**896**:
Applied, 07/1022
R. v Ley (Kerry) [2006] EWCA Crim 3063; [2007] 1 Cr. App. R. 25; [2007] Crim. L.R. 642, CA (Crim Div). . . . . *Digested*, 07/**996**
R. v LH (A Juvenile) (Manslaughter: Sentencing) see R. v Hamar (Laszlo)
R. v Liddle (Mark) (Appeal against Sentence); *joined case* R. v Hayes (Andrew Michael) [1999] 3 All E.R. 816; [2000] 1 Cr. App. R. (S.) 131; [1999] Crim. L.R. 847; (1999) 96(23) L.S.G. 34; *Times*, May 26, 1999; *Independent*, June 16, 1999, CA (Crim Div) . . . . *Digested*, 99/**1188**:
Applied, 01/1344: *Considered*, 01/1346, 02/3967, 05/3628, 05/3629,
05/3722, 06/3803, 07/3726: *Distinguished*, 04/3359
R. v Lincoln (Peter Alan) (1990-91) 12 Cr. App. R. (S.) 250, CA (Crim Div) . . . . *Digested*, 92/**1144**:
Considered, 00/1269: *Distinguished*, 07/3653
R. v Little (Liam John) see R. v Richardson (Jack Virgil)
R. v Littlefield (John) see R. v Aranguren (Jose de Jesus)
R. v Liverpool Justices Ex p. DPP [1993] Q.B. 233; [1992] 3 W.L.R. 20; [1992] 3 All E.R. 249; (1992) 95 Cr. App. R. 222; (1992) 156 J.P. 634; [1992] Crim. L.R. 294; [1992] C.O.D. 180; (1992) 156 J.P.N. 235; *Times*, December 10, 1991, QBD . . . . *Digested*, 92/**689**:
Applied, 01/1103, 03/829, 07/941
R. v Liversidge (Ian John) see R. v Cain (Alan John)
R. v Livesey (Mark Ivan) [2006] EWCA Crim 3344; [2007] 1 Cr. App. R. 35; [2007] Crim. L.R. 635; *Times*, January 8, 2007, CA (Crim Div) . . . . *Digested*, 07/**1004**
R. v Llewellyn (Gareth) see R. v O'Brien (Karl)
R. v Lloyd (Brian Paul), *Times*, March 26, 2007, CA (Crim Div)
R. v Lobban (Adrian Michael) see Attorney General's Reference (Nos.4 and 7 of 2002), Re
R. v Lochhead (William Stewart) see R. v Cuthbertson (Brian George)
R. v Logan (Andrew Danny) [2006] EWCA Crim 3007; [2007] 2 Cr. App. R. (S.) 7, CA (Crim Div) . . . . *Digested*, 07/**3730**
R. v Looseley (Grant Spencer) (No.2) see Attorney General's Reference (No.3 of 2000), Re
R. v Loosely (Grant Spencer) see Attorney General's Reference (No.3 of 2000), Re
R. v Loosley (Grant Spencer) (No.2) see Attorney General's Reference (No.3 of 2000), Re

R. v Lovegrove (David Lee) see R. v H
R. v Lowestoft Justices Ex p. DPP see R. v Warley Magistrates Court Ex p. DPP
R. v Lubwama (Abdul Musisi) see R. v Reynolds (Michael Edwin)
R. v Lucas (Dean Owen) [2007] EWCA Crim 708; [2007] 2 Cr. App. R. (S.) 81, CA
   (Crim Div) . . . .   *Digested*, 07/**3791**
R. v Lun Xi Tan see R. v Su Hua Liu
R. v M [2006] EWCA Crim 3055; [2007] 2 Cr. App. R. (S.) 10, CA (Crim Div) . . . . . .   *Digested*, 07/**3793**
R. v M; *joined cases* R. v Z; R. v I; R. v R; R. v B [2007] EWCA Crim 298, CA (Crim
   Div) . . . .   *Considered*, 07/1012:
                                        Not followed, 07/927
R. v M; *joined cases* R. v Z; R. v I; R. v R; R. v B [2007] EWCA Crim 970; [2007] 3
   All E.R. 53; [2007] 2 Cr. App. R. 17; (2007) 151 S.J.L.B. 610; *Times*, May 17,
   2007, CA (Crim Div) . . . .   *Digested*, 07/**1012**
R. v M [2007] EWCA Crim 1182; (2007) 151 S.J.L.B. 572, CA (Crim Div)
R. v M (Faisal Jamil) see R. v R (Amer)
R. v M (Michael) [2006] EWCA Crim 3408; [2007] Crim. L.R. 637, CA (Crim Div)
R. v M (Sarah Ruth) (A Juvenile) see Attorney General's Reference (Nos.78, 79 and
   85 of 1998), Re
R. v Mabee (Craig McCombs) [2007] EWCA Crim 3230; (2007) 104(47) L.S.G. 26,
   CA (Crim Div)
R. v McCallister (Gerard Martin) see Attorney General's Reference (Nos.88, 89, 90
   and 91 of 2006), Re
R. v McCann (Calvin) [2006] EWCA Crim 1078; [2007] 1 Cr. App. R. (S.) 4, CA
   (Crim Div)
R. v McCoy (Keith Thomas) see R. v Cuthbertson (Brian George)
R. v McDermott (Victor) [2006] EWCA Crim 1899; [2007] 1 Cr. App. R. (S.) 28, CA
   (Crim Div) . . . .   *Digested*, 07/**3576**
R. v McDonald (Kenneth Charles) [2007] EWCA Crim 1081; (2007) 151 S.J.L.B. 436,
   CA (Crim Div)
R. v McDonald (Michael Francis) [2007] EWCA Crim 1117; [2007] Crim. L.R. 737, CA
   (Crim Div)
R. v McDonnell (John Patrick) see R. v Cuthbertson (Brian George)
R. v McDowell (Thomas) [2006] EWCA Crim 1836; [2007] 1 Cr. App. R. (S.) 56, CA
   (Crim Div) . . . .   *Digested*, 07/**3702**
R. v McGarry (Michael) see Attorney General's Reference (Nos.98 and 99 of 2006),
   Re
R. v McGinlay (Alexander); *joined case* R. v Ballantyne (John) (1976) 62 Cr. App. R.
   156; [1976] Crim. L.R. 78, CA (Crim Div) . . . .   *Digested*, 76/**569**:
                       Applied, 92/1296: *Considered*, 07/967
R. v McGrady (Christian John) [2006] EWCA Crim 1547; [2007] 1 Cr. App. R. (S.)
   45; [2006] Crim. L.R. 940, CA (Crim Div) . . . .   *Digested*, 07/**3663**
R. v McGrady (John Joseph) [2007] EWCA Crim 192; [2007] 2 Cr. App. R. (S.) 56,
   CA (Crim Div) . . . .   *Digested*, 07/**3701**
R. v McGrath (Lee James) see R. v Lambert (John Ritchie)
R. v McInerney (William Patrick); *joined case* R. v Keating (Stephen James) [2002]
   EWCA Crim 3003; [2003] 1 All E.R. 1089; [2003] 1 Cr. App. R. 36; [2003] 2 Cr.
   App. R. (S.) 39; [2003] Crim. L.R. 209; (2003) 100(6) L.S.G. 25; *Times*,
   December 20, 2002, CA (Crim Div) . . . .   *Digested*, 03/**3636**:
             Applied, 05/3702, 07/3584: *Considered*, 03/835, 05/3525, 05/3545,
                                        06/992, 06/3690
R. v Mackie (William John) [2007] EWCA Crim 2486; (2007) 104(44) L.S.G. 32, CA
   (Crim Div)
R. v Mackney (George Frederick) [2006] EWCA Crim 1202; [2007] 1 Cr. App. R. (S.)
   20, CA (Crim Div)
R. v McManus (Kevin Peter) see R. v Gordon (Gavin Stephen)
R. v McNally (John Stephen) [2000] 1 Cr. App. R. (S.) 535; *Times*, December 1, 1999,
   CA (Crim Div) . . . .   *Digested*, 00/**1119**:
                    Applied, 06/3685: *Considered*, 07/3576
R. v McNee (Michael); *joined cases* R. v G; R. v Russell (John Paul); R. v X [2007]
   EWCA Crim 1529; *Times*, May 31, 2007, CA (Crim Div) . . . .   *Digested*, 07/**3616**
R. v MacPherson (Ian) [2005] EWCA Crim 3605; [2006] 1 Cr. App. R. 30; [2007]
   Crim. L.R. 504, CA (Crim Div) . . . .   *Digested*, 06/**817**
R. v Maguire (Robert) (Costs) [2006] 4 Costs L.R. 678, Sup Ct Costs Office . . . . . .   *Digested*, 07/**957**
R. v Mahmood (Zahid); *joined cases* R. v Karim (Shahid); R. v Iqbal (Javed); R. v Ali
   (Shaukat) [2006] EWCA Crim 3158; [2007] 2 Cr. App. R. (S.) 17, CA (Crim
   Div) . . . .   *Digested*, 07/**3618**
R. v Mahoney (Leianne) [2007] EWCA Crim 1553; [2007] 2 Cr. App. R. (S.) 103, CA
   (Crim Div)
R. v Maidstone Crown Court Ex p. Harrow LBC [2000] Q.B. 719; [2000] 2 W.L.R.
   237; [1999] 3 All E.R. 542; [2000] 1 Cr. App. R. 117; (2000) 53 B.M.L.R. 27;
   [1999] Crim. L.R. 838; (1999) 96(21) L.S.G. 38; *Times*, May 14, 1999, QBD . . .   *Digested*, 99/**99**:
             Considered, 02/3228: *Distinguished*, 01/1118, 07/21
R. v Majewski (Robert Stefan) see DPP v Majewski

R. _v_ Maka (Shaban) [2005] EWCA Crim 3365; [2006] 2 Cr. App. R. (S.) 14, CA
(Crim Div) . . . .   _Digested_, 06/**3857**:
                                               Applied, 07/3796: _Distinguished_, 06/3856
R. _v_ Makai (Atilla) [2007] EWCA Crim 1652; (2007) 151 S.J.L.B. 989, CA (Crim Div)
R. _v_ Makeid (Bashir) [2007] EWCA Crim 792; [2007] 2 Cr. App. R. (S.) 97, CA (Crim
Div)
R. _v_ Manchester Crown Court Ex p. DPP; _sub nom_ Huckfield, Re [1993] 1 W.L.R.
1524; [1993] 4 All E.R. 928; (1994) 98 Cr. App. R. 461; [1994] 1 C.M.L.R. 457;
(1993) 143 N.L.J. 1711; _Times_, November 26, 1993; _Independent_, December 7,
1993, HL; reversing [1993] 1 W.L.R. 693; [1993] 1 All E.R. 801; (1993) 96 Cr.
App. R. 210; [1992] 3 C.M.L.R. 329; [1993] Crim. L.R. 377; [1993] C.O.D. 123;
(1992) 136 S.J.L.B. 235; _Times_, July 29, 1992; _Independent_, July 3, 1992, QBD   _Digested_, 94/**19**:
                        Applied, 05/71, 07/940: _Considered_, 94/35, 94/35, 95/23, 95/969:
                                                Followed, 96/1550, 98/96
R. _v_ Manchester Crown Court Ex p. M (A Child) see R. (on the application of
McCann) _v_ Manchester Crown Court
R. _v_ Manchester Stipendiary Magistrate Ex p. Hill; _sub nom_ R. _v_ Leeds Justices Ex p.
Hanson; Hill _v_ Anderton; _joined cases_ Moody _v_ Anderton; R. _v_ Dartford Justices
Ex p. Dhesi; R. _v_ Gateshead Justices Ex p. Ives; R. _v_ Edmonton Justices Ex p.
Hughes; Hughes _v_ Hill; Dhesi _v_ Chief Constable of Kent [1983] 1 A.C. 328;
[1982] 3 W.L.R. 331; [1982] 2 All E.R. 963; (1982) 75 Cr. App. R. 346; [1982]
R.T.R. 449; [1982] Crim. L.R. 755; (1982) 126 S.J. 526, HL; affirming [1981]
Q.B. 892; [1981] 3 W.L.R. 315; [1981] 3 All E.R. 72; (1982) 74 Cr. App. R. 109;
[1982] R.T.R. 144; [1981] Crim. L.R. 711; (1981) 125 S.J. 464; _Times_, June 25,
1981, DC . . . .   _Digested_, 82/**1963**:
                   Applied, 88/610, 92/934, 07/1026: _Considered_, 86/2069, 93/2628, 94/949:
                                                    Referred to, 87/2463
R. _v_ Manir (Majid Ali) [2006] EWCA Crim 2188; [2007] 1 Cr. App. R. (S.) 94; (2006)
103(36) L.S.G. 33; (2006) 150 S.J.L.B. 1154, CA (Crim Div)
R. _v_ Mansfield (John) [2005] EWCA Crim 927, CA (Crim Div) . . . .   _Applied_, 07/3600
R. _v_ Mansha (Abu Baker) [2006] EWCA Crim 2051; [2007] 1 Cr. App. R. (S.) 70, CA
(Crim Div) . . . .   _Digested_, 07/**3759**
R. _v_ Marland (James Andrew) [2006] EWCA Crim 2474; [2007] 1 Cr. App. R. (S.)
105, CA (Crim Div)
R. _v_ Marquez (Shaun) see R. _v_ Avis (Tony)
R. _v_ Marr (Fraser) (1990) 90 Cr. App. R. 154; [1989] Crim. L.R. 743, CA (Crim Div) . .   _Digested_, 90/**904**:
                                         Applied, 92/774: _Considered_, 07/932
R. _v_ Marriott (Robert Scott) [2006] EWCA Crim 1000; [2006] 2 Cr. App. R. (S.) 101,
CA (Crim Div) . . . .   _Digested_, 07/**3648**
R. _v_ Marsh (Terence Colin) see R. _v_ Graham (Hemamali Krishna)
R. _v_ Marshall (James) [2007] EWCA Crim 1193; [2007] Crim. L.R. 994, CA (Crim
Div) . . . .   _Digested_, 07/**3725**
R. _v_ Marshall (Jay David); _joined case_ R. _v_ Crump (Robert John) [2007] EWCA Crim
35; [2007] Crim. L.R. 562; (2007) 151 S.J.L.B. 122, CA (Crim Div) . . . .   _Digested_, 07/**991**
R. _v_ Martin (Costs) [2007] 1 Costs L.R. 128, Sup Ct Costs Office
R. _v_ Martin (Nathan) see R. _v_ Davis (Iain)
R. _v_ Martin (Patrick Hugh) [1999] 1 Cr. App. R. (S.) 477; [1999] Crim. L.R. 97; _Times_,
November 5, 1998; _Independent_, November 6, 1998, CA (Crim Div) . . . .   _Digested_, 98/**1213**:
                                             Considered, 07/3691
R. _v_ Martin (Selina Elizabeth) [2006] EWCA Crim 1035; [2007] 1 Cr. App. R. (S.) 3;
Times, June 6, 2006, CA (Crim Div) . . . .   _Digested_, 06/**3691**
R. _v_ Mashaollahi (Behrooz); _sub nom_ R. _v_ Mashaolli [2001] 1 Cr. App. R. 6; [2001] 1
Cr. App. R. (S.) 96; [2000] Crim. L.R. 1029; (2000) 97(37) L.S.G. 39; _Times_,
August 4, 2000; _Independent_, October 12, 2000, CA (Crim Div) . . . .   _Digested_, 00/**1216**:
                                             Considered, 07/3634
R. _v_ Mashaolli see R. _v_ Mashaollahi (Behrooz)
R. _v_ Mason (Carl) [1988] 1 W.L.R. 139; [1987] 3 All E.R. 481; (1988) 86 Cr. App. R.
349; (1987) 151 J.P. 747; [1987] Crim. L.R. 757; (1987) 151 J.P.N. 542; (1987)
131 S.J. 973, CA (Crim Div) . . . .   _Digested_, 87/**561**:
                         Applied, 91/662, 07/853: _Considered_, 94/683: _Distinguished_, 88/562
R. _v_ Massey (Steven John) [2007] EWCA Crim 2664; _Times_, December 4, 2007, CA
(Crim Div) . . . .   _Digested_, 07/**915**
R. _v_ Masud (Umar) see R. _v_ Vernett-Showers (Michael)
R. _v_ Matthews (Rosalind) (Costs) [2007] 2 Costs L.R. 328, Sup Ct Costs Office
R. _v_ Maxwell (Unreported, February 9, 1995), CA (Crim Div) . . . .   _Applied_, 07/**981**:
                                                     Followed, 96/1611
R. _v_ Maxwell (Andrew Robert); _joined cases_ R. _v_ Coles (Robert); R. _v_ Coles (Lyndon)
[1990] 1 W.L.R. 401; [1990] 1 All E.R. 801; (1990) 91 Cr. App. R. 61; [1991]
Crim. L.R. 64; (1990) 140 N.L.J. 401; (1990) 134 S.J. 885, HL; affirming [1988]
1 W.L.R. 1265; [1989] 88 Cr. App. R. 173; [1988] Crim. L.R. 760; (1988) 132
S.J. 1063, CA (Crim Div) . . . .   _Digested_, 90/**846**:
                     Applied, 07/862: _Considered_, 91/3155, 95/1145, 96/1683, 97/1384:
                                                     Doubted, 06/986

R. *v* May (John) (1990) 91 Cr. App. R. 157; [1990] Crim. L.R. 415; *Times*, November
　21, 1989, CA (Crim Div) . . . .　　*Digested*, 90/**1059**:
　　　　　　　　　　　　　　　　　　　　　　　　　　　　　　　　　　Considered, 07/916
R. *v* May (Raymond George); *joined cases* R. *v* Lawrence (Steven); R. *v* Fowles
　(Herbert); R. *v* Bravard (Jacques); R. *v* Stapleton (Vincent) [2005] EWCA Crim
　97; [2005] 1 W.L.R. 2902; [2005] 3 All E.R. 523; [2005] 2 Cr. App. R. (S.)
　67; (2005) 149 S.J.L.B. 176; *Times*, February 15, 2005, CA (Crim Div) . . . . . .　　*Digested*, 05/**840**:
　　　　　　　　　　　　　　　　　　Applied, 05/926, 05/3901: *Considered*, 07/949
R. *v* Mayling (Cyril) [1963] 2 Q.B. 717; [1963] 2 W.L.R. 709; [1963] 1 All E.R. 687;
　(1963) 47 Cr. App. R. 102; (1963) 127 J.P. 269; (1963) 107 S.J. 177, CCA . . . .　　*Digested*, 63/**737**:
　　　　　　　　　　　　　Applied, 07/917: *Considered*, 95/1268, 07/916: *Distinguished*, 90/1059
R. *v* Mayron Multimedia Ltd see R. *v* Johnstone (Robert Alexander)
R. *v* Meade (Lee) [2006] EWCA Crim 2880; [2007] 1 Cr. App. R. (S.) 123, CA (Crim
　Div) . . . .　　*Digested*, 07/**3659**
R. *v* Meakin (Joel) see Attorney General's Reference (No.98 of 2004), Re
R. *v* Mee (Jason David) [2004] EWCA Crim 629; [2004] 2 Cr. App. R. (S.) 81;
　[2004] Crim. L.R. 487; (2004) 148 S.J.L.B. 267; *Times*, April 1, 2004, CA (Crim
　Div). . . . .　　*Digested*, 04/**3458**:
　　　　　　　　　　　　　　　　Considered, 05/3588, 07/3635: *Followed*, 06/3858
R. *v* Meehan (Brian John) see Attorney General's Reference (Nos.88, 89, 90 and 91 of
　2006), Re
R. *v* Merritt (Lisa Anne) [2005] EWCA Crim 2313; [2006] 1 Cr. App. R. (S.) 105, CA
　(Crim Div) . . . .　　*Digested*, 06/**3789**:
　　　　　　　　　　　　　　　　　　　　　　　　　　　　　　　　　Considered, 07/3712
R. *v* Miah (Costs) (No.2) see R. *v* Cheng (Costs) (No.2)
R. *v* Miah (Tutu) see Attorney General's Reference (Nos.108, 109, 110 and 111 of 2006),
　Re
R. *v* Miles (Timothy James) [2006] EWCA Crim 2958; [2007] 2 Cr. App. R. (S.) 5,
　CA (Crim Div) . . . .　　*Digested*, 07/**3761**
R. *v* Milford Haven Port Authority see Environment Agency *v* Milford Haven Port
　Authority (The Sea Empress)
R. *v* Millberry (William Christopher); *joined cases* R. *v* Lackenby (Ian Stuart); R. *v*
　Morgan (Paul Robert) [2002] EWCA Crim 2891; [2003] 1 W.L.R. 546; [2003]
　2 All E.R. 939; [2003] 1 Cr. App. R. 25; [2003] 2 Cr. App. R. (S.) 31; [2003]
　Crim. L.R. 207; (2003) 100(7) L.S.G. 34; (2003) 147 S.J.L.B. 28; *Times*,
　December 11, 2002, CA (Crim Div) . . . .　　*Digested*, 03/**3829**:
　　　　　　　　　　　　Applied, 03/3826, 03/3827, 03/3835, 03/3866, 04/3285, 04/3373,
　　　　　　　　　　04/3443, 05/3718, 05/3721, 05/3734, 06/3662, 06/3839, 06/3845,
　　　　　　　06/3899, 07/3725, 07/3749, 07/3792: *Cited*, 04/3444: *Considered*, 03/3828,
　　　　　　　　　　04/3422, 04/3423, 04/3426, 05/3638, 05/3714, 05/3717, 05/3719,
　　　　　　　　　　05/3739, 05/3741, 05/3776, 06/964, 06/3664, 06/3842, 06/3844,
　　　　　　　　　　06/3846, 06/3847, 06/3849, 06/3894, 06/3897, 06/3898, 07/3575,
　　　　　　　　　　　　07/3604, 07/3724, 07/3752, 07/3773: *Distinguished*, 07/3740:
　　　　　　　　　　　　Followed, 03/3825, 03/3836, 04/3421, 04/3427, 05/3536
R. *v* Miller (Gordon) see R. *v* Havell (Darren)
R. *v* Milling (Arthur Paul) see R. *v* Jones (Margaret)
R. *v* Mills (Gary) [2004] EWCA Crim 1466; [2005] 1 Cr. App. R. (S.) 38, CA (Crim
　Div). . . . .　　*Digested*, 05/**3706**:
　　　　　　　　　　　　　　　　　　　　　　　　　　　　　　　　　Considered, 07/3631
R. *v* Millward (David Samuel) [1999] 1 Cr. App. R. 61; [1999] Crim. L.R. 164, CA
　(Crim Div) . . . .　　*Digested*, 99/**1061**:
　　　　　　　　　　　　　　　　　　Considered, 07/992: *Followed*, 01/1145
R. *v* Mirza (Shabbir Ali); *joined cases* R. *v* Connor (Ben); R. *v* Rollock (Ashley
　Kenneth) [2004] UKHL 2; [2004] 1 A.C. 1118; [2004] 2 W.L.R. 201; [2004] 1
　All E.R. 925; [2004] 2 Cr. App. R. 8; [2004] H.R.L.R. 11; 16 B.H.R.C. 279;
　(2004) 101(7) L.S.G. 34; (2004) 154 N.L.J. 145; (2004) 148 S.J.L.B. 117;
　Times, January 23, 2004, HL; affirming [2002] EWCA Crim 1235; [2002] Crim.
　L.R. 921, CA (Crim Div) . . . .　　*Digested*, 04/**694**:
　　　　　　　　　Applied, 05/827, 05/832, 05/849: *Considered*, 07/5072: *Explained*, 05/895
R. *v* Mitchell (John) see R. *v* Czyzewski (Jozef Eugene) (Appeal against Sentence)
R. *v* MJ see R. *v* J
R. *v* Mohamed (Abdi Ahmed) see Attorney General's Reference (No.93 of 2006), Re
R. *v* Mohammed (Farida Said); *joined case* R. *v* Osman (Abdullah Mohamed) [2007]
　EWCA Crim 2332; *Times*, December 17, 2007, CA (Crim Div) . . . .　　*Digested*, 07/**897**
R. *v* Mohammed (Liban) see Attorney General's Reference (Nos.24, 25, 26, 27, 28
　and 29 of 2006), Re
R. *v* Mohammed (Raza) [2006] EWCA Crim 1107; [2007] 1 Cr. App. R. (S.) 16, CA
　(Crim Div) . . . .　　*Digested*, 07/**3600**
R. *v* Molcher (Andrew Alan) [2006] EWCA Crim 1522; [2007] 1 Cr. App. R. (S.) 48,
　CA (Crim Div) . . . .　　*Digested*, 07/**3760**
R. *v* Momoh (Ahmed) [2006] EWCA Crim 2489; [2007] 1 Cr. App. R. (S.) 100, CA
　(Crim Div) . . . .　　*Digested*, 07/**3779**

R. v Monfries (Karen) [2003] EWCA Crim 3348; [2004] 2 Cr. App. R. (S.) 3, CA
(Crim Div) . . . . *Digested*, 04/**3398**:
Considered, 07/3646

R. v Monopolies and Mergers Commission Ex p. Argyll Group Plc; *sub nom* R. v
Secretary of State for Trade and Industry Ex p. Argyll Group Plc [1986] 1 W.L.R.
763; [1986] 2 All E.R. 257; (1986) 2 B.C.C. 99086, CA (Civ Div) . . . . *Digested*, 86/**3397**:
Applied, 91/89, 95/142, 07/3967: *Considered*, 87/21, 88/3552

R. v Monopolies and Mergers Commission Ex p. South Yorkshire Transport Ltd; *sub
nom* South Yorkshire Transport v Monopolies and Mergers Commission [1993] 1
W.L.R. 23; [1993] 1 All E.R. 289; [1993] B.C.C. 111; [1994] E.C.C. 231; (1993)
143 N.L.J. 128; *Times*, December 17, 1992, HL; reversing [1992] 1 W.L.R. 291;
[1992] 1 All E.R. 257; [1992] B.C.C. 340; [1992] E.C.C. 432; (1992) 4 Admin.
L.R. 385; [1992] C.O.D. 259; (1992) 156 L.G. Rev. 741; *Times*, December 9,
1991; *Financial Times*, December 6, 1991, CA (Civ Div); affirming [1991] B.C.C.
347; [1992] E.C.C. 1; [1991] C.O.D. 432; *Times*, April 9, 1991; *Daily Telegraph*,
April 25, 1991, QBD . . . . *Digested*, 93/**416**:
Applied, 07/2892

R. v Monteanu (Adrian) see R. v Chirila (Remus Tenistocle)
R. v Montgomery (David John) [2007] EWCA Crim 2157; *Times*, September 6, 2007,
CA (Crim Div) . . . . *Digested*, 07/**886**

R. v Montgomery (James) [1995] 2 All E.R. 28; [1995] 2 Cr. App. R. 23; (1995) 16
Cr. App. R. (S.) 274; [1994] Crim. L.R. 869; (1994) 144 N.L.J. 1445; *Times*, July
19, 1994; *Independent*, July 25, 1994, CA (Crim Div) . . . . *Digested*, 95/**3961**:
Applied, 07/3619: *Referred to*, 97/1484

R. v Montila (Steven William); *sub nom* R. v Montilla (Steven William) [2004] UKHL
50; [2004] 1 W.L.R. 3141; [2005] 1 All E.R. 113; [2005] 1 Cr. App. R. 26; [2005]
Crim. L.R. 479; (2005) 102(3) L.S.G. 30; (2004) 148 S.J.L.B. 1403; *Times*,
November 26, 2004; *Independent*, November 30, 2004, HL; reversing [2003]
EWCA Crim 3082; [2004] 1 W.L.R. 624; [2004] 1 All E.R. 877; [2004] 1 Cr.
App. R. 32; (2003) 100(46) L.S.G. 24; (2003) 147 S.J.L.B. 1305; *Times*,
November 12, 2003, CA (Crim Div) . . . . *Digested*, 05/**806**:
Applied, 05/768, 06/834, 07/872: *Considered*, 06/1731

R. v Montilla (Steven William) see R. v Montila (Steven William)
R. v Moore (Deborah Jayne) [1995] Q.B. 353; [1995] 2 W.L.R. 728; [1995] 4 All E.R.
843; (1995) 16 Cr. App. R. (S.) 748; [1995] Crim. L.R. 347; (1995) 159 J.P.N.
101; (1995) 92(6) L.S.G. 38; (1995) 139 S.J.L.B. 44; *Times*, December 26, 1994,
CA (Crim Div) . . . . *Digested*, 95/**1475**:
Applied, 07/3620

R. v Moran (Kevin John) (1985) 81 Cr. App. R. 51; (1985) 7 Cr. App. R. (S.) 101, CA
(Crim Div) . . . . *Digested*, 85/**529**:
Considered, 89/623, 89/747, 95/1090, 96/29: *Followed*, 07/943:
Referred to, 88/892

R. v Morgan (Paul Robert) see R. v Millberry (William Christopher)
R. v Morris (Emmanuel) see R. v Anderson (Lascelles Fitzalbert)
R. v Morris (Kenneth Morleen) [1972] 1 W.L.R. 228; [1972] 1 All E.R. 384; (1972) 56
Cr. App. R. 175; [1972] R.T.R. 201; [1972] Crim. L.R. 116; [1971] 116 S.J. 17;
Times, November 23, 1971, CA (Crim Div) . . . . *Digested*, 72/**3015**:
Considered, 79/2311: *Disapproved*, 05/902: *Distinguished*, 73/2933, 07/1006

R. v Morrison (Matthew James) see Attorney General's Reference (No.92 of 2006),
Re
R. v Moss (Edgar) see R. v O'Brien (Karl)
R. v Most (1880-81) L.R. 7 Q.B.D. 244, Crown Cases Reserved . . . . *Applied*, 07/849
R. v Mujuru (Sandra) see R. v Stephens (Jerry)
R. v Multani (Hardeep Singh) see Jones (Setting of Minimum Term), Re
R. v Munro (Andrew) see R. v Cuthbertson (Brian George)
R. v Murray (James) [2007] N.I. 49, CA (NI)
R. v Murray (Jason Martin) [2006] EWCA Crim 2251; (2006) 103(36) L.S.G. 33;
(2006) 150 S.J.L.B. 1191, CA (Crim Div) . . . . *Digested*, 07/**943**
R. v Murray (Richard Alexander) see R. v Pepper (Jeremy Paul)
R. v Musone (Ibrahim) [2007] EWCA Crim 1237; [2007] 1 W.L.R. 2467; [2007] 2 Cr.
App. R. 29; (2007) 171 J.P. 425; [2007] Crim. L.R. 972; (2007) 171 J.P.N. 689;
(2007) 151 S.J.L.B. 709; *Times*, June 11, 2007, CA (Crim Div) . . . . *Digested*, 07/**825**
R. v Mutede (Lindiwe) [2005] EWCA Crim 3208; [2006] 2 Cr. App. R. (S.) 22, CA
(Crim Div) . . . . *Digested*, 07/**3644**:
Considered, 07/3716

R. v Myers (Dean Earl); *joined case* R. v Ennis-Simpson (Michael) [2007] EWCA Crim
599; [2007] 2 Cr. App. R. 19; [2007] R.T.R. 34, CA (Crim Div) . . . . *Digested*, 07/**1005**
R. v N (Kenneth) [2006] EWCA Crim 3309; (2007) 171 J.P. 158; (2007) 171 J.P.N.
382, CA (Crim Div) . . . . *Digested*, 07/**833**
R. v Nafei (Abdelkhalek) [2004] EWCA Crim 3238; [2005] 2 Cr. App. R. (S.) 24;
[2006] M.H.L.R. 176; [2005] Crim. L.R. 409, CA (Crim Div) . . . . *Digested*, 05/**3632**:
Considered, 07/3617

R. v National Insurance Commissioner Ex p. Hudson see Jones v Secretary of State for
Social Services

R. *v* National Insurance Commissioner Ex p. Jones see Jones *v* Secretary of State for
Social Services

R. *v* National Insurance Commissioner Ex p. Lloyd-Jones see Jones *v* Secretary of
State for Social Services

R. *v* National Lottery Commission Ex p. Camelot Group Plc [2001] E.M.L.R. 3; *Times*,
October 12, 2000, QBD . . . . *Digested*, 00/**4072**:
Considered, 07/1946

R. *v* Navabi (Fraydon); *joined case* R. *v* Embaye (Senait Tekie) [2005] EWCA Crim
2865; *Times*, December 5, 2005, CA (Crim Div) . . . . *Digested*, 06/**857**:
Applied, 06/804: *Considered*, 07/2323

R. *v* Nazifi (Elida) [2006] EWCA Crim 1743; [2007] 1 Cr. App. R. (S.) 66, CA (Crim
Div) . . . . *Digested*, 07/**3712**
Followed, 07/877

R. *v* Neary (Graham Robert) [2002] EWCA Crim 1736, CA (Crim Div) . . . .

R. *v* Neaven (Damian James) [2006] EWCA Crim 955; [2007] 2 All E.R. 891; [2006]
Crim. L.R. 909, CA (Crim Div) . . . . *Digested*, 07/**830**

R. *v* Nelson (Ashley George) [2006] EWCA Crim 3412; [2007] Crim. L.R. 709, CA
(Crim Div)

R. *v* Nelson (Patrick Alan) [2001] EWCA Crim 2264; [2002] 1 Cr. App. R. (S.) 134;
[2001] Crim. L.R. 999; *Times*, December 10, 2001; *Independent*, October 30,
2001, CA (Crim Div) . . . . *Digested*, 01/**1369**:
Applied, 05/3743: *Considered*, 02/3984, 03/3840, 04/3367, 05/3648,
05/3741, 07/3639

R. *v* Neuberg (Karen Jayne) [2007] EWCA Crim 1994; (2007) 104(36) L.S.G. 31;
(2007) 151 S.J.L.B. 1164, CA (Crim Div)

R. *v* Neville (Daniel John) see Attorney General's Reference (No.2 of 2004), Re

R. *v* Newman (Lee) see R. *v* Foster (Mark)

R. *v* Norman (Shane Martin); *joined cases* R. *v* Cory (Rodney Phillip); R. *v* Igbanoi
(Ambrose Otsemobor); R. *v* Walton (Lee Alan); R. *v* Egan (Jason); R. *v* Hussain
(Jameed) [2006] EWCA Crim 1792; [2007] 1 Cr. App. R. (S.) 82; [2006]
Crim. L.R. 1072; *Times*, August 4, 2006, CA (Crim Div) . . . . *Digested*, 06/**3833**:
Considered, 07/3735

R. *v* North and East Devon HA Ex p. Coughlan [2001] Q.B. 213; [2000] 2 W.L.R.
622; [2000] 3 All E.R. 850; (2000) 2 L.G.L.R. 1; [1999] B.L.G.R. 703; (1999) 2
C.C.L. Rep. 285; [1999] Lloyd's Rep. Med. 306; (2000) 51 B.M.L.R. 1; [1999]
C.O.D. 340; (1999) 96(31) L.S.G. 39; (1999) 143 S.J.L.B. 213; *Times*, July 20,
1999; *Independent*, July 20, 1999, CA (Civ Div); affirming (1999) 2 C.C.L. Rep.
27; (1999) 47 B.M.L.R. 27; [1999] C.O.D. 174; *Times*, December 29, 1998,
QBD . . . . *Digested*, 99/**2643**:
Applied, 00/4526, 01/5879, 02/46, 02/4293, 03/1917, 03/2837, 03/3399,
03/4101, 03/4713, 04/1905, 04/2643, 04/3859, 05/1837, 06/40, 06/1927,
07/3937: *Considered*, 03/3399, 05/2154, 06/1163, 06/1436, 06/2224, 07/45,
07/57, 07/1946: *Distinguished*, 03/4091, 05/4121: *Followed*, 99/3931,
00/1915

R. *v* North East Suffolk Magistrates Court Ex p. DPP see R. *v* Warley Magistrates
Court Ex p. DPP

R. *v* Northallerton Magistrates Court Ex p. Dove [2000] 1 Cr. App. R. (S.) 136; (1999)
163 J.P. 657; [1999] Crim. L.R. 760; [1999] C.O.D. 598; (1999) 163 J.P.N. 894;
Times, June 17, 1999, QBD . . . . *Digested*, 99/**985**:
Applied, 07/961: *Cited*, 00/4296: *Considered*, 05/729

R. *v* O (Claire) see R. *v* R (Amer)

R. *v* O (Jason Patrick) (A Juvenile) see Attorney General's Reference (Nos.78, 79 and
85 of 1998), Re

R. *v* O (Seun) see Attorney General's Reference (Nos.24, 25, 26, 27, 28 and 41 of
2006), Re

R. *v* O'Brien (Barry Paul) [2006] EWCA Crim 1419; [2007] 1 Cr. App. R. (S.) 35, CA
(Crim Div) . . . . *Digested*, 07/**3752**

R. *v* O'Brien (Karl); *joined cases* R. *v* Llewellyn (Gareth); R. *v* Moss (Edgar); R. *v* Harris
(Christopher) [2006] EWCA Crim 1741; [2007] 1 W.L.R. 833; [2006] 4 All
E.R. 1012; [2007] 1 Cr. App. R. (S.) 75; [2006] Crim. L.R. 1074; *Times*, August
30, 2006, CA (Crim Div) . . . . *Digested*, 06/**3681**:
Applied, 07/3650, 07/3660: *Considered*, 07/3639

R. *v* O'Leary (Gregory Patrick) [2007] EWCA Crim 186; [2007] 2 Cr. App. R. (S.) 51,
CA (Crim Div) . . . . *Digested*, 07/**3684**

R. *v* O'Mahoney (Michael Jon) see R. *v* Sheehan (Denny John)

R. *v* O'Reilly (Darren) see R. *v* Ashton (John)

R. *v* Oakley (Andrew) (1990-91) 12 Cr. App. R. (S.) 215, CA (Crim Div) . . . . *Digested*, 92/**1420**:
Considered, 97/1456, 07/3743

R. *v* Odewale (Ayodele); *joined cases* R. *v* Awofadeju (Moses); R. *v* Oshungbure
(Kazeem) [2004] EWCA Crim 145; [2004] 2 Cr. App. R. (S.) 47, CA (Crim
Div) . . . . *Digested*, 04/**3361**:
Considered, 07/3618

R. *v* Okine (Melanie) [2006] EWCA Crim 1158; [2007] 1 Cr. App. R. (S.) 15, CA (Crim
Div)

R. *v* Olditch (Toby) see R. *v* Jones (Margaret)

R. *v* Oliver (Mark David); *joined cases* R. *v* Hartrey (Michael Patrick); R. *v* Baldwin (Leslie) [2002] EWCA Crim 2766; [2003] 1 Cr. App. R. 28; [2003] 2 Cr. App. R. (S.) 15; [2003] Crim. L.R. 127; *Times*, December 6, 2002, CA (Crim Div) . . . *Digested*, 03/**3745**: *Applied*, 04/3376, 05/3349: *Considered*, 04/838, 04/3377, 05/3645, 05/3647, 06/3740, 07/3665: *Followed*, 04/849, 05/3646

R. *v* Olubitan (Ayodele Olusegun) [2003] EWCA Crim 2940; [2004] 2 Cr. App. R. (S.) 14; [2004] Crim. L.R. 155; *Times*, November 14, 2003, CA (Crim Div) . . . . *Digested*, 04/**3309**: *Applied*, 05/840, 06/909, 07/3615: *Distinguished*, 06/3676

R. *v* Olugboja (Stephen) [1982] Q.B. 320; [1981] 3 W.L.R. 585; (1981) 73 Cr. App. R. 344, CA (Crim Div) . . . . *Digested*, 81/**520**: *Applied*, 07/919

R. *v* Onung (Andrew Okon) [2006] EWCA Crim 2813; [2007] 2 Cr. App. R. (S.) 3, CA (Crim Div) . . . . *Digested*, 07/**3636**

R. *v* Orr (Ross) see Attorney General's Reference (Nos.24, 25, 26, 27, 28 and 29 of 2006), Re

R. *v* Osbourne (Gary Ozzy) [2007] EWCA Crim 481; [2007] Crim. L.R. 712; *Times*, April 24, 2007, CA (Crim Div) . . . . *Digested*, 07/**827**

R. *v* Oshungbure (Kazeem) see R. *v* Odewale (Ayodele)

R. *v* Osieh (Joseph) [1996] 1 W.L.R. 1260; [1996] 2 Cr. App. R. 145; [1997] Crim. L.R. 133; *Times*, March 5, 1996, CA (Crim Div) . . . . *Digested*, 96/**1615**: *Considered*, 07/994

R. *v* Osman (Abdullah Mohamed) see R. *v* Mohammed (Farida Said)

R. *v* Overton (Nicholas Andrew) [2007] EWCA Crim 811; [2007] 2 Cr. App. R. (S.) 102, CA (Crim Div)

R. *v* Owen (Henry Geoffrey) see Board of Trade *v* Owen

R. *v* Owens (Mark James); *joined case* R. *v* Owens (Patrick Gary) [2006] EWCA Crim 2206; (2006) 103(36) L.S.G. 33; (2006) 150 S.J.L.B. 1188, CA (Crim Div) . . . *Digested*, 07/**829**

R. *v* Owens (Patrick Gary) see R. *v* Owens (Mark James)

R. *v* Owoola (Donga James) see R. *v* Gbedje (Nanguy Ruddy)

R. *v* Oxford CC Ex p. Doyle (1998) 30 H.L.R. 506, QBD . . . . *Digested*, 97/**2670**: *Applied*, 05/2007, 07/2153

R. *v* Ozen (Costs) [2006] 5 Costs L.R. 847, Sup Ct Costs Office . . . . *Digested*, 07/**960**

R. *v* P see R. *v* H

R. *v* P; *joined case* R. *v* Blackburn (Derek Stephen) [2007] EWCA Crim 2290; (2007) 151 S.J.L.B. 1438; *Times*, December 24, 2007, CA (Crim Div)

R. *v* P; *sub nom* R. *v* P Ltd; R. *v* E [2007] EWCA Crim 1937; (2007) 151 S.J.L.B. 987; *Times*, August 13, 2007, CA (Crim Div) . . . . *Digested*, 07/**2075**

R. *v* P (Courtney) see Attorney General's Reference (Nos.24, 25, 26, 27, 28 and 41 of 2006), Re

R. *v* P Ltd see R. *v* P

R. *v* Palmer (Daniel Roy) see R. *v* Peters (Benjamin)

R. *v* Panel on Takeovers and Mergers Ex p. Datafin Plc [1987] Q.B. 815; [1987] 2 W.L.R. 699; [1987] 1 All E.R. 564; (1987) 3 B.C.C. 10; [1987] B.C.L.C. 104; [1987] 1 F.T.L.R. 181; (1987) 131 S.J. 23, CA (Civ Div) . . . . *Digested*, 87/**21**: *Applied*, 91/83, 92/13, 01/5140, 03/68, 06/4713, 07/55: *Considered*, 86/2054, 90/3912, 91/76, 92/12, 92/38, 93/31, 93/32, 93/33, 95/47, 95/55

R. *v* Parole Board Ex p. Gordon see R. (on the application of Gordon) *v* Parole Board

R. *v* Parole Board Ex p. Oyston [2000] Prison L.R. 45; *Independent*, April 17, 2000, CA (Civ Div) . . . . *Considered*, 07/2988

R. *v* Parole Board Ex p. Watson [1996] 1 W.L.R. 906; [1996] 2 All E.R. 641; (1996) 8 Admin. L.R. 460; [1997] C.O.D. 72; *Times*, March 11, 1996, CA (Civ Div); affirming *Independent*, November 2, 1995, QBD . . . . *Digested*, 96/**4576**: *Applied*, 01/4570, 07/2988: *Considered*, 03/2894

R. *v* Parole Board Ex p. White, *Times*, December 30, 1994, DC . . . . *Digested*, 95/**116**: *Considered*, 07/2975

R. *v* Parry (Neil Edward) [2006] EWCA Crim 1924; [2007] 1 Cr. App. R. (S.) 62, CA (Crim Div) . . . . *Digested*, 07/**3610**

R. *v* Parsons (John David) see R. *v* S

R. *v* Passmore (Paul Darren) [2007] EWCA Crim 2053; (2007) 171 J.P. 519; (2007) 171 J.P.N. 888; *Times*, June 28, 2007, CA (Crim Div) . . . . *Digested*, 07/**922**

R. *v* Patel (Rupal) [2006] EWCA Crim 2689; [2007] 1 Cr. App. R. 12; [2007] I.C.R. 571; [2007] Crim. L.R. 476, CA (Crim Div) . . . . *Digested*, 07/**3620**

R. *v* Patel (Taru) [2006] EWCA Crim 1480; [2007] 1 Cr. App. R. (S.) 33, CA (Crim Div)

R. *v* Paton (James Daniel) see R. *v* Brady (Carl Jason)

R. *v* Pattison (Leslie Dennis) see R. *v* Griffiths (Philip)

R. *v* Payne (John) [2007] EWCA Crim 157; [2007] 2 Cr. App. R. (S.) 45, CA (Crim Div) . . . . *Digested*, 07/**3592**

R. *v* Pearce (Stephen John) (1981) 72 Cr. App. R. 295; [1981] Crim. L.R. 639, CA (Crim Div) . . . . *Digested*, 81/**462**: *Applied*, 07/2908: *Distinguished*, 00/1097

R. v Pepper (Jeremy Paul); *joined cases* R. v Barber (Kenneth Leslie); R. v Lamont (Martin); R. v G; R. v Murray (Richard Alexander) [2005] EWCA Crim 1181; [2006] 1 Cr. App. R. (S.) 20; *Times*, May 10, 2005, CA (Crim Div) . . . . *Digested*, 05/**3743**: *Considered*, 07/3639, 07/3736

R. v Perry (Darren Michael) see Attorney General's Reference (Nos.59 and 60 of 2007), Re

R. v Peters (Benjamin); *joined cases* R. v Palmer (Daniel Roy); R. v Campbell (Shantelle Jamie) [2005] EWCA Crim 605; [2005] 2 Cr. App. R. (S.) 101; [2005] Crim. L.R. 492; *Times*, March 29, 2005, CA (Crim Div) . . . . *Digested*, 05/**3682**: *Applied*, 05/3735, 06/3754, 07/863: *Considered*, 05/3764, 06/3779, 06/3782, 07/3682, 07/3690, 07/3783, 07/3784: *Distinguished*, 06/3770

R. v Phelps (David) see Attorney General's Reference (Nos.104, 105 and 106 of 2006), Re

R. v Phillips (Costs) [2007] 1 Costs L.R. 121, Sup Ct Costs Office

R. v Pickstock (Christopher David) [2007] EWCA Crim 299; [2007] 2 Cr. App. R. (S.) 48, CA (Crim Div) . . . . *Digested*, 07/**3596**

R. v Pintori (Andrei) [2007] EWCA Crim 1700; [2007] Crim. L.R. 997; (2007) 151 S.J.L.B. 984, CA (Crim Div)

R. v Pluck (Perry) [2006] EWCA Crim 1394; [2007] 1 Cr. App. R. (S.) 9, CA (Crim Div)

R. v Plymouth Justices Ex p. Rogers [1982] Q.B. 863; [1982] 3 W.L.R. 1; [1982] 2 All E.R. 175; (1982) 75 Cr. App. R. 64; [1982] 3 C.M.L.R. 221; (1982) 126 S.J. 308, QBD . . . . *Digested*, 82/**560**: *Applied*, 07/1330

R. v Poel (Karel) see R. v Richardson (Jack Virgil)

R. v Pollard (Stephen) see Attorney General's Reference (No.149 of 2006), Re

R. v Pollin (Steven Lee) [1997] 2 Cr. App. R. (S.) 356, CA (Crim Div) . . . . *Digested*, 98/**1403**: *Applied*, 06/3770: *Considered*, 98/1407, 00/1267, 03/3729, 07/3798

R. v Pontypridd Juvenile Magistrates Court Ex p. B (1989) 153 J.P. 213; [1988] Crim. L.R. 842; (1989) 153 J.P.N. 78; *Times*, July 28, 1988; *Independent*, August 1, 1988, QBD . . . . *Digested*, 89/**682**: *Considered*, 07/1026

R. v Porter (Kye James) [2006] EWCA Crim 2857; [2007] 1 Cr. App. R. (S.) 115, CA (Crim Div) . . . . *Digested*, 07/**3673**

R. v Porter (Ross Warwick) [2006] EWCA Crim 560; [2006] 1 W.L.R. 2633; [2007] 2 All E.R. 625; [2006] 2 Cr. App. R. 25; [2006] Crim. L.R. 748; (2006) 103(14) L.S.G. 28; *Times*, June 21, 2006, CA (Crim Div). *Digested*, 06/**858**

R. v Potter see R. v D

R. v Powell (Anthony Glassford); *joined cases* R. v Daniels (Antonio Eval); R. v English (Philip) [1999] 1 A.C. 1; [1997] 3 W.L.R. 959; [1997] 4 All E.R. 545; [1998] 1 Cr. App. R. 261; (1998) 162 J.P. 1; [1998] Crim. L.R. 48; (1997) 161 J.P.N. 1100; (1998) 162 J.P.N. 26; (1997) 147 N.L.J. 1654; *Times*, October 31, 1997; *Independent*, November 11, 1997, HL; affirming [1996] 1 Cr. App. R. 14; *Times*, June 2, 1995; *Independent*, June 26, 1995, CA (Crim Div) . . . . *Digested*, 97/**1220**: *Applied*, 00/5468, 00/5481, 06/862, 06/1606: *Considered*, 97/1327, 98/959, 04/855: *Followed*, 98/1035, 07/877

R. v Pressdee (Robert Christopher) [2007] EWCA Crim 1289; [2007] Crim. L.R. 739, CA (Crim Div)

R. v Price (Graham John) [2006] EWCA Crim 972; [2007] 1 Cr. App. R. (S.) 6, CA (Crim Div) . . . . *Digested*, 07/**3762**

R. v Price (Margaret); *joined case* R. v Stephenson (Lawrence) [2006] EWCA Crim 1478; [2007] 1 Cr. App. R. (S.) 23, CA (Crim Div) . . . . *Digested*, 07/**3657**

R. v Price (Paul Graham) see R. v Graham (Hemamali Krishna)

R. v Price (Robert William) see R. v C

R. v Pritchard (Philip) see R. v Jones (Margaret)

R. v Purdy (Gary Mark) [2007] EWCA Crim 295; (2007) 151 S.J.L.B. 196, CA (Crim Div). . . . . *Digested*, 07/**1024**

R. v Purvis (Paul Nigel) see R. v Jones (Anthony William)

R. v Pusey (Lloyd Aaron) see R. v Gordon (Gavin Stephen)

R. v PW see Attorney General's Reference (No.77 of 2006), Re

R. v Q (Steven James) (A Juvenile) see Attorney General's Reference (Nos.4 and 7 of 2002), Re

R. v Qayyum (Abdul) [2006] EWCA Crim 1127; [2007] Crim. L.R. 160, CA (Crim Div)

R. v Quillan (Edward Steven) see R. v Last (Emma)

R. v Quillan (James Angus) see R. v Last (Emma)

R. v Qureshi (Sajad) [2006] EWCA Crim 2092; [2007] 1 Cr. App. R. (S.) 85, CA (Crim Div) . . . . *Digested*, 07/**3668**

R. v R see R. v M

R. v R see R. v M

R. v R see Attorney General's Reference (Nos.66 and 67 of 2006), Re

R. v R; *sub nom* Prosecution Right of Appeal (No.23 of 2007), Re [2007] EWCA Crim 3312; (2007) 104(46) L.S.G. 27, CA (Crim Div)

R. *v* R (Amer); *joined cases* R. *v* V (Abolghasem); R. *v* L (Abraham); R. *v* S (Imran); R. *v* C (James); R. *v* O (Claire); R. *v* M (Faisal Jamil) [2006] EWCA Crim 1974; [2007] 1 Cr. App. R. 10; [2007] Crim. L.R. 79, CA (Crim Div) . . . .   *Digested*, 07/**870**: *Followed*, 07/871

R. *v* R (Malcolm James) see Attorney General's Reference (No.27 of 2001), Re

R. *v* Rahman (Islamur); *joined cases* R. *v* Akram (Kamer); R. *v* Amin (Anjum Nisa); R. *v* Ali (Liaquat) [2007] EWCA Crim 342; [2007] 1 W.L.R. 2191; [2007] 3 All E.R. 396; [2007] 2 Cr. App. R. 16; [2007] Crim. L.R. 721; *Times*, March 2, 2007, CA (Crim Div) . . . .   *Digested*, 07/**877**

R. *v* Rainford (Craig Martin) [2006] EWCA Crim 3226; [2007] 2 Cr. App. R. (S.) 18, CA (Crim Div) . . . .   *Digested*, 07/**3776**

R. *v* Ralph (John Andrew) see Ralph (Setting of Minimum Term), Re

R. *v* Rampley (Kim) [2006] EWCA Crim 2203; [2007] 1 Cr. App. R. (S.) 87; [2007] Crim. L.R. 84, CA (Crim Div) . . . .   *Digested*, 07/**3754**

R. *v* Ramzan (Mohammed) see R. *v* Vernett-Showers (Michael)

R. *v* Rance (Ryan) see Attorney General's Reference (Nos.52 and 53 of 2006), Re

R. *v* Ranson (Raymond); *sub nom* R. *v* Kerr (Andrew John) [2007] EWCA Crim 153; [2007] 2 Cr. App. R. (S.) 55, CA (Crim Div) . . . .   *Digested*, 07/**3683**

R. *v* Rayworth (Paul Michael) [2003] EWCA Crim 2887; [2004] 1 Cr. App. R. (S.) 75, CA (Crim Div) . . . .   *Digested*, 04/**3406**: *Applied*, 07/3714

R. *v* Redfern (David Christopher) see R. *v* Jordan (Andrew James)

R. *v* Rehman (Fazal) [2006] EWCA Crim 1900; [2007] Crim. L.R. 101, CA (Crim Div)

R. *v* Rehman (Zakir); *joined case* R. *v* Wood (Gary Dominic) [2005] EWCA Crim 2056; [2006] 1 Cr. App. R. (S.) 77; [2005] Crim. L.R. 878; *Times*, September 27, 2005, CA (Crim Div) . . . .   *Digested*, 05/**3693**: *Applied*, 06/3717: *Considered*, 07/3718: *Distinguished*, 07/3791

R. *v* Revell (Adam John) [2006] EWCA Crim 676; [2006] 2 Cr. App. R. (S.) 95, CA (Crim Div) . . . .   *Digested*, 07/**3775**

R. *v* Reynolds (Michael Edwin); *joined cases* R. *v* Thompson (Amelio); R. *v* S; R. *v* D; R. *v* L; R. *v* Honore (James); R. *v* Webb (John Paul); R. *v* Lubwama (Abdul Musisi) [2007] EWCA Crim 538; [2007] 4 All E.R. 369; [2007] 2 Cr. App. R. (S.) 87; [2007] Crim. L.R. 493; *Times*, March 21, 2007, CA (Crim Div) . . . .   *Digested*, 07/**966**: *Considered*, 07/21

R. *v* RG; *sub nom* R. *v* Gazzard (Royston John) [2007] EWCA Crim 405; [2007] 2 Cr. App. R. (S.) 70; [2007] Crim. L.R. 489, CA (Crim Div) . . . .   *Digested*, 07/**3742**

R. *v* Richards (Christopher Andrew) [2006] EWCA Crim 2519; [2007] 1 W.L.R. 847; [2007] 1 Cr. App. R. (S.) 120; [2007] Crim. L.R. 173; *Times*, November 13, 2006, CA (Crim Div) . . . .   *Digested*, 07/**2990**

R. *v* Richards (Ian) see Attorney General's Reference (Nos.90 and 91 of 2006), Re

R. *v* Richards (Josh) see R. *v* Jones (Margaret)

R. *v* Richards (Natalie) see R. *v* Jones (Barry John)

R. *v* Richards (Nelson) see Attorney General's Reference (Nos.42, 43 and 44 of 2006), Re

R. *v* Richardson (Jack Virgil); *joined cases* R. *v* Sheppard (Dionne); R. *v* Abery (Lee Alan); R. *v* Little (Liam John); R. *v* Poel (Karel); R. *v* Robertson (Karen Ann) [2006] EWCA Crim 3186; [2007] 2 All E.R. 601; [2007] 2 Cr. App. R. (S.) 36; [2007] R.T.R. 29; [2007] Crim. L.R. 315; *Times*, January 15, 2007, CA (Crim Div) . . . .   *Digested*, 07/**3590**: *Applied*, 07/3588, 07/3589, 07/3592, 07/3595: *Considered*, 07/3591, 07/3596, 07/5512

R. *v* Richardson (John Mark) see R. *v* Saltmarsh (Richard)

R. *v* Richer (Joseph) see Attorney General's Reference (No.58 of 2006), Re

R. *v* Riding (Ashley Cuncliffe) see Attorney General's Reference (No.32 of 2006), Re

R. *v* Rigby (Carl); *joined case* R. *v* Bailey (Gareth Scott) [2006] EWCA Crim 1653; [2006] 1 W.L.R. 3067; [2007] 1 Cr. App. R. (S.) 73; *Times*, August 23, 2006, CA (Crim Div) . . . .   *Digested*, 06/**3672**

R. *v* Rigelsford (Costs) [2006] 3 Costs L.R. 518, Sup Ct Costs Office. . . . .   *Digested*, 06/**931**: *Applied*, 07/956

R. *v* Roberts (Darren) see R. *v* Lawson (Michael David)

R. *v* Roberts (David Wynne) (Application for Permission to Appeal) see Caines (Setting of Minimum Term), Re

R. *v* Robertson (David John) see R. *v* Cuthbertson (Brian George)

R. *v* Robertson (Karen Ann) see R. *v* Richardson (Jack Virgil)

R. *v* Robinson (Dean Phillip) [2006] EWCA Crim 613; [2006] 2 Cr. App. R. (S.) 88, CA (Crim Div) . . . .   *Digested*, 07/**3619**

R. *v* Robson (George) see R. *v* Robson (Thomas Anthony)

R. *v* Robson (Kevin) [2006] EWCA Crim 1414; [2007] 1 All E.R. 506; [2007] 1 Cr. App. R. (S.) 54; (2006) 170 J.P. 637; [2006] Crim. L.R. 935; (2007) 171 J.P.N. 123, CA (Crim Div) . . . .   *Digested*, 06/**3890**

R. *v* Robson (Thomas Anthony); *joined cases* R. *v* Wilson (Robert); R. *v* Robson (George) [2006] EWCA Crim 2754; [2007] Crim. L.R. 478; (2007) 151 S.J.L.B. 60, CA (Crim Div)

R. v Rochdale MBC Ex p. Milne (No.1); *joined case* R. v Rochdale MBC Ex p. Tew
  [2000] Env. L.R. 1; [1999] 3 P.L.R. 74; [2000] J.P.L. 54; [1999] E.G. 70 (C.S.);
  (1999) 96(20) L.S.G. 41, QBD . . . . *Digested,* 00/**4479**:
                Applied, 02/3717: *Approved,* 03/3420: *Considered,* 07/3272:
                              Distinguished, 03/3414, 04/3102
R. v Rochdale MBC Ex p. Milne (No.2) [2001] Env. L.R. 22; (2001) 81 P. & C.R. 27;
  [2001] J.P.L. 229 (Note); [2001] J.P.L. 470; [2000] E.G. 103 (C.S.), QBD . . . . *Digested,* 01/**4680**:
                  Applied, 03/3416, 07/1500: *Approved,* 03/3420
R. v Rochdale MBC Ex p. Schemet [1993] 1 F.C.R. 306; 91 L.G.R. 425; [1993] C.O.D.
  113; *Times,* September 9, 1992; *Independent,* November 9, 1992; *Guardian,*
  October 7, 1992, QBD . . . . *Digested,* 93/**1707**:
                Considered, 07/45: *Followed,* 95/1928: *Not followed,* 95/1909
R. v Rochdale MBC Ex p. Tew see R. v Rochdale MBC Ex p. Milne (No.1)
R. v Rochford Justices Ex p. Buck (1979) 68 Cr. App. R. 114; [1978] Crim. L.R. 492,
  DC . . . . *Digested,* 79/**1728**:
                         Considered, 07/934: *Followed,* 06/496
R. v Roci (Lorenc); *joined case* R. v Ismailaj (Vullnet) [2005] EWCA Crim 3404;
  [2006] 2 Cr. App. R. (S.) 15, CA (Crim Div) . . . . *Digested,* 06/**3856**:
                                     Considered, 07/3765
R. v Rodgers (Dennis) 2006 SCC 15; 22 B.H.R.C. 220, Sup Ct (Can)
R. v Rodgers (Stephen) see R. v Rogers (Stephen)
R. v Rodrigo De Oliveira (Werleson) see Attorney General's Reference (Nos.118 and
  119 of 2006), Re
R. v Rogers (Hone) [1979] 1 All E.R. 693; (1979) 69 Cr. App. R. 96, Sup Ct Taxing
  Office . . . . *Digested,* 79/**2127**:
                    Considered, 84/2004, 98/3706: *Distinguished,* 07/960
R. v Rogers (Philip) [2007] UKHL 8; [2007] 2 A.C. 62; [2007] 2 W.L.R. 280; [2007]
  2 All E.R. 433; [2007] 2 Cr. App. R. 7; 23 B.H.R.C. 88; [2007] Crim. L.R. 579;
  (2007) 151 S.J.L.B. 332; *Times,* March 1, 2007, HL; affirming [2005] EWCA
  Crim 2863; [2006] 1 W.L.R. 962; [2006] 1 Cr. App. R. 14; [2006] Crim. L.R.
  351; *Times,* November 22, 2005, CA (Crim Div). . . . .   *Digested,* 07/**911**
R. v Rogers (Stephen); *sub nom* R. v Rodgers (Stephen) [2003] EWCA Crim 945;
  [2003] 1 W.L.R. 1374; [2003] 2 Cr. App. R. 10; (2003) 100(19) L.S.G. 29;
  (2003) 147 S.J.L.B. 353; *Times,* March 20, 2003, CA (Crim Div) . . . . *Digested,* 03/**794**:
                                       Overruled, 07/899
R. v Rollock (Ashley Kenneth) see R. v Mirza (Shabbir Ali)
R. v Rowe (Andrew) [2007] EWCA Crim 635; [2007] Q.B. 975; [2007] 3 W.L.R. 177;
  [2007] 3 All E.R. 36; [2007] 2 Cr. App. R. 14; [2007] 2 Cr. App. R. (S.) 92;
  [2007] Crim. L.R. 744; *Times,* March 26, 2007, CA (Crim Div) . . . . *Digested,* 07/**927**:
                                       Followed, 07/1012
R. v Rowley (Michael) [1991] 1 W.L.R. 1020; [1991] 4 All E.R. 649; (1992) 94 Cr.
  App. R. 95; (1992) 156 J.P. 319; [1991] Crim. L.R. 785; (1991) 155 J.P.N. 672;
  (1991) 135 S.J.L.B. 84; *Times,* July 18, 1991, CA (Crim Div) . . . . *Digested,* 92/**1107**:
                                       Considered, 07/916
R. v Rumble (Jonathan Mark) [2003] EWCA Crim 770; (2003) 167 J.P. 205; (2003)
  167 J.P.N. 351, CA (Crim Div) . . . . *Digested,* 03/**786**:
                        Applied, 06/849: *Considered,* 07/886
R. v Russell (John Paul) see R. v McNee (Michael)
R. v Russell (Leon) see Attorney General's Reference (No.66 of 2007), Re
R. v Russell (Robert John) see Attorney General's Reference (Nos.78, 79 and 85 of
  1998), Re
R. v Russell (Sebastian Lee) (Costs) [2006] 5 Costs L.R. 841, Sup Ct Costs Office . . *Digested,* 07/**959**
R. v Ryan (John) see R. v Vernett-Showers (Michael)
R. v S see R. v Reynolds (Michael Edwin)
R. v S see R. v Harries (Michael John)
R. v S see R. v K
R. v S; *joined cases* R. v Burt (Scott-Rab John); R. v Parsons (John David); R. v Carr
  (Craig Edward); R. v Hargreaves (Stephen Lee); R. v Denton (Vincent); R. v
  Taylor (Timothy Nicholas); R. v Coyne (Timothy Malcolm); R. v H [2005] EWCA
  Crim 3616; [2006] 2 Cr. App. R. (S.) 35; (2006) 170 J.P. 145; [2006] Crim.
  L.R. 459; (2006) 170 J.P.N. 234; *Times,* December 30, 2005, CA (Crim Div) . . *Digested,* 06/**3709**:
                             Considered, 06/3890, 07/3640
R. v S [2007] EWCA Crim 2105; (2007) 151 S.J.L.B. 1260, CA (Crim Div)
R. v S (Andrew) [2006] EWCA Crim 1303; [2007] 1 W.L.R. 63; [2006] 2 Cr. App. R.
  31, CA (Crim Div). . . . .   *Digested,* 06/**778**
R. v S (Imran) see R. v R (Amer)
R. v S (Joe) see R. v D (Anthony)
R. v S (Jonathan Charles); *joined case* R. v W (Malcolm) [2006] EWCA Crim 1404;
  [2007] 2 All E.R. 974; *Independent,* July 4, 2006, CA (Crim Div) . . . . *Digested,* 06/**785**
R. v S (Maureen) (1993) 14 Cr. App. R. (S.) 788, CA (Crim Div) . . . . *Digested,* 94/**1274**:
                                       Considered, 07/3607
R. v S (Robert Michael) see R. v Harries (Michael John)

R. v S (Stephen Paul) [2006] EWCA Crim 756; [2006] 2 Cr. App. R. 23; (2006) 170
     J.P. 434; [2007] Crim. L.R. 296; (2006) 170 J.P.N. 760; *Times,* March 29, 2006,
     CA (Crim Div) . . . .   *Digested,* 06/**982**
R. v S (Susan) [2003] EWCA Crim 2300; [2004] 1 Cr. App. R. (S.) 51, CA (Crim Div)   *Digested,* 04/**3328**:
                                  Considered, 07/3607, 07/3741
R. v Sabir (Mohammed) see R. v Vernett-Showers (Michael)
R. v Sacco (Sigismonte) [2006] EWCA Crim 1391; [2007] 1 Cr. App. R. (S.) 39, CA
     (Crim Div) . . . .   *Digested,* 07/**3635**
R. v Saik (Abdulrahman) [2006] UKHL 18; [2007] 1 A.C. 18; [2006] 2 W.L.R. 993;
     [2006] 4 All E.R. 866; [2006] 2 Cr. App. R. 26; [2006] Crim. L.R. 998; (2006)
     103(20) L.S.G. 24; (2006) 150 S.J.L.B. 603; *Times,* May 5, 2006;
     Independent, May 5, 2006, HL; reversing [2004] EWCA Crim 2936; *Times,*
     November 29, 2004, CA (Crim Div) . . . .   *Digested,* 07/**872**:
                        Considered, 07/869, 07/870, 07/871, 07/971
R. v Sajid (Mohammed) see R. v Afonso (Americo Practicio)
R. v Saleem (Abdul); *joined cases* Javed (Umran); Muhid (Abdul) [2007] EWCA Crim
     2692; (2007) 104(44) L.S.G. 33, CA (Crim Div)
R. v Saltmarsh (Richard); *joined cases* R. v Richardson (John Mark); R. v Vasinoras
     (Anton) [2007] EWCA Crim 876; [2007] 2 Cr. App. R. (S.) 99, CA (Crim Div) .   *Digested,* 07/**3647**
R. v Sanders (Shaun Peters) [2006] EWCA Crim 1842; [2007] 1 Cr. App. R. (S.) 74;
     [2006] Crim. L.R. 1078, CA (Crim Div)
R. v Sandhu (Sukhwinder Singh) (Unreported, March 8, 1999), CA (Crim Div) . . . . . .   *Considered,* 07/3674
R. v Sandwell (David Anthony) (1985) 80 Cr. App. R. 78; [1985] R.T.R. 45; (1984) 81
     L.S.G. 2544, CA (Crim Div) . . . .   *Digested,* 85/**3008**:
                                       Considered, 07/3735
R. v Sangha (Bhovinder Singh) see Attorney General's Reference (Nos.88, 89, 90 and
     91 of 2006), Re
R. v Sant (Vicky) (1989) 11 Cr. App. R. (S.) 441, CA (Crim Div) . . . .   *Digested,* 91/**1141**:
                                   Considered, 00/1278, 07/3607
R. v Sargent (Reece) see R. v Case (Darren Lee)
R. v Sarmiento (Danielle); *joined case* R. v Gonzalez (Carmen Janeth) [2002] EWCA
     Crim 2685; [2003] 2 Cr. App. R. (S.) 9, CA (Crim Div) . . . .   *Digested,* 03/**3806**:
                                   Considered, 04/3398, 07/3685
R. v Sawyers (Christopher) see Attorney General's Reference (Nos.4 and 7 of 2002),
     Re
R. v Schumann (Angela) [2007] EWCA Crim 569; [2007] 2 Cr. App. R. (S.) 73, CA
     (Crim Div)
R. v Scunthorpe Justices Ex p. M (1998) 162 J.P. 635; *Times,* March 10, 1998, DC. . . .   *Digested,* 98/**1038**:
          Applied, 00/1047, 05/828, 07/988: *Followed,* 98/1037, 00/1048
R. v Secretary of State for Employment Ex p. Seymour-Smith (C-167/97) [1999] 2
     A.C. 554; [1999] 3 W.L.R. 460; [1999] All E.R. (E.C.) 97; [1999] E.C.R. I-623;
     [1999] 2 C.M.L.R. 273; [1999] C.E.C. 79; [1999] I.C.R. 447; [1999] I.R.L.R.
     253; *Times,* February 25, 1999, ECJ . . . .   *Digested,* 99/**2141**:
            Applied, 04/1268, 05/1268, 05/3886, 05/3886, 06/1306:
         Considered, 01/2319, 05/1265: *Followed,* 00/2160, 03/1307, 03/1341:
               Previous proceedings, 97/2265: *Referred to,* 07/1360:
                           Subsequent proceedings, 00/2210
R. v Secretary of State for Health Ex p. British American Tobacco (Investments) Ltd
     (C491/01) see R. (on the application of British American Tobacco (Investments)
     Ltd) v Secretary of State for Health (C-491/01)
R. v Secretary of State for Health Ex p. Imperial Tobacco Ltd (C-74/99) see Germany
     v European Parliament (C-376/98)
R. v Secretary of State for Health Ex p. United States Tobacco International Inc [1992]
     Q.B. 353; [1991] 3 W.L.R. 529; [1992] 1 All E.R. 212; (1991) 3 Admin. L.R. 735;
     (1992) 11 Tr. L.R. 1; [1991] C.O.D. 268; *Times,* January 4, 1991; *Independent,*
     January 4, 1991; *Guardian,* January 22, 1991; *Daily Telegraph,* January 21, 1991,
     DC . . . .   *Digested,* 92/**4109**:
                                       Considered, 07/1506
R. v Secretary of State for the Environment Ex p. Blake [1984] J.P.L. 101 . . . .   *Digested,* 84/**1617**:
                                  Considered, 04/1817, 07/3421
R. v Secretary of State for the Environment Ex p. Hillingdon LBC [1986] 1 W.L.R. 807;
     [1986] 2 All E.R. 273; (1988) 55 P. & C.R. 241; [1987] R.V.R. 6; [1987] J.P.L.
     717; (1986) 83 L.S.G. 2331; (1986) 130 S.J. 481, CA (Civ Div); affirming [1986]
     1 W.L.R. 192; [1986] 1 All E.R. 810; (1986) 52 P. & C.R. 409; [1987] R.V.R. 6;
     [1986] J.P.L. 363; (1986) 83 L.S.G. 525; (1986) 136 N.L.J. 16; (1986) 130 S.J.
     89; *Times,* November 20, 1985, QBD . . . .   *Digested,* 86/**2040**:
                                       Applied, 07/1183
R. v Secretary of State for the Environment Ex p. Royal Society for the Protection of
     Birds (RSPB) (C-44/95) [1997] Q.B. 206; [1997] 2 W.L.R. 123; [1996] E.C.R.
     I-3805; [1996] 3 C.M.L.R. 411; [1997] Env. L.R. 442; [1997] 2 P.L.R. 1; [1996]
     J.P.L. 844; *Times,* August 2, 1996, ECJ . . . .   *Digested,* 96/**2698**:
                                       Applied, 07/1470

R. v Secretary of State for the Environment, Transport and the Regions Ex p. Jarmain see Jarmain v Secretary of State for the Environment, Transport and the Regions (No.1)

R. v Secretary of State for the Environment, Transport and the Regions Ex p. Spath Holme Ltd see R. (on the application of Spath Holme Ltd) v Secretary of State for the Environment, Transport and the Regions

R. v Secretary of State for the Environment, Transport and the Regions Ex p. Walters; *joined case* R. v Brent LBC Ex p. O'Malley (1998) 30 H.L.R. 328; (1998) 10 Admin. L.R. 265; [1998] C.O.D. 121; *Times*, September 2, 1997, CA (Civ Div); affirming [1997] N.P.C. 41, QBD . . . . *Digested*, 97/**2701**:
Applied, 98/3000: *Considered*, 98/3025, 07/2048

R. v Secretary of State for the Environment, Transport and the Regions Ex p. West Sussex CC (1999) 77 P. & C.R. 263; [1999] P.L.C.R. 163; (1998) 95(32) L.S.G. 31; [1998] N.P.C. 133, QBD . . . . *Digested*, 99/**4274**:
Distinguished, 07/1527

R. v Secretary of State for the Home Department Ex p. Al-Mehdawi; *sub nom* Al-Mehdawi v Secretary of State for the Home Department [1990] 1 A.C. 876; [1989] 3 W.L.R. 1294; [1989] 3 All E.R. 843; [1990] Imm. A.R. 140; (1990) 2 Admin. L.R. 367; [1990] C.O.D. 188; (1990) 134 S.J. 50, HL; reversing [1989] 2 W.L.R. 603; [1989] 1 All E.R. 777; [1989] Imm. A.R. 125; [1989] C.O.D. 280; (1989) 86(10) L.S.G. 42; (1988) 138 N.L.J. Rep. 351; (1989) 133 S.J. 185; *Times*, November 26, 1988; *Independent*, December 6, 1988; *Independent*, November 28, 1988; *Daily Telegraph*, December 2, 1988, CA (Civ Div) . . . . *Digested*, 90/**66**:
Applied, 91/3108, 94/2467, 95/2677, 95/2710, 02/285, 05/430:
Considered, 92/4240, 95/4413, 97/6141: *Distinguished*, 02/2583, 07/2274:
Followed, 95/2284

R. v Secretary of State for the Home Department Ex p. Brind [1991] 1 A.C. 696; [1991] 2 W.L.R. 588; [1991] 1 All E.R. 720; (1991) 3 Admin. L.R. 486; (1991) 141 N.L.J. 199; (1991) 135 S.J. 250; *Times*, February 8, 1991; *Independent*, February 8, 1991; *Guardian*, February 8, 1991, HL; affirming [1990] 2 W.L.R. 787; [1990] 1 All E.R. 469; [1990] C.O.D. 190; (1989) 139 N.L.J. 1751; *Times*, December 7, 1989; *Independent*, December 7, 1989; *Guardian*, December 7, 1989, CA (Civ Div); affirming (1989) 2 Admin. L.R. 169; [1990] C.O.D. 49; *Times*, May 30, 1989; *Independent*, June 2, 1989; *Guardian*, May 27, 1989, QBD . . . . *Digested*, 91/**71**:
Applied, 90/3072, 92/2083, 92/2791, 93/2208, 94/7, 94/2504, 03/56,
07/27: *Considered*, 92/3, 92/3, 92/4455, 93/2567, 94/4462, 95/67,
95/3098, 00/5471: *Distinguished*, 92/2872: *Followed*, 96/3256, 96/4740,
97/2931, 98/3203, 98/3216, 01/5878: *Not followed*, 95/2713:
Referred to, 98/5998

R. v Secretary of State for the Home Department Ex p. Bugdaycay see Bugdaycay v Secretary of State for the Home Department

R. v Secretary of State for the Home Department Ex p. Cakabay (No.2) see R. v Special Adjudicator Ex p. Secretary of State for the Home Department

R. v Secretary of State for the Home Department Ex p. Doody; *joined cases* R. v Secretary of State for the Home Department Ex p. Pierson; R. v Secretary of State for the Home Department Ex p. Smart; R. v Secretary of State for the Home Department Ex p. Pegg [1994] 1 A.C. 531; [1993] 3 W.L.R. 154; [1993] 3 All E.R. 92; (1995) 7 Admin. L.R. 1; (1993) 143 N.L.J. 991; *Times*, June 29, 1993; *Independent*, June 25, 1993, HL; affirming [1993] Q.B. 157; [1992] 3 W.L.R. 956; [1993] 1 All E.R. 151; (1993) 5 Admin. L.R. 93; [1992] C.O.D. 458; *Times*, May 8, 1992; *Independent*, May 7, 1992; *Guardian*, May 13, 1992, CA (Civ Div); reversing [1991] C.O.D. 256, QBD . . . . *Digested*, 93/**1213**:
Applied, 94/3848, 95/960, 97/1335, 97/3929, 99/5437, 03/2058, 04/2772,
05/1785, 05/4967, 06/4534, 07/2173: *Considered*, 94/3841, 95/42, 95/162,
95/162, 95/162, 95/2534, 95/2617, 96/1954, 96/4579, 96/6855, 97/1595,
97/2443, 98/4079, 00/3334, 00/4326, 02/3234, 04/1904: *Followed*, 95/81,
96/1953, 96/3981, 97/1626, 97/2672, 97/2678, 99/5212:
Referred to, 95/1314

R. v Secretary of State for the Home Department Ex p. Jeyeanthan; *sub nom* R. v Immigration Appeal Tribunal Ex p. Jeyeanthan; Secretary of State for the Home Department v Ravichandran; *joined case* Ravichandran v Secretary of State for the Home Department [2000] 1 W.L.R. 354; [1999] 3 All E.R. 231; [2000] Imm. A.R. 10; [1999] I.N.L.R. 241; (1999) 11 Admin. L.R. 824; [1999] C.O.D. 349; *Times*, May 26, 1999; *Independent*, June 8, 1999, CA (Civ Div); affirming [1998] Imm. A.R. 369; [1998] I.N.L.R. 540; *Times*, April 23, 1998, QBD . . . . *Digested*, 99/**3162**:
Applied, 01/4380, 02/858, 04/4156, 06/582, 06/2699, 06/3291, 07/2372:
Considered, 04/2012, 05/2826, 07/3059: *Distinguished*, 02/4216:
Referred to, 01/4713

R. v Secretary of State for the Home Department Ex p. Mahmood (Amjad) see R. (on the application of Mahmood (Amjad)) v Secretary of State for the Home Department

R. v Secretary of State for the Home Department Ex p. Main see R. v Secretary of State for the Home Department Ex p. Simms

R. v Secretary of State for the Home Department Ex p. O'Brien see R. v Secretary of
    State for the Home Department Ex p. Simms
R. v Secretary of State for the Home Department Ex p. Onibiyo [1996] Q.B. 768;
    [1996] 2 W.L.R. 490; [1996] 2 All E.R. 901; [1996] Imm. A.R. 370; (1996)
    93(17) L.S.G. 30; (1996) 140 S.J.L.B. 109; *Times*, April 2, 1996, CA (Civ Div);
    affirming *Times*, January 29, 1996; *Independent*, January 24, 1996, QBD . . . . .   *Digested*, 96/**3242**:
                                    Applied, 00/3296, 00/3348, 04/2025: *Considered*, 96/3241, 97/2866,
                                    99/3153, 99/3177: *Followed*, 97/2865, 97/2867, 97/2869, 98/3196, 07/2295
R. v Secretary of State for the Home Department Ex p. Pegg see R. v Secretary of
    State for the Home Department Ex p. Doody
R. v Secretary of State for the Home Department Ex p. Pierson see R. v Secretary of
    State for the Home Department Ex p. Doody
R. v Secretary of State for the Home Department Ex p. Probyn; *joined cases* R. v
    Secretary of State for the Home Department Ex p. Walker; R. v Taylor (Adrian
    Edward) [1998] 1 W.L.R. 809; [1998] 1 All E.R. 357; [1998] 1 Cr. App. R. (S.)
    312; (1997) 161 J.P. 797; [1998] Crim. L.R. 76; (1997) 161 J.P.N. 1080; *Times*,
    August 11, 1997; *Times*, September 2, 1997; *Times*, October 30, 1997, DC . . . . .   *Digested*, 97/**1654**:
                                    Applied, 03/3871, 07/3627: *Considered*, 99/1184, 99/1231, 99/1281, 99/1348,
                                    00/1153, 00/1192, 02/3941, 06/3804
R. v Secretary of State for the Home Department Ex p. Ravichandran (No.1); *sub nom*
    R. v Immigration Appeal Tribunal Ex p. Sandralingam (No.1); *joined cases* R. v
    Secretary of State for the Home Department Ex p. Sandralingham (No.1); R. v
    Immigration Appeal Tribunal Ex p. Rajendrakumar [1996] Imm. A.R. 97; *Times*,
    October 30, 1995, CA (Civ Div) . . . .   *Digested*, 96/**3216**:
                                    Applied, 98/3174, 03/2234, 07/2277: *Cited*, 99/3202: *Considered*, 96/3225,
                                    97/2862, 98/3227, 99/3168, 05/2154, 07/2299: *Followed*, 97/2863,
                                    00/3322, 05/2215
R. v Secretary of State for the Home Department Ex p. Robinson [1998] Q.B. 929;
    [1997] 3 W.L.R. 1162; [1997] 4 All E.R. 210; [1997] Imm. A.R. 568; [1997]
    I.N.L.R. 182; (1997) 147 N.L.J. 1345; *Times*, August 1, 1997; *Independent*, July
    18, 1997, CA (Civ Div) . . . .   *Digested*, 97/**2857**:
                                    Applied, 99/3169, 99/3170, 02/2587, 06/2207, 06/2233, 07/2273, 07/2281:
                                    Considered, 99/3178, 99/3193, 00/3282, 04/2043, 06/2205, 06/2278,
                                    07/2285: *Distinguished*, 00/3278, 00/3294
R. v Secretary of State for the Home Department Ex p. Samaroo see R. (on the
    application of Samaroo) v Secretary of State for the Home Department
R. v Secretary of State for the Home Department Ex p. Sandralingham (No.1) see R. v
    Secretary of State for the Home Department Ex p. Ravichandran (No.1)
R. v Secretary of State for the Home Department Ex p. Shah see Islam v Secretary of
    State for the Home Department
R. v Secretary of State for the Home Department Ex p. Simms; *sub nom* R. v
    Secretary of State for the Home Department Ex p. Main; *joined cases* R. v
    Governor of Whitemoor Prison Ex p. Main; R. v Secretary of State for the Home
    Department Ex p. O'Brien [2000] 2 A.C. 115; [1999] 3 W.L.R. 328; [1999] 3
    All E.R. 400; [1999] E.M.L.R. 689; 7 B.H.R.C. 411; (1999) 11 Admin. L.R. 961;
    [1999] Prison L.R. 82; [1999] C.O.D. 520; (1999) 96(30) L.S.G. 28; (1999)
    149 N.L.J. 1073; (1999) 143 S.J.L.B. 212; *Times*, July 9, 1999, HL; reversing
    [1999] Q.B. 349; [1998] 3 W.L.R. 1169; [1998] 2 All E.R. 491; [1998] E.M.L.R.
    431; (1998) 95(1) L.S.G. 23; (1998) 142 S.J.L.B. 38; *Times*, December 9, 1997;
    Independent, December 10, 1997, CA (Civ Div); reversing [1997] E.M.L.R. 261;
    [1997] C.O.D. 217; *Times*, January 17, 1997, QBD . . . .   *Digested*, 99/**4105**:
                                    Applied, 02/4505, 06/2096, 07/2318: *Considered*, 99/335, 01/4578,
                                    03/2223: *Distinguished*, 05/2914: *Followed*, 99/4100
R. v Secretary of State for the Home Department Ex p. Smart see R. v Secretary of
    State for the Home Department Ex p. Doody
R. v Secretary of State for the Home Department Ex p. Thirukumar [1989] Imm. A.R.
    270; [1989] C.O.D. 459; *Times*, March 10, 1989; *Independent*, March 24, 1989;
    Guardian, March 10, 1989, CA (Civ Div); affirming [1989] C.O.D. 384; *Times*,
    December 27, 1988; *Independent*, January 11, 1989, QBD . . . .   *Digested*, 90/**2574**:
                                    Applied, 96/3220, 07/2344: *Considered*, 91/2024, 93/2233:
                                    Distinguished, 92/2444, 93/2238, 94/2493
R. v Secretary of State for the Home Department Ex p. Thornton (Andrew Paul)
    [1987] Q.B. 36; [1986] 3 W.L.R. 158; [1986] 2 All E.R. 641; (1986) 83 L.S.G.
    2493; (1986) 130 S.J. 246, CA (Civ Div) . . . .   *Digested*, 86/**2541**:
                                    Considered, 07/3620
R. v Secretary of State for the Home Department Ex p. Walker see R. v Secretary of
    State for the Home Department Ex p. Probyn
R. v Secretary of State for Trade and Industry Ex p. Argyll Group Plc see R. v
    Monopolies and Mergers Commission Ex p. Argyll Group Plc
R. v Secretary of State for Transport Ex p. Factortame Ltd (C-48/93) see Brasserie du
    Pecheur SA v Germany (C-46/93)
R. v Seed (Trigger Alan); *joined case* R. v Stark (Phillip) [2007] EWCA Crim 254;
    [2007] 2 Cr. App. R. (S.) 69; [2007] Crim. L.R. 501; (2007) 151 S.J.L.B. 262;
    Times, February 16, 2007, CA (Crim Div) . . . .   *Digested*, 07/**3621**

R. v Seepersad (Larissa Ann-Marie) [2006] EWCA Crim 2998; [2007] 2 Cr. App. R.
  (S.) 8, CA (Crim Div) . . . . *Digested,* 07/**3705**
R. v Sefton MBC Ex p. Help the Aged [1997] 4 All E.R. 532; [1997] 3 F.C.R. 573;
  (1997-98) 1 C.C.L. Rep. 57; (1997) 38 B.M.L.R. 135; [1998] C.O.D. 69; *Times,*
  August 23, 1997; *Independent,* October 3, 1997, CA (Civ Div); reversing [1997]
  3 F.C.R. 392; (1997) 36 B.M.L.R. 110; [1997] C.O.D. 387; (1997) 147 N.L.J.
  490; *Times,* March 27, 1997; *Independent,* April 18, 1997, QBD . . . . *Digested,* 97/**4721**:
  Applied, 99/4622, 02/4257, 05/3947, 07/1065: *Considered,* 99/3052,
  02/949
R. v Sellick (Carlo) see R. v Sellick (Santino)
R. v Sellick (Santino); *joined case* R. v Sellick (Carlo) [2005] EWCA Crim 651; [2005]
  1 W.L.R. 3257; [2005] 2 Cr. App. R. 15; [2005] Crim. L.R. 722; (2005)
  102(19) L.S.G. 33; *Times,* March 22, 2005, CA (Crim Div) . . . . *Digested,* 05/**888**:
  Applied, 06/304: *Considered,* 06/962, 06/984, 07/858
R. v Serrano (Raymond Samuel) [2006] EWCA Crim 3182; [2007] Crim. L.R. 569,
  CA (Crim Div)
R. v Serrant (Jordan Lee) [2007] EWCA Crim 717; [2007] 2 Cr. App. R. (S.) 80, CA
  (Crim Div) . . . . *Digested,* 07/**3602**
R. v Servite Houses Ex p. Goldsmith (2001) 33 H.L.R. 35; (2000) 2 L.G.L.R. 997;
  [2001] B.L.G.R. 55; (2000) 3 C.C.L. Rep. 325; [2001] A.C.D. 4, QBD . . . . *Digested,* 01/**5140**:
  Considered, 07/3912
R. v Seth-Smith (Patrick Sidney) see Board of Trade v Owen
R. v Seward (James Richard) [1970] 1 W.L.R. 323; (1970) 54 Cr. App. R. 85; [1970]
  R.T.R. 102; (1969) 113 S.J. 984, CA (Crim Div) . . . . *Digested,* 69/**3132**:
  Distinguished, 07/1006
R. v Shaffi (Zulfiqar) [2006] EWCA Crim 418; [2006] 2 Cr. App. R. (S.) 92; [2006]
  Crim. L.R. 665, CA (Crim Div) . . . . *Digested,* 06/**3755**:
  Considered, 07/3729: *Explained,* 07/3622
R. v Shahzad (Mohammed Khalid) see R. v Latif (Khalid)
R. v Shannon (John James); *sub nom* R. v Alford (John James) [2001] 1 W.L.R. 51;
  [2001] 1 Cr. App. R. 12; [2000] Crim. L.R. 1001; (2000) 97(40) L.S.G. 41;
  (2000) 144 S.J.L.B. 257; *Times,* October 11, 2000, CA (Crim Div) . . . . *Digested,* 00/**918**:
  Considered, 07/1953
R. v Sharkey (Bernard Lee) [2000] 1 W.L.R. 160; [2000] 1 All E.R. 15; [2000] 1 Cr.
  App. R. 409; [2000] 1 Cr. App. R. (S.) 541; (2000) 164 J.P. 256; [1999] Prison
  L.R. 134; [2000] Crim. L.R. 116; (2000) 164 J.P.N. 370; (1999) 96(43) L.S.G.
  32; *Times,* November 10, 1999; *Independent,* October 28, 1999, CA (Crim Div) . *Digested,* 99/**1279**:
  Applied, 01/1164, 07/3627
R. v Sharp (Charles) see Attorney General's Reference (No.123 of 2006), Re
R. v Sharrock (Michael Dean) see Attorney General's Reference (No.56 of 2006), Re
R. v Shaukat (Mirza Hamayou) see R. v Gordon (Gavin Stephen)
R. v Shaw (Dennis) see R. v Canavan (Darren Anthony)
R. v Shaw (Elvis Edward) [1980] 1 W.L.R. 1526; [1980] 2 All E.R. 433; (1980) 70 Cr.
  App. R. 313; [1980] Crim. L.R. 443; (1980) 124 S.J. 274, CA (Crim Div) . . . . . *Digested,* 80/**556**:
  Applied, 07/935
R. v Shaw (Michael Phillip) see Attorney General's Reference (No.86 of 2006), Re
R. v Sheehan (Denny John); *joined case* R. v O'Mahoney (Michael Jon) [2006]
  EWCA Crim 1459; [2007] 1 Cr. App. R. (S.) 29, CA (Crim Div) . . . . *Digested,* 07/**3768**
R. v Shepherd (Peter James) see Attorney General's Reference (Nos.14 and 24 of
  1993), Re
R. v Sheppard (Dionne) see R. v Richardson (Jack Virgil)
R. v Sheppard (James) see R. v Lang (Stephen Howard)
R. v Sherwood Ex p. Telegraph Group Plc see R. (on the application of Telegraph
  Group Plc) v Sherwood
R. v Shillibier (Marc James) [2006] EWCA Crim 793; [2007] Crim. L.R. 639, CA
  (Crim Div)
R. v Shivpuri (Pyare) [1987] A.C. 1; [1986] 2 W.L.R. 988; [1986] 2 All E.R. 334;
  (1986) 83 Cr. App. R. 178; (1986) 150 J.P. 353; [1986] Crim. L.R. 536; (1986)
  150 J.P.N. 510; (1986) 83 L.S.G. 1896; (1986) 136 N.L.J. 488; (1986) 130
  S.J. 392, HL; affirming [1985] Q.B. 1029; [1985] 2 W.L.R. 29; [1985] 1 All E.R.
  143; (1985) 80 Cr. App. R. 241; [1985] Crim. L.R. 43; (1984) 81 L.S.G. 3420;
  (1985) 129 S.J. 31, CA (Crim Div) . . . . *Digested,* 86/**482**:
  Applied, 86/484, 00/994, 07/849: *Considered,* 87/1113, 94/3984:
  Distinguished, 03/871
R. v Shrimpton (Alan) see Attorney General's Reference (Nos.59 and 60 of 2007), Re
R. v Shropshire CC Ex p. Abdullah see R. v Barnet LBC Ex p. Shah (Nilish)
R. v Simmons (Edward Matthew) [2006] EWCA Crim 1259; [2007] 1 Cr. App. R. (S.)
  27, CA (Crim Div) . . . . *Digested,* 07/**3694**
R. v Simms (Rodrigo Fernando) see R. v Davis (Iain)
R. v Simpson (Barry Alexander) see R. v Welcher (Anthony Frederick)

R. v Simpson (Ian McDonald) [2003] EWCA Crim 1499; [2004] Q.B. 118; [2003] 3
W.L.R. 337; [2003] 3 All E.R. 531; [2003] 2 Cr. App. R. 36; [2004] 1 Cr. App.
R. (S.) 24; [2003] Crim. L.R. 652; (2003) 100(27) L.S.G. 34; (2003) 147
S.J.L.B. 694; *Times*, May 26, 2003, CA (Crim Div) . . . .   *Digested*, 03/**900**:
Applied, 07/1672: *Considered*, 07/927: *Followed*, 05/3569

R. v Simpson (Moira) see Attorney General's Reference (Nos.86 and 87 of 1999), Re

R. v Simpson (Ronald Walker) see R. v Bentham (John Preston)

R. v Smith (Costs) [2004] 2 Costs L.R. 348, Sup Ct Costs Office . . . .   *Applied*, 05/851,
07/954

R. v Smith (Gary) see R. v Lang (Stephen Howard)

R. v Smith (Graham Westgarth); *joined case* R. v Jayson (Mike) [2002] EWCA Crim
683; [2003] 1 Cr. App. R. 13; [2002] Crim. L.R. 659; *Times*, April 23, 2002, CA
(Crim Div) . . . .   *Digested*, 02/**819**:
Applied, 07/5036

R. v Smith (Henry Lee) [2006] EWCA Crim 2307; [2007] Crim. L.R. 325, CA (Crim
Div)

R. v Smith (John) see R. v Ablewhite (Jonathan Charles)

R. v Smith (Leyford) see R. v Smith (Stephen)

R. v Smith (Paul Roger) [2003] EWCA Crim 2480; [2004] 1 Cr. App. R. (S.) 58, CA
(Crim Div) . . . .   *Digested*, 04/**3290**:
Considered, 07/3722

R. v Smith (Stephen); *joined case* R. v Smith (Leyford) [2006] EWCA Crim 901;
[2007] 1 Cr. App. R. (S.) 1, CA (Crim Div) . . . .   *Digested*, 07/**3687**:
Considered, 07/3616

R. v Smith (Stephen Gary) [2006] EWCA Crim 2366; [2007] 1 Cr. App. R. (S.) 98;
[2007] Crim. L.R. 92, CA (Crim Div)

R. v Solomka (Costs) [2007] 5 Costs L.R. 868, Sup Ct Costs Office

R. v Solomon (David) see R. v Cuthbertson (Brian George)

R. v Soneji (Kamlesh Kumar); *joined case* R. v Bullen (David Frederick) [2005] UKHL
49; [2006] 1 A.C. 340; [2005] 3 W.L.R. 303; [2005] 4 All E.R. 321; [2006] 2
Cr. App. R. 20; [2006] 1 Cr. App. R. (S.) 79; [2006] Crim. L.R. 167; (2005)
102(31) L.S.G. 26; (2005) 155 N.L.J. 1315; (2005) 149 S.J.L.B. 924; *Times*, July
22, 2005; *Independent*, July 26, 2005, HL; reversing [2003] EWCA Crim
1765; [2004] 1 Cr. App. R. (S.) 34; [2003] Crim. L.R. 738; (2003) 100(33)
L.S.G. 27; (2003) 147 S.J.L.B. 817; *Times*, July 1, 2003, CA (Crim Div) . . . .   *Digested*, 05/**842**:
Applied, 04/806, 06/912, 06/950, 06/3679: *Considered*, 07/3059:
Followed, 05/841

R. v Soroya (Naveed) [2006] EWCA Crim 1884; [2007] Crim. L.R. 181; (2006) 150
S.J.L.B. 1054, CA (Crim Div)

R. v Soule Ali (Adamou); *sub nom* R. v Bombatu (Eugene); *joined case* R. v Bonbatu
(Eugene) [2007] EWCA Crim 257; [2007] 1 W.L.R. 1599; [2007] 2 Cr. App. R.
2; [2007] Crim. L.R. 806; *Times*, February 7, 2007, CA (Crim Div) . . . .   *Digested*, 07/**896**

R. v Southampton University Hospital NHS Trust [2006] EWCA Crim 2971; [2007] 2
Cr. App. R. (S.) 9; (2007) 93 B.M.L.R. 160; (2006) 150 S.J.L.B. 1533, CA (Crim
Div). . . . .   *Digested*, 07/**3655**

R. v Spartley (Malcolm) [2007] EWCA Crim 1789; (2007) 151 S.J.L.B. 670, CA (Crim
Div)

R. v Special Adjudicator Ex p. Secretary of State for the Home Department; *joined
cases* R. v Secretary of State for the Home Department Ex p. Cakabay (No.2); R.
v Immigration Appellate Authority Ex p. Secretary of State for the Home
Department [1999] Imm. A.R. 176; [1998] I.N.L.R. 623; (1998) 142 S.J.L.B.
231; *Times*, July 13, 1998, CA (Civ Div); affirming [1998] Imm. A.R. 52; (1997)
94(44) L.S.G. 35; *Times*, November 25, 1997; *Independent*, November 5, 1997,
QBD . . . .   *Digested*, 98/**3196**:
Followed, 07/2295: *Previous proceedings*, 98/3199

R. v Special Commissioners of Income Tax Ex p. Morgan Grenfell & Co Ltd see R. (on
the application of Morgan Grenfell & Co Ltd) v Special Commissioners of
Income Tax

R. v Spence (Clinton Everton); *joined case* R. v Thomas (Vernon Walter) (1983) 5 Cr.
App. R. (S.) 413; [1984] Crim. L.R. 372, CA (Crim Div) . . . .   *Digested*, 84/**876**:
Applied, 03/3770: *Cited*, 91/1146, 94/1292: *Considered*, 87/986, 87/988,
92/1445, 96/1888, 96/1889, 97/1540, 04/3322, 04/3384, 05/3604,
05/3649, 07/3643: *Distinguished*, 86/842: *Followed*, 97/1604, 05/3536:
Referred to, 00/1262

R. v Spence (Colin Michael) (1999) 163 J.P. 754; [1999] R.T.R. 353; [1999] Crim.
L.R. 975; *Times*, May 24, 1999, CA (Crim Div) . . . .   *Digested*, 99/**958**:
Distinguished, 07/2493

R. v Spenceley (Russell Stephen) see R. v Cuthbertson (Brian George)

R. v Stacey [1982] R.T.R. 20, CA (Crim Div) . . . .   *Digested*, 82/**2772**:
Applied, 07/1006

R. v Staines Magistrates Court Ex p. DPP see R. v Warley Magistrates Court Ex p. DPP

R. *v* Stanley (Alan Basil) [1965] 2 Q.B. 327; [1965] 2 W.L.R. 917; [1965] 1 All E.R.
1035; (1965) 49 Cr. App. R. 175; (1965) 129 J.P. 279; (1965) 109 S.J. 193,
CCA . . . . *Digested,* 65/**871**:
Approved, 76/524: *Considered,* 07/916
R. *v* Stapleton (Vincent) see R. *v* May (Raymond George)
R. *v* Stapley (Michael) [2004] EWCA Crim 1139; [2004] 2 Cr. App. R. (S.) 99, CA
(Crim Div) . . . . *Digested,* 04/**3400**:
Considered, 07/3616
R. *v* Stark (Phillip) see R. *v* Seed (Trigger Alan)
R. *v* Steele (Michael); *joined cases* R. *v* Corry (Peter Thomas); R. *v* Whomes (Jack
Arthur) [2006] EWCA Crim 2000; [2007] 1 W.L.R. 222; [2007] 1 Cr. App. R. 3;
[2007] Crim. L.R. 168; (2006) 150 S.J.L.B. 1327; *Times,* September 5, 2006,
CA (Crim Div) . . . . *Digested,* 06/**941**
R. *v* Stephens (Jerry); *joined case* R. *v* Mujuru (Sandra) [2007] EWCA Crim 1249;
[2007] 2 Cr. App. R. 26; *Times,* June 20, 2007, CA (Crim Div) . . . . *Digested,* 07/**863**
R. *v* Stephenson (Lawrence) see R. *v* Price (Margaret)
R. *v* Stevens (Cyril John) see R. *v* H
R. *v* Stevens (Cyril John) [2007] EWCA Crim 1128; (2007) 171 J.P. 421; (2007) 171
J.P.N. 754, CA (Crim Div)
R. *v* Stewart 113 E.R. 1007; (1840) 12 Ad. & El. 773, QB . . . . *Applied,* 07/1972
R. *v* Stillwell (Kenneth Michael); *joined case* R. *v* Jewell (Ian John) (1992) 94 Cr. App.
R. 65; (1992) 13 Cr. App. R. (S.) 253; (1992) 156 J.P. 335; [1992] Crim. L.R.
922; (1991) 155 J.P.N. 690; *Times,* August 22, 1991; *Independent,* August 19,
1991, CA (Crim Div) . . . . *Digested,* 92/**1423**:
Applied, 94/1349: *Considered,* 07/966
R. *v* Stocker (David Paul) [2003] EWCA Crim 121; [2003] 2 Cr. App. R. (S.) 54;
[2003] Prison L.R. 229; [2003] Crim. L.R. 293; *Times,* January 30, 2003, CA
(Crim Div) . . . . *Digested,* 03/**3675**:
Applied, 03/3684, 07/3735
R. *v* Stockwell (Christopher James) (1993) 97 Cr. App. R. 260; *Times,* March 11, 1993,
CA (Crim Div) . . . . *Digested,* 94/**914**:
Applied, 96/1373, 02/738, 07/2960: *Considered,* 99/895
R. *v* Stredder (Nicholas Michael) [1997] 1 Cr. App. R. (S.) 209, CA (Crim Div). . . . . . . *Digested,* 97/**1485**:
Considered, 07/3610
R. *v* Stride (Ian Paul) see R. *v* Cooksley (Robert Charles)
R. *v* Su Hua Liu; *sub nom* R. *v* Lun Xi Tan [2006] EWCA Crim 3321; [2007] 2 Cr.
App. R. (S.) 12; (2006) 150 S.J.L.B. 1535, CA (Crim Div) . . . . *Digested,* 07/**3670**
R. *v* Suchedina (Hasnain); *joined cases* R. *v* Hadley (Paul); R. *v* Lehaney (Francis
Glen); R. *v* Hosier (Kevin James) [2006] EWCA Crim 2543; [2007] 1 Cr. App. R.
23; [2007] Crim. L.R. 301, CA (Crim Div) . . . . *Digested,* 07/**871**
R. *v* Sully (George Raymond) (2007) 151 S.J.L.B. 1564, CA (Crim Div)
R. *v* Sussex Justices Ex p. McCarthy [1924] 1 K.B. 256, KBD . . . . *Applied,* 68/**3372**,
75/741, 85/3432: *Considered,* 47-51/7724, 54/2011, 92/955:
Distinguished, 93/849, 99/3796, 07/248: *Followed,* 47-51/6074
R. *v* Swaby (Errol Rio) see Attorney General's Reference (Nos.117 and 118 of 2005),
Re
R. *v* Switchgear Engineering Services Ltd [2007] EWCA Crim 2758; (2007) 104(41)
L.S.G. 27, CA (Crim Div)
R. *v* Szypusz (Simeon); *sub nom* R. *v* Gaynor (David Anthony) [2006] EWCA Crim
1552; [2007] 1 Cr. App. R. (S.) 49, CA (Crim Div) . . . . *Digested,* 07/**993**
R. *v* T [2006] EWCA Crim 2006; [2007] 1 Cr. App. R. 4; (2007) 171 J.P. 265; [2007]
Crim. L.R. 165; (2007) 171 J.P.N. 596, CA (Crim Div) . . . . *Digested,* 07/**841**
R. *v* Tabassum (Naveed); *sub nom* R. *v* Tabassum (Navid) [2000] 2 Cr. App. R. 328;
[2000] Lloyd's Rep. Med. 404; [2000] Crim. L.R. 686; (2000) 97(22) L.S.G.
43; *Times,* May 26, 2000, CA (Crim Div) . . . . *Digested,* 00/**1003**:
Considered, 07/921
R. *v* Tabassum (Navid) see R. *v* Tabassum (Naveed)
R. *v* Tabnak (Masoud) [2007] EWCA Crim 380; [2007] 1 W.L.R. 1317; [2007] 2 Cr.
App. R. 4; *Times,* February 26, 2007, CA (Crim Div) . . . . *Digested,* 07/**2317**
R. *v* Taggart (Brendan) (1995) 16 Cr. App. R. (S.) 789, CA (Crim Div) . . . . *Digested,* 96/**2107**:
Distinguished, 07/3710
R. *v* Tailor (Farhad) [2005] EWCA Crim 3550; [2006] 2 Cr. App. R. (S.) 27, CA (Crim
Div) . . . . *Digested,* 07/**3642**
R. *v* Tarry (Derek Newton) [1970] 2 Q.B. 560; [1970] 2 W.L.R. 1034; [1970] 2 All E.R.
185; (1970) 54 Cr. App. R. 322; (1970) 114 S.J. 283, CA (Crim Div) . . . . *Digested,* 70/**512**:
Applied, 95/1475, 07/3620: *Considered,* 74/749, 86/894
R. *v* Taylor (Adrian Edward) see R. *v* Secretary of State for the Home Department Ex
p. Probyn
R. *v* Taylor (Gary Lee) (1994) 15 Cr. App. R. (S.) 120, CA (Crim Div) . . . . *Considered,* 07/3707
R. *v* Taylor (Joel Ison); *joined case* R. *v* Thomas (Joshua Declan) [2007] EWCA Crim
803; (2007) 104(17) L.S.G. 30, CA (Crim Div) . . . . *Digested,* 07/**3682**:
Considered, 07/3783
R. *v* Taylor (John) see Taylor (Setting of Minimum Term), Re
R. *v* Taylor (Mark William) see R. *v* Gordon (Gavin Stephen)

R. v Taylor (Morgan Dawson) [2006] EWCA Crim 3132; [2007] 2 Cr. App. R. (S.) 24;
    [2007] Crim. L.R. 491, CA (Crim Div) . . . .   *Digested*, 07/**852**
R. v Taylor (Paul Stephen) [2006] EWCA Crim 1777; [2007] 1 Cr. App. R. (S.) 59, CA
    (Crim Div) . . . .   *Digested*, 07/**3786**
R. v Taylor (Timothy Nicholas) see R. v S
R. v TF (Indecent Assault: Mental Health) [2000] 2 Cr. App. R. (S.) 292, CA (Crim
    Div) . . . .   *Digested*, 00/**1278**:
                                           Considered, 04/3328, 07/3607
R. v Thanh Hue Thi see Attorney General's Reference (Nos.129 and 132 of 2006), Re
R. v Thomas (Chris) (No.2) [2006] EWCA Crim 2036; [2007] 1 Cr. App. R. (S.) 84;
    [2007] Crim. L.R. 171, CA (Crim Div) . . . .   *Digested*, 07/**3662**
R. v Thomas (Derek) (1988) 10 Cr. App. R. (S.) 386, CA (Crim Div) . . . .   *Digested*, 90/**1193**:
                    Considered, 99/1079, 00/1132, 02/3995, 07/3578
R. v Thomas (Joshua Declan) see R. v Taylor (Joel Ison)
R. v Thomas (Richard Bartgerald) see R. v Avis (Tony)
R. v Thomas (Vernon Walter) see R. v Spence (Clinton Everton)
R. v Thompson (Amelio) see R. v Reynolds (Michael Edwin)
R. v Thompson (Glyn); *joined case* R. v Hanson (Brian) [2006] EWCA Crim 2849;
    [2007] 1 W.L.R. 1123; [2007] 2 All E.R. 205; [2007] 1 Cr. App. R. 15; [2007]
    Crim. L.R. 387; *Times*, December 6, 2006, CA (Crim Div) . . . .   *Digested*, 07/**985**
R. v Thwaites (Stefan Peter) see R. v Hardwicke (Joseph Philip)
R. v Tilley (Darren David) see Attorney General's Reference (Nos.104, 105 and 106 of
    2006), Re
R. v Times Newspapers Ltd; *sub nom* Times Newspapers Ltd, Re [2007] EWCA Crim
    1925; (2007) 157 N.L.J. 1319; *Times*, July 31, 2007, CA (Crim Div)
R. v Timmins (Mark) [2005] EWCA Crim 2909; [2006] 1 W.L.R. 756; [2006] 1 Cr.
    App. R. 18; *Times*, November 29, 2005, CA (Crim Div) . . . .   *Digested*, 06/**831**:
                                                Considered, 07/970
R. v Tirnaveanu (Cornel) [2007] EWCA Crim 1239; [2007] 1 W.L.R. 3049; [2007] 4
    All E.R. 301; [2007] 2 Cr. App. R. 23; (2007) 171 J.P. 621; [2007] Crim. L.R.
    969; *Times*, July 2, 2007, CA (Crim Div) . . . .   *Digested*, 07/**820**
R. v Tivnan (Michael) [1999] 1 Cr. App. R. (S.) 92; [1998] Crim. L.R. 591; (1998)
    95(21) L.S.G. 36; (1998) 142 S.J.L.B. 166; *Times*, May 6, 1998; *Independent*,
    May 11, 1998, CA (Crim Div) . . . .   *Digested*, 98/**1179**:
                                              Considered, 07/3612
R. v Todd (David Brown) see R. v Cuthbertson (Brian George)
R. v Todd (Henry Barclay) see R. v Cuthbertson (Brian George)
R. v Tomney (Jake Colin) see Attorney General's Reference (Nos.125 and 126 of 2006),
    Re
R. v Tomney (Simon) see Attorney General's Reference (Nos.125 and 126 of 2006), Re
R. v Tooth (David Christopher) (Costs) [2007] 2 Costs L.R. 302, Sup Ct Costs Office
R. v Topasna (Stephen George) [2006] EWCA Crim 1969; [2007] 1 Cr. App. R. (S.)
    76, CA (Crim Div) . . . .   *Digested*, 07/**3594**
R. v Torrington (Richard Edward) see R. v Avis (Tony)
R. v Toth (Mark) see Attorney General's Reference (Nos.52 and 53 of 2006), Re
R. v Tower Hamlets Healthcare NHS Trust Ex p. von Brandenburg see R. (on the
    application of von Brandenburg) v East London and the City Mental Health NHS
    Trust
R. v Townsend (Philip Henry); *joined cases* R. v Dearsley (Simon Robert); R. v
    Bretscher (Gordon Maxwell) [1997] 2 Cr. App. R. 540; [1998] Crim. L.R. 126,
    CA (Crim Div) . . . .   *Digested*, 98/**1034**:
                                              Considered, 07/923
R. v Toygun (Ismail) see R. v Ulcay (Erdogan)
R. v Tozer (Kerry Anne) (1994) 15 Cr. App. R. (S.) 807, CA (Crim Div) . . . .   *Digested*, 95/**1409**:
                         Considered, 00/1278, 04/3328, 07/3607
R. v Treacy (Eugene Anthony) see Treacy v DPP
R. v Tucker (Nicholas Guy) see Tucker (Setting of Minimum Term), Re
R. v Tully (Stephen); *joined case* R. v Wood (Kevin) [2006] EWCA Crim 2270; (2007)
    171 J.P. 25; (2007) 171 J.P.N. 306, CA (Crim Div) . . . .   *Digested*, 07/**839**
R. v Tunney (Reynolds Thomas) [2006] EWCA Crim 2066; [2007] 1 Cr. App. R. (S.)
    91, CA (Crim Div) . . . .   *Digested*, 07/**3714**
R. v Tuzzio (Daryll Dale) see Attorney General's Reference (No.133 of 2006), Re
R. v Twisse (Michael James) [2001] 2 Cr. App. R. (S.) 9; [2001] Crim. L.R. 151; *Times*,
    November 30, 2000, CA (Crim Div) . . . .   *Digested*, 01/**1282**:
                   Applied, 02/3922, 02/3932: *Considered*, 01/1279, 03/3695, 04/3412,
                   04/3450, 04/3452, 05/3700, 05/3707, 05/3748, 06/3695, 07/3632,
                   07/3633, 07/3757: *Distinguished*, 04/3454: *Followed*, 01/1490
R. v Uddin (Alim) see Attorney General's Reference (No.9 of 2004), Re
R. v Uddin (Rejan) [1999] Q.B. 431; [1998] 3 W.L.R. 1000; [1998] 2 All E.R. 744;
    [1999] 1 Cr. App. R. 319; [1999] Crim. L.R. 987; *Times*, April 2, 1998;
    Independent, April 24, 1998, CA (Crim Div) . . . .   *Digested*, 98/**959**:
                                              Considered, 07/877
R. v Ukpabio (Roland Thompson) [2007] EWCA Crim 2108; (2007) 171 J.P. 692;
    Times, September 6, 2007, CA (Crim Div) . . . .   *Digested*, 07/**856**

R. _v_ Ulcay (Erdogan); _joined case_ R. _v_ Toygun (Ismail) [2007] EWCA Crim 2379;
    (2007) 157 N.L.J. 1658; _Times_, November 7, 2007, CA (Crim Div) . . . .   _Digested_, 07/**935**
R. _v_ University of London Ex p. Vijayatunga see R. _v_ HM Queen in Council Ex p.
    Vijayatunga
R. _v_ V (Abolghasem) see R. _v_ R (Amer)
R. _v_ V (David Victor) see Attorney General's Reference (No.50 of 1997), Re
R. _v_ Van Nguyen (Dong) see R. _v_ Highton (Edward Paul)
R. _v_ Vandermeulen (Yvan) see Attorney General's Reference (No.146 of 2006), Re
R. _v_ Vasinoras (Anton) see R. _v_ Saltmarsh (Richard)
R. _v_ Vernett-Showers (Michael); _joined cases_ R. _v_ Sabir (Mohammed); R. _v_ Ahmad
    (Bakhtiar); R. _v_ Beg (Mohammed Akram); R. _v_ Khan (Mohammed Kurshid); R. _v_
    Ryan (John); R. _v_ Masud (Umar); R. _v_ Ahmed (Mumtaz); R. _v_ Ahmed (Nisar);
    R. _v_ Ahmed (Rizwan); R. _v_ Ramzan (Mohammed) [2007] EWCA Crim 1767;
    (2007) 104(31) L.S.G. 24, CA (Crim Div)
R. _v_ Vodden 169 E.R. 706; (1853) Dears. 229, QB . . . .   _Considered_, 07/992:
                Followed, 86/943

R. _v_ W; _joined case_ R. _v_ F [2006] EWCA Crim 686; [2007] 1 W.L.R. 339; [2006] 3
    All E.R. 562; [2006] 2 Cr. App. R. (S.) 110; (2006) 170 J.P. 406; [2006] Crim.
    L.R. 857; (2006) 170 J.P.N. 716, CA (Civ Div) . . . .   _Digested_, 06/**327**
R. _v_ W [2007] EWCA Crim 1251; [2007] 2 Cr. App. R. 31; (2007) 151 S.J.L.B. 671;
    Times, June 6, 2007, CA (Crim Div) . . . .   _Digested_, 07/**932**
R. _v_ W (2007) 151 S.J.L.B. 199, CA (Crim Div)
R. _v_ W (Malcolm) see R. _v_ S (Jonathan Charles)
R. _v_ Waddon (Graham) 99/5233/Z3, CA (Crim Div); affirming [1999] I.T.C.L.R. 422;
    [1999] Masons C.L.R. 396, Crown Ct (Southwark) . . . .   _Digested_, 00/**996**:
               Considered, 07/1017
R. _v_ Wake (Leslie) [1999] 2 Cr. App. R. (S.) 403, CA (Crim Div) . . . .   _Digested_, 00/**1377**:
            Considered, 06/3792, 07/3713: _Followed_, 03/3820
R. _v_ Walker (Lee Christian) [2003] EWCA Crim 154; [2003] 2 Cr. App. R. (S.) 58, CA
    (Crim Div) . . . .   _Digested_, 03/**3692**:
               Considered, 07/3631
R. _v_ Walker (Steven) [1996] 1 Cr. App. R. 111; [1995] Crim. L.R. 826; (1995) 159
    J.P.N. 406; (1995) 92(17) L.S.G. 47; (1995) 139 S.J.L.B. 118; _Times_, April 14,
    1995; _Independent_, May 8, 1995, CA (Crim Div) . . . .   _Digested_, 95/**1268**:
               Considered, 07/916
R. _v_ Wallace (James Andrew) [2007] EWCA Crim 1760; [2007] 2 Cr. App. R. 30;
    (2007) 171 J.P. 543; [2007] Crim. L.R. 976, CA (Crim Div) . . . .   _Digested_, 07/**821**
R. _v_ Walsh (Christopher) [2007] NICA 4; [2007] N.I. 154, CA (Crim Div) (NI)
R. _v_ Waltham Forest LBC Ex p. Baxter [1988] Q.B. 419; [1988] 2 W.L.R. 257; [1987]
    3 All E.R. 671; 86 L.G.R. 254; [1988] R.V.R. 6; (1987) 137 N.L.J. 947; (1988)
    132 S.J. 227, CA (Civ Div) . . . .   _Digested_, 88/**2187**:
            Considered, 91/54, 95/3252: _Followed_, 07/2867
R. _v_ Walton (Lee Alan) see R. _v_ Norman (Shane Martin)
R. _v_ Wandsworth LBC Ex p. O; _sub nom_ Bhikha _v_ Leicester City Council; O _v_
    Wandsworth LBC; _joined case_ R. _v_ Leicester City Council Ex p. Bhikha [2000] 1
    W.L.R. 2539; [2000] 4 All E.R. 590; (2001) 33 H.L.R. 39; [2000] B.L.G.R.
    591; (2000) 3 C.C.L. Rep. 237; _Times_, July 18, 2000; _Independent_, June 28,
    2000, CA (Civ Div) . . . .   _Digested_, 00/**4895**:
           Applied, 03/2049, 03/4069, 06/2216, 07/3908: _Considered_, 02/4289,
               07/2313: _Followed_, 03/4068
R. _v_ Ward (Brian) see R. _v_ Czyzewski (Jozef Eugene) (Appeal against Sentence)
R. _v_ Ward (Paul) [2005] EWCA Crim 1926; [2006] 1 Cr. App. R. (S.) 66, CA (Crim
    Div) . . . .   _Digested_, 06/**3650**:
               Considered, 07/3598
R. _v_ Warley Magistrates Court Ex p. DPP; _joined cases_ R. _v_ Staines Magistrates Court
    Ex p. DPP; R. _v_ North East Suffolk Magistrates Court Ex p. DPP; R. _v_ Lowestoft
    Justices Ex p. DPP [1999] 1 W.L.R. 216; [1999] 1 All E.R. 251; [1998] 2 Cr.
    App. R. 307; [1999] 1 Cr. App. R. (S.) 156; (1998) 162 J.P. 559; [1998] Crim.
    L.R. 684; (1998) 162 J.P.N. 565; (1998) 95(24) L.S.G. 33; (1998) 148 N.L.J.
    835; (1998) 142 S.J.L.B. 165; _Times_, May 18, 1998, DC . . . .   _Digested_, 98/**1009**:
            Applied, 00/1029, 00/1030, 02/859: _Considered_, 07/989:
               Distinguished, 01/1108
R. _v_ Warn (Peter John) see Secretary of State for Defence _v_ Warn
R. _v_ Warwick Crown Court Ex p. Smalley (No.1) see Smalley, Re
R. _v_ Warwood (Eugene Charles) [2006] EWCA Crim 842; [2006] 2 Cr. App. R. (S.)
    113, CA (Crim Div) . . . .   _Digested_, 06/**3744**:
               Considered, 07/3797
R. _v_ Waters (David) see Waters (Setting of Minimum Term), Re
R. _v_ Watson (1847) 2 Cox C.C. 376 . . . .   _Applied_, 63/737,
               07/917
R. _v_ Watts (Dale) see R. _v_ Fieldhouse (Paul Michael)
R. _v_ Watty (Stephen) [2007] EWCA Crim 123; [2007] 2 Cr. App. R. (S.) 44, CA (Crim
    Div) . . . .   _Digested_, 07/**3656**

R. v Webb 175 E.R. 391; (1848) 2 Car. & K. 933; (1848) 3 Cox C.C. 183, QB . . . .   *Applied*, 63/737, 07/917

R. v Webb (Ian David) see Attorney General's Reference (No.52 of 2003), Re
R. v Webb (John Paul) see R. v Reynolds (Michael Edwin)
R. v Webb (Robert Edward) see Attorney General's Reference (Nos.86 and 87 of 1999), Re
R. v Webster (Alan) see Attorney General's Reference (Nos.14 and 15 of 2006), Re
R. v Welcher (Anthony Frederick); *joined cases* R. v Simpson (Barry Alexander); R. v Harper (Roger) [2007] EWCA Crim 480; [2007] 2 Cr. App. R. (S.) 83; [2007] Crim. L.R. 804, CA (Crim Div) . . . .   *Digested*, 07/**834**
R. v Wells (Scott) see Attorney General's Reference (Nos.98 and 99 of 2006), Re
R. v Wernet (Robert Stewart) see Attorney General's Reference (Nos.14 and 24 of 1993), Re
R. v West (Melvin) see R. v Allsopp (Michael Nevin)
R. v Westminster City Council Ex p. A see R. v Hammersmith and Fulham LBC Ex p. M
R. v Wheatley (Jason); *joined case* R. v Fenton (Lee) [2007] EWCA Crim 835; [2007] 2 Cr. App. R. (S.) 77, CA (Crim Div) . . . .   *Digested*, 07/**3769**
R. v Wheeler (Glen) see Attorney General's Reference (No.1 of 1997), Re
R. v Wheeler (Ian) see Attorney General's Reference (No.1 of 1997), Re
R. v Whitburn (Kerry Deanian) see R. v Ablewhite (Jonathan Charles)
R. v White (Anthony Delroy) [2001] EWCA Crim 216; [2001] 1 W.L.R. 1352; [2001] Crim. L.R. 576; *Times*, March 13, 2001; *Independent*, March 26, 2001, CA (Crim Div). . . . .   *Digested*, 01/**1065**: *Approved*, 07/911: *Considered*, 04/771
R. v Whittaker (Steven Alan) see Attorney General's Reference (No.32 of 1996), Re
R. v Whitte (Adam George) see Attorney General's Reference (No.79 of 2006) (Application for Leave to Make Reference), Re
R. v Whittle (Martin) [2007] EWCA Crim 539; [2007] 2 Cr. App. R. (S.) 88; [2007] Crim. L.R. 499; (2007) 151 S.J.L.B. 398, CA (Crim Div) . . . .   *Digested*, 07/**3719**
R. v Whitton (Michael Peter) [2006] EWCA Crim 3229; [2007] 2 Cr. App. R. (S.) 15, CA (Crim Div) . . . .   *Digested*, 07/**2989**
R. v Whomes (Jack Arthur) see R. v Steele (Michael)
R. v Wigan MBC Ex p. Tammadge (1997-98) 1 C.C.L. Rep. 581, QBD . . . .   *Digested*, 99/**4622**: *Distinguished*, 07/2154
R. v Wilkinson (Edward John) (1983) 5 Cr. App. R. (S.) 105, CA (Crim Div) . . . .   *Digested*, 84/**880**: *Applied*, 01/1213: *Cited*, 94/1297: *Considered*, 89/1069, 94/3835, 94/3841, 96/1984, 96/1985, 96/1989, 96/2000, 98/1233, 07/3616: *Followed*, 95/1428, 96/1987
R. v Williams (Anthony Michael) see R. v Corran (Ben)
R. v Williams (Richard Thomas) (1995) 16 Cr. App. R. (S.) 191, CA (Crim Div) . . . .   *Digested*, 96/**2105**: *Considered*, 99/1289: *Distinguished*, 07/3710
R. v Williams (Robert Charles) [2006] EWCA Crim 2530; [2007] 1 Cr. App. R. (S.) 107, CA (Crim Div)
R. v Williamson (Kenneth Joseph) see R. v Abdroikov (Nurlon)
R. v Wilson (Craig) [2007] EWCA Crim 509; [2007] 2 Cr. App. R. (S.) 58, CA (Crim Div). . . . .   *Digested*, 07/**3743**
R. v Wilson (Robert) see R. v Robson (Thomas Anthony)
R. v Wingrove (Aaron Geoffrey) [2005] EWCA Crim 1392; [2006] 1 Cr. App. R. (S.) 41, CA (Crim Div). . . . .   *Digested*, 06/**3668**: *Considered*, 07/3740
R. v Winter (Malcolm John) [2007] EWCA Crim 3493; *Times*, December 20, 2007, CA (Crim Div)
R. v Winters (Keith) see R. v Lang (Stephen Howard)
R. v Wolf (Karl Christian) see R. v Allsopp (Michael Nevin)
R. v Wood (Gary Dominic) see R. v Rehman (Zakir)
R. v Wood (Kevin) see R. v Tully (Stephen)
R. v Wooley (Raymond) [2003] EWCA Crim 3458, CA (Crim Div) . . . .   *Considered*, 07/3598
R. v Woolley (Michael) [2005] EWCA Crim 2853; [2006] 1 Cr. App. R. (S.) 123, CA (Crim Div) . . . .   *Digested*, 06/**3871**: *Applied*, 07/3769
R. v Workman (David Paul) see Attorney General's Reference (No.85 of 2006), Re
R. v WR [2005] EWCA Crim 1907, CA (Crim Div) . . . .   *Followed*, 07/970
R. v Wright (Michael Anthony) [2006] EWCA Crim 2672; [2007] 1 Cr. App. R. (S.) 109, CA (Crim Div)
R. v Wright (Robert) see R. v Lang (Stephen Howard)
R. v Wynne (Stephen Alan) [2006] EWCA Crim 1943; [2007] 1 Cr. App. R. (S.) 68, CA (Crim Div) . . . .   *Digested*, 07/**3690**
R. v X see R. v McNee (Michael)
R. v X see R. v K
R. v X [2007] EWCA Crim 2498; (2007) 151 S.J.L.B. 1434, CA (Crim Div)
R. v X (Andrew Goldwyne) see Attorney General's Reference (Nos.24, 25, 26, 27, 28 and 41 of 2006), Re
R. v Xhelollari (Jetmir) [2007] EWCA Crim 2052; (2007) 151 S.J.L.B. 1265, CA (Crim Div)

R. v Yoonus (Naushad) [2004] EWCA Crim 1734; [2005] 1 Cr. App. R. (S.) 46, CA (Crim Div) . . . . *Digested,* 05/**3673**: *Considered,* 07/3685

R. v Yorkshire Water Services Ltd see Secretary of State for the Environment, Transport and the Regions v Yorkshire Water Services Ltd

R. v Youell (Mark John) [2007] EWCA Crim 225; [2007] 2 Cr. App. R. (S.) 43, CA (Crim Div) . . . . *Digested,* 07/**3597**

R. v Young (Stephen Andrew) [1995] Q.B. 324; [1995] 2 W.L.R. 430; [1995] 2 Cr. App. R. 379; (1995) 92(6) L.S.G. 38; (1995) 139 S.J.L.B. 32; *Times,* December 30, 1994; *Independent,* January 16, 1995, CA (Crim Div) . . . . *Digested,* 96/**1629**: *Considered,* 07/992: *Disapproved,* 04/694: *Distinguished,* 97/1327, 99/1061

R. v Z see R. v M

R. v Z see R. v M

R. v Z [2007] EWCA Crim 1473; [2007] Crim. L.R. 818, CA (Crim Div)

R. v Zammit (Godwin) see Attorney General's Reference (Nos.129 and 132 of 2006), Re

R. v Zielinski (Maciej) [2007] EWCA Crim 704; (2007) 151 S.J.L.B. 295, CA (Crim Div)

R. (on the application of A) v B Council [2007] EWHC 1529 (Admin); [2007] B.L.G.R. 813, QBD (Admin) . . . . *Digested,* 07/**1197**

R. (on the application of A) v Crown Prosecution Service see R. (on the application of A) v South Yorkshire Police

R. (on the application of A) v DPP see R. (on the application of A) v Governor of Huntercombe Young Offenders Institute

R. (on the application of A) v Governor of Huntercombe Young Offenders Institute; *joined case* R. (on the application of A) v DPP [2006] EWHC 2544 (Admin); (2007) 171 J.P. 65; (2007) 171 J.P.N. 345, QBD (Admin) . . . . *Digested,* 07/**3789**

R. (on the application of A) v Hackney LBC see R. (on the application of AW) v Croydon LBC

R. (on the application of A) v Hertfordshire CC; *sub nom* A v Hertfordshire CC; K v Hertfordshire CC [2006] EWHC 3428 (Admin); [2007] E.L.R. 95, QBD (Admin) . . . . *Digested,* 07/**1266**

R. (on the application of A) v Lambeth LBC see R. (on the application of G) v Barnet LBC

R. (on the application of A) v Lambeth LBC see R. (on the application of Lindsay) v Lambeth LBC

R. (on the application of A) v Liverpool City Council [2007] EWHC 1477 (Admin); (2007) 10 C.C.L. Rep. 716; *Times,* August 1, 2007, QBD (Admin) . . . . *Digested,* 07/**2302**

R. (on the application of A) v Lord Saville of Newdigate (Bloody Sunday Inquiry); *sub nom* R. (on the application of Widgery Soldiers) v Lord Saville of Newdigate; Lord Saville of Newdigate v Widgery Soldiers [2001] EWCA Civ 2048; [2002] 1 W.L.R. 1249; [2002] A.C.D. 22; *Times,* December 21, 2001; *Independent,* January 11, 2002; *Daily Telegraph,* January 11, 2002, CA (Civ Div); affirming [2001] EWHC Admin 888; (2001) 98(48) L.S.G. 29; (2001) 145 S.J.L.B. 262; *Times,* November 21, 2001; *Daily Telegraph,* November 20, 2001, DC . . . . *Digested,* 02/**38**: *Applied,* 03/2238, 04/35, 05/33: *Considered,* 07/544, 07/2238

R. (on the application of A) v Partnerships in Care Ltd [2002] EWHC 529 (Admin); [2002] 1 W.L.R. 2610; (2002) 5 C.C.L. Rep. 330; [2002] M.H.L.R. 298; (2002) 99(20) L.S.G. 32; (2002) 146 S.J.L.B. 117; *Times,* April 23, 2002, QBD (Admin) . . . . *Digested,* 02/**3232**: *Considered,* 07/3912

R. (on the application of A) v Secretary of State for the Home Department; *joined cases* R. (on the application of H) v Secretary of State for the Home Department; R. (on the application of AH) v Secretary of State for the Home Department [2006] EWHC 526 (Admin); [2006] Imm. A.R. 477, QBD (Admin) . . . . *Digested,* 07/**2299**

R. (on the application of A) v Secretary of State for the Home Department [2007] EWCA Civ 804; [2007] A.C.D. 93; *Times,* September 5, 2007, CA (Civ Div); reversing in part [2006] EWHC 3331 (Admin); [2007] A.C.D. 42, QBD (Admin) . . . . *Digested,* 07/**2319**

R. (on the application of A) v Secretary of State for the Home Department [2007] EWCA Civ 655; [2007] Imm. A.R. 817, CA (Civ Div); reversing [2006] EWHC 1489 (Admin); (2006) 150 S.J.L.B. 667, QBD (Admin)

R. (on the application of A) v South Staffordshire Magistrates Court; *sub nom* A v South Staffordshire Magistrates [2006] EWHC 1200 (Admin); (2007) 171 J.P. 36; (2007) 171 J.P.N. 305, QBD (Admin) . . . . *Digested,* 07/**984**

R. (on the application of A) v South Yorkshire Police; *joined case* R. (on the application of A) v Crown Prosecution Service [2007] EWHC 1261 (Admin); (2007) 171 J.P. 465; (2007) 171 J.P.N. 851, DC. . . . . *Digested,* 07/**979**

R. (on the application of AA (Afghanistan)) v Secretary of State for the Home Department [2006] EWCA Civ 1550; [2007] A.C.D. 32; (2006) 103(47) L.S.G. 30; (2006) 150 S.J.L.B. 1570; *Times,* November 29, 2006, CA (Civ Div); reversing [2006] EWHC 318 (Admin); [2006] A.C.D. 44, QBD (Admin) . . . . . *Digested,* 07/**2308**

R. (on the application of Abassi) *v* Secretary of State for Foreign and Commonwealth Affairs see R. (on the application of Abbasi) *v* Secretary of State for Foreign and Commonwealth Affairs

R. (on the application of Abbasi) *v* Secretary of State for Foreign and Commonwealth Affairs; *sub nom* R. (on the application of Abassi) *v* Secretary of State for Foreign and Commonwealth Affairs [2002] EWCA Civ 1598; [2003] U.K.H.R.R. 76; (2002) 99(47) L.S.G. 29; *Times*, November 8, 2002; *Independent*, November 8, 2002, CA (Civ Div) . . . . *Digested*, 02/**2934**:
Applied, 07/2234: *Considered*, 03/2676: *Followed*, 06/2621, 06/2622

R. (on the application of Abdi) *v* Lambeth LBC [2007] EWHC 1565 (Admin); [2007] N.P.C. 82; *Times*, July 11, 2007, QBD (Admin) . . . . *Digested*, 07/**2142**

R. (on the application of Abdi) *v* Secretary of State for the Home Department see R. (on the application of Nadarajah) *v* Secretary of State for the Home Department

R. (on the application of Abdulle) *v* Birmingham City Council see R. (on the application of Aweys) *v* Birmingham City Council

R. (on the application of Adam) *v* Birmingham City Council see R. (on the application of Aweys) *v* Birmingham City Council

R. (on the application of Adam) *v* Secretary of State for the Home Department see R. (on the application of Limbuela) *v* Secretary of State for the Home Department

R. (on the application of AH) *v* Secretary of State for the Home Department see R. (on the application of A) *v* Secretary of State for the Home Department

R. (on the application of Ahmad) *v* Newham LBC C1/2007/2245, CA (Civ Div); affirming [2007] EWHC 2332 (Admin); (2007) 151 S.J.L.B. 1227, QBD (Admin)

R. (on the application of Ahmad) *v* Waltham Forest LBC [2007] EWHC 957 (Admin); [2007] E.L.R. 445, QBD (Admin)

R. (on the application of Ahmadi) *v* Secretary of State for the Home Department [2005] EWCA Civ 1721; [2006] I.N.L.R. 318, CA (Civ Div); reversing [2005] EWHC 687 (Admin), QBD (Admin) . . . . *Digested*, 07/**2289**

R. (on the application of Akaroglu) *v* Secretary of State for the Home Department see Akaroglu *v* Romania

R. (on the application of Akyuz) *v* Secretary of State for the Home Department see R. (on the application of Ozturk) *v* Secretary of State for the Home Department

R. (on the application of Al-Fayed) *v* Deputy Coroner of the Queen's Household and Assistant Deputy Coroner for Surrey see Paul *v* Deputy Coroner of the Queen's Household and Assistant Deputy Coroner for Surrey

R. (on the application of Al-Jedda) *v* Secretary of State for Defence [2007] UKHL 58; *Times*, December 13, 2007, HL; affirming [2006] EWCA Civ 327; [2007] Q.B. 621; [2006] 3 W.L.R. 954; [2006] U.K.H.R.R. 27; [2006] U.K.H.R.R. 855; (2006) 103(15) L.S.G. 22; *Times*, April 25, 2006; *Independent*, April 4, 2006, CA (Civ Div); affirming [2005] EWHC 1809 (Admin); [2005] H.R.L.R. 39; [2006] U.K.H.R.R. 35; *Times*, September 12, 2005, QBD (Admin) . . . . *Digested*, 06/**2159**

R. (on the application of Al-Rawi) *v* Secretary of State for Foreign and Commonwealth Affairs [2006] EWCA Civ 1279; [2007] 2 W.L.R. 1219; [2006] H.R.L.R. 42; [2007] U.K.H.R.R. 58; (2006) 103(41) L.S.G. 33; *Times*, October 18, 2006, CA (Civ Div); affirming [2006] EWHC 972 (Admin); [2006] H.R.L.R. 30; [2006] U.K.H.R.R. 891; [2006] A.C.D. 79; (2006) 156 N.L.J. 797; *Times*, May 19, 2006, QBD (Admin) . . . . *Digested*, 06/**2622**

R. (on the application of Al-Skeini) *v* Secretary of State for Defence [2007] UKHL 26; [2007] 3 W.L.R. 33; [2007] 3 All E.R. 685; [2007] H.R.L.R. 31; [2007] U.K.H.R.R. 955; 22 B.H.R.C. 518; (2007) 104(26) L.S.G. 34; (2007) 157 N.L.J. 894; (2007) 151 S.J.L.B. 809; *Times*, June 14, 2007, HL [2005] EWCA Civ 1609; [2007] Q.B. 140; [2006] 3 W.L.R. 508; [2006] H.R.L.R. 7; [2006] U.K.H.R.R. 297; [2005] Inquest L.R. 205; [2006] A.C.D. 46; (2006) 103(4) L.S.G. 29; (2006) 156 N.L.J. 112; *Times*, January 6, 2006; *Independent*, January 17, 2006, CA (Civ Div); affirming [2004] EWHC 2911 (Admin); [2005] 2 W.L.R. 1401; [2005] H.R.L.R. 3; [2005] U.K.H.R.R. 427; [2004] Inquest L.R. 169; [2005] A.C.D. 51; (2005) 102(3) L.S.G. 30; (2005) 155 N.L.J. 58; *Times*, December 20, 2004, QBD (Admin) . . . . *Digested*, 07/**2239**

R. (on the application of Alem) *v* Secretary of State for the Home Department [2006] EWHC 899 (Admin), QBD (Admin) . . . . *Considered*, 07/2974

R. (on the application of Ali) *v* Birmingham City Council see R. (on the application of Aweys) *v* Birmingham City Council

R. (on the application of AM (Cameroon)) *v* Asylum and Immigration Tribunal [2007] EWCA Civ 131; *Times*, April 11, 2007, CA (Civ Div) . . . . *Digested*, 07/**2344**

R. (on the application of Amicus) *v* Secretary of State for Trade and Industry; *joined cases* R. (on the application of National Union of Teachers) *v* Secretary of State for Trade and Industry; R. (on the application of National Union of Rail, Maritime and Transport Workers) *v* Secretary of State for Trade and Industry; R. (on the application of Public & Commercial Services Union) *v* Secretary of State for Trade and Industry; R. (on the application of NASUWT) *v* Secretary of State for Trade and Industry; R. (on the application of UNISON) *v* Secretary of State for Trade and Industry; R. (on the application of National Association of Teachers in Further and Higher Education) *v* Secretary of State for Trade and Industry [2004] EWHC 860 (Admin); [2007] I.C.R. 1176; [2004] I.R.L.R. 430; [2004] E.L.R. 311; [2004] Pens. L.R. 261, QBD (Admin) . . . .   *Digested,* 04/**1292**:
Considered, 07/1405

R. (on the application of Amin (Imtiaz)) *v* Secretary of State for the Home Department; *sub nom* R. (on the application of Middleton) *v* HM Coroner for Western Somerset; *joined case* R. (on the application of Middleton) *v* West Somerset Coroner [2003] UKHL 51; [2004] 1 A.C. 653; [1998] 1 W.L.R. 972; [2003] 3 W.L.R. 1169; [2003] 4 All E.R. 1264; [2004] H.R.L.R. 3; [2004] U.K.H.R.R. 75; 15 B.H.R.C. 362; (2004) 76 B.M.L.R. 143; [2003] Inquest L.R. 1; [2004] Prison L.R. 140; (2003) 100(44) L.S.G. 32; (2003) 153 N.L.J. 1600; *Times,* October 17, 2003, HL; reversing [2002] EWCA Civ 390; [2003] Q.B. 581; [2002] 3 W.L.R. 505; [2002] 4 All E.R. 336; (2002) 166 J.P. 505; [2002] U.K.H.R.R. 846; [2002] Lloyd's Rep. Med. 187; (2003) 69 B.M.L.R. 35; [2002] Po. L.R. 100; [2002] A.C.D. 74; (2002) 166 J.P.N. 529; (2002) 99(19) L.S.G. 29; (2002) 146 S.J.L.B. 101; *Times,* April 18, 2002; *Independent,* April 12, 2002, CA (Civ Div); reversing [2001] EWHC Admin 719; [2001] Inquest L.R. 76; [2002] Po. L.R. 74; [2003] Inquest L.R. 1, QBD (Admin) . . . .   *Digested,* 03/**2167**:
Applied, 02/26, 03/12, 03/13, 03/2810, 06/18, 06/2933, 06/2934, 07/28:
Considered, 04/12, 04/36, 07/2980: *Overruled in part,* 04/37:
Previous proceedings, 02/26

R. (on the application of Amoako) *v* DPP; *sub nom* Amoako *v* DPP [2006] EWHC 1572 (Admin); [2006] 4 All E.R. 230; [2006] Extradition L.R. 97, QBD (Admin) . . .   *Digested,* 07/**541**

R. (on the application of AN) *v* Mental Health Review Tribunal (Northern Region) see R. (on the application of N) *v* Mental Health Review Tribunal (Northern Region)

R. (on the application of Anderson) *v* Customs and Excise Commissioners see Hughes *v* Customs and Excise Commissioners

R. (on the application of Andronati) *v* Criminal Injuries Compensation Appeals Panel [2006] EWHC 1420 (Admin); [2007] P.I.Q.R. P2, QBD (Admin) . . . .   *Digested,* 07/**48**

R. (on the application of Animal Defenders International) *v* Secretary of State for Culture, Media and Sport [2006] EWHC 3069 (Admin); [2007] E.M.L.R. 6; [2007] H.R.L.R. 9; [2007] U.K.H.R.R. 310; [2007] A.C.D. 46, QBD (Admin) . . . .   *Digested,* 07/**546**

R. (on the application of Anti-Waste Ltd) *v* Environment Agency; *sub nom* Environment Agency *v* Anti-Waste Ltd [2007] EWCA Civ 1377; [2007] N.P.C. 135, CA (Civ Div); reversing in part [2007] EWHC 717 (Admin); [2007] 1 W.L.R. 1977; [2007] Env. L.R. 28; [2007] J.P.L. 1585; (2007) 151 S.J.L.B. 502; [2007] N.P.C. 44, QBD (Admin) . . . .   *Digested,* 07/**1523**

R. (on the application of Anufrijeva) *v* Southwark LBC see Anufrijeva *v* Southwark LBC

R. (on the application of Arun DC) *v* First Secretary of State see Arun DC *v* First Secretary of State

R. (on the application of Ashworth Hospital Authority) *v* Mental Health Review Tribunal for West Midlands and North West Region see R. (on the application of H) *v* Ashworth Hospital Authority

R. (on the application of Association of British Travel Agents Ltd (ABTA)) *v* Civil Aviation Authority; *sub nom* Association of British Travel Agents Ltd *v* Civil Aviation Authority [2006] EWCA Civ 1356; [2007] 2 All E.R. (Comm) 898; [2007] 2 Lloyd's Rep. 249; (2006) 150 S.J.L.B. 1430, CA (Civ Div); affirming [2006] EWHC 13 (Admin); [2006] A.C.D. 49, QBD (Admin)

R. (on the application of AW) *v* Croydon LBC; *sub nom* R. (on the application of W) *v* Croydon LBC; *joined cases* R. (on the application of Y) *v* Hackney LBC; R. (on the application of D) *v* Hackney LBC; R. (on the application of A) *v* Hackney LBC [2007] EWCA Civ 266; [2007] 1 W.L.R. 3168; [2007] B.L.G.R. 417; (2007) 10 C.C.L. Rep. 225; *Times,* May 11, 2007, CA (Civ Div); affirming [2005] EWHC 2950 (Admin); [2006] B.L.G.R. 159; (2006) 9 C.C.L. Rep. 252, QBD (Admin) . . . .   *Digested,* 07/**2312**:
Applied, 07/3908: *Considered,* 06/2216, 07/2313

R. (on the application of AW (Kenya)) *v* Secretary of State for the Home Department [2006] EWHC 3147 (Admin); [2007] A.C.D. 33, QBD (Admin)

R. (on the application of Aweys) v Birmingham City Council; *sub nom* Birmingham City
Council v Aweys; *joined cases* R. (on the application of Omar) v Birmingham
City Council; R. (on the application of Ali) v Birmingham City Council; R. (on the
application of Abdulle) v Birmingham City Council; R. (on the application of
Sharif) v Birmingham City Council; R. (on the application of Mohammed) v
Birmingham City Council; R. (on the application of Adam) v Birmingham City
Council; 1/2007/0336, CA (Civ Div); affirming [2007] EWHC 52 (Admin);
[2007] 1 F.L.R. 2066; [2007] H.L.R. 27; [2007] Fam. Law 493; *Times,* February
21, 2007, QBD (Admin) . . . . *Digested,* 07/**2162**

R. (on the application of B) v Birmingham City Council Independent Appeal Panel see R.
(on the application of S) v Birmingham City Council Independent Appeal Panel

R. (on the application of B) v Criminal Injuries Compensation Appeals Panel [2007]
EWHC 180 (QB); [2007] P.I.Q.R. Q4, QBD (Admin) . . . . *Digested,* 07/**3069**

R. (on the application of B) v Haddock (Responsible Medical Officer) [2006] EWCA
Civ 961; [2006] H.R.L.R. 40; [2006] Lloyd's Rep. Med. 433; (2007) 93
B.M.L.R. 52; [2006] M.H.L.R. 306; *Independent,* July 13, 2006, CA (Civ Div);
affirming [2005] EWHC 921 (Admin); (2005) 85 B.M.L.R. 57; [2005] M.H.L.R.
317, QBD (Admin) . . . . *Digested,* 06/**2861**

R. (on the application of B) v Haringey LBC; *sub nom* PB v Haringey LBC; R. (on the
application of PB) v Haringey LBC [2006] EWHC 2255 (Admin); [2007] H.L.R.
13; (2007) 10 C.C.L. Rep. 99, QBD (Admin) . . . . *Digested,* 07/**2138**

R. (on the application of B) v Immigration Appeal Tribunal see R. (on the application of
Hoxha) v Special Adjudicator

R. (on the application of B) v Islington LBC see R. (on the application of H) v
Wandsworth LBC

R. (on the application of B) v Lambeth LBC; *sub nom* R (B by her Litigation Friend MB)
v Lambeth LBC [2006] EWHC 639 (Admin); [2007] 1 F.L.R. 2091; (2006) 9
C.C.L. Rep. 239; [2007] Fam. Law 118, QBD (Admin) . . . . *Digested,* 06/**367**

R. (on the application of B) v Lambeth LBC [2006] EWHC 2362 (Admin); (2007) 10
C.C.L. Rep. 84, QBD (Admin) . . . . *Digested,* 07/**2911**

R. (on the application of B) v Merton LBC [2003] EWHC 1689 (Admin); [2003] 4 All
E.R. 280; [2003] 2 F.L.R. 888; [2005] 3 F.C.R. 69; (2003) 6 C.C.L. Rep. 457;
[2003] Fam. Law 813; *Times,* July 18, 2003, QBD (Admin) . . . . *Digested,* 03/**2895**:
Applied, 07/2302: *Considered,* 06/1699: *Followed,* 05/2146

R. (on the application of B) v Stafford Combined Court; *sub nom* R. (on the application
of TB) v Stafford Crown Court [2006] EWHC 1645 (Admin); [2007] 1 W.L.R.
1524; [2007] 1 All E.R. 102; [2006] 2 Cr. App. R. 34; *Independent,* July 6, 2006,
QBD (Admin) . . . . *Digested,* 06/**990**

R. (on the application of Baiai) v Secretary of State for the Home Department [2006]
EWHC 1454 (Admin); [2007] 1 W.L.R. 735; [2006] 4 All E.R. 555; [2006]
H.R.L.R. 39, QBD (Admin) . . . . *Digested,* 06/**2276**

R. (on the application of Baiai) v Secretary of State for the Home Department; *joined
cases* R. (on the application of Trzcinska) v Secretary of State for the Home
Department; R. (on the application of Tilki) v Secretary of State for the Home
Department; R. (on the application of Bigoku) v Secretary of State for the Home
Department [2007] EWCA Civ 478; [2007] 3 W.L.R. 573; [2007] 4 All E.R.
199; [2007] 2 F.L.R. 627; [2007] 2 F.C.R. 421; [2007] H.R.L.R. 29; [2007]
U.K.H.R.R. 771; [2007] Imm. A.R. 730; [2007] Fam. Law 806; (2007) 104(23)
L.S.G. 33; (2007) 151 S.J.L.B. 711; *Times,* June 26, 2007, CA (Civ Div);
reversing in part [2006] EWHC 823 (Admin); [2007] 1 W.L.R. 693; [2006] 3
All E.R. 608; [2006] 2 F.L.R. 645; [2006] 2 F.C.R. 131; [2006] Fam. Law 535;
(2006) 150 S.J.L.B. 573; *Times,* April 14, 2006, QBD (Admin) . . . . *Digested,* 07/**2341**

R. (on the application of Balding) v Secretary of State for Work and Pensions; *sub nom*
Secretary of State for Work and Pensions v Balding [2007] EWCA Civ 1327;
[2007] B.P.I.R. 1669, CA (Civ Div); affirming [2007] EWHC 759 (Admin);
[2007] 1 W.L.R. 1805; [2007] 4 All E.R. 422; [2007] B.P.I.R. 864; *Times,* May 1,
2007, DC . . . . *Digested,* 07/**3885**

R. (on the application of Bamber) v Revenue and Customs Commissioners [2007]
EWHC 798 (Admin); [2007] B.T.C. 577; [2007] S.T.I. 1175, QBD (Admin) . . . . . *Digested,* 07/**4075**

R. (on the application of Bancoult) v Secretary of State for Foreign and Commonwealth
Affairs [2007] EWCA Civ 498; [2007] 3 W.L.R. 768; (2007) 104(23) L.S.G.
31; (2007) 151 S.J.L.B. 707; *Times,* May 31, 2007, CA (Civ Div); affirming [2006]
EWHC 1038 (Admin); [2006] A.C.D. 81; *Times,* May 23, 2006, QBD (Admin) . . *Digested,* 07/**716**

R. (on the application of Barhanu) v Hackney LBC see R. (on the application of H) v
Wandsworth LBC

R. (on the application of Barker) v Bromley LBC; *sub nom* R. v Bromley LBC Ex p.
Baker; R. v Bromley LBC Ex p. Barker [2006] UKHL 52; [2007] 1 A.C. 470;
[2006] 3 W.L.R. 1209; [2007] 1 All E.R. 1183; [2007] Env. L.R. 20; [2007]
J.P.L. 744; [2006] 50 E.G. 85 (C.S.); (2007) 151 S.J.L.B. 28; [2006] N.P.C. 129;
Times, December 7, 2006, HL; reversing [2001] EWCA Civ 1766; [2002] Env.
L.R. 25; [2002] 2 P. & C.R. 8; [2001] 49 E.G. 117 (C.S.); [2001] N.P.C. 170;
Independent, December 5, 2001, CA (Civ Div); affirming [2001] Env. L.R. 1;
[2000] P.L.C.R. 399; [2000] J.P.L. 1302 (Note); [2000] E.G. 51 (C.S.), QBD . . *Digested,* 07/**3272**:
Considered, 03/3420

R. (on the application of Barker) v Bromley LBC (C-290/03); *sub nom* Barker v Bromley LBC (C-290/03) [2006] Q.B. 764; [2006] 3 W.L.R. 492; [2006] E.C.R. I-3949; [2007] Env. L.R. 2; [2006] J.P.L. 1688; [2006] 19 E.G. 173 (C.S.); [2006] N.P.C. 53; *Times*, May 10, 2006, ECJ (1st Chamber). . . . .   *Digested*, 07/**3271**

R. (on the application of Barking and Dagenham LBC) v SENDIST see Barking and Dagenham LBC v Special Educational Needs and Disability Tribunal (SENDIST)

R. (on the application of Barnet LBC) v Parking Adjudicator [2006] EWHC 2357 (Admin); [2007] R.T.R. 14, QBD (Admin) . . . .   *Digested*, 07/**3496**

R. (on the application of Batantu) v Islington LBC; *sub nom* R. v Islington LBC Ex p. Batantu (2001) 33 H.L.R. 76; (2001) 4 C.C.L. Rep. 445, QBD (Admin) . . . . . .   *Digested*, 02/**4257**:
                      Considered, 03/2046: *Distinguished*, 07/2154

R. (on the application of BBC) v Information Tribunal see BBC v Sugar

R. (on the application of Beer (t/a Hammer Trout Farm)) v Hampshire Farmers Markets Ltd; *sub nom* Hampshire CC v Beer (t/a Hammer Trout Farm) [2003] EWCA Civ 1056; [2004] 1 W.L.R. 233; [2004] U.K.H.R.R. 727; [2003] 31 E.G. 67 (C.S.); (2003) 100(36) L.S.G. 40; (2003) 147 S.J.L.B. 1085; [2003] N.P.C. 93; *Times*, August 25, 2003; *Independent*, July 30, 2003, CA (Civ Div); affirming [2002] EWHC 2559 (Admin), QBD (Admin) . . . .   *Digested*, 03/**68**:
                Applied, 04/2652: *Considered*, 06/4044, 07/3912

R. (on the application of Begum) v Denbigh High School Governors; *sub nom* R. (on the application of SB) v Denbigh High School Governors [2006] UKHL 15; [2007] 1 A.C. 100; [2006] 2 W.L.R. 719; [2006] 2 All E.R. 487; [2006] 1 F.C.R. 613; [2006] H.R.L.R. 21; [2006] U.K.H.R.R. 708; 23 B.H.R.C. 276; [2006] E.L.R. 273; (2006) 103(14) L.S.G. 29; (2006) 156 N.L.J. 552; *Times*, March 23, 2006; *Independent*, March 24, 2006, HL; reversing [2005] EWCA Civ 199; [2005] 1 W.L.R. 3372; [2005] 2 All E.R. 396; [2005] 1 F.C.R. 530; [2005] H.R.L.R. 16; [2005] U.K.H.R.R. 681; 19 B.H.R.C. 126; [2005] E.L.R. 198; (2005) 102(17) L.S.G. 31; (2005) 155 N.L.J. 383; (2005) 149 S.J.L.B. 300; *Times*, March 4, 2005; *Independent*, March 8, 2005, CA (Civ Div); reversing [2004] EWHC 1389 (Admin); [2004] E.L.R. 374; [2004] A.C.D. 66; (2004) 101(27) L.S.G. 29; *Times*, June 18, 2004, QBD (Admin) . . . .   *Digested*, 06/**1145**:
            Applied, 07/2195, 07/2816: *Considered*, 07/2193, 07/2194

R. (on the application of Begum (Amirun)) v Tower Hamlets LBC; *sub nom* Begum (Amirun) v Tower Hamlets LBC [2002] EWHC 633 (Admin); [2003] H.L.R. 8; [2002] N.P.C. 60; *Independent*, June 17, 2002, QBD (Admin) . . . .   *Digested*, 03/**2060**:
               Considered, 07/3928: *Distinguished*, 06/2027

R. (on the application of Bennett) v HM Coroner for Inner South London [2007] EWCA Civ 617; (2007) 104(28) L.S.G. 26; (2007) 151 S.J.L.B. 891; *Times*, August 13, 2007, CA (Civ Div); affirming [2006] EWHC 196 (Admin); (2006) 170 J.P. 109; [2006] H.R.L.R. 22; [2006] Inquest L.R. 21; [2006] Po. L.R. 123; [2007] A.C.D. 2; (2006) 170 J.P.N. 395; (2006) 150 S.J.L.B. 224, QBD (Admin) . . . .   *Digested*, 07/**29**

R. (on the application of Benson) v Secretary of State for Justice [2007] EWHC 2055 (Admin); (2007) 104(35) L.S.G. 38, QBD (Admin)

R. (on the application of Bentham) v Governor of Wandsworth Prison [2006] EWHC 121; [2006] Crim. L.R. 855; [2007] A.C.D. 10, QBD

R. (on the application of Bermingham) v Director of the Serious Fraud Office; *joined case* Bermingham v United States of America [2006] EWHC 200 (Admin); [2007] Q.B. 727; [2007] 2 W.L.R. 635; [2006] 3 All E.R. 239; [2006] U.K.H.R.R. 450; [2006] Extradition L.R. 52; [2006] A.C.D. 55; *Times*, February 24, 2006, QBD (Admin). . . . .   *Digested*, 06/**1605**:
                 Applied, 06/1608: *Considered*, 07/1671

R. (on the application of Bibi) v Camden LBC [2004] EWHC 2527 (Admin); [2005] 1 F.L.R. 413; [2005] H.L.R. 18; [2005] A.C.D. 53; *Times*, October 25, 2004, QBD (Admin) . . . .   *Digested*, 05/**2007**:
                             Considered, 07/2153

R. (on the application of Bigoku) v Secretary of State for the Home Department see R. (on the application of Baiai) v Secretary of State for the Home Department

R. (on the application of Bishop) v Bromley LBC [2006] EWHC 2148 (Admin); (2006) 9 C.C.L. Rep. 635, QBD (Admin) . . . .   *Digested*, 07/**3937**

R. (on the application of Blackwood) v Birmingham Magistrates [2006] EWHC 1800 (Admin); (2006) 170 J.P. 613; (2007) 171 J.P.N. 19; [2007] Env. L.R. D3, QBD (Admin) . . . .   *Digested*, 06/**3330**

R. (on the application of Bleaklow Industries Ltd) v Peak District National Park Authority [2006] EWHC 3387 (Admin); [2007] J.P.L. 1484, QBD (Admin) . . . .   *Digested*, 07/**3291**

R. (on the application of Bloggs 61) v Secretary of State for the Home Department [2003] EWCA Civ 686; [2003] 1 W.L.R. 2724; [2003] Po. L.R. 221; [2003] Prison L.R. 426; [2007] Inquest L.R. 206; (2003) 100(33) L.S.G. 29; (2003) 147 S.J.L.B. 780; *Times*, July 4, 2003, CA (Civ Div); affirming [2002] EWHC 1921 (Admin); [2002] Prison L.R. 377, QBD (Admin) . . . .   *Digested*, 03/**3062**:
                             Considered, 07/2240

R. (on the application of Bontemps) v Secretary of State for Work and Pensions see R. (on the application of Couronne) v Crawley BC

R. (on the application of Boughton) v HM Treasury (Permission to Appeal) [2006] EWCA Civ 504; [2006] B.T.C. 460, CA (Civ Div) . . . .   *Digested*, 07/**2193**

R. (on the application of Bradley) *v* Secretary of State for Work and Pensions C1/2007/
0554;C1/2007/0556, CA (Civ Div); affirming [2007] EWHC 242 (Admin);
[2007] Pens. L.R. 87; [2007] A.C.D. 85; *Times*, February 27, 2007, QBD
(Admin) . . . .   *Digested, 07/***3029**

R. (on the application of Brayfal Ltd) *v* Revenue and Customs Commissioners see R. (on
the application of Just Fabulous (UK) Ltd) *v* Revenue and Customs
Commissioners

R. (on the application of Brewer) *v* Supreme Court Costs Office [2006] EWHC 1955
(Admin); [2007] 1 Costs L.R. 20; *Times*, August 16, 2006, DC . . . .   *Digested, 06/***405**

R. (on the application of Brinsons (A Firm)) *v* Financial Ombudsman Service Ltd [2007]
EWHC 2534 (Admin); [2007] N.P.C. 120, QBD (Admin)

R. (on the application of British American Tobacco (Investments) Ltd) *v* Secretary of State
for Health (C-491/01); *sub nom* R. *v* Secretary of State for Health Ex p. British
American Tobacco (Investments) Ltd (C491/01) [2003] All E.R. (EC) 604;
[2002] E.C.R. I-11453; [2003] 1 C.M.L.R. 14; [2003] C.E.C. 53; [2003]
E.T.M.R. CN10; [2003] E.T.M.R. CN5; *Times*, December 13, 2002, ECJ . . . .   *Digested, 03/***1455**:
                        Applied, 06/1556, 07/1552: Considered, 05/1448

R. (on the application of British Casino Association Ltd) *v* Secretary of State for Culture
Media and Sport [2007] EWHC 1312 (Admin); (2007) 104(26) L.S.G. 30;
(2007) 151 S.J.L.B. 811, QBD (Admin)

R. (on the application of British Union for the Abolition of Vivisection) *v* Secretary of State
for the Home Department [2006] EWHC 250 (Admin); [2007] A.C.D. 4, QBD
(Admin)

R. (on the application of British Union for the Abolition of Vivisection) *v* Secretary of State
for the Home Department; *sub nom* R. (on the application of Campaign to End
All Animal Experiments (t/a British Union for the Abolition of Vivisection)) *v*
Secretary of State for the Home Department; C1/2007/2139, CA (Civ Div)
[2007] EWHC 1964 (Admin); [2007] A.C.D. 69; *Times*, August 27, 2007, QBD
(Admin); affirming . . . .   *Digested, 07/***3574**

R. (on the application of Brooke) *v* Parole Board; *joined cases* R. (on the application of
Murphy) *v* Parole Board; R. (on the application of O'Connell) *v* Parole Board;
C1/2007/2229, CA (Civ Div); affirming [2007] EWHC 2036 (Admin); [2007]
H.R.L.R. 46; [2007] A.C.D. 99; (2007) 157 N.L.J. 1463; (2007) 151 S.J.L.B.
1167; *Times*, October 18, 2007, QBD (Admin)

R. (on the application of Brown) *v* Governor of Belmarsh Prison see Brown (formerly
Bajinya) *v* Governor of Belmarsh Prison

R. (on the application of Bruce) *v* Financial Ombudsman Services [2007] EWHC 1646
(Admin); [2007] Pens. L.R. 287, QBD (Admin)

R. (on the application of Buddington) *v* Secretary of State for the Home Department;
sub nom Buddington *v* Secretary of State for the Home Department [2006]
EWCA Civ 280; [2006] 2 Cr. App. R. (S.) 109; [2006] Crim. L.R. 765; (2006)
170 J.P.N. 262, CA (Civ Div); affirming [2005] EWHC 2198 (QB); [2006]
A.C.D. 18; *Times*, October 20, 2005, QBD . . . .   *Digested, 06/***2938**:
                        Applied, 06/2940, 07/2982

R. (on the application of Bullmore) *v* West Hertfordshire Hospitals NHS Trust [2007]
EWCA Civ 609; [2007] 5 Costs L.R. 844, CA (Civ Div)

R. (on the application of C) *v* Croydon Youth Court; *joined cases* R. (on the application
of S) *v* Croydon Youth Court; R. (on the application of S) *v* Croydon Youth
Court [2006] EWHC 2627 (Admin), DC . . . .   *Considered, 07/947*

R. (on the application of C) *v* Enfield LBC see R. (on the application of T) *v* Enfield LBC

R. (on the application of C) *v* London South and South West Region Mental Health
Review Tribunal see R. (on the application of C) *v* Mental Health Review
Tribunal

R. (on the application of C) *v* Mental Health Review Tribunal; *sub nom* R. (on the
application of C) *v* London South and South West Region Mental Health Review
Tribunal [2001] EWCA Civ 1110; [2002] 1 W.L.R. 176; [2002] 2 F.C.R. 181;
(2001) 4 C.C.L. Rep. 284; [2001] Lloyd's Rep. Med. 450; [2001] M.H.L.R. 110;
(2001) 98(29) L.S.G. 39; (2001) 145 S.J.L.B. 167; *Times*, July 11, 2001;
Independent, July 10, 2001, CA (Civ Div); reversing [2000] M.H.L.R. 220;
[2001] A.C.D. 63, QBD (Admin) . . . .   *Digested, 01/***4424**:
                        Applied, 07/2907: Considered, 05/2921

R. (on the application of Cali) *v* Waltham Forest LBC [2006] EWHC 302 (Admin);
[2007] H.L.R. 1; [2006] A.C.D. 76, QBD (Admin) . . . .   *Digested, 07/***2152**

R. (on the application of Campaign for Nuclear Disarmament) *v* Prime Minister; *sub nom*
Campaign for Nuclear Disarmament *v* Prime Minister of the United Kingdom
[2002] EWHC 2777 (Admin); [2003] A.C.D. 36; *Times*, December 27, 2002,
QBD (Admin) . . . .   *Digested, 03/***2676**:
                        Applied, 06/2396: Considered, 07/2234

R. (on the application of Campaign to End All Animal Experiments (t/a British Union for the
Abolition of Vivisection)) *v* Secretary of State for the Home Department see R.
(on the application of British Union for the Abolition of Vivisection) *v* Secretary
of State for the Home Department

R. (on the application of Campbell) v General Medical Council [2005] EWCA Civ 250; [2005] 1 W.L.R. 3488; [2005] 2 All E.R. 970; [2005] Lloyd's Rep. Med. 353; (2005) 83 B.M.L.R. 30; *Times*, April 18, 2005; *Independent*, April 12, 2005, CA (Civ Div); reversing [2004] EWHC 1301 (Admin), QBD (Admin) . . . . *Digested*, 05/**1802**:
　　　　　　　　　　　　　　　　　　　　　　　　　　　　　　　　　　　　　　Considered, 07/1950

R. (on the application of Care Principles Ltd) v Mental Health Review Tribunal [2006] EWHC 3194 (Admin); (2007) 94 B.M.L.R. 145; [2006] M.H.L.R. 365; [2007] A.C.D. 47, QBD (Admin) . . . . *Digested*, 07/**2910**

R. (on the application of Carson) v Secretary of State for Work and Pensions; *sub nom* Carson v Secretary of State for Work and Pensions; *joined case* R. (on the application of Reynolds) v Secretary of State for Work and Pensions [2005] UKHL 37; [2006] 1 A.C. 173; [2005] 2 W.L.R. 1369; [2005] 4 All E.R. 545; [2005] H.R.L.R. 23; [2005] U.K.H.R.R. 1185; 18 B.H.R.C. 677; *Times*, May 27, 2005, HL; affirming [2003] EWCA Civ 797; [2003] 3 All E.R. 577; [2003] H.R.L.R. 36; [2003] Pens. L.R. 215; [2003] A.C.D. 76; (2003) 100(34) L.S.G. 32; (2003) 147 S.J.L.B. 780; *Times*, June 28, 2003, CA (Civ Div); affirming [2002] EWHC 978 (Admin); [2002] 3 All E.R. 994; (2002) 99(26) L.S.G. 39; *Times*, May 24, 2002; *Daily Telegraph*, May 30, 2002, QBD (Admin) . . . . *Digested*, 05/**3835**:
　　　　　　　　　Applied, 04/2821, 04/3579, 05/1139, 06/2277, 07/2327, 07/3256:
　　　　　　　　　　　Considered, 04/1889, 06/3381, 06/4027, 07/2293

R. (on the application of Casey) v Crawley BC [2006] EWHC 301 (Admin); [2006] B.L.G.R. 239; [2006] A.C.D. 64; [2007] A.C.D. 12; [2006] N.P.C. 24, QBD (Admin) . . . . *Digested*, 06/**2823**

R. (on the application of Casey) v Restormel BC [2007] EWHC 2554 (Admin); [2007] N.P.C. 118, QBD (Admin)

R. (on the application of Cash) v HM Coroner for Northamptonshire [2007] EWHC 1354 (Admin); [2007] 4 All E.R. 903; [2007] U.K.H.R.R. 1037; (2007) 157 N.L.J. 895, QBD (Admin). . . . . *Digested*, 07/**13**

R. (on the application of Castle Cement Ltd) v Environment Agency see Castle Cement Ltd v Environment Agency

R. (on the application of Catt) v Brighton and Hove City Council [2007] EWCA Civ 298; [2007] Env. L.R. 32; [2007] B.L.G.R. 331; [2007] 2 P. & C.R. 11; [2007] J.P.L. 1517; [2007] N.P.C. 38, CA (Civ Div); affirming [2006] EWHC 1337 (Admin); [2007] Env. L.R. 6; [2007] B.L.G.R. 151; [2007] J.P.L. 70, QBD (Admin) . . . . . *Digested*, 07/**3270**

R. (on the application of Charlson) v Guildford Magistrates Court [2006] EWHC 2318 (Admin); [2006] 1 W.L.R. 3494; [2007] 3 All E.R. 163; (2006) 170 J.P. 739; [2007] R.T.R. 1; [2007] A.C.D. 6; (2007) 171 J.P.N. 193; *Times*, September 29, 2006, QBD (Admin) . . . . *Digested*, 06/**974**

R. (on the application of Chelmsford BC) v First Secretary of State; *sub nom* Chelmsford BC v First Secretary of State [2003] EWHC 2978 (Admin); [2004] 2 P. & C.R. 34; [2004] 2 P.L.R. 34, QBD (Admin) . . . . *Digested*, 06/**3370**:
　　　　　　　　　　　　　　　　　　　　　　　　Considered, 05/3264, 07/3235

R. (on the application of Chief Constable of the West Midlands) v Birmingham Justices see R. (on the application of Chief Constable of the West Midlands) v Birmingham Magistrates Court

R. (on the application of Chief Constable of the West Midlands) v Birmingham Magistrates Court; *sub nom* R. (on the application of Chief Constable of the West Midlands) v Birmingham Justices [2002] EWHC 1087 (Admin); [2002] Po. L.R. 157; [2003] Crim. L.R. 37; [2003] A.C.D. 18; (2002) 99(28) L.S.G. 32; (2002) 146 S.J.L.B. 159; *Times*, June 5, 2002, QBD (Admin) . . . . *Digested*, 02/**3761**:
　　　　　　　　　　　　　　　　　　　　　　　　　　　　　　　　　　　　　　Considered, 07/2811

R. (on the application of Christian) v Secretary of State for the Home Department [2006] EWHC 2152 (Admin); [2006] A.C.D. 101, QBD (Admin) . . . . *Digested*, 07/**2974**

R. (on the application of Clear Channel UK Ltd) v Southwark LBC [2007] EWCA Civ 1328; [2007] N.P.C. 133, CA (Civ Div); affirming [2006] EWHC 3325 (Admin); [2007] J.P.L. 927, QBD (Admin) . . . . *Digested*, 07/**3222**

R. (on the application of Cleary) v Highbury Corner Magistrates Court [2006] EWHC 1869 (Admin); [2007] 1 W.L.R. 1272; [2007] 1 All E.R. 270; [2007] A.C.D. 1; (2006) 150 S.J.L.B. 1052; *Times*, September 12, 2006, DC . . . . *Digested*, 06/**351**

R. (on the application of Clift) v Secretary of State for the Home Department; *sub nom* Hindawi v Secretary of State for the Home Department; Secretary of State for the Home Department v Hindawi; Secretary of State for the Home Department v Headley; *joined cases* R. (on the application of Headley) v Secretary of State for the Home Department; R. (on the application of Hindawi) v Secretary of State for the Home Department [2006] UKHL 54; [2007] 1 A.C. 484; [2007] 2 W.L.R. 24; [2007] 2 All E.R. 1; [2007] H.R.L.R. 12; [2007] U.K.H.R.R. 348; 21 B.H.R.C. 704; [2007] A.C.D. 27; *Times*, December 21, 2006, HL; affirming [2004] EWCA Civ 514; [2004] 1 W.L.R. 2223; [2004] 3 All E.R. 338; [2005] 1 Prison L.R. 51; (2004) 101(20) L.S.G. 34; (2004) 148 S.J.L.B. 569; *Times*, May 13, 2004; *Independent*, May 7, 2004, CA (Civ Div); affirming [2003] EWHC 1337 (Admin); [2003] Prison L.R. 389; [2003] A.C.D. 100; (2003) 100(32) L.S.G. 34; *Times*, June 25, 2003, QBD (Admin) . . . . *Digested*, 07/**2975**:
　　　　　　　　Applied, 07/3867: *Considered*, 07/2300, 07/2981:
　　　　　　　　　　　　　　Previous proceedings, 04/2776

R. (on the application of Cole) v Secretary of State for the Home Department; *joined cases* R. (on the application of Hawkes) v Secretary of State for the Home Department; R. (on the application of Rowland) v Secretary of State for the Home Department [2003] EWHC 1789 (Admin); [2003] Prison L.R. 342, QBD (Admin) . . . . *Approved*, 07/3692:
Considered, 06/3752, 07/3669

R. (on the application of Condron) v National Assembly for Wales; *sub nom* Condron v National Assembly for Wales; National Assembly for Wales v Condron [2006] EWCA Civ 1573; [2007] B.L.G.R. 87; [2007] 2 P. & C.R. 4; [2007] J.P.L. 938; [2006] 49 E.G. 94 (C.S.); [2006] N.P.C. 127; [2007] Env. L.R. D7; *Times*, December 13, 2006; *Independent*, November 29, 2006, CA (Civ Div); reversing [2005] EWHC 3007 (Admin); [2006] Env. L.R. 35, QBD (Admin) . . . . *Digested*, 07/**3264**

R. (on the application of Consumer Council for Postal Services (Postwatch)) v Postal Services Commission; *sub nom* Royal Mail Group v Consumer Council for Postal Services [2007] EWCA Civ 167; (2007) 104(12) L.S.G. 34; *Times*, April 20, 2007, CA (Civ Div); reversing in part [2005] EWHC 3163 (Admin); [2007] A.C.D. 67, QBD (Admin) . . . . *Digested*, 07/**3324**

R. (on the application of Cook) v General Commissioners of Income Tax [2007] EWHC 167 (Admin); [2007] S.T.C. 499; [2007] B.T.C. 626; [2007] S.T.I. 258, QBD (Admin)

R. (on the application of Cooke) v Revenue and Customs Commissioners [2007] EWHC 81 (Admin); [2007] B.T.C. 634; [2007] S.T.I. 256; *Times*, February 12, 2007, QBD (Admin)

R. (on the application of Cooper) v Parole Board [2007] EWHC 1292 (Admin); [2007] A.C.D. 101; *Times*, June 6, 2007, QBD (Admin) . . . . *Digested*, 07/**2983**

R. (on the application of Corby BC) v Secretary of State for Communities and Local Government; *joined case* R. (on the application of Slough BC) v Secretary of State for Communities and Local Government [2007] EWHC 1873 (Admin); [2007] R.V.R. 227; [2007] 33 E.G. 91 (C.S.), QBD (Admin) . . . . *Digested*, 07/**2877**

R. (on the application of Corner House Research) v Secretary of State for Trade and Industry [2005] EWCA Civ 192; [2005] 1 W.L.R. 2600; [2005] 4 All E.R. 1; [2005] C.P. Rep. 28; [2005] 3 Costs L.R. 455; [2005] A.C.D. 100; (2005) 102(17) L.S.G. 31; (2005) 149 S.J.L.B. 297; *Times*, March 7, 2005; *Independent*, March 4, 2005, CA (Civ Div); reversing [2004] EWHC 3011 (Admin), QBD (Admin) . . . . *Digested*, 05/**354**:
Applied, 05/373, 06/1706: *Considered*, 05/366, 06/5125, 07/402

R. (on the application of Costello) v North East Essex Magistrates [2006] EWHC 3145 (Admin); (2007) 171 J.P. 153; (2007) 171 J.P.N. 393, QBD (Admin) . . . . *Digested*, 07/**936**

R. (on the application of Council for the Regulation of Health Care Professionals) v General Medical Council [2005] EWHC 2973 (Admin), QBD (Admin) . . . . *Applied*, 07/2028

R. (on the application of Council for the Regulation of Health Care Professionals) v Nursing & Midwifery Council [2007] EWHC 1806 (Admin); (2007) 98 B.M.L.R. 60; [2007] A.C.D. 79, QBD (Admin) . . . . *Digested*, 07/**2028**

R. (on the application of Countryside Alliance) v Attorney General; *joined cases* R. (on the application of Derwin) v Attorney General; R. (on the application of Friend) v Attorney General [2007] UKHL 52; [2007] 3 W.L.R. 922; (2007) 104(48) L.S.G. 23; (2007) 157 N.L.J. 1730; (2007) 151 S.J.L.B. 1564; [2007] N.P.C. 127; *Times*, November 29, 2007, HL; affirming [2006] EWCA Civ 817; [2007] Q.B. 305; [2006] 3 W.L.R. 1017; [2007] Eu. L.R. 139; [2006] H.R.L.R. 33; [2006] U.K.H.R.R. 927; (2006) 150 S.J.L.B. 886; [2006] N.P.C. 73; *Times*, June 30, 2006, CA (Civ Div); affirming [2005] EWHC 1677 (Admin); [2006] Eu. L.R. 178; [2006] U.K.H.R.R. 73; (2005) 102(36) L.S.G. 29; (2005) 155 N.L.J. 1245; [2005] N.P.C. 107; *Times*, August 3, 2005, QBD (Admin) . . . . *Digested*, 07/**204**:
Applied, 07/1944, 07/3977: *Distinguished*, 06/1812

R. (on the application of Couronne) v Crawley BC; *sub nom* Couronne v Crawley BC; *joined case* R. (on the application of Bontemps) v Secretary of State for Work and Pensions [2007] EWCA Civ 1086, CA (Civ Div); affirming [2006] EWHC 1514 (Admin); [2007] B.L.G.R. 274, QBD (Admin) . . . . *Digested*, 07/**3875**

R. (on the application of Crown Prosecution Service) v Bow Street Magistrates Court [2006] EWHC 1763 (Admin); [2007] 1 W.L.R. 291; [2006] 4 All E.R. 1342; [2007] 1 Cr. App. R. 18, DC . . . . *Digested*, 07/**2810**

R. (on the application of Crown Prosecution Service) v Guildford Crown Court [2007] EWHC 1798 (Admin); [2007] 1 W.L.R. 2886; *Times*, July 16, 2007, DC . . . . *Digested*, 07/**21**

R. (on the application of Crown Prosecution Service) v Uxbridge Magistrates [2007] EWHC 205 (Admin); (2007) 171 J.P. 279; (2007) 171 J.P.N. 596, DC . . . . *Digested*, 07/**1029**

R. (on the application of Culley) v Dorchester Crown Court [2007] EWHC 109 (Admin); (2007) 171 J.P. 373; (2007) 171 J.P.N. 706, QBD (Admin) . . . . *Digested*, 07/**941**

R. (on the application of D) v Bromley LBC see R. (on the application of D) v Independent Education Appeal Panel of Bromley LBC

R. (on the application of D) v Hackney LBC see R. (on the application of AW) v Croydon LBC

R. (on the application of D) v Independent Education Appeal Panel of Bromley LBC; *sub nom* R. (on the application of D) v Bromley LBC [2007] EWCA Civ 1010; (2007) 104(38) L.S.G. 36; (2007) 151 S.J.L.B. 1226; *Times*, November 20, 2007, CA (Civ Div) . . . . *Digested*, 07/**1185**

R. (on the application of D) v Secretary of State for Health; *sub nom* D v Secretary of State for Health [2006] EWCA Civ 989; [2006] Lloyd's Rep. Med. 457; *Times*, August 28, 2006, CA (Civ Div); affirming [2005] EWHC 2884 (Admin), QBD (Admin) . . . . *Digested*, 06/**1809**: *Applied*, 07/1197

R. (on the application of D) v Secretary of State for the Home Department [2006] EWCA Civ 143; [2006] 3 All E.R. 946; [2006] H.R.L.R. 24; [2006] Inquest L.R. 35; [2006] A.C.D. 66; *Times*, March 21, 2006; *Independent*, March 2, 2006, CA (Civ Div); reversing in part [2005] EWHC 728 (Admin); [2005] U.K.H.R.R. 917; [2005] Inquest L.R. 54, QBD (Admin) . . . . *Digested*, 06/**2934**: *Applied*, 07/2980

R. (on the application of D) v Southwark LBC; *sub nom* D v Southwark LBC; R. (on the application of ED) v Southwark LBC [2007] EWCA Civ 182; [2007] 1 F.L.R. 2181; [2007] 1 F.C.R. 788; (2007) 10 C.C.L. Rep. 280; [2007] Fam. Law 701, CA (Civ Div); affirming [2006] EWHC 2280 (Admin), QBD (Admin) . . . . *Digested*, 07/**1777**: *Considered*, 07/3940

R. (on the application of Da Silva) v DPP [2006] EWHC 3204 (Admin); [2006] Inquest L.R. 224; [2006] Po. L.R. 176; (2007) 157 N.L.J. 31, DC . . . . *Digested*, 07/**980**

R. (on the application of Daniels) v Barnet LBC [2007] EWHC 1885 (Admin); [2007] R.V.R. 300, QBD (Admin) . . . . *Digested*, 07/**2839**

R. (on the application of Dari) v Secretary of State for the Home Department (C-16/05) see Tum v Secretary of State for the Home Department (C-16/05)

R. (on the application of Datta) v Secretary of State for the Home Department see R. (on the application of Vovk) v Secretary of State for the Home Department

R. (on the application of Debt Free Direct Ltd) v Advertising Standards Authority Ltd [2007] EWHC 1337 (Admin); [2007] A.C.D. 82, QBD (Admin)

R. (on the application of Dennis) v DPP [2006] EWHC 3211 (Admin); [2006] Po. L.R. 343; (2007) 104(4) L.S.G. 35; (2007) 157 N.L.J. 143, QBD (Admin) . . . . *Digested*, 07/**2072**

R. (on the application of Dennis) v Legal Services Commission see R. (on the application of Southwark Law Centre) v Legal Services Commission

R. (on the application of Department for Constitutional Affairs) v Miles [2005] EWHC 744 (Admin), QBD (Admin) . . . . *Disapproved*, 07/368

R. (on the application of Derwin) v Attorney General see R. (on the application of Countryside Alliance) v Attorney General

R. (on the application of DF) v Chief Constable of Norfolk [2002] EWHC 1738 (Admin); [2002] Prison L.R. 396, QBD (Admin) . . . . *Considered*, 07/2240

R. (on the application of Dimmock) v Secretary of State for Education and Skills see Dimmock v Secretary of State for Children, Schools and Families

R. (on the application of Director of Revenue and Customs Prosecutions) v Criminal Cases Review Commission [2006] EWHC 3064 (Admin); [2007] 1 Cr. App. R. 30; [2007] Crim. L.R. 383; [2007] A.C.D. 39, DC . . . . *Digested*, 07/**971**: *Doubted*, 07/970

R. (on the application of DJ) v Mental Health Review Tribunal see R. (on the application of N) v Mental Health Review Tribunal (Northern Region)

R. (on the application of Donnachie) v Cardiff Magistrates' Court [2007] EWHC 1846 (Admin); [2007] 1 W.L.R. 3085; (2007) 171 J.P. 612; *Times*, August 22, 2007, QBD (Admin) . . . . *Digested*, 07/**780**

R. (on the application of Doshi) v Southend-on-Sea PCT [2007] EWHC 1361 (Admin); [2007] LS Law Medical 418; [2007] A.C.D. 70, QBD (Admin) . . . . *Digested*, 07/**1949**

R. (on the application of DPP) v Everest see DPP v Everest

R. (on the application of Drain) v Secretary of State for the Environment, Food and Rural Affairs see R. (on the application of Godmanchester Town Council) v Secretary of State for the Environment, Food and Rural Affairs

R. (on the application of E) v Newham LBC see E v Newham LBC

R. (on the application of E) v Secretary of State for the Home Department [2007] EWHC 1731 (Admin); [2007] A.C.D. 83, QBD (Admin)

R. (on the application of East Hertfordshire DC) v First Secretary of State [2007] EWHC 834 (Admin); [2007] J.P.L. 1304, QBD (Admin) . . . . *Digested*, 07/**3225**

R. (on the application of ED) v Southwark LBC see R. (on the application of D) v Southwark LBC

R. (on the application of Edwards) v Environment Agency (No.2); *sub nom* Edwards v Environment Agency [2006] EWCA Civ 877; [2007] Env. L.R. 9; [2007] J.P.L. 82; (2006) 103(30) L.S.G. 32, CA (Civ Div); affirming [2005] EWHC 657 (Admin); [2006] Env. L.R. 3; [2005] J.P.L. 1576; [2005] N.P.C. 53; [2006] N.P.C. 74, QBD (Admin) . . . . *Digested*, 07/**1506**: *Considered*, 07/57

R. (on the application of Eisai Ltd) v National Institute for Health and Clinical Excellence see Eisai Ltd v National Institute for Health and Clinical Excellence (NICE)

R. (on the application of Ekinci) v Secretary of State for the Home Department [2003]
EWCA Civ 765; [2004] Imm. A.R. 15, CA (Civ Div) . . . .   *Digested, 04/2049*:
                                        Applied, 07/2364: *Considered*, 06/2286

R. (on the application of Elias) v Secretary of State for Defence; *sub nom* Secretary of
State for the Home Department v Elias; Elias v Secretary of State for Defence
[2006] EWCA Civ 1293; [2006] 1 W.L.R. 3213; [2006] I.R.L.R. 934; *Times*,
October 17, 2006; *Independent*, October 18, 2006, CA (Civ Div); affirming
[2005] EWHC 1435 (Admin); [2005] I.R.L.R. 788; [2006] A.C.D. 10; (2005)
102(30) L.S.G. 30; *Times*, August 25, 2005, QBD (Admin) . . . .   *Digested, 06/44*:
                                                Considered, 07/1399

R. (on the application of Elite Mobile Plc) v Customs and Excise Commissioners [2004]
EWHC 2923 (Admin); [2005] S.T.C. 275; [2005] B.T.C. 5113; [2005] B.V.C.
144; [2005] S.T.I. 21, QBD (Admin) . . . .   *Digested, 05/4374*:
                                       Considered, 06/4464, 07/4359

R. (on the application of Energy Financing Team Ltd) v Bow Street Magistrates Court; *sub
nom* Energy Financing Team Ltd v Director of the Serious Fraud Office [2005]
EWHC 1626 (Admin); [2006] 1 W.L.R. 1316; [2005] 4 All E.R. 285; [2006]
A.C.D. 8, QBD (Admin) . . . .   *Digested, 05/930*:
                                                Considered, 07/1931

R. (on the application of Equal Opportunities Commission) v Secretary of State for Trade
and Industry see Equal Opportunities Commission v Secretary of State for Trade
and Industry

R. (on the application of Errington) v Metropolitan Police Authority [2006] EWHC 1155
(Admin); (2007) 171 J.P. 89; [2006] Po. L.R. 203; [2006] A.C.D. 68; (2007)
171 J.P.N. 362; (2006) 103(17) L.S.G. 24, QBD (Admin) . . . .   *Digested, 07/945*:
                                                Considered, 07/375

R. (on the application of Essex CC) v Secretary of State for Transport see R. (on the
application of Wandsworth LBC) v Secretary of State for Transport

R. (on the application of Essex CC) v Secretary of State for Transport, Local Government
and the Regions see R. (on the application of Medway Council) v Secretary of
State for Transport, Local Government and the Regions

R. (on the application of Esterson) v Revenue and Customs Commissioners [2005]
EWHC 3037 (Admin); 77 T.C. 629; [2006] B.T.C. 170; [2007] S.T.I. 2215, QBD
(Admin) . . . .   *Digested, 06/4215*

R. (on the application of Evolution Export Trading Ltd) v Revenue and Customs
Commissioners see R. (on the application of Just Fabulous (UK) Ltd) v Revenue
and Customs Commissioners

R. (on the application of Ewing) v Davis; *sub nom* Ewing v Davis [2007] EWHC 1730
(Admin); [2007] 1 W.L.R. 3223; (2007) 171 J.P. 645; [2007] A.C.D. 73, QBD
(Admin) . . . .   *Digested, 07/1015*

R. (on the application of Ewing) v Department for Constitutional Affairs [2006] EWHC
504 (Admin); [2006] 2 All E.R. 993; [2007] A.C.D. 20, QBD (Admin) . . . .   *Digested, 06/345*

R. (on the application of Ewing) v Office of the Deputy Prime Minister; *sub nom* Ewing
v Office of the Deputy Prime Minister [2005] EWCA Civ 1583; [2006] 1
W.L.R. 1260; [2005] N.P.C. 146; *Independent*, January 20, 2006, CA (Civ Div);
affirming [2005] EWHC 825 (Admin), QBD (Admin) . . . .   *Digested, 06/417*:
                                                Considered, 07/402

R. (on the application of F (Mongolia)) v Asylum and Immigration Tribunal see F
(Mongolia) v Secretary of State for the Home Department

R. (on the application of Fatnani) v General Medical Council see Fatnani v General
Medical Council

R. (on the application of Faulkner) v Secretary of State for the Home Department
[2005] EWHC 2567 (Admin); [2006] I.N.L.R. 502, QBD (Admin) . . . .   *Digested, 07/2292*

R. (on the application of FD (Zimbabwe)) v Secretary of State for the Home Department
[2007] EWCA Civ 1220; (2007) 151 S.J.L.B. 1438, CA (Civ Div); reversing in
part [2006] EWHC 2975 (Admin), QBD (Admin)

R. (on the application of Federation of Tour Operators) v HM Treasury; *sub nom*
Federation of Tour Operators v HM Treasury [2007] EWHC 2062 (Admin);
[2007] U.K.H.R.R. 1210; [2007] A.C.D. 105; (2007) 151 S.J.L.B. 1168; *Times*,
October 9, 2007, QBD (Admin) . . . .   *Digested, 07/3977*

R. (on the application of Fogg) v Secretary of State for Defence; *sub nom* Fogg v
Secretary of State for Defence [2006] EWCA Civ 1270; [2007] Q.B. 96; [2006]
3 W.L.R. 931; [2006] 2 Lloyd's Rep. 576; [2007] A.C.D. 21; (2006) 103(40)
L.S.G. 33; *Times*, October 10, 2006; *Independent*, October 10, 2006, CA (Civ
Div); affirming [2005] EWHC 2888 (Admin); [2006] 3 W.L.R. 53; [2006] 1
Lloyd's Rep. 579; [2006] A.C.D. 48; (2006) 156 N.L.J. 23; *Times*, January 13,
2006, QBD (Admin) . . . .   *Digested, 06/230*

R. (on the application of Friend) v Attorney General see R. (on the application of
Countryside Alliance) v Attorney General

R. (on the application of Fudge) v South West Strategic HA [2007] EWCA Civ 803;
(2007) 10 C.C.L. Rep. 599; [2007] LS Law Medical 645; (2007) 98 B.M.L.R.
112, CA (Civ Div); affirming in part [2007] EWHC 1195 (Admin); (2007) 10
C.C.L. Rep. 387, QBD (Admin) . . . .   *Digested, 07/2048*

R. (on the application of Furness) v Brighton and Hove City Council [2006] EWHC
2075 (Admin); [2007] J.P.L. 577, QBD (Admin) . . . .   *Digested*, 07/**3242**

R. (on the application of G) v Barnet LBC; *joined cases* R. (on the application of W) v
Lambeth LBC; R. (on the application of A) v Lambeth LBC [2003] UKHL 57;
[2004] 2 A.C. 208; [2003] 3 W.L.R. 1194; [2004] 1 All E.R. 97; [2004] 1 F.L.R.
454; [2003] 3 F.C.R. 419; [2004] H.R.L.R. 4; [2004] H.L.R. 10; [2003]
B.L.G.R. 569; (2003) 6 C.C.L. Rep. 500; [2004] Fam. Law 21; (2003) 100(45)
L.S.G. 29; [2003] N.P.C. 123; *Times*, October 24, 2003; *Independent*, October
29, 2003, HL; affirming [2001] EWCA Civ 540; [2001] 2 F.L.R. 877; [2001] 2
F.C.R. 193; (2001) 33 H.L.R. 59; [2002] B.L.G.R. 34; (2001) 4 C.C.L. Rep. 128;
[2001] Fam. Law 662; (2001) 98(24) L.S.G. 43; *Times*, June 5, 2001;
Independent, April 25, 2001, CA (Civ Div); reversing [2001] EWHC Admin 5;
[2001] 1 F.C.R. 743; (2001) 4 C.C.L. Rep. 33; [2001] A.C.D. 59, QBD (Admin)   *Digested*, 04/**3643**:
                       Applied, 05/2004, 07/2165, 07/3941: *Considered*, 06/1654:
            Distinguished, 06/2021: *Followed*, 04/3636: *Previous proceedings*, 01/3434,
                                                   02/2339

R. (on the application of G) v Burnley Magistrates Court; *joined case* G v Burnley
Magistrates Court [2007] EWHC 1033 (Admin); (2007) 171 J.P. 445; (2007)
171 J.P.N. 789, DC . . . .   *Digested*, 07/**947**

R. (on the application of G) v Chief Constable of West Yorkshire; *sub nom* G v Chief
Constable of West Yorkshire; C1 2007/0343, CA (Civ Div); reversing [2006]
EWHC 3485 (Admin); [2007] A.C.D. 41, DC

R. (on the application of G) v Immigration Appeal Tribunal; *joined case* R. (on the
application of M) v Immigration Appeal Tribunal [2004] EWCA Civ 1731; [2005]
1 W.L.R. 1445; [2005] 2 All E.R. 165; [2005] Imm. A.R. 106; [2005] I.N.L.R.
329; (2005) 102(6) L.S.G. 32; (2005) 149 S.J.L.B. 59; *Times*, December 23,
2004; *Independent*, January 11, 2005, CA (Civ Div); affirming [2004] EWHC
588 (Admin); [2004] 1 W.L.R. 2953; [2004] 3 All E.R. 286; [2004] A.C.D. 85;
Times, May 13, 2004, QBD (Admin) . . . .   *Digested*, 05/**2170**:
                              Considered, 07/2344: *Followed*, 07/2300

R. (on the application of G (A Child)) v Westminster City Council [2004] EWCA Civ 45;
[2004] 1 W.L.R. 1113; [2004] 4 All E.R. 572; [2005] B.L.G.R. 64; [2004]
E.L.R. 135; (2004) 101(7) L.S.G. 35; (2004) 148 S.J.L.B. 179; *Times*, February
5, 2004; *Independent*, February 3, 2004, CA (Civ Div) . . . .   *Digested*, 04/**999**:
                                            Applied, 07/1179

R. (on the application of Galandauer) v Snaresbrook Crown Court see Galandauer v
Snaresbrook Crown Court

R. (on the application of Gambier) v Secretary of State for Health see R. (on the
application of Wright) v Secretary of State for Health

R. (on the application of Gardner) v Parole Board [2006] EWCA Civ 1222; (2006)
103(36) L.S.G. 35; (2006) 156 N.L.J. 1401; (2006) 150 S.J.L.B. 1187; *Times*,
September 29, 2006, CA (Civ Div); affirming [2005] EWHC 2981 (Admin),
QBD (Admin) . . . .   *Digested*, 07/**2979**

R. (on the application of GB) v Oxfordshire CC see Oxfordshire CC v B

R. (on the application of Gentle) v Prime Minister [2006] EWCA Civ 1689; [2007] Q.B.
689; [2007] 2 W.L.R. 195; [2007] H.R.L.R. 10; *Times*, January 1, 2007, CA
(Civ Div); affirming [2005] EWHC 3119 (Admin); [2007] A.C.D. 52, QBD
(Admin) . . . .   *Digested*, 07/**2234**:
                                   Considered, 07/2980

R. (on the application of Ghosh) v Northumberland NHS Care Trust see R. (on the
application of S) v Knowsley NHS Primary Care Trust

R. (on the application of Gibbs) v Bishop of Manchester [2007] EWHC 480 (Admin);
(2007) 104(14) L.S.G. 22; *Times*, April 25, 2007, QBD (Admin) . . . .   *Digested*, 07/**1083**

R. (on the application of Gilboy) v Liverpool City Council; *sub nom* Gilboy v Liverpool
City Council [2007] EWHC 2335 (Admin); [2007] B.L.G.R. 837; [2007] A.C.D.
91; [2007] N.P.C. 105, QBD (Admin) . . . .   *Digested*, 07/**2772**

R. (on the application of Giles) v Parole Board [2003] UKHL 42; [2004] 1 A.C. 1;
[2003] 3 W.L.R. 736; [2003] 4 All E.R. 429; [2003] H.R.L.R. 37; [2003]
U.K.H.R.R. 1035; (2003) 153 N.L.J. 1426; (2003) 147 S.J.L.B. 936; *Times*,
August 1, 2003, HL; affirming [2002] EWCA Civ 951; [2003] 2 W.L.R. 196;
[2002] 3 All E.R. 1123; [2003] 1 Cr. App. R. (S.) 78; [2002] Po. L.R. 11; [2004]
Prison L.R. 13; [2002] Crim. L.R. 743; (2002) 99(35) L.S.G. 38; (2002) 152
N.L.J. 1239; *Times*, July 23, 2002; *Independent*, October 14, 2002, CA (Civ Div);
reversing [2001] EWHC Admin 834; [2002] 1 W.L.R. 654; [2002] Po. L.R. 1;
Independent, December 17, 2001, QBD (Admin) . . . .   *Digested*, 03/**3067**:
            Applied, 03/3070, 04/2776, 07/2988: *Distinguished*, 04/3349

R. (on the application of Gillan) v Commissioner of Police of the Metropolis; *joined case* R. (on the application of Quinton) v Commissioner of Police of the Metropolis [2006] UKHL 12; [2006] 2 A.C. 307; [2006] 2 W.L.R. 537; [2006] 4 All E.R. 1041; [2006] 2 Cr. App. R. 36; [2006] H.R.L.R. 18; [2006] U.K.H.R.R. 740; 21 B.H.R.C. 202; [2006] Po. L.R. 26; [2006] Crim. L.R. 752; (2006) 150 S.J.L.B. 366; *Times*, March 9, 2006, HL; affirming [2004] EWCA Civ 1067; [2005] Q.B. 388; [2004] 3 W.L.R. 1144; [2005] 1 All E.R. 970; [2004] U.K.H.R.R. 1108; [2005] Crim. L.R. 414; [2004] A.C.D. 94; (2004) 101(35) L.S.G. 35; *Times*, August 12, 2004; *Independent*, October 5, 2004, CA (Civ Div); affirming [2003] EWHC 2545 (Admin); [2003] Po. L.R. 397; *Times*, November 5, 2003, DC ...   *Digested*, 06/**3409**:
Considered, 06/3407: *Previous proceedings*, 06/3409

R. (on the application of Gillan) v Crown Court at Winchester see Gillan v DPP

R. (on the application of Gillan) v DPP see Gillan v DPP

R. (on the application of Girling) v Parole Board; *sub nom* R. (on the application of Girling) v Secretary of State for the Home Department; Girling v Parole Board; Girling (Deceased) v Secretary of State for the Home Department [2006] EWCA Civ 1779; [2007] Q.B. 783; [2007] 2 W.L.R. 782; [2007] 2 All E.R. 688; [2007] A.C.D. 65; (2007) 104(2) L.S.G. 32; *Times*, January 19, 2007, CA (Civ Div); reversing [2005] EWHC 546 (Admin); [2006] 1 W.L.R. 1917; [2006] 1 All E.R. 11; [2005] 2 Prison L.R. 136, QBD (Admin) ....   *Digested*, 07/**2988**

R. (on the application of Girling) v Secretary of State for the Home Department see R. (on the application of Girling) v Parole Board

R. (on the application of Gladstone Plc) v Manchester City Magistrates' Court [2004] EWHC 2806 (Admin); [2005] 1 W.L.R. 1987; [2005] 2 All E.R. 56; *Times*, November 26, 2004, QBD (Admin) ....   *Digested*, 05/**919**:
Doubted, 07/1015

R. (on the application of GM) v Mental Health Review Tribunal see R. (on the application of KB) v Mental Health Review Tribunal

R. (on the application of Godmanchester Town Council) v Secretary of State for the Environment, Food and Rural Affairs; *joined case* R. (on the application of Drain) v Secretary of State for the Environment, Food and Rural Affairs [2007] UKHL 28; [2007] 3 W.L.R. 85; [2007] 4 All E.R. 273; [2007] J.P.L. 1691; [2007] 26 E.G. 163 (C.S.); (2007) 104(27) L.S.G. 29; (2007) 151 S.J.L.B. 858; [2007] N.P.C. 74; *Times*, June 22, 2007, HL; reversing [2005] EWCA Civ 1597; [2006] Q.B. 727; [2006] 2 W.L.R. 1179; [2006] 2 All E.R. 960; [2006] 2 P. & C.R. 1; [2006] J.P.L. 1541; [2006] 1 E.G. 98 (C.S.); [2005] N.P.C. 149; *Times*, December 27, 2005; *Independent*, January 18, 2006, CA (Civ Div); affirming [2004] EWHC 1217 (Admin); [2005] 1 W.L.R. 926; [2004] 4 All E.R. 342; [2005] A.C.D. 28; [2004] N.P.C. 127; *Independent*, October 11, 2004, QBD (Admin) ....   *Digested*, 07/**3421**

R. (on the application of Gordon) v Parole Board; *sub nom* R. v Parole Board Ex p. Gordon [2000] Prison L.R. 275; [2001] A.C.D. 47, QBD (Admin) ....   *Considered*, 07/2988

R. (on the application of Gorlov) v Institute of Chartered Accountants of England and Wales [2001] EWHC Admin 220; [2001] A.C.D. 73, QBD (Admin) ....   *Applied*, 07/2800

R. (on the application of Gosport BC) v Fareham Magistrates Court [2006] EWHC 3047 (Admin); [2007] 1 W.L.R. 634; (2007) 171 J.P. 102; (2007) 171 J.P.N. 363; *Times*, December 18, 2006, QBD (Admin)..................   *Digested*, 07/**356**

R. (on the application of Governor of Wandsworth Prison) v Kinderis see Governor of Wandsworth Prison v Kinderis

R. (on the application of Green) v City of Westminster Magistrates' Court [2007] EWHC 2785 (Admin); (2007) 157 N.L.J. 1767, QBD (Admin)

R. (on the application of Greenpeace Ltd) v Secretary of State for Trade and Industry [2007] EWHC 311 (Admin); [2007] Env. L.R. 29; [2007] J.P.L. 1314; [2007] N.P.C. 21; *Times*, February 20, 2007, QBD (Admin) ....   *Digested*, 07/**57**:
Applied, 07/1946

R. (on the application of Greenwich LBC) v Secretary of State for Health [2006] EWHC 2576 (Admin); (2007) 10 C.C.L. Rep. 60, QBD (Admin) ....   *Digested*, 07/**3910**

R. (on the application of Grendon) v First Secretary of State see Grendon v First Secretary of State

R. (on the application of Gulliver) v Parole Board [2007] EWCA Civ 1386; (2007) 151 S.J.L.B. 928; *Times*, August 20, 2007, CA (Civ Div); affirming [2006] EWHC 2976 (Admin), QBD (Admin)

R. (on the application of Gurung) v Ministry of Defence [2002] EWHC 2463 (Admin); (2003) 100(6) L.S.G. 25; *Times*, December 28, 2002, QBD (Admin) ....   *Digested*, 03/**57**:
Considered, 07/266

R. (on the application of H) v Ashworth Hospital Authority; *joined case* R. (on the application of Ashworth Hospital Authority) v Mental Health Review Tribunal for West Midlands and North West Region [2002] EWCA Civ 923; [2003] 1 W.L.R. 127; (2002) 5 C.C.L. Rep. 390; (2003) 70 B.M.L.R. 40; [2002] M.H.L.R. 314; [2002] A.C.D. 102; (2002) 99(34) L.S.G. 29; (2002) 146 S.J.L.B. 198; *Times*, July 10, 2002; *Daily Telegraph*, July 11, 2002, CA (Civ Div); affirming in part [2001] EWHC Admin 901; (2002) 5 C.C.L. Rep. 78; [2002] M.H.L.R. 13, QBD (Admin) ....   *Digested*, 02/**3230**:
Applied, 03/2953, 05/2822, 07/2910

R. (on the application of H) v Cornwall CC [2005] EWHC 3313 (Admin); [2006] E.L.R.
577, QBD (Admin) . . . .   *Digested*, 07/**1178**
R. (on the application of H) v DPP see H v DPP
R. (on the application of H) v Mental Health Review Tribunal [2007] EWHC 884
(Admin); (2007) 10 C.C.L. Rep. 306, QBD (Admin) . . . .   *Digested*, 07/**2898**
R. (on the application of H) v Secretary of State for Health; *sub nom* H v Secretary of
State for Health; R. (on the application of MH) v Secretary of State for Health
[2005] UKHL 60; [2006] 1 A.C. 441; [2005] 3 W.L.R. 867; [2005] 4 All E.R.
1311; [2006] H.R.L.R. 1; [2006] Lloyd's Rep. Med. 48; (2005) 86 B.M.L.R. 71;
[2005] M.H.L.R. 60; *Times*, October 25, 2005; *Independent*, October 26, 2005,
HL; reversing [2004] EWCA Civ 1609; [2005] 1 W.L.R. 1209; [2005] 3 All
E.R. 468; (2005) 8 C.C.L. Rep. 75; (2005) 82 B.M.L.R. 168; [2004] M.H.L.R.
345; (2004) 101(48) L.S.G. 26; (2004) 148 S.J.L.B. 1437; *Times*, December 8,
2004; *Independent*, December 7, 2004, CA (Civ Div); reversing [2004] EWHC
56 (Admin); [2004] M.H.L.R. 155, QBD (Admin) . . . .   *Digested*, 06/**2863**:
                                                    Applied, 07/2907
R. (on the application of H) v Secretary of State for the Home Department see R. (on
the application of A) v Secretary of State for the Home Department
R. (on the application of H) v Southampton Youth Court [2004] EWHC 2912 (Admin);
[2005] 2 Cr. App. R. (S.) 30; (2005) 169 J.P. 37; [2005] Crim. L.R. 395;
[2005] A.C.D. 45; (2005) 169 J.P.N. 159, QBD (Admin) . . . .   *Digested*, 05/**939**:
                   Applied, 05/940, 06/993, 07/947
R. (on the application of H) v Wandsworth LBC; *joined cases* R. (on the application of
Barhanu) v Hackney LBC; R. (on the application of B) v Islington LBC [2007]
EWHC 1082 (Admin); [2007] 2 F.L.R. 822; [2007] 2 F.C.R. 378; (2007) 10
C.C.L. Rep. 439; [2007] Fam. Law 802, QBD (Admin) . . . .   *Digested*, 07/**2165**:
                               Applied, 07/**3940**
R. (on the application of H) v West Sussex CC [2006] EWHC 1275 (Admin); [2006]
E.L.R. 471, QBD (Admin) . . . .   *Digested*, 07/**1262**
R. (on the application of H) v Wood Green Crown Court [2006] EWHC 2683 (Admin);
[2007] 1 W.L.R. 1670; [2007] 2 All E.R. 259; [2007] H.R.L.R. 2; [2007] Crim.
L.R. 727; (2006) 156 N.L.J. 1722; *Times*, November 9, 2006, DC . . . .   *Digested*, 07/**54**
R. (on the application of Hackney LBC) v Rottenberg; *sub nom* Hackney LBC v
Rottenberg [2007] EWHC 166 (Admin); [2007] Env. L.R. 24; *Times*, February 9,
2007, DC . . . .   *Digested*, 07/**2960**
R. (on the application of Hafner) v Secretary of State for the Home Department; *sub
nom* Hafner v Secretary of State for the Home Department [2006] EWHC 1259
(Admin); [2007] 1 W.L.R. 950; [2006] 3 All E.R. 382; *Independent*, June 9,
2006, QBD (Admin) . . . .   *Digested*, 06/**45**
R. (on the application of Hall) v First Secretary of State; *joined case* Potter v Hillingdon
LBC [2007] EWCA Civ 612; [2007] N.P.C. 83, CA (Civ Div); affirming [2006]
EWHC 2393 (Admin), QBD (Admin)
R. (on the application of Hall Hunter Partnership) v First Secretary of State [2006]
EWHC 3482 (Admin); [2007] 2 P. & C.R. 5; [2007] J.P.L. 1023, QBD (Admin)   *Digested*, 07/**3263**
R. (on the application of Hampshire CC) v Independent Appeal Panel for Hampshire
[2006] EWHC 2460 (Admin); [2007] E.L.R. 266, QBD (Admin)
R. (on the application of Hancock) v Security Industry Authority see Nicholds v Security
Industry Authority
R. (on the application of Hanson) v Middlesbrough BC see Hanson v Middlesbrough BC
R. (on the application of Harrison) v Secretary of State for the Home Department; *sub
nom* Harrison v Secretary of State for the Home Department [2003] EWCA Civ
432; [2003] I.N.L.R. 284; *Times*, April 15, 2003, CA (Civ Div) . . . .   *Digested*, 03/**2122**:
                           Considered, 07/856
R. (on the application of Havard) v South Kesteven DC [2006] EWHC 1373 (Admin);
[2006] J.P.L. 1734, QBD (Admin). . . . .   *Digested*, 07/**3276**
R. (on the application of Havering LBC) v Special Educational Needs and Disability
Tribunal see Havering LBC v Special Educational Needs and Disability Tribunal
R. (on the application of Haward) v General Medical Council [2007] EWHC 2236
(Admin); [2007] A.C.D. 102, QBD (Admin)
R. (on the application of Hawkes) v Secretary of State for the Home Department see R.
(on the application of Cole) v Secretary of State for the Home Department
R. (on the application of Haynes) v Stafford BC [2006] EWHC 1366 (Admin); [2007] 1
W.L.R. 1365; (2006) 170 J.P. 666; [2006] A.C.D. 85; (2007) 171 J.P.N. 123,
QBD (Admin) . . . .   *Digested*, 06/**191**
R. (on the application of Headley) v Secretary of State for the Home Department see R.
(on the application of Clift) v Secretary of State for the Home Department
R. (on the application of Headley) v Secretary of State for the Home Department see R.
(on the application of Hindawi) v Secretary of State for the Home Department
R. (on the application of Heath and Hampstead Society) v Camden LBC [2007] EWHC
977 (Admin); [2007] 2 P. & C.R. 19; [2007] J.P.L. 1529, QBD (Admin) . . . . . .   *Digested*, 07/**3286**
R. (on the application of Heffernan) v Rent Service; *sub nom* Rent Service v Heffernan
[2007] EWCA Civ 544; [2007] N.P.C. 72, CA (Civ Div); reversing [2006]
EWHC 2478 (Admin); [2007] A.C.D. 30; [2006] N.P.C. 108, QBD (Admin)

R. (on the application of Hertfordshire CC) v Department for the Environment, Food and Rural Affairs; *sub nom* Hertfordshire CC v Department for the Environment, Food and Rural Affairs [2006] EWCA Civ 1718; [2007] J.P.L. 1207; [2007] 1 E.G. 93 (C.S.); [2006] N.P.C. 133; *Times*, January 12, 2007, CA (Civ Div); affirming [2005] EWHC 2363 (Admin); [2006] J.P.L. 1338; [2005] N.P.C. 129, QBD (Admin) . . . . *Digested*, 07/**3460**

R. (on the application of Hickey) v Independent Assessor see R. (on the application of O'Brien) v Independent Assessor

R. (on the application of Hide) v Staffordshire CC [2007] EWHC 2441 (Admin); (2007) 157 N.L.J. 1543, QBD (Admin)

R. (on the application of Hill) v Secretary of State for the Home Department [2007] EWHC 2164 (Admin); (2007) 104(38) L.S.G. 32, QBD (Admin)

R. (on the application of Hindawi) v Secretary of State for the Home Department see R. (on the application of Clift) v Secretary of State for the Home Department

R. (on the application of Hindawi) v Secretary of State for the Home Department; *sub nom* Hindawi v Secretary of State for the Home Department; Secretary of State for the Home Department v Hindawi; *joined case* R. (on the application of Headley) v Secretary of State for the Home Department [2004] EWCA Civ 1309; [2005] 1 W.L.R. 1102; [2004] U.K.H.R.R. 1146; [2005] 1 Prison L.R. 56; [2005] A.C.D. 88; (2004) 101(43) L.S.G. 33; (2004) 148 S.J.L.B. 1214; *Times*, October 26, 2004, CA (Civ Div); reversing [2004] EWHC 78 (Admin); [2004] Prison L.R. 317; *Times*, February 5, 2004, QBD (Admin) . . . . *Digested*, 04/**2776**: *Reversed*, 07/2975

R. (on the application of Holloway) v Oxfordshire CC [2007] EWHC 776 (Admin); [2007] B.L.G.R. 891; (2007) 10 C.C.L. Rep. 264, QBD (Admin) . . . . *Digested*, 07/**2897**

R. (on the application of Horner) v Lancashire CC; *sub nom* Horner v Lancashire CC [2007] EWCA Civ 784; [2007] N.P.C. 99, CA (Civ Div); affirming [2005] EWHC 2273 (Admin); [2006] Env. L.R. 14; [2006] J.P.L. 664, QBD (Admin). . *Digested*, 07/**3268**

R. (on the application of Horvath) v Secretary of State for the Environment, Food and Rural Affairs [2007] EWCA Civ 620; [2007] Eu. L.R. 770; [2007] N.P.C. 83; *Times*, July 30, 2007, CA (Civ Div); affirming [2006] EWHC 1833 (Admin); [2006] Eu. L.R. 1231, QBD (Admin) . . . . *Digested*, 07/**108**

R. (on the application of Howes) v Child Support Commissioners [2007] EWHC 559 (admin); [2007] Fam. Law 980, QBD (Admin)

R. (on the application of Hoxa) v Special Adjudicator see R. (on the application of Hoxha) v Special Adjudicator

R. (on the application of Hoxha) v Special Adjudicator; *sub nom* R. (on the application of Hoxa) v Special Adjudicator; Hoxha v Secretary of State for the Home Department; B v Secretary of State for the Home Department; B, Re; *joined case* R. (on the application of B) v Immigration Appeal Tribunal [2005] UKHL 19; [2005] 1 W.L.R. 1063; [2005] 4 All E.R. 580; 19 B.H.R.C. 676; [2005] Imm. A.R. 272; [2005] I.N.L.R. 440; (2005) 149 S.J.L.B. 358; *Times*, March 11, 2005, HL; affirming [2002] EWCA Civ 1403; [2003] 1 W.L.R. 241; [2003] Imm. A.R. 211; [2002] I.N.L.R. 559; (2002) 99(44) L.S.G. 32; *Times*, October 31, 2002, CA (Civ Div); affirming [2001] EWHC Admin 708, QBD (Admin) . . . . *Digested*, 05/**2177**: *Applied*, 06/2227: *Considered*, 07/2296, 07/2303

R. (on the application of Hughes) v Customs and Excise Commissioners see Hughes v Customs and Excise Commissioners

R. (on the application of Hughes) v Office of the Deputy Prime Minister; *sub nom* Hughes v First Secretary of State [2006] EWCA Civ 838; [2007] B.L.G.R. 320; [2007] E.L.R. 1; [2006] N.P.C. 76, CA (Civ Div); reversing [2005] EWHC 2850 (Admin), QBD (Admin) . . . . *Digested*, 07/**3274**

R. (on the application of Hurst) v HM Coroner for Northern District London; *sub nom* R. (on the application of Hurst) v London Northern District Coroner; R. (on the application of Hurst) v Northern District of London Coroner; Commissioner of Police of the Metropolis v Hurst [2007] UKHL 13; [2007] 2 A.C. 189; [2007] 2 W.L.R. 726; [2007] 2 All E.R. 1025; [2007] H.R.L.R. 23; [2007] U.K.H.R.R. 797; (2007) 157 N.L.J. 519; (2007) 151 S.J.L.B. 466; *Times*, March 29, 2007, HL; reversing [2005] EWCA Civ 890; [2005] 1 W.L.R. 3892; [2005] H.R.L.R. 31; [2005] U.K.H.R.R. 1259; [2005] Inquest L.R. 115; [2006] A.C.D. 20; (2005) 102(31) L.S.G. 27; (2005) 155 N.L.J. 1207; *Times*, August 11, 2005; *Independent*, July 28, 2005, CA (Civ Div); affirming [2003] EWHC 1721 (Admin); [2004] U.K.H.R.R. 139; [2003] Inquest L.R. 112; [2003] A.C.D. 88, QBD (Admin) . . . . *Digested*, 07/**27**: *Disapproved*, 04/1976

R. (on the application of Hurst) v London Northern District Coroner see R. (on the application of Hurst) v HM Coroner for Northern District London

R. (on the application of Hurst) v Northern District of London Coroner see R. (on the application of Hurst) v HM Coroner for Northern District London

R. (on the application of Hussain) v Peterborough Magistrates Court [2007] EWHC 667 (Admin); (2007) 171 J.P. 339; (2007) 171 J.P.N. 628, DC. . . . . *Digested*, 07/**1011**

R. (on the application of Hwez) v Secretary of State for the Home Department see R. (on the application of Secretary of State for the Home Department) v Immigration Appeal Tribunal

R. (on the application of I) v Secretary of State for the Home Department [2002] EWCA Civ 888; [2003] I.N.L.R. 196, CA (Civ Div) . . . . *Digested,* 03/**2236**: *Considered,* 07/2319

R. (on the application of Ibrahimi) v Secretary of State for the Home Department see R. (on the application of Rudi) v Secretary of State for the Home Department

R. (on the application of Independent Panel for Special Educational Advice Ltd) v Secretary of State for Education and Skills; *sub nom* R. (on the application of IPSEA Ltd) v Secretary of State for Education and Schools [2003] EWCA Civ 7; [2003] E.L.R. 393; (2003) 147 S.J.L.B. 144; *Independent,* January 30, 2003, CA (Civ Div); affirming [2002] EWHC 504 (Admin), QBD (Admin) . . . . *Digested,* 03/**1124**: *Followed,* 07/1264

R. (on the application of Independent Police Complaints Commission) v Chief Constable of West Midlands [2007] EWHC 2715 (Admin); *Times,* December 17, 2007, QBD (Admin) . . . . *Digested,* 07/**3303**

R. (on the application of Inland Revenue Commissioners) v Aberdeen General Commissioners of Income Tax see Revenue and Customs Commissioners, Petitioners

R. (on the application of International Air Transport Association (IATA)) v Department of Transport (C-344/04) [2006] E.C.R. I-403; [2006] 2 C.M.L.R. 20; (2006) 156 N.L.J. 113; *Times,* January 16, 2006, ECJ. . . . . *Digested,* 06/**1522**: *Applied,* 07/1561, 07/3809: *Previous proceedings,* 05/1475

R. (on the application of International Association of Independent Tanker Owners (INTERTANKO)) v Secretary of State for Transport [2006] EWHC 1577 (Admin); [2007] Env. L.R. 8; [2006] A.C.D. 89; [2006] N.P.C. 79, QBD (Admin) . . . . . . *Digested,* 07/**3809**

R. (on the application of International Masters Publishers Ltd) v Revenue and Customs Commissioners see International Masters Publishers Ltd v Revenue and Customs Commissioners

R. (on the application of IPSEA Ltd) v Secretary of State for Education and Schools see R. (on the application of Independent Panel for Special Educational Advice Ltd) v Secretary of State for Education and Skills

R. (on the application of Ireneschild) v Lambeth LBC; *sub nom* Lambeth LBC v Ireneschild [2007] EWCA Civ 234; [2007] H.L.R. 34; [2007] B.L.G.R. 619; (2007) 10 C.C.L. Rep. 243; [2007] N.P.C. 31, CA (Civ Div); reversing [2006] EWHC 2354 (Admin); (2006) 9 C.C.L. Rep. 686, QBD (Admin) . . . . *Digested,* 07/**3928**: *Considered,* 07/3941

R. (on the application of Islamic Human Rights Commission) v Civil Aviation Authority [2006] EWHC 2465 (Admin); [2007] A.C.D. 5, QBD (Admin)

R. (on the application of Island Farm Development Ltd) v Bridgend CBC [2006] EWHC 2189 (Admin); [2007] B.L.G.R. 60; (2006) 103(36) L.S.G. 36; (2006) 150 S.J.L.B. 1153; [2006] N.P.C. 100, QBD (Admin) . . . . *Digested,* 07/**2867**

R. (on the application of J) v Southend BC [2005] EWHC 3457 (Admin); (2007) 10 C.C.L. Rep. 407; (2005) 102(33) L.S.G. 25, QBD (Admin)

R. (on the application of James) v Secretary of State for Justice [2007] EWHC 2027 (Admin); (2007) 104(34) L.S.G. 29, QBD (Admin)

R. (on the application of JD Wetherspoon Plc) v Guildford BC [2006] EWHC 815; [2007] 1 All E.R. 400; [2006] B.L.G.R. 767; [2006] J.P.L. 1710; [2006] A.C.D. 82; [2006] 16 E.G. 147 (C.S.); (2006) 150 S.J.L.B. 541; [2006] N.P.C. 48; *Times,* April 14, 2006, QBD (Admin) . . . . *Digested,* 06/**2780**

R. (on the application of Jeeves) v Gravesham BC [2006] EWHC 1249 (Admin); [2007] 1 P. & C.R. 15; [2006] J.P.L. 1743; [2006] A.C.D. 98, QBD (Admin) . . . . *Digested,* 07/**3261**

R. (on the application of Jefferey) v First Secretary of State see Jefferey v First Secretary of State

R. (on the application of JL) v Secretary of State for the Home Department [2007] EWCA Civ 767; [2007] H.R.L.R. 39; [2007] A.C.D. 95; *Times,* October 2, 2007, CA (Civ Div); affirming [2006] EWHC 2558 (Admin); [2006] Inquest L.R. 200; [2007] A.C.D. 31, QBD (Admin). . . . . *Digested,* 07/**2980**

R. (on the application of Johns) v Bracknell Forest DC see R. (on the application of McLellan) v Bracknell Forest BC

R. (on the application of Johnson) v Havering LBC see L v Birmingham City Council

R. (on the application of Johnson) v Secretary of State for the Home Department; *sub nom* Johnson v Parole Board; Johnson v Secretary of State for the Home Department [2007] EWCA Civ 427; [2007] 1 W.L.R. 1990; [2007] 3 All E.R. 532; [2007] U.K.H.R.R. 824; (2007) 104(21) L.S.G. 25; (2007) 157 N.L.J. 707; (2007) 151 S.J.L.B. 671; *Times,* May 30, 2007, CA (Civ Div); reversing [2006] EWHC 1772 (Admin), QBD (Admin) . . . . *Digested,* 07/**2981**

R. (on the application of Jones) v Ceredigion CC see Ceredigion CC v Jones

R. (on the application of Jones) v Ceredigion CC (No.2) see Ceredigion CC v Jones

R. (on the application of Jones) v Isleworth Crown Court; *sub nom* Jones v Isleworth Crown Court [2005] EWHC 662 (QB); [2005] M.H.L.R. 93, QBD . . . . *Applied,* 07/**3585**

R. (on the application of Jones) v Southend-on-Sea BC [2005] EWHC 1439 (Admin); (2007) 10 C.C.L. Rep. 428, QBD (Admin)

R. (on the application of Jorgensen (Listing Officer)) v Gomports see Jorgensen (Listing Officer) v Gomports

R. (on the application of JR) v Mental Health Review Tribunal see R. (on the application of KB) v Mental Health Review Tribunal

R. (on the application of Jummun) v Secretary of State for Health see R. (on the application of Wright) v Secretary of State for Health

R. (on the application of Just Fabulous (UK) Ltd) v Revenue and Customs Commissioners; *joined cases* R. (on the application of Brayfal Ltd) v Revenue and Customs Commissioners; R. (on the application of Evolution Export Trading Ltd) v Revenue and Customs Commissioners [2007] EWHC 521 (Admin); [2007] B.T.C. 5522; [2007] B.V.C. 490; [2007] S.T.I. 542, QBD (Admin) . . . . .   *Digested,* 07/**4317**

R. (on the application of K) v Manchester City Council [2006] EWHC 3164 (Admin); (2007) 10 C.C.L. Rep. 87, QBD (Admin) . . . .   *Digested,* 07/**1753**

R. (on the application of K) v Mental Health Review Tribunal see R. (on the application of KB) v Mental Health Review Tribunal

R. (on the application of K) v Special Educational Needs and Disability Tribunal (SENDIST); *sub nom* K v X School; K v Special Educational Needs and Disability Tribunal [2007] EWCA Civ 165; [2007] E.L.R. 234; *Times,* April 11, 2007, CA (Civ Div); affirming [2006] EWHC 622 (Admin); [2006] E.L.R. 488, QBD (Admin) . . . .   *Digested,* 07/**1255**

R. (on the application of Kapoor) v Secretary of State for the Home Department see Madan v Secretary of State for the Home Department

R. (on the application of Kashamu) v Bow Street Magistrates Court see R. (on the application of Kashamu) v Governor of Brixton Prison (No.2)

R. (on the application of Kashamu) v Governor of Brixton Prison (No.2); *sub nom* R. (on the application of Maklulif) v Bow Street Magistrates Court; *joined cases* R. (on the application of Makhlulif) v Bow Street Magistrates Court; R. (on the application of Kashamu) v Bow Street Magistrates Court [2001] EWHC Admin 980; [2002] Q.B. 887; [2002] 2 W.L.R. 907; [2002] A.C.D. 36; (2002) 99(5) L.S.G. 29; (2001) 145 S.J.L.B. 277; *Times,* December 12, 2001, DC . . . .   *Digested,* 02/**1593**: *Considered,* 07/1663

R. (on the application of Kay) v Commissioner of Police of the Metropolis see Kay v Commissioner of Police of the Metropolis

R. (on the application of KB) v Mental Health Review Tribunal; *sub nom* R. (on the application of K) v Mental Health Review Tribunal; *joined cases* R. (on the application of TB) v Mental Health Review Tribunal; R. (on the application of PD) v Mental Health Review Tribunal; R. (on the application of LB) v Mental Health Review Tribunal; R. (on the application of GM) v Mental Health Review Tribunal; R. (on the application of JR) v Mental Health Review Tribunal; R. (on the application of MK) v Mental Health Review Tribunal [2002] EWHC 639 (Admin); (2002) 5 C.C.L. Rep. 458; [2003] M.H.L.R. 1; [2002] A.C.D. 85; (2002) 152 N.L.J. 672, QBD (Admin) . . . .   *Digested,* 03/**2951**: *Considered,* 07/2983: *Subsequent proceedings,* 03/2955

R. (on the application of Kehoe) v Secretary of State for Work and Pensions; *sub nom* Secretary of State for Work and Pensions v Kehoe; Kehoe v Secretary of State for Work and Pensions [2005] UKHL 48; [2006] 1 A.C. 42; [2005] 3 W.L.R. 252; [2005] 4 All E.R. 905; [2005] 2 F.L.R. 1249; [2005] 2 F.C.R. 683; [2005] H.R.L.R. 30; [2006] U.K.H.R.R. 360; [2005] Fam. Law 850; (2005) 155 N.L.J. 1123; (2005) 149 S.J.L.B. 921; *Times,* July 15, 2005; *Independent,* July 19, 2005, HL; affirming [2004] EWCA Civ 225; [2004] Q.B. 1378; [2004] 2 W.L.R. 1481; [2004] 1 F.L.R. 1132; [2004] 1 F.C.R. 511; [2004] U.K.H.R.R. 443; [2004] Fam. Law 399; (2004) 101(13) L.S.G. 33; (2004) 148 S.J.L.B. 301; *Times,* March 10, 2004; *Independent,* March 19, 2004, CA (Civ Div); reversing [2003] EWHC 1021 (Admin); [2003] 2 F.L.R. 578; [2003] 3 F.C.R. 481; [2003] U.K.H.R.R. 702; [2003] Fam. Law 718; (2003) 100(26) L.S.G. 37; *Times,* May 21, 2003, QBD (Admin) . . . .   *Digested,* 05/**1553**: *Considered,* 07/1755

R. (on the application of Kelly) v Warley Magistrates' Court [2007] EWHC 1836 (Admin); (2007) 171 J.P. 585; [2007] A.C.D. 89; (2007) 157 N.L.J. 1155, QBD (Admin) .   *Digested,* 07/**999**

R. (on the application of Kemp) v Denbighshire Local Health Board [2006] EWHC 181 (Admin); [2007] 1 W.L.R. 639; [2006] 3 All E.R. 141; (2006) 9 C.C.L. Rep. 354; [2006] A.C.D. 63, QBD (Admin) . . . .   *Digested,* 06/**360**

R. (on the application of Kenneally) v Rampton Hospital Authority see R. (on the application of Kenneally) v Snaresbrook Crown Court

R. (on the application of Kenneally) v Snaresbrook Crown Court; *joined case* R. (on the application of Kenneally) v Rampton Hospital Authority [2001] EWHC Admin 968; [2002] Q.B. 1169; [2002] 2 W.L.R. 1430; [2002] M.H.L.R. 53; [2002] A.C.D. 46; *Times,* December 17, 2001, DC . . . .   *Digested,* 02/**3228**: *Distinguished,* 07/21

R. (on the application of Kides) v South Cambridgeshire DC [2002] EWCA Civ 1370; [2003] 1 P. & C.R. 19; [2002] 4 P.L.R. 66; [2003] J.P.L. 431; [2002] 42 E.G. 160 (C.S.); (2002) 99(43) L.S.G. 35; (2002) 146 S.J.L.B. 230; [2002] N.P.C. 121; *Times,* October 15, 2002; *Independent,* October 16, 2002, CA (Civ Div); affirming [2001] EWHC Admin 839; [2003] 1 P. & C.R. 4; [2002] J.P.L. 832; [2001] N.P.C. 153, QBD (Admin) . . . .   *Digested,* 02/**3662**: *Considered,* 07/3264

R. (on the application of Kilby) *v* Basildon DC see Kilby *v* Basildon DC

R. (on the application of Knight) *v* Comptroller General of Patents, Trade Marks and Designs [2007] EWHC 2264 (Admin); (2007) 30(10) I.P.D. 30063, QBD (Admin)

R. (on the application of Kola) *v* Secretary of State for Work and Pensions see Kola *v* Secretary of State for Work and Pensions

R. (on the application of Kumar) *v* Secretary of State for Constitutional Affairs [2006] EWCA Civ 990; [2007] 1 W.L.R. 536; [2006] C.P. Rep. 43; (2006) 150 S.J.L.B. 982; *Independent*, July 18, 2006, CA (Civ Div); reversing [2004] EWHC 3362 (Admin), QBD (Admin) . . . . *Digested*, 07/**368**

R. (on the application of L) *v* Commissioner of Police of the Metropolis [2007] EWCA Civ 168; [2007] 4 All E.R. 128; (2007) 104(11) L.S.G. 32; (2007) 151 S.J.L.B. 336; *Times*, March 28, 2007, CA (Civ Div); affirming [2006] EWHC 482 (Admin), QBD (Admin) . . . . *Digested*, 07/**3301**

R. (on the application of L) *v* Nottinghamshire CC [2007] EWHC 2364 (Admin); [2007] A.C.D. 92, QBD (Admin)

R. (on the application of L) *v* Waltham Forest LBC [2003] EWHC 2907 (Admin); [2004] E.L.R. 161, QBD (Admin) . . . . *Digested*, 04/**1087**:
Applied, 05/1061, 06/1226, 07/1260

R. (on the application of L) *v* Waltham Forest LBC [2007] EWHC 2060 (Admin); (2007) 151 S.J.L.B. 1164, QBD (Admin)

R. (on the application of L (A Child)) *v* J School Governors; *sub nom* R. *v* B School Governors Ex p. W; R. *v* J School Governors Ex p. L; L *v* J; W *v* B; L (A Child), Re; *joined case* R. (on the application of W (A Child)) *v* B School Governors [2003] UKHL 9; [2003] 2 A.C. 633; [2003] 2 W.L.R. 518; [2003] 1 All E.R. 1012; [2003] 1 F.C.R. 548; [2003] B.L.G.R. 343; [2003] E.L.R. 309; (2003) 100(18) L.S.G. 34; *Times*, March 6, 2003, HL; affirming [2001] EWCA Civ 1199; [2001] B.L.G.R. 561; [2002] E.L.R. 105; *Times*, August 20, 2001; *Independent*, July 26, 2001, CA (Civ Div); affirming [2001] EWHC Admin 318; [2001] E.L.R. 411, QBD (Admin) . . . . *Digested*, 03/**1056**:
Cited, 07/1186: *Considered*, 02/1102: *Previous proceedings*, 00/1929

R. (on the application of Laporte) *v* Chief Constable of Gloucestershire [2006] UKHL 55; [2007] 2 A.C. 105; [2007] 2 W.L.R. 46; [2007] 2 All E.R. 529; [2007] H.R.L.R. 13; [2007] U.K.H.R.R. 400; 22 B.H.R.C. 38; [2006] Po. L.R. 309; [2007] Crim. L.R. 576; [2007] A.C.D. 25; (2007) 151 S.J.L.B. 26; *Times*, December 14, 2006, HL; reversing in part [2004] EWCA Civ 1639; [2005] Q.B. 678; [2005] 2 W.L.R. 789; [2005] 1 All E.R. 473; [2005] H.R.L.R. 6; [2005] Crim. L.R. 467; [2005] A.C.D. 57; (2005) 102(6) L.S.G. 32; *Times*, December 13, 2004; *Independent*, December 14, 2004, CA (Civ Div); affirming [2004] EWHC 253 (Admin); [2004] 2 All E.R. 874; [2004] U.K.H.R.R. 484; [2004] Po. L.R. 123; [2004] A.C.D. 34; (2004) 154 N.L.J. 308; *Times*, February 26, 2004, QBD (Admin) . . . . *Digested*, 07/**3317**:
Applied, 07/3316

R. (on the application of Law Society) *v* Legal Services Commission; *joined case* Dexter Montague & Partners *v* Legal Services Commission [2007] EWCA Civ 1264; (2007) 104(48) L.S.G. 22; *Times*, December 3, 2007, CA (Civ Div); reversing in part [2007] EWHC 1848 (Admin); [2007] A.C.D. 97; (2007) 151 S.J.L.B. 1061, QBD (Admin) . . . . *Digested*, 07/**2795**

R. (on the application of Lawson) *v* Stafford Magistrates' Court [2007] EWHC 2490 (Admin); (2007) 104(40) L.S.G. 26, DC

R. (on the application of LB) *v* Mental Health Review Tribunal see R. (on the application of KB) *v* Mental Health Review Tribunal

R. (on the application of Leask) *v* South Western Magistrates Court [2007] EWHC 1233 (Admin); (2007) 171 J.P. 489; (2007) 171 J.P.N. 837, QBD (Admin) . . . . *Digested*, 07/**539**

R. (on the application of Legal Remedy UK Ltd) *v* Secretary of State for Health [2007] EWHC 1252 (Admin); (2007) 96 B.M.L.R. 191; (2007) 151 S.J.L.B. 742; *Times*, June 29, 2007, QBD (Admin) . . . . *Digested*, 07/**1946**

R. (on the application of Leicestershire CC) *v* Secretary of State for Communities and Local Government [2007] EWHC 1427 (Admin); [2007] N.P.C. 76, QBD (Admin)

R. (on the application of Limbuela) *v* Secretary of State for the Home Department; *joined cases* R. (on the application of Tesema) *v* Secretary of State for the Home Department; R. (on the application of Adam) *v* Secretary of State for the Home Department [2005] UKHL 66; [2006] 1 A.C. 396; [2005] 3 W.L.R. 1014; [2007] 1 All E.R. 951; [2006] H.R.L.R. 4; [2006] H.L.R. 10; (2006) 9 C.C.L. Rep. 30; (2005) 102(46) L.S.G. 25; (2005) 149 S.J.L.B. 1354; *Times*, November 4, 2005, HL; affirming [2004] EWCA Civ 540; [2004] Q.B. 1440; [2004] 3 W.L.R. 561; [2005] 3 All E.R. 29; [2004] H.L.R. 38; (2004) 7 C.C.L. Rep. 267; [2004] A.C.D. 70; (2004) 101(23) L.S.G. 32; *Times*, May 26, 2004; *Independent*, May 25, 2004, CA (Civ Div); affirming [2004] EWHC 219 (QB); *Times*, February 9, 2004, QBD . . . . *Digested*, 06/**2217**:
Applied, 06/2235: *Considered*, 05/2157, 07/3908: *Distinguished*, 06/844

R. (on the application of Lin) *v* Barnet LBC see R. (on the application of Mei Ling Lin) *v* Barnet LBC

R. (on the application of Lindo) v Secretary of State for the Home Department [2004]
EWCA Civ 491; [2005] 1 Prison L.R. 40; (2004) 148 S.J.L.B. 388; *Times*, April
26, 2004, CA (Civ Div); affirming [2003] EWHC 2918 (Admin), QBD (Admin) — *Digested*, 04/**3327**:
Considered, 07/2976

R. (on the application of Lindsay) v Lambeth LBC; *sub nom* Lambeth LBC v A; Lambeth
LBC v Lindsay; *joined case* R. (on the application of A) v Lambeth LBC
[2002] EWCA Civ 1084; [2002] H.L.R. 57, CA (Civ Div); affirming [2002]
EWHC 809 (Admin); [2002] N.P.C. 64, QBD (Admin) . . . . *Digested*, 03/**2054**:
Applied, 07/2152: *Considered*, 04/1902

R. (on the application of Ling (Bridlington) Ltd) v East Riding of Yorkshire Council
[2006] EWHC 1604 (Admin); [2007] J.P.L. 396, QBD (Admin) . . . . *Digested*, 07/**3273**:
Considered, 07/3284

R. (on the application of London Fire and Emergency Planning Authority) v Secretary of
State for Communities and Local Government (formerly Secretary of State for
the Office of the Deputy Prime Minister) [2007] EWHC 1176 (Admin); [2007]
B.L.G.R. 591, QBD (Admin)

R. (on the application of Louden) v Bury School Organisation Committee [2002] EWHC
2749 (Admin), QBD (Admin) . . . . *Followed*, 07/2867

R. (on the application of Lovelock) v First Secretary of State see Lovelock v First
Secretary of State

R. (on the application of Lowther) v Durham CC; *sub nom* R. v Durham CC Ex p.
Lowther [2001] EWCA Civ 781; [2002] Env. L.R. 13; [2002] 1 P. & C.R. 22;
[2001] 3 P.L.R. 83; [2002] J.P.L. 197; [2001] 22 E.G. 154 (C.S.); (2001) 98(23)
L.S.G. 42; *Times*, June 22, 2001, CA (Civ Div); affirming [2001] Env. L.R. 18;
(2001) 81 P. & C.R. 4; [2001] J.P.L. 354, QBD . . . . *Digested*, 01/**4659**:
Considered, 07/1506

R. (on the application of Lunn) v Governor of Moorland Prison [2006] EWCA Civ 700;
[2006] 1 W.L.R. 2870; [2006] 1 Prison L.R. 251; *Times*, June 27, 2006;
Independent, June 7, 2006, CA (Civ Div); reversing [2005] EWHC 2558 (QB);
Times, November 2, 2005, QBD . . . . *Digested*, 07/**2976**

R. (on the application of Lynch) v Lambeth LBC [2006] EWHC 2737 (Admin); [2007]
H.L.R. 15, QBD (Admin) . . . . *Digested*, 07/**2134**

R. (on the application of M) v Commissioner for Local Administration in England [2006]
EWHC 2847 (Admin); [2007] E.L.R. 42; (2006) 103(44) L.S.G. 30, QBD
(Admin)

R. (on the application of M) v Gateshead MBC [2006] EWCA Civ 221; [2006] Q.B.
650; [2006] 3 W.L.R. 108; [2007] 1 All E.R. 1262; [2006] 2 F.L.R. 379; (2006)
9 C.C.L. Rep. 337; [2006] Fam. Law 444; (2006) 103(13) L.S.G. 25; [2006]
N.P.C. 31; *Times*, April 27, 2006; *Independent*, March 17, 2006, CA (Civ Div) . . *Digested*, 06/**2824**

R. (on the application of M) v Hammersmith and Fulham LBC [2006] EWCA Civ 917;
[2007] 1 F.L.R. 256; [2006] 2 F.C.R. 647; [2007] H.L.R. 6; [2007] B.L.G.R.
127; (2006) 9 C.C.L. Rep. 418; [2006] Fam. Law 1028; *Independent*, July 7,
2006, CA (Civ Div) . . . . *Digested*, 06/**2030**:
Considered, 07/3940

R. (on the application of M) v HM Treasury see M v HM Treasury

R. (on the application of M) v Immigration Appeal Tribunal see R. (on the application of
G) v Immigration Appeal Tribunal

R. (on the application of M) v Inner London Crown Court; *sub nom* M v Inner London
Crown Court [2006] EWHC 2497 (QB); [2006] 1 W.L.R. 3406, DC . . . . *Digested*, 07/**942**

R. (on the application of M) v Islington LBC; *sub nom* M v Islington LBC [2004] EWCA
Civ 235; [2005] 1 W.L.R. 884; [2004] 4 All E.R. 709; [2004] 2 F.L.R. 867;
[2004] 2 F.C.R. 363; [2004] B.L.G.R. 815; (2004) 7 C.C.L. Rep. 230; [2004]
Fam. Law 645; *Times*, April 22, 2004, CA (Civ Div); reversing [2003] EWHC
1388 (Admin); [2003] 2 F.L.R. 903; [2003] H.L.R. 73; [2004] A.C.D. 8;
[2003] Fam. Law 729; (2003) 100(31) L.S.G. 32; *Times*, June 12, 2003, QBD
(Admin) . . . . *Digested*, 04/**2072**:
Applied, 04/2076: *Distinguished*, 07/3941

R. (on the application of M) v Secretary of State for the Home Department see
Anufrijeva v Southwark LBC

R. (on the application of M) v Secretary of State for the Home Department; *sub nom* R.
(on the application of MM) v Secretary of State for the Home Department
[2007] EWCA Civ 687; (2007) 98 B.M.L.R. 130; [2007] A.C.D. 98; (2007) 151
S.J.L.B. 927, CA (Civ Div); affirming [2006] EWHC 3056 (Admin); [2006]
M.H.L.R. 358; [2007] A.C.D. 50, QBD (Admin) . . . . *Digested*, 07/**2913**

R. (on the application of M) v Secretary of State for Work and Pensions [2007] EWCA
Civ 614; [2007] 1 W.L.R. 3067; [2007] H.R.L.R. 35; [2007] U.K.H.R.R. 1061;
[2007] A.C.D. 104; (2007) 151 S.J.L.B. 894, CA (Civ Div); affirming [2006]
EWHC 1761 (Admin), QBD (Admin) . . . . *Digested*, 07/**3867**

R. (on the application of M) v Slough BC [2006] EWCA Civ 655; [2007] B.L.G.R. 225;
(2006) 9 C.C.L. Rep. 438; *Times*, June 13, 2006, CA (Civ Div); affirming
[2004] EWHC 1109 (Admin); [2004] B.L.G.R. 657, QBD (Admin) . . . . *Digested*, 06/**2216**

R. (on the application of M) v Suffolk CC [2006] EWHC 2366 (Admin); [2007] E.L.R.
158; (2006) 9 C.C.L. Rep. 704, QBD (Admin) . . . . *Digested*, 07/**3909**

R. (on the application of M) v Sutton LBC [2007] EWCA Civ 1205; (2007) 151 S.J.L.B. 1532, CA (Civ Div); reversing [2007] EWHC 267 (Admin); [2007] E.L.R. 377; *Times*, March 1, 2007, QBD (Admin) . . . . *Digested*, 07/**1265**

R. (on the application of M) v Wiltshire CC [2006] EWHC 3337 (Admin); [2007] E.L.R. 171, QBD (Admin) . . . . *Digested*, 07/**1260**

R. (on the application of M (A Child)) v Manchester Crown Court see R. (on the application of McCann) v Manchester Crown Court

R. (on the application of Madan) v Secretary of State for the Home Department see Madan v Secretary of State for the Home Department

R. (on the application of Mahajan) v Central London CC see R. (on the application of Mahajan) v Department for Constitutional Affairs

R. (on the application of Mahajan) v Department for Constitutional Affairs; *sub nom* R. (on the application of Mahajan) v Central London CC [2004] EWCA Civ 946; (2004) 101(31) L.S.G. 26; *Times*, July 13, 2004, CA (Civ Div) . . . . *Digested*, 04/**281**: *Considered*, 07/**368**

R. (on the application of Mahmood) v General Medical Council see Mahmood v GMC

R. (on the application of Mahmood (Amjad)) v Secretary of State for the Home Department; *sub nom* R. v Secretary of State for the Home Department Ex p. Mahmood (Amjad); Mahmood (Amjad) v Secretary of State for the Home Department [2001] 1 W.L.R. 840; [2001] 1 F.L.R. 756; [2001] 2 F.C.R. 63; [2001] H.R.L.R. 14; [2001] U.K.H.R.R. 307; [2001] Imm. A.R. 229; [2001] I.N.L.R. 1; (2001) 3 L.G.L.R. 23; [2001] A.C.D. 38; [2001] Fam. Law 257; *Times*, January 9, 2001; *Independent*, January 24, 2001, CA (Civ Div); affirming CO/254/98, QBD . . . . *Digested*, 01/**3684**: *Applied*, 01/3646, 03/2255, 04/2076, 06/2276, 06/5522: *Considered*, 01/3660, 01/4578, 07/2330: *Distinguished*, 04/2051

R. (on the application of Main) v Minister for Legal Aid [2007] EWCA Civ 1147; (2007) 104(47) L.S.G. 27; *Times*, December 18, 2007, CA (Civ Div); reversing [2007] EWHC 742 (Admin); (2007) 96 B.M.L.R. 61; (2007) 151 S.J.L.B. 504; *Times*, May 9, 2007, QBD (Admin) . . . . *Digested*, 07/**2787**

R. (on the application of Makhlulif) v Bow Street Magistrates Court see R. (on the application of Kashamu) v Governor of Brixton Prison (No.2)

R. (on the application of Maklulif) v Bow Street Magistrates Court see R. (on the application of Kashamu) v Governor of Brixton Prison (No.2)

R. (on the application of Malik) v Central Criminal Court; *sub nom* Malik v Central Criminal Court [2006] EWHC 1539 (Admin); [2007] 1 W.L.R. 2455; [2006] 4 All E.R. 1141, DC . . . . *Digested*, 07/**940**

R. (on the application of Malik) v Chief Constable of Greater Manchester [2006] EWHC 2396 (Admin); [2007] A.C.D. 15, QBD (Admin)

R. (on the application of Malik) v Waltham Forest Primary Care Trust [2007] EWCA Civ 265; [2007] 1 W.L.R. 2092; [2007] 4 All E.R. 832; [2007] I.C.R. 1101; [2007] I.R.L.R. 529; [2007] H.R.L.R. 24; [2007] U.K.H.R.R. 1105; [2007] LS Law Medical 335; *Times*, April 10, 2007, CA (Civ Div); reversing [2006] EWHC 487 (Admin); [2006] 3 All E.R. 71; [2006] I.C.R. 1111; [2006] I.R.L.R. 526; [2006] Lloyd's Rep. Med. 298; (2006) 90 B.M.L.R. 49; [2006] A.C.D. 59; *Times*, May 26, 2006, QBD (Admin) . . . . *Digested*, 07/**1944**

R. (on the application of Marper) v Chief Constable of South Yorkshire see R. (on the application of S) v Chief Constable of South Yorkshire

R. (on the application of Marsh) v DPP see Marsh v DPP

R. (on the application of Martin) v Secretary of State for the Home Department [2006] EWHC 799 (Admin); [2006] Imm. A.R. 463, QBD (Admin) . . . . *Digested*, 07/**2290**

R. (on the application of McCann) v Manchester Crown Court; *sub nom* R. v Manchester Crown Court Ex p. M (A Child); R. (on the application of M (A Child)) v Manchester Crown Court; *joined case* Clingham v Kensington and Chelsea RLBC [2002] UKHL 39; [2003] 1 A.C. 787; [2002] 3 W.L.R. 1313; [2002] 4 All E.R. 593; [2003] 1 Cr. App. R. 27; (2002) 166 J.P. 657; [2002] U.K.H.R.R. 1286; 13 B.H.R.C. 482; [2003] H.L.R. 17; [2003] B.L.G.R. 57; [2003] Crim. L.R. 269; (2002) 166 J.P.N. 850; (2002) 146 S.J.L.B. 239; *Times*, October 21, 2002; *Independent*, October 23, 2002, HL; affirming [2001] EWCA Civ 281; [2001] 1 W.L.R. 1084; [2001] 4 All E.R. 264; (2001) 165 J.P. 545; [2001] H.R.L.R. 37; (2001) 166 J.P.N. 150; *Times*, March 9, 2001; *Independent*, March 20, 2001, CA (Civ Div); affirming [2001] 1 W.L.R. 358; (2001) 165 J.P. 225; (2001) 165 J.P.N. 204; (2001) 98(2) L.S.G. 40; (2000) 144 S.J.L.B. 287; *Times*, December 22, 2000; *Daily Telegraph*, December 12, 2000, DC . . . . *Digested*, 02/**3**: *Applied*, 01/41, 02/1579, 02/1579, 04/366, 04/1020, 06/902, 07/1949, 07/2171: *Considered*, 03/831, 04/790, 05/1073, 06/304, 06/304, 06/327, 07/4974: *Distinguished*, 04/1458, 06/316: *Followed*, 05/342

R. (on the application of McCarthy & Stone Developments Ltd) v First Secretary of State [2006] EWHC 390 (Admin); [2007] 1 P. & C.R. 11, QBD (Admin) . . . . *Digested*, 07/**3285**

R. (on the application of McLellan) v Bracknell Forest BC; *sub nom* R. (on the application of Johns) v Bracknell Forest DC; Forrest v Reigate and Banstead BC; McLellan v Bracknell Forest BC; *joined case* Reigate and Banstead BC v Benfield [2001] EWCA Civ 1510; [2002] Q.B. 1129; [2002] 2 W.L.R. 1448; [2002] 1 All E.R. 899; [2002] H.R.L.R. 12; [2002] U.K.H.R.R. 45; (2001) 33 H.L.R. 86; [2002] B.L.G.R. 191; [2002] A.C.D. 54; (2001) 98(46) L.S.G. 35; (2001) 145 S.J.L.B. 258; [2001] N.P.C. 149; *Times*, December 3, 2001; *Independent*, October 24, 2001, CA (Civ Div); affirming (2001) 33 H.L.R. 45; (2001) 3 L.G.L.R. 22; *Daily Telegraph*, February 13, 2001, QBD (Admin) . . . . . .   *Digested*, 01/**4170**:
           Applied, 01/4171, 02/2337, 02/3055, 03/2738, 03/2773, 07/2772:
           Considered, 02/2353: *Followed*, 02/1526

R. (on the application of Mead) v Secretary of State for Transport, Local Government and the Regions see R. (on the application of Medway Council) v Secretary of State for Transport, Local Government and the Regions

R. (on the application of Medway Council) v Secretary of State for Transport, Local Government and the Regions; *joined cases* R. (on the application of Essex CC) v Secretary of State for Transport, Local Government and the Regions; R. (on the application of Mead) v Secretary of State for Transport, Local Government and the Regions [2002] EWHC 2516 (Admin); [2003] J.P.L. 583; [2002] 49 E.G. 123 (C.S.); [2002] N.P.C. 152, QBD (Admin) . . . .   *Digested*, 03/**3363**:
           Considered, 06/40, 07/57

R. (on the application of Mei Ling Lin) v Barnet LBC; *sub nom* R. (on the application of Lin) v Barnet LBC; *joined case* Hassan v Barnet LBC [2007] EWCA Civ 132; [2007] H.L.R. 30; [2007] B.L.G.R. 454; (2007) 104(10) L.S.G. 28; (2007) 151 S.J.L.B. 297, CA (Civ Div); reversing in part [2006] EWHC 1041 (Admin); [2006] H.L.R. 44, QBD (Admin) . . . .   *Digested*, 07/**2139**

R. (on the application of Mendy) v Crown Prosecution Service [2007] EWHC 1765 (Admin); [2007] A.C.D. 90, QBD (Admin)

R. (on the application of Meredith) v Harwich Justices [2006] EWHC 3336 (Admin); (2007) 171 J.P. 249; (2007) 171 J.P.N. 547, QBD (Admin) . . . .   *Digested*, 07/**832**

R. (on the application of MH) v Secretary of State for Health see R. (on the application of H) v Secretary of State for Health

R. (on the application of MH) v Secretary of State for the Home Department; *joined case* R. (on the application of SH) v Secretary of State for the Home Department [2007] EWHC 2134 (Admin); (2007) 151 S.J.L.B. 1228, QBD (Admin)

R. (on the application of Midcounties Co-operative Ltd) v Forest of Dean DC [2007] EWHC 1714 (Admin); [2007] 2 P. & C.R. 30; [2007] 30 E.G. 133 (C.S.), QBD (Admin) . . . .   *Digested*, 07/**3284**

R. (on the application of Middleton) v HM Coroner for Western Somerset see R. (on the application of Amin (Imtiaz) v Secretary of State for the Home Department

R. (on the application of Middleton) v HM Coroner for Western Somerset; *sub nom* R. (on the application of Middleton) v West Somerset Coroner; R. v HM Coroner for Western Somerset Ex p. Middleton [2004] UKHL 10; [2004] 2 A.C. 182; [2004] 2 W.L.R. 800; [2004] 2 All E.R. 465; (2004) 168 J.P. 329; [2004] H.R.L.R. 29; [2004] U.K.H.R.R. 501; 17 B.H.R.C. 49; [2004] Lloyd's Rep. Med. 288; (2004) 79 B.M.L.R. 51; [2004] Inquest L.R. 17; (2004) 168 J.P.N. 479; (2004) 101(15) L.S.G. 27; (2004) 154 N.L.J. 417; (2004) 148 S.J.L.B. 354; *Times*, March 12, 2004; *Independent*, March 16, 2004, HL . . . .   *Digested*, 04/**37**:
           Applied, 05/34, 06/18, 06/2108, 07/27: *Considered*, 05/17, 06/17, 07/13,
           07/28, 07/2980: *Followed*, 04/38: *Previous proceedings*, 02/25

R. (on the application of Middleton) v West Somerset Coroner see R. (on the application of Amin (Imtiaz)) v Secretary of State for the Home Department

R. (on the application of Middleton) v West Somerset Coroner see R. (on the application of Middleton) v HM Coroner for Western Somerset

R. (on the application of MK) v Mental Health Review Tribunal see R. (on the application of KB) v Mental Health Review Tribunal

R. (on the application of MM) v Secretary of State for the Home Department see R. (on the application of M) v Secretary of State for the Home Department

R. (on the application of Mobile Export 365 Ltd) v Revenue and Customs Commissioners (No.1) [2006] EWHC 311 (Admin); [2006] S.T.C. 1069; [2007] B.T.C. 5717; [2007] B.V.C. 685; [2006] S.T.I. 456, QBD (Admin) . . . .   *Digested*, 06/**4464**:
           Considered, 07/4311, 07/4359

R. (on the application of Mohammed) v Birmingham City Council see R. (on the application of Aweys) v Birmingham City Council

R. (on the application of Mohammed) v Secretary of State for Defence (2007) 104(20) L.S.G. 32; (2007) 151 S.J.L.B. 610; *Times*, May 9, 2007, CA (Civ Div); affirming [2006] EWHC 2098 (Admin); (2006) 150 S.J.L.B. 1111, QBD (Admin) . . . . . .   *Digested*, 07/**266**

R. (on the application of Mondelly) v Commissioner of Police of the Metropolis [2006] EWHC 2370 (Admin); (2007) 171 J.P. 121; [2006] Po. L.R. 134; [2007] Crim. L.R. 298; (2007) 171 J.P.N. 529; *Times*, November 7, 2006, DC . . . .   *Digested*, 07/**3314**

R. (on the application of Mooney) v Southwark LBC [2006] EWHC 1912 (Admin); (2006) 9 C.C.L. Rep. 670; [2006] N.P.C. 94, QBD (Admin) . . . .   *Digested*, 07/**2154**

R. (on the application of Moreton) *v* Medical Defence Union Ltd [2006] EWHC 1948 (Admin); [2007] LS Law Medical 180; [2006] A.C.D. 102; (2006) 156 N.L.J. 1253, QBD (Admin) . . . . *Digested*, 07/**1976**

R. (on the application of Morgan Grenfell & Co Ltd) *v* Special Commissioners of Income Tax; *sub nom* R. *v* Inland Revenue Commissioners Ex p. Morgan Grenfell & Co Ltd; R. *v* Special Commissioners of Income Tax Ex p. Morgan Grenfell & Co Ltd [2002] UKHL 21; [2003] 1 A.C. 563; [2002] 2 W.L.R. 1299; [2002] 3 All E.R. 1; [2002] S.T.C. 786; [2002] H.R.L.R. 42; 74 T.C. 511; [2002] B.T.C. 223; 4 I.T.L. Rep. 809; [2002] S.T.I. 806; (2002) 99(25) L.S.G. 35; (2002) 146 S.J.L.B. 126; [2002] N.P.C. 70; *Times*, May 20, 2002; *Independent*, May 21, 2002, HL; reversing [2001] EWCA Civ 329; [2002] 2 W.L.R. 255; [2002] 1 All E.R. 776; [2001] S.T.C. 497; [2001] S.T.I. 281; (2001) 98(18) L.S.G. 45; [2000] N.P.C. 54; *Times*, April 17, 2001; *Independent*, March 15, 2001, CA (Civ Div); affirming [2001] 1 All E.R. 535; [2000] S.T.C. 965; [2000] S.T.I. 1609; (2000) 97(48) L.S.G. 37; (2000) 150 N.L.J. 1717; *Times*, November 22, 2000, QBD (Admin) . .   *Digested*, 02/**4505**: *Applied*, 06/839, 06/4304: *Considered*, 01/5320, 07/999

R. (on the application of Morris) *v* Trafford Healthcare NHS Trust [2006] EWHC 2334 (Admin); (2006) 9 C.C.L. Rep. 648; [2006] Lloyd's Rep. Med. 529; [2007] A.C.D. 11; (2006) 150 S.J.L.B. 1290, QBD (Admin) . . . . *Digested*, 07/**2019**

R. (on the application of Mortell) *v* Oldham MBC [2007] EWHC 1526 (Admin); [2007] J.P.L. 1679, QBD (Admin)

R. (on the application of Mount Cook Land Ltd) *v* Westminster City Council; *sub nom* Mount Cook Land Ltd *v* Westminster City Council [2003] EWCA Civ 1346; [2004] C.P. Rep. 12; [2004] 2 Costs L.R. 211; [2004] 2 P. & C.R. 22; [2004] 1 P.L.R. 29; [2004] J.P.L. 470; [2003] 43 E.G. 137 (C.S.); (2003) 147 S.J.L.B. 1272; [2003] N.P.C. 117; *Times*, October 16, 2003, CA (Civ Div); affirming [2002] EWHC 2125 (Admin), QBD (Admin) . . . . *Digested*, 04/**367**: *Applied*, 04/1387: *Considered*, 05/3307, 06/417, 07/402, 07/489

R. (on the application of Munaneza) *v* Governor of Belmarsh Prison see Brown (formerly Bajinya) *v* Governor of Belmarsh Prison

R. (on the application of Murphy) *v* Parole Board see R. (on the application of Brooke) *v* Parole Board

R. (on the application of N) *v* Lambeth LBC [2006] EWHC 3427 (Admin); [2007] A.C.D. 49, QBD (Admin) . . . . *Digested*, 07/**3908**

R. (on the application of N) *v* Mental Health Review Tribunal (Northern Region); *sub nom* R. (on the application of AN) *v* Mental Health Review Tribunal (Northern Region); *joined case* R. (on the application of DJ) *v* Mental Health Review Tribunal [2005] EWCA Civ 1605; [2006] Q.B. 468; [2006] 2 W.L.R. 850; [2006] 4 All E.R. 194; (2006) 88 B.M.L.R. 59; [2006] M.H.L.R. 59; *Times*, January 12, 2006, CA (Civ Div); affirming [2005] EWHC 587 (Admin); [2005] M.H.L.R. 56; [2005] A.C.D. 92; *Times*, April 18, 2005, QBD (Admin) . . . .   *Digested*, 06/**2859**: *Applied*, 07/1949: *Considered*, 06/316

R. (on the application of N) *v* Secretary of State for the Home Department see Anufrijeva *v* Southwark LBC

R. (on the application of NA) *v* Secretary of State for Foreign and Commonwealth Affairs [2007] EWCA Civ 759; *Times*, August 29, 2007, CA (Civ Div); reversing [2007] EWHC 286 (Admin), QBD (Admin) . . . . *Digested*, 07/**2329**

R. (on the application of Nadarajah) *v* Secretary of State for the Home Department see R. (on the application of Razgar) *v* Secretary of State for the Home Department (No.2)

R. (on the application of Nadarajah) *v* Secretary of State for the Home Department; *sub nom* Abdi *v* Secretary of State for the Home Department; Nadarajah *v* Secretary of State for the Home Department; *joined case* R. (on the application of Abdi) *v* Secretary of State for the Home Department [2005] EWCA Civ 1363; *Times*, December 14, 2005, CA (Civ Div) . . . .   *Digested*, 06/**2224**: *Applied*, 07/57

R. (on the application of Nasseri) *v* Secretary of State for the Home Department see Nasseri *v* Secretary of State for the Home Department

R. (on the application of NASUWT) *v* Secretary of State for Trade and Industry see R. (on the application of Amicus) *v* Secretary of State for Trade and Industry

R. (on the application of National Association of Teachers in Further and Higher Education) *v* Secretary of State for Trade and Industry see R. (on the application of Amicus) *v* Secretary of State for Trade and Industry

R. (on the application of National Grid Gas Plc (formerly Transco Plc)) *v* Environment Agency [2007] UKHL 30; [2007] 1 W.L.R. 1780; [2007] Bus. L.R. 1708; [2007] 3 All E.R. 877; [2007] 41 E.G. 202; [2007] J.P.L. 1737; [2007] 27 E.G. 302 (C.S.); (2007) 157 N.L.J. 974; (2007) 151 S.J.L.B. 893; [2007] N.P.C. 77; *Times*, June 28, 2007, HL; reversing [2006] EWHC 1083 (Admin); [2006] 1 W.L.R. 3041; [2007] 1 All E.R. 1163; [2006] Env. L.R. 49; [2006] J.P.L. 1823; [2006] A.C.D. 88; [2006] 21 E.G. 130 (C.S.); (2006) 150 S.J.L.B. 703; [2006] N.P.C. 59; *Times*, May 31, 2006, QBD (Admin) . . . . *Digested*, 07/**1477**

R. (on the application of National Union of Rail, Maritime and Transport Workers) *v* Secretary of State for Trade and Industry see R. (on the application of Amicus) *v* Secretary of State for Trade and Industry

R. (on the application of National Union of Teachers) v Secretary of State for Trade and Industry see R. (on the application of Amicus) v Secretary of State for Trade and Industry

R. (on the application of Naylor) v Secretary of State for the Home Department see R. (on the application of Ramsden) v Secretary of State for the Home Department

R. (on the application of Neptune Wharf Ltd) v Secretary of State for Trade and Industry [2007] EWHC 1036 (Admin); [2007] 3 All E.R. 676; [2007] 2 P. & C.R. 20; [2007] N.P.C. 55, QBD (Admin) . . . .   *Digested,* 07/**3229**

R. (on the application of Newsmith Stainless Ltd) v Secretary of State for the Environment, Transport and the Regions [2001] EWHC Admin 74, QBD (Admin) . . . .   *Applied,* 07/3223

R. (on the application of Niazi) v Secretary of State for the Home Department [2007] EWHC 1495 (Admin); [2007] A.C.D. 75; *Times,* July 9, 2007, DC . . . .   *Digested,* 07/**45**

R. (on the application of Nicholds) v Security Industry Authority see Nicholds v Security Industry Authority

R. (on the application of Nikonovs) v Brixton Prison Governor; *sub nom* Nikonovs v Governor of Brixton Prison [2005] EWHC 2405 (Admin); [2006] 1 W.L.R. 1518; [2006] 1 All E.R. 927; [2005] Extradition L.R. 125, QBD (Admin) . . . .   *Digested,* 06/**1601**:

                                                    Considered, 07/1661, 07/1664

R. (on the application of Noorkoiv) v Secretary of State for the Home Department (No.2) [2002] EWCA Civ 770; [2002] 1 W.L.R. 3284; [2002] 4 All E.R. 515; [2002] H.R.L.R. 36; [2002] Prison L.R. 311; [2002] A.C.D. 66; (2002) 99(27) L.S.G. 34; (2002) 146 S.J.L.B. 145; *Times,* May 31, 2002; *Independent,* June 14, 2002; *Daily Telegraph,* June 13, 2002, CA (Civ Div); reversing in part [2001] EWHC Admin 345; [2001] Prison L.R. 280; *Independent,* July 2, 2001, QBD (Admin) . . . .   *Digested,* 02/**3339**:

                 Applied, 04/2783, 07/2981: *Considered,* 05/2921, 07/2983

R. (on the application of Northern Foods Plc) v Department for the Environment, Food and Rural Affairs see Northern Foods Plc v Department for the Environment, Food and Rural Affairs

R. (on the application of Norton) v Lambeth LBC (2007) 151 S.J.L.B. 860, QBD (Admin)

R. (on the application of Nteziryayo) v Governor of Belmarsh Prison see Brown (formerly Bajinya) v Governor of Belmarsh Prison

R. (on the application of O) v Crown Court at Harrow see R. (on the application of O) v Harrow Crown Court

R. (on the application of O) v Governing Body of Park View Academy see R. (on the application of O) v Parkview Academy Governors

R. (on the application of O) v Hackney LBC [2006] EWHC 3405 (Admin); [2007] E.L.R. 405, QBD (Admin) . . . .   *Digested,* 07/**1179**

R. (on the application of O) v Harrow Crown Court; *sub nom* O (Writ of Habeas Corpus), Re; R. (on the application of O) v Crown Court at Harrow [2006] UKHL 42; [2007] 1 A.C. 249; [2006] 3 W.L.R. 195; [2006] 3 All E.R. 1157; [2007] 1 Cr. App. R. 9; [2006] H.R.L.R. 35; [2006] U.K.H.R.R. 1062; [2007] Crim. L.R. 63; (2006) 103(32) L.S.G. 22; (2006) 150 S.J.L.B. 1021; *Times,* August 10, 2006, HL; affirming [2003] EWHC 868 (Admin); [2003] 1 W.L.R. 2756; [2004] A.C.D. 3; *Times,* May 29, 2003; *Independent,* July 14, 2003, QBD (Admin) . . . .   *Digested,* 06/**905**

R. (on the application of O) v Mental Health Review Tribunal [2006] EWHC 2659 (Admin); (2007) 93 B.M.L.R. 110; [2006] M.H.L.R. 326; [2007] A.C.D. 16; [2007] A.C.D. 59, QBD (Admin) . . . .   *Digested,* 07/**2909**

R. (on the application of O) v Parkview Academy Governors; *sub nom* R. (on the application of O) v Governing Body of Park View Academy [2007] EWCA Civ 592; [2007] E.L.R. 454, CA (Civ Div); affirming [2007] EWHC 730 (Admin); [2007] E.L.R. 388, QBD (Admin) . . . .   *Digested,* 07/**1186**

R. (on the application of O) v Tower Hamlets LBC Independent Appeal Panel [2007] EWHC 1455 (Admin); [2007] E.L.R. 468, QBD (Admin) . . . .   *Digested,* 07/**1180**

R. (on the application of O'Brien) v Basildon DC [2006] EWHC 1346 (Admin); [2007] 1 P. & C.R. 16; (2006) 150 S.J.L.B. 1291, QBD (Admin) . . . .   *Digested,* 07/**2879**:

                                             Considered, 07/3259

R. (on the application of O'Brien) v Independent Assessor; *sub nom* Independent Assessor v O'Brien; O'Brien v Independent Assessor; *joined case* R. (on the application of Hickey) v Independent Assessor [2007] UKHL 10; [2007] 2 A.C. 312; [2007] 2 W.L.R. 544; [2007] 2 All E.R. 833; (2007) 151 S.J.L.B. 394, HL; affirming [2004] EWCA Civ 1035; [2005] P.I.Q.R. Q7; [2004] Po. L.R. 298; *Times,* September 7, 2004, CA (Civ Div); reversing [2003] EWHC 855 (Admin); [2003] Po. L.R. 183; (2003) 100(26) L.S.G. 36; (2003) 153 N.L.J. 668; *Times,* May 5, 2003, QBD (Admin) . . . .   *Digested,* 07/**1003**

R. (on the application of O'Connell) v Parole Board see R. (on the application of Brooke) v Parole Board

R. (on the application of O'Shea) v Coventry Magistrates Court [2004] EWHC 905 (Admin); [2004] A.C.D. 50; (2004) 101(17) L.S.G. 30; *Times,* April 22, 2004, QBD (Admin) . . . .   *Digested,* 04/**686**:

                                             Considered, 07/1017

R. (on the application of Omar) v Birmingham City Council see R. (on the application of Aweys) v Birmingham City Council

R. (on the application of OSS Group Ltd) v Environment Agency see OSS Group Ltd v Environment Agency

R. (on the application of OSS Group Ltd) v Environment Agency; *joined case* R. (on the application of Solvent Resource Management Ltd) v Environment Agency [2006] EWHC 2390 (Admin); [2007] A.C.D. 8, QBD (Admin)

R. (on the application of Otley) v Barking and Dagenham NHS Primary Care Trust [2007] EWHC 1927 (Admin); (2007) 10 C.C.L. Rep. 628; [2007] LS Law Medical 593; (2007) 98 B.M.L.R. 182; [2007] A.C.D. 78, QBD (Admin) . . . .　　　*Digested*, 07/**1983**

R. (on the application of Oyeyi-Effiong) v Bridge NDC Seven Sisters Partnership [2007] EWHC 606 (Admin); [2007] B.L.G.R. 669, QBD (Admin)

R. (on the application of Ozturk) v Secretary of State for the Home Department; *sub nom* Ozturk v Secretary of State for the Home Department; Akyuz v Secretary of State for the Home Department; *joined cases* R. (on the application of Payir) v Secretary of State for the Home Department; R. (on the application of Akyuz) v Secretary of State for the Home Department [2006] EWCA Civ 541; [2007] 1 W.L.R. 508; [2006] I.C.R. 1314; [2006] Imm. A.R. 553; [2006] I.N.L.R. 558, CA (Civ Div); reversing in part [2005] EWHC 1433 (Admin); [2005] 3 C.M.L.R. 26; [2006] I.C.R. 178; [2005] Imm. A.R. 677; [2006] A.C.D. 25; *Times*, July 20, 2005, QBD (Admin). . . . .　　　*Digested*, 06/**2289**:
Previous proceedings, 05/2206

R. (on the application of P (A Child)) v Oxfordshire CC Exclusion Appeals Panel see R. (on the application of S (A Child)) v Brent LBC

R. (on the application of P (A Juvenile)) v Barking Youth Court [2002] EWHC 734 (Admin); [2002] 2 Cr. App. R. 19; (2002) 166 J.P. 641; [2002] M.H.L.R. 304; [2002] Crim. L.R. 657; (2002) 166 J.P.N. 778, QBD (Admin) . . . .　　　*Considered*, 07/934,
07/1023

R. (on the application of Page) v Secretary of State for Justice [2007] EWHC 2026 (Admin); [2007] A.C.D. 100, QBD (Admin)

R. (on the application of Parker) v Bradford Crown Court [2006] EWHC 3213 (Admin); [2007] R.T.R. 30; [2007] A.C.D. 44; (2007) 104(5) L.S.G. 31, QBD (Admin) . .　　　*Digested*, 07/**3527**

R. (on the application of Parmak) v Secretary of State for the Home Department [2006] EWHC 244 (Admin); [2006] 2 C.M.L.R. 56, QBD (Admin) . . . .　　　*Digested*, 06/**2279**:
Applied, 07/2282

R. (on the application of Paul) v Assistant Deputy Coroner of Inner West London [2007] EWCA Civ 1259; *Times*, December 11, 2007, CA (Civ Div); affirming [2007] EWHC 2721 (Admin), QBD (Admin). . . . .　　　*Digested*, 07/**11**

R. (on the application of Paul) v Deputy Coroner of the Queen's Household and Assistant Deputy Coroner for Surrey see Paul v Deputy Coroner of the Queen's Household and Assistant Deputy Coroner for Surrey

R. (on the application of Payir) v Secretary of State for the Home Department see R. (on the application of Ozturk) v Secretary of State for the Home Department

R. (on the application of PB) v Haringey LBC see R. (on the application of B) v Haringey LBC

R. (on the application of PD) v Mental Health Review Tribunal see R. (on the application of KB) v Mental Health Review Tribunal

R. (on the application of Peacock) v General Medical Council [2007] EWHC 585 (Admin); [2007] LS Law Medical 284, QBD (Admin) . . . .　　　*Digested*, 07/**32**

R. (on the application of Playfoot) v Millais School Governing Body [2007] EWHC 1698 (Admin); [2007] 3 F.C.R. 754; [2007] H.R.L.R. 34; [2007] B.L.G.R. 851; [2007] E.L.R. 484; [2007] A.C.D. 80; *Times*, July 23, 2007, QBD (Admin). . . .　　　*Digested*, 07/**2194**

R. (on the application of Port Regis School Ltd) v North Dorset DC [2006] EWHC 742 (Admin); [2006] B.L.G.R. 696; [2007] 1 P. & C.R. 29; [2006] J.P.L. 1695; (2006) 156 N.L.J. 644; *Times*, April 14, 2006, QBD (Admin) . . . .　　　*Digested*, 06/**2803**

R. (on the application of Pretty) v DPP (2346/02) see Pretty v United Kingdom (2346/ 02)

R. (on the application of ProLife Alliance) v BBC; *sub nom* ProLife Alliance v BBC; R. (on the application of Quintavalle) v BBC [2003] UKHL 23; [2004] 1 A.C. 185; [2003] 2 W.L.R. 1403; [2003] 2 All E.R. 977; [2003] E.M.L.R. 23; [2003] H.R.L.R. 26; [2003] U.K.H.R.R. 758; [2003] A.C.D. 65; (2003) 100(26) L.S.G. 35; (2003) 153 N.L.J. 823; (2003) 147 S.J.L.B. 595; *Times*, May 16, 2003, HL; reversing [2002] EWCA Civ 297; [2002] 3 W.L.R. 1080; [2002] 2 All E.R. 756; [2002] E.M.L.R. 41; [2002] U.K.H.R.R. 1096; (2002) 152 N.L.J. 433; *Times*, March 19, 2002; *Daily Telegraph*, March 21, 2002, CA (Civ Div); reversing [2001] EWHC Admin 607, QBD (Admin) . . . .　　　*Digested*, 03/**2934**:
Considered, 07/898

R. (on the application of Public & Commercial Services Union) v Secretary of State for Trade and Industry see R. (on the application of Amicus) v Secretary of State for Trade and Industry

R. (on the application of Quark Fishing Ltd) v Secretary of State for Foreign and
Commonwealth Affairs (No.2) [2005] UKHL 57; [2006] 1 A.C. 529; [2005] 3
W.L.R. 837; [2006] 3 All E.R. 111; [2006] Eu. L.R. 424; [2005] H.R.L.R. 41;
[2006] U.K.H.R.R. 535; *Times,* October 17, 2005, HL; reversing in part [2004]
EWCA Civ 527; [2005] Q.B. 93; [2004] 3 W.L.R. 1; [2004] H.R.L.R. 28; *Times,*
May 10, 2004, CA (Civ Div); affirming [2003] EWHC 1743 (Admin); [2003]
A.C.D. 96, QBD (Admin) . . . .   *Digested,* 06/**2114**:
               Applied, 06/2163, 07/2239: *Considered,* 06/39, 06/2159, 07/2815:
                                          Distinguished, 07/1944

R. (on the application of Quinn) v Secretary of State for Health see R. (on the
application of Wright) v Secretary of State for Health

R. (on the application of Quintavalle) v BBC see R. (on the application of ProLife
Alliance) v BBC

R. (on the application of Quinton) v Commissioner of Police of the Metropolis see R. (on
the application of Gillan) v Commissioner of Police of the Metropolis

R. (on the application of R) v DPP [2006] EWHC 1375 (Admin); (2006) 170 J.P. 661;
(2007) 171 J.P.N. 140, QBD (Admin) . . . .   *Digested,* 06/**827**

R. (on the application of Raines) v Orange Grove Foster Care Agency Ltd [2006] EWHC
1887 (Admin); [2007] 1 F.L.R. 760; [2006] 2 F.C.R. 746; (2006) 9 C.C.L.
Rep. 541; [2006] Fam. Law 1027, QBD (Admin) . . . .   *Digested,* 06/**1712**

R. (on the application of Raissi) v Secretary of State for the Home Department C1/2007/
0694/QBACF, CA (Civ Div); reversing [2007] EWHC 243 (Admin); [2007] 4
All E.R. 225; (2007) 157 N.L.J. 330; *Times,* February 28, 2007, QBD (Admin)

R. (on the application of Ramsden) v Secretary of State for the Home Department;
joined case R. (on the application of Naylor) v Secretary of State for the Home
Department [2006] EWHC 3502 (Admin); [2007] A.C.D. 51, QBD (Admin)

R. (on the application of Rashid) v Secretary of State for the Home Department; *sub
nom* Rashid v Secretary of State for the Home Department [2005] EWCA Civ
744; [2005] Imm. A.R. 608; [2005] I.N.L.R. 550; *Times,* July 12, 2005;
Independent, June 21, 2005, CA (Civ Div); affirming [2004] EWHC 2465
(Admin); *Times,* November 17, 2004, QBD (Admin) . . . .   *Digested,* 05/**2154**:
                             Considered, 07/1946: *Followed,* 07/2299

R. (on the application of Rayner) v Secretary of State for the Home Department; *sub
nom* Secretary of State for Justice v Rayner; Rayner v Secretary of State for the
Home Department; C/2007/1099, CA (Civ Div); affirming [2007] EWHC 1028
(Admin); [2007] 1 W.L.R. 2239; (2007) 10 C.C.L. Rep. 464, QBD (Admin) . . .   *Digested,* 07/**2907**

R. (on the application of Razgar) v Secretary of State for the Home Department (No.2);
sub nom Secretary of State for the Home Department v Razgar; *joined cases* R.
(on the application of Soumahoro) v Secretary of State for the Home
Department; R. (on the application of Nadarajah) v Secretary of State for the
Home Department [2004] UKHL 27; [2004] 2 A.C. 368; [2004] 3 W.L.R. 58;
[2004] 3 All E.R. 821; [2004] H.R.L.R. 32; [2004] Imm. A.R. 381; [2004]
I.N.L.R. 349; [2004] M.H.L.R. 218; [2004] A.C.D. 83; (2004) 101(28) L.S.G.
33; (2004) 154 N.L.J. 986; (2004) 148 S.J.L.B. 761; *Times,* June 21, 2004;
Independent, June 23, 2004, HL; affirming [2003] EWCA Civ 840; [2003]
Imm. A.R. 529; [2003] I.N.L.R. 543; [2003] A.C.D. 81, CA (Civ Div); affirming
[2002] EWHC 2554 (Admin); [2003] Imm. A.R. 269, QBD (Admin) . . . .   *Digested,* 04/**2029**:
       Applied, 04/2032, 04/2041, 04/2052, 05/2159, 05/2181, 05/2192, 06/2229,
               06/2233, 06/2244, 06/2245, 06/2286, 07/2301, 07/2307, 07/2340:
           Considered, 04/839, 05/2179, 05/2213, 05/5431, 06/2246, 07/2295:
     Explained, 06/2223: *Followed,* 07/2313: *Previous proceedings,* 03/2234

R. (on the application of RD) v Mental Health Review Tribunal [2007] EWHC 781
(Admin); (2007) 104(18) S.G. 29; (2007) 151 S.J.L.B. 506, QBD (Admin)

R. (on the application of Reprotech (Pebsham) Ltd) v East Sussex CC; *sub nom*
Reprotech (Pebsham) Ltd v East Sussex CC; R. v East Sussex CC Ex p.
Reprotech (Pebsham) Ltd; East Sussex CC v Reprotech (Pebsham) Ltd [2002]
UKHL 8; [2003] 1 W.L.R. 348; [2002] 4 All E.R. 58; [2003] 1 P. & C.R. 5;
[2002] 2 P.L.R. 60; [2002] J.P.L. 821; [2002] 10 E.G. 158 (C.S.); [2002] N.P.C.
32; *Times,* March 5, 2002, HL; reversing [2001] Env. L.R. 14; [2001] 1 P.L.R.
12; [2001] J.P.L. 815; [2000] E.G. 79 (C.S.); [2000] N.P.C. 67, CA (Civ Div);
affirming [2000] Env. L.R. 381; [2000] J.P.L. 511; [1999] N.P.C. 109; *Times,*
September 14, 1999, QBD. . . . .   *Digested,* 02/**3695**:
               Applied, 04/3050, 07/3222: *Considered,* 06/3293

R. (on the application of Revenue and Customs Commissioners) v General Income Tax
Commissioners (Berkshire) [2007] EWHC 871 (Admin); [2007] B.T.C. 497;
[2007] S.T.I. 1396, QBD (Admin) . . . .   *Digested,* 07/**4156**

R. (on the application of Revenue and Customs Commissioners) v Teesside Crown Court
see Revenue and Customs Commissioners v Berriman

R. (on the application of Reynolds) v Secretary of State for Work and Pensions see R.
(on the application of Carson) v Secretary of State for Work and Pensions

R. (on the application of Roberts) *v* Parole Board; *sub nom* Roberts *v* Parole Board [2005] UKHL 45; [2005] 2 A.C. 738; [2005] 3 W.L.R. 152; [2006] 1 All E.R. 39; [2005] H.R.L.R. 38; [2005] U.K.H.R.R. 939; (2005) 155 N.L.J. 1096; *Times*, July 8, 2005; *Independent*, July 12, 2005, HL; affirming [2004] EWCA Civ 1031; [2005] Q.B. 410; [2005] 2 W.L.R. 54; [2004] 4 All E.R. 1136; [2005] 2 Prison L.R. 262; [2004] A.C.D. 79; (2004) 148 S.J.L.B. 1150; *Times*, September 6, 2004; *Independent*, October 7, 2004, CA (Civ Div); affirming [2003] EWHC 3120 (Admin); [2004] 2 All E.R. 776; [2004] Prison L.R. 257; [2004] A.C.D. 60, QBD (Admin) . . . . *Digested*, 05/**2916**:
Applied, 07/2173

R. (on the application of Robinson) *v* Torridge DC [2006] EWHC 877 (Admin); [2007] 1 W.L.R. 871; [2006] 3 All E.R. 1148; [2006] Env. L.R. 40; (2006) 156 N.L.J. 760, QBD (Admin). . . . . *Digested*, 06/**1484**

R. (on the application of Rockware Glass Ltd) *v* Chester City Council; *sub nom* R. (on the application of Rockware Glass Ltd) *v* Quinn Glass Ltd [2006] EWCA Civ 992; [2007] Env. L.R. 3; [2007] J.P.L. 217, CA (Civ Div); affirming [2005] EWHC 2250 (Admin); [2006] Env. L.R. 30; [2006] J.P.L. 699; [2006] A.C.D. 11; [2005] N.P.C. 120, QBD (Admin). . . . . *Digested*, 07/**1505**

R. (on the application of Rockware Glass Ltd) *v* Quinn Glass Ltd see R. (on the application of Rockware Glass Ltd) *v* Chester City Council

R. (on the application of Romer) *v* First Secretary of State; *sub nom* Romer *v* Haringey LBC [2006] EWHC 3480 (Admin); [2007] J.P.L. 1354; [2006] 50 E.G. 84 (C.S.), QBD (Admin) . . . . *Digested*, 07/**3232**

R. (on the application of Rose) *v* DPP see Rose *v* DPP

R. (on the application of Rowland) *v* Secretary of State for the Home Department see R. (on the application of Cole) *v* Secretary of State for the Home Department

R. (on the application of Rowley) *v* Secretary of State for Work and Pensions see Rowley *v* Secretary of State for Work and Pensions

R. (on the application of RSPCA) *v* Chester Crown Court; *sub nom* RSPCA *v* Chester Crown Court [2006] EWHC 1273 (Admin); (2006) 170 J.P. 725; (2007) 171 J.P.N. 179, QBD (Admin) . . . . *Digested*, 07/**860**

R. (on the application of Rudi) *v* Secretary of State for the Home Department; *joined case* R. (on the application of Ibrahimi) *v* Secretary of State for the Home Department [2007] EWCA Civ 1326, CA (Civ Div); affirming [2007] EWHC 60 (Admin); [2007] A.C.D. 57, QBD (Admin)

R. (on the application of S) *v* Birmingham City Council Independent Appeal Panel; *joined case* R. (on the application of B) *v* Birmingham City Council Independent Appeal Panel [2006] EWHC 2369 (Admin); [2007] E.L.R. 57; [2007] A.C.D. 7, QBD (Admin) . . . . *Digested*, 07/**1183**:
Considered, 07/1180

R. (on the application of S) *v* Chief Constable of South Yorkshire; *joined case* R. (on the application of Marper) *v* Chief Constable of South Yorkshire [2004] UKHL 39; [2004] 1 W.L.R. 2196; [2004] 4 All E.R. 193; [2004] H.R.L.R. 35; [2004] U.K.H.R.R. 967; 21 B.H.R.C. 408; [2004] Po. L.R. 283; [2005] Crim. L.R. 136; (2004) 101 (34) L.S.G. 29; (2004) 154 N.L.J. 1183; (2004) 148 S.J.L.B. 914; *Times*, July 23, 2004; *Independent*, July 29, 2004, HL; affirming [2002] EWCA Civ 1275; [2002] 1 W.L.R. 3223; [2003] 1 All E.R. 148; [2003] 1 Cr. App. R. 16; [2003] H.R.L.R. 1; 13 B.H.R.C. 569; [2002] Po. L.R. 284; [2003] Crim. L.R. 39; [2003] A.C.D. 8; (2002) 99 (40) L.S.G. 32; (2002) 152 N.L.J. 1483; (2002) 146 S.J.L.B. 207; *Times*, October 3, 2002; *Independent*, October 1, 2002, CA (Civ Div); affirming [2002] EWHC 478 (Admin); [2002] Po. L.R. 273; *Times*, April 4, 2002; *Daily Telegraph*, April 11, 2002, QBD (Admin) . . . . *Digested*, 04/**710**:
Applied, 05/3835, 06/4009, 07/1731, 07/3867: *Considered*, 05/190, 06/4027, 07/2293

R. (on the application of S) *v* Croydon Youth Court see R. (on the application of C) *v* Croydon Youth Court

R. (on the application of S) *v* Croydon Youth Court see R. (on the application of C) *v* Croydon Youth Court

R. (on the application of S) *v* Edu Action (Waltham Forest) [2006] EWHC 3144 (Admin); [2007] E.L.R. 185, QBD (Admin) . . . . *Digested*, 07/**1196**

R. (on the application of S) *v* Kent CC [2007] EWHC 2135 (Admin); [2007] E.L.R. 648, QBD (Admin)

R. (on the application of S) *v* Knowsley NHS Primary Care Trust; *joined case* R. (on the application of Ghosh) *v* Northumberland NHS Care Trust [2006] EWHC 26 (Admin); [2006] Lloyd's Rep. Med. 123; [2006] A.C.D. 60; *Times*, February 2, 2006, QBD (Admin) . . . . *Digested*, 06/**1820**:
Considered, 07/32

R. (on the application of S) *v* Secretary of State for the Home Department [2003] EWCA Civ 426; [2003] M.H.L.R. 264; [2003] Prison L.R. 112; (2003) 100(25) L.S.G. 46; (2003) 147 S.J.L.B. 506; *Times*, April 25, 2003, CA (Civ Div); affirming [2002] EWHC 2424 (Admin); [2003] M.H.L.R. 114; [2003] Prison L.R. 108; (2003) 100(1) L.S.G. 25; *Times*, November 13, 2002, QBD (Admin) . *Digested*, 03/**3071**:
Considered, 07/2976

R. (on the application of S) *v* Secretary of State for the Home Department [2007] EWCA Civ 546; [2007] Imm. A.R. 781; [2007] I.N.L.R. 450; [2007] A.C.D. 94; (2007) 104(27) L.S.G. 30; (2007) 151 S.J.L.B. 858, CA (Civ Div); affirming [2007] EWHC 51 (Admin), QBD (Admin)

R. (on the application of S) *v* Sutton LBC [2007] EWCA Civ 790; (2007) 10 C.C.L. Rep. 615, CA (Civ Div); reversing in part [2007] EWHC 1196 (Admin); [2007] 2 F.L.R. 849; (2007) 10 C.C.L. Rep. 485; [2007] Fam. Law 699, QBD (Admin) . . . . *Digested, 07/3940*

R. (on the application of S) *v* Waltham Forest Youth Court [2004] EWHC 715 (Admin); [2004] 2 Cr. App. R. 21; (2004) 168 J.P. 293; (2004) 168 J.P.N. 438, QBD (Admin) . . . . *Digested, 04/864*: *Considered, 07/856*

R. (on the application of S (A Child)) *v* Brent LBC; *sub nom* R. (on the application of P (A Child)) *v* Oxfordshire CC Exclusion Appeals Panel; *joined case* R. (on the application of T (A Child)) *v* Wembley High School Head Teacher [2002] EWCA Civ 693; [2002] E.L.R. 556; [2002] A.C.D. 90; (2002) 99(26) L.S.G. 38; (2002) 146 S.J.L.B. 137; *Times*, June 4, 2002; *Independent*, May 30, 2002, CA (Civ Div); affirming [2001] EWHC Admin 384; [2002] E.L.R. 57, QBD (Admin)   *Digested, 02/1101*: *Considered, 03/1055, 07/1183*: *Previous proceedings, 01/1899, 02/1100*

R. (on the application of Saad) *v* Secretary of State for the Home Department see Saad *v* Secretary of State for the Home Department

R. (on the application of Sacker) *v* HM Coroner for West Yorkshire; *sub nom* R. *v* HM Coroner for West Yorkshire Ex p. Sacker; Sacker *v* West Yorkshire Coroner [2004] UKHL 11; [2004] 1 W.L.R. 796; [2004] 2 All E.R. 487; [2004] H.R.L.R. 30; [2004] U.K.H.R.R. 521; [2004] Lloyd's Rep. Med. 281; (2004) 79 B.M.L.R. 40; [2003] Inquest L.R. 15; [2004] Inquest L.R. 28; (2004) 101(16) L.S.G. 28; (2004) 148 S.J.L.B. 354; *Times*, March 12, 2004, HL; affirming [2003] EWCA Civ 217; [2003] 2 All E.R. 278; [2003] Lloyd's Rep. Med. 326; (2003) 73 B.M.L.R. 46; [2003] Inquest L.R. 15; [2003] Prison L.R. 273, CA (Civ Div) . . .   *Digested, 04/38*: *Applied, 07/28: Considered, 06/17, 07/28*

R. (on the application of Sager House (Chelsea) Ltd) *v* First Secretary of State; *sub nom* Kensington and Chelsea RBC *v* Sager House (Chelsea) Ltd [2006] EWHC 1251 (Admin); [2007] J.P.L. 413, QBD (Admin); affirming [2005] P.A.D. 47, Planning Inspector . . . . *Digested, 07/3223*

R. (on the application of Samaroo) *v* Secretary of State for the Home Department; *sub nom* R. *v* Secretary of State for the Home Department Ex p. Samaroo; Samaroo *v* Secretary of State for the Home Department; *joined case* Sezek *v* Secretary of State for the Home Department [2001] EWCA Civ 1139; [2001] U.K.H.R.R. 1150; [2002] I.N.L.R. 55; (2001) 98(34) L.S.G. 40; (2001) 145 S.J.L.B. 208; *Times*, September 18, 2001, CA (Civ Div); affirming [2001] Imm. A.R. 324; *Daily Telegraph*, January 23, 2001, QBD (Admin) . . . .   *Digested, 01/3660*: *Applied, 04/3040, 05/3340, 06/2277: Considered, 03/2232, 03/3068, 04/3042, 07/2879: Distinguished, 05/2027: Followed, 04/2051*

R. (on the application of Save Britain's Heritage) *v* Westminster City Council [2007] EWHC 807 (Admin); (2007) 104(15) L.S.G. 22, QBD (Admin)

R. (on the application of SB) *v* Denbigh High School Governors see R. (on the application of Begum) *v* Denbigh High School Governors

R. (on the application of Scholes) *v* Secretary of State for the Home Department; *sub nom* Scholes *v* Secretary of State for the Home Department [2006] EWCA Civ 1343; [2006] H.R.L.R. 44; [2007] U.K.H.R.R. 112; (2007) 93 B.M.L.R. 136; [2006] Inquest L.R. 180; [2007] A.C.D. 24; *Times*, November 10, 2006, CA (Civ Div); affirming [2006] EWHC 1 (Admin); (2006) 170 J.P. 243; [2006] H.R.L.R. 11; [2006] Inquest L.R. 1; [2006] A.C.D. 77; (2006) 170 J.P.N. 494, QBD (Admin) . . . .   *Digested, 07/28*

R. (on the application of Searle) *v* Secretary of State for the Environment [2006] EWHC 1908 (Admin), QBD (Admin) . . . .   *Digested, 07/3226*

R. (on the application of Secretary of State for the Home Department) *v* Chief Asylum Support Adjudicator (2003) 147 S.J.L.B. 1276; *Times*, November 13, 2003, CA (Civ Div); affirming [2002] EWHC 2218 (Admin); (2002) 99(49) L.S.G. 19; *Times*, November 29, 2002, QBD (Admin) . . . .   *Digested, 03/2271*: *Considered, 07/2288*

R. (on the application of Secretary of State for the Home Department) *v* Chief Asylum Support Adjudicator [2006] EWHC 3059 (Admin); [2007] A.C.D. 68; *Times*, December 22, 2006, QBD (Admin) . . . .   *Digested, 07/2288*

R. (on the application of Secretary of State for the Home Department) *v* Immigration Appeal Tribunal; *joined case* R. (on the application of Hwez) *v* Secretary of State for the Home Department [2001] EWHC Admin 1067; [2002] Imm. A.R. 491; [2002] I.N.L.R. 116; *Times*, January 7, 2002, QBD (Admin) . . . .   *Digested, 02/2552*: *Applied, 07/2277*

R. (on the application of Secretary of State for the Home Department) *v* Information Tribunal [2006] EWHC 2958 (Admin); [2007] 2 All E.R. 703; [2007] A.C.D. 45; (2006) 156 N.L.J. 1883, DC. . . . .   *Digested, 07/2174*

R. (on the application of SH) *v* Secretary of State for the Home Department see R. (on the application of MH) *v* Secretary of State for the Home Department

R. (on the application of Sharif) *v* Birmingham City Council see R. (on the application of Aweys) *v* Birmingham City Council

R. (on the application of Sharman) *v* HM Coroner for Inner North London; *sub nom* Sharman *v* HM Coroner for Inner North London [2005] EWCA Civ 967; [2005] Inquest L.R. 168, CA (Civ Div); affirming [2005] EWHC 857 (Admin); [2005] Inquest L.R. 77; [2005] A.C.D. 96, QBD (Admin) . . . .   *Applied*, 07/29: *Considered*, 07/13

R. (on the application of Sills) *v* DPP [2006] EWHC 3383 (Admin); (2007) 171 J.P. 201; (2007) 171 J.P.N. 514, QBD (Admin). . . . .   *Digested*, 07/**905**

R. (on the application of Singapore Medical Council) *v* General Medical Council [2006] EWHC 3277 (Admin); *Times*, January 12, 2007, QBD (Admin)

R. (on the application of Singh) *v* Chief Constable of the West Midlands [2006] EWCA Civ 1118; [2006] 1 W.L.R. 3374; [2007] 2 All E.R. 297; (2006) 170 J.P. 765; [2006] Po. L.R. 261; [2007] Crim. L.R. 243; (2007) 171 J.P.N. 290; (2006) 156 N.L.J. 1400; *Times*, August 15, 2006, CA (Civ Div); affirming [2005] EWHC 2840 (Admin); [2006] Po. L.R. 1; [2006] Crim. L.R. 442, QBD . . . .   *Digested*, 06/**839**: *Considered*, 07/3313

R. (on the application of Singh) *v* Solihull MBC see Singh *v* Solihull MBC

R. (on the application of Singh) *v* Stratford Magistrates' Court [2007] EWHC 1582 (Admin); [2007] 1 W.L.R. 3119; [2007] 4 All E.R. 407; (2007) 171 J.P. 557; [2007] A.C.D. 72; *Times*, August 13, 2007, QBD (Admin). . . . .   *Digested*, 07/**934**

R. (on the application of Sinn Fein) *v* Secretary of State for Northern Ireland [2007] EWHC 12 (Admin); [2007] A.C.D. 58, DC

R. (on the application of Sinnarasa) *v* Secretary of State for the Home Department [2005] EWHC 1126 (Admin), QBD (Admin) . . . .   *Distinguished*, 07/2290

R. (on the application of Slator) *v* Bow Street Magistrates Court; *sub nom* Slator *v* Bow Street Magistrates Court [2006] EWHC 2628 (Admin); [2006] Extradition L.R. 243; [2007] A.C.D. 28; *Times*, October 25, 2006, DC. . . . .   *Digested*, 07/**1662**

R. (on the application of Slough BC) *v* Secretary of State for Communities and Local Government see R. (on the application of Corby BC) *v* Secretary of State for Communities and Local Government

R. (on the application of Smith) *v* North Eastern Derbyshire Primary Care Trust see Smith *v* North Eastern Derbyshire Primary Care Trust

R. (on the application of Smith) *v* Parole Board; *sub nom* Smith *v* Parole Board; *joined case* R. (on the application of West) *v* Parole Board [2005] UKHL 1; [2005] 1 W.L.R. 350; [2005] 1 All E.R. 755; [2005] H.R.L.R. 8; 18 B.H.R.C. 267; [2005] 2 Prison L.R. 14; (2005) 102(12) L.S.G. 26; (2005) 149 S.J.L.B. 145; *Times*, January 28, 2005; *Independent*, February 2, 2005, HL; reversing [2003] EWCA Civ 1269; [2004] 1 W.L.R. 421; [2004] Prison L.R. 216; [2004] Prison L.R. 31; (2003) 100(38) L.S.G. 34; (2003) 153 N.L.J. 1427; *Times*, September 2, 2003, CA (Civ Div) . . . .   *Digested*, 05/**2920**: *Applied*, 04/2776, 05/2734, 06/345, 06/2937: *Considered*, 05/2907, 07/2981: *Distinguished*, 04/3349: *Followed*, 04/2782: *Previous proceedings*, 02/3349

R. (on the application of Smith) *v* South Norfolk Council [2006] EWHC 2772 (Admin); [2006] 46 E.G. 209 (C.S.), QBD (Admin) . . . .   *Digested*, 07/**3259**

R. (on the application of Software Solutions Partners Ltd) *v* HM Commissioners for Customs and Excise see R. (on the application of Software Solutions Partners Ltd) *v* Revenue and Customs Commissioners

R. (on the application of Software Solutions Partners Ltd) *v* Revenue and Customs Commissioners; *sub nom* R. (on the application of Software Solutions Partners Ltd) *v* HM Commissioners for Customs and Excise [2007] EWHC 971 (Admin); [2007] B.T.C. 5699; [2007] B.V.C. 667; [2007] S.T.I. 1399, QBD (Admin) . . . . .   *Digested*, 07/**4324**

R. (on the application of Solvent Resource Management Ltd) *v* Environment Agency see R. (on the application of OSS Group Ltd) *v* Environment Agency

R. (on the application of Soumahoro) *v* Secretary of State for the Home Department see R. (on the application of Razgar) *v* Secretary of State for the Home Department (No.2)

R. (on the application of Southwark Law Centre) *v* Legal Services Commission; *sub nom* Southwark Law Centre *v* Legal Services Commission; *joined case* R. (on the application of Dennis) *v* Legal Services Commission [2007] EWHC 1715 (Admin); [2007] 4 All E.R. 754; (2007) 157 N.L.J. 1119; [2007] N.P.C. 97; *Times*, August 20, 2007, QBD (Admin) . . . .   *Digested*, 07/**2786**

R. (on the application of Spain) *v* Bow Street Magistrates Court see R. (on the application of United States) *v* Bow Street Magistrates Court

R. (on the application of Spath Holme Ltd) v Secretary of State for the Environment, Transport and the Regions; *sub nom* R. v Secretary of State for the Environment, Transport and the Regions Ex p. Spath Holme Ltd [2001] 2 A.C. 349; [2001] 2 W.L.R. 15; [2001] 1 All E.R. 195; (2001) 33 H.L.R. 31; [2001] 1 E.G.L.R. 129; [2000] E.G. 152 (C.S.); (2001) 98(8) L.S.G. 44; (2000) 150 N.L.J. 1855; (2001) 145 S.J.L.B. 39; [2000] N.P.C. 139; *Times*, December 13, 2000, HL; reversing [2000] 3 W.L.R. 141; [2000] 1 All E.R. 884; (2000) 32 H.L.R. 495; [2000] E.G. 10 (C.S.); (2000) 144 S.J.L.B. 100; [2000] N.P.C. 4; *Times*, February 15, 2000; *Independent*, March 6, 2000, CA (Civ Div) . . . . *Digested*, 01/**4206**:
Applied, 00/5095, 01/5632, 03/1962, 04/3189: *Considered*, 07/3064

R. (on the application of Springhall) v Richmond upon Thames LBC [2006] EWCA Civ 19; [2006] B.L.G.R. 419; [2007] 1 P. & C.R. 30; [2006] J.P.L. 970; [2006] A.C.D. 50; (2006) 103(8) L.S.G. 26; (2006) 150 S.J.L.B. 165; [2006] N.P.C. 7; *Times*, February 13, 2006, CA (Civ Div); affirming [2005] EWHC 52 (Admin), QBD (Admin) . . . . *Digested*, 06/**3356**

R. (on the application of Stace) v Milton Keynes Magistrates Court [2006] EWHC 1049 (Admin); (2007) 171 J.P. 1; [2007] A.C.D. 14, QBD (Admin). . . . . *Digested*, 07/**4220**

R. (on the application of Steele) v Birmingham City Council [2005] EWCA Civ 1824; [2006] 1 W.L.R. 2380; [2007] 1 All E.R. 73; [2006] I.C.R. 869; [2006] B.P.I.R. 856; [2006] R.V.R. 120; *Times*, April 26, 2006, CA (Civ Div); reversing [2005] EWHC 783 (Admin); [2005] R.V.R. 374, QBD (Admin) . . . . *Digested*, 06/**4022**

R. (on the application of Stellato) v Secretary of State for the Home Department; *sub nom* Stellato v Secretary of State for the Home Department [2007] UKHL 5; [2007] 2 A.C. 70; [2007] 2 W.L.R. 531; [2007] 2 All E.R. 737; (2007) 151 S.J.L.B. 395, HL; affirming [2006] EWCA Civ 1639; [2007] 1 W.L.R. 608; [2007] 2 Cr. App. R. (S.) 21; [2007] Crim. L.R. 246; [2007] A.C.D. 64; (2006) 150 S.J.L.B. 1607; *Times*, December 6, 2006, CA (Civ Div); reversing [2006] EWHC 608 (Admin); [2006] 2 Cr. App. R. (S.) 114; [2006] Crim. L.R. 767; (2006) 170 J.P.N. 262, QBD (Admin). . . . . *Digested*, 07/**2982**

R. (on the application of Strickson) v Preston County Court; *sub nom* Strickson v Preston County Court [2007] EWCA Civ 1132, CA (Civ Div); affirming [2006] EWHC 3300 (Admin); [2007] A.C.D. 37, QBD (Admin)

R. (on the application of Stubbs) v Central Criminal Court see R. (on the application of Thomas) v Central Criminal Court

R. (on the application of Sugar) v Information Commissioner see BBC v Sugar

R. (on the application of Supportways Community Services Ltd) v Hampshire CC; *sub nom* Hampshire CC v Supportways Community Services Ltd; Supportways Community Services Ltd v Hampshire CC [2006] EWCA Civ 1035; [2006] B.L.G.R. 836; (2006) 9 C.C.L. Rep. 484, CA (Civ Div); reversing [2005] EWHC 3101 (Admin); (2006) 9 C.C.L. Rep. 227, QBD (Admin) . . . . *Digested*, 07/**796**

R. (on the application of Swords) v Secretary of State for Communities and Local Government see Swords v Secretary of State for Communities and Local Government

R. (on the application of Synthon BV) v Licensing Authority [2006] EWHC 1759 (Admin); [2006] Eu. L.R. 1180; [2007] A.C.D. 9, QBD (Admin) . . . . *Digested*, 07/**1643**

R. (on the application of Szklanny) v City of Westminster Magistrates Court see Szklanny v City of Westminster Magistrates Court

R. (on the application of T) v Enfield LBC; *sub nom* R. (on the application of C) v Enfield LBC [2004] EWHC 2297 (Admin); [2005] 3 F.C.R. 55, QBD (Admin) . . . . *Digested*, 05/**2146**:
Applied, 07/2302

R. (on the application of T) v Independent Appeal Panel for Devon CC [2007] EWHC 763 (Admin); [2007] E.L.R. 499, QBD (Admin) . . . . *Digested*, 07/**1181**

R. (on the application of T) v Secretary of State for the Home Department see R. (on the application of Temiz) v Secretary of State for the Home Department

R. (on the application of T (A Child)) v Wembley High School Head Teacher see R. (on the application of S (A Child)) v Brent LBC

R. (on the application of Takeley Parish Council) v Stansted Airport Ltd [2005] EWHC 3312 (Admin); [2007] J.P.L. 126, QBD (Admin) . . . . *Digested*, 07/**3256**

R. (on the application of Takoushis) v HM Coroner for Inner North London [2005] EWCA Civ 1440; [2006] 1 W.L.R. 461; (2006) 9 C.C.L. Rep. 90; [2006] Lloyd's Rep. Med. 57; (2006) 87 B.M.L.R. 149; [2005] Inquest L.R. 185; (2006) 103(2) L.S.G. 30; *Times*, December 8, 2005, CA (Civ Div); reversing [2004] EWHC 2922 (Admin); [2004] Inquest L.R. 248; [2004] M.H.L.R. 365, QBD (Admin) . . . . *Digested*, 06/**16**:
Applied, 07/2238: *Considered*, 06/2108, 07/2980

R. (on the application of Tapecrown Ltd) v First Secretary of State see Tapecrown Ltd v First Secretary of State

R. (on the application of TB) v Mental Health Review Tribunal see R. (on the application of KB) v Mental Health Review Tribunal

R. (on the application of TB) v Stafford Crown Court see R. (on the application of B) v Stafford Combined Court

R. (on the application of Telegraph Group Plc) v Sherwood; *sub nom* Telegraph Group Plc, Ex p.; R. v Sherwood Ex p. Telegraph Group Plc [2001] EWCA Crim 1075; [2001] 1 W.L.R. 1983; [2002] E.M.L.R. 10; (2001) 98(28) L.S.G. 42; (2001) 145 S.J.L.B. 159; *Times*, June 12, 2001, CA (Crim Div) . . . . *Digested*, 01/**1182**; *Followed*, 07/1018

R. (on the application of Teleos Plc) v Customs and Excise Commissioners (C-409/04) [2007] S.T.I. 2216; *Times*, October 5, 2007, ECJ (3rd Chamber)

R. (on the application of Temiz) v Secretary of State for the Home Department; *sub nom* R. (on the application of T) v Secretary of State for the Home Department [2006] EWHC 2450 (Admin); [2007] A.C.D. 56; *Times*, November 8, 2006, QBD (Admin) . . . . *Digested*, 06/**2228**

R. (on the application of Tesema) v Secretary of State for the Home Department see R. (on the application of Limbuela) v Secretary of State for the Home Department

R. (on the application of Thames Water Utilities Ltd) v Bromley Magistrates' Court (C-252/05); *sub nom* Thames Water Utilities Ltd v Bromley Magistrates Court (C-252/05) [2007] 1 W.L.R. 1945; [2007] 3 C.M.L.R. 2; [2007] 20 E.G. 295 (C.S.); *Times*, May 25, 2007, ECJ

R. (on the application of Thangarasa) v Secretary of State for the Home Department see R. (on the application of Yogathas) v Secretary of State for the Home Department

R. (on the application of the Secretary of State for the Home Department) v Chief Asylum Support Adjudicator see Dogan v Secretary of State for the Home Department

R. (on the application of Thomas) v Central Criminal Court; *sub nom* Thomas v Central Criminal Court; *joined case* R. (on the application of Stubbs) v Central Criminal Court [2006] EWHC 2138; [2006] 1 W.L.R. 3278; [2007] 1 Cr. App. R. 7; [2006] Crim. L.R. 1061; *Times*, August 11, 2006, DC . . . . *Digested*, 06/**983**

R. (on the application of Thorpe) v Security Industry Authority see Nicholds v Security Industry Authority

R. (on the application of Thurman) v Lewisham LBC (Unreported), QBD (Admin) . . . . *Approved*, 07/402

R. (on the application of Tilki) v Secretary of State for the Home Department see R. (on the application of Baiai) v Secretary of State for the Home Department

R. (on the application of Tofik) v Immigration Appeal Tribunal [2003] EWCA Civ 1138; [2003] I.N.L.R. 623, CA (Civ Div); reversing [2002] EWHC 2889 (Admin), QBD (Admin) . . . . *Considered*, 07/2284

R. (on the application of Tottman) v Hertfordshire CC; *sub nom* T (A Child) v Hertfordshire CC [2004] EWCA Civ 927; [2005] B.L.G.R. 262, CA (Civ Div); affirming [2003] EWHC 1725 (Admin); [2003] E.L.R. 763, QBD (Admin) . . . . *Digested*, 04/**1080**; *Considered*, 07/1262

R. (on the application of Trailer & Marina (Leven) Ltd) v Secretary of State for the Environment, Food and Rural Affairs; *sub nom* Trailer & Marina (Leven) Ltd v Secretary of State for the Environment, Food and Rural Affairs [2004] EWCA Civ 1580; [2005] 1 W.L.R. 1267; [2005] Env. L.R. 27; [2005] 1 P. & C.R. 28; [2005] J.P.L. 1086; (2005) 102(5) L.S.G. 26; (2005) 149 S.J.L.B. 60; *Times*, December 28, 2004, CA (Civ Div); affirming [2004] EWHC 153 (Admin); [2004] Env. L.R. 40; [2004] J.P.L. 1512; (2004) 101(7) L.S.G. 37; [2004] N.P.C. 14; *Times*, February 19, 2004, QBD (Admin) . . . . *Digested*, 05/**1410**; *Applied*, 07/3256

R. (on the application of Transport for London) v Parking Adjudicator [2007] EWHC 1172 (Admin); [2007] R.T.R. 39; (2007) 104(15) L.S.G. 23, QBD (Admin)

R. (on the application of Tratt) v Horsham DC [2007] EWHC 1485 (Admin), QBD (Admin) . . . . *Applied*, 07/3284

R. (on the application of Traves) v DPP [2005] EWHC 1482 (Admin); (2005) 169 J.P. 421; (2005) 169 J.P.N. 659, QBD (Admin) . . . . *Digested*, 05/**817**; *Doubted*, 07/944

R. (on the application of Tree and Wildlife Action Committee Ltd) v Forestry Commissioners [2007] EWHC 1623 (Admin); [2007] 2 P. & C.R. 31; *Times*, July 17, 2007, QBD (Admin) . . . . *Digested*, 07/**3234**

R. (on the application of Trzcinska) v Secretary of State for the Home Department see R. (on the application of Baiai) v Secretary of State for the Home Department

R. (on the application of Tum) v Secretary of State for the Home Department (C-16/05) see Tum v Secretary of State for the Home Department (C-16/05)

R. (on the application of Ugirashebuja) v Governor of Belmarsh Prison see Brown (formerly Bajinya) v Governor of Belmarsh Prison

R. (on the application of UK Tradecorp Ltd) v Customs and Excise Commissioners [2004] EWHC 2515 (Admin); [2005] S.T.C. 138; [2005] B.T.C. 5097; [2005] B.V.C. 128; [2004] S.T.I. 2376; *Times*, November 17, 2004, QBD (Admin) . . . . . *Digested*, 05/**4373**; *Considered*, 07/4312

R. (on the application of Ullah) *v* Special Adjudicator; *sub nom* Do *v* Secretary of State for the Home Department; R. (on the application of Ullah (Ahsan)) *v* Secretary of State for the Home Department; Ullah (Ahsan) *v* Special Adjudicator; *joined case* Do *v* Immigration Appeal Tribunal [2004] UKHL 26; [2004] 2 A.C. 323; [2004] 3 W.L.R. 23; [2004] 3 All E.R. 785; [2004] H.R.L.R. 33; [2004] U.K.H.R.R. 995; [2004] Imm. A.R. 419; [2004] I.N.L.R. 381; (2004) 101(28) L.S.G. 33; (2004) 154 N.L.J. 985; (2004) 148 S.J.L.B. 762; *Times*, June 18, 2004; *Independent*, June 22, 2004, HL; affirming [2002] EWCA Civ 1856; [2003] 1 W.L.R. 770; [2003] 3 All E.R. 1174; [2003] H.R.L.R. 12; [2003] U.K.H.R.R. 302; [2003] Imm. A.R. 304; [2003] I.N.L.R. 74; [2003] A.C.D. 30; (2003) 100(10) L.S.G. 28; (2003) 147 S.J.L.B. 28; *Times*, December 18, 2002; *Independent*, December 20, 2002, CA (Civ Div); affirming [2002] EWHC 1584 (Admin); [2002] Imm. A.R. 601; *Times*, September 5, 2002; *Independent*, October 14, 2002, QBD (Admin) . . . . *Digested*, 04/**2009**:

Applied, 04/2052, 05/401, 05/2195, 06/1598, 06/2223, 07/2309: *Considered*, 04/839, 04/2038, 05/2140, 05/5431, 06/1605, 07/5169, 07/5432

R. (on the application of Ullah (Ahsan)) *v* Secretary of State for the Home Department see R. (on the application of Ullah) *v* Special Adjudicator

R. (on the application of UMBS Online Ltd) *v* Serious Organised Crime Agency [2007] EWCA Civ 406; [2007] Bus. L.R. 1317; (2007) 104(20) L.S.G. 29; (2007) 151 S.J.L.B. 608; *Times*, May 15, 2007, CA (Civ Div) . . . . *Digested*, 07/**1931**

R. (on the application of UNISON) *v* First Secretary of State; *sub nom* UNISON *v* First Secretary of State [2006] EWHC 2373 (Admin); [2006] I.R.L.R. 926; [2007] B.L.G.R. 188; [2006] Pens. L.R. 239; [2007] A.C.D. 26, QBD (Admin) . . . . . . *Digested*, 06/**3024**: *Considered*, 07/1310

R. (on the application of UNISON) *v* Secretary of State for Trade and Industry see R. (on the application of Amicus) *v* Secretary of State for Trade and Industry

R. (on the application of United States) *v* Bow Street Magistrates Court; *sub nom* United States of America *v* Tollman; Central Examining Court, Madrid *v* Sander; *joined case* R. (on the application of Spain) *v* Bow Street Magistrates Court [2006] EWHC 2256 (Admin); [2007] 1 W.L.R. 1157; [2006] Extradition L.R. 216; (2006) 103(37) L.S.G. 33; (2006) 156 N.L.J. 1440; (2006) 150 S.J.L.B. 1189; *Times*, September 19, 2006, QBD (Admin) . . . . *Digested*, 06/**1608**: *Cited*, 07/1665

R. (on the application of von Brandenburg) *v* East London and the City Mental Health NHS Trust; *sub nom* R. *v* East London and the City Mental Health NHS Trust Ex p. von Brandenburg; R. *v* Tower Hamlets Healthcare NHS Trust Ex p. von Brandenburg [2003] UKHL 58; [2004] 2 A.C. 280; [2003] 3 W.L.R. 1265; [2004] 1 All E.R. 400; [2004] H.R.L.R. 6; (2004) 7 C.C.L. Rep. 121; [2004] Lloyd's Rep. Med. 228; (2004) 76 B.M.L.R. 168; [2004] M.H.L.R. 44; (2004) 101(5) L.S.G. 28; (2003) 147 S.J.L.B. 1366; *Times*, November 14, 2003; *Independent*, November 19, 2003, HL; affirming [2001] EWCA Civ 239; [2002] Q.B. 235; [2001] 3 W.L.R. 588; (2001) 4 C.C.L. Rep. 105; (2001) 61 B.M.L.R. 206; [2001] M.H.L.R. 36; [2002] A.C.D. 9; (2001) 98(15) L.S.G. 33; (2001) 145 S.J.L.B. 107; *Times*, February 28, 2001; *Independent*, March 1, 2001, CA (Civ Div); affirming (2000) 3 C.C.L. Rep. 189; [2000] M.H.L.R. 131; *Independent*, October 2, 2000, QBD. . . . . *Digested*, 04/**2683**: *Applied*, 07/2910: *Followed*, 02/3230

R. (on the application of Vovk) *v* Secretary of State for the Home Department; *joined case* R. (on the application of Datta) *v* Secretary of State for the Home Department [2006] EWHC 3386 (Admin); [2007] I.N.L.R. 538; [2007] A.C.D. 48, QBD (Admin)

R. (on the application of W) *v* Commissioner of Police of the Metropolis [2006] EWCA Civ 458; [2007] Q.B. 399; [2006] 3 W.L.R. 1098; [2006] 3 All E.R. 458; (2006) 170 J.P. 500; [2006] Po. L.R. 102; (2006) 170 J.P.N. 876; (2006) 103(21) L.S.G. 26; (2006) 156 N.L.J. 844; *Times*, May 22, 2006; *Independent*, May 16, 2006, CA (Civ Div); reversing [2005] EWHC 1586 (Admin); [2005] 1 W.L.R. 3706; [2005] 3 All E.R. 749; (2005) 169 J.P. 473; [2005] Po. L.R. 202; (2005) 169 J.P.N. 718; (2005) 155 N.L.J. 1184; *Times*, July 21, 2005; *Independent*, July 22, 2005, QBD (Admin) . . . . *Digested*, 06/**3407**

R. (on the application of W) *v* Croydon LBC see R. (on the application of AW) *v* Croydon LBC

R. (on the application of W) *v* Lambeth LBC see R. (on the application of G) *v* Barnet LBC

R. (on the application of W (A Child)) *v* B School Governors see R. (on the application of L (A Child)) *v* J School Governors

R. (on the application of Wahid) *v* Tower Hamlets LBC [2002] EWCA Civ 287; [2003] H.L.R. 2; [2002] B.L.G.R. 545; (2002) 5 C.C.L. Rep. 239, CA (Civ Div); affirming [2001] EWHC Admin 641; (2001) 4 C.C.L. Rep. 455, QBD (Admin). . *Digested*, 03/**2046**: *Applied*, 07/2154: *Considered*, 05/3947, 07/3908

R. (on the application of Walker) v Secretary of State for the Home Department; *sub nom* Wells v Parole Board; Walker v Secretary of State for the Home Department; Secretary of State for Justice v Walker; *joined cases* R. (on the application of Wells) v Parole Board; Secretary of State for Justice v James; C1/2007/1959;C1/2007/2091, CA (Civ Div); affirming [2007] EWHC 1835 (Admin); [2007] A.C.D. 86; (2007) 157 N.L.J. 1275; *Times*, October 11, 2007, DC

R. (on the application of Wall) v Brighton and Hove City Council [2004] EWHC 2582 (Admin); [2005] 1 P. & C.R. 33; [2004] 4 P.L.R. 115; [2005] J.P.L. 807; [2004] 46 E.G. 150 (C.S.); (2004) 101(44) L.S.G. 33; *Times*, November 16, 2004, QBD (Admin) . . . . *Digested*, 05/**3300**:
Considered, 07/3273, 07/3284

R. (on the application of Wandsworth LBC) v Secretary of State for Transport; *joined case* R. (on the application of Essex CC) v Secretary of State for Transport [2005] EWHC 20 (Admin); [2006] 1 E.G.L.R. 91; [2005] 8 E.G. 191 (C.S.); *Times*, February 22, 2005, QBD (Admin) . . . . *Digested*, 05/**58**:
Considered, 07/57

R. (on the application of Wandsworth LBC) v Secretary of State for Transport, Local Government and the Regions see Wandsworth LBC v Secretary of State for Transport, Local Government and the Regions (Enforcement Notice)

R. (on the application of Wani) v Secretary of State for the Home Department [2005] EWHC 2815 (Admin); [2006] Imm. A.R. 125; [2006] I.N.L.R. 234, QBD (Admin) . . . . *Digested*, 06/**2207**:
Applied, 07/2275

R. (on the application of Ware) v Neath Port Talbot CBC; *sub nom* Neath Port Talbot CBC v Ware [2007] EWCA Civ 1359; [2007] N.P.C. 138, CA (Civ Div); reversing [2007] EWHC 913 (Admin); [2007] J.P.L. 1615, QBD (Admin) . . . . *Digested*, 07/**3252**

R. (on the application of Watson) v Dartford Magistrates' Court [2005] EWHC 905 (QB), QBD. . . . . *Considered*, 07/934

R. (on the application of Watts) v Bedford Primary Care Trust (C-372/04) [2006] Q.B. 667; [2006] 3 W.L.R. 213; [2006] All E.R. (EC) 835; [2006] E.C.R. I-4325; [2006] 3 C.M.L.R. 5; [2006] C.E.C. 884; (2006) 90 B.M.L.R. 150; *Times*, May 19, 2006, ECJ . . . . *Digested*, 07/**1981**:
Applied, 07/1632, 07/3977

R. (on the application of Wellington) v Secretary of State for the Home Department [2007] EWHC 1109 (Admin); (2007) 104(24) L.S.G. 28, DC

R. (on the application of Wells) v Parole Board see R. (on the application of Walker) v Secretary of State for the Home Department

R. (on the application of Wells) v Secretary of State for Transport, Local Government and the Regions (C-201/02); *sub nom* Wells v Secretary of State for Transport, Local Government and the Regions (C-201/02) [2005] All E.R. (EC) 323; [2004] E.C.R. I-723; [2004] 1 C.M.L.R. 31; [2004] Env. L.R. 27; [2004] N.P.C. 1, ECJ (5th Chamber) . . . . *Digested*, 04/**1397**:
Applied, 07/3269, 07/3271, 07/3272: *Considered*, 06/3364

R. (on the application of West) v Lloyd's of London [2004] EWCA Civ 506; [2004] 3 All E.R. 251; [2004] 2 All E.R. (Comm) 1; [2004] 2 C.L.C. 649; [2004] H.R.L.R. 27; [2004] Lloyd's Rep. I.R. 755; (2004) 148 S.J.L.B. 537, CA (Civ Div) . . . . . *Digested*, 04/**2221**:
Applied, 07/4193

R. (on the application of West) v Parole Board see R. (on the application of Smith) v Parole Board

R. (on the application of West London Waste Authority) v Mayor of London [2007] EWHC 757 (Admin); [2007] Env. L.R. 27; [2007] J.P.L. 1715, QBD (Admin) . . *Digested*, 07/**1527**

R. (on the application of Western Power Distribution Investments Ltd) v Countryside Council for Wales; *sub nom* Western Power Distribution Investments Ltd v Countryside Council for Wales [2007] EWHC 50 (Admin); [2007] Env. L.R. 25; [2007] N.P.C. 11, QBD (Admin) . . . . *Digested*, 07/**3292**

R. (on the application of Westminster City Council) v National Asylum Support Service; *sub nom* R. (on the application of Westminster City Council) v Secretary of State for the Home Department; Westminster City Council v National Asylum Support Services [2002] UKHL 38; [2002] 1 W.L.R. 2956; [2002] 4 All E.R. 654; [2002] H.L.R. 58; [2003] B.L.G.R. 23; (2002) 5 C.C.L. Rep. 511; (2002) 146 S.J.L.B. 241; *Times*, October 18, 2002, HL; affirming [2001] EWCA Civ 512; (2001) 33 H.L.R. 83; [2001] 4 C.C.L. Rep. 143, CA (Civ Div); affirming [2001] EWHC Admin 138, QBD (Admin) . . . . *Digested*, 02/**4288**:
Applied, 03/2237, 04/2020, 07/2312: *Considered*, 03/4069

R. (on the application of Westminster City Council) v Secretary of State for the Home Department see R. (on the application of Westminster City Council) v National Asylum Support Service

R. (on the application of Widgery Soldiers) v Lord Saville of Newdigate see R. (on the application of A) v Lord Saville of Newdigate (Bloody Sunday Inquiry)

R. (on the application of Williams) v Secretary of State for the Home Department; *sub nom* Williams v Secretary of State for the Home Department [2002] EWCA Civ 498; [2002] 1 W.L.R. 2264; [2002] 4 All E.R. 872; [2002] Prison L.R. 280; (2002) 99(20) L.S.G. 33; (2002) 146 S.J.L.B. 108; *Times*, May 1, 2002; *Independent*, April 24, 2002, CA (Civ Div); reversing [2001] EWHC Admin 516, QBD (Admin) . . . .   *Digested*, 02/**3337**: *Applied*, 07/**2988**

R. (on the application of Williamson) v Secretary of State for Education and Employment; *sub nom* Williamson v Secretary of State for Education and Employment [2005] UKHL 15; [2005] 2 A.C. 246; [2005] 2 W.L.R. 590; [2005] 2 All E.R. 1; [2005] 2 F.L.R. 374; [2005] 1 F.C.R. 498; [2005] H.R.L.R. 14; [2005] U.K.H.R.R. 339; 19 B.H.R.C. 99; [2005] E.L.R. 291; [2005] Fam. Law 456; (2005) 102(16) L.S.G. 27; (2005) 155 N.L.J. 324; (2005) 149 S.J.L.B. 266; *Times*, February 25, 2005; *Independent*, March 1, 2005, HL; affirming [2002] EWCA Civ 1926; [2003] Q.B. 1300; [2003] 3 W.L.R. 482; [2003] 1 All E.R. 385; [2003] 1 F.L.R. 726; [2003] 1 F.C.R. 1; [2003] H.R.L.R. 10; [2003] U.K.H.R.R. 800; [2003] E.L.R. 176; [2003] Fam. Law 227; (2003) 100(9) L.S.G. 27; *Times*, December 18, 2002; *Independent*, December 19, 2002, CA (Civ Div); affirming [2001] EWHC Admin 960; [2002] 1 F.L.R. 493; [2002] H.R.L.R. 14; [2002] E.L.R. 214; [2002] A.C.D. 32; [2002] Fam. Law 257; *Times*, December 12, 2001, QBD (Admin) . . . .   *Digested*, 05/**1019**: *Applied*, 04/4349: *Considered*, 03/1114, 04/1925, 06/1145, 07/1400, 07/2194

R. (on the application of Wilson) v Wychavon DC; *sub nom* Wilson v Wychavon DC [2007] EWCA Civ 52; [2007] Q.B. 801; [2007] 2 W.L.R. 798; [2007] H.R.L.R. 16; [2007] U.K.H.R.R. 835; [2007] B.L.G.R. 540; [2007] 2 P. & C.R. 13; [2007] J.P.L. 1158; [2007] 7 E.G. 142 (C.S.); [2007] N.P.C. 15; *Times*, February 9, 2007, CA (Civ Div); affirming [2005] EWHC 2970 (Admin); [2006] 2 P. & C.R. 24; [2006] J.P.L. 1530; (2006) 103(5) L.S.G. 31; [2005] N.P.C. 151; *Times*, January 18, 2006, QBD (Admin) . . . .   *Digested*, 07/**3293**

R. (on the application of Winchester College) v Hampshire CC C1/2008/0060, CA (Civ Div); reversing [2007] EWHC 2786 (Admin); [2007] N.P.C. 129, QBD (Admin)

R. (on the application of Wright) v Secretary of State for Health; *joined cases* R. (on the application of Jummun) v Secretary of State for Health; R. (on the application of Quinn) v Secretary of State for Health; R. (on the application of Gambier) v Secretary of State for Health [2007] EWCA Civ 999; *Times*, November 16, 2007, CA (Civ Div); reversing in part [2006] EWHC 2886 (Admin); [2007] 1 All E.R. 825; [2007] I.R.L.R. 507; [2007] H.R.L.R. 5; [2007] U.K.H.R.R. 675; (2007) 10 C.C.L. Rep. 34; (2007) 94 B.M.L.R. 160; [2007] A.C.D. 23; *Times*, November 28, 2006; *Independent*, November 22, 2006, QBD (Admin) . . . .   *Digested*, 07/**3915**

R. (on the application of X) v Headteachers and Governors of Y School [2007] EWHC 298 (Admin); [2007] H.R.L.R. 20; [2007] B.L.G.R. 698; [2007] E.L.R. 278, QBD (Admin) . . . .   *Digested*, 07/**2195**: *Considered*, 07/2194

R. (on the application of Y) v Hackney LBC see R. (on the application of AW) v Croydon LBC

R. (on the application of Yogathas) v Secretary of State for the Home Department; *joined case* R. (on the application of Thangarasa) v Secretary of State for the Home Department [2002] UKHL 36; [2003] 1 A.C. 920; [2002] 3 W.L.R. 1276; [2002] 4 All E.R. 800; 14 B.H.R.C. 185; [2003] Imm. A.R. 227; [2002] I.N.L.R. 620; (2002) 146 S.J.L.B. 240; *Times*, October 18, 2002, HL; affirming [2001] EWCA Civ 1611; *Times*, November 15, 2001, CA (Civ Div); affirming [2001] EWHC Admin 377; *Times*, July 25, 2001, QBD (Admin) . . . .   *Digested*, 02/**2595**: *Applied*, 03/2225, 06/2229: *Considered*, 07/2306: *Followed*, 04/2049

RA (Iraq) v Secretary of State for the Home Department; *sub nom* A v Secretary of State for the Home Department [2006] EWCA Civ 1144; [2007] Imm. A.R. 1, CA (Civ Div) . . . .   *Digested*, 07/**2310**

Rabaiotti 1989 Settlement, Re; *sub nom* Latour Trust Co Ltd and Latour Trustees (Jersey) Ltd's Representation, Re [2000] W.T.L.R. 953; (1999-2000) 2 I.T.E.L.R. 763; [2001] Fam. Law 808, Royal Ct (Jer) . . . .   *Digested*, 01/**5512**: *Applied*, 07/4254

RAC Motoring Services Ltd, Re; *sub nom* Royal Automobile Club Ltd, Re [2000] 1 B.C.L.C. 307, Ch D (Companies Ct) . . . .   *Digested*, 00/**676**: *Considered*, 07/2447

Racecourse Association v Office of Fair Trading (Costs) [2006] CAT 1; [2006] Comp. A.R. 438, CAT . . . .   *Digested*, 06/**359**: *Applied*, 07/393

Rachevi v Bulgaria (47877/99) (Unreported, September 23, 2004), ECHR . . . .   *Considered*, 07/2225

Radio Twist AS v Slovakia (62202/00) 22 B.H.R.C. 396, ECHR

Rae v International Insurance Brokers (Nelson Marlborough) Ltd (Unreported) . . . . . .   *Applied*, 07/363

Raglan Housing Association Ltd v Fairclough [2007] EWCA Civ 1087; [2007] 45 E.G. 163 (C.S.); (2007) 104(44) L.S.G. 30; (2007) 151 S.J.L.B. 1436; [2007] N.P.C. 113; *Times*, November 28, 2007, CA (Civ Div) . . . .   *Digested*, 07/**2763**

Raglan Housing Association Ltd v Southampton City Council [2007] EWCA Civ 785; (2007) 157 N.L.J. 1391, CA (Civ Div)

Rahman *v* Arearose Ltd [2001] Q.B. 351; [2000] 3 W.L.R. 1184; (2001) 62 B.M.L.R. 84, CA (Civ Div) . . . . *Applied*, 04/2731, 07/2928

Rai *v* CPS see Blum *v* DPP

Raiffeisen Zentralbank Osterreich AG *v* Commission of the European Communities (T-259/02) [2007] 5 C.M.L.R. 13, CFI (2nd Chamber)

Raja *v* Van Hoogstraten [2007] EWHC 1743 (Ch); *Times*, August 23, 2007, Ch D . . . . *Digested*, 07/**465**

Rajapakse, Re [2007] B.P.I.R. 99, Ch D . . . . *Digested*, 07/**2433**

Ralph Henry Pickett (Deceased), Re see Pickett *v* British Rail Engineering Ltd

Ralph (Setting of Minimum Term), Re; *sub nom* R. *v* Ralph (John Andrew) [2006] EWHC 2966 (QB); [2007] 1 All E.R. 1048, QBD

Ralston *v* Scottish Ministers see Somerville *v* Scottish Ministers

Ramazanova *v* Azerbaijan (44363/02) 22 B.H.R.C. 120, ECHR . . . . *Digested*, 07/**2181**

Ramirez Sanchez *v* France (59450/00) (2007) 45 E.H.R.R. 49, ECHR (Grand Chamber)

Ramos *v* Immigration Appeal Tribunal [1989] Imm. A.R. 148, CA (Civ Div) . . . . *Digested*, 91/**2014**: *Applied*, 00/3356: *Considered*, 07/2325

Ramsay *v* Rivers see Heil *v* Rankin

Ramstedt *v* Riksskatteverket (C-422/01) see Forsakringsaktiebolaget Skandia *v* Riksskatteverket (C-422/01)

Ranbaxy UK Ltd *v* Warner-Lambert Co; *joined case* Arrow Generics Ltd *v* Warner-Lambert Co [2006] EWCA Civ 876; [2007] R.P.C. 4, CA (Civ Div); affirming [2005] EWHC 2142 (Pat); [2006] F.S.R. 14; (2006) 29(1) I.P.D. 29005, Ch D (Patents Ct) . . . . *Digested*, 07/**2554**

Randall (Barry Victor) *v* Queen, The [2002] UKPC 19; [2002] 1 W.L.R. 2237; [2002] 2 Cr. App. R. 17; [2002] Crim. L.R. 928; *Times*, April 24, 2002, PC (CI) . . . . *Digested*, 02/**905**: *Applied*, 07/1027: *Considered*, 06/958

Randhawa *v* Official Receiver; *sub nom* Official Receiver *v* Randhawa [2006] EWHC 2946 (Ch); [2007] 1 W.L.R. 1700; [2007] 1 All E.R. 755; [2006] B.P.I.R. 1435, Ch D . . . . *Digested*, 07/**2418**: *Applied*, 07/2416

Rank Film Distributors Ltd *v* Video Information Centre [1982] A.C. 380; [1981] 2 W.L.R. 668; [1981] 2 All E.R. 76; [1981] Com. L.R. 90; [1981] E.C.C. 365; [1981] F.S.R. 363; *Times*, April 9, 1981, HL; affirming [1980] 3 W.L.R. 487; [1980] 2 All E.R. 273; [1980] F.S.R. 242, CA (Civ Div) . . . . *Digested*, 81/**2148**: *Applied*, 94/3679: *Considered*, 81/2115, 83/574, 83/924, 84/445, 84/2625, 85/888, 86/3414, 93/3211, 94/678, 06/499: *Distinguished*, 87/723, 88/2770: *Explained*, 91/2777: *Followed*, 91/777, 07/855: *Referred to*, 83/2859, 84/2568

Rao *v* Central Liverpool Primary Care Trust [2007] EWHC 773 (QB); [2007] LS Law Medical 319, QBD (Liverpool) . . . . *Digested*, 07/**1959**

Rapiscan Systems Ltd *v* Revenue and Customs Commissioners [2006] EWHC 2067 (QB); [2007] Eu. L.R. 129, QBD . . . . *Digested*, 07/**814**

RAS I Trust, Re (2006-07) 9 I.T.E.L.R. 798, Royal Ct (Jer)

Raschid *v* General Medical Council see Fatnani *v* General Medical Council

Raschid *v* General Medical Council [2006] EWHC 886 (Admin), QBD (Admin) . . . . . *Reversed*, 07/1943

Rasciclal *v* Boyce (Unreported, November 2, 2006), CC (Willesden) [*Ex rel.* Angela Frost, Barrister, 12 King's Bench Walk, London] . . . . *Digested*, 07/**426**

Rashid *v* Secretary of State for the Home Department see R. (on the application of Rashid) *v* Secretary of State for the Home Department

Rasmussen *v* Denmark (8777/79) see Rasmussen *v* Denmark (A/87)

Rasmussen *v* Denmark (A/87); *sub nom* Rasmussen *v* Denmark (8777/79) (1985) 7 E.H.R.R. 371, ECHR (1984) 6 E.H.R.R. CD94, Eur Comm HR . . . . *Applied*, 98/3155, 02/2527, 06/1685, 07/2254

Ratcliffe *v* North Yorkshire CC see British Coal Corp *v* Smith

Ratcliffe *v* North Yorkshire CC; *sub nom* North Yorkshire CC *v* Ratcliffe [1995] 3 All E.R. 597; [1995] I.C.R. 833; [1995] I.R.L.R. 439; (1995) 159 L.G. Rev. 1009; (1995) 145 N.L.J. 1092; (1995) 139 S.J.L.B. 196; *Times*, July 7, 1995; *Independent*, July 7, 1995, HL . . . . *Digested*, 95/**1995**: *Considered*, 07/1360

Ratcliffe *v* Sandwell MBC; *joined case* Lee *v* Leeds City Council [2002] EWCA Civ 6; [2002] 1 W.L.R. 1488; [2002] H.L.R. 17; [2002] B.L.G.R. 305; [2002] 2 P. & C.R. 23; [2002] L. & T.R. 35; [2002] 1 E.G.L.R. 103; (2002) 99(10) L.S.G. 31; (2002) 146 S.J.L.B. 46; [2002] N.P.C. 12; [2003] Env. L.R. D3; *Times*, January 29, 2002, CA (Civ Div); affirming (Unreported, November 2, 2000), CC (Birmingham) [*Ex rel.* Tracy Lakin, Barrister, Victoria Chambers, 177 Corporation Street, Birmingham] . . . . *Digested*, 02/**3059**: *Applied*, 07/2738

Ratel *v* Cecile Holding France [2007] I.L.Pr. 30, Cass (F) . . . . *Digested*, 07/**665**

Ratiopharm GmbH's Trade Mark Application [2007] R.P.C. 28, App Person

Ratten *v* Ultra Vehicle Design Ltd; *sub nom* Ultra Motorhomes International Ltd, Re [2006] EWHC 3415 (Ch); [2007] B.P.I.R. 214, Ch D . . . . *Digested*, 07/**2423**

Ravengate Estates Ltd *v* Horizon Housing Group Ltd [2007] EWCA Civ 1368; [2007] N.P.C. 140, CA (Civ Div)

Ravenhart Service (Holdings) Ltd, Re see Reiner v Gershinson

Ravennavi SpA v New Century Shipbuilding Co Ltd [2007] EWCA Civ 58; [2007] 2 All E.R. (Comm) 756; [2007] 2 Lloyd's Rep. 24; [2007] 1 C.L.C. 176, CA (Civ Div); affirming [2006] EWHC 733 (Comm); [2006] 2 Lloyd's Rep. 280, QBD (Comm) . . . . *Digested*, 07/**3812**

Ravichandran v Secretary of State for the Home Department see R. v Secretary of State for the Home Department Ex p. Jeyeanthan

Rayner v Secretary of State for the Home Department see R. (on the application of Rayner) v Secretary of State for the Home Department

Raytheon Co v Comptroller General of Patents, Designs and Trade Marks [2007] EWHC 1230 (Pat); [2007] Bus. L.R. D98, Ch D (Patents Ct)

RB v Secretary of State for the Home Department; *sub nom* RB (Maintenance: Income Support: Schedules: Morocco), Re [2004] UKIAT 142, IAT . . . . *Considered*, 07/2326

RB (Algeria) v Secretary of State for the Home Department see MT (Algeria) v Secretary of State for the Home Department

RB (Maintenance: Income Support: Schedules: Morocco), Re see RB v Secretary of State for the Home Department

Re-establishment of rights (J17/05) [2006] E.P.O.R. 58, EPO (Legal Bd App) . . . . . . *Digested*, 07/**2603**

Reader v Molesworths Bright Clegg (A Firm) see Reader v Molesworths Bright Clegg Solicitors

Reader v Molesworths Bright Clegg Solicitors; *sub nom* Reader v Molesworths Bright Clegg (A Firm) [2007] EWCA Civ 169; [2007] 1 W.L.R. 1082; [2007] 3 All E.R. 107; [2007] C.P. Rep. 25; [2007] P.N.L.R. 22; (2007) 157 N.L.J. 367; *Times*, April 5, 2007, CA (Civ Div). . . . . *Digested*, 07/**496**

Reading v Bill Chippington Haulage Ltd (Unreported, January 15, 2007), CC (Northampton) [*Ex rel.* Andrew Granvill Stafford, Barrister, 4 King's Bench Walk, Temple, London] . . . . *Digested*, 07/**3161**

Reading BC v D (Angela); *sub nom* BC v A; D, Re [2006] EWHC 1465 (Fam); [2007] 1 W.L.R. 1932; [2007] 1 All E.R. 293; [2006] 2 F.L.R. 1053; [2007] 1 F.C.R. 105; (2006) 92 B.M.L.R. 1; [2006] Fam. Law 738, Fam Div . . . . *Digested*, 07/**1722**

Ready Mixed Concrete (South East) Ltd v Minister of Pensions and National Insurance; *joined cases* Minister for Social Security v Greenham Ready Mixed Concrete Ltd; Minister for Social Security v Ready Mixed Concrete (South East) Ltd [1968] 2 Q.B. 497; [1968] 2 W.L.R. 775; [1968] 1 All E.R. 433; 4 K.I.R. 132; (1967) 112 S.J. 14; *Times*, December 11, 1967, QBD . . . . *Digested*, 68/**2550**:
Applied, 77/1124, 82/1010, 01/2263, 01/2264, 04/2263, 05/1330, 06/4196, 07/4132: *Approved*, 76/871, 78/1116, 04/1315: *Considered*, 69/2338, 82/1011, 01/6467, 01/6468, 05/4128: *Followed*, 71/3945, 76/878

Real Estate Opportunities Ltd v Aberdeen Asset Managers Jersey Ltd [2007] EWCA Civ 197; [2007] Bus. L.R. 971; [2007] 2 All E.R. 791; *Times*, April 6, 2007, CA (Civ Div); affirming [2006] EWHC 3249 (Ch); *Times*, January 23, 2007, Ch D . *Digested*, 07/**439**

Reardon Smith Line v Australian Wheat Board [1956] A.C. 266; [1956] 2 W.L.R. 403; [1956] 1 All E.R. 456; [1956] 1 Lloyd's Rep. 1, PC (Aus); reversing [1953] 1 Lloyd's Rep. 131, Sup Ct (WA) (Full Ct) . . . . *Digested*, 56/**8208**:
Considered, 80/2458, 07/3817: *Not followed*, 54/3086, 55/2559

Reavey v United Kingdom (34640/04) see Brecknell v United Kingdom (32457/04)

Rechnungshof v Osterreichischer Rundfunk (C-465/00) [2003] E.C.R. I-4989; [2003] 3 C.M.L.R. 10, ECJ. . . . . *Digested*, 04/**1206**:
Applied, 07/1552

Reckitt & Colman Products Ltd v Borden Inc (No.3); *sub nom* Jif Lemon case [1990] 1 W.L.R. 491; [1990] 1 All E.R. 873; [1990] R.P.C. 341; (1990) 134 S.J. 784; *Times*, February 9, 1990; *Independent*, March 13, 1990; *Guardian*, February 13, 1990, HL; affirming [1988] F.S.R. 601; (1988) 8 Tr. L.R. 97; *Times*, April 23, 1988; *Independent*, April 25, 1988; *Guardian*, April 26, 1988; *Daily Telegraph*, April 28, 1988, CA (Civ Div); affirming [1987] F.S.R. 505, Ch D . . . . *Digested*, 90/**3465**:
Applied, 93/3802, 00/3590, 02/2785, 07/2546: *Considered*, 95/4739, 96/5715, 07/2674: *Distinguished*, 95/4735: *Followed*, 96/6663:
Referred to, 99/3593

Reckitt & Colman Products Ltd v Richardson-Vicks Inc see Richardson-Vicks Inc's Patent

Redbus LMDS Ltd v Jeffrey Green & Russell (A Firm) [2006] EWHC 2938 (Ch); [2007] P.N.L.R. 12, Ch D . . . . *Digested*, 07/**2944**

Redcar and Cleveland BC v Bainbridge [2007] EWCA Civ 929; [2007] I.R.L.R. 984; (2007) 104(39) L.S.G. 32; *Times*, November 28, 2007, CA (Civ Div); affirming [2007] I.R.L.R. 91, EAT . . . . *Digested*, 07/**1366**:
Distinguished, 07/1364

Redcar and Cleveland BC v Williams see Bainbridge v Redcar and Cleveland BC

Redrow Plc v Pedley [2002] EWHC 983 (Ch); [2003] O.P.L.R. 29; [2002] Pens. L.R. 339, Ch D . . . . *Digested*, 03/**3082**:
Applied, 07/3043: *Considered*, 06/2993

Redworth Construction Ltd v Brookdale Healthcare Ltd [2006] EWHC 1994 (TCC); [2006] B.L.R. 366; 110 Con. L.R. 77; [2006] C.I.L.L. 2373, QBD (TCC) . . . . . *Digested*, 06/**667**

Reed Employment Plc *v* M Gaze & Co Ltd (Unreported, November 9, 2006), CC (Norwich) [*Ex rel.* Shona Harvey, Barrister, Octagon Chambers, 19 Colegate, Norwich] . . . .   *Digested,* 07/**424**

Reed Executive Plc *v* Reed Business Information Ltd (Costs: Alternative Dispute Resolution) [2004] EWCA Civ 887; [2004] 1 W.L.R. 3026; [2004] 4 All E.R. 942; [2005] C.P. Rep. 4; [2004] 4 Costs L.R. 662; [2005] F.S.R. 3; (2004) 27(7) I.P.D. 27067; (2004) 148 S.J.L.B. 881; *Times,* July 16, 2004, CA (Civ Div) . . . .   *Digested,* 04/**266**: *Considered,* 07/1078

REEF Trade Mark; *sub nom* Bessant *v* South Cone Inc; South Cone Inc *v* Bessant (t/a REEF) [2002] EWCA Civ 763; [2003] R.P.C. 5; *Times,* May 31, 2002, CA (Civ Div); reversing [2002] R.P.C. 19; (2001) 24(11) I.P.D. 24072; (2001) 98(38) L.S.G. 39; [2001] E.T.M.R. CN19; *Times,* October 9, 2001, Ch D . . . .   *Digested,* 02/**2897**: *Applied,* 02/2859, 05/2568, 07/2684: *Followed,* 02/2861

Reemtsma Cigarettenfabriken GmbH *v* Ministero delle Finanze (C-35/05) [2007] 2 C.M.L.R. 34; [2007] S.T.I. 543, ECJ (2nd Chamber)

Rees *v* Mabco (102) Ltd (Non-Pecuniary Damages) see Heil *v* Rankin

Reeves *v* Sprecher [2007] EWHC 117 (Ch); [2007] 2 B.C.L.C. 614, Ch D

Reeves (Valuation Officer), Re [2007] R.A. 168, Lands Tr

Refco Inc *v* Eastern Trading Co [1999] 1 Lloyd's Rep. 159, CA (Civ Div) . . . .   *Digested,* 98/**563**: *Considered,* 00/490, 07/437

Refusal of Social Security Benefits, Re (CIS/3182/2005) [2007] 2 C.M.L.R. 9, SS Comm   *Digested,* 07/**3868**

Regan *v* Paul Properties Ltd [2006] EWCA Civ 1391; [2007] Ch. 135; [2006] 3 W.L.R. 1131; [2007] 4 All E.R. 48; [2007] B.L.R. 56; [2007] 2 P. & C.R. 14; [2006] 3 E.G.L.R. 94; [2006] 46 E.G. 210; [2007] C.I.L.L. 2411; [2006] 44 E.G. 197 (C.S.); (2006) 103(43) L.S.G. 27; [2007] 2 P. & C.R. DG5, CA (Civ Div); reversing [2006] EWHC 1941 (Ch), Ch D . . . .   *Digested,* 07/**2962**

Regent Co *v* Ukraine (773/03) (2007) 45 E.H.R.R. SE8, ECHR

Regent Leisuretime Ltd *v* Skerrett [2006] EWCA Civ 1184; [2007] P.N.L.R. 9, CA (Civ Div); affirming [2005] EWHC 2255 (QB), QBD . . . .   *Digested,* 07/**2949**

Regent Leisuretime Ltd *v* Skerrett (Wasted Costs) [2006] EWCA Civ 1032; [2006] C.P. Rep. 42; (2006) 103(29) L.S.G. 29; (2006) 150 S.J.L.B. 918, CA (Civ Div) . . . .   *Digested,* 07/**427**

Regent Security Services Ltd *v* Power see Power *v* Regent Security Services Ltd

REGENTS OF THE UNIVERSITY OF CALIFORNIA/Endovascular electrolytically detachable guidewire tip (T1208/05) [2007] E.P.O.R. 51, EPO (Technical Bd App)

Regione Siciliana *v* Commission of the European Communities (C-15/06 P) [2007] 2 C.M.L.R. 32, ECJ (5th Chamber) . . . .   *Digested,* 07/**1591**

Regione Siciliana *v* Commission of the European Communities (C-417/04 P) [2006] E.C.R. I-3881; [2006] 2 C.M.L.R. 64, ECJ . . . .   *Digested,* 07/**1647**: *Applied,* 07/1591

Regione Toscana *v* Commission of the European Communities (C-180/97) [1997] E.C.R. I-5245, ECJ . . . .   *Followed,* 00/2408, 07/1647

Regus (UK) Ltd *v* Epcot Solutions Ltd A3/2007/1092, CA (Civ Div); reversing [2007] EWHC 938 (Comm); [2007] 2 All E.R. (Comm) 766, QBD (Merc) . . . .   *Digested,* 07/**794**

Rehman *v* Benfield [2006] EWCA Civ 1392; [2007] 2 P. & C.R. 16; [2006] N.P.C. 118, CA (Civ Div) . . . .   *Digested,* 07/**3355**

Reichling *v* Institut National d'Assurance Maladie-Invalidite (INAMI) (C-406/93) [1994] E.C.R. I-4061, ECJ . . . .   *Digested,* 95/**4626**: *Applied,* 07/1626

Reichman *v* Beveridge; *sub nom* Reichman *v* Gauntlett [2006] EWCA Civ 1659; [2007] Bus. L.R. 412; [2007] 1 P. & C.R. 20; [2007] L. & T.R. 18; [2007] 8 E.G. 138; [2007] 1 E.G. 92 (C.S.); (2007) 104(4) L.S.G. 35; [2006] N.P.C. 132; *Times,* January 4, 2007, CA (Civ Div) . . . .   *Digested,* 07/**2726**

Reichman *v* Gauntlett see Reichman *v* Beveridge

Reigate and Banstead BC *v* Benfield see R. (on the application of McLellan) *v* Bracknell Forest BC

Reiner *v* Gershinson; *sub nom* Ravenhart Service (Holdings) Ltd, Re [2004] EWHC 76 (Ch); [2004] 2 B.C.L.C. 376, Ch D (Companies Ct) . . . .   *Digested,* 04/**457**: *Applied,* 07/456

Reinprecht *v* Austria (67175/01) (2007) 44 E.H.R.R. 39, ECHR. . . . .   *Digested,* 07/**2232**

Reinwood Ltd *v* L Brown & Sons Ltd 116 Con. L.R. 1, HL; affirming [2007] EWCA Civ 601; [2007] 1 C.L.C. 959; [2007] B.L.R. 305; 114 Con. L.R. 211; [2007] C.I.L.L. 2486; (2007) 151 S.J.L.B. 855, CA (Civ Div); reversing [2007] B.L.R. 10; [2007] C.I.L.L. 2413, QBD (TCC) . . . .   *Digested,* 07/**743**

Reisch *v* Burgermeister der Landeshauptstadt Salzburg (C-515/99) [2002] E.C.R. I-2157; [2004] 1 C.M.L.R. 44, ECJ (6th Chamber). . . . .   *Digested,* 04/**3258**: *Applied,* 07/1602: *Followed,* 06/3504

Reisch Montage AG *v* Kiesel Baumaschinen Handels GmbH (C-103/05) [2006] E.C.R. I-6827; [2007] I.L.Pr. 10, ECJ (2nd Chamber). . . . .   *Digested,* 07/**657**

Remia BV *v* Commission of the European Communities (42/84) [1985] E.C.R. 2545; [1987] 1 C.M.L.R. 1; [1987] F.S.R. 190, ECJ (5th Chamber) . . . .   *Digested,* 87/**1503**: *Applied,* 05/549, 07/1550

Remice v Governor of Belmarsh Prison [2007] EWHC 936 (Admin); [2007] Crim.
L.R. 796; [2007] A.C.D. 76, QBD (Admin)
Rennie v Westbury Homes (Holdings) Ltd [2007] EWCA Civ 1401, CA (Civ Div);
affirming [2007] EWHC 164 (Ch); [2007] 2 P. & C.R. 12; [2007] 20 E.G. 296;
[2007] N.P.C. 16, Ch D . . . .   *Digested*, 07/**807**
Rent Service v Heffernan see R. (on the application of Heffernan) v Rent Service
Reprotech (Pebsham) Ltd v East Sussex CC see R. (on the application of Reprotech
(Pebsham) Ltd) v East Sussex CC
Research in Motion UK Ltd v Inpro Licensing Sarl [2007] EWCA Civ 51; [2007] Info.
T.L.R. 1; (2007) 30(3) I.P.D. 30017; (2007) 104(8) L.S.G. 37, CA (Civ Div);
affirming [2006] EWHC 70 (Pat); [2006] R.P.C. 20; (2006) 29(4) I.P.D.
29036, Ch D (Patents Ct) . . . .   *Digested*, 07/**2620**:
Applied, 07/2632: *Considered*, 07/2615
Research in Motion UK Ltd v Visto Corp [2007] EWHC 1921 (Pat); (2007) 30(10) I.P.D.
30066, Ch D (Patents Ct)
Retail Systems Technology Ltd v McGuire [2007] IEHC 13; [2007] E.C.D.R. 14, HC (Irl)
Retirement Care Group Ltd v Revenue and Customs Commissioners [2007] S.T.C.
(S.C.D.) 539, Sp Comm . . . .   *Digested*, 07/**4079**
Reunion Europeenne SA v Spliethoff's Bevrachtingskantoor BV (C51/97) [2000] Q.B.
690; [2000] 3 W.L.R. 1213; [1998] E.C.R. I-6511; [1999] C.L.C. 282; [1999]
I.L.Pr. 205; *Times*, November 16, 1998, ECJ (3rd Chamber) . . . .   *Digested*, 98/**769**:
Applied, 04/559, 05/470: *Considered*, 06/630, 07/657: *Followed*, 01/4290
Revenue and Customs Commissioners v Bank of Ireland Britain Holdings Ltd A3/2007/
1074, CA (Civ Div); affirming [2007] EWHC 941 (Ch); [2007] B.T.C. 389;
[2007] S.T.I. 1397, Ch D; affirming [2006] S.T.C. (S.C.D.) 477; [2006] S.T.I.
1793, Sp Comm . . . .   *Digested*, 07/**4147**
Revenue and Customs Commissioners v Barclays Bank Plc see Barclays Bank Plc v
Revenue and Customs Commissioners
Revenue and Customs Commissioners v Berriman; *joined case* R. (on the application of
Revenue and Customs Commissioners) v Teesside Crown Court [2007] EWHC
1183 (Admin); [2007] 4 All E.R. 925, DC . . . .   *Digested*, 07/**1048**
Revenue and Customs Commissioners v BUPA Purchasing Ltd see BUPA Purchasing
Ltd v Revenue and Customs Commissioners
Revenue and Customs Commissioners v Church of Scientology Religious Education
College Inc [2007] EWHC 1329 (Ch); [2007] S.T.C. 1196; [2007] B.T.C. 5796;
[2007] B.V.C. 743; [2007] S.T.I. 1690, Ch D . . . .   *Digested*, 07/**446**
Revenue and Customs Commissioners v Crossman [2007] EWHC 1585 (Ch); [2007]
B.P.I.R. 1068, Ch D . . . .   *Digested*, 07/**2413**
Revenue and Customs Commissioners v D'Arcy; *sub nom* D'Arcy v Revenue and
Customs Commissioners [2007] EWHC 163 (Ch); [2007] B.T.C. 257; [2007]
S.T.I. 337, Ch D; affirming [2006] S.T.C. (S.C.D.) 543; [2006] S.T.I. 1856, Sp
Comm . . . .   *Digested*, 07/**4102**
Revenue and Customs Commissioners v Decadt [2007] EWHC 1659 (Ch); [2007]
B.T.C. 586; [2007] S.T.I. 1434; *Times*, June 4, 2007, Ch D . . . .   *Digested*, 07/**4057**
Revenue and Customs Commissioners v Dempster (t/a Boulevard); *sub nom* Dempster
(t/a Boulevard) v Revenue and Customs Commissioners; CH/2007/APP/0380,
Ch D; affirming [2007] S.T.I. 2242, V&DTr (London)
Revenue and Customs Commissioners v Denyer see Denyer v Revenue and Customs
Commissioners
Revenue and Customs Commissioners v Dunwood Travel Ltd see Dunwood Travel Ltd v
Revenue and Customs Commissioners
Revenue and Customs Commissioners v EB Central Services Ltd (formerly Excess
Baggage Plc) see EB Central Services Ltd v Revenue and Customs
Commissioners
Revenue and Customs Commissioners v Egleton [2006] EWHC 2313 (Ch); [2007]
Bus. L.R. 44; [2007] 1 All E.R. 606; [2007] B.C.C. 78; [2006] S.T.I. 2233;
(2006) 103(38) L.S.G. 35; (2006) 150 S.J.L.B. 1252, Ch D . . . .   *Digested*, 07/**456**
Revenue and Customs Commissioners v Empowerment Enterprises Ltd see
Empowerment Enterprises Ltd v Customs and Excise Commissioners
Revenue and Customs Commissioners v Facilities & Maintenance Engineering Ltd
[2006] EWHC 689 (Ch); [2006] S.T.C. 1887; 77 T.C. 575; [2007] B.T.C. 231;
[2006] S.T.I. 1149; *Times*, April 18, 2006, Ch D . . . .   *Digested*, 06/**4136**
Revenue and Customs Commissioners v Gracechurch Management Services Ltd see
Gracechurch Management Services Ltd v Revenue and Customs
Commissioners
Revenue and Customs Commissioners v Household Estate Agents Ltd [2007] EWHC
1684 (Ch); [2007] S.T.I. 1815, Ch D
Revenue and Customs Commissioners v Isle of Wight Council see Isle of Wight Council
v Revenue and Customs Commissioners
Revenue and Customs Commissioners v Kearney [2007] EWHC 640 (Admin), DC . . .   *Considered*, 07/950
Revenue and Customs Commissioners v La Senza Ltd [2006] EWHC 1331 (Ch);
[2007] S.T.C. 901; [2006] S.T.I. 1148, Ch D . . . .   *Digested*, 07/**4160**

Revenue and Customs Commissioners *v* Leisure Employment Services Ltd; *sub nom* Leisure Employment Services Ltd *v* Revenue and Customs Commissioners [2007] EWCA Civ 92; [2007] I.C.R. 1056; [2007] I.R.L.R. 450; *Times*, March 7, 2007, CA (Civ Div); affirming [2006] I.C.R. 1094; *Times*, May 17, 2006, EAT. . . *Digested*, 07/**1383**

Revenue and Customs Commissioners *v* Limitgood Ltd see Limitgood Ltd *v* Revenue and Customs Commissioners

Revenue and Customs Commissioners *v* Longborough Festival Opera (Leave to Appeal) see Bournemouth Symphony Orchestra *v* Revenue and Customs Commissioners

Revenue and Customs Commissioners *v* Loyalty Management UK Ltd; *sub nom* Loyalty Management UK Ltd *v* Revenue and Customs Commissioners; Customs and Excise Commissioners *v* Loyalty Management UK Ltd [2007] EWCA Civ 965; [2007] B.T.C. 5854; [2007] B.V.C. 823; [2007] S.T.I. 2230; (2007) 151 S.J.L.B. 1300; *Times*, October 10, 2007, CA (Civ Div); reversing [2006] EWHC 1498 (Ch); [2007] S.T.C. 536; [2006] B.T.C. 5706; [2006] B.V.C. 776; [2006] S.T.I. 1792, Ch D [2005] B.V.C. 2628; [2005] V. & D.R. 377, V&DTr (London) . . . . . *Digested*, 07/**4310**

Revenue and Customs Commissioners *v* Maco Door & Window Hardware (UK) Ltd see Maco Door and Window Hardware (UK) Ltd *v* Revenue and Customs Commissioners

Revenue and Customs Commissioners *v* Mayor [2007] EWHC 3147 (Ch); [2007] S.T.I. 1774, Ch D

Revenue and Customs Commissioners *v* Mobilix Ltd [2007] S.T.C. 443, Ch D

Revenue and Customs Commissioners *v* Oriel Support Ltd [2006] EWHC 3217 (Ch); [2007] S.T.C. 1148; [2007] B.T.C. 465; [2007] S.T.I. 111, Ch D . . . . *Digested*, 07/**3997**

Revenue and Customs Commissioners *v* Pal (t/a Tapas Bar Cerveceria) see Pal (t/a Tapas Bar Cerveceria) *v* Revenue and Customs Commissioners

Revenue and Customs Commissioners *v* Peter Clay Discretionary Trust Trustees see Peter Clay Discretionary Trust Trustees *v* Revenue and Customs Commissioners

Revenue and Customs Commissioners *v* Premier Foods Ltd; *sub nom* Premier Foods (Holdings Ltd) *v* Revenue and Customs Commissioners [2007] EWHC 3134 (Ch); [2007] S.T.I. 2462, Ch D; reversing [2007] S.T.I. 1697, V&DTr

Revenue and Customs Commissioners *v* Prizedome Ltd see Limitgood Ltd *v* Revenue and Customs Commissioners

Revenue and Customs Commissioners *v* RBS Deutschland Holdings GmbH [2006] CSIH 10; [2007] S.T.C. 814; 2006 S.C. 515; 2006 S.L.T. 615; [2006] Eu. L.R. 917; [2007] B.T.C. 5980; [2006] S.T.I. 578; 2006 G.W.D. 19-387, IH (Ex Div) . . *Digested*, 06/**5131**

Revenue and Customs Commissioners *v* Robertson's Electrical Ltd see Robertson's Electrical Ltd *v* Customs and Excise Commissioners

Revenue and Customs Commissioners *v* RSPCA see RSPCA *v* Revenue and Customs Commissioners

Revenue and Customs Commissioners *v* Seymour Caravan Sales Ltd see Seymour Caravan Sales Ltd *v* Revenue and Customs Commissioners

Revenue and Customs Commissioners *v* Smallwood see Smallwood *v* Revenue and Customs Commissioners

Revenue and Customs Commissioners *v* Smith; *sub nom* Customs and Excise Commissioners *v* Smith [2006] EWHC 3435 (Ch), Ch D . . . . *Followed*, 07/1041

Revenue and Customs Commissioners *v* Smith [2007] EWHC 488 (Ch); 78 T.C. 424; [2007] S.T.I. 537, Ch D

Revenue and Customs Commissioners *v* Stringer (Reference to ECJ) see Inland Revenue Commissioners *v* Ainsworth (Reference to ECJ)

Revenue and Customs Commissioners *v* Tallington Lakes Ltd [2007] EWHC 1955 (Ch); [2007] S.T.I. 2019; [2007] S.T.I. 2063, Ch D

Revenue and Customs Commissioners *v* Thompson [2005] EWHC 3388; [2007] S.T.C. 240; [2005] S.T.I. 1812; *Times*, January 4, 2006, Ch D

Revenue and Customs Commissioners *v* Thorn Baker Ltd [2007] EWCA Civ 626; (2007) 104(28) L.S.G. 29; (2007) 151 S.J.L.B. 890; *Times*, July 27, 2007, CA (Civ Div); affirming (Unreported, July 14, 2006), Ch D . . . . *Digested*, 07/**3901**

Revenue and Customs Commissioners *v* Total Network SL see Customs and Excise Commissioners *v* Total Network SL

Revenue and Customs Commissioners *v* Total UK Ltd see Total UK Ltd *v* Revenue and Customs Commissioners

Revenue and Customs Commissioners *v* ToTel Ltd see RSPCA *v* Revenue and Customs Commissioners

Revenue and Customs Commissioners *v* UBS AG see UBS AG *v* Revenue and Customs Commissioners

Revenue and Customs Commissioners *v* Valentine Marketing Holdings Ltd [2006] EWHC 2820 (Ch); [2007] S.T.C. 1631; 78 T.C. 413; [2006] S.T.I. 2504, Ch D . . *Digested*, 07/**4096**

Revenue and Customs Commissioners *v* Vodafone 2 see Vodafone 2 *v* Revenue and Customs Commissioners

Revenue and Customs Commissioners *v* Weald Leasing Ltd see Weald Leasing Ltd *v* Revenue and Customs Commissioners

Revenue and Customs Commissioners *v* Weller; *sub nom* Customs and Excise Commissioners *v* Weller [2006] EWHC 237 (Ch); [2006] V. & D.R. 163, Ch D . *Digested*, 07/**1041**: *Considered*, 07/1042

Revenue and Customs Commissioners v William Grant & Sons Distillers Ltd (Scotland); *sub nom* William Grant & Sons Distillers Ltd v Inland Revenue Commissioners; Inland Revenue Commissioners v William Grant & Sons Distillers Ltd; *joined case* Small (Inspector of Taxes) v Mars UK Ltd [2007] UKHL 15; [2007] 1 W.L.R. 1448; [2007] 2 All E.R. 440; [2007] S.T.C. 680; 2007 S.C. (H.L.) 105; 2007 S.L.T. 522; 2007 S.C.L.R. 468; 78 T.C. 442; [2007] B.T.C. 315; [2007] S.T.I. 1165; (2007) 151 S.J.L.B. 470; 2007 G.W.D. 17-306; *Times*, April 2, 2007, HL; reversing [2005] CSIH 63; [2006] S.T.C. 69; 2006 S.C. 17; 2005 S.L.T. 888; [2005] B.T.C. 483; [2005] S.T.I. 1647; 2005 G.W.D. 29-536, IH (Ex Div) . . . . .   *Digested,* 07/**4019**

Revenue and Customs Commissioners v Wood; *sub nom* Wood v Revenue and Customs Commissioners [2007] S.T.I. 105, Ch D

Revenue and Customs Commissioners v Wright [2007] EWHC 526 (Ch); [2007] S.T.C. 1684; [2007] B.T.C. 596; [2007] S.T.I. 337, Ch D . . . .   *Digested,* 07/**4073**

Revenue and Customs Commissioners v Zurich Insurance Co see Zurich Insurance Co v Revenue and Customs Commissioners

Revenue and Customs Commissioners Application (Section 20 Notice: Financial Institution No.1), Re (SpC 580) [2007] S.T.C. (S.C.D) 202; [2007] W.T.L.R. 777; [2007] S.T.I. 351, Sp Comm . . . .   *Digested,* 07/**4086**

Revenue and Customs Commissioners Application (Section 20 Notice: Financial Institution No.2), Re (SpC 581) [2007] S.T.C. (S.C.D.) 208; [2007] S.T.I. 295, Sp Comm . . . .   *Digested,* 07/**4087**

Revenue and Customs Commissioners Application (Section 20 Notice: Financial Institution No.3), Re (SpC 582) [2007] S.T.C. (S.C.D.) 216; [2007] S.T.I. 297, Sp Comm

Revenue and Customs Commissioners Application (Section 20 Notice: Financial Institution No.4), Re (SpC 583) [2007] S.T.C. (S.C.D.) 222; [2007] S.T.I. 352, Sp Comm

Revenue and Customs Commissioners Application (Section 20(1) Notice: Subsidiary Co), Re (SpC 647) see Revenue and Customs Commissioners Application (Section 20(3) Notice: Plc), Re (SpC 647)

Revenue and Customs Commissioners Application (Section 20(3) Notice: Plc), Re (SpC 647); *sub nom* Revenue and Customs Commissioners Application (Section 20(1) Notice: Subsidiary Co), Re (SpC 647) [2007] S.T.I. 2851, Sp Comm

Revenue and Customs Commissioners, Petitioners; *sub nom* Inland Revenue Commissioners, Petitioners; R. (on the application of Inland Revenue Commissioners) v Aberdeen General Commissioners of Income Tax; Advocate General for Scotland v General Commissioners for Aberdeen City [2005] CSOH 135; [2006] S.T.C. 1218; 2005 S.L.T. 1061; 77 T.C. 391; [2006] B.T.C. 846; [2005] S.T.I. 1755; 2005 G.W.D. 33-634, OH . . . .   *Digested,* 06/**5702**: *Considered,* 07/4001

Revenue and Customs Prosecution Office v Stokoe Partnership [2007] EWHC 1588 (Admin); [2007] A.C.D. 84, QBD (Admin)

Revenue and Customs Prosecutions Office v Briggs-Price [2007] EWCA Civ 568; (2007) 104(26) L.S.G. 32, CA (Civ Div)

Revitt v DPP; *joined cases* Borg v DPP; Barnes v DPP [2006] EWHC 2266 (Admin); [2006] 1 W.L.R. 3172; [2007] 1 Cr. App. R. 19; (2006) 170 J.P. 729; [2007] R.T.R. 23; [2007] Crim. L.R. 238; (2007) 171 J.P.N. 251; (2006) 156 N.L.J. 1476; *Times*, September 14, 2006, QBD (Admin) . . . .   *Digested,* 06/**969**

Revival Properties Ltd v Edinburgh City Council see Edinburgh City Council v Secretary of State for Scotland

Rewe Zentralfinanz eG v Finanzamt Koln-Mitte (C-347/04) [2007] 2 C.M.L.R. 42; [2007] S.T.I. 1169, ECJ (2nd Chamber)

Rewe Zentralfinanz eG v Landwirtschaftskammer fur das Saarland (33/76) [1976] E.C.R. 1989; [1977] 1 C.M.L.R. 533, ECJ . . . .   *Digested,* 77/**1248**: *Applied,* 00/2406, 00/4462, 07/1641: *Considered,* 95/2112: *Referred to,* 97/3983

Rey v FNCB Ltd [2006] EWHC 1386 (Ch); [2006] B.P.I.R. 1260; [2006] N.P.C. 71, Ch D . . . .   *Digested,* 07/**2459**

Reynolds v Times Newspapers Ltd [2001] 2 A.C. 127; [1999] 3 W.L.R. 1010; [1999] 4 All E.R. 609; [2000] E.M.L.R. 1; [2000] H.R.L.R. 134; 7 B.H.R.C. 289; (1999) 96(45) L.S.G. 34; (1999) 149 N.L.J. 1697; (1999) 143 S.J.L.B. 270; *Times*, October 29, 1999; *Independent*, November 3, 1999, HL; affirming [1998] 3 W.L.R. 862; [1998] 3 All E.R. 961; [1998] E.M.L.R. 723; (1998) 95(32) L.S.G. 30; (1998) 148 N.L.J. 1051; (1998) 142 S.J.L.B. 218; *Times*, July 9, 1998; *Independent*, July 14, 1998, CA (Civ Div) . . . .   *Digested,* 99/**1630**: *Applied,* 99/1625, 00/1761, 00/1763, 01/1823, 01/1829, 01/1831, 02/953, 02/959, 04/935, 05/980, 06/1047, 06/1051, 07/1075, 07/1076: *Considered,* 01/1824, 01/1832, 01/1834, 05/973, 05/977, 06/1049, 06/1050: *Distinguished,* 06/1044: *Followed,* 99/1626, 02/960

RG (Ethiopia) v Secretary of State for the Home Department [2006] EWCA Civ 339; [2006] I.N.L.R. 379, CA (Civ Div) . . . .   *Digested,* 07/**2303**

RH v United Bristol Healthcare NHS Trust [2007] EWHC 1441 (QB); [2007] LS Law Medical 535, QBD . . . .   *Digested,* 07/**3065**

RH (Para 289A/HC395: No Discretion: Bangladesh), Re [2006] UKAIT 43, AIT . . . . .   *Disapproved,* 07/2353

RHJ Ltd *v* FT Patten (Holdings) Ltd A3/7007/1795/CHANF, CA (Civ Div); affirming
[2007] EWHC 1655 (Ch); [2007] 4 All E.R. 744; [2007] 44 E.G. 182; [2007] 29
E.G. 143 (C.S.); [2007] N.P.C. 90, Ch D .... *Digested,* 07/**2757**
Rhodia International Holdings Ltd *v* Huntsman International LLC [2007] EWHC 292
(Comm); [2007] 2 All E.R. (Comm) 577; [2007] 2 Lloyd's Rep. 325; [2007] 1
C.L.C. 59; [2007] Bus. L.R. D22; *Times,* April 6, 2007, QBD (Comm)........ *Digested,* 07/**786**
Rhondda Cynon Taff CBC *v* Watkins; *sub nom* Watkins *v* Rhondda Cynon Taff BC
[2003] EWCA Civ 129; [2003] 1 W.L.R. 1864; [2003] 2 P. & C.R. 19; [2003] 1
E.G.L.R. 117; [2003] R.V.R. 224; [2003] 8 E.G. 130 (C.S.); [2003] N.P.C. 20,
CA (Civ Div); reversing PD000191, Ch D .... *Digested,* 03/**3548**:
Considered, 07/51
Rhone Poulenc SA *v* Commission of the European Communities (T-1/89) [1991] E.C.R.
II-867, CFI (1st Chamber) .... *Digested,* 92/**4712**:
Applied, 01/760: *Considered,* 07/1551
Rhone-Poulenc Rorer International Holdings Inc *v* Yeda Research & Development Co
Ltd; *sub nom* Yeda Research & Development Co Ltd *v* Rhone-Poulenc Rorer
International Holdings Inc [2007] UKHL 43; [2007] Bus. L.R. 1796; (2007)
104(43) L.S.G. 31; (2007) 151 S.J.L.B. 1402; *Times,* October 30, 2007, HL;
reversing [2006] EWCA Civ 1094; [2007] Bus. L.R. 1; [2007] R.P.C. 9; (2007)
30(1) I.P.D. 30001; *Times,* September 5, 2006, CA (Civ Div); affirming [2006]
EWHC 160 (Pat); [2006] R.P.C. 24; (2006) 29(3) I.P.D. 29026, Ch D (Patents
Ct) .... *Digested,* 07/**2557**:
Considered, 07/2623
Rialas *v* Mitchell (1984) 128 S.J. 704, CA (Civ Div) .... *Digested,* 84/**1013**:
Applied, 05/3072: *Considered,* 07/3062
Ribitsch *v* Austria (A/336) (1996) 21 E.H.R.R. 573, ECHR .... *Digested,* 96/**3138**:
Applied, 07/2203
Rice *v* Secretary of State for Trade and Industry; *joined case* Thompson *v* Secretary of
State for Trade and Industry [2007] EWCA Civ 289; [2007] I.C.R. 1469; [2007]
P.I.Q.R. P23; (2007) 104(16) L.S.G. 23; (2007) 151 S.J.L.B. 469, CA (Civ
Div); affirming [2006] EWHC 1257 (QB), QBD .... *Digested,* 07/**2939**
Rice's Application for Judicial Review, Re [1998] N.I. 265, CA (NI) .... *Digested,* 99/**5206**:
Considered, 07/4518
Richard *v* United Kingdom (63475/00) see Hobbs *v* United Kingdom (63684/00)
Richard Parsons Ltd *v* Bristol City Council [2007] 47 E.G. 174; [2007] R.V.R. 341,
Lands Tr
Richards *v* Buckle (Unreported, September 12, 2006), CC (Stockport) [*Ex rel.* David
Calvert, Barrister, St James's Chambers, 68 Quay Street, Manchester] .... *Digested,* 07/**3110**
Richards *v* Somerset CC (Renewed Application for Permission to Appeal) [2006]
EWCA Civ 350; [2006] R.V.R. 232, CA (Civ Div) .... *Digested,* 07/**3387**
Richards *v* Swansea NHS Trust [2007] EWHC 487 (QB); (2007) 96 B.M.L.R. 180,
QBD .... *Digested,* 07/**2929**
Richardson *v* Blackmore; *joined case* Capital Cabs Ltd *v* Blackmore [2005] EWCA Civ
1356; [2006] B.C.C. 276, CA (Civ Div); affirming (Unreported, November 1,
2004), Ch D .... *Digested,* 07/**594**
Richardson *v* MacNab (Unreported, April 20, 1999), CA...................... *Applied,* 07/3365
Richardson *v* U Mole Ltd [2005] I.C.R. 1664; [2005] I.R.L.R. 668, EAT .... *Digested,* 06/**1391**:
Applied, 07/1349, 07/1399
Richardson *v* Watson [2006] EWCA Civ 1662; [2007] C.P. Rep. 13; [2007] R.T.R. 21;
[2007] P.I.Q.R. P18; *Times,* December 13, 2006, CA (Civ Div) .... *Digested,* 07/**445**
Richardson-Vicks Inc's Patent; *sub nom* Reckitt & Colman Products Ltd *v* Richardson-
Vicks Inc [1997] R.P.C. 888; (1997) 20(8) I.P.D. 20075, CA (Civ Div); affirming
[1995] R.P.C. 568, Ch D (Patents Ct)......................... *Digested,* 98/**3453**:
Applied, 07/2629: *Referred to,* 99/3466
Richco International Ltd *v* International Industries Food Co SAL (The Fayrouz III)
[1989] 1 All E.R. 613; [1989] 2 Lloyd's Rep. 106; (1988) 138 N.L.J. Rep. 271;
Financial Times, July 13, 1988, QBD (Comm) .... *Digested,* 90/**198**:
Distinguished, 07/241
Richmond *v* Burch [2006] EWHC 921 (Ch); [2007] 1 All E.R. 658, Ch D .... *Digested,* 07/**434**
Richmond Adult Community College *v* McDougall A2/2007/19/13, CA (Civ Div);
affirming [2007] I.C.R. 1567; [2007] I.R.L.R. 771, EAT
Richmond Court (Swansea) Ltd *v* Williams; *sub nom* Williams *v* Richmond Court
(Swansea) Ltd [2006] EWCA Civ 1719; [2007] H.L.R. 22; [2007] 1 P. & C.R.
21; [2007] L. & T.R. 19; [2007] 9 E.G. 204; (2007) 151 S.J.L.B. 26; *Times,*
December 29, 2006, CA (Civ Div) .... *Digested,* 07/**2765**
Richmond upon Thames LBC *v* Secretary of State for Communities and Local
Government [2006] EWHC 3324 (Admin); [2007] J.P.L. 1146; [2007] A.C.D.
61, QBD (Admin) .... *Digested,* 07/**3289**
Ricketts *v* Colquhoun (Inspector of Taxes) [1926] A.C. 1; 10 T.C. 118, HL; affirming
[1925] 1 K.B. 725, CA; affirming [1924] 2 K.B. 347, KBD .... *Applied,* 54/1574,
55/1300, 07/4055: *Considered,* 61/4235, 69/1741, 70/1313, 74/1867,
90/2668: *Distinguished,* 69/1741: *Followed,* 68/1903

Rickless v United Artists Corp [1988] Q.B. 40; [1987] 2 W.L.R. 945; [1987] 1 All E.R. 679; [1987] F.S.R. 362, CA (Civ Div); affirming [1986] F.S.R. 502; *Times*, June 17, 1985, QBD . . . . *Digested*, 87/**516**:
Considered, 95/2901, 07/2527: *Distinguished*, 94/4300
Riddle v Riddle 85 C.L.R. 202, HC (Aus) . . . . *Applied*, 07/4240
Ridgeons Bulk Ltd v Customs and Excise Commissioners [1994] S.T.C. 427; [1994] S.T.I. 449; [1994] E.G. 68 (C.S.); *Independent*, April 25, 1994, QBD . . . . *Digested*, 94/**4562**:
Applied, 06/4426: *Overruled in part*, 07/4282
Ridgwell v Ridgwell [2007] EWHC 2666 (Ch); (2007-08) 10 I.T.E.L.R. 754; [2007] S.T.I. 2655, Ch D
Riemann & Co v Linco Care Ltd [2007] E.C.C. 23, Ch D . . . . *Digested*, 07/**2654**
Riener v Bulgaria (46343/99) (2007) 45 E.H.R.R. 32; 9 I.T.L. Rep. 1013, ECHR
Rienks (HG), Re (C-5/83) [1983] E.C.R. 4233; [1985] 1 C.M.L.R. 144, ECJ (2nd Chamber) . . . . *Digested*, 85/**1404**:
Applied, 07/1620
RIETER/Textile machines (T726/93) [1996] E.P.O.R. 72, EPO (Technical Bd App) . . . . *Considered*, 07/2575
Rigby v MFI UK Ltd (Unreported, November 23, 2006), CC (Leeds) [*Ex rel.* Tom Nossiter, Barrister, Park Lane Chambers, 19 Westgate, Leeds] . . . . *Digested*, 07/**3206**
Rigsadvokaten v Ryborg (C-297/89) [1991] E.C.R. I-1943; [1993] 1 C.M.L.R. 218; *Times*, May 2, 1991, ECJ (6th Chamber) . . . . *Digested*, 91/**4130**:
Applied, 07/1575
Riksskatteverket v Gharehveran (C-441/99) [2001] E.C.R. I-7687, ECJ (5th Chamber) . . . *Applied*, 07/2496
Ringway Infrastructure Services Ltd v Vauxhall Motors Ltd [2007] EWHC 2507 (TCC); 115 Con. L.R. 149; [2007] C.I.L.L. 2532, QBD (TCC)
Riniker v University College London, *Times*, April 17, 1999; *Independent*, April 29, 1999, CA (Civ Div) . . . . *Digested*, 99/**578**:
Considered, 07/477
Ritchie Brothers (PWC) Ltd v David Philp (Commercials) Ltd [2005] CSIH 32; 2005 1 S.C. 384; 2005 S.L.T. 341; 2005 S.C.L.R. 829; [2005] B.L.R. 384; 2005 G.W.D. 11-169; *Times*, May 24, 2005, IH (2 Div); reversing 2004 S.L.T. 471; [2004] B.L.R. 379; 2004 G.W.D. 13-282, OH . . . . *Digested*, 05/**5068**:
Applied, 07/433
Ritter-Coulais v Finanzamt Germersheim (C-152/03) [2006] All E.R. (EC) 613; [2006] S.T.C. 1111; [2006] E.C.R. I-1711; [2006] 2 C.M.L.R. 31; [2006] C.E.C. 531; [2006] S.T.I. 529, ECJ . . . . *Digested*, 06/**1573**:
Applied, 07/1580
River Thames Society v First Secretary of State [2006] EWHC 2829 (Admin); [2007] J.P.L. 782; (2006) 150 S.J.L.B. 1253, QBD (Admin) . . . . *Digested*, 07/**536**
Riverside Housing Association Ltd v Revenue and Customs Commissioners [2006] EWHC 2383 (Ch); [2006] S.T.C. 2072; [2007] B.T.C. 5084; [2006] S.T.I. 2277; [2006] 41 E.G. 225 (C.S.); [2006] N.P.C. 106; *Times*, November 1, 2006, Ch D; affirming [2006] B.V.C. 2314; [2006] S.T.I. 515, V&DTr (Manchester) . . . . *Digested*, 07/**4364**
Riverside Housing Association Ltd v White see White v Riverside Housing Association Ltd
Riyad Bank v Ahli United Bank (UK) Plc [2006] EWCA Civ 780; [2006] 2 All E.R. (Comm) 777; [2006] 2 Lloyd's Rep. 292; [2006] 1 C.L.C. 1007; [2007] P.N.L.R. 1, CA (Civ Div); affirming [2005] EWHC 279 (Comm); [2005] 2 Lloyd's Rep. 409; [2006] 1 B.C.L.C. 311, QBD (Comm) . . . . *Digested*, 06/**2882**:
Applied, 06/2881
Rizeni Letoveho Provozu CR sp v Bundesamt fur Finanzen (C-335/05) [2007] S.T.C. 1509; [2007] 3 C.M.L.R. 14; [2007] S.T.I. 1691, ECJ (1st Chamber)
RJ Knapman Ltd v Richards [2006] EWHC 2518 (TCC); 108 Con. L.R. 64; [2006] C.I.L.L. 2400, QBD (TCC) . . . . *Digested*, 07/**726**
RJ Reynolds Tobacco Holdings Inc v Commission of the European Communities (C-131/ 03 P) [2006] E.C.R. I-7795; [2007] 1 C.M.L.R. 1, ECJ . . . . *Digested*, 07/**1587**:
Previous proceedings, 03/1431
RJ Reynolds Tobacco Holdings Inc v Commission of the European Communities (T-379/ 00) see Philip Morris International Inc v Commission of the European Communities (T-377/00)
RJT Consulting Engineers Ltd v DM Engineering (Northern Ireland) Ltd [2002] EWCA Civ 270; [2002] 1 W.L.R. 2344; [2002] C.L.C. 905; [2002] B.L.R. 217; [2002] T.C.L.R. 21; 83 Con. L.R. 99; (2002) 18 Const. L.J. 425; [2002] C.I.L.L. 1841; (2002) 99(15) L.S.G. 33; (2002) 146 S.J.L.B. 78, CA (Civ Div) . . . . *Applied*, 03/649,
04/591, 07/433
RK v Oldham NHS Trust see JD v East Berkshire Community Health NHS Trust
RM v Secretary of State for the Home Department; *sub nom* RM (Kwok On Tong: HC 395 Para 320: India), Re [2006] UKAIT 39; [2006] Imm. A.R. 496, AIT . . . . . . *Digested*, 07/**2337**
RM (Kwok On Tong: HC 395 Para 320: India), Re see RM v Secretary of State for the Home Department
RMCA Reinsurance Ltd, Re [1994] B.C.C. 378, Ch D (Companies Ct) . . . . *Digested*, 95/**2831**:
Considered, 07/2449
Roadchef Motorways Ltd v Secretary of State for Transport [2007] R.V.R. 5, Lands Tr . . *Digested*, 07/**412**
Robb v M&I Salamis Ltd (formerly Salamis Marine & Industrial Ltd) see Robb v Salamis (M&I) Ltd

Robb v Salamis (M&I) Ltd; *sub nom* Robb v M&I Salamis Ltd (formerly Salamis
Marine & Industrial Ltd) [2006] UKHL 56; [2007] 2 All E.R. 97; 2007 S.C.
(H.L.) 71; 2007 S.L.T. 158; 2007 S.C.L.R. 176; [2007] I.C.R. 175; (2007) 151
S.J.L.B. 25; 2007 G.W.D. 2-33; *Times*, December 22, 2006, HL; reversing 2005
S.L.T. 523; 2005 S.C.L.R. 676; 2005 Rep. L.R. 42; 2005 G.W.D. 16-290, IH
(Ex Div); affirming 2004 S.C.L.R. 672; 2003 G.W.D. 33-949, Sh Ct (Grampian)   *Digested*, 07/**5269**
Roberts v Crown Estate Commissioners see Roberts v Swangrove Estates Ltd
Roberts v Gable [2007] EWCA Civ 721; [2007] E.M.L.R. 16; (2007) 151 S.J.L.B. 988,
CA (Civ Div); affirming [2006] EWHC 1025 (QB); [2006] E.M.L.R. 23, QBD. .   *Digested*, 07/**1075**
Roberts v Johnstone [1989] Q.B. 878; [1988] 3 W.L.R. 1247; (1989) 86(5) L.S.G. 44;
(1989) 132 S.J. 1672; *Times*, April 15, 1988, CA (Civ Div); reversing in part
(Unreported, July 25, 1986), HC. . . . .   *Digested*, 89/**1202**:
              Applied, 94/1542, 99/1415, 00/1515, 01/1554: *Cited*, 05/5587:
              Considered, 89/1185, 92/5639, 02/3412, 07/3071: *Not followed*, 87/1171:
              Referred to, 90/1578
Roberts v Listing Officer [2006] R.V.R. 330, VT . . . .   *Digested*, 07/**2831**
Roberts v Parole Board see R. (on the application of Roberts) v Parole Board
Roberts v Skelmersdale College [2003] EWCA Civ 954; [2003] I.C.R. 1127; [2004]
I.R.L.R. 69, CA (Civ Div) . . . .   *Digested*, 03/**1260**:
              Considered, 07/1319
Roberts v Swangrove Estates Ltd; *sub nom* Roberts v Crown Estate Commissioners;
A3/2007/0970, CA (Civ Div); affirming [2007] EWHC 513 (Ch); [2007] 2 P. &
C.R. 17; [2007] N.P.C. 35, Ch D . . . .   *Digested*, 07/**3356**
Roberts v West Coast Trains Ltd [2004] EWCA Civ 900; [2005] I.C.R. 254; [2004]
I.R.L.R. 788; (2004) 101(28) L.S.G. 33; *Times*, June 25, 2004, CA (Civ Div);
affirming EAT/0312/03/ZT, EAT. . . . .   *Digested*, 04/**1310**:
              Applied, 06/1383, 07/1339
Robertson v Department for the Environment, Food and Rural Affairs; *sub nom*
Department for the Environment, Food and Rural Affairs v Robertson [2005]
EWCA Civ 138; [2005] I.C.R. 750; [2005] I.R.L.R. 363; (2005) 102(15) L.S.G.
33; *Times*, March 2, 2005; *Independent*, February 24, 2005, CA (Civ Div);
affirming [2004] I.C.R. 1289, EAT. . . . .   *Digested*, 05/**1258**:
              Considered, 07/1360
Robertson's Electrical Ltd v Customs and Excise Commissioners; *sub nom* Customs
and Excise Commissioners v Robertson's Electrical Ltd; Revenue and Customs
Commissioners v Robertson's Electrical Ltd [2005] CSIH 75; [2007] S.T.C. 612;
2006 S.C. 261; 2005 S.L.T. 1149; 2006 S.C.L.R. 493; [2007] B.T.C. 5763;
[2007] B.V.C. 710; [2005] S.T.I. 1813; 2005 G.W.D. 37-699, IH (2 Div); reversing
[2005] B.V.C. 2070; [2004] V. & D.R. 481; [2004] S.T.I. 2570, V&DTr
(Edinburgh) . . . .   *Digested*, 06/**5742**
Robertson's Trustees v Inland Revenue Commissioners 1987 S.L.T. 534; 1987 S.C.L.R.
433, IH (1 Div) . . . .   *Digested*, 87/**3983**:
              Considered, 07/5561
Robin Hood Cemetery, Solihull, Re see Pearson (Deceased), Re
Robins v Secretary of State for Work and Pensions (C-278/05) [2007] All E.R. (EC)
648; [2007] 2 C.M.L.R. 13; [2007] I.C.R. 779; [2007] I.R.L.R. 270; [2007]
Pens. L.R. 55; *Times*, January 30, 2007, ECJ (2nd Chamber) . . . .   *Digested*, 07/**3021**
Robinson v Abergavenny Magistrates' Court; *joined case* Fine v Abergavenny
Magistrates' Court [2007] EWHC (Admin); (2007) 171 J.P. 683; (2007)
104(36) L.S.G. 30, DC
Robinson v AIG Europe UK Ltd see Manning v AIG Europe UK Ltd
Robinson v Hammersmith and Fulham LBC [2006] EWCA Civ 1122; [2006] 1 W.L.R.
3295; [2007] H.L.R. 7; [2006] B.L.G.R. 822; (2006) 150 S.J.L.B. 1022; *Times*,
September 5, 2006, CA (Civ Div). . . . .   *Digested*, 06/**2045**
Robinson v Secretary of State for Northern Ireland; *sub nom* Robinson's Application
for Judicial Review, Re [2002] UKHL 32; [2002] N.I. 390; *Times*, July 26, 2002;
Independent, November 4, 2002, HL (NI); affirming [2002] N.I. 206, CA (NI);
affirming [2002] N.I. 64, QBD (NI) . . . .   *Digested*, 02/**4905**:
              Considered, 07/3064
Robinson v St Helens MBC [2002] EWCA Civ 1099; [2002] E.L.R. 681; [2003]
P.I.Q.R. P9; (2002) 99(39) L.S.G. 39, CA (Civ Div) . . . .   *Applied*, 03/1163,
            04/372: *Considered*, 07/474, 07/475, 07/3076: *Followed*, 04/2719
Robinson Jarvis & Rolf v Cave see Cave v Robinson Jarvis & Rolf
Robinson's Application for Judicial Review, Re see Robinson v Secretary of State for
Northern Ireland
Roche v United Kingdom (32555/96) (2006) 42 E.H.R.R. 30; 20 B.H.R.C. 99; *Times*,
October 27, 2005, ECHR (Grand Chamber). . . . .   *Digested*, 06/**2185**:
            Applied, 07/2212: *Considered*, 06/2395
Roche Diagnostics Ltd v Kent Pharmaceuticals Ltd see Roche Products Ltd v Kent
Pharmaceuticals Ltd
Roche Nederland BV v Primus (C-539/03) [2006] E.C.R. I-6535; [2007] I.L.Pr. 9;
[2007] F.S.R. 5, ECJ (1st Chamber) . . . .   *Digested*, 07/**2584**

Roche Products Ltd v Kent Pharmaceuticals Ltd; *sub nom* Roche Diagnostics Ltd v
Kent Pharmaceuticals Ltd [2006] EWCA Civ 1775; [2007] E.C.C. 20; [2007]
E.T.M.R. 27; (2007) 93 B.M.L.R. 123; (2007) 30(2) I.P.D. 30011, CA (Civ Div);
affirming [2006] EWHC 335 (Ch); [2006] E.T.M.R. 81; (2006) 29(6) I.P.D.
29047, Ch D . . . . *Digested,* 07/**2651**
Rockall v Department for the Environment, Food and Rural Affairs; *sub nom*
Department for the Environment, Food and Rural Affairs v Rockall [2007]
EWHC 614 (Admin); [2007] 1 W.L.R. 2666; [2007] 3 All E.R. 258; (2007) 171
J.P. 380; (2007) 171 J.P.N. 690; [2007] N.P.C. 34; [2007] Env. L.R. D16;
Times, May 11, 2007, DC . . . . *Digested,* 07/**1026**
Rockfon A/S v Specialarbejderforbundet i Danmark [1995] E.C.R. I-4291; [1996]
C.E.C. 224; [1996] I.C.R. 673; [1996] I.R.L.R. 168; *Times,* January 17, 1996,
ECJ. . . . . *Digested,* 96/**2589**:
Applied, 02/1402, 07/1554
Roddy (A Child) (Identification: Restriction on Publication), Re; *sub nom* Torbay BC v
News Group Newspapers [2003] EWHC 2927 (Fam); [2004] E.M.L.R. 8;
[2004] 2 F.L.R. 949; [2004] 1 F.C.R. 481; [2004] Fam. Law 793, Fam Div . . . *Digested,* 04/**1924**:
Considered, 06/454: *Followed,* 07/1721
Rodriguez v Instituto Nacional de la Seguridad Social (INSS) (C-153/97) [1998]
E.C.R. I-8645; [2001] 1 C.M.L.R. 42, ECJ (5th Chamber) . . . . *Digested,* 01/**5076**:
Applied, 07/1626
Rogers v Merthyr Tydfil CBC [2006] EWCA Civ 1134; [2007] 1 W.L.R. 808; [2007] 1
All E.R. 354; [2007] 1 Costs L.R. 77; [2006] Lloyd's Rep. I.R. 759; (2006) 150
S.J.L.B. 1053, CA (Civ Div) . . . . *Digested,* 06/**2421**
ROHM/Withdrawal of a European patent application (J11/80) [1979-85] E.P.O.R. A48;
[1981] O.J. E.P.O. 141, EPO (Legal Bd App) . . . . *Applied,* 07/2574:
Distinguished, 99/3469
Rolfe (Inspector of Taxes) v Wimpey Waste Management Ltd [1989] S.T.C. 454; 62 T.C.
399; [1989] B.T.C. 191; *Times,* April 7, 1989; *Independent,* April 24, 1989, CA
(Civ Div); affirming [1988] S.T.C. 329, Ch D . . . . *Digested,* 90/**761**:
Considered, 07/4002
Rolled Steel Products (Holdings) Ltd v British Steel Corp [1986] Ch. 246; [1985] 2
W.L.R. 908; [1985] 3 All E.R. 52; (1984) 1 B.C.C. 99158, CA (Civ Div); affirming
[1982] Ch. 478; [1982] 3 W.L.R. 715; [1982] 3 All E.R. 1057, Ch D . . . . *Digested,* 85/**306**:
Applied, 95/2589, 00/2324, 07/574: *Considered,* 87/321, 90/549
Rolls-Royce Plc v Director of Income Tax 10 I.T.L. Rep. 327, ITAT (Ind)
Rolph v Zolan [1993] 1 W.L.R. 1305; [1993] 4 All E.R. 202; [1993] N.P.C. 77; *Times,*
May 7, 1993; *Independent,* May 19, 1993, CA (Civ Div) . . . . *Digested,* 93/**3319**:
Applied, 94/3827, 07/516
Romanov v Russia (63993/00) (2007) 44 E.H.R.R. 23; [2006] M.H.L.R. 7, ECHR
Romer v Haringey LBC see R. (on the application of Romer) v First Secretary of State
Ron Grundy (Melbourne) Ltd v Bonehevo see Omar Parks Ltd v Elkington
Ronson International Ltd v Patrick; *sub nom* Patrick v Royal London Mutual Insurance
Society Ltd [2006] EWCA Civ 421; [2006] 2 All E.R. (Comm) 344; [2006] 1
C.L.C. 576; [2007] Lloyd's Rep. I.R. 85; *Times,* May 8, 2006, CA (Civ Div);
affirming [2005] EWHC 1767 (QB); [2005] 2 All E.R. (Comm) 453; [2006]
Lloyd's Rep. I.R. 194, QBD . . . . *Digested,* 06/**2403**
Roper v Tussauds Theme Parks Ltd [2007] EWHC 624 (Admin); [2007] Env. L.R. 31,
QBD (Admin) . . . . *Digested,* 07/**2963**
Roquette Freres v Ministre de l'Agriculture, de l'Alimentation, de la Peche et de la
Ruralite (C-441/05) [2007] 2 C.M.L.R. 29, ECJ (2nd Chamber) . . . . *Digested,* 07/**1644**
Rose v Director of the Assets Recovery Agency [2006] S.T.C. (S.C.D.) 472; [2006]
S.T.I. 1631, Sp Comm . . . . *Digested,* 07/**4050**
Rose v Director of the Assets Recovery Agency [2007] S.T.I. 2020, Sp Comm
Rose v DPP; *sub nom* R. (on the application of Rose) v DPP [2006] EWHC 852
(Admin); [2006] 1 W.L.R. 2626; [2006] 2 Cr. App. R. 29; (2007) 171 J.P. 57;
[2006] Crim. L.R. 993; (2007) 171 J.P.N. 323; *Times,* April 12, 2006, QBD
(Admin) . . . . *Digested,* 07/**917**
Rose v Revenue and Customs Commissioners [2007] S.T.C. (S.C.D.) 129; [2007]
S.T.I. 201, Sp Comm . . . . *Digested,* 07/**4131**
Rosebell Holdings v Newton see Brickfield Properties v Newton
Rosengren v Riksaklagaren (C-170/04) [2007] 3 C.M.L.R. 10, ECJ (Grand Chamber)
Rosewood Trust Ltd v Schmidt see Schmidt v Rosewood Trust Ltd
Ross v Ross (Process Appeal) 1927 S.C. (H.L.) 4; 1927 S.L.T. 2, HL . . . . *Applied,* 07/**4855**:
Followed, 61/10874
Ross River Ltd v Cambridge City Football Club Ltd [2007] EWHC 2115 (Ch); [2007]
41 E.G. 201 (C.S.); (2007) 157 N.L.J. 1507, Ch D
Rosser v Inland Revenue Commissioners [2003] S.T.C. (S.C.D.) 311; [2003] W.T.L.R.
1057; [2003] S.T.I. 1152, Sp Comm. . . . . *Digested,* 03/**4258**:
Applied, 07/4105
Rossi v Lalili (Unreported, September 12, 2006), CC (Brentford) [*Ex rel.* Weightmans
Solicitors, India Buildings, Water Street, Liverpool] . . . . *Digested,* 07/**330**
Rossi v Rossi [2006] EWHC 1482 (Fam); [2007] 1 F.L.R. 790; [2006] 3 F.C.R. 271;
[2007] Fam. Law 104, Fam Div . . . . *Digested,* 07/**1704**

Rotaru v Romania (28341/95) 8 B.H.R.C. 449, ECHR . . . .   *Digested*, 00/**3248**:
                                                                                      Applied, 07/2188, 07/2258
Roth (J4/03) . . . .   *Applied*, 07/2574
Rothwell v Chemical & Insulating Co Ltd see Grieves v FT Everard & Sons Ltd
Rouf (t/a New Balaka Restaurant), Petitioner [2006] CSOH 195; [2007] S.T.I. 113, OH
Roux v Belgium (C-363/89) [1991] E.C.R. I-273; [1993] 1 C.M.L.R. 3, ECJ (3rd
    Chamber) . . . .   *Considered*, 07/1652:
                                                                                      Followed, 05/1462
Rowallan Group Ltd v Edgehill Portfolio No 1 Ltd [2007] EWHC 32 (Ch); [2007] 4
    E.G. 187 (C.S.); [2007] N.P.C. 9, Ch D
Rowe v Clarke (Costs) [2006] EWHC 1292 (Ch); [2007] W.T.L.R. 373, Ch D . . . .   *Digested*, 07/**429**
Rowlands v Chief Constable of Merseyside [2006] EWCA Civ 1773; [2007] 1 W.L.R.
    1065; [2006] Po. L.R. 187; (2007) 151 S.J.L.B. 28; (2007) 151 S.J.L.B. 64;
    Times, January 11, 2007, CA (Civ Div) . . . .   *Digested*, 07/**1053**
Rowley v Rugby BC [2007] EWCA Civ 483; [2007] H.L.R. 40; (2007) 104(19)
    L.S.G. 27, CA (Civ Div) . . . .   *Digested*, 07/**2136**
Rowley v Secretary of State for Work and Pensions; *sub nom* R. (on the application of
    Rowley) v Secretary of State for Work and Pensions [2007] EWCA Civ 598;
    [2007] 1 W.L.R. 2861; [2007] 2 F.L.R. 945; [2007] 3 F.C.R. 431; [2007] Fam.
    Law 896; (2007) 151 S.J.L.B. 856; *Times*, July 6, 2007, CA (Civ Div) . . . .   *Digested*, 07/**1755**
Roy v Kensington and Chelsea and Westminster Family Practitioner Committee [1992]
    1 A.C. 624; [1992] 2 W.L.R. 239; [1992] 1 All E.R. 705; [1992] I.R.L.R. 233;
    (1992) 4 Admin. L.R. 649; [1992] 3 Med. L.R. 177; (1992) 142 N.L.J. 240;
    (1992) 136 S.J.L.B. 63; *Times*, February 10, 1992; *Independent*, February 11,
    1992, HL; affirming (1990) 2 Admin. L.R. 669; *Times*, March 27, 1990, CA (Civ
    Div); reversing (1990) 2 Admin. L.R. 29; *Times*, March 7, 1989, QBD . . . .   *Digested*, 92/**30**:
                                              Applied, 97/4055, 98/98, 98/4129, 07/1959: *Considered*, 92/2, 95/3907,
                                              96/3087, 96/5692, 04/1236: *Distinguished*, 92/2267, 96/3913, 96/5578:
                                                                                      Not followed, 94/1978, 04/1236
Royal & Sun Alliance Insurance Plc v Dornoch Ltd; *sub nom* Dornoch Ltd v Royal &
    Sun Alliance Insurance Plc [2005] EWCA Civ 238; [2005] 1 All E.R. (Comm)
    590; [2005] 1 C.L.C. 466; [2005] Lloyd's Rep. I.R. 544, CA (Civ Div); affirming
    [2004] EWHC 803 (Comm); [2004] 2 C.L.C. 133; [2004] Lloyd's Rep. I.R.
    826, QBD (Comm) . . . .   *Digested*, 05/**2402**:
                                                                                      Followed, 07/2502
Royal & Sun Alliance Insurance Plc v MK Digital FZE (Cyprus) Ltd [2006] EWCA Civ
    629; [2006] 2 All E.R. (Comm) 145; [2006] 2 Lloyd's Rep. 110; [2006] 1 C.L.C.
    787; [2007] I.L.Pr. 3, CA (Civ Div); reversing [2005] EWHC 1408; [2005] 2
    Lloyd's Rep. 679; [2005] 2 C.L.C. 146; [2005] I.L.Pr. 51, QBD (Comm) . . . . . .   *Digested*, 06/**638**
Royal Automobile Club Ltd, Re see RAC Motoring Services Ltd, Re
Royal Bank of Scotland Group Plc v Revenue and Customs Commissioners 2007 S.C.
    401; 2007 S.L.T. 265; [2007] B.T.C. 5410; [2007] B.V.C. 429; [2007] S.T.I. 535;
    2007 G.W.D. 7-131, IH (2 Div); affirming [2006] V. & D.R. 68; [2006] S.T.I.
    1368, V&DTr (Edinburgh)
Royal Bank of Scotland Group Plc v Revenue and Customs Commissioners [2007]
    B.V.C. 2295, V&DTr (Edinburgh)
Royal Bank of Scotland Plc v Etridge (No.2); *joined cases* Barclays Bank Plc v Coleman;
    Barclays Bank Plc v Harris; Midland Bank Plc v Wallace; National Westminster
    Bank Plc v Gill; UCB Home Loans Corp Ltd v Moore; Bank of Scotland v
    Bennett; Kenyon-Brown v Desmond Banks & Co (Undue Influence) (No.2)
    [2001] UKHL 44; [2002] 2 A.C. 773; [2001] 3 W.L.R. 1021; [2001] 4 All E.R.
    449; [2001] 2 All E.R. (Comm) 1061; [2002] 1 Lloyd's Rep. 343; [2001] 2
    F.L.R. 1364; [2001] 3 F.C.R. 481; [2002] H.L.R. 4; [2001] Fam. Law 880;
    [2001] 43 E.G. 184 (C.S.); (2001) 151 N.L.J. 1538; [2001] N.P.C. 147; [2002] 1
    P. & C.R. DG14; *Times*, October 17, 2001; *Daily Telegraph*, October 23, 2001,
    HL; affirming in part [1998] 4 All E.R. 705; [1998] 2 F.L.R. 843; [1998] 3 F.C.R.
    675; (1999) 31 H.L.R. 575; [1998] Fam. Law 665; (1998) 95(32) L.S.G. 31;
    (1998) 148 N.L.J. 1390; (2001) 151 N.L.J. 1538; [1998] N.P.C. 130; (1998) 76 P.
    & C.R. D39; *Times*, August 17, 1998, CA (Civ Div) . . . .   *Digested*, 01/**4880**:
                                              Applied, 00/4664, 01/4879, 03/2379, 03/3556, 03/3587, 03/3588,
                                              03/3612, 03/4118, 03/4122, 03/4124, 04/3671, 05/1423, 05/2673, 05/3402,
                                              05/3438, 05/3442, 05/3968, 06/4094, 07/2415: *Considered*, 00/2333,
                                              01/4878, 02/3840, 02/3841, 02/3841, 02/5794, 03/233, 03/5680, 04/1526,
                                              05/4291, 05/4301: *Followed*, 00/2334, 00/4273, 04/3246:
                                              Previous proceedings, 00/4273: *Referred to*, 99/4030
Royal Bank of Scotland Plc v McAdie; *sub nom* McAdie v Royal Bank of Scotland Plc
    [2007] EWCA Civ 806; [2007] I.R.L.R. 895; (2007) 104(32) L.S.G. 27; (2007)
    157 N.L.J. 1355; (2007) 151 S.J.L.B. 1060, CA (Civ Div); affirming
    (Unreported, November 29, 2006), EAT . . . .   *Digested*, 07/**1430**

Royal Brompton Hospital NHS Trust v Hammond (No.3) [2002] UKHL 14; [2002] 1
W.L.R. 1397; [2002] 2 All E.R. 801; [2002] 1 All E.R. (Comm) 897; [2003] 1
C.L.C. 11; [2002] B.L.R. 255; [2002] T.C.L.R. 14; 81 Con. L.R. 1; [2002] P.N.L.R.
37; *Times*, April 26, 2002, HL; affirming 69 Con. L.R. 145; [2000] Lloyd's Rep.
P.N. 643, CA (Civ Div); affirming [1999] B.L.R. 385, QBD (TCC)..........   *Digested*, 02/**326**:
              Applied, 03/3613: *Considered*, 07/4248: *Followed*, 03/4957

Royal Brompton Hospital NHS Trust v Hammond (No.5) [2001] EWCA Civ 550; [2001]
B.L.R. 297; [2001] Lloyd's Rep. P.N. 526; (2001) 98(23) L.S.G. 39; (2001)
145 S.J.L.B. 118; *Times*, May 11, 2001, CA (Civ Div); reversing 1993-ORB-No.46,
QBD (TCC) . . . .   *Digested*, 01/**680**:
       Considered, 07/3433

Royal Brunei Airlines Sdn Bhd v Philip Tan Kok Ming see Royal Brunei Airlines Sdn Bhd
  v Tan

Royal Brunei Airlines Sdn Bhd v Tan; *sub nom* Royal Brunei Airlines Sdn Bhd v Philip
Tan Kok Ming [1995] 2 A.C. 378; [1995] 3 W.L.R. 64; [1995] 3 All E.R. 97;
[1995] B.C.C. 899; (1995) 92(27) L.S.G. 33; (1995) 145 N.L.J. 888; [1995]
139 S.J.L.B. 146; (1995) 70 P. & C.R. D12; *Times*, May 29, 1995; *Independent*,
June 22, 1995, PC (Bru). . . . .   *Digested*, 95/**2193**:
       Applied, 99/294, 00/3566, 02/249: *Considered*, 97/692, 97/3828, 01/721,
       02/4666, 06/4380, 07/4237: *Followed*, 95/2191, 98/4871, 99/2217,
       00/2316: *Referred to*, 00/3713, 00/3768

Royal Canin, Re [2007] E.C.C. 1, C Concurrence (F)

Royal Life Insurance v Phillips (1991) 61 P. & C.R. 182; [1990] 2 E.G.L.R. 135; [1990]
43 E.G. 70; [1990] E.G. 32 (C.S.), QBD . . . .   *Digested*, 91/**2273**:
       Considered, 07/2728

Royal Life Saving Society v Page see Cheryl Investments Ltd v Saldanha

Royal Mail Group v Consumer Council for Postal Services see R. (on the application of
Consumer Council for Postal Services (Postwatch)) v Postal Services
Commission

Royal Mail Group Plc v Postal Services Commission [2007] EWHC 1205 (Admin);
[2007] A.C.D. 81, QBD (Admin)

Royle v Greater Manchester Police Authority [2007] I.C.R. 281, EAT . . . .   *Digested*, 07/**1319**

Rozanski v Poland (55339/00) [2006] 2 F.L.R. 1163; [2006] 2 F.C.R. 178; (2007) 45
E.H.R.R. 26; [2006] Fam. Law 844, ECHR . . . .   *Digested*, 06/**2190**

RP v RP [2006] EWHC 3409 (Fam); [2007] 1 F.L.R. 2105; [2007] Fam. Law 581,
Fam Div. . . . .   *Digested*, 07/**1699**

RSPCA v Chester Crown Court see R. (on the application of RSPCA) v Chester
Crown Court

RSPCA v Revenue and Customs Commissioners; *sub nom* Revenue and Customs
Commissioners v RSPCA; *joined case* Revenue and Customs Commissioners v
ToTel Ltd [2007] EWHC 422 (Ch); [2007] B.T.C. 5578; [2007] B.V.C. 546;
[2007] S.T.I. 486, Ch D; reversing in part [2006] V. & D.R. 460; [2006] S.T.I.
1371, V&DTr (London) . . . .   *Digested*, 07/**4359**

Rubber Chemicals, Re (COMP/F/38.443) [2007] C.E.C. 2058, CEC

Ruddy v Oakfern Properties Ltd see Oakfern Properties Ltd v Ruddy

Ruiz-Mateos v Spain (A/262) (1993) 16 E.H.R.R. 505, ECHR. . . . .   *Digested*, 94/**2406**:
         Applied, 98/3121, 98/3135, 98/3136: *Considered*, 07/1774:
       Referred to, 02/2409

Ruiz-Picasso v Office for Harmonisation in the Internal Market (Trade Marks and
Designs) (OHIM) (T-185/02) [2004] E.C.R. II-1739; [2005] E.T.M.R. 22, CFI
(2nd Chamber) . . . .   *Digested*, 05/**2551**:
       Applied, 07/2660: *Subsequent proceedings*, 06/2555

Runkee v United Kingdom (42949/98) [2007] 2 F.C.R. 178, ECHR. . . . .   *Digested*, 07/**2208**:
       Considered, 07/2207

Rusby v Harr [2006] EWCA Civ 865; [2007] J.P.L. 262; [2006] 24 E.G. 177 (C.S.),
CA (Civ Div) . . . .   *Digested*, 07/**3533**

Ruscillo v Council for the Regulation of Health Care Professionals see Council for the
Regulation of Health Care Professionals v General Medical Council

Rush & Tompkins Ltd v Greater London Council [1989] A.C. 1280; [1988] 3 W.L.R.
939; [1988] 3 All E.R. 737; 43 B.L.R. 1; 22 Con. L.R. 114; [1988] E.G. 145 (C.S.);
(1988) 138 N.L.J. Rep. 315; (1988) 132 S.J. 1592, HL; reversing [1988] 2
W.L.R. 533; [1988] 1 All E.R. 549; 40 B.L.R. 53; (1988) 138 N.L.J. Rep. 22;
(1988) 132 S.J. 265, CA (Civ Div) . . . .   *Digested*, 89/**1701**:
       Applied, 91/2870, 94/2817, 99/309, 99/349, 03/287, 04/260, 06/280:
       Considered, 92/106, 94/3674: *Distinguished*, 00/337, 04/390:
       Followed, 92/3288, 00/319, 07/343

Russell v Pal Pak Corrugated Ltd (No.1) see Callery v Gray (No.1)

Russell v Stubbs Ltd see Stubbs Ltd v Russell

Russell Cooke Trust Co Ltd v Elliott [2007] EWHC 1443 (Ch); [2007] 2 B.C.L.C. 637,
Ch D

Russian Conservative Party of Entrepreneurs v Russia (55066/00) 22 B.H.R.C. 1, ECHR   *Digested*, 07/**2264**

Rustal Trading Ltd v Gill & Duffus SA [2000] 1 Lloyd's Rep. 14; [2000] C.L.C. 231,
QBD (Comm) . . . .   *Digested*, 00/**224**:
       Applied, 05/199, 07/248

Rutherford v Harvest Towncircle Ltd (In Liquidation) see Rutherford v Secretary of
    State for Trade and Industry
Rutherford v Secretary of State for Trade and Industry; *sub nom* Rutherford v Harvest
    Towncircle Ltd (In Liquidation); Secretary of State for Trade and Industry v
    Rutherford; *joined case* Bentley v Secretary of State for Trade and Industry
    [2006] UKHL 19; [2006] 4 All E.R. 577; [2006] I.C.R. 785; [2006] I.R.L.R. 551;
    (2006) 103(20) L.S.G. 24; (2006) 150 S.J.L.B. 604; *Times*, May 8, 2006, HL;
    affirming [2004] EWCA Civ 1186; [2004] 3 C.M.L.R. 53; [2005] I.C.R. 119;
    [2004] I.R.L.R. 892; (2004) 148 S.J.L.B. 1065; *Times*, November 4, 2004, CA
    (Civ Div); affirming [2003] 3 C.M.L.R. 27; [2003] I.R.L.R. 858; [2004] Pens.
    L.R. 1; (2003) 100(42) L.S.G. 31; (2003) 153 N.L.J. 1633; *Times*, October 8,
    2003, EAT; reversing [2003] 2 C.M.L.R. 28; [2002] I.R.L.R. 768, ET . . . .   *Digested*, 06/**1306**:
                                 Followed, 07/1360: *Previous proceedings*, 01/2308
Ruttle Plant Hire Ltd v Department for the Environment, Food and Rural Affairs [2007]
    EWHC 1633 (QB); [2007] 5 Costs L.R. 750, QBD
Ruttle Plant Hire Ltd v Secretary of State for the Environment, Food and Rural Affairs
    [2007] EWHC 2870 (TCC); [2007] B.P.I.R. 1652, QBD (TCC)
Ruxley Electronics & Construction Ltd v Forsyth; *joined case* Laddingford Enclosures
    Ltd v Forsyth [1996] A.C. 344; [1995] 3 W.L.R. 118; [1995] 3 All E.R. 268;
    [1995] C.L.C. 905; 73 B.L.R. 1; 45 Con. L.R. 61; (1995) 14 Tr. L.R. 541; (1995) 11
    Const. L.J. 381; [1995] E.G. 11 (C.S.); (1995) 145 N.L.J. 996; (1995) 139
    S.J.L.B. 163; *Times*, July 3, 1995; *Independent*, July 12, 1995, HL; reversing
    [1994] 1 W.L.R. 650; [1994] 3 All E.R. 801; 66 B.L.R. 23; 36 Con. L.R. 103;
    (1994) 91(7) L.S.G. 31; (1994) 138 S.J.L.B. 31; *Times*, January 7, 1994, CA (Civ
    Div) . . . .   *Digested*, 95/**1561**:
              Applied, 01/4501, 03/943, 03/5323: *Considered*, 03/670, 07/2948:
                         Distinguished, 95/4508, 07/794: *Followed*, 96/1131
Ryde International Plc v London Regional Transport [2004] EWCA Civ 232; [2004] 2
    E.G.L.R. 1; [2004] 30 E.G. 108; [2004] R.V.R. 60; [2004] 12 E.G. 170 (C.S.);
    (2004) 101(12) L.S.G. 38; (2004) 148 S.J.L.B. 301; [2004] N.P.C. 36, CA (Civ
    Div); affirming [2003] R.V.R. 49, Lands Tr . . . .   *Digested*, 05/**3256**:
             Applied, 06/3286, 07/3248: *Previous proceedings*, 01/4662
Rye v Rye [2002] EWHC 956 (Fam); [2002] 2 F.L.R. 981; [2002] Fam. Law 736,
    Fam Div . . . .   *Digested*, 03/**1592**:
                                         Applied, 07/1686
Rysaffe Trustee Co (Cd) Ltd v Ataghan Ltd [2006] EWHC 2324 (Ch); [2007] 1 P. &
    C.R. DG18, Ch D
Rysaffe Trustee Co (CI) Ltd v Customs and Excise Commissioners see Rysaffe Trustee
    Co (CI) Ltd v Inland Revenue Commissioners
Rysaffe Trustee Co (CI) Ltd v Inland Revenue Commissioners; *sub nom* Rysaffe Trustee
    Co (CI) Ltd v Customs and Excise Commissioners; Customs and Excise
    Commissioners v Rysaffe Trustee Co (CI) Ltd [2003] EWCA Civ 356; [2003]
    S.T.C. 536; [2003] B.T.C. 8021; [2003] W.T.L.R. 481; (2002-03) 5 I.T.E.L.R.
    706; [2003] S.T.I. 452; (2003) 100(22) L.S.G. 31; (2003) 147 S.J.L.B. 388;
    [2003] N.P.C. 39; *Times*, April 29, 2003, CA (Civ Div); affirming [2002] EWHC
    1114 (Ch); [2002] S.T.C. 872; [2002] B.T.C. 8019; [2002] W.T.L.R. 1077;
    (2002-03) 5 I.T.E.L.R. 53; [2002] S.T.I. 855, Ch D; reversing [2001] S.T.C.
    (S.C.D.) 225; [2002] W.T.L.R. 65; [2001] S.T.I. 1504, Sp Comm. . . . .   *Digested*, 03/**4271**:
                                         Considered, 07/4106

S v DPP [2006] EWHC 1207 (Comm); (2006) 170 J.P. 707; (2007) 171 J.P.N. 161,
    QBD (Comm) . . . .   *Digested*, 07/**982**
S v Essex CC [2000] Ed. C.R. 471; [2000] E.L.R. 718; *Times*, May 10, 2000, QBD . . . .   *Digested*, 00/**1960**:
                                         Applied, 07/1258
S v Hertfordshire CC see A v Essex CC
S v S [2006] EWCA Civ 1617; [2006] 3 F.C.R. 604; [2007] Fam. Law 212; (2006)
    150 S.J.L.B. 1604, CA (Civ Div) . . . .   *Digested*, 07/**1782**:
                               Previous proceedings, 06/1681
S v S [2007] EWCA Civ 454; [2007] 2 F.L.R. 1103; [2007] 3 F.C.R. 552; [2007]
    Fam. Law 795, CA (Civ Div). . . . .   *Digested*, 07/**1703**
S v S (Ancillary Relief: Importance of FDR) [2007] EWHC 1975 (Fam); (2007) 151
    S.J.L.B. 1165, Fam Div
S v S (Ancillary Relief after Lengthy Separation) [2006] EWHC 2339 (Fam); [2007] 1
    F.L.R. 2120; [2007] 2 F.C.R. 762; [2007] Fam. Law 482, Fam Div . . . .   *Digested*, 07/**1694**
S v S (Divorce: Distribution of Assets) see S v S (Non-Matrimonial Property:
    Conduct)
S v S (Non-Matrimonial Property: Conduct); *sub nom* S v S (Divorce: Distribution of
    Assets) [2006] EWHC 2793 (Fam); [2007] 1 F.L.R. 1496; [2007] Fam. Law
    106; *Times*, January 15, 2007, Fam Div . . . .   *Digested*, 07/**1695**
S v Secretary of State for the Home Department see S (Ethiopia) v Secretary of State
    for the Home Department
S Schneiders & Sons Ltd v Abrahams [1925] 1 K.B. 301, CA. . . . .   *Applied*, 47-51/**8866**,
                               71/6689: *Considered*, 07/2763

S (A Child), Re see Newcastle City Council v Z
S (A Child), Re [2007] EWCA Civ 356; (2007) 151 S.J.L.B. 435, CA (Civ Div)
S (A Child) v B; sub nom K (A Child), Re [2007] 1 F.L.R. 1116; [2007] Fam. Law 217, Fam Div
S (A Child) v National Car Parks Ltd (Unreported, March 15, 2006), CC (Preston) [Ex rel. Blackhurst Swainson Goodier, 9 Cannon Street, Preston] . . . .   Digested, 07/**3189**
S (A Child) (Adoption Order or Special Guardianship Order), Re; sub nom DO v LP [2007] EWCA Civ 54; [2007] 1 F.L.R. 819; [2007] 1 F.C.R. 271; [2007] Fam. Law 390; Times, February 9, 2007, CA (Civ Div) . . . .   Digested, 07/**1799**:
            Applied, 07/1681
S (A Child) (Adoption Order or Special Guardianship Order), Re (Addendum) [2007] EWCA Civ 90; [2007] 1 F.L.R. 855; [2007] 1 F.C.R. 340; [2007] Fam. Law 390; (2007) 104(9) L.S.G. 32, CA (Civ Div) . . . .   Digested, 07/**1797**:
            Previous proceedings, 07/1799
S (A Child) (Identification: Restrictions on Publication), Re [2004] UKHL 47; [2005] 1 A.C. 593; [2004] 3 W.L.R. 1129; [2004] 4 All E.R. 683; [2005] E.M.L.R. 2; [2005] 1 F.L.R. 591; [2004] 3 F.C.R. 407; [2005] H.R.L.R. 5; [2005] U.K.H.R.R. 129; 17 B.H.R.C. 646; [2005] Crim. L.R. 310; (2004) 154 N.L.J. 1654; (2004) 148 S.J.L.B. 1285; Times, October 29, 2004; Independent, November 2, 2004, HL; affirming [2003] EWCA Civ 963; [2004] Fam. 43; [2003] 3 W.L.R. 1425; [2003] 2 F.L.R. 1253; [2003] 2 F.C.R. 577; [2003] H.R.L.R. 30; [2003] Fam. Law 818; (2003) 100(34) L.S.G. 29; (2003) 153 N.L.J. 1120; (2003) 147 S.J.L.B. 873; Times, July 21, 2003; Independent, July 15, 2003, CA (Civ Div); affirming [2003] EWHC 254 (Fam), Fam Div . . . .   Digested, 05/**2121**:
    Applied, 05/1686, 05/2049, 05/4191, 06/445, 06/1665, 06/2853, 07/1732,
    07/1806, 07/2189: Considered, 05/923, 06/1711
S (A Child) (Residence Order: Condition) (No.1), Re [2001] EWCA Civ 847; [2001] 3 F.C.R. 154, CA (Civ Div) . . . .   Digested, 01/**2667**:
        Considered, 07/1788: Followed, 05/1576
S (A Child) (Unmarried Parents: Financial Provision), Re see Walker v Jeffries
S (A Patient) v Hopal (Unreported, January 6, 2006), CC (Romford) [Ex rel. Richard Menzies, Barrister, Lamb Chambers, Lamb Building, Temple, London] . . . .   Digested, 07/**3083**
S (Child Proceedings: Urgent Appeals), Re [2007] EWCA Civ 958; [2007] 2 F.L.R. 1044, CA (Civ Div)
S (Children), Re; sub nom W v Hull City Council [2006] EWCA Civ 981; [2007] 1 F.L.R. 90; [2006] Fam. Law 831; (2006) 150 S.J.L.B. 705, CA (Civ Div) . . . . .   Digested, 07/**1728**
S (Children), Re; sub nom Cheshire CC v S; joined case W (A Child), Re [2007] EWCA Civ 232; [2007] 2 F.L.R. 275; [2007] 1 F.C.R. 721; [2007] Fam. Law 488; Times, March 30, 2007, CA (Civ Div) . . . .   Digested, 07/**1719**
S (Children), Re; sub nom S (Omission from Judgment: Duty of Counsel), Re [2007] EWCA Civ 694; [2007] C.P. Rep. 37; (2007) 104(26) L.S.G. 33; (2007) 151 S.J.L.B. 807; Times, July 2, 2007, CA (Civ Div) . . . .   Digested, 07/**466**
S (Children) (Permission to Seek Relief), Re; joined case E (A Child), Re [2006] EWCA Civ 1190; [2007] 1 F.L.R. 482; [2006] 3 F.C.R. 50; [2006] Fam. Law 1022; (2006) 103(34) L.S.G. 33; (2006) 150 S.J.L.B. 1112; Times, September 13, 2006, CA (Civ Div) . . . .   Digested, 06/**1681**:
        Applied, 07/1781: Followed, 07/1782
S (David Vincent) v S (now M) (Susan Ann) [2006] EWHC 2892 (Fam); [2007] 1 F.L.R. 1123; [2007] Fam. Law 108, Fam Div . . . .   Digested, 07/**3419**
S (Ethiopia) v Secretary of State for the Home Department; sub nom S v Secretary of State for the Home Department [2006] EWCA Civ 1153; [2007] Imm. A.R. 7; [2007] I.N.L.R. 60, CA (Civ Div) . . . .   Digested, 07/**337**
S (Minors) (Abduction: Custody Rights), Re see H (Minors) (Abduction: Custody Rights), Re
S (Omission from Judgment: Duty of Counsel), Re see S (Children), Re
S (Practice : Muslim Women Giving Evidence), Re [2006] EWHC 3743 (Fam); [2007] 2 F.L.R. 461; [2007] Fam. Law 986, Fam Div
S (Vulnerable Adult), Re [2007] 2 F.L.R. 1095, Fam Div
S&I Electronics Plc v Revenue and Customs Commissioners [2007] S.T.I. 1698, V&DTr (London)
SA v Secretary of State for the Home Department; sub nom SA (Ambit of s.85(5) of 2002 Act: Pakistan), Re [2006] UKAIT 18; [2006] Imm. A.R. 313, AIT . . . .   Digested, 07/**2330**
SA (Ambit of s.85(5) of 2002 Act: Pakistan), Re see SA v Secretary of State for the Home Department
SA (Somalia) v Secretary of State for the Home Department [2006] EWCA Civ 1302; [2007] Imm. A.R. 236; (2006) 103(41) L.S.G. 35, CA (Civ Div)
SA (Vulnerable Adult with Capacity: Marriage), Re; sub nom A Local Authority v MA [2005] EWHC 2942 (Fam); [2006] 1 F.L.R. 867; [2007] 2 F.C.R. 563; (2007) 10 C.C.L. Rep. 193; [2006] Fam. Law 268, Fam Div . . . .   Digested, 07/**1832**:
        Considered, 07/1834

Saad v Secretary of State for the Home Department; *sub nom* R. (on the application of Saad) v Secretary of State for the Home Department; *joined cases* Diriye v Secretary of State for the Home Department; Osorio v Secretary of State for the Home Department [2001] EWCA Civ 2008; [2002] Imm. A.R. 471; [2002] I.N.L.R. 34; [2002] A.C.D. 59; *Times*, January 7, 2002; *Independent*, January 24, 2002, CA (Civ Div) . . . . *Digested*, 02/**2551**:
Applied, 07/2277, 07/2286: *Considered*, 02/2552: *Distinguished*, 03/2211:
Followed, 03/2252

Saadi v United Kingdom (13229/03) (2007) 44 E.H.R.R. 50; [2007] Imm. A.R. 38; [2006] I.N.L.R. 638; *Times*, August 3, 2006, ECHR . . . . *Digested*, 07/**2229**

Sabaf SpA v Meneghetti SpA see Sabaf SpA v MFI Furniture Centres Ltd

Sabaf SpA v MFI Furniture Centres Ltd; *sub nom* Sabaf SpA v Meneghetti SpA [2004] UKHL 45; [2005] R.P.C. 10; (2004) 148 S.J.L.B. 1217, HL; reversing [2002] EWCA Civ 976; [2003] R.P.C. 14; *Times*, July 24, 2002, CA (Civ Div); reversing (2001) 24(10) I.P.D. 24069, Ch D (Patents Ct) . . . . *Digested*, 05/**2480**:
Distinguished, 05/2481, 07/2530

Sabel BV v Puma AG (C-251/95) [1997] E.C.R. I-6191; [1998] 1 C.M.L.R. 445; [1998] C.E.C. 315; [1998] E.T.M.R. 1; [1998] R.P.C. 199, ECJ . . . . *Digested*, 98/**3512**:
Applied, 00/3777, 00/3778, 01/4025, 01/4036, 02/2870, 04/2379, 04/2414, 05/2562, 06/2594, 07/1560, 07/2639: *Considered*, 98/3501, 98/3509, 00/3701, 03/2657, 05/2509, 06/2585: *Followed*, 99/3539, 99/3541, 06/2556: *Referred to*, 99/3542, 99/3562, 99/3568, 99/3581, 99/3587, 01/3987, 01/4024

Sacker v West Yorkshire Coroner see R. (on the application of Sacker) v HM Coroner for West Yorkshire

Sadler v General Medical Council [2003] UKPC 59; [2003] 1 W.L.R. 2259; [2004] H.R.L.R. 8; [2004] Lloyd's Rep. Med. 44; *Times*, September 29, 2003, PC (UK) . . . . *Digested*, 03/**1721**:
Considered, 05/1807, 07/1952

Sadler v Imperial Life Assurance Co of Canada Ltd [1988] I.R.L.R. 388; *Times*, January 8, 1988, QBD . . . . *Digested*, 89/**3674**:
Applied, 07/1327: *Followed*, 96/2600

Saffron Walden Building Society v Rayner see Saffron Walden Second Benefit Building Society v Rayner

Saffron Walden Second Benefit Building Society v Rayner; *sub nom* Saffron Walden Building Society v Rayner (1880) L.R. 14 Ch. D. 406, CA; reversing (1878-79) L.R. 10 Ch. D. 696, Ch D . . . . *Applied*, 70/2866, 07/2755: *Approved*, 66/11052

Safir v Skattemyndigheten i Dalarnas Lan (formerly Skattemyndigheten i Kopparbergs Lan) (C-118/96) [1999] Q.B. 451; [1999] 2 W.L.R. 66; [1998] S.T.C. 1043; [1998] E.C.R. I-1897; [1998] 3 C.M.L.R. 739; [1998] B.T.C. 8028; *Times*, May 1, 1998, ECJ . . . . *Digested*, 98/**4699**:
Applied, 07/1618

Sage v Double A Hydraulics Ltd; *joined case* Chambers v Starkings *Times*, April 2, 1992, CA (Civ Div) . . . . *Digested*, 92/**3630**:
Applied, 07/347

Sage (UK) Ltd v Bacco, *Times*, October 11, 2007, EAT

Sager v Dennemeyer & Co Ltd (C-76/90) [1991] E.C.R. I-4221; [1993] 3 C.M.L.R. 639, ECJ (6th Chamber) . . . . *Considered*, 07/**1634**:
Followed, 97/2446, 02/1582

Saggar v Ministry of Defence; *joined cases* Ministry of Defence v Gandiya; Lucas v Ministry of Defence [2005] EWCA Civ 413; [2005] I.C.R. 1073; [2005] I.R.L.R. 618; (2005) 102(23) L.S.G. 27; *Times*, May 9, 2005, CA (Civ Div); reversing [2004] I.C.R. 1708, EAT . . . . *Digested*, 05/**1252**:
Considered, 07/4518

Sahin v Turkey (44774/98) (2007) 44 E.H.R.R. 5; 19 B.H.R.C. 590; [2006] E.L.R. 73, ECHR (Grand Chamber) . . . . *Digested*, 06/**2103**:
Applied, 06/1145

Sainsbury Supermarkets Ltd v First Secretary of State see MR Dean & Sons (Edgware) Ltd v First Secretary of State

Sainsbury's Supermarkets Ltd v Hitt see Sainsbury's Supermarkets Ltd v Hitt

Sainsbury's Supermarkets Ltd v Hitt; *sub nom* J Sainsbury Ltd v Hitt; Sainsbury's Supermarkets Ltd v Hitt; J Sainsbury Plc v Hitt [2002] EWCA Civ 1588; [2003] I.C.R. 111; [2003] I.R.L.R. 23; [2002] Emp. L.R. 1273; (2002) 146 S.J.L.B. 238; *Times*, November 14, 2002, CA (Civ Div); reversing EAT/887/00, EAT . . . *Digested*, 02/**1440**:
Applied, 07/1422

Sainsbury's Supermarkets Ltd v HM Courts Service (South West Region, Devon & Cornwall Area); *joined case* J Sainsbury Plc v HM Courts Service (South West Region, Devon & Cornwall Area) [2006] EWHC 1749 (Admin); (2006) 170 J.P. 690; (2007) 171 J.P.N. 219, DC

Salah v Netherlands (8196/02) (2007) 44 E.H.R.R. 55, ECHR . . . . *Digested*, 07/**2170**

Salah Sheekh v Netherlands (1948/04) see Sheekh v Netherlands (1948/04)

Sale v Sale (Unreported, December 14, 2006), CC (Cardiff) [*Ex rel*. Andrew Arentsen, Barrister, 33 Park Place, Cardiff] . . . . *Digested*, 07/**3177**

Salford City Council v Garner [2004] EWCA Civ 364; [2004] H.L.R. 35; (2004) 148
S.J.L.B. 295; [2004] N.P.C. 35; *Times*, March 10, 2004, CA (Civ Div) . . . . *Digested*, 04/**2516**:
Distinguished, 07/373

Salisbury DC v Hall [2007] P.A.D. 9, Planning Inspector
Sallinen v Finland (50882/99) (2007) 44 E.H.R.R. 18, ECHR
Salman v Turkey (21986/93) (2002) 34 E.H.R.R. 17, ECHR . . . . *Digested*, 02/**2492**:
Considered, 06/2105, 07/2980

Salomon v Customs and Excise Commissioners; *sub nom* Solomon v Customs and
Excise Commissioners [1967] 2 Q.B. 116; [1966] 3 W.L.R. 1223; [1966] 3 All
E.R. 871; [1966] 2 Lloyd's Rep. 460; (1966) 110 S.J. 833; *Times*, October 27,
1966; *Guardian*, October 27, 1966, CA; reversing [1966] 3 W.L.R. 36; [1966] 2
All E.R. 340; [1966] 1 Lloyd's Rep. 642; (1966) 110 S.J. 290, QBD . . . . *Digested*, 67/**990**:
Applied, 70/2644, 71/10748, 71/10859, 72/796, 90/4: *Considered*, 69/138,
77/174, 78/2678, 92/2847, 07/3824: *Followed*, 68/3668

Salov v Ukraine (65518/01) (2007) 45 E.H.R.R. 51, ECHR
Saluja, Re see Council for the Regulation of Healthcare Professionals v General Medical
Council
Salvat Editores SA v Badillo (C-242/98) see Oceano Grupo Editorial SA v Quintero (C-
240/98)
Salvat Editores SA v Berroane (C-243/98) see Oceano Grupo Editorial SA v Quintero
(C-240/98)
Salvat Editores SA v Feliu (C-244/98) see Oceano Grupo Editorial SA v Quintero (C-
240/98)
Salvat Editores SA v Prades (C-241/98) see Oceano Grupo Editorial SA v Quintero (C-
240/98)
Salvesen v Simons [1994] I.C.R. 409; [1994] I.R.L.R. 52, EAT . . . . *Digested*, 94/**1910**:
Applied, 07/1427

Salzgitter Mannesmann GmbH (formerly Mannesmannrohren-Werke AG) v Commission
of the European Communities (C-411/04 P) [2007] 4 C.M.L.R. 17, ECJ (1st
Chamber) . . . . *Digested*, 07/**1544**

Sam McCauley Chemists (Blackpool) Ltd v Pharmaceutical Society of Ireland (C-221/
05) [2006] E.C.R. I-6869; [2006] 3 C.M.L.R. 42; [2007] C.E.C. 135, ECJ (3rd
Chamber) . . . . *Digested*, 07/**1623**

Samaroo v Secretary of State for the Home Department see R. (on the application of
Samaroo) v Secretary of State for the Home Department
Samengo-Turner v J&H Marsh & McLennan (Services) Ltd [2007] EWCA Civ 723;
[2007] 2 All E.R. (Comm) 813; [2007] C.P. Rep. 45; [2007] 2 C.L.C. 104;
[2007] I.L.Pr. 52, CA (Civ Div) . . . . *Digested*, 07/**351**

Sampson, Re; *sub nom* Sampson's Application, Re; Sampson v Croydon Crown Court
[1987] 1 W.L.R. 194; [1987] 1 All E.R. 609; (1987) 84 Cr. App. R. 376; [1987]
Crim. L.R. 570; (1987) 84 L.S.G. 825; (1987) 137 N.L.J. 169; (1987) 131 S.J.
225, HL . . . . *Digested*, 87/**2282**:
Applied, 93/12, 93/15, 05/71: *Considered*, 91/613, 92/39, 93/10, 95/23,
07/54: *Followed*, 01/3539: *Referred to*, 93/11

Sampson v Croydon Crown Court see Sampson, Re
Sampson's Application, Re see Sampson, Re
SAMSUNG/Combined DVD/CD ECC decoder (T940/03) [2007] E.P.O.R. 24, EPO
(Technical Bd App) . . . . *Digested*, 07/**2608**

Samuel v Jarrah Timber & Wood Paving Corp Ltd; *sub nom* Jarrah Timber & Wood
Paving Corp Ltd v Samuel [1904] A.C. 323, HL; affirming [1903] 2 Ch. 1, CA;
affirming [1902] 2 Ch. 479, Ch D . . . . *Applied*, 61/**5596**:
Considered, 07/4257

Sanchez Cardenas v Norway (12148/03) [2007] 3 F.C.R. 403; [2007] Fam. Law
1062, ECHR
Sanczyk v Revenue and Customs Commissioners [2006] V. & D.R. 411, V&DTr
(London) . . . . *Digested*, 07/**1042**

Sanders v Templar see Giles v Thompson
Sanders v Van der Putte (73/77) [1977] E.C.R. 2383; [1978] 1 C.M.L.R. 331, ECJ. . . . *Digested*, 78/**1297**:
Considered, 00/773, 07/666

Sanders BVBA v Belgium (C-47/96) see Garage Molenheide BVBA v Belgium (C-286/
94)
Sandford v Sandford [1986] 1 F.L.R. 412; [1986] Fam. Law 104, CA (Civ Div);
affirming [1985] Fam. Law 230, QBD. . . . . *Digested*, 86/**1089**:
Considered, 87/1745, 07/1690

Sandhu v Jan de Rijk Transport Ltd [2007] EWCA Civ 430; [2007] I.C.R. 1137; [2007]
I.R.L.R. 519; (2007) 104(21) L.S.G. 27; (2007) 151 S.J.L.B. 672, CA (Civ Div);
reversing UKEAT/0451/05/LA, EAT . . . . *Digested*, 07/**1435**

SanDisk Corp v Koninklijke Philips Electronics NV [2007] EWHC 332 (Ch); [2007]
Bus. L.R. 705; [2007] U.K.C.L.R. 1539; [2007] I.L.Pr. 22; [2007] F.S.R. 22;
(2007) 30(5) I.P.D. 30033; *Times*, March 21, 2007, Ch D . . . . *Digested*, 07/**662**

Sandwell BC v Preece [2007] EWCA Civ 1009; (2007) 151 S.J.L.B. 1260, CA (Civ
Div)
Sandwell MBC v Hensley [2007] EWCA Civ 1425; (2007) 151 S.J.L.B. 1436, CA (Civ
Div)

Sandwell MBC v Jones see Barber v Somerset CC
Sanles v Spain (Admissibility) (48335/99) (Unreported, October 26, 2000), ECHR .. *Considered*, 07/2233
Sapunarescu v Germany (Admissibility) (22007/03) (2007) 44 E.H.R.R. SE3, ECHR
Saramati v France (Admissibility) (78166/01) see Behrami v France (Admissibility) (71412/01)
Sardar v Watford BC [2006] EWHC 1590 (Admin); [2007] A.C.D. 19, QBD (Admin)
Sargin v Turkey (A/319) see Yagci v Turkey (A/319)
Sarrio SA v Commission of the European Communities (C-291/98 P) [2000] E.C.R. I-9991, ECJ; reversing in part . . . . *Applied*, 07/603:
Considered, 03/1430: *Distinguished*, 04/522
Sarrio SA v Kuwait Investment Authority [1999] 1 A.C. 32; [1997] 3 W.L.R. 1143; [1997] 4 All E.R. 929; [1998] 1 Lloyd's Rep. 129; [1998] Lloyd's Rep. Bank. 57; [1997] C.L.C. 1640; [1998] I.L.Pr. 319; (1997) 141 S.J.L.B. 248; *Times*, November 17, 1997; *Independent*, November 19, 1997, HL; reversing [1997] 1 Lloyd's Rep. 113; [1997] C.L.C. 280; [1997] I.L.Pr. 481; *Independent*, October 3, 1996, CA (Civ Div); reversing [1996] 1 Lloyd's Rep. 650; [1996] C.L.C. 211, QBD (Comm) . . . . *Digested*, 97/**900**:
Applied, 01/809, 07/501: *Considered*, 00/738
Sarwar v Ali [2007] EWHC 1255 (QB); [2007] LS Law Medical 375, QBD . . . . *Digested*, 07/**3066**:
Considered, 07/3065
SASOL CHEMICAL INDUSTRIES/Porous prilled ammonium nitrate (T1912/03) [2007] E.P.O.R. 37, EPO (Technical Bd App)
Saturn Leisure Ltd v Revenue and Customs Commissioners [2007] S.T.I. 2249, V&DTr (London)
Saunders v United Kingdom (19187/91); *sub nom* Saunders v United Kingdom (43/1994/490/572) [1997] B.C.C. 872; [1998] 1 B.C.L.C. 362; (1997) 23 E.H.R.R. 313; 2 B.H.R.C. 358; *Times*, December 18, 1996; *Independent*, January 14, 1997, ECHR; affirming (1994) 18 E.H.R.R. CD23; *Independent*, September 30, 1994, Eur Comm HR . . . . *Digested*, 97/**2816**:
Applied, 01/1047, 05/2092: *Considered*, 97/2818, 98/3150, 00/5473, 00/6043, 01/974, 01/6319, 02/849, 02/2664, 07/855:
Distinguished, 00/667, 00/2300, 04/1951, 05/765: *Followed*, 97/817, 00/3234: *Not applied*, 98/682
Saunders v United Kingdom (43/1994/490/572) see Saunders v United Kingdom (19187/91)
Saunders v Vautier 41 E.R. 482; 49 E.R. 282; (1841) 4 Beav. 115; (1841) Cr. & Ph. 240, Ct of Chancery. . . . . *Applied*, 61/6608,
02/4332, 03/3103, 07/4261: *Considered*, 47-51/9387, 67/410, 04/2823, 04/3672, 06/4403, 06/4404: *Distinguished*, 98/2301, 07/3036:
Followed, 75/3116
Saunders (A Bankrupt), Re; *sub nom* Bristol and West Building Society v Saunders; Bearman (A Bankrupt), Re [1997] Ch. 60; [1996] 3 W.L.R. 473; [1997] 3 All E.R. 992; [1997] B.C.C. 83; [1996] B.P.I.R. 355, Ch D . . . . *Digested*, 96/**3444**:
Considered, 05/2826, 07/374: *Followed*, 98/3319
Savage v South Essex Partnership NHS Foundation Trust [2007] EWCA Civ 1375, CA (Civ Div); affirming [2006] EWHC 3562 (QB); [2007] LS Law Medical 291; [2006] Inquest L.R. 235; *Times*, February 16, 2007, QBD. . . . . *Digested*, 07/**2238**
Save Group Plc (In Liquidation), Re see Manning v AIG Europe UK Ltd
Savil v Chase Holdings (Wellington) Ltd (Unreported) . . . . *Applied*, 07/363
Sawyer v Atari Interactive Inc [2007] EWCA Civ 170; [2007] Bus. L.R. D34, CA (Civ Div)
Sayers v Cambridgeshire CC [2006] EWHC 2029 (QB); [2007] I.R.L.R. 29, QBD. . . . *Digested*, 07/**2941**
Sayers v Clarke Walker [2002] EWCA Civ 645; [2002] 1 W.L.R. 3095; [2002] 3 All E.R. 490; [2002] C.P. Rep. 61; *Times*, June 3, 2002; *Independent*, May 22, 2002, CA (Civ Div) . . . . *Digested*, 02/**304**:
Considered, 07/3368
SB v Dunbar see Beattie v Dunbar
SB (Bangladesh) v Secretary of State for the Home Department [2007] EWCA Civ 28; [2007] 1 F.L.R. 2153; [2007] Imm. A.R. 491; [2007] I.N.L.R. 259; [2007] Fam. Law 494; (2007) 104(7) L.S.G. 27; (2007) 151 S.J.L.B. 198, CA (Civ Div). . . . . *Digested*, 07/**2298**
SC Packaging Ltd v Customs and Excise Commissioners see SCA Packaging Ltd v Revenue and Customs Commissioners
SC (A Minor) (Leave to Seek Residence Order), Re [1994] 1 F.L.R. 96; [1994] 1 F.C.R. 609; [1993] Fam. Law 618, Fam Div. . . . . *Digested*, 95/**3548**:
Applied, 95/3554: *Approved*, 07/1679
SCA Holding Ltd v Commission of the European Communities (C-297/98 P) [2000] E.C.R. I-10101; [2001] 4 C.M.L.R. 13, ECJ (5th Chamber); affirming . . . . *Digested*, 03/**552**:
Applied, 07/606
SCA Packaging Ltd v Revenue and Customs Commissioners; *sub nom* SC Packaging Ltd v Customs and Excise Commissioners [2007] EWHC 270 (Ch); [2007] S.T.C. 1640; [2007] B.T.C. 308; [2007] S.T.I. 414, Ch D; affirming [2006] S.T.C. (S.C.D.) 426; [2006] S.T.I. 1625, Sp Comm. . . . . *Digested*, 07/**4071**
Scamp v Maidstone BC [2007] P.A.D. 5, Planning Inspector

Scarce Skills Ltd v Revenue and Customs Commissioners [2007] S.T.I. 390, V&DTr
Schepens v Belgium (C-340/95) see Garage Molenheide BVBA v Belgium (C-286/94)
SCHERING/Combination therapy (T1117/05) [2007] E.P.O.R. 55, EPO (Technical Bd App)
Schiesser v Switzerland (1979-80) 2 E.H.R.R. 417, ECHR . . . .   *Considered,* 07/**2231**
Schindler v Pigault (1975) 30 P. & C.R. 328; (1975) 119 S.J. 273; *Times,* January 22,
    1975, Ch D . . . .   *Digested,* 76/**2862**:
                   Approved, 79/2775: *Considered,* 07/3394: *Followed,* 89/452
Schmidt v Germany (13580/88) (1994) 18 E.H.R.R. 513, ECHR . . . .   *Digested,* 95/**2666**:
                   Applied, 97/2823, 98/3076, 07/2265
Schmidt v Rosewood Trust Ltd; *sub nom* Angora Trust, Re; Everest Trust, Re;
    Rosewood Trust Ltd v Schmidt [2003] UKPC 26; [2003] 2 A.C. 709; [2003] 2
    W.L.R. 1442; [2003] 3 All E.R. 76; [2003] Pens. L.R. 145; [2003] W.T.L.R.
    565; (2002-03) 5 I.T.E.L.R. 715; (2003) 100(22) L.S.G. 31; *Times,* March 29,
    2003, PC (IoM); reversing [2001] W.T.L.R. 1081; (2000-01) 3 I.T.E.L.R. 734, HC
    (IoM) . . . .   *Digested,* 03/**4485**:
               Applied, 04/2815, 04/3950, 05/4303: *Considered,* 07/4242:
                              Followed, 05/4293
Schofield v Saunders & Taylor Ltd see Heil v Rankin
Scholes v Secretary of State for the Home Department see R. (on the application of
    Scholes) v Secretary of State for the Home Department
Schulte v Germany (C-188/94) see Dillenkofer v Germany (C-178/94)
Schwarcz v Aeresta and Customs and Excise Commissioners [1989] S.T.C. 230;
    [1989] B.T.C. 5003; *Independent,* November 28, 1988, QBD . . . .   *Digested,* 89/**3735**:
                              Considered, 07/4301
Schwarz v Finanzamt Bergisch Gladbach (C-76/05) [2007] 3 C.M.L.R. 47; [2007]
    S.T.I. 2188; *Times,* October 11, 2007, ECJ (Grand Chamber)
Scope v Thornett see Thornett v Scope
Scordino v Italy (36813/97) (2007) 45 E.H.R.R. 7, ECHR (Grand Chamber) . . . .   *Applied,* 07/**2222**
Score Draw Ltd v Finch [2007] EWHC 462 (Ch); [2007] Bus. L.R. 864; [2007]
    E.T.M.R. 54; [2007] F.S.R. 20; (2007) 30(7) I.P.D. 30045; *Times,* April 9,
    2007, Ch D . . . .   *Digested,* 07/**2689**
Scott v Belfast Education and Library Board [2007] NICh 4; 114 Con. L.R. 209;
    [2007] C.I.L.L. 2510, Ch D (NI)
Scott v Billett (1956) 167 E.G. 485; (1957) 1 R.R.C. 29; 49 R. & I.T. 379; [1956] J.P.L.
    464; (1956) 106 L.J. 316, Lands Tr . . . .   *Digested,* 56/**7257.21**:
                              Applied, 07/4705
Scott v Chief Constable of South Yorkshire [2006] EWCA Civ 598; [2006] Po. L.R.
    86, CA (Civ Div) . . . .   *Digested,* 07/**333**
Scott v Formica [1975] I.R.L.R. 104, IT . . . .   *Digested,* 75/**1171.57**:
                              Considered, 07/1435
Scott (aka Morgan) v Scott [1913] A.C. 417, HL; reversing [1912] P. 241, CA; affirming
    [1912] P. 4, PDAD . . . .   *Applied,* 52/494,
           57/2759, 63/1807, 93/3033, 94/5047, 01/564, 01/2622, 06/315, 06/353,
           07/940: *Considered,* 53/1034, 53/2752, 63/1092, 63/1092, 65/203, 75/955,
           77/1965, 79/2120, 81/2144, 84/866, 84/2250, 88/692, 89/784, 92/693,
           92/969, 93/2835, 95/3545, 95/3959, 01/2622, 02/1695:
          Distinguished, 47-51/7548, 04/185, 04/809: *Followed,* 58/2473, 96/2980:
                              Referred to, 53/1034
Scott-Davies v Redgate Medical Services [2007] I.C.R. 348, EAT . . . .   *Digested,* 07/**1407**
Scottish & Newcastle International Ltd v Othon Ghalanos Ltd [2006] EWCA Civ 1750;
    [2007] 1 All E.R. (Comm) 1027; [2007] 2 Lloyd's Rep. 341; [2006] 2 C.L.C.
    1015; [2007] I.L.Pr. 44, CA (Civ Div) . . . .   *Digested,* 07/**671**
Scottish & Newcastle Plc v Lancashire Mortgage Corp Ltd [2007] EWCA Civ 684;
    [2007] N.P.C. 84, CA (Civ Div)
Scottish & Newcastle Plc v Raguz (No.3) [2007] EWCA Civ 150; [2007] Bus. L.R.
    841; [2007] 2 All E.R. 871; [2007] L. & T.R. 20; [2007] 15 E.G. 148; [2007] 11
    E.G. 161 (C.S.); (2007) 104(12) L.S.G. 35; [2007] N.P.C. 29, CA (Civ Div);
    affirming [2006] EWHC 821 (Ch); [2006] 4 All E.R. 524; [2007] 1 P. & C.R. 1;
    [2006] L. & T.R. 25; [2006] 3 E.G.L.R. 119; [2006] N.P.C. 49, Ch D
    (Birmingham) . . . .   *Digested,* 07/**2774**
Scottish & Newcastle Retail Ltd v Williams (Valuation Officer) see Williams (Valuation
    Officer) v Scottish & Newcastle Retail Ltd
Scottish Coal Co Ltd v Crouch Mining Ltd see Scottish Coal Co Ltd v McCormack
Scottish Coal Co Ltd v McCormack; *sub nom* Scottish Coal Co Ltd v Crouch Mining
    Ltd 2006 S.C. 105, IH (Ex Div) . . . .   *Considered,* 07/1415
Scottish Exhibition Centre Ltd v Customs and Excise Commissioners see Scottish
    Exhibition Centre Ltd v Revenue and Customs Commissioners
Scottish Exhibition Centre Ltd v Revenue and Customs Commissioners; *sub nom*
    Scottish Exhibition Centre Ltd v Customs and Excise Commissioners [2006]
    CSIH 42; 2006 S.C. 702; 2006 S.C.L.R. 849; [2007] B.T.C. 5769; [2007] B.V.C.
    716; [2006] S.T.I. 1918, IH (Ex Div); reversing [2005] B.V.C. 2529; [2005]
    S.T.I. 896, V&DTr (Edinburgh) . . . .   *Digested,* 07/**5568**

Scottish Ministers *v* Scottish Information Commissioner; *sub nom* Alexander's
　Application, Re; Elstone's Application, Re [2007] CSIH 8; 2007 S.C. 330; 2007
　S.L.T. 274; 2007 S.C.L.R. 253; 2007 G.W.D. 3-48; *Times,* January 29, 2007, IH
　(1 Div) . . . . *Digested,* 07/**4888**
Scottish Power Generation Ltd *v* Scottish Environment Protection Agency (No.1) 2005
　S.L.T. 98; [2005] Eu. L.R. 449; [2005] Env. L.R. 38; 2005 G.W.D. 1-1, OH . . . . *Digested,* 05/**4970**:
　　　 Applied, 07/1518

Scottish Widows Plc *v* Stewart [2006] EWCA Civ 999; [2007] 1 P. & C.R. DG5, CA
　(Civ Div); reversing in part [2005] EWHC 1831, QBD
Scrace *v* Revenue and Customs Commissioners [2006] EWHC 2646 (Ch); [2007]
　S.T.C. 269; [2007] B.T.C. 5822; [2007] B.V.C. 791; [2006] S.T.I. 1886, Ch D . . *Digested,* 07/**4355**
Scrivner *v* Centre d'Aide Sociale de Chastre (122/84) [1985] E.C.R. 1027, ECJ . . . . . . *Followed,* 07/3830
SCRL Societe Belge des Auteurs, Compositeurs et Editeurs *v* SA Scarlet [2007] E.C.D.R.
　19, RB (Brussels)
Scully UK Ltd *v* Lee [1998] I.R.L.R. 259, CA (Civ Div); affirming 1997-S-No.711, QBD . *Digested,* 98/**2192**:
　　　　　　　　　　　　　　　　　　　　　　　　 Applied, 07/1328: *Distinguished,* 98/727
Sea Trade Maritime Corp *v* Hellenic Mutual War Risks Association (Bermuda) Ltd (The
　Athena) [2006] EWHC 2530 (Comm); [2007] 1 All E.R. (Comm) 183; [2007] 1
　Lloyd's Rep. 280; [2006] 2 C.L.C. 710; [2007] Bus. L.R. D5, QBD (Comm). . . *Digested,* 07/**791**
Seaconsar (Far East) Ltd *v* Bank Markazi Jomhouri Islami Iran (Service Outside
　Jurisdiction) [1994] 1 A.C. 438; [1993] 3 W.L.R. 756; [1993] 4 All E.R. 456;
　[1994] 1 Lloyd's Rep. 1; [1994] I.L.Pr. 678; (1993) 143 N.L.J. 1479; (1993) 137
　S.J.L.B. 239; *Times,* October 15, 1993; *Independent,* October 20, 1993, HL;
　reversing [1993] 1 Lloyd's Rep. 236; *Times,* November 25, 1992, CA (Civ Div) . *Digested,* 94/**3763**:
　　　　　　　　　 Applied, 95/398, 98/582, 03/310, 04/566, 05/2293: *Considered,* 95/703:
　　　　　　　　　　　　　　　　　　　　　　 Followed, 98/4394, 07/2548: *Referred to,* 95/399
Seafield Holdings Ltd (t/a Seafield Logistics) *v* Drewett [2006] I.C.R. 1413, EAT . . . . . *Digested,* 07/**1316**
Seagrave (Deceased), Re; *sub nom* O'Brien *v* Seagrave [2007] EWHC 788 (Ch);
　[2007] 1 W.L.R. 2002; [2007] 3 All E.R. 633; [2007] W.T.L.R. 1037; *Times,* May
　2, 2007, Ch D . . . . *Digested,* 07/**3953**
Seal *v* Chief Constable of South Wales [2007] UKHL 31; [2007] 1 W.L.R. 1910;
　[2007] 4 All E.R. 177; [2007] H.R.L.R. 37; 22 B.H.R.C. 769; [2007] B.P.I.R.
　1396; (2007) 10 C.C.L. Rep. 695; (2007) 97 B.M.L.R. 172; (2007) 104(29)
　L.S.G. 25; (2007) 151 S.J.L.B. 927; *Times,* July 5, 2007, HL; affirming [2005]
　EWCA Civ 586; [2005] 1 W.L.R. 3183; [2005] B.P.I.R. 993; (2005) 8 C.C.L.
　Rep. 372; [2005] M.H.L.R. 137; [2005] Po. L.R. 177; *Times,* May 31, 2005, CA
　(Civ Div) . . . . *Digested,* 07/**2908**:
　　 Considered, 07/374
Seamer *v* Medway Council [2007] P.A.D. 27, Planning Inspector
SEC Corp *v* Commission of the European Communities (T251/01) see Tokai Carbon Co
　Ltd *v* Commission of the European Communities (T-236/01)
Secic *v* Croatia (40116/02) 23 B.H.R.C. 24, ECHR
Secretary of State for Defence *v* MacDonald see Advocate General for Scotland *v*
　MacDonald
Secretary of State for Defence *v* Pensions Appeal Tribunal [2007] EWHC 1177 (Admin);
　[2007] Pens. L.R. 195, QBD (Admin) . . . . *Digested,* 07/**3059**
Secretary of State for Defence *v* Warn; *sub nom* R. *v* Warn (Peter John) [1970] A.C.
　394; [1968] 3 W.L.R. 609; [1968] 2 All E.R. 300; (1968) 52 Cr. App. R. 366;
　(1968) 112 S.J. 461, HL; affirming [1968] 1 Q.B. 718; [1968] 2 W.L.R. 131;
　[1968] 1 All E.R. 339; (1967) 111 S.J. 943; *Times,* November 21, 1967, CMAC . . *Digested,* 68/**135**:
　　　　　　　　　　　　　　　　　　　　 Applied, 79/575, 07/2908: *Considered,* 68/135
Secretary of State for Education and Science *v* Tameside MBC [1977] A.C. 1014; [1976]
　3 W.L.R. 641; [1976] 3 All E.R. 665; (1976) 120 S.J. 735, HL; affirming (1976)
　120 S.J. 539, CA (Civ Div) . . . . *Digested,* 76/**829**:
　　　　　　　　 Applied, 78/861, 82/1453, 83/359, 83/3723, 94/4593, 98/1901, 00/3115,
　　　　　　　　 00/5397, 07/1485: *Considered,* 79/198, 79/810, 81/1535, 87/31, 89/3586,
　　　　　　　　　　　　　　　 95/1911: *Distinguished,* 91/67, 99/4248: *Followed,* 80/1378
Secretary of State for Health *v* Clark see Secretary of State for Health *v* Rance
Secretary of State for Health *v* Maddocks see Secretary of State for Health *v* Rance
Secretary of State for Health *v* Rance; *joined cases* Secretary of State for Health *v* Clark;
　Secretary of State for Health *v* Maddocks; Secretary of State for Health *v*
　Wheeler [2007] I.R.L.R. 665; [2007] Pens. L.R. 313, EAT . . . . *Digested,* 07/**1359**
Secretary of State for Health *v* Wheeler see Secretary of State for Health *v* Rance
Secretary of State for Industry *v* McLean (Unreported, October 29, 1996), Ch D . . . . *Applied,* 07/436
Secretary of State for Justice *v* James see R. (on the application of Walker) *v* Secretary
　of State for the Home Department
Secretary of State for Justice *v* Rayner see R. (on the application of Rayner) *v* Secretary
　of State for the Home Department
Secretary of State for Justice *v* Walker see R. (on the application of Walker) *v* Secretary
　of State for the Home Department
Secretary of State for Scotland *v* Revival Properties Ltd see Edinburgh City Council *v*
　Secretary of State for Scotland

Secretary of State for the Environment v Beresford Trustees [1996] N.P.C. 128, CA (Civ Div)...... *Digested*, 96/**5019**: *Applied*, 07/3421

Secretary of State for the Environment, Food and Rural Affairs v Feakins; *sub nom* Department for Environment, Food and Rural Affairs v Feakins; Feakins v Department for Environment, Food and Rural Affairs [2005] EWCA Civ 1513; [2007] B.C.C. 54; [2006] Env. L.R. 44; [2006] B.P.I.R. 895; (2006) 103(4) L.S.G. 28; *Times*, December 22, 2005, CA (Civ Div); reversing in part [2004] EWHC 2735 (Ch); [2005] Eu. L.R. 207; [2005] B.P.I.R. 292; [2004] 49 E.G. 135 (C.S.); (2005) 102(5) L.S.G. 28; *Times*, December 29, 2004, Ch D ...... *Digested*, 06/**65**

Secretary of State for the Environment, Transport and the Regions v Thurrock BC (No.2) see Thurrock BC v Secretary of State for the Environment, Transport and the Regions

Secretary of State for the Environment, Transport and the Regions v Yorkshire Water Services Ltd; *sub nom* R. v Yorkshire Water Services Ltd [2001] EWCA Crim 2635; [2002] 2 Cr. App. R. (S.) 13; [2002] Env. L.R. 18; [2002] E.H.L.R. 11; *Times*, December 12, 2001, CA (Crim Div)...... *Digested*, 02/**4821**: *Considered*, 03/1416, 07/986

Secretary of State for the Home Department v AF see Secretary of State for the Home Department v MB

Secretary of State for the Home Department v AF T1/2007/2839, CA (Civ Div); reversing [2007] EWHC 2828 (Admin); *Times*, December 17, 2007, QBD (Admin) ..... *Digested*, 07/**926**

Secretary of State for the Home Department v AF [2007] EWHC 651 (Admin); *Times*, April 18, 2007, QBD (Admin) ...... *Digested*, 07/**2173**: *Reversed*, 07/2171

Secretary of State for the Home Department v AH (Sudan) see AH (Sudan) v Secretary of State for the Home Department

Secretary of State for the Home Department v Ahmed (Iftikhar) see Ahmed (Iftikhar) v Secretary of State for the Home Department

Secretary of State for the Home Department v Akaeke see Akaeke v Secretary of State for the Home Department

Secretary of State for the Home Department v Akrich (C-109/01) [2004] Q.B. 756; [2004] 2 W.L.R. 871; [2004] All E.R. (EC) 687; [2003] E.C.R. I-9607; [2003] 3 C.M.L.R. 26; [2004] I.N.L.R. 36; *Times*, September 26, 2003, ECJ .... *Digested*, 04/**2071**: *Distinguished*, 07/1652

Secretary of State for the Home Department v AR (Afghanistan) see WM (Democratic Republic of Congo) v Secretary of State for the Home Department

Secretary of State for the Home Department v E [2007] UKHL 47; [2007] 3 W.L.R. 720; (2007) 157 N.L.J. 1578; (2007) 151 S.J.L.B. 1433; *Times*, November 13, 2007, HL; affirming [2007] EWCA Civ 459; [2007] 3 W.L.R. 1; [2007] H.R.L.R. 27; (2007) 151 S.J.L.B. 676; *Times*, June 1, 2007, CA (Civ Div) [2007] EWHC 233 (Admin); [2007] H.R.L.R.18, QBD (Admin) ...... *Digested*, 07/**953**: *Applied*, 07/2171, 07/2173

Secretary of State for the Home Department v Elias see R. (on the application of Elias) v Secretary of State for Defence

Secretary of State for the Home Department v GG see Secretary of State for the Home Department v JJ

Secretary of State for the Home Department v Headley see R. (on the application of Clift) v Secretary of State for the Home Department

Secretary of State for the Home Department v HH see Secretary of State for the Home Department v JJ

Secretary of State for the Home Department v Hindawi see R. (on the application of Clift) v Secretary of State for the Home Department

Secretary of State for the Home Department v Hindawi see R. (on the application of Hindawi) v Secretary of State for the Home Department

Secretary of State for the Home Department v JJ; *sub nom* JJ, Re; *joined cases* Secretary of State for the Home Department v KK; Secretary of State for the Home Department v GG; Secretary of State for the Home Department v HH; Secretary of State for the Home Department v NN; Secretary of State for the Home Department v LL [2007] UKHL 45; [2007] 3 W.L.R. 642; (2007) 157 N.L.J. 1576; (2007) 151 S.J.L.B. 1432; *Times*, November 5, 2007, HL; affirming [2006] EWCA Civ 1141; [2007] Q.B. 446; [2006] 3 W.L.R. 866; [2006] H.R.L.R. 38; [2006] U.K.H.R.R. 1081; *Times*, August 18, 2006, CA (Civ Div) [2006] EWHC 1623 (Admin); [2006] A.C.D. 97; (2006) 103(28) L.S.G. 27, QBD (Admin) ...... *Digested*, 07/**2172**: *Applied*, 07/2171: *Distinguished*, 07/953

Secretary of State for the Home Department v KK see Secretary of State for the Home Department v JJ

Secretary of State for the Home Department v LL see Secretary of State for the Home Department v JJ

Secretary of State for the Home Department *v* MB; *sub nom* MB, Re; *joined case* Secretary of State for the Home Department *v* AF [2007] UKHL 46; [2007] 3 W.L.R. 681; (2007) 157 N.L.J. 1577; (2007) 151 S.J.L.B. 1437; *Times*, November 6, 2007, HL; affirming [2006] EWCA Civ 1140; [2007] Q.B. 415; [2006] 3 W.L.R. 839; [2006] H.R.L.R. 37; [2006] U.K.H.R.R. 1133; (2006) 156 N.L.J. 1288; (2006) 150 S.J.L.B. 1055; *Times*, August 18, 2006, CA (Civ Div) [2006] EWHC 1000 (Admin); [2006] H.R.L.R. 29; (2006) 150 S.J.L.B. 539; *Times*, April 17, 2006, QBD (Admin) . . . .   *Digested*, 07/**2171**:
            Applied, 07/953, 07/2173

Secretary of State for the Home Department *v* NN see Secretary of State for the Home Department *v* JJ

Secretary of State for the Home Department *v* Ravichandran see R. *v* Secretary of State for the Home Department Ex p. Jeyeanthan

Secretary of State for the Home Department *v* Razgar see R. (on the application of Razgar) *v* Secretary of State for the Home Department (No.2)

Secretary of State for Trade and Industry *v* Aaron see David M Aaron (Personal Financial Planners) Ltd, Re

Secretary of State for Trade and Industry *v* Aaron [2007] EWHC 1720 (Ch); [2007] Bus. L.R. D95, Ch D

Secretary of State for Trade and Industry *v* Arnold [2007] EWHC 1933 (Ch); (2007) 104(33) L.S.G. 28, Ch D (Manchester)

Secretary of State for Trade and Industry *v* Aviss; *sub nom* Mea Corp, Re [2006] EWHC 1846 (Ch); [2007] B.C.C. 288; [2007] 1 B.C.L.C. 618, Ch D

Secretary of State for Trade and Industry *v* Bairstow; *sub nom* Queens Moat Houses Plc, Re [2003] EWCA Civ 321; [2004] Ch. 1; [2003] 3 W.L.R. 841; [2004] 4 All E.R. 325; [2003] C.P. Rep. 46; [2003] B.C.C. 682; [2003] 1 B.C.L.C. 696; (2003) 100(18) L.S.G. 36; (2003) 153 N.L.J. 440; *Times*, March 31, 2003; *Independent*, March 20, 2003, CA (Civ Div); reversing 751 of 2000, Ch D . . . .   *Digested*, 03/**509**:
            Applied, 07/339, 07/345

Secretary of State for Trade and Industry *v* Bottrill; *sub nom* Bottrill *v* Secretary of State for Trade and Industry [2000] 1 All E.R. 915; [1999] B.C.C. 177; [2000] 2 B.C.L.C. 448; [1999] I.C.R. 592; [1999] I.R.L.R. 326; (1999) 96(10) L.S.G. 30; (1999) 143 S.J.L.B. 73; *Times*, February 24, 1999; *Independent*, February 17, 1999, CA (Civ Div); affirming [1998] I.C.R. 564; [1998] I.R.L.R. 120, EAT . . . .   *Digested*, 99/**2019**:
       Applied, 03/2506, 07/1348: *Considered*, 01/2265, 07/1352:
            Followed, 99/2110

Secretary of State for Trade and Industry *v* Carr; *sub nom* TransTec Plc, Re [2005] EWHC 1723 (Ch); [2006] B.C.C. 295; [2007] 1 B.C.L.C. 93, Ch D (Companies Ct) . .   *Digested*, 07/**436**

Secretary of State for Trade and Industry *v* Carr; *sub nom* TransTec Plc, Re [2006] EWHC 2110 (Ch); [2007] B.C.C. 313; [2007] 2 B.C.L.C. 495, Ch D (Companies Ct) . .   *Digested*, 07/**570**

Secretary of State for Trade and Industry *v* Gee see City Truck Group Ltd, Re

Secretary of State for Trade and Industry *v* Gee see City Truck Group Ltd, Re

Secretary of State for Trade and Industry *v* Gray see Grayan Building Services Ltd (In Liquidation), Re

Secretary of State for Trade and Industry *v* Grove see Vintage Hallmark Plc, Re

Secretary of State for Trade and Industry *v* Hall [2006] EWHC 1995 (Ch); *Times*, August 2, 2006, Ch D (Companies Ct) . . . .   *Digested*, 07/**569**

Secretary of State for Trade and Industry *v* Hollier [2006] EWHC 1804 (Ch); [2007] Bus. L.R. 352; [2007] B.C.C. 11, Ch D . . . .   *Digested*, 07/**566**

Secretary of State for Trade and Industry *v* Rutherford see Rutherford *v* Secretary of State for Trade and Industry

Secretary of State for Trade and Industry *v* Slater [2007] I.R.L.R. 928, EAT . . . .   *Digested*, 07/**1417**

Secretary of State for Trade and Industry *v* Swan; *sub nom* Finelist Ltd, Re [2003] EWHC 1780 (Ch); [2004] B.C.C. 877; (2003) 100(36) L.S.G. 37; *Times*, August 18, 2003, Ch D (Companies Ct) . . . .   *Digested*, 03/**512**:
            Applied, 07/397: *Followed*, 06/539

Secretary of State for Trade and Industry *v* Vohora [2007] EWHC 2656 (Ch); *Times*, December 10, 2007, Ch D . . . .   *Digested*, 07/**373**

Secretary of State for Transport *v* Pell Frischmann Consultants Ltd [2006] EWHC 2909 (TCC); [2007] B.L.R. 46, QBD (TCC) . . . .   *Digested*, 07/**492**

Secretary of State for Work and Pensions *v* Balding see R. (on the application of Balding) *v* Secretary of State for Work and Pensions

Secretary of State for Work and Pensions *v* Borrowdale see Secretary of State for Work and Pensions *v* Morina

Secretary of State for Work and Pensions *v* Kehoe see R. (on the application of Kehoe) *v* Secretary of State for Work and Pensions

Secretary of State for Work and Pensions *v* M see M *v* Secretary of State for Work and Pensions

Secretary of State for Work and Pensions *v* Morina; *sub nom* Morina *v* Secretary of State for Work and Pensions; Borrowdale *v* Secretary of State for Work and Pensions; *joined case* Secretary of State for Work and Pensions *v* Borrowdale [2007] EWCA Civ 749; [2007] 1 W.L.R. 3033; (2007) 157 N.L.J. 1318; *Times*, August 24, 2007, CA (Civ Div) . . . .   *Digested*, 07/**3897**

Secretary of State for Work and Pensions v Roach [2006] EWCA Civ 1746; [2007] 1
F.L.R. 2167; [2007] 1 F.C.R. 238; [2007] Fam. Law 395; *Times*, January 5,
2007, CA (Civ Div) . . . . *Digested*, 07/**1758**
Secretary of State for Work and Pensions v Wilson [2006] EWCA Civ 882; [2006] 1
W.L.R. 2682; [2007] 1 All E.R. 281; [2006] 2 F.C.R. 700; [2007] H.L.R. 11;
(2006) 103(28) L.S.G. 30; *Times*, July 4, 2006, CA (Civ Div) . . . . *Digested*, 06/**3998**
Securicor Omega Express Ltd v GMB (A Trade Union); *joined case* GMB (A Trade
Union) v Securicor Omega Express Ltd [2004] I.R.L.R. 9, EAT . . . . *Digested*, 04/**1284**:
Considered, 07/1394
SEE SHELL/Bloodflow (T182/90) [1994] E.P.O.R. 320, EPO (Technical Bd App) . . . . *Considered*, 07/2596
Seele Austria GMBH & Co v Tokio Marine Europe Insurance Ltd A3/2007/1540, CA (Civ
Div); reversing [2007] EWHC 1411 (Comm); [2007] 1 C.L.C. 972; [2007]
B.L.R. 337, QBD (Comm) . . . . *Digested*, 07/**2482**
Seeling v Finanzamt Starnberg (C-269/00) [2003] S.T.C. 805; [2003] E.C.R. I-4101;
[2004] 2 C.M.L.R. 32; [2003] C.E.C. 381; [2003] B.T.C. 5343; [2003] B.V.C.
399; [2003] S.T.I. 967, ECJ (5th Chamber) . . . . *Digested*, 03/**4272**:
Applied, 06/4430, 06/4458, 06/4493: *Considered*, 07/4309
Segal v Pasram [2007] B.P.I.R. 881; [2007] Fam. Law 892, Ch D (Bankruptcy Ct) . . . *Digested*, 07/**2408**
Segelman (Deceased), Re [1996] Ch.171; [1996] 2 W.L.R.173; [1995] 3 All E.R. 676, Ch D *Digested*, 96/**5557**:
Applied, 07/3966
Segerstedt-Wiberg v Sweden (62332/00) (2007) 44 E.H.R.R. 2; 21 B.H.R.C. 155,
ECHR . . . . *Digested*, 07/**2258**
Segi v Council of the European Union (C-355/04 P) [2007] 2 C.M.L.R. 23, ECJ . . . . *Digested*, 07/**1593**
Segi v Council of the European Union (T-338/02); *sub nom* Sigi v Council of the
European Union (T-338/02) [2004] E.C.R. II-1647; [2007] 1 C.M.L.R. 8, CFI
SEIKO/Divisional of divisional (T720/02) [2006] E.P.O.R. 2, EPO (Technical Bd App) . *Considered*, 07/2579
SEIKO/Divisional of divisional (T797/02) [2006] E.P.O.R. 34, EPO (Technical Bd App) *Considered*, 07/2579
SEIKO/Sequence of divisionals (T1409/05) [2006] E.P.O.R. 32, EPO (Technical Bd App) *Digested*, 07/**2579**
SEIKO/Sequences of divisionals (G1/06) [2007] E.P.O.R. 47, EPO (Enlarged Bd App)
Sekanina v Austria (A/266-A) (1994) 17 E.H.R.R. 221, ECHR . . . . *Digested*, 94/**2388**:
Applied, 02/2453, 07/2227: *Followed*, 03/2143
Selby DC v UK Coal Ltd [2007] P.A.D. 72, Planning Inspector
Seldon v Davidson [1968] 1 W.L.R. 1083; [1968] 2 All E.R. 755; (1968) 112 S.J. 463,
CA (Civ Div) . . . . *Digested*, 68/**612**:
Applied, 07/2415: *Approved*, 81/1272
Select Commodities Ltd v Valdo SA (The Florida) [2006] EWHC 1137 (Comm); [2006]
2 All E.R. (Comm) 493; [2007] 1 Lloyd's Rep. 1, QBD (Comm) . . . . *Digested*, 06/**3919**
Selex Sistemi Integrati SpA v Commission of the European Communities (T-155/04)
[2007] 4 C.M.L.R. 10, CFI (2nd Chamber) . . . . *Digested*, 07/**652**
Selkent Bus Co Ltd v Moore [1996] I.C.R. 836; [1996] I.R.L.R. 661, EAT . . . . *Digested*, 96/**2661**:
Applied, 00/2207: *Considered*, 05/1278: *Distinguished*, 07/1339
Sellars Arenascene Ltd v Connolly see Sellars Arenascene Ltd v Connolly (No.2)
Sellars Arenascene Ltd v Connolly (No.2); *sub nom* Connolly v Sellars Arenascene Ltd
(No.2); Sellars Arenascene Ltd v Connolly [2001] EWCA Civ 184; [2001]
I.C.R. 760; [2001] I.R.L.R. 222; [2001] Emp. L.R. 295; (2001) 98(8) L.S.G. 44;
(2001) 145 S.J.L.B. 37; *Times*, March 8, 2001, CA (Civ Div) . . . . *Digested*, 01/**2265**:
Applied, 07/1348: *Followed*, 07/1352
Selmouni v France (25803/94) (2000) 29 E.H.R.R. 403; 7 B.H.R.C. 1, ECHR . . . . *Digested*, 00/**3260**:
Applied, 07/2170: *Considered*, 06/2105, 06/2162
Sempra Metals Ltd (formerly Metallgesellschaft Ltd) v Inland Revenue Commissioners
[2007] UKHL 34; [2007] 3 W.L.R. 354; [2007] 4 All E.R. 657; [2007] S.T.C.
1559; [2007] B.T.C. 509; [2007] S.T.I. 1865; (2007) 104(31) L.S.G. 25; (2007)
157 N.L.J. 1082; (2007) 151 S.J.L.B. 985; *Times*, July 25, 2007, HL; affirming
in part [2005] EWCA Civ 389; [2006] Q.B. 37; [2005] 3 W.L.R. 521; [2005]
S.T.C. 687; [2005] 2 C.M.L.R. 30; [2005] Eu. L.R. 773; [2005] B.T.C. 202;
[2005] S.T.I. 831; [2005] N.P.C. 52; *Times*, April 26, 2005; *Independent*, April
22, 2005, CA (Civ Div); affirming [2004] EWHC 2387 (Ch); [2004] S.T.C. 1178;
[2004] Eu. L.R. 939; [2004] B.T.C. 358; [2004] S.T.I. 1495; *Times*, June 25,
2004, Ch D . . . . *Digested*, 07/**1052**:
Applied, 07/4311, 07/4359
Sen v Steelform Engineering Co Ltd see Lagden v O'Connor
Senanayake v Secretary of State for the Home Department [2005] EWCA Civ 1530;
[2006] Imm. A.R. 155, CA (Civ Div) . . . . *Digested*, 07/**2342**
Sendo International Ltd (In Administration), Re [2006] EWHC 2935 (Ch); [2007] B.C.C.
491; [2007] 1 B.C.L.C. 141, Ch D (Companies Ct) . . . . *Digested*, 07/**2394**
Senergy (UK) Ltd v Revenue and Customs Commissioners [2007] B.V.C. 2109; [2006]
S.T.I. 2580, V&DTr (London)
Senior Engineering Investments BV v Staatssecretaris van Financien (C-494/03)
[2007] S.T.C. 93; [2006] E.C.R. I-525; [2006] S.T.I. 201, ECJ (1st Chamber) . . *Digested*, 07/**3985**
Sensornet Ltd's Trade Mark Application (No.2375067) [2007] R.P.C. 10, App Person . *Digested*, 07/**2687**
Sepia Logistics Ltd (formerly Double Quick Supplyline Ltd) v Office of Fair Trading
[2007] CAT 13; [2007] Comp. A.R. 747, CAT
Sepia Logistics Ltd (formerly Double Quick Supplyline Ltd) v Office of Fair Trading
(Costs) [2007] CAT 14; [2007] Comp. A.R. 779, CAT

Sequential Trust, Re see Toland Trust, Re
Seray-Wurie v Charity Commissioners for England and Wales [2006] EWHC 3181
    (Ch); [2007] 1 W.L.R. 3242; [2007] 3 All E.R. 60, Ch D . . . .   *Digested*, 07/**321**
Serbeh v Governor of Brixton Prison [2002] EWHC 2356 (QB), QBD. . . . .   *Considered*, 07/1671
Serco Ltd v Lawson see Lawson v Serco Ltd
Serhan Estate v Johnson & Johnson (2006-07) 9 I.T.E.L.R. 326, CJ (Gen Div) (Ont) .   *Digested*, 07/**4198**
Servizi Ausiliari Dottori Commercialisti Srl v Calafiori (C-451/03) [2006] E.C.R. I-2941;
    [2006] 2 C.M.L.R. 45, ECJ (3rd Chamber). . . . .   *Digested*, 07/**1621**
SES Contracting Ltd v UK Coal Plc [2007] EWCA Civ 791; [2007] C.P. Rep. 46;
    [2007] 5 Costs L.R. 758; [2007] 33 E.G. 90 (C.S.); *Times*, October 16, 2007, CA
    (Civ Div); reversing [2007] EWHC 161 (QB), QBD . . . .   *Digested*, 07/**502**
Sevenoaks DC v Abbs [2007] P.A.D. 75, Planning Inspector
Sevenoaks Stationers (Retail) Ltd, Re [1991] Ch. 164; [1990] 3 W.L.R. 1165; [1991] 3 All
    E.R. 578; [1990] B.C.C. 765; [1991] B.C.L.C. 325; (1990) 134 S.J. 1367, CA (Civ
    Div); reversing [1990] B.C.L.C. 668, Ch D . . . .   *Digested*, 91/**401**:
                        Applied, 93/360, 00/662, 00/2243, 02/547, 05/518, 06/539, 07/3597:
                            Cited, 93/359, 93/374: *Considered*, 92/390, 94/408, 98/670, 98/671,
                                    06/540: *Followed*, 01/712: *Referred to*, 01/706
Seymour Caravan Sales Ltd v Revenue and Customs Commissioners [2007] S.T.I. 379,
    V&DTr
Seymour Caravan Sales Ltd v Revenue and Customs Commissioners; *sub nom*
    Revenue and Customs Commissioners v Seymour Caravan Sales Ltd [2007]
    EWHC 442 (Ch); [2007] S.T.C. 309; [2007] S.T.I. 409, Ch D . . . .   *Digested*, 07/**4360**
Sezek v Secretary of State for the Home Department see R. (on the application of
    Samaroo) v Secretary of State for the Home Department
SFU Barbers Ltd v Revenue and Customs Commissioners [2007] S.T.I. 377, V&DTr
    (Manchester)
SGL Carbon AG v Commission of the European Communities (C-308/04 P); *sub nom*
    Graphite Electrodes Cartel Appeal, Re (C-308/04 P) [2006] E.C.R. I-5977;
    [2006] 5 C.M.L.R. 16, ECJ (2nd Chamber). . . . .   *Digested*, 07/**604**:
                                                    Previous proceedings, 05/552
SGL Carbon AG v Commission of the European Communities (C-328/05) [2007] 5
    C.M.L.R. 1, ECJ . . . .   *Digested*, 07/**606**
SGL Carbon AG v Commission of the European Communities (T-239/01) see Tokai
    Carbon Co Ltd v Commission of the European Communities (T-236/01)
Shabpar v Barnet LBC see R. v Barnet LBC Ex p. Shah (Nilish)
Shackell v United Kingdom (45851/99) (Unreported, April 27, 2000), ECHR . . . .   *Applied*, 07/2205
Shaer v DPP see Blum v DPP
Shah v Baverstock; *sub nom* Baverstock (A Bankrupt), Re [2007] B.P.I.R. 1191, CC
    (Bournemouth)
Shah (Jitendra) v Barnet LBC see R. v Barnet LBC Ex p. Shah (Nilish)
Shala v Birmingham City Council [2007] EWCA Civ 624; [2007] LS Law Medical 517;
    (2007) 104(28) L.S.G. 28; (2007) 151 S.J.L.B. 895; *Times*, July 6, 2007, CA
    (Civ Div) . . . .   *Digested*, 07/**2151**
Shala v Secretary of State for the Home Department [2003] EWCA Civ 233; [2003]
    I.N.L.R. 349, CA (Civ Div) . . . .   *Digested*, 03/**2270**:
                        Applied, 07/2307: *Considered*, 04/2049, 06/2249: *Distinguished*, 04/2048,
                                                    05/2159, 06/2233
Shamil Bank of Bahrain EC v Beximco Pharmaceuticals Ltd (No.1); *sub nom* Beximco
    Pharmaceuticals Ltd v Shamil Bank of Bahrain EC [2004] EWCA Civ 19; [2004]
    1 W.L.R. 1784; [2004] 4 All E.R. 1072; [2004] 2 All E.R. (Comm) 312; [2004]
    2 Lloyd's Rep. 1; [2004] 1 C.L.C. 216; (2004) 101(8) L.S.G. 29; *Times*, February
    3, 2004, CA (Civ Div); affirming [2003] EWHC 2118 (Comm); [2003] 2 All
    E.R. (Comm) 849, QBD (Comm) . . . .   *Digested*, 04/**569**:
                                                    Considered, 07/799
Shamoon v Chief Constable of the Royal Ulster Constabulary [2003] UKHL 11;
    [2003] 2 All E.R. 26; [2003] N.I. 174; [2003] I.C.R. 337; [2003] I.R.L.R. 285;
    (2003) 147 S.J.L.B. 268; *Times*, March 4, 2003, HL (NI); affirming [2001]
    I.R.L.R. 520, CA (NI) . . . .   *Digested*, 03/**4767**:
                        Applied, 03/1297, 05/1337, 06/1303, 07/1388, 07/1402:
                            Considered, 04/1275, 05/1291, 06/1349, 06/1365, 07/1401
Shang v Zhang [2007] NSWSC 856; (2007-08) 10 I.T.E.L.R. 521, Sup Ct (NSW)
Sharkey v De Croos (Inspector of Taxes) see Sharkey v Revenue and Customs
    Commissioner
Sharkey v De Cross (Inspector of Taxes) see Sharkey v Revenue and Customs
    Commissioner
Sharkey v Revenue and Customs Commissioner; *sub nom* Sharkey v De Croos
    (Inspector of Taxes); Sharkey v De Cross (Inspector of Taxes) [2006] EWHC
    300 (Ch); [2006] S.T.C. 2026; 77 T.C. 484; [2007] B.T.C. 650; [2006] S.T.I.
    455, Ch D; affirming [2005] S.T.C. (S.C.D.) 336; [2005] S.T.I. 223, Sp Comm .   *Digested*, 06/**4267**:
                                                    Applied, 07/4067
Sharma v Brown-Antoine [2006] UKPC 57; [2007] 1 W.L.R. 780, PC (Trin) . . . .   *Digested*, 07/**53**
Sharma v Integrity Commission Registrar [2007] UKPC 42; [2007] 1 W.L.R. 2849, PC
    (Trin) . . . .   *Digested*, 07/**46**

Sharma v Trinidad and Tobago [2007] UKPC 41; [2007] 1 W.L.R. 2223, PC (Trin) . . . . .   *Digested*, 07/**692**
Sharman v HM Coroner for Inner North London see R. (on the application of
     Sharman) v HM Coroner for Inner North London
Sharp v Adam [2006] EWCA Civ 449; [2006] W.T.L.R. 1059; (2007-08) 10 I.T.E.L.R.
     419, CA (Civ Div); affirming [2005] EWHC 1806 (Ch), Ch D . . . .   *Digested*, 06/**4093**:
     Applied, 07/**3958**
Sharp v Dawes (1876-77) L.R. 2 Q.B.D. 26, CA . . . .   *Applied*, 69/**388**:
     Considered, 07/**2449**
Sharpe v Heighway (Unreported, November 20, 2006), CC (Telford) [*Ex rel.* Adam
     Farrer, Barrister, 5 Fountain Court, Steelhouse Lane, Birmingham] . . . .   *Digested*, 07/**3101**
Sharratt v London Central Bus Co Ltd (No.3) see Hollins v Russell
Shaw v DPP [2007] EWHC 207 (Admin); (2007) 171 J.P. 254; (2007) 171 J.P.N. 460,
     DC . . . .   *Digested*, 07/**988**
Shaw v Hutton-Shaw [2006] EWCA Civ 1235; [2007] 1 F.L.R. 1839; [2007] Fam.
     Law 497, CA (Civ Div) . . . .   *Digested*, 07/**1841**
Shaw v Revenue and Customs Commissioners [2006] EWHC 3699 (Ch); [2007]
     S.T.C. 1525; [2007] B.T.C. 5885; [2007] B.V.C. 854; [2006] S.T.I. 2509, Ch D;
     reversing [2006] S.T.I. 2108, V&DTr (Manchester)
Shaw v Royce Ltd [1911] 1 Ch. 138, Ch D . . . .   *Distinguished*, 07/**2422**
Shaw v Travel West Midlands (Unreported, February 15, 2006), CC (Birmingham) [*Ex*
     rel. Andrew Granville Stafford, Barrister, 4 King's Bench Walk, Temple, London] .   *Digested*, 07/**3136**
Shears v Mendeloff (1914) 30 T.L.R. 342. . . . .   *Considered*, 07/**4197**
Sheehan v London Fire and Civil Defence Authority see Cullin v London Fire and Civil
     Defence Authority
Sheekh v Netherlands (1948/04); *sub nom* Salah Sheekh v Netherlands (1948/04)
     (2007) 45 E.H.R.R. 50; [2007] I.N.L.R. 547, ECHR
Sheerin v Gallagher [2006] NICA 21; [2007] N.I. 1, CA (NI) . . . .   *Digested*, 07/**4518**
Sheffield v Oxford Controls Co Ltd [1979] I.C.R. 396; [1979] I.R.L.R. 133, EAT . . . . . .   *Digested*, 79/**1012**:
     Considered, 97/2225, 03/1224, 07/1435
Sheffield City Council v Shaw [2007] EWCA Civ 42; [2007] H.L.R. 25; (2007) 151
     S.J.L.B. 126, CA (Civ Div) . . . .   *Digested*, 07/**497**
Sheffield City Council v V see V (A Child), Re
Sheikh v Law Society [2006] EWCA Civ 1577; [2007] 3 All E.R. 183; (2006)
     103(47) L.S.G. 27; (2006) 156 N.L.J. 1846; *Times*, December 1, 2006;
     Independent, November 28, 2006, CA (Civ Div); reversing in part [2005]
     EWHC 1409 (Ch); [2005] 4 All E.R. 717; (2005) 102(30) L.S.G. 30; (2005) 155
     N.L.J. 1095, Ch D . . . .   *Digested*, 07/**2801**
Sheiling Trust (Ringwood Waldorf School) v Revenue and Customs Commissioners
     [2006] B.V.C. 2566; [2006] V. & D.R. 1; [2006] S.T.I. 1377; (2006) 150 S.J.L.B.
     570, V&DTr (London) . . . .   *Digested*, 07/**4336**
Sheldon v RHM Outhwaite (Underwriting Agencies) Ltd [1996] A.C. 102; [1995] 2
     W.L.R. 570; [1995] 2 All E.R. 558; [1995] 2 Lloyd's Rep. 197; [1995] C.L.C.
     655; [1995] 4 Re. L.R. 168; (1995) 92(22) L.S.G. 41; (1995) 145 N.L.J. 687;
     (1995) 139 S.J.L.B. 119; *Times*, May 5, 1995; *Independent*, May 9, 1995; *Lloyd's*
     List, May 24, 1995, HL; reversing [1994] 3 W.L.R. 999; [1994] 4 All E.R. 481;
     [1994] C.L.C. 703; [1995] 4 Re. L.R. 20; *Times*, July 1, 1994; *Independent*, July
     8, 1994, CA (Civ Div); reversing [1994] 1 W.L.R. 754; *Times*, December 8,
     1993, QBD . . . .   *Digested*, 95/**3159**:
     Applied, 96/839, 03/438, 07/471: *Considered*, 00/534, 02/3290
Shelfer v City of London Electric Lighting Co (No.1); *joined case* Meux's Brewery Co v
     City of London Electric Lighting Co [1895] 1 Ch. 287, CA . . . .   *Applied*, 57/3609,
     61/6344, 65/3985, 67/3170, 80/2251, 84/1150, 93/4040, 94/622, 95/4142,
     07/3425: *Considered*, 70/2290, 80/2007, 91/2676, 91/2976, 92/3602,
     96/1267, 00/5127, 07/2962: *Distinguished*, 69/2866, 70/2882, 82/2671:
     Followed, 95/3766
Shell UK Ltd v Revenue and Customs Commissioners [2007] S.T.I. 2122, Sp Comm
Shendish Manor Ltd v Customs and Excise Commissioners [2004] V. & D.R. 64,
     V&DTr (London) . . . .   *Digested*, 05/**4413**:
     Overruled, 07/**4321**
Shephard, Re see Shephard v Cartwright
Shephard v Cartwright; *sub nom* Shephard, Re [1955] A.C. 431; [1954] 3 W.L.R.
     967; [1954] 3 All E.R. 649; (1954) 98 S.J. 868, HL; reversing [1953] Ch. 728;
     [1953] 3 W.L.R. 378; [1953] 2 All E.R. 608; (1953) 97 S.J. 524, CA; affirming
     [1953] 1 W.L.R. 460; [1953] 1 All E.R. 569; (1953) 97 S.J. 151, Ch D . . . .   *Digested*, 54/**1600**:
     Applied, 07/4236: *Considered*, 70/138, 79/2414: *Distinguished*, 65/1562,
     03/4479: *Explained*, 70/138
Shepherd v Inland Revenue Commissioners see Shepherd v Revenue and Customs
     Commissioners
Shepherd v Official Receiver [2006] EWHC 2902 (Ch); [2007] B.P.I.R. 101, Ch D . . .   *Digested*, 07/**2444**
Shepherd v Revenue and Customs Commissioners; *sub nom* Shepherd v Inland
     Revenue Commissioners [2006] EWHC 1512 (Ch); [2006] S.T.C. 1821; 78 T.C.
     389; [2007] B.T.C. 426; [2006] S.T.I. 1518, Ch D; affirming [2005] S.T.C.
     (S.C.D.) 644, Sp Comm . . . .   *Digested*, 07/**4098**

Shepherd Homes Ltd v Encia Remediation Ltd [2007] EWHC 70 (TCC); [2007] B.L.R.
135; 110 Con. L.R. 90, QBD (TCC) . . . . *Digested, 07/***801**
Shepherds Investments Ltd v Walters [2006] EWHC 836 (Ch); [2007] 2 B.C.L.C. 202;
[2007] I.R.L.R. 110; [2007] F.S.R. 15; (2006) 150 S.J.L.B. 536, Ch D . . . . *Digested, 07/***573**
Shepherds Investments Ltd v Walters [2007] EWCA Civ 292; [2007] C.P. Rep. 31;
[2007] 5 Costs L.R. 837; (2007) 104(16) L.S.G. 25, CA (Civ Div) . . . . *Digested, 07/***525**
Sheppard v Glossop Corp [1921] 3 K.B. 132, CA . . . . *Applied,* 60/1692:
Considered, 07/2870: Distinguished, 78/1550, 80/1333, 94/4517
Shergold v Fieldway Medical Centre [2006] I.C.R. 304; [2006] I.R.L.R. 76, EAT . . . . *Digested, 07/***1408**:
Applied, 06/1334: *Followed,* 06/1335
Sherrin v Brand [1956] 1 Q.B. 403; [1956] 2 W.L.R. 131; [1956] 1 All E.R. 194; (1956)
100 S.J. 34, CA . . . . *Digested,* 56/**7612**:
Applied, 57/3065: *Considered, 07/2718: Distinguished,* 88/1801
Sherwin-Williams Co v Office for Harmonisation in the Internal Market (Trade Marks
and Designs) (OHIM) (T-190/05) (2007) 30(10) I.P.D. 30068, CFI (5th
Chamber)
Shevchenko v Ukraine (32478/02) (2007) 45 E.H.R.R. 27, ECHR
Shield Mark BV v Kist (t/a Memex) (C-283/01) [2004] Ch. 97; [2004] 2 W.L.R. 1117;
[2004] All E.R. (EC) 277; [2003] E.C.R. I-14313; [2005] 1 C.M.L.R. 41; [2004]
C.E.C. 228; [2004] E.T.M.R. 33; [2004] R.P.C. 17; *Times,* December 4, 2003,
ECJ (6th Chamber) . . . . *Digested, 04/***2420**:
Distinguished, 07/1580
Shierson v Rastogi (A Bankrupt) [2007] EWHC 1266 (Ch); [2007] B.P.I.R. 891;
(2007) 104(25) L.S.G. 39, Ch D (Bankruptcy Ct)
Shiloh Spinners Ltd v Harding [1973] A.C. 691; [1973] 2 W.L.R. 28; [1973] 1 All E.R.
90; (1973) 25 P. & C.R. 48; (1972) 117 S.J. 34, HL; reversing [1972] Ch. 326;
[1971] 3 W.L.R. 34; [1971] 2 All E.R. 307; (1971) 22 P. & C.R. 447; (1971) 115
S.J. 248, CA (Civ Div) . . . . *Digested,* 73/**1867**:
Applied, 85/1878, 99/3290, 07/3420: *Considered,* 74/2023, 81/1503, 83/421,
83/3405, 84/1326, 84/1901, 84/1931, 86/1841, 87/2959, 89/2128, 91/2226,
91/2232, 97/3293, 00/2326, 05/3793: *Distinguished,* 00/4658
Shilton v Wilmshurst (Inspector of Taxes) [1991] 1 A.C. 684; [1991] 2 W.L.R. 530;
[1991] 3 All E.R. 148; [1991] S.T.C. 88; 64 T.C. 78; (1991) 135 S.J. 250; *Times,*
February 13, 1991; *Independent,* February 20, 1991; *Financial Times,* February 12,
1991; *Guardian,* February 12, 1991, HL; reversing [1990] 1 W.L.R. 373; [1990]
S.T.C. 55; (1990) 87(4) L.S.G. 43; (1990) 134 S.J. 50, CA (Civ Div); affirming
[1989] 1 W.L.R. 179; [1988] S.T.C. 868; (1988) 132 S.J. 1755, Ch D . . . . *Digested,* 91/**2092**:
Applied, 93/2275, 99/4729, 05/4071: *Distinguished,* 07/4070
Shirley Children's Settlement Trustees v Crabtree [2007] EWHC 1532 (Admin); (2007)
157 N.L.J. 975; *Times,* July 30, 2007, QBD (Admin)
Shofman v Russia (74826/01) [2006] 1 F.L.R. 680; [2005] 3 F.C.R. 581; (2007) 44
E.H.R.R. 35; [2006] Fam. Law 185, ECHR . . . . *Digested, 06/***1685**:
Considered, 07/1787
Shopalotto.com Ltd's Patent Application (GB 0017772.5) [2005] EWHC 2416 (Pat);
[2006] R.P.C. 7, Ch D (Patents Ct) . . . . *Digested, 06/***2521**:
Applied, 07/2627, 07/2632: *Cited,* 06/2529
Showa Denko KK v Commission of the European Communities (C-289/04 P); *sub
nom* Graphite Electrodes Cartel Appeal, Re (C-289/04 P) [2006] E.C.R. I-
5859; [2006] 5 C.M.L.R. 14, ECJ (2nd Chamber) . . . . *Digested, 07/***603**:
Applied, 07/606: Previous proceedings, 05/552
Showa Denko KK v Commission of the European Communities (T245/01) see Tokai
Carbon Co Ltd v Commission of the European Communities (T-236/01)
Shree Vishwakarma Association of the UK, Re [2007] W.T.L.R. 829, Charity Comm. . . *Digested, 07/***4243**
Shruth Ltd (In Liquidation), Re see International Brands USA Inc v Goldstein
Shum Kwok Sher v HKSAR (Unreported), CFA (HK) . . . . *Applied,* 07/**962**:
Considered, 04/753
Shuttari v Solicitors Indemnity Fund [2007] EWCA Civ 244; [2007] 1 C.L.C. 303, CA
(Civ Div) . . . . *Digested, 07/***243**
SI (Ethiopia) v Secretary of State for the Home Department; *sub nom* SI (Reported
Cases as Evidence: Ethiopia), Re [2007] UKAIT 12; [2007] Imm. A.R. 505, AIT
SI (Reported Cases as Evidence: Ethiopia), Re see SI (Ethiopia) v Secretary of State for
the Home Department
SIAC Construction Ltd v Mayo CC [2002] IESC 37; [2003] Eu. L.R. 1, Sup Ct (Irl);
affirming [1999] Eu. L.R. 535, HC (Irl) . . . . *Digested,* 99/**5078**:
Applied, 07/3329
Sialkowska v Poland (8932/05) 22 B.H.R.C. 695, ECHR
Sidhu v British Airways Plc see Abnett v British Airways Plc
Sidhu v Memory Corp Plc (No.1) see Memory Corp Plc v Sidhu (No.1)
Sidney G Jones Ltd v Martin Bencher Ltd [1986] 1 Lloyd's Rep. 54, QBD . . . . *Considered,* 07/**4215**

Sieckmann v Deutsches Patent- und Markenamt (C-273/00) [2003] Ch. 487; [2003]
     3 W.L.R. 424; [2004] All E.R. (EC) 253; [2002] E.C.R. I-11737; [2005] 1
     C.M.L.R. 40; [2004] C.E.C. 404; [2003] E.T.M.R. 37; [2003] R.P.C. 38; *Times*,
     December 27, 2002, ECJ . . . . *Digested*, 03/**2637**:
              Applied, 04/2370, 05/2536: *Considered*, 04/2420: *Distinguished*, 07/1580:
              Followed, 06/2578
Siemens Schweiz AG v Thorn Security Ltd [2007] EWHC 2242 (Ch); (2007) 30(10)
     I.P.D. 30062, Ch D
Siemianowski v Poland (45972/99) (2007) 44 E.H.R.R. 24, ECHR
Sierney v DPP; *sub nom* Sierny v DPP [2006] EWHC 716 (Admin); (2006) 170 J.P.
     697; [2006] Po. L.R. 10; [2007] Crim. L.R. 60; [2006] A.C.D. 71, QBD
     (Admin) . . . . *Digested*, 07/**3313**
Sierny v DPP see Sierney v DPP
Sifri v Clough & Willis (A Firm) [2007] EWHC 985 (Ch); [2007] W.T.L.R. 1453, Ch D
Sigi v Council of the European Union (T-338/02) see Segi v Council of the European
     Union (T-338/02)
SIGLA SA v Office for Harmonisation in the Internal Market (Trade Marks and Designs)
     (OHIM) (T-215/03) [2007] E.T.M.R. 79; [2007] Bus. L.R. D53, CFI (5th
     Chamber)
Sika AG (T670/95) . . . . *Considered*, 07/2611
Sildedzis v Poland (45214/99) (2007) 44 E.H.R.R. 13, ECHR
Silicon Graphics Finance SA (formerly Silicon Graphics Manufacturing SA) v Revenue and
     Customs Commissioners [2006] EWHC 1889 (Admin); [2007] B.T.C. 5827;
     [2007] B.V.C. 796; [2006] S.T.I. 1986, QBD (Admin)
Sillett v Meek [2007] EWHC 1169 (Ch); (2007-08) 10 I.T.E.L.R. 617, Ch D
Silver Line Reiseburo GmbH v Zentrale zur Bekampfung Unlauteren Wettbewerbs eV
     (66/86) see Ahmed Saeed Flugreisen v Zentrale zur Bekampfung Unlauteren
     Wettbewerbs eV (66/86)
Silversafe Ltd (In Liquidation) v Hood [2006] EWHC 1849 (Ch); [2007] S.T.C. 871;
     [2006] S.T.I. 1988, Ch D . . . . *Digested*, 07/**493**
Silverton v Goodall [1997] P.I.Q.R. P451, CA (Civ Div) [*Ex rel*. Linda Atherstone,
     Solicitor, Cole & Cole, Reading] . . . . *Digested*, 97/**769**:
              Applied, 98/590: *Considered*, 07/3458
Sim v Stretch [1936] 2 All E.R. 1237, HL . . . . *Applied*, 57/1978,
              62/1749, 63/1998, 67/2281, 70/1575, 07/5098
Simion v Brown; *joined case* Brown v Simion [2007] EWHC 511 (Ch); [2007] B.P.I.R.
     412, Ch D . . . . *Digested*, 07/**2457**
Simms v Conlon see Conlon v Simms
Simonds Farsons Cisk Plc v Office for Harmonisation in the Internal Market (Trade
     Marks and Designs) (OHIM) (T-3/04) [2006] E.T.M.R. 49, CFI (5th Chamber)   *Applied*, 07/2658
Simpson v Bowker [2007] EWCA Civ 772; [2007] 5 Costs L.R. 850, CA (Civ Div)
Simpson v Worron (Unreported, May 4, 2007), CC (Brighton) [*Ex rel*. Richard
     Wheeler, 3 Paper Buildings, 4 St Peters Street, Winchester, Hants] . . . . *Digested*, 07/**3142**
Simtel Communications Ltd v Rebak [2006] EWHC 572 (QB); [2006] 2 B.C.L.C. 571,
     QBD . . . . *Digested*, 07/**2398**
Sinclair v Woods of Winchester Ltd [2006] EWHC 3003 (TCC); 109 Con. L.R. 14,
     QBD (TCC)
Sinclair Gardens Investments (Kensington) Ltd v Poets Chase Freehold Co Ltd [2007]
     EWHC 1776 (Ch); [2007] 49 E.G. 104; [2007] 32 E.G. 89 (C.S.); (2007) 157
     S.J.L.B. 1427; [2007] N.P.C. 96, Ch D
Sinclair Investment Holdings SA v Versailles Trade Finance Ltd (In Administrative
     Receivership) [2007] EWHC 915 (Ch); [2007] 2 All E.R. (Comm) 993; (2007-
     08) 10 I.T.E.L.R. 58, Ch D . . . . *Digested*, 07/**4246**
Singer v Beckett; *sub nom* Continental Assurance Co of London Plc (In Liquidation),
     Re [2007] 2 B.C.L.C. 287; [2001] B.P.I.R. 733, Ch D . . . . *Digested*, 01/**728**
Singh v Bhakar [2007] 1 F.L.R. 880; [2006] Fam. Law 1026; (2006) 150 S.J.L.B.
     1112, CC (Nottingham) . . . . *Digested*, 07/**1828**
Singh v Solihull MBC; *sub nom* R. (on the application of Singh) v Solihull MBC
     [2007] EWHC 552 (Admin); [2007] 2 C.M.L.R. 47, QBD (Admin) . . . . *Digested*, 07/**3458**
Singh v United Kingdom see Hussain v United Kingdom
Singla v Brown [2007] EWHC 405 (Ch); [2007] B.P.I.R. 424, Ch D . . . . *Digested*, 07/**2407**
Sir Christopher Wren's House Ltd v Revenue and Customs Commissioners [2006] V. &
     D.R. 399, V&DTr (London) . . . . *Digested*, 07/**4327**
Sir Lindsay Parkinson & Co v Triplan Ltd [1973] Q.B. 609; [1973] 2 W.L.R. 632; (1973)
     117 S.J. 146, CA (Civ Div); affirming [1973] 2 All E.R. 273; (1972) 117 S.J. 36,
     QBD . . . . *Digested*, 73/**2632**:
           Applied, 82/591.u, 07/416, 07/512: *Considered*, 86/2696, 92/3442, 01/5711:
              Followed, 97/563
Sir WG Armstrong Whitworth & Co Ltd v Redford [1920] A.C. 757, HL; affirming [1919]
     W.N. 153, CA . . . . *Considered*, 66/7943,
              77/2001, 07/2082
Sisojeva v Latvia (60654/00) (2007) 45 E.H.R.R. 33, ECHR (Grand Chamber)
Sison v Council of the European Union (C-266/05 P) [2007] 2 C.M.L.R. 17, ECJ (1st
     Chamber) . . . . *Digested*, 07/**1561**

Sison v Council of the European Union (T-47/03) [2007] 3 C.M.L.R. 39, CFI (2nd Chamber)

Sisu Capital Fund Ltd v Tucker; *joined case* Sisu Capital Fund Ltd v Wallace [2005] EWHC 2170 (Ch); [2006] B.C.C. 463; [2006] B.P.I.R. 154, Ch D (Companies Ct) . . . . *Digested,* 06/**2356**:
Considered, 07/2422

Sisu Capital Fund Ltd v Wallace see Sisu Capital Fund Ltd v Tucker

SITA UK Ltd v Hope UKEAT/0787/04/MAA, EAT. . . . . *Considered,* 07/1366

SITMA/Apparatus for applying adhesive (T986/04) [2007] E.P.O.R. 43, EPO (Technical Bd App)

SK (Adoption Not Recognised in UK: India), Re see SK (India) v Secretary of State for the Home Department

SK (Illegal Entrant: Leave to Enter: Nigeria), Re see SK (Nigeria) v Secretary of State for the Home Department

SK (India) v Secretary of State for the Home Department; *sub nom* SK (Proof of Indirect Racial Discrimination: India), Re [2006] UKAIT 67; [2007] Imm. A.R. 163, AIT . . . . *Digested,* 07/**2338**

SK (India) v Secretary of State for the Home Department; *sub nom* SK (Adoption Not Recognised in UK: India), Re [2006] UKAIT 68; [2007] Imm. A.R. 142, AIT . . . *Digested,* 07/**2324**

SK (Nigeria) v Secretary of State for the Home Department; *sub nom* SK (Illegal Entrant: Leave to Enter: Nigeria), Re [2007] UKAIT 3; [2007] I.N.L.R. 395, AIT

SK (Proof of Indirect Racial Discrimination: India), Re see SK (India) v Secretary of State for the Home Department

Skalka v Sozialversicherungsanstalt der Gewerblichen Wirtschaft (C-160/02) [2004] E.C.R. I-5613, ECJ. . . . . *Applied,* 07/1609

Skanska Construction Ltd v Egger (Barony) Ltd [2002] EWCA Civ 310; [2002] B.L.R. 236; 83 Con. L.R. 132; [2003] Lloyd's Rep. I.R. 479, CA (Civ Div) . . . . *Considered,* 07/2479

Skanska Rasleigh Weatherfoil Ltd v Somerfield Stores Ltd; *sub nom* Somerfield Stores Ltd v Skanska Rasleigh Weatherfoil Ltd [2006] EWCA Civ 1732; [2007] C.I.L.L. 2449; (2006) 150 S.J.L.B. 1567, CA (Civ Div); affirming [2006] EWHC 947 (TCC), QBD (TCC)

Skatteministeriet v Aktieselskabet Forsikringsselskabet Codan (C-236/97) [1998] E.C.R. I-8679; [2001] 1 C.M.L.R. 36, ECJ (6th Chamber) . . . . *Applied,* 07/3985

Skerrits of Nottingham Ltd v Secretary of State for the Environment, Transport and the Regions (No.2) see Skerritts of Nottingham Ltd v Secretary of State for the Environment, Transport and the Regions (No.2)

Skerritts of Nottingham Ltd v Secretary of State for the Environment, Transport and the Regions (No.2); *sub nom* Skerrits of Nottingham Ltd v Secretary of State for the Environment, Transport and the Regions (No.2) [2000] 2 P.L.R. 102; [2000] J.P.L. 1025; [2000] E.G. 43 (C.S.), CA (Civ Div); reversing (2000) 79 P. & C.R. 251; [1999] 4 P.L.R. 1; [2000] J.P.L. 281; *Times,* October 20, 1999, QBD . . *Digested,* 00/**4415**:
Applied, 02/3693, 07/3263

Skjevesland v Geveran Trading Co Ltd (No.4) [2002] EWHC 2898 (Ch); [2003] B.C.C. 391; [2003] B.P.I.R. 924, Ch D . . . . *Digested,* 03/**2362**:
Applied, 07/2411

Skowera v Revenue and Customs Commissioners [2007] V. & D.R. 128, V&DTr (London)

Skurcak v Slovakia (58708/00) [2007] B.P.I.R. 440, ECHR

Skuse v Granada Television Ltd [1996] E.M.L.R. 278; *Independent,* April 2, 1993, CA (Civ Div) . . . . *Digested,* 93/**2584**:
Applied, 01/1830, 05/982, 07/1070: *Considered,* 02/953, 02/955:
Followed, 95/3131

SL v Pembrokeshire CC see Lawrence v Pembrokeshire CC

Slack v Leeds Industrial Cooperative Society Ltd see Leeds Industrial Cooperative Society v Slack (No.2)

Slade v Corus (UK) Ltd (Unreported, December 18, 2006), CC (Cardiff) [*Ex rel.* Andrew Arentsen, Barrister, 33 Park Place, Cardiff] . . . . *Digested,* 07/**3175**

Slater v Lewisham LBC [2006] EWCA Civ 394; [2006] 2 F.C.R. 90; [2006] H.L.R. 37; (2006) 150 S.J.L.B. 539; *Times,* May 3, 2006, CA (Civ Div). . . . . *Digested,* 06/**2028**:
Applied, 07/2140

Slater v Simm [2007] EWHC 951 (Ch); [2007] W.T.L.R. 1043, Ch D . . . . *Digested,* 07/**3358**

Slator v Bow Street Magistrates Court see R. (on the application of Slator) v Bow Street Magistrates Court

Sledmore v Dalby (1996) 72 P. & C.R. 196; [1996] N.P.C. 16, CA (Civ Div) . . . . *Digested,* 96/**4949**:
Applied, 06/3494, 07/2762

Slingsby v Doncaster Community Transport (Unreported, November 29, 2006), CC (Rotherham) [*Ex rel.* James Hogg, Pupil Barrister, St James's Chambers, 68 Quay Street, Manchester] . . . . *Digested,* 07/**3144**

Sloan v Atkins (Unreported, March 21, 2007), CC (Maidstone) [*Ex rel.* Alison Griffiths, Barrister, 4 King's Bench Walk, Temple, London]. . . . . *Digested,* 07/**3130**

Small (Inspector of Taxes) v Mars UK Ltd see Revenue and Customs Commissioners v William Grant & Sons Distillers Ltd (Scotland)

Smalley, Re; *sub nom* Smalley *v* Warwick Crown Court; R. *v* Warwick Crown Court Ex
    p. Smalley (No.1) [1985] A.C. 622; [1985] 2 W.L.R. 538; [1985] 1 All E.R. 769;
    (1985) 80 Cr. App. R. 205; (1985) 149 J.P. 319; [1985] Crim. L.R. 371; (1985)
    82 L.S.G. 1638; (1985) 135 N.L.J. 229; (1985) 129 S.J. 172, HL; reversing
    (1984) 148 J.P. 708, DC. . . . . *Digested*, 85/**555**:
                    Applied, 86/604, 86/625, 88/587, 91/613, 93/12, 93/15, 05/71:
            Considered, 87/2282, 92/39, 93/10, 93/1082, 95/23, 95/3098, 07/54:
                           Distinguished, 93/11: *Followed*, 93/14
Smalley *v* Warwick Crown Court see Smalley, Re
Smallwood *v* Revenue and Customs Commissioners; *sub nom* Trustees of Trevor
    Smallwood Trust *v* Revenue and Customs Commissioners 10 I.T.L. Rep. 574, Sp
    Comm
Smallwood *v* Revenue and Customs Commissioners; *sub nom* Revenue and Customs
    Commissioners *v* Smallwood [2007] EWCA Civ 462; [2007] S.T.C. 1237; 78
    T.C. 560; [2007] B.T.C. 347; [2007] S.T.I. 1562; [2007] N.P.C. 63; *Times*, June 7,
    2007, CA (Civ Div); affirming [2006] EWHC 1653 (TCC); [2006] S.T.C. 2050;
    [2006] B.T.C. 741; [2006] S.T.I. 1852; *Times*, August 23, 2006, Ch D; affirming
    [2006] S.T.C. (S.C.D.) 12; [2005] S.T.I. 1998, Sp Comm . . . . *Digested*, 07/**3988**
Smart *v* East Cheshire NHS Trust [2003] EWHC 2806 (QB); [2004] 1 Costs L.R. 124;
    (2004) 80 B.M.L.R. 175, QBD . . . . *Considered*, 07/385:
                            Followed, 05/327, 07/383
Smart-Tel (UK) Ltd, Re; *sub nom* Official Receiver *v* Doshi [2007] B.C.C. 896; [2007]
    B.P.I.R. 1135, Ch D (Companies Ct)
Smirnova (Irina) *v* Russia (48183/99) see Smirnova (Yelena) *v* Russia (46133/99)
Smirnova (Yelena) *v* Russia (46133/99); *joined case* Smirnova (Irina) *v* Russia (48183/
    99) (2004) 39 E.H.R.R. 22, ECHR . . . . *Digested*, 05/**2110**:
                                  Applied, 07/2201
Smith *v* Baxter [1900] 2 Ch. 138, Ch D . . . . *Applied*, 07/3425
Smith *v* Brough [2005] EWCA Civ 261; [2006] C.P. Rep. 17, CA (Civ Div) . . . . *Digested*, 06/**518**:
                                     Applied, 07/446
Smith *v* Chief Superintendent of Woking Police Station (1983) 76 Cr. App. R. 234;
    [1983] Crim. L.R. 323, QBD . . . . *Digested*, 83/**544**:
                        Applied, 07/1028: *Considered*, 96/1437
Smith *v* DPP [2007] EWHC 100 (Admin); [2007] 4 All E.R. 1135; (2007) 171 J.P. 321;
    [2007] R.T.R. 36; (2007) 171 J.P.N. 612; (2007) 171 J.P.N. 642, QBD (Admin) . *Digested*, 07/**846**
Smith *v* Hampshire CC [2007] EWCA Civ 246; [2007] E.L.R. 321; (2007) 151 S.J.L.B.
    433, CA (Civ Div); affirming [2006] EWHC 743 (QB), QBD . . . . *Digested*, 07/**474**
Smith *v* Henniker-Major & Co [2002] EWCA Civ 762; [2003] Ch. 182; [2002] 3
    W.L.R. 1848; [2002] B.C.C. 768; [2002] 2 B.C.L.C. 655; (2002) 99(37) L.S.G.
    36; *Times*, August 29, 2002; *Independent*, October 21, 2002, CA (Civ Div);
    affirming [2002] B.C.C. 544, Ch D . . . . *Digested*, 02/**559**:
                              Applied, 04/472, 07/2920
Smith *v* Howell 155 E.R. 739; (1851) 6 Ex. 730, Ex Ct . . . . *Considered*, 07/2774
Smith *v* Hughes see Cranfield *v* Bridgegrove Ltd
Smith *v* Kvaerner Cementation Foundations Ltd [2006] EWCA Civ 242; [2007] 1
    W.L.R. 370; [2006] 3 All E.R. 593; [2006] C.P. Rep. 36; [2006] B.L.R. 244;
    [2006] A.C.D. 51; (2006) 103(14) L.S.G. 33; (2006) 156 N.L.J. 721; [2006]
    N.P.C. 35; *Times*, April 11, 2006, CA (Civ Div) . . . . *Digested*, 06/**19**
Smith *v* Littlewoods Organisation Ltd see Maloco *v* Littlewoods Organisation Ltd
Smith *v* Mental Health Tribunal for Scotland; *sub nom* Smith, Petitioner 2006 S.L.T.
    347; [2007] M.H.L.R. 17; 2006 G.W.D. 10-178, OH . . . . *Digested*, 06/**5006**
Smith *v* North East Derbyshire Primary Care Trust see Smith *v* North Eastern
    Derbyshire Primary Care Trust
Smith *v* North Eastern Derbyshire Primary Care Trust; *sub nom* Smith *v* North East
    Derbyshire Primary Care Trust; R. (on the application of Smith) *v* North Eastern
    Derbyshire Primary Care Trust [2006] EWCA Civ 1291; [2006] 1 W.L.R. 3315;
    (2006) 9 C.C.L. Rep. 663; [2007] LS Law Medical 188; (2006) 150 S.J.L.B.
    1152; *Times*, September 11, 2006, CA (Civ Div); reversing [2006] EWHC 1338
    (Admin); [2006] Lloyd's Rep. Med. 425; (2006) 90 B.M.L.R. 139; [2006]
    A.C.D. 75, QBD (Admin) . . . . *Digested*, 06/**1940**
Smith *v* North Somerset Council [2007] EWHC 1767 (Admin); (2007) 171 J.P. 509;
    (2007) 171 J.P.N. 906, DC . . . . *Digested*, 07/**3898**
Smith *v* Oliver [1989] 2 P.L.R. 1, DC. . . . . *Digested*, 90/**4479**:
                                   Followed, 07/3294
Smith *v* Parole Board see R. (on the application of Smith) *v* Parole Board
Smith *v* Revenue and Customs Commissioners [2007] EWHC 2304 (Ch); [2007]
    B.T.C. 8010; [2007] S.T.I. 2560; (2007) 157 N.L.J. 1506, Ch D; affirming [2007]
    S.T.C. (S.C.D.) 506; [2007] W.T.L.R. 1281; [2007] S.T.I. 1335; [2007] S.T.I.
    2409, Sp Comm . . . . *Digested*, 07/**4106**
Smith *v* Scott [2007] CSIH 9; 2007 S.C. 345; 2007 S.L.T. 137; 2007 S.C.L.R. 268;
    2007 G.W.D. 3-46; *Times*, February 5, 2007, Registration App Ct (SC) . . . . *Digested*, 07/**5431**
Smith *v* Secretary of State for Trade and Industry [2007] EWHC 1013 (Admin); [2007]
    N.P.C. 56, QBD (Admin)
Smith *v* Secretary of State for Work and Pensions see Smith *v* Smith

Smith v Smith; *sub nom* Smith v Secretary of State for Work and Pensions [2006]
   UKHL 35; [2006] 1 W.L.R. 2024; [2006] 3 All E.R. 907; [2007] 1 F.L.R. 166;
   [2006] 2 F.C.R. 487; [2006] Fam. Law 834; (2006) 103(30) L.S.G. 31; (2006)
   150 S.J.L.B. 986; *Times*, July 14, 2006; *Independent*, July 19, 2006, HL;
   reversing [2004] EWCA Civ 1318; [2005] 1 W.L.R. 1318; [2005] 1 F.L.R. 606;
   [2005] Fam. Law 204; (2004) 101(43) L.S.G. 34; *Times*, November 2, 2004;
   Independent, October 26, 2004, CA (Civ Div) . . . . *Digested*, 06/**1646**
Smith v South Staffordshire DC [2007] R.V.R. 16, Lands Tr . . . . *Digested*, 07/**3248**
Smith v South Wales Switchgear Co Ltd see Smith v UMB Chrysler (Scotland) Ltd
Smith v Southampton University Hospitals NHS Trust [2007] EWCA Civ 387; (2007)
   96 B.M.L.R. 79, CA (Civ Div); reversing (2006) 150 S.J.L.B. 1114, QBD
Smith v UMB Chrysler (Scotland) Ltd; *sub nom* Smith v South Wales Switchgear Co
   Ltd [1978] 1 W.L.R. 165; [1978] 1 All E.R. 18; 1978 S.C. (H.L.) 1; 1978 S.L.T. 21; 8
   B.L.R. 1; (1978) 122 S.J. 61, HL; reversing 1977 S.C. 93; 1977 S.L.T. (Notes) 37,
   IH (2 Div); affirming 1976 S.L.T. (Notes) 42, OH . . . . *Digested*, 80/**359**:
                                          Applied, 83/4038, 93/499, 96/1216, 98/5546, 07/5012:
                                          Considered, 92/1553, 03/730: *Followed*, 86/223, 96/5302
Smith v United Kingdom (Admissibility) (39658/05) (2007) 44 E.H.R.R. SE18, ECHR
Smith Hayden & Co Ltd's Application, Re (1946) 63 R.P.C. 97 . . . . *Applied*, 47-51/10364,
                                          93/3991, 96/5721, 07/2662: *Considered*, 93/3990, 96/5723, 97/4897,
                                          98/3534, 98/3539: *Followed*, 78/2957, 95/4946, 97/4899
Smith Kline & French Laboratories Ltd v Evans Medical Ltd (Amendment of Patent)
   [1989] 1 F.S.R. 561, Ch D (Patents Ct) . . . . *Applied*, 02/2786:
                                          Considered, 95/3752, 07/2613, 07/2633
Smith Kline & French Laboratories Ltd v Netherlands (Admissibility) (12633/87)
   (Unreported, October 4, 1990), Eur Comm HR . . . . *Applied*, 07/2636
Smith New Court Securities Ltd v Citibank NA; *sub nom* Smith New Court Securities
   Ltd v Scrimgeour Vickers (Asset Management) Ltd [1997] A.C. 254; [1996] 3
   W.L.R. 1051; [1996] 4 All E.R. 769; [1997] 1 B.C.L.C. 350; [1996] C.L.C. 1958;
   (1996) 93(46) L.S.G. 28; (1996) 146 N.L.J. 1722; (1997) 141 S.J.L.B. 5; *Times*,
   November 22, 1996; *Independent*, November 27, 1996, HL; reversing [1994] 1
   W.L.R. 1271; [1994] 4 All E.R. 225; [1994] 2 B.C.L.C. 212; [1994] C.L.C. 203;
   (1994) 91(15) L.S.G. 35; (1994) 91(22) L.S.G. 32; (1994) 138 S.J.L.B. 77;
   Times, March 8, 1994, CA (Civ Div); reversing [1992] B.C.L.C. 1104; *Times*, April
   7, 1992, Ch D . . . . *Digested*, 96/**996**:
                                          Applied, 00/1452, 01/965, 03/535, 04/920, 07/2918: *Followed*, 97/3370
Smith New Court Securities Ltd v Scrimgeour Vickers (Asset Management) Ltd see
   Smith New Court Securities Ltd v Citibank NA
Smith (Letitia) v Smith (Richard) [2000] 3 F.C.R. 374, CA (Civ Div) . . . . *Digested*, 00/**2519**:
                                          Considered, 05/1688, 07/1830
Smith, Petitioner see Smith v Mental Health Tribunal for Scotland
SmithKline Beecham Plc v Apotex Europe Ltd [2006] EWCA Civ 658; [2007] Ch. 71;
   [2006] 3 W.L.R. 1146; [2006] 4 All E.R. 1078; [2006] C.P. Rep. 39; [2007]
   F.S.R. 6; (2006) 29(10) I.P.D. 29072; (2006) 103(23) L.S.G. 32; (2006) 156
   N.L.J. 952; *Times*, June 9, 2006, CA (Civ Div); affirming [2005] EWHC 1655
   (Ch); [2006] 1 W.L.R. 872; [2006] 2 All E.R. 53; [2005] F.S.R. 44; (2005)
   28(10) I.P.D. 28077; *Times*, August 10, 2005, Ch D . . . . *Digested*, 06/**522**
SmithKline Beecham Plc v H (A Child) see Horne-Roberts v SmithKline Beecham Plc
SmithKline Beecham Plc v Horne-Roberts see Horne-Roberts v SmithKline Beecham
   Plc
SmithKline Beecham Plc's (Paroxetine Methanesulfonate) Patent (No.2) see Synthon BV v
   SmithKline Beecham Plc (No.2)
SMITHKLINE BEECHAM/Amoxycillin-clavulanate formulation (T214/04) [2007] E.P.O.R.
   56, EPO (Technical Bd App)
Smolen v Tower Hamlets LBC [2006] EWHC 3628 (Ch); [2007] B.P.I.R. 448, Ch D
Smurthwaite v Simpson-Smith [2006] B.P.I.R. 1483, Ch D . . . . *Subsequent proceed-*
                                          ings, 07/2437
Smurthwaite v Simpson-Smith; *joined case* Mond v Smurthwaite [2006] EWCA Civ
   1183; [2006] B.P.I.R. 1504, CA (Civ Div); affirming [2005] EWHC 447 (Ch);
   [2006] B.P.I.R. 1469, Ch D . . . . *Digested*, 07/**2437**:
                                          Reversed, 07/2437
Snell v Revenue and Customs Commissioners [2006] EWHC 3350 (Ch); [2007]
   S.T.C. 1279; 78 T.C. 294; [2007] B.T.C. 62; [2007] S.T.I. 115; (2007) 104(3)
   L.S.G. 30, Ch D; affirming [2006] S.T.C. (S.C.D.) 296; [2006] S.T.I. 1412, Sp
   Comm . . . . *Digested*, 07/**3993**
Sneyd v DPP [2006] EWHC 560; (2006) 170 J.P. 545; [2007] R.T.R. 6; (2006) 170
   J.P.N. 998, QBD (Admin) . . . . *Digested*, 06/**799**
Snook v London and West Riding Investments Ltd [1967] 2 Q.B. 786; [1967] 2
   W.L.R. 1020; [1967] 1 All E.R. 518; (1967) 111 S.J. 71, CA (Civ Div) . . . . *Digested*, 67/**1836**:
                                          Applied, 99/4764, 00/3879, 01/5319, 04/3954, 07/3396:
                                          Considered, 84/1915, 88/2043, 89/2112, 89/2145: *Followed*, 99/2485,
                                          02/5841, 05/4313

Snowdon *v* Charnock (Inspector of Taxes); *sub nom* Snowdon *v* Inland Revenue
    Commissioners (SpC 282) [2001] S.T.C. (S.C.D.) 152; [2001] S.T.I. 1111, Sp
    Comm . . . . *Digested, 02/***4423**:
                                Applied, 06/4197: *Approved,* 07/4057
Snowdon *v* Inland Revenue Commissioners (SpC 282) see Snowdon *v* Charnock
    (Inspector of Taxes)
Sobota-Gajic *v* Bosnia and Herzegovina (27966/06) [2007] 3 F.C.R. 591, ECHR
Sociedad General de Autores y Editores de Espana (SGAE) *v* Rafael Hoteles SL (C-306/
    05) [2007] Bus. L.R. 521; [2007] E.C.D.R. 2, ECJ (3rd Chamber) . . . . *Digested,* 07/**2518**
Sociedad Operadora de Telecomunicaciones de Castilla y Leon SA (RETECAL) *v*
    Commission of the European Communities (T-443/03) [2005] E.C.R. II-1803;
    [2007] 4 C.M.L.R. 28, CFI (5th Chamber) . . . . *Digested,* 07/**1542**
Societe Baxter *v* Premier Ministre (C-254/97) [2000] All E.R. (EC) 945; [1999]
    E.C.R. I-4809; [2000] 2 C.M.L.R. 899; [2000] C.E.C. 707, ECJ . . . . *Digested, 00/***4913**:
                                          Applied, 07/1616
Societe Belvedere *v* BAT Group Poland Sp ZO O [2007] E.T.M.R. 58, Cass (F)
Societe des Auteurs Dans les Arts Graphiques et Plastiques (ADAGP) *v* Editions Fernand
    Hazan [2007] E.C.C. 19; [2007] E.C.D.R. 18, Cass (F)
Societe France Antilles *v* Minister for the Economy, Finance and Industry [2007] E.C.C.
    16, CE (F)
Societe Keller Grundbau *v* Electricite de France (EDF) [2007] I.L.Pr. 1, Cass (F)
Societe ND Conseil SA *v* Societe Le Meridien Hotels et Resorts World Headquarters
    [2007] I.L.Pr. 39, Cass (F)
Societe Technique Miniere *v* Maschinenbau Ulm GmbH (56/65) [1966] E.C.R. 235;
    [1966] C.M.L.R. 357, ECJ . . . . *Digested, 66/***4781**:
                         Considered, 94/2765, 94/2766, 07/618
Societe Thermale d'Eugenie-les-Bains *v* Ministere de l'Economie, des Finances et de
    l'Industrie (C-277/05) [2007] 3 C.M.L.R. 38; [2007] C.E.C. 784; [2007] S.T.I.
    1866, ECJ (1st Chamber)
Society of Lloyd's *v* Buckley see Society of Lloyd's *v* Henderson
Society of Lloyd's *v* Henderson; *sub nom* Society of Lloyd's *v* Lowe; *joined cases*
    Society of Lloyd's *v* Buckley; Society of Lloyd's *v* Richardson; Society of Lloyd's
    v Stockwell [2007] EWCA Civ 930; *Times,* October 9, 2007, CA (Civ Div);
    affirming [2005] EWHC 850 (Comm), QBD (Comm) . . . . *Digested,* 07/**4193**
Society of Lloyd's *v* Lowe see Society of Lloyd's *v* Henderson
Society of Lloyd's *v* Richardson see Society of Lloyd's *v* Henderson
Society of Lloyd's *v* Stockwell see Society of Lloyd's *v* Henderson
Society of Medical Officers of Health *v* Hope (Valuation Officer) [1960] A.C. 551;
    [1960] 2 W.L.R. 404; [1960] 1 All E.R. 317; (1960) 124 J.P. 128; 58 L.G.R. 165;
    5 R.R.C. 388; 53 R. & I.T. 102; (1960) 104 S.J. 147, HL; affirming [1959] 1 Q.B.
    462; [1959] 2 W.L.R. 377; [1959] 1 All E.R. 509; (1959) 123 J.P. 211; 57
    L.G.R. 57; 4 R.R.C. 102; 52 R. & I.T. 165; (1959) 103 S.J. 200, CA . . . . *Digested, 60/***2706**:
                    Applied, 79/2121: *Considered,* 61/943, 61/943, 88/3028:
                                    Distinguished, 07/4001
Soderback *v* Sweden [1999] 1 F.L.R. 250; (2000) 29 E.H.R.R. 95; 1999 Fam. L.R.
    104; [1998] H.R.C.D. 958; [1999] Fam. Law 87, ECHR . . . . *Digested, 99/***2302**:
                                         Applied, 07/2246
Sodium Gluconate Cartel, Re (T-329/01) see Archer Daniels Midland Co *v* Commission of
    the European Communities (T-329/01)
Soe Thet *v* DPP see Thet *v* DPP
Software 2000 Ltd *v* Andrews [2007] I.C.R. 825; [2007] I.R.L.R. 568, EAT . . . . *Digested, 07/***1426**:
                                          Applied, 07/1427
Software Cellular Network Ltd *v* T-Mobile (UK) Ltd [2007] EWHC 1790 (Ch); [2007]
    U.K.C.L.R. 1663, Ch D
Sogbetun *v* Hackney LBC [1998] I.C.R. 1264; [1998] I.R.L.R. 676; *Times,* October 8,
    1998, EAT . . . . *Digested, 98/***2160**:
                Considered, 07/1352: *Doubted,* 01/2270: *Referred to,* 99/2050
Sohal *v* Sohal (Application for Permission to Appeal) [2002] EWCA Civ 1297, CA (Civ
    Div) . . . . *Considered,* 04/255,
                                          07/510
Sokoya *v* Revenue and Customs Commissioners [2007] S.T.I. 2021, Sp Comm
Sole *v* Secretary of State for Trade and Industry [2007] EWHC 1527 (Admin); (2007)
    104(24) L.S.G. 28; (2007) 151 S.J.L.B. 746, QBD (Admin)
Solicitor No.7 of 2007, Re (2007) 104(37) L.S.G. 36, CA (Civ Div)
Solinas *v* Societe Fabrica Textil Riopele [2007] I.L.Pr. 7, Cass (F) . . . . *Digested,* 07/**668**
Solleveld *v* Staatssecretaris van Financien (C-443/04); *joined case* Van den Hout-van
    Ejinsbergen *v* Staatssecretaris van Financien (C-444/04) [2007] S.T.C. 71;
    [2006] E.C.R. I-3617; [2006] C.E.C. 829; [2006] S.T.I. 1438, ECJ (3rd
    Chamber) . . . . *Digested,* 07/**4346**
Solomon *v* Customs and Excise Commissioners see Salomon *v* Customs and Excise
    Commissioners
Solutia UK Ltd (formerly Monsanto Chemicals UK Ltd) *v* Griffiths see Griffiths *v* Solutia
    UK Ltd

Solvay et Cie SA v Commission of the European Communities (C27/88) see Orkem SA (formerly CdF Chimie SA) v Commission of the European Communities (C374/87)

Solvay et Cie SA v Commission of the European Communities (T-12/89) [1992] E.C.R. II-907, CFI . . . . *Applied*, 07/610, 07/1546

Solvent Resource Management Ltd v Environment Agency see OSS Group Ltd v Environment Agency

Somerfield Stores Ltd v Skanska Rasleigh Weatherfoil Ltd see Skanska Rasleigh Weatherfoil Ltd v Somerfield Stores Ltd

Somerset CC v Barber see Barber v Somerset CC

Somerset CC v D see Somerset CC v SD

Somerset CC v DFM see F (A Child) (Care Proceedings), Re

Somerset CC v John Wainwright and Co Ltd [2007] P.A.D. 86, Planning Inspector

Somerset CC v SD; *sub nom* Somerset CC v D [2007] EWCA Civ 722; [2007] Fam. Law 894, CA (Civ Div)

Somerville v Scottish Ministers; *joined cases* Ralston v Scottish Ministers; Henderson v Scottish Ministers; Blanco v Scottish Ministers [2007] UKHL 44; [2007] 1 W.L.R. 2734; 2007 S.L.T. 1113; 2007 S.C.L.R. 830; (2007) 151 S.J.L.B. 1398; 2007 G.W.D. 37-656, HL; reversing in part [2006] CSIH 52; 2007 S.C. 140; 2007 S.L.T. 96; 2007 G.W.D. 4-67, IH (1 Div) . . . . *Digested*, 07/**5436**

Sonatacus Ltd, Re; *sub nom* CI Ltd v Joint Liquidators of Sonatacus Ltd [2007] EWCA Civ 31; [2007] B.C.C. 186; [2007] 2 B.C.L.C. 627; [2007] B.P.I.R. 106; (2007) 104(6) L.S.G. 30; (2007) 151 S.J.L.B. 162, CA (Civ Div) . . . . *Digested*, 07/**2425**

Sony Computer Entertainment Ltd v RH Freight Services Ltd [2007] EWHC 302 (Comm); [2007] 2 Lloyd's Rep. 463; [2007] I.L.Pr. 21, QBD (Comm) . . . . *Digested*, 07/**667**

Sooner Foods Ltd v Customs and Excise Commissioners see Customs and Excise Commissioners v Sooner Foods Ltd

Sorrell v Smith [1925] A.C. 700, HL; affirming [1924] 1 Ch. 506, CA; reversing [1923] 2 Ch. 32, Ch D . . . . *Applied*, 52/3507, 58/3441, 62/3063: *Considered*, 64/3703, 70/2739, 07/4298

Soulos v Korkontzilas [1997] 2 S.C.R. 217, Sup Ct (Can) . . . . *Applied*, 07/4198

Soulsbury v Soulsbury [2007] EWCA Civ 969; [2007] 3 F.C.R. 811; [2007] W.T.L.R. 1841; *Times*, November 14, 2007, CA (Civ Div)

South African Broadcasting Corp Ltd v National Director of Public Prosecutions 21 B.H.R.C. 533, Const Ct (SA) . . . . *Digested*, 07/**2217**

South Australia Asset Management Corp v York Montague Ltd; *joined cases* United Bank of Kuwait Plc v Prudential Property Services Ltd; Nykredit Mortgage Bank Plc v Edward Erdman Group Ltd [1997] A.C. 191; [1996] 3 W.L.R. 87; [1996] 3 All E.R. 365; [1996] 5 Bank. L.R. 211; [1996] C.L.C. 1179; 80 B.L.R. 1; 50 Con. L.R. 153; [1996] P.N.L.R. 455; [1996] 2 E.G.L.R. 93; [1996] 27 E.G. 125; [1996] E.G. 107 (C.S.); (1996) 93(32) L.S.G. 33; (1996) 146 N.L.J. 956; (1996) 140 S.J.L.B. 156; [1996] N.P.C. 100; *Times*, June 24, 1996; *Independent*, July 2, 1996, HL; affirming [1995] E.G. 71 (C.S.); [1995] N.P.C. 66, QBD (Comm) . . *Digested*, 96/**4519**: *Applied*, 97/3846, 98/4005, 98/4027, 98/4031, 98/4384, 99/1389, 99/4053, 00/1486, 00/4249, 00/4280, 01/4504, 01/4532, 03/2994, 03/3014, 06/2897, 06/2901, 07/2480: *Considered*, 97/3827, 97/3839, 98/3999, 98/4032, 98/5724, 00/4009, 00/4247, 00/4279, 01/2511, 01/4263, 06/2451: *Distinguished*, 02/3292: *Followed*, 98/3959, 98/3987, 99/804, 99/4018, 99/4057, 01/4529: *Not followed*, 00/4275: *Previous proceedings*, 98/1432: *Referred to*, 97/4871

South Buckinghamshire DC v Porter (No.1); *sub nom* South Bucks DC v Porter; *joined cases* Chichester DC v Searle; Wrexham CBC v Berry; Hertsmere BC v Harty [2003] UKHL 26; [2003] 2 A.C. 558; [2003] 2 W.L.R. 1547; [2003] 3 All E.R. 1; [2003] H.R.L.R. 27; [2003] U.K.H.R.R. 1344; [2003] B.L.G.R. 449; [2003] 2 P.L.R. 101; [2003] J.P.L. 1412; [2003] 23 E.G. 135 (C.S.); (2003) 100(22) L.S.G. 32; (2003) 147 S.J.L.B. 626; [2003] N.P.C. 70; *Times*, May 23, 2003, HL; affirming [2001] EWCA Civ 1549; [2002] 1 W.L.R. 1359; [2002] 1 All E.R. 425; [2002] B.L.G.R. 443; [2002] 2 P. & C.R. 16; [2002] 3 P.L.R. 1; [2002] J.P.L. 608; (2001) 98(46) L.S.G. 35; *Times*, November 9, 2001, CA (Civ Div) . . *Digested*, 03/**3381**: *Applied*, 02/3675, 03/3384, 05/3285, 06/3332, 06/3379: *Considered*, 03/3382, 03/3485, 05/3283, 07/2879: *Distinguished*, 06/3378: *Followed*, 07/3258

South Buckinghamshire DC v Porter (No.2); *sub nom* South Buckinghamshire DC v Secretary of State for Transport, Local Government and the Regions [2004] UKHL 33; [2004] 1 W.L.R. 1953; [2004] 4 All E.R. 775; [2005] 1 P. & C.R. 6; [2004] 4 P.L.R. 50; [2004] 28 E.G. 177 (C.S.); (2004) 101(31) L.S.G. 25; (2004) 148 S.J.L.B. 825; [2004] N.P.C. 108; *Times*, July 2, 2004; *Independent*, July 6, 2004, HL; reversing [2003] EWCA Civ 687; [2004] 1 P. & C.R. 8; [2004] J.P.L. 207; (2003) 147 S.J.L.B. 628; [2003] N.P.C. 68; *Times*, May 23, 2003; *Independent*, May 23, 2003, CA (Civ Div); reversing [2002] EWHC 2136 (Admin), QBD (Admin) . . . . *Digested*, 04/**3087**: *Applied*, 05/3296, 07/1157, 07/3277: *Followed*, 05/3304

South Buckinghamshire DC v Secretary of State for Transport, Local Government and the Regions see South Buckinghamshire DC v Porter (No.2)
South Buckinghamshire DC v Smith; *sub nom* South Bucks DC v Smith [2006] EWHC 281 (QB); [2006] J.P.L. 1519; [2006] N.P.C. 22, QBD . . . .   *Digested,* 06/**3379**:
       Distinguished, 07/3258

South Bucks DC v Porter see South Buckinghamshire DC v Porter (No.1)
South Bucks DC v Smith see South Buckinghamshire DC v Smith
South Cambridgeshire DC v Flynn [2006] EWHC 1320 (QB); [2007] B.L.G.R. 471; [2007] J.P.L. 440; [2006] N.P.C. 65, QBD . . . .   *Digested,* 07/**3258**:
       Considered, 07/3260

South Cone Inc v Bessant (t/a REEF) see REEF Trade Mark
South Gloucestershire Council v Clothier see South Gloucestershire Council vTitley
South Gloucestershire Council v Titley; *joined case* South Gloucestershire Council v Clothier [2006] EWHC 3117 (Admin); [2007] R.A. 27; [2007] N.P.C. 3, QBD (Admin) . . . .   *Digested,* 07/**2841**
South Herefordshire Golf Club v Revenue and Customs Commissioners [2007] B.V.C. 2003; [2006] S.T.I. 2224, V&DTr. . . . .   *Digested,* 07/**4292**
South Holland DC vTicketgrange Ltd [2007] P.A.D. 22, Planning Inspector
South Lakeland DC v Carlisle Diocesan Parsonages Board see South Lakeland DC v Secretary of State for the Environment
South Lakeland DC v Secretary of State for the Environment; *joined case* South Lakeland DC v Carlisle Diocesan Parsonages Board [1992] 2 A.C. 141; [1992] 2 W.L.R. 204; [1992] 1 All E.R. 573; 90 L.G.R. 201; (1992) 64 P. & C.R. 128; [1992] 1 P.L.R. 143; (1992) 156 L.G. Rev. 602; (1992) 142 N.L.J. 159; (1992) 136 S.J.L.B. 61; [1992] N.P.C. 16; *Times,* February 3, 1992; *Independent,* February 13, 1992; *Guardian,* February 5, 1992, HL; affirming [1991] 1 W.L.R. 1322; [1992] 1 All E.R. 45; 89 L.G.R. 857; (1991) 62 P. & C.R. 617; [1991] 2 P.L.R. 97; [1991] J.P.L. 654; (1992) 156 L.G. Rev. 143; [1991] E.G. 41 (C.S.); *Times,* March 21, 1991; *Daily Telegraph,* April 12, 1991, CA (Civ Div); reversing [1991] J.P.L. 149, QBD . . . .   *Digested,* 92/**4186**:
       Applied, 03/3434, 07/3266: *Followed,* 92/6514, 93/3925
South Oxfordshire DC v SITA UK Ltd [2006] EWHC 2459 (Comm); [2007] Env. L.R. 13, QBD (Comm) . . . .   *Digested,* 07/**798**
South Tyneside MBC v Anderson [2007] EWCA Civ 654; [2007] I.C.R. 1581; [2007] I.R.L.R. 715; (2007) 151 S.J.L.B. 892, CA (Civ Div); affirming UKEAT/0684/05/ ZT, UKEAT/0525/06/ZT, EAT . . . .   *Digested,* 07/**1362**
South Tyneside MBC v Revenue and Customs Commissioners see Isle of Wight Council v Revenue and Customs Commissioners
South West London Strategic HA v De Haas see Tameside and Glossop Acute Services NHS Trust vThompstone
South Yorkshire Strategic HA v Corbett see Tameside and Glossop Acute Services NHS Trust vThompstone
South Yorkshire Transport v Monopolies and Mergers Commission see R. v Monopolies and Mergers Commission Ex p. South Yorkshire Transport Ltd
Southampton Container Terminals Ltd v Hansa Schiffahrts GmbH (The Maersk Colombo); *sub nom* Southampton Container Terminals Ltd v Schiffahrtsgesellschaft Hansa Australia MGH & Co [2001] EWCA Civ 717; [2001] 2 Lloyd's Rep. 275; (2001) 98(24) L.S.G. 43; (2001) 145 S.J.L.B. 149; *Times,* June 13, 2001, CA (Civ Div); affirming [1999] 2 Lloyd's Rep. 491; [1999] C.L.C. 1814, QBD (Admlty) . . . .   *Digested,* 01/**4501**:
       Considered, 05/374, 07/1059: *Followed,* 03/939
Southampton Container Terminals Ltd v Schiffahrtsgesellschaft Hansa Australia MGH & Co see Southampton Container Terminals Ltd v Hansa Schiffahrts GmbH (The Maersk Colombo)
Southard v DPP [2006] EWHC 3449 (Admin); [2007] A.C.D. 53, QBD (Admin)
Southco Inc v Dzus Fastener Europe Ltd (No.2) [1992] R.P.C. 299, CA (Civ Div); affirming [1990] R.P.C. 587, Ch D (Patents Ct) . . . .   *Digested,* 93/**3040**:
       Applied, 93/3041, 95/3777, 07/2549: *Considered,* 93/3041:
       Followed, 95/3758
Southwark Law Centre v Legal Services Commission see R. (on the application of Southwark Law Centre) v Legal Services Commission
Southwark LBC v Dennett [2007] EWCA Civ 1091; [2007] N.P.C. 115, CA (Civ Div)
Southwark LBC v Onayomake; *sub nom* Lambeth LBC v Onayomake [2007] EWCA Civ 1426; *Times,* November 2, 2007, CA (Civ Div)
Sovereign Marine & General Insurance Co Ltd, Re [2006] EWHC1335 (Ch); [2006] B.C.C. 774; [2007] 1 B.C.L.C. 228, Ch D (Companies Ct) . . . .   *Digested,* 07/**2448**
Sovereign Trustees Ltd v Glover [2007] EWHC 1750 (Ch); [2007] Pens. L.R. 277, Ch D
Sowden v Lodge; *sub nom* Crookdake v Drury [2004] EWCA Civ 1370; [2005] 1 W.L.R. 2129; [2005] 1 All E.R. 581; [2005] Lloyd's Rep. Med. 86; (2004) 148 S.J.L.B. 1282, CA (Civ Div); reversing in part [2003] EWHC 588 (QB), QBD . .   *Digested,* 05/**3072**:
       Applied, 05/3071, 07/3069: *Considered,* 04/2845, 06/3063, 07/1065:
       Distinguished, 06/3065

SP (Serbia) *v* Secretary of State for the Home Department see DK (Serbia) *v* Secretary of State for the Home Department

Spackman *v* London Metropolitan University [2007] I.R.L.R. 744, CC . . . . *Digested,* 07/**1436**

Spain *v* Commission of the European Communities (C-312/90) [1992] E.C.R. I-4117; *Financial Times,* July 7, 1992, ECJ . . . . *Digested,* 92/**4852**: *Considered,* 07/1587

Spain *v* Council of the European Union (C-310/04); *sub nom* New Cotton Support Scheme, Re (C-310/04) [2006] E.C.R. I-7285; [2006] 3 C.M.L.R. 47, ECJ (2nd Chamber) . . . . *Digested,* 07/**107**

Spain *v* United Kingdom (C-145/04); *sub nom* Gibraltar European Elections, Re (C-145/04) [2007] All E.R. (EC) 486; [2006] E.C.R. I-7917; [2007] 1 C.M.L.R. 3; *Times,* November 6, 2006, ECJ. . . . . *Digested,* 07/**1553**

Spandeck Engineering (S) Pte Ltd *v* Defence Science & Technology Agency 114 Con. L.R. 166, CA (Sing)

Sparekassernes Datacenter (SDC) *v* Skatteministeriet (C-2/95) [1997] All E.R. (EC) 610; [1997] S.T.C. 932; [1997] E.C.R. I-3017; [1997] 3 C.M.L.R. 999; [1997] B.T.C. 5395; [1997] B.V.C. 509, ECJ (5th Chamber) . . . . *Digested,* 97/**4987**: *Applied,* 98/4900, 02/4755, 03/4538, 06/4435: *Considered,* 00/5294, 07/5568: *Followed,* 98/4921

Spargo *v* North Essex DHA [1997] P.I.Q.R. P235; [1997] 8 Med. L.R. 125; (1997) 37 B.M.L.R. 99; (1997) 94(15) L.S.G. 26; (1997) 141 S.J.L.B. 90; *Times,* March 21, 1997, CA (Civ Div); reversing [1996] 7 Med. L.R. 219, QBD. . . . . *Digested,* 97/**663**: *Applied,* 01/4461, 03/3001: *Considered,* 97/658, 00/4197, 07/474: *Followed,* 98/550, 01/603

Spargos Mining NL *v* Atlantic Capital Corp, *Times,* December 11, 1995, QBD. . . . . *Digested,* 96/**772**: *Applied,* 03/599, 07/347

Sparrow *v* HM Coroner for East Somerset [2006] EWHC 2718 (Admin); [2006] Inquest L.R. 194; [2007] A.C.D. 3, QBD (Admin)

Spearmint Rhino Ventures (UK) Ltd *v* Revenue and Customs Commissioners [2007] EWHC 613 (Ch); [2007] S.T.C. 1252; [2007] B.T.C. 5418; [2007] B.V.C. 437; [2007] S.T.I. 1051, Ch D; reversing [2006] S.T.I. 1371, V&DTr . . . . *Digested,* 07/**4344**

Special Effects Ltd *v* L'Oreal SA [2007] EWCA Civ 1; [2007] Bus. L.R. 759; [2007] E.T.M.R. 51; [2007] R.P.C. 15; (2007) 151 S.J.L.B. 126; *Times,* January 24, 2007, CA (Civ Div); reversing [2006] EWHC 481 (Ch); [2006] R.P.C. 33; (2006) 29(5) I.P.D. 29041; *Times,* May 1, 2006, Ch D . . . . *Digested,* 07/**2677**

Spectrum Computer Supplies Ltd *v* Revenue and Customs Commissioners [2006] S.T.C. (S.C.D.) 668; [2006] S.T.I. 2209, Sp Comm. . . . . *Digested,* 07/**4085**

Spencer Jones *v* Timmens Freeman [1974] I.R.L.R. 325, IT . . . . *Digested,* 75/**1171.99**: *Considered,* 07/1435

Spiers *v* Ruddy [2007] UKPC D2; 2007 G.W.D. 40-700; *Times,* December 31, 2007, PC (Sc)

Spiralglobe Ltd, Re . . . . *Followed,* 07/2395

Spirerose Ltd *v* Transport for London; *sub nom* 64-70 Holywell Lane, London, EC2, Re [2007] 49 E.G. 102 (C.S.), Lands Tr

Sporting Kicks Ltd's Trade Mark Application (O-302-05) [2007] E.T.M.R. 10, TMR

Sportswear Co SpA *v* Ghattaura (t/a GS3) see Sportswear Co SpA *v* Stonestyle Ltd

Sportswear Co SpA *v* Stonestyle Ltd; *sub nom* Sportswear Co SpA *v* Ghattaura (t/a GS3) [2006] EWCA Civ 380; [2006] U.K.C.L.R. 893; [2006] E.C.C. 27; [2006] Eu. L.R. 1014; [2006] E.T.M.R. 66; [2007] F.S.R. 2, CA (Civ Div); reversing [2005] EWHC 2087 (Ch); [2006] U.K.C.L.R. 1; [2006] E.C.C. 26; [2006] E.T.M.R. 25; [2006] F.S.R. 11; (2005) 28(10) I.P.D. 28076; (2005) 102(40) L.S.G. 26, Ch D . . . . *Digested,* 06/**2592**

Springboard Sunderland Trust *v* Robson [1992] I.C.R. 554; [1992] I.R.L.R. 261, EAT . . *Digested,* 92/**1934**: *Considered,* 07/1365

Springette *v* Defoe [1992] 2 F.L.R. 388; [1992] 2 F.C.R. 561; (1992) 24 H.L.R. 552; (1993) 65 P. & C.R. 1; [1992] Fam. Law 489; [1992] N.P.C. 34; *Independent,* March 24, 1992; *Guardian,* April 29, 1992, CA (Civ Div) . . . . *Digested,* 92/**2031**: *Considered,* 96/4996, 00/3941, 05/3378, 05/3407: *Doubted,* 07/3367: *Followed,* 93/1876, 96/2887

Sprung *v* Royal Insurance (UK) Ltd [1997] C.L.C. 70; [1999] 1 Lloyd's Rep. I.R. 111, CA (Civ Div) . . . . *Digested,* 97/**3121**: *Applied,* 07/2486: *Followed,* 05/2358

SQUARE D CO/Integrated control module (T1107/03) [2006] E.P.O.R. 57, EPO (Technical Bd App) . . . . *Digested,* 07/**2587**

Square Mile Partnership Ltd *v* Fitzmaurice McCall Ltd [2006] EWCA Civ 1690; [2007] 2 B.C.L.C. 23, CA (Civ Div); affirming [2005] EWHC 1565 (Ch), Ch D . . . . . . *Digested,* 07/**584**

Squires *v* AIG Europe UK Ltd see Manning *v* AIG Europe UK Ltd

SR (Iran) *v* Secretary of State for the Home Department [2007] EWCA Civ 460; (2007) 151 S.J.L.B. 673, CA (Civ Div)

Sreenath *v* General Medical Council [2002] UKPC 56, PC (UK) . . . . *Considered,* 07/1950

SS *v* Secretary of State for the Home Department; *sub nom* SS (Jurisdiction: Rule 62(7): Refugee's Family: Policy: Somalia), Re [2005] UKIAT 167; [2006] Imm. A.R. 100, IAT . . . . *Applied,* 07/2281

SS Global Ltd *v* Sava (2007) 104(40) L.S.G. 27, Ch D

SS (Ankara Agreement: No In-Country Right of Appeal: Turkey), Re see SS (Turkey) *v* Secretary of State for the Home Department

SS (Jurisdiction: Rule 62(7): Refugee's Family: Policy: Somalia), Re see SS *v* Secretary of State for the Home Department

SS (Turkey) *v* Secretary of State for the Home Department; *sub nom* SS (Ankara Agreement: No In-Country Right of Appeal: Turkey), Re [2006] UKAIT 74; [2007] Imm. A.R. 193, AIT . . . . *Digested,* 07/**2282**

SSSL Realisations (2002) Ltd (formerly Save Service Stations Ltd) (In Liquidation), Re see Manning *v* AIG Europe UK Ltd

St Clair-Ford (Youlden's Executor) *v* Ryder [2007] R.V.R. 12; [2006] W.T.L.R. 1647, Lands Tr . . . . *Digested,* 07/**4110**

St George's Investment Co *v* Gemini Consulting Ltd [2004] EWHC 2353 (Ch); [2005] 1 E.G.L.R. 5; [2005] 01 E.G. 96; [2005] 1 P. & C.R. DG12, Ch D . . . . *Digested,* 05/**2678**: *Considered,* 07/252

St Gregory Tredington, Re see St Gregory's, Tredington, Re

St Gregory's, Tredington, Re; *sub nom* St Gregory Tredington, Re [1972] Fam. 236; [1971] 2 W.L.R. 796; [1971] 3 All E.R. 269; (1971) 115 S.J. 284, Arches Ct . . . . *Digested,* 71/**3773**: *Applied,* 76/822, 85/1094, 87/1241, 07/1086: *Considered,* 95/1868, 05/990

St Helen's School Northwood Ltd *v* Revenue and Customs Commissioners [2006] EWHC 3306 (Ch); [2007] S.T.C. 633; [2007] B.T.C. 5059; [2007] B.V.C. 58; [2007] S.T.I. 117, Ch D; affirming [2006] S.T.I. 1374, V&D Tr . . . . *Digested,* 07/**4307**: *Considered,* 07/5569

St Helens BC *v* PE [2006] EWHC 3460 (Fam); [2007] 2 F.L.R. 1115; [2007] Fam. Law 1072, Fam Div

St Helens MBC *v* Barnes see Barnes *v* St Helens MBC

St Helens MBC *v* Derbyshire; *sub nom* Derbyshire *v* St Helens MBC [2007] UKHL 16; [2007] 3 All E.R. 81; [2007] I.C.R. 841; [2007] I.R.L.R. 540; (2007) 104(19) L.S.G. 26; (2007) 157 N.L.J. 635; (2007) 151 S.J.L.B. 573; *Times,* April 27, 2007, HL; reversing [2005] EWCA Civ 977; [2006] I.C.R. 90; [2005] I.R.L.R. 801; *Times,* August 26, 2005, CA (Civ Div); reversing [2004] I.R.L.R. 851, EAT   *Digested,* 05/**1235**: *Applied,* 07/1390

St John the Baptist, Halifax, Re (Unreported, December 19, 2000), Cons Ct (Wakefield)   *Applied,* 07/1086: *Considered,* 05/990

St John the Baptist, Stainton by Langworth, Re, *Times,* May 26, 2006, Cons Ct (Lincoln)   *Digested,* 07/**1086**

St John's College, Cambridge *v* Cambridge City Council [2007] P.A.D. 38, Planning Inspector

St Mary and St Michael Parish Advisory Co Ltd *v* Westminster Roman Catholic Diocese Trustee [2006] EWHC 762 (Ch); [2006] W.T.L.R. 881, Ch D . . . . *Digested,* 07/**4265**

St Mary's Church, Sledmere, Re [2007] 1 W.L.R. 1538; [2007] 3 All E.R. 74; *Times,* February 16, 2007, Cons Ct (York) . . . . *Digested,* 07/**1084**

ST Microelectronics NV *v* Condor Insurance Ltd [2006] EWHC 977 (Comm); [2006] 2 Lloyd's Rep. 525, QBD (Comm) . . . . *Digested,* 07/**804**

St Modwen Developments (Edmonton) Ltd *v* Tesco Stores Ltd [2006] EWHC 3177 (Ch); [2007] 6 E.G. 166, Ch D . . . . *Digested,* 07/**2732**

St Nicholas, Sevenoaks, Re [2005] 1 W.L.R. 1011; (2004) 101(44) L.S.G. 31; *Times,* October 29, 2004, Arches Ct . . . . *Digested,* 05/**993**: *Considered,* 07/1084

St Paul Travelers Insurance Co Ltd *v* Dargan see Ballast Plc, Re

St Peter and St Paul's, Chingford, Re [2007] Fam. 67; [2007] 3 W.L.R. 748; *Times,* October 8, 2007, Arches Ct

Staatssecretaris van Financien *v* Arthur Andersen & Co Accountants CS (C-472/03) [2005] S.T.C. 508; [2005] E.C.R. I-1719; [2005] 2 C.M.L.R. 51; [2007] Lloyd's Rep. I.R. 484; [2006] B.T.C. 5159; [2006] B.V.C. 228; [2005] S.T.I. 363, ECJ (1st Chamber) . . . . *Digested,* 05/**4350**

Staatssecretaris van Financien *v* Joustra (C-5/05) [2006] E.C.R. I-11075; [2007] 1 C.M.L.R. 30; [2007] C.E.C. 581; *Times,* November 24, 2006, ECJ (3rd Chamber) . . . . *Digested,* 07/**1034**

Staatssecretaris van Financien *v* Lipjes (C-68/03) [2004] S.T.C. 1592; [2004] E.C.R. I-5879; [2004] 2 C.M.L.R. 43; [2007] B.T.C. 5101; [2004] S.T.I. 1322, ECJ (1st Chamber) . . . . *Digested,* 05/**4402**

Staatssecretaris van Financien *v* Shipping & Forwarding Enterprise Safe BV (C-320/88) [1991] S.T.C. 627; [1990] E.C.R. I-285; [1993] 3 C.M.L.R. 547; *Times,* March 21, 1990, ECJ (6th Chamber) . . . . *Digested,* 90/**2242**: *Applied,* 05/4395, 06/4468, 06/4468, 07/4305

Staatssecretaris van Financien *v* Stichting Kinderopvang Enschede (C-415/04) [2007] S.T.C. 294; [2006] 2 C.M.L.R. 57; [2006] C.E.C. 590; [2006] S.T.I. 385, ECJ (3rd Chamber) . . . . *Digested,* 07/**4295**

Staatssecretaris van Financien *v* Verkooijen (C-35/98) [2002] S.T.C. 654; [2000] E.C.R. I-4071; [2002] 1 C.M.L.R. 48; 2 I.T.L. Rep. 727; [2000] S.T.I. 884, ECJ . .   *Digested,* 02/**4433**: *Applied,* 05/4028, 06/4291, 07/1600, 07/1601: *Considered,* 05/4134

Stack v Dowden; *sub nom* Dowden v Stack [2007] UKHL 17; [2007] 2 A.C. 432; [2007] 2 W.L.R. 831; [2007] 2 All E.R. 929; [2007] 1 F.L.R. 1858; [2007] 2 F.C.R. 280; [2007] B.P.I.R. 913; [2007] W.T.L.R. 1053; (2006-07) 9 I.T.E.L.R. 815; [2007] Fam. Law 593; [2007] 18 E.G. 153 (C.S.); (2007) 157 N.L.J. 634; (2007) 151 S.J.L.B. 575; [2007] N.P.C. 47; [2007] 2 P. & C.R. DG11; *Times*, April 26, 2007, HL; affirming [2005] EWCA Civ 857; [2006] 1 F.L.R. 254; [2005] 2 F.C.R. 739; [2006] 1 P. & C.R. 15; [2006] W.T.L.R. 511; (2005-06) 8 I.T.E.L.R. 174; [2005] Fam. Law 864; [2005] N.P.C. 93; [2006] 1 P. & C.R. DG3, CA (Civ Div) . . . . *Digested,* 07/**3367**:
Applied, 07/3362, 07/3366: *Considered,* 07/2408
Stadler v Finanzlandesdirektion fur Vorarlberg (C-409/99) see Metropol Treuhand Wirtschaftstreuhand GmbH v Finanzlandesdirektion fur Steiermark (C-409/99)
Stadt Halle v Arbeitsgemeinschaft Thermische Restabfall- und Energieverwertungsanlage TREA Leuna (C-26/03) [2006] 1 C.M.L.R. 39, ECJ (1st Chamber) . . . . *Digested,* 06/**3419**:
Applied, 06/3420, 07/1642, 07/3328: *Followed,* 07/3325
Staffordshire CC v Challinor [2007] EWCA Civ 864; [2007] N.P.C. 101, CA (Civ Div)
Staffordshire CC v Donovan; *sub nom* Donovan v Staffordshire CC [1981] I.R.L.R. 108, EAT . . . . *Digested,* 81/**813**:
Considered, 07/1435
Stallwood v David [2006] EWHC 2600 (QB); [2007] 1 All E.R. 206; [2007] R.T.R. 11; *Times*, December 27, 2006, QBD . . . . *Digested,* 07/**336**
Stamatelaki v NPDD Organismos Asfaliseos Eleftheron Epangelmation (OAEE) (C444/ 05) [2007] 2 C.M.L.R. 44, ECJ (2nd Chamber) . . . . *Digested,* 07/**1632**
Standard Bank London Ltd v Apostolakis (No.1) [2002] C.L.C. 933; [2000] I.L.Pr. 766, QBD (Comm) . . . . *Digested,* 01/**816**:
Applied, 07/766: *Subsequent proceedings,* 01/822
Standard Chartered Bank v Pakistan National Shipping Corp (Assessment of Damages) [2001] EWCA Civ 55; [2001] 1 All E.R. (Comm) 822; [2001] C.L.C. 825, CA (Civ Div); affirming [1999] 1 All E.R. (Comm.) 417; [1999] 1 Lloyd's Rep. 747; [1999] C.L.C. 761, QBD (Comm) . . . . *Digested,* 01/**1522**:
Applied, 07/1059
Standard Commercial Property Securities Ltd v Glasgow City Council [2006] UKHL 50; 2007 S.C. (H.L.) 33; 2006 S.L.T. 1152; 2007 S.C.L.R. 93; [2007] J.P.L. 758; [2006] 47 E.G. 181 (C.S.); (2006) 103(46) L.S.G. 31; (2006) 150 S.J.L.B. 1534; [2006] N.P.C. 122; 2006 G.W.D. 38-748; *Times*, November 20, 2006, HL; reversing 2005 S.L.T. 144; 2005 S.C.L.R. 423; [2005] 4 P.L.R. 1; 2005 G.W.D. 3-21, IH (1 Div); reversing 2004 S.L.T. 655; 2004 G.W.D. 18-395, OH . . . . *Digested,* 07/**5451**
Standesamt Stadt Niebull, Re (C-96/04) [2006] E.C.R. I-3561; [2006] 2 C.M.L.R. 58; [2006] C.E.C. 759, ECJ (1st Chamber) . . . . *Digested,* 07/**1595**
Stanford Marsh Ltd v Secretary of State for the Environment [1997] 1 E.G.L.R. 178; [1997] 17 E.G. 170; [1997] R.V.R. 34, Lands Tr . . . . *Digested,* 97/**4056**:
Considered, 07/3384
Stankiewicz v Poland (46917/99) (2007) 44 E.H.R.R. 47, ECHR . . . . *Digested,* 07/**2215**
Stankov v Bulgaria (29221/95); *joined case* United Macedonian Organisation Ilinden v Bulgaria (29225/95); (Unreported, October 2, 2001), ECHR . . . . *Considered,* 07/2177
Stanley J Holmes & Sons Ltd v Davenham Trust Plc [2006] EWCA Civ 1568; [2007] B.C.C. 485, CA (Civ Div) . . . . *Digested,* 07/**440**
Stansbury v Datapulse Plc; *sub nom* Stansby v Datapulse Plc [2003] EWCA Civ 1951; [2004] I.C.R. 523; [2004] I.R.L.R. 466; [2004] U.K.H.R.R. 340; (2004) 101(6) L.S.G. 32; (2004) 148 S.J.L.B. 145; *Times*, January 28, 2004, CA (Civ Div); reversing EAT/1255/01/RN, EAT . . . . *Digested,* 04/**1249**:
Applied, 07/1343
Stansby v Datapulse Plc see Stansbury v Datapulse Plc
Stansill (Peter) v DPP see Knuller (Publishing, Printing and Promotions) Ltd v DPP
Star Amusements Ltd v Brentwood BC [2007] P.A.D. 61, Planning Inspector
Star Fruit Co SA v Commission of the European Communities (C-247/87) [1989] E.C.R. 291; [1990] 1 C.M.L.R. 733, ECJ (2nd Chamber) . . . . *Digested,* 91/**3926**:
Applied, 07/1542
Starbucks Corp (t/a Starbucks Coffee Co of Seattle, United States) v Iakovos Photiades Foodstuff Suppliers Ltd [2007] E.T.M.R. 49, ED (Cy)
Starkey v Rotherham NHS Foundation Trust [2007] LS Law Medical 456, CC (Sheffield)
Starlight Developers Ltd, Re; *sub nom* Bryan v Arpan [2007] EWHC 1660 (Ch); [2007] B.C.C. 929, Ch D
Starlight Shipping Co v Tai Ping Insurance Co Ltd (Hubei Branch) [2007] EWHC 1893 (Comm); [2007] 2 C.L.C. 440, QBD (Comm)
STARLINGER/Weft thread monitoring (T64/02) [2007] E.P.O.R. 19, EPO (Technical Bd App)
Starside Properties v Mustapha [1974] 1 W.L.R. 816; [1974] 2 All E.R. 567; (1974) 28 P. & C.R. 95; (1974) 118 S.J. 388, CA (Civ Div) . . . . *Digested,* 74/**3940**:
Distinguished, 07/3420
State Central Authority v Ayob . . . . *Considered,* 07/1736
State Central Authority v CR . . . . *Considered,* 07/1736

Steadman-Byrne v Amjad; *sub nom* Amjad v Steadman-Byrne [2007] EWCA Civ 625;
[2007] 1 W.L.R. 2484; [2007] C.P. Rep. 38; (2007) 151 S.J.L.B. 890; *Times,*
July 30, 2007, CA (Civ Div) . . . . *Digested,* 07/**467**

Steamship Mutual Underwriting Association Ltd v Trollope & Colls (City) Ltd 33 B.L.R.
77; 6 Con. L.R. 11; (1986) 2 Const. L.J. 224, CA (Civ Div); affirming 11 Con.
L.R. 91; (1986) 2 Const. L.J. 75, DC . . . . *Digested,* 89/**3050**:
Applied, 90/3795, 97/3592: *Considered,* 93/3300, 07/492:
Distinguished, 97/734, 99/3944

Stec v United Kingdom (65731/01) (2006) 43 E.H.R.R. 47; 20 B.H.R.C. 348; *Times,*
May 26, 2006, ECHR (Grand Chamber) . . . . *Digested,* 06/**2089**:
Applied, 07/2208

Stec v United Kingdom (Admissibility) (65731/01) (2005) 41 E.H.R.R. SE18, ECHR . . *Considered,* 07/3867,
07/3875

Steedman v BBC [2001] EWCA Civ 1534; [2002] E.M.L.R. 17; (2001) 98(47) L.S.G.
27; (2001) 145 S.J.L.B. 260; *Times,* December 13, 2001, CA (Civ Div); affirming
HQ 0003940, QBD . . . . *Digested,* 02/**461**:
Considered, 07/1073

Steeds v Peverel Management Services Ltd [2001] EWCA Civ 419; *Times,* May 16,
2001; *Daily Telegraph,* April 10, 2001, CA (Civ Div) . . . . *Digested,* 01/**601**:
Considered, 07/1389: *Followed,* 05/1301

Steel v United Kingdom (24838/94) (1999) 28 E.H.R.R. 603; 5 B.H.R.C. 339; [1998]
Crim. L.R. 893; [1998] H.R.C.D. 872; *Times,* October 1, 1998, ECHR . . . . *Digested,* 98/**3068**:
Considered, 02/3768, 06/5238, 07/3317: *Distinguished,* 00/3185, 01/10

Steele (Inspector of Taxes) v European Vinyls Corp (Holdings) BV see Steele (Inspector
of Taxes) v EVC International NV (formerly European Vinyls Corp (Holdings)
BV)

Steele (Inspector of Taxes) v EVC International NV (formerly European Vinyls Corp
(Holdings) BV); *sub nom* Steele (Inspector of Taxes) v European Vinyls Corp
(Holdings) BV; Steeple v European Vinyls Corp (Holdings) BV [1996] S.T.C. 785;
69 T.C. 88; [1996] B.T.C. 425, CA (Civ Div); affirming [1995] S.T.C. 31; [1995]
B.T.C. 32, Ch D . . . . *Digested,* 96/**1291**:
Considered, 07/3989

Steeple v European Vinyls Corp (Holdings) BV see Steele (Inspector of Taxes) v EVC
International NV (formerly European Vinyls Corp (Holdings) BV)

Stein v Sybmore Holdings [2006] NSWSC 1004; (2006-07) 9 I.T.E.L.R. 258, Sup Ct
(NSW) . . . . *Digested,* 07/**4240**

Stellato v Secretary of State for the Home Department see R. (on the application of
Stellato) v Secretary of State for the Home Department

Stemson v AMP General Insurance (NZ) Ltd [2006] UKPC 30; [2006] Lloyd's Rep.
I.R. 852, PC (NZ) . . . . *Digested,* 07/**363**

Stenhouse Australia v Phillips [1974] A.C. 391; [1974] 2 W.L.R. 134; [1974] 1 All E.R.
117; [1974] 1 Lloyd's Rep. 1; (1973) 117 S.J. 875, PC (Aus) . . . . *Digested,* 74/**1271**:
Applied, 98/2193, 07/1327: *Considered,* 91/447, 97/2257

Stephens v Avery [1988] Ch. 449; [1988] 2 W.L.R. 1280; [1988] 2 All E.R. 477;
[1988] F.S.R. 510; (1988) 85(25) L.S.G. 45; (1988) 138 N.L.J. Rep. 69; (1988)
132 S.J. 822; *Times,* February 27, 1988; *Independent,* February 27, 1988, Ch D . . *Digested,* 88/**3403**:
Applied, 01/3851: *Considered,* 01/4415, 07/2189: *Followed,* 97/3588

Stephens v Cannon [2005] EWCA Civ 222; [2005] C.P. Rep. 31; [2006] R.V.R. 126;
Times, May 3, 2005, CA (Civ Div) . . . . *Digested,* 05/**292**:
Applied, 07/2680

Stephens v Doncaster HA [1996] 7 Med. L.R. 357, QBD . . . . *Digested,* 97/**1770**:
Applied, 07/3071

Stere v Romania (25632/02) (2007) 45 E.H.R.R. 6; 8 I.T.L. Rep. 636, ECHR . . . . *Digested,* 06/**2116**

Steria Ltd v Hutchison [2006] EWCA Civ 1551; [2007] I.C.R. 445; [2006] Pens. L.R.
291; (2006) 150 S.J.L.B. 1571; [2007] 2 P. & C.R. DG8, CA (Civ Div); reversing
[2005] EWHC 2993 (Ch); [2006] Pens. L.R. 13, Ch D . . . . *Digested,* 07/**3044**

Stericycle International LLC v Competition Commission [2006] CAT 21; [2007] Comp.
A.R. 281, CAT . . . . *Digested,* 07/**640**

Stericycle International LLC v Competition Commission [2007] CAT 9; [2007] Comp.
A.R. 662, CAT

Stericycle International LLC v Competition Commission (Costs) [2006] CAT 22;
[2007] Comp. A.R. 322, CAT . . . . *Digested,* 07/**629**

Sterling Developments (London) Ltd v Pagano [2007] I.R.L.R. 471, EAT . . . . *Digested,* 07/**1353**

Sterling Hydraulics Ltd v Dichtomatik Ltd [2006] EWHC 2004 (QB); [2007] 1 Lloyd's
Rep. 8, QBD . . . . *Digested,* 07/**3569**

Sterman v EW&WJ Moore (A Firm) [1970] 1 Q.B. 596; [1970] 2 W.L.R. 386; [1970]
1 All E.R. 581, CA (Civ Div) . . . . *Digested,* 71/**9446**:
Considered, 07/369

Stern Settlement Trustees v Levy [2007] EWHC 1187 (TCC); 113 Con. L.R. 92, QBD
(TCC)

Stevens v Parkhouse (Unreported, July 11, 2007), CC (Bristol) . . . . *Digested,* 07/**2779**

Stevens v Yorkhill NHS Trust [2006] CSOH 143; 2006 S.L.T. 889; 2007 S.C.L.R. 606;
(2007) 95 B.M.L.R. 1; 2006 G.W.D. 30-659, OH . . . . *Digested,* 06/**5590**

Steward v Kingston upon Thames RLBC [2007] EWCA Civ 565; [2007] H.L.R. 42;
    (2007) 151 S.J.L.B. 711, CA (Civ Div) . . . .   *Digested*, 07/**2137**
Stewart v PEM Stainless Steel Ltd (Unreported, December 7, 2006), CC (Sheffield)
    [*Ex rel.* John Collins, Barrister, Zenith Chambers, 10 Park Square, Leeds] . . . . . .   *Digested*, 07/**3188**
Stichting Goed Wonen v Staatssecretaris van Financien (C-376/02) [2006] S.T.C. 833;
    [2005] E.C.R. I-3445; [2005] 2 C.M.L.R. 41; [2007] B.T.C. 5989; [2005]
    S.T.I. 890, ECJ (Grand Chamber) . . . .   *Digested*, 06/**4443**
Stichting Regionaal Opleidingen Centrum Noord-Kennemerland/West-Friesland (Horizon
    College) v Staatssecretaris van Financien (C-434/05) [2007] 3 C.M.L.R. 18;
    [2007] C.E.C. 855; [2007] S.T.I. 1735, ECJ (3rd Chamber)
Stichting ROM-Projecten v Staatssecretaris van Economische Zaken (C-158/06)
    [2007] 3 C.M.L.R. 21, ECJ (3rd Chamber)
Stirk v Bridgnorth DC (1997) 73 P. & C.R. 439; [1996] E.G. 159 (C.S.); [1996] N.P.C.
    140, CA (Civ Div); affirming [1995] E.G. 131 (C.S.); [1995] N.P.C. 134, QBD . . .   *Digested*, 97/**4071**:
                            Applied, 97/4072, 99/4225, 00/4465: *Considered*, 99/4215, 99/4226,
                            07/3247: *Distinguished*, 00/4444, 00/4474, 02/3739: *Followed*, 98/4190
Stirling (t/a M&S Contracts) v Westminster Properties Scotland Ltd [2007] B.L.R. 537;
    2007 G.W.D. 24-396, OH
STJERNFJADRAR/Mattress (T1313/04) [2006] E.P.O.R. 51, EPO (Technical Bd App) .   *Digested*, 07/**2580**
Stockport MBC v Fan [2007] P.A.D. 53, Planning Inspector
Stoichkov v Bulgaria (9808/02) (2007) 44 E.H.R.R. 14, ECHR
Stojevic v Komercni Banka AS; *sub nom* Stojevic v Official Receiver [2006] EWHC
    3447 (Ch); [2007] B.P.I.R. 141, Ch D (Bankruptcy Ct) . . . .   *Digested*, 07/**2411**
Stojevic v Official Receiver see Stojevic v Komercni Banka AS
Stoke on Trent City Council v Walley see Walley v Stoke on Trent City Council
Stoll v Switzerland (69698/01) (2007) 44 E.H.R.R. 53, ECHR . . . .   *Digested*, 07/**2187**
Stone v Bolton see Bolton v Stone
Stone v Chataway see Yorke (Deceased), Re
Stone v Revenue and Customs Commissioners [2007] S.T.I. 2254, V&DTr (London)
Stone v South East Coast Strategic HA (formerly Kent and Medway Strategic HA)
    [2006] EWHC 1668 (Admin); [2007] U.K.H.R.R. 137; [2006] M.H.L.R. 288,
    QBD (Admin)
Stone and Rolls Ltd (In Liquidation) v Moore Stephens (A Firm) [2007] EWHC 1826
    (Comm); (2007) 157 N.L.J. 1154, QBD (Comm)
Stone Heritage Developments Ltd v Davis Blank Furniss [2007] EWCA Civ 765;
    [2007] 31 E.G. 80 (C.S.), CA (Civ Div); affirming (Unreported, June 1, 2006), Ch
    D
Storbraten v Norway (Admissibility) (12277/04) (2007) 44 E.H.R.R. SE24, ECHR
Storck v Germany (61603/00) (2006) 43 E.H.R.R. 6; [2005] M.H.L.R. 211, ECHR . . .   *Applied*, 07/**3913**
Storey v Clellands Shipbuilders Ltd see Grieves v FT Everard & Sons Ltd
Stovin v Wise [1996] A.C. 923; [1996] 3 W.L.R. 388; [1996] 3 All E.R. 801; [1996]
    R.T.R. 354; (1996) 93(35) L.S.G. 33; (1996) 146 N.L.J. 1185; (1996) 140
    S.J.L.B. 201; *Times*, July 26, 1996; *Independent*, July 31, 1996, HL; reversing
    [1994] 1 W.L.R. 1124; [1994] 3 All E.R. 467; [1994] R.T.R. 225; 92 L.G.R. 577;
    159 J.P.N. 722; (1994) 91(14) L.S.G. 48; (1994) 138 S.J.L.B. 60; *Times*, March
    8, 1994, CA (Civ Div) . . . .   *Digested*, 96/**4058**:
                            Applied, 97/3778, 01/4483, 01/4499, 04/1442, 04/2752, 05/2891, 07/4144:
                            Considered, 97/4087, 07/2870, 07/2939: *Distinguished*, 00/4232, 01/4495:
                            Followed, 99/2889, 99/2889
Stradasfalti Srl v Agenzia delle Entrate Ufficio di Trento (C-228/05) [2007] S.T.C. 508;
    [2006] E.C.R. I-8391; [2006] S.T.I. 2207, ECJ (3rd Chamber) . . . .   *Digested*, 07/**4304**
Strain (Deceased), Re see Allnutt v Wilding
Straker v Tudor Rose (A Firm) [2007] EWCA Civ 368; [2007] C.P. Rep. 32; (2007)
    151 S.J.L.B. 571, CA (Civ Div) . . . .   *Digested*, 07/**411**
Stran Greek Refineries v Greece (A/301-B) (1995) 19 E.H.R.R. 293, ECHR . . . .   *Digested*, 95/**2620**:
                            Applied, 02/2444, 07/2209: *Followed*, 01/3544, 02/2497
Strbac v Secretary of State for the Home Department [2005] EWCA Civ 848; [2005]
    Imm. A.R. 504, CA (Civ Div) . . . .   *Digested*, 06/**2249**:
                                                                                                            Applied, 07/2307
Streamserve Inc v Office for Harmonisation in the Internal Market (Trade Marks and
    Designs) (OHIM) (T-106/00) [2002] E.C.R. II-723; [2003] E.T.M.R. 59; (2002)
    25(4) I.P.D. 25026, CFI (4th Chamber) . . . .   *Digested*, 04/**2368**:
                            Applied, 05/2506, 07/2660: *Subsequent proceedings*, 05/2546
Streekgewest Westelijk Noord-Brabant v Staatssecretaris van Financien (C-174/02)
    [2007] S.T.C. 692; [2005] E.C.R. I-85; [2005] S.T.I. 136, ECJ (1st Chamber)
Street v Derbyshire Unemployed Workers Centre [2004] EWCA Civ 964; [2004] 4 All
    E.R. 839; [2005] I.C.R. 97; [2004] I.R.L.R. 687; *Times*, September 6, 2004, CA
    (Civ Div); affirming [2004] I.C.R. 213; (2004) 101(2) L.S.G. 29; *Times*,
    December 1, 2003, EAT . . . .   *Digested*, 04/**1308**:
                                                                                                            Applied, 07/1441
Streletz v Germany (34044/96); *joined cases* Kessler v Germany (35532/97); Krenz v
    Germany (44801/98) (2001) 33 E.H.R.R. 31, ECHR . . . .   *Digested*, 02/**2390**:
                                                                                                            Applied, 07/2237

Stretford v Football Association Ltd [2007] EWCA Civ 238; [2007] Bus. L.R. 1052;
   [2007] 2 All E.R. (Comm) 1; [2007] 2 Lloyd's Rep. 31; [2007] 1 C.L.C. 256;
   (2007) 151 S.J.L.B. 437; *Times*, April 13, 2007, CA (Civ Div); affirming [2006]
   EWHC 479 (Ch), Ch D . . . .   *Digested*, 07/**236**
Strickland v Hertfordshire CC [2003] EWHC 287 (QB); [2003] Po. L.R. 252, QBD. . .   *Considered*, 07/2937
Strickson v Preston County Court see R. (on the application of Strickson) v Preston
   County Court
Stringman v McArdle [1994] 1 W.L.R. 1653; [1994] P.I.Q.R. P230; [1994] J.P.I.L. 69;
   Times, November 19, 1993; *Independent*, December 6, 1993, CA (Civ Div) . . . .   *Digested*, 94/**1482**:
                        Applied, 00/1459, 07/3070: *Considered*, 97/1759, 98/1437
Stryker Corp (t/a Stryker Howmedica Osteonics) v Sulzer Metco AG [2006] IEHC 60;
   [2007] I.L.Pr. 47, HC (Irl)
Stuart-Hutcheson v Spread Trustee Co Ltd; *sub nom* Peter Acatos No.2 Settlement, Re
   [2002] W.T.L.R. 1213; (2002-03) 5 I.T.E.L.R. 140, CA (Gue); reversing (2000-
   01) 3 I.T.E.L.R. 683, Royal Ct (Gue) . . . .   *Digested*, 03/**4498**:
                                           Considered, 07/4242
Stubbs v Revenue and Customs Commissioners [2007] Pens. L.R. 407; [2007] S.T.I.
   2416; (2007) 151 S.J.L.B. 1263, Sp Comm . . . .   *Digested*, 07/**4091**
Stubbs Ltd v Russell; *sub nom* Russell v Stubbs Ltd [1913] A.C. 386; 1913 S.C. (H.L.)
   14; 1913 1 S.L.T. 428, HL. . . . .   *Applied*, 03/5452,
                         07/5098: *Considered*, 62/1749, 63/1998
Sturesson v Sweden (A/171) see Hakansson v Sweden (A/171)
Stylianakis v Greece (C-92/01) [2004] All E.R. (EC) 215; [2003] E.C.R. I-1291;
   [2004] 2 C.M.L.R. 21, ECJ (6th Chamber) . . . .   *Digested*, 04/**1420**:
                                           Applied, 07/3977
Styranowski v Poland (28616/95) [1998] H.R.C.D. 1001, ECHR (1996) 22 E.H.R.R.
   CD111, Eur Comm HR . . . .   *Considered*, 07/**2219**:
                                           Referred to, 01/3517
Suen Wah Ling (t/a Kong Luen Construction Engineering Co) v China Harbour
   Engineering Co [2007] B.L.R. 435, CA (HK)
Sugden v Davidoff (Unreported, September 11, 2006), CC (Edmonton) [*Ex rel.*
   Matthew Gullick, Barrister, 3 Paper Buildings, Temple, London] . . . .   *Digested*, 07/**3131**
Suiker Unie v Commission of the European Communities (40/73) see Cooperatieve
   Vereniging Suiker Unie UA v Commission of the European Communities (40/
   73)
Suisse Security Bank & Trust Ltd v Francis [2006] UKPC 41; [2007] 2 Costs L.R. 222,
   PC (Bah). . . . .   *Digested*, 07/**379**:
                                           Considered, 07/387
Sukhovetskyy v Ukraine (13716/02) (2007) 44 E.H.R.R. 57, ECHR. . . . .   *Digested*, 07/**2263**
Sukuman Ltd v Commonwealth Secretariat see Sumukan Ltd v Commonwealth
   Secretariat
Sullivan v Moody 207 C.L.R. 562, HC (Aus) . . . .   *Applied*, 07/**2934**:
                                           Considered, 05/2848
Sumitomo Metal Industries Ltd v Commission of the European Communities (C-403/
   04 P) [2007] 4 C.M.L.R. 16, ECJ (1st Chamber) . . . .   *Digested*, 07/**1545**
SUMITOMO/Retraction of withdrawal of request (T824/00) [2004] E.P.O.R. 25, EPO
   (Technical Bd App) . . . .   *Digested*, 04/**2284**:
                                           Applied, 07/2568
Summers v Kitson [2006] EWHC 3655 (Ch); [2007] W.T.L.R. 1645, Ch D
Summit Property Ltd v Pitmans (Costs) [2001] EWCA Civ 2020; [2002] C.P.L.R. 97,
   CA (Civ Div); affirming CH 1998 1500, Ch D . . . .   *Digested*, 03/**374**:
                                           Applied, 07/386
Sumsion v BBC (Scotland) [2007] I.R.L.R. 678, EAT (SC) . . . .   *Digested*, 07/**5143**
Sumukan Ltd v Commonwealth Secretariat; *sub nom* Sukuman Ltd v Commonwealth
   Secretariat [2007] EWCA Civ 243; [2007] Bus. L.R. 1075; [2007] 3 All E.R.
   342; [2007] 2 All E.R. (Comm) 23; [2007] 2 Lloyd's Rep. 87; [2007] 1 C.L.C.
   282; (2007) 157 N.L.J. 482; (2007) 151 S.J.L.B. 430; *Times*, April 13, 2007, CA
   (Civ Div); affirming [2006] EWHC 304 (Comm); [2006] 1 All E.R. (Comm)
   621; [2006] 2 Lloyd's Rep. 53; [2006] 1 C.L.C. 394, QBD (Comm) . . . .   *Digested*, 07/**233**
Sumukan Ltd v Commonwealth Secretariat [2007] EWCA Civ 1148; [2007] 2 C.L.C.
   821; 116 Con. L.R. 17; (2007) 104(46) L.S.G. 26; *Times*, December 18, 2007, CA
   (Civ Div); reversing [2007] EWHC 188 (Comm); [2007] 1 Lloyd's Rep. 370,
   QBD (Comm) . . . .   *Digested*, 07/**246**
Sun Alliance & London Assurance Co Ltd v Hayman [1975] 1 W.L.R. 177; [1975] 1 All
   E.R. 248; (1975) 29 P. & C.R. 422; (1975) 119 S.J. 84, CA (Civ Div) . . . .   *Digested*, 75/**1881**:
            Applied, 76/1537, 03/2757: *Considered*, 78/1769, 81/1516, 89/2160, 89/2162:
                                           Followed, 07/2764
Sun Alliance & London Insurance Plc v PT Asuransri Dayin Mitra TBK (The No 1 Dae Bu)
   [2006] EWHC 812 (Comm); [2006] Lloyd's Rep. I.R. 860, QBD (Comm) . . . .   *Digested*, 07/**2492**
Sun Chemical Group BV v Commission of the European Communities (T-282/06)
   [2007] 5 C.M.L.R. 6, CFI (2nd Chamber)
Sunderland City Council v Conn see Conn v Sunderland City Council

Sunderland City Council v P; *sub nom* Sunderland City Council v PS; PS (Incapacitated or Vulnerable Adult), Re [2007] EWHC 623 (Fam); [2007] 2 F.L.R. 1083; (2007) 10 C.C.L. Rep. 295; [2007] LS Law Medical 507; [2007] Fam. Law 695, Fam Div . . . .   *Digested*, 07/**3911**
Sunderland City Council v PS see Sunderland City Council v P
Sunderland Marine Mutual Insurance Co Ltd v Wiseman (The Seaward Quest) [2007] EWHC 1460 (Comm); [2007] 2 All E.R. (Comm) 937; [2007] 2 Lloyd's Rep. 308; [2007] 1 C.L.C. 989, QBD (Comm) . . . .   *Digested*, 07/**672**
Sunny Metal and Engineering Pte Ltd v Ng Khim Ming Eric [2007] SGCA 36; 113 Con. L.R. 112, CA (Sing); reversing [2006] SGHC 222; 110 Con. L.R. 115, HC (Sing)   *Digested*, 07/**733**
Sunrider Corp v Office for Harmonisation in the Internal Market (Trade Marks and Designs) (OHIM) (T-203/02) [2004] E.C.R. II-2811; [2004] C.E.C. 424, CFI (2nd Chamber) . . . .   *Digested*, 05/**2540**: *Applied*, 07/2686
Sunrider Corp (t/a Sunrider International) v Vitasoy International Holdings Ltd; *sub nom* VITALITE Trade Mark [2007] EWHC 37 (Ch); [2007] Bus. L.R. 602; [2007] R.P.C. 29; (2007) 30(2) I.P.D. 30014; *Times*, February 27, 2007, Ch D . . . .   *Digested*, 07/**2684**
Sunrider Corp (t/a Sunrider International) v Vitasoy International Holdings Ltd (Supplemental Judgement) (2007) 30(3) I.P.D. 30020, Ch D
Sunrock Aircraft Corp Ltd v Scandinavian Airlines System Denmark-Norway-Sweden [2007] EWCA Civ 882; [2007] 2 Lloyd's Rep. 612; (2007) 104(35) L.S.G. 39, CA (Civ Div); reversing [2006] EWHC 2834 (Comm), QBD (Comm)
Sunworld Ltd v Hammersmith and Fulham LBC; *joined case* R. v Blackfriars Crown Court Ex p. Sunworld Ltd [2000] 1 W.L.R. 2102; [2000] 2 All E.R. 837; [2000] Crim. L.R. 593, QBD . . . .   *Applied*, 07/**989**: *Considered*, 07/356
Supperstone v Hurst [2006] EWHC 2147 (Ch); [2006] B.P.I.R. 1263, Ch D . . . .   *Digested*, 07/**2409**
Supple v Pender [2007] EWHC 829 (Ch); [2007] W.T.L.R. 1461, Ch D
Supportways Community Services Ltd v Hampshire CC see R. (on the application of Supportways Community Services Ltd) v Hampshire CC
Surdonja v Ealing LBC see Mohamed v Hammersmith and Fulham LBC
Suresh v Canada (Minister of Citizenship and Immigration) 2002 SCC 1; [2002] 1 S.C.R. 3, Sup Ct (Can) . . . .   *Applied*, 06/657, 07/2362
Surmeli v Germany (75529/01) (2007) 44 E.H.R.R. 22, ECHR (Grand Chamber)
Surrendra Overseas Ltd v Sri Lanka (The Apj Akash) [1977] 1 W.L.R. 565; [1977] 2 All E.R. 481; [1977] 1 Lloyd's Rep. 653; (1977) 121 S.J. 13; *Times*, December 2, 1976, QBD (Comm) . . . .   *Digested*, 77/**1798**: *Considered*, 07/3813
Surrey CC v P [1997] E.L.R. 516; [1997] C.O.D. 118, QBD . . . .   *Digested*, 98/**1969**: *Considered*, 06/1217, 07/1267
Surrey Heath BC v Windlesham Community Home Trust [2007] P.A.D. 33, Planning Inspector
Surrey Homes Ltd v Secretary of State for the Environment, Transport and the Regions [2001] J.P.L. 379 (Note), QBD . . . .   *Applied*, 07/3286
Sutcliffe v BMI Healthcare Ltd [2007] EWCA Civ 476; (2007) 98 B.M.L.R. 211, CA (Civ Div); affirming (Unreported, July 5, 2006), QBD . . . .   *Digested*, 07/**2923**
Sutcliffe v Lloyd see Lloyd v Sutcliffe
Sutherland v Hatton see Barber v Somerset CC
Sutradhar v Natural Environment Research Council [2006] UKHL 33; [2006] 4 All E.R. 490; [2007] Env. L.R. 10; [2006] P.N.L.R. 36; (2006) 150 S.J.L.B. 922; *Times*, July 7, 2006, HL; affirming [2004] EWCA Civ 175; [2004] P.N.L.R. 30; (2004) 101(13) L.S.G. 36; [2004] Env. L.R. D8; *Times*, March 19, 2004, CA (Civ Div); reversing [2003] EWHC 1046 (QB); [2003] P.I.Q.R. P34; [2003] N.P.C. 61, QBD. . . . .   *Digested*, 06/**2878**
Sutton v Bridgend CBC (Unreported, December 2, 2005), CC (Bridgend) [*Ex rel.* Andrew Arentsen, 33 Park Place, Cardiff] . . . .   *Digested*, 07/**3169**
Sutton LBC v Sutton Islamic Centre [2007] P.A.D. 18, Planning Inspector
Svenska Petroleum Exploration AB v Lithuania (No.2) [2006] EWCA Civ 1529; [2007] Q.B. 886; [2007] 2 W.L.R. 876; [2007] 1 All E.R. (Comm) 909; [2007] 1 Lloyd's Rep. 193; [2006] 2 C.L.C. 797; *Times*, November 17, 2006; *Independent*, November 16, 2006, CA (Civ Div); affirming [2005] EWHC 2437 (Comm); [2006] 1 All E.R. (Comm) 731; [2006] 1 Lloyd's Rep. 181; [2005] 2 C.L.C. 965; (2005) 102(47) L.S.G. 26, QBD (Comm) . . . .   *Digested*, 07/**239**: *Affirmed*, 07/239
Swain v DPP see R. v Jones (Margaret)
Swainland Builders Ltd v Freehold Properties Ltd [2002] EWCA Civ 560; [2002] 2 E.G.L.R. 71; [2002] 23 E.G. 123; [2002] 17 E.G. 154 (C.S.), CA (Civ Div) . . . . .   *Digested*, 02/**3856**: *Distinguished*, 07/2748
Swansea City Council v Grove [2007] P.A.D. 66, Planning Inspector
Swash v Secretary of State for the Home Department [2006] EWCA Civ 1093; [2007] 1 W.L.R. 1264; [2007] 1 All E.R. 1033; [2006] Imm. A.R. 633; [2006] I.N.L.R. 655; *Times*, August 14, 2006, CA (Civ Div) . . . .   *Digested*, 06/**2213**
Sweeney v Boylan Nominees Pty Ltd [2006] B.L.R. 440, HC (Aus) . . . .   *Digested*, 07/**2943**

Sweetman *v* Nathan see Sweetman *v* Shepherd
Sweetman *v* Russell Jones Walker see Sweetman *v* Shepherd
Sweetman *v* Shepherd; *joined cases* Sweetman *v* Nathan; Sweetman *v* Russell Jones
    Walker [2007] EWHC 137 (QB); [2007] B.P.I.R. 455, QBD . . . .   *Digested,* 07/**531**
SWI Ltd *v* P&I Data Services Ltd [2007] EWCA Civ 663; [2007] B.L.R. 430, CA (Civ
    Div). . . . .   *Digested,* 07/**753**
Swift *v* Securicor Case Services Ltd (Unreported, April 26, 2007), CC (Tunbridge
    Wells) [*Ex rel.* Justyn Turner, Barrister, 4 King's Bench Walk, Temple, London] . . .   *Digested,* 07/**3150**
Swiggs *v* Nagarajan (No.2) see Nagarajan *v* London Regional Transport
Swindale *v* Forder; *sub nom* Forder *v* Forder [2007] EWCA Civ 29; [2007] 1 F.L.R.
    1905; [2007] 1 F.C.R. 220; [2007] Fam. Law 392; (2007) 151 S.J.L.B. 197, CA
    (Civ Div) . . . .   *Digested,* 07/**1838**
Swindon BC (formerly Thamesdown BC) *v* Aston; *sub nom* Aston *v* Swindon BC
    [2002] EWCA Civ 1850; [2003] H.L.R. 42; [2003] 2 P. & C.R. 22; [2003] L. &
    T.R. 18; [2003] 2 E.G. 104 (C.S.); (2003) 100(3) L.S.G. 35; [2002] N.P.C. 169;
    [2003] 1 P. & C.R. DG25, CA (Civ Div) . . . .   *Digested,* 03/**2770**:
                                              Applied, 07/2769: *Considered,* 06/2719
Swiss Commercial Loan, Re (XI ZR 82/05) [2007] E.C.C. 13, BGH (Ger) . . . .   *Digested,* 07/**676**
Swords *v* Secretary of State for Communities and Local Government; *sub nom* R. (on
    the application of Swords) *v* Secretary of State for Communities and Local
    Government [2007] EWCA Civ 795; [2007] B.L.G.R. 757; (2007) 151 S.J.L.B.
    1022, CA (Civ Div); affirming [2007] EWHC 771 (Admin), QBD (Admin)
Sydenhams (Timber Engineering) Ltd *v* CHG Holdings Ltd [2007] EWHC 1129 (TCC);
    112 Con. L.R. 49, QBD (TCC) . . . .   *Digested,* 07/**737**
Symphony Group Plc *v* Hodgson [1994] Q.B. 179; [1993] 3 W.L.R. 830; [1993] 4 All
    E.R. 143; (1993) 143 N.L.J. 725; (1993) 137 S.J.L.B. 134; *Times,* May 4, 1993;
    Independent, May 14, 1993, CA (Civ Div) . . . .   *Digested,* 93/**3153**:
                     Applied, 95/3994, 95/3995, 96/710, 99/389, 00/416, 00/423, 00/455,
                     01/474, 05/363, 06/369: *Approved,* 99/749: *Considered,* 94/3623, 96/701,
                     97/3113, 97/3343, 99/390, 99/391, 02/393, 02/394, 07/428:
                                  Followed, 96/3464, 99/387, 99/392
Syndesmos ton en Elladi Touristikon kai Taxidiotikon Grafeion *v* Ergasias (C398/95)
    [1997] E.C.R. I-3091; [1998] 1 C.M.L.R. 420; [1997] C.E.C. 1291, ECJ (6th
    Chamber) . . . .   *Digested,* 98/**2139**:
                     Applied, 98/4517, 07/617: *Considered,* 02/1561, 02/4420
Syndicat des Professionels Europeens de l'Automobile (SPEA) *v* Groupement des
    Concessionnaires Automobiles Peugeot (GCAP) [2007] E.C.C. 5, Cass (F);
    affirming [2005] E.C.C. 49, C d'A (Paris)
Synectiv Ltd *v* Revenue and Customs Commissioners [2006] V. & D.R. 183; [2006]
    S.T.I. 2577, V&DTr (London) . . . .   *Digested,* 07/**4315**
Synthon BV *v* SmithKline Beecham Plc (No.2); *sub nom* SmithKline Beecham Plc's
    (Paroxetine Methanesulfonate) Patent (No.2) [2005] UKHL 59; [2006] 1 All
    E.R. 685; [2006] R.P.C. 10; (2005) 86 B.M.L.R. 130, HL; reversing [2003]
    EWCA Civ 861; [2003] R.P.C. 43; (2003) 147 S.J.L.B. 814, CA (Civ Div);
    reversing [2002] EWHC 2573 (Pat); [2003] E.N.P.R. 10; [2003] R.P.C. 33;
    (2003) 26(1) I.P.D. 26004, Ch D (Patents Ct) . . . .   *Digested,* 06/**2525**:
                                     Applied, 07/2614
Szechter *v* Szechter [1971] P. 286; [1971] 2 W.L.R. 170; [1970] 3 All E.R. 905, PDAD .   *Digested,* 71/**3603**:
                 Applied, 71/3605, 97/2034: *Considered,* 71/1557, 83/1118, 07/1834
Szepietowski *v* Director of Assets Recovery Agency (Costs) [2007] EWCA Civ 766;
    Times, August 21, 2007, CA (Civ Div); affirming [2006] EWHC 3228 (Admin),
    QBD (Admin)
Szklanny *v* City of Westminster Magistrates Court; *sub nom* R. (on the application of
    Szklanny) *v* City of Westminster Magistrates Court [2007] EWHC 2646
    (Admin); *Times,* December 21, 2007, QBD (Admin)
Szoma *v* Secretary of State for Work and Pensions [2005] UKHL 64; [2006] 1 A.C.
    564; [2005] 3 W.L.R. 955; [2006] 1 All E.R. 1; [2006] Imm. A.R. 48; [2006]
    I.N.L.R. 88; (2005) 102(43) L.S.G. 31; *Times,* November 1, 2005, HL; reversing
    [2003] EWCA Civ 1131; *Times,* August 22, 2003, CA (Civ Div) . . . .   *Digested,* 05/**3882**:
                                   Considered, 07/3824
Szula *v* United Kingdom (Admissibility) (18727/06) (2007) 44 E.H.R.R. SE19, ECHR

T *v* BBC [2007] EWHC 1683 (QB); (2007) 10 C.C.L. Rep. 737; [2007] Fam. Law
    904, QBD
T *v* Devon CC [2006] EWHC 395 (Admin); [2007] E.L.R. 79, QBD (Admin) . . . .   *Digested,* 07/**1264**
T *v* DPP [2007] EWHC 1793 (Admin); (2007) 171 J.P. 605, DC
T *v* Finland (25702/94) (No.2) see K *v* Finland (25702/94) (No.2)
T *v* T see NMT *v* MOT
T *v* T (Joinder of Third Parties) [1996] 2 F.L.R. 357; [1997] 1 F.C.R. 98; [1996] Fam.
    Law 669, Fam Div . . . .   *Digested,* 96/**2876**:
                                     Considered, 07/1704
T and J (Children) (Abduction: Recognition of Foreign Judgment), Re [2006] EWHC 1472
    (Fam); [2006] 2 F.L.R. 1290; [2006] 3 F.C.R. 363; [2006] Fam. Law 919, Fam Div   *Digested,* 07/**1741**

T Comedy (UK) Ltd v Easy Managed Transport Ltd [2007] EWHC 611 (Comm); [2007] 2 All E.R. (Comm) 242; [2007] 2 Lloyd's Rep. 397; [2007] 1 C.L.C. 503, QBD (Comm) . . . . *Digested*, 07/**3567**

T (A Child) v Hertfordshire CC see R. (on the application of Tottman) v Hertfordshire CC

T (Adult: Refusal of Treatment), Re; *sub nom* T (Consent to Medical Treatment) (Adult Patient), Re [1993] Fam. 95; [1992] 3 W.L.R. 782; [1992] 4 All E.R. 649; [1992] 2 F.L.R. 458; [1992] 2 F.C.R. 861; [1992] 3 Med. L.R. 306; [1993] Fam. Law 27; (1992) 142 N.L.J. 1125; *Times*, August 21, 1992; *Independent*, July 31, 1992; *Guardian*, August 5, 1992, CA (Civ Div) . . . . *Digested*, 92/**2918**:
Applied, 94/3063, 95/4266, 03/58, 07/2898: *Considered*, 95/3535, 95/4104, 95/4105, 05/1850: *Referred to*, 94/3803

T (Children) (Abuse: Standard of Proof), Re; *sub nom* T (Children) (Sexual Abuse: Standard of Proof), Re [2004] EWCA Civ 558; [2004] 2 F.L.R. 838; [2004] Fam. Law 709; *Independent*, May 27, 2004, CA (Civ Div) . . . . *Digested*, 04/**1463**:
Applied, 07/1754

T (Children) (Sexual Abuse: Standard of Proof), Re see T (Children) (Abuse: Standard of Proof), Re

T (Consent to Medical Treatment) (Adult Patient), Re see T (Adult: Refusal of Treatment), Re

T&N Ltd, Re see Altitude Scaffolding Ltd, Re

T&N Ltd, Re [2006] EWHC 1447 (Ch); [2007] Bus. L.R. 1411; [2007] 1 All E.R. 851; [2007] 1 B.C.L.C. 563; [2006] B.P.I.R. 1283; [2006] Lloyd's Rep. I.R. 817, Ch D (Companies Ct) . . . . *Digested*, 07/**2450**

Tackaberry v Hollis [2007] EWHC 2633 (Ch); [2007] N.P.C. 121, Ch D

Tagg v Countess of Chester Hospital Foundation Trust [2007] EWHC 509 (QB); (2007) 95 B.M.L.R. 76, QBD . . . . *Digested*, 07/**2930**

Tague v Lancaster City Council [1999] 2 E.G.L.R. 103; [1999] 20 E.G. 156; [1998] R.V.R. 253, Lands Tr . . . . *Digested*, 99/**4196**:
Considered, 07/3384

Tahmassebi v Persia International Bank Plc [2007] EWHC 1751 (QB); [2007] Pens. L.R. 297, QBD

Taiga v Taiga see Moses-Taiga v Taiga

TAKASAGO/Reimbursement of appeal fee (T21/02) [2006] E.P.O.R. 36, EPO (Technical Bd App) . . . . *Digested*, 07/**2605**

Talacre Beach Caravan Sales Ltd v Customs and Excise Commissioners (C-251/05) [2006] S.T.C. 1671; [2006] E.C.R. I-6269; [2006] 3 C.M.L.R. 31; [2006] C.E.C. 1000; [2007] B.T.C. 5455; [2007] B.V.C. 366; [2006] S.T.I. 1855; [2006] N.P.C. 80, ECJ (1st Chamber) . . . . *Digested*, 07/**4362**

Talisman Property Co (UK) Ltd v Norton Rose [2006] EWCA Civ 1104; [2006] 3 E.G.L.R. 59; [2006] 45 E.G. 192; [2007] 1 P. & C.R. DG13, CA (Civ Div); reversing [2005] EWHC 2793 (Ch); [2006] 1 E.G.L.R. 145, Ch D . . . . *Digested*, 07/**1057**

Tallington Lakes Ltd v Reilly see Muschett v Hounslow LBC

Talotta v Belgium (C-383/05) [2007] 2 C.M.L.R. 36; [2007] C.E.C. 741; [2007] S.T.I. 1053, ECJ (1st Chamber) . . . . *Digested*, 07/**1616**

Tamares (Vincent Square) Ltd v Fairpoint Properties (Vincent Square) Ltd [2006] EWHC 3589 (Ch); [2007] 1 W.L.R. 2148; [2007] 2 P. & C.R. 3; [2006] 3 E.G.L.R. 87; [2006] 41 E.G. 226; (2006) 103(36) L.S.G. 35; (2006) 150 S.J.L.B. 1191; [2007] 1 P. & C.R. DG19, Ch D . . . . *Digested*, 07/**3425**

Tamares (Vincent Square) Ltd v Fairpoint Properties (Vincent Square) Ltd [2007] EWHC 212 (Ch); [2007] 1 W.L.R. 2167; [2007] 14 E.G. 106; [2007] 7 E.G. 143 (C.S.); *Times*, February 14, 2007, Ch D . . . . *Digested*, 07/**1061**

Tameside and Glossop Acute Services NHS Trust v Thompstone; *sub nom* Thompstone v Tameside and Glossop Acute Services NHS Trust; *joined cases* South West London Strategic HA v De Haas; United Bristol Healthcare NHS Trust v RH; South Yorkshire Strategic HA v Corbett; B3/2007/0077; B3/2007/1371; B3/2007/1519; B3/2007/0076, CA (Civ Div); affirming [2006] EWHC 2904 (QB); [2007] LS Law Medical 71, QBD . . . . *Digested*, 07/**3067**:
Applied, 07/3063, 07/3065

Tamil Nadu Electricity Board v ST-CMS Electric Co Private Ltd [2007] EWHC 1713 (Comm); [2007] 2 All E.R. (Comm) 701, QBD (Comm)

Tan v Sitkowski see Phaik Seang Tan v Sitkowski

Tan Te Lam v Superintendent of Tai A Chau Detention Centre [1997] A.C. 97; [1996] 2 W.L.R. 863; [1996] 4 All E.R. 256; (1996) 140 S.J.L.B. 106, PC (HK) . . . . *Digested*, 96/**3278**:
Considered, 07/2319

Tapecrown Ltd v First Secretary of State; *sub nom* R. (on the application of Tapecrown Ltd) v First Secretary of State [2006] EWCA Civ 1744; [2007] 2 P. & C.R. 7; (2007) 151 S.J.L.B. 64; [2007] N.P.C. 4, CA (Civ Div); affirming [2006] EWHC 1012 (Admin); [2006] J.P.L. 1816, QBD (Admin) . . . . *Digested*, 07/**3262**

Tarbuck v Sainsbury Supermarkets Ltd [2006] I.R.L.R. 664, EAT . . . . *Digested*, 06/**1297**:
Applied, 07/1334

Target Fixings Ltd v Brutt Beteiligungsgesellschaft MBH; *sub nom* BRUTT Trade Marks [2007] R.P.C. 19, App Person . . . . *Digested*, 07/**2680**

Tas-Hagen v Raadskamer WUBO van de Pensioen- en Uitkeringsraad (C-192/05) [2007] All E.R. (EC) 129; [2006] E.C.R. I-10451; [2007] 1 C.M.L.R. 23; [2007] C.E.C. 270, ECJ (2nd Chamber) . . . .   *Digested*, 07/**1608**

Tasarruf Mevduati Sigorta Fonu v Demirel; *sub nom* Tasarruff Mevduati Sigorta Fonu (A Firm) v Demirel (Application to Set Aside); Demirel v Tasarruff Mevduati Sigorta Fonu [2007] EWCA Civ 799; [2007] 1 W.L.R. 2508; [2007] 4 All E.R. 1014; [2007] 2 All E.R. (Comm) 925; [2007] 2 Lloyd's Rep. 440; [2007] C.P. Rep. 47; *Times*, August 24, 2007, CA (Civ Div); affirming [2006] EWHC 3354 (Ch); [2007] 2 All E.R. 815; [2007] 1 All E.R. (Comm) 649; [2007] 1 Lloyd's Rep. 223; [2007] I.L.Pr. 8; (2007) 104(5) L.S.G. 30, Ch D . . . .   *Digested*, 07/**521**

Tasarruff Mevduati Sigorta Fonu (A Firm) v Demirel (Application to Set Aside) see Tasarruf Mevduati Sigorta Fonu v Demirel

Tate Gallery Board of Trustees v Duffy Construction Ltd [2007] EWHC 361 (TCC); [2007] 1 All E.R. (Comm) 1004; [2007] B.L.R. 216; [2007] Lloyd's Rep. I.R. 758, QBD (TCC) . . . .   *Digested*, 07/**740**

Tatishvili v Russia (1509/02) (2007) 45 E.H.R.R. 52, ECHR

Tavli v Turkey (11449/02) [2007] 1 F.L.R. 1136; [2006] 3 F.C.R. 542; [2007] Fam. Law 120, ECHR . . . .   *Digested*, 07/**1787**

Tavoulareas v Alexander G Tsavliris & Sons see Tavoulareas v Tsavliris (The Atlas Pride)

Tavoulareas v Tsavliris (The Atlas Pride); *joined case* Tavoulareas v Alexander G Tsavliris & Sons [2006] EWCA Civ 1772; [2007] 1 W.L.R. 1573; [2007] 2 All E.R. (Comm) 356; [2007] C.P. Rep. 16; [2006] 2 C.L.C. 1034; *Times*, January 5, 2007, CA (Civ Div); affirming [2006] EWHC 414 (Comm); [2006] 1 C.L.C. 466; [2006] I.L.Pr. 33, QBD (Comm) . . . .   *Digested*, 07/**507**

Taxation of Pension Contributions, Re (C-150/04) see Commission of the European Communities v Denmark (C-150/04)

Taylor v British Legal Life Assurance Co Ltd [1925] Ch. 395, Ch D . . . .   *Considered*, 07/3400

Taylor v Chief Constable of Thames Valley [2004] EWCA Civ 858; [2004] 1 W.L.R. 3155; [2004] 3 All E.R. 503; (2004) 101(32) L.S.G. 36; (2004) 148 S.J.L.B. 877; *Times*, July 13, 2004, CA (Civ Div) . . . .   *Digested*, 04/**891**:
                                                                                      Applied, 07/2292

Taylor v Crotty [2006] EWCA Civ 1364; (2006) 150 S.J.L.B. 1330; [2007] 2 P. & C.R. DG9, CA (Civ Div)

Taylor v Director of the Serious Fraud Office; *sub nom* Taylor v Serious Fraud Office [1999] 2 A.C. 177; [1998] 3 W.L.R. 1040; [1998] 4 All E.R. 801; [1999] E.M.L.R. 1; *Times*, November 4, 1998; *Independent*, November 3, 1998, HL; affirming [1997] 4 All E.R. 887; [1998] E.M.L.R. 463; (1997) 94(36) L.S.G. 44; (1997) 147 N.L.J. 1309; (1997) 141 S.J.L.B. 216; *Times*, August 27, 1997; *Independent*, July 24, 1997, CA (Civ Div) . . . .   *Digested*, 98/**1768**:
                                     Applied, 07/438, 07/1073: *Considered*, 99/4296, 00/934, 00/2627:
                                                                                      Distinguished, 99/878

Taylor v Glasgow & Robinson (Unreported, September 27, 2006), CC (Lincoln) [*Ex rel.* Hodgkinsons, Solicitors, The Bracings, 7 Heath Road, Skegness, Lincolnshire] . . . .   *Digested*, 07/**3160**

Taylor v Lawrence (Appeal: Jurisdiction to Reopen) [2002] EWCA Civ 90; [2003] Q.B. 528; [2002] 3 W.L.R. 640; [2002] 2 All E.R. 353; [2002] C.P. Rep. 29; (2002) 99(12) L.S.G. 35; (2002) 152 N.L.J. 221; (2002) 146 S.J.L.B. 50; *Times*, February 8, 2002; *Independent*, February 14, 2002; *Daily Telegraph*, February 14, 2002, CA (Civ Div) . . . .   *Digested*, 02/**294**:
                                     Applied, 02/296, 03/443, 04/255, 05/464, 06/30: *Considered*, 03/453,
                                                        06/518, 07/510, 07/3387: *Explained*, 04/870: *Followed*, 03/842

Taylor v Perkins (Unreported, June 6, 2006), CC (Macclesfield) [*Ex rel.* David Calvert, Barrister, St James's Chambers, 68 Quay Street, Manchester] . . . .   *Digested*, 07/**3124**

Taylor v Serious Fraud Office see Taylor v Director of the Serious Fraud Office

Taylor v United Kingdom (Admissibility) (23412/94) (1994) 18 E.H.R.R. CD215, Eur Comm HR . . . .   *Applied*, 06/18:
                                                                                      Considered, 07/28, 07/2234

Taylor Walton (A Firm) v Laing see Laing v Taylor Walton (A Firm)

Taylor Woodrow Holdings Ltd v Barnes & Elliott Ltd [2006] EWHC 1693 (TCC); [2006] 2 All E.R. (Comm) 735; [2006] B.L.R. 377; 110 Con. L.R. 169; [2006] C.I.L.L. 2375, QBD (TCC) . . . .   *Digested*, 06/**689**

Taylor (A Bankrupt), Re see Davenham Trust Plc v CV Distribution (UK) Ltd

Taylor (Inspector of Taxes) v MEPC Holdings Ltd; *sub nom* MEPC Holdings Ltd v Taylor (Inspector of Taxes) [2003] UKHL 70; [2004] 1 W.L.R. 82; [2004] 1 All E.R. 536; [2004] S.T.C. 123; 75 T.C. 632; [2004] B.T.C. 20; [2004] S.T.I. 50; (2004) 101(4) L.S.G. 31; (2004) 148 S.J.L.B. 29; *Times*, January 9, 2004, HL; reversing [2002] EWCA Civ 883; [2002] S.T.C. 997; [2002] B.T.C. 276; [2002] S.T.I. 934; (2002) 99(31) L.S.G. 34; *Times*, July 3, 2002, CA (Civ Div); affirming [2002] S.T.C. 430; [2002] B.T.C. 162; [2001] S.T.I. 834; *Times*, June 12, 2001; *Independent*, June 25, 2001, Ch D; reversing [2000] S.T.C. (S.C.D.) 504; [2000] S.T.I. 1468, Sp Comm . . . .   *Digested*, 04/**3725**:
                                                                                      Applied, 07/4023

Taylor (Setting of Minimum Term), Re; *sub nom* R. v Taylor (John) [2006] EWHC 2944 (QB); [2007] 1 W.L.R. 3029; [2007] 3 All E.R. 441, QBD . . . .   *Digested*, 07/**3700**

TD *v* Secretary of State for the Home Department; *sub nom* TD (Paragraph 297 (I) (E): Sole Responsibility: Yemen), Re [2006] UKAIT 49; [2006] Imm. A.R. 569, AIT　　*Digested*, 07/**2325**
TD (Paragraph 297 (I) (E): Sole Responsibility: Yemen), Re see TD *v* Secretary of State for the Home Department
Technische Glaswerke Ilmenau GmbH *v* Commission of the European Communities (T-237/02) [2007] 1 C.M.L.R. 39, CFI (5th Chamber) . . . .　　*Digested*, 07/**1539**
Technotrade Ltd *v* Larkstore Ltd see Offer-Hoar *v* Larkstore Ltd
Teckal Srl *v* Comune di Viano (Reggio Emilia) (C-107/98) [1999] E.C.R. I-8121, ECJ . .　　*Applied*, 07/1642, 07/3328: *Distinguished*, 06/3419
Tegni Cymru Cyf *v* Denbighshire CC [2007] P.A.D. 73, Planning Inspector
Tehrani *v* Secretary of State for the Home Department; *sub nom* Tehrani, Petitioner [2006] UKHL 47; [2007] 1 A.C. 521; [2006] 3 W.L.R. 699; [2007] 1 All E.R. 559; 2007 S.C. (H.L.) 1; 2006 S.L.T. 1123; 2006 S.C.L.R. 879; [2007] I.N.L.R. 80; (2006) 103(42) L.S.G. 34; (2006) 150 S.J.L.B. 1395; 2006 G.W.D. 38-756; *Times*, October 24, 2006, HL; reversing 2004 S.L.T. 461; 2004 G.W.D. 13-281, IH (Ex Div); affirming 2003 S.L.T. 808; 2003 S.C.L.R. 448; 2003 G.W.D. 13-382, OH . . . .　　*Digested*, 06/**24**: *Followed*, 04/4482
Tehrani, Petitioner see Tehrani *v* Secretary of State for the Home Department
Teignbridge DC *v* Midas Homes [2007] P.A.D. 17, Planning Inspector
Telefonaktiebolaget LM Ericsson *v* Samsung Electronics UK Ltd [2007] EWHC 1047 (Pat); (2007) 30(7) I.P.D. 30047, Ch D (Patents Ct)
Telegraph Group Plc, Ex p. see R. (on the application of Telegraph Group Plc) *v* Sherwood
Telent Plc *v* Revenue and Customs Commissioners [2007] S.T.I. 2234, Sp Comm
Telent Plc *v* Revenue and Customs Commissioners [2007] V. & D.R. 81, V&DTr (London)
Telepharmacy Solutions Inc *v* Office for Harmonisation in the Internal Market (Trade Marks and Designs) (OHIM) (T-289/02) [2004] E.C.R. II-2851; [2006] E.T.M.R. 10, CFI (4th Chamber) . . . .　　*Digested*, 06/**2561**: *Applied*, 07/2645
Telford and Wrekin BC *v* Ahmed [2006] EWHC 1748 (Admin), DC . . . .　　*Applied*, 07/3458
Tempelman *v* Directeur van de Rijksdienst voor de Keuring van Vee en Vlees (C-96/03) [2005] E.C.R. I-1895, ECJ . . . .　　*Applied*, 07/1566
Templeton Insurance Ltd *v* Penningtons Solicitors [2006] EWHC 685 (Ch); [2007] W.T.L.R. 1103, Ch D . . . .　　*Digested*, 07/**4251**
Temporary Importation of Motor Vehicles, Re (C-156/04) see Commission of the European Communities *v* Greece (C-156/04)
Tennero Ltd *v* Arnold [2006] EWHC 1530 (QB); [2007] 1 W.L.R. 1025, QBD . . . .　　*Digested*, 07/**362**
Terhoeve *v* Inspecteur van de Belastingdienst Particulieren/Ondernemingen Buitenland (C-18/95) [1999] E.C.R. I-345; [2001] 1 C.M.L.R. 12; (1999) 96(19) L.S.G. 30; *Times*, February 25, 1999, ECJ . . . .　　*Digested*, 99/**4547**: *Considered*, 06/1573, 07/1627
Terry *v* Tonbridge and Malling DC [2007] P.A.D. 60, Planning Inspector
Tesco Stores Ltd *v* Constable A3/2007/2313QBCMF, CA (Civ Div); affirming [2007] EWHC 2088 (Comm); [2007] 2 C.L.C. 493; [2007] C.I.L.L. 2522; (2007) 104(38) L.S.G. 32, QBD (Comm)
Tesco Stores Ltd *v* Elogicom Ltd [2006] EWHC 403; [2006] E.T.M.R. 91; [2007] F.S.R. 4; (2006) 29(5) I.P.D. 29040, Ch D . . . .　　*Digested*, 06/**2593**
Tesco Stores Ltd *v* Liverpool City Council [2007] P.A.D. 39, Planning Inspector
Tesco Stores Ltd *v* Secretary of State for the Environment; *joined cases* Tesco Stores Ltd *v* West Oxfordshire DC; Tesco Stores Ltd *v* Tarmac Provincial Properties Ltd [1995] 1 W.L.R. 759; [1995] 2 All E.R. 636; 93 L.G.R. 403; (1995) 70 P. & C.R. 184; [1995] 2 P.L.R. 72; [1995] 2 E.G.L.R. 147; [1995] 27 E.G. 154; [1995] E.G. 82 (C.S.); (1995) 92(24) L.S.G. 39; (1995) 145 N.L.J. 724; (1995) 139 S.J.L.B. 145; [1995] N.P.C. 89A; *Times*, May 13, 1995, HL; affirming (1994) 68 P. & C.R. 219; [1994] 1 P.L.R. 97; [1994] E.G. 103 (C.S.); [1994] N.P.C. 80, CA (Civ Div); reversing (1994) 67 P. & C.R. 216; [1993] 2 P.L.R. 108; [1994] J.P.L. 227; [1993] E.G. 133 (C.S.), QBD . . . .　　*Digested*, 95/**4784**: *Applied*, 96/4779, 99/4215, 01/4682, 01/4731, 03/2057: *Considered*, 99/3049, 07/2988: *Followed*, 03/3438
Tesco Stores Ltd *v* Tarmac Provincial Properties Ltd see Tesco Stores Ltd *v* Secretary of State for the Environment
Tesco Stores Ltd *v* West Oxfordshire DC see Tesco Stores Ltd *v* Secretary of State for the Environment
Tesco Supermarkets Ltd *v* Nattrass [1972] A.C. 153; [1971] 2 W.L.R. 1166; [1971] 2 All E.R. 127; 69 L.G.R. 403; (1971) 115 S.J. 285, HL; reversing [1971] 1 Q.B. 133; [1970] 3 W.L.R. 572; [1970] 3 All E.R. 357; 68 L.G.R. 722; (1970) 114 S.J. 664, QBD . . . .　　*Digested*, 71/**10538**: *Applied*, 72/594, 72/3464, 82/2783, 85/3116, 87/4197, 93/3642, 96/969, 04/4634: *Considered*, 71/10538, 73/3036, 84/958, 88/851, 02/837, 07/2814: *Distinguished*, 88/175, 93/3559, 95/5132, 96/3020: *Followed*, 74/3441

Test Claimants in Class IV of the ACT Group Litigation *v* Inland Revenue Commissioners (C-374/04) [2007] All E.R. (EC) 351; [2007] S.T.C. 404; [2007] 1 C.M.L.R. 36; [2007] C.E.C. 498; 9 I.T.L. Rep. 360; [2006] S.T.I. 2748, ECJ . . . .
*Digested, 07/**3974**: Applied, 07/3975*

Test Claimants in the FII Group Litigation *v* Inland Revenue Commissioners (C-446/04) [2007] S.T.C. 326; [2007] 1 C.M.L.R. 35; 9 I.T.L. Rep. 426; [2006] S.T.I. 2750, ECJ . . . .
*Digested, 07/**3971**: Applied, 07/1614, 07/3972*

Test Claimants in the Thin Cap Group Litigation *v* Inland Revenue Commissioners (C-524/04) [2007] S.T.C. 906; [2007] 2 C.M.L.R. 31; 9 I.T.L. Rep. 877; [2007] S.T.I. 538, ECJ . . . .
*Digested, 07/**1614**: Applied, 07/1617*

Test Holdings (Clifton), Re; *sub nom* General Issue & Investment Co, Re; *joined case* General Issues and Investment Co, Re [1970] Ch. 285; [1969] 3 W.L.R. 606; [1969] 3 All E.R. 517; (1969) 113 S.J. 811, Ch D . . . .
*Digested, 69/**398**: Applied, 71/1415, 81/262: Distinguished, 07/2440*

TFB (Mortgages) Ltd *v* Anglo Petroleum Ltd see Anglo Petroleum Ltd *v* TFB (Mortgages) Ltd

TFB (Mortgages) Ltd *v* Sutton see Anglo Petroleum Ltd *v* TFB (Mortgages) Ltd

TFW Printers Ltd *v* Interserve Project Services Ltd [2006] EWCA Civ 875; [2006] 2 C.L.C. 106; [2006] B.L.R. 299; 109 Con. L.R. 1; (2006) 22 Const. L.J. 481; [2006] C.I.L.L. 2376; (2006) 103(28) L.S.G. 27, CA (Civ Div) . . . .
*Digested, 06/**690***

Thames Water Utilities Ltd *v* Bromley Magistrates Court (C-252/05) see R. (on the application of Thames Water Utilities Ltd) *v* Bromley Magistrates' Court (C-252/05)

Thames Water Utilities Ltd *v* Marcic see Marcic *v* Thames Water Utilities Ltd

Thames Water Utilities Ltd *v* Ministry of Defence see Ministry of Defence *v* Thames Water Utilities Ltd

Thane Investments Ltd *v* Tomlinson (No.3) [2006] EWHC 1182; [2007] 1 P. & C.R. DG3, Ch D

Thatcher *v* Middlesex University EAT/0134/05/DM, EAT . . . .
Applied, 07/1359

Thet *v* DPP; *sub nom* Soe Thet *v* DPP [2006] EWHC 2701 (Admin); [2007] 1 W.L.R. 2022; [2007] 2 All E.R. 425; [2007] I.N.L.R. 71; *Times*, November 1, 2006, DC.
*Digested, 07/**2323**: Applied, 07/897*

Thiermann *v* Norway (Admissibility) (71412/01) (2007) 45 E.H.R.R. SE13, ECHR

Thoday *v* Thoday [1964] P. 181; [1964] 2 W.L.R. 371; [1964] 1 All E.R. 341; (1964) 108 S.J. 15, CA . . . .
*Digested, 64/**1129**: Applied, 65/100, 67/3912, 77/1216, 80/933, 90/2019, 07/4001: Considered, 88/3432, 98/1981, 99/5146*

Thomas *v* Brighton HA see Wells *v* Wells

Thomas *v* Central Criminal Court see R. (on the application of Thomas) *v* Central Criminal Court

Thomas *v* Evans (Unreported, March 26, 2007), CC (Pontypridd) [*Ex rel.* Andrew Arentsen, Barrister, 33 Park Place, Cardiff] . . . .
*Digested, 07/**3106***

Thomas *v* Farr Plc [2007] EWCA Civ 118; [2007] I.C.R. 932; [2007] I.R.L.R. 419; (2007) 151 S.J.L.B. 296; *Times*, February 27, 2007, CA (Civ Div) . . . .
*Digested, 07/**1328***

Thomas *v* Home Office [2006] EWCA Civ 1355; [2007] 1 W.L.R. 230; [2007] C.P. Rep. 6; [2007] P.I.Q.R. P9; (2006) 103(42) L.S.G. 35, CA (Civ Div) . . . .
*Digested, 07/**372***

Thomas *v* Ken Thomas Ltd [2006] EWCA Civ 1504; [2007] Bus. L.R. 429; [2007] B.P.I.R. 959; [2007] L. & T.R. 21; [2007] 1 E.G. 94; [2006] 42 E.G. 244 (C.S.); (2006) 150 S.J.L.B. 1396, CA (Civ Div) . . . .
*Digested, 07/**2725***

Thomas *v* Kent [2006] EWCA Civ 1485; [2007] W.T.L.R. 177, CA (Civ Div)

Thomas & Agnes Carvel Foundation *v* Carvel [2007] EWHC 1314 (Ch); [2007] 4 All E.R. 81; [2007] W.T.L.R. 1297; (2007-08) 10 I.T.E.L.R. 455, Ch D . . . .
*Digested, 07/**3956**: Considered, 07/2447*

Thomas de la Rue & Co Ltd, Re [1911] 2 Ch. 361, Ch D . . . .

Thompson *v* Arnold [2007] EWHC 1875 (QB); (2007) 104(33) L.S.G. 27, QBD

Thompson *v* Commissioner of Police of the Metropolis; *joined case* Hsu *v* Commissioner of Police of the Metropolis [1998] Q.B. 498; [1997] 3 W.L.R. 403; [1997] 2 All E.R. 762; (1998) 10 Admin. L.R. 363; (1997) 147 N.L.J. 341; *Times*, February 20, 1997; *Independent*, February 28, 1997, CA (Civ Div) . . . . .
*Digested, 97/**1765**: Applied, 98/1451, 00/5118, 03/893, 07/1051, 07/1053, 07/4192: Approved, 97/4856: Considered, 99/5229, 01/1524: Distinguished, 05/4193: Followed, 99/1392*

Thompson *v* Secretary of State for Trade and Industry see Rice *v* Secretary of State for Trade and Industry

Thompstone *v* Tameside and Glossop Acute Services NHS Trust see Tameside and Glossop Acute Services NHS Trust *v* Thompstone

Thomson *v* Church Commissioners for England [2006] EWHC 1773 (Admin); [2006] 3 E.G.L.R. 1; [2006] 43 E.G. 180; [2006] N.P.C. 88, QBD (Admin) . . . .
*Digested, 07/**2714***

Thomson *v* Diosynth Ltd; *sub nom* Diosynth Ltd *v* Thomson; *joined cases* Watts *v* Diosynth Ltd; Fleming *v* Diosynth Ltd [2006] CSIH 5; 2006 S.C. 389; 2006 S.L.T. 323; [2006] I.R.L.R. 284; 2006 G.W.D. 4-81, IH (Ex Div); affirming EATS/0034/04, EAT (SC) . . . .
*Digested, 06/**5324**: Applied, 07/1432*

330

Thomson v Thomson Finance SA [2007] E.T.M.R. 32, PO (Irl)
Thorner v Curtis [2007] EWHC 2422 (Ch); [2007] N.P.C. 112, Ch D (Bristol)
Thornett v Scope; *sub nom* Scope v Thornett [2006] EWCA Civ 1600; [2007] I.C.R.
    236; [2007] I.R.L.R. 155, CA (Civ Div); reversing in part UKEAT/0477/05/CK,
    EAT. . . . .   *Digested,* 07/**1423**:
                        Applied, 07/1426: *Considered,* 07/1427
Thornton v Shoe Lane Parking [1971] 2 Q.B. 163; [1971] 2 W.L.R. 585; [1971] 1 All
    E.R. 686; [1971] 1 Lloyd's Rep. 289; [1971] R.T.R. 79; (1970) 115 S.J. 75; *Times,*
    December 19, 1970, CA (Civ Div) . . . .   *Digested,* 71/**1741**:
            Applied, 88/430, 99/2013: *Considered,* 88/61, 92/1553, 00/5250, 07/4324
Thorp v Hunt (Unreported, January 30, 2007), QBD (Canterbury) [*Ex rel.* John
    Gallagher, Barrister, Hardwicke Building, New Square, Lincolns Inn, London] . .   *Digested,* 07/**3081**
Thorpe v Listing Officer [2007] R.V.R. 5, VT . . . .   *Digested,* 07/**2833**
Thorpe v Poat UKEAT/0503/05/SM, EAT . . . .   *Considered,* 07/1408
Thorpe v Security Industry Authority see Nicholds v Security Industry Authority
Thrasyvoulou v Secretary of State for the Environment; *joined case* Oliver v Secretary
    of State for the Environment [1990] 2 A.C. 273; [1990] 2 W.L.R. 1; [1990] 1 All
    E.R. 65; 88 L.G.R. 217; (1990) 2 Admin. L.R. 289; (1990) 59 P. & C.R. 326;
    [1990] 1 P.L.R. 69; [1990] 13 E.G. 69; (1990) 154 L.G. Rev. 192; [1989] E.G.
    178 (C.S.), HL; affirming [1988] Q.B. 809; [1988] 3 W.L.R. 1; [1988] 2 All E.R.
    781; (1988) 56 P. & C.R. 259; [1988] 2 P.L.R. 37; [1988] 10 E.G. 131; [1988] 11
    E.G. 83; [1988] J.P.L. 689; (1988) 152 L.G. Rev. 946; (1988) 85(17) L.S.G.
    35; (1988) 138 N.L.J. Rep. 29; (1988) 132 S.J. 851, CA (Civ Div) . . . .   *Digested,* 90/**4426**:
                 Applied, 91/3509, 97/4075, 97/4109, 06/3293, 07/2677:
         Considered, 94/4363, 98/1981, 06/1949: *Distinguished,* 92/4216, 07/3225:
                                      Followed, 97/4039
Three Rivers DC v Acorn [2007] P.A.D. 44, Planning Inspector
Three Rivers DC v Bank of England (Disclosure) (No.4) [2004] UKHL 48; [2005] 1
    A.C. 610; [2004] 3 W.L.R. 1274; [2005] 4 All E.R. 948; (2004) 101(46) L.S.G.
    34; (2004) 154 N.L.J. 1727; (2004) 148 S.J.L.B. 1369; *Times,* November 12,
    2004; *Independent,* November 16, 2004, HL; reversing [2004] EWCA Civ 218;
    [2004] Q.B. 916; [2004] 2 W.L.R. 1065; [2004] 3 All E.R. 168; (2004) 101(11)
    L.S.G. 36; (2004) 154 N.L.J. 382; (2004) 148 S.J.L.B. 297; *Times,* March 3,
    2004; *Independent,* March 10, 2004, CA (Civ Div); affirming [2003] EWHC
    2565 (Comm), QBD (Comm) . . . .   *Digested,* 05/**299**:
                   Applied, 07/470: *Considered,* 04/257, 07/999:
                    Subsequent related litigation, 06/315, 06/332
Three Rivers DC v Bank of England (Indemnity Costs) [2006] EWHC 816 (Comm);
    [2006] 5 Costs L.R. 714, QBD (Comm) . . . .   *Digested,* 07/**398**
Three Rivers DC v Bank of England (No.3) (Summary Judgment) [2001] UKHL 16;
    [2003] 2 A.C. 1; [2001] 2 All E.R. 513; [2001] Lloyd's Rep. Bank. 125; (2001) 3
    L.G.L.R. 36; *Times,* March 23, 2001, HL . . . .   *Digested,* 01/**5355**:
          Applied, 03/509, 05/578, 07/4193: *Considered,* 01/669, 02/505, 03/2462,
         04/753, 05/4193, 05/4197, 06/4332, 06/4433: *Distinguished,* 05/461:
                                      Followed, 03/478
Three Rivers DC v Bank of England (No.3) [2003] 2 A.C. 1; [2000] 2 W.L.R. 1220;
    [2000] 3 All E.R. 1; [2000] Lloyd's Rep. Bank. 235; [2000] 3 C.M.L.R. 205;
    [2000] Eu. L.R. 583; (2000) 2 L.G.L.R. 769; (2000) 97(23) L.S.G. 41; *Times,*
    May 19, 2000, HL; affirming in part [2000] 2 W.L.R. 15; [1999] 4 All E.R. 800
    (Note); [1999] Lloyd's Rep. Bank. 283; [2000] 3 C.M.L.R. 1; [1999] Eu. L.R.
    211; (1999) 1 L.G.L.R. 645; (1999) 11 Admin. L.R. 281; (1999) 163 J.P.N. 314;
    Times, December 10, 1998, CA (Civ Div); affirming [1996] 3 All E.R. 558; [1997]
    3 C.M.L.R. 429; *Times,* April 22, 1996, QBD . . . .   *Digested,* 00/**270**:
            Applied, 03/4357, 05/4193, 06/4433, 07/2490: *Considered,* 00/5317,
                   02/4546, 04/753, 05/4197, 06/4332: *Reversed,* 01/5355
Three Rivers DC v Bank of England (Restriction on Cross Examination) [2005] EWCA
    Civ 889; [2005] C.P. Rep. 46, CA (Civ Div) . . . .   *Digested,* 06/**332**:
                     Subsequent related litigation, 07/398
Thurrock BC v Holding see Thurrock BC v Secretary of State for the Environment,
    Transport and the Regions
Thurrock BC v Secretary of State for the Environment, Transport and the Regions; *sub*
    nom Secretary of State for the Environment, Transport and the Regions v
    Thurrock BC (No.2); Holding v Thurrock BC; *joined case* Thurrock BC v Holding
    [2002] EWCA Civ 226; [2002] 2 P.L.R. 43; [2002] J.P.L. 1278; [2002] 10 E.G.
    157 (C.S.); (2002) 99(10) L.S.G. 34; [2002] N.P.C. 31, CA (Civ Div); affirming
    [2001] EWHC Admin 128; [2001] 3 P.L.R. 14; [2001] J.P.L. 1388; [2001] N.P.C.
    40; *Times,* April 3, 2001, QBD (Admin) . . . .   *Digested,* 03/**3377**:
                   Applied, 07/3227: *Considered,* 04/3075, 06/3300
Thyssen Canada Ltd v Mariana Maritime SA [2005] EWHC 219 (Comm); [2005] 1
    Lloyd's Rep. 640, QBD (Comm) . . . .   *Digested,* 05/**199**:
                    Applied, 06/208: *Followed,* 07/242
TI v United Kingdom [2000] I.N.L.R. 211, ECHR . . . .   *Digested,* 00/**3164**:
                   Applied, 07/2306: *Followed,* 02/2595
Tichband v Hurdman see Hollins v Russell

Tierney v News Group Newspapers Ltd (No.1) [2006] EWHC 50 (QB); [2006] 4
Costs L.R. 606, QBD . . . . *Digested*, 07/**384**
Tigana Ltd v Decoro Ltd [2003] EWHC 23 (QB); [2003] E.C.C. 23; [2003] Eu. L.R.
189, QBD . . . . *Digested*, 03/**79**:
Applied, 06/59: *Approved*, 04/89: *Considered*, 06/58, 06/61, 07/68
Tillack v Commission of the European Communities (T-193/04) [2007] 1 C.M.L.R. 5,
CFI (4th Chamber) . . . . *Digested*, 07/**1586**
TIME ART Uluslararasi Saat Ticareti ve dis Ticaret AS v Office for Harmonisation in the
Internal Market (Trade Marks and Designs) (OHIM) (C-171/06) [2007] E.T.M.R.
38, ECJ . . . . *Digested*, 07/**1560**
Time-Barred Appeal Against a Tax Assessment, Re (V R 67/05) [2007] 2 C.M.L.R.10, BFH
(Ger) . . . . *Digested*, 07/**1640**
Times Newspapers Ltd, Re see R. v Times Newspapers Ltd
Timishev v Russia (55762/00) (2007) 44 E.H.R.R. 37, ECHR . . . . *Digested*, 07/**2190**:
Distinguished, 07/3293
Timmins v Gormley see Locabail (UK) Ltd v Bayfield Properties Ltd (Leave to Appeal)
Tinker v Tinker (No.1) [1970] P. 136; [1970] 2 W.L.R. 331; [1970] 1 All E.R. 540;
(1970) 21 P. & C.R. 102; (1969) 114 S.J. 32; *Times*, December 4, 1969, CA (Civ
Div) . . . . *Digested*, 70/**1245**:
Applied, 98/3315: *Distinguished*, 71/5503, 99/4368, 07/3358
Tinsley v Milligan [1994] 1 A.C. 340; [1993] 3 W.L.R. 126; [1993] 3 All E.R. 65;
[1993] 2 F.L.R. 963; (1994) 68 P. & C.R. 412; [1993] E.G. 118 (C.S.); [1993]
N.P.C. 97; *Times*, June 28, 1993; *Independent*, July 6, 1993, HL; affirming [1992]
Ch. 310; [1992] 2 W.L.R. 508; [1992] 2 All E.R. 391; (1992) 63 P. & C.R. 152;
(1991) 88(33) L.S.G. 32; (1991) 135 S.J.L.B. 108; [1991] N.P.C. 100; *Times*,
August 22, 1991, CA (Civ Div) . . . . *Digested*, 93/**1839**:
Applied, 97/4730, 99/680, 99/4368, 02/3835, 03/4504, 04/3264:
Considered, 95/3660, 96/1489, 96/5554, 00/3879, 06/4377:
Distinguished, 93/1840, 03/1421: *Followed*, 96/5000, 01/5349, 07/3358:
Referred to, 94/5488
TINY PENIS Trade Mark see Ghazilian's Trade Mark Application
Titanium Dioxide Directive, Re (C-300/89) see Commission of the European Communities
v Council of the European Communities (C-300/89)
Tiverton and North Devon Railway Co v Loosemore; *sub nom* Loosemore v Tiverton and
North Devon Railway Co (1883-84) L.R. 9 App. Cas. 480, HL; reversing
(1883) L.R. 22 Ch. D. 25, CA . . . . *Applied*, 57/478,
62/405, 07/3418: *Considered*, 70/1500
Tiverton Estates Ltd v Wearwell Ltd [1975] Ch. 146; [1974] 2 W.L.R. 176; [1974] 1 All
E.R. 209; (1974) 27 P. & C.R. 24; (1978) 117 S.J. 913, CA (Civ Div) . . . . *Digested*, 74/**3952**:
Applied, 85/389, 07/3955: *Considered*, 75/1842, 75/3540, 78/2501,
79/2780, 83/3052, 83/3894, 87/2111, 88/2065, 90/3701:
Explained, 77/2374
TK (Consideration of Prior Determination: Directions: Georgia), Re see TK (Georgia) v
Secretary of State for the Home Department
TK (Georgia) v Secretary of State for the Home Department; *sub nom* TK
(Consideration of Prior Determination: Directions: Georgia), Re [2004] UKIAT
149, IAT . . . . *Considered*, 07/2305
TL v ML (Ancillary Relief: Claim against Assets of Extended Family) [2005] EWHC
2860 (Fam); [2006] 1 F.L.R. 1263; [2006] 1 F.C.R. 465; [2006] Fam. Law 183,
Fam Div . . . . *Digested*, 06/**1631**:
Approved, 07/1707: *Considered*, 07/1704
TM Kingdom Ltd (In Administration), Re [2007] EWHC 3272 (Ch); [2007] B.C.C. 480,
Ch D (Birmingham) . . . . *Digested*, 07/**2387**
TNT Global SpA v Denfleet International Ltd; *sub nom* Denfleet International Ltd v TNT
Global SpA [2007] EWCA Civ 405; [2007] 2 Lloyd's Rep. 504; [2007] 1
C.L.C. 710; [2007] R.T.R. 41; (2007) 104(20) L.S.G. 27; *Times*, May 11, 2007, CA
(Civ Div) . . . . *Digested*, 07/**4215**
Tobacco Advertising Directive 2003/33, R-e (C-380/03) see Germany v European
Parliament (C-380/03)
Todd (t/a Hygia Professional Training) v Cutter (2007) 151 S.J.L.B. 1297, EAT
Togher v Revenue and Customs Prosecution Office [2007] EWCA Civ 686; [2007]
U.K.H.R.R. 1079, CA (Civ Div)
Tokai Carbon Co Ltd v Commission of the European Communities (T-236/01); *joined
cases* Carbide/Graphite Group Inc v Commission of the European Communities
(T252/01); SEC Corp v Commission of the European Communities (T251/01);
GrafTech International Ltd v Commission of the European Communities (T246/
01); Showa Denko KK v Commission of the European Communities (T245/01);
Nippon Carbon Co Ltd v Commission of the European Communities (T-244/
01); SGL Carbon AG v Commission of the European Communities (T-239/01)
[2004] E.C.R. II-1181; [2004] 5 C.M.L.R. 28, CFI (2nd Chamber) . . . . *Digested*, 05/**552**:
Applied, 07/1546, 07/1589
Tokai Carbon Co Ltd v Commission of the European Communities (T-71/03) [2005]
E.C.R. II-10; [2005] 5 C.M.L.R. 13, CFI . . . . *Applied*, 07/1546
Toke UK Ltd's Trade Mark Application (O-119-06) [2007] E.T.M.R. 9, TMR . . . . *Digested*, 07/**2681**

Toland Trust, Re; *sub nom* Pennywise Trust, Re; Sequential Trust, Re (2006-07) 9
　I.T.E.L.R. 321, Royal Ct (Jer)
Tollgate Hotels Ltd *v* Secretary of State for Transport [2006] R.V.R. 315, Lands Tr . . . . .　　*Digested*, 07/**3228**
Tolsma *v* Inspecteur der Omzetbelasting, Leeuwarden (C-16/93) [1994] S.T.C. 509;
　[1994] E.C.R. I-743; [1994] 2 C.M.L.R. 908; [1994] B.V.C. 117; [1994] S.T.I. 424;
　Times, March 29, 1994, ECJ (6th Chamber) . . . .　　*Digested*, 94/**4962**:
　　　　　　　　　　　　Applied, 00/5347, 06/4469, 06/4488, 07/4284: *Considered*, 98/4891,
　　　　　　　　　　　　　　　　　　　　　　　　　　　　　　　02/4790, 02/4790
Tolstoy Miloslavsky *v* Aldington [1996] 1 W.L.R. 736; [1996] 2 All E.R. 556; [1996]
　P.N.L.R. 335; (1996) 93(1) L.S.G. 22; (1996) 140 S.J.L.B. 26; *Times*, December
　27, 1995; *Independent*, January 3, 1996, CA (Civ Div) . . . .　　*Digested*, 96/**3899**:
　　　　　　　　　　　Applied, 07/428: *Considered*, 02/393: *Followed*, 98/415, 02/363, 03/339,
　　　　　　　　　　　　　　　　　　　　　　　　　　　　　　　05/496
Tomasi *v* France (A/241-A) (1993) 15 E.H.R.R. 1, ECHR . . . .　　*Digested*, 93/**2131**:
　　　　　　　　　　Applied, 97/2764, 07/2203: *Considered*, 96/3138: *Distinguished*, 97/2809:
　　　　　　　　　　　　　　　　　　　　　　　　　　　　　　Doubted, 06/2141
Tomic *v* Serbia (25959/06) [2007] 2 F.C.R. 449, ECHR
Tomlakova *v* Slovakia (17709/04) [2006] 3 F.C.R. 747, ECHR . . . .　　*Digested*, 07/**2222**
Tonkin *v* UK Insurance Ltd [2006] EWHC 1120 (TCC); [2006] 2 All E.R. (Comm) 550;
　107 Con. L.R. 107; [2007] Lloyd's Rep. I.R. 283, QBD (TCC) . . . .　　*Digested*, 07/**2486**
Top Marques Car Rental, Re [2006] EWHC 746 (Ch); [2006] B.P.I.R. 1328, Ch D　. . .　　*Digested*, 07/**2396**
Topping *v* Benchtown Ltd (formerly Jones Bros (Preston) Ltd) see Grieves *v* FT
　Everard & Sons Ltd
Topps Tiles Plc *v* Revenue and Customs Commissioners [2007] B.V.C. 2167; [2006] V.
　& D.R. 480; [2006] S.T.I. 2585, V&DTr (Manchester)
Topsy Turvy World Holdings Ltd *v* Leahy (Valuation Officer) [2006] R.V.R. 275, VT . . . .　　*Digested*, 07/**3340**
Toray Textiles Europe Pension Scheme, Re; *sub nom* Hodgson *v* Toray Textiles Europe Ltd
　[2006] EWHC 2612 (Ch); [2006] Pens. L.R. 253, Ch D . . . .　　*Digested*, 07/**3043**
Toray Textiles Europe Pension Scheme, Re; *sub nom* Hodgson *v* Toray Textiles Europe Ltd
　[2007] EWHC 444 (Ch); [2007] Pens. L.R. 129, Ch D . . . .　　*Digested*, 07/**3042**
Torbay BC *v* News Group Newspapers see Roddy (A Child) (Identification: Restriction
　on Publication), Re
Toronto Dominion Bank *v* Oberoi [2002] EWHC 3216; [2004] S.T.C. 1197; 75 T.C. 244;
　[2007] B.T.C. 49; [2003] S.T.I. 171; [2002] N.P.C. 151, Ch D . . . .　　*Digested*, 04/**2530**
Toshiba Europe GmbH *v* Katun Germany GmbH (C-112/99) [2002] All E.R. (EC) 325;
　[2001] E.C.R. I-7945; [2002] 3 C.M.L.R. 7; [2002] C.E.C. 438; [2002] E.T.M.R.
　26; [2002] F.S.R. 39, ECJ (5th Chamber) . . . .　　*Digested*, 02/**2895**:
　　　　　　　　　　　　　　　　　　　　　Considered, 06/2615, 07/1571, 07/2671
Toshoku Finance UK Plc (In Liquidation), Re; *sub nom* Inland Revenue Commissioners *v*
　Kahn; Kahn *v* Inland Revenue Commissioners; Khan *v* Inland Revenue
　Commissioners [2002] UKHL 6; [2002] 1 W.L.R. 671; [2002] 3 All E.R. 961;
　[2002] S.T.C. 368; [2002] B.C.C. 110; [2002] 1 B.C.L.C. 598; [2002] B.P.I.R.
　790; [2003] R.V.R. 106; [2002] B.T.C. 69; [2002] S.T.I. 237; (2002) 99(12)
　L.S.G. 33; (2002) 146 S.J.L.B. 55; *Times*, February 25, 2002, HL; affirming
　[2000] 1 W.L.R. 2478; [2000] 3 All E.R. 938; [2000] S.T.C. 301; [2001] B.C.C.
　373; [2000] 1 B.C.L.C. 683; [2000] B.T.C. 96; [2000] S.T.I. 503; (2000)
　97(15) L.S.G. 39; (2000) 144 S.J.L.B. 165; *Times*, March 29, 2000, CA (Civ
　Div); reversing [1999] S.T.C. 922; [1999] 2 B.C.L.C. 777; [1999] B.T.C. 367,
　Ch D . . . .　　*Digested*, 02/**2718**:
　　　　　　　　　　　　　　Applied, 07/2393: *Distinguished*, 05/2260
Total E&P Soudan SA *v* Edmonds [2007] EWCA Civ 50; [2007] C.P. Rep. 20; (2007)
　104(9) L.S.G. 30; (2007) 151 S.J.L.B. 195, CA (Civ Div); reversing in part
　[2006] EWHC 1136 (Comm), QBD (Comm) . . . .　　*Digested*, 07/**499**:
　　　　　　　　　　　　　　　　　　　　　　　　　　　　Considered, 07/501
Total Network SL *v* Revenue and Customs Commissioners see Customs and Excise
　Commissioners *v* Total Network SL
Total Spares & Supplies Ltd *v* Antares SRL [2006] EWHC 1537 (Ch); [2006] B.P.I.R.
　1330; (2006) 150 S.J.L.B. 919, Ch D . . . .　　*Digested*, 07/**405**:
　　　　　　　　　　　　　　　　　　　　　　　　　　　　Considered, 07/387
Total UK Ltd *v* Revenue and Customs Commissioners; *sub nom* Revenue and Customs
　Commissioners *v* Total UK Ltd [2007] EWCA Civ 987; [2007] B.T.C. 5895;
　[2007] B.V.C. 762; [2007] S.T.I. 2562; (2007) 104(42) L.S.G. 32, CA (Civ Div);
　reversing [2006] EWHC 3422 (Ch); [2007] S.T.C. 564; [2007] B.T.C. 5276;
　[2007] B.V.C. 245; [2006] S.T.I. 2457; [2007] S.T.I. 2408; *Times*, December 8,
　2006, Ch D; reversing [2006] S.T.I. 1422, V&DTr . . . .　　*Digested*, 07/**4323**
Totel Ltd *v* Revenue and Customs Commissioners [2006] V. & D.R. 173; [2006] S.T.I.
　2106, V&DTr (Manchester) . . . .　　*Digested*, 07/**4311**
Touchwood Services Ltd *v* Revenue and Customs Commissioners [2007] EWHC 105
　(Ch); [2007] S.T.C. 1425; [2007] B.T.C. 5663; [2007] B.V.C. 631; [2007] S.T.I.
　292, Ch D . . . .　　*Digested*, 07/**4303**
Toussaint *v* Attorney General of St Vincent and the Grenadines [2007] UKPC 48;
　[2007] 1 W.L.R. 2825; 22 B.H.R.C. 790, PC (StV) . . . .　　*Digested*, 07/**693**
Tower Bridge Yacht & Boat Co *v* Southwark LBC [2007] P.A.D. 14, Planning Inspector
Tower Hamlets LBC *v* Begum (Runa) see Begum *v* Tower Hamlets LBC

Townsend Carriers Ltd *v* Pfizer Ltd (1977) 33 P. & C.R. 361; (1977) 242 E.G. 813;
(1977) 121 S.J. 375, Ch D . . . . *Digested*, 78/**1790**:
Considered, 89/2104, 89/2160, 89/2162, 93/2455: *Distinguished*, 86/358,
98/3608, 07/2755

TP *v* United Kingdom (28945/95) [2001] 2 F.L.R. 549; [2001] 2 F.C.R. 289; (2002)
34 E.H.R.R. 2; (2001) 3 L.G.L.R. 52; (2001) 4 C.C.L. Rep. 398; [2001] Fam.
Law 590; *Times*, May 31, 2001, ECHR (2000) 2 L.G.L.R. 181, Eur Comm HR . .   *Digested*, 01/**2571**:
Applied, 03/3004: *Considered*, 03/1522, 03/2198, 07/2934

TQ3 Travel Solutions Belgium SA *v* Commission of the European Communities (T-148/
04) [2005] E.C.R. II-2627; [2007] 1 C.M.L.R. 38, CFI (2nd Chamber) . . . . . .   *Digested*, 07/**3327**

TR *v* MR; *sub nom* R *v* R [2007] EWHC 496 (Fam); [2007] 2 F.L.R. 971; [2007]
Fam. Law 796, Fam Div

Tracey *v* Tracey [2006] EWCA Civ 734; [2007] 1 F.L.R. 196; [2006] 2 F.C.R. 481;
[2006] Fam. Law 838; (2006) 150 S.J.L.B. 666, CA (Civ Div) . . . .   *Digested*, 06/**1678**

Tracey *v* United Kingdom see Brogan *v* United Kingdom (A/145-B)

Tradigrain SA *v* Intertek Testing Services (ITS) Canada Ltd [2007] EWCA Civ 154;
[2007] 1 C.L.C. 188; [2007] Bus. L.R. D32; *Times*, March 20, 2007, CA (Civ
Div); affirming [2006] EWHC 778 (Comm), QBD (Comm) . . . .   *Digested*, 07/**2477**

Trafford MBC *v* Pollard (Valuation Officer) [2007] R.A. 49, LandsTr

Trafigura Beheer BV *v* Kookmin Bank Co [2006] EWHC 1921 (Comm); [2007] 1
Lloyd's Rep. 669; [2006] 2 C.L.C. 643, QBD (Comm) . . . .   *Digested*, 07/**354**

Trafigura Beheer BV *v* Mediterranean Shipping Co SA [2007] EWCA Civ 794; [2007]
2 Lloyd's Rep. 622; [2007] 2 C.L.C. 379, CA (Civ Div); affirming [2007] EWHC
944 (Comm); [2007] 2 All E.R. (Comm) 149; [2007] 1 C.L.C. 594, QBD
(Comm) . . . .   *Digested*, 07/**3800**

Traghetti del Mediterraneo SpA (In Liquidation) *v* Italy (C-173/03) [2006] All E.R. (EC)
983; [2006] E.C.R. I-5177; [2006] 3 C.M.L.R. 19, ECJ . . . .   *Digested*, 07/**1651**

Trailer & Marina (Leven) Ltd *v* Secretary of State for the Environment, Food and Rural
Affairs see R. (on the application of Trailer & Marina (Leven) Ltd) *v* Secretary of
State for the Environment, Food and Rural Affairs

Trailfinders *v* Razuki [1988] 30 E.G. 59 . . . .   *Digested*, 88/**2040**:
Considered, 07/3400

Training Consultant *v* Revenue and Customs Commissioners [2007] S.T.C. (S.C.D.)
231; [2007] S.T.I. 415, Sp Comm

Trans-World Investments Ltd *v* Dadarwalla [2007] EWCA Civ 480; [2007] N.P.C. 67,
CA (Civ Div)

Transalpine Olleitung in Osterreich GmbH *v* Finanzlandesdirektion fur Tirol (C-368/04)
[2006] E.C.R. I-9957; [2007] 1 C.M.L.R. 19, ECJ . . . .   *Digested*, 07/**646**

Transfield Shipping Inc *v* Mercator Shipping Inc (The Achilleas) [2007] EWCA Civ 901;
[2007] 2 Lloyd's Rep. 555; [2007] 2 C.L.C. 400, CA (Civ Div); affirming
[2006] EWHC 3030 (Comm); [2007] 1 All E.R. (Comm) 379; [2007] 1 Lloyd's
Rep. 19; [2006] 2 C.L.C. 1069, QBD (Comm) . . . .   *Digested*, 07/**1064**

Transport and General Workers Union *v* Brauer Coley Ltd (In Administration); *sub nom*
Transport and General Workers' Union *v* Brauer Coley Ltd [2007] I.C.R. 226;
[2007] I.R.L.R. 207, EAT . . . .   *Digested*, 07/**1395**

Transport & General Workers Union *v* Safeway Stores Ltd (2007) 151 S.J.L.B. 806, EAT

Transport and General Workers Union *v* Swissport (UK) Ltd (In Administration) [2007]
I.C.R. 1593; (2007) 151 S.J.L.B. 924, EAT

Transport and General Workers Union *v* Webber [1990] I.C.R. 711; [1990] I.R.L.R. 462,
EAT . . . .   *Digested*, 91/**3597**:
Considered, 07/1412

Transport and General Workers' Union *v* Brauer Coley Ltd see Transport and General
Workers Union *v* Brauer Coley Ltd (In Administration)

TransTec Plc, Re see Secretary of State for Trade and Industry *v* Carr

TransTec Plc, Re see Secretary of State for Trade and Industry *v* Carr

Trapp *v* Mackie [1979] 1 W.L.R. 377; [1979] 1 All E.R. 489; 1979 S.C. (H.L.) 38; 1979
S.L.T. 126; (1979) 123 S.J. 202, HL; affirming 1978 S.C. 283, IH (2 Div);
affirming 1977 S.L.T. 194, OH . . . .   *Digested*, 79/**3381**:
Applied, 85/1326, 03/949, 04/1221: *Considered*, 83/2203:
Followed, 00/2627, 07/1340

Travel West Midlands *v* Sandwell MBC (Unreported, July 5, 2006), CC (Walsall) . . . . .   *Digested*, 07/**3465**

Travelers Casualty & Surety Co of Canada *v* Sun Life Assurance Co of Canada (UK) Ltd
[2006] EWHC 2716 (Comm); [2007] Lloyd's Rep. I.R. 619, QBD (Comm) . . . .   *Digested*, 07/**2488**

Tre Traktorer AB *v* Sweden (10873/84) see Tre Traktorer AB *v* Sweden (A/159)

Tre Traktorer AB *v* Sweden (A/159); *sub nom* Tre Traktorer AB *v* Sweden (10873/84)
(1991) 13 E.H.R.R. 309, ECHR (1990) 12 E.H.R.R. CD128, Eur Comm HR . . . . .   *Considered*, 03/2838,
03/4413, 07/2815: *Distinguished*, 02/3277

Treacy *v* DPP; *sub nom* R. *v* Treacy (Eugene Anthony) [1971] A.C. 537; [1971] 2
W.L.R. 112; [1971] 1 All E.R. 110; (1971) 55 Cr. App. R. 113; (1971) 115 S.J. 12;
Times, December 16, 1970, HL; affirming [1970] 3 W.L.R. 592; [1970] 3 All E.R.
205; (1970) 114 S.J. 604, CA (Crim Div) . . . .   *Digested*, 71/**2188**:
Applied, 87/808, 07/923: *Considered*, 72/745, 75/603, 81/1204, 85/1515,
97/2441: *Not applied*, 74/676

Treasure & Son Ltd v Dawes [2007] EWHC 2420 (TCC); [2007] C.I.L.L. 2533; [2007] 44 E.G. 181 (C.S.), QBD (TCC)

Treasury Solicitors Department v Chenge [2007] I.R.L.R. 386, EAT . . . .   *Digested*, 07/**1392**

Tricarico v Assitalia SpA (C-297/04) see Manfredi v Lloyd Adriatico Assicurazioni SpA (C-295/04)

Tricell UK Ltd v Customs and Excise Commissioners [2003] V. & D.R. 333; [2003] S.T.I. 1516, V&DTr (Manchester) . . . .   *Digested*, 04/**4032**:
                                                                                         Applied, 07/**4286**

Trident Fashions Plc, Re see Exeter City Council v Bairstow

Trident Fashions Plc, Re; *sub nom* Exeter City Council v Bairstow [2006] EWCA Civ 203; [2007] 1 B.C.L.C. 491; [2006] R.V.R. 157; *Independent*, March 16, 2006, CA (Civ Div) . . . .   *Digested*, 06/**2320**

Trijonis v Lithuania (Admissibility) (2333/02) (Unreported, March 17, 2005), ECHR . .   *Considered*, 07/953

TRILUX Trade Mark [2007] E.T.M.R. 43, NSA (PL)

Triniti Corp v Commissioner of Income Tax 10 I.T.L. Rep. 357, Advance Rulings (Ind)

Tritton Development Fund Ltd v Fortis Bank (Cayman) Ltd (formerly Meespierson (Cayman) Ltd) [2007] W.T.L.R. 1483, Grand Ct (Cl)

Triumph Actuation Systems LLC (formerly Frisby Aerospace LLC) v Aeroquip-Vickers Ltd [2007] EWHC 1367 (Pat); (2007) 30(7) I.P.D. 30046, Ch D (Patents Ct)

Trojani v Centre Public d'Aide Sociale de Bruxelles (CPAS) (C-456/02) [2004] All E.R. (EC) 1065; [2004] E.C.R. I-7573; [2004] 3 C.M.L.R. 38; [2005] C.E.C. 139, ECJ . . . .   *Digested*, 05/**3856**:
                                                                                         Applied, 07/**3824**

Trouw UK Ltd v Mitsui & Co Plc [2007] EWHC 863 (Comm); [2007] U.K.C.L.R. 921, QBD (Comm)

Trow v Haydes (Unreported, September 19, 2006), CC (Cambridge) [*Ex rel*. Stephen Garner, Barrister, No. 8 Fountain Court, Steelhouse Lane, Birmingham] . . . . . .   *Digested*, 07/**3154**

Truex v Kitchin see David Truex (A Firm) v Kitchin

Trustee Solutions Ltd v Dubery; *sub nom* Cripps v Trustee Solutions Ltd [2007] EWCA Civ 771; [2007] Pens. L.R. 237; (2007) 157 N.L.J. 1354; (2007) 151 S.J.L.B. 1024; *Times*, August 17, 2007, CA (Civ Div); reversing [2006] EWHC 1426 (Ch); [2007] 1 All E.R. 308; [2007] I.C.R. 412; [2006] Pens. L.R. 177; *Times*, August 7, 2006, Ch D . . . .   *Digested*, 07/**3024**

Trustees of Abdul Gaffoor Trust v Income Tax Commissioner, Colombo see Caffoor (Trustees of the Abdul Gaffoor Trust) v Income Tax Commissioner (Colombo)

Trustees of Fairbairn's (aka Douglas's) Trust v Revenue and Customs Commissioners [2007] S.T.C. (S.C.D.) 338; [2007] W.T.L.R. 663; [2007] S.T.I. 1054, Sp Comm   *Digested*, 07/**5561**

Trustees of FD Fenston Will Trusts v Revenue and Customs Commissioners [2007] S.T.C. (S.C.D.) 316; [2007] S.T.I. 556, Sp Comm. . . . .   *Digested*, 07/**3992**

Trustees of Henry Smith's Charity Kensington Estate v Wagle see Wagle v Trustees of Henry Smith's Charity Kensington Estate

Trustees of Sir John Morden's Charity v Mayrick [2007] EWCA Civ 4; [2007] 1 P. & C.R. 17; [2007] 3 E.G. 125 (C.S.); (2007) 151 S.J.L.B. 127; [2007] N.P.C. 7, CA (Civ Div); affirming [2006] EWHC 574 (Ch), Ch D . . . .   *Digested*, 07/**3433**

Trustees of the Christian Brothers in Western Australia Inc v Attorney General of Western Australia [2007] W.T.L.R. 1375; (2006-07) 9 I.T.E.L.R. 212, Sup Ct (WA) (Sgl judge) . . . .   *Digested*, 07/**318**

Trustees of the Duke of Westminster's Estate v United Kingdom (8793/79) see James v United Kingdom (A/98)

Trustees of Trevor Smallwood Trust v Revenue and Customs Commissioners see Smallwood v Revenue and Customs Commissioners

TS&S Global Ltd v Fithian-Franks [2007] EWHC 1401 (Ch); [2007] B.P.I.R. 1166, Ch D . . . .   *Digested*, 07/**2451**

TSB Private Bank International SA v Chabra [1992] 1 W.L.R. 231; [1992] 2 All E.R. 245, Ch D . . . .   *Digested*, 92/**3545**:
              Applied, 01/45, 06/450, 07/456: *Considered*, 94/3738: *Distinguished*, 98/529

Tsfayo v United Kingdom (60860/00) [2007] H.L.R. 19; [2007] B.L.G.R. 1; *Times*, November 23, 2006, ECHR . . . .   *Considered*, 07/2772

Tsikata v Newspaper Publishing Plc [1997] 1 All E.R. 655; [1997] E.M.L.R. 117; (1996) 146 N.L.J. 1686; *Independent*, October 15, 1996, CA (Civ Div); affirming [1995] E.M.L.R. 8; *Times*, November 9, 1994; *Independent*, October 29, 1994, QBD . . .   *Digested*, 96/**5662**:
                                                                                         Considered, 07/1070

Tucker (Setting of Minimum Term), Re; *sub nom* R. v Tucker (Nicholas Guy) [2006] EWCA Crim 1885; [2007] 1 All E.R. 1043, CA (Crim Div) . . . .   *Digested*, 07/**3669**

Tudapetrol Mineralolerzeugnisse Nils Hansen KG v Conseil Europeen de l'Industrie Chimique (CEFIC) (R 214/2004-2) [2007] E.T.M.R. 36, OHIM (2nd Bd App) .   *Digested*, 07/**2646**

Tum v Secretary of State for the Home Department (C-16/05); *sub nom* R. (on the application of Tum) v Secretary of State for the Home Department (C-16/05); *joined case* R. (on the application of Dari) v Secretary of State for the Home Department (C-16/05) [2007] I.N.L.R. 473, ECJ (2nd Chamber)

Tumble Tots UK Ltd v Revenue and Customs Commissioners [2007] EWHC 103 (Ch); [2007] S.T.C. 1171; [2007] B.T.C. 5210; [2007] B.V.C. 179; [2007] S.T.I. 293, Ch D; reversing in part [2006] B.V.C. 2673; [2006] S.T.I. 1711, V&DTr (London) . . .   *Digested*, 07/**4332**

Tuquabo-Tekle v Netherlands (60665/00) [2006] 1 F.L.R. 798; [2005] 3 F.C.R. 649; [2006] Fam. Law 267, ECHR . . . . *Digested,* 06/**2177**: *Applied,* 07/2259

Turek v Slovakia (57986/00) (2007) 44 E.H.R.R. 43, ECHR . . . . *Digested,* 07/**2249**

Turkington v Times Newspapers Ltd see McCartan Turkington Breen v Times Newspapers Ltd

Turner v Commonwealth & British Minerals Ltd [2000] I.R.L.R. 114; *Independent,* November 29, 1999, CA (Civ Div) . . . . *Digested,* 00/**2201**: *Considered,* 07/1328

Turner v Turner [2006] EWHC 2023 (Ch); [2006] B.P.I.R. 1531, Ch D . . . . *Digested,* 07/**2452**

Turvey v CW Cheney & Son Ltd [1979] I.C.R. 341; [1979] I.R.L.R. 105, EAT . . . . *Digested,* 79/**932**: *Considered,* 97/2291: *Distinguished,* 07/1397

TW v Malta (2000) 29 E.H.R.R. 185, ECHR . . . . *Digested,* 00/**3175**: *Applied,* 00/6064, 07/2231

Tweed v Parades Commission for Northern Ireland [2006] UKHL 53; [2007] 1 A.C. 650; [2007] 2 W.L.R. 1; [2007] 2 All E.R. 273; [2007] N.I. 66; [2007] H.R.L.R. 11; [2007] U.K.H.R.R. 456; 22 B.H.R.C. 92; (2007) 151 S.J.L.B. 24; *Times,* December 15, 2006, HL (NI) . . . . *Digested,* 07/**4434**

Twinsectra Ltd v Yardley [2002] UKHL 12; [2002] 2 A.C. 164; [2002] 2 W.L.R. 802; [2002] 2 All E.R. 377; [2002] P.N.L.R. 30; [2002] W.T.L.R. 423; [2002] 38 E.G. 204 (C.S.); (2002) 99(19) L.S.G. 32; (2002) 152 N.L.J. 469; (2002) 146 S.J.L.B. 84; [2002] N.P.C. 47; *Times,* March 25, 2002, HL; reversing [1999] Lloyd's Rep. Bank. 438; [2000] Lloyd's Rep. P.N. 239; [2000] W.T.L.R. 527, CA (Civ Div) . . . . *Digested,* 02/**249**: *Applied,* 04/3940, 05/2732, 06/4381, 07/4251: *Considered,* 04/2408, 05/2325, 06/4380, 07/4237: *Distinguished,* 03/1421: *Followed,* 99/278, 05/2731

Twoh International BV v Staatssecretaris van Financien (C-184/05) [2007] S.T.I. 2219, ECJ (3rd Chamber)

TXU UK Ltd (In Administration), Re [2002] EWHC 2784 (Ch); [2003] 2 B.C.L.C. 341; [2003] B.P.I.R. 1062, Ch D (Companies Ct) . . . . *Digested,* 03/**2391**: *Considered,* 06/2326, 07/2395

Tyco Fire & Integrated Solutions (UK) Ltd (formerly Wormald Ansul (UK) Ltd) v Rolls Royce Motor Cars Ltd (formerly Hireus Ltd) A1/2007/1629/QBENF, CA (Civ Div); reversing [2007] EWHC 3159 (TCC); [2007] B.L.R. 419, QBD (TCC) . . . . *Digested,* 07/**739**

Tyne & Wear Passenger Transport Authority (t/a Nexus) v Best [2007] I.C.R. 523, EAT . . . . *Digested,* 07/**1361**

Tynewydd Labour Working Men's Club and Institute v Customs and Excise Commissioners [1979] S.T.C. 570; (1979) 123 S.J. 406 . . . . *Digested,* 79/**2744**: *Applied,* 07/4363

Tyrer v United Kingdom (A/26) (1979-80) 2 E.H.R.R. 1, ECHR . . . . *Digested,* 79/**1173**: *Considered,* 01/1147, 07/2196

Tysall Ltd v Snowdome (Unreported, July 28, 2006), CC (Coventry) [*Ex rel.* Davies Arnold Cooper Solicitors, 6-8 Bouverie Street, London] . . . . *Digested,* 07/**4196**

Tysiac v Poland (5410/03) [2007] 1 F.C.R. 666; (2007) 45 E.H.R.R. 42; 22 B.H.R.C. 155, ECHR . . . . *Digested,* 07/**2244**

U (Algeria) v Secretary of State for the Home Department see MT (Algeria) v Secretary of State for the Home Department

UA (Turkey) v Secretary of State for the Home Department [2007] EWCA Civ 72, CA (Civ Div) . . . . *Digested,* 07/**2304**

UASC/CSL Ltd v Deputy Commissioner of Income Tax 10 I.T.L. Rep. 13, ITAT (Ind)

UBS AG v Revenue and Customs Commissioners; *sub nom* Revenue and Customs Commissioners v UBS AG; USB AG v Revenue and Customs Commissioners [2007] EWCA Civ 119; [2007] S.T.C. 588; [2007] B.T.C. 285; 9 I.T.L. Rep. 767; [2007] S.T.I. 411, CA (Civ Div); affirming [2006] EWHC 117 (Ch); [2006] S.T.C. 716; [2006] B.T.C. 232; 8 I.T.L. Rep. 595; [2006] S.T.I. 379; *Times,* February 21, 2006, Ch D; reversing [2005] S.T.C. (S.C.D.) 589; 7 I.T.L. Rep. 893, Sp Comm. . . . *Digested,* 07/**4023**

UCB Home Loans Corp Ltd v Moore see Royal Bank of Scotland Plc v Etridge (No.2)

UCT (UK) Ltd v Dargan see UCT (UK) Ltd (In Administration), Re

UCT (UK) Ltd (In Administration), Re; *sub nom* UCT (UK) Ltd v Dargan [2001] 1 W.L.R. 436; [2001] 2 All E.R. 186; [2001] B.C.C. 734; [2001] 1 B.C.L.C. 443; [2002] B.P.I.R. 414, Ch D (Companies Ct) . . . . *Digested,* 01/**3708**: *Applied,* 03/2391, 07/2392: *Considered,* 07/2395: *Distinguished,* 04/2112

Udny v Udny (1866-69) L.R. 1 Sc. 441; (1869) 7 M. (H.L.) 89, HL . . . . *Applied,* 47-51/1583, 57/1076, 68/486, 68/487, 95/5872, 02/5386, 07/4068

Uecker v Land Nordrhein-Westfalen (C-64/96) see Land Nordrhein-Westfalen v Uecker (C-64/96)

Ufficio Distrettuale delle Imposte Dirette di Fiorenzuola d'Arda v Comune di Carpaneto Piacentino (231/87) [1991] S.T.C. 205; [1989] E.C.R. 3233; *Times,* November 15, 1989, ECJ . . . . *Digested,* 91/**3661**: *Applied,* 02/4739, 06/4498, 07/4351: *Considered,* 01/5579, 01/5609: *Followed,* 05/4411

UGE SA v Arezzo VAT Office 9 I.T.L. Rep. 345, It Cass (I) . . . . *Digested,* 07/**4119**

UIC Insurance Co Ltd (In Provisional Liquidation), Re see Jacob v UIC Insurance Co Ltd
UIC Insurance Co Ltd (In Provisional Liquidation), Re [2007] B.P.I.R. 589, Ch D
UK Channel Management Ltd v E! Entertainment Television Inc [2007] EWHC 2339 (Ch); (2007) 30(10) I.P.D. 30065, Ch D
UK Coal Mining Ltd v National Union of Mineworkers (Northumberland Area) (2007) 151 S.J.L.B. 1400; *Times*, November 23, 2007, EAT
UK Coal Mining Ltd v Raby EAT/1124/02, EAT . . . .   *Followed*, 07/**1432**
UK Working Time Guidelines, Re (C-484/04) see Commission of the European Communities v United Kingdom (C-484/04)
UK-Euro Group Plc, Re [2006] EWHC 2102 (Ch); [2007] 1 B.C.L.C. 812, Ch D (Companies Ct) . . . .   *Digested*, 07/**2462**
Ullah (Ahsan) v Special Adjudicator see R. (on the application of Ullah) v Special Adjudicator
Ullises Shipping Corp v Fal Shipping Co Ltd (The Greek Fighter) [2006] EWHC 1729 (Comm); [2006] 2 C.L.C. 497, QBD (Comm) . . . .   *Digested*, 07/**3814**
Ullusow v Secretary of State for Work and Pensions see Abdirahman v Secretary of State for Work and Pensions
Ulterra Ltd v Glenbarr (RTE) Co Ltd [2007] 48 E.G. 144 (C.S.), Lands Tr
Ultra Heat Treated Milk, Re (124/81) see Commission of the European Communities v United Kingdom (124/81)
Ultra Motorhomes International Ltd, Re see Ratten v Ultra Vehicle Design Ltd
Ultraframe (UK) Ltd v Fielding; *joined cases* Burnden Group Plc v Northstar Systems Ltd (In Liquidation); Northstar Systems Ltd (In Liquidation) v Fielding [2005] EWHC 1638 (Ch); [2006] F.S.R. 17; [2007] W.T.L.R. 835; (2005) 28(9) I.P.D. 28069, Ch D . . . .   *Digested*, 06/**543**
Ultraframe (UK) Ltd v Fielding (Costs); *sub nom* Ultraframe (UK) Ltd v Fielding (No.2); *joined case* Northstar Systems Ltd v Fielding (Costs) [2006] EWCA Civ 1660; [2007] 2 All E.R. 983; [2007] C.P. Rep. 12; [2007] 2 Costs L.R. 264; *Times*, January 8, 2007, CA (Civ Div); affirming [2005] EWHC 2506 (Ch), Ch D . . . .   *Digested*, 07/**391**
Ultraframe (UK) Ltd v Fielding (No.2) see Ultraframe (UK) Ltd v Fielding (Costs)
Umbro Holdings Ltd v Office of Fair Trading (Judgment on Penalty) [2005] CAT 22; [2005] Comp. A.R. 1060, CAT . . . .   *Subsequent related litigation*, 07/621
Unadkat & Co (Accountants) Ltd v Bhardwaj [2006] EWHC 2785 (Ch); [2007] B.C.C. 452, Ch D (Birmingham) . . . .   *Digested*, 07/**2440**
Uncompleted Loan Agreement, Re [2007] E.C.C. 3, BGH (Ger)
Underwood v Revenue and Customs Commissioners CH/2007/0415, Ch D; affirming [2007] S.T.C. (S.C.D.) 659; [2007] S.T.I. 1795, Sp Comm
Uner v Netherlands (46410/99) [2006] 3 F.C.R. 340; (2007) 45 E.H.R.R. 14; [2007] Imm. A.R. 303; [2007] I.N.L.R. 273, ECHR (Grand Chamber) . . . .   *Digested*, 07/**2252**: *Applied*, 07/2259, 07/2262
Unibet (London) Ltd v Justitiekanslern (C-432/05) [2007] 2 C.M.L.R. 30, ECJ (Grand Chamber) . . . .   *Digested*, 07/**1641**
UNIFI v Massey; *sub nom* Massey v UNIFI [2007] EWCA Civ 800; [2007] I.R.L.R. 902; (2007) 151 S.J.L.B. 1059, CA (Civ Div); reversing in part UKEAT/0223/04/ MAA, EAT . . . .   *Digested*, 07/**1413**
Unilever Bestfoods UK Ltd v Revenue and Customs Commissioners [2007] V. & D.R. 119, V&D Tr (London)
Unilever Bestfoods (Ireland) Ltd v Commission of the European Communities (C-552/ 03 P) [2006] E.C.R. I-9091; [2006] 5 C.M.L.R. 27; [2007] C.E.C. 760, ECJ (6th Chamber) . . . .   *Digested*, 07/**616**: *Applied*, 07/1547: *Previous proceedings*, 04/489
Unilever NV v Office for Harmonisation in the Internal Market (Trade Marks and Designs) (OHIM) (T-194/01) [2003] E.C.R. II-383; [2004] E.T.M.R. 31, CFI (2nd Chamber) . . . .   *Digested*, 04/**2391**: *Applied*, 07/2660
Unilever Plc v Procter & Gamble Co [2000] 1 W.L.R. 2436; [2001] 1 All E.R. 783; [2000] F.S.R. 344; (2000) 23(1) I.P.D. 23001; (1999) 96(44) L.S.G. 40; (1999) 143 S.J.L.B. 268; *Times*, November 4, 1999; *Independent*, November 5, 1999, CA (Civ Div); affirming [1999] 1 W.L.R. 1630; [1999] 2 All E.R. 691; [1999] F.S.R. 849; (1999) 22(5) I.P.D. 22042; (1999) 149 N.L.J. 370; *Times*, March 18, 1999, Ch D (Patents Ct) . . . .   *Digested*, 99/**349**: *Applied*, 00/334, 02/276, 03/277, 03/293, 04/251, 04/261, 05/289, 07/1078: *Considered*, 01/397, 01/3966, 03/288, 07/2555: *Followed*, 00/337
UNILEVER/Biocidal activity (T1429/04) [2006] E.P.O.R. 50, EPO (Technical Bd App).   *Digested*, 07/**2586**
UNILEVER/Hexagonal liquid crystal gel (T435/91) [1995] E.P.O.R. 314, EPO (Technical Bd App) . . . .   *Applied*, 07/2576
Unilin Beheer BV v Berry Floor NV [2007] EWCA Civ 364; [2007] Bus. L.R. 1140; [2007] F.S.R. 25, CA (Civ Div); reversing in part PAT 02010, PAT 02014, PCC .   *Digested*, 07/**2606**
UNILIN/Floor covering (T1040/04) [2006] E.P.O.R. 37, EPO (Technical Bd App) . . . .   *Digested*, 07/**2565**
Union Carbide Corp v BP Chemicals Ltd [1999] R.P.C. 409; (1999) 22(2) I.P.D. 22012, CA (Civ Div); reversing in part [1998] R.P.C. 1, Ch D (Patents Ct) . . . .   *Digested*, 99/**3480**: *Applied*, 07/2629

UNION CARBIDE/Indicator ligands (T1121/03) [2006] E.P.O.R. 49, EPO (Technical Bd App) . . . . *Digested*, 07/**2576**

Union de Pequenos Agricultores v Council of the European Union (C-50/00 P) [2003] Q.B. 893; [2003] 2 W.L.R. 795; [2002] All E.R. (EC) 893; [2002] E.C.R. I-6677; [2002] 3 C.M.L.R. 1; *Times*, August 16, 2002, ECJ . . . . *Digested*, 02/**1589**:
Applied, 07/608: *Followed*, 05/942, 05/1470

Union Discount Co Ltd v Zoller (Costs); *sub nom* Union Discount Ltd v Union Cal Ltd [2001] EWCA Civ 1755; [2002] 1 W.L.R. 1517; [2002] 1 All E.R. 693; [2002] C.L.C. 314; (2002) 99(3) L.S.G. 25; (2001) 151 N.L.J. 1769; (2001) 145 S.J.L.B. 276; *Times*, December 10, 2001; *Independent*, November 29, 2001, CA (Civ Div) . . . . *Digested*, 01/**478**:
Considered, 07/396

Union Discount Ltd v Union Cal Ltd see Union Discount Co Ltd v Zoller (Costs)

Union Francaise de l'Express (UFEX) v Commission of the European Communities (T-613/97) [2006] E.C.R. II-1531; [2006] 3 C.M.L.R. 17, CFI (3rd Chamber) . . . . . *Digested*, 07/**648**

Union of Clerical and Commercial Employees v Danish Employers Association Ex p. Danfoss A/S (109/88) see Handels- og Kontorfunktionaerernes Forbund i Danmark v Dansk Arbejdsgiverforening Ex p. Danfoss A/S (109/88)

Union of Refugee Women v Director of the Private Security Industry Regulatory Authority 21 B.H.R.C. 660, Const Ct (SA)

Union of Welsh Independents Inc, Re [2007] R.V.R. 205, Lands Tr

Union Pigments AS (formerly Waardals AS) v Commission of the European Communities (T62/02); *sub nom* Zinc Phosphate Cartel, Re (T62/02) [2006] 4 C.M.L.R. 20, CFI (5th Chamber) . . . . *Digested*, 06/**594**:
Considered, 07/605

UNISON v First Secretary of State see R. (on the application of UNISON) v First Secretary of State

UNISON v Leicestershire CC see Leicestershire CC v UNISON

Unison v Allen [2007] I.R.L.R. 975; [2007] Pens. L.R. 335, EAT

United Bank of Kuwait Plc v Prudential Property Services Ltd see South Australia Asset Management Corp v York Montague Ltd

United Bristol Healthcare NHS Trust v RH see Tameside and Glossop Acute Services NHS Trust v Thompstone

United Communist Party of Turkey v Turkey (19392/92) (1998) 26 E.H.R.R. 121; 4 B.H.R.C. 1; [1998] H.R.C.D. 247, ECHR . . . . *Digested*, 98/**3080**:
Applied, 98/3081, 98/3093, 03/2090, 07/2178

United Kingdom v European Parliament (C-217/04); *sub nom* Validity of Regulation 460/2004, Re (C-217/04) [2006] E.C.R. I-3771; [2006] 3 C.M.L.R. 2, ECJ . . *Digested*, 07/**1557**

United Kingdom v European Parliament (C-66/04); *sub nom* Validity of Regulation 2065/2003, Re (C-66/04) [2006] All E.R. (EC) 487; [2005] E.C.R. I-10553; [2006] 3 C.M.L.R. 1, ECJ . . . . *Digested*, 06/**1754**:
Applied, 07/1557

United Kingdom Atomic Energy Authority v Highland and Western Isles Valuation Joint Board Assessor [2006] CSIH 60; 2007 S.C. 252; 2007 S.L.T. 27; [2007] R.A. 65; 2007 G.W.D. 1-15, LVAC . . . . *Digested*, 07/**5489**:
Previous proceedings, 06/5657

United Macedonian Organisation Ilinden v Bulgaria (29225/95) see Stankov v Bulgaria (29221/95)

United Macedonian Organisation Ilinden-Pirin v Bulgaria (44079/98) (2007) 44 E.H.R.R. 4, ECHR

United States v Atkinson see Atkinson v United States

United States v Cobb [2001] 1 S.C.R. 587, Sup Ct (Can) . . . . *Distinguished*, 07/1667

United States v Hiley 10 I.T.L. Rep. 321, US Court

United States v Shulman [2001] 1 S.C.R. 616 . . . . *Distinguished*, 07/1667

United States of America v Tollman see R. (on the application of United States) v Bow Street Magistrates Court

United Trading Corp SA v Allied Arab Bank Ltd; *joined case* Murray Clayton v Rafidair Bank [1985] 2 Lloyd's Rep. 554; *Times*, July 23, 1984, CA (Civ Div) . . . . *Digested*, 84/**175**:
Applied, 87/203, 07/311: *Considered*, 96/407: *Followed*, 91/253

United Utilities Water Plc v Environment Agency [2007] UKHL 41; [2007] 1 W.L.R. 2707; 115 Con. L.R. 1; [2007] 43 E.G. 201 (C.S.); (2007) 104(42) L.S.G. 36; (2007) 151 S.J.L.B. 1366; [2007] N.P.C. 107; *Times*, October 26, 2007, HL; affirming [2006] EWCA Civ 633; [2006] Env. L.R. 42; [2006] 21 E.G. 131 (C.S.), CA (Civ Div); affirming [2006] EWHC 9 (QB); [2006] Env. L.R. 32; [2006] 4 E.G. 166 (C.S.); [2006] N.P.C. 3, QBD . . . . *Digested*, 07/**4275**

Universal Corp v Five Ways Properties [1979] 1 All E.R. 552; (1979) 38 P. & C.R. 687; (1978) 250 E.G. 447; (1979) 123 S.J. 33, CA (Civ Div); reversing [1978] 3 All E.R. 1131, Ch D . . . . *Digested*, 79/**2775**:
Applied, 80/2800, 84/2951: *Considered*, 01/4854, 02/2650, 07/3394

University Court of the University of Glasgow v Customs and Excise Commissioners [2007] S.T.I. 381, V&DTr (Edinburgh)

University Hospital Lewisham NHS Trust v Hamuth; *sub nom* Lewisham Hospital NHS Trust v Hamuth [2006] EWHC 1609 (Ch); [2006] Inquest L.R. 141; [2007] W.T.L.R. 309; (2006) 150 S.J.L.B. 168, Ch D . . . . *Digested*, 07/**1972**

University of Huddersfield Higher Education Corp v Customs and Excise Commissioners (C-223/03) [2006] Ch. 387; [2006] 2 W.L.R. 905; [2006] S.T.C. 980; [2006] E.C.R. I-1751; [2006] 2 C.M.L.R. 38; [2006] C.E.C. 743; [2006] B.T.C. 5308; [2006] B.V.C. 377; [2006] S.T.I. 501; [2006] N.P.C. 23, ECJ . . . . *Digested,* 06/**4462**:
Considered, 06/4462, 06/5131, 07/4159

University of Liverpool v Humber and Birch; *sub nom* Birch v University of Liverpool [1985] I.C.R. 470; [1985] I.R.L.R. 165; (1985) 82 L.S.G. 1250; (1985) 129 S.J. 245, CA (Civ Div); affirming [1984] I.R.L.R. 54; (1984) 134 N.L.J. 256, EAT . . *Digested,* 85/**1150**:
Applied, 07/1398: *Distinguished,* 97/2291

University of Nottingham v Fishel [2000] I.C.R. 1462; [2000] I.R.L.R. 471; [2001] R.P.C. 22; [2000] Ed. C.R. 505; [2000] E.L.R. 385; (2001) 24(2) I.P.D. 24009; *Times,* March 31, 2000, QBD . . . . *Digested,* 00/**2113**:
Applied, 07/1324

University of Reading v Miller Construction Ltd 75 B.L.R. 91; 52 Con. L.R. 31; (1995) 11 Const. L.J. 388, QBD (OR). . . . . *Digested,* 96/**1138**:
Considered, 07/229

University of Sheffield v Revenue and Customs Commissioners [2007] B.V.C. 2462, V&DTr (Manchester)

Uradex SCRL v Union Professionnelle de la Radio et de la Teledistribution (RTD) (C-169/05) [2006] E.C.R. I-4973; [2006] 3 C.M.L.R. 22; [2006] E.C.D.R. 23, ECJ (3rd Chamber) . . . . *Digested,* 07/**2513**

Uratemp Ventures Ltd v Carrell see Uratemp Ventures Ltd v Collins

Uratemp Ventures Ltd v Collins; *joined case* Uratemp Ventures Ltd v Carrell [2001] UKHL 43; [2002] 1 A.C. 301; [2001] 3 W.L.R. 806; [2002] 1 All E.R. 46; (2001) 33 H.L.R. 85; [2002] L. & T.R. 15; [2001] 3 E.G.L.R. 93; [2002] R.V.R. 162; 2001 Hous. L.R. 133; [2001] 43 E.G. 186 (C.S.); (2001) 98(41) L.S.G. 35; [2001] N.P.C. 145; [2002] 1 P. & C.R. DG15; *Times,* October 18, 2001; *Independent,* December 3, 2001; *Daily Telegraph,* October 16, 2001, HL; reversing (2001) 33 H.L.R. 4; [2000] L. & T.R. 369; [2000] 1 E.G.L.R. 156; (2000) 97(1) L.S.G. 23; [1999] N.P.C. 153; (2000) 79 P. & C.R. D18; *Times,* December 10, 1999, CA (Civ Div) . . . . *Digested,* 01/**4148**:
Applied, 05/2660: *Considered,* 06/2046, 07/3250

Urlaubs- und Lohnausgleichskasse der Bauwirtschaft v Amilcar Oliveira Rocha (C-50/98) see Finalarte Sociedade de Construcao Civil Lda v Urlaubs- und Lohnausgleichskasse der Bauwirtschaft (C-49/98)

Urlaubs- und Lohnausgleichskasse der Bauwirtschaft v Duarte dos Santos Sousa (C-68/98) see Finalarte Sociedade de Construcao Civil Lda v Urlaubs- und Lohnausgleichskasse der Bauwirtschaft (C-49/98)

Urlaubs- und Lohnausgleichskasse der Bauwirtschaft v Santos & Kewitz Construcoes Lda (C-69/98) see Finalarte Sociedade de Construcao Civil Lda v Urlaubs- und Lohnausgleichskasse der Bauwirtschaft (C-49/98)

Urlaubs- und Lohnausgleichskasse der Bauwirtschaft v Tecnamb-Tecnologia do Ambiante Lda (C-53/98) see Finalarte Sociedade de Construcao Civil Lda v Urlaubs- und Lohnausgleichskasse der Bauwirtschaft (C-49/98)

Urlaubs- und Lohnausgleichskasse der Bauwirtschaft v Tudor Stone Ltd (C-52/98) see Finalarte Sociedade de Construcao Civil Lda v Urlaubs- und Lohnausgleichskasse der Bauwirtschaft (C-49/98)

Urlaubs- und Lohnausgleichskasse der Bauwirtschaft v Turiprata Construcoes Civil SA (C-54/98) see Finalarte Sociedade de Construcao Civil Lda v Urlaubs- und Lohnausgleichskasse der Bauwirtschaft (C-49/98)

USB AG v Revenue and Customs Commissioners see UBS AG v Revenue and Customs Commissioners

Uttlesford DC v Eyers [2007] P.A.D. 50, Planning Inspector

Uzinterimpex JSC v Standard Bank Plc [2007] EWHC 1151 (Comm); [2007] 2 Lloyd's Rep. 187, QBD (Comm) . . . . *Digested,* 07/**4187**

V v M see M (A Child) (Abduction: Brussels II Revised), Re

V v V; *sub nom* L (Residence: Jurisdiction), Re [2006] EWHC 3374 (Fam); [2007] 1 F.L.R. 1686; [2007] Fam. Law 304, Fam Div. . . . . *Digested,* 07/**1790**

V (A Child), Re; *sub nom* Sheffield City Council v V [2006] EWHC 1861 (Fam); [2007] 1 F.L.R. 279; [2006] Fam. Law 833; *Times,* August 25, 2006, Fam Div. . . . . . . *Digested,* 07/**1725**

V (A Child) v Ward (Unreported, July 20, 2006), CC (Doncaster) [*Ex rel.* Leila Benyounes, Barrister, Park Lane Chambers, 19 Westgate, Leeds] . . . . *Digested,* 07/**3216**

Valent Biosciences Corp v Valent Pharmaceuticals International; *sub nom* Valent Biosciences' Trade Mark (No.2242946) [2007] R.P.C. 34, TMR

Valent Biosciences' Trade Mark (No.2242946) see Valent Biosciences Corp v Valent Pharmaceuticals International

Valentine v Bangla TV Ltd; *sub nom* Bangla Television Ltd (In Liquidation), Re [2006] EWHC 2292 (Ch); [2007] 1 B.C.L.C. 609, Ch D (Companies Ct) . . . . *Digested,* 07/**2455**

Validity of Directive 2003/86, Re (C-540/03) see European Parliament v Council of the European Union (C-540/03)

Validity of Regulation 1435/2003, Re (C-436/03) see European Parliament v Council of the European Union (C-436/03)

Validity of Regulation 2065/2003, Re (C-66/04) see United Kingdom v European
Parliament (C-66/04)
Validity of Regulation 460/2004, Re (C-217/04) see United Kingdom v European
Parliament (C-217/04)
Van Colle v Chief Constable of Hertfordshire [2007] EWCA Civ 325; [2007] 1 W.L.R.
1821; [2007] 3 All E.R. 122; [2007] 2 Cr. App. R. 32; [2007] 2 F.C.R. 469;
[2007] H.R.L.R. 25; [2007] U.K.H.R.R. 869; [2007] P.I.Q.R. Q7; (2007) 151
S.J.L.B. 576; *Times*, May 10, 2007, CA (Civ Div); affirming in part [2006] EWHC
360 (QB); [2006] 3 All E.R. 963; [2006] 1 F.C.R. 755; [2006] H.R.L.R. 25;
[2006] Inquest L.R. 68; [2006] Po. L.R. 47; *Times*, March 28, 2006;   *Digested*, 07/**2240**:
Independent, March 22, 2006, QBD . . . .   *Considered*, 07/2238

Van Dalfsen v Van Loon (C-183/90) [1991] E.C.R. I-4743; [1992] I.L.Pr. 5, ECJ (6th   *Digested*, 92/**4825**:
Chamber) . . . .   *Applied*, 07/508: *Followed*, 96/1103

Van den Bergh Foods Ltd v Commission of the European Communities (T65/98)
[2005] All E.R. (EC) 418; [2003] E.C.R. II-4653; [2004] 4 C.M.L.R. 1; *Times*,   *Digested*, 04/**489**:
November 7, 2003, CFI (5th Chamber) . . . .   *Subsequent proceedings*, 07/616

Van den Boogaard v Laumen (C-220/95) [1997] Q.B. 759; [1997] 3 W.L.R. 284;
[1997] All E.R. (E.C.) 517; [1997] E.C.R. I-1147; [1997] I.L.Pr. 278; [1997] 2
F.L.R. 399; [1997] 3 F.C.R. 493; [1997] Fam. Law 599; *Times*, March 26, 1997,   *Digested*, 97/**2454**:
ECJ (5th Chamber) . . . .   *Applied*, 07/1697: *Considered*, 98/2470, 07/5183

Van den Hout-van Ejinsbergen v Staatssecretaris van Financien (C-444/04) see
Solleveld v Staatssecretaris van Financien (C-443/04)
Van der Mussele v Belgium (8919/80) (1984) 6 E.H.R.R. 163, ECHR . . . .   *Applied*, 07/2265:
Considered, 06/4044

Van der Steen v Inspecteur van de Belastingdienst Utrecht-Gooi/Kantoor Utrecht (C-
355/06) [2007] S.T.I. 2406, ECJ (2nd Chamber)
Van der Ven v Netherlands (50901/99) (2004) 38 E.H.R.R. 46; [2003] Prison L.R.   *Digested*, 04/**1929**:
240, ECHR . . . .   *Followed*, 07/2170

Van der Wal v Commission of the European Communities (C-189/98 P) see
Netherlands v Commission of the European Communities (C-174/98 P)
Van der Weerd v Minister van Landbouw, Natuur en Voedselkwaliteit (C-222/05)
[2007] 3 C.M.L.R. 7, ECJ . . . .   *Digested*, 07/**1638**

Van Esbroeck v Openbaar Ministerie (C-436/04) see Criminal Proceedings against Van
Esbroeck (C-436/04)
Van Glabeke v France (38287/02) (2007) 45 E.H.R.R. 19, ECHR
Van Hilten-Van der Heijden's Heirs v Inspecteur van de Belastingdienst/Particulieren/
Ondernemingen Buitenland te Heerlen (C-513/03) [2006] E.C.R. I-1957;
[2006] W.T.L.R. 919; [2006] S.T.I. 535, ECJ (3rd Chamber) . . . .   *Digested*, 07/**4113**

Van Houten v Netherlands (25149/03) (2007) 45 E.H.R.R. 20, ECHR
Van Leuven v Belgium (A/43) see Le Compte v Belgium (A/43)
Van Marle v Netherlands (8543/79) see Van Marle v Netherlands (A/101)
Van Marle v Netherlands (A/101); *sub nom* Van Marle v Netherlands (8543/79) (1986)   *Applied*, 06/1812:
8 E.H.R.R. 483, ECHR (1985) 7 E.H.R.R. CD265, Eur Comm HR . . . .   *Considered*, 07/1944

Van Mellaert v Oxford University [2006] EWHC 1565 (QB); [2006] E.L.R. 617;
(2006) 103(29) L.S.G. 28, QBD . . . .   *Digested*, 07/**1281**

Van Riet v Onderlinge Waarborgmaatschappij OZ Zorgverzekeringen UA (C-385/99)
see Muller-Faure v Onderlinge Waarborgmaatschappij OZ Zorgverzekeringen UA
(C-385/99)
Van Schijndel v Stichting Pensioenfonds voor Fysiotherapeuten (C-430/93); *joined
case* Van Veen v Stichting Pensioenfonds voor Fysiotherapeuten (C-431/93)
[1996] All E.R. (E.C.) 259; [1995] E.C.R. I-4705; [1996] 1 C.M.L.R. 801; [1996]   *Digested*, 96/**2799**:
C.E.C. 240, ECJ . . . .   *Followed*, 07/1638

Van Uden Maritime BV (t/a Van Uden Africa Line) v Kommanditgesellschaft in Firma
Deco-Line (C-391/95) [1999] Q.B. 1225; [1999] 2 W.L.R. 1181; [1999] All E.R.
(E.C.) 258; [1999] 1 All E.R. (Comm.) 385; [1998] E.C.R. I-7091; [1999] I.L.Pr.   *Digested*, 99/**739**:
73; *Times*, December 1, 1998, ECJ . . . .   *Applied*, 07/457: *Followed*, 04/576, 05/428

Van Veen v Stichting Pensioenfonds voor Fysiotherapeuten (C-431/93) see Van
Schijndel v Stichting Pensioenfonds voor Fysiotherapeuten (C-430/93)
Vanbraekel v Alliance Nationale des Mutalites Chretiennes (ANMC) (C-368/98)
[2001] E.C.R. I-5363; [2002] 2 C.M.L.R. 20; *Times*, September 4, 2001, ECJ .   *Digested*, 01/**5134**:
Followed, 07/3854

Vance v Taylor [2007] EWHC 1602 (QB); [2007] LS Law Medical 676, QBD . . . .   *Digested*, 07/**3075**
Vanovitch v Ajeigb [*Ex rel.* Elliott Gold, Barrister, 5 Sussex Court, London]. . . . .   *Digested*, 07/**382**
Various Claimants v BACHL see KR v Bryn Alyn Community (Holdings) Ltd (In
Liquidation)

Various Claimants v Bryn Alyn Community (Holdings) Ltd (In Liquidation) see KR v
    Bryn Alyn Community (Holdings) Ltd (In Liquidation)
Various Claimants v Gower Chemicals Ltd [2007] 4 Costs L.R. 647, CC (Cardiff) .... *Digested*, 07/**380**
Vaughan v Jones (Costs) [2006] EWHC 2123 (Ch); [2006] B.P.I.R. 1538, Ch D ..... *Digested*, 07/**421**
Vaughan v Vaughan [2007] EWCA Civ 1085; [2007] 3 F.C.R. 533; (2007) 151
    S.J.L.B. 1435; (2007) 151 S.J.L.B. 1499, CA (Civ Div) .... *Digested*, 07/**1692**
Vaziri v Listing Officer [2006] R.V.R. 329, VT .... *Digested*, 07/**2834**
VBVB and VBBB v Commission of the European Communities (C-43/82 and C-63/
    82); *sub nom* Dutch Books, Re (C-43/82 and C-63/82) [1984] E.C.R. 19;
    [1985] 1 C.M.L.R. 27, ECJ .... *Digested*, 85/**1340**:
                                        Applied, 04/524, 07/1550
VC v Secretary of State for the Home Department see MG v Secretary of State for the
    Home Department
VDP Dental Laboratory NV v Staatssecretaris van Financien (C-401/05) [2007] S.T.C.
    474; [2007] S.T.I. 108, ECJ (3rd Chamber) .... *Digested*, 07/**4335**
Veba Oil Supply & Trading GmbH v Petrotrade Inc (The Robin); *sub nom* Veba Oil Supply
    & Trading Ltd v Petrotrade Inc (The Robin) [2001] EWCA Civ 1832; [2002] 1
    All E.R. 703; [2002] 1 All E.R. (Comm) 306; [2002] 1 Lloyd's Rep. 295; [2002]
    C.L.C. 405; [2002] B.L.R. 54; *Independent*, January 14, 2002, CA (Civ Div);
    affirming [2001] 1 All E.R. (Comm) 1051; [2001] 2 Lloyd's Rep. 731, QBD
    (Comm) .... *Digested*, 02/**707**:
                                          Considered, 07/1077
Veba Oil Supply & Trading Ltd v Petrotrade Inc (The Robin) see Veba Oil Supply &
    Trading GmbH v Petrotrade Inc (The Robin)
Vector Corp v Glatt Air Techniques Inc see Vector Corp v Glatt Air Techniques Ltd
Vector Corp v Glatt Air Techniques Ltd; *sub nom* Vector Corp v Glatt Air Techniques Inc
    [2007] EWCA Civ 805, CA (Civ Div); reversing [2006] EWHC 1638 (Pat);
    [2007] R.P.C. 12; (2006) 29(8) I.P.D. 29058, Ch D (Patents Ct) .... *Digested*, 07/**2613**
Vehicle and Operator Services Agency (VOSA) v F&S Gibbs Transport Services Ltd
    [2006] EWHC 1109 (Admin); (2006) 170 J.P. 586; [2007] R.T.R. 17; (2007) 171
    J.P.N. 35, QBD (Admin) .... *Digested*, 06/**4347**
Veitch v Avery [2007] EWCA Civ 711; 115 Con. L.R. 70; [2007] N.P.C. 89; *Times*,
    August 29, 2007, CA (Civ Div) .... *Digested*, 07/**2918**
Veldman v DPP (Witwatersrand Local Division) 21 B.H.R.C. 18, Const Ct (SA)
Velikova v Bulgaria (41488/98) (Unreported, May 18, 2000), ECHR .... *Applied*, 07/2197
Veliu v Mazrekaj [2006] EWHC 1710 (QB); [2007] 1 W.L.R. 495, QBD .... *Digested*, 07/**1074**
Velvet & Steel Immobilien und Handels GmbH v Finanzamt Hamburg-Eimsbuttel (C-455/
    05) [2007] S.T.I. 1359, ECJ (3rd Chamber)
Venema v Netherlands (35731/97) [2003] 1 F.L.R. 552; [2003] 1 F.C.R. 153; (2004)
    39 E.H.R.R. 5; [2003] Fam. Law 233, ECHR .... *Applied*, 05/1567:
            Considered, 07/1774, 07/2934: *Distinguished*, 07/1717
Vento v Chief Constable of West Yorkshire; *sub nom* Chief Constable of West Yorkshire
    v Vento (No.2) [2002] EWCA Civ 1871; [2003] I.C.R. 318; [2003] I.R.L.R. 102;
    [2003] Po. L.R. 171; (2003) 100(10) L.S.G. 28; (2003) 147 S.J.L.B. 181; *Times*,
    December 27, 2002, CA (Civ Div); affirming [2002] I.R.L.R. 177; [2002] Emp.
    L.R. 111, EAT .... *Digested*, 03/**1306**:
         Applied, 06/1363, 07/1413: *Considered*, 04/917, 04/1276, 06/1371:
                                   Followed, 04/1306, 05/1318
Veolia Water Operations Ireland Ltd v Dublin City Council [2007] E.T.M.R. 50, PO (Irl)
Veolia Water UK Plc v Fingal CC [2006] IEHC 137; [2007] Eu. L.R. 1, HC (Irl)
Verdoliva v JM van der Hoeven BV (C-3/05) [2006] E.C.R. I-1579; [2006] I.L.Pr. 31,
    ECJ (2nd Chamber) .... *Digested*, 07/**462**
Verein fur Konsumenteninformation v Commission of the European Communities (T-2/
    03) [2005] 1 W.L.R. 3302; [2005] All E.R. (EC) 813; [2005] E.C.R. II-1121;
    [2005] 4 C.M.L.R. 21; [2006] 2 C.M.L.R. 60; *Times*, May 20, 2005, CFI (1st
    Chamber) .... *Digested*, 06/**1523**:
                                        Applied, 07/1539
Vereinigung Bildender Kunstler v Austria (68354/01) [2007] E.C.D.R. 7, ECHR ...... *Digested*, 07/**2184**
Vereniging Dorpsbelang Hees v Directeur van de dienst Milieu en Water van de
    provincie Gelderland (C-419/97) see ARCO Chemie Nederland Ltd v Minister
    van Volkshuisvesting, Ruimtelijke Ordening en Milieubeheer (C-418/97)
Vereniging Werkgroep Commerciele Jachthavens Zuidelijke Randmeren v Commission of
    the European Communities (T-117/04) [2007] 1 C.M.L.R. 13, CFI (1st Chamber) *Digested*, 07/**1540**
Verimark (Pty) Ltd v Bayerische Motoren Werke AG [2007] F.S.R. 33, Sup Ct (SA)
Verlagsgruppe News GmbH v Austria (10520/02) [2007] E.M.L.R. 13, ECHR
Verlagsgruppe News GmbH v Austria (76918/01) [2007] E.M.L.R. 17, ECHR
Verrechia (t/a Freightmaster Commercials) v Commissioner of Police of the Metropolis
    see English v Emery Reimbold & Strick Ltd
Vertex Data Science Ltd v Powergen Retail Ltd [2006] EWHC 1340 (Comm); [2006] 2
    Lloyd's Rep. 591, QBD (Comm) .... *Digested*, 07/**245**
Vesely v Levy [2007] EWCA Civ 367; [2007] N.P.C. 52, CA (Civ Div)
Vesta Forsikring AS v Trygg-Hansa AB (HR-2006-01978-A) [2007] E.T.M.R. 31, HR
    (N)

Vetco Gray UK Ltd *v* FMC Technologies Inc [2007] EWHC 540 (Pat); (2007) 30(5) I.P.D. 30036, Ch D (Patents Ct)

Vetplus Ltd *v* Revenue and Customs Commissioners [2007] S.T.I. 376, V&DTr

Vicarage Gate Ltd *v* First Secretary of State [2007] EWHC 768 (Admin); [2007] N.P.C. 50, QBD (Admin)

Vicomtesse Montmort *v* Broers see Letterstedt *v* Broers

VIDEOJET TECHNOLOGIES/Jet ink composition (T234/03) [2007] E.P.O.R. 6, EPO (Technical Bd App) . . . .   *Digested*, 07/**2590**

Vie *v* Carrelages Menuiserie Produits du Batiment (CMPB) [2007] I.L.Pr. 26, Cass (F).   *Digested*, 07/**658**

Viertel (Deceased), Re [1996] QSC 66; [2003] W.T.L.R. 1075, Sup Ct (Qld) . . . .   *Digested*, 03/**4114**:   *Applied*, 07/3962

Vigla Olympou Dairy Products Aeve *v* Galaktoviomichania Larisis AE [2007] E.T.M.R. 48, ATMC (GR)

Vigreux *v* Michel see M (A Child) (Abduction: Brussels II Revised), Re

Villalba *v* Merrill Lynch & Co Inc [2007] I.C.R. 469; [2006] I.R.L.R. 437; (2006) 150 S.J.L.B. 742, EAT . . . .   *Digested*, 06/**1368**

Vinaver *v* Milton Ashbury Ltd [2006] EWCA Civ 363; [2006] W.T.L.R. 1675, CA (Civ Div). . . . .   *Digested*, 07/**3392**

Vince's Application, Re; *sub nom* Old Pinfold House, 16 The Green, Barby, Rugby, Warwickshire, CV23 8TS, Re (2007) 151 S.J.L.B. 1264, Lands Tr

Vine-Hall *v* Hazlems Fenton [2006] EWHC 2753 (Ch); [2007] P.N.L.R. 14, Ch D . . . .   *Digested*, 07/**491**

Vinos *v* Marks & Spencer Plc [2001] 3 All E.R. 784; [2001] C.P. Rep. 12; [2000] C.P.L.R. 570; *Independent*, July 17, 2000, CA (Civ Div) . . . .   *Applied*, 00/**535**,   01/641, 01/645, 04/391, 05/466: *Cited*, 03/456: *Considered*, 01/643, 01/644,   06/347: *Distinguished*, 01/654, 05/340, 07/468: *Followed*, 02/479

Vintage Hallmark Plc, Re; *sub nom* Secretary of State for Trade and Industry *v* Grove [2006] EWHC 2761 (Ch); [2007] 1 B.C.L.C. 788, Ch D (Companies Ct) . . . . .   *Digested*, 07/**568**

VIP Communications Ltd *v* Office of Communications (Costs) [2006] CAT 27; [2007] Comp. A.R. 324, CAT

VIP Communications Ltd (In Administration) *v* Office of Communications [2007] CAT 17; [2007] Comp. A.R. 808, CAT

VIP Communications Ltd (In Administration) *v* Office of Communications [2007] CAT 3; [2007] Comp. A.R. 666, CAT

VIP Communications Ltd (In Administration) *v* Office of Communications [2007] CAT 19; [2007] Comp. A.R. 895, CAT

VIP Communications Ltd (In Administration) *v* Office of Communications [2007] CAT 12; [2007] Comp. A.R. 781, CAT

VIP Communications Ltd (In Administration) *v* Office of Communications [2007] CAT 20; [2007] Comp. A.R. 897, CAT

Virdi *v* Commissioner of Police of the Metropolis [2007] I.R.L.R. 24, EAT . . . .   *Digested*, 07/**1389**

Virgin Enterprises Ltd *v* One in a Million Ltd see British Telecommunications Plc *v* One in a Million Ltd

Virtue (t/a Lammermuir Game Services) *v* Revenue and Customs Commissioners [2007] B.V.C. 2518, V&DTr (Edinburgh)

Vision Golf Ltd *v* Weightmans [2006] EWHC 1766 (Ch); [2007] P.N.L.R. 8, Ch D . . . .   *Digested*, 07/**1055**

Visserijbedrijf DJ Koornstra & Zn vof *v* Productschap Vis (C-517/04) [2006] E.C.R. I-5015; [2006] 3 C.M.L.R. 18, ECJ (2nd Chamber) . . . .   *Digested*, 07/**1603**

VITALITE Trade Mark see Sunrider Corp (t/a Sunrider International) *v* Vitasoy International Holdings Ltd

Vitamin Supplements, Re (C-387/99) see Commission of the European Communities *v* Germany (C-387/99)

Vitamins Cartel, Re (T-15/02) see BASF AG *v* Commission of the European Communities (T-15/02)

Vitamins Cartel, Re (T-26/02) see Daiichi Pharmaceutical Co Ltd *v* Commission of the European Communities (T-26/02)

Vo *v* France (53924/00) [2004] 2 F.C.R. 577; (2005) 40 E.H.R.R. 12; 17 B.H.R.C. 1; (2004) 79 B.M.L.R. 71; [2005] Inquest L.R. 129, ECHR (Grand Chamber) . . . .   *Digested*, 05/**2114**:   *Applied*, 07/2235

Vodafone 2 *v* Revenue and Customs Commissioners 10 I.T.L. Rep. 110, Sp Comm

Vodafone 2 *v* Revenue and Customs Commissioners; *sub nom* Revenue and Customs Commissioners *v* Vodafone 2 [2006] EWCA Civ 1132; [2006] S.T.C. 1530; [2006] B.T.C. 702; [2006] S.T.I. 1989; *Times*, August 8, 2006, CA (Civ Div); affirming [2005] EWHC 3040 (Ch); [2006] S.T.C. 483; [2006] B.T.C. 406; [2005] S.T.I. 1841, Ch D; affirming [2005] S.T.C. (S.C.D) 549; 8 I.T.L. Rep. 27, Sp Comm . . . .   *Digested*, 06/**4162**:   *Considered*, 07/4155

Voight *v* Regierungsprasidium Karlsruhe-Bretten (C-83/05) see Proceedings brought by Voigt (C-83/05)

Volkswagen AG *v* Commission of the European Communities (C-338/00 P) [2003] E.C.R. I-9189; [2004] 4 C.M.L.R. 7, ECJ (6th Chamber) . . . .   *Digested*, 04/**522**:   *Applied*, 07/1543: *Previous proceedings*, 01/775

Volkswagen AG *v* Commission of the European Communities (C-74/04 P) see Commission of the European Communities *v* Volkswagen AG (C-74/04 P)

Volkswagen AG v Commission of the European Communities (T62/98) [2000] E.C.R.
   II-2707; [2000] 5 C.M.L.R. 853, CFI . . . .   *Digested,* 01/**775**:
                                Affirmed, 04/522: *Applied,* 07/644: *Considered,* 06/572
Volokhy v Ukraine (23543/02) 9 I.T.L. Rep. 328, ECHR . . . .   *Digested,* 07/**2241**
Von Hannover v Germany (59320/00) [2004] E.M.L.R. 21; (2005) 40 E.H.R.R. 1; 16
   B.H.R.C. 545, ECHR. . . . .   *Applied,* 07/1072:
                                   Considered, 06/2853, 07/2247, 07/2250
Vortex v British Sky Broadcasting Ltd [2007] E.T.M.R. 64, Arbitration
Vranicki v Architects Registration Board [2007] EWHC 506 (Admin); [2007] 13 E.G.
   254 (C.S.), QBD (Admin)
VW-Audi Forhandlerforeningen v Skandinavisk Motor Co A/S (C-125/05) [2006]
   E.C.R. I-7637; [2007] R.T.R. 8; [2007] 4 C.M.L.R. 25, ECJ (3rd Chamber) . . . .   *Digested,* 07/**625**:
                                   Applied, 07/1568

W v B see R. (on the application of L (A Child)) v J School Governors
W v Commissioner of Police of the Metropolis [2000] 1 W.L.R. 1607; [2000] 4 All
   E.R. 934; [2000] I.C.R. 1064; [2000] I.R.L.R. 720; [2001] P.I.Q.R. P6; [2000]
   Po. L.R. 322; (2000) 97(39) L.S.G. 42; (2000) 144 S.J.L.B. 248; *Times,* August
   1, 2000; *Independent,* November 6, 2000, HL; reversing [1997] I.C.R. 1073;
   [1997] I.R.L.R. 589; *Times,* July 21, 1997, CA (Civ Div); affirming [1995] I.C.R.
   510; [1995] I.R.L.R. 531, EAT . . . .   *Digested,* 00/**4229**:
                                Applied, 00/2211: *Considered,* 07/2940
W v Essex CC [2001] 2 A.C. 592; [2000] 2 W.L.R. 601; [2000] 2 All E.R. 237;
   [2000] 1 F.L.R. 657; [2000] 1 F.C.R. 568; [2000] B.L.G.R. 281; (2000) 53
   B.M.L.R. 1; [2000] Fam. Law 476; (2000) 164 J.P.N. 464; (2000) 97(13) L.S.G.
   44; (2000) 144 S.J.L.B. 147; *Times,* March 17, 2000, HL; reversing in part
   [1999] Fam. 90; [1998] 3 W.L.R. 534; [1998] 3 All E.R. 111; [1998] 2 F.L.R.
   278; [1998] 2 F.C.R. 269; [1998] P.I.Q.R. P346; [1998] Fam. Law 455; (1998)
   95(20) L.S.G. 33; *Times,* April 9, 1998, CA (Civ Div); affirming [1997] 2 F.L.R.
   535; [1998] 2 F.C.R. 232; [1997] Fam. Law 720; (1997) 161 J.P.N. 1158; *Times,*
   July 16, 1997, QBD . . . .   *Digested,* 00/**4213**:
                          Considered, 07/1778: *Distinguished,* 03/5828
W v F see A (A Child) (Abduction: Habitual Residence), Re
W v H [2004] EWHC 526 (Fam); [2006] 2 F.L.R. 258; [2006] Fam. Law 356;
   [2006] Fam. Law 441, Fam Div . . . .   *Cited,* 07/1696
W v Hull City Council see S (Children), Re
W v Leeds City Council [2005] EWCA Civ 988; [2005] E.L.R. 617, CA (Civ Div);
   affirming [2004] EWHC 2513 (Admin); [2005] E.L.R. 459, QBD (Admin) . . . .   *Digested,* 06/**1221**:
                              Applied, 07/1254, 07/1264: *Considered,* 07/1262
W v Oldham MBC; *sub nom* GW v Oldham MBC; W (A Child) (Non-Accidental Injury:
   Expert Evidence), Re [2005] EWCA Civ 1247; [2006] 1 F.L.R. 543; [2005] 3
   F.C.R. 513; (2005) 149 S.J.L.B. 1351; *Times,* November 7, 2005; *Independent,*
   November 3, 2005, CA (Civ Div) . . . .   *Digested,* 06/**1663**:
                                   Distinguished, 07/1728
W v P see C Plc v P
W v Poole BC [2007] EWCA Civ 1145; *Times,* October 25, 2007, CA (Civ Div);
   affirming [2007] EWHC 1817 (Admin), QBD (Admin)
W v Staffordshire CC [2006] EWCA Civ 1676; [2007] E.L.R. 208, CA (Civ Div) . . . . .   *Digested,* 07/**1256**
W v United Kingdom (9749/82) see W v United Kingdom (A/121)
W v United Kingdom (A/121); *sub nom* W v United Kingdom (9749/82) (1988) 10
   E.H.R.R. 29, ECHR (1984) 6 E.H.R.R. CD565, Eur Comm HR. . . . .   *Applied,* 98/3104:
                    Considered, 03/1477, 03/1478, 03/2198: *Distinguished,* 07/1717
W v W (Preliminary Issue: Stay of Petition) [2002] EWHC 3049 (Fam); [2003] 1
   F.L.R. 1022; [2003] Fam. Law 307, Fam Div . . . .   *Digested,* 03/**600**:
                                   Considered, 07/1701
W Healthcare NHS Trust v H [2004] EWCA Civ 1324; [2005] 1 W.L.R. 834; *Times,*
   December 9, 2004; *Independent,* January 21, 2005, CA (Civ Div) . . . .   *Digested,* 05/**1850**:
                             Considered, 07/1984: *Distinguished,* 05/1794
W (A Child), Re see S (Children), Re
W (A Child), Re [2007] EWCA Civ 1255; (2007) 151 S.J.L.B. 1499, CA (Civ Div)
W (A Child), Re; *sub nom* W (A Child) (Care: Threshold Criteria), Re; L v A Local
   Authority [2007] EWCA Civ 102; [2007] 2 F.L.R. 98; [2007] 2 F.C.R. 160;
   [2007] Fam. Law 689; (2007) 151 S.J.L.B. 297, CA (Civ Div) . . . .   *Digested,* 07/**1715**
W (A Child) v Gwanzura (Unreported, February 12, 2007), CC (Peterborough) [*Ex rel.*
   Shabnam Walji, Barrister, Regency Chambers, Cathedral Square, Peterborough]   *Digested,* 07/**3103**
W (A Child) v Hinton (Unreported, May 12, 2006), CC (Walsall) [*Ex rel.* Stephen
   Garner, Barrister, No.8 Chambers, Fountain Court, Steelhouse Lane,
   Birmingham] . . . .   *Digested,* 07/**3214**
W (A Child) v Northern General Hospital NHS Trust see Heil v Rankin
W (A Child) v Southam (Unreported, September 7, 2006), CC (Bromley) [*Ex rel.*
   Nicholas J H Preston, Barrister, Clerksroom, 218 Strand, London] . . . .   *Digested,* 07/**3194**
W (A Child) (Care: Threshold Criteria), Re see W (A Child), Re
W (A Child) (Non-Accidental Injury: Expert Evidence), Re see W v Oldham MBC

W (An Infant), Re [1971] A.C. 682; [1971] 2 W.L.R. 1011; [1971] 2 All E.R. 49; (1971) 115 S.J.
286, HL; reversing [1970] 2 Q.B. 589; [1970] 3 W.L.R. 175; [1970] 3 All E.R. 990;
(1970) 114 S.J. 433, CA (Civ Div) . . . .   *Digested*, 71/**5831**:
Applied, 73/2142, 76/1752, 76/1753, 77/1919, 77/1920, 89/2416, 07/1681:
Considered, 74/2360, 75/2142, 75/2148, 76/1746, 85/2203, 85/2204,
86/2158, 86/2208, 88/2301, 90/3132, 96/468, 97/352, 98/2365, 00/2430,
07/4550: *Disapproved*, 70/1327: *Distinguished*, 94/3141: *Followed*, 76/1748,
83/2424, 87/2526
W (Children), Re [2007] EWCA Civ 786; [2007] Fam. Law 897; *Times*, August 2, 2007,
CA (Civ Div)
W (Children), Re [2007] EWCA Civ 753; [2007] 2 F.L.R. 1122; [2007] Fam. Law 899, CA
(Civ Div)
W (Children) (Identification: Restrictions on Publication), Re; *sub nom* A Local Authority
v W [2005] EWHC 1564 (Fam); [2006] 1 F.L.R. 1; [2007] 3 F.C.R. 69; [2005]
Fam. Law 868; *Times*, July 21, 2005, Fam Div . . . .   *Digested*, 05/**1686**:
Applied, 07/1806, 07/2189
W (China) *v* Secretary of State for the Home Department [2006] EWCA Civ 1494;
[2007] 1 W.L.R. 1514; [2007] 1 C.M.L.R. 17; [2007] Eu. L.R. 293; [2007] Imm.
A.R. 326; [2007] I.N.L.R. 115; (2006) 103(45) L.S.G. 27; *Times*, December 13,
2006; *Independent*, November 17, 2006, CA (Civ Div) . . . .   *Digested*, 07/**2367**
W's Application for Judicial Review, Re [2004] NIQB 67, QBD (NI) . . . .   *Applied*, 07/544
W's Parent and Guardian *v* Douglas [2006] CSOH 178; (2007) 93 B.M.L.R. 42; 2006
G.W.D. 37-737, OH . . . .   *Digested*, 07/**4980**
Wade *v* Turfrey [2007] LS Law Medical 352, QBD (Leeds) . . . .   *Digested*, 07/**3070**
Wadeson *v* Toole (Unreported, September 18, 2006), CC (Altrincham) [*Ex rel*. Elaine
Youshani, Barrister, St James's Chambers, 68 Quay Street, Manchester] . . . . . .   *Digested*, 07/**3112**
Wadham College Oxford *v* Revenue and Customs Commissioners [2007] B.V.C. 2480;
[2007] V. & D.R. 177, V&D Tr (London)
Wadlow *v* Samuel (aka Seal) [2007] EWCA Civ 155; (2007) 151 S.J.L.B. 331, CA
(Civ Div); affirming [2006] EWHC 1492, QBD
Wadsted *v* Q3 Media Ltd see Ice Media International Ltd (In Liquidation) *v* Q3 Media
Ltd
Waeco International GmbH *v* Cardon [2007] I.L.Pr. 38, Cass (F)
Wafer *v* Wright see Hicks *v* Chief Constable of South Yorkshire
Wagle *v* Trustees of Henry Smith's Charity Kensington Estate; *sub nom* Trustees of
Henry Smith's Charity Kensington Estate *v* Wagle [1990] 1 Q.B. 42; [1989] 2
W.L.R. 669; (1989) 21 H.L.R. 177; [1989] 11 E.G. 75; [1988] E.G. 162 (C.S.);
(1989) 133 S.J. 484; *Times*, December 12, 1988, CA (Civ Div) . . . .   *Digested*, 89/**2171**:
Applied, 89/2154, 07/2771: *Considered*, 89/2156
Wahr-Hansen *v* Compass Trust Co Ltd 10 I.T.L. Rep. 283; (2007-08) 10 I.T.E.L.R. 580,
Grand Ct (CI)
Wain *v* Guernsey Ship Management Ltd [2007] EWCA Civ 294; [2007] I.C.R. 1350;
(2007) 104(16) L.S.G. 24, CA (Civ Div); affirming UKEAT/0320/06/CEA, EAT   *Digested*, 07/**1416**
Wainwright *v* United Kingdom (12350/04) (2007) 44 E.H.R.R. 40; 22 B.H.R.C. 287;
(2006) 156 N.L.J. 1524; *Times*, October 3, 2006, ECHR. . . . .   *Digested*, 07/**2199**
Wakefield *v* Channel Four Television Corp [2006] EWHC 3289 (QB); (2007) 94
B.M.L.R. 1; (2007) 104(5) L.S.G. 28, QBD . . . .   *Digested*, 07/**438**
Wakeling *v* Harrington [2007] EWHC 1184 (Ch); [2007] 5 Costs L.R. 710; (2007) 151
S.J.L.B. 744, Ch D
Walden *v* Liechtenstein (Admissibility) (33916/96) (Unreported, March 16, 2000),
ECHR . . . .   *Considered*, 03/3059,
05/3926, 07/2261
Walderdorff *v* Finanzamt Waldviertel (C-451/06) [2007] S.T.I. 2850, ECJ (3rd
Chamber)
Walker *v* Birmingham City Council; *sub nom* Birmingham City Council *v* Walker [2007]
UKHL 22; [2007] 2 A.C. 262; [2007] 2 W.L.R. 1057; [2007] 3 All E.R. 445;
[2007] H.L.R. 38; [2007] L. & T.R. 24; [2007] 21 E.G. 131 (C.S.); (2007) 157
N.L.J. 742; (2007) 151 S.J.L.B. 673; [2007] N.P.C. 61; [2007] 2 P. & C.R. DG10;
Times, May 17, 2007, HL; affirming [2006] EWCA Civ 815; [2006] 1 W.L.R.
2641; [2006] 2 F.C.R. 623; [2007] H.L.R. 5; (2006) 103(27) L.S.G. 32; (2006)
150 S.J.L.B. 859; [2006] N.P.C. 72; [2007] 1 P. & C.R. DG7; *Independent*,
June 28, 2006, CA (Civ Div) . . . .   *Digested*, 07/**2768**
Walker *v* Chief Constable of the West Midlands see Hunter *v* Chief Constable of the
West Midlands
Walker *v* Dominey (Unreported, January 4, 2007), CC (Coventry) [*Ex rel*. Adam Farrer,
Barrister, No. 5 Fountain Court, Steelhouse Lane, Birmingham] . . . .   *Digested*, 07/**3181**
Walker *v* Hall [1984] Fam. Law 21; (1983) 80 L.S.G. 2139; (1983) 127 S.J. 550, CA
(Civ Div) . . . .   *Digested*, 84/**1675**:
Doubted, 07/3367: *Followed*, 86/1857, 87/1439
Walker *v* Hayton (Unreported, March 8, 2007), CC (Northampton) [*Ex rel*. David
McHugh, Barrister, Clerksroom, Tolworth] . . . .   *Digested*, 07/**3118**
Walker *v* Inter-Alliance Group Plc (In Administration) [2007] EWHC 1858 (Ch);
[2007] Pens. L.R. 347, Ch D

Walker v Jeffries; *joined case* S (A Child) (Unmarried Parents: Financial Provision), Re [2006] EWCA Civ 479; [2006] 2 F.L.R. 950; [2006] Fam. Law 633; (2006) 150 S.J.L.B. 361; *Times*, April 17, 2006, CA (Civ Div) . . . . *Digested*, 07/**1688**

Walker v Revenue and Customs Commissioners [2007] S.T.I. 2126, Sp Comm

Walker v Secretary of State for the Home Department see R. (on the application of Walker) v Secretary of State for the Home Department

Walker v Walker; *sub nom* Walker Wingsail Systems Plc, Re [2005] EWCA Civ 247; [2006] 1 W.L.R. 2194; [2005] 1 All E.R. 272; [2005] C.P. Rep. 33; [2005] 3 Costs L.R. 363; [2005] B.P.I.R. 454; *Times*, March 3, 2005, CA (Civ Div); reversing [2004] EWHC 1886 (Ch), Ch D . . . . *Digested*, 05/**362**:
Considered, 07/2722: *Followed*, 06/378

Walker Civil Engineering Pty Ltd v Sun Alliance & London Insurance Plc (Unreported), Sup Ct (NSW) . . . . *Considered*, 07/2479

Walker Residential Ltd v Davis [2005] EWHC 3483 (Ch), Ch D . . . . *Considered*, 07/403

Walker Wingsail Systems Plc, Re see Walker v Walker

Walker (Inspector of Taxes) v Centaur Clothes Group Ltd; *sub nom* Centaur Clothes Group Ltd v Walker (Inspector of Taxes) [2000] 1 W.L.R. 799; [2000] 2 All E.R. 589; [2000] S.T.C. 324; 72 T.C. 379; [2000] B.T.C. 121; [2000] S.T.I. 581; (2000) 97(16) L.S.G. 42; (2000) 144 S.J.L.B. 188; *Times*, April 7, 2000, HL; reversing [1998] S.T.C. 814; [1998] B.T.C. 277; (1998) 95(34) L.S.G. 31; *Times*, July 25, 1998, CA (Civ Div); affirming [1997] S.T.C. 72; [1997] B.T.C. 45, Ch D; reversing [1996] S.T.C. (S.C.D.) 222, Sp Comm . . . . *Digested*, 00/**4912**:
Applied, 00/820: *Considered*, 07/4003

WALKER/Text processor (T49/04) [2007] E.P.O.R. 34, EPO (Technical Bd App) . . . . *Digested*, 07/**2591**

Walkley v Precision Forgings Ltd [1979] 1 W.L.R. 606; [1979] 2 All E.R. 548; (1979) 123 S.J. 548, HL; reversing [1978] 1 W.L.R. 1228; [1979] 1 All E.R. 102; (1978) 122 S.J. 645, CA (Civ Div) . . . . *Digested*, 79/**1665**:
Applied, 80/1676, 83/2219, 89/2698, 95/3175, 03/435:
Considered, 80/1682, 81/328.u, 81/1618, 84/2416, 98/686, 07/445:
Distinguished, 82/1853, 89/2277, 92/413, 95/6098, 98/545, 03/437,
06/473: *Followed*, 93/2607, 97/653: *Not applied*, 99/475: *Overruled*, 06/475

Wall v Collins [2007] EWCA Civ 444; [2007] Ch. 390; [2007] 3 W.L.R. 459; (2007) 104(22) L.S.G. 26; (2007) 151 S.J.L.B. 675; [2007] N.P.C. 64, CA (Civ Div) . . *Digested*, 07/**3426**

Wall v Standard Telephones & Cables Ltd (No.2) see Alexander v Standard Telephones & Cables Ltd (No.2)

Wallace v Manchester City Council (1998) 30 H.L.R. 1111; [1998] L. & T.R. 279; [1998] 3 E.G.L.R. 38; [1998] 41 E.G. 223; [1998] E.G. 114 (C.S.); [1998] N.P.C. 115; *Times*, July 23, 1998; *Independent*, July 17, 1998, CA (Civ Div) . . . . *Digested*, 98/**3678**:
Applied, 03/2074, 05/2683, 07/2747: *Considered*, 99/3674, 00/4290

Wallach v Secretary of State for Trade and Industry see Genosyis Technology Management Ltd, Re

Wallbank v Aston Cantlow and Wilmcote with Billesley Parochial Church Council see Aston Cantlow and Wilmcote with Billesley Parochial Church Council v Wallbank

Waller v Wu (Unreported, February 23, 2007), CC (Gloucester) [*Ex rel.* Stephen Garner, Barrister, No. 8 Chambers, Fountain Court, Steelhouse Lane, Birmingham] . . . . *Digested*, 07/**3108**

Wallersteiner v Moir (No.2); *sub nom* Moir v Wallersteiner (No.2) [1975] Q.B. 373; [1975] 2 W.L.R. 389; [1975] 1 All E.R. 849; (1975) 119 S.J. 97, CA (Civ Div) . . *Digested*, 75/**2602**:
Applied, 94/3911, 95/2203, 95/3836, 96/4149: *Considered*, 78/2402,
87/334, 89/437, 98/481, 98/482, 01/481, 01/3803, 03/2420, 07/435:
Distinguished, 84/388, 86/316: *Followed*, 92/3525

Walley v Stoke on Trent City Council; *sub nom* Stoke on Trent City Council v Walley [2006] EWCA Civ 1137; [2007] 1 W.L.R. 352; [2006] 4 All E.R. 1230; [2006] C.P. Rep. 48; [2007] P.I.Q.R. P5; (2006) 103(33) L.S.G. 23; (2006) 150 S.J.L.B. 1051; *Times*, August 25, 2006, CA (Civ Div) . . . . *Digested*, 06/**492**:
Applied, 07/348

Walrave v Association Union Cycliste Internationale (36/74) [1974] E.C.R. 1405; [1975] 1 C.M.L.R. 320; *Times*, December 23, 1974, ECJ . . . . *Digested*, 75/**1253**:
Applied, 87/1569, 07/623: *Considered*, 06/2459

Walsh v United Kingdom (63484/00) see Hobbs v United Kingdom (63684/00)

Walter L Jacob & Co Ltd, Re (1989) 5 B.C.C. 244; [1989] B.C.L.C. 345; [1989] P.C.C. 47, CA (Civ Div); reversing (1987) 3 B.C.C. 532, Ch D (Companies Ct) . . . . *Digested*, 89/**350**:
Applied, 96/3552, 02/2725, 05/2305, 07/2462: *Followed*, 99/589, 07/2463

Waltham Forest LBC v Maloba [2007] EWCA Civ 1281; (2007) 151 S.J.L.B. 1597; [2007] N.P.C. 131, CA (Civ Div)

Waltham Forest LBC v Omilaju (No.2) see Omilaju v Waltham Forest LBC (No.2)

Walton v Zap Ltd [2007] E.C.D.R. 10, Designs Registry . . . . *Digested*, 07/**2536**

Walton International Ltd v Yong Teng Hing [2007] F.S.R. 32, HC (Mal)

Wandsworth BC v South Western Magistrates' Court [2007] EWHC 1079 (Admin); [2007] N.P.C. 60, DC

Wandsworth LBC v Randall [2007] EWCA Civ 1126; [2007] 46 E.G. 176 (C.S.); (2007) 104(45) L.S.G. 30; [2007] N.P.C. 116, CA (Civ Div)

Wandsworth LBC v Secretary of State for Transport, Local Government and the
  Regions (Enforcement Notice); *sub nom* R. (on the application of Wandsworth
  LBC) v Secretary of State for Transport, Local Government and the Regions
  [2003] EWHC 622 (Admin); [2004] 1 P. & C.R. 32; [2004] J.P.L. 291; [2003]
  N.P.C. 11, QBD (Admin) . . . . *Digested*, 04/**3050**:
                                   Applied, 07/3283: *Considered*, 06/3293
Wandsworth LBC v Winder (No.1) [1985] A.C. 461; [1984] 3 W.L.R. 1254; [1984] 3
  All E.R. 976; (1985) 17 H.L.R. 196; 83 L.G.R. 143; (1985) 82 L.S.G. 201; (1985)
  135 N.L.J. 381; (1984) 128 S.J. 838, HL; affirming [1984] 3 W.L.R. 563;
  [1984] 3 All E.R. 83; (1984) 15 H.L.R. 1; 82 L.G.R. 509; (1984) 81 L.S.G. 1684;
  (1984) 128 S.J. 384, CA (Civ Div) . . . . *Digested*, 85/**9**:
                       Applied, 88/593, 92/30, 92/79, 99/4749, 03/3548, 05/3951:
               Considered, 84/1344, 87/2378, 87/3052, 87/3097, 88/3432, 96/3087,
                       97/2691, 07/51: *Distinguished*, 88/2211, 88/2226, 89/35, 92/394, 93/2048:
                                   Followed, 00/5126, 03/5265: *Referred to*, 87/2385
Wang Laboratories Inc's Application [1991] R.P.C. 463, Ch D (Patents Ct) . . . . *Digested*, 92/**3280**:
                                                           Considered, 07/2632
Wanklin v Revenue and Customs Commissioners; *sub nom* Haresfield Court Tenants
  Association v Revenue and Customs Commissioners [2007] S.T.I. 2239, V&DTr
  (London)
Warborough Investments Ltd v Central Midland Estates Ltd [2006] EWHC 2622 (Ch);
  [2007] L. & T.R. 10, Ch D . . . . *Digested*, 07/**2764**
Warborough Investments Ltd v S Robinson & Sons (Holdings) Ltd [2003] EWCA Civ
  751; [2004] 2 P. & C.R. 6; [2003] 2 E.G.L.R. 149; (2003) 100(24) L.S.G. 38;
  (2003) 147 S.J.L.B. 748; [2003] N.P.C. 75; *Times*, July 9, 2003, CA (Civ Div);
  affirming [2002] EWHC 2502 (Ch), Ch D . . . . *Digested*, 03/**2778**:
                                   Applied, 06/196: *Considered*, 05/2678, 07/252
Ward v Perks see Hawkes Hill Publishing Co Ltd (In Liquidation), Re
Ward v Police Service of Northern Ireland [2007] UKHL 50; [2007] 1 W.L.R. 3013;
  (2007) 151 S.J.L.B. 1531; *Times*, November 22, 2007, HL (NI)
Ward v Ward 155 E.R. 1189; (1852) 7 Ex. 838, Ex Ct . . . . *Applied*, 07/**3428**:
                                   Considered, 72/352.1: *Distinguished*, 84/1152
Ward (A Child), Re; *sub nom* BBC v CAFCASS Legal [2007] EWHC 616 (Fam); [2007]
  2 F.L.R. 765; [2007] Fam. Law 704, Fam Div . . . . *Digested*, 07/**1711**
WARF/Stem cells (T1374/04) [2006] E.P.O.R. 31, EPO (Technical Bd App) . . . . *Digested*, 07/**2571**
Warnborough Ltd v Garmite Ltd [2003] EWCA Civ 1544; (2003) 147 S.J.L.B. 1307;
  [2003] N.P.C. 134; [2004] 1 P. & C.R. DG8, CA (Civ Div); reversing [2003]
  EWHC 282 (Ch), Ch D . . . . *Considered*, 07/3420
Warnborough Ltd v Garmite Ltd [2006] EWHC 10 (Ch); [2007] 1 P. & C.R. 2; [2006]
  3 E.G. 121 (C.S.); [2006] 2 P. & C.R. DG8, Ch D . . . . *Digested*, 07/**3420**
WARNER-LAMBERT/Taste of medicinal preparation (T400/05) [2007] E.P.O.R. 4, EPO
  (Technical Bd App) . . . . *Digested*, 07/**2578**
Warren (t/a WT Warren & Son) v Revenue and Customs Commissioners [2007] S.T.I.
  383, V&DTr (London)
Warwickshire CC v M; *sub nom* M (Children) (Placement Order), Re; M v
  Warwickshire CC [2007] EWCA Civ 1084; [2007] 3 F.C.R. 681; (2007) 104(44)
  L.S.G. 30; (2007) 151 S.J.L.B. 1435; *Times*, December 21, 2007, CA (Civ Div) . *Digested*, 07/**1679**
Wasa International Insurance Co Ltd v Lexington Insurance Co; *joined case* AGF
  Insurance Ltd v Lexington Insurance Co; A3/2007/0985;A3/2007/0984, CA
  (Civ Div); reversing [2007] EWHC 896 (Comm); [2007] 1 C.L.C. 570; [2007]
  Lloyd's Rep. I.R. 604, QBD (Comm) . . . . *Digested*, 07/**2504**
Waste Water Contract, Re (C-503/04) see Commission of the European Communities v
  Germany (C-503/04)
Watcham v Attorney General of East Africa Protectorate [1919] A.C. 533; [1918-19]
  All E.R. Rep. 455, PC (EA) . . . . *Applied*, 07/**3364**:
                       07/3365: *Considered*, 69/178, 72/475: *Distinguished*, 47-51/2733, 73/396,
                                                           73/955: *Doubted*, 04/3195
Watchman v Ipswich BC [2007] EWCA Civ 348; [2007] H.L.R. 33; (2007) 104(8)
  L.S.G. 37; (2007) 151 S.J.L.B. 260, CA (Civ Div)
Waterfront Shipping Co Ltd v Trafigura AG (The Sabrewing) [2007] EWHC 2482
  (Comm); [2007] 2 C.L.C. 763, QBD (Comm)
Waters (Setting of Minimum Term), Re; *sub nom* R. v Waters (David) [2006] EWHC 355
  (QB); [2006] 3 All E.R. 1251, QBD . . . . *Digested*, 06/**3753**:
                                                           Disapproved, 07/3692
Watkins v Home Office see Watkins v Secretary of State for the Home Department
Watkins v Rhondda Cynon Taff BC see Rhondda Cynon Taff CBC v Watkins
Watkins v Secretary of State for the Home Department; *sub nom* Watkins v Home
  Office [2006] UKHL 17; [2006] 2 A.C. 395; [2006] 2 W.L.R. 807; [2006] 2 All
  E.R. 353; [2006] 1 Prison L.R. 268; *Times*, April 3, 2006, HL; reversing [2004]
  EWCA Civ 966; [2005] Q.B. 883; [2005] 2 W.L.R. 1538; [2004] 4 All E.R.
  1158; [2005] 2 Prison L.R. 31; (2004) 101(34) L.S.G. 30; (2004) 148 S.J.L.B.
  912; *Times*, August 5, 2004, CA (Civ Div) . . . . *Digested*, 06/**4332**:
                                                           Applied, 07/4192
Watt v Northern Ireland Housing Executive [2007] R.V.R. 30, Lands Tr (NI) . . . . *Digested*, 07/**4432**

Watt (formerly Carter) v Ahsan see Carter v Ahsan (No.1)
Watts v Bell & Scott WS [2007] CSOH 108; 2007 S.L.T. 665; [2007] P.N.L.R. 30; 2007 G.W.D. 21-364, OH . . . . *Digested*, 07/**5015**
Watts v Diosynth Ltd see Thomson v Diosynth Ltd
Wawrzynczyk v Chief Constable of Staffordshire (2000) 97(12) L.S.G. 40; (2000) 144 S.J.L.B. 133; *Times*, March 16, 2000, DC . . . . *Digested*, 00/**999**: *Considered*, 07/3538
WE Black Ltd v First Secretary of State [2006] EWHC 1598 (Admin); [2007] 1 P. & C.R. 7; (2006) 150 S.J.L.B. 574, QBD (Admin) . . . . *Digested*, 07/**3281**
WEA/Admissibility of appeal (T591/05) [2006] E.P.O.R. 54, EPO (Technical Bd App) *Digested*, 07/**2568**
Weald Leasing Ltd v Revenue and Customs Commissioners; *sub nom* Revenue and Customs Commissioners v Weald Leasing Ltd; CH/2007/APP/0191, Ch D; affirming [2007] B.V.C. 2321, V&D Tr
Wealden DC v Secretary of State for the Environment 87 L.G.R. 1, CA (Civ Div) . . . . . . *Applied*, 07/3231
Webb v Barnet LBC (1989) 21 H.L.R. 228; [1989] 11 E.G. 80; [1988] E.G. 177 (C.S.), CA (Civ Div) . . . . *Digested*, 89/**2156**: *Applied*, 07/2771
Webb v Leadbetter [1966] 1 W.L.R. 245; [1966] 2 All E.R. 114; (1966) 130 J.P. 277; (1966) 110 S.J. 90, QBD . . . . *Digested*, 66/**7529**: *Applied*, 72/621, 73/2106, 05/817: *Considered*, 84/2079, 07/944
Webb v Webb (C-294/92) [1994] Q.B. 696; [1994] 3 W.L.R. 801; [1994] 3 All E.R. 911; [1994] E.C.R. I-1717; [1994] I.L.Pr. 389; [1994] N.P.C. 97; *Times*, June 27, 1994, ECJ . . . . *Digested*, 94/**4798**: *Applied*, 00/3490, 01/3736, 07/1710
Webber v Webber [2006] EWHC 2893 (Fam); [2007] 1 W.L.R. 1052; [2007] 2 F.L.R. 116; [2007] Fam. Law 209, Fam Div . . . . *Digested*, 07/**1696**
Webster v Brunel University see Wong v Igen Ltd (formerly Leeds Careers Guidance)
Webster (A Child), Re; *sub nom* Norfolk CC v Webster [2006] EWHC 2733 (Fam); [2007] E.M.L.R. 7; [2007] 1 F.L.R. 1146; [2007] H.R.L.R. 3; [2007] Fam. Law 399, Fam Div . . . . *Digested*, 07/**1732**
Webster (A Child), Re; *sub nom* Norfolk CC v Webster [2006] EWHC 2898 (Fam); [2007] 2 F.L.R. 415; [2007] Fam. Law 907, Fam Div . . . . *Digested*, 07/**1721**
Weeks v Magill see Porter v Magill
Weetwood Services Ltd v Ansvar Holdings Ltd [2007] EWCA Civ 736; (2007) 151 S.J.L.B. 924; [2007] N.P.C. 92, CA (Civ Div)
Weigel v Finanzlandesdirektion fur Vorarlberg (C-387/01) [2004] E.C.R. I-4981; [2004] 3 C.M.L.R. 42, ECJ (6th Chamber) . . . . *Digested*, 05/**4009**: *Applied*, 07/1580, 07/1607: *Followed*, 05/4008, 07/1044
WEIGHT WATCHERS/Slimmer's calculator (T537/04) [2007] E.P.O.R. 58, EPO (Technical Bd App)
Weightman v DPP [2007] EWHC 634 (Admin); [2007] R.T.R. 45, DC . . . . *Digested*, 07/**1016**
Weill v Mean Fiddler Holdings Ltd [2003] EWCA Civ 1058, CA (Civ Div) . . . . *Applied*, 07/525
Weir v Bettison; *sub nom* Weir v Chief Constable of Merseyside [2003] EWCA Civ 111; [2003] I.C.R. 708; [2003] Po. L.R. 32; (2003) 100(12) L.S.G. 32; (2003) 147 S.J.L.B. 145; *Times*, February 4, 2003, CA (Civ Div) . . . . *Digested*, 03/**4351**: *Distinguished*, 07/4201
Weir v Chief Constable of Merseyside see Weir v Bettison
Welch v United Kingdom (17440/90) see Welch v United Kingdom (A/307-A)
Welch v United Kingdom (A/307-A); *sub nom* Welch v United Kingdom (17440/90) (1995) 20 E.H.R.R. 247; *Times*, February 15, 1995, ECHR (1993) 16 E.H.R.R. CD42, Eur Comm HR . . . . *Digested*, 95/**2650**: *Applied*, 00/1169: *Considered*, 01/1062, 01/6327, 04/3428, 07/5429: *Followed*, 03/3862: *Not followed*, 03/3710
Welford v EDF Energy Networks (LPN) Plc [2007] EWCA Civ 293; [2007] 2 P. & C.R. 15; [2007] 24 E.G. 170; [2007] R.V.R. 172; [2007] 15 E.G. 147 (C.S.); [2007] N.P.C. 40; [2007] Bus. L.R. D63; *Times*, May 8, 2007, CA (Civ Div); affirming [2006] 3 E.G.L.R. 165; [2006] R.V.R. 245, Lands Tr . . . . *Digested*, 07/**3385**
Welford Road Cemetery (Leicester), Re [2007] Fam. 15; [2007] 2 W.L.R. 506; [2007] 1 All E.R. 426; *Times*, November 2, 2006, Arches Ct; reversing [2006] Fam. 62; [2006] 2 W.L.R. 1214; *Times*, February 15, 2006, Cons Ct . . . . *Digested*, 07/**1085**
Wellcome Trust Ltd v Hamad; *joined cases* Ebied v Hopkins; Church Commissioners for England v Baines [1998] Q.B. 638; [1998] 2 W.L.R. 156; [1998] 1 All E.R. 657; (1998) 30 H.L.R. 629; [1998] L. & T.R. 130; [1998] 1 E.G.L.R. 73; [1998] 02 E.G. 121; *Times*, October 13, 1997, CA (Civ Div) . . . . *Digested*, 97/**3334**: *Applied*, 98/3682: *Considered*, 06/2708, 07/2771
Wellington v Belmarsh Prison Governor; *joined case* Wellington v United States of America [2004] EWHC 418 (Admin); [2005] Extradition L.R. 1, QBD (Admin) . *Applied*, 07/1663
Wellington v DPP [2007] EWHC 1061 (Admin); (2007) 171 J.P. 497; (2007) 171 J.P.N. 868, QBD (Admin) . . . . *Digested*, 07/**836**
Wellington v Secretary of State for Transport [2007] R.V.R. 7, Lands Tr . . . . *Digested*, 07/**3391**
Wellington v United States of America see Wellington v Belmarsh Prison Governor
Wells v Parole Board see R. (on the application of Walker) v Secretary of State for the Home Department

Wells v Secretary of State for Transport, Local Government and the Regions (C-201/02) see R. (on the application of Wells) v Secretary of State for Transport, Local Government and the Regions (C-201/02)

Wells v United Kingdom (Admissibility) (37794/05) (2007) 44 E.H.R.R. SE20, ECHR

Wells v Wells; *joined cases* Thomas v Brighton HA; Page v Sheerness Steel Co Plc [1999] 1 A.C. 345; [1998] 3 W.L.R. 329; [1998] 3 All E.R. 481; [1998] I.R.L.R. 536; [1998] 2 F.L.R. 507; [1998] P.I.Q.R. Q56; (1998) 43 B.M.L.R. 99; [1998] Fam. Law 593; (1998) 95(35) L.S.G. 35; (1998) 148 N.L.J. 1087; (1998) 142 S.J.L.B. 245; *Times*, July 20, 1998; *Independent*, July 27, 1998, HL; reversing [1997] 1 W.L.R. 652; [1997] 1 All E.R. 673; [1997] P.I.Q.R. Q1; (1997) 37 B.M.L.R. 111; (1996) 93(40) L.S.G. 25; (1996) 140 S.J.L.B. 239; *Times*, October 24, 1996; *Independent*, November 13, 1996, CA (Civ Div); reversing [1996] P.I.Q.R. Q62, QBD . . . . *Digested*, 98/**1446**:
Applied, 98/1478, 98/1573, 00/1479, 00/1503, 01/1546, 03/3125, 04/2847, 05/3072, 07/3063: *Cited*, 00/1489, 00/6430: *Considered*, 98/1474, 99/1397, 99/5671, 04/910, 04/2848, 06/3067, 07/3064: *Distinguished*, 00/1470, 01/6222: *Followed*, 97/1833, 99/1422, 99/5950, 99/5972, 99/5974, 00/1464, 00/1490, 00/1492, 00/5905, 00/6161, 00/6164, 02/928

Wells (Personal Representative of Glowacki (Deceased)) v Revenue and Customs Commissioners [2007] W.T.L.R. 1863; [2007] S.T.I. 2232, Sp Comm

Welsby v Brelec Installations Ltd (In Liquidation); *sub nom* Brelec Installations Ltd, Re [2001] B.C.C. 421; [2000] 2 B.C.L.C. 576; [2001] B.P.I.R. 210; (2000) 97(20) L.S.G. 43; *Times*, April 18, 2000, Ch D . . . . *Digested*, 00/**3491**:
Considered, 07/2422

Welsh v Secretary of State for the Home Department [2006] EWHC 156 (Admin); [2007] 1 W.L.R. 1281; [2006] 3 All E.R. 204; [2006] Extradition L.R. 31; [2006] A.C.D. 56, QBD (Admin) . . . . *Digested*, 06/**1614**:
Considered, 07/1671

Welsh v Stokes [2007] EWCA Civ 796; [2007] P.I.Q.R. P27; (2007) 157 N.L.J. 1390; (2007) 151 S.J.L.B. 1020, CA (Civ Div)

Welsh Development Agency v Redpath Dorman Long Ltd [1994] 1 W.L.R. 1409; [1994] 4 All E.R. 10; 67 B.L.R. 1; 38 Con. L.R. 106; (1994) 10 Const. L.J. 325; (1994) 91(21) L.S.G. 42; (1994) 138 S.J.L.B. 87; *Times*, April 4, 1994; *Independent*, May 2, 1994, CA (Civ Div) . . . . *Digested*, 95/**4191**:
Applied, 97/1047, 07/491: *Considered*, 96/859, 97/2719, 99/481, 05/479:
Distinguished, 96/820, 99/542

Welwyn Hatfield Council v Dimant [2007] P.A.D. 21, Planning Inspector

Wembley National Stadium Ltd v Wembley (London) Ltd [2007] EWHC 756 (Ch); [2007] L. & T.R. 36; [2007] 16 E.G. 191 (C.S.); [2007] N.P.C. 43, Ch D

Wendenburg v Germany (Admissibility) (71630/01) (2003) 36 E.H.R.R. CD154, ECHR . . . . *Considered*, 07/1944

Wermuth v Wermuth [2003] EWCA Civ 50; [2003] 1 W.L.R. 942; [2003] 4 All E.R. 531; [2003] 1 F.C.R. 289; [2003] Fam. Law 308; *Times*, February 7, 2003, CA (Civ Div) . . . . *Digested*, 03/**1585**:
Applied, 07/1772

Wesley v Kleinwort Benson (Channel Islands) Trustees Ltd see Countess Bathurst v Kleinwort Benson (Channel Islands) Trustees Ltd

West v Newham LBC [2007] EWCA Civ 304; (2007) 151 S.J.L.B. 298, CA (Civ Div)

West v Revenue and Customs Commissioners [2006] V. & D.R. 252, V&DTr (London)   *Digested*, 07/**1032**

West Berkshire Council v Revenue and Customs Commissioners see Isle of Wight Council v Revenue and Customs Commissioners

West Bromwich Albion Football Club Ltd v El-Safty [2006] EWCA Civ 1299; [2007] P.I.Q.R. P7; [2007] LS Law Medical 50; (2006) 92 B.M.L.R. 179; (2006) 103(41) L.S.G. 34; (2006) 150 S.J.L.B. 1428, CA (Civ Div); affirming [2005] EWHC 2866 (QB); [2006] Lloyd's Rep. Med. 139; (2006) 88 B.M.L.R. 196; [2006] P.N.L.R. 18, QBD . . . . *Digested*, 07/**2952**

West Mercia Safetywear Ltd (In Liquidation) v Dodd see Liquidator of West Mercia Safetywear Ltd v Dodd

West Norwood Cemetery (No.1), Re [1994] Fam. 210; [1994] 3 W.L.R. 820; [1995] 1 All E.R. 387; *Times*, April 11, 1994, Cons Ct (Southwark) . . . . *Digested*, 94/**1790**:
Applied, 06/2822: *Disapproved*, 07/1085

West Tankers Inc v RAS Riunione Adriatica di Sicurta SpA (The Front Comor) [2007] UKHL 4; [2007] 1 All E.R. (Comm) 794; [2007] 1 Lloyd's Rep. 391; [2007] I.L.Pr. 20; (2007) 23 Const. L.J. 458; (2007) 104(10) L.S.G. 30; (2007) 151 S.J.L.B. 294, HL [2005] EWHC 454 (Comm); [2005] 2 All E.R. (Comm) 240; [2005] 2 Lloyd's Rep. 257; [2005] 1 C.L.C. 347, QBD (Comm) . . . . *Digested*, 07/**352**

Westacre Investments Inc v Jugoimport SPDR Holding Co Ltd [2000] Q.B. 288; [1999] 3 W.L.R. 811; [1999] 3 All E.R. 864; [1999] 1 All E.R. (Comm) 865; [1999] 2 Lloyd's Rep. 65; [1999] C.L.C. 1176; [1999] B.L.R. 279; *Times*, May 25, 1999; *Independent*, May 25, 1999, CA (Civ Div); affirming [1999] Q.B. 740; [1998] 3 W.L.R. 770; [1998] 4 All E.R. 570; [1998] 2 Lloyd's Rep. 111; [1998] C.L.C. 409, QBD (Comm) . . . . *Digested*, 99/**236**:
Applied, 99/230, 07/242

Westdeutsche Landesbank Girozentrale v Islington LBC; *sub nom* Islington LBC v Westdeutsche Landesbank Girozentrale; *joined case* Kleinwort Benson Ltd v Sandwell BC [1996] A.C. 669; [1996] 2 W.L.R. 802; [1996] 2 All E.R. 961; [1996] 5 Bank. L.R. 341; [1996] C.L.C. 990; 95 L.G.R. 1; (1996) 160 J.P. Rep. 1130; (1996) 146 N.L.J. 877; (1996) 140 S.J.L.B. 136; *Times*, May 30, 1996, HL; reversing [1994] 1 W.L.R. 938; [1994] 4 All E.R. 890; [1994] C.L.C. 96; 92 L.G.R. 405; (1994) 158 L.G. Rev. 981; (1994) 91(8) L.S.G. 29; (1994) 138 S.J.L.B. 26; *Times*, December 30, 1993; *Independent*, January 5, 1994, CA (Civ Div); affirming 91 L.G.R. 323; *Times*, February 23, 1993, QBD . . . . *Digested*, 96/**4149**:
Applied, 98/304, 00/2320, 02/4666, 03/1421, 03/2374, 04/1932, 05/3444, 07/3438: *Considered*, 97/712, 98/1433, 02/3386, 07/2388: *Distinguished*, 95/4151, 04/480, 07/1052: *Followed*, 98/231, 99/278

Westek Ltd v Revenue and Customs Commissioners [2007] S.T.I. 2145, Sp Comm

Western Broadcasting Services v Seaga [2007] UKPC 19; [2007] E.M.L.R. 18, PC (Jam) . . . . *Digested*, 07/**523**

Western Power Distribution Investments Ltd v Countryside Council for Wales see R. (on the application of Western Power Distribution Investments Ltd) v Countryside Council for Wales

Westfalen Gassen Nederland BV v Commission of the European Communities (T-303/02) [2007] 4 C.M.L.R. 9, CFI (5th Chamber) . . . . *Digested*, 07/**605**

Westminster City Council v National Asylum Support Services see R. (on the application of Westminster City Council) v National Asylum Support Service

Westminster Renslade Ltd v Secretary of State for the Environment (1984) 48 P. & C.R. 255; [1983] J.P.L. 454; (1983) 127 S.J. 454, QBD. . . . . *Digested*, 83/**3738**:
Applied, 07/3223: *Considered*, 93/431

Weston v Gribben [2006] EWCA Civ 1425; [2007] C.P. Rep. 10; (2006) 103(44) L.S.G. 27; (2006) 150 S.J.L.B. 1463; *Independent*, November 8, 2006, CA (Civ Div) . . . . *Digested*, 07/**490**:
Doubted, 07/534

Westone Wholesale Ltd v Revenue and Customs Commissioners [2007] EWHC 2676 (Ch); [2007] S.T.I. 2810, Ch D; affirming [2007] S.T.I. 1700, V&DTr (Manchester)

Westway Homes Ltd v Moores (1992) 63 P. & C.R. 480; [1991] 2 E.G.L.R. 193; [1991] 31 E.G. 57, CA (Civ Div) . . . . *Digested*, 92/**560**:
Considered, 02/3010: *Distinguished*, 07/2755

Wetherill v Birmingham City Council; *sub nom* Birmingham City Council v Wetherill [2007] EWCA Civ 599; [2007] I.R.L.R. 781; (2007) 151 S.J.L.B. 859, CA (Civ Div) . . . . *Digested*, 07/**1329**

WF Fearman, Re (No.2) (1988) 4 B.C.C. 141, Ch D (Companies Ct) . . . . *Digested*, 88/**292**:
Applied, 07/2440: *Considered*, 88/296

WHA Ltd v Customs and Excise Commissioners [2004] EWCA Civ 559; [2004] S.T.C. 1081; [2004] B.T.C. 5425; [2004] B.V.C. 485; [2004] S.T.I. 1202, CA (Civ Div); reversing [2003] EWHC 305 (Ch); [2003] S.T.C. 648; [2003] B.T.C. 5481; [2003] B.V.C. 537; [2003] S.T.I. 298, Ch D; reversing [2002] V. & D.R. 202; [2002] S.T.I. 1235, V&DTr (London) . . . . *Digested*, 04/**3992**:
Applied, 06/5741, 07/4345: *Considered*, 07/4310, 07/4349

WHA Ltd v Revenue and Customs Commissioners [2007] EWCA Civ 728; [2007] S.T.C. 1695; [2007] B.T.C. 5748; [2007] B.V.C. 695; [2007] S.T.I. 1869, CA (Civ Div) . . . . *Digested*, 07/**4308**

Whaley v Lord Advocate see Friend v Lord Advocate

Whalley v Doney (No.2) see MDA Investment Management Ltd (No.2), Re

Wheeldon v Burrows (1879) L.R. 12 Ch. D. 31; [1874-90] All E.R. Rep. 669; (1879) 48 L.J. Ch. 853; (1879) 41 L.T. 327, CA. . . . . *Applied*, 69/1158,
00/4631, 05/3403: *Considered*, 70/823, 72/1109, 77/333, 80/93.u, 81/743, 83/224, 87/1231, 88/1181, 88/2088, 95/3740, 96/5016, 00/4640, 07/3429: *Distinguished*, 68/1313: *Followed*, 47-51/3227, 93/3007: *Not followed*, 66/4176

Whig v Whig [2007] EWHC 1856 (Fam); [2007] B.P.I.R. 1418, Fam Div

Whipps Cross University NHS Trust v Iqbal see Iqbal v Whipps Cross University Hospital NHS Trust

White v Aldridge (President of the Special Educational Needs Tribunal); *sub nom* Ealing LBC v White; White v Ealing LBC (Striking out of Second Appeal) (1999) 1 L.G.L.R. 501; [1999] Ed. C.R. 612; [1999] E.L.R. 150; *Independent*, December 14, 1998, CA (Civ Div); reversing [1999] Ed. C.R. 488; [1999] E.L.R. 58, QBD . *Digested*, 99/**1901**:
Applied, 99/1880: *Considered*, 00/1950: *Distinguished*, 01/2037, 07/1178: *Previous proceedings*, 98/1977

White v Birmingham City Council (Unreported, April 3, 2006), CC (Birmingham) [*Ex rel.* Adam Walker, Barrister, Lamb Chambers, Temple, London] . . . . *Digested*, 07/**3163**

White v Chief Adjudication Officer [1986] 2 All E.R. 905; (1986) 83 L.S.G. 1319; (1986) 130 S.J. 448, CA (Civ Div) . . . . *Digested*, 86/**3142**:
Applied, 07/3897

White v Chief Constable of South Yorkshire; *joined cases* Frost v Chief Constable of
  South Yorkshire; Duncan v British Coal Corp [1999] 2 A.C. 455; [1998] 3
  W.L.R. 1509; [1999] 1 All E.R. 1; [1999] I.C.R. 216; [1999] I.R.L.R. 110; (1999)
  45 B.M.L.R. 1; (1999) 96(2) L.S.G. 28; (1998) 148 N.L.J. 1844; (1999) 143
  S.J.L.B. 51; *Times*, December 4, 1998; *Independent*, December 9, 1998, HL;
  reversing [1998] Q.B. 254; [1997] 3 W.L.R. 1194; [1997] 1 All E.R. 540; [1997]
  I.R.L.R. 173; (1997) 33 B.M.L.R. 108; (1996) 146 N.L.J. 1651; *Times*, November
  6, 1996; *Independent*, November 5, 1996, CA (Civ Div); reversing *Times*, July 3,
  1995, QBD . . . .   *Digested*, 99/**4059**:
                       Applied, 01/4462, 03/5828, 05/2884, 06/2891: *Considered*, 97/2615,
                       00/4213, 00/4220, 02/948, 02/3307, 06/2884, 07/3063, 07/4654:
                                      Followed, 99/3980: *Referred to*, 00/6598
White v Ealing LBC (Striking out of Second Appeal) see White v Aldridge (President of
  the Special Educational Needs Tribunal)
White v Greensand Homes Ltd [2007] EWCA Civ 643; [2007] C.P. Rep. 43; [2007] 1
  C.L.C. 1001; [2007] B.L.R. 313; *Times*, July 19, 2007, CA (Civ Div) . . . .   *Digested*, 07/**348**
White v Herefordshire Council; *sub nom* Herefordshire Council v White; 83 Tower Hill,
  Upper Dormington, Hereford, Re [2007] EWCA Civ 1204; [2007] N.P.C. 126,
  CA (Civ Div); reversing [2007] R.V.R. 164, Lands Tr
White v Knowsley Housing Trust see Knowsley Housing Trust v White
White v London Fire and Civil Defence Authority see Cullin v London Fire and Civil
  Defence Authority
White v Riverside Housing Association Ltd; *sub nom* Riverside Housing Association
  Ltd v White [2007] UKHL 20; [2007] 4 All E.R. 97; [2007] H.L.R. 31; [2007] L.
  & T.R. 22; [2007] 29 E.G. 144; [2007] 18 E.G. 152 (C.S.); (2007) 104(19)
  L.S.G. 25; (2007) 151 S.J.L.B. 574; [2007] N.P.C. 46; *Times*, May 7, 2007, HL;
  reversing [2005] EWCA Civ 1385; [2006] H.L.R. 15; [2006] L. & T.R. 13;
  [2006] 1 E.G.L.R. 45; [2006] 14 E.G. 176; [2005] 50 E.G. 91 (C.S.); [2005]
  N.P.C. 142, CA (Civ Div) . . . .   *Digested*, 07/**2717**
White v Shortall (2006-07) 9 I.T.E.L.R. 470, Sup Ct (NSW) . . . .   *Digested*, 07/**813**
White v Sweden (42435/02) [2007] E.M.L.R. 1, ECHR . . . .   *Digested*, 07/**1072**
White v Weston [1968] 2 Q.B. 647; [1968] 2 W.L.R. 1459; [1968] 2 All E.R. 842;
  (1968) 112 S.J. 217, CA (Civ Div) . . . .   *Digested*, 68/**618**:
                       Considered, 81/351.u, 94/3759, 94/3768, 03/448, 07/370:
                                   Distinguished, 69/576: *Not followed*, 98/417
White & Carter (Councils) Ltd v McGregor [1962] A.C. 413; [1962] 2 W.L.R. 17; [1961]
  3 All E.R. 1178; 1962 S.C. (H.L.) 1; 1962 S.L.T. 9; (1961) 105 S.J. 1104, HL;
  reversing 1960 S.C. 276; 1961 S.L.T. 144; 1960 S.L.T. (Notes) 96, IH (2 Div) . . .   *Digested*, 62/**501**:
                       Applied, 78/2023, 83/2089, 84/3173, 03/3901: *Considered*, 71/1838,
                       77/959, 79/658, 92/2758, 96/5327, 07/2726: *Distinguished*, 68/4013,
                                            68/4013, 70/2436, 75/3163, 04/661
White (Brian) v White; *joined cases* Mighell v Reading; Evans v Motor Insurers Bureau
  [2001] UKHL 9; [2001] 1 W.L.R. 481; [2001] 2 All E.R. 43; [2001] 1 All E.R.
  (Comm) 1105; [2001] 1 Lloyd's Rep. 679; [2001] R.T.R. 25; [2001] 2 C.M.L.R. 1;
  [2001] Lloyd's Rep. I.R. 493; [2001] P.I.Q.R. P20; (2001) 98(15) L.S.G. 33;
  (2001) 151 N.L.J. 350; (2001) 145 S.J.L.B. 67; *Times*, March 6, 2001;
  Independent, April 30, 2001, HL; reversing [1999] 1 C.M.L.R. 1251; [1999] Eu.
  L.R. 389; [1999] Lloyd's Rep. I.R. 30; [1999] P.I.Q.R. P101; *Times*, October 12,
  1998, CA (Civ Div); affirming [1997] 3 C.M.L.R. 1218; *Times*, November 10,
  1997, QBD (Comm) . . . .   *Digested*, 01/**3828**:
                       Applied, 05/5054, 07/2496: *Considered*, 04/2231, 06/2426:
                                                       Followed, 03/2472
White (Pamela) v White (Martin) [2001] 1 A.C. 596; [2000] 3 W.L.R. 1571; [2001] 1
  All E.R. 1; [2000] 2 F.L.R. 981; [2000] 3 F.C.R. 555; [2001] Fam. Law 12;
  (2000) 97(43) L.S.G. 38; (2000) 150 N.L.J. 1716; (2000) 144 S.J.L.B. 266;
  [2000] N.P.C. 111; *Times*, October 31, 2000; *Independent*, November 1, 2000;
  Daily Telegraph, November 7, 2000, HL; affirming [1999] Fam. 304; [1999] 2
  W.L.R. 1213; [1998] 4 All E.R. 659; [1998] 2 F.L.R. 310; [1998] 3 F.C.R. 45;
  [1998] Fam. Law 522; *Times*, July 13, 1998; *Independent*, June 29, 1998, CA
  (Civ Div) . . . .   *Digested*, 00/**2530**:
                       Applied, 01/2634, 01/5156, 02/1678, 02/1679, 02/1682, 02/1687, 02/1690,
                       03/1581, 03/1589, 05/1656, 06/1623, 06/1626, 07/1695, 07/1700:
                       Considered, 01/2632, 01/2635, 01/2639, 03/1579, 04/1515, 04/4216,
                       05/1688, 06/1633, 06/4090, 07/1691, 07/1706: *Followed*, 01/2633
White's Application for Judicial Review, Re [2000] N.I. 432, QBD (NI) . . . .   *Digested*, 01/**5651**:
                                                                   Considered, 07/4378
Whitehead v Searle; *sub nom* Hibbert Pownall & Newton (A Firm) v Whitehead;
  HQ05X00457, CA (Civ Div); reversing in part [2007] EWHC 1060 (QB); (2007)
  151 S.J.L.B. 810, QBD
Whitehead (Valuation Officer) v Bako (UK) Ltd [2007] R.A. 236, Lands Tr
Whitehill v McDermott (Unreported, August 25, 2006), CC (Salford) [*Ex rel.* David
  Calvert, Barrister, St James's Chambers, 68 Quay Street, Manchester] . . . .   *Digested*, 07/**3120**
Whitehouse v Wilson [2006] EWCA Civ 1688; [2007] B.C.C. 595; [2007] B.P.I.R.
  230; (2007) 104(1) L.S.G. 11, CA (Civ Div) . . . .   *Digested*, 07/**2424**

Wi-Fi Alliance's Trade Mark Application (No.80831) see WISI Trade Mark
Wielockx v Inspecteur der Directe Belastingen (C-80/94) [1996] 1 W.L.R. 84; [1995]
   All E.R. (E.C.) 769; [1995] S.T.C. 876; [1995] E.C.R. I-2493; [1995] 3 C.M.L.R.
   85; *Times*, October 3, 1995, ECJ . . . . *Digested*, 95/**2786**:
              Applied, 03/4226, 05/4028, 07/4026: *Considered*, 96/3341
Wieser v Austria (2293/03) (2007) 45 E.H.R.R. 44, ECHR
Wilcox v Tait [2006] EWCA Civ 1867; [2007] 2 F.L.R. 871; [2007] 3 F.C.R. 611;
   [2007] B.P.I.R. 262; [2007] W.T.L.R. 1109; [2007] Fam. Law 988, CA (Civ
   Div). . . . . *Digested*, 07/**3359**
Wilde v Queen, The 164 C.L.R. 365, HC (Aus) . . . . *Considered*, 07/1027
Wilderbrook Ltd v Olowu; *sub nom* Wilderbrook Ltd v Oluwu [2005] EWCA Civ 1361;
   [2006] 2 P. & C.R. 4; [2005] N.P.C. 133; [2006] 1 P. & C.R. DG18, CA (Civ
   Div); affirming 4LB02223, CC (Lambeth) . . . . *Digested*, 06/**2706**:
                                  Followed, 07/2764
Wilderbrook Ltd v Oluwu see Wilderbrook Ltd v Olowu
Wildgruber v Germany (Admissibility) (32817/02) (2007) 44 E.H.R.R. SE9, ECHR
Wilf Gilbert (Staffordshire) Ltd v Revenue and Customs Commissioners [2007] S.T.I.
   2247, V&D Tr (Manchester)
Wilkes v Jessop (Unreported, January 30, 2007), CC (Dudley) [*Ex rel.* Jack Harding,
   Barrister, No.1 Chancery Lane, London] . . . . *Digested*, 07/**795**
Wilkinson v Kitzinger; *sub nom* X v Y (Overseas Same-Sex Relationship) [2006]
   EWHC 2022 (Fam); [2007] 1 F.L.R. 295; [2007] 1 F.C.R. 183; [2006] H.R.L.R.
   36; [2007] U.K.H.R.R. 164; [2006] Fam. Law 1030; (2006) 103(33) L.S.G.
   25; *Times*, August 21, 2006, Fam Div . . . . *Digested*, 06/**1714**
Wilkinson v Revenue and Customs Commissioners [2007] S.T.C. (S.C.D.) 9; [2006]
   S.T.I. 2512, Sp Comm . . . . *Digested*, 07/**4130**
Wilkinson v West Coast Capital [2005] EWHC 3009 (Ch); [2007] B.C.C. 717, Ch D
   (Companies Ct)
Willey v My Travel UK Ltd (Unreported, April 18, 2006), CC (Walsall) [*Ex rel.* Anthony
   Verduyn, Barrister, St Phillips Chambers, 55 Temple Row, Birmingham]. . . . . . . *Digested*, 07/**3209**
William Grant & Sons Distillers Ltd v Inland Revenue Commissioners see Revenue and
   Customs Commissioners v William Grant & Sons Distillers Ltd (Scotland)
William Grant & Sons Ltd v Devlin EATS/0074/03, EAT . . . . *Followed*, 07/1432
William Morton & Co v Muir Bros & Co 1907 S.C. 1211; (1907) 15 S.L.T. 252; (1907) 44
   S.L.R. 885, IH (Ex Div). . . . . *Applied*, 68/4633,
                        92/5952: *Considered*, 07/3568
Williams, Re; *sub nom* Williams v Williams [1912] 1 Ch. 399, Ch D . . . . *Applied*, 07/4255
Williams v Birmingham City Council [2007] EWCA Civ 691; (2007) 104(26) L.S.G.
   30; (2007) 151 S.J.L.B. 808, CA (Civ Div)
Williams v Blaenau Gwent BC (1994) 67 P. & C.R. 393; [1994] 2 E.G.L.R. 201;
   [1994] 40 E.G. 139; [1996] R.V.R. 21, Lands Tr . . . . *Digested*, 95/**668**:
                                    Applied, 07/3418
Williams v Fawcett [1986] Q.B. 604; [1985] 1 W.L.R. 501; [1985] 1 All E.R. 787;
   [1986] Fam. Law 52; (1985) 135 N.L.J. 227; (1985) 129 S.J. 224, CA (Civ
   Div). . . . . *Digested*, 85/**471**:
       Applied, 07/4298: *Considered*, 86/458, 87/2927, 87/2930, 90/3162, 92/389:
                               Distinguished, 86/456
Williams v Hensman 70 E.R. 862; (1861) 1 John. & H. 546, QB . . . . *Applied*, 80/2256,
       07/3963: *Considered*, 55/2537, 73/3487, 85/2944, 95/2364
Williams v Inspector of Taxes see Locabail (UK) Ltd v Bayfield Properties Ltd (Leave
   to Appeal)
Williams v Pritchard see Pritchard (A Bankrupt), Re
Williams v Richmond Court (Swansea) Ltd see Richmond Court (Swansea) Ltd v
   Williams
Williams v Sandy Lane (Chester) Ltd [2006] EWCA Civ 1738; [2007] 1 P. & C.R. 27;
   [2007] 7 E.G. 144; [2007] 2 E.G. 125 (C.S.); *Times*, January 5, 2007, CA (Civ
   Div). . . . . *Digested*, 07/**3428**
Williams v Secretary of State for the Home Department see R. (on the application of
   Williams) v Secretary of State for the Home Department
Williams v Southampton Institute see Dunnachie v Kingston upon Hull City Council
Williams v University of Nottingham [2007] I.R.L.R. 660, EAT . . . . *Digested*, 07/**1355**
Williams v Williams see Williams, Re
Williams v Williams (1881-82) L.R. 20 Ch. D. 659, Ch D . . . . *Applied*, 07/1972
Williams v Wirral BC 79 L.G.R. 697; [1981] R.A. 189; (1981) 125 S.J. 398, CA (Civ
   Div). . . . . *Digested*, 82/**2652**:
                  Applied, 04/2605, 07/2841: *Considered*, 07/2842
Williams (Valuation Officer) v Scottish & Newcastle Retail Ltd; *sub nom* Scottish &
   Newcastle Retail Ltd v Williams (Valuation Officer); *joined case* Allied Domecq
   Retailing Ltd v Williams (Valuation Officer) [2001] EWCA Civ 185; [2001] 1
   E.G.L.R. 157; [2001] R.A. 41; [2001] 9 E.G. 227 (C.S.); (2001) 98(19) L.S.G. 37;
   [2001] N.P.C. 46; *Times*, March 6, 2001; *Independent*, February 21, 2001, CA
   (Civ Div); affirming [2000] 2 E.G.L.R. 171; [2000] R.A. 119, Lands Tr . . . . *Digested*, 01/**4833**:
      Applied, 01/4834, 03/3497, 03/3498, 07/3349: *Considered*, 03/3528:
                                 Followed, 03/3516

Williamson v Secretary of State for Education and Employment see R. (on the application of Williamson) v Secretary of State for Education and Employment

Willingale v Global Grange Ltd see Willingale v Globalgrange Ltd

Willingale v Globalgrange Ltd; *sub nom* Willingale v Global Grange Ltd (2001) 33 H.L.R. 17; (2000) 80 P. & C.R. 448; [2000] L. & T.R. 549; [2000] 2 E.G.L.R. 55; [2000] 18 E.G. 152; (2000) 97(12) L.S.G. 44; (2000) 80 P. & C.R. D12; *Times*, March 29, 2000; *Independent*, April 17, 2000, CA (Civ Div). . . . .   *Digested*, 00/**3899**:   *Applied*, 07/3368: *Considered*, 05/3386

Willis v Nicolson [2007] EWCA Civ 199; [2007] C.P. Rep. 24; [2007] P.I.Q.R. P22; (2007) 104(13) L.S.G. 26; (2007) 151 S.J.L.B. 394, CA (Civ Div) . . . .   *Digested*, 07/**385**

Willis v United Kingdom (36042/97) [2002] 2 F.L.R. 582; [2002] 2 F.C.R. 743; (2002) 35 E.H.R.R. 21; [2002] Fam. Law 661, ECHR. . . . .   *Digested*, 03/**2176**:   *Applied*, 06/2184, 07/2208

Willis v Vauxhall Centre (Unreported, November 1, 2006), CC (Central London) [*Ex rel.* Colm Nugent, Barrister, Hardwicke Building, New Square, Lincoln's Inn, London] . . . .   *Digested*, 07/**3122**

Willoughby v Eckstein [1937] Ch. 167, Ch D . . . .   *Considered*, 07/2757

Wills v Gibbs [2007] EWHC 3361 (Ch); [2007] S.T.I. 1970, Ch D

Willson v Ministry of Defence; *sub nom* Wilson v Ministry of Defence [2007] EWCA Civ 485; (2007) 151 S.J.L.B. 675, CA (Civ Div)

Wilson v Burnett [2007] EWCA Civ 1170; (2007) 151 S.J.L.B. 1399, CA (Civ Div)

Wilson v Commissioner of Valuation [2006] R.V.R. 335, Lands Tr (NI) . . . .   *Digested*, 07/**4705**

Wilson v First County Trust Ltd (No.2); *sub nom* Wilson v Secretary of State for Trade and Industry [2003] UKHL 40; [2004] 1 A.C. 816; [2003] 3 W.L.R. 568; [2003] 4 All E.R. 97; [2003] 2 All E.R. (Comm) 491; [2003] H.R.L.R. 33; [2003] U.K.H.R.R. 1085; (2003) 100(35) L.S.G. 39; (2003) 147 S.J.L.B. 872; *Times*, July 11, 2003; *Independent*, November 3, 2003, HL; reversing [2001] EWCA Civ 633; [2002] Q.B. 74; [2001] 3 W.L.R. 42; [2001] 3 All E.R. 229; [2001] 2 All E.R. (Comm) 134; [2001] E.C.C. 37; [2001] H.R.L.R. 44; [2001] U.K.H.R.R. 1175; (2001) 98(24) L.S.G. 44; (2001) 145 S.J.L.B. 125; *Times*, May 16, 2001; *Independent*, May 8, 2001; *Daily Telegraph*, May 8, 2001, CA (Civ Div) . . . .   *Digested*, 04/**628**:   *Applied*, 01/2315, 04/2222, 05/190, 05/672, 05/1410, 05/3376, 06/2735:   *Considered*, 01/100, 01/3504, 04/1312, 04/3581, 05/17: *Followed*, 07/3293

Wilson v Jaymarke Estates Ltd [2007] UKHL 29; 2007 S.C. (H.L.) 135; 2007 S.L.T. 958; 2007 S.C.L.R. 712; [2007] B.C.C. 883; (2007) 151 S.J.L.B. 854; 2007 G.W.D. 26-450; *Times*, June 28, 2007, HL; affirming 2006 S.C.L.R. 510, IH (1 Div); affirming 2002 G.W.D. 28-962, Sh Ct (Grampian) . . . .   *Digested*, 07/**4976**

Wilson v Ministry of Defence see Willson v Ministry of Defence

Wilson v Ordre des Avocats du Barreau de Luxembourg (C-506/04) [2007] All E.R. (EC) 403; [2006] E.C.R. I-8613; [2007] 1 C.M.L.R. 7; [2006] C.E.C. 1060; *Times*, October 6, 2006, ECJ . . . .   *Digested*, 07/**2798**

Wilson v Secretary of State for Trade and Industry see Wilson v First County Trust Ltd (No.2)

Wilson v Specter Partnership; *sub nom* Wilson Properties UK Ltd, Re [2007] EWHC 133 (Ch); [2007] 5 Costs L.R. 802; [2007] B.P.I.R. 649, Ch D . . . .   *Digested*, 07/**2460**

Wilson v Wychavon DC see R. (on the application of Wilson) v Wychavon DC

Wilson Properties UK Ltd, Re see Wilson v Specter Partnership

Wiluszynski v Tower Hamlets LBC [1989] I.C.R. 493; [1989] I.R.L.R. 259; 88 L.G.R. 14; (1989) 133 S.J. 628; *Times*, April 24, 1989, CA (Civ Div); reversing . . . .   *Digested*, 90/**1857.a**:   *Applied*, 07/1436: *Distinguished*, 89/1411

Winchester City Council v Handcock (Valuation Officer) [2006] R.A. 265, Lands Tr . . .   *Digested*, 07/**3345**

Winchester City Council v Secretary of State for Communities and Local Government [2007] EWHC 2303 (Admin); (2007) 104(38) L.S.G. 32, QBD (Admin)

Winchester City Council v Steele [2007] P.A.D. 12, Planning Inspector

Windsor and Maidenhead RLBC v Tom Jones Boatbuilders Ltd [2007] P.A.D. 76, Planning Inspector

Windsurfing International Inc v Tabur Marine (Great Britain) Ltd [1985] R.P.C. 59, CA (Civ Div) . . . .   *Applied*, 92/**3291**,   92/3319, 93/3041, 95/3758, 95/3777, 95/3778, 96/4568, 97/3902, 98/3477,   99/3506, 99/3519, 00/3639, 01/3902, 02/2816, 02/2840, 04/2273, 04/2308,   04/2341, 04/2346, 05/2481, 06/2503, 06/2530, 06/2531, 06/5538:   *Considered*, 94/2766, 95/3757, 01/3963, 02/2845, 03/5748, 04/2340,   07/2620: *Followed*, 96/4543, 97/3901, 00/3678, 01/3967:   *Referred to*, 94/3438, 99/3480, 99/3514

Wine Oh! LLC's Community Trade Mark Application (R1074/2005-4) [2006] E.T.M.R. 95, OHIM (4th Bd App) . . . .   *Digested*, 07/**2643**

Wingett v Knightsbridge (Unreported, January 19, 2007), CC (Croydon) [*Ex rel.* David McHugh, Barrister, Equity House, Blackbrook Park Avenue, Taunton] . . . .   *Digested*, 07/**3155**

Wingrove v United Kingdom (17419/90) (1997) 24 E.H.R.R. 1; 1 B.H.R.C. 509; *Times*, December 5, 1996; *Independent*, November 28, 1996, ECHR (1994) 18 E.H.R.R. CD54, Eur Comm HR . . . .   *Digested*, 96/**3143**:   *Applied*, 07/2187, 07/2189: *Considered*, 05/692: *Referred to*, 01/3479

Winter v First Secretary of State [2006] EWHC 491 (Admin); [2007] J.P.L. 250, QBD
(Admin) . . . . *Digested,* 07/**3277**
Winter v Traditional & Contemporary Contracts Ltd [2006] EWCA Civ 1740; [2007] 2
All E.R. 343; [2007] R.V.R. 122; [2007] 3 E.G. 124 (C.S.), CA (Civ Div). . . . . *Digested,* 07/**413**
Winter v Traditional & Contemporary Contracts Ltd [2007] EWCA Civ 1088; [2007]
R.V.R. 353; [2007] 46 E.G. 177 (C.S.); (2007) 104(45) L.S.G. 30; [2007] N.P.C.
117, CA (Civ Div)
Winters v Haq (Unreported, May 25, 2007), QBD [*Ex rel.* Andrew Ritchie, 9 Gough
Square, London] . . . . *Digested,* 07/**3176**
Winterwerp v Netherlands (A/33) (1979-80) 2 E.H.R.R. 387, ECHR . . . . *Digested,* 81/**1089**:
　　　　　　　　　　　　Applied, 04/2686, 06/2160, 06/5461, 07/2197: *Considered,* 02/3239:
　　　　　　　　　　　　　　　　　　　　　　　　　　　　　　　　　　　　Distinguished, 00/3171
Wippel v Peek & Cloppenburg GmbH & Co KG (C-313/02) [2004] E.C.R. I-9483;
[2005] 1 C.M.L.R. 9; [2005] I.C.R. 1604; [2005] I.R.L.R. 211, ECJ . . . . *Digested,* 05/**1197**:
　　　　　　　　　　　　　　　　　　　　　　　　　　　　　　　　　Applied, 06/1347, 07/1386
Wise v Metcalfe 109 E.R. 461; (1829) 10 B. & C. 299, KB . . . . *Followed,* 07/**1082**
WISI Trade Mark; *sub nom* Wi-Fi Alliance's Trade Mark Application (No.80831) [2007]
E.T.M.R. 5; [2006] R.P.C. 22, App Person . . . . *Applied,* 06/**2612**
Withers v Delaney (C-158/01) [2002] E.C.R. I-8301, ECJ . . . . *Applied,* 07/**1565**
Witkowska v Kaminski [2006] EWHC 1940 (Ch); [2007] 1 F.L.R. 1547; [2006] 3
F.C.R. 250; [2006] W.T.L.R. 1293; [2007] Fam. Law 115, Ch D . . . . *Digested,* 06/**4086**
Witt v Germany (Admissibility) (18397/03) (2007) 44 E.H.R.R. SE21, ECHR
Wittmann (UK) Ltd v Willdav Engineering SA [2007] EWCA Civ 824; [2007] B.L.R.
509, CA (Civ Div) . . . . *Digested,* 07/**310**
WJ Tatem Ltd v Gamboa [1939] 1 K.B. 132; (1938) 61 Ll. L. Rep. 149, KBD . . . . *Considered,* 07/**3815**
WK (Article 8: Expulsion Cases: Review of Case Law: Palestinian Territories), Re see WK
(Palestinian Territories) v Secretary of State for the Home Department
WK (Palestinian Territories) v Secretary of State for the Home Department; *sub nom*
WK (Article 8: Expulsion Cases: Review of Case Law: Palestinian Territories), Re
[2006] UKAIT 70; [2007] Imm. A.R. 115, AIT . . . . *Digested,* 07/**2301**
WM (Democratic Republic of Congo) v Secretary of State for the Home Department;
joined case Secretary of State for the Home Department v AR (Afghanistan)
[2006] EWCA Civ 1495; [2007] Imm. A.R. 337; [2007] I.N.L.R. 126; (2006)
103(45) L.S.G. 27; *Times,* December 1, 2006, CA (Civ Div) . . . . *Digested,* 07/**2295**
Wolfe v Hogan [1949] 2 K.B. 194; [1949] 1 All E.R. 570; 35 T.L.R. 525, CA . . . . *Digested,* 47-51/**8608**:
　　　　　　　　　Applied, 47-51/8501, 47-51/8539, 47-51/8673, 53/3156, 58/2916, 69/3075:
　　　　　　　　　　　　Considered, 47-51/7450, 68/2168, 82/29, 83/2121, 89/2169, 89/2171,
　　　　　　　　　　　　　　　　　　　　　　　　　　　　　　　　　97/2689, 07/2771
Wolman v Islington LBC [2007] EWCA Civ 823; (2007) 104(32) L.S.G. 24; *Times,*
August 20, 2007, CA (Civ Div) . . . . *Digested,* 07/**3495**
Wolsey Theatre Co Ltd, Re [2001] B.C.C. 486, Ch D . . . . *Digested,* 02/**2651**:
　　　　　　　　　　　　　　　　　　　　　　　　Applied, 03/2391: *Considered,* 07/2395
Wolverhampton City Council v Special Educational Needs and Disability Tribunal
[2007] EWHC 1117 (Admin); [2007] E.L.R. 418; *Times,* May 25, 2007, QBD
(Admin) . . . . *Digested,* 07/**1258**
Wong v Igen Ltd (formerly Leeds Careers Guidance); *sub nom* Chamberlin Solicitors v
Emokpae; Brunel University v Webster; Igen Ltd (formerly Leeds Careers
Guidance) v Wong; *joined cases* Webster v Brunel University; Emokpae v
Chamberlin Solicitors [2005] EWCA Civ 142; [2005] 3 All E.R. 812; [2005]
I.C.R. 931; [2005] I.R.L.R. 258; (2005) 102(13) L.S.G. 28; (2005) 149 S.J.L.B.
264; *Times,* March 3, 2005, CA (Civ Div); affirming UKEAT/0944/03/RN, EAT. *Digested,* 05/**1221**:
　　　　　　　　　　Applied, 06/1349, 06/1354, 06/1368, 07/1184, 07/1401: *Considered,* 07/1388,
　　　　　　　　　　　　　　　　　　　　　　　　　　　　　　　　　　　　　　　07/1433
Wong v Parkside Health NHS Trust [2001] EWCA Civ 1721; [2003] 3 All E.R. 932;
(2002) 99(2) L.S.G. 28; (2001) 145 S.J.L.B. 276; *Times,* December 7, 2001;
Independent, November 27, 2001, CA (Civ Div) . . . . *Digested,* 01/**5353**:
　　　　　　　　　　　　　　　　　　　　　　　　　　　　　　　　　　　　Applied, 07/4200
Woningen v Netherlands (20641/92) (1997) 24 E.H.R.R. 456, ECHR (1995) 20
E.H.R.R. CD1, Eur Comm HR. . . . . *Digested,* 98/**3120**:
　　　　　　　　　　　　　　　　　　　　　　　　　　　　　　　　　　　　Applied, 07/2214
Wood v Holden (Inspector of Taxes); *sub nom* R v Holden (Inspector of Taxes) [2006]
EWCA Civ 26; [2006] 1 W.L.R. 1393; [2006] S.T.C. 443; [2006] 2 B.C.L.C.
210; 78 T.C. 1; [2006] B.T.C. 208; 8 I.T.L. Rep. 468; [2006] S.T.I. 236; (2006)
150 S.J.L.B. 127; *Times,* February 20, 2006, CA (Civ Div); affirming [2005]
EWHC 547 (Ch); [2005] S.T.C. 789; [2005] B.T.C. 253; 7 I.T.L. Rep. 725;
[2005] S.T.I. 801; *Times,* May 10, 2005, Ch D [2004] S.T.C. (S.C.D.) 416;
[2004] S.T.I. 1868, Sp Comm . . . . *Digested,* 06/**4118**:
　　　　　　　　　　　　　　　　　　　　　　　　　　　　　　　　　Considered, 07/4006
Wood v Light (Unreported, January 16, 2007), CC (Brighton) [*Ex rel.* Nicholas J H
Preston, Barrister, Clerksroom, 218 Strand, London] . . . . *Digested,* 07/**3114**
Wood v Revenue and Customs Commissioners see Revenue and Customs
Commissioners v Wood
Wood v Rost [2007] EWHC 1511 (Fam); [2007] 2 F.C.R. 728, Fam Div. . . . . *Digested,* 07/**1690**

Wood Pulp Cartel, Re (C89/85) see A Ahlstrom Osakeyhtio v Commission of the European Communities (C89/85)

WoodHouse UK Plc v Architectural Lighting Systems (t/a Aquila Design) [2006] E.C.D.R. 11; [2006] R.P.C. 1; (2006) 29(1) I.P.D. 29008, PCC . . . . *Digested*, 06/**2461**: *Applied*, 07/2536

Woodman v French Connection Ltd; *sub nom* FCUK Trade Mark; French Connection Ltd's Trade Mark Application (No.81862) [2007] E.T.M.R. 8; [2007] R.P.C. 1, App Person; affirming (Unreported, December 20, 2005), TMR . . . . *Digested*, 06/**2583**

Woods v WM Car Services (Peterborough) Ltd [1982] Com. L.R. 208; [1982] I.C.R. 693; [1982] I.R.L.R. 413, CA (Civ Div); affirming [1981] I.C.R. 666; [1981] I.R.L.R. 347; *Times*, June 24, 1981, EAT . . . . *Digested*, 83/**1204**: *Applied*, 91/1612, 91/2725, 91/2725, 04/1196, 07/1320: *Considered*, 84/1194, 99/838, 99/838, 03/1221

Woods (Inspector of Taxes) v Lightpower Ltd [2005] EWHC 1799 (Ch); [2006] S.T.C. 759; 77 T.C. 641; [2007] B.T.C. 224; [2005] S.T.I. 1169, Ch D . . . . *Digested*, 06/**4209**: *Applied*, 06/4136

Woolfe v DPP [2006] EWHC 1497 (Admin); [2007] R.T.R. 16, DC . . . . *Digested*, 07/**845**: *Followed*, 07/882

Woolwich Equitable Building Society v Inland Revenue Commissioners [1993] A.C. 70; [1992] 3 W.L.R. 366; [1992] 3 All E.R. 737; [1992] S.T.C. 657; (1993) 5 Admin. L.R. 265; 65 T.C. 265; (1992) 142 N.L.J. 1196; (1992) 136 S.J.L.B. 230; *Times*, July 22, 1992; *Independent*, August 13, 1992; *Guardian*, August 19, 1992, HL; affirming [1991] 3 W.L.R. 790; [1991] 4 All E.R. 577; [1991] S.T.C. 364; (1991) 135 S.J.L.B. 46; *Times*, May 27, 1991, CA (Civ Div); reversing [1989] 1 W.L.R. 137; [1989] S.T.C. 111; (1989) 133 S.J. 291, QBD . . . . *Digested*, 92/**2508**: *Applied*, 94/4567, 07/3438: *Considered*, 94/3900, 94/6018, 05/4129, 06/4141, 07/3973: *Distinguished*, 96/5578, 01/5024: *Followed*, 97/1735

Wootton Trucks Ltd v Man ERF UK Ltd [2006] EWCA Civ 1042; [2007] R.T.R. 19; [2006] Eu. L.R. 1217, CA (Civ Div); reversing [2006] EWHC 943 (Ch); [2006] Eu. L.R. 967, Ch D . . . . *Digested*, 07/**817**

World Marine & General Insurances Pty Ltd, Re see HIH Casualty & General Insurance Ltd, Re

Worth v McKenna see Hollins v Russell

Worthing BC v Hayhoe [2007] P.A.D. 8, Planning Inspector

Wos v Poland (22860/02) (2007) 45 E.H.R.R. 28, ECHR

Wotherspoon (John Maxwell) v HM Advocate 1978 J.C. 74, HCJ . . . . *Digested*, 80/**3180**: *Applied*, 07/2075

Wouters v Algemene Raad van de Nederlandse Orde van Advocaten (C309/99) [2002] All E.R. (EC) 193; [2002] E.C.R. I-1577; [2002] 4 C.M.L.R. 27; [2002] C.E.C. 250, ECJ . . . . *Applied*, 07/623: *Considered*, 06/583: *Distinguished*, 05/3963,

WPP Holdings Italy Srl v Benatti; *sub nom* Benatti v WPP Holdings Italy Srl [2007] EWCA Civ 263; [2007] 1 W.L.R. 2316; [2007] 2 All E.R. (Comm) 525; [2007] 1 C.L.C. 324; [2007] I.L.Pr. 33; (2007) 104(15) L.S.G. 21; *Times*, April 16, 2007, CA (Civ Div); reversing in part [2006] EWHC 1641 (Comm); [2007] 1 All E.R. (Comm) 208; [2006] 2 Lloyd's Rep. 610; [2006] 2 C.L.C. 142, QBD (Comm) . . . . *Digested*, 07/**664**

Wren v Gramegna see Wren v Wren

Wren v Wren; *joined case* Wren v Gramegna [2006] EWHC 2243 (Ch); [2006] 3 F.C.R. 18; [2007] W.T.L.R. 531; (2006-07) 9 I.T.E.L.R. 223; (2006) 103(37) L.S.G. 30, Ch D . . . . *Digested*, 06/**4102**

Wrexham Associated Football Club Ltd (In Administration) v Crucialmove Ltd [2006] EWCA Civ 237; [2007] B.C.C. 139, CA (Civ Div); affirming (Unreported, October 20, 2005), Ch D . . . . *Digested*, 07/**574**

Wrexham CBC v Berry see South Buckinghamshire DC v Porter (No.1)

Wright v MGN Pension Trustees Ltd [2007] EWCA Civ 1247; (2007) 104(45) L.S.G. 29, CA (Civ Div)

Wright v North Norfolk DC [2007] P.A.D. 35, Planning Inspector

Wright v Paton Farrell [2006] CSIH 7; 2006 S.C. 404; 2006 S.L.T. 269; 2006 S.C.L.R. 371; [2007] P.N.L.R. 7; 2006 G.W.D. 8-139, IH (1 Div); reversing 2002 S.C.L.R. 1039; [2003] P.N.L.R. 20; 2002 G.W.D. 28-988, OH . . . . *Digested*, 06/**5562**

Wrigley v Lord (Unreported, July 16, 2007), CC (Oldham) [*Ex rel.* David Calvert, Barrister, St James's Chambers, 68 Quay Street, Manchester] . . . . *Digested*, 07/**3096**

Wroblewski v Poland (76299/01) [2006] 3 F.C.R. 739, ECHR . . . . *Digested*, 07/**2220**

Wrotham Park Estate Co Ltd v Parkside Homes Ltd [1974] 1 W.L.R. 798; [1974] 2 All E.R. 321; (1974) 27 P. & C.R. 296; (1973) 118 S.J. 420, Ch D . . . . *Digested*, 74/**3130**: *Applied*, 75/1017, 06/1018, 07/1054: *Considered*, 86/2827, 87/1227, 88/2729, 92/1513, 93/427, 95/2968, 95/3766, 98/4341, 03/717: *Distinguished*, 87/3654, 93/1368: *Explained*, 89/3422

WWF Italia v Lombardy (C-60/05) [2007] Env. L.R. D1, ECJ (2nd Chamber)

WWF World Wide Fund for Nature (formerly World Wildlife Fund) v Moniker Online Services LLC [2007] E.T.M.R. 21, Arbitration . . . . *Digested*, 07/**2540**

WWF World Wide Fund for Nature (formerly World Wildlife Fund) *v* World Wrestling
    Federation Entertainment Inc [2007] EWCA Civ 286; [2007] Bus. L.R. 1252,
    CA (Civ Div); reversing in part [2006] EWHC 184 (Ch); [2006] F.S.R. 38;
    (2006) 150 S.J.L.B. 263, Ch D . . . .   *Digested,* 07/**1054**
Wyatt (A Child) (Medical Treatment: Continuation of Order), Re see Portsmouth NHS Trust
    v Wyatt
Wynn-Jones *v* Bickley [2006] EWHC 1991 (Ch), Ch D . . . .   *Considered,* 07/1060
Wynn's Will Trusts, Re (No.1); *sub nom* Public Trustee *v* Baron Newborough [1952] Ch.
    271; [1952] 1 All E.R. 341; [1952] 1 T.L.R. 278; (1952) 96 S.J. 120, Ch D . . . . .   *Digested,* 52/**3648**:
        Applied, 07/4255
Wynne *v* Tempest [1897] 1 Ch. 110, Ch D . . . .   *Applied,* 07/4248

X, Re; *sub nom* Barnet LBC *v* Y [2006] 2 F.L.R. 998; [2006] Fam. Law 740, CC
    (Barnet) . . . .   *Digested,* 07/**1718**
X *v* Persons Unknown [2006] EWHC 2783 (QB); [2007] E.M.L.R. 10; [2007] 1
    F.L.R. 1567; [2007] 3 F.C.R. 223; [2007] H.R.L.R. 4, QBD . . . .   *Digested,* 07/**2183**
X *v* Secretary of State for the Home Department see A *v* Secretary of State for the
    Home Department
X *v* United Kingdom (Unreported, November 5, 1981), ECHR [*Ex rel.* Irwin Mitchell &
    Co, Solicitors] . . . .   *Digested,* 82/**1483**:
        Considered, 07/2907
X *v* Y (Overseas Same-Sex Relationship) see Wilkinson *v* Kitzinger
X City Council *v* MB [2006] EWHC 168 (Fam); [2006] 2 F.L.R. 968; [2007] 3 F.C.R.
    371; [2006] Fam. Law 637, Fam Div . . . .   *Digested,* 07/**1833**
X Council *v* B (Emergency Protection Orders) see X Local Authority *v* B (Emergency
    Protection Orders)
X Local Authority *v* B (Emergency Protection Orders); *sub nom* X Council *v* B
    (Emergency Protection Orders); B (Children) (Emergency Protection Orders), Re
    [2004] EWHC 2015 (Fam); [2005] 1 F.L.R. 341; [2007] 1 F.C.R. 512; [2005]
    Fam. Law 13, Fam Div . . . .   *Digested,* 05/**1530**:
        Applied, 06/1676
X Ltd *v* Morgan Grampian (Publishers) Ltd [1991] 1 A.C. 1; [1990] 2 W.L.R. 1000;
    [1990] 2 All E.R. 1; (1990) 87(17) L.S.G. 28; (1990) 140 N.L.J. 553; (1990) 134
    S.J. 546, HL; affirming [1990] 2 W.L.R. 421; [1990] 1 All E.R. 616; (1990) 140
    N.L.J. 17; (1990) 134 S.J. 861, CA (Civ Div); affirming [1990] 1 All E.R. 608;
    (1989) 139 N.L.J. 1634, Ch D . . . .   *Digested,* 90/**3698**:
        Applied, 97/2780, 99/16, 07/241: *Considered,* 96/3145, 02/415, 07/1698:
        Followed, 96/23
X Trust Co Ltd *v* RW; *sub nom* H Trust, Re [2007] W.T.L.R. 677; (2006-07) 9 I.T.E.L.R.
    133, Royal Ct (Jer) . . . .   *Digested,* 07/**4262**
X (A Child), Re; *sub nom* X (Emergency Protection Orders), Re [2006] EWHC 510
    (Fam); [2006] 2 F.L.R. 701; [2007] 1 F.C.R. 551; [2006] Fam. Law 627; *Times,*
    April 21, 2006, Fam Div . . . .   *Digested,* 06/**1676**
X (Emergency Protection Orders), Re see X (A Child), Re
X (Minors) *v* Bedfordshire CC; *joined cases* M (A Minor) *v* Newham LBC; E (A Minor)
    v Dorset CC (Appeal); Christmas *v* Hampshire CC (Duty of Care); Keating *v*
    Bromley LBC (No.2) [1995] 2 A.C. 633; [1995] 3 W.L.R. 152; [1995] 3 All E.R.
    353; [1995] 2 F.L.R. 276; [1995] 3 F.C.R. 337; 94 L.G.R. 313; (1995) 7
    Admin. L.R. 705; [1995] Fam. Law 537; (1996) 160 L.G. Rev. 103; (1996) 160
    L.G. Rev. 123; (1995) 145 N.L.J. 993; *Times,* June 30, 1995; *Independent,* June
    30, 1995, HL; affirming [1994] 2 W.L.R. 554; [1994] 4 All E.R. 602; [1994] 1
    F.L.R. 431; 92 L.G.R. 427; [1994] Fam. Law 434; (1994) 144 N.L.J. 357; *Times,*
    March 3, 1994; *Independent,* February 24, 1994; *Guardian,* February 28, 1994,
    CA (Civ Div); affirming [1993] 2 F.L.R. 575; [1994] P.I.Q.R. P515; [1993] Fam.
    Law 575; (1993) 143 N.L.J. 1783; *Times,* November 24, 1993; *Independent,*
    December 23, 1993, QBD . . . .   *Digested,* 95/**3452**:
        Applied, 98/2570, 98/3935, 98/3944, 98/3945, 99/1765, 99/3968,
        99/5435, 00/5662, 01/4470, 03/364, 05/976: *Considered,* 96/4140,
        96/4441, 97/2692, 97/2879, 97/3775, 98/3931, 98/3937, 98/3942,
        99/1889, 99/5434, 03/1118, 03/3004, 07/2937: *Distinguished,* 99/3966,
        05/2858: *Doubted,* 00/1947: *Followed,* 96/3913, 97/424, 97/2142, 97/4087,
        97/4860, 98/1965, 99/3967: *Previous proceedings,* 95/1927:
        Remitting to, 98/3943: *Subsequent related litigation,* 95/3452
X, Y and Z *v* United Kingdom (21830/93) [1997] 2 F.L.R. 892; [1997] 3 F.C.R. 341;
    (1997) 24 E.H.R.R. 143; (1998) 39 B.M.L.R. 128; [1997] Fam. Law 605; (1997)
    94(17) L.S.G. 25; *Times,* April 23, 1997; *Independent,* April 24, 1997, ECHR
    (1995) 20 E.H.R.R. CD6, Eur Comm HR . . . .   *Digested,* 97/**2822**:
        Applied, 07/2260: *Considered,* 02/914
X/Polysuccinate esters (G01/89 and G02/89) [1991] E.P.O.R. 239, EPO (Enlarged Bd
    App) . . . .   *Applied,* 07/**2593**:
        Followed, 00/3597
X/Same invention (G2/98) [2002] E.P.O.R. 17, EPO (Enlarged Bd App) . . . .   *Digested,* 03/**2567**:
        Applied, 07/2564: *Considered,* 03/2575: *Distinguished,* 04/2301

Xenides-Arestis v Turkey (46347/99) (2007) 44 E.H.R.R. SE13, ECHR
XL Insurance Ltd v Owens Corning [2001] 1 All E.R. (Comm) 530; [2000] 2 Lloyd's
    Rep. 500; [2001] C.P. Rep. 22; [2001] C.L.C. 914, QBD (Comm) . . . .   *Digested,* 00/**786**:
                  Applied, 07/353

XXX SA, Re 9 I.T.L. Rep. 176, C d'A (L)
XXX/Exclusion and objection (G1/05) [2007] E.P.O.R. 17, EPO (Enlarged Bd App) . . .   *Digested,* 07/**2558**
Xydhias v Xydhias [1999] 2 All E.R. 386; [1999] 1 F.L.R. 683; [1999] 1 F.C.R. 289;
    [1999] Fam. Law 301; (1999) 96(6) L.S.G. 34; (1999) 149 N.L.J. 52; *Times,*
    January 13, 1999; *Independent,* January 21, 1999, CA (Civ Div) . . . .   *Digested,* 99/**2416**:
                  Applied, 07/1709

Y v Union Bancaire du Nord (UBN) [2007] E.C.C. 30, Cass (F)
Y (Kevin Raymond) v Catholic Care (Diocese of Leeds) see Catholic Care (Diocese of
    Leeds) v Y (Kevin Raymond)
Y (Kevin Raymond) v South Tyneside MBC see Catholic Care (Diocese of Leeds) v Y
    (Kevin Raymond)
Yagci v Turkey (A/319); *joined case* Sargin v Turkey (A/319) (1995) 20 E.H.R.R. 505;
    Times, June 26, 1995, ECHR. . . . .   *Digested,* 96/**3134**:
         Applied, 07/2230: *Considered,* 97/2771: *Followed,* 98/3073
Yanah v General Medical Council [2006] EWHC 3843 (Admin); [2007] LS Law
    Medical 143, QBD (Admin) . . . .   *Digested,* 07/**1954**
Yanko-Weiss Holdings (1996) Ltd v Holon Assessing Office 10 I.T.L. Rep. 524, District
    Ct (Tel Aviv)
Yankov v Bulgaria (39084/97) (2005) 40 E.H.R.R. 36; 15 B.H.R.C. 592; [2004]
    Prison L.R. 424, ECHR . . . .   *Digested,* 04/**1974**:
                  Applied, 07/2199

Yarburgh Children's Trust v Customs and Excise Commissioners; *sub nom* Customs and
    Excise Commissioners v Yarburgh Children's Trust [2002] S.T.C. 207; [2001]
    B.T.C. 5651; [2002] B.V.C. 141; [2001] S.T.I. 1661; [2001] N.P.C. 173, Ch D;
    affirming [2001] B.V.C. 2307; [2001] V. & D.R. 342; [2001] S.T.I. 1170, V&DTr . .   *Digested,* 02/**4811**:
              Distinguished, 07/4307: *Followed,* 05/4383
Yarmouth Corp v Simmons (1878-79) L.R. 10 Ch. D. 518, Ch D . . . .   *Applied,* 06/2682:
                  Distinguished, 07/2752

Yavuz v Turkey (67137/01) (2007) 45 E.H.R.R. 16, ECHR
Yean v Dominican Republic 23 B.H.R.C. 601, IACHR
Yeboah v Crofton see Crofton v Yeboah
Yeda Research & Development Co Ltd v Rhone-Poulenc Rorer International Holdings Inc
    see Rhone-Poulenc Rorer International Holdings Inc v Yeda Research &
    Development Co Ltd
Yelland Wind Farm Ltd v West Devon BC [2007] P.A.D. 13, Planning Inspector
Yeoman's Row Management Ltd v Cobbe see Cobbe v Yeoman's Row Management Ltd
Yewbelle Ltd v London Green Developments Ltd [2007] EWCA Civ 475; [2007] 23
    E.G. 164 (C.S.), CA (Civ Div); reversing [2006] EWHC 3166 (Ch), Ch D
Yi Hui Tan v Liverpool City Council [2007] P.A.D. 64, Planning Inspector
YL v Birmingham City Council see L v Birmingham City Council
YMCA Training v Stewart [2007] I.R.L.R. 185, EAT . . . .   *Digested,* 07/**1421**
York v Murray (Unreported, January 2, 2007), CC (Birmingham) [*Ex rel.* Stephen
    Garner, Barrister, No. 8 Fountain Court, Steelhouse Lane, Birmingham] . . . . . .   *Digested,* 07/**3151**
Yorke (Deceased), Re; *sub nom* Stone v Chataway [1997] 4 All E.R. 907; (1997)
    94(33) L.S.G. 26; *Times,* August 11, 1997, Ch D . . . .   *Digested,* 97/**4724**:
               Applied, 01/625: *Followed,* 07/3957
Yorkshire Water Services Ltd v Sun Alliance and London Insurance Plc (No.1) [1997] 2
    Lloyd's Rep. 21; [1997] C.L.C. 213; (1996) 93(34) L.S.G. 34; (1996) 140
    S.J.L.B. 193; [1997] Env. L.R. D4; *Times,* August 20, 1996, CA (Civ Div) . . . . . .   *Digested,* 96/**3555**:
                  Applied, 07/2501
Youell v Bland Welch & Co Ltd (No.2) [1990] 2 Lloyd's Rep. 431, QBD (Comm) . . . . .   *Digested,* 91/**3288**:
      Applied, 00/4252: *Considered,* 02/2753, 06/2405, 07/2467
Young v Bristol Aeroplane Co Ltd [1946] A.C. 163; (1946) 79 Ll. L. Rep. 35, HL;
    affirming [1944] K.B. 718; (1945) 78 Ll. L. Rep. 6, CA . . . .   *Applied,* 47-51/2389,
        47-51/3047, 47-51/7882, 47-51/11049, 55/351, 56/6138, 56/6957, 57/3680,
              75/1906, 77/1527, 84/366, 85/471, 85/568, 85/2704, 90/3733, 01/814:
         Considered, 47-51/7868, 53/3472, 68/496, 68/647, 68/3317, 74/3952,
          75/2657, 78/1590, 84/366, 87/994, 89/631, 90/1522, 02/3096, 07/4518:
         Distinguished, 47-51/9934: *Followed,* 54/1583, 59/1052
Young v Lauretani [2007] EWHC 1244 (Ch); [2007] 2 F.L.R. 1211; [2007] Fam. Law
    906; [2007] 2 P. & C.R. DG12, Ch D
Young v Thomas [1892] 2 Ch. 134, CA . . . .   *Applied,* 07/46
Young v United Kingdom (60682/00) (2007) 45 E.H.R.R. 29, ECHR
Younger v Bellward see Younger v Molesworth
Younger v Dorset and Somerset Strategic HA [2006] Lloyd's Rep. Med. 489, CC
    (Southampton) . . . .   *Digested,* 07/**3076**
Younger v Molesworth; *joined case* Younger v Bellward [2006] EWHC 3088 (QB);
    [2006] N.P.C. 130; [2007] Env. L.R. D11, QBD

Younger *v* United Kingdom (Admissibility) (57420/00) [2003] Prison L.R. 204;
[2007] Inquest L.R. 176; (2003) 36 E.H.R.R. CD252, ECHR
Yudt *v* Leonard Ross & Craig (A Firm); *joined cases* Goodeve-Docker *v* Leonard Ross
& Craig; Kantor *v* Leonard Ross & Craig; Kedem *v* Leonard Ross & Craig
Independent, October 12, 1998; *Independent*, October 5, 1998, Ch D . . . .   *Digested*, 98/**3928**:
   Considered, 06/556: *Followed*, 07/2944
Yusuf *v* Council of the European Union (T-306/01) [2006] All E.R. (EC) 290; [2005]
E.C.R. II-3533; [2005] 3 C.M.L.R. 49, CFI (2nd Chamber) . . . .   *Considered*, 07/1645

Z *v* Odetoyinbo (Quantum) (Unreported, November 20, 2006), QBD [*Ex rel.* Timothy
Briden, Barrister, Lamb Chambers, Lamb Building, Temple, London] . . . .   *Digested*, 07/**3208**
Z *v* Secretary of State for the Home Department (No.2) [2004] EWCA Civ 1578;
[2005] Imm. A.R. 75, CA (Civ Div). . . . .   *Digested*, 05/**2140**:
   Applied, 06/2227, 07/2297: *Considered*, 05/2176
Z *v* United Kingdom (29392/95) [2001] 2 F.L.R. 612; [2001] 2 F.C.R. 246; (2002)
34 E.H.R.R. 3; 10 B.H.R.C. 384; (2001) 3 L.G.L.R. 51; (2001) 4 C.C.L. Rep. 310;
[2001] Fam. Law 583; *Times*, May 31, 2001, ECHR [2000] 2 F.C.R. 245;
(2000) 2 L.G.L.R. 212, Eur Comm HR . . . .   *Digested*, 01/**3459**:
   Applied, 03/3004, 04/665, 05/1553, 07/2212: *Considered*, 02/763, 07/2937
Z *v* Z (Abduction: Children's Views) [2005] EWCA Civ 1012; [2006] 1 F.L.R. 410;
[2006] 1 F.C.R. 387; [2005] Fam. Law 763, CA (Civ Div); reversing [2005]
EWHC 1234 (Fam); [2005] Fam. Law 691, Fam Div . . . .   *Digested*, 06/**1640**:
   Considered, 07/1744, 07/1746: *Doubted*, 07/1736
Z CC *v* R see R (A Child) (Adoption: Duty to Investigate), Re
Z Munter Farms Ltd *v* Pettitt (Listing Officer) [2006] R.V.R. 332, VT . . . .   *Digested*, 07/**2840**
Z (A Child) *v* Attridge (Unreported, February 9, 2006), CC (Dudley) [*Ex rel.* Stephen
Garner, No.8 Chambers, Fountain Court, Steelhouse Lane, Birmingham] . . . . .   *Digested*, 07/**3204**
Z (A Child) *v* Latif (t/a A1 Kebabish Restaurant) (Unreported, August 25, 2006), CC
(Clerkenwell) [*Ex rel.* Timothy Sharpe, Barrister, 1 Temple Gardens, Temple,
London] . . . .   *Digested*, 07/**3210**
Zafar *v* DPP [2004] EWHC 2468 (Admin); (2005) 169 J.P. 208; [2005] R.T.R. 18;
(2005) 169 J.P.N. 360; (2004) 148 S.J.L.B. 1315; *Times*, January 7, 2005, QBD
(Admin) . . . .   *Digested*, 05/**779**:
   Considered, 07/882
Zarb *v* Odetoyinbo [2006] EWHC 2880 (QB); (2007) 93 B.M.L.R. 166, QBD . . . . . .   *Digested*, 07/**2926**
Zawadka *v* Poland (48542/99); *sub nom* Zawadkaw *v* Poland (48542/99) [2005] 2
F.L.R. 897; [2006] 1 F.C.R. 371; (2007) 44 E.H.R.R. 9; [2005] Fam. Law 774,
ECHR . . . .   *Digested*, 06/**2189**
Zawadkaw *v* Poland (48542/99) see Zawadka *v* Poland (48542/99)
Zdanoka *v* Latvia (58278/00) (2007) 45 E.H.R.R. 17, ECHR (Grand Chamber)
Zellweger Analytics Ltd's Community Design [2006] E.C.D.R. 17, OHIM (Cancellation Div)   *Digested*, 07/**2532**
Zermalt Holdings SA *v* Nu-Life Upholstery Repairs Ltd [1985] 2 E.G.L.R. 14; (1985)
275 E.G. 1134, QBD (Comm) . . . .   *Digested*, 85/**95**:
   Applied, 05/202, 06/196, 06/203: *Approved*, 89/3857: *Considered*, 93/169,
   93/182, 94/208, 94/227, 96/3796, 97/3326, 05/2678, 07/250:
   Followed, 04/2522
ZEVEX/Pinch clip occluder (T636/05) [2007] E.P.O.R. 30, EPO (Technical Bd App) . .   *Digested*, 07/**2566**
Zhu *v* Secretary of State for the Home Department (C-200/02) see Chen *v* Secretary
of State for the Home Department (C-200/02)
Zielinski (Deceased), Re; *sub nom* Korab-Karpinski *v* Lucas-Gardiner [2007] W.T.L.R.
1655, Ch D
Ziliberberg *v* Moldova (Admissibility) (61821/00) (Unreported, May 4, 2004), ECHR .   *Applied*, 07/879
Zim Israel Navigation Co Ltd *v* Effy Shipping Corp [1972] 1 Lloyd's Rep. 18, QBD
(Comm) . . . .   *Digested*, 72/**3207**:
   Considered, 07/3420
Zinc Phosphate Cartel, Re (T62/02) see Union Pigments AS (formerly Waardals AS) *v*
Commission of the European Communities (T62/02)
Zino Davidoff SA *v* A&G Imports Ltd (C-414/99); *joined cases* Levi Strauss & Co *v*
Tesco Stores Ltd (C-415/99); Levi Strauss & Co *v* Costco Wholesale UK Ltd (C-
416/99) [2002] Ch. 109; [2002] 2 W.L.R. 321; [2002] All E.R. (EC) 55;
[2001] E.C.R. I-8691; [2002] 1 C.M.L.R. 1; [2002] C.E.C. 154; [2002] E.T.M.R.
9; [2002] R.P.C. 20; *Times*, November 23, 2001; *Daily Telegraph*, November 27,
2001, ECJ . . . .   *Digested*, 01/**4032**:
   Applied, 05/2572, 05/2573, 06/2581, 06/2595, 06/2605, 07/2651:
   Considered, 03/2621: *Subsequent proceedings*, 02/2905
Zipher Ltd *v* Markem Systems Ltd [2007] EWHC 154 (Pat); [2007] F.S.R. 18; (2007)
30(3) I.P.D. 30021, Ch D (Patents Ct) . . . .   *Digested*, 07/**2633**
Znamenskaya *v* Russia (77785/01) [2005] 2 F.C.R. 406; (2007) 44 E.H.R.R. 15,
ECHR . . . .   *Digested*, 06/**2199**
Zockoll Group Ltd (formerly Phonenames Ltd) *v* Controller of Patents, Designs and Trade
Marks [2006] IEHC 300; [2007] E.T.M.R. 26, HC (Irl)

Zoological Society of London *v* Customs and Excise Commissioners (C-267/00); *sub nom* Customs and Excise Commissioners *v* Zoological Society of London (C-267/00) [2002] Q.B. 1252; [2002] 3 W.L.R. 829; [2002] All E.R. (EC) 465; [2002] S.T.C. 521; [2002] E.C.R. I-3353; [2002] 2 C.M.L.R. 13; [2002] C.E.C. 316; [2002] B.T.C. 5224; [2002] B.V.C. 414; [2002] S.T.I. 356; *Times*, April 11, 2002, ECJ (5th Chamber) . . . . *Digested*, 02/**4758**:
Applied, 05/4356, 06/4441: *Considered*, 07/4291

Zurich Insurance Co *v* Gearcross Ltd [2007] EWHC 1318 (TCC); 112 Con. L.R. 82, QBD (TCC) . . . . *Digested*, 07/**748**

Zurich Insurance Co *v* Revenue and Customs Commissioners; *sub nom* Revenue and Customs Commissioners *v* Zurich Insurance Co [2007] EWCA Civ 218; [2007] S.T.C. 1756; [2007] 2 C.M.L.R. 53; [2007] B.T.C. 5314; [2007] B.V.C. 283; *Times*, April 5, 2007, CA (Civ Div); affirming [2006] EWHC 593 (Ch); [2006] S.T.C. 1694; [2006] B.T.C. 5389; [2006] B.V.C. 458; [2006] S.T.I. 1142; [2007] S.T.I. 1046; *Times*, April 26, 2006, Ch D; reversing [2006] B.V.C. 2003; [2005] S.T.I. 1733, V&DTr (London) . . . . *Digested*, 07/**4348**

Zvozskov *v* Belarus (1039/2001) 22 B.H.R.C. 114, UN HRC. . . . . *Digested*, 07/**2180**

ZYMOGENETICS/Hematopoietic cytokine receptor (T898/05) [2007] E.P.O.R. 2, EPO (Technical Bd App) . . . . *Digested*, 07/**2583**

This section contains:

(a) Details of cases decided or judicially considered in the Scottish courts during 2007.

(b) References to English Cases judicially considered in Scotland during 2007.

Scottish cases published in English Law Reports are included in both the English and Scottish sections.

Figures appearing in bold type indicate the main substantive paragraph.

A v A see A v N
A v Balkan Holidays Ltd 2007 G.W.D. 9-157, Sh Ct (Tayside)
A v East Ayrshire Council 2006 Fam. L.R. 112; 2006 G.W.D. 35-721, Sh Ct (North
    Strathclyde) . . . . *Digested*, 07/**5115**
A v HM Advocate; *sub nom* DA v HM Advocate [2007] HCJAC 8; 2007 J.C. 170;
    2007 S.C.C.R. 85; 2007 G.W.D. 4-53, HCJ . . . . *Digested*, 07/**5021**
A v N; *sub nom* A v A 2007 Fam. L.R. 43; 2007 G.W.D. 1-2, OH . . . . *Digested*, 07/**5190**
A v Secretary of State for the Home Department see HA v Secretary of State for the
    Home Department
A's Guardian, Applicant 2007 S.L.T. (Sh Ct) 69; 2006 G.W.D. 19-417, Sh Ct (Glasgow)   *Digested*, 07/**5539**
AB v CD see B v D
Abacus Estates Ltd v Bell Street Estates Ltd 2007 G.W.D. 2-31, OH
Abarquey v Secretary of State for the Home Department 2007 G.W.D. 7-117, OH
Abdulla v Secretary of State for the Home Department 2007 G.W.D. 15-289, OH
Abercromby Motor Group Ltd v Revenue and Customs Commissioners [2007] S.T.I.
    1702, V&D Tr (Edinburgh)
Aberdeen City Council v Fergus 2006 Hous. L.R. 90; 2006 G.W.D. 36-727, Sh Pr . . . .   *Digested*, 07/**4974**
Aberdeen City Council v Shauri 2006 Hous. L.R. 40; 2006 G.W.D. 22-468, Sh Pr . . . .   *Digested*, 07/**5336**
Aberdeen City Council v Wanchoo [2006] CSOH 196; 2007 S.L.T. 289; 2007 G.W.D.
    6-102, OH
AC Stoddart & Sons v Trustees of the Coulson Trust; *sub nom* Firm of AC Stoddart &
    Sons, Colstoun (1995) v Balfour Thomson CA [2007] CSIH 38; 2007 S.C. 655;
    2007 S.L.T. 593; 2007 Hous. L.R. 84; 2007 G.W.D. 18-314, IH (2 Div) . . . .   *Digested*, 07/**5326**
Accountant in Bankruptcy v Butler 2007 S.L.T. (Sh Ct) 200; 2007 G.W.D. 32-542, Sh
    Pr; reversing 2006 S.L.T. (Sh Ct) 2; 2005 G.W.D. 36-674, Sh Ct (North
    Strathclyde) . . . .   *Digested*, 06/**5129**
Accountant in Bankruptcy (Brown's Trustee) v Brown [2007] CSOH 133; 2007 G.W.D.
    25-425, OH
Advocate General for Scotland v General Commissioners for Aberdeen City see
    Revenue and Customs Commissioners, Petitioners
Advocate General for Scotland v Taylor 2004 S.C. 339; 2003 S.L.T. 1340; 2003 G.W.D.
    36-998, IH (Ex Div) . . . . *Digested*, 04/**4956**:
                                  Considered, 05/5025, 07/5017: *Followed*, 05/4967
AG v Mental Health Tribunal for Scotland [2007] M.H.L.R. 1, Sh Pr
Ainsworth v Inland Revenue Commissioners see Inland Revenue Commissioners v
    Ainsworth
Air & General Finance Ltd v RYB Marine Ltd 2007 G.W.D. 35-589, OH
Aitken v Lees 1993 J.C. 228; 1994 S.L.T. 182; 1993 S.C.C.R. 845, HCJ . . . .   *Digested*, 93/**5756**:
                                                   Applied, 07/5044
Akzo NV's European Patent (EP 0 389 035) see Arrow Generics Ltd, Petitioners
Alagon v Secretary of State for the Home Department 1995 S.L.T. 381; [1993] Imm.
    A.R. 336, OH . . . .   *Digested*, 95/**6024**:
                                   Considered, 07/2325: *Not followed*, 97/6141
Albert Bartlett & Sons (Airdrie) Ltd v Gilchrist & Lynn Ltd 2007 G.W.D. 27-472, OH
Albyn Realisations (Festival Cars) Ltd v Levenfleet Ltd 2007 G.W.D. 21-357, OH
Alexander's Application, Re see Scottish Information Commissioner v Scottish Information Commissioner
Allaway v Reilly [2007] I.R.L.R. 864, EAT (SC)
Alldays Stores Ltd v Central Fife Divisional Licensing Board 2007 G.W.D. 34-585, Sh
    Ct (Tayside)
Allen v McTaggart see Allen v MacTaggart

Allen *v* MacTaggart; *sub nom* Allen *v* McTaggart [2007] CSIH 24; 2007 S.C. 482;
    2007 S.L.T. 387; 2007 Hous. L.R. 29, IH (Ex Div) . . . .   *Digested*, 07/**5339**
Anderson *v* Christian Salvesen Plc [2006] CSOH 101; 2006 S.L.T. 815; 2007 S.C.L.R.
    552; 2006 Rep. L.R. 108; 2006 G.W.D. 24-525, OH . . . .   *Digested*, 06/**5599**
Anderson *v* Griffiths 2005 1 J.C. 169; 2005 S.L.T. 86; 2005 S.C.C.R. 41; 2004 G.W.D.
    38-778, HCJ . . . .   *Digested*, 05/**5107**:
                                                                                        Applied, 07/5044
Anderson *v* McKinnon 2007 G.W.D. 29-513, LandsTr (Scot)
Anderson (Colin) *v* HM Advocate [2007] HCJAC 50; 2007 S.L.T. 1232; 2007 S.C.C.R.
    507; 2007 G.W.D. 31-528, HCJ
Anderson (James McAulay) *v* HM Advocate 1996 J.C. 29; 1996 S.L.T. 155, HCJ
    Appeal . . . .   *Digested*, 96/**6764**:
                                Applied, 04/4679, 06/5173: *Considered*, 06/5192, 07/5078:
                                Distinguished, 00/6091: *Followed*, 03/5379: *Referred to*, 97/5804
Andrew *v* HM Advocate 1982 S.C.C.R. 539, HCJ Appeal . . . .   *Digested*, 83/**4160**:
                                Considered, 07/5051: *Distinguished*, 88/3952
Angus *v* Donaldson see Angus *v* Spiers
Angus *v* Spiers; *sub nom* Angus *v* Donaldson [2006] HCJAC 67; 2007 J.C. 19; 2006
    S.C.C.R. 603; 2006 G.W.D. 31-666, HCJ . . . .   *Digested*, 07/**5044**
Angus Braidwood & Sons Ltd *v* Revenue and Customs Commissioners [2007] CSIH
    63; 2007 S.L.T. 768; 2007 G.W.D. 24-399, IH (1 Div) . . . .   *Digested*, 07/**5095**
Anwar, Re 2007 G.W.D. 35-590, HCJ
APC Ltd *v* Amey Construction Ltd 2007 G.W.D. 24-402, OH
AppA UK Ltd *v* Clyde & Forth Press Ltd 2007 G.W.D. 4-52, OH
AppA UK Ltd *v* Scottish Daily Record & Sunday Mail Ltd 2007 G.W.D. 37-645, IH (1
    Div)
Ardenglen Developments Ltd *v* Revenue and Customs Commissioners [2007] S.T.I.
    385, V&DTr (Edinburgh)
Arrow Generics Ltd, Petitioners; *sub nom* Akzo NV's European Patent (EP 0 389 035)
    [2006] CSOH 146; 2006 S.L.T. 919; [2007] R.P.C. 11; 2006 G.W.D. 29-649,
    OH . . . .   *Digested*, 06/**5538**
Arsenal Football Club Plc *v* Reed (C-206/01) [2003] Ch. 454; [2003] 3 W.L.R. 450;
    [2003] All E.R. (EC) 1; [2002] E.C.R. I-10273; [2003] 1 C.M.L.R. 12; [2003]
    C.E.C. 3; [2003] E.T.M.R. 19; [2003] R.P.C. 9; (2002) 152 N.L.J. 1808; *Times*,
    November 18, 2002, ECJ . . . .   *Digested*, 02/**2912**:
                                Applied, 07/2653, 07/5324: *Considered*, 06/2595
Ashford & Thistle Securities LLP *v* Kerr 2007 S.L.T. (Sh Ct) 60; 2006 S.C.L.R. 873;
    2007 G.W.D. 8-150, Sh Pr. . . . .   *Digested*, 07/**5331**
Assessor for Grampian Valuation Joint Board *v* Fraser see Grampian Valuation Joint
    Board Assessor *v* Fraser
At.home Nationwide Ltd *v* Morris 2007 G.W.D. 31-535, LandsTr (Scot)
Attorney General's Reference (No.152 of 2002), Re see R. *v* Cooksley (Robert Charles)
Auchterarder Golf Club *v* Revenue and Customs Commissioners [2007] S.T.I. 386,
    V&DTr (Edinburgh)
Autolink Concessionaires (M6) Plc *v* Amey Construction Ltd 2007 G.W.D. 37-640, OH

B *v* A see B *v* Burns
B *v* B 2007 G.W.D. 12-238, Sh Pr
B *v* Burns; *sub nom* Bolam *v* Burns; B *v* A 1993 S.C. 232; 1994 S.L.T. 250; 1993
    S.C.L.R. 560; Scotsman, March 10, 1993, IH (2 Div); reversing 1992 S.L.T. (Sh.
    Ct.) 48, Sh Pr. . . . .   *Digested*, 93/**5741**:
                                                                                        Considered, 07/4979
B *v* D; *sub nom* AB *v* CD 2007 Fam. L.R. 53; 2007 G.W.D. 4-64, OH . . . .   *Digested*, 07/**5185**
B *v* Harrow LBC (No.1); *sub nom* F *v* Harrow LBC; F *v* Special Education Needs
    Tribunal; B *v* Special Educational Needs Tribunal [2000] 1 W.L.R. 223; [2000] 1
    All E.R. 876; [2000] 3 F.C.R. 1; [2000] B.L.G.R. 162; [2000] Ed. C.R. 188;
    [2000] E.L.R. 109; (2000) 97(6) L.S.G. 34; (2000) 144 S.J.L.B. 83; *Times*,
    January 28, 2000; *Independent*, February 2, 2000, HL; reversing [1998] 3
    F.C.R. 231; [1999] B.L.G.R. 144; [1998] Ed. C.R. 176; [1998] E.L.R. 351; (1998)
    42 B.M.L.R. 88; (1998) 95(17) L.S.G. 32; (1998) 142 S.J.L.B. 134; *Times*,
    March 26, 1998, CA (Civ Div); reversing [1998] Ed. C.R. 1; *Times*, December 29,
    1997, QBD . . . .   *Digested*, 00/**1946**:
                                Considered, 98/1983, 02/1165, 07/5121
B *v* Highland Council [2007] CSOH 126; 2007 S.L.T. 844; 2007 Fam. L.R. 115; 2007
    G.W.D. 23-381, OH
B *v* Murray (No.2); *sub nom* Bowden *v* Poor Sisters of Nazareth; S *v* Poor Sisters of
    Nazareth; *joined case* Whitton *v* Poor Sisters of Nazareth [2007] CSIH 39; 2007
    S.C. 688; 2007 S.L.T. 605; 2007 G.W.D. 21-362, IH (1 Div); affirming 2005
    S.L.T. 982, OH . . . .   *Digested*, 07/**4991**
B *v* Secretary of State for the Home Department [2007] CSOH 121; 2007 G.W.D. 24-
    409, OH
B *v* Special Educational Needs Tribunal see B *v* Harrow LBC (No.1)

B&Q Plc v Assessor for Dunbartonshire and Argyll and Bute Valuation Joint Board [2006] CSIH 50; 2007 S.C. 135; 2006 S.L.T. 1115; [2006] R.A. 420; 2006 G.W.D. 33-695, LVAC .... *Digested*, 07/**5490**

B, Petitioner [2007] CSOH 73; 2007 S.L.T. 566; 2007 G.W.D. 15-288, OH .... *Digested*, 07/**5432**

Babcock International Ltd v National Grid Co Plc see Fairchild v Glenhaven Funeral Services Ltd (t/a GH Dovener & Son)

Baillie (David) v HM Advocate [2006] HCJAC 91; 2007 J.C. 161; 2007 S.L.T. 2; 2007 S.C.C.R. 26; 2006 G.W.D. 40-777, HCJ .... *Digested*, 07/**5515**

Baillie (Stuart Malcolm) v HM Advocate [2006] HCJAC 75; 2006 S.L.T. 1117; 2007 S.C.C.R. 1; 2006 G.W.D. 34-702, HCJ .... *Digested*, 07/**5311**

Bain v Bain 2007 G.W.D. 6-84, OH

Bain v Brand (1875-76) L.R. 1 App. Cas. 762; (1876) 3 R. (H.L.) 16, HL; reversing (1874) 2 R. 258, IH (2 Div) .... *Considered*, 07/5285:
Explained, 86/4106: *Followed*, 81/3242, 89/4524

Balfour Beatty Ltd v Gilcomston North Ltd (formerly Gilcomstom Construction Ltd) 2006 S.C.L.R. 717, OH .... *Digested*, 07/**5012**

Banbury Visionplus Ltd v Revenue and Customs Commissioners [2006] EWHC 1024 (Ch); [2006] S.T.C. 1568; [2006] B.T.C. 5482; [2006] B.V.C. 552; [2006] S.T.I. 1511; *Times*, June 12, 2006, Ch D; affirming [2006] B.V.C. 2246; [2005] V. & D.R. 337; [2006] S.T.I. 283, V&DTr (London) .... *Digested*, 06/**4454**:
Applied, 07/4333: *Considered*, 07/5569

Bank of Scotland v Forman see Bank of Scotland v Tait

Bank of Scotland v Tait; *sub nom* Bank of Scotland v Forman [2007] CSIH 46; 2007 S.C. 731, IH (Ex Div)

Barclay v Lanarkshire Health Board 2007 G.W.D. 12-257, IH (1 Div)

Barker v Barker 2007 G.W.D. 38-660, Sh Ct (Tayside)

Barker v Lewis 2007 S.L.T. (Sh Ct) 48; 2007 G.W.D. 13-270, Sh Ct (Tayside) .... *Digested*, 07/**5281**

Barron (Vincent Paul) v HM Advocate [2007] HCJAC 39; 2007 S.C.C.R. 335; 2007 G.W.D. 26-455, HCJ

Barry D Trentham Ltd v Lawfield Investments Ltd 2002 S.C. 401; 2002 S.L.T. 1094; 2002 S.C.L.R. 704; 2002 G.W.D. 15-485, OH .... *Digested*, 02/**5324**:
Applied, 07/5017

Barvi v Secretary of State for the Home Department 2007 G.W.D. 9-166, IH (2 Div)

Bashir (Abdul Mutalub) v HM Advocate 2006 S.C.C.R. 99; 2006 G.W.D. 12-230, HCJ *Digested*, 07/**5502**

Beattie v Dunbar; *sub nom* SB v Dunbar 2006 S.C.L.R. 777; [2007] M.H.L.R. 7; 2006 G.W.D. 10-180, Sh Pr .... *Digested*, 07/**5413**

Beaumont v Scottish Solicitors Discipline Tribunal [2006] CSIH 27; 2006 S.C. 659, IH (Ex Div) .... *Digested*, 07/**5360**

Beggs v Scottish Ministers; *sub nom* Beggs, Petitioner [2006] CSIH 34; 2006 S.C. 649; 2007 S.C.L.R. 1, IH (Ex Div) .... *Digested*, 07/**4855**

Beggs v Scottish Ministers [2007] UKHL 3; [2007] 1 W.L.R. 455; 2007 S.L.T. 235; 2007 S.C.L.R. 287; (2007) 151 S.J.L.B. 258; 2007 G.W.D. 5-72; *Times*, February 8, 2007, HL .... *Digested*, 07/**717**

Beggs v Scottish Ministers (Contempt of Court) 2005 1 S.C. 342; 2005 S.L.T. 305; 2005 S.C.L.R. 640; 2005 G.W.D. 10-145, IH (1 Div) .... *Digested*, 05/**5026**:
Subsequent related litigation, 07/717

Beggs, Petitioner see Beggs v Scottish Ministers

Bell v Inkersall Investments Ltd [2007] CSIH 60; 2007 S.C. 823; 2007 S.L.T. 737; 2007 G.W.D. 23-382, IH (2 Div) .... *Digested*, 07/**5351**

Bell v North Ayrshire Council 2007 G.W.D. 3-39, OH

Bell v North Ayrshire Council 2007 Rep. L.R. 108; 2007 G.W.D. 25-444, OH

Bentley v United States [2005] EWHC 1078 (Admin); [2005] Extradition L.R. 65, QBD (Admin) .... *Considered*, 07/5169

Beriston Ltd v Dumbarton Motor Boat & Sailing Club [2006] CSOH 190; 2007 S.L.T. 227; 2007 G.W.D. 4-51, OH .... *Digested*, 07/**4854**

Besmel v Secretary of State for the Home Department 2007 G.W.D. 19-337, OH

Bibi, Petitioner [2006] CSOH 152; 2007 S.L.T. 173; 2006 G.W.D. 40-781, OH .... *Digested*, 07/**5407**

Bibi, Petitioner [2007] CSOH 151; 2007 G.W.D. 28-483, OH

Billig v Council of the Law Society of Scotland [2006] CSOH 148; 2007 S.C. 32; 2006 G.W.D. 32-673, OH .... *Digested*, 07/**5359**

Billig v Council of the Law Society of Scotland [2007] CSIH 86; 2007 G.W.D. 40-690, IH (1 Div)

Birrell, Petitioner 2007 S.L.T. 440; 2007 G.W.D. 1-5, OH .... *Digested*, 07/**5430**

Black v McGregor [2006] CSIH 45; 2007 S.C. 69; 2006 G.W.D. 31-668, IH (Ex Div); affirming 2006 G.W.D. 17-351, Sh Pr .... *Digested*, 07/**5275**

Blanco v Scottish Ministers see Somerville v Scottish Ministers

Bolam v Burns see B v Burns

Bookit Ltd v Customs and Excise Commissioners see Bookit Ltd v Revenue and Customs Commissioners

Bookit Ltd v Revenue and Customs Commissioners; *sub nom* Bookit Ltd v Customs
  and Excise Commissioners [2006] EWCA Civ 550; [2006] S.T.C. 1367; [2006]
  B.T.C. 5535; [2006] B.V.C. 605; [2006] S.T.I. 1513, CA (Civ Div); affirming
  [2005] EWHC 1689 (Ch); [2005] S.T.C. 1481; [2005] B.T.C. 5581; [2005]
  B.V.C. 612; [2005] S.T.I. 1337, Ch D; reversing [2004] B.V.C. 2229; [2004] V. &
  D.R. 421; [2004] S.T.I. 1949, V&DTr (London) . . . .   *Digested,* 06/**4435**:
                                                   Applied, 07/5568
Boskabelle Ltd v Laird [2006] CSOH 173; 2006 S.L.T. 1079; 2006 G.W.D. 36-734, OH   *Digested,* 07/**5285**
Bott v Riordan 2007 G.W.D. 29-505, Sh Ct (Lothian)
Bourhill v Young; *sub nom* Bourhill v Young's Executor [1943] A.C. 92; [1942] 2 All
  E.R. 396; 1942 S.C. (H.L.) 78; 1943 S.L.T. 105, HL; affirming 1941 S.C. 395; 1941
  S.L.T. 364, IH (2 Div) . . . .   *Applied,* 47-51/6897,
          52/917, 53/2525, 55/2194, 61/2343, 80/3416, 07/5426: *Approved,* 82/2153:
          Considered, 62/2033, 64/2520, 67/2674, 70/1849, 72/2397, 76/1858,
          81/1849, 87/2608, 87/4737, 92/3250, 94/3380, 95/3682:
          Distinguished, 47-51/6812, 59/886, 60/873, 68/2663, 84/2330:
                                            Followed, 53/964
Bourhill v Young's Executor see Bourhill v Young
Bowden v Poor Sisters of Nazareth see B v Murray (No.2)
Bowie v Argyll and Clyde Health Board 2007 G.W.D. 10-194, OH
Boyle (James Patrick) v HM Advocate 2007 S.C.C.R. 286, HCJ . . . .   *Digested,* 07/**5429**
Bremner (Robert John) v Westwater 1994 J.C. 25; 1994 S.L.T. 707; 1993 S.C.C.R. 1023,
  HCJ . . . .   *Digested,* 94/**6241**:
                                                 Approved, 07/1006
Britz (Julie Caroline) v HM Advocate [2006] HCJAC 90; 2007 J.C. 75; 2007 S.L.T. 78;
  2007 S.C.C.R. 21; 2006 G.W.D. 40-774, HCJ . . . .   *Digested,* 07/**5024**
Broadley (Rose) v HM Advocate [2005] HCJAC 96; 2005 S.C.C.R. 620; 2005 G.W.D.
  28-520, HCJ. . . . .   *Digested,* 06/**5175**:
                                         Distinguished, 07/5032
Brooks v Miller; *sub nom* Brooks (Matthew James) v HM Advocate [2007] HCJAC 9;
  2007 J.C. 79; 2007 S.L.T. 572; 2007 S.C.C.R. 75; 2007 G.W.D. 8-140, HCJ . . .   *Digested,* 07/**5067**
Brooks (Matthew James) v HM Advocate see Brooks v Miller
Brouwers v Tartaglia 2007 G.W.D. 22-374, OH
Brown v Donaldson [2007] HCJAC 40; 2007 S.C.C.R. 344; 2007 G.W.D. 26-453,
  HCJ
Brown v Glasgow Housing Authority Ltd 2007 Hous. L.R. 2; 2007 G.W.D. 9-156, OH .   *Digested,* 07/**5332**
Brown v JA Alexander & Son Ltd 2007 G.W.D. 35-610, Sh Ct (North Strathclyde)
Brown v Lindsay 2007 G.W.D. 35-609, Sh Ct (North Strathclyde)
Brown v McTaggart Construction Ltd 2007 G.W.D. 35-611, Sh Ct (North Strathclyde)
Brown v Richardson 2007 G.W.D. 28-490, Lands Tr (Scot)
Brown v Richardson (Expenses) 2007 G.W.D. 38-666, Lands Tr (Scot)
Bruce v Dignity Funerals Ltd; *sub nom* Dignity Funerals Ltd v Bruce 2005 1 S.C. 59;
  2004 S.L.T. 1223; 2005 S.C.L.R. 951; [2005] I.R.L.R. 189; (2004) 148 S.J.L.B.
  1313; 2004 G.W.D. 32-662, IH (2 Div); reversing EATS/0015/02, EAT (SC) . . .   *Digested,* 05/**5217**:
                                               Considered, 07/1317
Buchan v Bruce 2007 G.W.D. 26-468, Sh Ct (Grampian)
Burgon v Highland Council 2007 G.W.D. 19-339, OH
Burke v Bayne Services (Edinburgh) Ltd 2007 G.W.D. 37-639, OH
Burnett v Grampian Fire and Rescue Service [2007] CSOH 3; 2007 S.L.T. 61; 2007
  S.C.L.R. 192; 2007 G.W.D. 1-11, OH . . . .   *Digested,* 07/**5423**
Burns (George Francis) v HM Advocate [2007] HCJAC 66; 2007 S.L.T. 1177; 2007
  G.W.D. 37-641, HCJ
Burnside v Burnside 2007 Fam. L.R. 144; 2007 G.W.D. 24-404, Sh Ct (Lothian)
Bye v Fife Council 2007 Rep. L.R. 40, Sh Ct (Tayside) . . . .   *Digested,* 07/**5100**
Byrne v Mental Health Tribunal for Scotland [2007] M.H.L.R. 2; 2006 G.W.D. 10-179,
  Sh Pr

C v C 2007 G.W.D. 40-699, OH
C v C 2007 G.W.D. 8-148, Sh Ct (South Strathclyde)
C Czarnikow Ltd v Koufos (The Heron II) see Koufos v C Czarnikow Ltd (The Heron II)
Calder v Frame [2006] HCJAC 62; 2006 J.C. 4; 2006 S.L.T. 862; 2006 S.C.C.R. 487;
  2006 G.W.D. 28-622, HCJ. . . . .   *Digested,* 06/**5170**
Calder v Lord Advocate; *sub nom* Calder (David John) v HM Advocate; *joined case*
  Calder v Scottish Ministers 2006 S.C.C.R. 609; 2006 G.W.D. 30-658, HCJ . . .   *Digested,* 07/**5169**
Calder v Scottish Ministers see Calder v Lord Advocate
Calder (David John) v HM Advocate see Calder v Lord Advocate
Cameron v Gibson (Expenses); *sub nom* Cameron v MacIntyre's Executor (Expenses)
  [2006] CSIH 53; 2006 S.L.T. 1088; 2006 Fam. L.R. 128; 2006 G.W.D. 36-731,
  IH (1 Div). . . . .   *Digested,* 07/**4982**
Cameron v MacIntyre's Executor (Expenses) see Cameron v Gibson (Expenses)
Campbell v Aberdeen City Council 2007 Hous. L.R. 26; 2007 G.W.D. 9-168, Sh Ct
  (Grampian)

Campbell v Western Isles Islands Council 1989 S.L.T. 602, IH (1 Div); affirming 1988
S.L.T. (LandsTr.) 4, LandsTr (Scot) . . . . *Digested*, 89/**4542**:
Applied, 07/**5333**
Campbell Riddell Breeze Patterson v Council of the Law Society of Scotland 2007
G.W.D. 2-32, IH (1 Div)
Candleberry Ltd v West End Homeowners Association; *sub nom* Candleberry Ltd v
Westend Homeowners Association 2006 S.C. 638; 2007 S.C.L.R. 128; 2006
Hous. L.R. 45; 2006 G.W.D. 22-485, IH (Ex Div); reversing in part 2006 G.W.D.
21-457, Sh Pr . . . . *Digested*, 07/**5279**
Candleberry Ltd v Westend Homeowners Association see Candleberry Ltd v West End
Homeowners Association
Card Protection Plan Ltd v Customs and Excise Commissioners [2001] UKHL 4;
[2002] 1 A.C. 202; [2001] 2 W.L.R. 329; [2001] 2 All E.R. 143; [2001] 1 All E.R.
(Comm) 438; [2001] S.T.C. 174; [2001] 2 C.M.L.R. 2; [2001] B.T.C. 5083;
[2001] B.V.C. 158; [2001] S.T.I. 151; (2001) 98(9) L.S.G. 41; (2001) 145 S.J.L.B.
60; *Times*, February 6, 2001, HL; reversing [1994] S.T.C. 199; [1994] 1
C.M.L.R. 756, CA (Civ Div); affirming [1992] S.T.C. 797, QBD . . . . *Digested*, 01/**5600**:
Applied, 94/4602, 04/3992, 06/4449: *Considered*, 98/4961, 07/5568:
Preliminary ruling given, 99/4972: *Referred to*, 95/5039, 95/5093
Carling v WP Bruce Ltd [2007] CSOH 119; 2007 S.L.T. 743; 2007 G.W.D. 25-432, OH. *Digested*, 07/**5448**
Carltona Ltd v Commissioners of Works [1943] 2 All E.R. 560, CA . . . . *Applied*, 47-51/1530,
47-51/8203, 54/46, 61/7385, 68/3426, 69/276, 76/279, 96/7374, 02/2593,
02/3761, 03/4042, 07/717: *Cited*, 07/2811: *Considered*, 83/2708, 87/4112,
91/1981, 93/1662, 00/5396, 07/5436: *Distinguished*, 97/4123:
Followed, 90/4713, 96/2961
Carter v McIntosh (1862) 24 D. 925, IH (2 Div) . . . . *Applied*, 55/3507:
Considered, 97/6106, 07/5335
Castle Inns (Stirling) Ltd (t/a Castle Leisure Group) v Clark Contracts Ltd 2007 G.W.D.
12-237, OH
Cawdor v Cawdor see Ilona (Countess of Cawdor) v Vaughan (Earl of Cawdor)
Chalmers Trustee v Dick's Trustee 1909 S.C. 761; 1909 1 S.L.T. 324, IH (2 Div); affirming
1909 1 S.L.T. 240, OH. . . . . *Considered*, 07/5285
Charleston v News Group Newspapers Ltd [1995] 2 A.C. 65; [1995] 2 W.L.R. 450;
[1995] 2 All E.R. 313; [1995] E.M.L.R. 129; (1995) 145 N.L.J. 490; (1995) 139
S.J.L.B. 100; *Times*, March 31, 1995; *Independent*, March 31, 1995, HL;
affirming [1994] E.M.L.R. 186; *Times*, January 12, 1994, *Independent*, January
14, 1994; *Guardian*, February 26, 1994, CA (Civ Div) . . . . *Digested*, 95/**3126**:
Applied, 07/5098: *Considered*, 95/5: *Followed*, 99/1634
Chief Constable of Strathclyde v Cowie 2007 G.W.D. 2-24, Sh Ct (South Strathclyde)
Chief Constable of Tayside v Basterfield 2007 S.L.T. (Sh Ct) 129; 2007 G.W.D. 30-516,
Sh Ct (Tayside)
Chinn v Cyclacel Ltd 2007 G.W.D. 24-416, OH
Christie Owen & Davies Plc (t/a Christie & Co) v Campbell 2007 G.W.D. 24-397, Sh Ct
(Glasgow)
City Wall Properties (Scotland) Ltd v Pearl Assurance Plc [2007] CSIH 79; [2007]
N.P.C. 114, IH (Ex Div); affirming 2005 G.W.D. 35-666, OH
Clark v Clark see Clarke v Clarke
Clark v Clark; *sub nom* Clarke v Clarke 2007 S.L.T. (Sh Ct) 86; 2007 Fam. L.R. 34;
2007 G.W.D. 10-186, Sh Pr . . . . *Digested*, 07/**5189**
Clark v Kelly [2003] UKPC D 1; [2004] 1 A.C. 681; [2003] 2 W.L.R. 1586; [2003] 1
All E.R. 1106; 2003 S.C. (P.C.) 77; 2003 S.L.T. 308; 2003 S.C.C.R. 194; [2003]
H.R.L.R. 17; [2003] U.K.H.R.R. 1167; 14 B.H.R.C. 369; (2003) 100(17) L.S.G.
27; (2003) 147 S.J.L.B. 234; 2003 G.W.D. 7-164; *Times*, February 12, 2003;
Independent, March 17, 2003, PC (Sc); affirming 2001 J.C. 16; 2000 S.L.T. 1038;
2000 S.C.C.R. 821; 2000 G.W.D. 27-1041, HCJ. . . . . *Digested*, 03/**5167**:
Applied, 07/5049: *Disapproved*, 05/5123
Clark v Lindale Homes Ltd 1994 S.C. 210; 1994 S.L.T. 1053; 1994 S.C.L.R. 301, IH (1
Div). . . . . *Digested*, 94/**5897**:
Applied, 95/5568: *Distinguished*, 07/5286
Clark (James Roy) v HM Advocate [2007] HCJAC 92; 2007 J.C. 186; 2006 G.W.D.
40-776, HCJ Appeal
Clarke v Clarke see Clark v Clark
Clarke v Clarke; *sub nom* Clark v Clark 2007 S.L.T. (Sh Ct) 64; 2006 Fam. L.R. 91;
2006 G.W.D. 27-605, Sh Ct (Grampian) . . . . *Digested*, 07/**5186**
Clingham v Kensington and Chelsea RLBC see R. (on the application of McCann) v
Manchester Crown Court
Closure Order, [address], Fife; *sub nom* Superintendent of Fife Constabulary, Applicant
2007 G.W.D. 37-649, Sh Ct (Tayside)
Clow (Elizabeth) v HM Advocate [2007] HCJAC 24; 2007 S.L.T. 517; 2007 S.C.C.R.
201; 2007 G.W.D. 14-277, HCJ . . . . *Digested*, 07/**5070**
Clydeport Properties Ltd v Shell UK Ltd [2007] CSOH 92; 2007 S.L.T. 547; 2007
Hous. L.R. 49; 2007 G.W.D. 18-328, OH . . . . *Digested*, 07/**5484**
Cobb v General Chiropractic Council [2007] CSIH 66; 2007 G.W.D. 25-436, IH (1
Div)

Cochrane v HM Advocate 2007 G.W.D. 2-25, HCJ
Coleman v Clydesdale Bank 2007 G.W.D. 28-484, Sh Ct (Grampian)
Comhairle Nan Eilean Siar v Collins 2007 S.L.T. (Sh Ct) 122; 2007 S.C.L.R. 567; 2007
    G.W.D. 11-203, Sh Pr
Common Services Agency v Scottish Information Commissioner [2006] CSIH 58;
    2007 S.C. 231; 2007 S.L.T. 7; 2006 G.W.D. 39-766, IH (1 Div) . . . .   *Digested*, 07/**4889**
Connolly v Brown [2006] CSOH 187; 2007 S.L.T. 778; 2007 G.W.D. 9-155, OH . . . . .   *Digested*, 07/**4894**
Constance & Swinscoe, Re 2007 G.W.D. 27-479, Sh Pr
Conway v Griffiths see Gordon v Griffiths
Cook (John Wishart) v HM Advocate [2006] HCJAC 82; 2007 S.L.T. 81; 2006
    S.C.C.R. 687; 2006 G.W.D. 36-730, HCJ . . . .   *Digested*, 07/**5073**
Cooper v Dundee City Council 2007 G.W.D. 35-618, Sh Ct (Tayside)
Cosgrove (Richard William) v HM Advocate [2007] HCJAC 54; 2007 G.W.D. 32-551,
    HCJ
Coulter v HM Advocate see Montgomery v HM Advocate
Countess of Cawdor v Cawdor Castle (Tourism) Ltd 2007 G.W.D. 25-423, OH
Countrywide North Ltd v GWM Developments Ltd 2007 G.W.D. 13-260, OH
Cowie v Strathclyde RC (Unreported, July 8, 1986), IH (1 Div) . . . .   *Considered*, 07/5500
Coyle v Auditor of the Court of Session [2006] CSOH 169; 2006 S.L.T. 1045; 2006
    G.W.D. 34-698, OH . . . .   *Digested*, 07/**4986**
Coyle (James Thomas) v HM Advocate [2007] HCJAC 52; 2007 S.C.C.R. 479; 2007
    G.W.D. 29-508, HCJ
Craig v McCall 2007 G.W.D. 36-632, Sh Ct (Tayside)
Creighton v HM Advocate (1904) 6 F. (J.) 72; (1904) 12 S.L.T. 36, HCJ . . . .   *Considered*, 07/5051
Crichton (Raymond) v HM Advocate 2007 S.C.C.R. 339, HCJ
Curly Lloyds (Partnership) v Clackmannanshire Licensing Board 2007 G.W.D. 12-256,
    Sh Ct (Tayside)
Customs and Excise Commissioners v Hubbard Foundation Scotland [1981] S.T.C. 593;
    1981 S.C. 244; 1982 S.L.T. 277, IH (1 Div) . . . .   *Digested*, 82/**4440**:
                                    Considered, 07/4322: *Followed*, 98/4878
Customs and Excise Commissioners v Morrison's Academy Boarding Houses
    Association [1978] S.T.C. 1; 1977 S.C. 279; 1977 S.L.T. 197, IH (1 Div) . . . .   *Digested*, 77/**3812**:
                                    Applied, 79/2743, 95/5121, 07/4364: *Considered*, 01/5579:
                                                                 Distinguished, 98/6219
Customs and Excise Commissioners v Robertson's Electrical Ltd see Robertson's
    Electrical Ltd v Customs and Excise Commissioners
CW v Secretary of State for the Home Department; *sub nom* W v Secretary of State
    for the Home Department [2007] CSIH 71; 2007 G.W.D. 28-494, IH (Ex Div)

D v Glasgow City Council [2007] CSIH 72; 2007 S.L.T. 1057; 2007 Fam. L.R. 118;
    2007 G.W.D. 33-563, IH (1 Div); affirming [2007] CSOH 139; 2007 S.L.T. 881;
    2007 G.W.D. 26-457, OH
D v HM Advocate 2007 G.W.D. 29-504, HCJ
D v Secretary of State for the Home Department 2007 G.W.D. 19-336, OH
DA v HM Advocate see A v HM Advocate
Dacre v Aberdeenshire Council 2007 G.W.D. 27-478, Sh Ct (Grampian)
Dale v Lets Glasgow Ltd 2007 G.W.D. 1-4, Sh Pr
Dalfaber Action Group v Scottish Ministers 2007 G.W.D. 39-688, OH
Davidson v McIrvine 2007 S.L.T. (Sh Ct) 71; 2007 G.W.D. 8-151, Sh Ct (Grampian) . . .   *Digested*, 07/**5425**
Davidson v McIrvine 2007 G.W.D. 23-389, Sh Ct (Grampian)
Davidson v Midlothian Council 2007 G.W.D. 39-675, Sh Ct (Lothian)
Davidson v Scottish Ministers (Incidental Petition: Dismissal of Appeal); *sub nom*
    Davidson, Petitioner (No.3) 2005 1 S.C. (H.L.) 1, HL . . . .   *Digested*, 06/**5114**:
                                                                 Considered, 07/4855
Davidson, Petitioner (No.3) see Davidson v Scottish Ministers (Incidental Petition:
    Dismissal of Appeal)
DCM (Optical Holdings) Ltd v Revenue and Customs Commissioners [2007] CSIH 58;
    2007 S.C. 813; 2007 S.L.T. 705; [2007] B.T.C. 5786; [2007] B.V.C. 733;
    [2007] S.T.I. 1813; 2007 G.W.D. 22-377, IH (1 Div); reversing [2006] B.V.C.
    2708; [2006] S.T.I. 1716, V&DTr . . . .   *Digested*, 07/**5569**
De Lathouwer v Anderson [2007] CSOH 54; 2007 S.L.T. 437; 2007 G.W.D. 11-232,
    OH . . . .   *Digested*, 07/**5545**
Deighan v Edinburgh City Council 2004 Hous. L.R. 89, Sh Ct (Lothian) . . . .   *Digested*, 05/**5473**:
                                                                 Considered, 07/5332
DFR Properties Ltd v Glen House Properties 2007 S.C. 74; 2006 G.W.D. 38-749, IH
    (Ex Div) . . . .   *Digested*, 07/**5016**
Dickie v Flexcon Glenrothes Ltd 2007 G.W.D. 34-586, Sh Ct (Tayside)
Dickson v Dickson (Parent & Child: Evidence) 1990 S.C.L.R. 692, IH (Ex Div);
    affirming 1990 S.L.T. (Sh. Ct.) 80; 1990 S.C.L.R. 542, Sh Pr . . . .   *Digested*, 91/**4468**:
                                                   Applied, 07/5190: *Followed*, 97/5617
Dickson v Hastings 2007 S.L.T. (Sh Ct) 58; 2007 G.W.D. 11-214, Sh Ct (Tayside) . . . . .   *Digested*, 07/**5449**
Dickson v Hastings (No.1) 2007 S.L.T. (Sh Ct) 161; 2007 G.W.D. 21-355, Sh Ct
    (Tayside)

Dickson v Hastings (No.2) 2007 S.L.T. (Sh Ct) 164; 2007 G.W.D. 21-356, Sh Ct (Tayside)

Dickson (Kenneth Robert) v HM Advocate; *joined cases* McNaughton v Gilchrist; McHale v Miller [2006] HCJAC 74; 2006 S.L.T. 1027; 2006 S.C.C.R. 637; 2006 G.W.D. 33-689, HCJ . . . . *Digested*, 07/**5055**

Dickson (Kenneth Robert) v HM Advocate; *joined case* McNaughton (Iain) v HM Advocate [2007] HCJAC 65; 2007 G.W.D. 40-692, HCJ

Dignity Funerals Ltd v Bruce see Bruce v Dignity Funerals Ltd

Dillon v Inverclyde Leisure 2007 G.W.D. 15-292, OH

Din (Taher Javid) v HM Advcocate 2007 S.C.C.R. 299, HCJ . . . . *Digested*, 07/**5517**

Dineley v Lothian Health Board 2007 G.W.D. 28-498, OH

Dionsynth Ltd v Thomson see Thomson v Diosynth Ltd

DJS v Criminal Injuries Compensation Board see S v Criminal Injuries Compensation Appeal Panel

DL v HM Advocate 2007 S.C.C.R. 472, HCJ

DNG v JM 2007 Rep. L.R. 114, OH

Do v Immigration Appeal Tribunal see R. (on the application of Ullah) v Special Adjudicator

Do v Secretary of State for the Home Department see R. (on the application of Ullah) v Special Adjudicator

Dodd v Southern Pacific Personal Loans Ltd 2007 G.W.D. 21-352, OH

Dodds v Advocate General for Scotland 2007 G.W.D. 8-134, OH

Dodds (Brian) v HM Advocate 2003 J.C. 8; 2002 S.L.T. 1058; 2002 S.C.C.R. 838; 2002 G.W.D. 25-786, HCJ . . . . *Digested*, 02/**5434**: *Considered*, 07/5022

Donaldson v Fallon 2007 G.W.D. 35-608, Sh Ct (South Strathclyde)

Donaldson v Hays Distribution Services 2007 G.W.D. 6-97, OH

Donnelly v Advocate General for Scotland see Donnelly v Secretary of State for Works and Pensions

Donnelly v Central Demolition Ltd 2007 G.W.D. 35-605, Sh Ct (Tayside)

Donnelly v Graham 2007 G.W.D. 35-613, Sh Ct (Tayside)

Donnelly v Secretary of State for Works and Pensions; *sub nom* Donnelly v Advocate General for Scotland 2007 S.C.L.R. 746; 2007 G.W.D. 7-129, OH

Donnelly (Darryn) v HM Advocate see Donnelly (Francis) v HM Advocate

Donnelly (Francis) v HM Advocate; *joined case* Donnelly (Darryn) v HM Advocate [2007] HCJAC 59; 2007 S.C.C.R. 577; 2007 G.W.D. 40-693, HCJ

Donnet, Fatal Accident Inquiry 2007 G.W.D. 30-522, Sh Ct (Tayside)

Donoghue v Stevenson; *sub nom* McAlister v Stevenson [1932] A.C. 562; 1932 S.C. (H.L.) 31; 1932 S.L.T. 317; [1932] W.N. 139, HL . . . . *Applied*, 47-51/6681, 47-51/6693, 47-51/6761, 47-51/6881, 47-51/6897, 52/1563, 52/2362, 53/639, 53/2422, 56/904, 57/1415, 57/2371, 61/825, 62/2028, 62/2188, 63/2362, 64/1670, 65/416, 65/2669, 68/4511, 69/2403, 70/1493, 70/1850, 72/1104, 72/2350, 72/2352, 72/2408, 72/2409, 74/2579, 75/933, 75/3994, 77/2025, 78/2065, 78/3538, 81/1849, 82/2135, 85/2301, 87/2579, 88/3410, 89/1286, 01/4509, 04/2747, 07/5426: *Considered*, 47-51/351, 47-51/6734, 47-51/9691, 54/2200, 55/1839, 57/2369, 62/2083, 62/3080, 65/2663, 65/2671, 69/1157, 70/1849, 72/2528, 74/363, 74/3638, 75/2343, 76/228, 87/2580, 88/2418, 88/2433, 88/3376, 88/3409, 91/2657, 91/2661, 93/2983, 93/2997, 94/5335, 95/4519, 98/3995, 99/3960, 00/4227: *Distinguished*, 51/3988, 47-51/6584, 47-51/6705, 47-51/7886, 52/4290, 57/2366, 57/2639, 63/330, 63/2360, 64/2516, 66/6884, 72/2361, 83/2746: *Followed*, 76/3296, 85/4437: *Referred to*, 79/1866

Douglas Shelf Seven Ltd v Cooperative Wholesale Society Ltd 2007 G.W.D. 9-167, OH

Dow v West of Scotland Shipbreaking Co [2007] CSOH 71; 2007 Rep. L.R. 59, OH

Downie v Trustees of Earl of Stair's 1970 Trust [2007] CSIH 62; 2007 S.L.T. 827; 2007 Hous. L.R. 72; 2007 G.W.D. 26-463, IH (2 Div) . . . . *Digested*, 07/**5327**

DS v HM Advocate; *sub nom* HM Advocate v DS [2007] UKPC D1; 2007 S.C. (P.C.) 1; 2007 S.L.T. 1026; 2007 S.C.C.R. 222; [2007] H.R.L.R. 28; *Times*, June 12, 2007, PC (Sc) . . . . *Digested*, 07/**5019**

DTA Chartered Accountants v Clydeview Development Ltd 2007 G.W.D. 32-545, Sh Pr

Duncan v MFV Marigold PD 145 [2006] CSOH 128; 2006 S.L.T. 975; 2007 S.C.L.R. 155; 2006 G.W.D. 32-681, OH . . . . *Digested*, 06/**5601**

Duncan (t/a G Duncan Motor Services) v Revenue and Customs Commissioners [2007] V. & D.R. 114; [2007] S.T.I. 1704, V&DTr (Edinburgh)

Dundee City Council v D 2007 Fam. L.R. 157; 2007 G.W.D. 38-667, Sh Ct (Tayside)

Dunn (Christopher Gary) v HM Advocate see Mason (Lee) v HM Advocate

Dunnachie (Colin) v HM Advocate [2007] HCJAC 49; 2007 S.C.C.R. 446; 2007 G.W.D. 29-509, HCJ

Durant v Financial Services Authority (Disclosure) [2003] EWCA Civ 1746; [2004] F.S.R. 28; *Times*, January 2, 2004, CA (Civ Div) . . . . *Digested*, 04/**1551**: *Considered*, 07/4889

Dyer v Anderson 2007 G.W.D. 40-697, Sh Ct (Glasgow)

Dyer v Caledonian Industrial Ltd 2007 G.W.D. 5-78, Sh Ct (Glasgow)

Dyer v Gallacher [2007] HCJAC 19; 2007 J.C. 125; 2007 S.C.C.R. 152; 2007 G.W.D.
   10-197, HCJ Appeal; affirming 2006 G.W.D. 7-136, Sh Ct (Glasgow) . . . .   *Digested*, 07/**5324**
Dyer v Gallagher 2007 G.W.D. 36-627, Sh Ct (Glasgow)
Dyer v McHendry 2007 G.W.D. 36-628, Sh Ct (Glasgow)
Dyson v Leeds City Council (No.2) see Fairchild v Glenhaven Funeral Services Ltd (t/
   a GH Dovener & Son)

Earl of Cawdor, Petitioner [2006] CSOH 141; 2006 S.L.T. 1070; 2006 G.W.D. 30-662, OH   *Digested*, 07/**5562**
Early (Gerald Patrick) v HM Advocate [2006] HCJAC 65; 2007 J.C. 50; 2006 S.L.T.
   856; 2006 S.C.C.R. 583; 2006 G.W.D. 28-623, HCJ . . . .   *Digested*, 06/**5205**:
                                            Applied, 07/5046: *Considered*, 07/5068
East Ayrshire Council v Robertson [2007] R.V.R. 158; 2006 G.W.D. 26-581, Sh Pr. . . .   *Digested*, 07/**4977**
Eaton Ltd v King see King v Eaton Ltd (No.2)
Edinburgh City Council v Middlemiss 2007 Hous. L.R. 70; 2007 G.W.D. 38-670, Sh Ct
   (Lothian)
Edinburgh City Council v Salteri 2007 S.C. 463; 2007 S.C.L.R. 576; 2007 G.W.D. 11-
   220, IH (Ex Div); affirming 2006 G.W.D. 13-247, Sh Pr
Edinburgh City Council v Secretary of State for Scotland; *joined cases* Revival
   Properties Ltd v Edinburgh City Council; Secretary of State for Scotland v
   Revival Properties Ltd [1997] 1 W.L.R. 1447; [1998] 1 All E.R. 174; 1998 S.C.
   (H.L.) 33; 1998 S.L.T. 120; 1997 S.C.L.R. 1112; [1997] 3 P.L.R. 71; [1998] J.P.L.
   224; [1997] E.G. 140 (C.S.); (1997) 94(42) L.S.G. 31; (1997) 141 S.J.L.B. 228;
   [1997] N.P.C. 146; 1997 G.W.D. 33-1693; *Times*, October 31, 1997, HL; affirming
   in part 1996 S.C.L.R. 600, IH (2 Div). . . . .   *Digested*, 97/**6350**:
        Applied, 99/4178, 06/3289, 07/5464: *Considered*, 99/4218, 01/4743,
                              05/3295: *Followed*, 97/4116, 99/6411
Edinburgh Pharmaceutical Processes Ltd v Lothian see Lothian v Edinburgh
   Pharmaceutical Processes Ltd
Elshani v Secretary of State for the Home Department 2007 G.W.D. 31-537, OH
Elstone's Application, Re see Scottish Ministers v Scottish Information Commissioner
Emms' Application for Judicial Review, Re see Emms, Petitioner
Emms, Petitioner; *sub nom* Emms' Application for Judicial Review, Re [2007] CSOH
   184; 2007 G.W.D. 39-674, OH
Empowerment Enterprises Ltd v Customs and Excise Commissioners; *sub nom*
   Revenue and Customs Commissioners v Empowerment Enterprises Ltd [2006]
   CSIH 46; 2007 S.C. 123; 2006 S.L.T. 955; [2007] B.T.C. 5931; [2007] B.V.C.
   878; [2006] S.T.I. 2344; 2006 G.W.D. 32-682, IH (Ex Div); reversing [2005]
   B.V.C. 2445; [2005] S.T.I. 876, V&D Tr (Edinburgh). . . . .   *Digested*, 06/**5739**
Eriden Properties LLP v Falkirk Council [2007] CSOH 157; 2007 S.L.T. 966; 2007
   G.W.D. 29-501, OH
Euro Properties Scotland Ltd v Alam 2000 G.W.D. 23-896, OH. . . . .   *Considered*, 07/5330
Experno Ltd v Banks 2007 G.W.D. 20-343, Sh Pr

F v Harrow LBC see B v Harrow LBC (No.1)
F v Quarriers 2007 G.W.D. 11-208, OH
F v Quarriers 2007 G.W.D. 11-222, OH
F v Special Education Needs Tribunal see B v Harrow LBC (No.1)
Fairchild v Glenhaven Funeral Services Ltd (t/a GH Dovener & Son); *joined cases*
   Pendleton v Stone & Webster Engineering Ltd; Dyson v Leeds City Council
   (No.2); Matthews v Associated Portland Cement Manufacturers (1978) Ltd; Fox
   v Spousal (Midlands) Ltd; Babcock International Ltd v National Grid Co Plc;
   Matthews v British Uralite Plc [2002] UKHL 22; [2003] 1 A.C. 32; [2002] 3
   W.L.R. 89; [2002] 3 All E.R. 305; [2002] I.C.R. 798; [2002] I.R.L.R. 533;
   [2002] P.I.Q.R. P28; [2002] Lloyd's Rep. Med. 361; (2002) 67 B.M.L.R. 90;
   (2002) 152 N.L.J. 998; *Times*, June 21, 2002; *Independent*, June 25, 2002;
   Daily Telegraph, June 27, 2002, HL; reversing [2001] EWCA Civ 1881; [2002] 1
   W.L.R. 1052; [2002] I.C.R. 412; [2002] I.R.L.R. 129; [2002] P.I.Q.R. P27;
   Times, December 13, 2001; *Independent*, December 21, 2001; *Daily Telegraph*,
   December 20, 2001, CA (Civ Div); affirming 00/TLQ/1284, QBD. . . . .   *Digested*, 02/**2225**:
        Applied, 04/2693, 04/2755, 06/2867, 07/5100: *Considered*, 02/3245,
                02/3247, 03/2990, 05/2841, 05/4199: *Followed*, 06/2866
Falkirk Council v Central RC 1997 S.L.T. 1242, IH (Ex Div). . . . .   *Digested*, 97/**6252**:
                                              Considered, 07/5279
Farleyer House Hotel Ltd v Smart 2007 G.W.D. 14-275, OH
Fee v East Renfrewshire Council 2006 Hous. L.R. 99; 2006 G.W.D. 27-610, Lands Tr
   (Scot) . . . .   *Digested*, 07/**5337**
Fegan v Highland Regional Council [2007] CSIH 44; 2007 S.C. 723; 2007 S.L.T. 651;
   2007 Rep. L.R. 95; 2007 G.W.D. 18-323, IH (Ex Div); affirming 2006 G.W.D. 8-
   156, Sh Ct (Grampian) . . . .   *Digested*, 07/**5422**
Fernandez v Fernandez [2007] CSIH 6; 2007 S.C. 547; 2007 S.C.L.R. 244, IH (Ex
   Div); affirming 2006 G.W.D. 28-617, OH . . . .   *Digested*, 07/**4978**

Ferns v Scottish Homes 2007 S.L.T. (Sh Ct) 27; 2007 S.C.L.R. 632; 2007 Hous. L.R.
   8; 2007 G.W.D. 3-38, Sh Pr . . . .   *Digested,* 07/**5419**
Fiat Auto Financial Services v Connelly 2007 S.L.T. (Sh Ct) 111; 2007 G.W.D. 15-293,
   Sh Ct (Glasgow)
Findlay's Executor v West Lothian Council; *sub nom* Findlay's Executor, Petitioner
   [2006] CSOH 188; [2007] R.V.R. 263; 2006 G.W.D. 40-769, OH
Findlay's Executor, Petitioner see Findlay's Executor v West Lothian Council
Firm of AC Stoddart & Sons, Colstoun (1995) v Balfour Thomson CA see AC Stoddart &
   Sons v Trustees of the Coulson Trust
First People Solutions Group v Jack 2007 G.W.D. 32-547, OH
Fishers Bistro v Lothian Assessor [2007] CSIH 41; 2007 S.C. 671; [2007] R.A. 384;
   2007 G.W.D. 19-342, LVAC
Fitzpatrick v Inland Revenue Commissioners (No.2) 1992 S.C. 207; 1993 S.L.T. 54, IH
   (1 Div) . . . .   *Digested,* 93/**5419**:
                        Considered, 07/4057: *Subsequent proceedings,* 94/5928
Fleming v Diosynth Ltd see Thomson v Diosynth Ltd
Fleming v Xaniar Ltd (In Liquidation) 1998 S.C. 8; 1998 S.L.T. 703; [1997] I.R.L.R.
   682; 1997 G.W.D. 31-1582, IH (1 Div) . . . .   *Digested,* 98/**5812**:
                        Applied, 07/1348: *Followed,* 98/2188
Fleming (Douglas Colin) v HM Advocate [2006] HCJAC 64; 2007 J.C. 44; 2006
   S.C.C.R. 594, HCJ. . . . .   *Digested,* 07/**5046**
Fletcher v Argyll and Bute Council [2007] CSOH 174; 2007 S.L.T. 1047; 2007 G.W.D.
   33-567, OH
Forsyth v Aberdeen Licensing Board 2007 G.W.D. 39-683, OH
Fox v Spousal (Midlands) Ltd see Fairchild v Glenhaven Funeral Services Ltd (t/a GH
   Dovener & Son)
Frame v Trux + Ltd 2007 G.W.D. 35-606, Sh Ct (Grampian)
Fraser v Stewart see Stewart v Stewart
Fresh Catch Ltd v CGU Insurance Plc 2007 G.W.D. 10-173, OH
Friend v Lord Advocate; *sub nom* Whaley v Lord Advocate [2007] UKHL 53; 2007
   S.L.T. 1209; (2007) 151 S.J.L.B. 1565; 2007 G.W.D. 39-680, HL; affirming 2006
   S.C. 121; 2005 G.W.D. 30-577, IH (Ex Div); affirming 2004 S.C. 78; 2004 S.L.T.
   425; 2003 G.W.D. 22-651, OH . . . .   *Digested,* 04/**4480**
FSH Airport (Edinburgh) Services Ltd v Edinburgh City Council 2007 G.W.D. 39-687,
   OH

G v Quarriers 2007 G.W.D. 11-223, OH
G v S [2006] CSOH 88; 2006 S.L.T. 795; 2007 S.C.L.R. 137; 2006 Rep. L.R. 131;
   2006 G.W.D. 22-473, OH. . . . .   *Digested,* 06/**5113**
G v Secretary of State for the Home Department 2007 G.W.D. 39-682, OH
Gaffney (Derek Jerry) v HM Advocate 2007 S.C.C.R. 296, HCJ . . . .   *Digested,* 07/**5506**
Gallacher v Wood 2007 G.W.D. 37-647, Lands Tr (Scot)
Gardiner v HM Advocate 2007 G.W.D. 11-209, HCJ
Gardiner (John) v HM Advocate [2007] HCJAC 14; 2007 S.C.C.R. 379; 2007 G.W.D.
   28-486, HCJ
Gardner v Edinburgh City Council 2006 S.L.T. (Sh Ct) 166; 2006 G.W.D. 33-683, Sh
   Pr . . . .   *Digested,* 07/**5403**
Garty (James) v HM Advocate see Weir (Mark Lindsay) v HM Advocate
Geddes, Petitioner 2006 S.L.T. 664; 2007 S.C.L.R. 11; 2006 G.W.D. 21-460, OH . . . . .   *Digested,* 06/**5527**
Ghafoor (Choudry Naser) v HM Advocate 2007 S.C.C.R. 342, HCJ
Ghaidan v Godin-Mendoza; *sub nom* Mendoza v Ghaidan; Ghaidan v Mendoza;
   Godin-Mendoza v Ghaidan [2004] UKHL 30; [2004] 2 A.C. 557; [2004] 3
   W.L.R. 113; [2004] 3 All E.R. 411; [2004] 2 F.L.R. 600; [2004] 2 F.C.R. 481;
   [2004] H.R.L.R. 31; [2004] U.K.H.R.R. 827; 16 B.H.R.C. 671; [2004] H.L.R. 46;
   [2005] 1 P. & C.R. 18; [2005] L. & T.R. 3; [2004] 2 E.G.L.R. 132; [2004] Fam.
   Law 641; [2004] 27 E.G. 128 (C.S.); (2004) 101(27) L.S.G. 30; (2004) 154
   N.L.J. 1013; (2004) 148 S.J.L.B. 792; [2004] N.P.C. 100; [2004] 2 P. & C.R.
   DG17; *Times,* June 24, 2004, HL; affirming [2002] EWCA Civ 1533; [2003] Ch.
   380; [2003] 2 W.L.R. 478; [2002] 4 All E.R. 1162; [2002] 3 F.C.R. 591;
   [2003] U.K.H.R.R. 254; 13 B.H.R.C. 608; [2003] H.L.R. 35; [2003] L. & T.R.
   14; [2003] A.C.D. 12; [2003] Fam. Law 87; [2002] 46 E.G. 197 (C.S.); (2003)
   100(1) L.S.G. 24; (2002) 152 N.L.J. 1718; (2002) 146 S.J.L.B. 253; [2002]
   N.P.C. 138; [2003] 1 P. & C.R. DG14; *Times,* November 14, 2002; *Independent,*
   November 22, 2002, CA (Civ Div) . . . .   *Digested,* 04/**2538**:
           Applied, 04/1889, 05/2118, 05/2641, 06/4484, 07/3293, 07/4358:
       Considered, 04/707, 04/1312, 05/2129, 06/871, 06/1004, 06/1649, 06/4470,
                                   07/5431
Ghaidan v Mendoza see Ghaidan v Godin-Mendoza
Gibson v Scottish Ambulance Service EATS/0052/04, EAT (SC) . . . .   *Applied,* 07/**5145**
Gibson v Whyte 2007 Rep. L.R. 50; 2007 G.W.D. 4-66, OH
Giftex Corp v Divex Ltd 2007 G.W.D. 10-175, OH

Gilbert Ash (Northern) Ltd v Modern Engineering (Bristol) Ltd; *sub nom* Modern
   Engineering (Bristol) Ltd v Gilbert Ash (Northern) Ltd [1974] A.C. 689; [1973] 3
   W.L.R. 421; [1973] 3 All E.R. 195; 1 B.L.R. 73; 72 L.G.R. 1; (1973) 117 S.J. 745,
   HL; reversing 71 L.G.R. 162, CA (Civ Div) . . . . *Digested*, 73/**262**:
                                  Applied, 74/268, 81/188, 85/218, 88/461, 92/312, 93/2361:
                                  Considered, 75/3180, 85/2604, 93/2519, 94/2797, 07/5011:
                                  Distinguished, 74/267, 84/2722: *Followed*, 82/3441, 83/3961, 86/202,
                                                                                                 93/301
Gillespie v Toondale Ltd [2005] CSIH 92; 2006 S.C. 304, IH (Ex Div); affirming 2005
   G.W.D. 31-590, OH . . . . *Digested*, 07/**5017**
Gillon (Andrew Urquhart) v HM Advocate [2006] HCJAC 61; 2007 J.C. 24; 2006
   S.L.T. 799; 2006 S.C.C.R. 561; 2006 G.W.D. 27-601, HCJ . . . . *Digested*, 06/**5174**
Gilmour (Raymond McKenzie) v HM Advocate [2006] HCJAC 73; 2006 S.L.T. 1099;
   2006 S.C.C.R. 626; 2006 G.W.D. 32-679, HCJ . . . . *Digested*, 07/**5056**
Gilmour (Raymond McKenzie) v HM Advocate [2007] HCJAC 48; 2007 S.L.T. 893;
   2007 S.C.C.R. 417; 2007 G.W.D. 28-485, HCJ
Gilogley v HM Advocate 2007 G.W.D. 13-262, HCJ
Given v James Watt College [2006] CSOH 189; 2007 S.L.T. 39; 2007 Rep. L.R. 22;
   2007 G.W.D. 1-13, OH. . . . . *Digested*, 07/**5420**
Glasgow Airport v Kirkman & Bradford [2007] CSIH 47; 2007 S.C. 742; [2007]
   C.I.L.L. 2506; 2007 G.W.D. 18-316, IH (Ex Div); affirming 2007 G.W.D. 9-160,
   OH
Glasgow City Council v McNab [2007] I.R.L.R. 476, EAT (SC) . . . . *Digested*, 07/**5147**
Glasgow Housing Association Ltd v Gourlay 2006 Hous. L.R. 52, Sh Ct (Glasgow) . . *Digested*, 07/**5309**
Glasgow Housing Association Ltd v Marshall 2006 Hous. L.R. 56, Sh Ct (Glasgow) . . *Digested*, 07/**5310**
Gloag v Perth and Kinross Council 2007 S.C.L.R. 530, Sh Ct (Tayside)
Goatley (Stephen Maurice) v HM Advocate [2006] HCJAC 55; 2007 S.L.T. 14; 2006
   S.C.C.R. 463; [2007] Eu. L.R. 42; 2006 G.W.D. 33-690, HCJ . . . . *Digested*, 07/**5168**
Godin-Mendoza v Ghaidan see Ghaidan v Godin-Mendoza
Goodwin v Patent Office [1999] I.C.R. 302; [1999] I.R.L.R. 4; [1999] Disc. L.R. 104;
   Times, November 11, 1998, EAT. . . . . *Digested*, 98/**2114**:
                        Applied, 00/2125, 01/2242, 04/1209, 05/1147: *Considered*, 07/5115
Gordon v Argyll and Bute Council 2007 Fam. L.R. 76; 2007 G.W.D. 11-217, OH
Gordon v Griffiths; *joined case* Conway v Griffiths [2007] HCJAC 45; 2007 S.L.T.
   954; 2007 S.C.C.R. 349; 2007 G.W.D. 26-452, HCJ Appeal
Gough v McFadyen see Robertson (Stewart) v HM Advocate
Gough (Stephen Peter) v HM Advocate see Robertson (Stewart) v HM Advocate
Graham v HM Advocate 2007 G.W.D. 11-213, HCJ
Graham v Parker 2007 G.W.D. 30-524, Lands Tr (Scot)
Graham v Western Bank (1865) 3 M. 617 . . . . *Considered*, 07/4979
Grampian Housing Association v Pyper 2004 Hous. L.R. 22; 2004 G.W.D. 13-293, Sh
   Pr . . . . *Digested*, 05/**5425**:
                                                                                 Considered, 07/5336
Grampian Valuation Joint Board Assessor v Fraser; *sub nom* Assessor for Grampian
   Valuation Joint Board v Fraser [2006] CSIH 55; 2007 S.C. 210; 2007 S.L.T. 48;
   [2006] R.A. 449; 2006 G.W.D. 39-765, IH (2 Div) . . . . *Digested*, 07/**5394**
Grampian Valuation Joint Board Assessor v Macdonald 2002 S.L.T. 817; 2001 S.C.L.R.
   686; [2002] R.A. 63; 2001 G.W.D. 20-779, OH . . . . *Digested*, 02/**5971**:
                                                                                 Considered, 07/5394
Grant v Scottish Water 2007 G.W.D. 3-44, Sh Ct (Tayside)
Gray v Binny (1879) 7 R. 332, IH (1 Div) . . . . *Applied*, 00/6697,
                                                                                           07/5544
Gray v Dickson 2007 G.W.D. 31-540, Sh Ct (Tayside)
Gray v Welsh 2007 G.W.D. 11-205, OH
Gray Aitken Partnership Ltd v Link Housing Association Ltd see Link Housing
   Association Ltd v PBL Construction Ltd
Greenan v Courtney [2007] CSOH 58; 2007 S.L.T. 355; 2007 G.W.D. 11-233, OH . . . . *Digested*, 07/**5546**
Greenan v Courtney 2007 G.W.D. 40-702, OH
Greenan (Leonard Smith) v HM Advocate [2006] HCJAC 80; 2007 J.C. 181; 2006
   S.C.C.R. 659; 2006 G.W.D. 37-739, HCJ Appeal . . . . *Digested*, 07/**5029**
Greens v HM Advocate 2007 G.W.D. 32-552, HCJ
Greenwoods Ltd v Ans Homes Ltd [2007] CSOH 13; 2007 S.L.T. 149; 2007 S.C.L.R.
   563; 2007 G.W.D. 3-36, OH . . . . *Digested*, 07/**4998**
Griffiths v Scottish Water 2007 G.W.D. 7-111, Sh Ct (Tayside)
Guler v HM Advocate 2007 G.W.D. 13-263, HCJ
Gunn v MacDonald 2007 G.W.D. 11-230, HCJ

H v Secretary of State for the Home Department 2007 G.W.D. 37-652, OH
H, Applicant 2007 S.L.T. (Sh Ct) 5; 2006 G.W.D. 21-447, Sh Ct (Glasgow) . . . . *Digested*, 07/**5411**
HA v Secretary of State for the Home Department; *sub nom* A v Secretary of State for
   the Home Department [2007] CSIH 65; 2007 G.W.D. 27-480, IH (Ex Div)
Hadden Construction Ltd v Midway Services Ltd; *sub nom* Hadden Construction Ltd,
   Petitioners 2007 G.W.D. 34-580, Sh Pr

Hadden Construction Ltd, Petitioners see Hadden Construction Ltd v Midway Services Ltd

Haddow v WH Malcolm Ltd 2007 G.W.D. 6-98, Sh Ct (North Strathclyde)

Hakeem v Secretary of State for Work and Pensions 2007 S.L.T. (Sh Ct) 179; 2007 Fam. L.R. 108; 2007 G.W.D. 23-379, Sh Pr

Hallam Land Management Ltd v Scottish Ministers 2007 G.W.D. 16-295, OH

Hamilton v Allied Domecq Plc [2007] UKHL 33; 2007 S.C. (H.L.) 142; 2007 S.L.T. 697; (2007) 151 S.J.L.B. 984; 2007 G.W.D. 23-390, HL; affirming 2006 S.C. 221; 2005 S.L.T. 1151; 2005 G.W.D. 37-697, IH (2 Div); reversing 2004 S.L.T. 191; 2003 G.W.D. 31-877, OH . . . .　*Digested,* 06/**5162**

Hamilton v Dumfries and Galloway Council [2006] CSOH 110; 2006 S.C.L.R. 839, OH . . . .　*Digested,* 07/**5500**

Hamilton v Dumfries and Galloway Council 2007 G.W.D. 34-582, IH (Ex Div); affirming 2007 G.W.D. 20-347, OH

Hamilton v Ford 2007 G.W.D. 10-177, OH

Hammond v Commissioner of Police of the Metropolis [2004] EWCA Civ 830; [2004] I.C.R. 1467; [2005] P.I.Q.R. P1; (2004) 101(27) L.S.G. 30; (2004) 148 S.J.L.B. 758; *Times,* June 24, 2004, CA (Civ Div) . . . .　*Digested,* 04/**1814**: *Applied,* 07/5270: *Considered,* 07/2082

Harbachou v Secretary of State for the Home Department 2007 G.W.D. 12-252, OH

Harbinson v McTaggart (Expenses) 2007 G.W.D. 37-646, Lands Tr (Scot)

HarperCollins Publishers Ltd v Young 2007 G.W.D. 15-286, OH

Harris (Stuart) v HM Advocate see McGowan (Steven) v HM Advocate

Hart v Aberdeen City Council 2006 Hous. L.R. 93; 2006 G.W.D. 23-512, Sh Ct (Grampian) . . . .　*Digested,* 07/**5302**

Harvey (Steven) v HM Advocate see Weir (Mark Lindsay) v HM Advocate

Hasibi v Secretary of State for the Home Department 2007 G.W.D. 21-360, OH

HBOS Plc v Revenue and Customs Commissioners [2007] B.V.C. 2394, V&DTr (Edinburgh)

Helow v Advocate General for Scotland [2007] CSIH 5; 2007 S.C. 303; 2007 S.L.T. 201; 2007 S.C.L.R. 219; 2007 G.W.D. 2-17, IH (Ex Div) . . . .　*Digested,* 07/**5313**

Henderson v Sayer (t/a Chris Sayer Solicitors) 2007 G.W.D. 37-655, OH

Henderson v Scottish Ministers see Somerville v Scottish Ministers

Henderson v Sutherland 2007 Rep. L.R. 120; 2007 G.W.D. 35-604, OH

Hendry v Alexander Taylor & Sons 2007 G.W.D. 36-624, OH

Hennon v Cape Building Products Ltd 2006 Rep. L.R. 71; 2006 G.W.D. 5-98, OH . . . .　*Digested,* 07/**5426**

Herrity (Kevin) v HM Advocate [2006] HCJAC 39; 2007 J.C. 1; 2006 S.C.C.R. 262; 2006 G.W.D. 20-431, HCJ . . . .　*Digested,* 06/**5207**

Highland Council v Revenue and Customs Commissioners; *sub nom* Highland Council v VAT and Duties Tribunal [2007] CSIH 36; 2007 S.C. 533; 2007 S.L.T. 529; [2007] S.T.I. 1588; 2007 G.W.D. 17-312, IH (Ex Div); affirming [2006] B.V.C. 2693; [2006] S.T.I. 1714, V&DTr (Edinburgh) . . . .　*Digested,* 07/**5567**

Highland Council v VAT and Duties Tribunal see Highland Council v Revenue and Customs Commissioners

Hirst v United Kingdom (74025/01) (2006) 42 E.H.R.R. 41; 19 B.H.R.C. 546; [2006] 1 Prison L.R. 220; (2005) 155 N.L.J. 1551; *Times,* October 10, 2005, ECHR (Grand Chamber). . . . .　*Digested,* 06/**2150**: *Considered,* 07/5431

HM Advocate v A [2007] HCJT 15; 2007 G.W.D. 39-677, HCJ

HM Advocate v Amin (Rehan Ali) see HM Advocate v McPhee (David William)

HM Advocate v B; *sub nom* HM Advocate v GB 2006 S.L.T. 1093; 2006 S.C.C.R. 692; 2006 G.W.D. 36-729, HCJ . . . .　*Digested,* 07/**5064**

HM Advocate v B; *sub nom* HM Advocate v GB 2006 S.C.C.R. 692, HCJ. . . . .　*Digested,* 07/**5091**

HM Advocate v C 2007 S.L.T. 963; 2007 G.W.D. 37-646, HCJ

HM Advocate v Caledonian Alloys Ltd 2007 G.W.D. 2-29, Sh Ct (Lothian)

HM Advocate v Clark (John Archibald) 1935 J.C. 51; 1935 S.L.T. 143, HCJ . . . .　*Applied,* 55/532, 07/5050: *Distinguished,* 92/5440: *Followed,* 94/5585

HM Advocate v DS see DS v HM Advocate

HM Advocate v F 2007 S.C.C.R. 216; 2007 G.W.D. 15-287, HCJ. . . . .　*Digested,* 07/**5069**

HM Advocate v Frost (Martin) [2006] CSIH 56; 2007 S.C. 215; 2007 S.L.T. 345; 2006 G.W.D. 40-771, IH (Ex Div) . . . .　*Digested,* 07/**4999**

HM Advocate v GB see HM Advocate v B

HM Advocate v GB see HM Advocate v B

HM Advocate v Graham (John Gibson) 2007 S.C.C.R. 360, HCJ

HM Advocate v Headrick (Robert John) (No.2) 2005 S.C.C.R. 787, Sh Ct. . . . .　*Digested,* 06/**5337**: *Overruled,* 07/5168

HM Advocate v Jackson 2007 G.W.D. 30-519, HCJ

HM Advocate v Kirk (Charles George) 2007 S.C.C.R. 44; 2007 G.W.D. 8-142, HCJ . . .　*Digested,* 07/**5516**

HM Advocate v M 2007 S.L.T. 462; 2007 S.C.C.R. 124; 2007 G.W.D. 8-139, HCJ . . . .　*Digested,* 07/**5047**

HM Advocate v M 2007 G.W.D. 14-278, HCJ

HM Advocate v McGovern (James) [2007] HCJAC 21; 2007 S.L.T. 331; 2007 S.C.C.R. 173; 2007 G.W.D. 10-180, HCJ . . . .　*Digested,* 07/**5505**

HM Advocate v McLarty 2007 G.W.D. 31-529, HCJ

HM Advocate v McPhee (David William); *joined cases* HM Advocate v Amin (Rehan
    Ali); HM Advocate v McPhee (Hugh David) 2007 S.C.C.R. 91, HCJ . . . .   *Digested,* 07/**5068**
HM Advocate v McPhee (Hugh David) see HM Advocate v McPhee (David William)
HM Advocate v Macpherson (Thomas Donald) see HM Advocate v Macpherson
    (Thomas Macdonald)
HM Advocate v Macpherson (Thomas Macdonald); *sub nom* HM Advocate v
    Macpherson (Thomas Donald) 2005 S.L.T. 397; 2004 S.C.C.R. 579; 2004
    G.W.D. 34-702, HCJ . . . .   *Digested,* 05/**5657**:
                                          Considered, 04/3298, 07/5512
HM Advocate v McSween (John Edward) [2007] HCJAC 33; 2007 S.L.T. 645; 2007
    S.C.C.R. 310; 2007 G.W.D. 20-344, HCJ . . . .   *Digested,* 07/**5018**
HM Advocate v Montgomery (David Shields) see Montgomery v HM Advocate
HM Advocate v Mullen (Hugh) [2007] HCJT 6; 2007 J.C. 213; 2007 S.C.C.R. 330;
    2007 G.W.D. 24-398, HCJ . . . .   *Digested,* 07/**5508**
HM Advocate v Murray (Gavin Mitchell) 2007 S.C.C.R. 271, Sh Ct (South Strathclyde)
HM Advocate v P 2007 S.L.T. 949; 2007 S.C.C.R. 370; 2007 G.W.D. 29-507, HCJ
HM Advocate v Purcell (Isaac Michael) 2007 S.C.C.R. 520; 2007 G.W.D. 30-518, HCJ
HM Advocate v R; *sub nom* R v HM Advocate [2002] UKPC D 3; [2004] 1 A.C. 462;
    [2003] 2 W.L.R. 317; 2003 S.C. (P.C.) 21; 2003 S.L.T. 4; 2003 S.C.C.R. 19;
    [2003] U.K.H.R.R. 1; 2002 G.W.D. 39-1280; *Times,* December 6, 2002, PC (Sc);
    reversing 2002 S.L.T. 834; 2002 S.C.C.R. 697; 2002 G.W.D. 19-622, HCJ
    Appeal; affirming 2001 S.L.T. 1366; 2001 S.C.C.R. 915; 2001 G.W.D. 32-1275,
    HCJ . . . .   *Digested,* 03/**5410**:
                   Considered, 05/5137, 07/5436: *Not followed,* 04/884
HM Advocate v Ronald (Stephen) (No.1) 2007 S.L.T. 1170; 2007 S.C.C.R. 451; 2007
    G.W.D. 33-561, HCJ
HM Advocate v Ronald (Stephen) (No.2) 2007 S.C.C.R. 466, HCJ
HM Advocate v Shewan 2007 G.W.D. 38-664, Sh Ct (Grampian)
HM Advocate v Swift (James Aloysius) 1984 J.C. 83; 1985 S.L.T. 26; 1984 S.C.C.R.
    216, HCJ . . . .   *Digested,* 84/**3906**:
         Applied, 88/3921, 97/5801, 98/5594: *Considered,* 97/5862, 06/5205,
        07/5068: *Followed,* 97/5803, 01/6344, 03/5378: *Referred to,* 92/5423,
                                                 93/4935
HM Advocate v Turner (Robert James) [2007] HCJAC 23; 2007 S.C.C.R. 194; 2007
    G.W.D. 13-266, HCJ . . . .   *Digested,* 07/**5509**
HM Advocate v Voudouri (Michael George) 2007 S.L.T. 407; 2007 G.W.D. 4-61, HCJ .   *Digested,* 07/**5053**
HM Advocate v Ward (Francis) 1993 S.L.T. 1202; 1993 S.C.C.R. 595, HCJ . . . .   *Digested,* 93/**4970**:
                                                Considered, 07/4979
HM Advocate v Welch (David Nesbit) 2006 S.C.C.R. 87; 2006 G.W.D. 3-49, HCJ . . . .   *Digested,* 07/**5092**
HM Advocate v Wright (David) 2007 S.C.C.R. 134, Sh Ct (Glasgow) . . . .   *Digested,* 07/**5511**
HM Advocate v Wright (Joseph) 2007 S.L.T. 597; 2007 S.C.C.R. 258; 2007 G.W.D.
    18-317, HCJ . . . .   *Digested,* 07/**5052**
Hodge v Hodge 2007 G.W.D. 13-269, Sh Pr
Holms v Ashford Estates Ltd 2006 S.L.T. (Sh Ct) 161; 2007 S.C.L.R. 460; 2006
    G.W.D. 34-700, Sh Pr; affirming 2006 S.L.T. (Sh Ct) 70; 2006 G.W.D. 17-350,
    Sh Ct (Lothian) . . . .   *Digested,* 07/**5286**:
                                                Considered, 07/5332
Honer v Wilson [2006] CSOH 166; 2007 S.L.T. 54; 2006 G.W.D. 36-732, OH . . . .   *Digested,* 07/**4983**
Horban v Torith Ltd 2007 G.W.D. 36-623, Sh Ct (Tayside)
Houston v Doonin Plant Ltd (No.1) 2007 G.W.D. 35-616, Sh Ct (Lanark)
Houston v Doonin Plant Ltd (No.2) 2007 G.W.D. 35-615, Sh Ct (Lanark)
Houston v HM Advocate 2007 G.W.D. 10-182, HCJ
Houston v Renfrewshire Council 2007 G.W.D. 8-132, OH
Howarth v HM Advocate 1992 S.C.C.R. 364, HCJ Appeal . . . .   *Digested,* 92/**5361**:
               Distinguished, 97/5765: *Followed,* 02/5518: *Not applied,* 07/5024
Hughes v Grampian Country Food Group Ltd [2007] CSIH 32; 2007 S.L.T. 635;
    [2007] Eu. L.R. 719; 2007 Rep. L.R. 72; 2007 G.W.D. 18-324; *Times,* June 4,
    2007, IH (1 Div); affirming 2006 S.C.L.R. 682; 2006 Rep. L.R. 78; 2006 G.W.D.
    14-270, OH . . . .   *Digested,* 07/**5272**:
                                         Distinguished, 07/5273
Hughes v HM Advocate 2007 G.W.D. 26-454, HCJ
Hughes v Mental Health Tribunal [2007] M.H.L.R. 29, Sh Pr
Hume v Nursing and Midwifery Council [2007] CSIH 53; 2007 S.C. 644, IH (1 Div)
Hutchinson (Charles Henry) v HM Advocate 2007 S.C.C.R. 477, HCJ
Hutchison v North Lanarkshire Council 2007 G.W.D. 4-65, OH
Hutton v Jack 2007 G.W.D. 2-26, Sh Pr
Hyaltech Ltd, Petitioners 2007 G.W.D. 15-284, OH
Hynd v Armstrong [2007] CSIH 16; 2007 S.C. 409; 2007 S.L.T. 299; [2007] I.R.L.R.
    338; 2007 G.W.D. 8-145, IH (1 Div) . . . .   *Digested,* 07/**5149**

Ibbotson v United Kingdom [1999] Crim. L.R. 153; (1999) 27 E.H.R.R. CD332, Eur
    Comm HR . . . .   *Applied,* 07/5429:
                                                Considered, 03/866

Ibrahim *v* Secretary of State for the Home Department 2007 G.W.D. 14-281, IH (Ex Div)

Ilona (Countess of Cawdor) *v* Vaughan (Earl of Cawdor); *sub nom* Cawdor *v* Cawdor [2007] CSIH 3; 2007 S.C. 285; 2007 S.L.T. 152; 2007 S.C.L.R. 334; 2007 G.W.D. 3-41, IH (1 Div); affirming 2006 S.C.L.R. 212; 2006 G.W.D. 19-395, OH   *Digested,* 07/**5563**

Inland Revenue Commissioners *v* Ainsworth; *sub nom* Ainsworth *v* Inland Revenue Commissioners; *joined cases* Inland Revenue Commissioners *v* Kilic; Inland Revenue Commissioners *v* Stringer; Inland Revenue Commissioners *v* Thwaites [2005] EWCA Civ 441; [2005] I.C.R. 1149; [2005] I.R.L.R. 465; *Times,* May 16, 2005, CA (Civ Div); reversing UKEAT/0650/03/Tm, UKEAT/0745/03/TM, UKEAT/0798/03/TM, UKEAT/0901/03/TM, EAT . . . .   *Digested,* 05/**1273**:
                      Applied, 07/5143: *Cited,* 07/1443: *Considered,* 07/2941

Inland Revenue Commissioners *v* John M Whiteford & Son 1962 S.C. 229; 1962 S.L.T. 269; 40 T.C. 379; (1962) 41 A.T.C. 166; [1962] T.R. 157, IH (1 Div) . . . .   *Digested,* 62/**3466**:
                                    Applied, 07/4105

Inland Revenue Commissioners *v* Kilic see Inland Revenue Commissioners *v* Ainsworth

Inland Revenue Commissioners *v* Spencer-Nairn [1991] S.T.C. 60; 1991 S.L.T. 594, IH (1 Div) . . . .   *Digested,* 91/**4441**:
                               Considered, 07/4108

Inland Revenue Commissioners *v* Stringer see Inland Revenue Commissioners *v* Ainsworth

Inland Revenue Commissioners *v* Thwaites see Inland Revenue Commissioners *v* Ainsworth

Inland Revenue Commissioners *v* William Grant & Sons Distillers Ltd see Revenue and Customs Commissioners *v* William Grant & Sons Distillers Ltd (Scotland)

Inland Revenue Commissioners, Petitioners see Revenue and Customs Commissioners, Petitioners

J *v* Fife Council [2007] CSOH 18; 2007 S.L.T. 85; 2007 G.W.D. 2-27, OH . . . .   *Digested,* 07/**5096**

J *v* HM Advocate see James (Cliffroy) *v* HM Advocate

J *v* Quarriers 2007 G.W.D. 11-224, OH

J&H Ritchie Ltd *v* Lloyd Ltd; *sub nom* JH Ritchie Ltd *v* Lloyd Ltd [2007] UKHL 9; [2007] Bus. L.R. 944; [2007] 1 W.L.R. 670; [2007] 2 All E.R. 353; [2007] 1 All E.R. (Comm) 987; [2007] 1 Lloyd's Rep. 544; 2007 S.C. (H.L.) 89; 2007 S.L.T. 377; [2007] 1 C.L.C. 208; (2007) 157 N.L.J. 403; (2007) 151 S.J.L.B. 397; 2007 G.W.D. 9-171; *Times,* March 8, 2007, HL; reversing 2005 1 S.C. 155; 2005 S.L.T. 64; 2005 S.C.L.R. 447; 2005 G.W.D. 2-38, IH (Ex Div). . . . .   *Digested,* 07/**3568**

J&L Leisure Ltd *v* Shaw 2007 G.W.D. 28-489, Lands Tr (Scot)

Jacobs & Turner Ltd *v* Celsius Sarl [2007] CSOH 76; 2007 S.L.T. 722; 2007 G.W.D. 23-387, OH

Jaffray *v* Grampian Test & Certification Ltd 2007 S.L.T. (Sh Ct) 73; 2006 Rep. L.R. 112; 2006 G.W.D. 24-543, Sh Ct (Grampian) . . . .   *Digested,* 07/**5273**

James (Cliffroy) *v* HM Advocate; *sub nom* J *v* HM Advocate 2006 S.C.C.R. 170; 2006 G.W.D. 10-185, HCJ . . . .   *Digested,* 07/**5078**

JH Cunningham & Son (Haulage) Ltd *v* Smith 2007 G.W.D. 7-105, OH

JH Ritchie Ltd *v* Lloyd Ltd see J&H Ritchie Ltd *v* Lloyd Ltd

John Doyle Construction Ltd *v* Laing Management (Scotland) Ltd; *sub nom* Laing Management (Scotland) Ltd *v* John Doyle Construction Ltd 2004 S.C. 713; 2004 S.C.L.R. 872; [2004] B.L.R. 295; (2004) 20 Const. L.J. 477; [2004] C.I.L.L. 2135; 2004 G.W.D. 20-434; *Times,* June 18, 2004, IH (Ex Div); affirming 2004 S.L.T. 678; [2002] B.L.R. 393; [2002] T.C.L.R. 24; 85 Con. L.R. 98; (2003) 19 Const. L.J. 152; 2002 G.W.D. 14-461; *Times,* July 10, 2002, OH . . . .   *Digested,* 05/**5071**:
                               Considered, 07/254

Johnston *v* Dundee City Council 2006 Hous. L.R. 68; 2006 G.W.D. 27-609, Lands Tr (Scot) . . . .   *Digested,* 07/**5334**

Johnston *v* Dyer 2007 S.C.C.R. 494, HCJ

Johnston *v* Edinburgh DC 2007 G.W.D. 33-562, OH

Jones *v* Post Office; *sub nom* Post Office *v* Jones [2001] EWCA Civ 558; [2001] I.C.R. 805; [2001] I.R.L.R. 384; [2001] Emp. L.R. 527; *Times,* June 5, 2001; *Independent,* April 26, 2001, CA (Civ Div); affirming [2000] I.C.R. 388, EAT . .   *Digested,* 01/**2236**:
         Applied, 01/6463, 02/1329, 04/1220, 06/1299, 06/1300:
         Considered, 04/1215, 05/1227, 06/1136, 07/1331, 07/5115:
                            Distinguished, 04/1219

Jones (Brendan Noel) *v* HM Advocate 2003 S.C.C.R. 94; 2002 G.W.D. 40-1337, HCJ   *Digested,* 03/**5349**:
                        Applied, 07/5074: *Distinguished,* 06/5211

Jones (Grant) *v* HM Advocate [2007] HCJAC 35; 2007 S.L.T. 685; 2007 S.C.C.R. 291; 2007 G.W.D. 21-353, HCJ. . . . .   *Digested,* 07/**5474**

JS Cruickshank (Farmers) Ltd *v* Gordon & Innes Ltd (In Receivership) 2007 G.W.D. 38-673, OH

JT *v* Stirling Council; *sub nom* K's Legal Guardian *v* Stirling Council [2007] CSIH 52; 2007 S.C. 783; 2007 Fam. L.R. 88, IH (Ex Div); reversing 2007 G.W.D. 11-216, OH

K v HM Advocate 2007 G.W.D. 16-297, HCJ
K v Quarriers 2007 G.W.D. 11-225, OH
K v S 2007 Fam. L.R. 141; 2007 G.W.D. 29-512, Sh Ct (Tayside)
K v Secretary of State for the Home Department 2007 G.W.D. 12-253, IH (Ex Div)
K v Secretary of State for the Home Department 2007 G.W.D. 22-366, OH
K v Secretary of State for the Home Department 2007 G.W.D. 24-410, OH
K v Secretary of State for the Home Department 2007 G.W.D. 21-358, OH
K's Legal Guardian v Stirling Council see JT v Stirling Council
Kaniz v Secretary of State for the Home Department 2007 G.W.D. 7-116, OH
Kaur v Singh (No.1) 1999 S.C. 180; 1999 S.L.T. 412; 1998 S.C.L.R. 849; 1998 G.W.D.
　　24-1226, IH (1 Div); affirming 1998 S.C. 233; 1997 S.C.L.R. 1075; 1997 G.W.D.
　　37-1914, OH . . . . 　　*Digested*, 98/**5951**:
　　　　　　　　　　　　　　　　　　　　　　　　　　　　　　　　　　　　　　　Considered, 07/5278
Kearney v HM Advocate 2007 G.W.D. 6-85, HCJ
Kearney v Ramage; *sub nom* Kearney v Watt [2007] HCJAC 4; 2007 S.C.C.R. 35;
　　2007 G.W.D. 5-74, HCJ . . . . 　　*Digested*, 07/**5051**
Kearney v Watt see Kearney v Ramage
Kearney (Arthur) v HM Advocate [2006] UKPC D 1; 2006 S.C. (P.C.) 1; 2006 S.L.T.
　　499; 2006 S.C.C.R. 130; [2006] H.R.L.R. 15; 20 B.H.R.C. 157; 2006 G.W.D. 15-
　　284, PC (Sc); affirming 2005 S.L.T. 74; 2005 S.C.C.R. 79; 2005 G.W.D. 2-26,
　　HCJ . . . . 　　*Digested*, 06/**5003**:
　　　　　　　　　　　　　　　　　　　　　　　　　　　　　　　　　　　　　　　Applied, 07/5049
Kenny v Pollock (Scotrans) Ltd 2007 G.W.D. 5-80, OH
Kerr v Aberdeen City Council 2007 G.W.D. 36-631, IH (Ex Div)
Kerr (John) v HM Advocate 1958 J.C. 14; 1958 S.L.T. 82, HCJ . . . . 　　*Digested*, 58/**3660**:
　　　　　　　　　　　　　Disapproved, 07/5018: *Distinguished*, 91/4558: *Referred to*, 01/6305
Khosrowpour v Murray Beith Murray, WS 2007 G.W.D. 24-419, OH
Killen v Dundee City Council 2007 G.W.D. 35-619, Sh Ct (Tayside)
King v Eaton Ltd (No.2); *sub nom* Eaton Ltd v King 1999 S.L.T. 656; 1998 S.C.L.R.
　　1017; [1998] I.R.L.R. 686; 1998 G.W.D. 27-1381, IH (2 Div) . . . . 　　*Digested*, 99/**6048**:
　　　　　　　　　　　　　　　　Applied, 06/1387: *Considered*, 07/1426: *Followed*, 05/1333
King v T Tunnock Ltd 2000 S.C. 424; 2000 S.L.T. 744; [2001] E.C.C. 6; [2000] Eu.
　　L.R. 531; [2000] I.R.L.R. 569; 2000 G.W.D. 12-408; *Times*, May 12, 2000, IH
　　(Ex Div); reversing (Unreported, December 24, 1997), Sh Pr; affirming 1996
　　S.C.L.R. 742, Sh Ct . . . . 　　*Digested*, 00/**5846**:
　　　　　　　　　　　　Applied, 02/65: *Considered*, 06/60: *Distinguished*, 03/79: *Doubted*, 07/68
King's Prosecutor (Brussels) v Armas see Office of the King's Prosecutor (Brussels) v
　　Cando Armas
Kinnaird v Paton 2007 G.W.D. 19-333, OH
Koufos v C Czarnikow Ltd (The Heron II); *sub nom* C Czarnikow Ltd v Koufos (The
　　Heron II) [1969] 1 A.C. 350; [1967] 3 W.L.R. 1491; [1967] 3 All E.R. 686;
　　[1967] 2 Lloyd's Rep. 457; (1967) 111 S.J. 848, HL; affirming [1966] 2 Q.B. 695;
　　[1966] 2 W.L.R. 1397; [1966] 2 All E.R. 593; [1966] 1 Lloyd's Rep. 595, CA;
　　reversing [1966] 1 Lloyd's Rep. 259; (1966) 110 S.J. 287, QBD (Comm) . . . . . 　　*Digested*, 67/**3623**:
　　　　　　　　　　　　Applied, 70/924, 77/2881, 78/2821, 85/198, 88/1165, 96/3566, 97/6093,
　　　　　　　　　　　　　　　　　　　　99/5790, 03/3919, 07/1064: *Approved*, 66/3146: *Considered*, 67/3623,
　　　　　　　　　　　　　　　　　　　　　　68/1013, 69/3226, 72/990, 75/2324, 94/5413, 07/5015
KR v Bryn Alyn Community (Holdings) Ltd (In Liquidation); *sub nom* Various
　　Claimants v BACHL; Various Claimants v Bryn Alyn Community (Holdings) Ltd
　　(In Liquidation) [2003] EWCA Civ 85; [2003] Q.B. 1441; [2003] 3 W.L.R. 107;
　　[2004] 2 All E.R. 716; [2003] 1 F.L.R. 1203; [2003] 1 F.C.R. 385; [2003]
　　Lloyd's Rep. Med. 175; [2003] Fam. Law 482; *Times*, February 17, 2003, CA
　　(Civ Div); affirming HQ/99/01473, QBD . . . . 　　*Digested*, 03/**432**:
　　　　　　　　　　　　　　　　　Applied, 05/2859: *Considered*, 07/5096: *Doubted*, 07/473, 07/483:
　　　　　　　　　　　　　　　　　　　　　　　　　　　　　　　　　　　　　　　Followed, 06/476
Kunle (John Bamtefa) v HM Advocate [2007] HCJAC 41; 2007 S.L.T. 957; 2007
　　G.W.D. 25-430, HCJ

L Rowland & Co (Retail) Ltd v National Appeal Panel for Entry to the Pharmaceutical
　　Lists 2006 S.C.L.R. 759; 2006 G.W.D. 26-589, OH. . . . . 　　*Digested*, 07/**5264**
L, Petitioner 2007 G.W.D. 10-172, OH
La Torre (Antonio) v HM Advocate [2006] HCJAC 56; 2006 S.L.T. 989; 2006
　　S.C.C.R. 503; [2007] Eu. L.R. 70; 2006 G.W.D. 31-667, HCJ. . . . . 　　*Digested*, 06/**5339**:
　　　　　　　　　　　　　　　　　　　　　　　　　　　　　　　　　　　　　　　Considered, 07/5170
La Torre (Antonio) v Lord Advocate; *sub nom* La Torre, Petitioner [2006] HCJAC 81;
　　2007 S.L.T. 51; 2006 S.C.C.R. 673; 2006 G.W.D. 39-762, HCJ. . . . . 　　*Digested*, 07/**5170**
La Torre, Petitioner see La Torre (Antonio) v Lord Advocate
Laidlaw v Parole Board for Scotland 2007 G.W.D. 19-341, OH
Laing Management (Scotland) Ltd v John Doyle Construction Ltd see John Doyle
　　Construction Ltd v Laing Management (Scotland) Ltd
Laing (Paul David) v HM Advocate see Mason (Lee) v HM Advocate

Lamarra v Capital Bank Plc 2007 S.C. 95; 2006 S.L.T. 1053; 2007 S.C.L.R. 719; 2006 G.W.D. 33-686, IH (Ex Div); affirming 2005 S.L.T. (Sh Ct) 21; 2004 G.W.D. 40-817, Sh Pr . . . . *Digested,* 07/**5014**

Land Securities Group Plc v Scottish Ministers [2006] UKHL 48; 2007 S.C. (H.L.) 57; 2006 S.L.T. 1019; 2006 S.C.L.R. 908; [2007] J.P.L. 710; [2006] 45 E.G. 190 (C.S.); (2006) 103(43) L.S.G. 30; (2006) 150 S.J.L.B. 1429; [2006] N.P.C. 113; 2006 G.W.D. 35-723, HL . . . . *Digested,* 07/**5466**

Latham v Hunt 2007 G.W.D. 25-434, Sh Pr

Latimer, Petitioner 2007 G.W.D. 19-340, OH

Laurence McIntosh Ltd v Balfour Beatty Group Ltd 2007 G.W.D. 2-20, OH

Laurie v Mental Health Tribunal for Scotland 2007 G.W.D. 32-555, Sh Pr

Lavery v Strathclyde Joint Police Board [2007] CSIH 31; 2007 S.C. 509; 2007 G.W.D. 20-349, IH (Ex Div)

Lawson v Broomfield Holiday Park 2007 G.W.D. 25-443, Sh Ct (Grampian)

Legal Services Centre Ltd v Miller Samuel LLP 2007 G.W.D. 5-79, OH

Leonard v Houston [2007] HCJAC 46; 2007 S.C.C.R. 354; 2007 G.W.D. 27-473, HCJ

Lerwick Port Authority v Scottish Ministers [2007] CSOH 156; 2007 G.W.D. 31-525, OH

Leslie v Babcock Engineering Services Ltd 2007 G.W.D. 2-19, OH

Lessani v Lessani 2007 Fam. L.R. 81, Sh Pr . . . . *Digested,* 07/**5183**

Lindsay v Inland Revenue Commissioners 1953 S.L.T. (Notes) 14; 46 R. & I.T. 146; 34 T.C. 289; (1953) 32 A.T.C. 1; [1953] T.R. 5, IH (1 Div) . . . . *Digested,* 53/**4272**: *Applied,* 07/4105

Lindsay v Lindsay 2007 Fam. L.R. 18; 2007 G.W.D. 26-459, Sh Pr . . . . *Digested,* 07/**5184**

Lindsay v Walker 2007 G.W.D. 24-400, Sh Ct (Lothian)

Lindsay (Steven) v HM Advocate 2007 S.C.C.R. 377, HCJ

Link Housing Association Ltd v Gray Aitken Partnership Ltd see Link Housing Association Ltd v PBL Construction Ltd

Link Housing Association Ltd v PBL Construction Ltd; *sub nom* Gray Aitken Partnership Ltd v Link Housing Association Ltd; Link Housing Association Ltd v Gray Aitken Partnership Ltd [2007] CSIH 4; 2007 S.C. 294; 2007 S.C.L.R. 343; 2007 G.W.D. 17-305, IH (1 Div); reversing 2006 G.W.D. 15-280, OH

Liquidator of Bank of Credit and Commerce International SA, Noter see Morris, Petitioner

Lister v Hesley Hall Ltd [2001] UKHL 22; [2002] 1 A.C. 215; [2001] 2 W.L.R. 1311; [2001] 2 All E.R. 769; [2001] I.C.R. 665; [2001] I.R.L.R. 472; [2001] Emp. L.R. 819; [2001] 2 F.L.R. 307; [2001] 2 F.C.R. 97; (2001) 3 L.G.L.R. 49; [2001] E.L.R. 422; [2001] Fam. Law 595; (2001) 98(24) L.S.G. 45; (2001) 151 N.L.J. 728; (2001) 145 S.J.L.B. 126; [2001] N.P.C. 89; *Times,* May 10, 2001; *Independent,* June 11, 2001; *Daily Telegraph,* May 8, 2001, HL; reversing *Times,* October 13, 1999; *Independent,* November 22, 1999, CA (Civ Div) . . . . *Digested,* 01/**5359**: *Applied,* 02/1531, 03/432, 03/3033, 03/3046, 04/655, 05/4199, 05/4200, 06/1337, 07/4201: *Cited,* 02/5360, 03/2975: *Considered,* 05/5573, 06/476, 06/5592, 07/5427

Little v Little 1990 S.L.T. 785; 1991 S.C.L.R. 47, IH (1 Div); affirming 1990 S.L.T. 230; 1989 S.C.L.R. 613, OH . . . . *Digested,* 90/**5111**: *Approved,* 91/4936, 97/6053: *Considered,* 91/4936, 92/5679, 95/5884, 97/6039, 06/5353, 07/5182: *Followed,* 94/5784, 03/1559: *Referred to,* 95/5937

Little Cumbrae Estate Ltd v Island of Little Cumbrae Ltd [2007] CSIH 35; 2007 S.C. 525; 2007 S.L.T. 631; 2007 Hous. L.R. 40; 2007 G.W.D. 18-319, IH (Ex Div) . . . *Digested,* 07/**5329**

Lloyds Bank Plc v Bamberger 1993 S.C. 570; 1994 S.L.T. 424; 1993 S.C.L.R. 727, IH (2 Div) . . . . *Digested,* 93/**5387**: *Considered,* 07/5275: *Followed,* 97/6166

Lloyds Pharmacy Ltd v National Appeal Panel for Entry to the Pharmaceutical Lists 2004 S.C. 703; 2004 S.L.T. 687; 2004 S.C.L.R. 887; 2004 G.W.D. 20-437, IH (2 Div); reversing 2003 S.L.T. 830; 2003 S.C.L.R. 700; 2003 G.W.D. 21-639, OH . *Digested,* 04/**4895**: *Applied,* 07/5264

Lord Advocate v Harrison [2007] HCJAC 74; 2007 G.W.D. 40-694, HCJ Appeal

Lord Advocate's Reference (No.1 of 1983) 1984 J.C. 52; 1984 S.L.T. 337; 1984 S.C.C.R. 62, HCJ . . . . *Digested,* 84/**3850**: *Applied,* 92/5361: *Not applied,* 07/5024: *Referred to,* 95/5729

Lord Advocate, Petitioner [2007] CSOH 135; 2007 S.L.T. 849; 2007 S.C.L.R. 660; 2007 G.W.D. 26-446, OH

Lord Robertson of Port Ellen v Newsquest (Sunday Herald) Ltd see Robertson v Newsquest (Sunday Herald) Ltd

Lothian v Edinburgh Pharmaceutical Processes Ltd; *sub nom* Edinburgh Pharmaceutical Processes Ltd v Lothian [2007] CSIH 61; 2007 S.C. 777; 2007 G.W.D. 27-475, IH (Ex Div); affirming UKEATS/0085/05/RN, EAT (SC)

Lothian Health Board v M 2007 S.C.L.R. 478; 2007 G.W.D. 17-309, Sh Pr

Love v North Lanarkshire Council 2007 G.W.D. 7-123, OH

Low (Fatal Accident Inquiry), Re 2007 G.W.D. 36-633, Sh Ct (North Strathclyde)

Lowe v Yorkhill NHS Trust 2007 G.W.D. 32-557, OH

Lyon v Dean 2007 G.W.D. 10-183, Sh Ct (Tayside)

M v C (Children: Consent to Change of Name) 2002 S.L.T. (Sh Ct) 82; 2002 G.W.D.
    14-457, Sh Ct (Tayside) ....   *Digested*, 02/**5614**:
                                                             Distinguished, 07/5176
M v Hendron [2007] CSIH 27; 2007 S.C. 556; 2007 S.L.T. 467; 2007 S.C.L.R. 360;
    2007 G.W.D. 16-301, IH (Ex Div); reversing 2005 S.L.T. 1122; 2005 G.W.D. 35-
    663, OH ....   *Digested*, 07/**5427**
M v M; *sub nom* McG v McG 2007 Fam. L.R. 62; 2006 G.W.D. 25-548, OH ....   *Digested*, 07/**5178**
M v Secretary of State for the Home Department [2007] CSIH 55; 2007 S.C. 796;
    2007 G.W.D. 22-371, IH (1 Div)
M v Secretary of State for the Home Department 2007 G.W.D. 38-671, IH (Ex Div)
M v Secretary of State for the Home Department 2007 G.W.D. 22-370, IH (Ex Div)
M, Applicant 2007 S.L.T. (Sh Ct) 24; 2006 G.W.D. 19-418, Sh Ct (Glasgow).......   *Digested*, 07/**4990**
M, Petitioner [2007] CSOH 66; 2007 S.L.T. 433; 2007 G.W.D. 11-201, OH ....   *Digested*, 07/**5175**
McAlister v Stevenson see Donoghue v Stevenson
McAllister v Scottish Water 2007 G.W.D. 39-684, Sh Pr
McArthur v HM Advocate 2007 G.W.D. 12-242, HCJ
McAuley Catholic High School v C [2003] EWHC 3045 (Admin); [2004] 2 All E.R.
    436; [2004] I.C.R. 1563; [2004] E.L.R. 89; [2004] A.C.D. 24, QBD (Admin) .   *Digested*, 04/**1077**:
                                                             Considered, 07/5115
McCabe v Wilson 2006 Hous. L.R. 86, Sh Ct (South Strathclyde) ....   *Digested*, 07/**5328**
McClusky v Aberdeenshire Council 2007 G.W.D. 11-228, Sh Ct (Grampian)
MacColl v Crofters Commission 2007 Hous. L.R. 46; 2007 G.W.D. 27-481, OH
McColm v Borders General Hospital NHS Trust 2007 G.W.D. 38-672, Sh Ct (Lothian)
McCrindle v Gala Casinos Ltd 2007 G.W.D. 10-195, OH
McCrory v Hutchison's Coaches (Overtown) Ltd 2007 S.L.T. (Sh Ct) 187; 2007
    G.W.D. 34-579, Sh Ct (South Strathclyde)
McCulloch v Dunedin Independent Plc 2007 G.W.D. 11-229, OH
McDonagh v Pattison [2007] HCJAC 61; 2007 S.L.T. 1239; 2007 S.C.C.R. 482; 2007
    G.W.D. 34-578, HCJ
McDonald v Bain see McDonald v Dyer
McDonald v Dyer; *sub nom* McDonald v Bain [2007] HCJAC 58; 2007 S.C.C.R.
    488; 2007 G.W.D. 34-577, HCJ
MacDonald v EMAC Recycling Ltd 2007 G.W.D. 6-90, Sh Ct (Grampian)
McDonald v O'Donnell see O'Donnell v McDonald
MacDonald v United Kingdom Atomic Energy Authority 2007 G.W.D. 6-92, Sh Ct
    (Grampian)
Macdonald Estates Plc v Regenesis (2005) Dunfermline Ltd [2007] CSOH 123; 2007
    S.L.T. 791; 2007 G.W.D. 25-428, OH
McDonald (Felix Charles) v HM Advocate [2006] HCJAC 89; 2007 S.C.C.R. 10, HCJ   *Digested*, 07/**5032**
McDonald-Grant v Sutherland & Co [2007] CSIH 54; 2007 S.C. 651; 2007 G.W.D.
    21-351, IH (Ex Div); affirming 2006 G.W.D. 35-712, OH
McDougal-Inglis v Scottish Borders Council 2007 G.W.D. 27-482, OH
McFarlane v McFarlane 2007 G.W.D. 16-296, OH
MacFarlane v Samuel 2007 G.W.D. 29-510, Sh Ct (North Strathclyde)
McFarlane v Scottish Borders Council (Expenses) 2006 S.L.T. 721; 2007 S.C.L.R. 143;
    2006 G.W.D. 22-484, OH ....   *Digested*, 06/**5102**
McFarlane v Thain 2007 G.W.D. 38-665, OH
McG v McG see M v M
McGarvey Construction Ltd v Shanks [2007] CSOH 77; 2007 S.L.T. 537; 2007 G.W.D.
    16-294, OH ....   *Digested*, 07/**4993**
McGhee v Diageo Plc [2007] CSIH 68; 2007 S.L.T. 1016; 2007 G.W.D. 29-503, IH
    (Ex Div)
McGhee v HM Advocate 2007 G.W.D. 4-60, HCJ
McGhee v National Coal Board [1973] 1 W.L.R. 1; [1972] 3 All E.R. 1008; 1973 S.C.
    (H.L.) 37; 1973 S.L.T. 14; 13 K.I.R. 471; (1972) 116 S.J. 967, HL; reversing 1972
    S.L.T. (Notes) 61, IH (1 Div).................................   *Digested*, 73/**3841**:
                         Applied, 83/2548, 92/1552, 94/3399, 99/3987, 00/4187, 02/2225,
                         06/2866, 07/5100: *Considered*, 85/2319, 87/2604, 96/4426, 00/5114,
                        04/2693, 06/2867: *Distinguished*, 87/4758, 88/2415, 90/5497, 98/1501:
                                                Followed, 04/2714
McGhee (Colin) v HM Advocate [2006] HCJAC 87; 2006 S.C.C.R. 712, HCJ ......   *Digested*, 07/**5507**
McGirr (James) v HM Advocate 2007 J.C. 83; 2007 S.C.C.R. 80; 2007 G.W.D. 4-59,
    HCJ ....   *Digested*, 07/**5074**
McGlynn v Mental Health Tribunal for Scotland [2007] M.H.L.R. 16; 2006 G.W.D. 13-
    248, Sh Pr
McGowan v McQuaid 2007 G.W.D. 11-211, HCJ
McGowan v W&JR Watson Ltd [2006] CSIH 62; 2007 S.C. 272; 2007 S.L.T. 169;
    2007 S.C.L.R. 147; 2007 Rep. L.R. 18; 2007 G.W.D. 1-9, IH (Ex Div); affirming
    2006 Rep. L.R. 52; 2006 G.W.D. 16-320, OH ....   *Digested*, 07/**5417**
McGowan (Steven) v HM Advocate; *joined case* Harris (Stuart) v HM Advocate 2006
    S.C.C.R. 186; 2006 G.W.D. 11-204, HCJ ....   *Digested*, 07/**5075**
McGregor v LMRS Farm Ltd 2007 G.W.D. 27-474, OH

McGregor v Scottish Water 2007 G.W.D. 3-40, OH

McHale v Miller see Dickson (Kenneth Robert) v HM Advocate

McKelvie v Scottish Steel Scaffolding Co Ltd 1938 S.C. 278; 1938 S.L.T. 159, IH (1 Div)... *Applied*, 82/4350, 95/6341, 07/4978: *Considered*, 92/6408

Mackenzie v Co-operative Group (CWS) Ltd 2007 G.W.D. 17-311, Sh Ct (Grampian)

Mackenzie v Grant 2007 G.W.D. 25-433, Sh Pr

Mackenzie v Grant 2007 G.W.D. 16-298, Sh Ct (Grampian)

McKenzie v Nutter 2007 S.L.T. (Sh Ct) 17; 2007 S.C.L.R. 115; 2007 Fam. L.R. 69; 2006 G.W.D. 39-768, Sh Pr .... *Digested*, 07/**5494**

Mackintosh v Morrice's Executors [2005] CSOH 167; 2007 S.C. 6; 2006 S.L.T. 853; 2007 S.C.L.R. 708; 2006 G.W.D. 28-624, IH (1 Div); affirming [2006] CSIH 43; 2006 S.L.T. 580; 2006 S.C.L.R. 521; 2006 Rep. L.R. 57; 2006 G.W.D. 16-313, OH .... *Digested*, 06/**5245**

McLaughlin v Thenew Housing Association Ltd 2007 Hous. L.R. 18; 2007 G.W.D. 13-273, Sh Ct (Glasgow)

McLean v Rainbow Homeloans Ltd [2007] I.R.L.R. 14, EAT (SC) .... *Digested*, 07/**5150**

McLean (Sasha Linda) v HM Advocate [2007] HCJAC 51; 2007 S.C.C.R. 363; 2007 G.W.D. 30-517, HCJ

McLeod v Davidson 2007 G.W.D. 23-386, Sh Ct (Tayside)

MacLeod v Doonin Plant Ltd 2007 G.W.D. 35-612, Sh Ct (Lothian)

MacLeod v Newsquest (Sunday Herald) Ltd 2007 S.C.L.R. 555; 2007 Rep. L.R. 5; 2007 G.W.D. 1-6, OH .... *Digested*, 07/**5097**

McLeod (Alistair) v HM Advocate (No.2); *sub nom* McLeod (Alistair), Petitioner 1998 J.C. 67; 1998 S.L.T. 233; 1998 S.C.C.R. 77; 1998 G.W.D. 4-161, HCJ.......... *Digested*, 98/**5607**: *Applied*, 01/6347: *Considered*, 01/6314, 02/5518, 04/4671, 05/5136, 07/5064

McLeod (Alistair), Petitioner see McLeod (Alistair) v HM Advocate (No.2)

McLeod (Peter) v HM Advocate [2006] HCJAC 79; 2007 J.C. 66; 2006 S.L.T. 1113; 2006 S.C.C.R. 679; 2006 G.W.D. 35-718, HCJ .... *Digested*, 07/**5071**

MacLeod's Trustee v MacLeod 2007 Hous. L.R. 34, Sh Ct (Glasgow)

McMenemy v Capita Business Services Ltd 2007 S.C. 492; 2007 S.L.T. 428; [2007] I.R.L.R. 400; 2007 G.W.D. 13-267, IH (Ex Div); affirming [2006] I.R.L.R. 761; (2006) 150 S.J.L.B. 665, EAT (SC) .... *Digested*, 07/**5145**

McNab v Bluebird Buses Ltd 2007 Rep. L.R. 36; 2007 G.W.D. 7-121, OH........... *Digested*, 07/**5416**

McNally v McNally 2007 G.W.D. 9-164, Sh Ct (Tayside)

McNaughton v Gilchrist see Dickson (Kenneth Robert) v HM Advocate

McNaughton (Iain) v HM Advocate see Dickson (Kenneth Robert) v HM Advocate

McPherson v Mackie 2007 S.C.L.R. 351; 2007 G.W.D. 10-189, IH (Ex Div); reversing 2006 G.W.D. 27-606, Lands Tr (Scot)

MacPlant Services Ltd v Contract Lifting Services (Scotland) Ltd 2007 G.W.D. 22-373, Sh Pr

McQuarrie v McKinstray 2007 S.L.T. (Sh Ct) 120; 2007 G.W.D. 17-307, Sh Ct (South Strathclyde)

MacRitchie v MacRitchie (Divorce: Financial Provision) 1994 S.L.T. (Sh Ct) 72; 1994 S.C.L.R. 348, Sh Pr .... *Digested*, 94/**5779**: *Applied*, 07/5187

Magnet Ltd v Cape (t/a Briggate Investments) 2007 G.W.D. 25-427, Sh Ct (Tayside)

Mahmood v Mahmood 2007 S.L.T. (Sh Ct) 176; 2007 Fam. L.R. 94; 2007 G.W.D. 23-383, Sh Pr

Mair v Arshad 2007 G.W.D. 34-575, Sh Ct (Tayside)

Malcolm v Dundee City Council 2007 G.W.D. 7-119, OH

Mallon v General Medical Council [2007] CSIH 17; 2007 S.C. 426; 2007 S.L.T. 372; 2007 G.W.D. 9-169, IH (2 Div) .... *Digested*, 07/**5238**

Maloco v Littlewoods Organisation Ltd; *joined case* Smith v Littlewoods Organisation Ltd [1987] A.C. 241; [1987] 2 W.L.R. 480; [1987] 1 All E.R. 710; 1987 S.C. (H.L.) 37; 1987 S.L.T. 425; 1987 S.C.L.R. 489; (1987) 84 L.S.G. 905; (1987) 137 N.L.J. 149; (1987) 131 S.J. 226, HL; affirming 1986 S.L.T. 272, IH (1 Div); reversing 1982 S.L.T. 267, OH .... *Digested*, 87/**4737**: *Applied*, 95/3668, 04/2711: *Considered*, 88/2019, 93/2934, 94/3365, 96/1162, 98/4037: *Distinguished*, 90/250, 96/3699: *Followed*, 07/5419: *Not followed*, 85/4437

Maris v Banchory Squash Racquets Club Ltd; *sub nom* Sloane-Maris v Banchory Squash Racquets Club Ltd [2007] CSIH 30; 2007 S.C. 501; 2007 S.L.T. 447; 2007 Hous. L.R. 54; 2007 G.W.D. 13-272, IH (Ex Div) .... *Digested*, 07/**5330**

Marshall v Marshall 2007 Fam. L.R. 48; 2007 G.W.D. 10-188, OH .... *Digested*, 07/**5188**

Martin (Ronald O'Neill) v HM Advocate [2006] HCJAC 86; 2007 J.C. 70; 2006 S.C.C.R. 683; 2006 G.W.D. 37-740, HCJ .... *Digested*, 07/**5518**

Mason (Lee) v HM Advocate; *joined cases* Dunn (Christopher Gary) v HM Advocate; Laing (Paul David) v HM Advocate 2006 S.C.C.R. 96; 2006 G.W.D. 8-145, HCJ .... *Digested*, 07/**5519**

Matalan Retail Ltd v Renfrewshire Valuation Joint Board Assessor [2007] CSIH 40; 2007 S.C. 663; [2007] R.A. 339; 2007 G.W.D. 18-329, LVAC

Matthews v Associated Portland Cement Manufacturers (1978) Ltd see Fairchild v Glenhaven Funeral Services Ltd (t/a GH Dovener & Son)

Matthews v British Uralite Plc see Fairchild v Glenhaven Funeral Services Ltd (t/a GH Dovener & Son)

Mauchland, Fatal Accident Inquiry 2007 G.W.D. 30-521, Sh Ct (Tayside)

Melfort Pier Holidays Ltd v Melfort Club [2006] CSIH 61; 2007 S.C. 243; 2007 G.W.D. 7-115, IH (1 Div); affirming 2006 G.W.D. 28-627, OH

Melville v Thomson [2006] HCJAC 77; 2006 S.L.T. 1017; 2006 S.C.C.R. 663; 2006 G.W.D. 34-707, HCJ . . . . *Digested*, 07/**5496**

Melville Dundas Ltd v Hotel Corp of Edinburgh Ltd [2006] CSOH 136; 2007 S.C. 12; [2006] B.L.R. 474, OH . . . . *Digested*, 07/**5011**

Melville Dundas Ltd (In Receivership) v George Wimpey UK Ltd [2007] UKHL 18; [2007] Bus. L.R. 1182; [2007] 1 W.L.R. 1136; [2007] 3 All E.R. 889; 2007 S.C. (H.L.) 116; 2007 S.L.T. 413; 2007 S.C.L.R. 429; [2007] B.L.R. 257; 112 Con. L.R. 1; [2007] C.I.L.L. 2469; (2007) 104(19) L.S.G. 25; (2007) 151 S.J.L.B. 571; 2007 G.W.D. 14-276; *Times*, May 8, 2007, HL; reversing 2006 S.C. 310; 2006 S.L.T. 95; 2006 S.C.L.R. 356; [2006] B.L.R. 164; 2006 G.W.D. 2-26, IH (Ex Div); reversing 2005 S.L.T. 24; 2005 S.C.L.R. 116, OH . . . . *Digested*, 06/**5149**

Mendoza v Ghaidan see Ghaidan v Godin-Mendoza

Middlebank Ltd v University of Dundee 2007 G.W.D. 10-190, OH

Miller v Central Demolition Ltd 2007 G.W.D. 35-617, Sh Ct (North Strathclyde)

Miller v Jamieson [2007] HCJAC 56; 2007 S.L.T. 1180; 2007 S.C.C.R. 497; 2007 G.W.D. 32-548, HCJ

Miller v Sacone Environmental Ltd 2007 G.W.D. 40-696, Sh Ct (Tayside)

Miller v Scottish Water 2007 G.W.D. 35-614, Sh Ct (Tayside)

Miller, Petitioner 2007 G.W.D. 17-303, OH

Minshull v Advocate General 2007 G.W.D. 25-422, OH

Minto v Spiers 2007 G.W.D. 14-279, HCJ

Mitchell v North Lanarkshire Council [2007] CSOH 141; 2007 S.L.T. 765; 2007 G.W.D. 24-413, OH . . . . *Digested*, 07/**5399**

MM v HM Advocate see Moir (Mitchell John) v HM Advocate

MM v HM Advocate see Moir (Mitchell John) v HM Advocate

Modern Engineering (Bristol) Ltd v Gilbert Ash (Northern) Ltd see Gilbert Ash (Northern) Ltd v Modern Engineering (Bristol) Ltd

Moir (Mitchell John) v HM Advocate; *sub nom* MM v HM Advocate 2005 1 J.C. 102; 2004 S.C.C.R. 658, HCJ . . . . *Digested*, 05/**5084**: *Considered*, 06/5226, 07/5019

Moir (Mitchell John) v HM Advocate; *sub nom* MM v HM Advocate [2007] HCJAC 20; 2007 J.C. 131; 2007 S.L.T. 452; 2007 S.C.C.R. 159; 2007 G.W.D. 12-243, HCJ . . . . *Digested*, 07/**5023**: *Considered*, 07/5019

Moncrieff v Jamieson [2007] UKHL 42; [2007] 1 W.L.R. 2620; 2007 S.L.T. 989; 2007 S.C.L.R. 790; [2007] 43 E.G. 200 (C.S.); (2007) 151 S.J.L.B. 1368; [2007] N.P.C. 106; 2007 G.W.D. 33-564, HL; affirming 2005 1 S.C. 281; 2005 S.L.T. 225; 2005 S.C.L.R. 463; 2005 G.W.D. 5-66, IH (Ex Div); affirming 2004 S.C.L.R. 135, Sh Ct (Grampian) . . . . *Digested*, 07/**5277**

Montgomery v Cameron & Greig 2007 G.W.D. 26-467, OH

Montgomery v HM Advocate; *sub nom* HM Advocate v Montgomery (David Shields); *joined case* Coulter v HM Advocate [2003] 1 A.C. 641; [2001] 2 W.L.R. 779; 2001 S.C. (P.C.) 1; 2001 S.L.T. 37; 2000 S.C.C.R. 1044; [2001] U.K.H.R.R. 124; 9 B.H.R.C. 641; 2000 G.W.D. 40-1487; *Times*, December 6, 2000, PC (Sc) . . . . . *Digested*, 01/**6371**: *Applied*, 04/1629: *Considered*, 06/5552, 07/923: *Previous proceedings*, 00/6068

Montgomery v Lanarkshire Health Board [2007] CSOH 172; 2007 G.W.D. 33-568, OH

Moore v Scottish Daily Record & Sunday Mail Ltd [2007] CSOH 24; 2007 S.L.T. 217; 2007 G.W.D. 5-76, OH . . . . *Digested*, 07/**5099**

Moray Council v Scottish Ministers [2006] CSIH 41; 2006 S.C. 691; 2007 S.C.L.R. 55; 2006 G.W.D. 25-578, IH (2 Div) . . . . *Digested*, 07/**5464**

Moray Council v Scottish Ministers [2007] CSIH 2; 2007 S.C. 280, IH (2 Div)

Morris, Petitioner; *sub nom* Liquidator of Bank of Credit and Commerce International SA, Noter [2007] CSOH 165; 2007 S.L.T. 1149; 2007 G.W.D. 32-554, OH

Morrish v NTL Group Ltd [2007] CSIH 56; 2007 S.C. 805; 2007 S.L.T. 1074; 2007 G.W.D. 31-531, IH (Ex Div)

Morrison v BBC 2007 Rep. L.R. 2; 2007 G.W.D. 5-77, OH . . . . *Digested*, 07/**4988**

Morrison Sports Ltd v Scottish Power Plc; *joined cases* Singh v Scottish Power Plc; Pitchers v Scottish Power Plc [2007] CSOH 131; 2007 S.L.T. 1103; 2007 G.W.D. 31-538, OH

Morton v Glasgow City Council 2007 S.L.T. (Sh Ct) 81; 2007 Rep. L.R. 66; 2007 G.W.D. 15-291, Sh Ct (Glasgow) . . . . *Digested*, 07/**5424**

Muir (David Howard) v HM Advocate see Weir (Mark Lindsay) v HM Advocate

Muirhead v G 2007 Fam. L.R. 160; 2007 G.W.D. 34-571, IH (Ex Div)

Munnoch v Tay-Forth Foundries Ltd 2007 G.W.D. 31-530, OH

Murphy (Michael John) v HM Advocate [2007] HCJAC 57; 2007 S.L.T. 1079; 2007
    S.C.C.R. 532; 2007 G.W.D. 36-625, HCJ
Murray v J&E Shepherd 2007 G.W.D. 7-108, Sh Ct (Tayside)
Mushaka v Secretary of State for the Home Department 2007 G.W.D. 12-255, OH
Mycroft, Petitioner 1983 S.L.T. 342, OH . . . .   *Digested*, 83/**4032**:
                                                                                             Applied, 07/5011

N v Secretary of State for the Home Department see NAK v Secretary of State for the
    Home Department
Nabb v Kirkby 2007 S.C.L.R. 65; 2007 G.W.D. 7-114, Sh Pr . . . .   *Digested*, 07/**5276**
NAK v Secretary of State for the Home Department; *sub nom* N v Secretary of State
    for the Home Department [2007] CSIH 69; 2007 G.W.D. 28-495, IH (Ex Div)
National Galleries of Scotland v Revenue and Customs Commissioners [2007] V. &
    D.R. 234, V&DTr (Edinburgh)
Neil v HM Advocate 2007 G.W.D. 5-73, HCJ
Nelson v Barbour [2007] HCJAC 31; 2007 J.C. 195; 2007 S.C.C.R. 283; 2007 G.W.D.
    19-335, HCJ Appeal . . . .   *Digested*, 07/**5514**
Nelson v MacBeath 2007 G.W.D. 11-202, Sh Pr
Network Rail Infrastructure Ltd, Petitioner [2007] CSOH 169; 2007 G.W.D. 33-558, OH
Nevin (Patrick Joseph) v HM Advocate [2006] HCJAC 59; 2006 S.C.C.R. 460; 2006
    G.W.D. 25-557, HCJ . . . .   *Digested*, 07/**5034**
Newbould v MacEwan 2007 G.W.D. 8-153, Sh Ct (Lothian)
Newman Shopfitters Ltd v MJ Gleeson Group Plc 2003 S.L.T. (Sh Ct) 83; 2003
    S.C.L.R. 235; 2003 G.W.D. 10-271, Sh Pr . . . .   *Digested*, 03/**5291**:
                                                         Applied, 05/5036: *Considered*, 07/5184
Nisala v Glasgow City Council 2006 Hous. L.R. 66; 2006 G.W.D. 34-703, Sh Pr . . . . .   *Digested*, 07/**5333**
North Lanarkshire Council v Crossan 2007 S.L.T. (Sh Ct) 169; 2007 G.W.D. 32-543,
    Sh Ct (South Strathclyde)
North of Scotland Hydro-Electric Board v D&R Taylor 1956 S.C. 1; 1955 S.L.T. 373, IH
    (2 Div) . . . .   *Digested*, 55/**3036**:
                                                                                             Applied, 07/5012
NS v Scottish Legal Aid Board see S v Scottish Legal Aid Board
Nunn v Nunn 1997 S.L.T. 182, OH . . . .   *Digested*, 97/**5696**:
                                                                                             Applied, 07/5332

O'Brien v Pacitti Jones (A Firm) see Pacitti Jones (A Firm) v O'Brien
O'Donnell v McDonald; *sub nom* McDonald v O'Donnell 2007 S.L.T. 1227; 2007
    G.W.D. 36-620, IH (2 Div); reversing in part 2006 S.L.T. (Sh Ct) 107; 2006
    G.W.D. 28-615, Sh Pr . . . .   *Digested*, 06/**5543**
O'Halloran v CIBA Speciality Chemicals Plc 2007 Rep. L.R. 32; 2007 G.W.D. 7-126,
    OH . . . .   *Digested*, 07/**5421**
O'Hara v Murray [2007] HCJAC 34; 2007 J.C. 206; 2007 S.C.C.R. 322; 2007 G.W.D.
    23-380, HCJ Appeal . . . .   *Digested*, 07/**5520**
O'Neill v Dowding & Mills Plc 2007 G.W.D. 34-576, OH
O'Neill v Gilhooley 2007 Fam. L.R. 15; 2007 G.W.D. 8-136, Sh Pr
Office of the King's Prosecutor (Brussels) v Cando Armas; *sub nom* King's Prosecutor
    (Brussels) v Armas [2005] UKHL 67; [2006] 2 A.C. 1; [2005] 3 W.L.R. 1079;
    [2006] 1 All E.R. 647; [2005] Extradition L.R. 139; (2005) 155 N.L.J. 1809;
    Times, November 18, 2005; *Independent*, November 22, 2005, HL; affirming
    [2004] EWHC 2019 (Admin); [2005] 1 W.L.R. 1389; [2005] 2 All E.R. 181;
    [2005] Extradition L.R. 22; (2004) 154 N.L.J. 1498; *Times*, October 8, 2004,
    QBD (Admin) . . . .   *Digested*, 06/**1594**:
                                                         Applied, 06/1596, 07/1657: *Considered*, 06/1600, 07/5169:
                                                                                             Followed, 07/1670
Oxfordshire CC v B; *sub nom* R. (on the application of GB) v Oxfordshire CC;
    Oxfordshire CC v GB [2001] EWCA Civ 1358; [2002] B.L.G.R. 279; [2002]
    E.L.R. 8, CA (Civ Div); reversing in part [2001] EWHC Admin 378; [2001]
    E.L.R. 797, QBD (Admin) . . . .   *Digested*, 02/**1165**:
                                                                                             Considered, 07/5121
Oxfordshire CC v GB see Oxfordshire CC v B

P v Secretary of State for the Home Department 2007 G.W.D. 37-653, IH (Ex Div)
Pacitti Jones (A Firm) v O'Brien; *sub nom* O'Brien v Pacitti Jones (A Firm) [2005] CSIH
    56; 2006 S.C. 616; 2005 S.L.T. 793; [2005] I.R.L.R. 888; 2005 G.W.D. 25-
    483, IH (Ex Div); affirming EATS/0025/04, EAT (SC) . . . .   *Digested*, 05/**5214**:
                                                                                             Considered, 07/5328
Palmer v Revenue and Customs Commissioners [2006] CSIH 8; 2006 S.C. 464;
    2006 S.L.T. 259; 77 T.C. 738; [2007] B.T.C. 126; [2006] S.T.I. 580; 2006 G.W.D.
    6-117, IH (Ex Div) . . . .   *Digested*, 06/**5703**
Paterson v Advocate General for Scotland [2007] CSOH 112; 2007 S.L.T. 846; 2007
    Rep. L.R. 81; 2007 G.W.D. 24-395, OH

Paterson *v* Kent 2007 S.L.T. (Sh Ct) 8; [2007] M.H.L.R. 20; 2006 G.W.D. 24-541, Sh
Pr . . . .   *Digested*, 07/**5412**

Peacock Group Plc *v* Railston Ltd [2007] CSOH 26; 2007 S.L.T. 269; 2007 G.W.D. 5-
69, OH

Peart *v* Legge [2007] CSIH 70; 2007 S.L.T. 982; 2007 G.W.D. 28-499, IH (Ex Div);
reversing 2007 S.C.L.R. 86; 2007 G.W.D. 3-49, Sh Pr; affirming 2006 G.W.D.
18-377, Sh Ct (Lothian) . . . .   *Digested*, 07/**5483**

Peebles (Glen John) *v* HM Advocate [2007] HCJAC 6; 2007 J.C. 93; 2007 S.L.T. 197;
2007 G.W.D. 3-43, HCJ . . . .   *Digested*, 07/**5035**

Pendleton *v* Stone & Webster Engineering Ltd see Fairchild *v* Glenhaven Funeral
Services Ltd (t/a GH Dovener & Son)

Performing Right Society Ltd *v* Kwik-Fit Group Ltd 2007 G.W.D. 33-560, OH

Perth and Kinross Council *v* Secretary of State for Scotland 1999 S.C. 144; 1999 S.L.T.
1095; 1998 G.W.D. 38-1976, IH (2 Div) . . . .   *Digested*, 99/**6411**:
                          Applied, 07/5464

Pervez (Shahid) *v* HM Advocate [2006] HCJAC 85; 2007 J.C. 89; 2006 S.C.C.R.
707, HCJ . . . .   *Digested*, 07/**5473**

Pickett (Scott) *v* HM Advocate [2007] HCJAC 47; 2007 S.C.C.R. 389; 2007 G.W.D.
32-549, HCJ

Pirie *v* Clydesdale Bank Plc 2007 S.C.L.R. 18; 2006 G.W.D. 19-419, OH . . . .   *Digested*, 07/**5544**

Pitchers *v* Scottish Power Plc see Morrison Sports Ltd *v* Scottish Power Plc

Post Office *v* Jones see Jones *v* Post Office

Potter *v* Scottish Ministers see Potter *v* Scottish Prison Service

Potter *v* Scottish Prison Service; *sub nom* Potter *v* Scottish Ministers [2007] CSIH 67;
2007 S.L.T. 1019; [2007] U.K.H.R.R. 1361; 2007 G.W.D. 28-500, IH (1 Div);
reversing [2007] CSOH 56; 2007 S.L.T. 363; 2007 G.W.D. 10-196; *Times*, April
4, 2007, OH . . . .   *Digested*, 07/**5434**

Price *v* HM Advocate 2007 G.W.D. 25-429, HCJ

Principal Reporter (Scottish Children's Reporter Administration), Petitioner [2006] CSOH
172; 2006 S.L.T. 1090; 2006 Fam. L.R. 110; 2006 G.W.D. 36-726, OH . . . .   *Digested*, 07/**4849**

Procurator Fiscal, Dunoon *v* Dominick see Webster *v* Dominick

Project *v* Hutt (2006) 150 S.J.L.B. 702, EAT (SC) . . . .   *Applied*, 07/467

PS Independent Trustees Ltd *v* Kershaw 2007 G.W.D. 31-527, OH

PS Properties (2) Ltd *v* Callaway Homes Ltd 2007 G.W.D. 31-526, OH

R *v* Highland Council [2007] CSOH 51; 2007 S.L.T. 513; 2007 G.W.D. 9-158, OH . . . .   *Digested*, 07/**4857**

R *v* HM Advocate see HM Advocate *v* R

R. *v* Abery (Lee Alan) see R. *v* Richardson (Jack Virgil)

R. *v* Bowden (Jonathan) [2001] Q.B. 88; [2000] 2 W.L.R. 1083; [2000] 2 All E.R.
418; [2000] 1 Cr. App. R. 438; [2000] 2 Cr. App. R. (S.) 26; [2000] Crim. L.R.
381; (1999) 96(47) L.S.G. 29; (2000) 144 S.J.L.B. 5; *Times*, November 19,
1999; *Independent*, November 26, 1999, CA (Crim Div) . . . .   *Digested*, 99/**947**:
       Applied, 00/993, 01/1450: *Followed*, 00/6039, 02/819, 07/5036

R. *v* Connor (Ben) see R. *v* Mirza (Shabbir Ali)

R. *v* Cook (Neil Terence) see R. *v* Cooksley (Robert Charles)

R. *v* Cooksley (Robert Charles); *sub nom* Attorney General's Reference (No.152 of
2002), Re; *joined cases* R. *v* Stride (Ian Paul); R. *v* Cook (Neil Terence); R. *v*
Crump (Richard James) [2003] EWCA Crim 996; [2003] 3 All E.R. 40; [2003]
2 Cr. App. R. 18; [2004] 1 Cr. App. R. (S.) 1; [2003] R.T.R. 32; (2003) 100(23)
L.S.G. 36; *Times*, April 8, 2003; *Independent*, June 30, 2003, CA (Crim Div) . .   *Digested*, 04/**3333**:
       Applied, 04/3295, 04/3296, 04/3298, 05/3547, 05/3550, 06/3811,
06/3814, 06/3820, 06/3874, 06/3875, 06/3876, 07/862, 07/3588, 07/3595,
07/3775: *Considered*, 04/3294, 04/3297, 04/3467, 05/3546, 05/3549,
05/3551, 05/3552, 05/3553, 05/3581, 05/3766, 05/5657, 06/3805,
06/3806, 06/3807, 06/3808, 06/3809, 06/3810, 06/3812, 06/3813,
06/3815, 06/3873, 06/3877, 06/5669, 07/3589, 07/3590, 07/3591,
07/3592, 07/3594, 07/5512: *Followed*, 04/4371, 05/3548, 07/3593

R. *v* Croxson (Matthew Louis) see R. *v* Johnstone (Robert Alexander)

R. *v* Crump (Richard James) see R. *v* Cooksley (Robert Charles)

R. *v* Eley (Charles Thomas) see R. *v* Johnstone (Robert Alexander)

R. *v* Harrison (Richard James) see R. *v* Johnstone (Robert Alexander)

R. *v* Ho (Toon Chin) see R. *v* Johnstone (Robert Alexander)

R. *v* Jayson (Mike) see R. *v* Smith (Graham Westgarth)

R. *v* Johnstone (Robert Alexander); *joined cases* R. *v* Harrison (Richard James); R. *v* Mayron Multimedia Ltd; R. *v* Eley (Charles Thomas); R. *v* Ho (Toon Chin); R. *v* Croxson (Matthew Louis) [2003] UKHL 28; [2003] 1 W.L.R. 1736; [2003] 3 All E.R. 884; [2003] 2 Cr. App. R. 33; (2003) 167 J.P. 281; [2004] E.T.M.R. 2; [2003] H.R.L.R. 25; [2003] U.K.H.R.R. 1239; [2003] F.S.R. 42; [2004] Crim. L.R. 244; (2003) 167 J.P.N. 453; (2003) 100(26) L.S.G. 36; (2003) 147 S.J.L.B. 625; *Times*, May 29, 2003; *Independent*, June 5, 2003, HL; affirming [2002] EWCA Crim 194; [2003] E.T.M.R. 1; [2002] F.S.R. 56; (2002) 99(13) L.S.G. 25; (2002) 146 S.J.L.B. 60; *Times*, March 12, 2002, CA (Crim Div) . . . .   *Digested*, 03/**2644**:
Considered, 04/707, 04/800, 06/2546: *Distinguished*, 07/5324:
Doubted, 03/814

R. *v* Little (Liam John) see R. *v* Richardson (Jack Virgil)

R. *v* Manchester Crown Court Ex p. M (A Child) see R. (on the application of McCann) *v* Manchester Crown Court

R. *v* Mayron Multimedia Ltd see R. *v* Johnstone (Robert Alexander)

R. *v* Mirza (Shabbir Ali); *joined cases* R. *v* Connor (Ben); R. *v* Rollock (Ashley Kenneth) [2004] UKHL 2; [2004] 1 A.C. 1118; [2004] 2 W.L.R. 201; [2004] 1 All E.R. 925; [2004] 2 Cr. App. R. 8; [2004] H.R.L.R. 11; 16 B.H.R.C. 279; (2004) 101(7) L.S.G. 34; (2004) 154 N.L.J. 145; (2004) 148 S.J.L.B. 117; *Times*, January 23, 2004, HL; affirming [2002] EWCA Crim 1235; [2002] Crim. L.R. 921, CA (Crim Div) . . . .   *Digested*, 04/**694**:
Applied, 05/827, 05/832, 05/849: *Considered*, 07/5072: *Explained*, 05/895

R. *v* Poel (Karel) see R. *v* Richardson (Jack Virgil)

R. *v* Richardson (Jack Virgil); *joined cases* R. *v* Sheppard (Dionne); R. *v* Abery (Lee Alan); R. *v* Little (Liam John); R. *v* Poel (Karel); R. *v* Robertson (Karen Ann) [2006] EWCA Crim 3186; [2007] 2 All E.R. 601; [2007] 2 Cr. App. R. (S.) 36; [2007] R.T.R. 29; [2007] Crim. L.R. 315; *Times*, January 15, 2007, CA (Crim Div) . . . .   *Digested*, 07/**3590**:
Applied, 07/3588, 07/3589, 07/3592, 07/3595: *Considered*, 07/3591,
07/3596, 07/5512

R. *v* Robertson (Karen Ann) see R. *v* Richardson (Jack Virgil)

R. *v* Rollock (Ashley Kenneth) see R. *v* Mirza (Shabbir Ali)

R. *v* Sheppard (Dionne) see R. *v* Richardson (Jack Virgil)

R. *v* Smith (Graham Westgarth); *joined case* R. *v* Jayson (Mike) [2002] EWCA Crim 683; [2003] 1 Cr. App. R. 13; [2002] Crim. L.R. 659; *Times*, April 23, 2002, CA (Crim Div) . . . .   *Digested*, 02/**819**:
Applied, 07/5036

R. *v* Stride (Ian Paul) see R. *v* Cooksley (Robert Charles)

R. (on the application of GB) *v* Oxfordshire CC see Oxfordshire CC *v* B

R. (on the application of Inland Revenue Commissioners) *v* Aberdeen General Commissioners of Income Tax see Revenue and Customs Commissioners, Petitioners

R. (on the application of M (A Child)) *v* Manchester Crown Court see R. (on the application of McCann) *v* Manchester Crown Court

R. (on the application of McCann) *v* Manchester Crown Court; *sub nom* R. *v* Manchester Crown Court Ex p. M (A Child); R. (on the application of M (A Child)) *v* Manchester Crown Court; *joined case* Clingham *v* Kensington and Chelsea RLBC [2002] UKHL 39; [2003] 1 A.C. 787; [2002] 3 W.L.R. 1313; [2002] 4 All E.R. 593; [2003] 1 Cr. App. R. 27; (2002) 166 J.P. 657; [2002] U.K.H.R.R. 1286; 13 B.H.R.C. 482; [2003] H.L.R. 17; [2003] B.L.G.R. 57; [2003] Crim. L.R. 269; (2002) 166 J.P.N. 850; (2002) 146 S.J.L.B. 239; *Times*, October 21, 2002; *Independent*, October 23, 2002, HL; affirming [2001] EWCA Civ 281; [2001] 1 W.L.R. 1084; [2001] 4 All E.R. 264; (2001) 165 J.P. 545; [2001] H.R.L.R. 37; (2002) 166 J.P.N. 150; *Times*, March 9, 2001; *Independent*, March 20, 2001, CA (Civ Div); affirming [2001] 1 W.L.R. 358; (2001) 165 J.P. 225; (2001) 165 J.P.N. 204; (2001) 98(2) L.S.G. 40; (2000) 144 S.J.L.B. 287; *Times*, December 22, 2000; *Daily Telegraph*, December 12, 2000, DC . . . .   *Digested*, 02/**3**:
Applied, 01/41, 02/1579, 02/1579, 04/366, 04/1020, 06/902, 07/1949,
07/2171: *Considered*, 03/831, 04/790, 05/1073, 06/304, 06/304, 06/327,
07/4974: *Distinguished*, 04/1458, 06/316: *Followed*, 05/342

R. (on the application of Ullah) v Special Adjudicator; *sub nom* Do v Secretary of State
for the Home Department; R. (on the application of Ullah (Ahsan)) v Secretary
of State for the Home Department; Ullah (Ahsan) v Special Adjudicator; *joined
case* Do v Immigration Appeal Tribunal [2004] UKHL 26; [2004] 2 A.C. 323;
[2004] 3 W.L.R. 23; [2004] 3 All E.R. 785; [2004] H.R.L.R. 33; [2004]
U.K.H.R.R. 995; [2004] Imm. A.R. 419; [2004] I.N.L.R. 381; (2004) 101(28)
L.S.G. 33; (2004) 154 N.L.J. 985; (2004) 148 S.J.L.B. 762; *Times*, June 18,
2004; *Independent*, June 22, 2004, HL; affirming [2002] EWCA Civ 1856;
[2003] 1 W.L.R. 770; [2003] 3 All E.R. 1174; [2003] H.R.L.R. 12; [2003]
U.K.H.R.R. 302; [2003] Imm. A.R. 304; [2003] I.N.L.R. 74; [2003] A.C.D. 30;
(2003) 100(10) L.S.G. 28; (2003) 147 S.J.L.B. 28; *Times*, December 18, 2002;
Independent, December 20, 2002, CA (Civ Div); affirming [2002] EWHC 1584
(Admin); [2002] Imm. A.R. 601; *Times*, September 5, 2002; *Independent*,
October 14, 2002, QBD (Admin) . . . . *Digested*, 04/**2009**:
Applied, 04/2052, 05/401, 05/2195, 06/1598, 06/2223, 07/2309:
Considered, 04/839, 04/2038, 05/2140, 05/5431, 06/1605, 07/5169,
07/5432

R. (on the application of Ullah (Ahsan)) v Secretary of State for the Home Department
see R. (on the application of Ullah) v Special Adjudicator
RA Logan & Co v Maxwell 2007 G.W.D. 33-570, OH
Rainford v Aberdeenshire Council 2007 Rep. L.R. 126; 2007 G.W.D. 24-414, OH
Ralston v Scottish Ministers see Somerville v Scottish Ministers
Raza v Scottish Criminal Cases Review Commission [2007] CSOH 152; 2007
S.C.C.R. 403; 2007 G.W.D. 27-469, OH
Ready (Gary) v HM Advocate [2007] HCJAC 15; 2007 S.L.T. 340; 2007 G.W.D. 7-110,
HCJ . . . . *Digested*, 07/**5072**
Redpath Dorman Long Ltd v Cummins Engine Co Ltd 1981 S.C. 370; 1982 S.L.T. 489,
IH (2 Div) . . . . *Digested*, 82/**3441**:
Approved, 96/6702: *Considered*, 07/5011: *Followed*, 83/3961
Reid v Sundolitt Ltd [2007] CSIH 64; 2007 Rep. L.R. 90; 2007 G.W.D. 24-417, IH (Ex
Div)
Renewable Energy Systems Ltd v Moray Council 2007 G.W.D. 1-7, IH (2 Div)
Rennie v Society of Vincent de Paul [2007] CSOH 40; 2007 S.L.T. 308; 2007 G.W.D.
7-112, OH . . . . *Digested*, 07/**4981**
Response Handling Ltd v BBC [2007] CSOH 102; 2007 G.W.D. 22-367, OH
Revenue and Customs Commissioners v Empowerment Enterprises Ltd see
Empowerment Enterprises Ltd v Customs and Excise Commissioners
Revenue and Customs Commissioners v RBS Deutschland Holdings GmbH [2006]
CSIH 10; [2007] S.T.C. 814; 2006 S.C. 515; 2006 S.L.T. 615; [2006] Eu. L.R.
917; [2007] B.T.C. 5980; [2006] S.T.I. 578; 2006 G.W.D. 19-387, IH (Ex Div) . . *Digested*, 06/**5131**
Revenue and Customs Commissioners v Robertson's Electrical Ltd see Robertson's
Electrical Ltd v Customs and Excise Commissioners
Revenue and Customs Commissioners v William Grant & Sons Distillers Ltd (Scotland);
sub nom William Grant & Sons Distillers Ltd v Inland Revenue Commissioners;
Inland Revenue Commissioners v William Grant & Sons Distillers Ltd; *joined case*
Small (Inspector of Taxes) v Mars UK Ltd [2007] UKHL 15; [2007] 1 W.L.R.
1448; [2007] 2 All E.R. 440; [2007] S.T.C. 680; 2007 S.C. (H.L.) 105; 2007
S.L.T. 522; 2007 S.C.L.R. 468; 78 T.C. 442; [2007] B.T.C. 315; [2007] S.T.I.
1165; (2007) 151 S.J.L.B. 470; 2007 G.W.D. 17-306; *Times*, April 2, 2007, HL;
reversing [2005] CSIH 63; [2006] S.T.C. 69; 2006 S.C. 17; 2005 S.L.T. 888;
[2005] B.T.C. 483; [2005] S.T.I. 1647; 2005 G.W.D. 29-536, IH (Ex Div) . . . . . *Digested*, 07/**4019**
Revenue and Customs Commissioners, Petitioners; *sub nom* Inland Revenue
Commissioners, Petitioners; R. (on the application of Inland Revenue
Commissioners) v Aberdeen General Commissioners of Income Tax; Advocate
General for Scotland v General Commissioners for Aberdeen City [2005] CSOH
135; [2006] S.T.C. 1218; 2005 S.L.T. 1061; 77 T.C. 391; [2006] B.T.C. 846;
[2005] S.T.I. 1755; 2005 G.W.D. 33-634, OH . . . . *Digested*, 06/**5702**:
Considered, 07/4001
Revival Properties Ltd v Edinburgh City Council see Edinburgh City Council v Secretary
of State for Scotland
Ritchie Brothers (PWC) Ltd v David Philp (Commercials) Ltd [2005] CSIH 32; 2005 1
S.C. 384; 2005 S.L.T. 341; 2005 S.C.L.R. 829; [2005] B.L.R. 384; 2005
G.W.D. 11-169; *Times*, May 24, 2005, IH (2 Div); reversing 2004 S.L.T. 471;
[2004] B.L.R. 379; 2004 G.W.D. 13-282, OH . . . . *Digested*, 05/**5068**:
Applied, 07/433
Robb v M&I Salamis Ltd (formerly Salamis Marine & Industrial Ltd) see Robb v
Salamis (M&I) Ltd
Robb v Salamis (M&I) Ltd; *sub nom* Robb v M&I Salamis Ltd (formerly Salamis
Marine & Industrial Ltd) [2006] UKHL 56; [2007] 2 All E.R. 97; 2007 S.C.
(H.L.) 71; 2007 S.L.T. 158; 2007 S.C.L.R. 176; [2007] I.C.R. 175; (2007) 151
S.J.L.B. 25; 2007 G.W.D. 2-33; *Times*, December 22, 2006, HL; reversing 2005
S.L.T. 523; 2005 S.C.L.R. 676; 2005 Rep. L.R. 42; 2005 G.W.D. 16-290, IH
(Ex Div); affirming 2004 S.C.L.R. 672; 2003 G.W.D. 33-949, Sh Ct (Grampian)   *Digested*, 07/**5269**

Robbie the Pict *v* Wylie; *sub nom* Wylie *v* Robbie the Pict [2007] HCJAC 10; 2007 J.C.
   101; 2007 S.C.C.R. 114; 2007 G.W.D. 6-88, HCJ . . . . *Digested*, 07/**5049**
Robbins *v* Mitchell 2007 G.W.D. 22-375, Sh Pr
Robertson *v* Donaldson [2007] HCJAC 22; 2007 J.C. 175; 2007 S.C.C.R. 146; 2007
   G.W.D. 12-244, HCJ Appeal . . . . *Digested*, 07/**5503**
Robertson *v* Glasgow City Council 2007 G.W.D. 18-325, OH
Robertson *v* Horses in Scotland Ltd 2007 G.W.D. 11-215, OH
Robertson *v* Inspirations East Ltd 2007 G.W.D. 7-122, OH
Robertson *v* Newsquest (Sunday Herald) Ltd; *sub nom* Lord Robertson of Port Ellen
   v Newsquest (Sunday Herald) Ltd 2006 S.C.L.R. 792; 2006 Rep. L.R. 124;
   2006 G.W.D. 23-506, OH . . . . *Digested*, 07/**5098**
Robertson *v* Scottish Ministers 2007 G.W.D. 40-704, OH
Robertson (Scott Alexander) *v* HM Advocate [2007] HCJAC 12; 2007 S.L.T. 459;
   2007 S.C.C.R. 129; 2007 G.W.D. 7-109, HCJ . . . . *Digested*, 07/**5025**
Robertson (Stewart) *v* HM Advocate; *sub nom* Robertson, Petitioner; Gough *v*
   McFadyen; *joined case* Gough (Stephen Peter) *v* HM Advocate [2007] HCJAC
   63; 2007 S.L.T. 1153; 2007 G.W.D. 37-643, HCJ
Robertson's Electrical Ltd *v* Customs and Excise Commissioners; *sub nom* Customs
   and Excise Commissioners *v* Robertson's Electrical Ltd; Revenue and Customs
   Commissioners *v* Robertson's Electrical Ltd [2005] CSIH 75; [2007] S.T.C. 612;
   2006 S.C. 261; 2005 S.L.T. 1149; 2006 S.C.L.R. 493; [2007] B.T.C. 5763;
   [2007] B.V.C. 710; [2005] S.T.I. 1813; 2005 G.W.D. 37-699, IH (2 Div); reversing
   [2005] B.V.C. 2070; [2004] V. & D.R. 481; [2004] S.T.I. 2570, V&DTr
   (Edinburgh) . . . . *Digested*, 06/**5742**
Robertson's Trustees *v* Inland Revenue Commissioners 1987 S.L.T. 534; 1987 S.C.L.R.
   433, IH (1 Div) . . . . *Digested*, 87/**3983**:
                                                                                   Considered, 07/5561

Robertson, Petitioner see Robertson (Stewart) *v* HM Advocate
Robinson *v* HM Advocate 2007 G.W.D. 9-161, HCJ
Roeser *v* Edinburgh City Council see Roeser *v* Lothian Valuation Appeal Committee
Roeser *v* Lothian Valuation Appeal Committee; *sub nom* Roeser *v* Edinburgh City
   Council [2007] CSIH 37; 2007 S.C. 523; 2007 S.L.T. 656; 2007 G.W.D. 18-321,
   IH (2 Div) . . . . *Digested*, 07/**5397**
Rooney (Thomas) *v* HM Advocate [2007] HCJAC 1; 2007 S.C.C.R. 49; 2007 G.W.D.
   8-138, HCJ . . . . *Digested*, 07/**5093**
Rooney, Petitioner 2007 G.W.D. 7-127, OH
Ross *v* Gosselin's Executors 1926 S.C. 325; 1926 S.L.T. 239, IH (1 Div) . . . . *Applied*, 07/5544
Ross *v* Ross (Process Appeal) 1927 S.C. (H.L.) 4; 1927 S.L.T. 2, HL . . . . *Applied*, 07/4855:
                                                                                   Followed, 61/10874

Rouf *v* General Commissioners of Income Tax 2007 G.W.D. 1-16, OH
Rouf (t/a New Balaka Restaurant), Petitioner [2006] CSOH 195; [2007] S.T.I. 113, OH
Rowan *v* Partick Housing Association Ltd 2007 G.W.D. 36-636, Sh Ct (Glasgow)
Royal Bank of Scotland Group Plc *v* Revenue and Customs Commissioners 2007 S.C.
   401; 2007 S.L.T. 265; [2007] B.T.C. 5410; [2007] B.V.C. 429; [2007] S.T.I. 535;
   2007 G.W.D. 7-131, IH (2 Div); affirming [2006] V. & D.R. 68; [2006] S.T.I.
   1368, V&DTr (Edinburgh)
Royal Bank of Scotland Group Plc *v* Revenue and Customs Commissioners [2007]
   B.V.C. 2295, V&DTr (Edinburgh)
Royal Insurance (UK) Ltd *v* Amec Construction Scotland Ltd 2007 G.W.D. 25-424, OH
Russell *v* Stubbs Ltd see Stubbs Ltd *v* Russell
Ruxton *v* Starrs see Starrs *v* Ruxton

S *v* Criminal Injuries Compensation Appeal Panel; *sub nom* DJS *v* Criminal Injuries
   Compensation Board [2007] CSIH 49; 2007 S.C. 748; 2007 S.L.T. 575; 2007
   S.C.L.R. 502; 2007 G.W.D. 21-350, IH (Ex Div) . . . . *Digested*, 07/**5447**
S *v* D 2007 S.L.T. (Sh Ct) 37; 2006 S.C.L.R. 805; 2006 Fam. L.R. 66; 2006 G.W.D.
   24-539, Sh Ct (Lothian) . . . . *Digested*, 07/**5176**
S *v* Edinburgh City Council; *sub nom* S, Petitioner; SM, Appellant 2007 Fam. L.R. 2;
   2007 G.W.D. 2-28, OH . . . . *Digested*, 07/**5121**
S *v* Poor Sisters of Nazareth see B *v* Murray (No.2)
S *v* Scottish Legal Aid Board; *sub nom* NS *v* Scottish Legal Aid Board [2007] CSOH
   116; 2007 S.L.T. 711; 2007 Fam. L.R. 98; 2007 G.W.D. 22-365, OH
S *v* Secretary of State for the Home Department 2007 G.W.D. 24-411, IH (Ex Div)
S, Petitioner see S *v* Edinburgh City Council
Saeed *v* Secretary of State for the Home Department [2006] CSOH 120; 2006 S.L.T.
   1037; 2006 G.W.D. 27-608, OH . . . . *Digested*, 07/**5314**
Safeway Stores Plc *v* National Appeal Panel 1996 S.C. 37; 1996 S.L.T. 235, IH (2 Div);
   reversing 1995 S.L.T. 1083, OH . . . . *Digested*, 96/**7203**:
                                                                                   Applied, 07/5264

Sattar *v* HM Advocate 2007 G.W.D. 16-300, HCJ
SB *v* Dunbar see Beattie *v* Dunbar
Scottish Coal Co Ltd *v* Crouch Mining Ltd see Scottish Coal Co Ltd *v* McCormack

Scottish Coal Co Ltd v McCormack; *sub nom* Scottish Coal Co Ltd v Crouch Mining
    Ltd 2006 S.C. 105, IH (Ex Div) . . . . *Considered*, 07/1415
Scottish Exhibition Centre Ltd v Customs and Excise Commissioners see Scottish
    Exhibition Centre Ltd v Revenue and Customs Commissioners
Scottish Exhibition Centre Ltd v Revenue and Customs Commissioners; *sub nom*
    Scottish Exhibition Centre Ltd v Customs and Excise Commissioners [2006]
    CSIH 42; 2006 S.C. 702; 2006 S.C.L.R. 849; [2007] B.T.C. 5769; [2007] B.V.C.
    716; [2006] S.T.I. 1918, IH (Ex Div); reversing [2005] B.V.C. 2529; [2005]
    S.T.I. 896, V&DTr (Edinburgh) . . . . *Digested*, 07/**5568**
Scottish Ministers v Buchanan [2006] CSOH 121; 2007 S.C.L.R. 301, OH
Scottish Ministers v Doig [2006] CSOH 176; 2007 S.L.T. 313; 2007 G.W.D. 8-137, OH.   *Digested*, 07/**5048**
Scottish Ministers v McGuffie [2006] CSIH 54; 2006 S.L.T. 1166; 2006 G.W.D. 38-
    754, IH (Ex Div); affirming 2006 S.L.T. 401; 2006 G.W.D. 9-175, OH.   *Digested*, 07/**5082**
Scottish Ministers v Scottish Information Commissioner; *sub nom* Alexander's
    Application, Re; Elstone's Application, Re [2007] CSIH 8; 2007 S.C. 330; 2007
    S.L.T. 274; 2007 S.C.L.R. 253; 2007 G.W.D. 3-48; *Times*, January 29, 2007, IH
    (1 Div) . . . . *Digested*, 07/**4888**
Scottish Ministers, Petitioners 2007 G.W.D. 13-259, OH
Scottish Power Generation Ltd v Scottish Environment Protection Agency (No.1) 2005
    S.L.T. 98; [2005] Eu. L.R. 449; [2005] Env. L.R. 38; 2005 G.W.D. 1-1, OH . . . .   *Digested*, 05/**4970**:
                                                            Applied, 07/1518
Seabrokers Ltd v Riddell 2007 G.W.D. 26-451, OH
Secretary of State for Scotland v Revival Properties Ltd see Edinburgh City Council v
    Secretary of State for Scotland
Secretary of State for Trade and Industry v Coakley 2007 S.C. 1; 2006 G.W.D. 26-580, IH
    (Ex Div) . . . . *Digested*, 07/**4989**
Secretary of State for Trade and Industry v Gerard 2007 G.W.D. 38-662, IH (Ex Div);
    affirming 2006 G.W.D. 31-663, OH
Secretary of State for Work and Pensions v Runciman 2007 G.W.D. 27-470, Sh Pr
Sellars (Andrew) v HM Advocate see Weir (Mark Lindsay) v HM Advocate
Sheltered Housing Management Ltd v Jack 2007 G.W.D. 32-553, Lands Tr (Scot)
Sherwood v Hamilton-Gray 2007 G.W.D. 25-441, Sh Ct (Tayside)
Shetland Islands Council v Lerwick Port Authority 2007 G.W.D. 3-35, OH
Shipman v Lothian RC 1989 S.L.T. (Lands Tr.) 82, Lands Tr (Scot) . . . . *Digested*, 89/**4541**:
                                                            Applied, 07/5333
Sim v Stretch [1936] 2 All E.R. 1237, HL . . . . *Applied*, 57/1978,
                            62/1749, 63/1998, 67/2281, 70/1575, 07/5098
Simmers v Innes [2007] CSIH 12; 2007 G.W.D. 9-159, IH (Ex Div); reversing 2006
    S.C.L.R. 61, OH . . . . *Digested*, 06/**5155**
Simms v NHS Tayside 2007 G.W.D. 36-621, Sh Ct (Tayside)
Simpson v Simpson 2007 Fam. L.R. 134; 2007 G.W.D. 31-532, Sh Pr; reversing 2007
    S.L.T. (Sh Ct) 43; 2007 G.W.D. 12-250, Sh Ct (Grampian) . . . . *Digested*, 07/**5187**
Simpson v Thompson 2007 S.C.C.R. 503, HCJ
Simson v Aberdeenshire Council 2007 S.C. 366; 2007 S.L.T. 244; 2007 G.W.D. 6-100,
    IH (Ex Div); affirming 2006 G.W.D. 18-384, OH . . . . *Digested*, 07/**5463**
Sinclair Lockhart's Trustees v Central Land Board 1951 S.C. 258; 1951 S.L.T. 121; (1949-
    51) 1 P. & C.R. 320, IH (1 Div); affirming 1950 S.L.T. 283; (1949-51) 1 P. & C.R.
    195, OH. . . . . *Digested*, 47-51/**10107**:
                      Applied, 94/4335, 04/3091, 07/5337: *Approved*, 64/4524
Sinclair (Alvin Lee) v HM Advocate [2005] UKPC D 2; 2005 1 S.C. (P.C.) 28; 2005
    S.L.T. 553; 2005 S.C.C.R. 446; [2005] H.R.L.R. 26; 18 B.H.R.C. 527; 2005
    G.W.D. 17-306; *Times*, June 1, 2005, PC (Sc); reversing 2004 S.L.T. 794; 2004
    S.C.C.R. 499; 2004 G.W.D. 23-503, HCJ . . . . *Digested*, 05/**5136**:
                                 Applied, 06/5238: *Considered*, 07/5064
Singh v Scottish Power Plc see Morrison Sports Ltd v Scottish Power Plc
Skarpaas v Skarpaas (Divorce: Financial Provision) 1993 S.L.T. 343; 1992 S.C.L.R.
    398, IH (1 Div); affirming 1991 S.L.T. (Sh. Ct.) 15; 1991 S.C.L.R. 423, Sh Pr . . . .   *Digested*, 92/**5670**:
              Applied, 94/5779, 07/5187: *Considered*, 94/5779: *Overruled in part*, 93/5219
Slessor v Vetco Gray UK Ltd 2007 Rep. L.R. 83, OH
Slessor v Vetco Gray UK Ltd [2007] CSOH 59; 2007 S.L.T. 400; 2007 G.W.D. 11-204,
    OH . . . . *Digested*, 07/**5268**
Sloane-Maris v Banchory Squash Racquets Club Ltd see Maris v Banchory Squash
    Racquets Club Ltd
SM, Appellant see S v Edinburgh City Council
Small (Inspector of Taxes) v Mars UK Ltd see Revenue and Customs Commissioners v
    William Grant & Sons Distillers Ltd (Scotland)
Smart (Ronald Barbour) v HM Advocate [2006] HCJAC 12; 2006 J.C. 119; 2006
    S.C.C.R. 120; 2006 G.W.D. 12-229, HCJ . . . . *Digested*, 07/**5036**
Smith v Dumfries and Galloway Health Board 2007 G.W.D. 40-698, OH
Smith v Elrick 2007 G.W.D. 29-515, Lands Tr (Scot)
Smith v Golar-Nor Offshore A/S 2007 Rep. L.R. 127; 2007 G.W.D. 38-658, OH
Smith v Honda Motor Europe Ltd (t/a Honda (UK)) 2007 G.W.D. 26-456, OH
Smith v Littlewoods Organisation Ltd see Maloco v Littlewoods Organisation Ltd
Smith v Lothian University Hospitals NHS Trust 2007 G.W.D. 12-258, OH

Smith *v* Mental Health Tribunal for Scotland; *sub nom* Smith, Petitioner 2006 S.L.T.
347; [2007] M.H.L.R. 17; 2006 G.W.D. 10-178, OH . . . .   *Digested*, 06/**5006**
Smith *v* Nairn Golf Club; *sub nom* Smith, Petitioner [2007] CSOH 136; 2007 S.L.T.
909; 2007 G.W.D. 25-420, OH
Smith *v* Prior 2007 G.W.D. 30-523, Lands Tr (Scot)
Smith *v* Prior 2007 G.W.D. 28-487, Lands Tr (Scot)
Smith *v* Scott [2007] CSIH 9; 2007 S.C. 345; 2007 S.L.T. 137; 2007 S.C.L.R. 268;
2007 G.W.D. 3-46; *Times*, February 5, 2007, Registration App Ct (SC) . . . .   *Digested*, 07/**5431**
Smith *v* South Wales Switchgear Co Ltd see Smith *v* UMB Chrysler (Scotland) Ltd
Smith *v* Stewart (1884) 11 R. 921, CS . . . .   *Applied*, 07/5483
Smith *v* UMB Chrysler (Scotland) Ltd; *sub nom* Smith *v* South Wales Switchgear Co
Ltd [1978] 1 W.L.R. 165; [1978] 1 All E.R. 18; 1978 S.C. (H.L.) 1; 1978 S.L.T. 21; 8
B.L.R. 1; (1978) 122 S.J. 61, HL; reversing 1977 S.C. 93; 1977 S.L.T. (Notes) 37,
IH (2 Div); affirming 1976 S.L.T. (Notes) 42, OH. . . . .   *Digested*, 80/**359**:
Applied, 83/4038, 93/499, 96/1216, 98/5546, 07/5012:
Considered, 92/1553, 03/730: *Followed*, 86/223, 96/5302
Smith (Hugh Ian) *v* HM Advocate 1996 S.L.T. 1338; 1996 S.C.C.R. 49, HCJ Appeal. . .   *Digested*, 96/**6746**:
Applied, 07/5076
Smith, Petitioner see Smith *v* Mental Health Tribunal for Scotland
Smith, Petitioner see Smith *v* Nairn Golf Club
Somerville *v* Scottish Ministers; *joined cases* Ralston *v* Scottish Ministers; Henderson
v Scottish Ministers; Blanco *v* Scottish Ministers [2007] UKHL 44; [2007] 1
W.L.R. 2734; 2007 S.L.T. 1113; 2007 S.C.L.R. 830; (2007) 151 S.J.L.B. 1398;
2007 G.W.D. 37-656, HL; reversing in part [2006] CSIH 52; 2007 S.C. 140;
2007 S.L.T. 96; 2007 G.W.D. 4-67, IH (1 Div) . . . .   *Digested*, 07/**5436**
Southesk Trust Co Ltd *v* Angus Council 2007 G.W.D. 37-637, IH (Ex Div); affirming
2006 G.W.D. 5-97, OH
Sparekassernes Datacenter (SDC) *v* Skatteministeriet (C-2/95) [1997] All E.R. (EC)
610; [1997] S.T.C. 932; [1997] E.C.R. I-3017; [1997] 3 C.M.L.R. 999; [1997]
B.T.C. 5395; [1997] B.V.C. 509, ECJ (5th Chamber) . . . .   *Digested*, 97/**4987**:
Applied, 98/4900, 02/4755, 03/4538, 06/4435: *Considered*, 00/5294,
07/5568: *Followed*, 98/4921
Speirs *v* 1st Choice Building Contractors Ltd 2007 G.W.D. 35-607, Sh Ct (South
Strathclyde)
Spence *v* Ayrshire and Arran Health Board see Urquhart *v* Ayrshire and Arran Health
Board
Spence (Paul) *v* HM Advocate [2007] HCJAC 64; 2007 S.L.T. 1218; 2007 S.C.C.R.
592; 2007 G.W.D. 36-629, HCJ
Spencer-Franks *v* Kellog Brown & Root Ltd; *sub nom* Spencer-Franks *v* Kellogg
Brown and Root Ltd [2007] CSIH 23; 2007 S.C. 469; 2007 S.L.T. 392; 2007
S.C.L.R. 648; 2007 Rep. L.R. 52; 2007 G.W.D. 13-274, IH (2 Div); reversing in
part 2006 S.L.T. (Sh Ct) 9; 2006 G.W.D. 3-64, Sh Ct (Grampian) . . . .   *Digested*, 07/**5270**
Spencer-Franks *v* Kellogg Brown and Root Ltd see Spencer-Franks *v* Kellog Brown &
Root Ltd
Spiers *v* Ruddy [2007] UKPC D2; 2007 G.W.D. 40-700; *Times*, December 31, 2007,
PC (Sc)
St Helen's School Northwood Ltd *v* Revenue and Customs Commissioners [2006]
EWHC 3306 (Ch); [2007] S.T.C. 633; [2007] B.T.C. 5059; [2007] B.V.C. 58;
[2007] S.T.I. 117, Ch D; affirming [2006] S.T.I. 1374, V&DTr. . . . .   *Digested*, 07/**4307**:
Considered, 07/5569
Standard Commercial Property Securities Ltd *v* Glasgow City Council [2006] UKHL 50;
2007 S.C. (H.L.) 33; 2006 S.L.T. 1152; 2007 S.C.L.R. 93; [2007] J.P.L. 758;
[2006] 47 E.G. 181 (C.S.); (2006) 103(46) L.S.G. 31; (2006) 150 S.J.L.B.
1534; [2006] N.P.C. 122; 2006 G.W.D. 38-748; *Times*, November 20, 2006, HL;
reversing 2005 S.L.T. 144; 2005 S.C.L.R. 423; [2005] 4 P.L.R. 1; 2005 G.W.D.
3-21, IH (1 Div); reversing 2004 S.L.T. 655; 2004 G.W.D. 18-395, OH . . . .   *Digested*, 07/**5451**
Standard Life Assurance Co, Petitioner [2007] CSOH 137; 2007 S.C.L.R. 581; 2007 G.W.D.
26-449, OH
Starrs *v* Ruxton; *sub nom* Ruxton *v* Starrs 2000 J.C. 208; 2000 S.L.T. 42; 1999
S.C.C.R. 1052; [2000] H.R.L.R. 191; [2000] U.K.H.R.R. 78; 8 B.H.R.C. 1; 1999
G.W.D. 37-1793; *Times*, November 17, 1999, HCJ . . . .   *Digested*, 99/**5884**:
Considered, 00/6091, 00/6095, 01/6372, 02/5493, 04/4588, 06/5017,
07/5055: *Distinguished*, 01/92, 01/358, 06/5003: *Followed*, 00/478,
05/5137: *Referred to*, 00/5841
Stephen *v* Cawdor English Marriage Settlement Trust Trustees see Stephen *v* Innes Ker
Stephen *v* Innes Ker; *sub nom* Stephen *v* Cawdor English Marriage Settlement Trust
Trustees [2007] CSIH 42; 2007 S.C. 679; 2007 S.L.T. 625; 2007 G.W.D. 19-338,
IH (2 Div); affirming [2006] CSOH 66; 2006 S.L.T. 1105; 2006 G.W.D. 23-514,
OH . . . .   *Digested*, 07/**5325**
Stephen (William James) *v* HM Advocate [2006] HCJAC 78; 2007 J.C. 61; 2006
S.C.C.R. 667; 2006 G.W.D. 35-713, HCJ. . . . .   *Digested*, 07/**5020**
Stevens *v* Yorkhill NHS Trust [2006] CSOH 143; 2006 S.L.T. 889; 2007 S.C.L.R. 606;
(2007) 95 B.M.L.R. 1; 2006 G.W.D. 30-659, OH . . . .   *Digested*, 06/**5590**
Stewart *v* Henderson 2007 G.W.D. 4-50, OH

Stewart v Stewart; *sub nom* Fraser v Stewart [2007] CSIH 20; 2007 S.C. 451; 2007
  G.W.D. 34-581, IH (Ex Div)
Stewart (Dean) v HM Advocate [2007] HCJAC 32; 2007 J.C. 198; 2007 S.C.C.R.
  303; 2007 G.W.D. 20-345, HCJ . . . . *Digested, 07/5022*
Stirling v D 1995 S.C. 358; 1995 S.L.T. 1089; 1995 S.C.L.R. 460, IH (Ex Div) . . . . *Digested, 95/5526*:
                                                                            Considered, 07/5183
Stirling v McFadyen 2000 S.C.C.R. 239; 2000 G.W.D. 8-274, HCJ . . . . *Digested, 00/6005*:
                                                             Considered, 05/5092, 07/5020
Stirling (t/a M&S Contracts) v Westminster Properties Scotland Ltd [2007] B.L.R. 537;
  2007 G.W.D. 24-396, OH
Strachan v Railtrack Plc 2007 G.W.D. 19-331, OH
Strain v Premier Custodial Group Ltd [2007] CSOH 28; 2007 S.L.T. 262; 2007 G.W.D.
  6-82, OH . . . . *Digested, 07/4979*
Strathclyde Joint Police Board v Gordon Ritchie & Co 2007 S.L.T. (Sh Ct) 2; 2006
  G.W.D. 25-563, Sh Ct (North Strathclyde) . . . . *Digested, 07/4987*
Stubbs Ltd v Russell; *sub nom* Russell v Stubbs Ltd [1913] A.C. 386; 1913 S.C. (H.L.)
  14; 1913 1 S.L.T. 428, HL . . . . *Applied, 03/5452,*
                                                      07/5098: Considered, 62/1749, 63/1998
Sumsion v BBC (Scotland) [2007] I.R.L.R. 678, EAT (SC) . . . . *Digested, 07/5143*
Superintendent of Fife Constabulary, Applicant see Closure Order, [address], Fife
Sutherland v Advocate General for Scotland [2006] CSIH 38; 2006 S.C. 682; 2006
  G.W.D. 24-538, IH (1 Div); reversing 2006 G.W.D. 3-62, OH . . . . *Digested, 07/5321*
Swankie (Arthur Thomas) v HM Advocate 1999 J.C. 40; 1999 S.L.T. 1225; 1999
  S.C.C.R. 1; 1999 G.W.D. 2-86, HCJ . . . . *Digested, 99/5875*:
                                                                            Considered, 07/5072
Sweeney v Sweeney 2007 S.C. 396; 2007 Fam. L.R. 12; 2007 G.W.D. 12-248, IH (1
  Div) . . . . *Digested, 07/5182*
Symington v Milne 2007 Rep. L.R. 63; 2007 G.W.D. 14-280, Sh Pr
Systems Division Inc v Teknek Holdings Ltd 2007 G.W.D. 17-304, OH

T, Petitioner [2007] CSOH 43; 2007 S.L.T. 543; 2007 Fam. L.R. 66; 2007 G.W.D. 8-135, OH   *Digested, 07/5174*
T, Petitioner 2007 G.W.D. 11-200, OH
Taylor v Dumfries & Galloway Citizens Advice Services 2007 S.L.T. 425; 2007 G.W.D.
  12-247, IH (1 Div) . . . . *Digested, 07/5144*
Taylor v Taylor 2007 Fam. L.R. 139; 2007 G.W.D. 31-533, Sh Pr
Taylor v Yorkshire Building Society 2007 S.L.T. (Sh Ct) 117; 2007 G.W.D. 19-334, Sh Pr
Teale v Infrastructure Technologies Ltd 2007 G.W.D. 4-62, Sh Ct (Grampian)
Teale v Marine Harvest (Scotland) Ltd 2007 G.W.D. 40-695, Sh Ct (Grampian)
Tehrani v Secretary of State for the Home Department; *sub nom* Tehrani, Petitioner
  [2006] UKHL 47; [2007] 1 A.C. 521; [2006] 3 W.L.R. 699; [2007] 1 All E.R.
  559; 2007 S.C. (H.L.) 1; 2006 S.L.T. 1123; 2006 S.C.L.R. 879; [2007] I.N.L.R.
  80; (2006) 103(42) L.S.G. 34; (2006) 150 S.J.L.B. 1395; 2006 G.W.D. 38-756;
  Times, October 24, 2006, HL; reversing 2004 S.L.T. 461; 2004 G.W.D. 13-281,
  IH (Ex Div); affirming 2003 S.L.T. 808; 2003 S.C.L.R. 448; 2003 G.W.D. 13-
  382, OH . . . . *Digested, 06/24*:
                                                                             Followed, 04/4482
Tehrani, Petitioner see Tehrani v Secretary of State for the Home Department
Tennant v Dundee City Council 2007 G.W.D. 10-192, Sh Ct (Tayside)
Thompson v Crowe 2000 J.C. 173; 1999 S.L.T. 1434; 1999 S.C.C.R. 1003; 1999
  G.W.D. 37-1790, HCJ . . . . *Digested, 00/5996*:
                                              Applied, 07/5018: Considered, 07/5024: Followed, 03/5341
Thomson v Bank of Scotland 2007 G.W.D. 32-546, Sh Ct (Grampian)
Thomson v Diosynth Ltd; *sub nom* Dionsynth Ltd v Thomson; *joined cases* Watts v
  Diosynth Ltd; Fleming v Diosynth Ltd [2006] CSIH 5; 2006 S.C. 389; 2006
  S.L.T. 323; [2006] I.R.L.R. 284; 2006 G.W.D. 4-81, IH (Ex Div); affirming EATS/
  0034/04, EAT (SC) . . . . *Digested, 06/5324*:
                                                                             Applied, 07/1432
Thomson v H&A Wason (Kamehill) Ltd 2007 G.W.D. 6-91, Sh Ct (Lothian)
Thomson v HM Advocate 2007 G.W.D. 30-520, HCJ
Thorpe v Aberdeen City Council 2007 Rep. L.R. 105, Sh Ct (Grampian)
Tiffney v Flynn [2007] CSOH 149; 2007 S.L.T. 929; 2007 G.W.D. 28-496, OH
Tods Murray WS v McNamara [2007] CSIH 19; 2007 S.C. 435; 2007 S.L.T. 687, IH (2
  Div) . . . . *Digested, 07/4984*
Tonner v Reiach & Hall (A Firm) [2007] CSIH 48; 2007 S.L.T. 1183; 2007 S.C.L.R.
  754; 2007 G.W.D. 38-657, IH (Ex Div); reversing 2005 S.L.T. 936; 2005 G.W.D.
  25-463, OH . . . . *Digested, 05/5037*
Tor Corporate AS v Sinopec Group Star Petroleum Corp Ltd [2007] CSOH 86; 2007
  S.L.T. 552; 2007 G.W.D. 18-313, OH . . . . *Digested, 07/4992*
Tosh (Lee) v HM Advocate see Weir (Mark Lindsay) v HM Advocate
Toynar Ltd v Whitbread & Co Plc; *sub nom* Toynar Ltd (in Receivership), Petitioner
  1988 S.L.T. 433; 1988 S.C.L.R. 35; (1988) 4 B.C.C. 6, IH (2 Div) . . . . *Digested, 88/3821*:
                                                                            Considered, 07/5279
Toynar Ltd (in Receivership), Petitioner see Toynar Ltd v Whitbread & Co Plc

Treasure v McGrath; *sub nom* WT v RM 2007 S.C.L.R. 447; 2006 Fam. L.R. 100;
   2007 G.W.D. 5-68, Sh Ct (Lothian) . . . . *Digested,* 07/**5177**
Trueman vAberdeenshire Council 2007 G.W.D. 39-686, Sh Ct (Grampian)
Tuley v Highland Council 2007 S.L.T. (Sh Ct) 97; 2007 G.W.D. 23-385, Sh Ct
   (Grampian)

UCB Bank Plc v Dundas & Wilson CS (No.2) 1990 S.C. 377; 1991 S.L.T. 90; 1990
   S.C.L.R. 827, IH (1 Div); affirming 1990 S.C.L.R. 371, OH . . . . *Digested,* 91/**4997**:
   Applied, 07/4983: *Considered,* 98/5469: *Followed,* 95/5935
Ullah (Ahsan) v Special Adjudicator see R. (on the application of Ullah) v Special
   Adjudicator
UNISON, Petitioner 2007 G.W.D. 8-133, OH
United Co-operative Ltd v National Appeal Panel for Entry to the Pharmaceutical Lists
   [2007] CSOH 125; 2007 S.L.T. 831; 2007 G.W.D. 24-406, OH
United Kingdom Atomic Energy Authority v Highland and Western Isles Valuation Joint
   Board Assessor [2006] R.A. 153, Lands Tr (Scot) . . . . *Digested,* 06/**5657**:
   Subsequent proceedings, 07/5489
United Kingdom Atomic Energy Authority v Highland and Western Isles Valuation Joint
   Board Assessor [2006] CSIH 60; 2007 S.C. 252; 2007 S.L.T. 27; [2007] R.A.
   65; 2007 G.W.D. 1-15, LVAC . . . . *Digested,* 07/**5489**:
   Previous proceedings, 06/5657
University Court of the University of Glasgow v Customs and Excise Commissioners
   [2007] S.T.I. 381, V&D Tr (Edinburgh)
Urquhart v Ayrshire and Arran Health Board; *sub nom* Spence v Ayrshire and Arran
   Health Board 2000 S.L.T. 829; 2000 G.W.D. 20-812, OH . . . . *Digested,* 01/**6245**:
   Approved, 05/5042: *Distinguished,* 07/4983
Urquhart v Campbell [2006] HCJAC 76; 2006 S.L.T. 1097; 2006 S.C.C.R. 656; 2006
   G.W.D. 35-720, HCJ . . . . *Digested,* 07/**5513**
Urquhart v Fife Primary Care NHS Trust 2007 S.C.L.R. 317; 2007 Rep. L.R. 11; 2007
   G.W.D. 7-124, OH . . . . *Digested,* 07/**5274**

Van den Boogaard v Laumen (C-220/95) [1997] Q.B. 759; [1997] 3 W.L.R. 284;
   [1997] All E.R. (E.C.) 517; [1997] E.C.R. I-1147; [1997] I.L.Pr. 278; [1997] 2
   F.L.R. 399; [1997] 3 F.C.R. 493; [1997] Fam. Law 599; *Times,* March 26, 1997,
   ECJ (5th Chamber) . . . . *Digested,* 97/**2454**:
   Applied, 07/1697: *Considered,* 98/2470, 07/5183
Various Claimants v BACHL see KR v Bryn Alyn Community (Holdings) Ltd (In
   Liquidation)
Various Claimants v Bryn Alyn Community (Holdings) Ltd (In Liquidation) see KR v
   Bryn Alyn Community (Holdings) Ltd (In Liquidation)
Viewpoint Housing Association Ltd v Edinburgh City Council [2007] CSOH 114; 2007
   S.L.T. 772; 2007 Rep. L.R. 99; 2007 G.W.D. 24-415, OH . . . . *Digested,* 07/**5418**
Virtue (t/a Lammermuir Game Services) v Revenue and Customs Commissioners
   [2007] B.V.C. 2518, V&D Tr (Edinburgh)

W v Quarriers 2007 G.W.D. 11-226, OH
W v Secretary of State for the Home Department see CW v Secretary of State for the
   Home Department
W's Parent and Guardian v Douglas [2006] CSOH 178; (2007) 93 B.M.L.R. 42; 2006
   G.W.D. 37-737, OH . . . . *Digested,* 07/**4980**
Wadham vWadham 2007 G.W.D. 29-502, Sh Ct (Tayside)
Wali (Usman) v HM Advocate [2007] HCJAC 11; 2007 J.C. 111; 2007 S.C.C.R. 106;
   2007 G.W.D. 13-264, HCJ . . . . *Digested,* 07/**5076**
Walker (Andrew) v HM Advocate (Sentencing) 2003 S.L.T. 130; 2002 S.C.C.R. 1036;
   2002 G.W.D. 35-1170, HCJ . . . . *Digested,* 03/**5889**:
   Applied, 04/5108: *Considered,* 07/5509
Walsh vTNT UK Ltd [2006] CSOH 149; 2006 S.L.T. 1100; 2006 G.W.D. 30-660, OH . . *Digested,* 07/**5271**
Warren James (Jewellers) Ltd v Overgate GP Ltd 2007 G.W.D. 6-94, IH (Ex Div);
   affirming 2006 G.W.D. 12-235, OH
Watt v Ralph [2007] HCJAC 5; 2007 J.C. 191; 2007 S.L.T. 464; 2007 S.C.C.R. 70;
   2007 G.W.D. 6-87, HCJ Appeal . . . . *Digested,* 07/**5079**
Watts v Bell & Scott WS [2007] CSOH 108; 2007 S.L.T. 665; [2007] P.N.L.R. 30;
   2007 G.W.D. 21-364, OH . . . . *Digested,* 07/**5015**
Watts v Diosynth Ltd seeThomson v Diosynth Ltd
Waydale Ltd v DHL Holdings (UK) Ltd (No.2) 2000 S.C. 172; 2001 S.L.T. 207; 2000
   G.W.D. 1-7, IH (Ex Div); affirming 1999 S.L.T. 631; 1999 S.C.L.R. 23; 1998 G.W.D.
   40-2036, OH . . . . *Digested,* 00/**5937**:
   Considered, 00/5937, 07/5321
Weatherstone vT Graham & Son (Builders) Ltd 2007 G.W.D. 18-318, OH

Webster v Dominick; *sub nom* Procurator Fiscal, Dunoon v Dominick 2005 1 J.C. 65;
    2003 S.L.T. 975; 2003 S.C.C.R. 525; 2003 G.W.D. 26-734, HCJ . . . .   *Digested*, 03/**5371**:
                                     Applied, 06/5182, 07/5514: *Considered*, 05/5110
Weir (Mark Lindsay) v HM Advocate; *joined cases* Muir (David Howard) v HM
    Advocate; Garty (James) v HM Advocate; Harvey (Steven) v HM Advocate;
    Tosh (Lee) v HM Advocate; Sellars (Andrew) v HM Advocate [2007] HCJAC 2;
    2007 S.L.T. 284; 2007 S.C.C.R. 59; 2007 G.W.D. 5-75, HCJ . . . .   *Digested*, 07/**5050**
Welch v United Kingdom (17440/90) see Welch v United Kingdom (A/307-A)
Welch v United Kingdom (A/307-A); *sub nom* Welch v United Kingdom (17440/90)
    (1995) 20 E.H.R.R. 247; *Times*, February 15, 1995, ECHR (1993) 16 E.H.R.R.
    CD42, Eur Comm HR . . . .   *Digested*, 95/**2650**:
                     Applied, 00/1169: *Considered*, 01/1062, 01/6327, 04/3428, 07/5429:
                                Followed, 03/3862: *Not followed*, 03/3710
Wereszczynski v Bott 2006 S.C.C.R. 556; 2006 G.W.D. 26-586, HCJ . . . .   *Digested*, 07/**5510**
West Coast Property Developments Ltd v Clarke 2007 G.W.D. 29-511, Lands Tr (Scot)
Westbury Estates Ltd v Royal Bank of Scotland Plc [2006] CSOH 177; 2006 S.L.T.
    1143; 2006 G.W.D. 38-757, OH. . . . .   *Digested*, 07/**5341**
Whaley v Lord Advocate see Friend v Lord Advocate
Whillock v Henderson [2007] CSOH 175; 2007 S.L.T. 1222; 2007 G.W.D. 38-663, OH
Whitton v Poor Sisters of Nazareth see B v Murray (No.2)
Wiles (Christopher Ronald) v HM Advocate [2007] HCJAC 26; 2007 S.C.C.R. 191;
    2007 G.W.D. 13-265, HCJ . . . .   *Digested*, 07/**5077**
William Grant & Son Distillers Ltd v McClymont 2007 Hous. L.R. 76; 2007 G.W.D. 34-
    584, Sh Ct (South Strathclyde)
William Grant & Sons Distillers Ltd v Inland Revenue Commissioners see Revenue and
    Customs Commissioners v William Grant & Sons Distillers Ltd (Scotland)
William Lippe Architects Ltd v Innes 2007 G.W.D. 39-676, IH (Ex Div); reversing in part
    2007 G.W.D. 2-22, OH
William Morton & Co v Muir Bros & Co 1907 S.C. 1211; (1907) 15 S.L.T. 252; (1907) 44
    S.L.R. 885, IH (Ex Div). . . . .   *Applied*, 68/4633,
                                      92/5952: *Considered*, 07/3568
Williamson v Fife Special Housing Association 2006 Hous. L.R. 80; 2006 G.W.D. 25-
    570, Lands Tr (Scot) . . . .   *Digested*, 07/**5335**
Wilson v BAE Systems Plc 2007 G.W.D. 14-283, OH
Wilson v Dunbar Bank Plc A13/00, IH (Ex Div); reversing in part [2006] CSOH 105;
    2006 S.L.T. 775; 2007 S.C.L.R. 25; 2006 G.W.D. 25-567, OH . . . .   *Digested*, 06/**5497**
Wilson v Glasgow City Council 2007 G.W.D. 25-440, OH
Wilson v Jaymarke Estates Ltd [2007] UKHL 29; 2007 S.C. (H.L.) 135; 2007 S.L.T.
    958; 2007 S.C.L.R. 712; [2007] B.C.C. 883; (2007) 151 S.J.L.B. 854; 2007
    G.W.D. 26-450; *Times*, June 28, 2007, HL; affirming 2006 S.C.L.R. 510, IH (1
    Div); affirming 2002 G.W.D. 28-962, Sh Ct (Grampian) . . . .   *Digested*, 07/**4976**
Wilson v McNamee 2007 G.W.D. 39-678, Lands Tr (Scot)
Winter (Clive) v HM Advocate 2002 S.C.C.R. 720; 2002 G.W.D. 19-621, HCJ . . . . . .   *Digested*, 03/**5383**:
                                          Considered, 07/5078
Wotherspoon (John Maxwell) v HM Advocate 1978 J.C. 74, HCJ. . . . .   *Digested*, 80/**3180**:
                                          Applied, 07/2075
Wright v Paton Farrell [2006] CSIH 7; 2006 S.C. 404; 2006 S.L.T. 269; 2006
    S.C.L.R. 371; [2007] P.N.L.R. 7; 2006 G.W.D. 8-139, IH (1 Div); reversing 2002
    S.C.L.R. 1039; [2003] P.N.L.R. 20; 2002 G.W.D. 28-988, OH . . . .   *Digested*, 06/**5562**
Wright v Stoddard International Plc; *sub nom* Wright v Stoddart International 2007
    G.W.D. 26-464, OH
Wright v Stoddard International Plc 2007 G.W.D. 33-565, OH
Wright v Stoddart International see Wright v Stoddard International Plc
Wright (Fabian Buehrig) v HM Advocate [2007] HCJAC 16; 2007 J.C. 119; 2007
    S.C.C.R. 139; 2007 G.W.D. 8-154, HCJ Appeal . . . .   *Digested*, 07/**5512**
Wright (Paul Murray) v HM Advocate [2006] HCJAC 66; 2006 S.C.C.R. 455; 2006
    G.W.D. 29-639, HCJ . . . .   *Digested*, 07/**5081**
WT v RM see Treasure v McGrath
Wylie v Robbie the Pict see Robbie the Pict v Wylie

X v Scottish Ministers [2007] CSIH 45; 2007 S.C. 631; 2007 S.L.T. 657; 2007 G.W.D.
    20-348, IH (1 Div) . . . .   *Digested*, 07/**5433**
X v Y 2007 Fam. L.R. 153, Sh Ct (North Strathclyde)
Xerri v Direct Line Insurance 2007 G.W.D. 20-346, Sh Ct (South Strathclyde)

Yaxley v Glen see Yaxley v Morrison
Yaxley v Morrison; *sub nom* Yaxley v Glen [2007] CSOH 90; 2007 S.L.T. 756; 2007
    Hous. L.R. 59; 2007 G.W.D. 23-384, OH . . . .   *Digested*, 07/**5278**
Young v Thomson 2007 G.W.D. 11-212, HCJ
Yung v Thomson [2006] HCJAC 70; 2006 S.L.T. 1104; 2006 G.W.D. 30-655, HCJ . . .   *Digested*, 07/**5054**

Zhi Pen Lin v HM Advocate [2007] HCJAC 62; 2007 G.W.D. 35-591, HCJ
Zurich GSG Ltd v Gray & Kellas (A Firm) [2007] CSOH 91; 2007 S.L.T. 917; 2007
    G.W.D. 26-460, OH

PART III

SHIPS' NAMES INDEX

Fu Ning Hai, The [2006] EWHC 3250 (Comm); [2007] 1 All E.R. (Comm) 1127; [2007] 2
  Lloyd's Rep. 223, QBD (Comm) . . . . *Digested,* 07/**3802**

Golden Victory, The [2007] UKHL 12; [2007] 2 A.C. 353; [2007] Bus. L.R. 997; [2007] 2
  W.L.R. 691; [2007] 3 All E.R. 1; [2007] 2 All E.R. (Comm) 97; [2007] 2 Lloyd's Rep.
  164; [2007] 1 C.L.C. 352; (2007) 157 N.L.J. 518; (2007) 151 S.J.L.B. 468; *Times,*
  March 30, 2007, HL; affirming [2005] EWCA Civ 1190; [2006] 1 W.L.R. 533;
  [2006] 1 All E.R. (Comm) 235; [2005] 2 Lloyd's Rep. 747; [2005] 2 C.L.C. 576;
  (2005) 102(43) L.S.G. 31; *Times,* October 21, 2005, CA (Civ Div); affirming
  [2005] EWHC 161 (Comm); [2005] 1 All E.R. (Comm) 467; [2005] 1 Lloyd's
  Rep. 443; [2005] 1 C.L.C. 138; *Times,* March 4, 2005, QBD (Comm) . . . . *Digested,* 07/**3816**
Good Luck, The [1992] 1 A.C. 233; [1991] 2 W.L.R. 1279; [1991] 3 All E.R. 1; [1991] 2 Lloyd's
  Rep. 191; (1991) 141 N.L.J. 779; *Times,* May 17, 1991; *Independent,* May 31, 1991;
  Financial Times, May 21, 1991, HL; reversing [1990] 1 Q.B. 818; [1990] 2
  W.L.R. 547; [1989] 3 All E.R. 628; [1989] 2 Lloyd's Rep. 238; (1990) 87(10)
  L.S.G. 34; *Times,* April 20, 1989, CA (Civ Div); reversing [1988] 1 Lloyd's Rep.
  514, QBD (Comm) . . . . *Digested,* 91/**3261**:
        Applied, 02/2753, 06/2428: *Considered,* 95/4125, 96/681:
        Distinguished, 07/2470: *Followed,* 95/754, 03/2483
Greek Fighter, The [2006] EWHC 1729 (Comm); [2006] 2 C.L.C. 497, QBD (Comm) . *Digested,* 07/**3814**

Heron II, The [1969] 1 A.C. 350; [1967] 3 W.L.R. 1491; [1967] 3 All E.R. 686; [1967] 2
  Lloyd's Rep. 457; (1967) 111 S.J. 848, HL; affirming [1966] 2 Q.B. 695; [1966] 2
  W.L.R. 1397; [1966] 2 All E.R. 593; [1966] 1 Lloyd's Rep. 595, CA; reversing [1966]
  1 Lloyd's Rep. 259; (1966) 110 S.J. 287, QBD (Comm) . . . . *Digested,* 67/**3623**:
        Applied, 70/924, 77/2881, 78/2821, 85/198, 88/1165, 96/3566, 97/6093,
        99/5790, 03/3919, 07/1064: *Approved,* 66/3146: *Considered,* 67/3623,
        68/1013, 69/3226, 72/990, 75/2324, 94/5413, 07/5015
Hoegh Anapa, The [1983] 2 A.C. 570; [1983] 2 W.L.R. 778; [1983] 2 All E.R. 189; [1983] 2
  Lloyd's Rep. 1; [1983] I.C.R. 490; [1983] I.R.L.R. 218; (1983) 133 N.L.J. 577; (1983)
  127 S.J. 306, HL; affirming [1983] 2 W.L.R. 45; [1982] 1 All E.R. 334; [1983] 1
  Lloyd's Rep. 154; [1983] I.C.R. 178; [1982] I.R.L.R. 26; (1983) 80 L.S.G. 213; (1983)
  133 N.L.J. 186; (1982) 126 S.J. 745; *Times,* November 5, 1982, CA (Civ Div) . . *Digested,* 83/**3794**:
        Applied, 84/3553, 85/3384, 87/3769: *Considered,* 87/3759, 89/3519,
        05/4189: *Overruled in part,* 07/4190
Hull 553, The [2006] EWHC 1044; [2007] 1 All E.R. (Comm) 237; [2006] 2 Lloyd's Rep.
  400, QBD (Comm) . . . . *Digested,* 06/**214**

Kallang, The [2006] EWHC 2825 (Comm); [2007] 1 Lloyd's Rep. 160, QBD (Comm) . *Digested,* 07/**3803**
Kei, The [2007] S.T.I. 2254, V&DTr (London)
Krapan J, The [1999] 1 Lloyd's Rep. 688, QBD (Comm) . . . . *Digested,* 99/**244**:
        Considered, 07/745
Kriti Palm, The [2006] EWCA Civ 1601; [2007] 1 All E.R. (Comm) 667; [2007] 1 Lloyd's Rep.
  555; [2007] 2 C.L.C. 223; *Times,* December 21, 2006, CA (Civ Div); affirming
  [2005] EWHC 2122 (Comm); [2006] 1 Lloyd's Rep. 1; [2005] 2 C.L.C. 490,
  QBD (Comm) . . . . *Digested,* 07/**482**

Luxmar, The [2007] EWCA Civ 494; [2007] 2 All E.R. (Comm) 548; [2007] 2 Lloyd's Rep.
  542; [2007] 1 C.L.C. 807, CA (Civ Div); affirming [2006] EWHC 1322 (Comm);
  [2006] 2 All E.R. (Comm) 913; [2006] 2 Lloyd's Rep. 543, QBD (Comm) . . . . *Digested,* 07/**810**

Maersk Colombo, The [2001] EWCA Civ 717; [2001] 2 Lloyd's Rep. 275; (2001) 98(24)
  L.S.G. 43; (2001) 145 S.J.L.B. 149; *Times,* June 13, 2001, CA (Civ Div); affirming
  [1999] 2 Lloyd's Rep. 491; [1999] C.L.C. 1814, QBD (Admlty) . . . . *Digested,* 01/**4501**:
        Considered, 05/374, 07/1059: *Followed,* 03/939
Magdalena Oldenorff, The [2007] EWCA Civ 998; [2007] 2 C.L.C. 537; *Times,* October 31,
  2007, CA (Civ Div); affirming [2006] EWHC 2532 (Comm), QBD (Comm) . . . *Digested,* 07/**253**
Manzanillo II, The [2004] EWCA Civ 1007; [2005] 1 W.L.R. 144; [2004] 4 All E.R. 899;
  [2005] 1 All E.R. (Comm) 53; [2005] 1 Lloyd's Rep. 1; [2005] 1 C.L.C. 394; *Times,*
  August 19, 2004; *Independent,* October 8, 2004, CA (Civ Div); affirming
  [2003] EWHC 1802 (Admlty); [2004] 1 Lloyd's Rep. 647, QBD (Admlty) . . . . *Digested,* 04/**3495**:
        Applied, 07/2625: *Considered,* 05/3794
Mary Nour, The [2007] EWHC 2070 (Comm); [2007] 2 C.L.C. 518; (2007) 104(38) L.S.G.
  35, QBD (Comm)
Mary Nour, The [2007] EWHC 2340 (Comm); [2007] 2 C.L.C. 530, QBD (Comm)
Mediana, The [1900] A.C. 113, HL; affirming [1899] P. 127, CA . . . . *Applied,* 47-51/2554,
        03/943, 05/4193: *Considered,* 52/893, 78/44.u, 07/2497

Mihalis Angelos, The [1971] 1 Q.B.164; [1970] 3 W.L.R.601; [1970] 3 All E.R.125; [1970] 2
  Lloyd's Rep. 43; (1970) 114 S.J. 548, CA (Civ Div); reversing [1970] 2 W.L.R. 907;
  [1970] 1 All E.R. 673; [1970] 1 Lloyd's Rep. 118, QBD (Comm) . . . . *Digested*, 70/**357**:
Considered, 71/1838, 76/2547, 07/3816: *Followed*, 98/811, 00/4702

Nema, The (No.2) [1982] A.C. 724; [1981] 3 W.L.R. 292; [1981] 2 All E.R. 1030; [1981] 2
  Lloyd's Rep. 239; [1981] Com. L.R.197; (1981) 125 S.J. 542, HL; affirming [1980]
  Q.B. 547; [1980] 3 W.L.R. 326; [1980] 3 All E.R. 117; [1980] 2 Lloyd's Rep. 339;
  [1980] E.C.C. 467, CA (Civ Div); reversing [1980] 2 Lloyd's Rep. 83, QBD (Comm)   *Digested*, 81/**76**:
Applied, 82/82, 82/84, 82/85, 82/138, 85/113, 87/146: *Cited*, 84/96, 84/127,
84/243, 89/114, 90/193, 90/2850, 92/164, 92/2745: *Considered*, 82/83,
82/89, 82/115, 82/2856, 83/112, 83/131, 86/91, 86/92, 86/1907, 90/202,
90/206, 91/201, 91/203, 92/2734, 93/163, 07/254: *Distinguished*, 83/111,
89/104: *Followed*, 82/86, 82/87: *Not applied*, 86/1926: *Referred to*, 82/88,
83/125, 87/2216
Nestegas, The [1983] 2 Lloyd's Rep. 658; [1983] Com. L.R. 145; (1983) 133 N.L.J. 597,
  QBD (Comm) . . . . *Digested*, 83/**201**:
Applied, 97/5578, 00/3433, 07/2388: *Considered*, 92/489, 93/73
New Vanguard, The [1994] 1 W.L.R.1634; [1995] 1 All E.R. 641; [1995] 1 Lloyd's Rep. 191;
  Times, August 15, 1994; *Independent*, August 22, 1994, CA (Civ Div) . . . . *Digested*, 95/**4213**:
Applied, 06/692, 07/238: *Considered*, 05/206, 06/211
No 1 Dae Bu, The [2006] EWHC 812 (Comm); [2006] Lloyd's Rep. I.R. 860, QBD (Comm)   *Digested*, 07/**2492**
Norseman, The [2006] EWHC 3150 (Comm); [2007] Lloyd's Rep. I.R. 403, QBD (Comm)

Odenfeld, The [1978] 2 Lloyd's Rep. 357, QBD (Comm) . . . . *Digested*, 78/**2712**:
Considered, 07/2726
Oranie, The and Tunisie, The [1966] 1 Lloyd's Rep. 477; 116 N.L.J. 948, CA. . . . . *Digested*, 66/**380**:
Considered, 07/229

P Caland, The [1893] A.C. 207, HL; affirming [1892] P. 191, CA; affirming [1891] P. 313,
  PDAD . . . . *Applied*, 07/363:
Considered, 59/77, 76/2558
Pacifica, The [1994] 1 W.L.R.1634; [1995] 1 All E.R. 641; [1995] 1 Lloyd's Rep. 191; *Times*,
  August 15, 1994; *Independent*, August 22, 1994, CA (Civ Div) . . . . *Digested*, 95/**4213**:
Applied, 06/692, 07/238: *Considered*, 05/206, 06/211

Remmar, The [2007] EWHC 1821 (Comm); [2007] 2 Lloyd's Rep. 302, QBD (Comm)   *Digested*, 07/**250**
Rewia, The [1991] 2 Lloyd's Rep. 325; [1993] I.L.Pr. 507; *Financial Times*, July 12, 1991,
  CA (Civ Div); reversing [1991] 1 Lloyd's Rep. 69; *Lloyd's List*, September 21,
  1990, QBD (Admlty) . . . . *Digested*, 92/**3917**:
Applied, 03/484, 07/441
Robin, The [2001] EWCA Civ 1832; [2002] 1 All E.R. 703; [2002] 1 All E.R. (Comm) 306;
  [2002] 1 Lloyd's Rep. 295; [2002] C.L.C. 405; [2002] B.L.R. 54; *Independent*,
  January 14, 2002, CA (Civ Div); affirming [2001] 1 All E.R. (Comm) 1051;
  [2001] 2 Lloyd's Rep. 731, QBD (Comm) . . . . *Digested*, 02/**707**:
Considered, 07/1077

Sabrewing, The [2007] EWHC 2482 (Comm); [2007] 2 C.L.C. 763, QBD (Comm)
Sardinia Sulcis, The [1991] 1 Lloyd's Rep. 201; *Times*, November 21, 1990; *Independent*,
  December 3, 1990; *Financial Times*, November 13, 1990, CA (Civ Div) . . . . *Digested*, 91/**3204**:
Applied, 99/494, 05/89, 06/197, 07/534: *Followed*, 96/890:
Not followed, 05/315
Sea Angel, The [2007] EWCA Civ 547; [2007] 2 All E.R. (Comm) 634; [2007] 2 Lloyd's
  Rep. 517; [2007] 1 C.L.C. 876, CA (Civ Div); affirming [2006] EWHC 1713 (Comm);
  [2007] 1 All E.R. (Comm) 407; [2007] 1 Lloyd's Rep. 335; [2006] 2 C.L.C. 600,
  QBD (Comm) . . . . *Digested*, 07/**3815**
Sea Empress, The [2000] 2 Cr. App. R. (S.) 423; [2000] Env. L.R. 632; [2000] J.P.L. 943,
  CA (Crim Div); reversing in part [1999] 1 Lloyd's Rep. 673, Crown Ct (Cardiff) .   *Digested*, 00/**2291**:
Considered, 07/3655
Sea Tractor, The [2007] EWHC 31 (Admlty); [2007] 2 Lloyd's Rep. 363, QBD (Admlty)   *Digested*, 07/**3810**
Seaflower, The (No.2) [2000] 2 All E.R. (Comm) 169; [2000] 2 Lloyd's Rep. 37; [2000]
  C.L.C. 802, QBD (Comm) . . . . *Digested*, 00/**4702**:
Considered, 07/3816
Seaward Quest, The [2007] EWHC 1460 (Comm); [2007] 2 All E.R. (Comm) 937; [2007] 2
  Lloyd's Rep. 308; [2007] 1 C.L.C. 989, QBD (Comm) . . . . *Digested*, 07/**672**

Starsin, The [2003] UKHL 12; [2004] 1 A.C. 715; [2003] 2 W.L.R. 711; [2003] 2 All E.R. 785; [2003] 1 All E.R. (Comm) 625; [2003] 1 Lloyd's Rep. 571; [2003] 1 C.L.C. 921; 2003 A.M.C. 913; (2003) 100(19) L.S.G. 31; *Times*, March 17, 2003, HL; reversing [2001] EWCA Civ 56; [2001] 1 All E.R. (Comm) 455; [2001] 1 Lloyd's Rep. 437; [2001] C.L.C. 696, CA (Civ Div); reversing in part [1999] 2 All E.R. (Comm) 591; [2000] 1 Lloyd's Rep. 85; [1999] C.L.C. 1769, QBD (Comm) . . . .   *Digested,* 03/**3896**:
       Applied, 00/4679, 03/3900, 07/2748: *Considered,* 06/2673:
       Followed, 04/3480

Suhadiwarno Panjan (C440/97), The [2000] All E.R. (EC) 865; [1999] 2 All E.R. (Comm) 700; [1999] E.C.R. I-6307; [1999] C.L.C. 1976; [2000] I.L.Pr. 626, ECJ . . . . .   *Digested,* 00/**764**:
       Applied, 05/604, 07/657: *Considered,* 04/578

Tiiskeri, The [1983] 2 Lloyd's Rep. 658; [1983] Com. L.R. 145; (1983) 133 N.L.J. 597, QBD (Comm) . . . .   *Digested,* 83/**201**:
       Applied, 97/5578, 00/3433, 07/2388: *Considered,* 92/489, 93/73
Tramp, The [2007] EWHC 31 (Admlty); [2007] 2 Lloyd's Rep. 363, QBD (Admlty) . . .   *Digested,* 07/**3810**
Tutova, The [2006] EWHC 2223 (Comm); [2007] 1 Lloyd's Rep. 104, QBD (Comm) . .   *Digested,* 07/**2500**

UB Tiger, The [2006] EWCA Civ 1717; [2007] 1 W.L.R. 2288; [2007] 2 All E.R. (Comm) 401; [2007] 2 Lloyd's Rep. 231; [2006] 2 C.L.C. 985; 116 Con. L.R. 200; *Times*, January 15, 2007, CA (Civ Div); affirming [2006] EWHC 2433 (Comm), QBD (Comm)   *Digested,* 07/**472**
UB Tiger, The [2006] EWCA Civ 1300; [2007] 1 W.L.R. 2483; [2007] 2 Lloyd's Rep. 148, CA (Civ Div); reversing [2005] EWHC 1276 (Comm); [2005] 1 W.L.R. 3733; [2006] 1 Lloyd's Rep. 111; *Times*, August 3, 2005, QBD (Comm) . . . .   *Digested,* 05/**314**
UpYaws, The [2007] EWHC 210 (Admlty); [2007] 1 Lloyd's Rep. 719; [2007] 2 F.L.R. 444; [2007] 3 F.C.R. 515; [2007] Fam. Law 597, QBD (Admlty) . . . .   *Digested,* 07/**3363**

Vimeira, The (No.1) [1984] 2 Lloyd's Rep. 66, CA (Civ Div); reversing [1983] 2 Lloyd's Rep. 424; [1983] Com. L.R. 142; (1983) 133 N.L.J. 575, QBD (Comm) . . . .   *Digested,* 84/**114**:
       Applied, 98/233, 00/225, 06/196: *Considered,* 85/105, 07/250
Vimeira, The (No.2) [1986] A.C. 965; [1986] 2 W.L.R. 1051; [1986] 2 All E.R. 409; [1986] 2 Lloyd's Rep. 117; (1986) 130 S.J. 429, HL; reversing [1985] 1 W.L.R. 1222; [1985] 3 All E.R. 641; [1986] 1 Lloyd's Rep. 107; (1985) 82 L.S.G. 3529; (1985) 135 N.L.J. 1165; (1985) 129 S.J. 812; *Financial Times*, October 16, 1985, CA (Civ Div); reversing [1985] 2 Lloyd's Rep. 377, QBD (Comm) . . . .   *Digested,* 86/**2606**:
       Applied, 87/2991, 89/2938, 92/3454, 93/49, 94/3591, 95/3994, 96/710:
       Considered, 87/2942, 88/296, 90/3604, 91/2823, 92/2535, 92/2570,
       93/3153, 93/3175, 94/3579, 97/607, 97/3113, 99/390, 01/1817, 02/393,
       02/394, 07/361: *Followed,* 96/3541, 99/392, 99/417

Western Triumph, The [2002] EWCA Civ 405; [2002] 1 W.L.R. 2397; [2002] 4 All E.R. 390; [2002] 2 All E.R. (Comm) 193; [2002] 2 Lloyd's Rep. 1; [2002] C.L.C. 992; (2002) 99(20) L.S.G. 31; *Times*, April 18, 2002; *Daily Telegraph*, May 13, 2002, CA (Civ Div). . . . .   *Digested,* 02/**208**:
       Applied, 04/181: *Considered,* 07/240: *Distinguished,* 07/249:
       Followed, 06/204

Zephyr, The [1985] 2 Lloyd's Rep. 529; *Financial Times*, July 30, 1985, CA (Civ Div); reversing in part [1984] 1 W.L.R. 100; [1984] 1 All E.R. 35; [1984] 1 Lloyd's Rep. 58; (1984) 134 N.L.J. 35; (1983) 127 S.J. 733, QBD (Comm) . . . .   *Digested,* 86/**1785**:
       Applied, 86/2620, 06/429: *Considered,* 95/4184, 03/4558, 07/2467